Footprint Brazil

Alex Robinson
4th edition

Those whose aesthetic sense leans towards restraint... feel almost offended by this lavish display of colours and forms. An ascetic would be inclined to close his eyes, as though he had suddenly come face to face with a naked woman.

Peter Fleming, *Brazilian Adventure*

❶ Lençóis Maranhenses Vast coastal dunes dotted with clearwater lakes

❷ Delta do Parnaíba Rich culture, thousands of islands and abundant wildlife

❸ Serra da Capivara Bizarre beehive domes and 50,000-year-old rock art

❹ Festa de São João in Campina Grande The largest and most colourful festival in Brazil's interior

❺ Pirenópolis Pretty colonial town surrounded by waterfall-filled forest

❻ Chapada dos Veadeiros Waterfalls, canyons, mountains of rock crystal and great walking

❼ Chapada Diamantina Great hiking and caving, a hop away from Salvador

❽ Itacaré Idyllic beaches, great restaurants and a sophisticated crowd

❾ Salvador Brazil's pulsating African heart, liveliest urban carnival and some of the best nightlife

❿ Pantanal The best place for wildlife in South America

Brazil Highlights

See colour maps at back of book

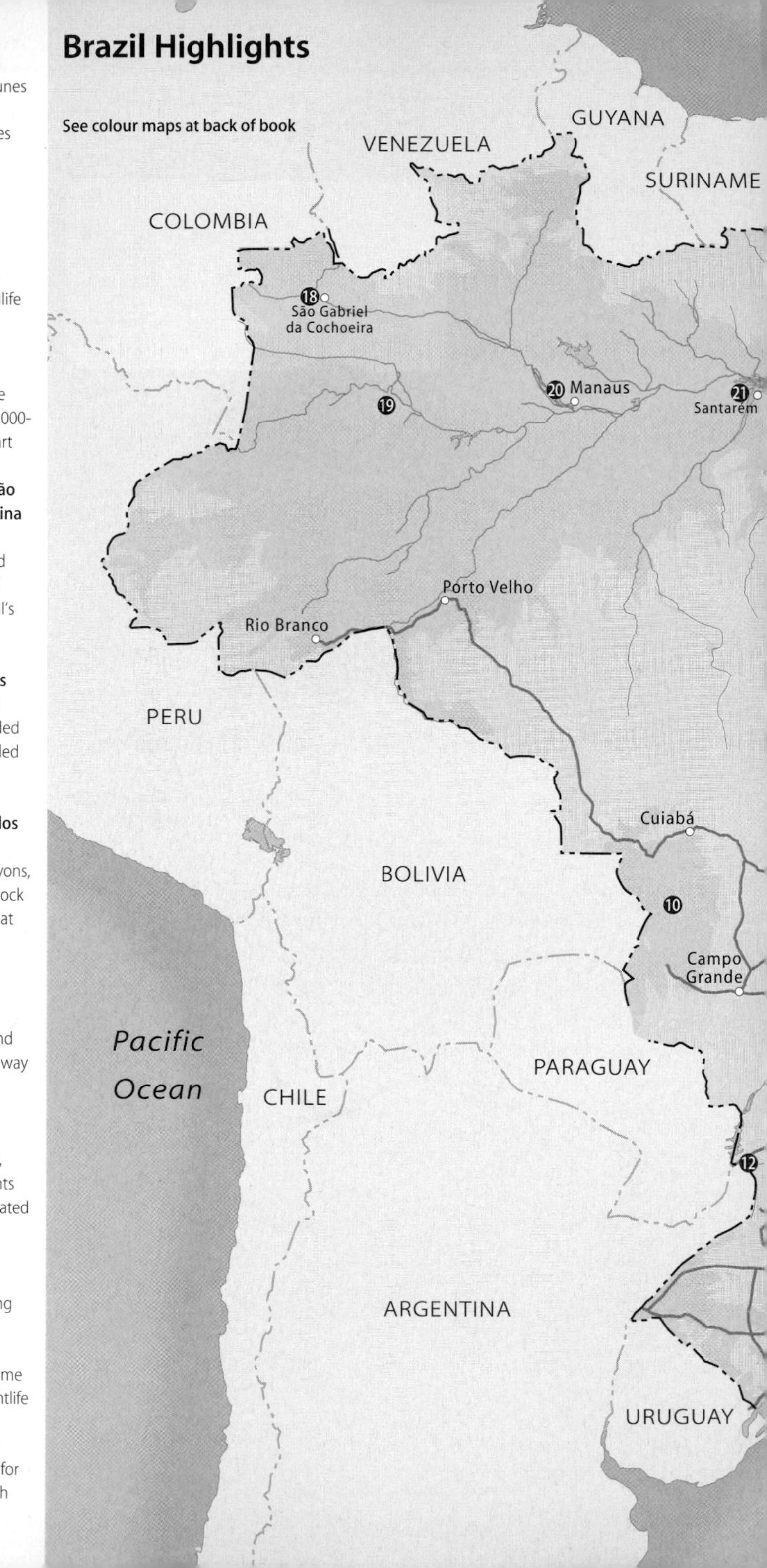

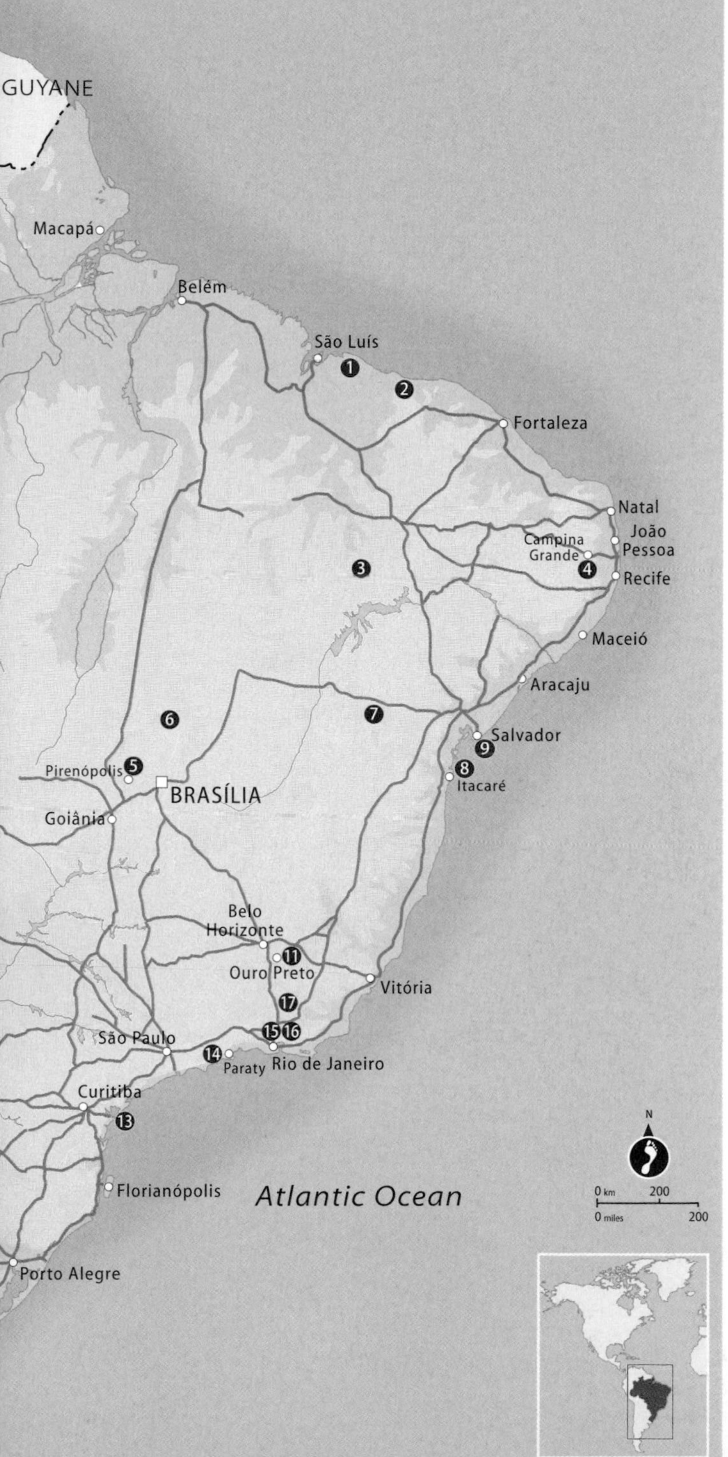

⑪ Ouro Preto
Splendid Baroque churches and fine religious art

⑫ Iguaçu Falls
The world's largest, most magnificent waterfalls

⑬ Superagüi and Ilha do Mel
A laid-back beach island on the edge of the wilderness

⑭ Costa Verde
Chocolate-box villages, pristine islands and beaches

⑮ Tijuca National Park
A green oasis in the metropolis with stunning views

⑯ Corcovado
The magnificent views of Rio from the statue of Christ

⑰ Serro dos Órgãos
Atlantic forests and bizarre rock formations

⑱ São Gabriel da Cachoeira
Black rivers, white beaches, thick forest and boulders the size of mountains

⑲ Mamirauá
One of the Amazon's remote and most beautiful wildernesses

⑳ Analvilhanas Islands
Rainforest lodges in the world's largest river archipelago

㉑ Alter do Chão, Santarem
Blue rivers, pink dolphins and 10-km- long beaches

Contents

Minas Gerais and Espirito Santo

Iguaçu Falls and the south

Bahia

Recife and the northeast coast

Fortaleza

The Amazon

Goiás, Brasília and the Pantanal

Brasília, the stark and impressive modernist capital, symbolizes the twin motifs of 'Order and Progress' which adorn the national flag.

Background

Footnotes

Inside front cover

Inside back cover

The glorious past

Ouro Preto testifies to the wealth of the gold rush era, which produced some of the world's finest Iberian Baroque architecture.

A foot in the door

There are few countries that can rival Brazil for sheer magnificence of landscape and diversity of culture. In the central Amazon, forest stretches unbroken in every direction for over 2,000 km. The table-top mountains of the Goiás Cerrado, covered in medicinal plants and bushes laden with wild fruits, are drained by rivers which tumble through gorges and rush over spectacular waterfalls. Thousands of kilometres of pristine beaches line the Atlantic coast, some fringing mountainous islands in a warm, emerald sea, others backed by dunes the size of deserts. And then there are the marshlands of the Pantanal where egrets fill the air like butterflies; the tiny cobble-and-whitewash gold mining towns of Minas Gerais; the 3-km-wide waterfalls at Iguaçu; the beaches and mountains of Rio and a continent's worth of sights which speckle a country big enough to swallow Australia and leave room for Germany and France combined.

Brazil's people are as diverse as its landscape. Bierfests, sushi bars, Bauhaus architecture, cowboys and capoeira are as Brazilian as Carnival and World Cup football. Portugal, France, Ireland, Holland and Britain all laid claims here and left their cultures to mingle with the indigenous nations and the greatest numbers of Africans in the Americas. The south was a haven for US confederates, while São Paulo has the largest population of ethnic Japanese outside Japan. In short, Brazilians are from everywhere; a fevered mingling of the world united by the lilting music of the Portuguese language, the rhythms of Africa and the spontaneity of a country bathed in perennial sunlight.

Brazil remains relatively undiscovered. There are still areas here where culture has not been re-packaged for the tourism market and where spontaneity is genuine. But things are changing – Brazil is becoming fashionable. Now is the time to visit.

Carnival

Carnival is poor Brazil's excuse to forget its problems and descend into a week of frenetic, unbounded Baccahanalia. The most famous is Rio's but there are Mardi Gras celebrations throughout the country – from street parties in Salvador and São Paulo to more traditional parades in Cidade de Goiás and Olinda, or middle-class hippy festivals on the beaches of Rio Grande de Norte and Bahia.

Sport

Sporting heroes are Homeric in Brazil. When Ayrton Senna died the country literally shut down and went into mourning. And when Brazil won the World Cup for the fifth time, millions of people flocked to the streets clad in yellow and green chanting 'Tudo o Mundo tenta mais so Brasil e Penta' (Everyone tried but only Brazil has won five times).

Religion

Brazil is nominally Catholic but in reality it is home to every kind of cult and creed. Fundamentalist Protestantism is growing rapidly among the urban poor, Rosicrucians advertise themselves with car bumper stickers, Brazilian voodoo is used to further careers, many of the São Paulo middle class are spiritists and members of Santo Daime get high on Amazonian hallucinogens.

The mighty waters
This is the translation of 'Iguaçu' in Tupi Guarani. And there are none mightier or more magnificent in the world.

Music

The Girl from Ipanema is only played in gringo restaurants in Brazil. Music here has moved on. The centre of the club and hip hop scene is São Paulo. Rio uses real instruments and funksters like Jorge Ben play on the beaches and in clubs throughout the summer. Salvador vibrates to *axê* music and further north the *mangue-beat* scene fuses Brazilian rhythms with *electronica*. Beaches all-over pulse with a barefoot, bar-floor dance called *forró* and the forests of the Amazon gyrate to *guitarrada*, which sounds like Dick Dale on acid at 78 rpm.

Television

Brazilians are transfixed by their national television which pours out tacky studio chat shows, sensationalist news and melodramatic soap operas or *telenovelas* by the daily dozen. At the forefront is *TV Globo* – an archetypally Brazilian company; set up by a great patriarch, Roberto Marinho, who planned and organized everything presented on the station with an attention to detail and ideological bent to rival Rupert Murdoch. When Marinho died in 2003 *Globo* presenters wept openly on the news and the station broadcast hourly hagiographies.

The daily grind
Rio's middle classes seem to order their working lives around trips to the beach rather than the other way around.

1
2
4
5
7
8
10
11

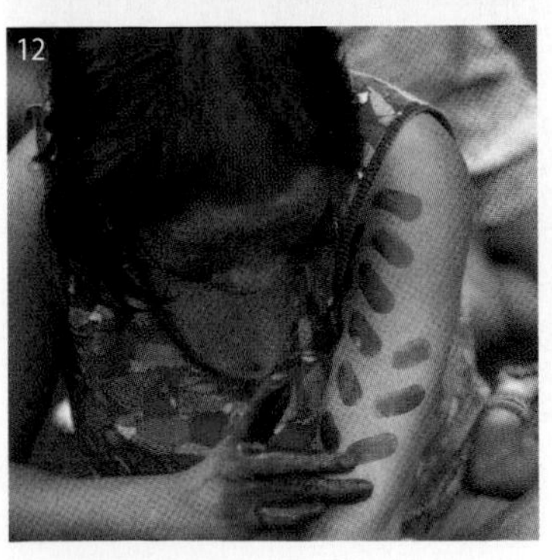

1 *There are nine species of toucan in Brazil. This one, the red-breasted toucan, can often be seen in Iguaçu or São Paulo's Botanical Gardens.* ▸▸ *See page 189.*

2 *Brazil has a long tradition of ceramics; pottery fragments dating back some 10,000 years have been found in Monte Alegre.* ▸▸ *See page 573.*

3 *The tram journey between Rio's Metropolitan Cathedral and the suburb of Santa Teresa is one of Brazil's most enchanting short journeys.* ▸▸ *See page 96.*

4 *The popular hillside retreat of Campos do Jordão near São Paulo offers good walking and some of the world's most risible mock-Alpine architecture.* ▸▸ *See page 190.*

5 *The Rio Carnival is a modern re-working of a medieval pageant, full of narrative and symbol.* ▸▸ *See page 122.*

6 *Brazil's northeastern coast is fringed by towering sandstone cliffs and shifting expanses of sand dune, like these at Genipabu near Natal.* ▸▸ *See page 489.*

7 *Brasília Cathedral was designed by the country's internationally celebrated architect, Oscar Niemeyer.* ▸▸ *See page 625.*

8 *The Pantanal, a tapestry of lakes, gallery forests, pastures and meadows the size of a European nation, is the wildlife capital of South America.* ▸▸ *See page 649.*

9 *As well as fish, the Sunday morning market at Ubajara sells all kinds of produce from the sertão.* ▸▸ *See page 511.*

10 *The Amazon is home to freshwater giants of all sorts: bullsharks, 3-m-long air-breathing fish, manatees and giant otters the size of a man.* ▸▸ *See page 543.*

11 *Pineapples grow wild in the Amazon from the centre of forest-floor bromeliads.* ▸▸ *See page 718.*

12 *The Kaiapó are one of several indigenous groups in Brazil who remain culturally strong.* ▸▸ *See page 692.*

Amazon

This vast wilderness may be disappearing at a frightening rate, but is still one of the few places left on Earth where mankind can feel dwarfed by the immensity of Nature. Think of it not as a forest or a river but as a continent with as much diversity of scenery, people and culture as any other. A visit here is a must, preferably with some knowledge of the indigenous people who know it best. Visit from Tefe, Manaus or Tabatinga.

Cerrado

Brazil's great forests are not all rainforests. Between the Amazon and the coast is a broad band of dry forest replete with strangely scented flowers and medicinal plants, and interspersed with clear-water rivers, canyons and some of the continent's most beautiful waterfalls. Visit from the pretty colonial town of Pirenópolis or São Jorge in the dramatic Chapada dos Veadeiros mountains.

Pantanal

The world's largest wetland is, in wildlife terms, the Serengeti of the Americas. The sheer abundance of birds, mammals and reptiles here is staggering, from metre-long indigo parrots, to guinea pig-like rodents the size of a labrador. Storks, ibis and egrets flock by the hundred thousand, while huge cayman bask in the sun alongside 7-m-long anacondas. Visit from Cuiabá or Corumbá.

The Amazon Forest is a network of thousands of rivers which stretch across Brazil like veins in the body. At least four of them hold volumes of water greater than any other river in the world.

Brazil's first capital, Salvador, was once the busiest slaving city in the world and thus the source of urban Brazilian culture which remains resolutely African at heart.

Beaches

Brazilians love their beaches and with good reason. There are stretches of sand to suit every taste – from little coves surrounded by lush forest in Rio de Janeiro state, to the sweeping surf beaches of Santa Catarina, and the endless expanse of sand along the coast of Maranhão, Ceara and Rio Grande de Norte.

Waterfalls

Iguaçu, the world's largest and most spectacular waterfall, lies on Brazil's border with Argentina. The falls stretch for almost 3 km and are surrounded on all sides by pristine rainforest filled with myriad bright butterflies and birds. You will need at least two days to see them.

Atlantic Coastal Forests

Brazil's most biodiverse forest is not the Amazon but the Mata Atlântica which extends for a tiny fraction of its original length but still shrouds the mountains which stretch along the country's southern coast. Views from Itatiaia National Park, the waterways around Cananeia and Superagui or the Serra da Graciosa are unforgettable. Visit from Rio, São Paulo or Curitiba.

Sertão

Northern Brazil's arid interior, often overlooked by tourists, holds countless treasures. From the rich wildlife of the Parque Nacional Grande Sertão Veredas, to the hulking escarpments of the Chapada Diamantina and the ancient rock art of the Serra de Capivara. Visit from Natal, Belo Horizonte or Salvador.

Carnival drums

African rhythms like Batucada, originally played by Brazil's slaves, lie behind most of the country's musical styles from axé to samba.

Essentials

Footprint features

Planning your trip

Where to go

Brazil is as big as the USA (without Alaska), or Australia together with France and Germany. It is important to bear this in mind when planning a visit. Try and allow plenty of time and/or consider flying.

Brazil is usually divided into five regions. The **Southeast**, which includes Rio and São Paulo, is the engine of the country, with the highest population and largest cities. It has fine beaches, good hiking in the mountains along the coast, and the best infrastructure. In the subtropical **South**, European immigration has had a strong influence and German and Italian culture is still strong; there are some beautiful natural sights including the Iguaçu Falls and the Ilha Santa Catarina. The **Northeast**, where Portuguese Brazil began, has the strongest African culture. In Bahia, there are many beautiful historical cites, fine beaches and a fascinating, little-visited interior. The **North** mostly comprises the Amazon forest and tropical savannahs and is Brazil's wild frontier; there are a number of cities which can serve as a base for visiting the forest. The **Centre West** was, for many decades, the country's forgotten interior, until Juscelino Kubitschek decided to build his new capital, Brasília, there. The capital's futuristic buildings sit on the edge of the beautiful *cerrado* forests; further south are the vast wetlands of the Pantanal which overflow with wildlife.

The Southeast

Many journeys to Brazil begin and end in **Rio de Janeiro**, Brazil's most famous and most beautiful city. Spend at least three days here. Much of the city's past has been buried under successive waves of architectural vandalism but there is still plenty to see, including Tijuca National Park, the world's largest stretch of urban forest, and the views from Corcovado and Pão de Açucar, which are absolutely breathtaking and exceed even the highest expectations.

Rio's ugly sister city is **São Paulo**, which many tourists do their utmost to avoid. However, Sampa, as it is lovingly called by locals, has by far the best restaurants, shopping, hotels and nightlife in the country and is, without question, the cultural capital.

The coast which runs between the two cities and up into the northern state of Espírito Santo is fringed by many of the country's best beaches, which are backed by rainforest covered mountains. Brazil's largest islands, Ilhabela and Ilha Grande, which lie a boat hop from shore, remain forested and unspoilt. The pretty colonial town of Paraty is a popular base for exploring the coast itself. Further north is the fashionable mock-Mediterranean resort town of Búzios. Itaunas, on the border of Bahia in Espírito Santo, offers a simpler, cheaper and more laid back beach experience. Just inland are the national parks of Itatiaia, Serra dos Órgãos, Caparaó and the Serra do Cipó, all of which preserve stunning mountain scenery and some of Brazil's areas of greatest biodiversity.

Minas Gerais, Brazil's second most powerful state lies to the north of Rio de Janeiro and São Paulo. It was founded when gold was discovered in its rugged hills. The prosperity this brought led to the construction of a series of fine colonial cities, a number of which have been listed by UNESCO as World Heritage sights. Ouro Preto is the most famous and beautiful, although it is suffering from the erosive power of traffic. Tiradentes and Diamantina are almost as pretty, and Congonhas preserves the single most remarkable monument – a reworking of the Sanctuario de Bom Jesus in Braga, Portugal, decorated with remarkable statues by one of Latin America's greatest sculptors, O Aleijadinho.

The South

The main attraction in the state of **Paranã** is Iguaçu, the world's most magnificent waterfalls. This state's coastline is one of the wildest in the country, with a long stretch of rainforest stretching north into São Paulo and a bay of broken islands many of which, like Ilha do Mel, are fringed by wonderful beaches. The little railway which winds and cuts its way down to the coast from Curitiba, through the Serra da Graciosa mountains, is one of the most delightful in South America.

Santa Catarina state, immediately to the south, has many of southern Brazil's best beaches, most of which are concentrated near the city of Florianópolis on the island of Santa Catarina. Inland are a series of towns with a strong residue of Bavarian culture; Blumenau even has a Bierfest with locals walking around in lederhosen.

Rio Grande do Sul, the land of the Brazilian cowboy, the *gaúcho*, is also an immigrant area with a strong Italian influence, evident in the wine-growing region around Caxias do Sul. The state capital, Porto Alegre, an important industrial city, gives access to yet more coastal areas: the beaches and the Lagoa dos Patos; one of the country's foremost marine bird sanctuaries. In the far west, near the border with Argentina, are the Sete Missões, all that remains of the Jesuit mission cities which flourished in this region in the 17th and 18th centuries.

Southern Brazil can be cold in the Antipodean winter and Santa Catarina's beaches can become very crowded in summer as they are popular with Argentine holidaymakers.

The Northeast

The Northeast is the country's poorest region and the country's cultural heartland. The coast is dotted with colonial cites, the most beautiful of which are crumbling São Luis, Olinda and Salvador – the capital of African Brazilian culture. In between are large cities like Fortaleza and Recife and long stretches of beach, some of them backed by Bounty advert coconut palms, others by vast shifting dunes.

The state of **Bahia** has, as its capital, one of Brazil's most famous cities, Salvador, whose windy, hilly streets lined with pastel-painted colonial buildings and topped by Baroque churches, are among Brazil's most photographed sights. The city is busy with cultural life: capoeira, a uniquely African-Brazilian martial art, is played in the squares of the old city; there is music on every corner; and restaurants serve the state's delicious seafood, cooked in spicy coconut or palm oil sauce.

The state has little resort towns to the south and north: Trancoso, Itacaré, Tinharé and Praia do Forte are fairly low key (out of season) and have wonderful beaches nearby. The larger and brasher resort towns of Port Seguro and Arraial d'Ajuda are given over to partying. The interior of Bahia is mostly a harsh land, but one town that attracts a great many visitors is Lençóis, a pretty little town close to the escarpments of Chapada Diamantina National Park – a great place for trekking, exploring caves and swimming in waterfalls and rivers.

Sergipe and **Alagoas** are two small states which do not usually figure as major stops on itineraries. However, they have good beaches and, being in the zone which was first colonized by the Portuguese and which was intensively cultivated for sugar, they have a smattering of historical attractions which are worth a look if you are in the area.

The capital of **Pernambuco** state, Recife, is a modern and architecturally uninteresting city with a lively music scene. Its neighbour, Olinda is far more beautiful, boasting one of the greatest concentrations of Portuguese architecture in the country. There are more great beaches close to both and a little resort, Porto de Galinhos, which is rapidly emerging as a new sight on the Brazilian beach trail. Unspoilt Fernando de Noronha, a small archipelago far out in the Atlantic, has some of Brazil's best diving and is the favourite honeymoon destination of Brazil's cultured middle classes. The beaches are, as ever, wonderful.

The beaches in **Rio Grande do Norte**, **Paraíba** and **Ceará** are similar to those in Pernambuco – long sweeping bays or endless straight stretches of broad sand backed by red and yellow sandstone cliffs broken by seas of shifting dunes. The best are Pipa, a laid back little resort town with some great restaurants and little bars, and Genipabu and Jericoacoara which have some of the best dune scenery in Brazil. There are plenty of quiet little escapes in between.

The coast gets wilder around **Piauí** and **Maranhão**; the little resort towns and fishing villages give way to the spectacular Delta do Parnaíba swamps – one of the richest wildlife habitats outside of the Amazon. Beyond these lie Lençóis Maranhenses, with its seemingly endless sand dunes pocked with perched lakes. The capital of Maranhão, São Luís, is a beautiful, though desperately poor city, many of whose Portuguese buildings are covered in 17th and 18th century *azulejo* tiles.

The interior of these far northern states are among there most fascinating and inaccessible parts of the region, looking more like the Australian outback than popular imaginings of South America. The dry *sertão* plains are broken by giant boulders, fossilised dinosaur prints and hulking sandstone hills, weathered into smooth domes by the wind and cut with canyons and caves. Many of these are covered in ritual art which may be older than any so far found in South America.

The North

This region is dominated by the **Amazon Basin** and, except for a handful of dirt roads which contributed heavily to Brazil's national debt, are accessible only by boat or air. But don't let that put you off. Travel here is a magical experience, whether it is on a long languid river journey, punctuated with stops at scruffy, busy river villages; or by light aircraft above a carpet of broccoli green stretching to every horizon and broken only by the occasional red gash of road or the sluggish, sinuous path of a giant black, blue or brown river.

The Amazon itself is divided by a myriad of islands, the largest of which, Marajó, is about as big as Denmark and was home to an advanced civilisation. Towns and cities line the rivers length: Belém and Manaus grew large and prosperous during 19th-century rubber boom and preserve interesting colonial buildings like the Theatro Amazonas Opera House, where the likes of Isadora Duncan and Enrico Caruso once sang. Parintins has one of Brazil's liveliest, wildest and most colourful festivals, the Boi Bumba. Tefe provides access to the unspoilt Ramsar-listed wetlands of Mamirauá and São Gabriel, spectacularly situated on black water river rapids beneath a giant granite boulder which would dwarf Rio's Sugar Loaf. Tabatinga is an important centre for indigenous culture and the gateway to Peru and Colombia.

Roraima to the north is dominated by Amazon savannah and some of the world's grandest and highest table-top mountains which mark the border with Guyana and Venezuela. **Rondônia** and **Acre**, to the south are semi-lawless frontier states with vast stretches of wilderness which is rapidly being chopped down by unscrupulous loggers and ranchers.

The Centre West

Salvador and the Pantanal wetlands, the best place in the Americas for seeing wildlife, are high on most visitors lists of Brazilian must-sees. Between the two, on a direct overland or air route, is the country's purpose-built capital, **Brasília** – a bizarre fusion of visionary post-modernism à la Le Corbusier and Milton Keynes. The best buildings here, the church of João Bosco and Niemeyer's convex and concave Parliamentary domes, are among the most daring and exciting in South America and should not be missed by any lovers of architecture. The city is also close to some spectacular natural sights, the best of which is the Chapada dos Veadeiros, a series of gentle *mesetas* flowing with rivers and waterfalls and covered in forests of medicinal plants and buriti palms. To the north are the wilds of **Tocantins** state, with virgin cerrado forest and deserts of sweeping dunes broken by large expanses of soya. To the south, in the state of **Goiás**, are the colonial towns of Pirenópolis and Cidade de Goiás. Both are set in forest-covered hills; the latter is listed as a UNESCO World Heritage sight. Many tourists who visit them find them less spoilt than the those in neighbouring Minas Gerais. Emas National Park in the extreme south of Goiás can easily be visited en route to the Pantanal and is one of the best places in the country to see Maned Wolf and Jaguar.

Essentials Planning your trip

The Pantanal itself is best reached from Cuiabá in Mato Grosso or Corumbá. The former is more comfortable with ranch-based stays and day-trips out on foot or horseback to see caiman, capybara and enormous quantities of birds. Trips from Corumbá are cheaper and are mostly camping based. Both are excellent for wildlife. Bonito, a much vaunted and now over-developed tourist town, lies close to Corumbá. The once abundant wildlife here has long fled.

When to go

The best time for a visit is from April to June, and August to October. Business visitors should avoid mid-December to the end of February, when it is hot and people are on holiday. In these months, hotels, beaches and transport tend to be very crowded. July is a school holiday month. If visiting tourist centres like Salvador, Rio and the colonial cities in Minas Gerais in the low season, be aware that some tourist sights may be closed for restoration.

Climate

In Rio de Janeiro conditions during the winter (May to September) are like those of a North European summer (including periods of rain and overcast skies), with temperatures from 14°C to the high 20s. It is more like a North European autumn in São Paulo and the southern states and it can get very cold in the far south. In São Paulo, which is in the Highlands, warmer clothing is required in the winter and the climate can be treacherous with large temperature changes in a brief space of time. It can get surprisingly cold south and west of Rio, and on high ground anywhere in Brazil, at night; warm clothes are needed. The season of heavy rains is from November to March in Rio and São Paulo, and from April to August around Recife (where irregular rainfall causes severe draughts). The rainy season in the north and Amazônia can begin in December and is heaviest from March to May, but it is getting steadily shorter, possibly as a result of deforestation. It is only in rare cases that the rainfall can be described as either excessive or deficient. Few places get more than 2,000 mm– the coast north of Belém, some of the Amazon Basin, and a small area of the Serra do Mar between Santos and São Paulo, where the downpour has been harnessed to generate electricity. Summer conditions all over the country are tropical, although temperatures rarely reach 40°C.

The average annual temperature increases steadily from south to north, but even on the equator, in the Amazon Basin, the average temperature is not more than 27°C. The highest recorded was 42°C, in the dry northeastern states. From the latitude of Recife south to Rio, the mean temperature is from 23° to 27°C along the coast, and from 18° to 21°C in the Highlands. South of Rio, towards the boundary with Uruguay, the mean temperature is from 17° to 19°C. Humidity is relatively high in Brazil, particularly along the coast. The luminosity is also very high, and sunglasses are advisable.

Festivals

The most famous festival in Brazil is Carnival, particularly that of Rio de Janeiro although there are other cities that have traditions just as interesting. Carnival dates vary between February and early March. New Year's Eve is another popular party with beaches all over the country becoming packed with revellers. June is a busy month with São João festivities, especially in the Northeast, as well as the bull festival of Bumba-meu-Boi held in the North and Maranhão. Brazilians need little excuse to hold a party and there are always plenty of festivities year-round. »» *See Holidays and festivals, page 60, for further information.*

Tour operators

Very few tour operators offer anything beyond the predictable on their Brazilian itineraries. Expect to arrive in Rio and be given the option of visiting the Pantanal, Amazon (invariably from Manaus), Iguaçu and the Bahia. More unusual destinations like the Goiás and the Chapada dos Veadeiros, Fernando da Nornonha, the Minas gold towns and the Sertão are gradually creeping onto itineraries.

In the UK

Austral Tours Ltd, 20 Upper Tachbrook St, London SW1V 1SH, T020-72335384, www.latinamerica.co.uk. Tours to Rio, the Amazon and the Northeast.

Condor Journeys and Adventures, 2 Ferry Bank, Colintraive, Argyll PA22 3AR, UK, T01700-841318, www.condorjourneys-adventures.com. Tailor-made journeys to the standard destinations listed above.

Encounter Overland , 2001 Camp Green, Debenham, Stowmarket, Suffolk 1P14 6LA, UK, T01728-862222, www.encounter.co.uk. Extended overland trips through the Amazon and throughout South America. Interesting routes.

Explore Worldwide, 1 Frederick St, Aldershot, Hants GU11 1LQ, UK, T01252-760000, www.exploreworldwide.com. Standard small-group trips to the Northeast, Amazon and Rio.

Journey Latin America, 12-13 Heathfield Terr, Chiswick, London W4 4JE, T020-87478315, and 12 St Ann's Square (2nd floor), Manchester M3 7HW, T0161-8321441, www.journeylatinamerica.co.uk. Long-established company running excellent escorted tours throughout Brazil including to some interesting new areas like Goiás and the Chapada Diamantina. They also offer a wide range of good-value flight options.

Last Frontiers Ltd, Fleet Marston Farm, Aylesbury, Bucks HP18 0QT, UK, T01296-653000, www.lastfrontiers.com. Imaginative tours to some interesting out-of-the-way locations including Fernando de Noronha.

Select Latin America (incorporating Galapagos Adventure Tours, UK), 79 Maltings Pl, 169 Tower Bridge Rd, London SE1 3LJ, T020-74071478, www.selectlatinamerica.com. Quality tailor-made holidays and small group tours.

South American Experience, 47 Causton St, Pimlico, London SW1P 4AT, T020-79765511, www.southamericanexperience.co.uk. Standard itineraries with a few more unusual options like the Chapada Diamantina.

Steppes Latin America, 51 Castle St, Cirencester, Glos GL7 1QD, T01285-885333, www.steppeslatinamerica.co.uk. Tailor-made and group itineraries throughout Brazil and Latin America.

Sunvil, Sunvil House, Upper Square, Old Isleworth, Middlesex, TW7 7BJ, T020-87584774, www.sunvil.co.uk. A good range of options throughout Brazil, including some out-of-the-way destinations.

Trips Worldwide, T0117-3114400, www.tripsworldwide.co.uk. Tailor-made trips throughout South America.

Trivium, T062-2126232, www.trivium.co.uk. Highly professional English-run company based in Goiás and offering an interesting range of general and specialist botanical tours throughout the state, especially to the Chapada dos Veadeiros and to the Atlantic coast rainforest. Much of the money goes back into local communities.

Veloso Tours, Ground Floor, 34 Warple Way, London W3 0RG, T020-87620616, www.veloso.com. An imaginative range of tours throughout Brazil and bespoke options on request.

Wildlife and birding specialists

Ornitholidays, 29 Straight Mile, Romsey, Hampshire, SO51 9BB, 01794 519445, www.ornitholidays.co.uk. Annual or biannual birdwatching trips throughout Brazil; usually to the Pantanal, Atlantic coast rainforest and Iguaçu.

Reef and Rainforest Tours Ltd, 1 The Plains, Totnes, Devon, TQ9 5DR, T01803-866965, www.reefandrainforest.co.uk. Wildlife tours to the Pantanal.

Trivium (see above), Specialist botanical tours in conjunction with the Eden Project.

In North America

4starSouth America, T1-800-8875686, www.4starSouthAmerica.com. Customized or scheduled tours throughout South America. Also has an office in Brazil at Av NS Copacabana 1066/907, Rio de Janeiro, T021-22676624.

Ela Brasil Tours, 14 Burlington Drive, Norwalk, CT 06851, T2038409010, www.elabrasil.com. Excellent bespoke tours throughout Brasil to some very imaginative destinations. Loving service and using only the best and most responsible small local operators.

Ladatco Tours, 3006 Aviation Av #4C, Coconut Grove, Florida 33133, USA, T1800-3276162, www.ladatco.com. Standard tours to Rio, Iguaçu and Manaus for the Amazon.

Mila Tours, 100 S Greenleaf Av, Gurnee, IL 60031-337, T847-2482111, T800-3877378 (USA and Canada), www.milatours.com. Standard itineraries to Rio, Iguaçu and the Northeast.

Wildlife and birding specialists

Field Guides, 9433 Bee Cave Rd, Building 1, Suite 150, Austin, Texas 78733, USA, T1-800-7284953, www.fieldguides.com. A range of interesting birdwatching tours to all parts of Brazil.

Focus Tours, 103 Moya Rd, Santa Fe, NM87508, USA, T505-4664688, www.focustours.com. Specialists in birdwatching and environmentally responsible travel.

In Brazil

Manary Ecotours, Rua Francisco Gurgel, 9067, Ponta Negra Beach, Natal T84219-2900, www.manary.com.br. If ecotourism means wildlife then Manary are not eco at all, but they do offer unusual, exciting tours to the northeastern *sertão*, including the spectacular Serra da Capivara (to see the rock paintings), Cariri and the fossilized dinosaur prints in Paraíba. Very professional service.

Open Door Tour Operator, R Barão do Rio Branco 314, Centro, Campo Grande/MS,

T067-3218303, www.opendoortur.com.br. Specialize in travel to the Pantanal and Amazon.
Tatur Turismo, Av Tancredo Neves 274, Centro Empresarial Iguatemi, Sala 228, Bloco B, Salvador, 41820-020, Bahia, Brazil, T0XX71-4507216, tatur@svn.com.br. Very helpful bespoke Bahia-based agency who can organize tours throughout Brazil, especially in Bahia, using many of the smaller hotels.

Finding out more

Tourist information

Tourist information can be obtained from Brazilian embassies and consulates. Other sources of information are: **South American Explorers**, formerly the **South American Explorers Club**, 126 Indina Creek Rd, Ithaca, NY 14850, T607-2770488, www.samexplo.org. A non-profit educational organization functioning primarily as an information network for South America. Useful for travellers to Brazil and the rest of the continent.
Latin American Travel Advisor, PO Box 17-17-908, Quito, Ecuador, F593-2562566, USA and Canada toll free T1-800-3273573, www.amerispan.com/lata/ is a complete travel information service offering up-to-date, detailed and reliable information about Brazil and countries throughout South and Central America. Public safety, health, weather and natural phenomena, travel costs, economics and politics are highlighted for each nation. You can subscribe to the comprehensive quarterly newsletter (a free sample is available), obtain country reports by email or fax and choose from a wide selection of Latin American maps. Individual travel planning assistance is available.

Business travellers

Specific information for UK exporters can be obtained from the **Department of Trade and Industry**'s Brazil Desk, Bay 828, Kingsgate House, 66-74 Victoria St, London SW1E 6SW, T020-72154262, www.trasdepartners.gov.uk. *Brazil Report*, published by Latin American Newsletters, has well-written articles on recent political and economic news. They can be contacted at 61 Old St, London EC1V 9HW, T020-72510012, www.latinnews.com. The **American Chamber of Commerce** in São Paulo is another good source of information on local markets, www.amcham.com.br.

Useful websites

See also under individual sections in this chapter. For embassy websites, see p32; newspaper and magazine websites, see p56. All the following websites are in English:
www.socioambiental.org Invaluable resource of up-to-the-minute, accurate information on environmental and indigenous issues.
www.survival-international.org The world's leading campaign organization for indigenous peoples with excellent info on various Brazilian indigenous groups.
www.gringos.com.br An excellent source of information on all things Brazilian for visitors and ex-pats.
www.brazil4you.com Comprehensive travel and tourism info on everything from sights to hotels and weather.
www.brazil.org.uk Provides a broad range of info on Brazilian history and culture from the UK Brazilian embassy.
www.roteirosdecharme.com.br Complete listing of the hotels in this group – all selected for their style and personality very much in emulation of Spain's *Parador* and Portugal's *Pousada* network.
www.brasembottawa.org Information on Brazil's national parks and links.
www.camacdonald.com/birding/sabrazil.htm Comprehensive birdwatching information including species lists and sites.
www.worldtwitch.com Birding information and comprehensive listings of rainforest lodges.
www.atbrazil.com Has a useful currency converter, general country information and details of hotels with email/websites.
www. ipanema.com A quirky, informative site on all things Rio de Janeiro.

www.brazil-brasil.com Wide-ranging, with a chat room and information on cinema, etc.
www.brazilianmusic.com Detailed information on all aspects and styles of Brazilian music and various aspects of Brazilian culture.
www.maria-brazil.org A wonderfully personal introduction to Brazil, specifically Rio, featuring Maria's cookbook and little black book, features and reviews.
http://plasma.nationalgeographic.com/mapmachine For maps anywhere in the world, by satellite or by street, or even historically.
www.rainforestweb.org Excellent accurate information on rainforest related issues with detailed comprehensive information on Brazil and extensive links.

Language

No quantity of dictionaries, phrase books or word lists will provide the same enjoyment of being able to converse directly with the people of Brazil. English is not widely spoken and it is definitely a good idea to learn some basic Portuguese before you go. As you travel you will pick up more of the language and the more you know, the more you will benefit from your stay. Efforts to speak Portuguese are greatly appreciated. Brazilians are very keen to communicate with foreigners and very patient generally. If you speak Spanish, you will probably be understood, but you will certainly have difficulty in understanding the answers. If you find yourself resorting to sign language, it might be useful to know that the 'ok' sign is actually an insult in Brazil and tugging your ear means 'delicious'. There are many differences between the Portuguese of Portugal and Brazil (particularly in the pronunciation) and, if learning Portuguese before you go to Brazil, you may want to get lessons with a Brazilian, or from a language course which teaches Brazilian Portuguese. There are Brazilian tutors in most cities (in London, see *Time Out* and *Leros*, the Brazilian magazine, for advertisements). For information on centres offering Portuguese courses in Brazil, see Directory text of the relevant towns and cities. » *See the glossary, page 726, for a list of useful words and phrases.*

Student travellers

If you are in full time education you will be entitled to an **ISIC** (International Student Identity Card), which is distributed by student travel offices and travel agencies in 77 countries. The ISIC card gives you special prices on all forms of transport (air, sea, rail etc), and access to a variety of other concessions and services. If you need to find the location of your nearest ISIC office contact: The **ISIC Association**, Box 15857, 1001 NJ Amsterdam, Holland, T+45-33939303. ISIC cards can be obtained in Brazil from **STB** agencies throughout the country such as Av Brig Faria Lima 1713, São Paulo, ToXX11-8700555. Remember to take photographs when having a card issued.

In practice, however, the ISIC card is rarely recognized or accepted for discounts outside of the South and Southeast of Brazil. It is nonetheless useful for obtaining half-price entry to the cinema. Youth hostels will often accept it in lieu of a IYHA card or at least give a discount, and some university accommodation (and subsidized canteens) will allow very cheap short-term stays to holders.

Disabled travellers

As in most Latin American countries, facilities for disabled travellers are severely lacking. Wheelchair ramps are a rare luxury and getting a wheelchair into a bathroom or toilet is practically impossible, except for some of the more modern hotels. Pavements are often in a poor state of repair or crowded with street vendors requiring passers-by to brave the passing traffic. Disabled Brazilians obviously have to cope with these problems and mainly rely on the help of others to get on and off public transport and generally move around.

But of course only a minority of disabled people are wheelchair-bound and it is now widely acknowledged that disabilities do not stop you from enjoying a great holiday. It is well worth taking a valid European disabled sticker with you if you are planning to travel by car as all shopping centres and some public areas in Rio and Petrópolis have disabled spaces available if the sticker is displayed. Some travel companies are now specializing in exciting holidays, tailor-made for individuals depending on their level of disability. **A Global Access – Disabled Travel Network Site**, www.geocities.com/Paris/1502, provides travel information for 'disabled adventurers' and includes a number of reviews and tips from the public. You might also want to read *Nothing Ventured*, edited by Alison Walsh (Harper Collins), which gives personal accounts of worldwide journeys by disabled travellers, plus advice and listings.

Gay and lesbian travellers

Brazil is a good country for gay and lesbian travellers as attitudes are fairly liberal, especially in the big cities. Opinions in the interior and rural areas are far more conservative and it is wise to adapt to this. There is a well-developed scene in Rio de Janeiro and São Paulo while Salvador is also a popular destination. Local information can be obtained from the *Rio Gay Guide*, www.riogayguide.com, and in Salvador from the **Centro Cultura** ⓘ *R do Sodre 45*, close to the Museu de Arte Sacra da Bahia, which publishes a guide to the gay scene in the city for US$4.

Travelling with children

Travel with children can bring you into closer contact with Brazilian families and, generally, presents no special problems. In fact the path is often smoother for family groups. Officials tend to be more amenable where children are concerned and they are pleased if your child knows a little Spanish or Portuguese. Moreover, even thieves and pickpockets seem to have some of the traditional respect for families, and may leave you alone because of it!

People contemplating overland travel in Brazil with children should remember that a lot of time can be spent waiting for buses, trains, and especially for aeroplanes. On bus journeys, if the children are good at amusing themselves, or can readily sleep while travelling, the problems can be considerably lessened. If your child is of an early reading age, take reading material with you as it is difficult and expensive to find. The website, www.babygoes2.com, doesn't feature Brazil specifically and tends to focus on package holidays, but has good general advice for planning and packing, 'toy tips' and ideas for entertaining on journeys.

Food

This can be a problem if the children are not adaptable. It is easier to take snacks and drinks with you on longer trips than to rely on meal stops where the food may not be to their taste. Avocados are safe, easy to eat and nutritious and can be fed to babies as young as six months. A small immersion heater and jug for hot drinks is invaluable, but remember that electric current varies. Try and get a dual-voltage one (110v and 220v).

Fares

On all long distance buses you pay for each seat, and there are no half-fares if the children occupy a seat each. For shorter trips it is cheaper, if less comfortable, to seat small children on your knee. Often there are spare seats which children can occupy after tickets have been collected. In city and local excursion buses, small children generally do not pay a fare, but are not entitled to a seat when paying customers are standing. On sightseeing tours you should always bargain for a family rate – often children can go free. On trains, reductions for children are general, but not universal.

On internal flights, airlines charge half for children under 12 (less for children under two), but some military services don't have half-fares, or have younger age limits. Note that a child travelling free on a long excursion is not always covered by the operator's travel insurance; it is advisable to pay a small premium to arrange cover.

Hotels

Try to negotiate family rates. If charges are per person, always insist that two children will occupy one bed only, therefore counting as one tariff. If rates are per bed, the same applies. In either case you can almost always get a reduced rate at cheaper hotels. Occasionally when travelling with a child you will be refused a room in a hotel that is 'unsuitable'. On river boat trips, unless you have very large hammocks, it may be more comfortable and cost effective to hire a two-berth cabin for two adults and a child. (In restaurants, you can normally buy children's helpings, or divide one full-size helping between two children.)

Working in Brazil

Volunteering

Contact **RioVoluntário** ⓘ *T021-22621110, ask for Isadora or Fábio, www.riovoluntario.org.br*, which supports 450 voluntary organizations, from environmental to healthcare. In the UK, **www.taskbrasil.org.uk**, T020–73941177, welcomes donations and volunteers (in the UK or Brazil) for its programme to help Brazilian street children. Similarly, **www.saomartinho.org.br**, T021-22422238, and its sister company in England (**Jubilee Action**, www.jubileecampaign.co.uk), seeks volunteers in both Brazil and abroad to assist in its project for street children.

Before you travel

Visas and immigration

Visas are not required for stays of up to 90 days by tourists from Andorra, Argentina, Austria, Bahamas, Barbados, Belgium, Bolivia, Chile, Colombia, Costa Rica, Denmark, Ecuador, Finland, France, Germany, Greece, Iceland, Ireland, Italy, Liechtenstein, Luxembourg, Malaysia, Monaco, Morocco, Namibia, the Netherlands, Norway, Paraguay, Peru, Philippines, Portugal, San Marino, South Africa, Spain, Suriname, Sweden, Switzerland, Thailand, Trinidad and Tobago, United Kingdom, Uruguay, the Vatican and Venezuela. For them, only the following documents are required at the port of disembarkation: a passport valid for at least six months (or *cédula de identidad* for nationals of Argentina, Chile, Paraguay and Uruguay); and a return or onward ticket, or adequate proof that you can purchase your return fare, subject to no remuneration being received in Brazil and no legally binding or contractual documents being signed. Venezuelan passport holders can stay for 60 days on filling in a form at the border.

Citizens of the United States, Canada, Australia, New Zealand and other countries not mentioned above, and anyone wanting to stay longer than 180 days, *must* get a visa before arrival, which may, if you ask, be granted for multiple entry. US

Emergency numbers

Credicard T0800-784411
Diners Club T0800-784444
MasterCard T000811-8870533
Visa T000811-9335589
American Express T011-2470966
Thomas Cook visa
T000811-7840553
Thomas Cook refund service, UK
F+44-1733-502370

citizens must be fingerprinted on entry to Brazil. Visa fees vary from country to country, so apply to the Brazilian consulate in your home country. The consular fee in the USA is US$55. Students planning to study in Brazil or employees of foreign companies can apply for a one- or two-year visa. Two copies of the application form, two photos, a letter from the sponsoring company or educational institution in Brazil, a police form showing no criminal convictions and a fee of around US$80 is required.

Extensions Foreign tourists may stay a maximum of 180 days in any one year. Ninety-day renewals are easily obtainable, but only at least 15 days before the expiry of your 90-day permit, from the Polícia Federal. The procedure varies, but generally you have to do the following: fill out three copies of the tax form at the Polícia Federal, take them to a branch of **Banco do Brasil**, pay US$15 and bring two copies back. You will then be given the extension form to fill in and be asked for your passport to stamp in the extension. According to regulations (which should be on display) you need to show a return ticket, cash, cheques or a credit card, a personal reference and proof of an address of a person living in the same city as the office (in practice you simply write this in the space on the form). Some offices will only give you an extension within 10 days of the expiry of your permit.

Some points of entry such as the Colombian border refuse entry for longer than 30 days, renewals are then for the same period, insist if you want 90 days. For longer stays you must leave the country and return (not the same day) to get a new 90-day permit. If your visa has expired, getting a new visa can be costly (US$35 for a consultation, US$30 for the visa itself) and may take anything up to 45 days, depending on where you apply. If you overstay your visa, or extension, you will be fined US$7 per day, with no upper limit. After paying the fine to Polícia Federal, you will be issued with an exit visa and must leave within eight days. If you cannot pay the fine you must pay when you next return to Brazil.

Officially, if you leave Brazil within the 90-day permission to stay and then re-enter the country, you should only be allowed to stay until the 90-day permit expires. If, however, you are given another 90-day permit, this may lead to charges of overstaying if you apply for an extension.

Identification You must always carry identification when in Brazil. It is a good idea to take a photocopy of the personal details in your passport, plus your Brazilian immigration stamp, and leave your passport in the hotel safe deposit. This photocopy, when authorized in a *cartório*, US$1, is a legitimate copy of your documents. Be prepared, however, to present the originals when travelling in sensitive areas such as near the borders. Always keep an independent record of your passport details. Also register with your consulate to expedite document replacement if yours gets lost or stolen.

Warning Do not lose the emigration permit they give you when you enter Brazil. Leaving the country without it, you may have to pay up to US$100 per person. It is suggested that you photocopy this form and have it authenticated at a *cartório*, US$1, in case of loss or theft.

Embassies

Argentina C Cerrito 1350, 1010 Buenos Aires, T005411-4515, www.brasil.org.ar.
Australia 19 Forster Cres, Yarralumla, Canberra ACT 2600, T00612-62732372, www.brazil.org.au.
Austria Am Lugeck 1/5/15, A-1010 Wien, T00431-5120631, F5138374.
Belgium 350 Av Louise, 6ème Étage, Boîte 5-1050 Bruxelles, T00322-6402015, F6408134.
Bolivia C Capitán Ravelo 2334, Ed Metrobol, Sopocachi, La Paz, Casilla 429, T005912-8112233, F8112733.
Canada 450 Wilbrod St, Sandyhill, Ottawa, ON K1N 6M8, T001613-2371090, www.brasembottawa.org.
Chile C Alonso Ovalle 1665, Santiago, T00562-6982486, www.brasembsantiago.cl.
Colombia C 93, No 14-20, 8th floor, Aptdo Aéreo 90540, Bogotá 8, T00571-2180800, F2188393.
Denmark Ryvangs Alle, 24-2100 Kobenhavn Ø, T00453-9206478, F9273607.
France 34 Cours Albert I, 75008 Paris, T00331-45616300, www.bresil.org.
Germany Kennedyallee 74-53175 Bonn, T0049228-959230, F373696.
Ireland Harcourt Centre, Europa House, 5th Floor, 41-54 Harcourt St, Dublin 2, T003531-4756000, F4751341.
Israel Beit Yachin, 2 Kaplin St, 8th floor, Tel Aviv, T009723-6963934, F6916060.
Italy 14 Piazza Navona, 00186 Roma, T003906-683981, www.ambasciatadelbrasile.it.
Japan 2-11-12 Kita-Aoyama, Minato-Ku, Tokyo 107-8633, T00813-34045211, www.braemb.or.jp.
Netherlands Mauritskade 19-2514 HD, The Hague, T003170-3023959, F3023950.
New Zealand 19 Brandon St, level 9, Wellington 1, T00644-4733516, F473357.
Norway Sigurd Syrs Gate 4, 1st floor, 0273 Oslo, T0047-22552029, F22443964.
Paraguay C Coronel Irrazábal esq , Av Mariscal López, 1521 Asunción, T0059521-214466, www.embajadabrasil.org.py.
Peru Av José Pardo 850, Miraflores, Lima 100, T00511-4212759, F4452421.
Portugal Estrada das Laranjeiras, 1649-021 Lisboa, T003511-217248510, www.emb-brasil.pt.
South Africa Hadefields, Block c, 1st floor, 1267 Pretorius St, Hatfield 0083, Pretoria, T002712-4269400, www.brazil.co.za.
Spain C Fernando El Santo, 6 DP 28010 Madrid, T00341-7004650, F7004660.
Sweden Sturgegatan 11, 2 Tr 114 36 Stockholm, T00468-234010, F234018.
Switzerland Monbijouster 68-3007 Berne, T004131-3718515, F3710525.
UK 32 Green St, London WIK 7AT, T020-7490877, www.brazil.org.uk.
USA 3006 Massachusetts Ave NW, Washington DC 20008-3699, T001202-2382700, www.brasilemb.org
Uruguay Blvd Artigas, 1328, Montevideo, Aptdo Postal 16022, T005982-7072119, www.brasmont.org.uy.
Venezuela Centro Gerencial Mohedano, 6th floor, C Los Chaguaramos con Av Mohedano, La Castellana, 1060 Caracas, T00582-2616529, F2619601.

Customs

Duty-free allowance Clothing and personal articles are free of import duty. Articles such as cameras, camcorders, portable radios, tape recorders, typewriters and binoculars are also admitted free if there is not more than one of each. Tourists may also bring in, duty-free, 24 alcoholic drinks (no more than 12 of any one type), 400 cigarettes, 25 cigars, 280 g of perfume, up to 10 units of cosmetics, up to three each of any electronic item or watch, up to a total value of US$500 monthly. There is a limit of US$150 at land borders and a written declaration must be made to this effect. Duty-free goods may only be purchased in foreign currency.

Vaccinations

You should be immunized against typhoid, polio, tetanus and hepatitis A. Visitors no longer require vaccination against smallpox. Poliomyelitis vaccination is required for children from three months to six years.

Proof of vaccination against **yellow fever** is necessary if you are visiting Amazônia and the Centre West, or are coming from countries with Amazonian territories, eg Bolivia, Colombia, Ecuador, or Peru. It is strongly recommended that you have a yellow fever inoculation before visiting northern Brazil since anyone without a certificate will be inoculated on entering any of the northern and centre-western states. Although yellow fever vaccination is free it might be administered in unsanitary conditions.

Yellow fever and some other vaccinations can be obtained from the Ministério da Saúde, R Cais de Pharoux, Rio de Janeiro. Less common vaccinations can be obtained at **Saúde de Portos**, Praça 15 de Novembro, Rio de Janeiro. » *See also page 68.*

What to take

Everybody has their own list. A **waterproof jacket** is recommended – it will probably rain several times on your trip. Take no more than two or three changes of clothes and one light sweater for chilly nights and overly air-conditioned buses. Light, natural fabrics are best in the heat. **Wax earplugs** (almost impossible to find outside large cities) and an airline-type **eye mask** can help you sleep in noisy and poorly curtained hotel rooms and on buses. Some people swear by inflatable **travel pillows** for long journeys. **Sports sandals** are much cooler than sweat-inducing trainers and can be worn in showers to avoid athlete's foot. A **sarong** or **sheet sleeping bag** is invaluable for use as a towel, a bedsheet or beach towel. (**Towels** are provided at even the cheapest hotels, although not always at youth hostels.) A **hat** is necessary to protect against sunstroke.

> *When packing, leave space in your bag; it makes it much quicker to re-pack and you will always accumulate more possessions on your way.*

Also useful are a **clothes line, nailbrush** (for scrubbing dirt off clothes as well as off oneself), a universal **plug** and a large **penknife**, preferably the famous Swiss Army knife. Possible extras include a **torch** (flashlight) – especially one that will clip on to a pocket or belt, and a **padlock** (combination lock is best) and **chain** for securing luggage to bed or bus/train seat.

It is wise to take a small **first aid kit**; useful medication is given in Health (see page 68). Also, lip salve with sun protection, and pre-moistened wipes. Major cities have a wide selection of products for **contact lens** wearers, so you don't need to take litres of lotions.

Insurance

Insurance companies have tightened up considerably over recent years and it is now almost impossible to claim successfully if you have not followed procedures closely. The problem is that these often involve dealing with the country's red tape which can lead to some inconvenience at best and to some quite long delays at worst. There is no substitute for suitable precautions against petty crime.

The level of insurance is inevitably the highest if you go through the USA. Don't forget to obtain sports extensions if you are going to go diving, rafting, climbing, etc. Most policies do not cover very high levels of baggage/cash. Don't forget to check whether you can claim on your household insurance. They often have worldwide all-risks extensions. Most policies exclude manual work whilst away, although working in bars or restaurants is usually alright. **Direct Line** in the UK offer comprehensive travel insurance, T0845 2468744, www.directline.com.

Tips Here are our tips: they apply to most types of policies but always check the details of your own policy before you leave.

1 Take the policy with you (a photocopy will do but make sure it is a complete one).
2 Do not travel against medical advice. It will invalidate the medical insurance part of the cover.
3 There is a 24-hour medical emergency service helpline associated with your insurance. You need to contact them if you require in-patient hospital treatment or you need to return home early. The telephone number is printed on the policy. Make sure you note the time of the call, the person you were talking to and get a reference number. Even better, get a receipt from the telephone company showing the number you called. Should you need to be airlifted home, this is always arranged through the insurance company's representative and the hospital authorities. Ironically, this can lead to quite intense discussions which you will not be aware of – the local hospital is often quite keen to keep you!
4 If you have to cancel your trip for whatever reason, contact your travel agent, tour operator or airline without delay.
5 If your property is damaged by an airline, report it immediately and always within three days, and get a 'property irregularity report' from them.
6 Claims for baggage left unattended are very rarely settled unless they were left in a securely locked hotel room or apartment; locked in the boot of a car and there is evidence of a forced entry; cash is carried on your person or is in a locked safe or security box.
7 All loss must be reported to the police and/or hotel authorities within 24 hours of discovery and a written report obtained.
8 If medical attention is received for injury or sickness, a medical certificate showing its nature must be obtained, although some companies waive this if only out-patient treatment is required. Keep all receipts in a safe place as they will be needed to substantiate the claim.
9 Check your policy carefully to see if there is a date before which claims must be submitted. This is often within 30 days of returning home. It is now usual for

companies to want your policy document, proof that you actually travelled (airline ticket or travel agent's confirmation of booking), receipts and written reports (in the event of loss). Photocopies are not accepted.

Money

Currency

The unit of currency is the real, R$ (plural reais) introduced on 1 July 1994 on a par with the US dollar, a link that was severed in 1999. In October 2004 the rate was R$2.86 = US$1. Any amount of foreign currency and 'a reasonable sum' in reais can be taken in, but sums over US$10,000 must be declared. Residents may only take out the equivalent of US$4,000. Notes in circulation are: 100, 50, 10, 5 and 1 real; coins: 1 real, 50, 25, 10, 5 and 1 centavo. **Note** The exchange rate has been fairly volatile recently.

ATMs

ATMs, or cash machines, are common in Brazil. As well as being the most convenient way of withdrawing money, they frequently offer the best available rates of exchange. They are usually closed after 9.30pm in large cities. There are two international ATM acceptance systems, **Plus** and **Cirrus.** Many issuers of debit and credit cards are linked to one, or both (eg Visa is Plus, MasterCard is Cirrus). **Banco do Brasil** and **HSBC** are the two main banks offering this service. Look for the relevant symbol on an ATM (there is usually only one international machine per bank) and draw cash using your PIN. **Red Banco 24 Horas** kiosks advertise that they take a long list of credit cards in their ATMs, including MasterCard and Amex, but international cards cannot always be used.

Find out before you leave what international 'functionality' your card has. Check if your bank or credit card company imposes handling charges. Obviously you must ensure that the account to which your debit card refers contains sufficient funds. With a credit card, obtain a credit limit sufficient for your needs, or pay money in to put the account in credit. If travelling for a long time, consider a direct debit to clear your account regularly. Internet banking is useful for monitoring your account or transferring funds. Do not rely on one card, in case of loss. If you do lose a card, immediately contact the 24-hour helpline of the issuer in your home country (keep this number in a safe place).

Exchange

Banks in major cities will change cash and travellers' cheques. If you keep the official exchange slips, you may convert back into foreign currency up to 50% of the amount you exchanged. The parallel market, found in travel agencies, exchange houses and among hotel staff, often offers marginally better rates than the banks. Many banks may only change US$300 minimum in cash, US$500 in travellers' cheques. Dollars cash (take US$5 or US$10 bills) are becoming more frequently used for tourist transactions and are useful for emergencies. Damaged dollar notes may be rejected. Parallel market and official rates are quoted in the papers and on TV news programmes.

Traveller's cheques

Rates for cheques are usually lower than for cash, they are harder to change and commission may be charged. Tourists cannot change US dollar traveller's cheques into dollar notes, but US dollar traveller's cheques can be obtained on an American Express card (against official policy). It is a good idea to take two kinds of cheque: if large numbers of one kind have recently been forged or stolen, making people suspicious, it is unlikely to have happened simultaneously with the other kind.

Credit cards

Credit cards are widely used but not always by who you'd expect. In Iguaçu we found that whilst the large tour company we had booked with would not take credit cards, the small pharmacy across the road would allow us to pay for a $0.50 bottle of water with our Visa. **Diners Club**, **MasterCard**, **Visa** and **American Express** are useful. MasterCard/Access Is accepted by **Banco Real**. Overseas credit cards need authorization from São Paulo, which can occasionally take a while. MasterCard and Diners are equivalent to Credicard, and Eurocheques can be cashed at **Banco Alemão** (major cities only). Cash advances on credit cards will only be paid in *reais* at the tourist rate, incurring a 1.5% commission. Banks in small remote places may still refuse to give a cash advance: try asking for the manager (*gerente*).

Money transfers

Money sent to Brazil is normally paid out in Brazilian currency, so do not have more money sent out than you need for your stay. A recommended method is, before leaving, to find out which local bank is correspondent to your bank at home, then when you need funds, telex your own bank and ask them to telex the money to the local bank (confirming by fax). Give exact information to your bank of the routing number of the receiving bank. Funds can be received within 48 banking hours.

To open a bank account in Brazil, you need to have a visa valid for more than one year.

In most large cities **Citibank** will hold US personal cheques for collection, paying the day's tourist dollar rate in *reais* with no charge. **Banco do Brasil** offers the same service with a small charge. From the UK the quickest method of having money sent is **Swift Air.** *See box on page 31 for a list of emergency telephone numbers to report card loss or theft.*

Cost of travelling

As a very rough guide, prices are about a third of those in Western Europe and the United States. The devaluation of the real in 1999 has greatly reduced costs, but Brazil is still more expensive than other countries in South America (including Argentina since the collapse of its economy).

Accommodation is good value in every price range. Budget hotels with few frills have rooms for as little as US$6, and you should have no difficulty finding a room costing US$10 wherever you are. Rooms are often pretty much the same price whether one or two people are staying, so travelling alone pushes costs up. Eating is generally inexpensive, especially in *comida a kilo* (pay by weight) restaurants, which offer a wide range of food (salads, meat, pasta, vegetarian). Although bus travel is very reasonable, because of the long distances, costs can soon mount up. Internal flights prices have come down dramatically in the last couple of years and some routes work out cheaper than taking a bus.

Getting there

Air

International flights into Brazil generally land at either Rio de Janeiro or São Paulo. São Paulo has better domestic and international flight connections. Both cities are good points to enter Brazil and there are excellent transport connections between the two, although tourists tend to choose Rio de Janeiro as their point of disembarkation. Prices are more competitive during the low season and cheap flights can be very difficult to find during the high season (generally between 15 December and 15 January, the

Thursday before Carnival to the Saturday after Carnival and 15 June to 15 August). Flight frequency changes regularly and you are advised to check current timetables.

If buying a ticket to another country but with a stopover in Brazil, check whether two tickets are cheaper than one. Airline tickets are expensive in Brazil, buy internal tickets with *reais* (you can pay by credit card). External tickets must be paid for in dollars. You cannot buy an air ticket in Brazil for use abroad unless you have a ticket out of Brazil.

Varig ⓘ *T0845-6037601, www.varig.co.uk*, also has an extensive 'Stopover' programme which gives reduced rates on transfers and hotel rooms in many cities in Brazil and throughout South America.

From Europe

Rio de Janeiro and São Paulo are connected to the principal European cities direct by **Aerolíneas Argentinas** (Amsterdam and Madrid), **Air France** (Paris), **Alitalia** (Rome), **British Airways** (London), **Iberia** (Barcelona and Madrid), **KLM** (Amsterdam), **LanChile** (Frankfurt and Madrid), **Lufthansa** (Frankfurt), **Pluna** (Madrid), **Swissair** (Zurich), **TAM** (Paris), **TAP Air Portugal** (Lisbon), **Varig** (Copenhagen, Frankfurt, London, Lisbon, Paris and Milan) and **Vasp** (Athens, Barcelona, Brussels, Frankfurt and Zurich).

Varig flies to Recife and Fortaleza from Milan and to Salvador from Rome. **TAP Air Portugal** flies to Fortaleza, Natal, Recife and Salvador from Lisbon. **Transbrasil** flies from Amsterdam and London to Recife and Salvador.

From the USA and Canada

Rio de Janeiro and São Paulo are connected to the USA direct by **American Airlines** (Chicago, Dallas, Miami), **Continental** (New York), **Delta** (Atlanta), **TAM** (Miami), **United Airlines** (Chicago, Miami), **Varig** (Los Angeles, Miami and New York) and **Vasp**. Other US gateways are Boston, Cincinnati, Denver, Detroit and San Francisco. The cheapest routes are probably from Miami.

American Airlines fly from Miami to Belo Horizonte. **Varig** fly from Miami to Belém, Fortaleza, Manaus and Recife. **Air Canada** flies direct to São Paulo from Toronto.

From Latin America

Most Latin American cities are connected by air to São Paulo and Rio de Janeiro. There are flights from Asunción with **American Airlines, TAM** and **Varig**; Bogotá with **Varig** and **Avianca**; Buenos Aires with **Aerolíneas Argentinas, TAM** and **Varig**; Caracas with **Varig**; Córdoba with **Varig**; Guayaquil with **Ecuatoriana** and **Vasp**; La Paz with **Varig**; Lima with **AeroMéxico, TAM** and **Varig**; Mexico City with **AeroMéxico** and **Varig**; Montevideo with **TAM, Pluna** and **Varig**; Santa Cruz with **LAB, TAM, Varig** and **Vasp**; San José, Costa Rica with **Lacsa**; Santiago with **LanChile, TAM** and **Varig**; Quito with **Ecuatoriana** and **Vasp**.

Penta fly from Cayenne to Belém and Macapá. **Pluna** fly from Montevideo to Porto Alegre. **Surinam Airways** fly from Paramaribo to Belém. **Varig** fly from Asunción to Curitiba, Florianópolis and Foz do Iguaçu; Buenos Aires to Porto Alegre; Mexico City to Manaus; Montevideo to Porto Alegre; Santiago to Porto Alegre.

From elsewhere

There are flights to São Paulo from Abidjan and Beirut with **Middle East Airlines**; Johannesburg with **South African Airways**; Nagoya, Japan with **Varig**; Osaka with **Vasp**; Tokyo with **JAL** and **Varig**.

Air passes

Aerolíneas Argentinas, Austral, Lan Chile, Lapa, Líneas Aéreas Paraguayas, Pluna, Varig and **Vasp** operate the **Mercosur Airpass**. Valid for a minimum of seven and a maximum of 30 days, the pass is for a maximum of eight flight coupons with no more than two stops allowed per country. At least two *Mercosur* member countries must be included; re-routing is not permitted. The airpass is available to all international return ticket holders travelling by air into the participating countries. Passes are price-banded according to mileage flown; fares range from US$225 to US$870. Children pay 67% whilst infants pay 10% of the adult fare and some of the carriers operate a blackout period between 17 December and 10 January.

LAB, Ecuatoriana and **Vasp** operate a **South American Airpass** valid for 90 days, available to non-residents of Brazil arriving in South America on long-haul flights. There is no child discount but infants pay 10% of the price, which varies between US$560 for up to four flights and US$1,100 for the maximum of nine flights. Up to two transfers of less than five hours are permitted and coverage is from northern Argentina, Chile, Bolivia, Peru, Ecuador and Brazil.

Baggage allowance

Airlines will only allow a certain weight of luggage without a surcharge; this is normally 30 kg for first class and 20 kg for business and economy classes, but these limits are often not strictly enforced when it is known that the plane is not going to be full. On some flights from the UK, special outbound concessions are offered (by Iberia, Air France) of a two-piece allowance up to 32 kg, but you may need to request this. Passengers seeking a larger baggage allowance can route via the USA, but with certain exceptions, the fares are slightly higher using this route. On the other hand, weight limits for internal flights are often lower; it is best to enquire beforehand.

Prices and discounts

1 Fares from Europe to Brazilian destinations vary from airline to airline, destination to destination, and according to the time of year. Check with an agency for the best deal for when you wish to travel. There is a wide range of offers to choose from in a highly competitive environment in the UK.

2 Most airlines offer discounted fares of one sort or another on scheduled flights. These are not offered by the airlines direct to the public, but through agencies which specialize in this type of fare. The very busy seasons are 7 December to 15 January and 1 July to 10 September. If you intend travelling during those times, book ahead. Between February and May, and from September to November, special offers may be available.

3 Other fares fall into three groups, and are all on scheduled services: **Excursion (return) fares** (A) With restricted validity, eg 5-90 days, but with certain flexibility on payment of a fee.

Yearly fares (B) These may be bought on a one-way or return basis. Some airlines require a specified return date, changeable upon payment of a fee. To leave the return completely open is possible for an extra fee. You must fix the route (some of the cheapest flexible fares now have six months validity).

Student (or under 26) fares Some airlines are flexible on the age limit, others strict. One-way and returns available, or 'Open Jaws' (see below). Do not assume that student tickets are the cheapest; though they are often very flexible, they are usually more expensive than A or B above. On the other hand, there is a wider range of cheap one-way student fares originating in Latin America than can be bought outside the continent.

4 'Open Jaw' fares For people intending to travel a linear route and return from a different point from that which they entered, these fares are available on student, yearly, or excursion tickets.

5 Multi-stop itineraries Many fares require a change of plane at an intermediate point, and a stopover may be permitted, or even obligatory, depending on schedules. However, simply because a flight stops at a given airport does not mean you can break your journey there. If you want a multi-stop itinerary, you can save hundreds of pounds by dealing with a specialized agency.

6 Because of high local taxes, a one-way ticket from Latin America is more expensive than a one-way in the other direction, so it's usually best to buy a return (but see Student fares, above). Taxes are calculated as a percentage of the full IATA fare; on a discounted fare the tax can therefore make up as much as 30-50% of the price.

7 If you buy discounted air tickets always check the reservation with the airline concerned to make sure the flight still exists. Also remember the IATA airlines' schedules change in March and October each year, so if you're going to be away for a long time it's best to reconfirm your flight well in advance or leave return flight coupons open.

8 Check whether you are entitled to any refund or re-issued ticket if you lose, or have stolen, a discounted air ticket. Some airlines require the repurchase of a ticket before you can apply for a refund, which will not be given until after the validity of the original ticket has expired. Travel insurance in some cases covers lost tickets.

9 Some South American carriers change departure times of short-haul or domestic flights at short notice and, in some instances, schedules shown in the computers of transatlantic carriers differ from those actually flown by smaller, local carriers.

Boat

Voyages on passenger-carrying cargo vessels between Brazilian ports and Europe, the USA, or elsewhere, are listed here: the **Grimaldi Line** sails from Tilbury to Brazil (Vitória, Santos, Paranaguá, Rio) and Buenos Aires via Hamburg, Amsterdam and Antwerp, Le Havre, Southampton and Bilbao, round trip about 51 days, US$3,040-5,400, also from Genoa to Paranaguá, Santos and Rio for US$1,100-1,400 (round trip or southbound only, no northbound-only passages). A number of German container ships sail the year round to the east coast of South America: Felixstowe, Hamburg, Antwerp, Bilbao or Algeciras, Santos, Buenos Aires, Montevideo, Rio Grande do Sul, Itajaí, Santos, Rio de Janeiro, Rotterdam, Felixstowe (about 45 days, £3,100-3,500 per person round trip). Four German vessels make a 49-day round trip: Tilbury, Hamburg, Antwerp, Le Havre, Suape, Rio de Janeiro, Santos, Buenos Aires, Montevideo, São Francisco do Sul, Paranaguá, Santos, Suape, Rotterdam, Tilbury. There are also German sailings from Genoa or Livorno (Italy), or Spain to the east coast of South America.

There is an 8% tax on international shipping line tickets bought in Brazil.

A cheaper option is **Polish Ocean Line**'s services to the east coast, Gdynia to Buenos Aires, Montevideo and Santos (2-2½ months).

From the USA, **Maritime Reederei** of Germany sails to Charleston, Miami, Puerto Cabello, Santos, Buenos Aires, Montevideo, Rio Grande do Sul, Santos, Puerto Cabello, Freeport, New York, from £3,540 per person on a 42-day round trip. A German consortium has a 48-day round trip to New York, Savannah, Miami, Rio, Santos, Buenos Aires, Montevideo, Rio Grande do Sul, Santos, Salvador, Fortaleza, Norfolk, Philadelphia, New York, £4,020 per person (one-way to Rio, 15 days £1,395).

Enquiries regarding passages should be made through agencies in your own country, or through John Alton of **Strand Voyages** ⓘ *Charing Cross Shopping Concourse, The Strand, London WC2N 4HZ, T020-78366363, F74970078*. Strand Voyages are booking agents for all the above. Advice can also be obtained from **Cargo Ship Voyages Ltd** ⓘ *Hemley, Woodbridge, Suffolk IP12 4QF, T/F01473-736265*. Also in London are **The Cruise People** ⓘ *88 York St W1H 1DP, T020-77232450, reservations 0800-526313*. In continental Europe, contact **Wagner Frachtschiffreisen** ⓘ *Stadlerstrasse 48, CH-8404, Winterthur, Switzerland, T052-2421442, F2421487*. In the USA, contact **Freighter World Cruises** ⓘ *180 South Lake Ave, Pasadena, CA 91101, T818-4493106*, **Traveltips Cruise and Freighter Travel Association** ⓘ *163-07 Depot Rd, PO Box 188, Flushing, NY 11358, T800-8728584*, or **Maris Freighter Travel Inc** ⓘ *215 Main St, Westport, CT06880-3210, T1-800-9962747*. It is not possible to get a passage on a non-passenger-carrying cargo ship to South America from a European port.

River

A popular entry point to the Amazon region is along the Rio Amazonas from Iquitos in Peru to Tabatinga in Brazil. Onward travel is then by river boat or air to Manaus. This border can also be crossed by land from Leticia in Colombia. Security is particularly tight on this triple border and there have been reports that Brazilian immigration often refuse to allow entry to Brazil for more than 30 days.

Road

International buses

There are good road connections between Argentina, Paraguay, Uruguay and the South of Brazil. Rio de Janeiro and São Paulo can easily be reached by international buses from Asunción, Buenos Aires, Santiago and Montevideo. Transport is not so easy in the north and west of the country, although a reasonable road now exists between Caracas and Manaus. Entry from Bolivia at Corumbá is fairly straightforward. Buses from here connect with the main Brazilian road system at Campo Grande. Other border crossings from French Guiana at Oiapoque and from Guyana at Bonfim require some effort to actually get to the Brazilian border. Once there, bus services are frequent, although heavy rains may make for slow going and can cause cancellations.

Driving

Foreign driving licences are acceptable in Brazil, although it may be worth taking an international licence as not all officials and rental companies are able to recognize foreign licences. If requested, tourists driving in Brazil should be able to present their licence and a passport to the police. Road accidents should be reported to the department of transport, **Detran** ⓘ *Av Presidente Vargas 817, 2nd floor, Rio de Janeiro, T5509744*.

There are agreements between Brazil and all South American countries (but check in the case of Bolivia) whereby a car can be taken into Brazil (or a Brazilian car out of Brazil) for a period of 90 days without any special documents; an extension of up to 90 days is granted by the Customs authorities on presentation of the paper received at the border, which must be retained; this may be done at most Customs posts and at the **Serviço de Controle Aduaneiro** ⓘ *Ministério da Fazenda, Av Presidente Antônio Carlos, Sala 1129, Rio de Janeiro*.

For cars registered in other countries, the requirements are proof of ownership and/or registration in the home country and valid driving licence (see above). A 90-day permit is given by Customs and procedure is very straightforward. Nevertheless, it is better to cross the border into Brazil when it is officially open because an official who knows all about the entry of cars is then present. You must specify which border station you intend to leave by, but application can be made to the Customs to change this.

Touching down

Airport information

For most visitors the point of arrival will either be **Tom Jobim international airport** (also known as **Galeão**) on the Ilha do Governador, some 16 km from the centre of Rio de Janeiro, or **Cumbica International Airport** at Guarulhos in São Paulo. Details of other entry airports are given in their respective sections. Make sure you arrive two hours before international flights and it is wise to reconfirm your flight as departure times may have changed. ➤➤ *See also pages 78 and 200 for detailed airport information in Rio de Janeiro and São Paulo respectively.*

Airport departure tax

The amount of tax depends on the class of airport. All airports charge R$69.50 (US$36) international departure tax. First class airports charge R$9.50 domestic tax; second class airports R$7; domestic rates are lower still in third and fourth class airports. Tax must be paid on checking in, in *reais* or US dollars. Tax is waived if you stay in Brazil less than 24 hours.

Tourist information

Embratur, the Brazilian Tourist Board, is at Setor Comercial Norte, Quadra 02, Bloco G, Brasília, DF, CEP 70710-500, Brazil, ToXX61-3289100, www.embratur.gov.br. Embratur also has an office in Rio de Janeiro at Rua Uruguaiana 174, 8 andar, Rio de Janeiro, RJ, CEP 20050-090, ToXX21-5096017, rio@embratur.gov.br. See also Tours and tour operators (page 23) for a list of specialist agencies operating from both inside and outside of Brazil.

Details of state and municipal tourist offices are given in the Essentials section of the respective towns and cities. They are not usually too helpful regarding information on cheap hotels. It is also difficult to get information on neighbouring states.

National parks are run by **Ibama**, the Instituto Brasileiro do Meio Ambiente e dos Recursos Naturais Renováveis (Brazilian Institute of Environmental Protection) ⓘ *SAIN, Avenida L-4, bloco B, Térreo, Edifiço Sede de Ibama, CEP 70800-200, Brasília, DF, ToXX61-226 8221/9014, www.ibama.gov.br*. The Institute is under-funded, often under-staffed and visitors may find it difficult to obtain information. National parks are open to visitors, usually with a permit from Ibama. For further details, see individual parks in the text. ➤➤ *See page 55 for an explanation of phone codes in Brazil.*

Touching down

Official time Brazil has four time zones: Brazilian standard time is three hours behind GMT; the Amazon time zone (Pará west of the Rio Xingu, Amazonas, Roraima, Rondônia, Mato Grosso and Mato Grosso do Sul) is four hours behind GMT; the State of Acre is five hours behind GMT; the Fernando de Noronha archipelago is two hours behind GMT. Clocks move forward one hour in summer for approximately five months (usually between October and February or March), but times of change vary. This does not apply to Acre.

IDD code 55.

Business hours Generally 0900-1800 Monday-Friday; closed for lunch some time between 1130 and 1400. Shops are open on Saturday till 1230 or 1300. Government offices: 1100-1800 Monday-Friday. Banks: 1000-1600 or 1630, closed on Saturday.

Voltage Generally 110 V 60 cycles AC, but in some cities and areas 220 V 60 cycles AC is used.

Weights and measures The metric system is used by all.

Local customs and laws

Clothing

In general, clothing requirements in Brazil are less formal than in the Hispanic countries. It is, however, advisable for men visiting restaurants to wear long trousers (women in shorts may also be refused entry) and jackets or pullovers in São Paulo. As a general rule, it is better not to wear shorts in official buildings, cinemas, interstate buses and on flights.

Colour

Racial discrimination is illegal in Brazil. There is, however, a complex class system which is informed both by heritage and by economic status. This effectively discriminates against the poor, who are chiefly (but by no means exclusively) black. There are very few black role models, television is dominated by white actors and there is no visible black political movement. In Salvador, where 80% of the population is black, television coverage still manages to be limited to white participants. Black visitors to the country may encounter racial prejudice. A surprising number of Brazilians are unaware that black Europeans exist, so you could become the focus of curiosity.

Conduct

Men should avoid arguments or insults (care is needed even when overtaking on the road); pride may be defended with a gun. Gay men, while still enjoying greater freedom than in many countries, should exercise reasonable discretion. It is normal for men to stare and comment on a woman's appearance, and if you happen to look different or to be travelling alone, you will undoubtedly attract attention. Be aware that Brazilian men can be extremely persistent, and very easily encouraged; it is safest to err on the side of caution until you are accustomed.

Prohibitions

Despite the wide distribution and use of drugs such as marijuana and cocaine, they are still illegal and you will face a heavy sentence if you are caught with them. Be especially aware when crossing borders and on no account bring coca leaves from Bolivia. A campaign against the exploitation of minors for sexual purposes gained wide publicity in 1997 (in Brazilian law a minor is considered to be under the age of

18). Although the local bikinis leave little to the imagination you will be prosecuted for nude bathing except on an official nudist beach of which there are very few. Never carry firearms; their possession could land you in serious trouble.

Time-keeping

Brazilians have a very 'relaxed' attitude towards time. It is quite normal for them to arrive an hour or so late even for business appointments. If you expect to meet someone more or less at an exact time, you can add *'em punto'* or *'a hora inglesa'* (English time) but be prepared to wait anyway.

Tipping

Tipping is usual, but less costly than in most other countries, that is except for porters. In restaurants, tip 10% of bill if no service charge is added, but give a small tip anyway if it is. Taxi drivers are not tipped. Give a small tip to cloakroom attendants; none to cinema usherettes; 10-15% to hairdressers; about US$0.50 per item for airport porters.

Responsible tourism

Travel to the furthest corners of the globe is now commonplace and the mass movement of people for leisure and business is a major source of foreign exchange and economic development in many parts of South America. The benefits of international travel are self-evident for both hosts and travellers – employment, increased understanding of different cultures, business and leisure opportunities. At the same time there is clearly a downside to the industry. Where visitor pressure is high and/or poorly regulated, adverse impacts on society and the natural environment may be apparent. Paradoxically, this is as true in undeveloped and pristine areas (where culture and the natural environment are less 'prepared' for even small numbers of visitors) as it is in major resort destinations.

The travel industry is growing rapidly and increasingly the impacts of this supposedly 'smokeless' industry are becoming apparent. These impacts can seem remote and unrelated to an individual trip or holiday (eg air travel is clearly implicated in global warming and damage to the ozone layer, resort location and construction can destroy natural habitats and restrict traditional rights and activities), but individual choice and awareness can make a difference in many instances (see box, page 44), and collectively, travellers are having a significant effect in shaping a more responsible and sustainable industry.

In an attempt to promote awareness of and credibility for responsible tourism, organizations such as **Green Globe** ⓘ *T020-79308333, greenglobe@compuserve.com* and the **Center for Environmentally Sustainable Tourism (CERT)** ⓘ *T01268-795772*, in the UK now offer advice on destinations and sites that have achieved certain commitments to conservation and sustainable development. Generally these are larger mainstream destinations and resorts, but they are still a useful guide and increasingly aim to provide information on smaller operations.

Of course travel can also have beneficial impacts and this is something to which every traveller can contribute – many national parks are part funded by receipts from visitors. Similarly, travellers can promote patronage and protection of important archaeological sites and heritage through their interest and contributions via entrance fees. They can also support small-scale enterprises by staying in locally run hotels and hostels, eating in local restaurants and by purchasing local goods, supplies and arts and crafts.

In fact, since the Responsible Travel section was first introduced in the *South American Handbook* in 1992 there has been a phenomenal growth in tourism that

How big is your footprint?

- Where possible choose a destination, tour operator or hotel with a proven ethical and environmental commitment – if in doubt ask.
- Spend money on locally produced (rather than imported) goods and services and use common sense when bargaining – your few dollars saved may be a week's salary to others.
- Use water and electricity carefully – travellers may receive preferential supply while the needs of local communities are overlooked.
- Learn about local etiquette and culture – consider local norms and behaviour and dress appropriately for local cultures and situations.
- Protect wildlife and other natural resources – don't buy souvenirs or goods made from wildlife unless they are clearly sustainably produced and are not protected under CITES legislation (CITES controls trade in endangered species).
- Always ask before taking photographs or videos of people.
- Consider staying in local rather than foreign-owned accommodation – the economic benefits for host communities are far greater, as are the opportunities to learn about local culture.

promotes and supports the conservation of natural environments and is also fair and equitable to local communities. This ecotourism segment is probably the fastest-growing sector of the travel industry and provides a vast and growing range of destinations and activities in South America. For example, the **Una Ecopark** ⓘ *T/FoXX73-6341118, Vrisea@bitsnet.com.br*, in Bahia offers visits and experiences in Brazil's Atlantic forest (one of the most endangered ecosystems in the world). A visit to the park provides opportunities to undertake walks in the forest canopy walkway suspended high above the forest floor. Other initiatives can be found in São Paulo state (amazonadv@aol.com).

While the authenticity of some ecotourism operators' claims need to be interpreted with care, there is clearly both a huge demand for this type of activity and also significant opportunities to support worthwhile conservation and social development initiatives.

Organizations such as **Conservation International** ⓘ *T202-4295660, www.ecotour.org*, the **Eco-Tourism Society** ⓘ *T802-4472121, www.ecotourism.org*, **Planeta** ⓘ *www2.planeta.com/mader*, and the UK-based **Tourism Concern** ⓘ *T020-77533330, www.gn.apc.org/tourismconcern*, have begun to develop and/or promote ecotourism projects and destinations and their websites are an excellent source of information and details for sites and initiatives throughout South America. Additionally, UK organizations such as **Earthwatch** ⓘ *T01865-311601, www.earthwatch.org*, and **Discovery International** ⓘ *T020-72299881, www.discoveryinitiatives.com*, offer opportunities to participate directly in scientific research and development projects throughout the region. ▸▸ *See also Ecotourism, page 64 and box, page 721.*

Safety

Although Brazil's big cities suffer high rates of violent crime, this is mostly confined to the *favelas* where poverty and drugs are the main cause. Visitors should not enter *favelas* except when accompanied by workers for NGOs, tour groups or other people who know the local residents well and are accepted by the community. Visitors may be targets of theft, but if you don't take anything you aren't prepared to lose and insure yourself adequately, it should not ruin your trip. If the worst does happen and you are threatened, don't panic, and hand over your valuables. Do not resist, but report the crime to the local tourist police later. It is extremely rare for a tourist to be hurt during a robbery in Brazil. Being aware of the dangers, acting confidently and using your common sense, will reduce many of the risks.

Certain parts of the country are areas of drug cultivation and should be avoided. These are mentioned where appropriate in the travelling text. All border areas should be regarded with some caution because of smuggling activities. Violence over land ownership in parts of the interior have resulted in a 'Wild West' atmosphere in some towns which should therefore be passed through quickly. Red-light districts should also be given a wide berth as there are reports of drinks being drugged with a substance popularly known as 'Good night Cinderella'. This leaves the victim easily amenable to having their possessions stolen, or worse.

Avoiding con tricks

Never trust anyone telling sob stories or offering 'safe rooms', and when looking for a hotel, always choose the room yourself. Be wary of 'plain-clothes policemen'; insist on seeing identification and on going to the police station by main roads. Do not hand over your identification (or money) until you are at the station. On no account take them directly back to your hotel. Be even more suspicious if they seek confirmation of their status from a passer-by.

Hotel security

Hotel safe deposits are generally, but not always, secure. If you cannot get a receipt for valuables in a hotel safe, you can seal the contents in a plastic bag and sign across the seal. Always keep an inventory of what you have deposited. If you don't trust the hotel, lock everything in your pack and secure it in your room when you go out. If you lose valuables, report to the police and note details of the report for insurance purposes.

Police

There are several types of police: **Polícia Federal,** civilian dressed, who handle all federal law duties, including immigration. A subdivision is the **Polícia Federal Rodoviária,** uniformed, who are the traffic police on federal highways. **Polícia Militar** are the uniformed, street police force, under the control of the state governor, handling all state laws. They are not the same as the Armed Forces' Internal police. **Polícia Civil,** also state-controlled, handle local laws and investigations. They are usually in civilian dress, unless in the traffic division. In cities, the **Prefeitura** controls the Guarda Municipal, who handle security. Tourist police operate in places with a strong tourist presence. In case of difficulty, visitors should seek them out in the first instance.

Protecting money and valuables

Apart from the obvious precautions of not wearing jewellery (wear a cheap, plastic, digital watch), take local advice about safety and do not assume that daytime is safer than night. If walking after dark, walk in the road, not on the pavement/sidewalk and do not go on to the beach. Don't take valuables to the beach.

Photocopy your passport, air ticket and other documents, make a record of travellers' cheque and credit card numbers. Keep them separately from the originals and leave another set of records at home. Keep all documents secure; hide your main cash supply in different places or under your clothes. Extra pockets sewn inside shirts and trousers, moneybelts (best worn below the waist), neck or leg pouches and elasticated support bandages for keeping money above the elbow or below the knee have been repeatedly recommended (the last by John Hatt in *The Tropical Traveller*).

Public transport

When you have all your luggage with you at a bus or railway station, be especially careful and carry any shoulder bags in front of you. To be extra safe, take a taxi between airport/bus station/railway station and hotel, keep your bags with you and pay only when you and your luggage are outside; avoid night buses and arriving at your destination at night.

Rape

This can happen anywhere in the world. If you are the victim of a sexual assault, you are advised firstly to contact a doctor (this can be your home doctor if you prefer). You will need tests to determine whether you have contracted any sexually transmitted diseases; you may also need advice on post-coital contraception. You should also contact your embassy, where consular staff are very willing to help in cases of assault.

Women travellers

These additional hints have mainly been supplied by women, but most apply to any single traveller. When you set out, err on the side of caution until your instincts have adjusted to the customs of a new culture. Be prepared for the exceptional curiosity extended to visitors, especially women and try not to overreact. If, as a single woman, you can befriend a local woman, you will learn much more about the country you are visiting. There is a definite 'gringo trail' which you can follow which can be helpful when looking for safe accommodation, especially if arriving after dark (which is best avoided). Remember that for a single woman a taxi at night can be as dangerous as wandering around on your own. It is easier for men to take the friendliness of locals at face value; women may be subject to unwanted attention. Do not disclose to strangers where you are staying. By wearing a wedding ring and saying that your 'husband' is close at hand, you may dissuade an aspiring suitor. If politeness fails, do not feel bad about showing offence and departing. A good rule is always to act with confidence, as though you know where you are going, even if you do not. Someone who looks lost is more likely to attract unwanted attention.

Sleeping

Hotels

Unless travelling in high season, always ask for a discount, especially if staying for more than one night. The best guide to hotels in Brazil is the *Guia Brasil Quatro Rodas*, with good maps of towns. Motels are specifically intended for very short-stay couples: there is no stigma attached and they usually offer good value (the rate for a full night is called the *pernoite*), though the decor can be a little unsettling. The type known as *hotel familiar*, to be found in the interior – large meals, communal washing, hammocks for children – is much cheaper, but only for the enterprising. *Pousadas* are the equivalent of bed-and-breakfast, often small and family run, although some are very sophisticated and correspondingly priced. Usually hotel prices include breakfast; there is no reduction if you don't eat it. In the better hotels (our category **A** and upwards), the breakfast is well worth eating: rolls, ham, eggs, cheese, cakes, fruit. Normally the *apartamento* is a room with a bath; a *quarto* is a room without a bath. Leave rooms in good time so frigobar bills can be checked.

For a quick reference price guide to our hotel categories, see inside the front cover.

The star rating system for hotels (five-star hotels are not price controlled) is not the standard used in North America or Europe.

Hotel prices and facilities

Prices include taxes and service charges, but are without meals unless otherwise stated. They are based on a double room, except in the **E** and **F** ranges where prices are almost always per person.

LL (over US$150) to **AL** (US$66-99) Hotels in these categories can be found in most of the large cities in Brazil, but especially in areas with a strong concentration of tourists or business travellers. They should offer pool, sauna, gym, jacuzzi, all business facilities (including email), several restaurants and bars. A safe box is usually provided in each room. In cities such as São Paulo and Rio de Janeiro the top hotels compare with the highest standards in the world, although service can sometimes still be very Brazilian.

A (US$46-65) and **B** (US$31-45) Hotels in these categories should provide more than the standard facilities and a fair degree of comfort. Most include a good breakfast and many offer extras such as colour TV, minibar, a/c and a swimming pool. They may also provide tourist information and their own transport for airport pick-ups. Service is generally good and most accept credit cards, although a lower rate for cash is often offered.

C (US$21-30) and **D** (US$12-20) Hotels in these categories range from very comfortable to functional and there are some real bargains to be had. You should expect your own bathroom, constant hot water, a towel, soap and toilet paper. There is sometimes a restaurant and a communal sitting area. In tropical regions rooms are usually equipped with a/c, although this may be rather old. Hotels used to catering for foreign tourists and backpackers often have luggage storage, money exchange and kitchen facilities.

E (US$7-11) and **F** (US$6 and under) Hotels in these categories are often extremely simple with bedside or ceiling fans, shared bathrooms and little in the way of furniture. Breakfast, when included, is very simple, usually no more than a bread roll and coffee. The best accommodation and facilities for under US$10 per night is generally found in the youth hostels, although tourist areas with high quantities of bed spaces such as Porto Seguro often have good quality rooms at this price during low season.

Business visitors are strongly recommended to book accommodation in advance, and this can easily be done for Rio or São Paulo hotels with representation abroad. **Varig** has a good hotel reservation service, with discounts of up to 50% for its passengers.

It's a good idea to book accommodation in advance in small towns which are popular at weekends with city dwellers (eg near São Paulo and Rio de Janeiro).

Roteiros de Charme, in some 30 locations in the Southeast and Northeast, is an association of hotels and *pousadas* which aims to give a high standard of accommodation in establishments which represent the town they are in. It is a private initiative. If you are travelling in the appropriate budget range (our **A** price range upwards), you can plan an itinerary which takes in these high-class hotels, with a reputation for comfort and good food, and some fine places of historical and leisure interest. Roteiros de Charme hotels are listed in the text and any one of them can provide information on the group. Alternatively, contact the office in the **Caesar Park Hotel** ⓘ *Av Vieira Souto 460, Ipanema, Rio de Janeiro, F021-2871592, www.roteirosdecharme.com.br.*

Advice and suggestions

1 The service stations (*postos*) and hostels (*dormitórios*) along the main roads provide excellent value in room and food, akin to truck-driver type accommodation in Europe, for those on a tight budget.

2 The electric showers used in many hotels should be checked for obvious flaws in the wiring; try not to touch the rose while it is producing hot water.

3 Some taxi drivers will try to take you to the expensive hotels, who pay them commission for bringing in custom. Beware!

4 Cockroaches are ubiquitous and unpleasant, but not dangerous. Take some insecticide powder if staying in cheap hotels; **Baygon** (Bayer) has been recommended. Stuff toilet paper in any holes in walls that you suspect of being parts of cockroach runs.

5 Away from the main commercial centres, many hotels, restaurants and bars have inadequate water supplies. Almost without exception, used toilet paper should not be flushed down the pan, but placed in the receptacle provided. This applies even in quite expensive hotels. Failing to observe this custom will block the pan or drain.

Youth hostels

For information about youth hostels contact **Federação Brasileira dos Albergues da Juventude** ① *R dos Andradas 1137, conj 214, Porto Alegre, Rio Grande do Sul, CEP 90.020-007, www.albergues.com.br*; its annual book provides a full list of good value accommodation, with the addresses of the regional representatives. Also see the **Internet Guide to Hostelling** which has a list of Brazilian youth hostels, www.hostels.com/br.html.

Low-budget travellers with student cards (photograph needed) can often use the **Casa dos Estudantes** (CEU) network.

Camping

Members of the Camping Clube do Brasil or those with an international campers' card pay only half the rate of a non-member, which is US$10-15 per person. The Clube has 43 sites in 13 states and 80,000 members. For enquiries, **Camping Clube do Brasil** ① *Divisão de Campings, R Senador Dantas 75, 29th floor, Centro, Rio de Janeiro, CEP 20037-900, ToXX21-2103171*. It may be difficult to get into some Camping Clube campsites during the high season (January to February). Private campsites charge about US$8 per person. For those on a very low budget and in isolated areas where there is no campsite, service stations can be used as camping sites (Shell stations recommended); they have shower facilities, watchmen and food; some have dormitories; truck drivers are a mine of information. There are also various municipal sites. Campsites often tend to be some distance from public transport routes and are better suited to those with their own transport. Never camp at the side of a road; wild camping is generally not possible.

Good camping equipment may be purchased in Brazil and there are several rental companies. Camping gas cartridges are easy to buy in sizeable towns in the South, eg in HM shops. *Guia de Camping* is produced by **Artpress** ① *R Araçatuba 487, São Paulo 05058*; it lists most sites and is available in bookshops in most cities. **Quatro Rodas'** *Guia Brasil* also lists main campsites.

Homestays

Experiment in International Living Ltd ① *287 Worcester Rd, Malvern, Worcestershire WR14 1AB, T01684-562577, F562212*, or **Friesdorferstrasse** ① *194A, 53175 Bonn 9, T0228-957220, F358282*, can arrange stays with families from one to four weeks in Brazil; EIL has offices in 38 countries. This has been recommended as an excellent way to meet people and learn the language.

Getting around

Public transport in Brazil is very efficient, especially compared to other South American countries. The main issue is the distances involved. Most visitors will find themselves travelling by buses and planes, except in the Amazon when a boat is often the only way to get around. Train routes are practically non-existent, car hire is expensive and hitchhiking not widely accepted. Taxis are very reasonable and easy to come by.

Air

Because of the size of the country, flying is often the most practical option and internal air services are highly developed. The larger cities are linked with each other several times a day and all national airlines offer excellent service. Internal flights used to be expensive, but recent deregulation of the airlines has reduced prices on some routes by about a third (although flights to and from the Amazon remain the most costly). In addition, no-frills airlines have been set up, offering fares that can be as cheap as travelling by bus. Gol is the main bargain airline; **BRA, Trip** and **ATA** are the three others. The largest airlines are **TAM, Varig** and **Vasp. Rio-Sul**and **Nordeste** (both allied to **Varig**), have extensive networks. Smaller airlines include **Penta**, who have recently built up a wide and cheap network throughout the Amazon region, and **Pantanal**, mainly operating flights between São Paulo state and Mato Grosso do Sul.

Double check all bookings and information given by ground staff. National toll-free numbers (except for **Gol**, which charges) for reservations and confirmations are detailed below. Most websites provide full information, including a booking service, although not all are in English. ▸▸ *For addresses and telephone numbers of airline offices, see directory of individual towns.*

Domestic airlines

Gol T0300 7892121 (US$0.10 per min), English-speaking operators, www.voegol.com.br, website in Portuguese only.
Nordeste T0800-992004, www.nordeste.com.
Pantanal T0800-125833, www.pantanal-airlines.com.br.
Rio-Sul T0800-992004, www.rio-sul.com.
TAM T0800-123100, www.tam.com.br.
Transbrasil T0800-151151, www.transbrasil.com.br.
Trip T0800-7018747; www.voetrip.com.br.
Varig T0800-997000, T0845-6037601 (UK), www.varig.com.br.
Vasp T0800-998277, www.vasp.com.br.

Airpasses

TAM, Varig and **Vasp** offer 21-day air passes for people resident outside of Brazil, but since deregulation they are not as good value as they used to be. They also offer limited flexibility; you must buy your airpass outside of Brazil in conjunction with an international scheduled flight and decide your itinerary at the time of purchase. There are no discounts for children and infants pay 10% of the price.

The **Varig Airpass** is US$530 for five flights, with a maximum of four extra coupons available for US$100 each and valid for 21 days. Amendments may be made once prior to commencement of travel at US$30 per change. The **Varig** pass is only available to travellers arriving in Brazil with **Varig** or **British Airways**.

The **Vasp Airpass** is valid for 21 days and costs US$440 for five flights with a maximum of four extra coupons available for US$100 each which must be bought with the airpass. It is available to anyone purchasing an international flight on any airline.

Like the Vasp airpass, the **TAM Airpass** allows you to arrive in Brazil on any airline. It costs US$530, is valid for 21 days and re-routing is permitted for US$50.

With airpasses, no journey may be repeated and none may be used on the Rio-São Paulo shuttle. Remember that domestic airport tax has to be paid at each departure. Hotels in the **Tropical** and **Othon** chains, and others, offer discounts of 10% to **Varig** airpass travellers. Promotions on certain destinations offer a free flight, hotel room, etc; enquire when buying the airpass. Converting the voucher can take some hours, do not plan an onward flight immediately, check at terminals that the airpass is still registered, faulty cancellations have been reported. Cost and restrictions on the airpass are subject to change.

Small scheduled domestic airlines operate Brazilian-built *bandeirante*, 16-seater prop-jets, into virtually every city and town with any semblance of an airstrip. Internal flights often have many stops and are therefore quite slow. Most airports have left-luggage lockers (US$2 for 24 hours). Seats are often unallocated on internal flights; board in good time.

Road

Though the best paved highways are heavily concentrated in the Southeast, those serving the interior are being improved to all-weather status and many are paved. Brazil has over 1,650, 000 km of highways, of which 150,000 km are paved, and several thousand are all-weather. Most main roads between principal cities are paved. Some are narrow and therefore dangerous and many are in poor condition.

Bus

There are three standards of bus: *Comum*, or *Convencional* are quite slow, not very comfortable and fill up quickly; *Executivo* are more expensive, comfortable (many have reclining seats), and don't stop en route to pick up passengers so are safer. *Leito* (literally, bed) run at night between the main centres, offering reclining seats with leg rests, toilets, and sometimes refreshments, at double the normal fare. For journeys over 100 km, most buses have chemical toilets (bring toilet paper). Air conditioning can make buses cold at night, so take a blanket or sweater; on some services blankets are supplied.

Buses stop fairly frequently (every two to four hours) at *postos* for snacks. Bus stations for interstate services and other long distance routes are usually called rodoviárias. They are frequently outside the city centres and offer snack bars, lavatories, left-luggage stores (*guarda volume*), local bus services and information centres. Buy bus tickets at rodoviárias (most now take credit cards), not from travel agents who add on surcharges. Reliable bus information is hard to come by, other than from companies themselves. Buses usually arrive and depart in very good time. Many town buses have turnstiles which can be inconvenient if you are carrying a large pack. Urban buses normally serve local airports.

Taxi

Rates vary from city to city, but are consistent within each city. At the outset, make sure the meter is cleared and shows 'tariff 1', except (usually) from 2300-0600, Sunday, and in December when '2' is permitted. Check that the meter is working; if not, fix the price in advance. The **radio taxi** service costs about 50% more but cheating is less likely. Taxis outside larger hotels usually cost twice as much. If you are seriously cheated note the number of the taxi and insist on a signed bill; threatening to take it to the police can work. **Moto-taxis** are much more economical, but many are unlicensed and there have been a number of robberies of passengers.

Car

Any foreigner with a passport can purchase a Brazilian car and travel outside Brazil. A letter in Spanish from your consul explaining your aims and that you will return the vehicle to Brazil can make life much easier at borders and check points. Foreigners do not need the CPF tax document (needed by Brazilians), and the official purchase receipt is accepted as proof of ownership. Don't buy an alcohol-driven car if you propose to drive outside Brazil. It is essential to have an external intake filter fitted, or dust can rapidly destroy an engine. VW kombi vans are cheapest in Brazil where they are made, they are equivalent to the pre-1979 model in Europe. If a lot of time is to be spent on dirt roads, the Ford Chevrolet pick-up is more robust.

Fuel It is virtually impossible to buy premium grades of petrol/gasoline anywhere. With alcohol fuel you need about 50% more alcohol than regular gasoline. Larger cars have a small extra tank for 'gasolina' to get the engine started; remember to keep this topped up. Fuel is only 85% octane (owing to high methanol content), so be prepared for bad consumption and poor performance and starting difficulties in non-Brazilian cars in winter. Diesel fuel is cheap and a diesel engine may provide fewer maintenance problems. Very few service stations open during Carnival week. Fuel prices vary from week to week and region to region: ordinary petrol, *gasolina comun*, is around US$1 per litre; *alcool comun* and diesel are cheaper. There is no unleaded fuel.

Preparation It's well worth installing extra heavy-duty shock-absorbers (such as Spax or Koni). Fit tubes on 'tubeless' tyres, since air plugs for tubeless tyres are hard to find, and if you bend the rim on a pothole, the tyre will not hold air. Take spare tubes, an extra spare tyre, spare plugs, fan-belts, radiator hoses and headlamp bulbs. Find out about your car's electrics and filters and what spares may be required. Similarly, know how to handle problems arising from dirty fuel. Take a 10-litre water container for self and vehicle. Note that in some areas gas stations are few and far between.

Security Spare no ingenuity in making your car secure. Try never to leave the car unattended except in a locked garage or guarded parking space. Remove all belongings and leave the empty glove compartment open. Also lock the clutch or accelerator to the steering wheel with a heavy, obvious chain or lock. Adult minders or street children will generally protect your car fiercely in exchange for a tip.

Documents Be very careful to keep *all* the papers you are given when you enter, to produce when you leave.

Insurance against accident and theft is very expensive. If the car is stolen or written off you will be required to pay very high import duty on its value. The legally required minimum cover for third party insurance is not expensive. If anyone is hurt, do not pick them up as you may become liable.

Car hire

Renting a car in Brazil is expensive – the cheapest rate for unlimited mileage for a small car is about US$50 per day. The minimum age is 21 and it is essential to have a credit card. Companies operate under the names *aluguel de automóveis* or *autolocadores*. Toll free numbers for nationwide firms are **Avis** ⓘ *T0800-558066* and **Localiza** ⓘ *T0800-992000, www.localiza.com.br*. Details of local companies are given in the text.

Car hire insurance Check exactly what the hirer's insurance policy covers. In many cases it will not apply to major accidents, or 'natural' damage (eg flooding). Ask if extra cover is available. Sometimes using a credit card automatically includes insurance. Beware of being billed for scratches which were on the vehicle before you hired it. » *See Driving, page 40, for required documents.*

Motorcycling

The machine you use should be off-road capable, eg the BMW R80/100/GS for its rugged and simple design and reliable shaft drive. A road bike can go most places an off-road bike can go, at the cost of greater effort.

Preparation Many roads are rough. Fit heavy-duty front fork springs, the best quality rebuildable shock absorber you can afford (Ohlins, White Power) and lockable luggage such as Krausers (reinforce luggage frames). A large capacity fuel tank (Acerbis), +300 mile/480 km range is essential if going off the beaten track. A washable air filter is a good idea (K&N), also fuel filters and fueltap rubber seals, a good set of trails-type tyres, as well as a high mudguard. Get to know the bike before you go, ask the dealers in your country what goes wrong with it and arrange a link whereby you can get parts flown out to you. If using a fully enclosed chaincase on a chain-driven bike, an automatic chain oiler is a good idea. The **Scott-Oiler** (106 Clober Road, Milngavie, Glasgow G62 7SS, Scotland) has been recommended. Fill it with Sae 90 oil. A hefty bash plate/sump guard is invaluable. A first-class tool kit is a must and if riding a bike with a chain then a spare set of sprockets and an 'o' ring chain should be carried. Parts are few and far between, but mechanics are skilled at making do and can usually repair things.

Security Try not to leave a fully laden bike on its own. An Abus D or chain will keep the bike secure. A cheap alarm can give you peace of mind. Look for hotels with a courtyard or secure parking and never leave luggage on the bike whilst unattended.

Documents Passport, International Driving Licence and bike registration document are necessary. Temporary import papers are given on entry, to be surrendered on leaving the country.

Cycling

A mountain bike is strongly recommended. The good quality ones (and the cast-iron rule is never to skimp on quality) are incredibly tough, with low gear ratios for difficult terrain, wide tyres with plenty of tread for good road-holding, cantilever brakes, and a low centre of gravity for improved stability. Although touring bikes – and to a lesser extent mountain bikes – and spares are available in the larger cities, most locally manufactured goods are shoddy and rarely last. Buy everything you possibly can before you leave home.

Equipment A small but comprehensive tool kit (to include chain rivet and crank removers, a spoke key and possibly a block remover), a spare tyre and inner tubes, a puncture repair kit with plenty of extra patches and glue, a set of brake blocks, brake and gear cables and all types of nuts and bolts, at least 12 spokes (best taped to the chain stay), a light oil for the chain (eg Finish-Line Teflon Dry-Lube), tube of waterproof grease, a pump secured by a pump lock, a Blackburn parking block (a most invaluable accessory, cheap and virtually weightless), a cyclometer, a loud bell, and a secure lock and chain. *Richard's Bicycle Book* makes useful reading for even the most mechanically minded.

Strong and waterproof front and back panniers are a must. When packed these are likely to be heavy and should be carried on the strongest racks available. Poor quality racks have ruined many a journey for they take incredible strain on unpaved roads. A top bag-cum-rucksack (eg Carradice) makes a good addition for use on and off the bike. A Cannondale front bag is good for maps, camera, compass, etc. (Other recommended panniers are Ortlieb – front and back – which is waterpoof and almost 'sandproof', Mac-Pac, Madden and Karimoor.) 'Gaffa' tape is excellent for protecting vulnerable parts of panniers and for carrying out all manner of repairs. Pack equipment and clothes in plastic bags to give extra protection against dust and rain.

Useful tips Wind, not hills, is the enemy of the cyclist. Avoid dehydration by drinking regularly and carry an ample supply of water. Give your bicycle a thorough daily check for loose nuts or bolts or bearings. See that all parts run smoothly. A good chain should last 3,200 km but keep it as clean as possible – an old toothbrush is good for this – and to oil it lightly from time to time. Traffic on main roads can be a nightmare; it is usually far more rewarding to keep to the smaller roads or to paths if they exist. A rearview mirror has been frequently recommended to forewarn you of vehicles which are too close behind. Also, watch out for oncoming, overtaking vehicles, unstable loads on trucks, protruding loads, etc. Make yourself conspicuous by wearing bright clothing and a helmet. Most towns have a bicycle shop of some description, but in an emergency it is amazing how one can improvise with wire, string, dental floss, nuts and bolts, odd pieces of tin or electrical 'Gaffa' tape!

The **Expedition Advisory Centre**, administered by the Royal Geographical Society, 1, Kensington Gore, London SW7 2AR, has published a useful monograph entitled *Bicycle Expeditions*, by Paul Vickers (March 1990), it is available direct from the Centre, price £6.50 (postage extra if outside the UK). In the UK there is also the **Cyclist's Touring Club** ⓘ *CTC, Cotterell House, 69 Meadrow, Godalming, Surrey GU7 3HS, T01483-417217, cycling@ctc.org.uk*, for touring and technical information.

Hitchhiking

Hitchhiking (*carona* in Portuguese) is difficult everywhere. This is partly because drivers are reluctant to give lifts because passengers are their responsibility. Try at the highway police check points on the main roads (but make sure your documents are in order) or at service stations (*postos*).

Boat

The main areas where travel by boat is practical (and often necessary) are the Amazon region, along the São Francisco River and along the Atlantic coast. There are also some limited transport services through the Pantanal. » *See also page 549 for details of river transport in the Amazon.*

Train

There are 30,379 km of railways which are not combined into a unified system. Brazil has two gauges and there is little transfer between them. Two more gauges exist for the isolated **Amapá** Railway and the tourist-only **São João del Rei** line. There are still passenger services in the state of São Paulo, but most passenger services have been withdrawn. Full details are given in the text.

Maps and guide books

A recommended series of general maps is published by **International Travel Maps** (ITM) ⓘ *345 West Broadway, Vancouver BC, V5Y 1P8, Canada, T604-8793621, F8794521*, compiled with historical notes, by the late Kevin Healey. Available are *South America*

South, *North East* and *North West* (1:4M), *Rio de Janeiro* (1:20,000). Also available is *New World Edition*, Bertelsmann, Neumarkter Strasse 18, 81673 München, Germany, *Mittelamerika, Südamerika Nord, Südamerika Sud, Brasilien* (all 1:4M). London's **Stanfords** ⓘ *12-14 Long Acre, Covent Garden, WC2E 9LP, UK, T020-78361321, www.stanfords.co.uk*, also sells a wide variety of guides and maps.

Quatro Rodas, a motoring magazine, publishes an excellent series of maps and guides in Portuguese and English from about US$10. Its annual *Guia Brasil* is a type of Michelin Guide to hotels, restaurants (not the cheapest), sights, facilities and general information on hundreds of cities and towns in the country, including good country and street maps. These guides can be purchased from street newspaper vendors throughout the country and at Av das Nações Unidas 7221, 14 andar, Pinheiros, CEP 05425-902, ToXX11-30376004, www.publiabril.com.br. *Quatro Rodas* guides may be bought in Europe from: 33, rue de Miromesnil, 75008 Paris, T00331-42663118, abrilparis@wanadoo.fr; and *Deltapress-Sociedade Distribuidora de Publicações*, Capa Rota, Tapada Nova, Linhó, 2710 Sintra, Portugal, T003511-9249940. In the USA: Lincoln Building, 60 East 42nd St, Suite 3403, New York, NY 10165/3403, T001212-5575990/3, abril@walrus.com.

Telephone yellow pages in most cities (but not Rio) contain good street maps which, together with the Quatro Rodas maps, are a great help for getting around.

Keeping in touch

Communications

Internet

Brazil is said to be seventh in the world in terms of internet use. Public internet access is available in all towns and cities and anywhere popular with tourists. There is usually an hourly charge of around US$3, but you can almost always use partial hours at a reduced rate. More and more hotels offer an internet service to their guests, while some government programmes even offer free use (notably in Manaus and Cuiaba). In some more remote locations, such as Lençios in Bahia, connections are so slow as to be almost pointless. For a regularly updated list of locations around the world, check www.netcafeguide.com.

The @ sign is known as ahoba in Brazil. For cybercafés see under Internet, in the Directory of individual towns.

Post

To send a **standard letter** or **postcard** to the USA costs US$0.75, to Europe US$0.85, to Australia or South Africa US$1. Air mail should take about seven days to or from Britain or the US. Franked and registered (insured) letters are normally secure, but check that the amount franked is what you have paid, or the item will not arrive. Aerogrammes are most reliable. To avoid queues and obtain higher denomination stamps go to the stamp desk at the main post office.

The post office sells cardboard boxes for sending **packages** internally and abroad. They must be submitted open; string and official sellotape are provided. You pay by the kilo and fill in a list of contents. Courier services such as **DHL, Federal Express** and **UPS** (recommended) are useful, but they may not necessarily operate under those names.

Postes Restantes usually only hold letters for 30 days. Identification is required and it's a good idea to write your name on a piece of paper to help the attendant find your letters. Charge is usually minimal but often involves queuing at another counter to buy stamps which are attached to your letter and franked before it is given to you. Poste Restante for Amex customers is dealt with by the Amex agents in most large towns.

Telephone

Important changes All ordinary phone numbers in Brazil are changing from seven-to eight-figure numbers. The process will last until 2005. Enquire locally for the new numbers as in many cases whole numbers will change while others will simply add an extra digit. Where confirmed, eight-digit numbers have been included in the text. A trunk dialling system (DDD) links all parts of Brazil. Recent privatization of the telephone system has led to increased competition. The consumer must now choose a telephone company for all calls by inserting a two-digit code between the zero and the area code. Phone numbers are now printed in this way: 0XX21 (0 for a national call, XX for the code of the phone company chosen, 21 for Rio de Janeiro, for example), followed by the seven- or eight-digit number of the subscriber.

For area codes see under individual towns, or look in the telephone directory.

Nationwide and international telephone operators and their codes are: **Embratel**, 21 (nationwide); **Telefônica**, 15 (state of São Paulo); **Telemar**, 31 (Alagoas, Amazonas, Amapá, Bahia, Ceará, Espírito Santo, Maranhão, most of Minas Gerais, Pará, Paraíba, Pernambuco, Piauí, Rio de Janeiro, Rio Grande do Norte, Roraima, Sergipe); **Tele Centro-Sul**, 14 (Acre, Goiás, Mato Grosso, Mato Grosso do Sul, Paraná, Rondônia, Santa Catarina, Tocantins and the cities of Brasília and Pelotas); **CTBC-Telecom**, 12 (some parts of Minas Gerais, Goiás, Mato Grosso do Sul and São Paulo state); **Intelig**, 23.

National calls Telephone boxes are easy to come by in towns and cities. Major cities have telephone kiosks, for both local and international calls (with an international calling card), in the shape of large orange shells, for which *fichas* can be bought from bars, cafés and newsvendors; in Rio they are known as *orelhões* (big ears). Local phone calls and telegrams are quite cheap.

Phone cards are available from telephone offices, newsstands, post offices and some chemists. They cost US$1.50 for 30 units and up to US$3 for 90 units. Public boxes for intercity calls are blue. To use the telephone office, tell the operator which city or country you wish to call, go to the booth whose number you are given; make your call and you will be billed on exit. Not all offices accept credit cards. Collect calls within Brazil can be made from any telephone – dial 9, followed by the number, and announce your name and city. Local calls from a private phone are normally free.

If you need to find a telephone number, you can dial 102 in any city (*auxílio à lista*) and the **operator** will connect you to a pre-recorded voice which will give the number. To find the number in a different city, dial the DDD code, followed by 121 (so, if you are in Salvador and want to know a Rio number, dial 021 121). If your Portuguese is not up to deciphering spoken numbers, ask a hotel receptionist, for example, to assist you.

International calls Make sure you buy at least one 90-unit card or pay at the desk after making your call from a booth. The rate to Europe is US$1-2 per minute, to USA around US$1 depending on which operator you use. Between 2000 and 0600, and all day Sunday, rates are normally reduced by about a fifth, although again this depends on which operator you use. **Embratel** offer a good service, covering most of the world, with very helpful English-speaking operators and international calls at less than a dollar a minute. Embratel cards are available from newsagents in large towns and cities, and have English instructions.

Brazil is linked to North America, Japan and most of Europe by trunk dialling (DDI). Codes are listed in the telephone directories. **Home Country Direct** is available from hotels, private phones or blue public phones to the following countries (prefix all numbers with 00080); Argentina 54, Australia 61, Belgium 03211, Bolivia 13, Canada 14, Chile 56 (**Entel**), 36 (**Chile Sat**), 37 (**CTC Mundo**), Colombia 57, Costa Rica 50, Denmark 45, France 33, Germany 49, Holland 31, Hong Kong 85212, Israel 97, Italy 39, Japan 81 (**KDD**), 83 (**ITJ**), 89 (**Super Japan**), Norway 47, Paraguay 18, Peru 51, Portugal

35, Singapore 65, Spain 34, Sweden 46, Switzerland 04112, UK 44 (**BT Direct**), USA 10 (**AT&T**), 12 (**MCI**), 16 (**Sprint**), 11 (**Worldcom**), Uruguay 59, Venezuela 58. For collect calls (*a cobrar*) from phone boxes, dial 107 and ask for the *telefonista internacional*. No collect calls are available to New Zealand.

Mobile phones Mobiles have made a big impact in Brazil owing to past difficulties in getting fixed lines, especially outside the main towns. When using a cellular telephone you do not drop the zero from the area code as you now have to when dialling from a fixed line. In Rio de Janeiro and São Paulo, mobile phones, or even a line for your own phone, can be hired. Pay-as-you-go phones are now available, which is another option for travellers. The systems in Brazil are mainly AMPS analog or TDMA digital.

Fax services These operate in main post offices in major cities, at telephone offices, or from private lines. Rates are around US$1.50 per page within Brazil, US$5 to Europe and the USA. To receive a fax costs US$1.40.

Media

Newspapers and magazines

There is no national newspaper although the news magazines (see below) are distributed nationally. The main papers in **Rio de Janeiro** are *Jornal do Brasil* (www.jb.com.br), *O Globo* (www.oglobo.com.br), *O Dia* (www.uol.com.br/odia) and *Jornal do Commércio* (www.jornaldocommercio.com.br). In **São Paulo** Morning: *O Estado de São Paulo* (www. estado.com.br), *Folha de São Paulo* (www.uol.com.br/fsp), *Gazeta Mercantil* (www.gazeta.com.br/) and *Diário de São Paulo*. Evening: *Jornal da Tarde*, *A Gazeta*, *Diário da Noite* and *Ultima Hora*. Around the country, the major cities have their own local press. Of particular note are *A Tarde* in **Salvador** (www.atarde.com.br), the *Diário de Pernambuco* in **Recife** (www.dpnet.com.br) and the *Estado de Minas* in **Belo Horizonte** (www.estaminas.com.br).

Foreign-language newspapers include *The Brazilian Post* and *Sunday News* in English, and *Deutsche Zeitung* in German. In Europe, the *Euro-Brasil Press* is available in most capitals; it prints Brazilian and some international news in Portuguese. London office: 23 Kings Exchange, Tileyard Rd, London N7 9AH, T020-77004033, F77003540, eurobrasilpress@compuserve.com

There are a number of good, informative weekly news magazines which are widely read: *Veja* (www.uol.com.br/veja), *Istoé* (www.uol.com.br/istoe), *Epoca* and *Exame*.

Television

Nationwide TV channels are *Globo* based in Rio de Janeiro and *SBT*, *Record*, *Bandeirantes* based in São Paulo. *Rede Amazônica* operates in the northern region. *TVE* is an educational channel showing documentaries and original-language films. Programming revolves around light entertainment, soap operas, foreign films dubbed in Portuguese and football.

Radio

South America has more local and community radio stations than practically anywhere else in the world; a shortwave (world band) radio offers a practical means to brush up on the language, sample popular culture and absorb some of the richly varied regional music. International broadcasters such as the *BBC World Service*, the *Voice of America* and Boston (Mass)-based *Monitor Radio International* (operated by **Christian Science Monitor**) keep the traveller abreast of news and events, in English, Portuguese and Spanish.

There are English-language radio broadcasts daily at 15290 kHz, 19 m Short Wave (Rádio Bras, Caixa Postal 04/0340, DF-70 323 Brasília).

Compact or miniature portables are recommended, with digital tuning and a full range of shortwave bands, as well as FM, long and medium wave. Detailed advice on radio models and wavelengths can be found in the annual publication, *Passport to World Band Radio* (Box 300, Penn's Park, PA 18943, USA), £14.99. Details of local stations is listed in *World TV and Radio Handbook* (WTRH), PO Box 9027, 1006 AA Amsterdam, The Netherlands, £19.99. Both of these, free wavelength guides and selected radio sets are available from the *BBC World Service Bookshop*, Bush House Arcade, Bush House, Strand, London WC2B 4PH, UK, T020-75572576.

Eating

Cuisine

The most common dish is *bife (ou frango) com arroz e feijão*, steak (or chicken) with rice and the excellent Brazilian black beans. However, due to Brazil's rich cultural mix many other influences are found in the various regions. São Paulo is by far the best place for international and foreign cuisines.

Feijoada The most famous dish with beans is the *feijoada completa*: several meat ingredients (jerked beef, smoked sausage, smoked tongue, salt pork, along with spices, herbs and vegetables) are cooked with the beans. Manioc flour is sprinkled over it, and it is eaten with *kale* (*couve*) and slices of orange, and accompanied by glasses of *aguardente* (unmatured rum), usually known as *cachaça* (booze), though *pinga* (drop) is a politer term. Most restaurants serve the *feijoada completa* for Saturday lunch (up to about 1630).

Churrasco A mixed grill, including excellent steak, served with roasted manioc flour is available throughout Brazil. Originating from the cattlemen of Rio Grande do Sul, it is normally served in restaurants known as *churrascarias* or *rodízios* (or *espeto corrido*). In *rodízios*, waiters ask you in advance what types of meat you want and then bring them round to you until you tell them to stop. Each one has its own variation on the red light/green light system for communicating to the staff. *Churrascarias* usually have a self-service salad bar. Both are good places for large appetites.

Minas Gerais has two delicious special dishes with pork, black beans, *farofa* and *kale*: *tutu á mineira* and *feijão tropeiro*. A white hard cheese (*queijo prata*) or a slightly softer one (*queijo Minas*) is often served for dessert with bananas, or guava or *quince* paste. *Comida mineira* is quite distinctive and very wholesome and you can often find restaurants serving this type of food in other parts of Brazil.

Bahia has some excellent fish dishes (see the note on page 386); some restaurants in most of the big cities specialize in them. *Vatapá* is a good dish in the North; it contains shrimp or fish in a sauce of palm oil or coconut milk. *Empadinhas de camarão*, shrimp patties, with olives and heart of palm, are worth trying.

Desserts and fruits

There is fruit all the year round, ranging from banana and orange to mango, pawpaw, custard-apple (*fruta do conde*) and guava. Try *manga de Ubá*, a non-fibrous small mango. Also good are *amora*, a raspberry that looks like a strawberry, *jaboticaba*, a small black damson-like fruit, and *jaca* (jackfruit), a large yellow/green fruit. Don't miss the exotic flavours of Brazilian ice-creams.

Eating out

Portions are usually for two and come with two plates. If you are on your own, you could ask for an *embalagem* (doggy bag) or get a takeaway called a *marmita* or *quentinha* and

Food and drink

Drinks Bebidas
beer cerveja
coffee café
fruit juice suco
hot chocolate chocolate quente
milk leite
mineral water água mineral
soft drink refrigerante
tea chá
tonic water água tónica
whisky uísque
wine vinho

Fruit Frutas
apple maçã
banana banana
coconut coco
grape uva
lime limão
mango manga
orange laranja
papaya mamão
passion fruit maracujá
pineapple abacaxi
strawberry morango
watermelon melancia

Meat Carne
beef bife
chicken frango/galinha
fish peixe
ham presunto
hot dog cachorro quente
kid cabrito
pork porco
toasted cheese and ham sandwich misto quente
sausages salsichas
steak filé
turkey peru

Vegetables Legumes
carrot cenoura
lettuce alface
onion cebola
potato batata
rice arroz
salad salada
sweetcorn milho
tomato tomate

Others
bread pão
butter manteiga
cake bolo
cheese queijo
egg ovo
ice-cream sorvete
mustard mostarda
peanut amendoim
pepper pimenta
pie pastel
salt sal
sandwich sanduiche
sugar açúcar
yoghurt iogurte

offer it to a person with no food (many Brazilians do). Many restaurants now serve *comida por kilo* where you serve yourself and pay for the weight of food on your plate. This is good news if your Portuguese is not up to much, if you want a cheap meal, and also if you don't want to spend time waiting for your food to be served.

The main meal is usually taken in the middle of the day; cheap restaurants tend not to be open in the evening. Always ask the price of a dish before ordering and, if travelling on a tight budget, ask for the *prato feito* or *sortido*, an excellent value set menu. The *prato comercial* is similar but rather better and a bit more expensive. *Lanchonetes* are cheap eating places where you generally pay before eating. *Salgados* (savoury pastries), *coxinha* (a pyramid of manioc filled with meat or fish and deep fried), *esfiha* (spicy hamburger inside an onion bread envelope), *empadão* (a filling – eg chicken – in sauce in a pastry case), *empadas* and *empadinhas* (smaller fritters of the same type), are the usual fare. *Pão de queijo* is a hot roll made with cheese. A *bauru* is a toasted sandwich which, in Porto Alegre, is filled with steak, while further north has tomato, ham and cheese filling. *Cocada* is a coconut and sugar biscuit.

Five of the best Brazilian drinks

→ **Agua de coco** (coconut milk), good for rehydration, perfect for hangovers.
→ **Caiprinha**, the national cocktail of firewater (*cachaça*) and fresh limes.
→ **Suco**, fresh juice such as *acerola*, an Amazonian cherry. Vitaminas also contain guarana
→ **Batida**, vodka or *cachaça* with fresh juice (maracuya, passion fruit, is delicious).
→ **Açai** (pronounced assayear), a fashionable Amazonian fruit drink.

Warning Avoid mussels, marsh crabs and other shellfish caught near large cities: they are likely to have lived in a highly polluted environment.

Drinks

The local firewater, *aguardente* (known as *cachaça* or *pinga*), made from sugar-cane, is cheap and strong; São Francisco, Praianinha, Nega Fulô, '51' and Pitu are some recommended makes. Mixed with fruit juice, sugar and crushed ice, *cachaça* becomes the principal element in a *batida*, a delicious and powerful drink. The most popular is a lime batida or *batida de limão*; a variant of which is the *caipirinha*, a *cachaça* with several slices of lime; a *caipiroska* is made with vodka. *Cachaça* with Coca-Cola is a *cuba*, while rum with Coca-Cola is a *cuba libre*.

Some genuine Scotch whisky brands are bottled in Brazil, which are very popular because of the high price of Scotch imported in the bottle. Teacher's is the most highly regarded brand. Locally made gin, vermouth and campari are very good.

Imported drinks are expensive, but there are some fair local wines. Among the better ones are Château d'Argent, Château Duvalier, Almadén, Dreher, Preciosa and Bernard Taillan. The red Marjolet from Cabernet grapes, and the Moselle-type white Zahringer, have been well spoken of. A new *adega* tends to start off well, but the quality gradually deteriorates with time; many vintners have switched to American Concorde grapes, producing a rougher wine. Greville Brut champagne-type is inexpensive and very drinkable. A white wine sangria, containing tropical fruits such as pineapple and papaya, is worth looking out for. Chilean and Portuguese wines are sometimes available at little more than the cost of local wines.

If you don't want sugar in your coffee, suco, or even caipirinha, *you must ask when you order it.*

The beers are good and there are plenty of brands: Antarctica, Brahma, Bohemia, Cerpa, Skol and Xingu black beer. Beers are cheaper by the bottle than on draught, which is known as *chope* or *chopp*, after the German Schoppen, and pronounced 'shoppi'.

There is an excellent range of non-alcoholic fruit juices, known as sucos. *Açai*, *acerola*, *caju* (cashew), *pitanga*, *goiaba* (guava), *genipapo*, *graviola* (*chirimoya*), *maracujá* (passion fruit), *sapoti* and *amarindo* are recommended. *Vitaminas* are thick fruit or vegetable drinks with milk. *Caldo de cana* is sugar-cane juice, sometimes mixed with ice. *Água de côco* or *côco verde* (coconut water from chilled, fresh green coconut) should not be missed. The best known of many local soft drinks is *Guaraná*, which is a very popular carbonated fruit drink, completely unrelated to the natural product from the Amazon. Apart from the ubiquitous coffee, good tea is grown and sold.

Bars

These can vary from basic neighbourhood bars open to the street, often known as *pésujos* or *botequins*, to sophisticated places with waiter service. Food and snacks are often served and there is usually some form of music for entertainment, whether a live band or the customers providing their own in an improvised samba session with guitars and drums.

Shopping

What to buy

Gold, diamonds and gemstones are good buys throughout Brazil and there are innovative designs in jewellery. Buy at reputable dealers (the best value is in Minas Gerais), but cheap, fun pieces can be bought from street traders. There are interesting furnishings made with gemstones, and marble. Clay figurines from the Northeast, lace from Ceará, leatherwork, strange pottery from Amazônia, carvings in soapstone and in bone, tiles and other ceramic work, African-type pottery and basketwork from Bahia, are all worth seeking out. Brazilian cigars are excellent for those who like the mild flavours popular in Germany, the Netherlands and Switzerland. Recommended purchases are musical instruments, such as guitars, other stringed instruments and percussion instruments.

There are excellent textiles and good hammocks from the Northeast (ironmongers sell hooks – *ganchos pararede* – for hanging your hammock at home). Design in clothing is impressive, though unfortunately not equalled by manufacturing quality. Buy your beachwear in Brazil: it is matchless.

For those who know how to use them, medicinal herbs, barks and spices can be bought from street markets. Coconut oil and local skin and haircare products (fantastic conditioners) are better and cheaper than in Europe, but known brands of toiletries are exorbitant. Other bad buys are film (including processing), cameras and any electrical goods (including batteries). Sunscreen, sold in all department stores and large supermarkets, is expensive.

Prices and bargaining

As a rule, shopping is easier, quality more reliable and prices higher in the shopping centres (mostly excellent) and in the wealthier suburbs. Prices are often confusingly displayed as 3X (figure) which means that customers can pay in three monthly installments, even for items like bikinis. Better prices are posted at the small shops and street traders. Shopping is most entertaining at markets and on the beach. Bargaining (with good humour) is expected in the latter.

Festivals and events

Festivals

The major festival is **Carnival**, which is held three days up to, and including, Ash Wednesday and is celebrated all over Brazil. See boxes under Rio de Janeiro page 122, São Paulo page 196, Salvador page 392 and Pernambuco page 460. **Semana Santa**, which ends on Easter Sunday, is celebrated with parades in many cities and towns. The **Festas Juninhas** throughout the country and **Bumba-meu-boi** in Maranhão are held throughout June, while the **Festa do Boi** is held in Parantins at the end of the month.

Bahia has many festivals throughout the year but some of the most interesting are the **Lavagem do Bomfim** in January, the **Presente para Iemanjá** in February and the **Festa da Boa Morte** in August.

In the South the **Festa Nacional da Uva**, a grape and wine festival, is held in Caxias do Sul during February. São Paulo has the Brazilian Grand Prix at the end of March or beginning of April and the **Festa do Peão Boiadeiro in Barretos** during August.

In May the **Festa do Divino Espírito Santo** is celebrated throughout Brazil, but the parades in Pirenópolis are especially interesting.

Towards the end of the year in October the **Oktoberfest** is held in Blumenau, whilst the **Círio de Nazaré** festival takes place in Belém.

The festival year ends on 31 December with the hugely popular **Reveillon** festivities being held particularly on beaches.

Carnival dates

- → **2005** 5-9 February
- → **2006** 25-29 February
- → **2007** 17-21 February
- → **2008** 2-6 February
- → **2009** 21-25 February

National holidays

Aside from the festivals listed above, the main holidays are: 1 January, **New Year;** 21 April, **Tiradentes;** 1 May, **Labour Day;** June, **Corpus Christi;** 7 September, **Independence Day;** 12 October, **Nossa Senhora Aparecida;** 2 November, **All Souls' Day;** 15 November, **Proclamation of the Republic;** and 25 December, **Christmas.** The local holidays in the main cities are given in the text. Other religious or traditional holidays (including Good Friday and, usually, 1 November, **All Saints' Day** and 24 December, **Christmas Eve**) must be fixed by the municipalities. Other holidays are usually celebrated on the Monday prior to the date.

Sport and activities

Archaeology and palaeontology

There are many sites where remains can be found of the continent's original inhabitants, whether human or other species such as dinosaurs. The best areas are probably in the Central West and the Northeast. Cave paintings are to be found in Serra do Roncador in Mato Grosso, Serra da Capivara in Piauí and near Xique-Xique in Bahia. Dinosaur tracks can be seen at Souza in the interior of Paraíba, whilst eggs have been found at Peirópolis in western Minas Gerais.

Birdwatching

Brazil has more endemic species than any other country in South America, including the world's rarest bird, Spix's macaw. The country is second only to Peru in the world for total numbers of bird families and second only to Bolivia in total numbers of endemic families. There are some 1,661 species – fewer than Colombia or Peru, but still an extraordinary number when you consider that the Andes do not pass through Brazil. Habitats range from freshwater wetlands to lowland rainforest, dry *cerrado* and *caatinga*, Atlantic coastal forest, mangrove forest and wet pampa grassland. There are patches of *Araucaria* pine forest in the South. The best time for birding is from September to October as it is quiet relatively dry and flights are at their cheapest. Some of the specialist tour agencies listed on page 23, such as **Ornitholidays, Focus Tours** and **Field Guides** offer packages to many good areas. Details of the following key birdwatching sites are given in the main travelling text.

The Amazon Together with the Atlantic coast rainforest this is the best destination in Brazil for serious birders although there are very few serious birding guides available and you may have to rely on your own resources. Birds are harder to see here than in the Pantanal and do not occur in the spectacular numbers but there are more rarities. The best spots are around Tefé in the Ramsar-listed Mamirauá reserve, along the Rio Javari (from Leticia) and around Alta Floresta in northern Mato Grosso.

Minas Gerais This state is host to a large number of accessible national and state parks which are excellent for viewing a variety of different bird species; especially

Atlantic coast rarities. Recommended are the Parque Natural de Caraça, Parque Nacional da Serra do Cipó, Parque Florestal de Ibitipoca, Parque Florestal do Rio Doce and the Parque Nacional da Serra Canastra, among many other lesser known areas.

The Northeast The interior of Bahia, Pernambuco and Ceará is home to a variety of rare endemics in the arid *caatinga* and *sertão*. Canudos in Bahia is typical – the red-rock escarpment of Raso da Catarina near here supports the world's sole population of Lear's macaw as well as other rare endemics like white-browed guan and great xenops. Many new species have recently been found in the Atlantic forests of Alagoas; rarities here include pygmy nightjar and alogoas foliage-gleaner. The south of Bahia around Itacaré is good for Atlantic rainforest species like red-browed parrot and plain parakeet as well as various rare cotingas and tanagers.

The Pantanal This large area of swampland on the Bolivian and Brazilian borders is home to more than 600 species of bird including two species of rhea and the world's largest parrot, the hyacinth macaw. The birding here is spectacular – if only for the sheer quantity of avifauna. Jabiru storks, wood ibises and egrets occur in ridiculous quantities, there arecanary-winged parakeets by the thousand and raptors on every telegraph pole.

The southern Atlantic coastal forests This mountain range runs parallel to the coast from Rio Grande do Sul to Espírito Santo and still has some remains of the once mighty Atlantic rainforest. It is excellent birding territory and a favourite destination for birding tour companies. The best areas are the Serra dos Órgãos, Itatiaia and the mountains around Ubatuba. Endemics include seven-coloured tanager, Itatiaia thistletail, black and gold cotinga, grey-winged cotinga (which occurs only in the Serra dos Órgãos), tawny-browed owl and black-capped manakin. » *For more information on flora and fauna, see page 717.*

Canoeing

Canoeing is supervised by the **Confederação Brasileira de Canoagem** (R Fernando Abott 582/703, Estrela, CEP 95880-000, Rio Grande do Sul, ToXX51-7122600), founded in 1989. It covers all aspects of the sport, speed racing, slalom, downriver, surfing and ocean kayaking. For downriver canoeing, go to **Visconde de Mauá** (Rio de Janeiro state – see page 161 where the Rio Preto is famous for the sport); also the Rio Formoso at **Bonito** (Mato Grosso do Sul – see page 646). A recommended river for slalom is the Paranhana, **Três Coroas**, Rio Grande do Sul. For kayak surfing the best places are Rio, the Ilha de Santa Catarina and Ubatuba, while ocean kayaking is popular in Rio, Búzios and Santos (São Paulo).

Caving

There are some wonderful cave systems in Brazil, and **Ibama** (see national parks, page 720) has a programme for the protection of the national speleological heritage. National parks such as **Ubajara** (see page 511) and **Chapada Diamantina** (page 420) and the state park of **PETAR** (page 218) have easy access for the casual visitor, but there are also many options for the keen potholer in the states of São Paulo, Paraná, Minas Gerais and the federal district of Brasília.

Cave diving

Cave diving can be practised in many of the 200 underwater grottoes such as **Bonito, Mato Grosso do Sul, Lapa de São Jorge,** 280 km from Brasília, in Chapada Diamantina and **Vale do Ribeira** located between São Paulo and Paraná. **Gabriel Ganme,** Diving College, R Dr Mello Alves 700, São Paulo, To11-8814723, and **Rafael de Nicola,** Divers University, are instructors in this specialized sport.

Climbing

As Brazil has no mountain ranges of Alpine or Andean proportions, the most popular form of climbing (*escalada*) is rock-face climbing. In the heart of Rio, you can see, or join, climbers scaling the rocks at the base of **Pão de Açúcar** and on the Sugar Loaf itself. Not too far away, the **Serra dos Órgãos** provides plenty of challenges, not least the **Dedo de Deus** (God's Finger – see page 153). In the state of São Paulo a good location for climbing is **Pedra do Báu** near São Bento do Sapucaí, and **Brotas** is popular for abseiling (rappel). **Pedra Branca** and the **Serra do Cipó** are recommended locations in Minas Gerais. Mato Grosso has the **Serra do Roncador** and there are other good areas in Paraná and Rio Grande do Sul.

Cultural tourism

Several of the tour operators listed on page 23 offer customized packages for special interest groups. Local operators offering these more specialized tours are listed in the text under the relevant location.

Diving

The Atlantic coast offers many possibilities for scuba diving (*mergulho*). The best site is the archipelago of **Fernando de Noronha** (Pernambuco), 345 km off the northeast coast in the open Atlantic. The underwater landscape is volcanic, with cliffs, caverns and some corals, but the marine life that shelters here is magnificent. There are sharks, a protected breeding ground for hawksbill and green turtles and – the greatest draw for divers – a bay which is the home for a pod of several hundred spinner dolphin (diving with the dolphins is not allowed). In the archipelago there are a number of dive sites including the wreck of the corvette *Ipiringa* at a depth of 53 m (*Atlantis* is an operator that specializes in deep-water diving). Average visibility is 30 m with an average depth of 22 m. The best time of year is from January to February and July to October. Also in Pernambuco, **Recife** (from where planes leave for Fernando de Noronha) is a diving centre, particularly for wrecks. The reef that protects the shore up to Recife provides sheltered swimming, natural pools and many, very rewarding diving spots. Full of marine life, with warm, clear, greenish-blue sea. However, visiting sea anglers are urged to respect local traditions – many species are in danger of extinction, as is the coral, which is threatened by any disturbance and all forms of pollution.

> *In some areas in Brazil, diving includes underwater sport fishing; for details, contact a company which specializes in fishing.*

Moving south, Bahia's most popular dive sites are the marine park of **Abrolhos** and **Porto Seguro**. The best time to visit Abrolhos is from July to November, when whales come from the Antarctic to breed, and from January to February. Other attractions are Moray eels, Barracudas, a wide variety of corals and the wreck of the cargo ship Rosalina that sank in 1939. Visibility varies between 8 m and 20 m, with an average depth of 10 m in the archipelago.

In the Southeast, **Búzios, Arraial do Cabo**, visibility of 8 m to 15 m, depths of 7 m to 70 m, grottoes, ridges and the greatest number of wrecks in the country, and **Cabo Frio** are sites to the north of Rio. South of the state capital, the island-filled bay of **Angra dos Reis**, together with **Ilha Grande**, and **Paraty**, best from December to April, with calm seas, visibility from 5 m to 20 m and an average depth of 15 m, are all recommended sites. **Ilhabela/São Sebastião** in São Paulo state, best visited from January to May, offers good opportunities for wreck diving. Visibility is up to 12 m with depths from 6 m to 85 m. Other places in the state include **Ubatuba**, Laje de Santos, 22 km from the mainland with an anchor graveyard and rays has visibility up to 20 m and depths between 18 m to 40 m, and **Ilha de Alcatrazes**.

At Fernando de Noronha and Recife you can dive all year, although Recife (like anywhere on the coast) may be subject to strong currents. The further south you go, the lower the water temperatures become in winter (15-20°C). Visibility can also be affected by currents and weather. Many resorts have dive shops, some of which are listed in the Handbook. Whether you are already a qualified diver or a beginner seeking tuition, get local advice on which companies provide the level of expertise and knowledge of local waters that you need.

American/Brazilian Dive Club ⓘ *1645 SE 3 Road Court, Deerfield Bch, FL 33441, USA, T/F954-4200009, can be accessed through www.cris.com/apavan*, which has links to dive sites in Brazil. There is a diving magazine called *Mergulho*. **Océan** is a dive shop and tour operator based in Rio de Janeiro state (Rio, Angra dos Reis, Ilha Grande, Arraial do Cabo) which has a **Diving in Brasil** website, www.ocean.com.br (Portuguese only).

Ecotourism

Ecotourism is very slowly becoming important as a form of sustainable development in the parts of Brazil most threatened by deforestation and as a way of alleviating local unemployment in a way that doesn't harm the environment. Many opportunities for visiting the rainforest are to be found in the North and efforts are being made to save what is left of the Atlantic forest cover in the Southeast.

Useful organizations include the **Instituo Brasileiro de Ecoturismo** (IEB) ⓘ *R Minerva 156, Perdizes, São Paulo, ToXX11-36727571, www.ecoturismo.org.br*. In Minas Gerais, **Amo-Te** (Associação Mineira dos Organizadores do Turismo Ecológico) ⓘ *R Prof Morais 624, Apto 302, Savassi, Belo Horizonte, ToXX31-32815094*, is helpful. **Terra Virgem** ⓘ *R Galeno de Almeida 179, CEP 05410-030, T/F8837823*, terravirgem@originet.com.br, is a publishing house in São Paulo which publishes guides in Portuguese and English for adventure tourism, accompanied by books of photographs.

Fishing

Brazil has enormous potential for angling, given the number and variety of its rivers, lakes and reservoirs. Add to this the scope for sea-angling along the Atlantic coast and it is not difficult to see why the sport is gaining in popularity (but see under Diving above). Officially, the country's fish stocks are under the control of **Ibama** (see national parks, page 720) and a licence is required for fishing in any waters. The states of Mato Grosso and Mato Grosso do Sul require people fishing in their rivers to get the states' own fishing permit, which is not the same as an Ibama licence. All details on prices, duration and regulations concerning catches can be obtained from Ibama; the paperwork can be found at Ibama offices, some branches of the **Banco do Brasil** and some agencies which specialize in fishing. In Mato Grosso and Mato Grosso do Sul information is provided by **Sema**, the Special Environment Secretariat, and documents may be obtained at fishing agencies or Bamerindus in Mato Grosso do Sul.

Freshwater fishing can be practised in so many places that the best bet is to make local enquiries in the part of Brazil that you are visiting. You can then find out about the rivers, lakes and reservoirs, which fish you are likely to find and what types of angling are most suited to the conditions. Favoured rivers include tributaries of the **Amazon,** those in the **Pantanal** and the **Rio Araguaia,** but there are many others. Many agencies can arrange fishing trips and there are several local magazines on the subject. As an example, the best time to go fishing in the Araguaia and around the Ilha de Bananal is the dry season, May to October. In Aruanã, one of the towns which gives access to the river, the **Associação dos Barqueiros de Aruanã** (ABA), Praça Couto Magalhães, gives information about boat rentals and fishing tours. **Lages** in Santa Catarina is good for trout fishing, as is **Campos do Jordão** in São Paulo which also has good opportunities for salmon.

Information **Pura Pesca Tour** operates tours in the Pantanal, Rio Araguaia and elsewhere, in São Paulo, ToXX11-5355880/5435901, FoXX11-55616447, or Cuiabá ToXX65-6241660, FoXX65-6249966; **Eldorado Pantaneiro** operates tours in fishing boats with a/c apartments, bar and all equipment, ToXX11-4340283, or Corumbá

T067-2316369. **Fishing World**'s website, www.fishingworld.com.br, is not exclusively about Brazil and in Portuguese, but is informative and also includes diving.

Hang-gliding and paragliding

These are both covered by the **Associação Brasileira de Vôo Livre** (ABVL – Brazilian Hangliding Association, Rio de Janeiro, ToXX21-3220266). There are state associations affiliated with ABVL and there are a number of operators offering tandem flights for those without experience. Launch sites (called *rampas*) are growing in number. Among the best known are: Pedra Bonita at Gávea in **Rio**; Parque da Cidade in **Niterói**; in **São Paulo**, Pico do Urubu (Mogi das Cruzes), Serra de São Pedro, Pedra do Baú (Campos do Jordão), Pico Agudo (Santo Antônio do Pinhal), Pedra Grande (Atibaia); in **Espírito Santo**, Morro de Filette, Venda Nova do Imigrante; in **Minas Gerais**, Pico do Ibitiruna (Governador Valadares), Pico do Gavião (Andradas) and Serra de Santa Helena (Sete Lagoas); in **Paraná**, Morro do Picouto and Morro da Queixada at Foz do Iguaçu; **Santa Catarina**, Careca – Praia Brava (Itajaí), Pelado (Gaspar), Morro Azul, Morro da Turquia and Intermediário (all at Pomerode), Pico das Antenas (Jaraguá do Sul); in **Rio Grande do Sul**, Morro do Farrabraz (Sapiranga) and Ninho das Águias (Nova Petrópolis); in **Ceará**, Aratuba, Urucu (Meruoca) and Urucu (Queixada); Morro do Urucum, Corumbá, **Mato Grosso do Sul** (which offers views of the Pantanal); and the Vale do Paranã in **Brasília**.

Horse riding

Some of the best trails for horse riding are the routes that used to be taken by the mule trains that transported goods between the coast and the interior. A company like **Tropa Serrana** in Belo Horizonte (ToXX31-33448986, tropaserrana@hotmail.com) is an excellent place to start because their tours, including overnight horse treks, explore many aspects of the Minas Gerais countryside that visitors do not normally see.

Mountain biking

Brazil is well-suited to cycling, both on and off-road. On main roads it is important to obey the general advice of being on the look out for motor vehicles as cyclists are very much second-class citizens. Also note that when cycling on the coast you may encounter strong winds which will hamper your progress. There are endless roads and tracks suitable for mountain biking, and there are many clubs in major cities which organize group rides, activities and competitions. **Serra da Canastra** in Minas Gerais is a popular area. **Tamanduá** in São Roque de Minas offer personalized tours and equipment hire. (See also Getting around, page 49.)

Mystical tourism

Brazil has a number of locations that have been claimed by seekers of hidden knowledge, or those interested in unusual sciences. Some of the best sites are to be found in the central west such as **Alto Paraíso de Goiás**, north of Brasília, and **Barra do Garças** in Mato Grosso. In these places 'new age' communities have formed dedicated to natural healing, alternative religions, or the search for UFOs and alien life-forms. In the south of Minas Gerais, a similar ambience is found at **São Tomé das Letras**, but there are many other examples across the country.

Rafting

Whitewater rafting started in Brazil in 1992. There are companies offering trips in São Paulo state (eg on the rios **Juquiá, Jaguarí, do Peixe**, **Paraibuna**), in Rio de Janeiro (also on the Paraibuna, at **Três Rios** in the Serra dos Órgãos), Paraná (**Rio Ribeira**), Santa Catarina (**Rio Itajaí**) and Rio Grande do Sul (**Três Coroas**). **Serra da Canastra** in Minas Gerais is also popular for the local sport of **Bóia-cross** (rafting with rubber tubes).

Spas and alternative therapies

Like many other places in the world Brazil has a growing spa and alternative therapy scene. And whilst there are few resort spas as wonderful as the best of Thailand or Mexico there are a number of freelance practitioners as good as any in the world. They often bring skills learnt from Brazilian indigenous traditions to their work and charge prices at a fraction of those in Europe or the USA. On top of this come a number of interesting Health and Well Being programmes, the foremost of which have won several international tourism awards.

Resort spas

Kurotel Spa and Centre for Longevity, Nações Unidas, 533, Gramado, Rio Grande do Sul, T054-2862133. An old-fashioned, destination spa with dieting and medical consultation running alongside the various vanity treatments. There is comprehensive information on the web site if you can decipher the English.

Txai, Ilhéus-Itacaré road km 48, Itacaré, Bahia T073-6346936. More a resort than a spa; in an idyllic beach location near Itacaré, Bahia. Facilities and treatments include sauna, *ofuru* baths, *watsu* water therapy and various massages.

Casas Brancas, Alto do Humaitá 10, Búzios, Rio De Janeiro, T022-26231458. A newly opened spa in the prettiest hotel in Búzios, with stunning views out over the Ocean; offers a modest range of quality massages and treatments. Popular with jet setters.

Costa Brasilis Resort, Av. Beira Mar, 2000, Praia de Santo André, Santa Cruz Cabrália, T0800-7011413. A beach resort on a beautiful stretch of sand backed by coconut palms. The spa has a modest selection of treatments and massages.

Santa Clara, Boipeba, Bahia. Tiny little *pousada* with a great restaurant and a very special resident massage therapist, Norma Matos. Norma also works from Salvador and São Paulo and can be reached on T011-91547824 or via normalucia8@hotmail.com.

Heath and wellness programmes

Lambent do Brasil – Lambent Life, T011-30401698. Run by one of the world's leading experts on neuro-linguistic programming and life coaching, his partner and guests from a range of spiritual disciplines from Adhyatma (Advaita yoga) to Vipassana Meditation. Excellent programmes in a range of stunning locations on the Atlantic coast of Rio and São Paulo states, all of which provide real practical tools for change.

Body and Soul Adventures, USA T086-63413180, UK T0800-9175506. Light walking, kayaking and adventure activities preceded by yoga and followed by aromatherapy massages. The programmes take place on Ilha Grande in some of Brazil's most spellbinding scenery. Popular with celebs.

Individual therapists

Silvia Luz, T011-32073983. One of Brazil's very best Shitasu and Ayurvedic practitioners. Very special treatments.

Surfing

This can be enjoyed in just about every coastal state. It does not require a permit; all you need is a board and the right type of wave. Brazilians took up surfing in the 1930s and have been practising ever since. In this beach-obsessed country, with 8,000 km of coastline, all shore and watersports are taken seriously. Surfers associations include: **Associação Brasileira de Surfe Profissional,** ToXX48-2231226; **Associação Brasileira de Bodyboard,** ToXX21-2590669.

A favourite locale is **Fernando de Noronha,** a cluster of idyllic islands belonging to Pernambuco state, 345 km out in the Atlantic, but the best waves are found in the South, where long stretches of the Atlantic, often facing the swell head-on, give some excellent and varied breaks. The season is from November to March in the archipelago, but it is an expensive place to surf. Many Brazilian surf spots are firmly on the international championship circuit: best known is **Saquarema**, in Rio de Janeiro state.

There are many other good surf spots in Rio de Janeiro state. Most of the coastline faces south, head-on to the powerful swell, and is freshened by an early morning north-northeast offshore wind blowing off the mountains which run parallel to the coast. It receives a consistent winter swell, although in summer it stays flat for long periods. The urban beaches have good surf, and are friendly, but beware of thieves. Don't leave your board unattended; get straight in the water. The beautiful, mountainous coast between Ubatuba and Rio de Janeiro has no surf except to the ocean side of Ilha Grande, which protects the mainland coast.

In the state of São Paulo, on the coast between Santos and Rio de Janeiro (Linha Verde) the best-known and the busiest beach near the city is **Pitangueiras** where professional and amateur championships are held at the spot known as Maluf, where the waves consistently break at 8 ft. São Sebastião has 21 good beaches and an adequate, but not over-developed tourist infrastructure. The many small islands offshore are very good for scuba diving; there is also sailing, fishing and canoeing. During high season, lively watersports events are held at **Marésias**, with excellent surfing.

One of the best states for surfing, **Santa Catarina,** has a straight coastline with several islands offshore. Surfing is prohibited at some beaches from 15 May to 15 July, because of the *tainha* fish harvest. Ilha de Santa Catarina has more than 40 beaches, all different and all highly sought-after during the holiday season. The mInute Carnival has ended, the smaller villages to the south of the island are deserted by holidaymaking city-dwellers, leaving the beaches relatively uncrowded.

Considered one of Brazil's finest surfing spots, **Silveira** is 3 km east of Garopaba, 96 km south of Florianópolis: follow the SC-434 for about 1 km and take a left turn. Swimming can be risky here because of the surf and sudden drops in the ocean floor. There is also excellent fishing.

Surfing in the Northeast The majority of beaches in **Salvador** are polluted, but south of the city there is surfing near **Itaparica**, **Itacaré** and **Ilhéus**. Beaches **north of Bahia** are protected by the reef which runs off the northeast shore up the coast to Recife, waves tend to be smaller and much less powerful than on the southern coasts. There are some interesting reef breaks, however, and a chain of palm-fringed, white sand beaches that beg to be visited even without your board. This coast is also good for diving.

At **Recife** surf is weak in the urban area, and banned at Boa Viagem because of shark attacks. **Porto de Galinhas** has pretty beaches and a variety of surf spots.

Rio Grande do Norte and **Ceará** also have surfing beaches, but not of the quality or quantity of further south.

Swimming

The extensive coastline means there are plenty of opportunities for good bathing. Do, however, observe local warnings as strong undertows and currents can make it extremely dangerous to swim in places. A number of people are drowned every year from recklessness on Rio de Janeiro's beaches. **Triathlon** has become a popular sport in the south and southeast of Brazil with many organized competitions.

Trekking

Trekking is very popular, especially in Rio de Janeiro, São Paulo, Minas Gerais, Paraná and Rio Grande do Sul. There are plenty of hiking shops and agencies which handle hiking tours. Trails are frequently graded according to difficulty; this is noticeably so in areas where *trilhas ecológicas* have been laid out in forests or other sites close to busy tourist areas. Many national parks and other protected areas provide good opportunities for trekking (eg the Chapada Diamantina in Bahia) and local information can easily be found to get you on the right track.

Yachting

A popular sport along Brazil's Atlantic coastline. **Angra dos Reis** and **Paraty** in Rio de Janeiro state as well as **Bahia** are good locations among many others.

Health

Local populations in Brazil are exposed to a range of health risks not encountered in other parts of the world. Many of the diseases are major problems for the local communities and the risk to travellers, although remote, cannot be ignored. Obviously five-star travel is going to carry less risk than backpacking on a minimal budget. The healthcare in the region is varied. There are many excellent private and government clinics/hospitals. As with all medical care, first impressions count. If a facility is grubby, staff wear grey coats instead of white ones then be wary of the general standard of medicine and hygiene. A good tip is to contact your embassy or consulate on arrival and ask where the recommended clinics are (those used by diplomats). If you do get ill, you should also check with your medical insurer whether they are satisfied that the medical centre or hospital that you have been referred to is of a suitable standard.

Disease risk

The greater disease risk in tropical Brazil is caused by the greater volume of insect disease carriers in the shape of mosquitoes and sandflies. The key **viral disease** is dengue fever, which is transmitted by a day biting mosquito. The disease is like a very nasty form of the flu with two to three days of illness, followed by a short period of recovery, then a second attack of illness. Westerners very rarely get the worst haemorrhagic form of the disease.

Bacterial diseases include **tuberculosis** (TB) and some causes of traveller's diarrhoea. The **parasitic diseases** are many, but the two key ones are malaria and South American trypanosomiasis (known as Chagas's Disease).

Risk areas for malaria are in states of **Acre**, **Rondônia**, **Amapa**, **Amazonas**, **Roraima**, and **Tocantins**. Risk in parts of the states of **Maranhão** (western part), **Mato Grosso** (northern part), and **Pará** (except Belem City). There is also transmission in urban areas, including large cities such as **Porto Velho**, **Boa Vista**, **Macapá**, **Manaus**, **Santarém**, and **Marabá**. The coastal states from the 'horn' south to the Uruguay border, including Iguaçu Falls, are not risk areas.

Before you go

Ideally see your GP or travel clinic at least six weeks before the departure for general advice on travel risks, **malaria** and **vaccinations**. Make sure you have adequate **travel insurance**; get a **dental check**; know your own **blood group**; and if you suffer a long-term condition such as diabetes or epilepsy make sure someone knows or that you have a Medic Alert bracelet/necklace with this information.

Vaccinations

Hepatitis A	Recommended as the disease can be caught easily from food/water.
Polio	Recommended if nil in last 10 years.
Rabies	Recommended if travelling to jungle and/or remote areas.
Tetanus	Recommended if nil in last 10 years (but after five doses you've had enough for life).

Typhoid	Recommended if nil in last 3 years.
Yellow fever	Recommended if travelling around Brazil as it is needed for the Northern areas.

Malaria precautions

A for Awareness Brazil has areas with a risk of the deadly **falciparum** malaria. Always check with your doctor or travel clinic for the most up-to-date advice.

B for Bite avoidance Wear clothes that cover arms and legs and use effective insect repellents in areas with risks of insect spread disease. Use a mosquito net dipped in permethrin as both a physical and chemical barrier at night in the same areas.

C for Chemoprophylaxis Depending on the type of malaria and your previous medical condition/psychological profile, take the right drug before, during and after your trip. Always be sure to check with your doctor or travel clinic for the most up-to-date advice.

D for Diagnosis Remember that up to a year after your return an illness could be caused by malaria. Be forceful about asking for a malaria test, even if the doctor says it is 'only flu.' The symptoms of malaria are wide ranging from fever, lethargy, headache, muscle pains, flu-like illness, to diarrhoea, convulsions. Malaria can lead to coma and death.

Further information

When you arrive in each country let the Embassy or Consulate know. The information can be useful if a friend/relative gets ill at home and there is a desperate search for you around the globe. You can also ask them about locally recommended medical facilities and do's and don'ts.

Websites

Foreign and Commonwealth Office (FCO), **www.fco.gov.uk**, a key travel advice site, with useful Information on the country, people, climate and lists the UK embassies/consulates. It site also promotes the concept of 'Know Before You Go'. And encourages travel insurance and appropriate travel health advice. It has links to the Department of Health travel advice site, listed below.

Department of Health Travel Advice (UK), **www.doh.gov.uk/traveladvice**, is an excellent site also available as a free booklet, the *T6*, from UK post offices. It lists the vaccine advice requirements for each country.

Medic Alert (UK), **www.medicalalert.co.uk**, is the website of the foundation that produces bracelets and necklaces for those with existing medical problems. Once you have ordered your bracelet/necklace, write your key medical details on paper inside it, so that if you collapse, a medical person can identify you as someone with epilepsy, allergy to peanuts, etc.

Blood Care Foundation (UK), **www.bloodcare.org.uk**, is a charity 'dedicated to the provision of screened blood and resuscitation fluids in countries where these are not readily available.' They will dispatch certified non-infected blood of the right type to your hospital/clinic. The blood is flown in from various centres around the world.

Public Health Laboratory Service (UK), **www.phls.org.uk**, has the 2001 malaria advice guidelines for travel around the world. It gives specific advice about the right drugs for each location. It also has useful information for those who are pregnant, suffering from epilepsy or planning to travel with children.

Communicable Disease Control (USA), **www.cdc.gov**, is a US Government site with excellent advice on travel health, has useful disease maps and details of disease outbreaks.

World Health Organisation (WHO), **www.who.int**, has links to the WHO *Yellow Book* on travel advice. This lists the diseases in different regions of the world. It describes vaccination schedules and makes clear

which countries have Yellow Fever Vaccination certificate requirements.
Tropical Medicine Bureau, **www.tmb.ie**, is an Irish-based site with a good collection of general travel health information and disease risks.
Fit for Travel, **www.fitfortravel.scot.nhs.uk**, from Scotland, provides an A-Z of vaccine and travel health advice requirements for each country.
British Travel Health Association (UK), **www.btha.org**, is the official website of an organization of travel health professionals.
NetDoctor (UK), **www.Netdoctor.co.uk**, is a general health advice site with a useful section on travel and an 'ask the expert' interactive chat forum.
Travel Screening Services (UK), **www.travelscreening.co.uk**. A private clinic dedicated to integrated travel health. The clinic gives vaccine, travel health advice, email and SMS text vaccine reminders and screens returned travellers for tropical diseases.

Books and leaflets

The Travellers Good Health Guide, Dr Ted Lankester (ISBN 0-85969-827-0).
Expedition Medicine (The Royal Geographic Society), Editors David Warrell and Sarah Anderson (ISBN 1 86197 040-4).
International Travel and Health, World Health Organisation Geneva (ISBN 92 4 158026 7).
The World's Most Dangerous Places, Robert Young Pelton, Coskun Aral and Wink Dulles (ISBN 1-566952-140-9).
The Travellers Guide to Health (T6) can be obtained by calling the Health Literature Line on T0800-555 777.
Advice for travellers on avoiding the risks of HIV and AIDS (Travel Safe) is available from Department of Health, PO Box 777, London SE1 6XH.
The Blood Care Foundation, order from PO Box 7, Sevenoaks, Kent TN13 2SZ, UK, T01732-742 427.

What to take

Antibiotics Ciproxin (**Ciprofloaxcin**) is a useful antibiotic for traveller's diarrhoea (which can affect up to 70% of travellers). You take one 500 mg tablet when the diarrhoea starts and if you do not feel better in 24 hours the diarrhoea is likely to have a non-bacterial cause and may be viral. Viral causes of diarrhoea will settle on their own. However, with all diarrhoeas try to keep hydrated by taking the right mixture of salt and water. This is available as Oral Dehydration Salts (ORS) in ready made sachets or can be made up by adding a teaspoon of sugar and a half teaspoon of salt to a litre of clean water. Flat carbonated drinks can also be used.

Anti-malarials Specialist advice is required as to which type to take. General principles are that all except **Malarone** should be continued for four weeks after leaving the malarious area. Malarone needs to be continued for only seven days afterwards (if a tablet is missed or vomited seek specialist advice). The start times for the anti-malarials vary in that if you have never taken **Lariam** (Mefloquine) before it is advised to start it at least two to three weeks before the entry to a malarious zone (this is to help identify serious side effects early). **Chloroquine** and **Paludrine** are often started a week before the trip to establish a pattern, but **Doxycycline** and Malarone can be started only 1-2 days before entry to the malarious area. It is risky to buy medicinal tablets abroad because the doses may differ and there may be a trade in false drugs.

Diarrhoea treatment Immodium is a great standby or those diarrhoeas that occur at awkward times, that is before a long coach/train journey or on a trek. It helps stop the flow of diarrhoea and in the author's view is of more benefit than harm. It was believed that letting the bacteria or viruses flow out had to be more beneficial. However, with Immodium they still come out, just in a more solid form. **Pepto-Bismol** is used a lot by Americans for diarrhoea. It certainly relieves symptoms but it is not a cure for underlying disease. Be aware that it turns the stool black as well as making it more solid.

First-aid kit This should include water-sterilizing tablets, plasters/band-aids, antiseptic cream, etc. For longer trips involving jungle treks take a clean needle pack, clean dental pack and water filtration devices.

Insect bite relief If you are prone to insects' bites or develop lumps quite soon after being bitten, carry an **Aspivenin** kit. This syringe suction device is available in the UK from **Boots** chemists and draws out some of the allergic materials and provides quick relief.

Painkillers Paracetomol or a suitable painkiller can have multiple uses for symptoms but remember that more than eight paracetamol a day can lead to liver failure.

MedicAlert These simple bracelets, or an equivalent, should be carried or worn by anyone with a significant medical condition.

Mosquito repellents Remember that DEET (Di-ethyltoluamide) is the gold standard. Apply the repellent every four to six hours but more often if you are sweating heavily. If a non-DEET product is used check who tested it. Validated products (tested at the London School of Hygiene and Tropical Medicine) include **Mosiguard**, Non-DEET **Jungle Formula** and non-DEET **Autan.** If you want to use **Citronella** remember that it must be applied very frequently (ie hourly) to be effective.

Sun block The Australians have a great campaign which has reduced skin cancer. It is called **Slip, Slap, Slop:** Slip on a shirt, Slap on a hat, Slop on sun screen.

Washing Biodegradable soap for jungle areas or ordinary soap for emergencies. Washing your hands is the safest way of preventing unwanted muck-to-mouth transmission before you eat.

Health care A-Z

Altitude sickness

Symptoms This can creep up on you as just a mild headache with nausea or lethargy. The more serious disease is caused by fluid collecting in the brain in the enclosed space of the skull and can lead to coma and death. A lung disease with breathlessness and fluid infiltration of the lungs is also recognized.
Cures The best cure is to descend as soon as possible.
Prevention Get acclimatized. Do not try to reach the highest levels on your first few days of arrival. Try to avoid flying directly into the cities of highest altitude. Climbers like to take treatment drugs as protective measures but this can lead to macho idiocy and death. The peaks are still there and so are the trails, whether it takes you personally a bit longer than someone else does not matter as long as you come back down alive.

Chagas's Disease

Symptoms The disease occurs throughout Brazil, affects locals more than travellers but travellers can be exposed by sleeping in mud-constructed huts where the bug that carries the parasite bites and defecates on an exposed part of skin. You may notice nothing at all or a local swelling, with fever, tiredness and enlargement of lymph glands, spleen and liver. The seriousness of the parasite infection is caused by the long-term effects which include gross enlargement of the heart and/or guts.
Cures Early treatment is required with toxic drugs.
Prevention Sleep under a permethrin treated bed net and use insect repellents.

Dengue fever

Symptoms This disease can be acquired throughout Brazil. In travellers this can cause a severe flu like illness with fever, lethargy, enlarged lymph glands and muscle pains. It starts suddenly, lasts for 2-3 days, seems to get better for 2-3 days and then kicks in again for another 2-3 days. It is usually all over in an unpleasant week. The local children are prone to the much nastier haemorrhagic form of the disease, which causes them to bleed from internal organs, mucous membranes and often leads to their death.

Cures The traveller's disease is self-limiting and forces rest and recuperation on the sufferer.

Prevention The mosquitoes that carry the dengue virus bite during the day unlike the malaria mosquitoes. Sadly this means that repellent and covered limbs are a 24-hour issue. Check your accommodation for flower pots and shallow pools of water since these are were the dengue-carrying mosquitoes breed.

Diarrhoea and intestinal upset

Summary This is almost inevitable. One study showed that up to 70% of all travellers may suffer during their trip.

Symptoms Diarrhoea can refer either to loose stools or an increased frequency; both of these can be a nuisance. It should be short lasting and persistence beyond two weeks, blood or pain all require specialist medical attention.

Cures Ciproxin will cure many of the bacterial causes but none of the viral ones. Immodium and Pepto-Bismol provide symptomatic relief. Dehydration can be a key problem especially in hot climates and is best avoided by the early start of Oral Rehydration Salts (at least one large cup of drink for each loose stool).

Prevention The standard advice is to be careful with water and ice for drinking. Ask yourself where the water came from. If you have any doubts then boil it or filter and treat it. There are many filter/treatment devices now available on the market. Food can also transmit disease. Be wary of salads (what were they washed in, who handled them), re-heated foods or food that has been left out in the sun having been cooked earlier in the day. There is a simple adage that says 'wash it, peel it, boil it or forget it'. Also be wary of unpasteurized dairy products these can transmit a range of diseases from brucellosis (fevers and constipation), to listeria (meningitis) and tuberculosis of the gut (obstruction, constipation, fevers and weight loss).

Hepatitis

Symptoms Hepatitis means inflammation of the liver. Viral causes of Hepatitis can be acquired anywhere in Brazil. The most obvious sign is if your skin or the whites of your eyes become yellow. However, prior to this all you may notice is itching and tiredness.

Cures Early on depending on the type of Hepatitis a vaccine or immunoglobulin may reduce the duration of the illness.

Prevention Pre-travel Hepatitis A vaccine is the best bet. Hepatitis B is spread a different route by blood and unprotected sexual intercourse, both of these can be avoided. Unfortunately there is no vaccine for Hepatitis C or the increasing alphabetical list of other Hepatitis viruses.

Leishmaniasis

Symptoms A skin form of this disease occurs in Brazil. If infected, you may notice a raised lump, which leads to a purplish discolouration on white skin and a possible ulcer. The parasite is transmitted by the bite of a sandfly. Sandflies do not fly far and the greatest risk is at ground levels, if you can avoid sleeping on the jungle floor do so.

Cures Several weeks treatment is required under specialist supervision. The drugs themselves are toxic but if not taken in sufficient amounts recurrence of the disease is more likely.

Prevention Sleep above ground, under a permethrin treated net, use insect repellent and get a specialist opinion on any unusual skin lesions soon after return.

Malaria and insect bite prevention

Symptoms Malaria can cause death within 24 hours. It can start with something just resembling an attack of flu. You may feel tired, lethargic, headachy or worse develop fits, coma and then death. Have a low index of suspicion because it is very easy to write off vague symptoms, which may actually be malaria. Whilst abroad and on return get tested as soon as possible, the test could save your life.
Cures Treatment is with drugs and may be oral or into a vein depending on the seriousness of the infection.
Prevention Is best summarized by the B and C of the ABCD (see page 69). **Bite avoidance** and **Chemoprophylaxis**. Some would prefer to take test kits for malaria with them and have standby treatment available. However, the field test of the blood kits have had poor results, when you have malaria you do not perform well enough to do the tests correctly enough to make the right diagnosis. Standby treatment (treatment that you carry and take yourself for malaria) should still ideally be supervised by a doctor since the drugs themselves can be toxic if taken in correctly. The Royal Homeopathic Hospital does not advocate homeopathic options for malaria prevention or treatment.

Rabies

Symptoms Most of you will know when you have been bitten. It may take days or weeks before odd tingling sensations occur in the affected part, followed by a fear of drinking water and spasms which lead to death.
Cures There is no cure for rabies once it has hold of the Central Nervous System.
Prevention Avoid getting bitten. Dog lovers have to remember that this is a whole new ball game and you are the ball. A full course of rabies vaccine is 100% effective. If you get bitten you will need more vaccine and if you had no pre-exposure vaccine or an inadequate amount you will also need to be injected with something called immunoglobulin. It is always wise to wash the wound but animal bites should ideally not be stitched up in the early stages.

Sexual health

Unprotected sex can spread HIV, Hepatitis B and C, Gonorrhea (green discharge), chlamydia (nothing to see but may cause painful urination and later female infertility), painful recurrent herpes, syphilis and warts, just to name a few. You can cut down the risk by using condoms, a femidom or avoiding sex altogether.

Sun protection

Symptoms Particularly vulnerable are white-skinned people who travel to hot countries and stay out longer without using adequate skin protection. This can lead to sunburn, which is painful and followed by flaking of skin. Aloe vera gel is a good pain reliever for sunburn. Long-term sun damage leads to a loss of elasticity of skin and the development of pre-cancerous lesions. Many years later a mild or a very malignant form of cancer may develop. The milder basal cell carcinoma, if detected early, can be treated by either cutting it out or freezing it. The much nastier malignant melanoma may have already spread to the bone and brain at the time that it is first noticed.
Prevention Follow the Australians with their Slip, Slap, Slop campaign and use sun screen. **SPF** (Sunscreen Protection Factor) is measured by determining how long a given person takes to 'burn' with and without the sunscreen product on. If it takes 10 times longer with the sunscreen product then that product has an SPF of 10. If it only takes twice as long then that product has an SPF of 2. The higher the SPF the

 greater the protection. However, do not use higher factors just to stay out in the sun longer; 'flash frying' (desperate bursts of excessive exposure) is known to increase the risks of skin cancer.

Typhoid fever

Symptoms This a gut infection which can spread to the blood stream. You get it from someone else's muck getting into your mouth. A classic example would be the waiter who fails to wash his hands and then serves you a salad. The fever is an obvious feature, occasionally there is a mild red rash on the stomach and often you have a headache. Constipation or diarrhoea can occur. Gut pain and hearing problems may also feature.

Cures Antibiotics are required and you are probably best managed in hospital.

Prevention The vaccine is very effective and is best boosted every 3 years. Watch what you eat and the hygiene of the place or those serving your food.

Underwater health

If you go diving make sure that you are fit do so. The **British Scuba Association** (BSAC, Telford's Quay, South Pier Road, Ellesmere Port, Cheshire CH65 4FL, United Kingdom, T0151-350 6200, F0151-350 6215, www.bsac.com), can put you in touch with doctors who do medical examinations. Protect your feet from cuts, beach dog parasites (larva migrans) and sea urchins. The latter are almost impossible to remove but can be dissolved with lime or vinegar. Keep an eye out for secondary infection.

Antibiotics for secondary infections. Serious diving injuries may need time in a decompression chamber.

Check that the dive company know what they are doing, have appropriate certification from BSAC or Professional Association of Diving Instructors (PADI) and that the equipment is well maintained.

Water purification

There are a number of ways of purifying water in order to make it safe to drink. Dirty water should first be strained through a filter bag (available from camping shops) and then boiled or treated. Bringing water to a rolling **boil** at sea level is sufficient to make the water safe for drinking, but at higher altitudes you have to boil the water for a few minutes longer to ensure that all the microbes are killed. There are **sterilizing** methods that can be used and there are proprietary preparations containing chlorine (for example Puritabs) or iodine compounds. Chlorine compounds generally do not kill protozoa (for example giardia). There are a number of water **filters** now on the market available in personal and expedition size. They work either on mechanical or chemical principles, or may do both. Make sure you take the spare parts or spare chemicals with you and do not believe everything the manufacturers say.

Rio de Janeiro

Footprint features

Introduction

Even those who know nothing else of Brazil will have heard of Rio, its Mardi Gras carnival and its spectacular beach and mountain scenery. What many do not realize is that Rio de Janeiro is a state as well as a city, and that this state hides beaches, forests and mountains just as beautiful as those in its capital. The southern coast, or Costa Verde is fringed with emerald green coves and bays which rise steeply to rainforest-covered hills, pocked with national parks. Coffee-swathed mountains lie behind Rio itself, with hill retreats once favoured by the Imperial family dotted throughout their valleys and remnants of one of the world's most biodiverse forests covering parts of their slopes. And to the northeast of the city of Rio de Janeiro lie a string of surf beaches and little resorts, the most celebrated of which is Búzios; a fishing village put on the map by Brigitte Bardot in the late 1960s which has now grown to become a chic little retreat for the state's middle classes.

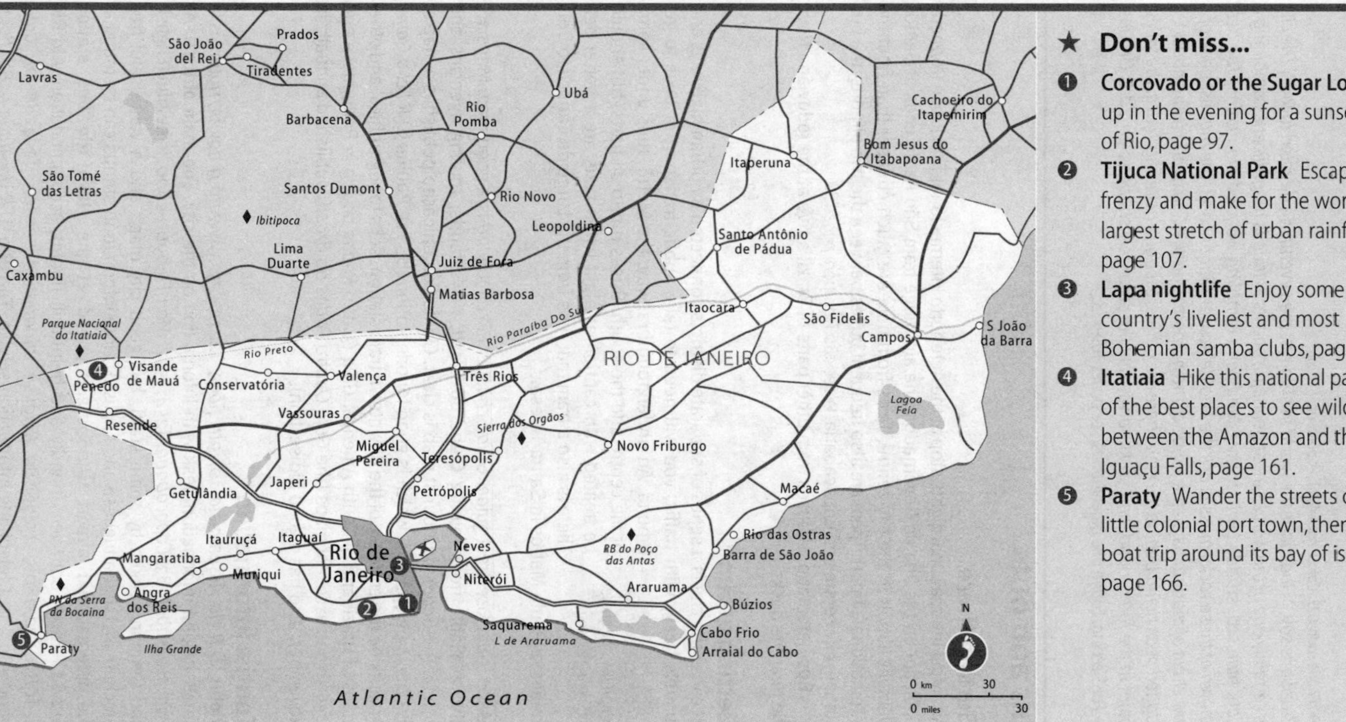

★ Don't miss...

1. **Corcovado or the Sugar Loaf** Go up in the evening for a sunset view of Rio, page 97.
2. **Tijuca National Park** Escape the frenzy and make for the world's largest stretch of urban rainforest, page 107.
3. **Lapa nightlife** Enjoy some of the country's liveliest and most Bohemian samba clubs, page 118.
4. **Itatiaia** Hike this national park, one of the best places to see wildlife between the Amazon and the Iguaçu Falls, page 161.
5. **Paraty** Wander the streets of the little colonial port town, then take a boat trip around its bay of islands, page 166.

Rio de Janeiro City

→ *Phone code: 021. Colour map 4, C3. Population: 8 million.*

Brazilians say, "God made the world in six days; the seventh he devoted to Rio". The city is certainly one of the world's most beautiful, and its setting is magnificent, combining a dark blue sea, studded with rocky islands and tumbling wooded mountains. The best known of these rocky masses are the Pão de Açúcar (Sugar Loaf), the highest peak of a low chain of mountains on the fringe of the harbour, and the Corcovado (Hunchback), a jagged peak rising behind the city. There are others, though, including Tijuca, the tallest point in the foreground, and 50 km away rise the strangely shaped Serra dos Órgãos.

▸▸ *For Sleeping, Eating and other listings, see pages 109-135.*

Ins and outs

Getting there

Air Most international flights stop at the Aeroporto Internacional Tom Jobim (formerly Galaeão) on the Ilha do Governador. The air bridge from São Paulo ends at Santos Dumont airport in the city centre. Taxis from here are much cheaper than from the international airport. There are also frequent buses between the two airports, the bus station, city centre and Copacabana. ▸▸ *See also Transport, page 130.*

Bus International buses from other parts of Brazil arrive at the rodoviária Novo Rio near the docks.

Getting around

Because the city is a series of separate districts connected by urban highways and tunnels heavy with traffic, you will need to take public transport or taxis to get around. An underground railway, the Metrô, runs under some of the centre and the south. Buses run to all parts, but should be treated with caution at night when taxis are a better bet. There is also a tram that runs from the Largo da Carioca to Dois Irmãos or Paula Mattos in Santa Teresa.

www.addresses.com.br/ for a comprehensive guide to addresses in the city.

Maps *Guia Rex* street guide. *Guia Schaeffer Rio de Janeiro* is a good map. Maps are also available from **Touring Clube do Brasil**, newsstands, touring agencies and hotels. The *Geomapas* tourist map is clear. **Cia de Comunicaçao** publishes a map of the city in perspective, which is good for orientation (US$2). **Paulini** ⓘ *R Lélio Gama 75*, outside the entrance of the downtown tram station, sells topographical and other maps of Brazil and of South America. *Guia Quatro Rodas do Rio* in Portuguese and English has excellent maps (the *Guia Quatro Rodas do Brasil*, published annually in November, also has a good Rio section).

Tourist information

Riotur ⓘ *R da Assembléia 10, 9th floor, T22177575, www.rio.rj.gov.br/riotur*, is a small, helpful information desk with information on the city. The **main office** ⓘ *Av Princesa Isabel 183, Copacabana, T25417522, Mon-Fri 0900-1800*, is helpful (English and German spoken by some staff), has good city maps and a very useful free brochure *RIO* (in Portuguese and English). More information stands can be found at the **international airport** ⓘ *0600-2400*, and at the **Novo Rio bus station** ⓘ *0800-2000*, both very friendly and helpful in finding accommodation. **Alo Rio** ⓘ *T0800 7071808, 25428080 (English information service, T22428000), daily 0900-1800*, is a telephone information service. **TurisRio** ⓘ *R da Ajuda 5, 8th floor,*

24 hours in Rio

Start with a *suco* from one of the many juice bars in Copacabana. Join the body-conscious locals and order an energy-giving *guarana* or a fashionable *açai*, both fruits from the Amazon, together with cereal they are an atom bomb of energy. Then make your way down to the theatre that is the beach. This is where real life is lived out in Rio, and where locals are most at home, sunbathing, but also playing volleyball and mostly socializing. Barra de Tijuca, a 40-minute bus ride away, is a much cleaner, quieter beach where those in the know go. Later, you can take the scenic tram ride to Santa Teresa, Rio's hilltop artistic enclave with its cobbled streets and cooler climate. Have lunch at Bar do Arnaudo, one of Rio's best restaurants and shop for handicrafts and works by local artists at La Vereda.

Head to Ipanema for a walk on the rocks and to watch the sunset over the water. Have a *chope* (draught beer) and delicious appetizers at A Garota de Ipanema, the 'Girl from Ipanema' bar, where the famous song was written. For an altogether classier early-evening drink, step into the elegant 1920s oasis that is the Copacabana Palace Hotel. The poolside bar here cries out for a gin and tonic. Then enjoy a lakeside dinner at one of the restaurants lining Avenida Epitácio Pessoa on the eastern side of Lagoa Rodrigo de Freitas. Bar Lagoa has a terrace overlooking the water. Take a taxi to Lapa and visit some of its funky bars with live music and dancing. Carioca da Gema is a 'musical café ', next door is Sacrilegio, a 'cultural café' with cutting-edge theatre. Semente is the venue for samba, choro and salsa. All are open until the early hours.

T22150011, www.turisrio.rj.gov.br, is very helpful and provides information for the state of Rio de Janeiro. **Embratur** ⓘ *R Uruguaiana 174, 8th floor, Centro, T25096017, www.embratur.gov.br*, has information on the whole country. **Touring Clube do Brasil** ⓘ *Pres Antônio Carlos 130 and Av Brasil 4294 (out of town)*, publish maps which are sold at newsstands and in some hotels.

Guidebooks *Trilhas do Rio*, by Pedro da Cunha e Meneses (Editora Salamandra, 2nd edition), US$22.50, describes walking trips around Rio. For a light-hearted approach to living in Rio, see *How to be a Carioca*, by Priscilla Ann Goslin. Many hotels provide guests with the weekly Itinerário, *Rio This Month*.

Newspapers and magazines *Balcão*, an advertising newspaper, US$2, twice weekly, offers apartments in and around Rio, language lessons, discounted tickets, items for sale and advertises shops; similar advertisements in the classified sections of dailies *O Globo* and *Jornal do Brasil*; both have entertainments pages too; *O Globo* has a travel section on Thursday; the *Jornal do Brasil's Programa* on Fri is an essential 'what's-on' magazine, as is the Rio supplement to *Veja*, a weekly news magazine (*Veja* publishes similar supplements in other major cities). **Riotur**'s fortnightly booklet lists the main attractions; *Rio This Month* (less reliable) is free from hotels. **TurisRio**'s free magazine about the state of Rio de Janeiro is interesting; if your hotel does not have these publications, just ask at the reception of one of the larger establishments.

Climate

Rio has one of the healthiest climates in the tropics. Trade winds cool the air. June, July and August are the coolest months, with temperatures ranging from 22°C (18° in a

Arriving at night

The airport is pretty safe, but watch your belongings. The excellent a/c bus doesn't run between 2300 and 0600, so if arriving in the early hours you will need to take a taxi or wait until morning – there is a 24-hour café in Terminal 1. Most hotels have someone on duty all night although they may not speak English.

cold spell) to 32°C on a sunny day at noon. December to March is hotter, from 32°C to 42°C. Humidity is high. October to March is the rainy season and the annual rainfall is about 1,120 mm. Carnival is a movable feast, running for five riotous days from the Friday afternoon before Shrove Tuesday to the morning hangover of Ash Wednesday.

History

The coast of Rio de Janeiro was first settled about 5,000 years ago. When the Europeans arrived in the region, the indigenous inhabitants belonged to the Tupi or Tupi-Guarani, Puri, Botocudos and Maxacali linguistic groups. Tragically, no Indian people in what is now Rio de Janeiro state survived the European incursions.

The Portuguese navigator, Gonçalo Coelho, arrived at what is now Rio de Janeiro on 1 January 1502. Thinking that the Baía de Guanabara (the name the local Indians used) was the mouth of a great river, they called the place the January River.

But the bay wasn't settled until 1555 when the French, under the Huguenot Admiral Nicholas Durand de Villegagnon, occupied Lage Island. They later transferred to Seregipe Island (now Villegagnon), where they built the fort of Coligny. The fort has been demolished to make way for the **Escola Naval** (Naval College) and the island itself, since the narrow channel was filled up, has become a part of the mainland. Villegagnon set up a colony as the starting point for what he called Antarctic France.

Rio de Janeiro orientation

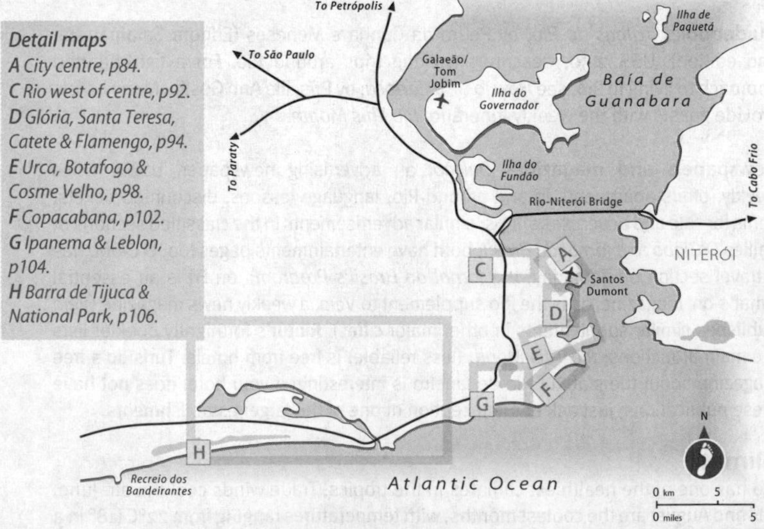

Safety in Rio

The majority of visitors enjoy Rio and all it has to offer without any problems. But Rio is one of the world's most densely populated cities and there are areas of extreme poverty; most robberies that occur are committed out of desperation.

Overseas visitors are an obvious target. Many crimes against tourists are avoidable. Avoid wearing expensive clothes and jewellery and if you are carrying a camera, keep it out of view. Don't leave things unattended on the beach. You have the most to lose when carrying all your belongings and as you go in and out of banks, exchange houses and expensive shops, so take extra care then. At other times, put your passport, travellers' cheques, etc in the hotel safe. In other words, don't take too much out with you, have some sense and relax.

Certain parts of the city are best avoided: the city centre on Sunday when it is deserted; tunnels, quiet alleyways, jostling crowds and dark corners. Locals don't walk on the beaches at night: if you must, do not go out of sight of the pavement. The Tijuca forest is best explored with a group of six or more, except the stretch between Afonso Vizeu square and Cascatinha which is well policed during the day; the tram to Santa Teresa (see page 96) attracts pickpockets; robberies sometimes happen on city buses, don't use them if guarding your property is essential (private *frescão* buses are more secure). The main bus station is patrolled Inside, but uncomfortable outside. If you go to the Zona Norte at night, use a taxi; wandering around *favelas* alone at any time of day is ill-advised. The 'red light' districts of the Zona Sul are unlikely to offend anyone walking about at night, even children or unaccompanied women. Do, however, be suspicious of any club that you are invited into by a stranger (have your drink opened in front of you) and of anyone offering drugs. When ordering drinks in red-light bars, check prices first.

The Tourist Police, Av Afrânio de Melo Franco, Leblon (in front of the Casa Grande theatre), T25115112, publish a sensible advice leaflet (available from hotels and consulates; consulates also issue safety guidelines). Tourist police officers are helpful, efficient and multilingual; they patrol all the main tourist areas and if you have any problems, contact them first.

In early 1559-1560, Mem de Sá, third governor of Brazil, mounted an expedition from Salvador to attack the French, who were supported by Tamoio Indians. The Portuguese succeeded in capturing the French fort and putting an end to Antarctic France, but did not colonize the area until 1567 when they transferred their settlement to the Morro de São Januário. This is generally considered the date of the founding of the city of São Sebastião do Rio de Janeiro, so called in honour of the Portuguese prince who would soon assume the throne.

Though constantly attacked by local indigenous groups, the new city grew rapidly and when King Sebastião divided Brazil into two provinces, Rio was chosen capital of the southern captaincies. Salvador became sole capital again in 1576, but Rio again became the southern capital in 1608 and the seat of a bishopric. There was a further French incursion in 1710-1711 as a result of the tension between France and Portugal during the war of Spanish Succession, and because of the flow of gold out of Minas Gerais through Rio.

Rio de Janeiro was by now becoming the leading city in Brazil. Not only was it the port out of which gold was shipped, but it was also the focus of the export/import trade of the surrounding agricultural lands. On 27 January 1763, it became the seat of the Viceroy. After Independence, in 1834, it was declared capital of the Empire and remained the capital for 125 years.

The shaping of a city

When the Portuguese royal family fled to Brazil in 1808, the ideas that were brought over from Europe started a major transformation of the city. True, works to beautify and clean up the place had been undertaken when the city acquired viceregal status, but the remodelling which occurred in the early 19th century was on a different scale (see Fine art and architecture on pages 707 and 710). The city also expanded beyond its historical boundaries. It grew north into São Cristóvão and Tijuca and south through Glória, Catete, Flamengo and Botafogo. The prosperous coffee barons and business class built their mansions and the Imperial court was the centre of the nation's attention. The decline of the coffee trade in Rio de Janeiro state and the proclamation of the Republic did not affect the city's dominance as political, economic and cultural heart of Brazil.

Growth continued into the 20th century and one of the most significant acts was the construction of a monumental new boulevard through the middle of the commercial district. The 33-m wide Avenida Central, later renamed Avenida Rio Branco, was driven through the old city's narrow streets in 1904-1905 as the principal means of access in Rio. Meanwhile, the city continued to expand outwards: north into industrial zones; south around the coast; and inland, up the hills, mainly in the form of the slums known as *favelas*.

When, in 1960, the nation's capital was moved to Brasília, Rio went into decline, especially the commercial centre, and began to suffer badly from poor urban planning decisions and too many high-rise buildings. However, in the late 1990s, the mayor of the city, Luiz Paulo Conde, embarked on a massive programme of regenerating the centre through remodelling and attracting residents to neglected districts. As an architect and urbanist he brought a social vision which encompasses the improvement of favelas and a plan to clean up the south of the city as far as Leblon.

In December 1997 a new 25-km expressway, the Linha Amarela, was opened from the Ilha do Fundão, near the international airport, to Barra de Tijuca, cutting by more than half the journey time to Barra.

Sights

Central Rio and Lapa

Known as 'Centro', this is the historical part of the city, which dates from 1567 when the Portuguese moved their settlement from the area now known as Urca to the Morro de São Januário. Today the centre stretches from the Mosteiro de São Bento to the Santos Dumont airport and inland as far as the Campo de Santana Park.

Check opening times in advance of all churches, museums and public buildings; they change frequently. All museums and the Jardim Botânico close over Carnival.

The hill on which the original city was located was removed in the 1920s, so the historical centre effectively ends at the São José Church. The 400 years following the founding of the city saw so many changes in architectural design and fashion that, today, the centre appears to be an incoherent collection of buildings, with the ultra-modern towering over the neoclassical, which in turn sits uneasily beside the colonial. Add to this the crowded streets and the constant traffic and it may seem a daunting place to explore. Don't give up! There is much to discover and your perseverance will be repaid.

An example of the juxtaposition of so many elements in close surroundings is the **Travessa do Comércio**, which runs between the Praça 15 de Novembro and the Rua do Ouvidor. On the northwest side of Praça 15 de Novembro is the Arco do Teles, all that remains of an 18th-century construction, now incorporated into a modern building. Through the arch is the Travessa do Comércio, a narrow, twisting street with neoclassical houses and wrought-iron arches over the street lamps. This is how the whole city was in the 19th century. The Travessa, now dwarfed by 20th-century office blocks, leads to the church of Nossa Senhora da Lapa dos Mercadores, another 18th-century construction sandwiched between the concrete and glass. On Friday nights the Travessa is very lively; along it are several restaurants, including the **Arco Imperial**, where Carmen Miranda (see page 697) lived between 1925 and 1930 (her mother kept a boarding house).

The city's main artery is the **Avenida Presidente Vargas**, 4½ km long and over 90 m wide. It starts at the waterfront, divides to embrace the famous Candelária Church, then crosses the **Avenida Rio Branco** in a magnificent straight stretch past the Central do Brasil railway station, with its imposing clock tower, until finally it incorporates a palm-lined, canal-divided avenue. Most of the Avenida Rio Branco's ornate buildings have been replaced by modern blocks; a few remain by Cinelândia and the Biblioteca Nacional. Some of the finest modern architecture is to be found along the **Avenida República do Chile**, such as the Petrobrás, the Banco Nacional de Desenvolvimento Econômico and the former Banco Nacional de Habitação buildings and the new cathedral.

Around Praça 15 de Novembro

Originally an open space at the foot of the Morro do Castelo, the **Praça 15 de Novembro** (often called Praça XV) has always been one of the focal points in Rio de Janeiro. Today it has one of the greatest concentrations of historic buildings in the city. Having been through various phases of development in its history, it had major remodelling in the late 1990s. The last vestiges of the original harbour, at the seaward end of the praça were restored. The steps no longer lead to the water and the Avenida Alfredo Agache now goes through an underpass, creating an open space between the praça and the seafront and giving easy access to the ferry dock for Niterói. The area is well illuminated and clean and the municipality has started to stage shows, music and dancing in the praça. At weekends there's an antiques, crafts, stamp and coin fair, **Feirarte II** ⓘ *0900-1900*.

On Rua 1 de Março, across from Praça 15 de Novembro, there are three buildings related to the Carmelite order. The convent of the **Ordem Terceira do Monte do Carmo**, started in 1611, is now used as the Faculdade Cândido Mendes. The Carmo Church was appropriated by the royal family in the early 19th century as a residence for the queen, Dona Maria I (nicknamed A Louca because of her mental illness). Such buildings were called PR, that is, taken over by the Príncipe Regente (or, in popular terminology, *Prédio Roubado* – stolen building). To prevent the members of the Imperial family sullying their feet on streets used by all and sundry, a covered bridge was built between the ex-convento and the cathedral when the Rua 7 de Setembro was driven between them in 1857.

Between the former convent and the Igreja da Ordem Terceira do Carmo is the old cathedral, the **Igreja de Nossa Senhora do Carmo da Antiga Sé**, separated from the Carmo Church by a passageway. It was the chapel of the Convento do Carmo from 1590 until 1754. A new church was built in 1761, which became the Capela Real with the arrival of the Portuguese royal family in 1808 and subsequently the city's cathedral. In the crypt are the alleged remains of Pedro Alvares Cabral, the Portuguese explorer (though Santarém, Portugal, also claims to be his last resting place).

The order's present church, the **Igreja da Ordem Terceira do Carmo** ⓘ *R Primeiro de Março, Mon-Fri 0800-1400, Sat 0800-1200*, the other side of the old cathedral from the convent, was built in 1754, consecrated in 1770 and rebuilt between 1797 and 1826. It has strikingly beautiful portals by Mestre Valentim (see Fine art and sculpture, page 709), the son of a Portuguese nobleman and a slave girl. He also created the main altar of fine moulded silver, the throne and its chair and much else. A fountain designed by Mestre Valentim stands in the praça: the **Chafariz do Mestre Valentim**, or Chafariz do Pirâmide.

At the rear of the old cathedral and the Carmo Church, on Rua do Carmo, is the **Oratório de Nossa Senhora do Cabo da Boa Esperança**, one of the few remaining public oratory from the colonial period in Rio.

The beautiful colonial **Paço Imperial** ⓘ *T25334407, Tue-Sun 1100-1830* (former Royal Palace), on the southeast corner of the Praça 15 de Novembro, was built in 1743 as the residence of the governor of the Capitania. It later became the king's storehouse and armoury (Armazens), then the Casa da Moeda, before being made into the Paço Real when the Portuguese court moved to Brazil. After Independence it became the Imperial Palace. During the Republic it was used as the post and telegraph office and fell into decline. In the 1980s it was completely restored as a cultural centre. It has several exhibition spaces, one theatre, one cinema for art films, a library, a section showing the original construction, a superb model of the city and the Bistro and the Atrium restaurants (recommended).

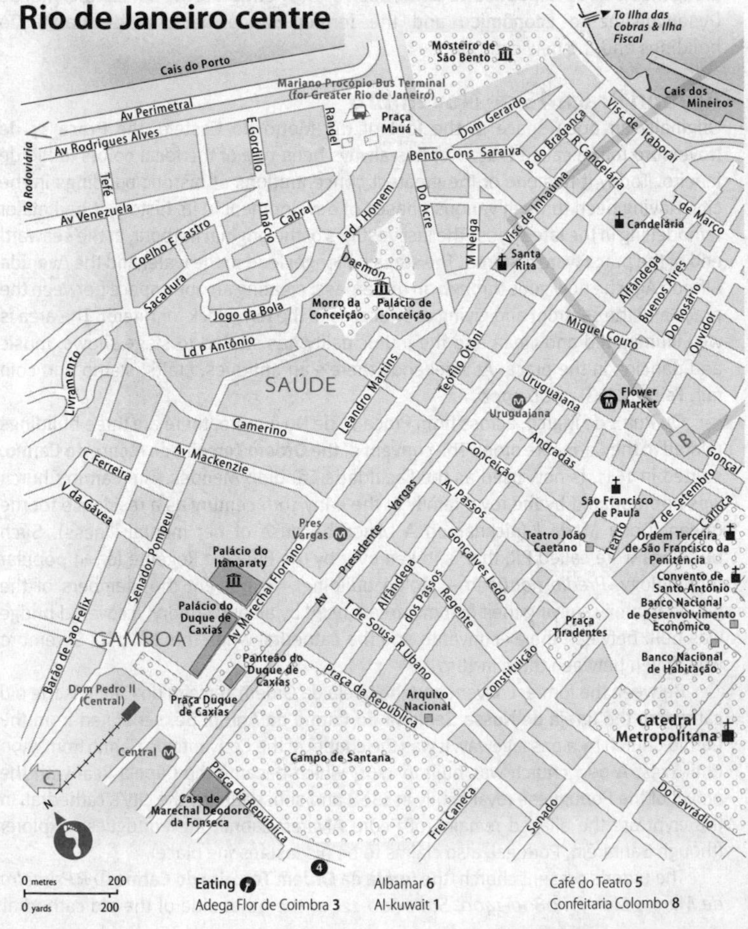

Beside the Paço Imperial, across Rua da Assembléia, is the **Palácio Tiradentes** ⓘ *T25881000, Mon-Fri 1300-1900 by prior appointment*, built between 1922 and 1926. It is now the legislative assembly of the State of Rio de Janeiro, but the building was closed twice in the 1930s as different administrations did not feel the need for a Chamber of Federal Deputies. The palace is in eclectic style (see Architecture, page 710), with a façade displaying heavy Greek influence. In front stands a statue of the Independence fighter, Tiradentes (see page 253), by Francisco de Andrade; the palace was given his name because it was on this spot, the site of the old prison, that the national hero was held prisoner while awaiting execution.

In the next block southeast is the **Igreja de São José** ⓘ *R São José e Av Presidente Antônio Carlos, Mon-Fri 0900-1200, 1400-1700, Sun 0900-1100*, considerably altered since its original construction in the 17th century. The current building dates from 1824 and was remodelled in 1969.

One block further northeast, at Rua Dom Manoel 15, is the **Museu Naval e Oceanográfico**. It had a collection of paintings and prints, as well as a display of weapons and figureheads, but most of the exhibits have been moved to the Espaço Cultural da Marinha.

Turning to the northwest side of Praça 15 de Novembro, you go through the Arco do Teles and the Travessa do Comércio (see above) to Rua do Ouvidor. The Igreja

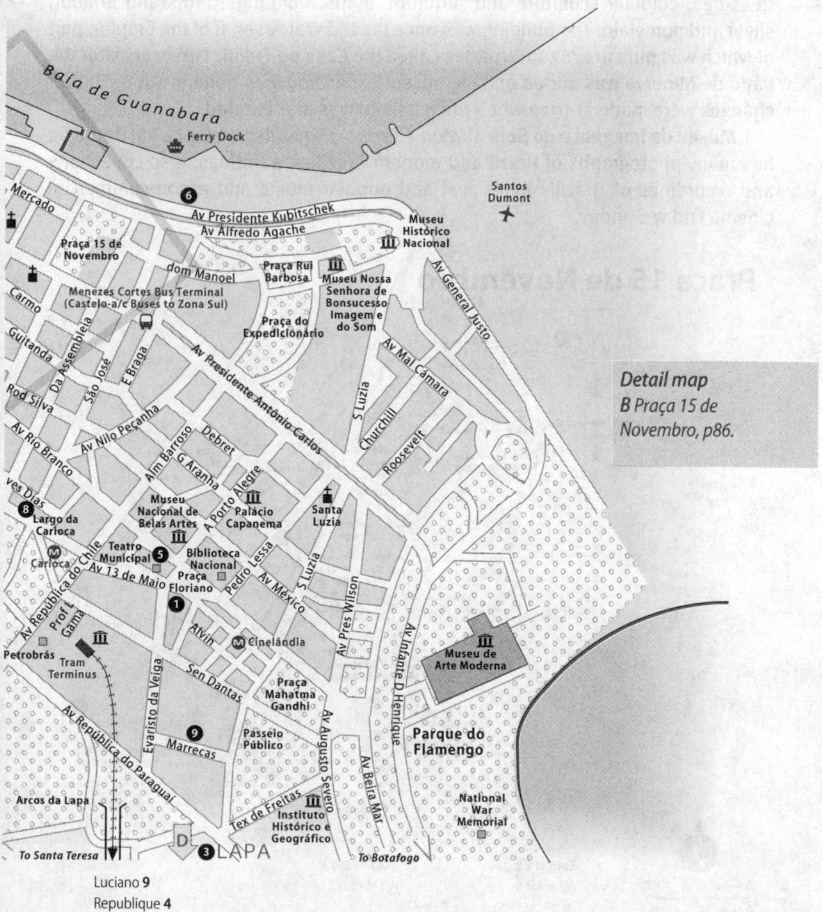

Luciano **9**
Republique **4**

Detail map
B Praça 15 de Novembro, p86.

Nossa Senhora da Lapa dos Mercadores ⓘ *R do Ouvidor 35, Mon-Fri 0800-1400*, was consecrated in 1750, remodelled in 1869-1872 and has been fully restored. Across the street, with its entrance at Rua 1 de Março 36, is the church of **Santa Cruz dos Militares**, built 1780-1811. It is large, stately and beautiful and the inside has been well renovated in a 'light' Baroque style.

Praça Marechal Âncora/Praça Rui Barbosa

In the corner of the centre bounded by Praça 15 de Novembro and the Esplanada do Castelo is an area which has changed significantly since colonial times. Most alterations were made in the 20th century, first with the removal of the old municipal fish market, for health reasons, then with the levelling of the Morro do Castelo in the 1920s. There are two squares here, Praça Marechal Âncora, or Praça Rui Barbosa, and Praça do Expedicionário. The only remnant of the Morro do Castelo is a short stretch of the Ladeira da Misericórdia, at the foot of which is the church of Nossa Senhora de Bonsucesso, also known as the church of the Santa Casa da Misericórdia. The Santa Casa itself is behind the church. The colonial hospital made way for a neoclassical building in the mid-19th century. The main focus here is the **Museu Histórico Nacional** ⓘ *T22409529, Tue-Fri 1000-1730, Sat, Sun and holidays 1400-1800, US$1*, which contains a collection of historical treasures, colonial sculpture and furniture, maps, paintings, arms and armour, silver and porcelain. The building was once the old War Arsenal of the Empire, part of which was built in 1762 (this part is called the Casa do Trem). Two years later the Pátio de Minerva was added and significant expansion was done in 1808. Further changes were made in 1922 when the museum was inaugurated.

Museu da Imagem e do Som ⓘ *Mon-Fri 1300-1800*, also on Praça Rui Barbosa, has many photographs of Brazil and modern Brazilian paintings; also collections and recordings of Brazilian classical and popular music and a non-commercial cinema Friday-Sunday.

Avenida Presidente Vargas

The church of **Nossa Senhora da Candelária** ⓘ *Praça Pio X (Dez), Mon-Fri 0730-1200, 1300-1630, Sat 0800-1200, Sun 0900-1300* (1775-1810), at the city end of Avenida Presidente Vargas where it meets Rua 1 de Março, has beautiful ceiling decorations and romantic paintings. It is on the site of a chapel founded in 1610 by Antônio da Palma after he had survived a shipwreck, an event depicted by paintings inside the present dome.

In this part of the city a number of cultural centres have opened in recent years. The **Espaço Cultural dos Correios** ⓘ *R Visconde de Itaboraí 20, T25038770, Tue-Sun 1300-1900*, holds temporary exhibitions and cultural events and a postage stamp fair on Saturdays. Opposite, with entrances on Avenida Presidente Vargas and Rua 1 de Março 66, is the **Centro Cultural Banco do Brasil (CCBB)** ⓘ *T38082000, Tue-Sun 1230-1900*, hlghly recommended for good exhibitions, with a library, multimedia facilities, a cinema, concerts (US$6 at lunchtime) and a restaurant. At the corner of Rua Visconde de Itaboraí (No 253) and Avenida Presidente Vargas is the **Casa França-Brasil** ⓘ *T22535366, Tue-Sun 1200-2000*. This building holds temporary exhibitions and is dedicated to cultural exchanges between the two countries, but is much more important for its history. Its construction dates from the first French Artistic Mission to Brazil (see Architecture and Fine Art and Sculpture, pages 707 and 710 respectively) and it was the first neoclassical building in Rio. The interior is entirely neoclassical, although the pillars and mouldings are made of wood. The roof, though, is a hybrid between the colonial Brazilian style and the newly introduced European fashion. It was built as a customs house and the strong-room can still be seen. The newest cultural centre here is the **Espaço Cultural da Marinha** ⓘ *Av Alfredo Agache at Av Presidente Kubitschek, Tue-Sun 1200-1700*. This former naval establishment now contains museums of underwater archaeology and navigation and the Galeota, the boat used by the Portuguese royal family for sailing around the Baía de Guanabara. Moored outside is the warship, *Bauru*.

Offshore, but connected to the mainland by a causeway to Ilha das Cobras, is the **Ilha Fiscal**. It was built as a customs house at the emperor's request, but he deemed it too beautiful, so he said that it should be used only for official parties. Only one was ever held, five days before the Republic began. It is now a museum, linked with the Naval Cultural Centre. Boats leave Friday, Saturday and Sunday at 1300, 1430 and 1600 (30 minutes later October to March) ⓘ *T38706879*. The island is passed by the ferry to Niterói.

Praça Mauá

The Praça Mauá marks the end of Centro and the beginning of the port zone. Many of the empty warehouses are used as workshops by the samba schools, where their beautiful floats are built.

Just north of Candelária, on a promontory overlooking the bay, is the World Heritage Site of **Mosteiro de São Bento** ⓘ *daily 0800-1230, 1400-1730, shorts not allowed*. The monastery's church, dedicated to Nossa Senhora de Monserrate, contains much of what is best in the 17th- and 18th-century art of Brazil. Monks of the Benedictine order arrived in Rio de Janeiro in 1586, five years after their installation in Salvador.

São Bento is reached either by a narrow road from Rua Dom Gerardo 68, or by a lift whose entrance is at Rua Dom Gerardo 40 (taxi to the monastery from centre US$5). Both routes lead to a praça with tall trees, but stepping out of the lift into this oasis increases the sense of escape from the city below. The church's façade is in the mannerist style, plain and undecorated. You go through the *galilé*, the antechamber for the unbaptized with its fine tiles, and enter the main body of the church. *Corta ventos*, doors which keep out the draughts so that the candles inside are not extinguished, are the last obstacle to the sight of the interior. The carving and gilding

Wild Jock of Skelater

The crypt of Convento de Santo Antônio contains the tomb of a Scottish soldier of fortune known as 'Wild Jock of Skelater'. He was in the service of the Portuguese government during the Napoleonic War, and had the distinction of being appointed the first Commander-in-Chief of the Army in Brazil. The statue of Santo Antônio was made a captain in the Portuguese army after his help had been sought to drive out the French in 1710, and his salary paid to the monastery. In 1810 the statue became a major, in 1814 a lieutenant-colonel, and was granted the Grand Cross of the Order of Christ. He was retired without pay in 1914. The church and convent are open Monday-Friday 1400-1700 .

is remarkable – not an inch is unadorned in gold and red – much of it by Frei Domingos da Conceição (see Fine Art and Sculpture, page 707). The paintings, too, should be seen; *O Salvador*, the masterpiece of Brazil's first painter, Frei Ricardo do Pilar, hangs in the sacristy. The lamps (*lampadarios* – two of which are attributed to Mestre Valentim) are of solid silver which, coming from Peru and Bolivia, was of greater value than Brazil's own gold. See also the two *anjos tocheiros*, angels carrying torches, common in many Baroque churches. On top of the main altar is a statue of Nossa Senhora de Monserrate, made by Frei Domingos da Conceição; the eyes of both the Virgin and her Child are made from painted birds' eggs. The Chapels of the Immaculate Conception (Nossa Senhora da Conceição) and of the Most Holy Sacrament (Santíssimo Sacramento) are masterpieces of colonial art. The organ, dating from the end of the 18th century, is very interesting.

Every Sunday at 1000, Mass is sung with Gregorian chant and music, which is free, but you should arrive an hour early to get a seat. On other days, mass is at 0715. At other times you may be lucky enough to hear the monks singing. The monastery is a few minutes' walk from Praça Mauá, turning left off Avenida Rio Branco; Rua Dom Gerardo 68 is behind the massive, new RBI building.

Also easily reached from Praça Mauá and requiring a climb is the **Morro da Conceição,** another hill from which the early Portuguese settlers could survey the bay. The first constructions on the hill were religious and a bishop's palace was built in 1702, the **Palácio da Conceição**. This and the subsequently built **Fortaleza da Conceição** are currently in the hands of the military. The Palácio has a small museum and the area is perfectly safe to visit as another remnant of colonial Rio. Above the door of the Fortaleza is another of the few remaining public oratories; it is lit at night.

Largo da Carioca

The Largo da Carioca, a remarkable ensemble of old and new plus the muddle of the street vendors who have occupied the praça between Rua da Carioca and the Metrô station, is another good location for seeing a variety of sites within a small area.

The second oldest convent in the city is the 17th-century **Convento de Santo Antônio**, on a hill off the Largo da Carioca, built between 1608 and 1615. Its church has a marvellous sacristy adorned with blue tiles and paintings illustrating the life of St Anthony. In the church itself, the Baroque decoration is concentrated in the chancel, the main altar and the two lateral altars. Santo Antônio is a particular object of devotion for women who want to find husbands and many will be seen in the precincts.

Separated from this church only by some iron railings is the charming church of the **Ordem Terceira de São Francisco da Penitência**, built in 1773. Currently closed for renovation, it contains much more carving and gilding of walls and altar than its neighbour. The workmanship is superb. In the ceiling over the nave is a fine panel painted by José de Oliveira. There is a museum attached to the church.

Across Rua da Carioca and Rua 7 de Setembro is the church of **São Francisco de Paula** ⓘ *Mon-Fri 0900-1300*, at the upper end of the Rua do Ouvidor. The first stone was laid in 1759 and construction was completed in 1801. It contains some of Mestre Valentim's work – the carvings in the main chapel and the lovely Capela da Nossa Senhora da Vitória (Our Lady of Victory). The beautiful fountain at the back of the church plays only at night.

One long block behind the Largo da Carioca and São Francisco de Paula is the **Praça Tiradentes**, old and shady, with a statue to Dom Pedro I. Erected in 1862, it is the work of Luís Rochet and shows the emperor on horseback, declaring Independence. At the northeast corner of the praça is the **Teatro João Caetano** ⓘ *T22210305*, named after a famous 19th-century actor. Shops in nearby streets specialize in selling goods for umbanda, the Afro-Brazilian religion.

South of the Largo da Carioca are the modern buildings on Avenida República do Chile mentioned above. The New Cathedral, the **Catedral Metropolitana** ⓘ *0800-1800*, was dedicated in November 1976. It is a cone-shaped building with an internal height of 68 m, diameter 104 m and external height 83 m; its capacity is 5,000 seated, 20,000 standing. The four enormous 60-m-high stained-glass windows are its most striking feature. It is still incomplete.

Crossing Avenida República do Paraguai from the east side of the Catedral Metropolitana, you come to an open area with the Petrobrás building and the station, with museum, for the tram to Santa Teresa (entrance on Rua Senador Dantas – see below). Soon after leaving the station the tram traverses the **Arcos da Lapa**, which were built as an aqueduct to take water from the Rio Carioca to the Largo da Carioca.

Avenida Rio Branco

Here are the last vestiges of the early 20th-century project of the grand Avenida Central. Facing Praça Marechal Floriano is the **Teatro Municipal** ⓘ *T25442900 for opera and orchestral performances, tickets from about US$10; to book a tour of the theatre (in English and Spanish, French or Portuguese) T22623501 in advance, Mon-Fri 0900-1700, US$1.20 per person*. It is one of the most magnificent buildings in Brazil in the so-called 'eclectic' style (see Architecture, page 710). It was built in 1905-1909, in imitation of the Opéra in Paris. On either side of the colonnaded façade are rotundas, surmounted by cupolas. Above the columns are statues of two women; Poetry and Music. The decorative features inside and out represent many styles, all lavishly executed. The tour is worth it to see front and back stage, the decorations and the machine rooms. The box office is at the right-hand side of the building.

Across the avenue is the **Biblioteca Nacional** ⓘ *Av Rio Branco 219, T22628255, Mon-Fri 0900-1700, US$1*. This building also dates from the first decade of the 20th century. The monumental staircase leads to a hall, off which lead the fine internal staircases of Carrara marble. The first national library was brought to Brazil by the Prince Regent, Dom João, in 1808 (the original collection coming from the Ajuda Palace in Lisbon); today the library houses over nine million pieces, including the 15th-century *Book of Hours*, paintings donated by Pedro II and scores by Mozart.

The third major building in this group, opposite the Teatro Municipal, is the **Museu Nacional de Belas Artes** ⓘ *Av Rio Branco 199, T22400068, Tue-Fri 1000-1800, Sat, Sun and holidays 1400-1800, US$1*. It was built between 1906 and 1908, also in 'eclectic' style. It has about 800 original paintings and sculptures and some thousand direct reproductions. There is a gallery dedicated to works by Brazilian artists from the 17th century onwards, including paintings by Frans Janszoon Post (Dutch 1612-1680), who painted Brazilian landscapes in classical Dutch style (see The Dutch in Brazil, page 444) and the Frenchmen Debret and Taunay (see Fine Art and sculpture, page 707, for these and other painters represented). Another gallery

Favelas, a numberless existence

Rio de Janeiro's *favelas*, the slums which creep up the city's hillsides and spread out across the flat lands, have been the source of much bad press for many years. They have been represented as no-go areas, where drug lords rule and fight for dominance, and out of which the city's criminals came. No sensible visitor would venture within their radius until *favela* tours were started in the mid-1990s. One such tour is to Vila Canoas and Rocinha, close to São Conrado. The tours are interesting and lead to a greater appreciation of Rio and its people. They have the same motivation as a major scheme, Favela-Bairro, designed to rehabilitate the favelas, to show that the *favelados* are hardworking, simple people, and that their communities deserve the same facilities and rights as other parts of the city. (It is unadvisable to visit the favelas unless on an organized tour.)

The name *favela* was first used at the end of the 19th century after soldiers on the Canudos campaign in Bahia set up their guns on a hill called the Morro das Favelas. The soldiers became known as favelados. When they returned to Rio after the campaign, the soldiers built their homes on the Morro da Providência, but the *favela* nickname stuck. In time, any temporary settlement acquired the name favela and, as urban and rural poor alike strove to make it in the city, many people stayed initially in the shanties before moving to better accommodation. Many, of course, were unable to better themselves. In the 1970s and 1980s, there were some attempts to improve conditions in the *favelas* and residents, given assurances that they would not be forcibly removed, began to make their dwellings more permanent. Electricity and water supplies can be tapped into, usually illegally, but waste disposal and other basic facilities are rare. One of Rio's problems is that the favelas are in the middle of the city, not on the outskirts as in other metropoli. Almost a million people live in these conditions. The huge number of entries and exits make them difficult to police.

Since 1993, an ambitious project has been underway to upgrade the majority of the city's *favelas*. A US$350 m programme, aided by the Inter-American Development Bank, is providing the shanties with streets in place of alleys, sewerage, lighting, day-care centres, recreational areas, rubbish collection and transport. The favelas will be integrated with the surrounding neighbourhoods. The work also includes reforestation and the prevention of hill slides. Residents are given a say in how their district should be improved and no family will be rehoused in a part of the city which is alien to it. Having accepted that the favelas are permanent, not transitory, the city's authorities' task is to incorporate them into the whole, not leave them marginalized. An IADB special report on the project quoted O Globo: "Every citizen ought to have the right to live on a street in a house with a number".

The Secretaria Municipal da Habitação and IplanRio, the Empresa Municipal de Informática e Planejamento, produce a magazine on Favela-Bairro, available from Avenida Afonso Cavalcanti 455, bloco B, 4 andar, CEP 20.211-110, Rio de Janeiro, T2732345, or R Gago Coutinho 52, Largo do Machado, CEP 22.221-070, Rio de Janeiro, T5563399. See Tour operators, page 23, for guides who can offer a safe, different and interesting experience.

charts the development of Brazilian art in the 20th century, including works by Cândido Portinari, Alberto da Veiga Guignard and others. A third gallery contains work by foreign artists. There is also a hall for temporary exhibitions.

Those interested in contemporary art should also visit the **Palácio Capanema**, the former Ministry of Education and Health building, then the Palácio da Cultura. It is on the Esplanada do Castelo, at the junction of Avenida Graça Arana and Rua Araújo Porto Alegre, and dates from 1937-1945 (UNESCO has declared it an International Monument). A team of architects led by Lúcio Costa and under the guidance of Le Corbusier designed it; Oscar Niemeyer and Affonso Reidy were in the group (see Architecture, page 710). Inside are the great murals of Cândido Portinari, as well as works by renowned artists. The gardens were laid out by Roberto Burle Marx (see page 108).

In the Rua de Santa Luzia, near the Palácio Capanema and overwhelmed by tall office buildings, is the attractive little church of **Santa Luzia**. When built in 1752 it had only one tower; the other was added late in the 19th century. Feast day is 13 December, when devotees bathe their eyes with holy water, which is considered miraculous.

Cinelândia

Praça Mahatma Gandhi, at the end of Avenida Rio Branco, is flanked on one side by the old cinema and amusement centre of the city, known as Cinelândia. The cast-iron fountain in the ornamental garden was moved here from Praça 15 de Novembro.

Next to the praça is the **Passeio Público** ⓘ *daily 0900-1700*, a garden planted in 1779-1783 by the artist Mestre Valentim, whose bust is near the old former gateway.

The **Museu do Instituto Histórico e Geográfico** ⓘ *Av Augusto Severo 8 (10th floor), just off Av Beira Mar, Mon-Fri 1200-1700*, is across the street from the Passeio Público. It has an interesting collection of historical objects, Brazilian products and artefacts.

Praça da República

Campo de Santana, Praça da República, is an extensive and picturesque public garden close to the Pedro II, or Central Railway Station. The Parque Júlio Furtado in the middle of the square is populated by agoutis (or gophers), best seen at dusk; there is also an artificial grotto, with swans.

A plaque at Praça da República 197 marks the house of Marechal Deodoro da Fonseca, who proclaimed Brazil a republic in 1889. On the opposite side of the praça is the **Arquivo Nacional** ⓘ *Praça da República e R Azeredo Coutinho, closed for repairs*, in the neoclassical former Casa da Moeda; and the **Faculdade de Direito** ⓘ *R Moncorvo Filho 8*, in the Solar do Conde dos Arcos. On the opposite side of Avenida Presidente Vargas from the praça are the **Palácio** and **Panteão do Duque de Caxias**.

Palácio do Itamaraty ⓘ *Av Marechal Floriano 196*, is in the next block east from the Palácio do Duque de Caxias. Built in neoclassical style in the 1850s for the coffee baron Francisco José da Rocha, it became the president's residence between 1889 and 1897 and then the Ministry of Foreign Affairs until the opening of Brasília. Now it houses the **Museu Histórico e Diplomático** ⓘ *T22532828, free guided tours on Mon, Wed and Fri hourly between 1315 and 1615*, which is recommended.

Northern Rio

Rua da Gamboa

Over the Morro da Providência, which is between the Estação Dom Pedro II and the bay, is the **Cemitério dos Ingleses** ⓘ *R da Gamboa 181*. The cemetery, the oldest in Rio, was granted to the British community by Dom João, Regent of Portugal, in 1810. Catholics who could afford a burial were laid to rest inside their churches (see the numbers on the church floors, marking the graves), but the British in Rio, being non-Catholic, were not allowed to be buried in the religious establishments.

Maracanã Stadium

ⓘ *T25689962, daily 0900-1700 (0800-1100 on match days); a guided tour of the stadium (in Portuguese) from Gate 16 costs US$2 and of the museum, US$0.50.*

Maracanã Stadium, officially called Estádio Mário Filho, is one of the largest sports centres in the world, with a capacity of 200,000. This is where Pelé scored his 1,000th goal in 1969. Matches are worth going to if only for the spectators' samba bands and the adrenalin-charged atmosphere. There are three types of ticket: *cadeiras* (individual chairs), the most expensive; *arquibancadas* (terraces), good for watching the game, but don't sit between rival groups of fans; *geral* (standing), the cheapest, not recommended, not safe. Prices vary according to the game, but it's more expensive to buy tickets from agencies than at the gate; it is cheaper to buy tickets from club sites on the day before the match.

Maracanã is now used only for major games; Rio teams play most matches at their home grounds (still a memorable experience). Hotels can arrange visits to football matches, a good idea on Sunday when the Metrô is closed and buses are very full.

Getting there Take the metro to Maracanã Metrô station on Linha 2, one stop beyond São Cristóvão. Buses Nos 238 and 239 from the centre, 434 and 464 from Glória, Flamengo and Botafogo, 455 from Copacabana, and 433 and 464 from Ipanema and Leblon all go to the stadium.

Useful information Don't take valuables or wear a watch; take special care when entering and leaving the stadium. The rivalry between the local clubs Flamengo and Vasco da Gama is intense, often leading to violence, so it is advisable to avoid their encounters. Don't be tempted to buy a club shirt or favour on match day; if you find yourself in the wrong place, you could be in trouble.

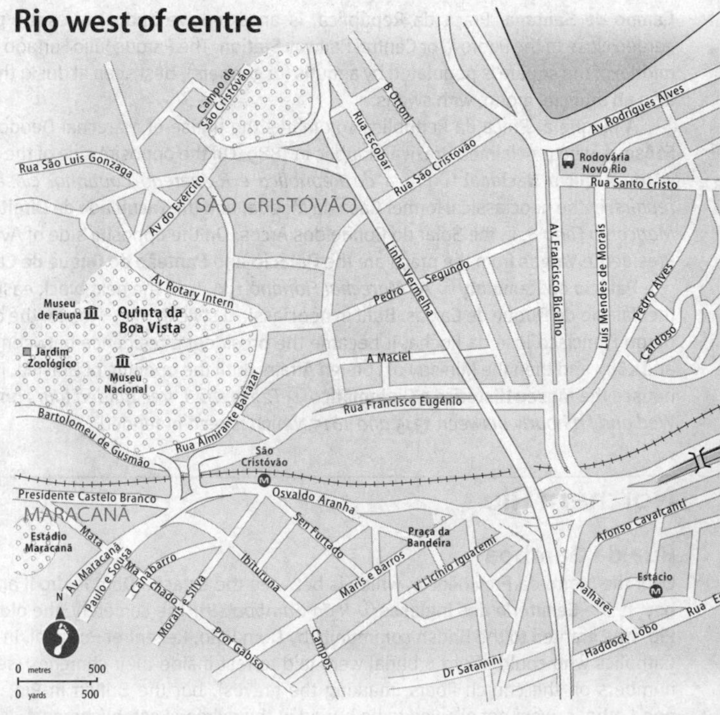

Quinta da Boa Vista

About 3 km west of the Praça da República (beyond the Sambódromo – see box on Carnival, page 122) is the Quinta da Boa Vista, formerly the emperor's private park, from 1809 to 1889. The palace in which the Imperial family lived now houses the Museu Nacional (see below). In recent years the Quinta da Boa Vista has had the problem of thieves operating by the park entrance and in the park itself. If you are comfortable in crowds, perhaps the best time to visit is Saturday, or better still, Sunday afternoon. There are more people and therefore more police because it is full of Cariocas looking for fun and relaxation. It is a good time for people-watching (but don't take an expensive camera). The park becomes a noisy mixture of colours, smells of hot dogs and corn, people playing football, preachers warning of the end of the world and street sellers.

The **Museu Nacional** ⓘ *Tue-Sun 1000-1600, US$2*, in the Quinta da Boa Vista has important collections which are poorly displayed. The building was the principal palace of the emperors of Brazil, but only the unfurnished Throne Room and Ambassadorial Reception Room on the second floor reflect past glories. In the Entrance Hall is the famous Bendegó meteorite, found in the state of Bahia in 1888; its original weight, before some of it was chipped, was 5,360 kg. Besides several foreign collections of note (for example, of Peruvian and Mexican archaeology, Graeco-Roman ceramics and Egyptian mummies), the museum contains collections of Brazilian Indian weapons, dresses, utensils, etc, of minerals and of historical documents. There are also collections of birds, beasts, fish and butterflies. Despite the need for conservation work, the museum is still worth visiting. Some of the collections are open to qualified research students only. To get there it is safest to take a taxi to the main door, but the museum can be reached by taking the Metrô to São Cristóvão, crossing the railway line and walking a few metres to the park. This is safer than taking a bus.

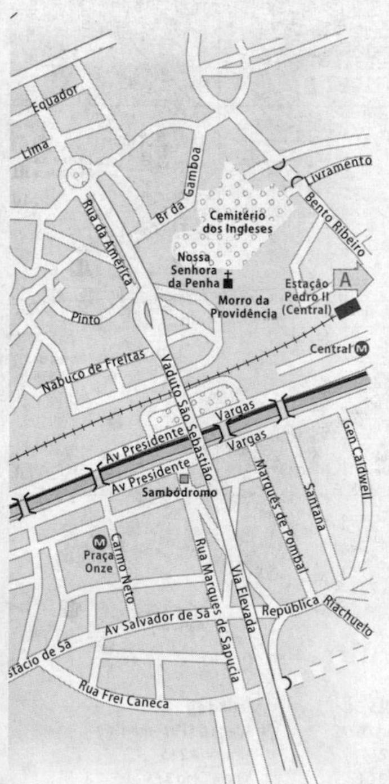

Museu de Fauna ⓘ *Tue-Sun 1200-1700*, also in the Quinta da Boa Vista, contains a most interesting collection of Brazilian fauna.

The church of **Nossa Senhora da Penha**, in the northern suburb of Penha, is on a bare rock in which 365 steps are cut. This staircase is ascended by pilgrims on their knees during the festival month of October; there is a funicular for those unable to do this. The church in its present form dates from the early 20th century, based on an early 18th-century chapel. The first religious building, a hermitage, was built in 1632. Its prominent position makes Nossa Senhora da Penha a major landmark and its balustrade provides fine views. To get there, take bus No 497 from Copacabana, or Nos 340 and 346 from the centre.

Glória, Catete and Flamengo

This commercial district ends where Avenida Rio Branco meets Avenida Beira Mar, with its royal palms and bougainvilleas, coasting the Botafogo and Flamengo beaches.

On the Glória and Flamengo waterfront, with a view of the Pão de Açúcar and Corcovado, is the **Parque do Flamengo**, designed by Burle Marx (see page 108), opened in 1965 during the 400th anniversary of the city's founding and landscaped on 100 ha reclaimed from the bay. The park (officially called Parque Brigadeiro Eduardo Gomes) runs from the aterro on which Santos Dumont Airport stands to the

Glória, Santa Teresa, Catete & Flamengo

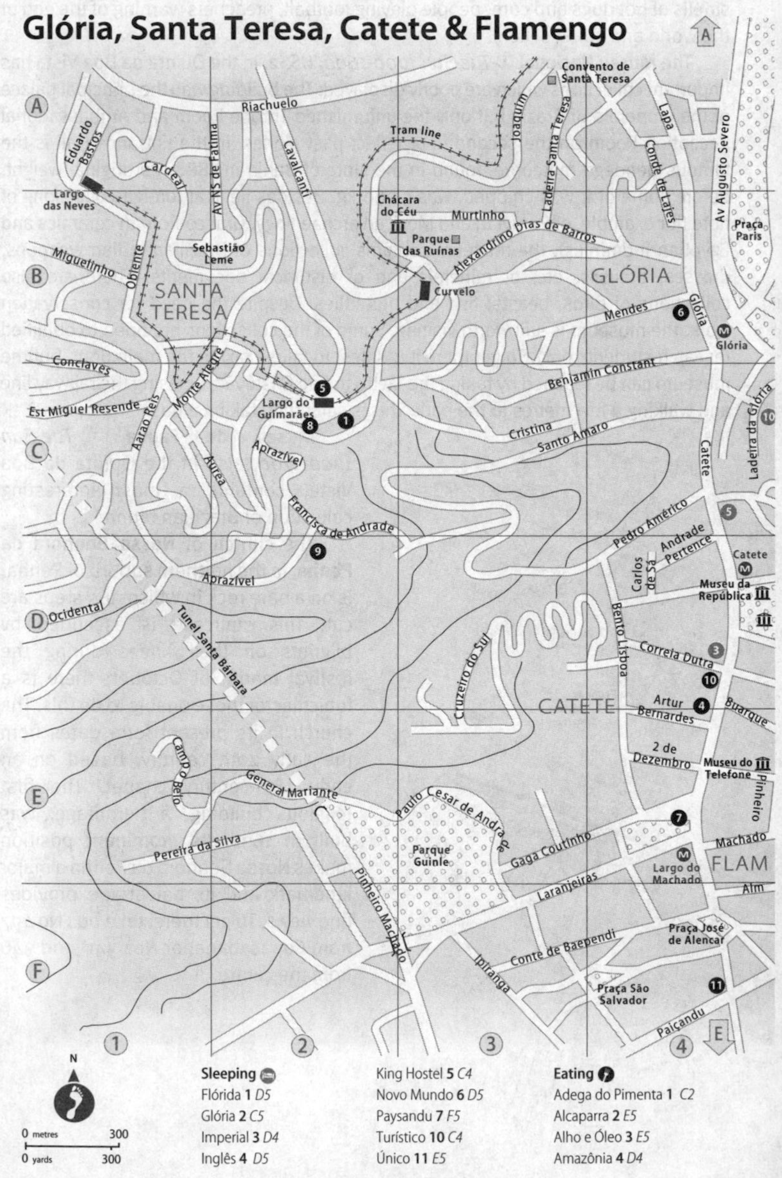

Morro da Viúva and Botafogo beach. The area was reclaimed from the sea using 1.2 million metric tonnes of earth. Behind the War Memorial (see below) is the public yacht marina. In the park are many sports fields; there is a sailboat basin and model plane-flying field, as well as night amusements, such as bandstands and areas for dancing. There is also a marionette theatre, a miniature village and a staffed nursery. Security in the park is in the hands of vigilante policemen and it is a popular recreation area. On Sunday and holidays between 0700 and 1800 the avenues through the park are closed to traffic.

At the city end of the Parque Flamengo is the **Museu de Arte Moderna** ⓘ *Av Infante Dom Henrique 85, T22404944, www.mamrio.com.br, Tue-Sun 1200-1700 (last entry 1630), US$2*, a spectacular building near the War Memorial. It suffered a disastrous fire in 1978; the collection is now being rebuilt and several countries have donated works of art. There is also a non-commercial cinema. The collection of contemporary Brazilian art includes drawings by Cândido Portinari from the 1940s and 1950s and drawings and etchings of everyday work scenes by Gregório Gruber, made in the 1970s.

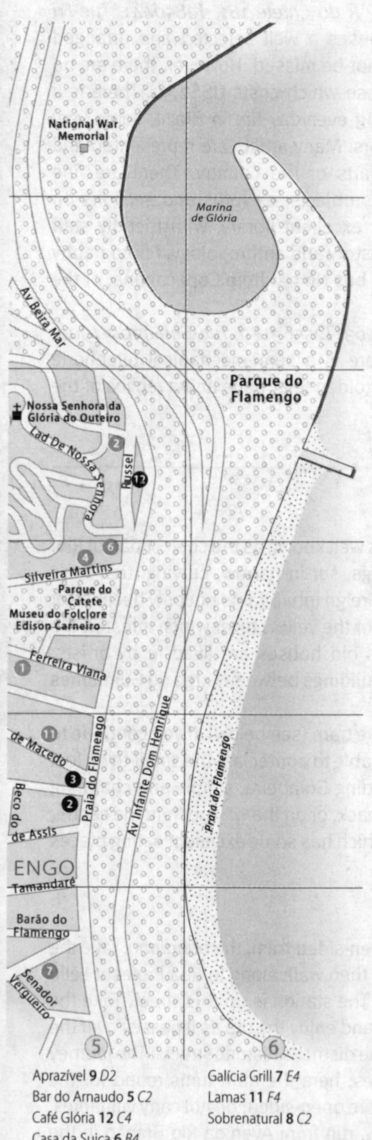

Praça Paris, built on reclaimed ground near the Largo da Glória, is much admired for the beauty of its formal gardens and illuminated fountains. Opposite Praça Paris is the **Monumento aos Mortos da Segunda Guerra Mundial** (National War Memorial to Brazil's dead in the Second World War) ⓘ *Av Infante Dom Henrique 75, Tue-Sun 1000-1700 (crypt and museum)*. The memorial is two slender columns supporting a slightly curved slab, representing two palms uplifted to heaven. In the crypt are the remains of the Brazilian soldiers killed in Italy in 1944-1945. Beach clothes and rubber-thonged sandals are not permitted.

The beautiful little church on the Glória Hill, overlooking the Parque do Flamengo, is **Nossa Senhora da Glória do Outeiro** ⓘ *Mon-Fri 1300-1700, Sat and Sun 0800-1200*. It was the favourite church of the Imperial family, and Dom Pedro II was baptized here. The building is polygonal, with a single tower. Construction began in 1735 and was completed in 1791. It contains some excellent examples of blue-faced Brazilian tiling. Its main altar, of wood, was carved by Mestre Valentim. Adjacent is the **Museum of Religious Art** ⓘ *T25566434, same hours, but closed on Mon*. To get there, take bus No 119 if going from the centre or No 571 if heading there from Copacabana.

The **Museu da República** ⓘ *R do Catete 153, T25573150, Tue-Sun 1200-1700, US$2.50*, is the former palace of a coffee baron, the Barão de Nova Friburgo. The palace was built in 1858-1866 and, in 1887, it was converted into the presidential seat, until the move to Brasília. The ground floor of this museum consists of the sumptuous rooms of the coffee baron's mansion. The first floor is devoted to the history of the Brazilian republic. You can also see the room where former president Getúlio Vargas shot himself. The museum is highly recommended. Behind the museum is the **Parque do Catete** with many birds and monkeys. To get there, take bus 571 from Copacabana, or the Metrô to Catete station.

The **Museu do Folclore Edison Carneiro** ⓘ *R do Catete 181, T2850441, Tue-Fri 1100-1800, Sat and Sun 1500-1800, free*, houses a well selected and arranged collection of interesting objects which should not be missed. However, there are no explanations other than in a book in Portuguese which costs US$2.50. There is a collection of small ceramic figures representing everyday life in Brazil, some very funny, some scenes animated by electric motors. Many artists are represented and displays show the way of life in different parts of the country. There are fine Candomblé and Umbanda costumes, religious objects, ex-votos and sections on many of Brazil's festivals. It has a small, but excellent library, with friendly staff helpful for finding books on Brazilian culture, history and anthropology. Photography is allowed, but without flash. To get there, take bus No 571 from Copacabana, or the Metrô to Catete station.

The **Museu do Telefone** ⓘ *R 2 de Dezembro 63, T25563189, Tue-Sun 0900-1900*, exhibits old telephones. On the top floor there is a semi-mechanical telephone exchange from the 1940s plus Getúlio Vargas' golden telephone and a replica of the telephone of Dom Pedro II. Recommended.

Santa Teresa

This hilly inner suburb southwest of the centre is well known as the coolest part of Rio. It has many colonial and 19th-century buildings, set in narrow, curving, tree-lined streets. Santa Teresa attracted well-to-do and foreign inhabitants not only because of its cooler climate, but also because it was free of the yellow fever which infested the lower parts of the city. Today, Santa Teresa's old houses are lived in by artists, intellectuals and makers of handicrafts. Many buildings between Largo do Guimarães and Largo das Neves are being restored.

Most visitors in the daytime will arrive on the tram (see below). If you continue to the end of the line, Largo das Neves, you will be able to appreciate the small-town feel of the place. There are several bars here, including Goiabeira, simple and charming with a nice view of the praça. Either on the way back, or on the way up from the centre, the essential stop is the **Largo do Guimarães**, which has some excellent eating places (see Eating, page 115) and a great atmosphere.

Ins and outs

Santa Teresa is best visited on the traditional open-sided **tram**, the *bondinho*: take the Metrô to Cinelândia, go to Rua Senador Dantas then walk along to Rua Profesor Lélio Gama (look for **Banco do Brasil** on the corner). The station is up this street. Take the Paula Mattos line (a second line is Dois Irmãos) and enjoy the trip as it passes over the **Arcos da Lapa** aqueduct, winding its way up to the district's historic streets. The journey ends at the round praça called Largo das Neves; here the tram turns round for the journey back to Rua Profesor L Gama. The trams are open-sided; do not carry valuables. Fare US$0.40 one way. **Buses** Nos 206 and 214 run from Avenida Rio Branco in the centre to Santa Teresa. At night, be careful only to take a **taxi** (about US$7).

History

In 1624, Antônio Gomes do Desterro erected a hermitage dedicated to Nossa Senhora do Desterro on the hill which was to become Santa Teresa. The name was changed from Morro do Desterro to Santa Teresa after the construction in 1750 of a convent in honour of two Carmelite sisters, Jacinta and Francisca. The Convento da Santa Teresa, at Joaquim Murtinho e Ladeira de Santa Teresa, can only be seen from the outside; the Carmelite nuns do not admit visitors. From the 17th to the mid-18th century, work was done in various stages to bring water from the Rio Carioca to the city. The final project was the Aqueduto dos Arcos (**Arcos da Lapa**), which carried water from Santa Teresa to the Chafariz da Carioca, with its 16 fountains, in the city centre. The aqueduct's use changed at the end of the 19th century with the introduction of electric trams in Rio. The first run along the tracks laid on the arches was on 1 September 1896. It has been a major task to preserve the Santa Teresa tram, called the *bondinho*, the last such service in Rio.

Sights

Some of the fine historical residences that can be seen include the **Casa de Valentim** (a castle-like house in Vista Alegre), the tiled **Chácara dos Viegas** in Rua Monte Alegre and the **Chalé Murtinho** ⓘ *R Murtinho Nobre 41*. This was the house in which Dona Laurinda Santos Lobo held her famous artistic, political and intellectual salons at the turn of the 20th century. The house was in ruins until it was partially restored and turned into a cultural centre called **Parque das Ruínas** ⓘ *daily 1000-1700*. It has superb views of the city, an exhibition space, an open-air stage (live music Thursday) and a snack bar. A bridge connects it to the Chácara do Céu (see below). Also in the district is the old hotel known as the **Hotel das Paineiras**. See also the **Rua Aprazível** and **Largo de Guimarães**.

The **Chácara do Céu**, or **Fundação Raymundo Ottoni de Castro Maia** ⓘ *R Murtinho Nobre 93, T22850891, Wed-Mon 1200-1700, US$1*, has a wide range of art objects and works by modern painters, including Brazilian; exhibitions change through the year. To get there, take the Santa Teresa tram to Curvelo station, walk along Rua Dias de Barros, following the signposts to Parque das Ruínas. Castro Maia's former residence, **Museu Açude** ⓘ *Estrada do Açude 764, Alto da Boa Vista, Floresta da Tijuca, T2380368*, is also a museum. Every Sun it has a 'brunch' with music (1230-1700).

Security In recent years, visitors have been put off going to Santa Teresa because of a reputation for crime which has spilled over from neighbouring *favelas*. It would, however, be a great shame to miss this unique 'town within a city'. The crime rate has been reduced and normally a policeman rides each *bondinho*, but you are advised not to take valuables or look 'wealthy'. A T-shirt, shorts and enough money for a meal is sufficient. Avoid long walks on streets that are far from Largo das Neves and Largo do Guimarães. The area around the **Hotel das Paineiras** is well patrolled.

Pão de Açúcar and Corcovado

The district of Botafogo sits roughly midway between the Pão de Açúcar and Corcovado, as the crow flies. On the ground, access to either peak from this part of the city is quite straightforward, but involves many more twists and turns than a bird would take. There are also plenty of other attractions at ground level.

Pão de Açúcar

At 396 m, the Pão de Açúcar, or **Sugar Loaf**, is a massive granite cone at the entrance to Guanabara Bay. The bird's eye view of the city and beaches is very beautiful. There is a restaurant (excellent location, terrible food, closes 1900) and a playground for children on the Morro da Urca, halfway up, where there are also shows at night (consult the cultural sections in the newspapers). You can get refreshments at the top.

The sea level cable-car station is in a military area and is safe to visit. At Praia Vermelha, the beach to the south of the rock, is the **Círculo Militar da Praia Vermelha** restaurant, which is open to the public (no sign). It has wonderful views, but is not so good for food or service; stop there for a drink anyway. From Praia Vermelha, the **Pista Cláudio Coutinho** runs around the foot of the rock. It is a paved path for walking, or jogging, and for access to various climbing places. It is open until 1800, but you can stay on the path after that. Here you have mountain, forest and sea side-by-side, right in the heart of the city. You can also use the Pista Coutinho as a way of getting up the Pão de Açúcar more cheaply than the US$12.50 cable-car ride. About 350 m from the path entrance is a track to the left which leads though the forest to **Morro de Urca**, from where the cable car can be taken for US$10 (you can come down this way, too, but if you take the cable-car from sea level you must pay full fare). You can save more money, but use more energy, by climbing the **Caminho da Costa**, a path to the summit of the Pão de Açúcar. One stretch, of 10 m, requires climbing gear (even then, some say it is not necessary), but if you wait at the bottom of the path, a group going up will let you tag along. You can then descend to Morro de Urca by cable-car for free and walk down.

There are 35 **rock routes** up the mountain, with various degrees of difficulty. The best months for climbing are April to August. See Activities and tours, page 129, for climbing clubs; there is also a book on climbing routes.

Getting there **Buses** Nos 107 (from the centre, Catete or Flamengo) and 511 from Copacabana (512 to return) take you to the cable-car station, Av Pasteur 520, at the foot. **Cable-cars** From Praia Vermelha to Morro de Urca. The first car goes up at 0800,

Urca, Botafogo & Cosme Velho

then every 30 minutes (or when full), until the last comes down at 2200. From Urca to Sugar Loaf, the first connecting cable-car goes up at 0815 then every 30 minutes (or when full), until the last leaves the summit at 2200; the return trip costs US$8 (US$6 to Morro da Urca, halfway up). The old cableway has been completely rebuilt. Termini are ample and efficient and the present Italian cable-cars carry 75 passengers. Even on the most crowded days there is little queuing.

Urca and Botafogo

The suburb of Urca was built in 1922 when an *aterro* was made at the base of the Pão de Açúcar on its north side. It is mostly residential. Note the small statue of São Pedro holding the keys to heaven on a rock in the sea in front of the church. From the esplanade there are lovely views of the sunset behind Corcovado.

In the district is the Morro do Pasmado, which has fine views of the bay. Also in Botafogo is one of the city's main shopping malls, Rio Sul, a good place to go for entertainment, services, eating and, of course, shopping. It has been totally refurbished and is completely safe (more details are given under Shopping, page 125). As well as a **Theatre Museum** ⓘ *R São João Batista 103-105, T22863234, Mon-Fri 1100-1630*, there are three important museums in Botafogo.

The **Museu do Índio** ⓘ *R das Palmeiras 55, T22868899, Mon-Fri 1000-1730, Sat and Sun 1300-1700 (shop closes 1200-1400), US$1.75*, houses 12,000 objects from many Brazilian-Indian groups, including basketry, ceramics, masks and weapons. There is also a small, well-displayed handicraft shop. It belongs to the **Fundação Nacional do Índio** (Funai) and was set up by Marechal Rondon. To get there, it's a 10-minute walk from Botafogo Metrô; from Catete, bus 571 (Glória-Leblon) passes Ruas Bento Lisboa and São Clemente. There is also a **library of ethnology** ⓘ *weekdays only*, at the same location, which is friendly and helpful.

Museu Villa-Lobos ⓘ *R Sorocaba 200, T22663845, Mon-Fri 1000-1700*, houses a collection of personal objects belonging to the great composer, with a various number of instruments, scores, books and recordings.

Corcovado

ⓘ *T/F5581329, www.corvocado.com.br, daily 0830-1900.*

To reach the statue of the Cristo Redentor at the summit of Corcovado, you have to go through Laranjeiras and Cosme Velho. The road through these districts heads west out of Catete. Near the station for the cog railway which climbs to the statue are two important cultural sites.

The **Museu Internacional de Arte Naif do Brasil** (**MIAN**) ⓘ *R Cosme Velho 561, T22058612, Tue-Fri 1000-1800, Sat, Sun and holidays 1200-1800, US$3.20, discounts for groups, students and senior citizens*, is one of the most comprehensive museums of Naive and Folk paintings in the world. It is only 30 m

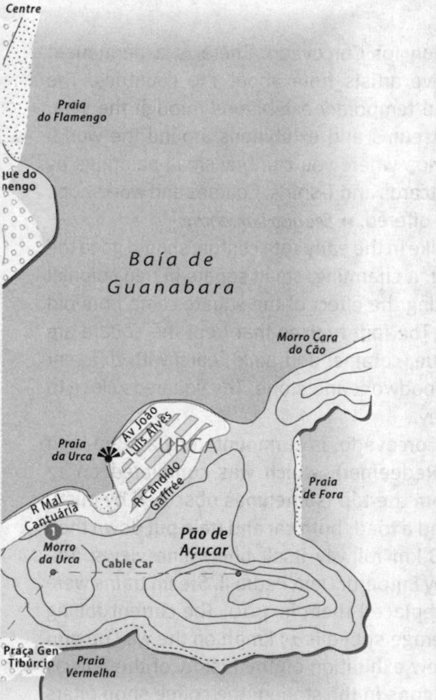

Carême Bistrô **3**
Chez Michou & Habib's **4**
Cobal Humaitá **5**
Raajmahal **6**

Brazil's International Museum of Naive Art

MIAN, the Museu Internacional de Arte Naif do Brasil, grew out of the private collection of Lucien Finkelstein, a French jewellery designer who lives in Brazil and who, about 40 years ago, started to buy Naive paintings all over Brazil and abroad, on his frequent international trips. As the collection grew so large, he decided to create a foundation and in October 1995 the museum opened its doors to the public. The current director is Jaqueline Finkelstein. The museum is located in a huge, spacious old house surrounded by gardens and trees.

The museum's international section gathers together works from several countries, from the 17th century to today, including the world-famous paintings on glass from former Yugoslavia (Hlebine School) and impressive campesino paintings on leather from Ecuador.

The Brazilian section is remarkable for the vibrant tropical colours and the diversity of subjects. Among the most representative Brazilian Naive painters, the museum has several works by Antônio Poteiro, José Antônio da Silva, Rosina Becker do Vale, Lia Mittarakis and others (including our own Fábio Sombra). One of the most interesting works is an enormous painting (4 m by 7 m) by Lia Mittarakis, in the main hall, showing the city of Rio de Janeiro. This colourful work, full of funny details, is considered the biggest Naive painting in the world and took five years to complete.

uphill, on the same street as the station for Corcovado. There is a permanent collection of some 8,000 works by Naive artists from about 130 countries. The museum also hosts several thematic and temporary exhibitions through the year. Parts of its collection travel to other museums and exhibitions around the world. There is a coffee shop and a souvenir shop where you can buy small paintings by some of the artists on display, books, postcards and T-shirts. Courses and workshops on painting and related subjects are also offered. » *See also box above.*

Those who want to see what Rio was like in the early 19th century should go to the **Largo do Boticário** ⓘ *R Cosme Velho 822*, a charming, small square in neo-colonial style. Much of the material used in creating the effect of the square came from old buildings demolished in the city centre. The four houses that front the square are painted different colours (white, pale blue, caramel and pink), each with different features picked out in decorative tiles, woodwork and stone. The square is close to the terminus for the Corcovado cog railway.

A hunch-backed peak 710 m high, Corcovado, is surmounted by a 38-m high statue of **Cristo Redentor** (Christ the Redeemer), which was completed on 12 October 1931. There is a superb view from the top (sometimes obscured by mist), which can be reached by a cog railway and a road; both car and train put down their passengers behind the statue. The 3.8-km railway itself offers fine views. The railway was opened on 9 October 1884 by Emperor Dom Pedro II. Steam trains were used to begin with, but electric trains replaced them in 1910. The current rolling stock is Swiss and dates from 1979. Average speed is 15 kmph on the way up and 12 kmph on the way down. There is a new exhibition on the history of the railway with photos, videos, models and old wagons in the station; the coffee shop offers free coffee and mineral water. From the upper terminus there is a climb of 220 steps to the top (although an escalator is being installed), near which there is a café. Mass is held on Sunday in a small chapel in the statue pedestal. The floodlighting was designed in 1931 by Marconi and came into operation during the following year.

Getting there The train runs every 20-30 minutes according to demand between 0800 and 1830, journey time 10 minutes (cost: US$8 return; single tickets available). Also, No 206 bus does the very attractive run from Praça Tiradentes (or No 407 from Largo do Machado) to Silvestre (the railway has no stop here now). An active 9-km walk will take you to the top and the road is shady. Take the narrow street to the right of the station, go through the gate used by people who live beside the tracks and continue to the national park entrance. Walkers are not usually charged entrance fees. Allow a minimum of two hours (up to four depending on fitness) for the climb. If going by car to Corcovado, the entrance fee is US$2.20 for the vehicle, plus US$2.20 for each passenger. For safety reasons go in company, or at weekends when more people are about. To get there, take a Cosme Velho bus to the cog railway station at Rua Cosme Velho 513: from the centre or Glória/Flamengo No 180; from Copacabana take No 583, from Botafogo or Ipanema/Leblon No 583 or 584; from Santa Teresa Microônibus Santa Teresa. Coach trips tend to be rather brief; taxis which wait in front of the station also offer tours of Corcovado and Mirante Dona Marta.

To see the city by day and night go up at 1500 or 1600 and descend on the last train, at about 1815.

Copacabana, Ipanema and Leblon

Copacabana began to develop when the **Túnel Velho** (Old Tunnel) was built in 1891 and an electric tram service reached it. Weekend villas and bungalows sprang up; all have now gone. In the 1930s the **Copacabana Palace Hotel** was the only tall building; it is now one of the lowest on the beach. The opening of the **Túnel Novo** (New Tunnel) in the 1940s led to an explosion of population which shows no sign of fading. Unspoilt art deco blocks at the Leme (city) end of Copacabana are now under preservation order.

There is almost everything in this 'city within a city'. The shops, mostly in **Avenida Nossa Senhora de Copacabana** and the **Rua Barata Ribeiro**, are excellent. Even more stylish shops are to be found in Ipanema and Leblon. It is at Copacabana and beyond, facing the open Atlantic Ocean, that Rio de Janeiro's true *praia* culture comes to the fore. The beach is divided into numbered *postos*, where the lifeguards are based. Different sections attract different types of people, whether young mothers, elderly card players or serious intellectuals. 'Where do you go on the beach?' is the defining question for Cariocas.

A Carioca is said to be someone who goes to the beach before, after or instead of work.

The safest places are in front of the major hotels which have their own security, for instance the **Meridien** on Copacabana beach or the **Caesar Park** on Ipanema. The Caesar Park also has 24-hour video surveillance during the summer season, which makes it probably the safest patch of sand in Rio. Also outside this hotel, Brazil's Olympic beach volleyball players practise. Sports of all types, however, can be seen or played all along the beaches: volleyball, football, aerobics, jogging and so on.

Getting there Buses to and from the city centre to Copacabana are plentiful and cost US$0.40. The buses to take are Nos 119, 154, 413, 415, 455 and 474 from Avenida Nossa Senhora de Copacabana. If you are going to the centre from Copacabana, look for 'Castelo', 'Praça 15', 'E Ferro' or 'Praça Mauá' on the sign by the front door. 'Aterro' means the expressway between Botafogo and downtown Rio (not open on Sunday). From the centre to Copacabana is easier as all buses in that direction are clearly marked. The 'Aterro' bus does the journey in 15 minutes.

Built on a narrow strip of land between mountain and sea, Copacabana has one of the highest population densities in the world: 62,000 per sq km, or 250,000 in all.

Buses run from Botafogo Metrô terminal to Ipanema: some take integrated Metrô-Bus tickets; look for the blue signs on the windscreen. Many buses from Copacabana run to Ipanema and Leblon.

Copacabana

A fort at the far end of the beach, **Forte de Copacabana**, was once an important part of Rio's defences and prevents a seashore connection with the Ipanema and Leblon beaches. Parts of the military area are now being handed over to civilian use, the first being the **Parque Garota de Ipanema** at Arpoador, the fashionable Copacabana end of the Ipanema beach. Tourist police patrol Copacabana beach until 1700.

Ipanema and Leblon

Like Copacabana and Leme, Ipanema and Leblon are essentially one long curving beach integrated by the monolithic **Dois Irmãos** rocks at the western end and the **Arpoador** rocks at the eastern. And like them they have few sights beyond the sand, the landscape and the beautiful people who inhabit them. Comparisons, however end there. Ipanema and Leblon are as fashionable and cool as Copacabana is grungy and frenetic. If Copacabana is samba, then Ipanema is bossa nova: wealthy, sealed off from the realities of Rio in a neat little fairytale strip of streets and watched over by

Copacabana

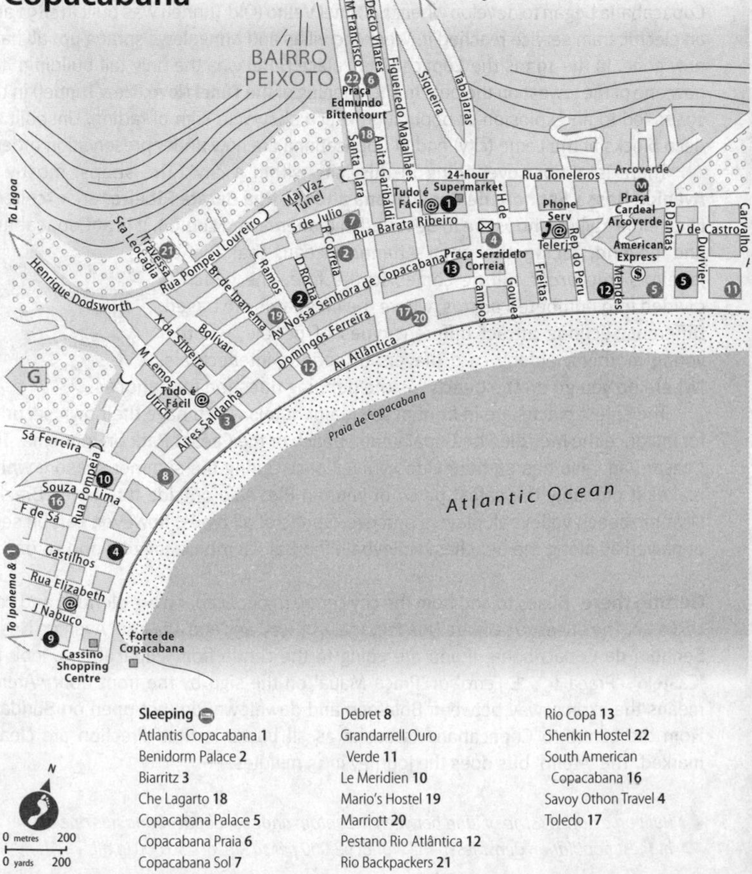

To Botafogo via Túnel Velho

Sleeping

Atlantis Copacabana **1**
Benidorm Palace **2**
Biarritz **3**
Che Lagarto **18**
Copacabana Palace **5**
Copacabana Praia **6**
Copacabana Sol **7**
Debret **8**
Grandarrell Ouro Verde **11**
Le Meridien **10**
Mario's Hostel **19**
Marriott **20**
Pestano Rio Atlântica **12**
Rio Backpackers **21**
Rio Copa **13**
Shenkin Hostel **22**
South American Copacabana **16**
Savoy Othon Travel **4**
Toledo **17**

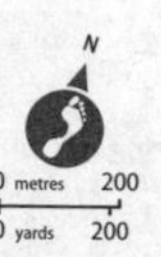

twinkling lights high up on the flanks of the Morro Dois Irmãos rocks. They look so romantic that it is easy to forget that they come from the world's largest *favela*.

Closeted and cosseted though it may be, this is the suburb in which to base yourself whilst in Rio. Almost all of the city's best restaurants and bars lie here (and in the suburbs of Gávea and Lagoa which lie behind). The streets are fairly clean and usually walked by nothing more dangerous than a small white poodle, there is plenty of reasonable accommodation which doesn't rent by the hour at the lower end of the market and the sea is good for swimming.

Like Copacabana, Ipanema/Leblon are places for people-watching. A half day wandering Ipanema/Leblon followed by a half day wandering Copacabana/Leme can be most interesting. The crowds are quite different. Whilst Copacabana attracts a real cross section of Rio society from the poor to the wealthy, Ipanema/Leblon are predominantly haunts of the fashionable peacocks, who emerge early to strut in small swimming gear and fan out their pectorals along the beachfront promenade, especially around Posto Nove. This is a Vanity Fair which should not be missed, especially if you like photography. Beyond the people and the breathtaking landscape, there is little to see here. But there is plenty to do, especially for avid consumers. Shopping is best on and around Garcia D'Avila and the Feira Hippy (see page 125), where you will find everything from high-quality Brazilian designer swimwear to seed bracelets and T-shirts with pictures of Bob Marley smoking a reefer on their front. Those seeking culture but unwilling to leave the beach should head for the **Casa de Cultura Laura Alvim** ⓘ *Av Vieira Souto 176, T2671647*, a complex comprising an arts cinema, art galleries (with some temporary exhibitions), a number of workshop spaces and a bookshop.

Eating

A Marisquera **1**
Aipo & Aipim **2**
Casarão **10**
Cervantes **3**
Chon Kou **4**
Churrascaria Palace **5**
La Tratoria **12**
Marakesh **13**
Siri Mole & Cia **9**
Taberna do Leme **14**

Gávea, Lagoa and Jardim Botânico

Just inland from Ipanema/Leblon, nestled under the forested slopes of Corcovado and the Tijuca National Park and spread around the picturesque saltwater lagoon, **Lagoa Rodrigo de Freitas** are these three mainly residential suburbs. All have lively top-end nightlife. Gávea tends to attract the young and wealthy, whilst the thirty-somethings dine in the restaurants in Lagoa, overlooking the lagoon and go out to clubs in Leblon or the exclusive **Jardim Botânico Jóquei Clube**. See page 119 for further details.

Lagoa de Freitas and around

The Lagoa de Freitas is yet another of Rio de Janeiro's beautiful natural sights and has long been admired. Darwin and German naturalists Spix and Martius mention it in their accounts. It is best seen in the early evening light, when thick golden sunlight bathes the rainforest-clad slopes of the Serra da Carioca which rise high above it to reach their spectacular pinnacle with the distant xenon white statue of Christ, and the sky fades to peacock blue through shades of subtropical orange and violet. Like Copacabana and Guanabara Bay it could be even more beautiful if only it were looked after a little better. The canal linking the lake to the sea is too narrow for sufficient exchange of water, pollution makes it unsafe for swimming and occasional summer algal blooms have led to mass fish deaths.

The lake is surrounded by a series of parks. Immediately surrounding it is the **Parque Tom Jobim** and contiguous are **Brigadeiro Faria Lima, Parque do Cantagalo** and **Parque das Taboas.** All have extensive leisure areas popular with roller skaters and volleyball players. There are live shows and *forró* dancing in the **Parque dos Patins** and kiosks serve a variety of food from Arabic to Japanese. Nearby is the **Parque Carlos Lacerda** in the **Parque da Catacumba** ⓘ *Av Epitacio Pessoa, daily 0800-1900*, an open-air art gallery with sculptures by local artists in a landscaped park.

Jardim Botânico (Botanic Gardens)

ⓘ *R Jardim Botânico 1008, T2947494, www.jbrj.gov.br, daily 0800-1700, US$2, to get to the gardens, take bus No 170 from the centre, or any bus to Leblon, Gávea or São*

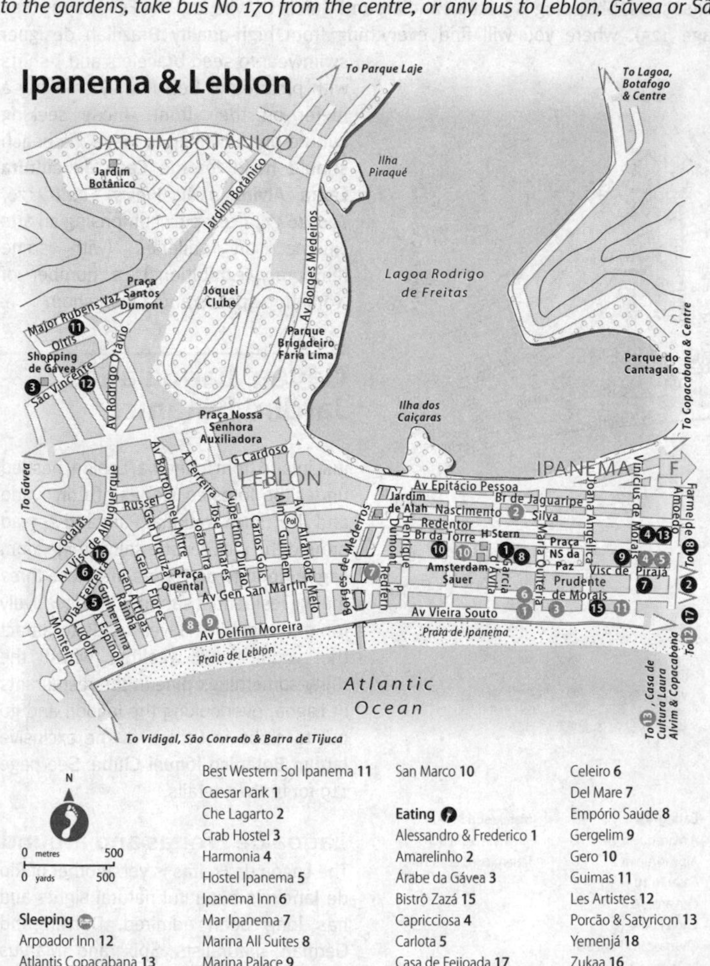

Sleeping
Arpoador Inn 12
Atlantis Copacabana 13
Best Western Sol Ipanema 11
Caesar Park 1
Che Lagarto 2
Crab Hostel 3
Harmonia 4
Hostel Ipanema 5
Ipanema Inn 6
Mar Ipanema 7
Marina All Suites 8
Marina Palace 9
San Marco 10

Eating
Alessandro & Frederico 1
Amarelinho 2
Árabe da Gávea 3
Bistrô Zazá 15
Capricciosa 4
Carlota 5
Casa de Feijoada 17
Celeiro 6
Del Mare 7
Empório Saúde 8
Gergelim 9
Gero 10
Guimas 11
Les Artistes 12
Porcão & Satyricon 13
Yemenjá 18
Zukaa 16

The essential Rio beach kit

To get the best out of Rio dress as the locals do – become a Carioca. Leave your board shorts, sense of shame and awareness of time in the hotel and go out in search of the essential Carioca uniform. If you are a man, the first thing you will need is a **sunga**, a tiny piece of square lycra that will barely cover the essentials; if you are a woman you'll need a tiny **bikini**, which contrary to popular belief, is not a 'dental floss' thong. The most fashionable places for these are in Ipanema: Salinas (Rua Visconde de Pirajá 547,) or Lenny (Rua Visconde de Pirajá 351, www.lenny.com.br). The next essential is a **canga** – a sarong of the kind ubiquitous in Asia; which is used as a wrap, towel and beach mat. You will then need a **frescobol kit** – a wooden racket and a rubber ball to hit back and forth across the sand – and a pair of **Havaianas** – Brazilian flip flops. Both are available for next to nothing in the supermarket. A small **white poodle** (for women) and pair of **cheap sunglasses** (for men) complete the outfit.

Conrado marked 'via Jóquei'; from Glória, Flamengo or Botafogo take No 571, or 172 from Flamengo; from Copacabana, Ipanema or Leblon take No 572 (584 back to Copacabana. Visitors needing information in English should ask for Beatriz Heloisa Guimaraes, of the Society of Friends of the Garden.

These extensive 137-ha gardens, which protect some 70,000 rare vascular plants, are home to some 140 species of birds, and butterflies including brilliant blue Morphos. There are stately stands of 40-m high royal palms, large tropical ficus and ceiba trees and Pau Brasil, from whom Brazil gets its name. Giant Amazonian victoria regia lilies cover many of the ponds.

The gardens were founded in 1808 by the king, Dom Joao VI as a nursery for European plants and new specimens from throughout the world. When the electric tram line arrived in this part of the city, housing and industries soon followed, but the gardens, then as now, remained a haven of peace. There is a herbarium, an aquarium and a library as well as the Museu Botânico, housing exhibitions on the conservation of Brazilian flora, and the Casa dos Pilões, the first gunpowder factory in Brazil. A new pavilion contains sculptures by Mestre Valentim transferred from the centre. Many improvements were carried out before the 1992 Earth Summit, including a new Orquidario, an enlarged book shop and a smart café.

Birdwatchers can expect to see rarities including the social flycatcher, great and boat-billed kiskadees, cattle tyrants, sayaca, palm and seven coloured (green headed) tanagers as well as over 20 different kinds of hummingbird, roadside hawks, the laughing falcons and various toucans and parakeets. There are marmosets in the trees.

Leblon to Barra da Tijuca

The Pedra Dois Irmãos overlooks Leblon; on the slopes is **Vidigal favela**. From Leblon, two inland roads take traffic west to the outer seaside suburb of Barra da Tijuca.

Parque da Cidade ⓘ *daily 0700-1700, free*, a pleasant park a short walk beyond the Gávea bus terminus, has a great many trees and lawns, with views over the ocean. However, the proximity of the Rocinha *favela* (see below) means the park is not very safe. It is advisable to have a copy of your passport here because of frequent police checks. The buses 170, 174, 546, 592 and 593 leave you just short of the entrance, but it should be OK to walk the last part if in a group. Do not walk the trails in the park alone.

In the park is the **Museu Histórico da Cidade** ⓘ *Tue-Sun 1100-1700, US$1*, a former coffee *fazenda* with historical exhibits. Every third Sunday in the month it holds a gastronomic event with music from 1400. See the **Capela de São João Bautista** whose murals by Carlos Bastos so scandalized the patrons for their inclusion of famous people into the life of Christ that they were never finished (only open weekends). » *For favela tours, see box page 90.*

Beyond Leblon the coast is rocky. A third route to Barra da Tijuca is the Avenlda Niemeyer, which skirts the cliffs on the journey past Vidigal, a small beach where the **Sheraton** is situated. Avenida Niemeyer carries on round the coast to **São Conrado**, with its Fashion Mall and the Gávea golf club; a very exclusive neighbourhood where few tourists stop. On the slopes of the Pedra da Gávea, through which the Avenida Niemeyer has two tunnels, is the **Rocinha favela**.

The flat-topped **Pedra da Gávea** can be climbed or scrambled up for magnificent views, but beware of snakes. Some say that the rock is sphinx-like and from the Tijuca Forest side there is clearly a conformation similar to a face with a beard. Claims have been made that Phoenician inscriptions have been found and many other legends surround the rock.

Behind the Pedra da Gávea is the **Pedra Bonita**. The Estrada das Canoas, climbs up past these rocks on to the Tijuca National Park. There is a spot on this road which is one of the chief hang-glider launch sites in the area (see Activities and tours, page 128).

Barra da Tijuca

This rapidly developing residential area is also one of the principal recreation zones of Rio, with its 20-km sandy beach and good waves for surfing. At the westernmost end is the small beach of **Recreio dos Bandeirantes**, where the ocean can be very

Barra da Tijuca & National Park

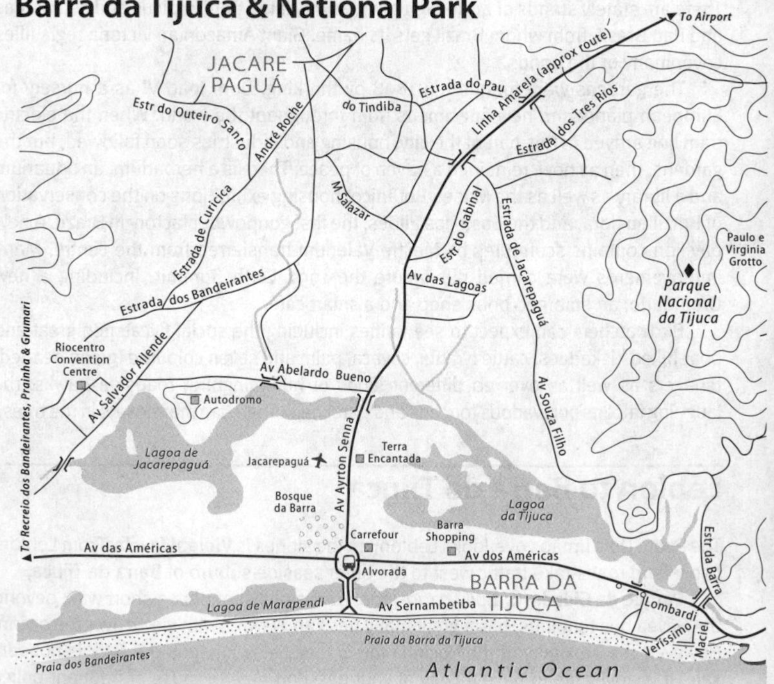

rough. The channels behind the Barra are popular with jet-skiers. It gets very busy on Sundays. There are innumerable bars and restaurants, clustered at both ends, as well as campsites (see page 114), motels and hotels: budget accommodation tends to be self-catering. The facilities include **Riocentro**, a 600,000-sq m convention complex, and the huge **Barra Shopping** and **Carrefour** shopping centres.

The **Bosque da Barra/Parque Arruda Câmara** ⓘ *daily 0700-1700*, at the junction of Avenida das Américas and Avenida Ayrton Senna, preserves the vegetation of the sandbanks which existed on this part of the coast before the city took over.

The **Autódromo** (motor racing track) is behind Barra and the Lagoa de Jacarepaguá, in the district of the same name. The Brazilian Grand Prix was held here during the 1980s before returning to Interlagos, São Paulo.

Terra Encantada ⓘ *Av Ayrton Senna 2800, T24309800, www.terra-encantada.com.br, Thu-Sun 1000-2300*, is a 300,000-sq m theme park in Barra whose attractions are based on the different cultural heritages of Brazil: the indigenous, African and European. Among the attractions are roller coasters, river rapids, a cinema and shows. Rides close at 2200 and on the main street restaurants, bars and nightspots open.

A bit further out is the **Museu Casa do Pontal** ⓘ *Estrada do Pontal 3295, Recreio dos Bandeirantes, Tue-Sun 0900-1930*. This is another collection of Brazilian folk art, put together by the French designer Jacques van de Beuque. Recommended.

Getting there Buses from the city centre to Barra are Nos 175, 176; from Botafogo, Glória or Flamengo take No 179; Nos 591 or 592 from Leme; and from Copacabana via Leblon No 523 (45 minutes to one hour). A taxi to Zona Sul costs US$15 (US$22.50 after 2400). A comfortable bus, **Pegasus**, goes along the coast from the Castelo bus terminal to Barra da Tijuca and continues to Campo Grande or Santa Cruz, or take the free 'Barra Shopping' bus. Bus 700 from Praça São Conrado (terminal of bus 553 from Copacabana) goes the full length of the beach to Recreio dos Bandeirantes.

Although buses do run as far as Barra, getting to and around here is best by car. A cycleway links Barra do Tijuca with the centre of the city.

Tijuca National Park

ⓘ *0600-2100. Maps of the park are available. If hiking in the national park other than on the main paths, a guide may be useful if you do not want to get lost: Sindicato de Guías, T22674582. Allow at least five or six hours for the excursion.*

The vegetation in the Parque Nacional da Tijuca, for all its abundance, is not primeval. Most of what is now the largest urban, forested national park in the world is reforested. The first Europeans in the area cut down trees for use in construction and as firewood. The lower areas were cleared to make way for sugar plantations. When coffee was introduced to Rio de Janeiro in 1760, the logical place to start cultivating it was on the hillsides surrounding the city. Huge tracts of the forest were cut down and coffee estates created. Conditions for the bushes were ideal, but for the city itself, it did not prove ideal. Although many people made lots of money, deforesting the hills disrupted the rainfall pattern and the water supply for the expanding city became insufficient. In 1861, therefore, the Imperial government decided that the whole area should be reforested. The job was given to Major Manuel Gomes Archer who, with just six slaves, completed the task in 13 years. They used saplings taken from neighbouring areas, but added to the native species many exotic varieties. The work was continued by Tomás de Gama. A national park of 3,300 ha, which united various different forests, was set up in 1961.

The **Pico da Tijuca** (1,022 m) gives a good idea of the tropical vegetation of the interior and a fine view of the bay and its shipping. A two- to three-hour walk leads to the summit: on entering the park at **Alto da Boa Vista**, follow the signposts (maps are displayed) to **Bom Retiro**, a good picnic place (1½ hours' walk). At Bom Retiro the road ends and there is another hour's walk up a fair footpath to the summit (take the path from the right of the Bom Retiro drinking fountain; not the more obvious steps from the left). The last part consists of steps carved out of the solid rock; look after children at the summit as there are several sheer drops, invisible because of bushes. The route is shady for almost its entire length. The main path to Bom Retiro passes the **Cascatinha Taunay** (a 30-m waterfall) and the **Mayrink Chapel** (built 1860). Panels painted in the Chapel by Cândido Portinari have been replaced by copies and the originals will probably be installed in the Museu de Arte Moderna. Beyond the chapel is the restaurant **A Floresta** and **Major Archer's house**, although this is now in ruins.

Other places of interest not passed on the walk to the peak are the **Paulo e Virginia Grotto**, the **Vista do Almirante** and the **Mesa do Imperador** (viewpoints).

Getting there Bus No 221 from Praça 15 de Novembro, No 233 (which continues to Barra da Tijuca) or No 234 from the rodoviária or from Praça Sáens Pena, Tijuca (the city suburb, not Barra – reached by Metrô), or No 454 from Copacabana to Alto da Boa Vista, for the park entrance. Jeep tours are run by **Atlantic Forest Jeep Tour** daily; T24959827, T99740218 (mob), or contact through travel agencies.

Western Rio

Almost half of the municipal area of Rio de Janeiro is in what is referred to as the **Zona Oeste** (the West Zone). On the coast, this stretches from Barra de Tijuca past the beaches at **Prainha** (a little cove, good for surfing) and **Grumari** (very attractive, rustic beach bars), not accessible by public transport, but attracting heavy traffic at weekends. Further west still are the **Barra de Guaratiba** and **Pedra de Guaratiba** beaches and, finally, those at **Sepetiba** (on the bay, with calm sea and medicinal mud). This stunning coastal road (the start of the Costa Verde highway) is becoming obliterated by executive housing developments – visit soon, if you can.

Inland are suburbs such as **Campo Grande** and **Santa Cruz**, the **Parque Estadual da Pedra Branca** ⓘ *T24453387*, and sites such as the 19th-century **Capela Magdalena** ⓘ *T24107183*. The authorities are planning to develop the Zona Oeste. A **Centro Cultural** (**NOPH**) ⓘ *Praça Dom Romualdo 11, Santa Cruz, T3950260*, in the Igreja Matriz, can supply information.

Two museums in the northwest of the city are well established. **Capão do Bispo Estate** ⓘ *Av Suburbana 4616, del Castilho, Mon-Fri 1400-1700*, is an 18th-century estate house with an archaeological exhibition. **Museu Aeroespacial** ⓘ *Av Marechal Fontenele 2000, Campo dos Afonsos, Tue-Fri 0930-1500, Sat, Sun and holidays 0930-1600*, has early Brazilian aircraft, historic weapons and documents.

Sítio Roberto Burle Marx ⓘ *Estrada da Barra de Guaratiba 2019, Barra de Guaratiba, T24101171, daily 0930-1330 (by prior appointment only)*, was, from 1949 to 1994, the home of the great Roberto Burle Marx (1909-1994), world famous as a landscape designer and artist. His projects achieved a rare harmony between nature, architecture and man-made landscapes. He created many schemes in Brazil and abroad; in Rio alone his work includes the Parque do Flamengo, the pavements of the Avenida Atlântica in Copacabana, Praça Júlio de Noronha in Leme, the remodelling of the Largo da Carioca, the gardens of the Museu Nacional de Belas Artes and of the Biblioteca Nacional and the complex at the Santa Teresa tram station near the Catedral Metropolitana.

Covering 350,000 sq m, the estate contains an estimated 3,500 species of plants, mostly Brazilian. It is run now by the Instituto do Patrimônio Histórico e Artístico Nacional and one of its main aims is to produce seedlings of the plants in its collection. Also on view are Burle Marx's collection of paintings, ceramics, sculptures and other objets d'art, plus examples of his own designs and paintings. The library houses 2,500 volumes on botany, architecture and landscape design.

Ilha de Paquetá

Paquetá Island, the second largest in Guanabara Bay, is noted for its gigantic pebble-shaped rocks, butterflies and orchids. Its name means 'many shells' in Tupi, but it has also been called the **Ilha dos Amores**. The house of **José Bonifáclo**, the opponent of slavery, may be seen. Another historical building is the **Solar D'El Rel**, which today houses the Biblioteca Popular de Paquetá and has recently been refurbished. At the southwest tip is the interesting **Parque Darke de Mattos**, with beautiful trees, lots of birds and a lookout on the Morro da Cruz. The island has several beaches, but ask about the state of the water before bathing. The only means of transport are bicycles and horse-drawn carriages (many have harnesses which cut into the horse's flesh). Neither is allowed into the Parque Darke de Mattos. A tour by *trenzinho*, a tractor pulling trailers, costs US$1.25, or just wander around on foot (quieter and free); bicycles can be hired. The island is crowded at weekends and on public holidays, but is quieter during the week. Food and drink prices are reasonable.

Getting there Paquetá Island can be visited by ferry services that leave more or less every 2 hours from Praça 15 de Novembro, where there is a general boat terminal; there are boats from 0515 (0710 on Sunday and holidays) to 2300, T25337524, or hydrofoils between 1000 and 1600, Saturday and Sunday 0800-1630 hourly, T33970656 (US$1 by boat, 1 hour; US$4 by hydrofoil, 20 minutes' journey, which more than doubles its price Sat, Sun and holidays). Buses to Praça 15 de Novembro: No 119 from Glória, Flamengo or Botafogo; Nos 154, 413, 455, 474 from Copacabana; or No 415 passing from Leblon via Ipanema.

Several companies offer trips to Paquetá. There are day cruises, including lunch, to Jaguanum Island (see page 164, under Itacuruçá) and a sundown cruise around Guanabara Bay. **Saveiros Tour** ⓘ *Rua Conde de Lages 44, Glória, T22246990, www.saveiros.com.br*, offers tours in sailing schooners around the bay and down the coast, also 'Baía da Guanabara Histórica' historical tours.

Sleeping

The best and safest places to stay in Rio are Ipanema and southern Copacabana. Those on a budget will find a number of decent new hostels in these areas. However, with a few exceptions, Rio's other hotels are a disappointment. Aside from the Copacabana Palace, those in the higher and mid-range bracket are a mix of anonymous business chain towers and fading leftovers from the 1970s, complete with period decor. Those at the lower end are almost invariably dubious hot-pillow establishments in equally dubious areas.

All accommodation is considerably pricier over New Year and Carnival. Reserve well in advance, especially budget accommodation.

Youth Hostel Associations ALBERJ (for Rio), R da Assembleia 10, I 16, T25312234. **Federação Brasileira** (Brazil), at **Chave do Rio de Janeiro** hostel, T22860303. For web bookings see www.hostelworld.com.

Self-catering apartments This is a popular form of accommodation in Rio, available at all price levels: eg furnished apartments for short-term let, accommodating up to 6, cost US$300 per month; in **Flamengo**. **Copacabana**, **Ipanema** and **Leblon** prices range from about US$25 a day for a simple studio, starting at US$500-600 a month up to US$2,000 a month for a luxurious residence sleeping 4-6. Heading south past **Barra da Tijuca**, virtually all the accommodation available is self-catering. Renting a small flat, or sharing a larger one, can be much better value than a hotel room. Blocks consisting entirely of short-let apartments can attract thieves, so check the (usually excellent) security arrangements; residential buildings are called *prédio familial*. Higher floors (alto andar) are considered quieter.

'Apart-Hotels' are listed in the Guia 4 Rodas and Riotur's booklet. Agents and private owners advertise under 'Apartamentos – Temporada' in publications like *Balcão* (twice weekly), *O Globo* or *Jornal do Brasil* (daily); advertisements are classified by district and size of apartment: *vagas e quartos* means shared accommodation; *conjugado* (or *conj*) is a studio with limited cooking facilities; *3 quartos* is a 3-bedroom flat. There should always be a written agreement when renting.

Glória, Catete and Flamengo

p94, map p94, phone code 021

Primarily residential areas between the centre and Copacabana. Catete and Glória to the north and Flamengo to the south lie next to a park landscaped by Burle Marx and a beautiful beach lapped by a filthy sea. They have good bus and Metrô connections but are not as safe as Ipanema.

L Glória, R do Russel 632, Glória, T25557572, www.hotelgloriario.com.br. Rio's other stylish and elegant 1920s hotel. Not as grand as the **Copacabana Palace** but with far more charm than any others in Copacabana or Ipanema. Rooms have mock-Edwardian decoration. The hotel has 2 pools, a spa and an in-house theatre. Highly recommended. Good for business travellers.

L Novo Mundo, Praia Flamengo 20, Catete, T25574355, www.hotelnovomundo-rio.com.br. Standard 4-star rooms, suites with balcony views of the Sugar Loaf. Recommended but noisy. Reasonable business services.

AL Flórida, Ferreira Viana, 71/81, Catete, T25565242, www.windsorhoteis.com. Business-orientated hotel with a well-equipped business centre, one of the city's largest convention centres, bars (for private hire), a restaurant and modestly decorated no-nonsense modern rooms.

B Imperial, R do Catete 186, Catete, T25565212, www.imperialhotel.com.br. One of the city's very first grand hotels – built in the late 19th century. Rooms are divided between the grander older main building and the annex whose modern US-style motel rooms are better equipped but look over the car park.

B Paysandu, Paysandu, R Paissandu 23, Flamengo, T25587270, www.paysandu hotel.com.br. Wonderful old art deco tower next to the Palacio de República and Flamengo gardens, with spartan rooms but helpful staff, good location, organized tours available.

B Turístico, Ladeira da Glória 30, Glória, T25577698, F25585815. With breakfast, a/c, tourist information provided, mixed reports, some highly favourable.

C Inglês, R Silveira Martins 20, Glória, T25583052, www.hotelingles.com.br. Popular cheapie next to the metro and in front of the Museu da República. The better rooms have been refurbished and have a/c.

C Único, R Buarque de Macedo 54, Catete, T22059932, F22058149. Plain rooms with TV, a/c and fridges. Recommended.

D-E King Hostel, R Barão de Guaratiba 20, Catete, www.kingalbergue.hpg.ig.com.br. Cheap and cheerful hostel with dorms and doubles a stroll from Catete metro.

Camping

If travelling by trailer, you can park at the Marina Glória car park, where there are showers and toilets, a small shop and snack bar. Pay the guards to look after your vehicle. See also www.camping-club.com.br.

Santa Teresa *p96, map p94, phone code 021*

Camaecafe. Many great bed and breakfast deals and charming options can be found on www.camaecafe.com.br.

Urca and Botafogo *p99, map p98, phone code 021*

B-D **Carioca Easy**, R Marechal Cantuaria 168, Urca, T22957805, www.cariocahostel.com.br. Bright little hostel in a colonial house in one of the safest and most spectacular neighbourhoods in Rio; at the base of Sugar Loaf. Pool, kitchen, bike rental, boat trips and dorms and doubles.

D **Chave do Rio de Janeiro**, R Gen Dionísio 63, Botafogo, T22860303, www.riohostel.com.br. IYHA, cheaper for members, clean, laundry and cooking facilities. Superb breakfast. Noisy but frequently recommended.

E **El Misti Hostel**, Praia de Botafogo 462 casa 9, T22260991, www.elmistihostel.com. A converted colonial house with 6 dorms, shared bathrooms and a kitchen, internet, *capoeira* classes and tour service. Convenient for public transport.

Copacabana *p101, map p102, phone code 021*

Once the place to stay in Rio but now increasingly sleazy. Ipanema is a better option. Many hotels charge about 30% more for a seaview, but some town-side upper rooms have good views of the mountains.

LL **Copacabana Palace**, Av Atlântica 1702, T25487070, www.copacabanapalace.com.br. The best hotel in Rio for leisure or business and one of the best in the world; dripping in 1920s elegance. *Flying Down to Rio* in which Fred Astaire and Ginger Rogers first danced together was filmed here and celebrities have been visiting ever since. The plushest rooms are the 6th-floor suites. Cipriani has the best cooking in Rio: come for cocktails and dinner if you can't afford to stay.

LL **Marriott**, Av Atlântica 2600, T25456500, www.marriott.com. Rio's newest top-end business hotel with 245 guest rooms specifically designed for the business traveller, an Executive Floor, 12 meeting rooms and a gamut of other business services.

LL-L **Le Meridien**, Av Atlântica 1020, T0800111554, www.meridien-br.com. Air France hotel with pool, smallish rooms, and breakfasts with a wonderful view. Good for business travellers.

L **Pestana Rio Atlântica**, Av Atlântica 2964, T25486332, www.pestana.com. The best option on Copacabana after the **Palace**, with spacious bright rooms and a rooftop pool and terrace with sweeping views. Part of the well-managed Portuguese Pestana group. Very high standards. Highly recommended.

L-A **South American Copacabana**, R Francisco de Sá 90, T25220040, southamerican@uol.com.br. 2 blocks from the beach but in the Arpoador, which is safer than Copacabana. The front rooms are noisy, others are garishly decorated but well maintained. Helpful staff. Recommended.

AL **Grandarell Ouro Verde**, Av Atlântica 1456, T25421887, www.grandarell.com.br. The best small hotel in Copacabana with spacious well-decorated rooms and a decent restaurant. Good for families – the hotel has a Kids' Club.

AL-A **Benidorm Palace**, R Barata Ribeiro 547, T25488880, www.benidorm.com.br. Rather tacky, though well-maintained hotel whose rooms look very B-grade *Saturday Night Fever*.

A **Debret**, Av Atlântica 3564, T25220132, www.debret.com. Bright, spacious, modern seafront rooms; others are a little dark.

A **Rio Copa**, Av Princesa Isabel 370, T22756644, www.riocopa.com.br. Simple, plain rather grubby rooms 2 blocks back from beach. English-speaking staff.

A **Savoy Othon Travel**, Av Nossa Senhora de Copacabana 552, T/F25250282, www.othon.com.br. Spacious, anonymous early 1990s rooms 2 blocks from the beach. Absurd rack-rates; good corporate rates.

A-B **Atlantis Copacabana**, Av Bulhões de Carvalho 61, T25211142, atlantishotel@uol.com.br. Fading Arpoador hotel in a quiet, safe street very close to the beach. Small rooftop pool, sauna, and excellent rates.

A-B Biarritz, R Aires Saldanha 54, T25220542, www.hoteisgandara.com.br. Large fading rooms a block from the beach.

A-B Copacabana Sol, R Santa Clara 141, T25494577, www.copacabanasolhotel.com.br. A/c, safe, helpful, quiet, good breakfast, simple rooms and a cheesy marble lobby.

B Toledo, R Domingos Ferreira 71, T22571990, www.hoteisgandara.com.br. Garishly decorated rather gloomy rooms a block from the beach.

C-D Copa Chalet, R Henrique Oswald 103, T22360047, www.copachalet.com.br. Pleasant hostel with mock-Moorish touches and a little garden area. A range of rooms and dorms including a suite. Very friendly. Recommended.

D Che Lagarto, R Anita Garibaldi 87, T22562778, www.chelagarto.com. Sister party hostel to the **Che Lagarto** in Ipanema.

D-E Mario's Hostel, R Leopoldo Miguez 10, T31856604, www.marioshostel.com. Dorms, singles and doubles, 2 mins from the beach. Airport pick-up, kitchen, internet and a shared sitting room.

D-E Rio Backpackers, Travessa Santa Leocadia 38, T22363803, www.riobackpackers.com.br. Another new party hostel popular with Brazilians. Bright clean with small dorms, singles and doubles. Recommended.

D-E Shenkin Hostel, R Santa Clara 304, T22573133, www.shenkinhostel.com. Party hostel with its own bar 5 mins' walk from the beach, dorms (some with a/c) singles and doubles. Good value.

E Copacabana Praia, R Tte Marones de Gusmão 85, Bairro Peixoto, T22353817, www.wcenter.com.br/copapraia. Dorms and doubles in a quiet residential area 600 m from beach.

Self-catering apartments

Copacabana Holiday, R Barata Ribeiro 90A, Copacabana, T25421525, www.copacabanaholiday.com.br. Recommended, well-equipped small apartments from US$500 per month, minimum 30 days let.

Fantastic Rio, Av Atlântica 974, Suite 501, Copacabana, BR-22020-000, T/F25432667, hpcorr@hotmail.com, all types of furnished accommodation from US$20 per day. Owned by Peter Corr. Recommended.

Holidays in Copacabana, Av Atlântica 4066, Apt 605, T25130281. Rents apartments, all with phone, near beach, a/c, maid service, English, French, German spoken, all apartments owned by the agency, prices around US$50 per flat.

Paulo de Tarso, Av Princesa Isabel, 236, Apto 102, T25425635, pauldetarso@ig.com.br. Apartments near Copacabana beach from US$25 per person. Several languages spoken, very helpful.

Rio Residences, Av Prado Júnior 44, apto 508, T25414568, F25416462. Swiss-run, includes airport transfer.

Ipanema and Leblon *p102, map p104, phone code 021*

LL **Caesar Park**, Av Vieira Souto 460, T25252525, www.caesar-park.com. Anonymous chain hotel with mock 19th-century flourishes in a beachfront tower. Some rooms have beach views. Decent service includes beach patrol and child minding. Pool, sauna, restaurant and business facilities.

L **Best Western Sol Ipanema**, Av Vieira Souto, 320, T26252020, www.bestwestern.com. Part of the US group and world's largest chain, with the usual hotel catalogue rooms. Popular with agencies and business travellers.

L **Marina Palace and Marina All Suites**, Av Delfim Moreira 630 and 696, T22941794, www.hotelmarina.com.br. Two 1980s towers almost next door to each other. The former has smart, modern but standard 4-star rooms and a rooftop pool, the latter is a luxury boutique with 'designer' suites and is favoured by the likes of Giselle Bundchen. By international standards it is shabby. But it has an excellent and fashionable seaview restaurant and bar which is great for breakfast and a light lunch or dinner.

AL-A Arpoador Inn, Francisco Otaviano 177, T25230060, F25115094. One of the best deals on the seafront. Well maintained, with off-season special offers. Recommended.

AL-A Mar Ipanema, R Visconde de Pirajá 539, T38759190, www.maripanema.com. Simple, smart, modern rooms a block from the beach. The front rooms on the lower floors are noisy.

A Ipanema Inn, Maria Quitéria 27, behind Caesar Park, T25233092, F25115094. Good value and location.

B San Marco, R Visconde de Pirajá 524, T25405032, www.sanmarcohotel.net. Newly renovated 2-star with plain and simple rooms and a free *caipirinha* for every internet booking. Price includes breakfast. 2 blocks from beach. Recommended.

C-D Che Lagarto, R Barão de Jaguaripe 208, T22474582, www.chelagarto.com. Bright red party hostel with young staff and a terrace with views of Corcovado. Dorms and doubles. See also **Atlantis Copacabana**.

C-D Crab Hostel, R Prudente de Morais 903, T22677353, www.crabhostel.com.br. Brand new hostel a block from the beach with a pool, sauna, cable TV and all rooms with en suites. Excellent value.

D Hostel Ipanema, R Barão da Torre 175, casa 14, T22477269, www.geocities.com/hostelipanema. Little residential house with dorms, singles and doubles. English spoken.

D-E Casa 6, R Barão da Torre 175, casa 6, T22471384, www.casa6ipanema.com. Charming, colourful but simple French-owned B&B in a townhouse 3 blocks from the beach. Good long-stay rates.

D-E Harmonia, R Barão da Torre 175, casa 18, T25234905, www.hostelharmonia.com. 3 blocks from beach, doubles or dorms, kitchen facilities, English, Spanish, German and Swedish spoken, good internet, very welcoming and helpful. There are several other hostels in this building including **Hostel Ipanema**, T22477269.

Leblon to Barra da Tijuca *p105, phone code 021*

Spectacular settings, but isolated and far from centre.

LL Sheraton, Av Niemeyer 121 (Vidigal), T22741122, www.sheraton-rio.com. One of the **Sheraton**'s poorer hotels – a 1970s slab of concrete in painful need of restyling and refurbishing. Wonderful beach views though and a decent pool area.

Camping

Camping Clube do Brasil, Av Sen Dantas 75, 29th floor, Centro, CEP 20037-900, T22103171, has 2 beach sites at Barra da Tijuca: Av Sernambetiba 3200, T24930628 (bus 233 from centre, 702 or 703 from the airport via Zona Sul, US$5 – a long way from the centre), sauna, pool, bar, café, US$12 (half price for members). During Jan and Feb this site is often full and sometimes restricted to members of the Camping Clube do Brasil. A simpler site at Estrada do Pontal 5900, T24378400, lighting, café, good surfing, US$6. Both have trailer plots.

Eating

There are many restaurants in Rio and the very few good ones are owned and run by people from São Paulo and situated in Copacabana, Ipanema or Leblon. Don't be taken in either by appearances or hotel concierges. At the cheaper end of the spectrum Rio lacks that almost ubiquitous Brazilian institution, the corner bakery and a decent breakfast which isn't mock-French in appearance and price can be hard to find. But there are plenty of stand-up juice bars serving fruit juices made from as many as 25 different fruits from orange to *açai* and carrot to *cupuaçu*, all of which are wonderful. You can eat well for an average US$5 per person, less if you choose the *prato feito* at lunchtime (US$1.50-6), or eat in a place that serves food by weight (starting at about US$0.65 per gram). Expect to pay US$30+ per person in the better restaurants. Avoid mussels! Most restaurants are closed on 24 and 25 Dec.

For fast food fans, there are plentiful hamburger stands and lunch counters all over the city. Grill or barbecue houses (*churrascarias*) are relatively cheap, especially by European standards. There are many at São Conrado and Joá, on the road out to Barra da Tijuca (see p106). Look for the **Churrascaria Rodízio**, where you are served as much as you can eat. *Galetos* are very reasonable lunch counters specializing in chicken and grilled meat. In the shopping centres there is usually a variety of restaurants and snack bars grouped around a central plaza where you can shop around for a good meal. Most less-expensive restaurants in Rio have basically the same type of food (based on steak, fried potatoes and rice) and serve large portions; those with small appetites, especially families with children, can ask for a spare plate and split helpings. **La Mole**, at 11 locations, serves good, cheap Italian food and is very popular.

Central Rio and Lapa *p82, maps p84 and p86, phone code 021*

Many restaurants in the business district are open only for weekday lunch. Many *lanchonetes* in this area offer good, cheap meals.

R **Miguel Couto** (opposite Santa Rita church) is called the **Beco das Sardinhas** because on Wed and Fri in particular it is full of people eating sardines and drinking beer.

There are several Arab restaurants on **Av Senhor dos Passos**, which are also open Sat and Sun. In addition to those listed there are plenty of cafés, including a few new chic options on R Lavradio in Lapa, where the lively Sat antiques market is held.

ΨΨΨ Republique, Praça da República 63 (2nd floor), T25329000. Newly refurbished and designed by the architect Chicô Gouveia. Chef Paulo Carvalho cooks a mix of Portuguese, Italian and French dishes.

ΨΨ Adega Flor de Coimbra, R Teotônio Regadas 34, Lapa. Founded 1938, serving Portuguese food and wines, speciality *bacalhau* (dried cod). Very good.

ΨΨ Café do Teatro, Rio Branco, Teatro Municipal. Traditional Portuguese and Brazilian cooking cuisine for a mostly business clientele. No shorts or sandals. Weekday lunch only.

ΨΨ Casa da Suiça, R Cândido Mendes 157, Lapa, T22525182. Bar/restaurant with good atmosphere.

ΨΨ Café Glória, R do Russel 734, Lapa, T22059647. Open daily for lunch and dinner. Beautiful art nouveau building, helpful staff, excellent food.

ΨΨ Confeitaria Colombo, R Gonçalves Dias 32, near Carioca Metrô station, is highly recommended for atmosphere and the only one of its kind in Rio. Over 100 years old, it has the original belle époque decor, open 0900-1800, lunch available, no service charge so tip the excellent waiters. More modern but similar establishments in some of the main hotels.

Ψ Albamar, Praça Marechal Âncora 184-6, T22408428. Good, reasonably priced fish and seafood, with lovely views of the bay. Open Mon 1130-1600, Tue-Sat 1130-2200.

Ψ Al-kuwait, Av Treze de Maio, T22401114. Charming Middle Eastern fan-cooled restaurant with wood panelling in unprepossessing alley off 13 de Maio. No English menu but helpful staff. Try a traditional kofta or the daily special. Mon-Fri 1100-2300.

Ψ Bistro do Paço, Praça 15 de Novembro 48 (Paço Imperial), T22623613. Excellent, good-value food in attractive surroundings, Swiss-run. Recommended. Mon-Fri 1130-2000, Sat and Sun 1200-1830.

Ψ Fiorino, Av Heitor Beltrão 126, Tijuca, T25674476. Delicious, home-cooked Italian food with indulgent desserts. Recommended.

Ψ Luciano, R das Marrecas 44. One of several functional, fairly cheerless all-you-can-eat buffets on this street.

Ψ Mala e Cuia, R Candelária 92, T22534032. For *comida mineira*. Recommended – also in Ipanema and Copacabana.

Ψ Rio Minho, R do Ouvidor 10, T25092338. Excellent seafood in a historic building.

Glória, Catete and Flamengo

p94, map p94, phone code 021

There are many cheap and mid-range eating places on R do Catete; all much of a muchness.

Ψ Alcaparra, Praia do Flamengo 144, Flamengo, T25577236. Elegant traditional Italian popular with politicians and business people. Overlooking the sea.

Ψ Alho E Óleo, R Buarque de Macedo 13, Flamengo, T25578541. Fashionable Italian with a strong emphasis on pasta. Recommended.

Ψ Amazônia, R do Catete 234B, Catete. Downstairs for 1-price counter service, upstairs for good, reasonably priced evening meals. Recommended.

Ψ Catelandia, R do Catete 204, Catete. Excellent and cheap, pay by weight.

Ψ Galícia Grill, R do Catete 265 at Largo do Machado, Catete. Very good pizza and service.

Ψ Lamas, Marquês de Abrantes 18A, Flamengo. Steak, seafood and general Brazilian fare have been served here for over 130 years. Excellent value, great atmosphere, opens late, popular with Brazilian arts/media people. Recommended.

Santa Teresa

p96, map p94, phone code 021

ΨΨΨ Aprazível, R Aprazível 62, Santa Teresa, T38524935. Decent but unspectacular Brazilian dishes and seafood with one of the best restaurant table views in the city: tables are outdoors in a tropical garden overlooking the Guanabara Bay. This is a good Sun lunch spot when they have *choro* and samba performed by Rio's equivalent of the Buena Vista Social Club.

Ψ Adega do Pimenta, R Almte Alexandrino 296, Santa Teresa. Mon and Wed-Fri 1130-2200, Sun 1100-1800. A very small German restaurant in the Largo do Guimarães with excellent sausages, sauerkraut and cold beer.

Ұ **Bar do Arnaudo**, in the Largo do Guimarães, R Almte Alexandrino 316, Santa Teresa, T22527246. A modest-looking restaurant decorated with handicrafts but serving generous portions of wonderful northeast Brazilian cooking. Try the carne do sol (sun-dried beef, or jerky) with feijão de corda (brown beans and herbs), or the queijo coalho (a country cheese, grilled).

Ұ **Sobrenatural**, R Almirante Alexandrino 432, T22241003, lunchtime only, closed Mon. A charming rustic restaurant serving fish caught daily from owner's boat. For a light lunch, order a mix of excellent appetizers. Recommended. On the same square as the Adega do Pimenta.

Urca and Botafogo *p99, map p98, phone code 021*

ҰҰҰ **Carême Bistrô**, R Visconde de Caravelas 113, Botafogo, T25375431. An elegant and intimate little restaurant serving the best French bistro food in Rio. Recommended.

ҰҰ **Raajmahal**, R Gen Polidoro 29, in Baixo Botafogo, T25426242, www.raajmahal.com.br. One of the few restaurants offering authentic Indian food.

Ұ **Aurora**, corner of R Capitão Salomão 43, and **Botequim**, R Capitão Salomão 184. Two of several enticing bars and restaurants on R Visconde de Caravelas, both with varied menus, and good-value simple fare.

Ұ **Chez Michou**, Shopping Rio Sul. Crêpes.

Ұ **Cobal Humaitá**, is a daytime fruit market with many popular restaurants (Mexican tacos, pizzeria, etc).

Ұ **Habib's**, Shopping Rio Sul. One of the ubiquitous chain serving Arabic fast food.

Copacabana, Ipanema and Leblon *p101, maps p102 and p104, phone code 021*

ҰҰҰ **Alessandro and Frederico**, R Garcia D'Ávila, 134 loja D, Ipanema, T25210828. Upmarket café with decent café latte and breakfasts. Great juice bar next door.

ҰҰҰ **Bar D'Hotel**, **Hotel Marina All Suites** (see p113). Light but very well-flavoured fish dishes served to people with tiny waists in casual designer cool surrounds. Very good cocktails. The best for breakfast or lunch with a beach view.

ҰҰҰ **Bistrô ZaZá**, R Joana Angélica 40, Ipanema, T2479101. Hippy chic pseudo-Moroccan/French restaurant that attracts a mix of tourist and Bohemian Zona Sul Cariocas. Good fish dishes and cocktails and good fun. Evenings are best for intimate dining when the tables are lit by candles.

ҰҰҰ **Capricciosa**, R Vinicius de Morais 134, Ipanema, T25233394. The best pizzeria in town and a lynchpin in the TV and fashion scene – the famous and wealthy gather here to gossip and catch up. Queues can be long.

ҰҰҰ **Carlota**, R Dias Ferreira 64, Leblon, T25406821. The best of many on a street lined with restaurants and bars. Great, unpretentious Mediterranean food in an elegant casual all-white dining room.

ҰҰҰ **Cipriani**, **Copacabana Palace** (see p111). The best restaurant for formal evening dining in Rio with a chef from the **Hotel Cipriani** in Venice. Very good seafood and modern Italian fare.

ҰҰҰ **Gero**, R Aníbal de Mendonça 157, Ipanema, T22398158. Light Italian fare strong with excellent fish served to TV Globo novella stars and the like in a beautiful, minimalist space.

ҰҰҰ **Porcão**, Barão de Torre 218, Ipanema, T25220999. One of the city's best *churrascaria*, serving all manner of meat in unlimited quantities for a set price.

ҰҰҰ **Satyricon**, R Barão da Torre 192, Ipanema, T25210627. The best seafood in Rio; especially the squid. Lively crowd in a large dining room which precludes intimacy. A favourite with businessmen and politicians and Ronaldo. Avoid Sat when there is a seafood buffet.

ҰҰҰ **Zukaa**, R Dias Ferreira 233, Leblon, T32057154. One of the most fashionable restaurants in Rio with an exciting and eclectic fusion of everything – French and Japanese, American fast food and Italian... all presented on huge rectangular plates and prepared by Felipe Bronze, formerly of **Nobu** and **Le Bernardin**. The fusions include delights like teriyaki-glazed foie gras.

ҰҰ **Casa da Feijoada**, Prudente de Morais 10, Ipanema, T25234994. Serves an excellent *feijoada* all week. Generous portions.

ҰҰ **Chon Kou**, Av Atlântica 3880, Copacabana, T22873956. A traditional Chinese restaurant which bizarrely also offers an extensive sushi menu. A/c with piped music; sit upstairs for good views over Copacabana beach. A welcome change from most of the other options in this area.

Churrascaria Palace, R Rodolfo Dantas 16B, Copacabana. 20 different kinds of barbecued meat served on a spit at your table with buffet salads to accompany. Good value.

Gergelim, R Vinícius de Moraes 121, Ipanema, T25237026. Vegetarian whole food in an a/c café atmosphere. Good puddings.

Mala e Cuia, R Barata Ribeiro 638, Copacabana, T25457566. *Comida mineira* at another of the restaurants in this recommended chain (also in the centre).

Siri Mole and Cia, R Francisco Otaviano 90, T22330107. Excellent Bahian seafood and Italian coffee in elegant a/c. At the upper end of this price bracket.

Yemenjá, R Visconde de Pirajá 128, T22477004. Bahian cooking such as *moqueca*, *vatapa* and various other dishes cooked in dende palm or coconut oil.

Aipo and Aipim, Av Nossa Senhora de Copacabana 391b and 599, Copacabana and R Visconde de Pirajá 145, Ipanema, T22678313. Plentiful tasty food sold by weight at this popular chain.

Amarelinho, R Farme de Amoedo 62, Ipanema. Great corner *lanchonete* with tables outside, fresh food, good value, friendly, open until 0300. Recommended.

A Marisquera, Barata Ribeiro 232, Copacabana, T25473920. Reasonable seafood dishes and Brazilian standard meals.

Casarão, Souza Lima 37A, Copacabana Cheap but decent café food and breakfasts.

Celeiro, R Dias Ferreira 199, Leblon. Some of the best salads and light food by weight.

Cervantes, Barata Ribeiro 07-B e Prado Júnior 335B, Copacabana. Stand-up bar or sit-down, a/c restaurant, open all night, queues after 2200. Said to serve the best sandwiches in town, a local institution.

Del Mare, on the corner of Prudente de Morais and Vinícius de Morais. Recommended.

Empório Saúde, R Visconde de Pirajá, 414, Ipanema, T25221494, closed Sun and evenings. A large variety of vegetarian comfort cooking from quiches to stews.

La Tratoria, Av Atlântica, opposite Hotel Excelsior. Italian. Good food and service very reasonable. Recommended.

Marakesh, Av NS de Copacabana 599. Good-value pay-by-weight food.

Taberna do Leme, corner of Princesa Isabel and Av NS Copacabana. A simple, friendly bar/restaurant with helpful waiters and tables on pavement. Comprehensive menu all in English includes delicious crab pancakes. Recommended for eating as well as drinking.

Traiteurs de France, Av NS de Copacabana 386, Copacabana. Delicious tarts and pastries, not expensive.

There are stand-up bars selling snacks all around Copacabana and Ipanema.

Gávea, Lagoa and Jardim Botânico *p103, map p104, phone code 021*

Gávea is the grungy heartland of trendy twenty-something Rio. The neighbourhoods of Jardim Botânico and Lagoa appear, at first sight to offer no end of exciting upmarket dining opportunities. But the restaurants are mostly mutton dressed up as lamb. They look great, cost loads and serve dreadful food. Here are a very few exceptions:

Claude Troisgros, R Custódio Serrão 62, Lagoa, T25378582. Elegant French restaurant named after its French chef who cooks a mixture of traditional cuisine and Franco-Brazilian fusions. Recommended.

Árabe da Gávea, Gávea shopping mall, R Marquês de São Vicente 52, T22942439. By far the best Arabic restaurant in Rio.

Dom João, R Pacheco Leão, Jardim Botânico, T38742819. Elegant colonial building with a mixed menu of respectable dishes. Good if you are in the area.

Guimas, R José Roberto Macedo Soares, Baixo Gávea, T22597996. This is one of the places where the under 30s come to be seen in Rio – especially after 2200 towards the end of the week and on Mon. There's nothing to the restaurant though – simple, traditionally Portuguese, with only a handful of tables, a modest front and decent *bacalhau* (cod). But Rio's trendiest gather before moving down the street to the 2 tatty bars on the corner of the street and Praça Santos Dumont.

Mistura Fina, Av Borges de Medeiros 3207, T25372844. See Bars and clubs, below.

Les Artistes, R Marquês de São Vicente 75, Baixo Gávea, T22394242. Another bar/restaurant most notable for who goes there, not what is served; but only after 2200 on Fri when there's drum 'n bass.

Bars and clubs

Rio nightlife is young and vivacious. **Lapa** is a current hotspot at weekends – once a down-at-heel area and still not entirely safe but undergoing a great renaissance, with a string of clubs along **Mem do Sa** and **Lavradio** with dance steps from samba and forro to techno and hip-hop. Similarly busy, even on Sun and Mon, is **Baixa Gávea**, where beautiful twenty-somethings gather around **Praça Santos Dumont**.

In **Ipanema/Leblon**, there is always activity on and around **Av General San Martin** and **R Dias Ferreira**. **Copacabana** nightlife is mostly seedy and tawdry. Discos like **Help** are sad places full of large fat visiting males panting after the lowest common denominator. The exception to this rule are the clubs like **Bunker** – the only to play European club music in Rio. The guidebook *O Guia dos Botequins do Rio de Janeiro*, describes Rio's best, most traditional bars and their history, US$20. You can find it in the **Livraria da Travessa** (see p125), together with similar books; some in English.

Wherever you are in Rio, there's a bar near you. Beer costs around US$1.50 for a large bottle, but up to US$5 in the plusher venues, where you are often given a card which includes 2 drinks and a token entrance fee. A cover charge of US$3-7 may be made for live music, or there might be a minimum consumption charge of around US$3, sometimes both. Snack food is always available. Copacabana, Ipanema and Leblon have many beach *barracas*, several open all night. The seafront bars on Av Atlântica are great for people-watching; but avoid those towards Leme as some may offer more than beer. The big hotels have good cocktail bars.

Clubs in Rio are either fake Europe (eg **Melt** and **Bunker**) and US (eg **Nuth** and **00**) or samba halls undergoing a renaissance (eg **Scenarium** and **Carioca da Gema**).

Central Rio and Lapa *p82, maps p84 and 86, phone code 021*

Lapa is without doubt the centre of Rio nightlife and shouldn't be missed if you are in Rio over a weekend. Ideally come early on a Sat for the afternoon market and live street tango, eat here and stay for a bar and club crawl later. Always be wary of pickpockets.

Carioca da Gema, Av Mem de Sa 79, Centro, T22210043. Great samba club café second only to **Rio Scenarium**.

Club 6, R das Marrecas 38, Lapa. Huge pounding European/NYC dance club with everything from hip-hop to ambient house.

Dama da Noite, R Gomes Freire 773, Lapa. Samba, *chorinho* and crêpes on the patio.

Mercado, R do Mercado 32, Centro. A little bar with live *chorinho* every Thu from 2030.

Rio Scenarium, R do Lavradio 20, Lapa, T38525516, www.rioscenarium.com.br. 3-storey samba club in a colonial house used as a movie prop warehouse. Overflowing with Brazilian exuberance and joie de vivre, with people dancing furiously, to the bizarre backdrop of a 19th-century apothecary's shop or mannequins wearing 1920s outfits. This is Rio at its bohemian best. Buzzes with beautiful people of all ages on Fri. Come after 2300.

Sacrilegio, Av Mem de Sa 81, Lapa, T25073898. Samba, *chorinho*, *pagode* and occasional theatre. Close to many other bars

Semente, R Joaquim Silva 138, T22425165. Popular for samba, *choro* and salsa Mon-Sat from 2200, US$2.50 cover; minimum consumption US$2. Book at weekends. Great atmosphere inside and out. Recommended.

See also Samba schools (p124).

Glória, Catete and Flamengo

p94, map p94, phone code 021

Look out for the frequent free live music performances at the **Marina da Gloria** and along **Flamengo beach** during the summer.

Urca and Botafogo *p99, map p98, phone code 021*

Casa de Matriz, R Enrique de Novais 107, Botafogo. Great grungy club with a bar, Atari room, small cinema and 2 dance floors. Full of Rio students.

Porão, under the Anglican church hall, R Real Grandeza 99, Botafogo. British ex-pats meet here on Fri nights.

Copacabana, Ipanema and Leblon *p101, maps p102 and p104, phone code 021*

There is frequent live music on the beaches of Copacabana and Ipanema, and along the Av Atlântica throughout the summer; especially around New Year.

A Garota de Ipanema, R Vinícius de Morais 49, Ipanema. Where the song *Girl from Ipanema* was written. Now packed with foreigners on the package Rio circuit listening to bossa. For the real thing head to **Toca do Vinicius** on a Sun afternoon (see p121).

Academia da Cachaça, R Conde de Bernadotte 26-G, Leblon; with another branch at Av Armando Lombardi 800, Barra da Tijuca. The best *cachacas*, great *caipirinhas* and traditional Brazilian dishes. Good on Fri.

Bar D'Hotel, Hotel Marina All Suites (see p113). Models and media people drink the excellent house cocktails here at the cool long bar before dining on light Mediterranean fare. Beach views. Good for sunset in smart casual.

Barril 1800, Av Vieira Souto 110, Ipanema. Nice place to watch sunset. Highly recommended.

Bip Bip, R Almirante Gonçalves 50, Copacabana. **Botequim** bar which attracts a crowd of jamming musicians every Tue.

Bom Bar, R General San Martin 1011, Leblon. A downstairs bar and an upstairs club. Packed after 2300, especially Sat.

Bunker, R Raul Pompéia 94, Copacabana. European-style dance club where the likes of DJs Marky and Patife play. Busy Wed-Sat. Gets going around 0200. The queues have become a party in themselves – at the bar next door.

Caroline Café, R JJ Seabra 10, Jardim Botânico, T25400705, www.carolinecafe.com. Popular with Rio's young and good-looking middle classes. Kicks off after 2100. Food too.

Devassa, Av General San Martin 1241, Leblon. A 2-floor pub/restaurant/bar which is always heaving. Brews its own beer.

Empório, R Maria Quitéria 37, Ipanema. Street bar which attracts hordes. Mon is busiest.

Melt, R Rita Ludolf 47, T22499309. Downstairs bar and upstairs sweaty club. Occasional performances by the cream of Rio's new samba funk scene – usually on a Sun. Always heaving on Thu.

Shenanigans, R Visconde de Pirajá 112, Ipanema. Obligatory mock-Irish bar with Guinness and Newcastle Brown. Not a place to meet the locals.

Vinícius, R Vinícius de Morais 39, Ipanema, 2nd floor. Mirror image of the **Garota de Ipanema** with slightly better acts and food.

Gávea, Lagoa and Jardim Botânico *p103, phone code 021*

Bar Lagoa, Av Epitácio Pessoa 1674, Lagoa. Attracts a slightly older arty crowd on weekday evenings.

Clan Café, R Cosme Velho 564 (in front of the Corcovado train station), T25582322, closed Sun, Mon. Great little sit-down *choro* and samba club almost unknown to tourists with live music and decent bar food.

Cozumel, Av Lineu de Paula Machado 696, Jardim Botânico. The Rio equivalent of a Cairns foam disco – with free margaritas, tacky music and a tacky crowd, most of whom are looking not to go home alone.

El Turf (aka Jockey Club), opposite the Jardim Botânico, Praça Santos Dumont 31. Opens at 2200, gets going at 2300, you may have to wait to get in at the weekend if you arrive after 2400, no T-shirts allowed, very much a Rio rich-kid singles and birthday-party place; another in Rio Sul Shopping Centre.

Mistura Fina. Downstairs restaurant upstairs jazz and bossa nova club. One of the few places not orientated solely to the young. Liza Minelli came here when she was in Rio.

Sitio Lounge, R Marques de Sao Vicente 10, Gávea. The nearest thing Rio has to a lounge bar. Good for a chilled out Sat night.

00 (Zero Zero), Av Padre Leonel Franca 240, Gávea. Mock-LA bar/restaurant/club with a small outdoor area. Currently the trendiest club in Rio for Brazil's equivalent of sloanes or valley girls. Gay night on Sun.

Barra da Tijuca *p106, phone code 021*

Nuth, R Armando Lombardi 999, Barra da Tijuca, www.nuth.com.br. Barra's slickest club; very mock-Miami and frequented by a mixed crowd of rich-kid surfers, footballers (Romario comes here) and women with surgically enhanced beauty. The music is a mix of tacky Brazilian and Eurotrash with occasional samba funk live acts.

Pepe, Posto 2, Barra da Tijuca beach. One of a string of very popular beach bars frequented by toned, tanned surfers.

Brazilian football – a beautiful game

The world's favourite national team has done more than any other to elevate a sport involving 22 players and a round leather ball into an art form, more akin to ballet than the usual sweaty exertions of lesser nations.

It has been more than 100 years since Charles Miller, an English expatriate, returned to São Paulo from a trip to the UK and brought with him a couple of leather footballs and arranged a kickabout with some fellow Englishmen. For the first decades of the 20th century Brazilian football was a white middle-class game. Then, in 1923, Vasco da Gama, with a team of black and poor white players, won the Rio championship in the first year of their promotion to the first division. Other local clubs responded by forming their own league and barring Vasco from joining.

Brazilian football has come a long way since then. Players now come from all walks of life, colours and creeds, and they become national heroes. When Garrincha, one of the heroes of the 1962 World Cup finals, died in 1983, millions of Brazilians mourned. The most famous Brazilian footballer remains Edson Arantes do Nascimento, better known as Pelé. He played for Brazil for the first time when he was 17 in 1958 when Brazil won its first World Cup and was still playing for the national squad when it claimed the Jules Rimet trophy, in Mexico 1970, for a third time, thus earning the right to keep it.

Such heady credentials have led to an impossibly hard-to-please, football-crazy population threatening revolution every time the national team falls even marginally below the superhuman standards set by the 1970 side. Brazilians not only expect their national team to win the World Cup, but to do so samba-style, with all the panache exhibited in 1970 and the early 1980s. The 1994 World Cup-winning squad were criticized for not playing the *jogo bonito*, or 'beautiful game' and 'only' managed to squeeze past Sweden in the semi-finals and eventually win the tournament thanks to a woeful penalty miss in the final by Italy's Roberto Baggio.

But if that was bad, worse was to come in France 1998. It all started so well. Brazil were flowing, playing with an effortless abandon not seen for many a year. And there were new gods to worship, most notably the young Ronaldo, a buck-toothed genius who could embarrass opponents with his speed and skill and score seemingly at will. After blowing away Holland in the semis, Brazil met an improving but still less than impressive host side in the final. It should have been a classic Brazil victory but Ronaldo had suffered a mysterious fit the previous night and there were doubts over his inclusion. In the end, he played, but the Brazilians were clearly shell-shocked by what had happened to their talented talisman and were a shadow of their real selves. In a one-sided match France ran out 3-0 winners.

And so to 2002. For once Brazil were underdogs, having only just scraped through their South American qualifying group. With the team – and country – in disarray and still not fully recovered from the trauma of the previous World Cup, football pundits across the globe dismissed them. But what took place in the next four weeks was a revelation and, for the neutral observer, a joy to watch as the 'three R's' – Ronaldo, Rivaldo and the latest star, Ronaldinho – wreaked havoc on their opponents, including England, and swept majestically towards a record fifth win. In the process they have reaffirmed the world's faith in the 'beautiful game'.

Entertainment

Cinema

There are cinemas serving subtitled Hollywood fare and major Brazilian releases on the top floor of almost all the malls. The normal seat price is around US$3. Discounts on Wed and Thu (students pay half price any day of the week).

Other films are shown in the following theatres:

Centro Cultural do Banco do Brasil, R Primeiro de Março 66, Centro, T28082020. One of Rio's better arts centres with the best of the art films and exhibitions from fine art to photography (Mêtro Uruguaiana).

Cinemateca do MAM, Infante Dom Henrique 85, Aterro do Flamengo, T22102188. Cinema classics, art films and roving art exhibitions and a good café with live music. Views of Guanabara Bay from the balconies.

Estaçao Ipanema, R Visconde de Pirajá 605, Ipanema. European art cinema, less mainstream US and Brazilian releases.

Horse racing

Jockey Club Racecourse, by Jardim Botânico and Gávea, meetings on Mon and Thu evenings and Sat and Sun 1400, entrance US$1-2, long trousers required, a table may be booked. Take any bus marked 'via Jóquei'. Betting is by tote only.

Music

Many young Cariocas congregate in Botafogo for live music. There are free concerts throughout the summer, along the Copacabana and Ipanema beaches, in Botafogo and at the parks: mostly samba, reggae, rock and MPB (Brazilian pop): there is no advance schedule, information is given in the local press (see below). Rio's famous jazz, in all its forms, is performed in lots of enjoyable venues too, see the local press. See www.samba-choro.com.br for more info.

Centro Cultural Carioca, R do Teatro 37, T22429642, www.centroculturalcarioca.com, for advance information, 1830-late. This restored old house with wrap-around balconies and exposed brick walls is a dance school and music venue that attracts a lovely mix of people. Professional dancers perform with musicians; after a few tunes the audience joins in. Thu is impossibly crowded; Sat is calmer. Bar food available. US$3 cover charge. Highly recommended.

Canecão, R Venceslau Brás 215, Botafogo, T22953044. A big, inexpensive venue for live concerts, most nights, and a taste of some purely local entertainment on Mon nights. See local press for listings.

Praia do Vermelha, Urca. Residents bring musical instruments and chairs onto the beach for an informal night of samba from around 2100-2400. Free. Bus No 511 from Copacabana.

Rhapsody, Av Epitácio Pessoa 1104, Lagoa, T22472104. Piano-bar restaurant with a mixture of Brazilian and Diana Kraal-style crooning.

Toca do Vinicius, R Vinícius de Moraes 129C, Ipanema. Rio's leading bossa nova and *choro* record shop has live concerts from some of the finest past performers every Sun lunchtime.

See also **Clan Café**, **Melt**, **Nuth** and **Mistura Fina** in Bars and Clubs, above.

Theatre

There are about 40 theatres in Rio, presenting a variety of classical and modern performances in Portuguese. Seat prices start at about US$15; some children's theatre is free.

Festivals and events

Carnival *See also box page 122*

Tickets

The Sambódromo parades start at 1900 and last about 12 hrs. Gates (which are not clearly marked) open at 1800. There are *cadeiras* (seats) at ground level, *arquibancadas* (terraces) and *camarotes* (boxes). The best

Carnival

Carnival in Rio is spectacular. On the Friday before Shrove Tuesday, the mayor of Rio hands the keys of the city to Rei Momo, the Lord of Misrule, signifying the start of a five-day party. Imagination runs riot, social barriers are broken and the main avenues, full of people and children wearing fancy dress, are colourfully lit. Areas throughout the city such as the Terreirão de Samba in Praça Onze are used for shows, music and dancing. Bandas and blocos (organized carnival groups) seem to be everywhere, dancing, drumming and singing.

There are numerous samba schools in Rio divided into two leagues both of which parade in the Sambódromo. The 14 schools of the Grupo Especial parade on Sunday and Monday whilst the Grupos de Acesso A and B parade on Saturday and Friday respectively. There is also a mirins parade (younger members of the established schools) on Tuesday. The judging takes place on Wednesday afternoon and the winners of the various groups parade again on the following Saturday.

Every school presents 2,500-6,000 participants divided into alas (wings) each with a different costume and 5-9 carros alegóricos, beautifully designed floats. Each school chooses an enredo (theme) and composes a samba (song) that is a poetic, rhythmic and catchy expression of the theme. The enredo is further developed through the design of the floats and costumes. A bateria (percussion wing) maintains a reverberating beat that must keep the entire school, and the audience, dancing throughout the parade. Each procession follows a set order with the first to appear being the comissão de frente, a choreographed group that presents the school and the theme to the public. Next comes the abre alas, a magnificent float usually bearing the name or symbol of the school. The alas and other floats follow as well as porta bandeiras and mestre salas, couples dressed in 18th-century costumes bearing the school's flag, and passistas, groups traditionally of mulata dancers. An ala of bahianas, elderly women with circular skirts that swirl as they dance is always included as is the velha guarda, distinguished members of the school who close the parade. Schools are given between 65 and 80 minutes and lose points for failing to keep

boxes are reserved for tourists and VIPs and are very expensive or by invitation only. Seats are closest to the parade, but you may have to fight your way to the front. Seats and boxes reserved for tourists have the best view, sectors 4, 7 and 11 are preferred (they house the judging points); 6 and 13 are least favoured (being at the end when dancers might be tired) but have more space. The terraces, while uncomfortable, house the most fervent fans, tightly packed; this is the best place to soak up the atmosphere but it's too crowded to take pictures. Tickets start at US$40 for *arquibancadas* and are sold at travel agencies as well as the Maracanã Stadium box office. Tickets should be bought as far as possible in advance – they are usually sold out before Carnival weekend but touts outside can generally sell you tickets at inflated prices. Samba schools have an allocation of tickets which members sometimes sell, if you are offered one of these check its date. Tickets for the champions' parade on the Sat following Carnival are much cheaper. Many tour companies offer Rio trips including Carnival; with those tickets at rather inflated prices. Taxis to the Sambódromo are negotiable and will find your gate, the nearest Metrô is Praça Onze and this can be an enjoyable ride in the company of costumed samba school members. You can follow the participants to the *concentração*, the assembly and formation on Av Presidente Vargas, and within this time. Judges award points to each school for components of their procession, such as costume, music and design, and make deductions for lack of energy, enthusiasm or discipline. The winners of the Grupos de Acesso are promoted to the next-higher group while the losers, including those of the Grupo Especial, are relegated to the next-lowest group. Competition is intense and the winners gain a monetary prize funded by entrance fees.

The Carnival parades are the culmination of months of intense activity by community groups, mostly in the city's poorest areas. To understand the traditions of the schools, the meanings of the different parts of the parade, and carnival as a whole, visit the **Museu do Carnaval** in the Sambódromo; although small, it has lots of photographs and the English-speaking staff are very informative (entrance in R Frei Caneca, T5026996. Monday-Friday 1100-1700, free). The **Sambódromo**, a permanent site at R Marquês de Sapucai, Cidade Nova, is 600 m long with seating for 43,000 people. Designed by Oscar Niemeyer and built in 1983-1984, it handles sporting events, conferences and concerts during the year.

Rio´s bailes (fancy-dress balls) range from the sophisticated to the wild. The majority of clubs and hotels host at least one. The Copacabana Palace hotel´s is elegant and expensive whilst the Scala club has licentious parties. It is not necessary to wear fancy dress; just join in, although you will feel more comfortable if you wear a minimum of clothing to the clubs (crowded, hot and rowdy). The most famous are the Red & Black Ball (Friday) and the Gay Ball (Tuesday) which are both televised.

Bandas and blocos can be found in all neighbourhoods and some of the most popular and entertaining are Cordão do Bola Preta (meets at 0900 on Saturday in Rua 13 de Maio 13, Centro), Simpatia é Quase Amor (meets at 1600 Sunday in Praça General Osório, Ipanema) and the transvestite Banda da Ipanema (meets at 1600 on Saturday and Tuesday in Praça General Osorio, Ipanema). It is necessary to join a bloco in advance to receive their distinctive T-shirts, but anyone can join in with the bandas.

The expensive hotels offer special Carnival breakfasts from 0530. Caesar Park is highly recommended for a wonderful meal and a top-floor view of the sunrise over the beach.

mingle while they queue to enter the Sambódromo. Ask if you can take photos.

Sleeping and security

Visitors wishing to attend the Carnival are advised to reserve accommodation well in advance. Virtually all hotels raise their prices during Carnival, although it is usually possible to find a room. Your property should be safe inside the Sambódromo, but the crowds outside can attract pickpockets; as ever, don't brandish your camera, and only take the money you need for fares and refreshments (food and drink are sold in the Sambódromo). It gets hot! Wear as little as possible (shorts and a T-shirt).

Taking part

Most samba schools will accept a number of foreigners and you will be charged upwards of US$125 for your costume as your money helps to fund poorer members of the school. You should be in Rio for at least 2 weeks before Carnival. It is essential to attend fittings and rehearsals on time, to show respect for your section leaders and to enter into the competitive spirit of the event. For those with the energy and the dedication, it will be an unforgettable experience.

Rehearsals

Ensaios are held at the schools' *quadras* from Oct onwards and are well worth seeing. It is wise to go by taxi, as most schools are in

Samba across the globe

The samba, an utterly Brazilian art form, has, in recent years, become an irrepressible musical force across the world. Samba percussion is now regarded as the community art form par excellence. From Sweden to Japan, from France to Israel, professionals and aficionados have joined forces to recreate the collective abandon of the blocos and escolas.

In the UK alone there are more than 100 groups playing some form of samba, meeting regularly to beat out their rhythms on the surdo and tamborim, practise their dance steps and prepare for the local carnival parade.

Some are small percussion workshops, others form huge parades modelled on the classical forms of Rio, with 200-strong baterias and dancers of all types, Bahianas and Passistas all moving to the sound of a specially composed story-samba. In Helsinki, there is a carnival devoted entirely to samba where a select few of the hundreds of Scandinavian bands take to the streets. Street parades across the US are set alight by the American escolas; San Francisco alone boasts 10 or more samba groups. Mexicans, Italians, Austrians, Germans, Danes, all have fallen under the spell of the samba, getting together at regular encontros to share techniques, learn from Brazilian mestres and celebrate their particular brand of samba.

Many groups are striving to produce their own sound by incorporating such influences as jazz, Jamaican reggae and even Punjabi bhangra. The development of samba-jungle rhythms in London and beyond demonstrates that groups are often committed to innovation as well as celebration.

It's not hard to see why the samba school idea has proved so popular. Providing a focus for collective activity, the samba carnival is open to all who want to participate, a non-stop creative party. Whether struggling with the complex batucada rhythms, building carros alegóricos, sewing bahiana skirts or cooking a feijoada, making a parade involves a group effort where for one day in a year the streets of Tokyo, Brighton and Berlin ring to the irresistible rhythms of the samba.

You can find out about samba worldwide through the internet and email. The UK samba website is at www.farrie.demon.co.uk/samba/bands/htm. To subscribe to the UK samba email address, contact tardis.ed.ac.uk and send on sambistas@tardis.ed.ac.uk. The worldwide samba home page is at www.worldsamba.org/.

poorer districts. Tour agents sell tickets for glitzy samba shows, which are not like the real thing. When buying a Carnival video, make sure the format is compatible (Brazilian format matches the USA; VHS PAL for most of Europe).

Samba schools

Acadêmicos de Salgueiro, R Silva Teles 104, Andaraí, T22385564, www.salgueiro.com.br; **Beija Flor de Nilópolis**, Pracinha Wallace Paes Leme 1025, Nilópolis, T27912866, www.beija-flor.com.br; **Imperatriz Leopoldinense**, R Prof Lacê 235, Ramos, T22708037, www.love-rio.com/imperatriz/; **Mocidade Independente de Padre Miguel**, R Coronel Tamarindo 38, Padre Miguel, T33325823, www.mocidade. com; **Portela**, R Clara Nunes 81, Madureira, T33900471, www.gresportela.com.br; **Primeira Estação de Mangueira**, R Visconde de Niterói 1072, Mangueira, T25674637, www.mangueira.com.br; **Unidos da Viradouro**, Av do Contorno 16, Niterói, T27177540, www.databrasil.com/viradouro.

Useful information
Carnival week comprises an enormous range of official and unofficial contests and events which reach a peak on the Tue. **Riotur's** guide booklet gives concise information on these in English. The entertainment sections of newspapers and magazines such as *O Globo*, *Jornal do Brasil*, *Manchete* and *Veja Rio* are worth checking. *Liga Independente das* Escolas de Samba do Rio de Janeiro, www.liesa.com.br, is useful. *Felipe Ferreira's Rio Carnival Guide* has good explanations of the competition, rules, schools, a map and other practical details.

Other festivals

20 Jan The festival of **São Sebastião**, patron saint of Rio, is celebrated by an evening procession, leaving Capuchinhos Church, Tijuca and arriving at the cathedral of São Sebastião. On the same evening, an *umbanda* festival is celebrated at the Caboclo Monument in Santa Teresa.
Jun The **Festas Juninas** are celebrated throughout Brazil. In Rio they start with the festival of **Santo Antônio** on **13 Jun**, when the main event is a Mass, followed by celebrations at the Convento do Santo Antônio and the Largo da Carioca. All over the state, the festival of **São João** is a major event, marked by huge bonfires on the night of **23-24 Jun**. It is traditional to dance the *quadrilha* and drink *quentão*, *cachaça* and sugar, spiced with ginger and cinnamon, served hot. The Festas Juninas close with the festival of **São Pedro** on **29 Jun**. Being the patron saint of fishermen, his feast is normally accompanied by processions of boats.
Oct This is the month of the feast of **Nossa Senhora da Penha** (see p93).

Many people look for **umbanda** religious ceremonies. Those offered on the night tours sold at hotels are not genuine and are a disappointment. You need a local contact to see the real ones, which are usually held in *favelas* and are none too safe for unaccompanied tourists.
30 Dec Less hectic than Carnival, but very atmospheric, is the festival of **Yemanjá** (see Religion, p694), when devotees of the *orixá* of the sea dress in white and gather at night on Copacabana, Ipanema and Leblon beaches, singing and dancing around open fires and making offerings. The elected Queen of the Sea is rowed along the seashore. At midnight small boats are launched as offerings to Yemanjá. The religious event is dwarfed, however, by a massive New Year's Eve party, called **Reveillon** at Copacabana. The beach is packed as thousands of revellers enjoy free outdoor concerts by big-name pop stars, topped with a lavish midnight firework display. It is most crowded in front of Copacabana Palace Hotel. Another good place to see the fireworks is in front of Le Meridien, famous for its fireworks waterfall at about 0010. Many followers of Yemanjá are now making their offerings on 29 or 30 Dec and at Barra da Tijuca or Recreio dos Bandeirantes to avoid the crowds and noise of Reveillon.

Shopping

Bookshops

Anglican Church, R Real Grandeza 99, Botafogo. Second-hand English books.
Argumento, R Dias Ferreira 417, Leblon, sells imported English books, including Footprint.
Casa dos Artistas, on the south side of Praça Tiradentes. Trades in second-hand paperbacks.
Da Vinci, Av Rio Branco 185 lojas 2, 3 and 9, all types of foreign books, Footprint Handbooks available.
Eldorado, Av das Américas 4666, loja 207. Second-hand books.
Livraria Antiquário, 7 de Setembro 207 and in R Pedro I, in centre. Also on Av Marechal Floriano, near Av Rio Branco, especially at No 63. Second-hand books.
Livraria da Travessa, R Visconde de Pirajá 572, Ipanema, T32059002. Classy little bookshop with broad selection of novels, general books, magazines and guidebooks in English. Great café upstairs for a coffee whilst you read.
Saraiva, R do Ouvidor 98, T25079500, a massive (megastore) bookshop which also

includes a music and video shop and a café; other branches in Shopping Iguatemi and Shopping Tijuca.

Siciliano, Av Rio Branco 156, loja 26. European books, also at Nossa Senhora de Copacabana 830 and branches; French books at No 298.

Unilivros, Largo do Machado 29C. French and English bestsellers (7 branches).

Camping equipment

On **R 1 de Março**, north of Av Pres Vargas, are military shops which sell jungle equipment, such as hammocks, mosquito nets and clothing, eg **Casa do Militar**, No 145 and **London**, No 155; you can also buy the Brazilian flag in any size you want here.

Malamada, R da Carioca 13, recommended for rucksacks.

Fashion

Fashion is one of the best buys in Brazil; with a wealth of Brazilian designers selling clothes of the same quality as European or US famous names at a fraction of the price. Rio is the best place in the world for buying high-fashion **bikinis**. The best shops in Rio are on **Garcia D'Ávila** and **R Nascimento Silva** in Ipanema which runs off it. This is where some of the best Brazilian designers like **Andrea Saletto** and **Rosana Bernardes**, together with international big-name stalwarts like **Louis Vuitton** and **Cartier** and Brazil's classiest jeweller, **Antonio Bernardo**. Most of the international names, together with all the big Brazilian names like **Lenny** (Brazil's best bikinis), **Alberta**, **Salinas**, **Club Chocolate** and so on are housed in the Fashion Mall in **São Conrado**.

Andrea Saletto, R Nascimento Silva 244, T25225858, and in the Fashion Mall, Loja 211 T332254235. One of the most sophisticated labels in Rio – elegant and low-profile style, classical cuts and the use of light and tropical fabrics: cotton, linen and silk.

Blue Man, São Conrado Fashion Mall. Tiny bright bikinis beloved of those with perfect bodies.

Bum Bum, R Visconde de Piraja 351, Ipanema, T22879951, www.bumbum.com.br. Together with **Rosa Cha**, Brazil's most internationally renowned bikini designers, tiny and beautifully cut.

Carlos Tufvesson, R Nascimento Silva 304, Ipanema, T2523920, www.carlostufvesson.com. Brazil's latest bright young star who received a standing ovation for his collection at the Barra fashion week in Rio. Sensual long evening wear in high-quality fabric.

Lenny, R Visconde de Pirajá, 351, Ipanema, T22879951, and in the Fashion Mall. Lenny Niemeyer is widely regarded as Brazil's most sophisticated bikini designer.

Maria Bonita, R Aníbal de Mendonça 135, Ipanema, T25405354. Impeccably cut, elegantly simple, sophisticated women's wear in high-quality fabrics. One of the oldest labels in Rio de Janeiro.

Saara is a multitude of little shops along R Alfândega and R Senhor dos Passos (between the city centre and Campo Santana), where clothing bargains can be found (especially jeans, kanga beach wraps and bikinis); it is known popularly as *Shopping a Céu Aberto*.

Salinas, R Visconde de Pirajá 547, Ipanema, T22740644, and Fashion Mall, T24220677. The most highly regarded Brazilian bikinis on the international scene – small, exquisitely made with great attention to detail and using only the best fabrics in a variety of contemporary styles from hand crochet and beading to reversibles in multiple colour combinations.

Little shops on Aires Saldanha, Copacabana (1 block back from beach), are good for bikinis and cheaper than in shopping centres.

Jewellery

Buy precious and semi-precious stones from reputable dealers.

Antônio Bernado, R Garcia d'Ávila 121, Ipanema, T25127204, and in the Fashion Mall. Brazil's foremost jeweller who has been making beautifully understated jewellery with contemporary designs for nearly 30 years. Internationally well known but available only in Brazil.

H Stern, R Visconde de Pirajá 490/R Garcia d'Ávila 113, Ipanema. Have 10 outlets, plus branches in major hotels throughout the city (as well as branches elsewhere in Brazil and worldwide).

Amsterdam Sauer, R Garcia D'Ávila 105. Have 10 shops in Rio and others throughout Brazil, plus St Thomas (US Virgin Islands) and New York; they offer free

taxi rides to their main shop.
Mineraux, Av NS de Copacabana 195. For mineral specimens rather than cut stones. Belgian owner.

There are several good jewellery shops at the Leme end of Av NS de Copacabana.

Markets

Northeastern market at Campo de São Cristóvão, with music and magic, on Sun 0800-2200 (bus 472 or 474 from Copacabana or centre). Sat antiques market on the waterfront near Praça 15 de Novembro, 1000-1700. Also in Praça 15 de Novembro is **Feirarte II**, Thu-Fri 0800-1800. **Feirarte I** is a Sun open-air handicrafts market (everyone calls it the **Feira Hippy**) at Praça Gen Osório, Ipanema, 0800-1800, touristy but fun: items from all over Brazil. **Babilônia Feira Hype** is held every other weekend at the Jockey Club 1400-2300. This lively and popular market has lots of stalls selling clothes and crafts, as well as massage and live music and dance performances. A **stamp and coin market** is held on Sun in the Passeio Público. **Markets** on Wed 0700-1300 on R Domingos Ferreira and on Thu, same hours, on Praça do Lido, both Copacabana (Praça do Lido also has a **Feirarte** on Sat-Sun 0800-1800). There is an **artesania market** nightly near the **Othon hotel**, near R Miguel Lemos: one part for paintings, one part for everything else. **Sunday market** on R da Glória, colourful, cheap fruit, vegetables and flowers; **early-morning food market**, 0600-1100, R Min Viveiros de Castro, Ipanema. Excellent **food and household-goods markets** at various places in the city and suburbs (see newspapers for times and places). **Feira do Livro** is a book market that moves around various locations (Largo do Machado, Cinelândia, Nossa Senhora da Paz – Ipanema), selling books at 20% discount.

Music

Modern Sound Música Equipamentos, R Barata Ribeiro 502D, Copacabana. For a large selection of Brazilian music, jazz and classical.
Toca do Vinicius R Vinícius de Moraes 129C, Ipanema. Specializes in Bossa Nova books, CDs and souvenirs, doubles as a performance space (see also Music, p121).

Photography

Slide film is difficult to get in Rio.
For processing, **Flash Studio**, R Visconde de Pirajá 156, expensive; **One Hour Foto**, in the Rio Sul and Barra shopping centres, is recommended; **Honório**, R Vinícius de Moraes 146E. Stocks lithium batteries. Nikon camera repairs, **T Tanaka Cia Ltda**, Av Franklin Roosevelt 39, office 516, T22201127. Also **Mecánica de Precisão**, R da Conceição 31, shop 202, good.

Shopping centres

Rio Sul, at the Botafogo end of Túnel Novo, has almost everything the visitor may need. It has been refurbished and is convenient and very safe. Some of the services available are: **Telemar** (phone office) for international calls at A10-A, Mon-Sat 1000-2200; next door is **Belle Tours Câmbio**, A10. There is a **post office** at G2. A good branch of **Livraria Sodiler** is at A03. Entertainment includes the **Fun Club** nightclub on the 4th floor, open all night, very young crowd (see under Entertainment above); live music at the **Terraço**; the Ibeas **Top Club** gym; and a **cinema**. Eating places include fast food restaurants, 2 branches of **Kotobuki** sushi bar (another branch on the road to Praia Vermelha, recommended) and **Chaika** for milkshakes, ice creams and sandwiches (4th floor, original branch on Praça Nossa Senhora da Paz, Ipanema). A US$5 bus service runs as far as the **Sheraton** passing the main hotels, every 2 hrs between 1000 and 1800, then 2130.
São Conrado Fashion Mall. The best designers and an excellent restaurant at the **Clube Chocolate** shop.

Other shopping centres, which include a wide variety of shops and services, include: **Cassino** (Copacabana), **Norte Shopping** (Todos os Santos), **Plaza Shopping** (Niterói), **Barra** in Barra da Tijuca (see p106).

Activities and tours

There are hundreds of excellent gyms and sports clubs; most will not grant temporary (less than 1 month) membership: big hotels may allow use of their facilities for a small deposit. **Paissandu Athletic Club**, Av Afrânio de Melo Franco 330, Leblon – tennis, bowls, swimming, Scottish dancing, Tue, Apr-Oct, 2000-2230, may admit non-members.

Cycling

Rio Bikers, R Domingos Ferreira 81, room 201, T22745872. Tours (hire available).

Diving

Squalo, Av Armando Lombardi 949-D, Barra de Tijuca, T/F24933022, squalo1@hotmail.com. Offers courses at all levels, NAUI and PDIC training facilities, also snorkelling and equipment rental.

Golf

Itanhangá Golf Club, Jacarepaguá. Both 18-hole and 9-hole courses, visiting cards from Av Rio Branco 26, 16th floor.

Gávea Club, São Conrado, T33994141, and **Teresópolis Golf Club**, Estr Imbuí (Várzea), both have 18 holes.

Petrópolis Country Club, Nogueira. 9 holes.

Hang-gliding

Delta Flight, T96938800, www.deltaflight.com.br. Flight tours above Rio from Padro Bonito Mountain with instructors licensed by Brazilian Hang-Gliding Association. Contact Richard Hamond.

Just Fly, T/F22680565, T99857540 (mob), www.justfly.com.br. US$80 for tandem flights with Paulo Celani (licensed by Brazilian Hang-Gliding Association), pick-up and drop-off at hotel included, in-flight pictures US$15 extra, flights all year, best time of day 1000-1500 (5% discount for South American and Brazil Handbook readers on presentation of book at time of reservation).

Tandem Flight and Rio by Jeep, T96938800, www.riobyjeep.com. Tandem flight tours above Rio from Pedro Bonita mountain with instructors licensed by the Brazilian Hang-Gliding Association. Contact Ricardo Hamond.

Ultra Força Ltda, Av Sernambetiba 8100, Barra da Tijuca, T33993114; 15-min tandem hang-gliding flights.

Rejane Reis, Exotic Tours (see Tour operators, below) also arranges hang-gliding, as well as paragliding, ultra-light flights, walks and other activities.

Parachuting and paragliding

Barra Jumping, Aeroporto de Jacarepaguá, Av Ayrton Senna 2541, T33252494, www.barrajumping.com.br. Tandem jumping (*Vôo duplo*).

Sr Ruy Marra, T33222286, or find him at the beach. Paragliding from Leblon beach with Brazilian paragliding champion (US$75). Several other people offer tandem jumping; check that they are accredited with the Associação Brasileira de Vôo Livre.

Riding

Sociedade Hípico Brasileiro, Av Borges de Medeiros 2448, T25278090, Jardim Botânico.

Rock climbing and hillwalking

ECA, Av Erasmo Braga 217, room 305, T22426857. Personal guide US$100 per day, owner Ralph speaks English.
Clube Excursionista Carioca, R Hilário Gouveia 71, room 206, T22551348. Recommended for enthusiasts, meets Wed and Fri.

Sailing

Federação Brasileira de Vela e Motor, R Alcindo Guanabara 15, sl 801, Centro, T22203738. For information.
Federação de Vela, Praça Mahatma Gandhi 2, 12th floor, T22208785. For information.
Iate Clube do Rio de Janeiro, Av Pasteur, Urca, T22954482. Yachting.

Surfing

For the state of the waves on the beaches in Rio de Janeiro and its environs, see Surfing, p66.
Associação Brasileira de Bodyboard, T22743614.
Federação de Bodyboard do Estado do Rio de Janeiro, T22565653.

Federação de Surf do Estado do Rio de Janeiro, T22872385.
Organização dos Surfistas Profissionais do Rio de Janeiro, T24932472.

Swimming

On all Rio's beaches you should take a towel or mat to protect you against sandflies. In the water stay near groups of other swimmers. There is a strong undertow. See also Tour operators, below.

Tour operators

Regular sightseeing tours are operated by **American Sightseeing**, T22363551; **Sul América**, T22574235; **Canbitur** (of Copacabana); **Passamar Turismo**, Av Rio Branco 25, T2338883, also at **Hotel Nacional**.
Adrianotour, T22085103. For guided tours, reservations and commercial services (English, French, German and Spanish spoken).
Atlantic Forest Jeep Tour, T24959827, T99740218 (mob). As well as running jeep tours to Tijuca National Park (see above), they offer trips to coffee *fazendas* in the Paraíba Valley, to Angra dos Reis and to offshore islands and the Serra dos Órgãos.
Blumar, R Visconde de Pirjajá 550, Subsolo 108/109, Ipanema, T25113636, www.blumar.com.br. Run extensive tours throughout Brazil as well as reservations for Rio.
Cultural Rio, R Santa Clara 110/904, Copacabana, T33224872 or T99113829 (mob), www.culturalrio.com. Tours escorted personally by Professor Carlos Roquette, English and French spoken, almost 200 options available.
Dantur, Largo do Machado 29 (Galeria Condor) loja 47, T25577144. Helena speaks English and is friendly and helpful.
Favela Tour, Estr das Canoas 722, Bl 2, apt 125, CEP 22610-210, T33222727, T99890074 (mob), www.favelatour.com.br. Guided tours of Rio's *favelas*; safe, different and interesting, US$20, 3 hrs. Also ask Marcelo Armstrong, the owner, about eco tours, river-rafting and other excursions. He speaks English, French, Spanish, Italian and can provide guides in German and Swedish. For the best attention and price call Marcelo direct rather than through a hotel desk.
Fábio Sombra, T22959220, T97295455 (mob), fabiosombra@hotmail.com. Offers private and tailor-made guided tours focusing on the cultural aspects of Rio and Brazil.

Fenician Tours, Av NS de Copacabana 335, T22353843. Cheaper than some at US$30 including transport from/to hotel.
Guanatur Turismo, R Dias da Rocha 16A, Copacabana, T22353275, F22353664. Sells long-distance bus tickets.
Hanseatic, R 7 de Setembro 111/20, T22246672. German-run (English, French, Portuguese spoken). Recommended.
Helisight, R Visconde de Pirajá 580, loja 107, Térreo, Ipanema, T35112141, www.helisight.com.br. Helicopter sightseeing tours. Prices from US$43 per person for 6-7 mins from Morro de Urca over Sugar Loaf and Corcovado, to US$148 per person for 30 mins over the city.
Marlin Tours, Av NS de Copacabana 605, office 1204, T25484433, bbm.robin@openlink.com.br. Recommended for hotel, flights and tours, Robin and Audrey speak English.
Metropol, R São José 46, T25335010, www.metro polturismo.com.br. Eco, adventure and culture tours to all parts of Brazil.
Rejane Reis, Exotic Tours, also has *favela* tours, 2½ hrs, US$30 (transport included) – tours are combined with a guide-training programme. English spoken.
Rio by Jeep, T78115912, www.riobyjeep. 5-hour tours in open or closed jeeps with local guides, US$45 per person. Contact Richard Hamond.
South American Experience, R Raimundo Correa 36a, Copacabana, T25488813, www.southamericanexperience.com. Backpacker bus trips south to Paraty and Trindade with stops along the Costa Verde. Part of the Oz Experience bus group. Trips Brazil-wide can be booked through their travel agency.
Travel Café, R Cosme Velho 513, T22858302. City tours, rafting, sky diving, horse riding, night tours and packages along the Costa Verde. Speak English.
Turismo Clássico, Av NS de Copacabana 1059/805, T25233390, classico@infolink.com.br. Recommended. Organized trips to Samba shows cost US$50 including dinner, good, but it's cheaper to go independently.

Transport

See also Ins and outs, p78.

Air

Antônio Carlos Jobim International Airport

Previously called Galeão, the Antônio Carlos Jobim International Airport is situated on Governador Island some 16 km from the centre of Rio. It is in 2 sections: international and domestic.

Transport from the airport There are a/c taxis; Cootramo and Transcopass have fixed rates (US$19 Copacabana), buy a ticket at the counter near the arrivals gate before getting into the car. The hire is for the taxi, irrespective of the number of passengers. Make sure you keep the ticket, which carries the number to phone in case of difficulty. Ordinary taxis also operate with the normal metre reading (about US$12.50, but some may offer cheaper rates from Copacabana to the airport, US$7-8.50). Do not negotiate with a driver on arrival, unless you are a frequent visitor. Beware of pirate taxis which are unlicensed. It is better to pay extra for an official vehicle than run the risk of robbery. The a/c Real bus runs very frequently from the 1st floor of the airport to Recreio dos Bandeirantes via the municipal rodoviária and city centre, Santos Dumont Airport, Flamengo, Copacabana, Ipanema and Leblon. Luggage is secured in the hold (receipted), passengers are given a ticket and fares are collected during the journey; to anywhere in Rio it costs US$3.50. The driver will stop at requested points (the bus runs along the seafront from Leme to Leblon), so it's worth checking a map beforehand so that you can specify your required junction. The bus returns by the same route. Town buses M94 and M95, Bancários/Castelo, take a circular route passing through the centre and the interstate bus station. They leave from the 2nd floor of the airport.

Money exchange There are câmbios in the departure hall of the airport. There is also a câmbio on the 1st floor of the international arrivals area, but it gives worse rates than the Banco do Brasil, 24-hr bank, 3rd floor, which has Visa ATMs and will give cash advances against a Visa card.

Shops Duty-free shops are well stocked, but not especially cheap and are open to arrivals as well as departures. Only US dollars or credit cards are accepted on the air-side of the departure lounge. There is a wider choice of restaurants outside passport control.

Tourist information Check at the Riotur counter before leaving, for folders, maps and advice, T33984073. They will give help in booking hotels if required.

Tourist packs sold at the international airport are completely unnecessary.

Nationwide tickets The best deals on flights within Brazil are available through Gol, T08007012131, www.voegol.com.br. See also www.varig.com.br, www.vasp.com.br and www.tam.com.br.

Santos Dumont Airport

Situated on Guanabara Bay, right in the city, the Santos Dumont Airport is used for Rio-São Paulo shuttle flights (US$150 single, US$300 return), other domestic routes, air taxis and private planes. The shuttle services operate every 30 mins throughout the day from 0630-2230. Sit on the right-hand side for views to São Paulo, the other side coming back, book flights in advance.

Airline offices

Aerolíneas Argentinas, R São José 70, 8th floor, Centro, T22924131, airport T33983520. **Air France**, Av Pres Antônio Carlos 58, 9th floor, T25323642, airport T33983488. **Alitalia**, Av Pres Wilson 231, 21st floor, T22924424, airport T33983143. **American**, Av Pres Wilson 165, 5th floor, T0800 7034000. **Avianca**, Av Pres Wilson 165, offices 801-03, T22404413, airport T33983778. **British Airways**, airport T33983889. **Iberia**, Av Pres Antônio Carlos 51, 8th and 9th floors, T22821336, airport T33983168. **Japan Airlines**, Av Rio Branco 156, office 2014, T22206414. **KLM**, Av Rio Branco 311A, T25427744, airport T33983700. **LAB**, Av Calógeras 30A, T22209548. **Lan Chile**, R da Assambléia 92, office 1301, T2220972, T0800 5549000, airport T33983797. **Lufthansa**, Av Rio Branco 156D, T22176111, airport T33985855. **RioSul/Nordeste**, Av Rio Branco 85, 10th floor, T25074488 (has an advance check-in desk in Rio Sul Shopping). **Swissair**, Av Rio Branco 108, 10th floor, T22975177, airport T33984330. **TAP**, Av Rio Branco 311-B, T22101287, airport, T33983455. **United**, Av Pres Antônio Carlos 51, 5th floor, T0800 245532. **Varig**, Av Rio Branco 277G, T22203821 information, T0800 997000 bookings; airport T33982122. Most staff speak English. **Vasp**, R Santa Luzia 735, T0800 998277.

Bus

Local

There are good services to all parts, but buses are very crowded and not for the aged and infirm during rush hours. Buses have turnstiles which are awkward if you are carrying luggage. Hang on tight, drivers live out Grand Prix fantasies. At busy times allow about 45 mins to get from Copacabana to the centre by bus. The fare on standard buses is US$0.40 and suburban bus fares are US$0.75. Bus stops are often not marked. The route is written on the side of the bus, which is hard to see until the bus has actually pulled up at the stop.

Private companies operate a/c *frescão* buses which can be flagged down practically anywhere: **Real, Pegaso, Anatur**. They run from all points in Rio Sul to the city centre, rodoviária and the airports. Fares are US$1.50 (US$1.80 to the international airport).

City Rio, T0800 258060, is an a/c tourist bus service with security guards which runs between all the major parts of the city. Good maps show what sites of interest are close to each bus stop – marked by grey poles and found where there are concentrations of hotels.

Long distance

Buses run from Rio to all parts of the country; it is advisable to book tickets in advance. Details of journey times and fares are given under destinations throughout the chapter.

Rodoviária Novo Rio, Av Rodrigues Alves, corner with Av Francisco Bicalho, just past the docks, T22915151. Some travel agents sell interstate tickets, or will direct you to a bus ticket office in the centre. Agencies include **Dantur Passagens e Turismo**, Av Rio Branco 156, subsolo loja 134, T22623424/3624; **Itapemirim Turismo**, R Uruguaiana 10, loja 24, T25098543, both in the centre; **Guanatur**, R Dias da Rocha 16A,

Copacabana, T22353275; and an agency at R Visconde de Pirajá 303, loja 114, Ipanema. They charge about US$1 for bookings.

The rodoviária has a **Riotur** information centre, which is very helpful. Left luggage costs US$3. There are *câmbios* for cash only. The local bus terminal is just outside the rodoviária: turn right as you leave and run the gauntlet of taxi drivers – best ignored. The bus station attracts thieves, so exercise caution. The a/c **Real** bus (opposite the exit) goes along the beach to São Conrado and will secure luggage. If you need a taxi collect a ticket, which ensures against overcharging, from the office inside the entrance (to Flamengo US$6).

International buses

Asunción, 1,511 km via Foz do Iguaçu, 30 hrs (Pluma), US$70; **Buenos Aires** (Pluma), via Porto Alegre and Santa Fe, 48 hrs, US$100 (book 2 days in advance); **Uruguaiana**, US$90, cheaper and quicker to get a through ticket; **Santiago de Chile**, (Pluma) US$135, or Gen Urquiza, about 70 hrs.

The main bus station is reached by buses M94 and M95, Bancários/Castelo, from the centre and the airport; 136, 172, rodoviária/Glória/Flamengo/Botafogo; 127, 128, 136, rodoviária/Copacabana; 170, rodoviária/Gávea/São Conrado; 128, 172, rodoviária/Ipanema/Leblon.

Car

Service stations are closed in many places on Sat and Sun. Road signs are notoriously misleading in Rio and you can end up in a *favela* (take special care if driving along the Estr da Gávea to São Conrado as it is possible to unwittingly enter Rocinha, Rio's biggest slum).

Car hire

Many agencies on Av Princesa Isabel, Copacabana. A credit card is virtually essential for hiring a car. Recent reports suggest it is cheaper to hire outside Brazil, you may also obtain fuller insurance this way. **Avis**, Antônio Carlos Jobim International Airport, T33985060, Santos Dumont Airport, T38147378, Av Princesa Isabel 150A and B, Copacabana, T25438481; **Hertz**, international airport, T3984338, Av Princesa Isabel 273-A, Copacabana, T22757440; **Interlocadora**, international airport, T33983181; **Localiza**, international airport and Santos Dumont Airport, T0800 992000, Av Princesa Isabel 150, Copacabana, T22753340; **Nobre**, Av Princesa Isabel 7, Copacabana, T25414646; Telecar, R Figueiredo Magalhães 701, Copacabana, T22356778.

Car repairs

Kyoso Team Mecânico Siqueira Campos, at the entrance to the old tunnel, T22550506. A good mechanic who enjoys the challenge of an unusual car. Recommended.

Distances and journey times

Juiz de Fora, 184 km (2¾ hrs); **Belo Horizonte**, 434 km (7 hrs); **São Paulo**, 429 km (6 hrs); **Vitória**, 521 km (8 hrs); **Curitiba**, 852 km (12 hrs); **Brasília**, 1,148 km (20 hrs); **Florianópolis**, 1,144 km (20 hrs); **Foz do Iguaçu**, 1,500 km (21 hrs); **Porto Alegre**, 1,553 km (26 hrs); **Salvador**, 1,649 km (28 hrs); **Recife**, 2,338 km (38 hrs); **Fortaleza**, 2,805 km (48 hrs); **São Luís**, 3,015 km (50 hrs); **Belém**, 3,250 km (52 hrs).

Hitchhiking

To hitch to **Belo Horizonte** or **Brasília**, take a C-3 bus from Av Pres Antônio Carlos to the railway station, cross through the station to a bus station and catch the Nova Iguaçu bus. Ask to be let off at the Belo Horizonte turn-off. For the **motorway entrance** north and south, take bus No 392 or 393 from Praça São Francisco.

Metro

The Metrô provides a good service; it is clean, a/c and fast. **Line 1** operates between the inner suburb of Tijuca (station Saens Peña) and Arcoverde (Copacabana), via the railway station (Central), Glória and Botafogo. **Line 2** runs from Pavuna, passing Engenho da Rainha and the Maracanã stadium, to Estácio. It operates 0600-2300, Sun 1400-2000; closed holidays. The fare is US$0.50 single; multi-tickets and integrated bus/Metrô tickets are available.

Substantial changes in bus operations are

taking place because of the extended Metrô system; buses connecting with the Metrô have a blue-and-white symbol in the windscreen.

Taxi

The fare between Copacabana and the centre is US$7. Between 2300 and 0600 and on Sun and holidays, 'tariff 2' is used. Taxis have red number plates with white digits (yellow for private cars, with black digits) and have meters. Smaller ones (mostly Volkswagen) are marked TAXI on the windscreen or roof. Make sure meters are cleared and on 'tariff 1', except at those times mentioned above. Only use taxis with an official identification sticker on the windscreen. Don't hesitate to argue if the route is too long or the fare too much. Radio Taxis are safer but almost twice as expensive, eg **Cootramo**, T25605442; **Coopertramo**, T22602022; **Centro de Táxi**, T25932598; **Transcoopass**, T25604888. Luxury cabs are allowed to charge higher rates; **Inácio de Oliveira**, T22254110, is a reliable taxi driver for excursions, he only speaks Portuguese. Recommended; **Grimalde**, T22679812, has been recommended for talkative daytime and evening tours, English and Italian spoken, negotiate a price.

Train

There are suburban trains to **Nova Iguaçu**, **Nilópolis**, **Campo Grande** and elsewhere. Buses marked 'E Ferro' go to the railway station.

Tram

See also Ins and outs, p78.

The last remaining tram runs from near the Largo da Carioca (there is a museum open 0830-1700 Fri only) across the old aqueduct (Arcos) to Dois Irmãos or Paula Mattos in Santa Teresa – historical and interesting, US$0.40. For more details see above, Santa Teresa, p96.

Rio de Janeiro Metrô

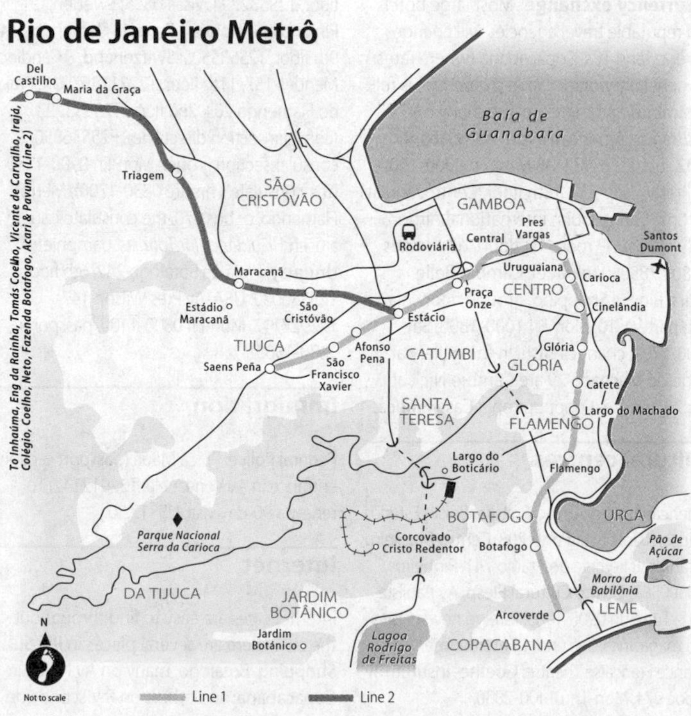

Directory

Banks

Lloyds Bank, R da Alfândega 332, 7th floor. **Banco Internacional** (Bank of America and Royal Bank of Canada), R do Ouvidor 90; **Banco Holandês Unido**, R do Ouvidor 101; **Citibank**, R Assembléia 100, changes large US$ TCs into smaller ones, no commission; **Banco do Brasil**, there are only 2 branches in Rio which will change US$ TCs, Praia de Botafogo, 384A, 3rd floor (minimum US$200) and the central branch at R Sen Dantas 105, 4th floor (minimum US$500 – good rates). The international airport is probably the only place to change TCs at weekends. Visa cash withdrawals at **Banco do Brasil** (many ATMs at the R Sen Dantas branch, no queues) and **Bradesco** (personal service or machines). MasterCard, Visa and Cirrus cash machines at **HSBC** branches throughout the city; **Itaú**, on Av Atlântica (next to Copacabana Palace), R Visconde de Pirajá, close to Praça Gen Osório (Ipanema) and other locations. Also at Santos Dumont Airport.

Currency exchange Most large hotels and reputable travel agencies will change currency and TCs. Copacabana (where rates are generally worse than in the centre) is full of **câmbios** and there are also many on Av Rio Branco. **American Express**, Av Atlântica 1702, loja 1, T25482148 Mon-Fri 0900-1600, Av Pres Wilson 231, 18th floor, Centro, and at Antônio Carlos Jobim International Airport, T33984251 (VIP room 1st floor), good rates (T0800 785050 toll-free); **Câmbio Belle Tours**, Rio Sul Shopping, ground floor, loja 101, parte A-10, Mon-Fri 1000-1800, Sat 1000-1700, changes cash. In the gallery at Largo do Machado 29 are **Câmbio Nick** at loja 22 and, next door but one, **Casa Franca**.

Cultural centres

American Library, União Cultural Brasil- Estados Unidos, R Col Oscar Porto 208; **Centro Brasileiro Britânico**, R Ferriera de Araújo 741, Pinheiros, T30390567; **Centro Cultural Fiesp**, Av Paulista 1313, Tue-Sun 0900-1900, foreign newspapers and magazines. See under Entertainment for Alliance Française Theatre; **Goethe- Instituto**, R Lisboa 974, Mon-Thu 1400-2030.

Dentist

Amílcar Werneck de Carvalho Vianna, Av Pres Wilson 165, suite 811. English-speaking; **Dr Mauro Suartz**, R Visconde de Pirajá 414, room 509, T22876745. Speaks English and Hebrew, helpful.

Embassies and consulates

Argentina, Praia de Botafogo 228, T25531646. Very helpful over visas, 1130-1600; **Australia**, Av Presidente Wilson, T38244624. Mon-Fri 0900-1300, 1430-1800; **Austria**, Av Atlântica 3804, T25222286; **Canada**, R Lauro Müller 116, T25433004; **Denmark**, Praia do Flamengo 66, T25586050; **France**, Av Pres Antônio Carlos 58, T22101272; **Germany**, R Pres Carlos de Campos 417, T25536777; **Greece**, Praia do Flamengo 344, T25526799; **Israel**, Av NS de Copacabana 680, T25485432; **Netherlands**, Praia de Botafogo 242, 10th floor, T25529028 (Dutch newspapers here and at KLM office on Av Rio Branco); **Paraguay**, same address, 2nd floor, T25532294. Visas US$5; **Sweden, Finland** and **Norway**, Praia do Flamengo 344, 9th floor, T25535505; **Switzerland**, R Cândido Mendes 157, 11th floor, T22211867; **UK**, Praia do Flamengo 284, 2nd floor, T25533223 (consular section direct line), F25536850, consular section is open Mon-Fri 0900-1230 (the consulate's hrs are 0830-1700), Metrô Flamengo, or bus 170, the consulate issues a useful '*Guidance for Tourists*' pamphlet; **Uruguay**, Praia de Botafogo 242, 6th floor, T25536030; **USA**, Av Pres Wilson 147, T22927117, Mon-Fri 0800-1100, passports 1330-1500.

Immigration

Federal Police, Praça Mauá (passport section), entrance in Av Venezuela, T22912142. To renew a 90-day visa, US$12.50.

Internet

Internet cafés are easy to find throughout the city. There are several places in **Rio Sul Shopping**, Botafogo; many on **Av NS de Copacabana**; and others on R Visconde de

Pirajá, Ipanema. **Phone Serv**, Av N S de Copacabana 454, loja B. US$3 per hr internet, telephone service; **Tudo é Fácil**, 3 branches in Copacabana: R Xavier da Silveira 19; Av Prado Júnior 78 and R Barata Ribeiro 396. Well-organized, with identification cards so once registered you can bypass the front desk, telephone booths and scanners, US$2 per hr, discounts for extended use.

Language courses

Instituto Brasil-Estados Unidos, Av Copacabana 690, 5th floor, 8-week course, 3 classes a week, US$150, 5-week intensive course US$260. Good English library at same address; **IVM Português Prático**, R do Catete 310, sala 302, US$18 per hr for individual lessons, cheaper for groups. Helpful staff. Recommended; **Cursos da UNE** (União Nacional de Estudantes), R Catete 243, include cultural studies and Portuguese classes for foreigners.

Laundry

Lavanderia, Visconde de Pirajá 631A, Ipanema, T22948142; **Fénix**, R do Catete 214, loja 20; **Laundromat** at Av NS de Copacabana 1216. In Rio Sul there are self-service laundrettes such as **Lavelev**, about US$7 for a machine, including detergent and drying, 1 hr. Also at R Buarque de Macedo 43B, Catete, R Voluntários da Patria 248, Botafogo, Av Prado Júnior 63B, Copacabana; **Lavlev Flamengo**, RC de Baependi 78, or R das Laranjeiras 43, L28.

Medical services

Vaccinations at **Saúde de Portos**, Praça Mcal Âncora, T22408628/8678, Mon-Fri 1000-1100, 1500-1800 (international vaccination book and ID required); **Policlínica**, Av Nilo Peçanha 38. Recommended for diagnosis and investigation. A good public hospital for minor injuries and ailments is **Hospital Municipal Rocha Maia**, R Gen Severiano 91, Botafogo, T22952295/2121, near Rio Sul Shopping Centre. Free, but there may be queues; **Hospital Miguel Couto**, Mário Ribeiro 117, Gávea, T22746050. Has a free casualty ward.

Post

Central Post Office is on R 1 de Março 64, at the corner of R do Rosário. Also at Av N S de Copacabana 540 and many other locations. All handle international post. There is a post office at Antônio Carlos Jobim International Airport; **Poste Restante** at Correios, Av N S de Copacabana 540 and all large post offices (letters held for a month, recommended, US$0.10 per letter); **Federal Express**, Av Calógeras 23 (near Santa Luzia Church) T22628565, is reliable.

Students

Student Travel Bureau, Av Nilo Peçanha 50, SL 2417, Centro, T/F25442627, and R Visconde de Pirajá 550, lj 201, Ipanema, T25128577, www.stb.com.br (with offices throughout the country) has details of travel, discounts and cultural exchanges for ISIC holders.

Telephone

International telephone booths are blue. International telephone calls can be made at larger **Correios**, eg Av NS de Copacabana 540; larger **Embratel** offices also have telex and fax; at the **airports** and the **Novo Rio rodoviária**; at R Dias da Cruz 192, Méier-4 (24 hrs, 7 days a week); in **Urca**, near the Pão de Açúcar cable car; at **Praça Tiradentes 41**, a few mins' walk from Metrô Carioca; at **R Visconde de Pirajá 111**, Ipanema; and at **R do Ouvidor 60**, Centro.

Telephone numbers often change in Rio de Janeiro and other Brazilian cities. If in doubt, phone 102, **Auxilio à Lista**, which is the current daily updated directory of telephone numbers. This number can be used all over the country, but if you want to find out a Rio phone number from outside Rio, dial the city code 021, then 121. If you do not understand Portuguese, you should seek assistance from a hotel receptionist or similar because the numbers are only spoken in Portuguese.

Toilets

There are very few public toilets in Rio de Janeiro, but shopping centres, many bars and restaurants (eg McDonald's) offer facilities. Just ask for the banheiro.

Niterói, Búzios and the Costa do Sol

East of Rio the country gets drier and more Mediterranean in appearance, and the coast which is lined by fabulous beaches all the way to Búzios is backed by a long series of saltwater lakes and drifting sand dunes. Most visitors ignore Niterói, the city immediately opposite Rio across Guanabara Bay, despite it having ocean beaches as good or better than Rio's. Instead, they head straight for the surf towns around Cabo Frio or the fashionable little resort of Búzios which has good beaches and lively summer nightlife. ➞ *For Sleeping, Eating and other listings, see pages 142-149.*

Niterói ➔ *Phone code: 021. Colour map 4, C3. Population: 460,000.*

Just across Guanabara Bay is Niterói, the old capital of Rio de Janeiro state. Cariocas often joke that the best thing about Niterói is its views back to Rio, which are spectacular. It is also a pleasant excursion with some good beaches nearby and a star attraction in the futuristic Museu de Arte Contemporânea, designed by Oscar Niemeyer.

When the French under Villegagnon, with their Tamoio allies, established their colony on the western side of the mouth of the Baía de Guanabara, the Portuguese and the Temiminós set up camp on the eastern shore. The formal founding of a settlement here was in 1573 and once the Portuguese had established sovereignty, the area became a centre for sugar growing in the 17th century. It only really became important after Dom João VI's visit in 1816, when it was given the name of Vila Real da Praia Grande. In 1834 it was renamed Niterói ('hidden waters' in Tupi-Guarani) and was capital of the province (later state) of Rio de Janeiro until 1975 when the capital moved to Rio.

Sights

Many buildings associated with the city's period as state capital are grouped around the Praça da República (none is open to the public). The main avenue is Av Ernâni do Amaral Peixoto, with buildings similar to those on Avenida Presidente Vargas in Rio. At the end of the avenue is the dock for Rio, a statue of the Indian chief Araribóia and Bay Market shopping centre. The main green area in the centre is Campo de São Bento, which has many trees and handicraft stalls at weekends. **Tourist information** is at **Neltur** ⓘ *Estrada Leopoldo Fróes 773, São Francisco, T27102727, www.neltur.com, open daily*. A monthly newspaper, *Niterói, Esporte, Lazer, Turismo e Cultura*, is free.

The centre of Niterói is easily explored on foot.

Colonial churches include **São Lourenço dos Índios**, Praça General Rondon, which dates from at least 1627 and the **Capela da Boa Viagem** (1663), which stands on a fortified island, attached by a causeway to the mainland (open one day a month for mass). By Gragoatá beach in the city is the **Capela São Domingos** (1662) and the **Forte de Gragoatá**, from the same period (closed to the public).

The **Basílica de Nossa Senhora Auxiliadora** ⓘ *R Santa Rosa 207, daily 0600-1100, 1500-2000*, is an early 20th-century church. Its famous organ, made in Italy, was bought by the Salesian order during the Second World War and is one of the largest pipe organs in the world, certainly the largest in Latin America.

The most important historical monument, however, is the 16th-century **Fortaleza Santa Cruz** ⓘ *T27107840, daily 0900-1600, US$1.50, tours have a compulsory guide, Portuguese only*, which is still a military establishment. It is situated on a promontory

Villa-Lobos – Rio's greatest musical son

One of the many contradictory beauties of Brazil is that whilst the country as a whole is entrenchantly institutionalized and socially stratified, its best music has always burst forth spontaneously from the various roots of Brazil, and been loved by all. Gilberto Gil says in one song that it comes from 'beneath the soil at our feet'; the feet of Bahia. African feet. Marlui Miranda celebrates it as indigenous, Hermeto Pascoal and Egberto Gismonti as bursting from Nature. And none of these composers, revered though they are throughout Brazil, move within set traditions – their music defies labels. This attitude to music within Brazil is as much a product of the vision of one man as it is a lucky fluke. Heitor Villa-Lobos, the country's most distinguished composer once famously stated: 'one foot in the academy and you are changed for the worst'. He went on to change the academy; founding a system of education, still used today which fused classical training with a love and appreciation for popular and traditional musical forms.

Like so many other great Brazilian musicians from Djavan to Tom Jobim, Villa-Lobos began his musical career in Rio's cafes. You could have seen him at the turn of the 19th century playing cello in places like Bar Luiz in the city centre. He then secured a place in the Rio Symphony Orchestra, where he played under the Strauss's baton, and where he began to compose. His early concerts enchanted Cariocas and by 1923, he had attracted enough official favour to win a government grant to study in Paris; a considerable amount of money at that time. Here, he met and became friends with Milhaud, was strongly influenced by Satie and composed many of his most famous works – like the Bachianas Brasileiras, which re-invented and Brazilianized baroque music. On his return to Brazil Villa-Lobos founded the Conservatório Nacional de Canto Orfeónico and the Brazilian Academy of Music, where he invented and instilled his much revered system of musical education.

Villa-Lobos was a magnetic personality and a Carioca through and through. Julian Bream, the foremost European interpreter of his guitar music remembers him as 'larger than life, quite extraordinary. He dldn't seem to be a composer. He wore loud checked shirts, smoked a cigar, and always kept the radio on, listening to the news or light music or whatever.' He was famous for his anecdotes which were told with a cigar in one hand a glass of brandy in the other. These were full of unlikely accounts of encounters with tribes of cannibalistic Indians and giant snakes, met on his numerous travels throughout the Amazon and North East, in search of Nature and traditional folk music.

His music too is idiosyncratic; anecdotal; visual and thoroughly Brazilian. Bachianas Brasileiras and Little Caipira Train are celebrations of daily Brazilian life. Green Mansions and Saudades das Selvas Brasileiras (Longing for the Brazilian Forest) are dedicated to the beauty of the natural landscape. He even wrote a series of Choros; a musical style which fused Portugal and Africa and which would later produce Samba. He died, on November 17, 1959, in his beloved Rio de Janeiro.

Villa-Lobos' house is now a museum – see page 99.

which commands a fine view of the entrance to the bay. Tours show the Capela de Santa Bárbara, whose statue was destined for Santa Cruz dos Militares in Rio. All attempts to move the saint were accompanied by great storms, which was taken as a sign to leave her at the fortress. Also shown are the dungeons, fortifications, execution sites and gun batteries. It is about 13 km from the centre of Niterói, on the Estrada General Eurico Gaspar Dutra, by Adão e Eva beach.

Museu de Arqueologia de Itaipu ⓘ *T27094079, Wed-Sun 1300-1800*, is in the ruins of the 18th-century Santa Teresa Convent and also covers the archaeological site of Duna Grande on Itaipu beach. It is 20 km from the city.

Museu de Arte Contemporânea ⓘ *Mirante da Praia da Boa Viagem s/n, T26202400, www.macniteroi.com, Tue-Sun 1100-1900, US$1, Sat 1300-2100, free*, is an Oscar Niemeyer project and worth visiting for the building itself as much as for its exhibitions. It is best seen at night, especially when the pond beneath the spaceship design is full of water. The exhibition inside changes.

Beaches

The beaches closest to the city centre are unsuitable for bathing (Gragoatá, Vermelha, Boa Viagem, das Flechas). The next ones, also in the city and with polluted water, have more in the way of restaurants, bars and nightlife (**Icaraí**, the smartest district, with the best hotels has good nightlife; **São Francisco** – for example Rua das Pedras and Charitas – is even better). The road continues round the bay, past Preventório and Samanguaiá to **Jurujuba**, a fishing village at the end of the bus line (take bus No 33 from the boat dock; sit on the right-hand side, it's a beautiful ride). About 2 km from Jurujuba along a narrow road are the attractive twin beaches of **Adão** and **Eva** beneath the Fortaleza da Santa Cruz, with lovely views of Rio across the bay.

To get to the ocean beaches, take a 38 or 52 bus from Praça general Gomes Carneiro.

Piratininga, **Camboinhas**, **Itaipu** (note the archaeology museum, above) and **Itacoatiara**, four fabulous stretches of sand, are the best in the area, about 40 minutes' ride through picturesque countryside. Buses leave from the street directly ahead of the ferry entrance, at right angles to the coast street. The undertow at Itacoatiara is dangerous, but the waves are popular with surfers and the beach itself is safe. Itaipu is also used by surfers.

The Costa do Sol

To the east of Niterói lie a series of saltwater lagoons, the **Lagos Fluminenses.** Two small lakes lie behind the beaches of Piratininga, Itaipu and Itacoatiara, but they are polluted and ringed by mud. The next lakes, **Maricá** and **Saquarema**, are much larger. Although they are still muddy, the waters are relatively unpolluted and wildlife abounds in the scrub and bush around the lagoons. This is a prime example of the *restinga* environment. The RJ-106 road runs behind the lakes en route to Cabo Frio and Búzios, but an unmade road goes along the coast between Itacoatiara and Cabo Frio, giving access to the many long, open beaches of Brazil's Costa do Sol. The whole area is perfect for camping.

Maricá → *Phone code: 022. Population: 60,500.*

The 36-km Itaipu-Açu, with many wild, lonely stretches, leads to Maricá, a sleepy fishing village with sand streets on its own lagoon. There is good walking in the Serra do Silvado, 14 km away on the road to Itaboraí. Between Maricá and Saquarema are Ponta Negra and Jaconé, both surfing beaches. There's a **tourist office** ⓘ *Av Ver Francisco Sabino da Costa 477, www.marica.rj.gov.br.*

Saquarema → *Phone code: 022. Colour map 4, C3. Population: 44,000.*

Saquarema is a fishing and holiday village, known as the centre for surfing in Brazil. Its cold, open seas provide consistent, crashing waves of up to 3 m. Frequent national and international championships take place here. Beware of strong currents, though. The lovely white church of **Nossa Senhora de Nazaré** (1675) is on a green promontory jutting into the ocean. Local legend has it that on 8 September 1630, fishermen, saved from a terrible storm, found an image of the Virgem de Nazaré in the rocks. A chapel was founded on the spot and subsequent attempts to relocate the Virgin (as when the chapel was falling into disrepair) resulted in her miraculously returning to the original site. **Tourist information** ⓘ *www.saquarema.rj.gov.br*.

Araruama → *Phone code: 022. Colour map 4, C4. Population: 66,500.*

Araruama (220 sq km), is one of the largest lakes in Brazil and famous for its medicinal mud. The salinity is high, the waters calm and almost the entire lake is surrounded by sandy beaches, making it popular with families looking for unpolluted bathing. The constant breeze makes the lake perfect for windsurfing and sailing. The major industry of the area is salt, and all around are saltpans and wind pumps used to carry the water into the pans. The town itself is at the western end of the lake on the inland shore, 116 km from Rio.

At the eastern end of the lake, also inland, is **São Pedro de Aldeia**, which has a population of 55,500, and which, despite intensive development, still retains much of its colonial charm. There is a lovely Jesuit church built in 1723, and a **tourist information office** ⓘ *Ton Av São Pedro; www.araruama.rj.gov.br.*

Arraial do Cabo → *Phone code: 022. Population: 21,500.*

This rather ugly little salt-industry town near Cabo Frio is considerably less busy than the resort at Cabo Frio a little to the north, and provides access to equally good beaches and dunes. The lake and the ocean here are divided by the Restinga de Massambaba, a long spit of sand whose lengths are mostly deserted except for the beaches of **Massambaba** and **Seca** at the western end and **Grande** in the east at Arraial do Cabo town itself. Arraial has lots of other small beaches on the bays and islands which form the cape, round which the line of the coast turns north, including the long, busy stretch at **Anjos, Praia do Forno** and **Prainha.** Excursions can be made by boat around the islets and by jeep or buggy over the sand dunes.

Diving and adventure sports Though this is not a dive destination in its own right of international-quality diving, Arraial proclaims itself the scuba diving capital of Brazil. Diving here is worth exploring, with a number of sites of varying difficulty with caverns and swim-throughs. Cold and warm currents meet here just off the coast and the marine life is more abundant than almost anywhere else on mainland southern Brazil. Expect to see schools of tropical and subtropical reef fish like batfish and various tangs and butterfly fish, the occasional turtle and colonies of gorgonians and beautiful, though invasive soft corals probably brought here on oil tankers from the Indo-Pacific. Dolphins are frequent visitors. The best visibility is between November and May. Water temperature is always below 20°C. The little town is also establishing itself as an adventure sports destination with activities like dune boarding, parachuting, kite surfing and kayaking available. ⏩ *See Tour operators page 148.*

Praia do Farol, on Ilha do Cabo Frio, is considered one of Brazil's best beaches. It has dunes and crystal-clear water. **Zarany tours** at the Marina dos Pescadores, 2º Pier on Praia dos Anjos, T26225837, www.arraialdocabo-rj.com.br/zarony and **Barco Lindo Olhar,** T26474493, ask for Vadinho or Eraldo in the town's main Marina, offer trips here. **Tourist information** ⓘ *T26205039, www.arraialdocabo-rj.com.br*, is at Praça da Bandeira. See also Activities and tours, page 148.

Cabo Frio → *Phone code: 022. Colour map 4, C4. Population: 127,000.*

This busy tourist town, 168 km from Rio, is a popular middle-class Brazilian seaside resort, overflowing at the weekend with Cariocas and Mineiras from Juiz da Fora. Although the town itself is very touristy, there are some attractive white-sand beaches, some with dunes and good surf and windsurfing, with accommodation nearby, . Bring mosquito repellent.

Cabo Frio vies with Porto Seguro for the title of Brazil's first city. The navigator Americo Vespucci landed here in 1503 and returned to Portugal with a boatload of pau-brasil. Since the wood in these parts was of better quality than that further north, the area subsequently became the target for loggers from France, the Netherlands and England. The Portuguese failed to capitalize on their colony here and it was the French who established the first defended settlement. Eventually the Portuguese took it by force but it was not until the second decade of the 17th century that they planned their own fortification, the **Forte São Mateus** ⓘ *daily 0800-1800*, which was started in 1618 on the foundations of the French fort. It is now a ruin at the mouth of the Canal de Itajuru, with rusting cannons propped up against its whitewashed ramparts.

The canal, which connects the Lagoa Araruama and the ocean, has a small headland at its mouth, which protects the nearest beach to the busy town; the heavily developed **Praia do Forte** and Cabo Frio town, with Forte São Mateus watching over it on a rocky promontory. The town beach stretches south for about 7½ km to Arraial do Cabo, its name changing to **Praia das Dunas** (after the dunes) and **Praia do Foguete**. These waters are much more suited to surfing. North of the canal entrance and town is the small underdeveloped surf and naturist beach at **Praia Brava** (and the wine glass bay of **Praia das Conchas**, which has a few shack restaurants). Next is **Praia do Peró**, 7 km of surf and sand on the open sea with a small town behind it and cheap accommodation. The best **dunes** are at Peró, Dama Branca (on the road to Arraial) and the Pontal dunes at Praia do Forte. **Tourist information** ⓘ *Av Contorno 200, Praia do Forte, T26471689, www.cabofrio.tur.br*, a large orange building.

Búzios → *Phone code: 022. Colour map 4, C4. Population: 18,000.*

Some 25 km up the coast from Cabo Frio is the sophisticated yet informal Búzios. This charming seaside town (full name Armação de Búzios) is spread out with low-rise, attractive development. It is situated on a peninsula with more than enough beaches to choose from and is the perfect choice for those who want to enjoy the sun and the sea by day and, after dark, its internationally famous nightlife and gastronomy.

Búzios, 192 km from Rio and 37 km from Arraial do Cabo, is the principal resort of choice for Carioca and Mineira upper-middle classes searching for their idea of St Tropez sophistication. When it was discovered by Brigitte Bardot in 1964 it was little more than a collection of colonial fishermen's huts and a series of pristine beaches hidden beneath steep hills covered in maquis-like vegetation. Now there are strings of hotels behind all of those beaches and the huts have been lost within a designated tourist village of bars, bikini boutiques and restaurants; most of which are strung along the pretty little main street – **Rua das Pedras**. Bardot sits here too – cheesily immortalized in brass and subsequently in tens of thousands of pictures taken by the troops of cruise-line passengers who fill Búzios's streets in high season. St Tropez this is not, but it can be fun for twenty-somethings who are single and looking not to stay that way.

For most of the hotels and services on the peninsula check www.Búziosonline.com.br.

The golden lion tamarin

The tamarin, or *mico-leão* in Portuguese, is a small primate, about the size of a squirrel, which lives off fruit, flowers, tender vegetation and insects. In Brazil there are three species of tamarin, all under threat of extinction: the golden lion tamarin; the black lion tamarin; and the golden-headed lion tamarin. The main problem for the tamarins is that their habitat, the mata atlântica of São Paulo, Rio de Janeiro, Espírito Santo and Bahia, has all but been destroyed and there has been further threat from predation by man.

These engaging creatures are quite beautiful, so much so that they were popular pets with European royalty in the 17th and 18th centuries. The golden lion tamarin, with its face surrounded by a bright, silky mane, was considered the most beautiful. It has been described as having a coat that "shines like gold dust in the light." And thereby hangs another of the animal's problems; its attractiveness made it a prize pet for non-royal collectors and demand in the trade soon contributed to the golden lion tamarin's dwindling numbers. By the 1970s it seemed a foregone conclusion that the golden lion tamarin and its Brazilian relatives were doomed to extinction.

Fortunately, the Golden Lion Tamarin Conservation Project, set up in 1983 at the Poço das Antas Biological Reserve (which was created in 1974), has been successful in breeding tamarins in captivity and returning them to the wild. Around the world, zoos have been helping with the breeding programme. In 1997, a WWF estimate for the number of golden lion tamarins living in the wild in Poço das Antas was put at 800, but other figures suggest 550 (some even as low as 150). Whatever the number, the severest test for the survival of the species is the creation of more forest in which the tamarins can live. Corridors of suitable vegetation have to be set up so that the tamarins can move about safely and breed freely in their natural surroundings. This goal was undermined during the drought of 1997 which led to an increase in forest fires in Brazil (the majority started by man), posing a renewed threat to the tamarin's habitat. So the *mico-leão-dourado*'s future is by no means secured; despite this, the animal has become a symbol of hope for forest conservation throughout Brazil. Many Brazilian and international agencies and specialist centres have contributed to its survival, but as with all such projects, the work never stops.

Besides the *mico-leão-dourado* population at Poço das Antas, there is a conservation project for the mico-leão-da cara-dourada at Una in Bahia, and the *mico-leão-preto* can be seen near Praia do Forte, north of Salvador.

Sources WWF Update (World Wide Fund for Nature), Summer 1997, website www.wwf-uk.org; in the UK T01483-426444, F01483-426409, or contact your local office. Marya Rowan, 'Breeds Apart', South American Explorer (25 May 1990), pages 32-3. Wildlife Fact File, International Masters Publishers Ltd (London), No120.

During the daytime, the best option is to head for the beaches, of which there are 25. The most visited are **Geribá** (many bars and restaurants; popular with surfers), **Ferradura** (deep blue sea and calm waters), **Ossos** (the most famous and close to the centre), **Tartaruga** and **João Fernandes**. The better surf beaches like **Praia de**

Manguinhos and **Praia de Tucuns** are further from the town centre. To help you decide which beach suits you best, you can join one of the local two- or three-hour schooner trips which pass many of the beaches, or else hire a beach buggy. These trips cost around US$10-15 and can be arranged through **Escuna Queen Lory** (T26231179).

Traffic back to Rio can be appalling on Sunday nights and during the peak holiday season.

There are two **tourist offices**: the main office at **Manguinhos** ⓘ *T0800 249999, 24-hour*, on the western edge of the peninsula, which has lots of information and helpful staff, some of whom speak English, and **Praça Santos Dumont** ⓘ *T26232099*, in the centre of town is more limited.

Macaé → *Phone code: 022. Colour map 4, C4. Population: 120,500.*

Further north, is Barra de São João, **Rio das Ostras** and Macaé. These beaches, at the northern end of the Costa do Sol, all have sheltered coves with good swimming and OK scuba diving.

Macaé is the supply centre for the offshore oil industry but is attempting to develop tourism as well; not very successfully it seems as most of the oil people seem to take breaks in Búzios. Cavaleiros beach has some surf and many bars and restaurants. **Tourist information** ⓘ *www.macaetur.com*.

North to Espírito Santo

From Rio and Niterói, the BR-101 runs northeast past Campos and the border with Espírito Santo. There are many *fazenda* hotels around **Rio Bonito**, 64 km from Niterói.

At Km 222 is the **Biological Reserve of Poço das Antas** ⓘ *Ibama, Av Pres Antônio Carlos 607-12°, CEP 20000, Rio de Janeiro*, is the only natural habitat of the *mico- leão*, golden lion tamarin; it is a two-hour drive from Rio and not open to the general public.

Campos dos Goytacases → *Phone code: 022. Colour map 4, C4. Population: 390,500.*

Campos (dos Goytacases – after the Indian tribe which used to inhabit the area) is a busy industrial city, 276 km from Rio de Janeiro and 70 km from Macaé which few choose to visit but which can be used as a stopping-off point on the journey to or from Rio. There are OK beaches to the south at **Farol de São Tomé**, **Barra do Furrado** and **Quissamã**. And north of the Rio Paraíba there are several beaches in the vicinity of **São Francisco** and **Itabapoana**.

Santo Antônio de Pádua → *Phone code: 024. Population: 36,000.*

As an alternative to taking the BR-101 to Vitória, you can take a detour inland, going through São Fidélis, Cambiasca, Itoacara and on to Santo Antônio de Pádua, 106 km from Campos, a pleasant town on the Rio Pomba. The large number of rapids in this area means canoeing is popular. The **hydromineral spring** ⓘ *Av Dr Themístocles de Almeida, Mon-Fri 0700-1100, 1300-1600, Sat 0700-1100*, is unique for the chemical composition of its waters. The **bus station** ⓘ *T38510823*, is at Rua José de Alencar Leite.

Sleeping

Niterói *p136, phone code 021*

AL-A Tower Hotel, Av Almirante Ari Parreiras 12, Icaraí, T26122121, www.towerhotel.com.br. Niterói's smartest hotel with ordinary 3-star hotel rooms, an indoor pool and reasonable business facilities.

A Icaraí Praia, R Belisário Augusto 21, T27102323, www.icaraipraiahotel.com.br. Plain rooms in a 1980s beachfront tower. A little faded.

B Pousada Suba and Veja, R Mal Raul Albuquerque (Mirante de Piratininga), Km 18, T26190823. Wonderful views out over one of the most beautiful beaches on the Costa do Sol. Facilities include bar, restaurant, pool and sauna.

Camping

Piratininga, Estr Frei Orlando Km 2, T26094581.

Saquarema *p138, phone code 022*

B **Pousada Pedra d'Água Maasai**, Trav de Itaúna 17, T/F26511092, www.maasai.com.br. Good little beachfront hotel with 18 apts, pool, sauna and a reasonable seafood restaurant.

C **Pousada do Holandês**, Av Vilamar 377, Itaúna beach. Recommended, many languages spoken by Dutch owner and his Brazilian wife. Good meals – follow the signs, or take a taxi, from Saquarema.

C-D **Pousada Canto da Vila**, Av Min Salgado 52, T26511563, www.pousadacantodavila.com.br. 14 little rooms and 2 larger ones. Overlooking the beach. Poky but well maintained.

D-E **Garota de Itaúna**, Av Oceânica 165, Itaúna, T26512321. Very simple rooms next to the beach and a good seafood restaurant.

D-E **Ilhas Gregas**, R do Prado 671, Itaúna, T26511008. Youth hostel with a pool, sauna, bar and restaurant.

Camping

Itaúna's, R dos Tatuís 999, access from Av Oceânica, T26511711.

Araruama *p139, phone code 022*

A **Enseada das Garças**, R José Costa 1088, Ponta da Areia, about 5 km from São Pedro de Aldeia, T26211924, www.roteirosdecharme.com.br. Beautiful little hotel overlooking the sea with access to good walking trails.

A **Ver a Vista**, R São Sebastião 400, São Pedro de Aldeia, T26654721, www.veravistahotel.com.br. Small apartment hotel with a sauna, bar and swimming pool.

C **Pousada do Peu**, RJ-132, Km 12, T26653614. Basic *pousada* popular with families.

E **Praia do Sudoeste**, R Pedro Américo, Lt 27, T26212763. Youth hostel with simple rooms available in high season only.

Camping

Camping Clube do Brasil, R RJ106, Marica Km 81.5, Ponte dos Leites beach.

Camping da Colina, RJ-106, Km 108, Praia da Teresa, São Pedro de Aldeia, T26211919. Not much shade.

Arraial do Cabo *p139, phone code 022*

A **Pousada Nautillu's**, R Marcílio Dias 100, T26221611, www.pousadanautillus.com. Medium-sized *pousada* with a pool, sauna, bar and restaurant. Recommended.

B **Pousada dos Atobás**, R José Pinto Macedo 270, T26222461, www.pousadadosatobas.com.br. Small newly built hostel with a pool, sauna and bar.

C **Orlamar**, Av Beiramar 111, Recanto da Prainha, T/F6222410, www.pousadaorlamar.hpg.com.br. Literally on the beach – with car access only at low tide. Reasonable restaurant and bar.

Camping

Camping Clube do Brasil, Praia dos Anjos, T26221023. Crowded beach. Plenty of places to eat along the beach.

Maricá *p142, phone code 022*

B **Pousada Colonial**, Ponta Negra, T/F7481707. Simple suites and bungalows with breakfast.

B **Solar Tabaúna**, Ponta Negra, T26481626. Similar to the **Colonial** but with a pool.

Cabo Frio *p140, phone code 022*

AL-B **La Plage**, R das Badejos 40, Peró, T26471746, www.redebela.com.br. Price falls in low season. Newly refurbished with fully equipped suites; those upstairs have sea view, excellent for families. Right on the beach, services include pool and bar, à la carte restaurant, hydromassage, sauna, 24-hr cyber café, garage.

B **Othon Sítio do Portinho**, R Cnel Ferreira 281, T26449264, www.pousadasitiodoportinho.hpg.com.br. Cheaper in low season. A good *pousada* with very nice rooms set in gardens in this residential suburb, a/c and all usual facilities, pool and bar. You can get to Portinho district from Av Excelsior or along the canal (go underneath the bridge). (See www.hoteis-othon.com.br for all Othon hotels, including Othon Travel hotels.)

B-C **Pousada Água Marinha**, R Rui Barbosa 996b, Centre, T26438447, p.aguamarinha@uol.com.br. Cheaper in low season. Plain white rooms with comfortable beds, a/c, fan, TV, frigobar, breakfast, pool and parking. Good choice in the centre, about 4 blocks from Praia do Forte.

B-C **Pousada Espírito do Mar**, R Anequim s/n, Peró, T26443077, www.espiritodomar.com.br. Cheaper in low season. Bright orange building with central swimming pool around which the rooms are built. Good, spacious but simple rooms, with extra bed available. Breakfast included, a/c, frigobar, TV and fan. A friendly place. The bus to Cabo Frio passes outside.

B-C **Pousada La Bela**, R Prof Miguel Couto 192, Centre, T26431970, pousadalabela@ig.com.br. Cheaper in low season, a/c, TV, frigobar. In the centre, close to the canal, but not so convenient for the rodoviária.

B-D **Pousada Suzy**, Av Júlia Kubitschek 48, T26431742. 100 m from the rodoviária. Cheaper in low season and with fan. Also has shared rooms for 8. Price includes breakfast, frigobar, plain rooms but not spartan, pool, sauna, covered garage.

C **Pousada Restaurant Mar e Luz**, R Jorge Lóssio 1435, Centre, T26454025. Simple, with fan, frigobar, TV, hot shower, also has a/c rooms, breakfast included, with lunch and dinner available at extra cost, 3 blocks from Praia do Forte.

C **Pousada Velas ao Vento**, Av Júlia Kubitschek 5, T26441235. Between rodoviária and centre. Cheaper in low season, clean, comfortable and convenient, set back from the main road but still a bit of traffic noise. Hot water, a/c, breakfast included. Helpful and friendly owner and staff.

C-E **Pousada São Lucas**, R Goiás 266, Jardim Excelsior, T26453037 (formerly youth hostel). 3 mins from rodoviária. Price is for double room with TV. Also has dormitories, with hot shower, breakfast and fan (a little cheaper in low season).

E **Albergue da Juventude São Lucas**, R Goiás 266, Jardim Excelsior, 3 mins from the rodoviária, T26453037. IYHA youth hostel. Price per person.

E **Albergue Internacional da Juventude de Muxarabi**, R Leonor Santa Rosa, 13 – Jardim Flamboyant, T26430369. Youth hostel. Price per person.

E **Albergue Peró**, R Coutrim 13, Peró, T26477605, www.perohostel.com.br. IYHA youth hostel a stroll from the Peró beach with bike rental a restaurant, dorms and doubles.

E **Albergue Praia das Palmeiras**, Praia das Palmeiras 1, T26432866. Youth hostel. Price per person.

Camping

Camping Clube do Brasil, Estr dos Passageiros 700, 2 km from town, T26433124.

Camping da Estação, Estr dos Passageiros 370, T26431786.

Dunas do Peró, Estr do Gurirl 1001, T26292323. Small *pousada* with a campsite on Praia do Peró.

Búzios *p140, phone code 022*

The best rooms on the peninsula are not on the beaches but are those with a superb view, on the **Morro do Humaita** hill, 10 mins walk from the town centre. Hire a beach buggy. Prior reservations are needed in summer, during holidays such as Carnival and New Year's Eve, and at weekends. For cheaper options and better availability, try Cabo Frio.

Several private houses rent rooms, especially in summer and holidays. Look for the signs: 'Alugo Quartos'.

LL **Boca do Ceu**, Mirante de Joao Fernandes, Rua Hum s/n, T26234713, www.bocadoceu.com. Super luxurious private home/mini *pousada* (owned by a famous Uruguayan interior designer) with the best views on the peninsula out across a carefully designed swimming pool and garden. All the fittings are by famous names – sofas by Roger Dubois, etc. Nonetheless somewhat overpriced.

LL-L **Casas Brancas**, Alto do Humaita 8, T26231458, www.casasbrancas.com.br. Far and away the best hotel in Búzios; a series of rooms perched on the hill in mock-Mykonos buildings with separate terraces for the pool and spa areas. Sweeping views over the bay. Wonderfully romantic at night when all is lit by candlelight. If you can't afford to stay come for dinner.

LL-L **El Cazar**, Alto do Humaitá 6, T26231620. Next door to **Casas Brancas** and almost as luxurious; though a little darker inside. Beautiful artwork on the walls and Central Asian kelims on the ipe wood floors. Tasteful and relaxing.

L-AL **Pousada Byblos**, Alto do Humaitá 14, T26231162, www.byblos.com.br. Wonderful views out over the bay and bright, light rooms with tiled floors and balconies.

AL **Pousada Pedra da Laguna**, R 6, lote 6, praia da ferradura, T/F26231965, www.pedra

dalaguna.com.br. Spacious rooms, the best with a view 150 m from the beach. Part of the **Roteiros do Charme** (see p47).

A Pousada Hibiscus Beach, R 1 No 22, Quadra C, Praia de João Fernandes, T26236221, www.hibiscusbeach.com.br. A peaceful spot, run by its British owners, overlooking Praia de João Fernandes, 15 pleasant bungalows, a/c, satellite TV, garden, pool, light meals available, help with car/buggy rentals and local excursions. One of the best beach hotels.

A-B Brigitta's Guest House, R das Pedras 131, T/F26236157, www.Búziosonline.com.br/brigitta. Beautifully decorated little *pousada* where Bardot once stayed with just 4 rooms on the main street. Its delightful restaurant, bar and tea house overlooking the water are worth a visit.

A-B Casa da Ruth, R dos Gravatás, Geribá, T26232242, www.Búziosturismo.com/casadaruth. Simple mock-Greek rooms in lilac overlooking the beach and pool.

C-E Praia dos Amores, Av José Bento Ribeiro Dantas 92, T26232422, www.Búziosturismo.com/auberge. IYHA, not far from the bus station, next to Praia da Tartaruga and just under 1 km from the centre. The best value in Búzios. Recommended.

Camping and Chalets

E Country Camping Park, R Maria Joaquina Justiniano 895, (off Praca da Rasa), Praia Rasa, km12, T26291155, www.Búzioscamping.com.br. Chalets and a well-run shady campsite 1km from the beach. Arrival directions on website.

Macaé *p142, phone code 022*

A Colonial, Av Elias Agostinho 140, Praia de Imbetiba, T/F27225155. Helpful, comfortable.

B Hotel Mirante do Poeta, T2641910. Standard mid-range hotel with pleasant views and decent service.

Camping

Costazul, Av Heleno Nunes, Costa Azul, T27641389.

Campos dos Goytacases *p142, phone code 022*

A Antares, R Vig João Carlos 19, T27334055, www.hotelantares.com.br. Anonymous 1980s tower with standard B-grade business hotel rooms a sauna and restaurant.

C Planície, R 13 de Maio 56, T27234455. Simple business-orientated hotel, friendly staff.

Santo Antônio de Pádua *p142, phone code 024*

C Hotel das Águas, R Luís da Silva Magacho 170, T38510805. A short walk from the centre of town, it is set in a park and associated with the health centre and bottling plant for the local mineral water.

Eating

Niterói *p136, phone code 021*

Bicho Papão, Jurujuba, good seafood.

Caranguejo e Cia, Estr do Boqueirão (road to beach, car needed). Seafood served overlooking the lake. Warm service. Recommended.

La Sagrada Familia, R Domingues de Sá, Jd Icaraí, T26101683. The best restaurant in Niterói, varied menu and reasonable wine list.

T Tio Cotó, **Vila Real** and **Zia Amélia**. 3 good-value restaurants opposite the Ruínas de Estação da Cantareira (which has occasional shows and handicraft market).

Saquarema *p138, phone code 022*

TTT Le Bistrô, Av São Rafael 1134, Itaúna. The best restaurant in the area with good seafood.

TT Tem Uma Né Chama Teré, on the main square, decent Brazilian standards and fish.

Araruama *p139, phone code 022*

TT-T O Pirata, RJ-106 Amaral Peixoto) 16, São Pedro de Aldeia. A varied menu including reasonable seafood.

TT Don Roberto, Av Getúlio Vargas 272, São Pedro de Aldeia, T26213913. Wood-fired pizzas.

Arraial do Cabo *p139, phone code 022*

T Todos os Prazeres, R José Pinto Macedo, T26222365. A decent varied menu of Franco-Brazilian fusion; closed on Mon and Wed off season.

Cabo Frio *p140, phone code 022*

The neat row of restaurants on Av dos Pescadores are worth a browse for good-value seafood and pasta. They have French-style seating on the pavement under awnings.

TTT-TT Picolino, R Mcal F Peixoto 319, T26432436. In a nice old building, very smart, mixed menu of seafood and a few international dishes.

TT Do Zé, Av dos Pescadores, T26434277. Brazilian specialities.

TT Hippocampo, R Mcal F Peixoto 283, next door but one, T26455757. One of the better seafood restaurants with good *robalo* and *badejo*.

TT Gaijin, R José Bonifácio 28, T26434922. Reasonable Japanese food in generous portions.

TT-T Chico's, Av Teixeira e Souza 30, upstairs in Centro Comercial Víctor Nunes da Rocha, town centre, T26457454. Clean, smart, does breakfast, self-service, some more expensive dishes. On the ground floor is the **Coffee Shop.** More a stand than a shop, cheap; but better coffee in **Branca**.

TT-T "In" Sônia, Av dos Pescadores 140 loja 04. Good service and tasty fish, many dishes offered for 2 people.

TT-T Tonto, Av dos Pescadores, next door to "In" Sônia, T26451886 for delivery. Also serves pizza and has a bar, too.

T Bacalhauzinho, Praça Porto Rocha, in the town centre. Portuguese food.

T Branca, Praça Porto Rocha, in the centre of town. Lunches à kilo 1100-1700, also fast food, pizza after 1800, coffee, pastries and cakes, good, a big, popular place.

T Chez Michou, Av dos Pescadores. For crêpes (as in Rio Sul shopping centre in Rio de Janeiro – closed Mon). Upstairs are a number of bars and nightclubs, eg **Eleven**, above San Francisco restaurant, and others.

T Galeto do Zé, Av Maçonica 100, T26441269 (on the canal quayside). Cheap Brazilian standards – chicken, rice, beans and chips; steak, rice, beans and chips etc…

T Kilo-Kura, Av Teixeira e Souza 121-A, town centre. Good self-service lunches, very popular.

T Tia Maluca, Av dos Pescadores 102, T26433286. Also serving Brazilian food.

Búzios *p140, phone code 022*

See also **Casas Brancas** p144 (fine views and romantic dining) and **Brigitta's** p145 (funky seafood bistro). There are many restaurants on and around R das Pedras and one of the charms of Búzios is browsing here. The cheaper options tend to be off the main drag. There are plenty of beachside barracas all over the peninsula serving the usual x and beans, rice and chips combinations outside of the low season.

TTT Acquerello, R das Pedras 130, T26236576. Smart a/c seafood and Italian restaurant with a reasonable wine list. The best on the street.

TTT Satyricon, Av José Bento Ribeiro Dantas 500, Praia da Armação (in front of Morro da Humaitá), T26231595. Búzios's most illustrious restaurant specializing in Italian seafood. Decent wine list.

TT Moqueca Capixaba, R Manoel de Carvalho 116, Centro, T26231155. Bahian seafood, with dishes cooked in coconut or dende oil.

For an explanation of the sleeping and eating price codes used in this guide, see the inside front cover. Other relevant information is provided in the Essentials chapter, pages 47 and 57.

🍴 **Banana Land**, R Manoel Turíbio de Farias 50, T26230855. Cheap and cheerful per kilo buffet.
🍴 **Chez Michou**, R das Pedras, 90, Centro, T26232169. An open-air bar with videos, music and dozens of choices of pancakes accompanied by ice-cold beer. Always crowded.
🍴 **Fashion Café**, R das Pedras 151, T26232697. Fast food and pizzas with a young crowd and a live band.
🍴 **La Prima**, Av Manuel Turibo de Farias, homely, serving sandwiches and self-service food; doubles as a bakery.

There are a few other very cheap places on Praça Santos Dumont, off R das Pedras and a small supermarket a couple of doors away from La Prima.

Campos dos Goytacases *p142, phone code 022*
🍴 **Kantão do Líbano**, Av Pelinca 101. Arabic.

Bars and clubs

Búzios *p140, phone code 022*
In season Búzios nightlife is young, beautiful and buzzing. Out of season it is non-existent. The bulk of the bars and the handful of clubs are on R das Pedras. These include **Guapo Loco**, a bizarrely shaped Mexican theme-bar and restaurant with dancing. **Privelege**, Av José Bento Ribeiro Dantas 550, R Orla Bardot, Búzios's main club and one of Brazil's best European-style dance clubs with pumping techno, house and hip-hop and 5 rooms, including a cavernous dance floor, sushi bar and lounge. **Ta-ka-ta ka-ta**, R das Pedras 256, is strewn with motorbike parts and has its walls covered completely with graffiti. The Dutch owner obstinately refuses to say where he comes from. There are plenty of others including more upscale wine bar-style options like **Café Concerto**.

Shopping

Búzios *p140, phone code 022*
Many of Brazil's fashionable and beautiful come here for their holidays and Búzios is therefore a good place to pick up the kind of beach clothes and tropical cuts which they would wear. Although seemingly expensive these clothes are a fraction of what you would pay for labels of this quality in Europe, the US or Australia. Shopping is best on R das Pedras. Aside from the boutiques, there is little else of interest beyond the expected gamut of tourist tack shops. Of the boutiques the best are as follows:
Alice Capella, R das Pedras. Very sexy sophisticated dresses, skirts and tops. This is their only shop in Brazil.
Tenda, R das Pedras. A little boutique with the pick of Brazilian designers including the supermodels' bikini choice – Rosa Chá.
Lenny, R das Pedras. For Brazil's most à la mode bikinis – from the point of view of Brazilians.
Bum Bum Ipanema, R das Pedras. Bright young bikinis in gorgeous cuts.
Salinas, R das Pedras. Beautifully crafted bikinis and beachwear. Together with Rosa Cha, Brazil's most à la mode bikinis – from the point of view of foreigners.
Farm, R das Pedras. Elegant and cool beachwear and light clothes for women.

Festivals and events

Niterói *p136, phone code 021*
Mar, Apr and May Festa do Divino, a festival which traditionally begins on Easter Sun and continues for the next 40 days, in which the *Bandeira* (banner) *do Divino* is taken around the local municipalities. The festival ends at Pentecost with sacred and secular celebrations.
24 Jun São João, lots of parades forro dancing and barn dance costumes.
22 Nov Founding of the town. Parades, concerts and dancing.

Saquarema *p138, phone code 022*
Mar, Apr and May Festa do Divino, as above under Niterói.
8 May Founding of the town. Dancing, concerts and plenty of drinking.
29 Jun Festival of São Pedro, at the end of the Festas Juninas.
7 Sep Nossa Senhora de Nazaré, the town's patron saint's day.

Araruama *p139, phone code 022*
16 May Founding of the town.
29 Jun São Pedro São Pedro de Aldeia celebrates the feast of its patron saint.

Arraial do Cabo *p139, phone code 022*
13 May Founding of the town.
May/Jun Corpus Christi.

Activities and tours

Niterói *p136, phone code 021*
Rio Cricket Associação Atlética (RCA), R Fagundes Varela 637, T27175333. Bus 57 from ferry.
Rio Sailing Club (late Clube de Niterói), Estr Leopoldo Fróes 418, lote 338, T26105810. Bus 33 marked 'via Fróes'.

Arraial do Cabo *p139, phone code 022*
K-Kite School, R da Alegria 15, T26629465, www.kkite.hpg.ig.com.br. Wind and kite surfing and classes.
Deep Trip, Av Getulio Vargas 93, Praia Grande, Arraial do Cabo, T26221800, www.deeptrip.com.br. The only PADI-affiliated dive operator in Arraial, with a range of courses and dive trips.
Gas, Av Litoranea 80, Praia Grande, T99561222, www.arraialdocabo-rj.com.br/gas. Various adventure sports including parachuting, dune boarding and kayak surfing. Has dive trips but is not PADI accredited.

Cabo Frio *p140, phone code 022*
Tour operators
Planeta Costa Azul, Square Shopping loja 21, T26452023, www.planetacostadosol.com.br. For flights and local packages.

Búzios *p140, phone code 022*
Tour operators
Malizia, R das Pedras, T26232022. Money exchange, car hire and other tourist services.
Mister Tours, R Germiniano J Luis 3, Centro, T26232100.

Transport

Niterói *p136, phone code 021*
Boat Niterói, across Guanabara Bay, is reached by ferry boats and launches crossing every 10 mins (15-20 mins, US$0.50) from the 'Barcas' at Praça 15 de Novembro (ferry museum at the terminal). There are also catamarans (*aerobarcas*) every 10 mins (about 3 mins, US$2.45; the fare is US$1.25 between 0700 and 1000 Rio-Niterói and after 1700 Niterói-Rio). The slow, cheaper ferry gives the best views. Ferries and catamarans to Rio de Janeiro leave from the terminal at Praça Araribóia.

Bus No 996 Gávea-**Jurujuba**, 998 Antônio Carlos Jobim International Airport-**Charitas**, 740-D and 741 Copacabana-**Charitas**, 730-D Castelo-**Jurujuba**, US$0.60-0.75.

Saquarema *p138, phone code 022*
Bus To **Rio de Janeiro** (Mil e Um, 1001), every 2 hrs 0730-1800, 2 hrs, US$3.40.

Arraial do Cabo *p139, phone code 022*
A very steep road connects the beaches of Itaipu and Itacoatiara with RJ-106 (and on to Bacaxá and Araruama) via the village of Itaipu-Açu. Most maps do not show a road beyond Itaipu-Açu; it is certainly too steep for buses. An alternative to the route from Niterói to Araruama through the lagoons is further inland than the RJ-106, via Manilha, Itaboraí and Rio Bonito on the BR-101 and RJ-124; this is a fruit-growing region.

Bus Rio de Janeiro to **Arraial do Cabo** US$6.

Cabo Frio *p140, phone code 022*
Air A new airport has opened linking the area with **Belo Horizonte**, **Brasília**, **Rio de Janeiro** and **São Paulo**.

Bus
Local Salineira and Montes Brancos lines run the local services. US$0.75 to places like **Búzios**, **São Pedro da Aldeia**, **Saquarema**, **Araruama**, **Arraial do Cabo**. US$0.50 for closer destinations. The urban bus terminal is near Largo de Santo Antônio, opposite the BR petrol station.
Long distance The rodoviária is 2 km from the centre. Bus from **Rio** every 30 mins, 2½ hrs, US$8.To **Búzios**, from the local bus terminus in the town centre, every hr, US$1. Útil to **Belo Horizonte** US$20. **Unifac** to **Belo Horizonte**, **Juiz da Fora**, **Petrópolis**. Macaense runs to **Macaé** all the time. To **São Paulo** US$22.60 at 2100.

The route from Cabo Frio to **Vitória**: either take Macaense bus to **Macaé** and take 1900 bus (about 5¼ hrs), or take 1001 to **Campos**, 3½ hrs, US$5.60 (R$14), and change. 1001 stops in Campos first at the Shopping Estrada rodoviária, which is the one where the bus connection is made, but it's outside town (US$3 taxi to the centre, or local bus US$0.35). The **1001** then goes on to local rodoviária, closer to the centre, but there are no long-distance services from that terminal. Shopping Estrada rodoviária has a tourist office, but no cheap hotels nearby. Aguia Branca buses to **Vitória** at 0900 and 1900, US$8.10, 3 hrs 40 mins.

Búzios *p140, phone code 022*
Beach buggies A popular way to get around the cobbled streets of Búzios. Buggy rental available at Malízia, T26232022 or Rent Buggy, T26236421.

Bus from Rio's rodoviária Novo Rio, go to the **1001** counter, T25161001. **Rio**-Búzios US$8, 2½ hrs (be at the bus terminal 20 mins before departure). 4 departures daily 0815 from Rio a/c, 1300 from Búzios a/c. You can also take any bus to **Cabo Frio** (many more during the day), from where it's 30 mins to Búzios and vice versa. Buying the ticket in advance is only recommended on major holidays. The Búzios rodoviária is a few blocks' walk from the centre. Some *pousadas* are within 10 mins on foot, eg La Coloniale and Brigitta's, while others need a local bus (US$0.50) or taxi. The buses from Cabo Frio run the length of the peninsula and pass several *pousadas*.

Car By car via BR-106 takes about 2½ hrs from Rio and far more on Brazilian public holidays.

Macaé *p142, phone code 022*
Air Air taxis with Líder, T27723202, and Aeróleo, T27725995.

Bus Bus station, Av Ver Abreu Lima, T27724500. To **Rio de Janeiro** 2½-3 hrs, every 30 mins, Mil e Um or Rápido Macaense. To **Campos**, 1¾ hrs, US$4.

Campos dos Goytacases *p142, phone code 022*
Air Airport, BR-101, Km 5, T27330144. Flights to **Rio de Janeiro**.

Bus Bus station, BR 101, T27331001. To **Rio de Janeiro** (Mil e Um), hourly, 4 hrs, US$10.

Directory

Niterói *p136, phone code 021*
Banks Banco 24 Horas, Niterói Shopping, R da Conceição 188; Bradesco, R Gavião Peixoto 108. **Internet** O Lido Cyber C@fé, Av Rui Barbosa 29, lj 124, São Francisco. **Laundry** Lavlev, R Pres Backer 138. **Medical services** Universitário Antônio Pedro, Av Marques do Paraná, T26202828.

Saquarema *p138, phone code 022*
Banks Bradesco, Rod Amaral Peixoto 83.

Araruama *p139, phone code 022*
Banks Bradesco, Av São Pedro 120, São Pedro de Aldeia.

Arraial do Cabo *p139, phone code 022*
Banks Unibanco, R Dom Pedro. Will not change cheques and has no ATM.

Maricá *p142, phone code 022*
Banks Bradesco, R Sen Macedo Soares 44, Ponta Negra.

Cabo Frio *p140, phone code 022*
Banks Banco do Brasil, Praça Porto Rocha 44, The only bank with exchange. *Câmbio* 1100-1430; Bradesco, Av Assunção 904, has Visa ATM; HSBC, Av Assunção 793, has ATM for AmEx, Visa/Plus, MasterCard/Cirrus. **Internet** Aç@i, Av João Pessoa, near R Casemiro de Abreu, US$0.75 per 30 mins, older machines. Not always open; Cyber Mar, CC V Nunes da Rocha, Av Teixeira e Souza 30. New, a/c, minimum US$1.50 for 30 mins, US$2.20 per hr, daily 0800-2000; Cyber Tel, Praça Porta Rocha 56, T26497575, in gallery next to Banco do Brasil. Only 3 machines, but good and fast, US$2 per hr.

Búzios *p140, phone code 022*
Banks Banco do Brasil, R Manuel de Carvalho 70, Centro, T25232302. **Internet** Búzios@internet, Av J B Ribeiro Dantas 97, close to Shopping One, US$1.20 per ½ hr.

Inland resorts and coffee towns

The three mountain resorts of Petrópolis, Teresópolis and Nova Friburgo are set high in the scenic Serra do Mar behind Rio. The Imperial city of Petrópolis boasts perhaps Brazil's finest museum, and all three are lovely mountain retreats with accommodation in charming fazendas. *This is a beautiful area that is becoming increasingly popular for walking, as well as horse riding and other activities.*

These resorts became established originally because the cool mountain air offered an escape from the heat of Rio and meant an escape from yellow fever and other diseases which festered in the unhealthy port on the bay in the 19th century. Also, they provided the routes which brought first gold, then coffee from the interior to the coast. » *For Sleeping, Eating and other listings, see pages 157-160.*

Petrópolis → *Phone code: 024. Colour map 4, C3. Population: 290,000.*

Standing at 809 m in the Serra da Estrela range of mountains in the Serra do Mar, Petrópolis is reached by bus along a steep, scenic mountain road 68 km north of Rio. For about 80 years this Imperial city was the 'summer capital' of Brazil. Now it combines manufacturing industry (particularly textiles) and tourism with floral beauty and hill scenery. The town, with its distinctly European feel, is considered to be one of the gastronomic centres of Brazil.

The pleasant **climate** which attracted the Imperial family has an average high temperature of 23°C and a low of 14°C. The warmest months are September to December. The wettest months are January-March, although it can start getting wet in November and rain can be expected at any time. It can get chilly at night all year round, but especially in winter. The area is prone to dense fog, called *o ruço*, which usually forms in the late afternoon. While this can be atmospheric, it can also be dangerous for drivers as the fog can descend very quickly.

Tourist information Petrotur ⓘ *Praça da Confluência 03, T22433561, F2420639, Mon-Fri 0900-1830*, is in the Prefeitura de Petrópolis, at the rear of the Casa do Barão de Mauá. It has a list of tourist sites and of hotels and a good, free coloured map of the city. There's also a **tourist kiosk** ⓘ *Praça Dom Pedro II, Mon-Sat 0900-1800, Sun and holidays 0900-1700.*

History

Because the Emperor Pedro I abdicated in 1831, he never realized his dream of building a summer palace in the Serra. But after his abdication, Júlio Frederico Koeler, a German engineer who worked on the construction of a road to Minas Gerais, proposed building a German colony in the hills above Rio. When the new emperor, Dom Pedro II, approved this plan in 1843, he stipulated that a summer palace should be built in addition to a town and the settlement scheme. Petrópolis dates its founding from 1843 and in little over a decade had become an important place. Once the Imperial palace was built, the emperor and his family began to spend six months of each year there (November-April). His court had to accompany him, so other fine residences sprang up in the city that Koeler had designed.

In April 1854, Brazil's first railway line was opened, from Porto Mauá on Guanabara Bay to Raiz da Serra, which greatly shortened the journey time between Rio and Petrópolis. By the 1880s the railway had crossed the mountains to Petrópolis itself. So by the time the Republic was proclaimed in 1889, Petrópolis was administrative capital of the country for half the year, an intellectual centre for the same months, had its own commercial importance and was connected to Brazil's rapidly growing transport links.

In the early 20th century it became the official summer seat of the president of the republic (the residence being the Palácio Rio Negro). In the 1940s it had a brief flirtation with gambling, when the **Hotel e Cassino Quitandinha** attracted Hollywood stars like Bing Crosby and other members of the international jet set until the banning of gaming in 1946. Since then, the city has thrived industrially and, most recently it has become a centre for tourism.

Sights

Three rivers are dominant features in the design of Petrópolis: the Piabanha, Quitandinha and Palatino. In the historic centre (Centro Histórico), where most of the sites of tourist interest are to be found, the rivers have been channelled to run down the middle of the main avenues. Their banks, especially the Quitandinha, are planted with fine trees and flowers and the overall aspect is completely different from elsewhere in Brazil. You quickly get a sense that this was a city built with a specific purpose and at a specific time in Brazil's history.

The **Museu Imperial** (Imperial Palace) ⓘ *R da Imperatriz 220, T22378000, Tue-Sun 1100, last entry 1700, US$2*, Brazil's most visited museum, is so well kept you might think the Imperial family had left the day before, rather than in 1889. The modest but elegant building, neoclassical in style, is fully furnished, but it's worth a visit just to see the Crown Jewels of both Pedro I and Pedro II. In the palace gardens is a pretty French-style tearoom, the **Petit Palais**. Descendants of the original family live in a house behind the palace. Horse-drawn carriages wait to be hired outside the gate (not all the horses are in good shape). To get in, you pay at a small kiosk outside the entrance, then queue to deposit any bags and be admitted.

On Sun during Easter and high season, you can expect long queues to get into the palace.

The Gothic-style **Catedral de São Pedro de Alcântara** ⓘ *Tue-Sat 0800-1200, 1400-1800*, completed in 1925, contains the tombs of the emperor and empress. The Imperial Chapel is to the right of the entrance.

The summer home of air pioneer **Alberto Santos Dumont** ⓘ *Tue-Sun 0900-1700, US$1*, who was responsible for the first powered flight in Europe, is at Rua do Encanto 22. The small house was designed in 1918 as a mock-Alpine chalet. Santos Dumont

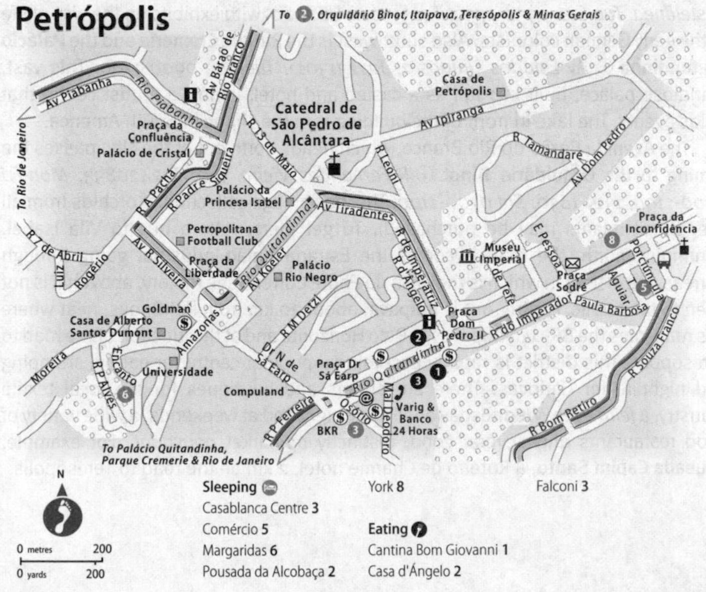

Sleeping
Casablanca Centre 3
Comércio 5
Margaridas 6
Pousada da Alcobaça 2
York 8
Falconi 3

Eating
Cantina Bom Giovanni 1
Casa d'Ángelo 2

called it 'the enchanted one', and it is a delightful example of an inventor's house. Steps to the roof lead to an observation point, a desk doubled as his bed and the alcohol-heated shower is said to be the first in Brazil.

The **Palácio de Cristal** in Praça da Confluência was designed in the same style as several similar crystal palaces in Europe. This one was built in France in 1879, with the original intention of being an exhibition hall for local products, but it became the Imperial ballroom, and is now sadly empty.

The exteriors of fine mansions built by the aristocracy of both the Imperial and republican eras can be seen on Avenida Koeler and Avenida Ipiranga. Among them are the neoclassical **Palácio Rio Negro** ⓘ *Av Koeler 255*, the summer palace of the current president, and the **Palácio da Princesa Isabel** ⓘ *Av Koeler 42*, and the **Casa de Rui Barbosa** ⓘ *Av Ipiranga 405*, in the eclectic style. Another palace is the mid-19th-century **Casa do Barão do Rio Branco** ⓘ *Av Barão do Rio Branco 279*. It was here that the Treaty of Petrópolis was signed, settling with Bolivia the issue of the annexation of Acre (1903). None of these houses are open to the public, but **Casa de Petrópolis – Instituto de Cultura** ⓘ *R Ipiranga 716, T22372133, Tue-Fri and Sun 1100-1900, Sat 1100-1300, US$2, US$1.20 when no exhibition*, has recently thrown open its doors to visitors as a cultural centre and is not to be missed. The completely original, over-the-top interior has been lovingly restored by family members and impressive art exhibitions and classical concerts take place. A charming restaurant in the old stables is worth a stop for coffee, if not for lunch.

The twin praças of **dos Expedicionários** and **Dom Pedro II** (in which there is a tourist kiosk) are at the junction of Rua do Imperador and Rua da Imperatriz. A short distance up Rua da Imperatriz, on the same side as Praça Dom Pedro II, is the **Praça Visconde de Mauá**, in which is a statue of an eagle and a snake. On one side of the praça is the Palácio Amarelo (1850), now the Câmara Municipal, and on another the modern Palácio da Cultura. On Sundays in the square is a small antiques market. **Praça da Liberdade** (formerly known as Praça Rui Barbosa) is very busy on Sunday, with goat-drawn carriages for children and occasional open-air concerts.

Excursions from Petrópolis

Southwest of the centre is the **Museu Casa do Colono** ⓘ *R Cristóvão Colombo 1034, Castelânea, Tue-Sun 0930-1730, T22313011, US$1.20*, with exhibits on the way of life of the early German colonists. Also southwest is the **Parque Cremerie** and the **Palácio Quitandinha** ⓘ *Av Estados Unidos 2, T212313011, Tue-Sun 0900-1700*. This vast, grandiose palace, built in 1944 as a casino and hotel, is now a tourist centre that holds events. The lake in front of the building is in the shape of South America.

The Avenida Barão do Rio Branco, which heads north out of the city, passes the turning to the **Orquidário Binot** ⓘ *R Fernandes Vieira 390, T22420833, Mon-Fri 0800-1100, 1315-1630, Sat 0700-1100*. This has a huge collection of orchids from all over Brazil (plants may be purchased). To get there, take a bus to Vila Isabel. Continuing north, the road becomes the Estrada União-Indústria, going through Corrêas, the district in which is the Casa do Padre Correia (see History, above); it is not open to the public. Further out is **Itaipava**, about 20 km from Petrópolis, near where this road joins the BR-040 highway to Belo Horizonte and at the junction of the road to Teresópolis. This district is rapidly becoming a popular centre for eating, shopping and nightlife for Cariocas. There are outlets and boutiques for the local textile industry, a *feira* every Wednesday and Friday night and at weekends, a wide variety of good restaurants and several good, distinctly upmarket *pousadas*. For example, **Pousada Capim Santo**, a Roteiro de Charme hotel, 2 km on the road to Teresópolis.

Teresópolis → *Phone code: 021. Colour map 4, C3. Population: 140,000.*

At 910 m this is the highest city in the state of Rio de Janeiro. It is named after Empress Teresa Cristina, whose favourite summer residence it was. Building in recent years has destroyed some of the city's character, but most visitors do not go only to see the town. Its location, at the foot of the Serra dos Órgãos, with the associated outdoor activities, is an essential part of its charm. There are two **tourist offices**: **Secretaria de Turismo** ⓘ *Praça Olímpica, T27423352, ext 2082*, and **Terminal Turístico Tancredo Neves** ⓘ *Av Rotariana, T27423352, ext 2106*, at the entrance to town from Rio.

History

Because of its altitude and the relatively low temperatures, the area was not exploited by the early colonists since they could not grow the tropical crops which were in demand in Europe. The existence of *fazendas* in the region was first documented in the early 19th century, the best known being that belonging to an Englishman, George March. To accommodate a constant stream of visitors, March added lodgings to his farm and, not long after, other landowners followed suit. Before taking the name of the empress, the parish was called Santo Antônio de Paquequer.

Sights

The **Colina dos Mirantes** hill is a 30-minute steep climb from Rua Jaguaribe (2 km from the centre; an inexpensive taxi ride), with sweeping views of the city and surroundings. Around the town are various attractions, such as the Sloper and Iaci lakes, the Imbui and Amores waterfalls and the Fonte Judith, which has mineral-rich water, access from Avenida Oliveira Botelho, 4 km southwest. Just off the road to Petrópolis is the **Orquidário Aranda** ⓘ *Alameda Francisco Smolka, T27420628*, 5 km from the centre.

The road to Nova Friburgo (see below) is known as the **Vale das Hortaliças** because it passes through a zone where vegetables and some flowers are cultivated. There is a rock formation called **A Mulher de Pedra**, 12 km out of Teresópolis on this road.

Serra dos Órgãos

ⓘ *Entrance to the park is US$1, with an extra charge for the path to the top of the Pedra do Sino; for information from Ibama for the state of Rio de Janeiro, ToXX21-22311772.*

Some 11,000 ha of the Serra dos Órgãos, so called because their strange shapes are said to recall organ-pipes, have been a national park since 1939 (the second oldest in the country). The main attraction is the precipitous peak **Dedo de Deus** ('God's Finger', 1,692 m) and the highest point is **Pedra do Sino** ('Bell Rock', 2,263 m), up which winds a 14-km path, a climb of three to four hours. The west face of this mountain is one of the hardest climbing pitches in Brazil. Another well-known peak is the **Pedra do Açu** (2,245 m, the name is a Tupi word meaning 'large'). Many others have names evocative of their shape: for example, O Escalavrado ('The Scarred One'), O Dedo de Nossa Senhora ('Our Lady's Finger'), A Cabeça de Peixe ('Fish Head'), A Agulha do Diabo ('The Devil's Needle') and A Verruga do Frade ('The Friar's Wart'). Near the Sub-Sede (see below) is the **Von Martius Natural History Museum** ⓘ *0800-1700*, named after a German naturalist, Karl Friedrich Philipp Von Martius (1794-1868), who visited Brazil in 1817-1820.

> *The Serra dos Órgãos is considered Brazil's climbing capital and the park is also good for trekking.*

There are **natural swimming pools** at both the Sede and Sub-Sede, although between May and October the temperature may be a little too chilly for bathing. In the Sub-Sede they are called **Poço Verde**, **Poço da Preguiça** and **Ponte Velha**. It is possible to trek right through the park, from Teresópolis to Petrópolis, a distance of 42 km, but it is essential to take a guide; contact **Campo de Aventuras Paraíso Açu** (see Sleeping, page 157).

The park has 2 dependencies, both accessible from the BR-116: the **Sede** (headquarters) ⓘ *T/F26421070*, is closer to Teresópolis (from town take Avenida Rotariana), while the **Sub-Sede** is just outside the park proper, off the BR-116. By the Sede entrance is the Mirante do Soberbo, with views to the Baía de Guanabara. Anyone can enter the park and hike the trails from the Teresópolis gate, but if you intend to climb the Pedra do Sino, you must sign a register (those under 18 must be accompanied by an adult and have authorization from the park authorities).

Flora and fauna

The park belongs to the Mata Atlântica ecosystem which, as frequently mentioned, is seriously threatened. There are 20-30-m-high trees, such as *paineiras* (floss-silk tree), *ipês* and *cedros*, rising above palms, bamboos and other smaller trees. Flowers include begonias, bromeliads, orchids and *quaresmeiras* (glorybushes). The park is the home of the very rare and endemic grey-winged cotinga, as well as a number of other cotingas, berryeaters and other endemic birds. Less rare birds include hummingbirds, guans, *araçaris* and tinamous. Mammals include some species of monkey, wild cat, deer, armadillo, agouti and peccary. There are also a number of frogs and toads, including the *sapo-pulga* (the flea-toad, at 10 mm claimed by local literature to be the smallest amphibian in the world; although other sources say that the Cuban pygmy frog is the smallest).

A good way to see the park is to do the Rio-Teresópolis-Petrópolis-Rio circuit, a scenic day trip by car. It can also be hiked in two or three days (take a tent).

Nova Friburgo → *Phone code: 024. Colour map 4, C3. Population: 175,000.*

This town, standing at 846 m in a beautiful valley with excellent walking and riding, is a popular resort during the summer months. It was founded by Swiss settlers from Fribourg, the first families arriving in 1820. Apart from tourism, Nova Friburgo has an important textile industry, specializing in lingerie, and also produces cheeses, preserves, sweets and liqueurs. **Centro de Turismo** ⓘ *Praça Demerval Barbosa Moreira, T25238000, ext 236.*

A cable car from Praça dos Suspiros goes 650 m up the **Morro da Cruz**, for a magnificent view of the rugged country (US$5). Most of the interesting sites are in the surrounding countryside, so a car may be necessary to see everything. About 10 km northeast are the **Furnas do Catete**, an area of forest, caves, waterfalls and rock formations, one of which is called the Pedra do Cão Sentado ('The Seated Dog'); there is a small entry fee. Other natural attractions are the Pico da Caledônia (2,310 m) 15 km southwest, and the Véu de Noiva waterfall, 9 km north. The district of **Lumiar**, 34 km southeast, has beautiful scenery, waterfalls, natural swimming pools and good canoeing in the Rios Macaé and Bonito. These two rivers meet at a point called Poço do Alemão, or Poço Verde, 4½ km south of Lumiar.

Towns in the coffee zone

Although coffee no longer dominates this part of Brazil, as it did in the 19th century, there are still many reminders of the wealth of this trade. It can be seen in the towns of Vassouras and Valença, and especially in the *fazendas*, which were the homes and production headquarters of the coffee barons. Today many of these plantations have been well and truly incorporated into a rural, cultural and historic tourist circuit, with some small towns in the Vale do Rio Paraíba do Sol such as Conservatória maintaining the serenading street tradition. Nearer to Rio, the train journey from Miguel Pereira has spectacular views of this mountainous terrain whilst the Museu da Cachaça at Pati doe Alferes is a shrine to this strong sugar cane spirit.

The coffee zone covered the valley of the Rio Paraíba do Sul and neighbouring hills and valleys. Before the coming of the railways in the second half of the 19th century, mule trains carried the coffee from the interior to the coast on roads such as the Estrada do Comércio from Minas Gerais, through Valença and Vassouras, to the town of Iguaçu on the river of the same name. At the end of the 19th century, the abolition of slavery, the exhaustion of the land and lower international prices for coffee caused the collapse of the coffee trade. The towns had to adapt to new economic activities or die, but many of the *fazendas* remain, and although not easy to get to, a visit is worth the effort. (*Fazendas: As Casas Grandes Rurais do Brasil*, by Fernando Tasso Frajoso Pires, Abbeville Press, is a beautiful book showing these magnificent houses.)

Miguel Pereira → *Phone code: 024. Population: 24,000.*

This town, 113 km north of Rio de Janeiro, has an excellent mountain climate. In the mid-19th century the area was entirely given over to coffee; other industries were introduced when a railway branch line reached here in the late 19th century. The town was named after a doctor who, in the 1930s, promoted the region for holidays away from the coast. About 3 km from town on the road to Rio is the **Javari lake**, a popular recreational spot. Mountain roads through the Serra do Mar head east to Petrópolis (see above) and Vassouras (see below), but ask about their condition before using either of them. For tourist information, go to **Setur** ⓘ *Av Manuel Guilherme Barbosa 375, T24841616*. There are a few cheap hotels in town and a number of mid-range options stretched along the main road and in the countryside on the outskirts.

The **Miguel Pereira-Conrado railway** ⓘ *56 km round trip, 4½ hrs, US$25, 0930 on Sat, Sun and public holidays*, a tourist train, also known as the Trem Azul, started operations in 1993 and affords beautiful views of mountains, rivers and waterfalls. The diesel train follows a metre-gauge line constructed to take coffee to the port of Rio. Among the attractions of the journey is the Paulo de Frontin iron bridge, built in 1889 and said to be the only railway bridge built in a curve. The line is operated by **Montmar Turismo of Angra dos Reis**. At the railway station there is a **museum** ⓘ *T24844877, Tue-Fri 1200-1700, Sat-Sun 0900-1400*.

Vassouras → *Phone code: 024. Colour map 4, C3. Population: 32,000.*

It is hard to believe that the small town of Vassouras was once one of the most important cities of the Brazilian Empire. During the coffee boom in the 19th century, it was surrounded by coffee farms whose owners became immensely rich. These coffee barons acquired noble titles and, as their power increased, they built enormous, opulent town houses in Vassouras. The majority of these buildings are still there, surrounding the beautiful main Praça Barão de Campo Belo. The Emperor Pedro II visited the city several times.

In 1875 the railway station was opened in Vassouras, allowing the local farmers to send their produce directly to Rio de Janeiro. But the town went into decline when the coffee boom ended. For many years it had almost no economic activity, except for some cattle ranching and small-scale agriculture. Nowadays, it has a university and is being rediscovered by the tourism industry. It still retains its small-town calm, but the reminders of its golden past mix with the student nightlife in the bars along a street called, unofficially, 'The Broadway'.

Sights

The best way to explore Vassouras is on foot. Starting at the rodoviária, walk as far as the **Estação Ferroviária**, the former railway station. Recently restored, it is now the headquarters of the Universidade de Vassouras. Carry straight on to the **Praça Barão de Campo Belo**, where you will find the most important old houses and public buildings, all dating from the 19th century. Note the neoclassical influence. One of these old 'baronial' houses, at Rua Custódio Guimarães 65, on the left-hand side of the square as you enter, houses the **Casa da Cultura**, a municipal cultural centre which has tourist information and temporary exhibitions of local art and folklore. Ask if you can go upstairs and on the second floor, at the top of some of the internal walls, look for where the paint has peeled. You can see the 19th-century method of house construction, using clay over a frame of interwoven wood and bamboo.

At the top end of the praça is the church of **Nossa Senhora da Conceição**, the most important in the city, finished in 1853 in neoclassical style. Behind the church is the small Praça Sebastião Lacerda, surrounded by huge fig trees. The story goes that there is one fig tree for each of the rich coffee barons who lived in Vassouras in the last century. Keep on walking until you come to the cemetery. A visit is recommended; most of the wealthiest men of Brazil's second empire are buried here. Rich mausoleums decorated with Italian and Portuguese marble sculptures show the competition among the families. Two of the most important clans are represented: the Teixeira Leite family and the Correa e Castro family. On the grave of a Catholic priest who died in 1866, Monsenhor Rios, a strange purple flower blooms every year in November on the 'Day of the Dead'. Its intense smell is reminiscent of rotting flesh. Scientists have studied it, but have reached no conclusion as to what it is. The flower vanishes after a few days and the small bush lives on until January or February. It is now protected by a small iron fence and a number of miracles are reported to have occurred there.

Back at Praça Barão de Campo Belo, on Rua Barão de Vassouras, is the **Palacete do Barão do Ribeirão**, the former residence of a coffee baron, later converted into the town's court. Nowadays it is closed for restoration as it has been badly attacked by termites. Turn right and at the end of Rua Dr Fernandes Junior (No 160) you will find the fascinating **Casa da Hera Museum** ⓘ *T24712342, Wed-Sun 1100-1700*, an old country house covered with ivy, which belonged in the 19th century to one of the richest men in the town, Joaquim Teixeira Leite. After his death the house was inherited by his daughter, Eufrásia Teixeira Leite, who lost interest in the coffee business. She went to Paris, living a life of parties and luxury for many years. After she died in 1930 the house was made into a museum, in accordance with her will. All the furniture, decoration and architecture is original, from the golden years of coffee. The wide variety of imported tapestries, pianos and porcelain contrasts with very rough building materials: a fantastic portrait of life in the 1850s. On some Sundays, depending on the number of visitors, they serve tea in a recreation of the atmosphere of the old coffee *fazendas*.

Because Vassouras is a university centre, it has more variety than in other towns of a similar size. The action is concentrated in Rua Expedicionário Oswaldo de Almeida Ramos, but you won't need to pronounce that: simply ask for the 'Broadway' and everybody will direct you to the right place. Here there are enough bars and open-air restaurants to suit all tastes and budgets.

Another possibility is a guided visit to the food technology centre at the **Senai**, close to the main praça. Here students learn how to process fruit, vegetables, meat and also how to work in a brewery. Most of the hotels can arrange a weekend guided visit.

Excursions from Vassouras

As yet, Vassouras lacks a well-developed tourist infrastructure. There is a lot to see around the city, especially the old *fazendas*, but they are only just starting to open to the public. The majority of them are privately owned and can only be visited with a prior appointment. The bigger hotels can arrange guided tours with transport at weekends. During the week, the only option is to go by car, as some of the *fazendas* are a long way away, down dirt roads. The best *fazendas* in the vicinity are: **Fazenda Santa Mônica**, **Fazenda São Fernando**, **Fazenda Paraíso** and **Fazenda Oriente.** More information can be obtained from the Casa da Cultura or from the **Tourism Secretary** ⓘ *Municipalidade, Praça Barão de Campo Belo, T24711367*.

Valença and Conservatória

Like Vassouras, **Valença** is a historical monument and its history follows much the same pattern, with wealth from the coffee trade followed by some small-scale industry and agriculture. There are a number of *fazendas* nearby and in the town a Faculty of Medicine. **Secretaria de Turismo** ⓘ *T24420102*.

About 35 km from Valença is **Conservatória**, another town in the coffee zone. Although it did not become as wealthy as Vassouras or Valença, it still has some fine 19th-century houses and is much more peaceful. In Conservatória, local farm produce can be bought, as well as blankets, macrame and crochet work. A local custom is the serenade through the streets; serenaders meet at the **Museu da Seresta** ⓘ *R Osvaldo Fonseca*, on Friday and Saturday. This region can also be reached via the Japeri turn-off on the BR-116, a beautiful mountain drive.

Secretaria de Turismo ⓘ *T34381188*, is in the centre of town. There are a few moderate and cheap hotels in town and the Secretaria can advise on stays in *fazendas*.

Sleeping

Petrópolis *p150, map p151**, phone code 024*
Good, budget accommodation is hard to find, but bargaining is possible Mon-Fri (see p47)

L **Pousada da Alcobaça**, R Agostinho Goulão 298, Correas, T22211240, www.pousadadaalcobaca.com.br. In the

Roteiros de Charme group (see p47). Delightful, family-run large country house set in flower-filled gardens leading down to a river, with pool and sauna. Worth stopping by for tea on the terrace, or for dinner at the restaurant. Recommended.

A Margaridas, R Bispo Dom José Pereira Alves 235, Trono de Fátima, T22424686. A chalet-type hotel set in lovely gardens with a swimming pool, charming proprietors.

A Riverside Parque, R Hermogéneo Silva 522, Retiro, 5 mins from the centre, T0800248011, T22310730, F22432312, www.hoteis-riverside.com.br. Mock colonial hotel with a nice outdoor pool set in attractive gardens and with views of the surrounding countryside. The helpful owner can arrange tours.

B Casablanca Centre, R General Osório 28, T22422612. Old 1960s block, reasonable rooms and restaurant. Somewhat faded.

B York, R do Imperador 78, a short walk from the rodoviária, T22432662, F22428220. Convenient, helpful, the fruit and milk at breakfast come from the owners' own farm. Recommended.

C Comércio, R Dr Porciúncula 55, opposite rodoviária, T22423500. One of the cheapest options. Very basic with shared bath.

Camping

Associação Brasileira de Camping and YMCA, Araras district. Space can be reserved through Rio YMCA, T2319860.

Teresópolis *p153, phone code 021*

There are many cheap hotels in R Delfim Moreira, near the praça.

L Fazenda Rosa dos Ventos, Km 22 on the road to Nova Friburgo, T27428833. In the Roteiros de Charme group (see p47). One of the best hotels in inland Rio with a range of chalets set in 1 million sq m of private forest and with wonderful views.

A Fazenda Montebello, at Km 17 on the Petrópolis road, T/F26446313. Modern hotel with pool, price includes 3 meals. Recommended.

C Várzea Palace, R Sebastião Teixeira 41, T27420878. Simple hotel with very friendly staff. Highly recommended.

D-E Retiro da Inglesa, 20 km on road to Nova Friburgo, Fazenda Boa Esperança, in the beautiful Vale dos Frades, T27423109. Youth hostel. Book in advance in Jan-Feb, dormitory accommodation and family rooms, camping beside the hostel.

Camping

Quinta de Barra, R Antônio Maria 100, Km 3 on Petrópolis Rd, T26431050.

Serra dos Órgãos *p153, phone code 021*

Ibama has some hostels, US$5 full board, or US$3 1st night, US$2 thereafter, a bit rough.

A Cabanas Açu, Estr do Bonfim, T0XX21-29835041, Km 3.5 inside the park, cabins, restaurant, sports include riding, canoeing and fishing (credit cards accepted).

A Campo de Aventuras Paraíso Açu, Estr do Bonfim 3511, at the Petrópolis side of the park, T0XX24-21426275. Various types of accommodation, from rooms to chalets, specializes in adventure sports (credit cards not accepted).

Camping

2 sites in the Sub-Sede part, 1 close to the museum, the other not far from the natural swimming pool at Poço da Ponte Velha; 1 site in the Sede part. The Sede has a restaurant and the Sub-Sede a *lanchonete*.

Nova Friburgo *p155, phone code 024*

AL Bucsky, 5 km out on the Niterói Rd, T25225052. With meals, tours and guided walks available.

AL Pousada do Riacho, Estr Nova Friburgo Km 8, Cardinot, T25222823, www.pousadadoriacho.com. A **Roteiro de Charme** hotel (see p47). Charming upmarket hotel extensive gardens and surrounded by gentle mountains.

A Fazenda São João, 11 km from Garlipp (under the same ownership) up a side road, T25421304. Riding, swimming, sauna, tennis, hummingbirds and orchids. The owner will meet guests in Nova Friburgo or even in Rio.

A Garlipp, at Muri, 8 km south, Km 70.5 from Rio, T/F25421173. German-run, in chalets, with meals.

B Fabris, Av Alberto Browne 148, T25222852. Central, with plain rooms with TVs and en suites with hot showers. Plentiful breakfast buffet.

C-D Maringá, R Monsenhor Miranda 110, T25222309. Cheaper without bath. Very standard but with a very good breakfast. Recommended.

Camping

Camping Clube do Brasil has sites on the Niterói Rd, at Caledônia (7 km out, T25220169) and Muri (10 km out, T25422275). There is a private site at **Fazenda Sanandu**, 20 km out on the same road.

Vassouras *p156, phone code 024*

AL Santa Amália, Av Sebastião Manoel Furtado 526, T/F24711897, close to the rodoviária. Located in a very pleasant and quiet park, swimming pool, sauna, volleyball and soccer pitches, 1 of the best in town, try to negotiate in the low season (Mar-Jun and Aug-Nov) and during the week.

B Gramado da Serra, R Aldo Cavalcanti 7, T/F24712314. With bar, restaurant, pool, sauna.

B Mara Palace, R Chanceler Dr Raul Fernandes 121, T24711993. In a house built in 1870, fully and tastefully preserved, swimming pool, bar, sauna, sports, nice atmosphere and good service, owner (Gerson) can arrange visits to *fazendas*; also

C-D Pousada Bougainville, T24712451. Modest little guesthouse with breakfast included in the price.

D Pousada Veredas, T24712728. Basic but with helpful staff and breakfast included.

Eating

Petrópolis *p150, map p151, phone code 024*

Falconi, R do Imperador 757, T22421252. Traditional restaurant with rustic elegance that has been serving Italian food since 1914. Good value, with pasta and pizza for US$3. Recommended.

Cantina Bom Giovanni, R do Imperador 729, T22425588. A 1st-floor simple, canteen-style Italian restaurant that is justifiably popular for self-service lunch and dinner.

Casa d'Ângelo, R do Imperador 700, by Praça Dom Pedro II. A traditional, long-standing teahouse with self-service food that doubles as a bar at night.

Pavelka, Rod Washington Luiz, T22427990, 0800-2100 (Fri 0800- 0200), see Shopping, below. Locals in the know stock up at the deli with the German, Austrian and Czech specialities such as sausages and trout smoked on the premises and tuck into the éclairs and mille-feuilles fresh from the bakery in the little attached café. Recommended.

Teresópolis *p153, phone code 021*

Da Irene, R Tte Luís Meireles 1800, T27422901. Very popular upmarket Russian restaurant. Reservations necessary.

Bar Gota d'Água, Praça Baltasar da Silveira 16. A little bar, simple fish dishes and *feijoada*.

Taberna Alpina, Duque de Caxias 131. Excellent German cuisine.

There are cheap eats and a good café in the ABC supermarket.

Nova Friburgo *p155, phone code 024*

There are many options to choose from, several in European styles which reflect the background of the people who settled in the area. You can also find Brazilian food, pizzas and confeitarias.

Chez Gigi, Av Euterpe Friburguense 21, T25230107. Excellent Brazilian-French fusion cooking with dishes like duck's breast in *jabuticaba*, pear and damson sauce.

Auberge Suisse, R 10 de Outubro, T25411270. Fondue, *roschti* and other Swiss options alongside very good steak.

Vassouras *p156, phone code 024*

The best and best-value restaurants are located in the centre, on R Expedicionário Oswaldo de Almeida Ramos 'The Broadway'.

Festivals and events

Petrópolis *p150, map p151, phone code 024*

16 Mar Foundation day.

29 Jun São Pedro de Alcântara, patron saint of Petrópolis.

Jun Bohemia Beer Festival. Brazil's oldest beer dates from 1853; it was originally brewed in the city, and although production has now been moved to Rio the festival is still celebrated in Petrópolis.

Teresópolis *p153, phone code 021*

May Festa das Colônias.

13 Jun Santo Antônio, patron saint of Teresópolis.

29 Jun São Pedro is celebrated with fireworks.

7 Jul Foundation day.

15 Oct Santa Terezinha.

Nova Friburgo *p155, phone code 024*

May Maifest festival throughout the month.

16 May Founding of Nova Friburgo.

24 Jun São João Batista, patron saint's day.

Vassouras *p156, phone code 024*
Feb/Mar Carnival is one of the best in the region, with its own samba schools and balls. **Jun** Santo Antônio, São Pedro and São João are celebrated with traditional parties. **8 Dec** Feast of Nossa Senhora da Conceição, the city's patron saint, with a Mass and procession.

Shopping

Petrópolis *p150, map p151, phone code 024*
R Teresa, southeast of the centre, is where the textile industry exhibits its wares. In common with **Itaipava**, it draws buyers from all over the country and is a good place to find good-quality knitwear and bargain clothes. Closed Mon morning and Sun.

Activities and tours

Petrópolis *p150, map p151, phone code 024*
Tour operators
Coopetur, R 16 de Março 155, Centro. T/F22318498, www.coopetur.com.br. Offers horse riding, trekking (including a 3-day mountain trek to Teresópolis), whitewater rafting and a range of trips into the scenic mountain area as well as cultural tours around the city with enthusiastic, multi-lingual guides. Warmly recommended. There are also possibilities for climbing and cycling in the vicinity.

Serra dos Órgãos *p153, phone code 024*
Tour operators
Lazer Tours, T27427616. Tours of the park are offered by Francisco (find him at the grocery shop on R Sloper 1). Recommended. **Focus Tours** (see p26) offer birdwatching tours.

Transport

Petrópolis *p150, map p151, phone code 024*
Bus From **Rio** every 15 mins throughout the day (US$3) with **Única Fácil**, Sun every hr, 1½ hrs, sit on the left-hand side for best views. Return tickets are not available, so buy tickets for the return on arrival in Petrópolis. The ordinary buses leave from the rodoviária in Rio; a/c buses, hourly from 1100, from Av Nilo Peçanha, US$4. Bus to **Niterói**, US$4.50; to **Cabo Frio**, US$10. To **Teresópolis**, Viação Teresópolis, 8 a day, US$3. Salutário to **São Paulo** daily at 2330.

Teresópolis *p153, phone code 021*
Bus **Rio**-Teresópolis buses leave every 30 mins from the Novo Rio rodoviária. Book the return journey as soon as you arrive at Teresópolis; rodoviária at R 1 de Maio 100. Fare US$3.60. From Teresópolis to **Petrópolis**, 8 a day, US$3.

Nova Friburgo *p155, phone code 024*
Bus Bus station, Ponte da Suadade, T25220400. To **Rio**, every hr, 2 hrs, US$4.

Vassouras *p156, phone code 024*
Bus Several buses daily from **Rio de Janeiro**'s rodoviária Novo Rio with Normandy. Around 1½ hrs between departures 0615-2030, 2 hrs, US$6.50. More buses during summer and holidays.

Directory

Petrópolis *p150, map p151, phone code 024*
Banks Banco do Brasil, R Paulo Barbosa 81; a Banco 24 Horas ATM is located by the Varig office at R Mcal Deodoro 98. Travel agencies with exchange; **BKR**, R Gen Osório 12; **Goldman**, R Barão de Amazonas 46 (between Praça da Liberdade and the Universidade) and **Vert Tur**, R 16 de Março 244, from 1000-1630; **Internet** Compuland, R do Imperador opposite Praça Dr Sá Earo, US$1.50 per hr. **Post office** R do Imperador 350 in the Palácio dos Correios. **Telephones** R Mcal Deodoro, just above Praça Dr Nelson de Sá Earp, no fax.

Teresópolis *p153, phone code 021*
Banks Cash or TCs at **Teretur**, Trav Portugal 46. English spoken. **Internet** Cott@ge Cybercafe, R Alfredo Rebello Filho 996, 2nd floor. US$3 per hr.

Nova Friburgo *p155, phone code 024*
Banks Bradesco, Praça Demerval Barbosa Moreira.

Vassouras *p156, phone code 024*
Banks Banco do Brasil, R Caetano Furquim, in the centre; has an ATM but does not change money.

West of Rio de Janeiro

Towns to the west of Rio are mostly spread along the ugly Rio-São Paulo motorway known as the Dutra. None are appealing. But the mountains which watch over them preserve important tracts of Atlantic coast rainforest, particularly around Itatiaia. This is one of the best places close to Rio for seeing wild animals and virgin rainforest and is the country's oldest protected area. The little mock-alpine resort of Visconde de Mauá sits in the same mountain chain a little further towards São Paulo, although the forest here is less well preserved. » *For Sleeping, Eating and other listings, see pages 162-164.*

Penedo → *Phone code: 024. Altitude: 600 m. Population: 8,000.*

In the same region, 175 km from Rio, is the small town of Penedo which in the 1930s attracted Finnish settlers who brought the first saunas to Brazil. There is a Finnish museum, a cultural centre and Finnish dancing on Saturdays. This popular weekend resort also provides horse riding and swimming in the Portinho River.

There are five buses a day from Resende. **Tourist information** ⓘ *Av Casa das Pedras, T33511876*, and there are plenty of mid-range and cheap hotels in town.

Visconde de Mauá → *Phone code: 024. Altitude: 1,200 m. Colour map 4, C3.*

About 33 km beyond Penedo (part of the road unpaved) is the charming small village of Visconde de Mauá in the **Serra da Mantiqueira**. In the early 20th century Swiss and German immigrants settled in the town which is popular with tourists today. The surrounding scenery is lovely, with green valleys, clear rivers, wild flowers and opportunities for good walks and other outdoor activities. Many places offer acupuncture, shiatsu massage and macrobiotic food and there is a hippy feel to the crafts on sale. Horses can be rented in Visconde de Mauá from Berto (almost opposite Vendinha da Serra), or Pedro (Lote 10) and many places in Maringá arrange riding. The Rio Preto is good for canoeing and there is an annual national event (dates change; check in advance). The **tourist office** ⓘ *T33871283*, is closed out of season.

Three other small hill towns are nearby: **Mirantão**, at 1,700 m, with semitropical vegetation; **Maringá**, just across the state border in Minas Gerais and a delightful two hours' walk; and **Maromba**. On the way to Maromba is the Mirante do Posto da Montanha, a lookout with a view of the Rio Preto, which runs through the region and is the border between Rio de Janeiro and Minas Gerais states. Also in Minas Gerais, 6 km upriver from Maringá but on a different road, are the Santa Clara falls (turn off before Maromba). Between Visconde de Mauá and Maringá is a natural pool in the river (turn left before crossing the bridge). After Maromba follow the signs to Cachoeira e Escorrega, a small fall and waterslide with a cold natural swimming pool, a 2-km walk. A turning off this road leads to another waterfall, the Cachoeira Véu da Noiva.

Although served by buses from both São Paulo and Rio *pousadas* are spread out and the area is best visited with a car. For **tourist info** ⓘ *www.guiamaua.com.br*, lists many of the hotels and restaurants and gives a good overview of the area (in Portuguese but with pictures).

Itatiaia National Park

ⓘ *Information and maps can be obtained at the park office. The Administração do Parque Nacional de Itatiaia operates a refuge in the park which acts as a starting point for climbs and treks. Information can be obtained from Ibama, T02433521461, for the local headquarters, or T02132246463 for the Rio de Janeiro state department. Information on treks can be obtained from Clube Excursionista Brasileira, Av*

Almirante Barroso 2, 8th floor, Rio de Janeiro, T02122203695. Although buses do run through the park calling at the hotels, hiring a car to visit Itatiaia will save time and sweat in summer, or chill in winter. Entry per day is $10 per car. Avoid weekends and Brazilian holidays if you want to see wildlife.

Deep valleys shrouded in pristine rainforest hiding rocky clear-water rivers and icy waterfalls; one-hour, four-hour, one-day and two-day walks are possible on little winding trails watched over by some of world's rarest birds and mammals; there's a whole swathe of different ecosystems (and hotels and guesthouses to suit all budgets from which to explore them); and all is within easy reach of Rio or São Paulo. Itatiaia is a must for those who wish to see Brazilian forest and animals and have a limited itinerary or time. This 30,000-ha mountainous park is Brazil's oldest. It was founded in 1937 to protect Atlantic coast rainforest in the Serra de Mantiqueira mountains, and important species still find a haven here, including jaguars and pumas, brown capuchin and black-faced titi monkeys. The park is particularly good for birds. It has a list of over 350 species with scores of spectacular tanagers, hummingbirds (including the ultra-rare Brazilian ruby, with emerald wings and a dazzling red chest), cotingas (included the black and gold cotinga; which as far as we are aware has never been photographed) and manakins. Guans literally squawk and flap next to the park roads.

The vegetation is stratified by altitude so that the plateau at 800-1,100 m is covered by forest, ferns and flowering plants (such as orchids, bromeliads, begonias), giving way on the higher escarpments to pines and bushes. Higher still, over 1,900 m, the distinctive rocky landscape has low bushes and grasses, isolated trees and unique plants adapted to high winds and strong sun. There are also a great variety of lichens.

This is good hiking country with walks through subtropical and temperate forests, grasslands and paramo to a few peaks just under 3,000m. The best trails head for Pedra de Taruga and Pedra de Maçã and the Poranga and Véu de Noiva waterfalls. The Pico das Agulhas Negras and Serra das Prateleiras (up to 2,540 m) offer good rock climbing.

There is a **Museu de História Natural** ⓘ *Tue-Sun 1000-1600*, near the headquarters with a depressing display of stuffed animals from the 1940s.

Itatiaia lies just off the main Sao Paulo-Rio motorway, the Dutra. There are bus connections to **Itatiaia town** or nearby **Resende** from both Rio and São Paulo. There is only one way into the park from Itatiaia town and one main road within it – which forks off to the various hotels, all of which are signposted. Four times a day (variable hours), a bus marked '504 Circular' leaves Itatiaia town for the park, calling at the hotels and stopping at the Simon. Coming from Resende this may be caught at the crossroads before Itatiaia. Through tickets to São Paulo are sold at a booth in the large bar in the middle of Itatiaia main street. Basic accommodation in cabins and dormitories is available in the village strung along the road leading to the park. There are some delightful options inside the park but they are more expensive.

Engenheiro Passos → *Phone code: 024. Population: 3,500.*

Further along the Dutra highway (186 km from Rio) is the small town of Engenheiro Passos, from which a road (BR-354) leads to São Lourenço and Caxambu in Minas Gerais (see page 277). By turning off this road at the Registro pass (1,670 m) on the Rio-Minas border, you can reach the **Pico das Agulhas Negras**. The mountain can be climbed from this side from the **Abrigo Rebouças** refuge at 2,350 m which is manned all year round. Take your own food, US$2.50 to stay.

Sleeping

Visconde de Mauá *p161, phone code 024*
There are many *fazendas, pousadas* and chalets in the vicinity, but very little budget accommodation.

LL Fronteira, Estr Visconde de Mauá-Campo Lindo, Km 4, T33871219. A **Roteiro de Charme** hotel (see p47). Huge cabins with tiny private gardens set in a forested garden with wonderful views. Sauna, pool and a good restaurant and bar.

C-D **Encanto**, Road to Maringa, km 7, T33871155, www.guiamaua.com.br/encanto. 7 chalets in woodland and a sauna. Popular with 20- and 30-somethings.

C-D **Fazenda Boa Vista**, Vale das Flores, Road to Maringa, Km 15, T99983614, www.fazendaboavista.com.br. Great views, a pool and a range of organized activities. The simple chalets sit in a private rainforest reserve. Minimum 2-day stay.

C-D **Sitio Portal da Travessia**, Road to Maringa, Km 7, T33871154, www.portaldatravessia.com.br. 6 chalets next to a mountain stream and with a spring water natural pool. The range of activities include hikes and horse riding.

Camping

Barragen's, Maringá, T33871354. One of several campsites in the area.

Itatiaia National Park *p161, phone code 024*

A **Hotel Donati**, T33521110, www.hoteldonati.com.br. One of the most delightful hotels in the country – mock-Swiss chalets and rooms, set in tropical gardens visited by animals every night and early morning. A series of trails lead off from the main building and the hotel can organize professional birding guides. Decent restaurant and 2 pools. Highly recommended. Map on website.

A **Simon**, Km 13 on the road in the park, T33521122, www.hotelsimon.com.br. A 1970s concrete block with *Hawaii Five 0* decor at the top of the park which marks the trailhead for the higher walks to Agulhas Negras and Três Picos. Wonderful views from fading rooms.

B **Pousada do Elefante**, 15 mins' walk back downhill from **Hotel Simon**. Good food, swimming pool, lovely views, may allow camping; cheap lodging at R Maricá 255, T33521699. Possibility of pitching a tent on the premises, located close to the national park.

B-C **Hotel Cabanas de Itatiaia**, T33521252. Magical views from these comfortable but ridiculously Swiss chalets on a hillside. Pool and good restaurant too.

C-D **Cabanas da Itatiaia**, T33521152, www.hotelcabanasitatiaia.com.br. Price per person in these simple chalets in secondary forest overlooking a stream in the lower reaches of the park. The sister hotel (**Aldeia dos Passaros**) opposite has a pool. Both share facilities and are very friendly and helpful. Great breakfasts, good off-season rates and a riverside sauna.

D **Hotel Alsene**, at 2,100 m, 2 km from the side entrance to the park, take a bus to São Lourenço and Caxambu, get off at Registro, walk or hitch from there (12 km). Very popular with climbing and trekking clubs, dormitory or camping, chalets available, hot showers, fireplace, evening meal after everyone returns, drinks but no snacks.

E **Ipê Amarelo**, R João Maurício Macedo Costa 352, Campo Alegre, T/F0XX24-33521232. IYHA youth hostel.

Camping

Camping Clube do Brasil site is entered at Km 148 on the Vla Dutra.

Engenheiro Passos *p162, phone code 024*

Around Engenheiro Passos there are many *fazenda* hotels.

L **Fazenda Villa Forte**, 1 km from town, T/F33571122. With meals, bar, sauna, massage, gym and other sports facilities.

A **Fazenda Palmital**, Km 11 BR-354 towards Caxambu, T/F33571108. Chalets on the wedge of the national park, arranged around a lake in a garden and with a waterfall nearby. Facilities include a pool, sauna, horse riding and a play area for kids.

Eating

Visconde de Mauá *p161, phone code 024*

ŸŸ **Gosto com Gosto**, R Wenceslau Brás, Mineiro. Self-service Minas Gerais dishes which are heavy on meat and flavour.

Ÿ **Bar do Jorge**. Café. Everywhere in town shuts at about 2200.

Itatiaia National Park *p161, phone code 024*

The hotels in the park all have restaurants. Hotel Donati and **Cabanas de Itatiaia**, the latter with a view, have the best (see Sleeping).

ŸŸ-Ÿ **Via Park**, 1441 Estrada Parque, in the village some 4 km before the park entrance, T92687934. Delicious trout with Brazilian accompaniments, in super generous portions.

Bars and clubs

Visconde de Mauá *p161, phone code 024*
Adega Bar, open till 2400, live music and dancing (Sat only).
Forró da Marieta for *forró* dancing.

Activities and tours

Itatiaia National Park *p161, phone code 024*
Tour operators
Wildlife Guides Ralph Salgueiro, T33511823, www.ecoralph.com; Edson Endrigo, T37428374, www.avesfoto.com.br – birding trips in Itatiaia and throughout Brazil, English spoken.

Transport

Visconde de Mauá *p161, phone code 024*
Bus To Visconde de Mauá from **Resende**, 1500 and 1630, 2 hrs, return 0900-0830, US$5. Direct bus **Rio**-Visconde de Mauá, **Cidade de Aço**, 0900 daily, plus 1 in evening, 3½ hrs, US$7.

The Costa Verde

The Rio de Janeiro-Santos section of the BR-101 is one of the world's most beautiful highways, hugging the forested and hilly Costa Verde southwest of Rio. The coast is littered with islands, beaches, colonial settlements and mountain fazendas. *Unmissables here include the Paraty, whose colonial façade seen from the harbour in the morning light is one of Brazil's most photographed sights, and the rainforest-covered island of Ilha Grande, which has some of the state's best beaches.*
▸▸ *For Sleeping, Eating and other listings, see pages 152-174.*

Ins and outs

The BR-101 is paved all the way to Santos (see page 209), which has good links with São Paulo. Buses run from Rio to Angra dos Reis, Paraty, Ubatuba, Caraguatatuba and São Sebastião, where it may be necessary to change for Santos or São Paulo. Hotels and *pousadas* have sprung up all along the road, as have expensive housing developments, though these have not spoiled the views. The drive from Rio to Paraty should take four hours, but it would be better to break the journey and enjoy some of the attractions. The coast road has lots of twists and turns so, if prone to motion sickness, get a seat at the front of the bus to make the most of the views.

Itacuruçá → *Phone code: 021. Population: 3,500.*

The BR-101 does not take the coastal route through Barra da Tijuca out of the city, but goes around the north side, eventually hitting the coast at **Coroa Grande**. This fishing village with summer houses and beach (the sea is polluted), together with Itacuruçá and Mangaratiba, are all on the shore of the Baía de Sepetiba, which is protected from the open sea by a long sandspit, the Restinga da Marambaia. At the spit's western end is the **Ilha da Marambaia**, while the mouth of the bay is protected by Ilha Grande.

Itacuruçá, 91 km from Rio, is a delightful place, offering fine scenery, peace and quiet and islands off its coast. The sea in the town is too polluted for bathing, but you can walk along the railway to Castelo where the beach is cleaner. Separated from the town by a channel is the **Ilha de Itacuruçá**, the largest of a string of islands stretching into the bay. Further offshore is **Ilha de Jaguanum**, around which there are lovely walks. Both islands have beaches from which bathing is possible. *Saveiros* (schooners) sail around the bay and to the islands from Itacuruçá (**Passamar**, T99792429). Ilha de Itacuruçá can also be reached from **Muriqui**, a beach resort 9 km from Itacuruçá; bathing is also possible in the Véu de Noiva waterfall. The next beach along the coast is Praia Grande, then **Praia do Saí** which has the ruins of an old port. There are a few basic hotels in the and around town.

Mangaratiba → *Phone code: 021. Population: 25,000.*

About 22 km down the coast, this fishing village is halfway from Rio to Angra dos Reis. It stands on a little bay within the Baia de Sepetiba and in the 18th century was a port for the export first of gold, later coffee and for the import of slaves. During the coffee era, it was the terminus for the Estrada São João Marcos from the Rio Paraíba do Sul. Mangaratiba's beaches are muddy, but the surroundings are pleasant and better beaches can be found outside town, for example **Ibicuí** (2 km) and **Brava** (between Ibicuí and Saí) to the east, at the head of the bay **Saco**, **Guiti** and **Cação**, and further west **São Brás**. There are numerous hotels in town. Boats run to Ilha Grande several times a day. Times vary according to the season but the last usually departs around 1400.

Angra dos Reis and around

→ *Phone code: 024. Colour map 4, C3. Population: 120,000.*

Said to have been founded on 6 January 1502 (O Dia dos Reis – The Day of Kings), Angra dos Reis is 151 km southwest of Rio by road. A small port with an important fishing and shipbuilding industry, it has several small coves with good swimming within easy reach and is situated on an enormous bay full of islands. The town itself is very ugly but the islands are home to some of the plushest private homes in southern Brazil and there are a string of exclusive resorts on the forested peninsula to the south.

Angra is the best place from which to catch a boat to Ilha Grande. The city is well connected by bus to Rio and Santos. **Tourist information** ⓘ *Largo da Lapa, opposite the bus station, T33651175 ext 2186*, is very helpful.

Several buildings remain from Angra's heyday. Of particular note are the church and convent of **Nossa Senhora do Carmo**, built in 1593 (Praça General Osório), the Igreja Matriz de **Nossa Senhora da Conceição** (1626) in the centre of town and the church and convent of **São Bernardino de Sena** (1758-1763) on the Morro do Santo Antônio. On the Largo da Lapa is the church of **Nossa Senhora da Lapa da Boa Morte** (1752) and a **Museum of Sacred Art** ⓘ *Thu-Sun 1000-1200, 1400-1800*.

On the Península de Angra, west of the town, is the **Praia do Bonfim**, a popular beach; offshore is the island of the same name, on which is the hermitage of **Senhor do Bonfim** (1780). Some 15 km east are the ruins of the **Jacuecanga** seminary (1797).

Boat trips around the bay are offered, some stop for lunch on the island of **Gipóia** (five hours). Boats run tours from the **Cais de Santa Luzia** and there are agencies for *saveiros* in town.

Ilha Grande → *Phone code: 021. Colour map 4, C3.*

Ilha Grande is a mountain ridge covered in tropical forest sticking out of an emerald sea and fringed by some of the world's most beautiful beaches. As there are no cars and no roads either, just trails through the forest, the island is still relatively undeveloped. And with luck it will remain so, as much of Ilha Grande forms part of a State Park and Biological Reserve, and cannot even be visited. That the island has so much forest is largely a fluke of history; or as Brazilians say – 'a strange protection afforded by the forces of evil'. The island was a notorious pirate lair in the 16th and 17th centuries and then a landing port for slaves. By the 20th century it was the site of an infamous prison for the country's most notorious criminals, including the writer Graciliano Ramos (see Literature, page 706), whose *Memórias do cárcere* relate his experiences. The prison closed in 1994 and is now overgrown, since then Ilha Grande has been a well-kept Brazilian treasure, which is now being discovered by the international backpacker circuit.

Ins and outs

Ferries and fishing boats take two hours or so to reach **Vila do Abraão** from Angra do Reis or Mangaratiba. Accommodation is simple; *pousada*-based at the island's only real village – Vila do Abraão and camping-based elsewhere. There is one upmarket secret reachable only by boat and frequented by those who read exclusive magazines like the *NB Review*. The weather is best from March to June and is overrun during the Christmas, New Year and Carnival period. There is a helpful **tourist office** on the jetty at Abraão. Further information and pictures on www.ilhagrande.com.

Beaches and walks

The beach at **Abraão** may look beautiful to first arrivals but those further afield are far more spectacular. The two most famous are **Lopes Mendes** – a long stretch of sand on the eastern, ocean side, backed by flatlands and patchy forest – and **Aventureiro** – fringed by coconut palms and tropical forest, and whose powder-fine sand is pocked with boulders and washed by transparent aquamarine. Lopes Mendes is two hours' walk from Abraão. Aventureiro is over six hours, but it can be reached via the **Maria Isabel** or **Mestre Ernani** boats (T33619895 or T92695877), which leave from the quay in front of the BR petrol station in Angra dos Reis. A few fishermen's huts and *barracas* provide food here and allow camping. Good beaches closer to Abraão include the half-moon bay at **Abraãoozinho** (15 minutes' walk) and **Grande das Palmas**, which has a delightful tiny whitewashed chapel (1 hour 20 minutes' walk). Both lie east of the town past the **Hotel Sagu**. **Lagoa Azul**, with crystal-clear water and reasonable snorkelling, **Freguesia de Santana** and **Saco do Céu** are all boat trips.

There are a couple of good treks over the mountains to **Dois Rios**, where the old jail was situated. There is still a settlement of former prison guards here who have nowhere to go. The walk is about 13 km one way, takes about three hours and affords beautiful scenery and superb views. You can also hike to **Pico do Papagaio** (980 m) through forest; a stiff, three hours' climb for which a guide is essential. The view from the top is breathtaking. **Pico da Pedra d'Água** (1,031 m) can also be climbed.

Paraty → *Phone code: 024. Colour map 4, C2. Population: 30,000.*

Paraty is one of Brazil's prettiest colonial towns and one of Rio de Janeiro's most popular tourist destinations. It is at its most captivating at dawn, when all but the dogs and chickens are sleeping. As the sun peeps over the horizon the little rectilinear streets are infused with a rich golden light which warms the whitewash and brilliant blue and yellow window frames of the colonial townhouses and the façade of the Manueline churches. Brightly coloured fishing boats bob up and down in the water in the foreground and behind the town the deep green of the rainforest-covered mountains of the Serra da Bocaina sit shrouded in their self-generated wispy cloud.

At the weekend Paraty buzzes with tourists who browse in the little boutiques and art galleries or buy souvenirs from the Guarani Indians who proffer their wares on the cobbles. At night they fill the numerous little bars and restaurants, many of which like the *pousadas* are owned by the bevy of expat Europeans who live in Paraty and who are determined to preserve its charm. During the week, especially off season the town is quiet, its atmosphere unspoilt by the increasing numbers of travellers who arrive.

The town's environs are as beautiful as Paraty itself. Just a few kilometres away lie the forests of the Ponta do Juatinga peninsula, fringed by wonderful beaches, washed by little waterfalls and still home to communities of Caicara fishermen who live much as they have done for centuries. Islands pepper the bay, some of them home to ultra-rare animals like the tiny golden lion tamarin monkey which is found nowhere else. The best way to visit these destinations is on a boat trip, operated from the quay by fishermen.

Ins and outs

Paraty has direct bus connections to Rio and São Paulo and destinations along the coast. The town centre is out of bounds for motor vehicles; heavy chains are strung

“” Paraty is at its most captivating at dawn, when all but the dogs and chickens are sleeping.

across the entrance to the streets but it occupies only about 2 sq km and is easily negotiable on foot. Staff at the **Centro de Informações Turísticas** ⓘ *Av Roberto Silveira, near the entrance to the historical centre, T33711266*, are friendly and helpful and some speak English. The best town map is in the *Welcome to Paraty* brochure, www.eco-paraty.com. More information is available at www.paraty.com.br. The wettest times of year are January to February and June to July. In spring streets in the colonial centre may flood, but the houses remain above the water line.

History

Paraty was officially founded in the first half of the 17th century. Its name is usually said to derive from the indigenous word for a small fish common in these waters, called *paratii*, but others say it comes from language of the local tupi-guarani people in which it means ‘gulf’ or ‘chasm’. Having a good harbour and a well-worn trail into the interior (used by the Guiana people before the Portuguese colonizers), Paraty was a natural choice for a port. Some parts of the old trail can still be walked; ask tour operators (see page 174). It became the chief port for the export of gold in the 17th century and thus grew rich. Most of its colonial churches date from this period, as do the fortresses which were built to prevent pirates and foreign ships stealing the valuable cargo (see the Forte do Defensor Perpétuo, below). Walls protected the

Paraty

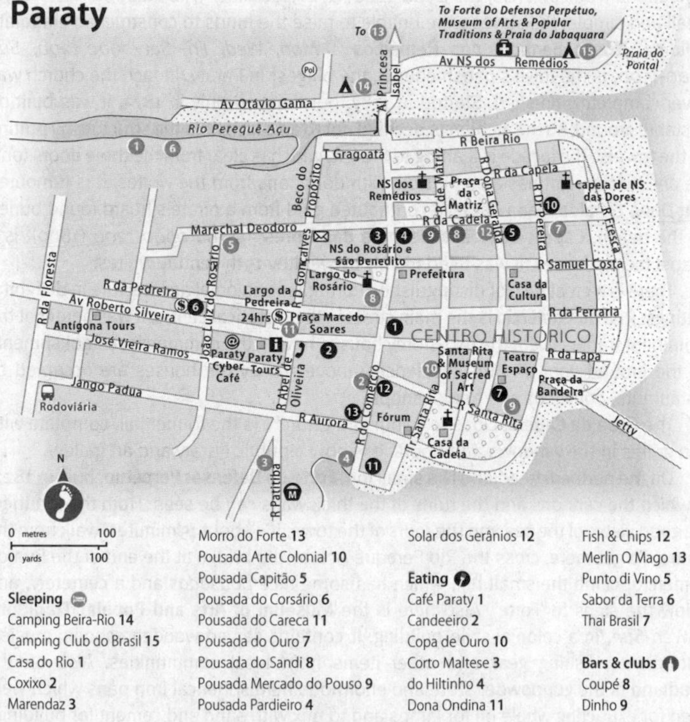

landward side and the ruins of an old gate can be seen close to the football field at the entrance to town. Commerce prospered and farms around the city produced sugar and fine brands of *cachaça* (the name Paraty is still synonymous with *cachaça*). When a road was built to Rio de Janeiro from the mining regions at the beginning of the 18th century, shortening the journey by some 15 days, Paraty's importance declined.

It recovered in the 19th century as a coffee-exporting port for the *fazendas* of the valley of the Paraíba do Sul. At the same time, through its wharf came imported European luxuries which furnished the barons' houses. It is hard to imagine that slaves carried French furniture, pianos and fine porcelain over the hills through dense forest.

In the second half of the 19th century, the opening of the railway from the Paraíba Valley to Rio led to Paraty being effectively isolated again. The port became redundant and almost all its inhabitants left; those that remained grew bananas, but the old sugar plantations were mostly abandoned. Because so few people stayed in the town, there was no urge to modernize. In this way, Paraty has become an open-air museum.

Only in the 1950s was the town 'rediscovered' as a tourism and cultural centre. It was declared a national historic monument in 1966. Whereas in colonial times Paraty was dependent for its livelihood on the roads across the mountains, in the late 20th century the Rio-Santos road brought a new prosperity.

Sights

In keeping with all Brazilian colonial towns, Paraty's churches were built according to social status and race. There are four churches in the town, one for the 'freed coloured men', one for the blacks and two for the whites. **Santa Rita** (1722), built by the 'freed coloured men' in elegant Brazilian Baroque, faces the bay and the port. It is probably the most famous 'picture postcard' image of Paraty. It houses a small **Museum of Sacred Art** ⓘ *Wed-Sun 0900-1200, 1300-1800, US$1*. **Nossa Senhora do Rosário e São Benedito** ⓘ *R do Comércio, Tue 0900-1200*, (1725, rebuilt 1757) built by black slaves, is small and simple; the slaves were unable to raise the funds to construct an elaborate building. **Nossa Senhora dos Remédios** ⓘ *Mon, Wed, Fri, Sat 0900-1200, Sun 0900-1500*, is the town's parish church, the biggest in Paraty. In fact, the church was never completely finished. Started in 1787, but finished only in 1873, it was built on unstable ground, so the architects decided not to add weight to the structure by putting up the towers. The façade is leaning to the left, which is clear from the three doors (only the one on the right has a step). Built with donations from the whites, it is rumoured that Dona Geralda Maria da Silva contributed gold from a pirate's hoard found buried on the beach. **Capela de Nossa Senhora das Dores** ⓘ *Thu 0900-1200* (1800), is a chapel facing the sea. It was used mainly by wealthy 19th century whites.

There is a great deal of distinguished Portuguese colonial architecture in delightful settings. **Rua do Comércio** is the main street in the historical centre. It was here that the prominent traders lived, the two-storey houses having the commercial establishments on the ground floor and the residences above. Today the houses are occupied by restaurants, *pousadas* and tourist shops.

The **Casa da Cadeia**, close to Santa Rita Church, is the former jail, complete with iron grilles in the windows and doors. It is now a public library and art gallery.

On the northern headland is a small fort, **Forte do Defensor Perpétuo**, built in 1822, of which the cannons and the ruins of the thick walls can be seen. From the fort there are good views of the sea and the roofs of the town. It's about 15 minutes' walk from the centre. To get there, cross the Rio Perequê Açu by the bridge at the end of the Rua do Comércio; climb the small hill, which has some nice *pousadas* and a cemetery, and follow the signs to 'Forte'. Also here is the **Museum of Arts and Popular Traditions** ⓘ *Wed-Sun*, in a colonial-style building. It contains carved wooden canoes, musical instruments, fishing gear and other items from local communities. Also on the headland is the gunpowder store and enormous hemispherical iron pans which were used for extracting whale oil for lamps and to mix with sand and cement for building.

Excursions from Paraty

The most popular trip, and highly recommended, is a five-hour **schooner tour** around the bay with three stops at beaches for swimming and lunch on board, US$10, lunch (optional) extra. Smaller boats available for US$10 for an hour or US$20 for three hours.

Praia do Pontal is the town beach, five minutes' walk from the historic centre – cross the bridge and turn right along the river. The water and sand is not very clean but its handful of *barracas* under the trees are a nice place to hang out. **Praia do Jabaquara** is about 20 minutes away on foot – cross the bridge and continue straight up the hill. There are a few *barracas* here and the sand is cleaner, but the water tends to be muddy.

There are other beaches further from town, many of which make worthwhile excursions. Scruffy **Boa Vista** is just south of town and, further south still (reachable only by boat), are in order: the long, broad and clean stretches of **Praia da Conçeicao**, **Praia Vermelha** and **Praia da Lula**, all of which have simple restaurants and are backed by forest and washed by gentle waves. The **Saco da Velha**, further south still is small and intimate, protected by an island and surrounded by rainforested slopes.

The small town of **Paraty Mirím**, is 17 km away and has a vast sweeping beach with a Manueline church sitting on the sand and some ruined colonial buildings. It is reached by boat or four buses a day (three on Sunday) and has simple restaurants and spots to camp. Fishing boats leave from here for other islands and beaches including the **Praia do Pouso da Cajaíba**, which has lodgings of the same name and the spectacular sweep at **Martim do Sá**. The **Saco do Mamanguá** Is a long sleeve of water which separates the Ponta da Juatinga and Paraty Mirím, which has good snorkelling.

The partly cobbled **Gold Trail** through the mountains was built by slaves in the 18th century to bring gold down from Ouro Preto before transporting it to Portugal. Recently restored, it can be visited, along with the ruins of a toll house, on foot or horse on a day trip. Tours leave from **Teatro Espaço** ⓘ *R Dona Geralda 327, T33711575,* at 1000.

There are several waterfalls (*cachoeiras*) in the area, such as the **Cachoeira da Penha**, near the church of the same name. It is 10 km from town on the road to Cunha; take a local bus from the rodoviária, US$1, there are good mountain views on the way. The tourist office and travel agencies have details on trips to waterfalls and other hikes.

Fazenda Murycana ⓘ *T33713930 for information and organized tours*, an old sugar estate and 17th-century *cachaça* distillery with original house and water-wheel, is a recommended excursion. You can taste and buy the different types of *cachaça*; some are aged in oak barrels for 12 years (try the *cachaça com cravo e canela*, with clove and cinnamon). There is an excellent restaurant and horse riding is available but English is not spoken by the employees. Mosquitoes can be a problem at the *fazenda*, take repellent and don't wear shorts. Take a Penha/Ponte Branca bus from the rodoviária, four a day; alight where it crosses a small white bridge and then walk 10 minutes along a signed, unpaved road. Returning to Paraty, there is a good chance of hitching a lift.

Trindade

Ramshackle little Trindade may not be as beautiful in its own right as Paraty but its setting, sandwiched between rainforested slopes and emerald sea, is equally spectacular. And unlike Paraty it has a long, broad beach. The town has long been a favourite hang out for young middle-class surf hippies from São Paulo and Rio, who still come here in droves over Christmas and New Year. Now it is gradually finding its place on the international backpacker circuit. It is easy to see why. The beach is spectacular, the *pousadas* and restaurants cheap and cheerful, and there are a number of campsites. Sadly there is no sewage treatment and when the town is full foul black water flows from the town onto the sand. There are plenty of fairly unprepossessing restaurants along the town's main drag, **Avenida Principal**. All serve the usual 'and beans and rice and chips combinations'. Avoid coming here during Brazilian holidays (Christmas, New Year, Carnival and Easter).

 There are even more beautiful beaches outside of town – beyond the upmarket condo at Laranjeiras. The most famous is **Praia do Sono**; one of the most impressive stretches of sand in the country. To get there take a bus to Laranjeiras and walk east along the trail for one or two hours. There are restaurant *barracas* here and a campsite.

Trindade is 30 km south of Paraty. It is reached by a steep, winding 7-km road lying off the Rio-Santos road (Br 101). It has no banks. **Tourist information** ⓘ *www.paraty.com.br*, is available at the booth at the entrance to town (no English) or through the Paraty website and tourist office. There are plenty of simple restaurants.

Sleeping

Angra dos Reis and around *p165, phone code 024*

Only stay in Angra town if you miss your bus or boat. There are a few cheap hotels near the port and main praça.

L do Frade, on the road to Ubatuba, Km 123 BR-101, 33 km from Angra, T33692244. Luxury hotel on the Praia do Frade with restaurants, bar, sauna, sports facilities on land and sea.

AL Pestana, Estr. Do Contorno 3700, Km 13, T33672754, www.pestanahotels.com.br. A range of bungalows on a forested hillside overlooking an emerald green sea. Very pretty, peaceful and secluded with a decent open-sided restaurant and bar overlooking the water and excellent service.

B Caribe, R de Conceição 255, T33650033. Central, well kept and a good option if you miss your bus or boat. Recommended.

Ilha Grande *p165, phone code 021*

Abraão

There are many *pousadas* in Abraão and reservations are only necessary in peak season or on holiday weekends.

B Ancoradouro, R da Praia 121, T33615153, www.ancoradouro.ilhagrande.com. Clean, simple rooms with en suítes in a beachfront building. 10 mins' walk east of the jetty.

B-C Farol dos Borbas, Praia do Abraão, T33615260, www.ilhagrandetour.com.br. A minute from the jetty. Simple, well-maintained, fan-cooled rooms with tiled floors and breakfast tables and chairs. The best have balconies. The worst have no windows. Boat trips organized.

C Porto Girassol, R do Praia 65, T3361527, portogirasol@ilhagrande.com. Simple rooms in a mock-colonial beach house 5 mins east of the jetty.

C-E Pousada Cachoeira, T33615083, www.cachoeira.com. Price per person. Great little *pousada* full of character; with little rooms in chalets in a forest garden. Run by German-Brazilian couple; English spoken. Good breakfasts. Map on website.

D Colibri, R da Assembléia 70, T33615033, www.colibriresort.com. Smart little Swedish-owned resort with rooms decorated with a personal touch and an outdoor breakfast area. Tours around the island offered. Map and directions on the confusing website.

D Estalagem Costa Verde, R Amâncio Felicio de Souza 239a, ½ a block behind the church, T31047490, www.estalagemcostaverde.com.br. Bright hostel with light, well-maintained rooms decorated with a little thought. Great value. Map on website.

F Albergue Holdandes, R Assembleia de Deus, T33615034. Price per person. 4 little chalets and rooms lost in the forest. Great atmosphere. Be sure to reserve.

Camping

Emilia Ecocamping, R Amâncio F de Souza 18, T33615094, www.ecocamping.com.br. Hot showers, lockers, fridges, communal living area (with table tennis) a campsite with lots of shade and cabins (**E** per person) for those who don't want to camp.

Outside Abraão

LL-L Sitio do Lobo, T22274138, www.sitiodolobo.com.br. An architect-commissioned house converted into a small boutique hotel and sitting on an isolated peninsula with its own little dock. The views are marvellous: emerald sea, rainforest, mountains in the distance, fiery red sunsets. The best rooms are the suites; the others which overlook the pool are boxy. Access to the rest of the island is only by boat. Restaurant serves the best food on the island.

AL-A Sankay, Enseada do Bananal (1 hr by boat from Angra or Abraão), T33651090, www.pousadasankay.com.br. Another beautiful little *pousada* perched on a peninsula with wonderful views. Simple rooms with brick or stone walls. The best is the Cavalo Marinho (seahorse) suite. Sauna and bar. Dinner included. Used for much of the year by **Body and Soul Adventures** (see p66).

Paraty *p166, map p167, phone code 024*
There are many options in Paraty and 2 beautiful places in the hills nearby. Browse through www.paraty.com.br/frame.htm, for still more options.

AL Pousada do Ouro, R Dr Pereira (or da Praia) 145, T/F3712221, www.pousadaouro.com.br. Near Parati's eastern waterfront and built as a private home from a fortune made on the gold route. Plain rooms in an annex and suites in the main building. The grounds house an open-air poolside pavilion, in a tropical garden. Icons of previous guests like Mick Jagger, Tom Cruise and Linda Evangelista, adorn the lobby.

AL Pousada do Sandi, Largo do Rosário 1, T33712100, www.pousadadosandi.com.br. An 18th-century building with a grand lobby, comfortable mock-colonial rooms and an adjoining restaurant and pool area.

AL Pousada Pardieiro, R do Comércio 74, T33711370, www.pousadapardieiro.com.br. Tucked away in a quiet corner, with a calm, sophisticated atmosphere. Attractive colonial building with lovely gardens, delightful rooms facing internal patios and a little swimming pool. Always full at weekends. Does not take children under 15.

AL-A Bromelias Pousada and Spa, Rodovia Rio Santos, Km 562, Graúna T/F33712791, www.pousadabromelias.com.br. An Asian-inspired spa *pousada* with its own aromatherapy products and a range of massage treatments. Accommodation is in tastefully decorated chalets perched on a hillside forest garden overlooking the sea and islands. Pool, sauna and restaurant.

A-B Hotel Coxixo, R do Comércio 362, T33711460, www.hotelcoxixo.com.br. A converted colonial building in the heart of the 17-century town, which has been turned into a temple to its Brazilian movie-star owner, Maria Della Costa. Black and white pictures of her from the 1950s adorn every corner. Rooms are decked out in Catholic kitsch. The best rooms in the hotel and in Paraty are the plush colonial suites.

A-B Le Gite d'Indaitiba, Rodovia Rio-Santos (BR-101) Km 562, Graúna, T33717174, www.legitedindaiatiba.com.br. French-owned *pousada* with chalets with carefully designed stylish chalets set in gardens on a hillside. Sweeping views of the sea and bay of islands. French food to match the location.

A-B Morro do Forte, R Orlando Carpinelli, T/F3711211, www.pousadamorrodoforte.com.br. Lovely garden, good breakfast, pool, German owner Peter Kallert offers trips on his yacht. Out of the centre. Recommended.

B Pousada Capitão, R Luiz do Rosário 18, T33711815, www.paraty.com.br/capitao. Converted colonial building, close to the historical centre, swimming pool, English and Japanese spoken.

B Pousada do Corsário, Beco do Lapeiro 26, T33711866, www.pousadadocorsario.com.br. New building with a pool and its own gardens; next to the river and 2 blocks from the centre. Simple, stylish rooms, most with hammocks outside. Highly recommended.

B Pousada Mercado do Pouso, Largo de Santa Rita 43, T/F33711114, www.paraty.com.br/mercadodepouso. Historic building close to waterfront decked out in lush wood, good sea views. Family atmosphere, no pool.

B-C Pousada Arte Colonial, R da Matriz 292, T33717231, www.paraty.com.br/artecolonial. One of the best deals in Paraty – colonial building in the centre decorated with style and a genuine personal touch; artefacts and antiques from all over the world by its French owner. Friendly, helpful, beautiful and with breakfast. Highly recommended.

C-D Solar dos Gerânios, Praça da Matriz, T/F33711550, www.paraty.com.br/geranio. Beautiful colonial family house on main square in traditional rustic style that is a welcome antidote to the more polished *pousadas*. Rooms have lovely wooden lattice balconies – ask for the corner one which has two. Very reasonably priced, English spoken. Warmly recommended.

D Marendaz, R Patitiba 9, T33711369. Family run, simple, charming, near historical centre.

D-E Casa do Rio, R Antônio Vidal 120, T33712223, www.paraty.com.br/casadorio. Youth hostel in a little house with riverside courtyard and hammocks. There's a kitchen and price includes breakfast. Offers jeep and horse riding trips to waterfalls, mountains and beaches. Dorms a little crowded.

D-E **Pousada do Careca**, Praça Macedo Soares, T33711291. Simple rooms. Those without street windows are musty.

Camping

Camping Beira-Rio, just across the bridge, before the road to the fort.
Camping Club do Brasil, Av Orlando Carpinelli, Praia do Pontal, T33711877. Small, good, very crowded in Jan and Feb, US$8 per person.
Praia Jabaquara, T33712180.

Trindade *p169, phone code 024*

Expect no frills in Trindade.
D-F **Ponta da Trindade Pousada and Camping**, T33715113. Simple fan-cooled rooms and a sand-floored campsite with cold water showers and no power.
D **Chalé e Pousada Magia do Mar**, T33715130. Thatched-roofed hut with space for four. Views out over beach.
D **Pousada Marimbá**, R Principal, T33715147. Simple colourful rooms and a breakfast area.

Eating

Ilha Grande *p165, phone code 024*

Aside from **Sito do Lobo** (guests only, see Sleeping, above), food on the island is fairly basic – fish, chicken or meat with beans, rice and chips. There are plenty of restaurants serving these exciting combinations in Abraão. We list the very few better options.
TTT **Lua e Mar**, Abraão, on the waterfront, T33615113. A few more adventurous fish-based options than the other restaurants.
TT **Fogão de Lenha**, R Projetada A, Abraão, T33615097. Wood-fired pizzas and *caipirinhas*.

Paraty *p166, map p167, phone code 024*

The best restaurants in Paraty are in the historic part of town and are almost as good as any you will find in Rio or São Paulo. Watch out for surreptitious cover charges for live music which are often very discreetly displayed. If you are looking for budget options look outside the city centre.

Paraty's regional specialities include *peixe à Parati* – local fish cooked with herbs, green bananas and served with *pirão*, a mixture of manioc flour and the sauce that the fish was cooked in. Also popular is the *filé de peixe ao molho de camarão* – fried fish fillet with a shrimp and tomato sauce. There is plenty of choice in Paraty and browsing is a good option. Also see **Le Gite d'Indaitiba**, p171.
TTT **Copa de Ouro**, (next to the Ouro), R Dr Pereira 145, historical centre, T33711311. Very good seafood and Brazilian dishes and a reasonable wine list. Recommended.
TTT **do Hiltinho**, R Mcal Deodoro 233, historical centre, T3711432. Decent seafood, including local dishes.
TTT **Merlin O Mago**, (next to Coxixo), R do Comercio 376, historical centre, T33712157, www.paraty.com.br/merlin.htm. Franco-Brazilian cooking in an intimate dining room/bar, by a German cordon bleu-trained chef and illustrious photojournalist. Decent wine list. Highly recommended.
TT **Café Paraty**, R da Lapa and Comércio, historical centre. Sandwiches, appetizers, light meals, also bar with live music nightly (cover charge). A local landmark. Open 0900-2400.
TT **Corto Maltese**, R do Comércio 130. Italian.
TT **Dona Ondina**, R do Comércio 2, by the river, historical centre. Family restaurant with well-prepared simple food (closed on Mon Mar and Nov). Good value.
TT **Punto Di Vino**, R Mcal Deodoro 129, historical centre, T33711348. Wood-fired pizza and *calzoni* served with live music and a good selection of wine.
TT **Thai Brasil**, R Dona Geralda 345, historical centre, T33710127, www.thaibrasil.com.br. Beautiful restaurant ornamented with handicrafts and furnished with handpainted chairs and tables. The cooking loosely resembles Thai without spices (Brazilians yelp in pain at the sight of a chilli).
T The less expensive restaurants, those offering *comida a quilo* (pay by weight) and the fast food outlets are outside the historical centre, mainly on Av Roberto Silveira.
T **Fish and Chips**, R do Comercio 95, T33712747. A British chippie owned by an expat from Tunbridge Wells. Good…er fish and chips. And some veggie options.
T **Sabor da Terra**, Av Roberto Silveira, next to Banco do Brasil. Reliable, if not bargain-priced self-service food. Closes 2200.
T **Kontiki**, Ilha Duas Irmãs, T9999599, www.paraty.com.br/kontiki.htm, a tiny island 5 mins from the pier where a small speed boat runs a (free) shuttle service. Wonderful island setting. Ordinary food. 1000-1500 daily and Fri and Sat for dinner (reservations recommended) boat taxi from Paraty.

Bars and clubs

Paraty *p166, map p167, phone code 024*
The best way to sample Paraty's nightlife is wander its handful of streets.
Bar Coupé, Matriz Square. A popular hang-out with outside seating. Good bar snacks and breakfast.
Bar Dinho, Praça da Matriz at R da Matriz. Good bar with live music at weekends, sometimes mid-week.
Umoya, R Comendador José Luiz. Video bar and café, live music at weekends.

Entertainment

Paraty *p166, map p166, phone code 024*
Theatre Teatro Espaço, The Puppet Show, R Dona Geralda 327, T33711575, ecparati@ax.apc.org. Wed, Sat 2100, US$12. This world-famous puppet show should not be missed. The puppets tell stories, without words, which are funny, sad, even shocking, with incredible realism. The series of short pieces (lasting 1 hr) are works of pure imagination and emotion and a moving commentary on the human condition.

Festivals and events

Angra dos Reis and around *p165, phone code 024*
New Year Festa do Mar, with boat processions.
5 Jan Folia dos Reis, the Three Kings, culmination of a religious festival that begins at Christmas.
6 Jan Founding of Angra dos Reis.
May Festa do Divino and, on the 2nd Sun, the **Senhor do Bonfim** maritime procession.
Jun As elsewhere in the state, the Festas Juninas are celebrated.
8 Dec Festival of Nossa Senhora da Conceição.

Paraty *p166, map p167, phone code 024*
Feb/Mar **Carnival**, hundreds of people cover their bodies in black mud and run through the streets yelling like prehistoric creatures (anyone can join in).
Mar/Apr Semana Santa (Easter Week) with religious processions and folk songs.
Mid-Jul Semana de Santa Rita, traditional foods, shows, exhibitions and dances.
Aug **Festival da Pinga**, the *cachaça* fair at which local distilleries display their products and there are plenty of opportunities to over-indulge.
Sep (around the 8th) **Semana da Nossa Senhora dos Remédios**, processions and religious events.
Sep/Oct **Spring Festival of Music**, concerts in front of Santa Rita Church.
31 Dec **New Year's**, a huge party with open-air concerts and fireworks (reserve accommodation in advance).

As well as the **Dança dos Velhos** (see Music and dance, 698), another common dance in these parts is the *ciranda*, in which everyone, young and old, dances in a circle to songs accompanied by guitars.

Shopping

Paraty *p166, map p167, phone code 024*
Shopping here is by and large a disappointment. There are many shops but most sell the kind of tack you'd expect to find in any tourist town anywhere in the world; key rings, fridge magnets, cheesy T-shirts and so on... The best items are fine art (which tends to be overpriced), and artisan ware – fish trays, small, wooden canoes and boats and similar. The Guarani people sell their arts and crafts on the R da Matriz. Paraty *cachaça* is some of the best in the state; although it can't compare with bottles from Minas.

Activities and tours

Angra dos Reis and around *p165, phone code 024*
Diving **Aquamaster**, Praia da Enseada, T33652416, take 'Retiro' bus from the port in Angra. US$60 for 2 dives with drinks and food.

Ilha Grande *p165, phone code 021*
Boat trips US$10 without food or drinks, includes fruit. Recommended boats: *Victória Régia* (contact Carlos at **Pousada Tropicana**), *Papyk* or *André Maru* (owned by André).
Scuba diving There is some good diving around the coast; instructor Alexandre at Bougainville shop No 5.

Tour operators

Antígona, Praça da Bandeira 2, Centro Histórico, T/F33711165. Daily schooner tours, 5 hrs, bar and lunch on board. Recommended. **Fausto Goyos**, T99145506, offers off-road tours in an ex-US military jeep to rainforest, waterfalls, historical sites, also photo safaris, He has horse riding tours and offers youth-hostel style rooms for US$5, or US$7.50 with 2 meals. **Paraty Tours**, Av Roberto Silveira 11, T/F3711327. English and Spanish spoken. **Soberana da Costa**, R Dona Geraldo 43, in Pousada Mercado do Pouso, T/F33711114, others offer schooner trips in the bay. Recommended.

Transport

Angra dos Reis and around *p165, phone code 024*

Bus At least hourly from **Rio**'s rodoviária with Costa Verde, several direct, T22901484, accepts credit cards, new comfortable buses, several go through Copacabana, Ipanema and Barra then take the 'via litoral', sit on the left, US$5.75, 2½ hrs (you can flag the bus down in Flamengo, Copacabana, Ipanema, Barra de Tijuca, but it may well be full at weekends).

Ferry Ferries to **Ilha Grande** 1½ hrs, US$6.75, daily at 1530, return 1000. For day trips, go from **Mangaratiba**, see p165. Fishing boats take passengers from Angra for US$5.

Ilha Grande *p165, phone code 021*

Bicycles Can be hired and tours arranged; ask at *pousadas*.

Ferry For boats to Ilha Grande, see above under Angra dos Reis, above. There are 5 ferries called *Isabel*, check which is going to the mainland destination you want.

Paraty *p166, map p167, phone code 024*

Bus On holidays and in high season, the frequency of bus services usually increases. Paraty has a new rodoviária at the corner of R Jango Padua and R da Floresta. 9 buses a day go to **Rio** (241 km, 3¾ hrs, US$8.10, Costa Verde – see under Angra dos Reis for details – only the 0630 from Rio and the 1730 from Paraty go through Barra da Tijuca); to **Angra dos Reis** (98 km, 1½ hrs, every 1 hr 40 mins, US$4); 3 a day to **Ubatuba** (75 km, just over 1 hr, São José company, US$4), **Taubaté** (170 km) and **Guaratinguetá** (210 km); 2 a day to **São Paulo**, 1100 and 2335 (304 km via São José dos Campos, 5½ hrs, US$8.50 (**Reunidas** book up quickly and are very busy at weekends), and **São Sebastião**.

Taxi Set rate of US$4 for historic centre.

Trindade *p169*

Paraty-Ubatuba bound buses all pass the turn off to Trindade and will drop you here. Ask for 'Patrimonio' or 'Estrada para Trindade' (pronounced *Tringdajee*). In high season there are vans from here to Trindade (US$2). In low season you'll have to hitch or walk. Frequent cars pass and hitching here is normal. Trindade is the last stop on the South American Experience jump-on-jump- off backpacker bus tour (see p130).

Directory

Angra dos Reis and around *p165, phone code 024*

Banks There are several banks in town, with ATMs and money-changing facilities. These include Banco 24 Horas, R do Comércio 250 and Bradesco, R do Comércio 196.

Ilha Grande *p165, phone code 021*

Banks Only open at weekends.

Paraty *p166, map p167, phone code 024*

Banks Banco do Brasil, Av Roberto Silveira, just outside historic centre. ATM. Exchange 1100-1430, ask for the manager. **Internet** Internet connections are plentiful, but neither fast nor cheap. Paraty Cyber Café, Av Roberto Silveira 17. Friendly, 0900-2300, coffee and snacks served. US$3, 30 mins.

Laundry Paraty Wash Shopping Martins, Loja 15, opposite bus station. **Medical services** Hospital Municipal São Pedro de Alcântara (Santa Casa), Av Dom Pedro de Alcântara, T33711623. **Post office** R da Cadeia and Beco do Propósito, Mon-Sat 0800-1700, Sun 0800-1200. **Telephone** International calls, Praça Macedo Soares, opposite the tourist office. Local and long-distance calls can be made from public phones; buy phone cards from newspaper stands in the centre.

São Paulo

Footprint features

Introduction

São Paulo is as famous for its ugliness as Rio is for its beauty. But whilst Rio looks marvellous from a distance and less than perfect close to; São Paulo is the opposite. Restaurants, shops, hotels, nightlife and general services here are infinitely better than in Rio. And in neighbourhoods like Jardins it is even possible to forget that few cities in the world have quite so much relentless concrete punctuated with quite so few green spaces or rivers as disgraceful as the Tietê. Marlene Dietrich perhaps summed it up when she said – "Rio is a beauty – but São Paulo; ah... São Paulo is a city."

São Paulo is more than a city, it is also a state a little larger than the UK; and whilst most of its interior is dull agricultural hinterland its coast is magnificent; just as beautiful as Rio de Janeiro's but far less visited by international tourists. The northern beaches are long and glorious and pounded by some of South America's finest surf. Brazil's largest island, which is every bit as pristine and romantic as Ilha Grande, lies a short boat ride off shore. Beaches further south are less beautiful but far wilder and behind them and stretching into the neighbouring state of Paraná are the largest expanses of primary forest on Brazil's Atlantic coast.

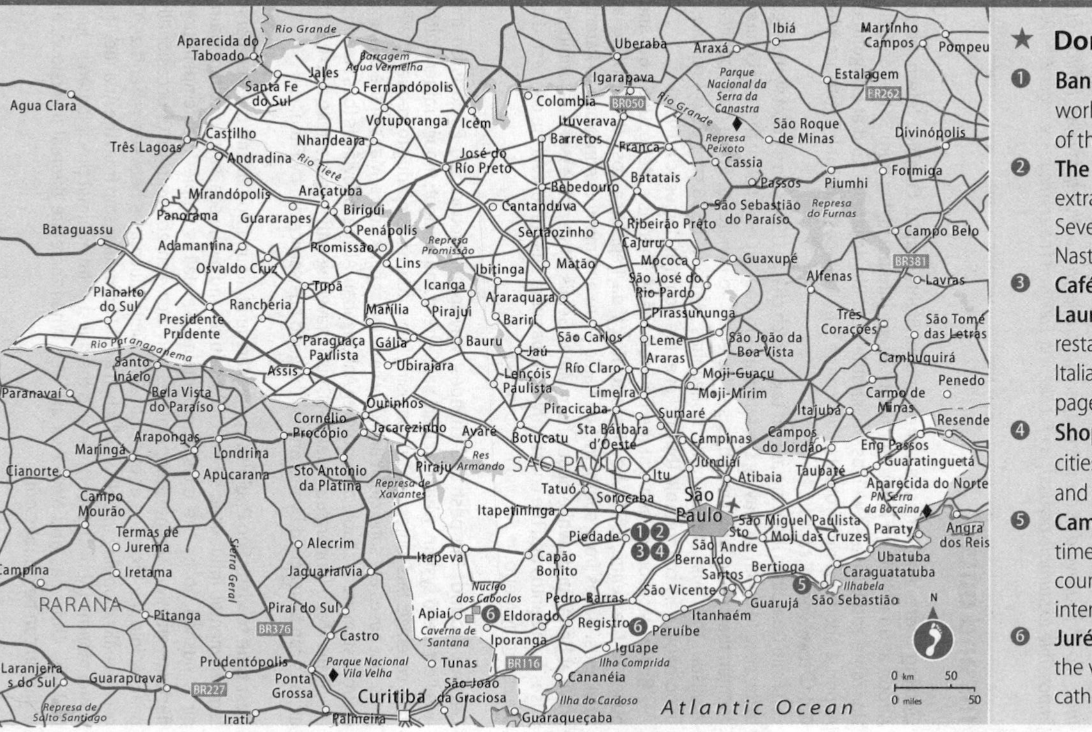

★ Don't miss...

❶ **Banespa Tower** Take in the view of the world's second largest city from the top of the tower, page 183.

❷ **The Unique** Marvel at the luxury of this extraordinary hotel, voted as one of new Seven Wonders of the World by Conde Nast Traveller Magazine, page 191.

❸ **Café Antique, Fasano, Sakamoto or Laurent** Enjoy a meal in one of the best restaurants in the Americas - for French, Italian, Japanese or exciting fusion cusine, page 192.

❹ **Shopping** Stock up at one of the best cities anywhere for quality clothes, shoes and designer goods, page 196.

❺ **Camburi, Maresias & Ilhabela** Spend time on some of the best beaches in the country and the least visited by international tourists, pages 210 and 211.

❻ **Juréia and the Vale do Ribeiro** Explore the virgin forests, deserted beaches and cathedral-sized caves, pages 217 and 218.

São Paulo City

➔ *Phone code: 011. Colour map 5, A5. Altitude: 850 m. Population: 18-20 million.*

São Paulo is vast and can feel Intimidating on first arrival. But this is a city of separate neighbourhoods, only a few of which are interesting for visitors and once you have your base it is easy to negotiate. São Paulo is the intellectual capital of Brazil. Those who don't flinch at the city's size and leave, who are instead prepared to spend time (and money) here, and who get to know Paulistanos are seldom disappointed and often end up preferring the city to Rio. Nowhere in Brazil is better for concerts, clubs, theatre, ballet, classical music, all-round nightlife, restaurants and beautifully designed hotels. And you will not be seen as a gringo *in São Paulo. The city is safer than Rio if you avoid the centre after dark and the outlying* favelas *(which are impossible to stumble across).* ▸▸ *For Sleeping, Eating and other listings, see pages 219-226.*

Ins and outs

Getting there Air Almost all international flights stop at Cumbica International Airport at Guarulhos 30 km from the city. Some internal flights from Salvador, Belo Horizonte and Vitória as well as the shuttle from Rio de Janeiro land at Congonhas Airport a short taxi ride from the city centre. The cheapest internal flights are with **Gol** ⓘ *www.voegol.com.br.*

From Guarulhos there are airport taxis which charge US$25 on a ticket system (go to the second booth on leaving the terminal and book a Co-op taxi at the Taxi Comum counter, the best value). **Emtu** bus service every 30 minutes to Praça da República, Paulista, the bus station and Congonhas Airport, US$6.50, 30-45 minutes, 0500-0200, very comfortable (buy ticket at the booth in domestic arrivals).

Buses Most buses arrive at the Tietê rodoviária. There is a Metrô, US$0.60, and buses to the centre, US$0.80. Taxis to Praça da República cost US$5, US$9 at weekends. Buses from southern São Paulo state and many destinations in Paraná arrive at **Barra Funda** while buses from Minas Gerais arrive at **Bresser** bus terminals. Buses from Santos and the coast arrive at **Jabaquara** bus station. All are connected to the centre by Metrô. ▸▸ *See also Transport, page 200.*

Getting around The best and cheapest way to get around São Paulo is on the excellent Metrô system, which is clean, safe, cheap and efficient; though rather limited in its coverage. Bus routes can be confusing for visitors and slow due to frequent traffic jams. But buses are safe, clean and only crowded at peak hours. Maps of the bus and Metrô system are available at depots, eg Anhangabaú. All the rodoviárias (bus stations) are on the Metrô (underground railway), but if travelling with luggage, take a taxi. Both airports can be reached by taxi and by the good bus service run by Emtu.

Best time to visit São Paulo sits on a plateau at around 800 m and the weather is temperamental, influenced by the city's altitude and by the sea, whose cold or warm air is pushed up by the coastal mountains. Rainfall is ample and temperatures fluctuate greatly. Summer temperatures vary between 20° and 30°C, occasionally peaking into the high 30s or even 40s. The winter fluctuates between 15° and 25°C, occasionally dropping to below 10° when a cold front comes up from the Atlantic. The winter months (April-October) are also the driest, with minimal precipitation in June and July. Christmas and New Year are wet. When there are thermal inversions, air pollution can be troublesome.

24 hours in São Paulo

Start the day with a stroll along the 3-km **Avenida Paulista**, a cross between Oxford Street and Wall Street and home to designer boutiques and multinationals. It was once lined with the huge colonial mansions of the coffee barons. Few of these homes survive and some have been turned into offices; one has become perhaps the most beautiful McDonald's in the world.

On this avenue, don't miss **Museu de Arte de São Paulo** and you might want to take a look at **Shopping Ibirapuera**, one of the city's oldest and biggest shopping centres. For lunch, look for the **Praça da Alimentação**, found in most shopping centres, serving fast, good food.

At the very heart of the city, **Praça da Sé** is a lively place. Here, the **Catedral Metropolitana** is an oasis in the mayhem. Visit the **Pátio Colégio**, a little to the north, in the old downtown part of São Paulo. This is where the Jesuits founded the original settlement, although what you see today is only a reconstruction.

São Paulo is famous for its international cuisine, so spend the evening enjoying some of the gastronomic delights in the bohemian area of **Bixiga**, famous for its Italian restaurants and many bars, some with live music. The city has the best nightlife in Brazil; pick up a copy of *Veja* for weekly listings. São Paulo pretty much never sleeps so you could easily keep going until the early hours of the next day.

Tourist information There are tourist information booths with English-speaking staff in international and domestic arrivals (ground floor) at Guarulhos Airport (Cumbica); and tourist information booths in the bus station and in the following locations throughout the city: **Praça da República** ⓘ *T2312922, daily 0900-1800*, very helpful; **Praça Dom José Gaspar** ⓘ *on the corner of Av São Luís, T2573422, Mon-Fri 0900-1800*; Av Paulista **at Parque Trianon** ⓘ *T2510970, Sun-Fri 0900-1800*; and on **Av Brig Faria Lima** ⓘ *opposite the Iguatemi Shopping Center, T2111277, Mon-Fri 0900-1800*. An excellent map is available free at all these offices. Tourist offices have free maps and pamphlets in English and Portuguese. **Editora Abril** also publish maps, an excellent *Guide to São Paulo – Sampa* (in Portuguese) – and a guide to cheap travel – *Viajar Bem e Barato*. Both are available at newsstands and bookshops all over the city and are in their *Quatro Rodas* series. For online info see www.guiasp.com.br and www.gringoes.com.br. **Tourist Police Deatur** ⓘ *R São Bento 398, T31075642, Centro*; **Aeroporto de Cumbica** ⓘ *T64453045*.

Orientation

The **Old Centre** (Praça da República, Sé, Santa Cecilia) is a place to visit but not to stay. There are a number of sights here – the vast, cavernous Catedral Metropolitana, the ornate Basilica and Mosteiro do São Bento, the Baroque municipal theatre, the city's best museum, the Pinacoteca. The Banespa tower has spectacular views and is the best place to go to see the extent of the city, which stretches all round as far as the eye can see. The central commercial district, containing banks, offices and shops, is known as the Triângulo, bounded by Ruas Direita, 15 (Quinze) de Novembro, São Bento and Praça Antônio Prado, but it is rapidly spreading towards the Praça da República. A large part of the Triângulo and the area between it and Praça da República is mostly closed to cars. There are plenty of budget hotels near here but with the exception of one or two hostels, they are generally seedy and not used for sleeping; parts of the centre can be unsafe at night.

Jardins, just south of Avenida Paulista and to the west of the Centre, is a good place to stay and to visit; especially if you want to shop well and eat well. This is the city's most affluent inner neighbourhood with elegant little streets hiding hundreds of wonderful restaurants including the city's best. All of Brazil's best clothing designers have shops here and there are plenty of funky little corner cafés and bars to while away the hours. Accommodation ranges from the luxurious to the top end of the budget range. You are safe here at night.

Avenida Paulista, immediately to the southwest of the Centre, is one of São Paulo's grandest modern avenues, and is lined with skyscrapers, shops and a few churches and museums including MASP (Museu de Arte de São Paulo). There are Metrô connections from here and a number of good hotel options in all price categories. **Bela Vista**, which was once the centre of Italian São Paulo is just north of Avenida Paulista as is **Liberdade**, which was once the centre of Japanese culture in the city but is now also home to large numbers of Koreans and Chinese. The Praça da

São Paulo orientation

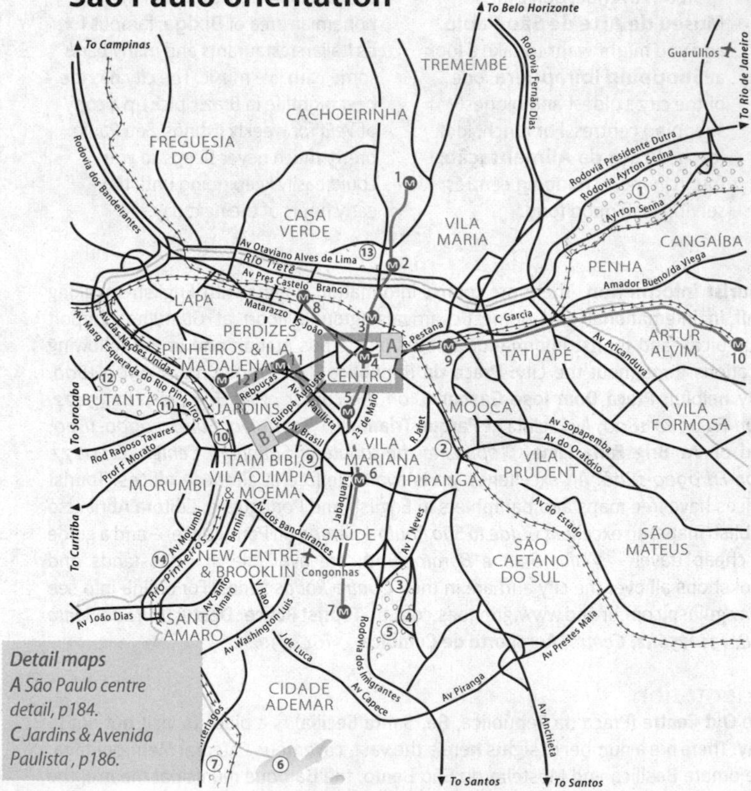

Detail maps
A São Paulo centre detail, p184.
C Jardins & Avenida Paulista , p186.

Open spaces
Parque Ecológico do Tietê 1
Parque da Independência 2
Jardim Botânico 3
Jardim Zoológico & Simba Safári 4
Parque do Estado 5
Represa Billings 6
Autodromo de Interlagos 7
Represa de Guarapiranga 8
Parque do Ibirapuera 9
Jóquei Clube 10
Instituto Butantã 11
Ciudad Universitária 12
Campo de Marte 13
Parque Burle Marx 14

Metro stations
Tucuruvi 1
Tietê 2
Luz 3
Sé 4
Paraíso 5
Vila Mariana 6
Jabaquara 7
Barra Funda 8
Bresser 9
Corinthians-Itaquera 10
Clinicas 11
Vila Madalena 12

Arriving at night

São Paulo's airport has 24-hour facilities (for food, banking and of course taxis) if you arrive late at night or in the early hours of the morning. It is a long drive from the airport to the city and the a/c bus to Praça da República does not operate between 0200 and 0500 and the service to Avenida Paulista does not run from 2315 to 0645.

Liberdade is one of the best places in the city for cheap but good Japanese food. There is an interesting museum of Japanese immigration here.

Ibirapuera Park, some 5 km south of the Centre, is the inner city's largest green space. It is home to a handful of museums, including the modern art museum which exhibits important shows from Picasso to the Terracotta Army, and the Bienal, the largest art fair in South America. There are running tracks, a lake and a sculpture garden as well as frequent free live concerts here on Sundays. The adjoining neighbourhoods of Moema and Vila Mariana have a few hotel options. Moema has good nightlife.

Situated between Ibirapuera and the river, **Italm**, **Moema** and **Vila Olimpia** are, along with Vila Madalena, the nightlife centres of São Paulo with a wealth of streetside bars, ultra-chic designer restaurants and European-style dance clubs. Hotels tend to be expensive as these areas abut on the new business centre on Avenidas Brigadeiro Faria Lima and Luis Carlos Berrini where companies like MIcrosoft and Lloyds are based.

Pinheiros and Vila Madalena, immediately to the west of the Centre, are hippier and more studenty than Itaim and Vila Olimpia but equally lively at night and with the funkiest shops.

History

The history of São Paulo state and São Paulo city were very much one and the same from the arrival of the Europeans until the coffee boom transformed the region's economic and political landscape. According to John Hemming (Red Gold, see page 692), there were approximately 196,000 indigenous inhabitants living in what is now São Paulo state. Today their numbers have been vastly diminished and you will be lucky to see any; but of those few who have survived a number live in villages within the city of São Paulo itself and can be seen selling handicrafts in the centre.

The first official settlement in the state was at São Vicente on the coast, near today's port of Santos. It was founded in 1532 by Martim Afonso de Sousa, who had been sent by King João III to drive the French from Brazilian waters, explore the coast and lay claim to all the lands apportioned to Portugal under the Treaty of Tordesillas.

In 1554 two Jesuit priests from São Vicente founded São Paulo as a colégio, a combined mission and school. The Jesuits chose to settle inland because they wished to distance themselves from the civil authority, which was based in Bahia, but was extending up and down the coast to form a defendable colony. Moreover, on the plateau there was much easier access to Indians to convert to Catholicism. Pioneers seeking to found farms followed in the Jesuits' wake and as the need for workers on these farms grew, expeditions were sent into the interior of the country to capture and enslave the indigenous people. These marauders were known as *bandeirantes* after the flag wielder who ostensibly walked at their head to claim territory. And their ignominious expeditions were responsible for the opening up of the country's interior. An ugly brutalist monument worthy of Soviet Russia and sitting next to Parque Ibirapuera, celebrates the bandeirantes (see also box, page 208).

In a sense, the bandeirantes' success in discovering gold led to a demise of São Paulo in the 18th century. Like everywhere else, the inhabitants rushed to the gold fields in the *sertão*, causing ruin at home and allowing São Paulo to fall under the influence of Rio de Janeiro. The relative backwardness of the region lasted until the second half of the 19th century when coffee spread west from Rio de Janeiro. Landowners became immensely rich. São Paulo changed from a little town into a financial and residential centre. Exports and imports flowed through Santos and the industrial powerhouse of the country was born. As the city boomed, industries and agriculture fanned outwards to the far reaches of the state.

Between 1885 and the end of the century the boom in coffee and the arrival of large numbers of Europeans transformed the state out of all recognition. By the end of the 1930s there had arrived in São Paulo state a million Italians, 500,000 each of Portuguese and immigrants from the rest of Brazil, nearly 400,000 Spaniards and nearly 200,000 Japanese. It is the world's largest Japanese community outside Japan and their main contribution to the economy of São Paulo has been in horticulture, raising poultry and in cotton farming, especially around cities such as Marília. Significant numbers of Syrian-Lebanese came too, adding an extra dimension to the cultural diversity of the city.

Much of the immigrant labour which flooded in during the early years of the 20th century was destined for the coffee *fazendas* and farms. Others went to work in the industries which were opening up in the city. By 1941 there were 14,000 factories and today the city covers more than 1,500 sq km – three times the size of Paris.

Sights

City centre

Since much of the centre is pedestrianized, there is no option other than to walk if you wish to explore it. This may seem a daunting prospect with the streets permanently crowded and the buildings towering above, but it is a challenge worth taking.

A focal point in the centre is the **Parque Anhangabaú**, an open space between the Triângulo and the streets which lead to Praça da República (Metrô Anhangabaú is at its southern end). Beneath Anhangabaú, north-south traffic is carried by a tunnel. Crossing it are two viaducts: **Viaduto do Chá**, which is open to traffic and links Rua Direita and Rua Barão de Itapetininga. Along its length sellers of potions, cures, fortunes and trinkets set up their booths, an incongruous sight in the middle of a district so dedicated to modern commerce. The **Viaduto Santa Ifigênia**, an iron bridge for pedestrians only, was constructed of 1,100 tonnes of Belgian iron in 1913. As a backdrop to the viaduct and its thousands of pedestrians is the massive frontage of the Sharp building.

The **Largo de São Bento** is a square in front of the Capela São Bento, which was built in 1598 on the site of the village of chief Tibiriça. Originally it was a public place where fish and vegetables were sold and where travelling circuses set up.

Facing the Largo is the **Igreja e Mosteiro de São Bento** (1910-1922) on the site of the 16th-century Capela São Bento. In 1635 the building was enlarged and a new church and monastery was built in 1650, financed by the *bandeirante* Fernão Dias Paes Leme. It was demolished in 1907 to make way for the new church and college. On the ceiling of the main nave are religious portraits and carved wooden pillars support the organ, which has 6,000 pipes. When the São Bento Metrô station was built, the church had to be reinforced and the Largo was remodelled; the station itself has an exhibition and concert space.

South of São Bento on the junction of Rua Líbero Badaró and Avenida São João is the **Martinelli building** ⓘ *Mon-Sat 0900-1600, entry to 26th floor, free*, the city's first skyscraper, built in 1929 by Comendador Giuseppe Martinelli, a businessman. Just around the corner is one of the city's 'must sees', the **Banespa Tower** ⓘ *24 Rua João Brícola, T32497180, Mon-Fri 1000-1700, US$1.50*, whose observation deck on the top floor has by far the best views in the city. Come at around 1600 and wait to see the city lights come on as sunset approaches.

On Praça Antônio Prado stands the **Antigo Prédio do Banco do São Paulo** ⓘ *Mon-Fri 0900-1800*. This building, which is two interlinked office blocks, has some art nouveau elements and was constructed in the 1930s. The ground floor is now used for fairs and exhibitions. From Praça Antônio Prado go down Rua 15 de Novembro to Praça Padre Manuel da Nóbrega.

The **Pátio do Colégio**, just east of Praça Padre Manuel da Nóbrega, is the site of the founding of São Paulo. It houses the **Capela de Anchieta** and the **Museu Casa de Anchieta** ⓘ *Mon-Fri 0730-1700, US$0.50*. The original chapel collapsed in 1896; some of this building has been preserved in the new complex. The **Museu Casa de Anchieta** ⓘ *Tue-Sun 1300-1630, US$1*, houses items from the Jesuit era, including paintings and relics. It also has a model of Piratininga/São Paulo in the 16th-century museum.

A short distance southeast of the Pátio do Colégio is the **Solar da Marquesa de Santos**, an 18th-century residential building, which now contains the **Museu da Cidade** ⓘ *R Roberto Simonsen 136, T2304238, Tue-Sun 0900-1700*.

The **Praça da Sé** is a huge open space south of the Pátio do Colégio, dominated by the Catedral Metropolitana. The Praça has been, since colonial times, the heart of São Paulo. Around it were the cathedral and other churches; it was where religious processions started and finished. Over the years its aspect was altered, but most appreciably in 1911 when the whole area was remodelled into a monumental square. Today, with its avenue of palms, it is alive with stalls, music, hawkers, buses, fumes and people constantly on the move. Others sit on the steps or sleep on the grass.

The **Catedral Metropolitana** was inaugurated during the 1954 festivities commemorating the fourth centenary of the city and was fully completed in 1970. This enormous building in neo-Gothic style has a capacity for 8,000 worshippers in its five naves. Its twin towers are 97 m high and the central, octagonal cupola is supported by 12 columns a staggering 30 m high. There are two gilt mosaic pictures in the trancepts: on the north side is the Virgin Mary (1952, by Gigotti) and on the south St Paul (1953, by M Avenali, Ravenna Gruppo Mosaicisti). The marble surround to the steps which lead up to the main altar is carved with biblical scenes.

West of the Praça da Sé, along Rua Benjamin Constant, is the Largo de São Francisco. Here is the **Igreja da Ordem Terceira de São Francisco**. The convent was inaugurated in 1647 and reformed in 1744. Note the blue-and-white tile decorations in the chancel and behind the font (up the left-hand passageway). To the right is the Igreja das Chagas do Seráphico Pai São Francisco (1787), painted like its neighbour in blue and gold. To the left is the Faculdade do Direito (Law Faculty) of São Paulo.

North is the Praça do Patriarca, on which stands the church of **Santo Antônio** ⓘ *Mon-Fri 0600-1830*, next to the Hotel Othon. Dating from 1717, the church has a beautifully painted wooden ceiling. Across the Viaduto do Chá on Praça Ramos de Azevedo is the **Teatro Municipal** ⓘ *T2233022*, one of the few distinguished early 20th-century survivals that São Paulo can boast. Inaugurated in 1911, many famous international and national stars have played at the theatre. Viewing the interior may only be possible during a performance; as well as the full evening performances. Look out for midday, string quartet and vesperais líricas concerts (all free, usually once a week).

Praça da República

Praça da República is filled with tall trees and birds and is always busy. There are also lots of police. Nearby is the city's tallest building, the **Edifício Itália** on the corner of

Avenida Ipiranga and Avenida São Luís. There is a restaurant on top, Terraço Itália, and a sightseeing balcony (see Eating). Also here is Oscar Niemeyer's famous curving **Edifício Copan**. Two blocks northwest of the Praça is the **Largo do Arouche**, by which is a large flower market, which is worth seeing.

North of the centre

About 10 minutes' walk from the centre of the city is the old **Mercado Municipal**, ⓘ *Mon-Sat 0400-1600*, covering 27,000 sq m at Rua Cantareira 306. A new Mercado Municipal has been built in the outskirts.

Worth a visit is the **Parque da Luz** on Avenida Tiradentes, formerly a botanical garden. Be careful here after 1700 or at weekends. On the same avenue is the **State Art Collection** (**Pinacoteca do Estado**) ⓘ *Av Tiradentes 141, T2299844, Tue-Sun 1000-1800, free*. Nearby, the **Igreja e Convento Nossa Senhora da Luz** ⓘ *Av Tiradentes 676*, is one of the few colonial buildings left in São Paulo, although the chapel dates from 1579 and is an example of *taipa de pilão* construction (see Architecture, page 710). It houses the **Museu de Arte Sacra** ⓘ *T2277694, Tue-Sun 1300-1800*, which has a large collection of sacred objects from the 17th to 20th centuries; not all are on show at one time.

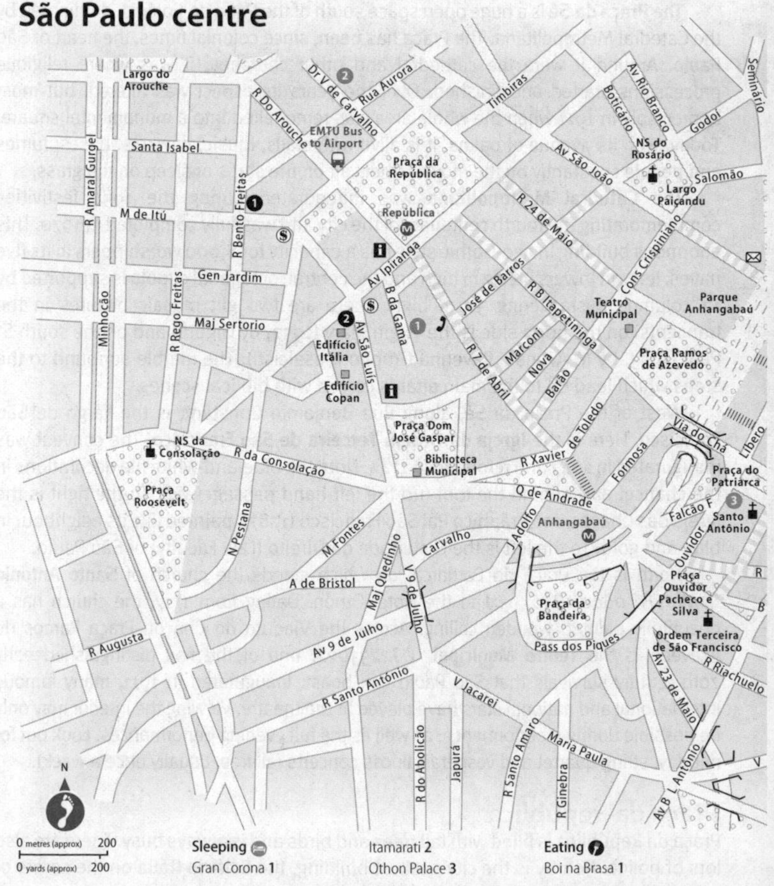

Liberdade

Directly south of the Praça da Sé, Liberdade is the central Japanese district. An oriental market is held every Sunday (see Shopping) in the Praça da Liberdade Metrô station. Here you can buy traditional arts and crafts and sample all types of oriental foods, not just Japanese. On the streets of the quarter are Japanese stores, plenty of places to eat and street lights designed like oriental lanterns.

Museu da Imigração Japonesa ⓘ *R São Joaquim 381, T2795465, Tue-Sun 1330-1730, US$1.50*, is excellent, with a nice roof garden; ask at the desk for an English translation of the exhibits.

The next stop south on the Metrô is Vergueiro, near which is the **Centro Cultural São Paulo** ⓘ *R Vergueiro 1000, T2773611, daily until 2200*, which has art and photographic exhibitions, a library, music and dance shows (often regional) and films.

Avenida Paulista and the Jardins District

Either Metrô station Vergueiro or Paraíso is convenient for the southeastern end of **Avenida Paulista**. This famous avenue was inaugurated in 1891 by the Uruguayan engineer Joaquim Eugênio de Lima, who wanted to construct an avenue similar to those found in European capitals. In no time, the wealthy built their elegant houses, many in the fashionable eclectic style (see Architecture, page 710), and transformed this into the grandest part of the city. The industrial explosion in the 1930s and 1940s brought a new role to the avenue as offices for commercial houses and service industries were put up. Land prices rose and residents relocated to other districts. In the 1970s the avenue was widened to cope with the ever increasing flow of traffic and in the 1980s the international finance companies, the banks and the multinationals erected the latest architectural towers that rise up on either side today. Immediately west of Paulista and an easy ten minute walk from Consolação Metro along Rua Hadoock Lobo, is the plush neighbourhood of **Jardins**. There are no sights of note here, but it is far and away the most pleasant area to stay in São Paulo, is the best area for shopping and has excellent casual and fine dining.

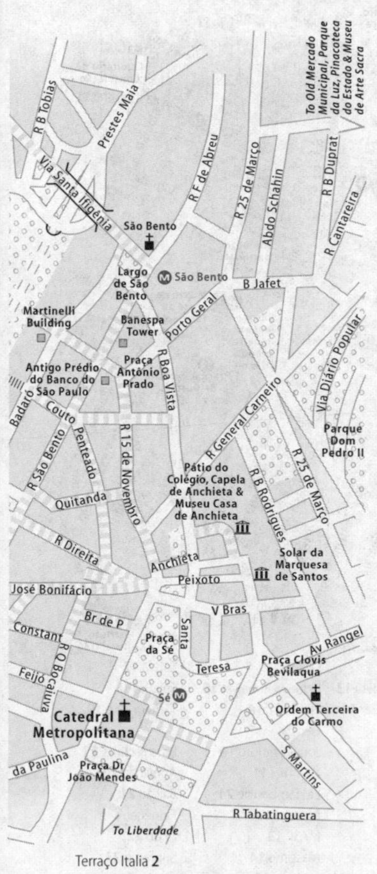

Terraço Italia 2

The highlight of Avenida Paulista is **MASP**, or **Museu de Arte de São Paulo** ⓘ *T2515644, Tue-Sun 1100-1800, US$8 (first you must buy a ticket from the booth, then enter the building)*. The present building was designed in 1957 and opened in 1968 by Queen Elizabeth II. It is at Avenida Paulista 1578 (immediately above the 9 de Julho tunnel) and the nearest Metrô is Trianon-MASP. The building is a simple parallelepiped, but instead of resting on the ground it is suspended from two red, concrete arches so that the lowest floor spans a 74-m open space. The museum has major collections of European painters and sculptors, and some interesting work by Brazilian artists, including Portinari. Particularly interesting are the pictures of northeastern Brazil done by Dutch artists during the Dutch occupation (1630-1654): the exotic tropical landscapes have been made to look incredibly temperate. Exhibitions vary, not all the artists above may be on view. Temporary exhibitions are also held and when a popular show is on, it can take up to an hour to get in. In this case, the later you go the better. Bus 805A from Praça da República goes by MASP.

On Sunday, an antiques fair is held in the open space beneath the museum, see Shopping. Opposite MASP is **Parque Tenente Siqueira Campos** ⓘ *R Peixoto Gomide 949 and Av Paulista, daily 0700-1830*, also known as Parque Trianon, covering two blocks on either side of Alameda Santos. It is a welcome, luxuriant, green area that is located in what is now the busiest part of the city. The vegetation includes native plants typical of the Mata Atlântica. Next to the park is the smaller Praça Alexandre de Gusmão.

Avenida Paulista & Jardins

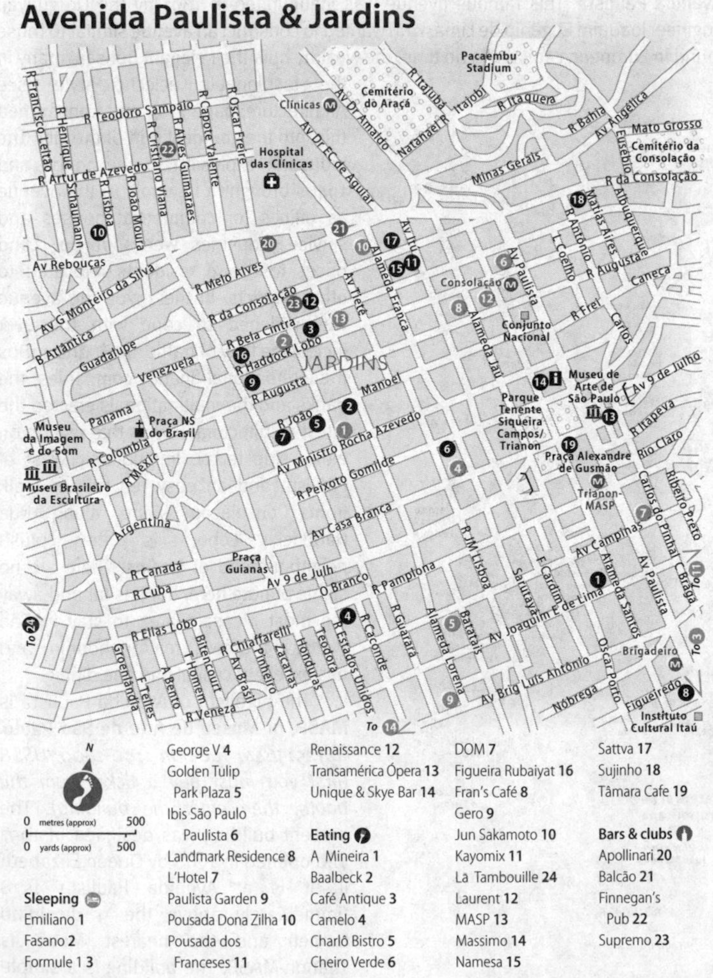

The **Museu da Imagem e do Som** ⓘ *Av Europa 158, Tue-Fri 1400-1800*, has photographic exhibitions, archives of Brazilian cinema, video and music, and a nice café on the ground floor.

At Avenida Europa 218 and Rua Alemanha 221, the **Museu Brasileiro da Escultura** (**MuBE**) holds temporary exhibitions and offers courses in sculpture, painting, engraving and art history. Entry to the various temporary exhibitions and to recitals in the afternoons is free.

Avenida Europa continues to Avenida Brigadeiro Faria Lima, on which is the **Casa Brasileira** ⓘ *Av Faria Lima 774, T2102564, Tue-Sun 1300-1800*, a museum of Brazilian furniture. It also holds temporary exhibitions. A little further up the avenue is **Shopping Iguatemi**.

Memorial da América Latina ⓘ *Tue-Fri 0900-2100, Sat 0900-1800, Sun 1000-1800, free*, designed by Oscar Niemeyer, built in March 1989, at Avenida Mário de Andrade 664, next to Barra Funda Metrô station, has a relief map of Central and South America under a glass floor in the section which houses a permanent exhibition of handicrafts from all over Latin America; there is a photo library, books, magazines, newspapers and films shown on video. A few blocks west is **SESC Pompeia** ⓘ *R Clélia 93*, a sports and arts complex with a library, designed by Lina Bo Bardi in 1982-1986. It is a vibrant place, with a theatre, exhibitions, workshops, restaurant and café, as well as areas for sunbathing and television watching.

Parque Água Branca ⓘ *Av Francisco Matarazzo 455, daily 0700-1800*, not far west of Barra Funda, has beautiful gardens with specimens of tropical plants, Brazilian birds and wildlife. Pavilions house a well-stocked aquarium, a zoo, and exhibitions of food produce. It is also popular with children.

Ibirapuera

The **Parque do Ibirapuera** ⓘ *entrance on Av Pedro Álvares Cabral, daily 0600-1730*, was designed by architect Oscar Niemeyer and landscape artist Roberto Burle Marx for the city's fourth centenary in 1954. Bicycles can be hired. Within its 1.6 million sq m is the new architecturally impressive **Assembléia Legislativa**. There is also a **Planetarium** ⓘ *T5755206, shows at 1530 and 1730 at weekends and on holidays, US$5, half price for under 18s*; a Japanese pavilion; a velodrome for cycle and motorcycle racing; an all-aluminium covered stadium for indoor sports which seats 20,000 people; outdoor sports fields; children's play areas; and weekend concerts in the Praça da Paz.

In this park, too, is the **Museu de Arte Moderna** (**MAM**) ⓘ *T55496688, www.mam.org.br, Tue, Wed, Fri 1200-1800, Thu 1200-2200, Sat and Sun 1000-1800, US$2, students half price, free all Tue and Fri after 1700*, with a collection of contemporary paintings, sculptures and photographs, a library specializing in Brazilian and international art and an exciting sculpture garden (look out for Nuno Ramos' Craca made of real fish, bones and shell. The recently refurbished and spectacular building now known as the **Oca** was designed by Niemeyer in the style of a simple Amazonian roundhouse. It houses temporary exhibitions. Bicycles can be hired from local character Maizena beside the city hall, Prodam (US$1.25 for a bike without gears, US$2 with gears, leave document as security). To get to Ibirapuera, take bus No 574R from Paraíso Metrô station or No 6364 from Praça da Bandeira; to Cidade Universitária take No 702U or 7181 from Praça da República.

Every even-numbered year the **Bienal Internacional de São Paulo** (São Paulo Biennial) at Ibirapuera has the most important show of modern art in Latin America, usually open from the beginning of September till November.

Cidade Universitária

Instituto Butantã/The Butantã Snake Farm and Museum ⓘ *Av Dr Vital Brasil 1500, T8137222, Tue-Sun 0900-1700, US$1, children and students half price*, on the Cidade Universitária university campus, is one of the most popular tourist attractions in São

Paulo. The snakes are milked for their poison six times a day but you may not witness this. The antidotes made from the venom have greatly reduced deaths from snakebite in Brazil. The centre also deals with spider and scorpion venom, has a small hospital and is a biomedical research institute. What visitors see is the museum of poisonous animals and public health, which is well organized and educational, with explanations in Portuguese and English. To get there from Praça da República take the bus marked 'Butantã' or 'Cidade Universitária' (Nos 701U or 792U) along Avenida Paulista, and ask to be let out at Instituto Butantã.

The **Museu de Arte Contemporâneo (MAC)** ⓘ *T38183039, Tue-Sat 1200-1800, Sun 1000-1800, free*, with an important collection of Brazilian and European modern art, is in the Prédio Novo da Reitoria. Also in the university is the **Museu de Arqueologia e Etnologia (MAE)** ⓘ *R Reitoria 1466, T38124001*, with a collection of Amazonian and ancient Mediterranean material.

Not far from the Butantã Institute, just inside the Cidade Universitária, is the **Casa do Bandeirante** ⓘ *Praça Monteiro Lobato, T2110920*, the reconstructed home of a pioneer from 400 years ago.

On the west bank of the Rio Pinheiros, just southeast of the campus, is the palatial **Jóquei Clube/Jockey Club** ⓘ *Av Lineu de Paula Machado 1263, T8164011*, a racecourse in the Cidade Jardim area. Race meetings are held on Monday and Thursday at 1930 and Saturday and Sunday at 1430. The racecourse is easily accessible by bus (Butantã from República, among others). It has a **Museu do Turfe** ⓘ *Av Lineu de Paula Machado 1263, T8164011, Tue-Sun, but closed Sat and Sun mornings*.

Morumbi

Morumbi is a smart residential district with some very imposing houses due south of the Cidade Universitária. In the area are the state government building, **Palácio dos Bandeirantes** ⓘ *Av Morumbi 4500*, the small, simple **Capela de Morumbi** ⓘ *Av Morumbi 5387*, and the **Parque Alfredo Volpi** ⓘ *R Oscar Americano 480, 0600-2000*. This small park has native plants which are the last vestiges of the time when this was a farm; there are also paths and a playground. No public transport goes there. Morumbi is most famous for the stadium of **São Paulo Football Club**, holding 100,000 people (it is known as Morumbi). Motor racing fans might like to visit the Morumbi cemetery, last resting place of Ayrton Senna. To get there, take bus No 6291 to Rua Profesor Benedito Montenegro.

Museu da Fundação Maria Luisa e Oscar Americano ⓘ *Av Morumbi 3700, Morumbi, Tue-Fri 1100-1830, Sat-Sun 1000-1830*, close to the Palácio dos Bandeirantes, is a well-displayed, private collection of Brazilian and Portuguese art and furniture. The garden has fascinating plants, patios and native plants.

Parque da Independência

In the suburb of Ipiranga (a Tupi-Guarani word meaning 'red clay'), 5½ km southeast of the city centre, the **Parque da Independência** contains the famous **Monumento à Independência** to commemorate the declaration of Brazilian Independence; beneath the monument is the **Imperial Chapel** ⓘ *Tue-Sun 1300-1700*, with the tomb of the first emperor, Dom Pedro I, and Empress Leopoldina. The monument was the second to be built, in time for the centenary of Independence in 1922. The **Casa do Grito** ⓘ *Tue-Sun 0930-1700*, the little house in which Dom Pedro I spent the night before his famous Cry of Ipiranga – 'Independence or Death' – is preserved in the park. When Independence was declared, Ipiranga was outside the city's boundaries, in an area where bricks were made, on the main trade route between Santos and São Paulo.

The **Museu Paulista** ⓘ *Tue-Sun 0900-1645, US$1*, is housed in a huge palace at the top of the park. The original building, later altered, was the first Monument to Independence. The museum contains old maps, traditional furniture, collections of old coins and of religious art and rare documents, and a department of indigenous ethnology. Behind the museum is the **Horto Botânico/ Ipiranga Botanical Garden** ⓘ *Tue-Sun 0900-1700*, and the **Jardim Francês**, designed as a garden for plant study, now a recreational area. There is a light and sound show on Brazilian history in the park on Wednesday, Friday and Saturday at 2030. To get there, take either bus No 478P (Ipiranga-Pompéia for return) from Ana Rosa, or take bus No 4612 from the Praça da República.

Parque do Estado (Jardim Botânico)

This large park is a long way south of the centre, at **Água Funda** ⓘ *Av Miguel Estefano, T30313687*. It contains both the Botanical and Zoological Gardens and a game reserve called Simba Safári. The **Jardim Botânico** ⓘ *T55846300, Wed-Sun 0900-1700*, has a vast garden esplanade surrounded by magnificent stone porches, with lakes and trees and places for picnics, and a very fine orchid farm worth seeing during the flowering season, November-December. Over 19,000 different kinds of orchids are cultivated. There are orchid exhibitions in April and November. The astronomical observatory nearby is open to the public on Thursday afternoons. To get there, take the Metrô to São Judas on the Jabaquara line, then take a bus.

Burle Marx Park ⓘ *Av Dona Helena Pereira de Moraes 200, daily 0700-1900*, was designed by famous landscape designer Burle Marx. It is the only place in the city where you can walk along trails in the Mata Atlântica (Atlantic rainforest).

Nearby, over 200 animals roam free at the wildlife park, **Simba Safári** ⓘ *Av do Cursino 6338, T9466249, Tue-Fri 1000-1630, Sat-Sun 0900-1630, entry is by car only and price of admission depends on the number of people in the vehicle (eg US$25 for a car with 2 adults); children under 12 free.*

Excursions from São Paulo

Horto Florestal

ⓘ *R do Horto 931, T9528555, daily 0600-1800.*

In Tremembé, a little beyond Cantareira, 30 minutes north from the downtown area, is the Horto Florestal, in Parque Estadual Alberto Löfgren. The park contains examples of nearly every species of Brazilian woodland flora, 15 km of natural trails, a museum with exhibits of regional flora and fauna and a view of São Paulo from Pedra Grande on the right of the entrance to the park.

Pico de Jaraguá

This is the highest peak (1,135 m) in the neighbourhood and, on a fine day, has good views of Greater São Paulo. Lots of hang-gliders fly here at weekends. It is reached from Km 18 on the Campinas highway (Via Anhangüera) by a good road through Taipas and Pirituba.

Miraporanga Botanical and Wildlife Sanctuary

ⓘ *Contact Sr Samuel Jorge de Mello, T8160817, weekends T4766716, for information and prices.*

Situated in the foothills of the Serra do Mar, this is one hour's drive from São Paulo city centre. It has a vast collection of orchids, carnivorous and aquatic plants, waterlily pools, a lake and 20 glasshouses. It also contains armadillos, deer and other mammals, monitor lizards and a variety of hummingbirds.

Santo Amaro Dam (Old Lake) and Interlagos

About 3 km from the centre of Santo Amaro suburb (a 30-minute bus ride from São Paulo) is this popular boating resort with several sailing clubs and many attractive cottages along the shore.

São Paulo's lake resort on the Santo Amaro Dam, **Avenida Interlagos** ⓘ *T5770522* has an 18-km motor-racing circuit. It can be reached from Santo Amaro by bus. Close to the track, where the **Brazilian Grand Prix** takes place, is the 32-km long **Guarapiranga** ⓘ *Av Guarapiranga 575, daily 0600-1700*, an artificial lake with good restaurants and several luxurious sailing and sports clubs. There is a **Camping Clube do Brasil** site. Guarapiranga is less polluted than the other artificial lake, **Billings**, which also has restaurants. ›› *See box, page 199, for more on the Brazilian Grand Prix.*

Embu

This colonial town, 28 km from São Paulo, has become a centre for artists and craftsmen. The town itself, on a hill, is surrounded by industry and modern developments and the colonial centre is quite small. Many of the old houses are brightly coloured and most contain arts, furniture, souvenir or antiques shops. To get to Embu take an São Paulo-Pinheiros bus from Clínicas, which takes the main highway to Embu; 40 minutes, it costs US$0.80. Get out at Largo 21 de Abril in Embu. To return to São Paulo, walk up Rua da Matriz from 21 de Abril, turn left down Avenida Junior, then left again on Rua Solano Trindade to a junction where the buses stop.

Campos do Jordão → *Phone code: 012. Colour map 5, A6. Population: 38,000.*

This cheesy mountain resort between Rio de Janeiro and São Paulo 1,628 m high in the Serra da Mantiqueira is full of very ugly mock-Alpine hotels set in denuded hills. Although it is much beloved of Paulistanos there is little reason to come here except perhaps for the classical music and dance festivals in June and July. Walking is far better in Itatiaia or Visconde de Mauá.

The **tourist office** ⓘ *T2622755, F2624100*, is in the alpine-looking gateway to the city, the **Portal da Cidade**. There are plenty of hotels and restaurants on and around the main street and banks with ATMs and money-changing services. Regular buses run to and from São Paulo.

Sleeping

Both for business and for leisure, São Paulo has by far the best hotels in Latin America and by far the best in Brazil. There are design hotels which Ian Shrager would be proud of and business towers with all the requisite facilities together with an almost personal touch. These rooms are expensive however and although there are some reasonable budget options they are not in the best locations. Like most of the New World's larger cities, Sampa is a place where you have to spend money to enjoy yourself. The best places to stay are Jardins (the most affluent area), Paulista and around (close to one of the business centres). Business travellers will find good hotels on Faria Lima and Av Luis Carlos Berrini in the new centre in the south of the city. There are cheapies in the centre but this is an undesirable area at night. Some of the better hostels are around the city in seemingly random locations or are in the seedy centre.

The youth hostel association, **Associação Paulista de Albergues da Juventude**, is at R 7 de Abril 386, Conj 22, T/F2580388, www.alberguesp.com.br.

City centre *p182, map p184, phone code 011*

AL **Othon Palace**, R Líbero Badaró 190, T32915000, www.othon.com.br. The only business hotel of quality in the Triângulo; in a 1950s heritage building.

A **Gran Corona**, Basílio da Gama 101, T2140043, F2144503, in a small street. Comfortable, good services, good restaurant. Warmly recommended.

B **Itamarati**, Av Dr Vieira de Carvalho 150, T2224133, F2221878. Good location, safe. Highly recommended and very popular.

Liberdade *p185, phone code 011*

B **Banri**, R Galvão Bueno 209, T2708877, F2789225. Good. Chinese owners. Recommended.

E **Ikeda**, R dos Estudantes. With breakfast, shared bath, quiet. Both near Metrô station.

Av Paulista and the Jardins District
p185, map p186, phone code 011

LL**Emiliano**, R Oscar Freire 384, T30694369, www.emiliano.com.br. Bright, light and beautifully designed, with attention to every detail and the best suites in the city. No pool but a relaxing small spa. Excellent Italian restaurant, location and service.

LL**L'Hotel**, Av Campinas 266, T/F2830500, all suites. Part of the **Roteiros de Charme** group, see p47. Decorated in mock-French style and convenient for Paulista.

LL**Fasano**, R Vittorio Fasano 88, T38964077, www.fasano.com.br. One of the world's great hotels with decor like a modernist gentleman's club designed by Armani, a fabulous pool and the best formal haute cuisine restaurant in Brazil. The lobby bar is a wonderful place to arrange a meeting. Excellently positioned in Jardins.

LL**Renaissance**, Alameda Santos 2233 (at Haddock Lobo), T30692233, www.marriott.com/property/propertyPage/Sãobr. The best business hotel off Av Paulista with standard business rooms, a good spa, gym, pool and 2 squash courts. The excellent business and conference facilities include a full business centre, secretarial services and airline booking.

LL**Unique**, Av Brigadeiro Luis Antonio 4700, Jardim Paulista, T30554700, www.hotelunique.com. The most ostentatiously designed hotel in the country – an enormous half moon on concrete uprights with curving floors, circular windows and beautiful use of space and light. The bar on the top floor is São Paulo's answer to the LA Sky Bar and is always filled with the beautiful and famous after 2130. The rock stars' choice; Coldplay stayed here on their last world tour.

LL-AL**George V**, R Jose Maria Lisboa 1000, T30889822, www.george-v.com.br. Proper apartments of over 60-180 sq m, with living rooms, fully equipped kitchens (with dish washers and washing machines), huge bathrooms, closets and comprehensive business services. Shared facilities include sauna, indoor pool and modern gym. Special deals through the website.

A**Golden Tulip Park Plaza**, Alameda Lorena 360, T30584055, www.parkplaza.com.br. Modern tower with apartments of 30 sq m, spa and well-equipped modern gym. Good value.

A**Transamérica Ópera**, Alameda Lorena 1748, T30622666, www.transamericaflats.com.br. Conservatively decorated but elegant and well-maintained modern flats of 42 sq m in a tower between the heart of Jardins and Av Paulista. At the bottom end of this price range.

B**The Landmark Residence**, Alameda Jaú 1607, T30828677, www.landmarkresidence.com.br. Spacious apartments with hotel catalogue furnishings and a shared gym, gardens and modest business centre. Good location.

B-C**Ibis São Paulo Paulista**, Av Paulista 2355, T35233000, www.accorhotels.com.br. Great value – modern, business-standard rooms with a/c in a tower right on Paulista. Cheaper at weekends. Online reservations.

C**Formule 1**, R Vergueiro 1571, T50855699, www.accorhotels.com.br. Another great value business-style hotel built in 2001, with apts big enough for 3, making this an E option for those in a group. Right next to Paraíso Metrô in a safe area. Rooms have a/c.

C**Paulista Garden**, Alameda Lorena 21, T/F38858498, www.paulistagardenhotel.com.br. Small, simple rooms with a/c, cable TV and fridges. Close to Ibirapuera Park.

C**Pousada Dona Zilha**, Alameda Franca 1621, Jardim Paulista, T30621444, www.zilah.com. Little *pousada* in a renovated colonial house with plain but well-maintained rooms and common areas decorated with thought and a personal touch. Excellent location, bike rental and generous breakfast included in the price. Triple rooms available in D category per person.

D-F**Pousada dos Franceses**, R dos Franceses 100, Bela Vista, T32624026, www.pousadadosfranceses.com.br. Price per person. A plain little *pousada* 10 mins' walk from Brigadeiro Metrô, with dorms, doubles and singles. Free internet, TV room and breakfast included in the price.

Elsewhere *phone code 011*

The New Centre, Av Br Faria Lima and Av Luis Carlos Berrini

LL-L**Grand Hyatt São Paulo**, Av das Nações Unidas 13301, T68381234, www.sãopaulo.hyatt.com. A superb business hotel close to Berrini, which successfully fuses corporate efficiency and requisite services with designer cool. Spa, pool, state-of-the-art business centre and marvellous views from the upper-floor suites.

AL-L **Blue Tree Towers**, Av Brigadeiro Faria Lima 3989, Vila Olímpia, T38967544, www.bluetree.com.br. Modern business hotel with discreetly designed rooms and excellent service. Ideally positioned for Faria Lima's business district and the restaurants and nightlife of Vila Olímpia and Itaim. Pool, massage, gym, sauna and well-equipped business centre.

D **ACE Hostel**, R Gastão da Cunha 253, Congonhas Airport, T50342472, www.bedandbreakfast.com.br. Friendly pocket-sized hostel in a brightly painted residential house near to Congonhas. Services include, TV, DVD and movies, broadband internet, kitchen, laundry book exchange and pick-up. Tours of São Paulo available.

E **Primavera**, R Mariz e Barros 346, Vila Santa Eulália (bus 4491 from Parque Dom Pedro in the centre), T2153144. Hostel with cooking and laundry facilities, friendly staff.

E-F **Praça da Árvore IYHA**, R Pageú 266, Saúde, T50715148, www.spalbergue.com.br. Well-kept *pousada* in a quiet back street. Friendly and helpful. 2 mins from Praça do Arvore Metrô. kitchen, laundry and internet service (overpriced).

Eating

Those on a budget can eat to their stomach's content in per kilo places or if looking for cheaper still, in bakeries (*padarias*). There is one of these on almost every corner. They all serve sandwiches like Misto Quentes, Beirute's and Americanos – delicious Brazilian burgers made from decent meat and served with ham, egg, cheese or salad. They always have good coffee, juices, cakes and set lunches (*almoços*) for a very economical price. Most have a designated sitting area – either at the *padaria* bar or in an adjacent room; you aren't expected to eat on your feet as you are in Rio. Restaurants in São Paulo are safe on the stomach. Juices are made with mineral or filtered water.

City centre *p182, map p184, phone code 011*

Restaurants in the old centre tend to be lunchtime only; there are many per kilo options and *padarias*.

TTT **Terraço Italia**, Av Ipiranga 344, T32576566. Average and overpriced Italian food with the best restaurant views in the city – out over an infinity of skyscrapers. Come for a coffee.

TTT **Boi na Brasa**, R Bento Freitas by Praça da República. Very good meat dishes and feijoada at a reasonable price.

T **Café da Pinacoteca**, Pinacoteca Museum, Praça da Luz 2, T33260350. Portuguese-style café with marble floors and mahogany balconies. Great coffee, sandwiches and cakes.

Liberdade *p185, phone code 011*

TT **Gombe**, R Tomas Gonzaga 22, T32098499. Renowned for grilled tuna and various noodle dishes.

TT **Sushi Yassu**, R Tomas Gonzaga 98, T32096622. The best of Liberdade's traditional Japanese restaurants. Excellent sushi/sashimi combinations.

Av Paulista and the Jardins District *p185, map p186, phone code 011*

TTT **Café Antique**, R Haddock Lobo 1416, Jardins, T30620882. French cooking by Erick Jacquin, a Maitre Cuisinier de France in an informal but traditional dining room atmosphere – a long corridor-like room lined with 19th-century oil paintings. Wonderful foie gras and an excellent, though expensive, wine list.

TTT **Charlô Bistro**, R Barão de Capanema 440 (next to DOM), Jardins, T30886790 (with another branch at the high-society set Jockey Club, Av Lineu de Paula Machado 1263, Cidade Jardim, T30343682). One of the premier VIP and old family haunts in the city run by, a scion of one of the city's establishment families. Decked out in tribute to a Paris brasserie and with food to imitate.

TTT **DOM**, R Barão de Capanema 549, Jardins, T30880761. São Paulo's evening restaurant of the moment – Alex Attala has won the coveted Veja best chef of the year award twice. Contemporary food, fusing Brazilian ingredients with French and Italian styles and served in a large open modernist dining room to the sharply dressed.

TTT **Fasano**, Hotel Fasano, R Fasano, T38964077, www.fasano.com.br. Long regarded as the best restaurant for gourmets in São Paulo. A huge choice of modern

Italian and French cooking, modelled on the best of Milan from chef Salvatore Loi. Intimate space – diners have their own lowly-lit booths, in a magnificent dining room, populated by flocks of black-tie waiters. Exemplary wine list. Formal dress.

¥¥¥ **Figueira Rubaiyat**, R Haddock Lobo 1738, T30633888. The most interesting of the **Rubaiyat** restaurant group, with Argentinian steaks prepared by Argentinian chef Francis Mallman. Very lively for lunch on a Sun and remarkable principally for the space – open walled, light and airy and under a huge tropical fig tree.

¥¥¥ **Gero**, R Haddock Lobo 1629, T30640005. Fasano's version of a French bistrô, but serving pasta and light Italian. Ever so casual design by architect Aurelio Martinez Flores and an evening clientele which includes a mix of the best-known faces in São Paulo high society. Be prepared for a long wait at the bar alongside people who are there principally to be seen. Reservations are not accepted.

¥¥¥ **Jun Sakamoto**, R Lisboa 55, Jardins, T30886019. Japanese with a touch of French; superb fresh ingredients, (some of it flown in especially from Asia and the USA). The dishes of choice are the dégustation menu and the duck breast teppaniyaki.

¥¥¥ **La Tambouille**, Av 9 de Julho 5925, Jardim Europa, T30796276. The favourite Franco-Italian restaurant of the city's old money. Chef Andre Fernandes's signature dishes are the saffron linguini with fresh mussels and prawn sauce and the brie ravioli with rocket and pinoli infused with white truffles. Excellent wine list.

¥¥¥ **Laurent**, Alameda Lorena 1899, Cerqueira César, Jardins, T30621452. The best French cooking in the country, served to a discerning and eclectic clientele. French style, Brazilian ingredients.

¥¥¥ **Massimo**, Alameda Santos 1826, Cerqueira César, Jardins, T32840311. One of São Paulo's longest-established Italian restaurants serving northern Italian food to the city's politicians and business executives. Credit cards are not accepted, despite the costly price.

¥¥ **A Mineira**, Alameda Joaquim Eugenio de Lima 697, Jardins, T32832349. Self-service Minas food by the kilo. Lots of choice. *Cachaca* and pudding included in the price.

¥¥ **Baalbeck**, Alameda Lorena 1330, Jardins, T30884820. Lebanese cooking vastly superior to its luncheonette setting. Great falafel.

¥¥ **Camelo**, R Pamplona 1873, Jardins, T38878764. A menu of over 40 superior pizzas with a choice of dough as well.

¥¥ **Fran's Café**, open 24 hrs, Av Paulista 358, and all over the city. The Brazilian equivalent of Starbuck's only with proper coffee and a menu of light eats.

¥¥ **Kayomix**, R da Consolação 3215, Jardins, T30822769. Brazilian-Oriental fusions like salmon taratare with shimeji and shitake.

¥¥ **Namesa**, R da Consolação 2967, Jardins, T30887498. Great little gourmet snacky dishes created by the chef from DOM like wild boar pâté with pistachio pesto.

¥¥ **Restaurante do MASP**, Av Paulista 1578, T32532829. In the basement of the museum, reasonably priced standards like lasagna and stroganoff often with a garnish of live music.

¥¥ **Sattva**, R da Consolação 2904, Jardins, T30836237. Light vegetarian curries, stir fries, salads and pastas. Very Neal's Yard.

¥¥ **Sujinho**, R da Consolação 2068, Consolação, T32568026. South American beef in large portions. Other carnivorous options also available.

¥ **Cheiro Verde**, R Peixoto Gomide 1413, Jardins, T2896853 (lunchtimes only). Hearty vegetarian food – like vegetable crumble in gorgonzola sauce and wholewheat pasta with buffalo mozzarella and sundried tomato.

¥ **Tâmara Cafe**, Alameda Santos 1518, Jardins, T2881248 (lunchtimes only). Arabic cooking with good kibe, kafta and falafel.

Elsewhere *phone code 011*

Vila Olimpia Moema and Itaim

Restaurants here are ultra, ultra trendy; full of the beautiful posing in beautiful surroundings. We include only a handful of the best.

¥¥¥ **Boo**, R Viradouro 132, T30787477. Opposite **Kosushi**, with a carbon-copy crowd, Luso-Asian cooking and a beautiful garden setting.

¥¥¥ **Kosushi**, R Viradouro 139, Itaim Bibi, T31677272. The first of São Paulo's chic Japanese restaurants which began life in Liberdade and is now housed in a beautifully designed Asian modernist space. Full of the famous sitting to be seen. Great sushi combinations.

ǂǂǂ **Parigi**, R Amauri 275, Itaim, T31671575. One of the city's premier evening places to be seen; celebrity couples come here for intimate public view Franco-Italian dining. The menu also has classical French dishes like coq au vin. Attractive dining room – beautlfully lit and decked out in lush dark wood.

Bars and clubs

São Paulo has a bit more nocturnal panache than Rio and DJs like Marky and the sadly deceased Suba have made the São Paulo club scene world famous. Marky is resident DJ at the **Love Club** (see below). Fri's biggest party is **Vapour at the Prime Club** (see below). Other fashionable spots include **30Hz at Jive**, Alameda Barros, 376, Higienópolis on Sat, T11 3824 0097, and **The Bass**, R Vitória 810, City Centre, T1133371915, on Sun.

Av Paulista and the Jardins District

p185, map p186, phone code 011

Jardins has a few bars, the most famous of which are in the better hotels.

Apollinari, R Oscar Freire 1206, T30619965. Smart restaurant-bar frequented by the city's glitterati.

Barretto, in the **Fasano Hotel**, feels rather conservative with its heavy dark wood, mirrors and cool live bossa jazz. The crowd is mostly the Cuban cigar with a sprinkling of the tanned and toned-in figure-enhancing designer labels.

Bar Balcão, R Doutor Melo Alves 150, T30636091. After-work meeting place, very popular with young professionals and media types who gather on either side of the long low wooden bar which winds its way around the room like a giant snake.

Emiliano Bar, Hotel Emiliano. Similar crowd to **Skye** (see below) but despite its popularity, it can feel like a sterile corridor rather than an intimate space. DJs play on Fri nights.

Finnegan's Pub, R Cristiano Viana 358, Pinheiros, T30623232, www.finnegan.com.br. One of São Paulo's Irish bars; every city has one. This one is actually run and owned by an Irishman and is very popular with ex-pats.

Plataforma 1, Av Paulista 424. Dinner and folkloric show, very touristy but extremely popular.

Skye, the rooftop bar at **Hotel Unique**. Another fashionable spot with a definite door policy. The views of glistening skyscrapers pocked by patches of green and red tile are wonderful. Coldplay had their after-gig party here on their 2003 tour.

Supremo, R Oscar Freire 1000, T30620950. Down-at-heel cellar bar on the smartest street in Jardins, which despite its frayed decor hosts some of the city's most interesting and sophisticated acts from Badi Assad to Maria Rita Mariano, the daughter of legendary bossa singer, Elis Regina.

Elsewhere *phone code 011*

Vila Madalena/Pinheiros

Vila Madalena and adjacent Pinheiros lie just northeast of Jardins. A taxi from Jardins is about $7; there is also a Metrô station, but this closes by the time the bars get going. These suburbs are the favourite haunts of São Paulo twenty- somethings, more hippy chic than Itaim, less stuffy than Jardins. This is the best part of town for live, Brazilian music and uniquely Brazilian close dances such as *forró*; as opposed to international club sounds. It can feel grungy and informal but is undoubtedly buzzing. The liveliest streets are Aspicuelta and Girassol and the current bars of choice are **Grazie A Dio!** and **A Marcenaria** (see below).

AMP Galaxy, R Fradique Coutinho 352, T30857867, www.ampgalaxy.com.br. A fusion of retro 50s bar and café, clothing boutique and after 2300 packed dancefloor with alternate live music and DJs. The crowd is twenty-something and bohemian.

Grazie a Dio, R Girassol, 67, T30316568, www.grazieadio.com.br. The best bar in Vila Madalena to hear live music – there's a different band every night with samba on Sun. Great for dancing. Always packed.

A Marcenaria, R Fradique Coutinho 1378, T30329006, www.amarcenaria.com.br. This is the bar of choice for the young, single and hippy chic who gather here from around 2130, until the dancefloor fills up at around 2300.

Mood, R Teodoro Sampaio 1109, T30609010. European-style club with the latest sounds and DJs like Mau Mau and Felipe Venancio.

Posto 6, R Aspicuelta 644, Vila Madalena, T38127831. An imitation Rio de Janeiro *boteco* with attractive crowds and backdrop of bossa nova and MPB. Busy from 2100 onwards.

Urbano R Cardeal Arcoverde 614, Pinheiros, T30851001, www.urbano.com.br. São Paulo's premiere dance club – modelled on a London club with a lounge bar area, huge dancefloor and a combination of live bands and DJs. Popular with musicians and creative industry twenty- and thirty-somethings.
Vapour at the Prime Club, R dos Pinheiros 783, Pinheiros, T0113087466. Big party on Fri.

Vila Olimpia Moema and Italm

This area, just south of Ibirapuera and north of the new centre, is about US$10 by taxi from Jardins and US$15 from the Centre, but well worth the expense of getting here. It is packed with street-corner bars which are great for a browse. The bars here, although informal, have a style of their own, lively and varied crowds and decent service. The busiest streets for a bar wander are **R Atilio Inocenti** near the junction of **Av Juscelino Kubitschek** and **Av Brigadeiro Faria Lima**, **Av Hélio Pellegrino** and **R Araguari** which runs behind it. Take a taxi here.
Liquid Lounge, Av Hélio Pellegrino 801, Vila Olímpia, T38495014, www.liquidlounge.com.br. Pulsing European-style dance club with a smart bar area. Always busy.
Love Club and Lounge, R Pequetita 189, Vila Olímpia, T30441613. Trance, house, drum 'n' bass; big-name DJs. The most famous night is Thu's **Vibe**, which is played by the top local and international DJs. This year Marcus Intalex, Calibre, Bryan Gee and EZ Rollers played there.
Na Mata Café, Rua da Mata 70, Itaim, T30790300, www.namata.com.br. Popular flirting and pick-up spot for twenty- and thirty-something rich kids who gyrate in the dark dance room to a variety of Brazilian and European dance tunes and select live bands.
Columbia, upstairs, R Estados Unidos 1570. Lively. **Hell's Club** downstairs. Opens 0400, techno, wild.
Cha-Cha-Cha, R Tabapuã 1236. Closed Mon, no Brazilian music, art on walls, candles, gay and straight.
Balafon, R Sergipe 160. Wed-Sun, small, Afro-Brazilian.
Reggae Night, Av Robert Kennedy 3880, Interlagos. Thu-Sun, outdoors on lakeside.
Limelight Industry, R Franz Schubert 93. Pop hits, Japanese restaurant upstairs. 5 other nightspots on this street.

Entertainment

See the *Guia da Folha* section of *Folha de São Paulo* and *Veja São Paulo* section of the weekly news magazine *Veja* for listings of concerts, theatre, museums, galleries, cinema, bars and restaurants.

Art galleries

Casa da Fazenda, Morumbi, exhibits in 19th-century house. Espaço Cultural Ena Beçak, R Oscar Freire 440. Galeria São Paulo, R Estados Unidos 1456.

Cinema

In cinemas entrance is usually half price on Wed; normal seat price is US$3 in the centre, US$5-6 in R Augusta, Av Paulista and Jardins. There is no shortage of cinemas in the city showing the latest releases, eg **Belas Artes**, R da Consolação 2423. Multiscreen. There are also cine clubs, eg **Cine SESC**, R Augusta 2075; **Espaço Unibanco**, R Augusta 1470/1475, and cinemas at the **Museu da Imagem e do Som**, **Centro Cultural Itaú** and **Centro Cultural São Paulo**.

Motor racing

See box p199 for information on the Brazilian Grand Prix.

Theatre

The **Teatro Municipal** (see Sights, p183) is used by visiting theatrical and operatic groups, as well as the **City Ballet Company** and the **Municipal Symphony Orchestra** who give regular performances. There are several first-class theatres: **Aliança Francesa**, R Gen Jardim 182, Vila Buarque, T2590086. **Itália**, Av Ipiranga 344, T2579092. **Paiol**, R Amaral Gurgel 164, Santa Cecília, T2212462. Free concerts at **Teatro Popular do Sesi**, Av Paulista 1313, T2849787, at midday, under MASP (Mon-Sat).

Festivals and events

See also box on Carnival, p196. Throughout the year, though, there are countless anniversaries, religious feasts, international fairs and exhibitions, so it would be wise to look in the press or the monthly tourist magazines to see what is on while you are in town. See p187 for the São Paulo Biennial.

Carnival in São Paulo

Carnival in São Paulo follows the lead of Rio de Janeiro and is improving in quality every year. The Samba Schools' parades take place in the Sambódromo, Avenida Olavo Fontoura 1209, Anhembi, T69715000. The **Grupo 1** (Saturday), **Grupo Especial** (Sunday and Monday) and the **Parade of the Champions** on the following Saturday are the ones to watch. Tickets can be obtained from the Sambódromo, from the Saraiva chain of bookshops or on T8294559.

To take part or to visit a practice session at a **quadra** contact the Samba Schools directly: **Gaviões da Fiel Torcida**, Rua Cristina Tomás 183, Bom Retiro, T2212066 (Friday 2200); **Mocidade Alegre**, Avenida Casa Verde 3498, Bairro do Limão, T8577525 (Wednesday and Friday 2000); **Rosas de Ouro**, Avenida Coronel Euclides Machado 1066, near Ponte da Freguesia do Ó, T8574555 (Wednesday, Friday and Sunday 2030); **Vai-Vai**, Rua São Vicente 276, Bela Vista, T31058725 (Sunday 2100); **X-9 Paulistana**, Av Luiz Dumont Villares 324, Carandiru, T2677081 (Wednesday and Sunday 2000).

25 Jan Foundation of the city.
Feb Carnival in *Escolas de samba* parade in the Anhembi Sambódromo, note that during Carnival most museums and attractions are closed.
Jun Festas Juninas and the Festa de São Vito, the patron saint of the Italian immigrants.
Sep Festa da Primavera.
Dec Various Christmas and New Year festivities.

Shopping

Bookshops

Livraria Cultura, Av Paulista 2073, loja 153, Conjunto Nacional. New books in English.
Livraria Freebook, R da Consolação 1924. Ring bell for entry, wide collection of art books and imported books in English.
Livraria Triângulo, R Barão de Itapetininga 255, loja 23, Centro. Sells books in English.
Livraria Kosmos, Av São Luís 258, loja 6. International stock.
Livrarias Saraiva and **Laselva**, in various shopping malls and at airports, sell books in English.
Sodiler, Shopping Market Place, Av Nações Unidas 13947, Brooklin, loja 121A, floor T.
Librairie Française, R Barão de Itapetininga 275, ground floor. Wide selection, also at R Prof Atilio Innocenti 920, Jardins.
Letraviva, Av Rebouças 1986. Mon-Fri 0900-1830, Sat 0900-1400, specializes in books and music in Spanish.
Book Centre, R Gabus Mendes 29, between Basílio da Gama and 7 de Abril (Praça da Republica). Has books in English and German.
Duas Cidades, R Bento Freitas 158, near República. Good selection of Brazilian and Spanish-American literature.
Cinema Elétrico, R Augusta 973, Centro, and **Sola Cinemateca**, R Fradique Coutinho 361. Sell postcards and books on cinema and art.
Gusto, Gôsto, Gusta, R Augusta 2161. Art books and CDs

Fashion stores and boutiques

São Paulo is one of the new hot spots on the global fashion circuit and the designers based here have collections as chic as any in Europe or North America, but at a fraction of the price. Best buys include smart casual day wear, bikinis, shoes, jeans and leather jackets. *Havaiana* flip flops, made famous by Gisele Bundchen and Fernanda Tavares, are as much as a tenth the price of Europe. The best areas for fashion shopping are Jardins (around R Oscar Freire) and the **Iguatemi shopping centre** (on Av Faria Lima). The city's most exclusive shopping emporium is **Daslu**.
Daslu, R Domingos Leme 284, Vila Nova Conçeição, T1138423785. This temple to snobbery is worth visiting if only for

anthropological reasons. It is the fashion store of choice for South America's high society: it's not uncommon for customers to fly in from Argentina or Mato Grosso on private planes and spend up to $50,000 in a single shopping spree. Collections include that of **Daslu** itself, alongside Brazilian names like **Ricardo Almeida** and international names. These sit alongside boutiques selling everything from high-class wines to beautiful coffee-table books.

Shopping Iguatemi, Av Brigadeiro Faria Lima 2232.The leading shopping mall in the city with a healthy representation of most of Brazil's foremost labels.

Hotel Lycra, R Oscar Freire 1055, Jardins, T38974401, www.hotellycra.com. A favourite shopping spot for the Jardins teenybopper set who park their expensive open-top 18th birthday presents outside and pop in to browse the collection from a rotating selection of young, new Brazilian designers.

Adriana Barra, R Peixoto Gomide, 1801, casa 5, Jardins, T1130643691. Elegantly whimsical clothing in beautiful fabrics displayed in an artsy little boutique.

Alexandre Herchcowitz, R Haddock Lobo 1151, T1130632889. The most famous Brazilian designer – using brightly colou red materials to create avante garde designs strongly influenced by what is in vogue in Europe.

Andre Lima, R Dr Cardoso de Mello 474, Vila Olímpia, T1138493444. One of the brightest new stars on the SP fashion scene. André grew up in the Amazon and his collections are light, tropical and sensual.

Fause Haten, Alameda Lorena 1731, Jardins, T1130818685. One of Brazil's most internationally renowned designers who works in laminate plastic, lace, leather, mohair and denim with laminate appliqués, selling through, amongst others, Giorgio Beverly Hills.

Forum, R Oscar Freire 916, Jardins T1130856269, www.forum.com.br. A huge white space attended by beautiful pouting shop assistants helping impossibly thin twenty-something Brazilians to squeeze into tight, but beautifully cut jeans and other fashion items.

Iodice, R Oscar Freire 940, T30859310, and Shopping Iguatemi, T1138132622, www.iodice.com.br. Sophisticated and innovative knitwear designs sold abroad in boutiques like **Barney's NYC**.

Lenny, Shopping Iguatemi. T1130322663, and R Escobar Ortiz 480, Vila Nova Conceicao, T3846-6594, www.lenny.com.br. Rio de Janeiro's premiere swimwear designer and Brazil's current favourite.

Mario Queiroz, R Alameda Franca 1166, T1130623982, www.marioqueiroz.com.br. Casual and elegant clothes for twenty-something men with a strong gay chic element.

Ocimar Versolato Luxo, Bela Cintra 2190, Jardins and in Shopping Iguatemi. Brazil's foremost and most famous fashion figure made his name in Paris as the creative director of **Lanvin**, and is still based there. He is famous for his uninhibited haute couture evening gowns ('my dresses bear the mark of a country where people are not ashamed of their bodies'), which sell in Paris for around $15,000. His São Paulo shop sells his range of sexy, flirty, luxury, ready-to-wear clothes and jeans.

Ricardo Almeida, Daslu and Shopping Iguatemi, T1138126947. One of the few Brazilian designers who styles for men. His clothes are a range of dark suits and slick leather jackets aimed at would-be bit-part actors from *The Matrix*.

Rosa Chá, R Oscar Freire 977, T1130812793, and Shop X76, Shopping Iguatemi, T30323078. The premier fashion label in designer swimwear in the world: beautifully cut bikinis in the very best materials.

Victor Hugo, R Oscar Freire 816, T1130821303. Brazil's most fashionable handbag designer.

Walter Rodrigues, R Natingui 690/696, Vila Madalena, T1130318562. Haute couture for women – renowned for evening gowns which are fluid, sensual and very much inspired by the belle epoque.

Zoomp, R Oscar Freire 995, T30641556, Shopping Iguatemi, T1130325372, www.zoomp.com.br. **Zoomp** have been famous for their figure-hugging jeans for nearly 3 decades and have grown to become a nationwide and now international brand.

Handicrafts and souvenirs

Casa dos Amazonas, Av Jurupis 460.

Ceará Meu Amor, R Pamplona 1551, loja 7. Good-quality lace from the northeast.

Galeria Arte Brasileira, Av Lorena 2163,

galeria@dialdata.com.br. Good value.
Sutaco, República Metrô station. Handicrafts shop promoting items from the state of São Paulo, Tue-Fri 1000-1900, Sat 1000-1500; there is a showroom at R Augusta 435, 6th floor.
Arts and handicrafts are also sold in **Parque Tte Siqueira Campos/Trianon** on Sun from 0900-1700.

Jewellery

There are many shops selling precious stones.
H Stern, Praça da República 242, R Augusta 2340, R Oscar Freire 652 and at Iguatemi, Ibirapuera, Morumbi, Paulista and other shopping centres, hotels **Hilton**, Sheraton and **Maksoud Plaza**, and at the international airport.
Amsterdam Sauer, has outlets at Av São Luís 29, hotels **Maksoud Plaza and Sheraton**, shopping centres Iguatemi, Morumbi, and at the international airport.

Maps

Mapolândia, 7 de Abril 125, shop 40.
Geo Mapas, R Gen Jardim 645, 3rd floor, Consolação, T2592166 (40% discount for volume purchases, excellent 1988 1:5,000,000 map of Brazil, town maps).
Editorial Abril, R do Cartume 585, Bl C, 3rd floor, Lapa, T8716004, F8716270.

Markets

The '**Hippy Fair**' that used to take place in Praça da República was moved to Tiradentes Metrô station but is not nearly as lively or colourful. **Oriental Fair**, Praça de Liberdade Sun 1000-1900, good for Japanese snacks, plants and some handicrafts, very picturesque, with remedies on sale, tightrope walking, gypsy fortune tellers, etc. Below the Museu de Arte de São Paulo, an **Antiques Market** takes place Sun 1000-1700. **Av Lorena**, which is one of the upmarket shopping streets off R Augusta in Jardins, has an open-air market on Sun selling fruits and juices. There are **flea markets** Sun in **Praça Don Orione** (main square of the Bixiga district) and in **Praça Benedito Calixto** (Pinheiros). São Paulo is relatively cheap for film and clothes (especially shoes). The **Ceasa flower market**, Av Doutor Gastão Vidigal 1946, Jaguaré, Tue and Fri 0700-1200, should not be missed.

Photography

Cine Camera Service, R Conselheiro Crispiniano 97, 2nd floor. For repairs to Canon and other makes.

Supermarkets and malls

Typical of modern development are the huge **Iguatemi**, **Ibirapuera** and **Morumbi** shopping centres. They include luxurious cinemas, snack bars and most of the best shops in São Paulo. Other malls include **Paulista** and **Butantã**. On a humbler level are the big supermarkets of **El Dorado** (Av Pamplona 1704) and **Pão de Açúcar** (Praça Roosevelt, near the Hilton); the latter is open 24 hrs a day (except Sun).

Activities and tours

Football

The most popular local teams are Corinthians, Palmeiras and São Paulo who generally play in the Morumbi and Pacaembu stadiums.

Golf courses

The following 18-hole golf courses are about half an hour's drive from the centre:
São Paulo Golf Club, Praça Dom Francisco Souza 635, in Santo Amaro, in beautiful surroundings.
Clube de Golf de Campinas, Via Anhangüera, Km 108, Campinas.
Clube de Campo São Paulo and **Guarapiranga Golf e Country**, both at Reprêsa Guarapiranga, Estr Paralheiros, Km 34.
São Fernando Golf Club, Estr de Cotia, Km 29. There is a lakeside club at Km 50 on the Santos road.
There are 9-hole courses at:
São Francisco Club, Estr de Osasco, Km 15.
Anglo Sports Center, Barretos.
International Golf Club, Via Dutra Km 232, Guaratinguetá.

Tour operators

Ambiental Viagens e Expedições, Av Prudente Morais 344, conj 5, T8148809. English and Spanish spoken, helpful. Recommended for trips to less well known places.
AmEx office in **Hotel Sheraton Mofarrej**, Av Santos 1437, T2843515.
Kontik-Franstur (American Express

The Brazilian Grand Prix

Motor racing has had a long and distinguished history in Brazil and the first race day for cars and motorcycles at Interlagos was held on 12 May 1940. The first Brazilian Grand Prix was held there in 1972 and Emerson Fittipaldi won in 1973 driving a Lotus in a time of one hour 43 minutes at an average speed of 183 kph. He repeated this with an even faster time of one hour 24 minutes the following year in a McLaren and in 1975 another Brazilian José Carlos Pace (after whom the track is named) won in a Brabham. During the 1980s the race was held at the Jacarepaguá racetrack in Rio de Janeiro where the outspoken Nelson Piquet won twice in 1983 and 1986 with some of the fastest lap times seen on this track.

The race returned to the reformed Interlagos during the 1990s, and the legendary Aryton Senna was the last Brazilian driver to win here in 1991 and 1993. After his tragic death in 1994 as a result of mechanical failure, Brazilian viewing figures for motor racing fell drastically. Today, however, there are still many very capable Brazilians driving for the Formula One teams such as Pedro Paulo Diniz (Sauber), Ricardo Zonta (BAR) and Rubens Barrichello (Ferrari) who is probably only waiting for the right car to be up there with his fellow countrymen.

The Brazilian Grand Prix is usually the second of the year being held over a weekend at the end of March or the beginning of April. The race consists of 72 laps of the 4.292-km circuit for a total distance of 309.024 km. Approximately 55,000 people attend the race in addition to the millions watching around the world. The training session takes place on Friday morning; the time trial on Saturday morning and the race itself on Sunday afternoon with warm ups and the drivers' parade in the morning. Tickets can be bought from the racetrack during the whole week or by contacting ABN Amro Bank on T01155072500 from abroad and T0800170200 inside Brazil. Minimum ticket price is US$75 rising to US$350 depending on the viewing sector. Sectors A and G are uncovered and the cheapest, whilst sector D (S do Senna) is covered, provides a better view and is more expensive. Tickets for the training sessions are cheaper and can be bought from 0700 on the day from the box office at the circuit. VIP hospitality is readily available but at a high price.

Private cars are banned from the racetrack but park and ride facilities (US$5) are available on Saturday from Shopping SP Market, Avenida das Nações Unidas 22540, and on Sunday from Hipermercado, Avenida das Nações Unidas 4403 and Shopping Interlagos, Avenida Interlagos 2255. There are also buses (Saturday-Sunday) from Praça da República, between Rua do Arouche and Rua Marquês de Itu (295), from Praça Com Linneu Gomes at Congonhas Airport and from Rua dos Jequitibás in front of the Jabaquara bus station (189). All buses have different coloured stickers to indicate which drop-off point they serve. Further general information about the Grand Prix in English can be obtained from www.gpbrasil.org.

representative), R Marconi 71, T2597566.

Lema Turismo, Av Marquês de Itú 837, T231519. Personalized excursions, Marta Schneider speaks 8 languages, including Hungarian.

STB, Av Brig Faria Lima 1713, T8700555. ISIC cards and student discounts.

Terra Expedições, Osmar e Valdir, R Silva Jardim 429, Santa Terezinha, Santo André, T4463381, recommended for motorcycle tours and information, Spanish and Italian spoken (English improving). Visits to coffee *fazendas* (May-Jun) and round trips to the surrounding country organized by agencies.

Walking

Free Way, R Leôncio de Carvalho 267, Paraíso, T2854767. For nature trails, etc.

Yachting, sailing and rowing

See Santo Amaro reservoir (see p189).

Transport

See also Ins and outs, p178.

Air

Cumbica International Airport (also known as **Guarulhos**, T64452945) operates services to all parts of the world and much of the rest of Brazil from here. **Varig** has its own terminal for international flights, adjoining the old terminal and shared with only a handful of other airlines. There is a helpful English-speaking tourist office in each terminal on the ground floor which gives advice on hotels and transport and hands out free maps and listings of events. **Emtu** bus service every 30 mins to Guarulhos from Praça da República 343 (northwest side, corner of R Arouche) 0530-2300, and from Tietê rodoviária, US$6.50, 30-45 mins. Buses also run from Bresser bus station to Guarulhos and there are other buses from Jabaquara bus terminal to Guarulhos, without luggage space, usually crowded. Taxi fares from the city to the airport are between US$35-40 and vary from cab to cab. Rush-hour traffic can easily turn this 30-min journey into an hour. There are plenty of banks and money changers in the arrivals hall open 0800-2200 daily. There is a post office on the 3rd floor of Asa A and tourist information is also available from the airport branch of Secretaria de Esportes e Turismo open 0800-2200, Sat-Sun and holidays 0900-2100.

The domestic airport of **Congonhas**, 14 km from the city centre on Av Washington Luiz, T50909000, is used for the Rio-São Paulo shuttle (about 400 flights a week US$100 one-way) and some other domestic services. The airport at Campo de Marte, Av Santos Dumont 1979, T2902699, is used for charter flights and helicopters.

Airline offices Aerolíneas Argentinas, Araújo 216, 6th floor, T2590319 (Guarulhos T64453806); **Alitalia**, Av São Luís 50, cj 291, T2571922 (Guarulhos T64453791); **American Airlines**, Araújo 216, 1st floor, T568010; **Avianca**, R da Consolação 293, 10th floor T2576511 (Guarulhos T64453798); **British Airways**, Av São Luís 50, 32nd floor, T2596144 (Guarulhos T64452462); **Continental**, R da Consolação 247, 13th floor, T0800554777 (Guarulhos T64454187); Delta, R Marquês de Itu 61, T2585866; **Iberia**, Araújo 216, 3rd floor, T25076711 (Guarulhos T64452060); **JAL**, Av Paulista 542, 2nd floor, T2515222 (Guarulhos T64452040); **KLM**, Av São Luís 86, T2571363 (Guarulhos T64452011); **LanChile**, R da Consolação 247, 12th floor, T2592900 (Guarulhos T64452824); **Lufthansa**, R Gomes de Carvalho 1356, 2nd floor, T30485868 (Guarulhos T64452220); **Rio-Sul**, R Bráulio Gomes 151, T55612161; **TAM**, R da Consolação 247, 3rd floor, T55828631 (Guarulhos T64452220); **TAP**, Av São Luís 187, T2555366 (Guarulhos T64452400); **United**, Av Paulista 777, 9-10th floor, T2532323 (Guarulhos T64453283); **Varig**, R da Consolação 362/372, Av Paulista 1765, T50917000 (Guarulhos T64452825, Congonhas T5350216); **Vasp**, Praça L Gomes/Aurora 974, Av São Luís 72, T0800998277.

Bus

There is a convenient Metrô connection to the main rodoviária at **Tietê**, T2350322, but the only way to the platforms is by stairs. This is very difficult for people with heavy luggage and, for the disabled, almost impossible. Tietê handles buses to the interior of São Paulo state, to all state capitals and international destinations (see below). The left luggage charges US$0.80 per day per item. You can sleep in the bus station after 2200 when the guards have gone; tepid showers cost US$2.

Buses to **Rio**, 6 hrs, every 30 mins, US$12.50 (*leito* US$25), special section for this route in the rodoviária, request the coastal route via Santos (*via litoral*) unless you wish to go the direct route. To **Florianópolis**, 11 hrs (US$23.75, *leito* US$36.25). To **Porto Alegre**, 18 hrs, US$36.50 (*leito* US$60). To **Curitiba**, 6 hrs, US$10.25-12.50. To **Salvador**, 30 hrs, US$51 (*leito* US$64). To **Recife**, 40 hrs,

US$60-70. To **Campo Grande**, 14 hrs, US$33. To **Cuiabá**, 24 hrs, US$42. To **Porto Velho**, 60 hrs (or more), US$75. To **Brasília**, 16 hrs, US$30 (*leito* US$60). To **Foz do Iguaçu**, 16 hrs, US$30. To **São Sebastião**, 4 hrs, US$8.85 (say 'via Bertioga' if you want to go by the coast road, beautiful journey but few buses take this route).

International buses To **Montevideo**, via Porto Alegre, with TTL, departs Mon, Thu, Sat 2200, 31 hrs, US$100, cold a/c at night, plenty of meal stops, bus stops for border formalities, passengers disembark only to collect passport and tourist card on the Uruguayan side (also EGA, same price, US$67 to **Chuy**, Tue, Fri, Sun). To **Buenos Aires**, Pluma, 36 hrs, US$145. To **Santiago**, Pluma or Chilebus, 56 hrs, US$130, Chilebus, poor meals, but otherwise good, beware overbooking. To **Asunción** (1,044 km), 18 hrs with Pluma (US$57, *leito* US$112), Brújula (US$64) or RYSA (US$110), all stop at Ciudad del Este (US$43, 50 and 84 respectively, Pluma *leito* US$84). Cometa del Amambay runs to Pedro Juan Caballero and Concepción.

There are 3 other bus terminals, Barra Funda, T664682 (as described above), to cities in southern São Paulo state and many destinations in Paraná, including **Foz do Iguaçu** (check for special prices on buses to **Ciudad del Este**, which can be cheaper than buses to Foz). Bresser (Metrô Bresser), T66925191, for Cometa (T69677255) or Transul (T66938061) serving destinations in Minas Gerais. **Belo Horizonte**, 10 hrs, US$15.60, 11 a day (*leito* US$31.20), 9 a day with Gontijo. Translavras and Util also operate out of this station. Prices are given under destinations. Buses from Jabaquara, at the southern end of the Metrô line for **Santos**, US$3.60, leave every 15 mins, taking about 50 mins, last bus at 0100. Also serves destinations on the southern coast of São Paulo state.

Car

The *rodízio* which curbs traffic pollution by restricting car use according to number plate functions between 0800-1000 and 1700-2000. Check which day restricts your number plate.

Car hire Avis, Araújo 232 and at the airports, T0800118066; Budget, R da Consolação 328, loja 1, and at Guarulhos, T2564355; Hertz, Araújo 216, 1st floor, and at the airports, T8837300 or T0800147300; Interlocadora, several branches, São Luís T2555604, M Fontes T2573544, Guarulhos T64453838, Congonhas T2409287; Localiza,

Sao Paulo metrô

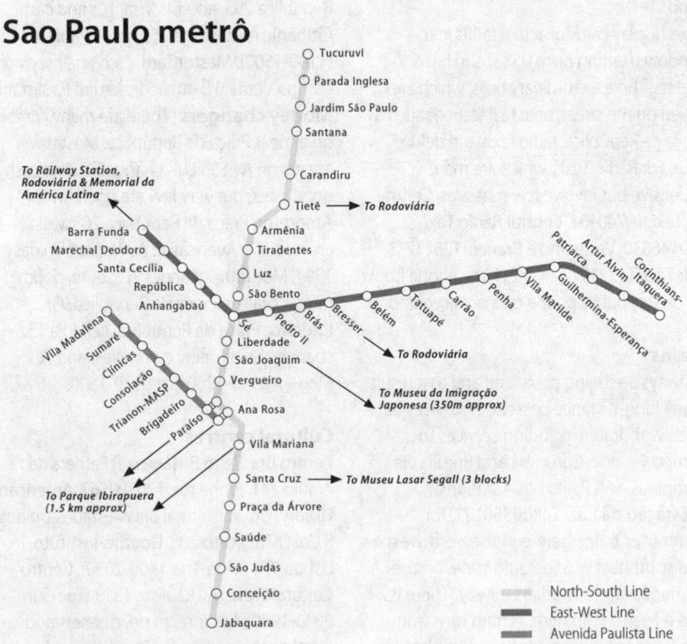

T0800-992000, or www.localiza.com.br, for all reservations, 8 branches in the city.

Hitchhiking

To hitch to Rio, take the Metrô to Armênia, then a bus to Guarulhos, alighting where the bus turns off the Rio road for Guarulhos.

Metrô

The first Metrô in Brazil, it began operating in 1975 and has 2 main lines intersecting at **Praça de Sé**: north-south from **Tucuruvi** to **Jabaquara**; east-west from **Corinthians Itaquera** to **Barra Funda** (the interchange with Fepasa and RFFSA railways and site of the São Paulo and Paraná rodoviária). An extension east to Guaianases is to open soon. A 3rd line runs from **Vila Madalena** in the west, along **Av Paulista**, to **Ana Rosa** in the south, joining the Jabaquara line at Paraíso and Ana Rosa. A 4th line, **Vila Sônia** to **Luz**, is projected. The 2 main lines operate from 0500-2400, **Vila Madalena** to **Ana Rosa** 0600-2200. Stations are well-policed and safe. Fare US$0.75, US$6 for a book of 10 tickets; backpacks are allowed. Combined bus and Metrô ticket are available, US$1, eg to Congonhas Airport.

Taxi

Taxis display cards of actual tariffs in the window (starting price US$3) and have meters. There are ordinary taxis, which are hailed on the street, or at taxi stations such as Praça da República, radio taxis and deluxe taxis. For Radio Taxis, which are more expensive but involve fewer hassles, **Central de Táxi**, T9740182; **Central Rádio Táxi**, T69146630; **Vermelho e Branco**, T2511733; **TeleTáxi**, T2331977, or check the phone book for others; public phone calls not accepted.

Trains

Railways are being privatized and as a result many long-distance passenger services have been withdrawn including services to Campo Grande, Corumbá and Brasília via Campinas. São Paulo has 4 stations:

Estação da Luz, T0800550121, for commuter trains between the northwest and southeast of São Paulo state, on the former Santos a Jundiaí Railway. There is also a Metrô stop here. A train runs from Luz 8 times a day to connect with the **tourist train** from Paranapiaçaba to Rio Grande da Serra, US$0.50.

Barra Funda, T0800550121, handles commuter destinations on the former Sorocabana and former Santos a Jundlaí railway lines. Services go to **São José do Rio Preto** (overnight), **Barretos**, **Ourinhos**, **Londrina**, **Maringá**, **Sorocaba** and **Ponta Grossa**. There is also a Metrô station and a rodoviária at Barra Funda.

Júlio Prestes, T0800550121, for commuter services to the west on the former Sorocabana metre-gauge railway.

Roosevelt, T9421132, for commuter trains to east on former Central do Brasil and Santos a Jundiaí railways.

Directory

Banks

Banking hours are generally 1000-1600, although times differ for foreign exchange transactions (check at individual branches). **Banco do Brasil** will change cash and TCs and will advance cash against Visa. All transactions are done in the foreign exchange department of any main branch (eg Av São João 32, Centro), but queues are long. **Banespa**, eg at R Duque de Caxias 200, Centro, or Praça da República 295, accepts Visa, TCs and cash. **Citibank**, Av Ipiranga 855, or Av Paulista 1111 (1100-1500). **MasterCard**, cash against card, R Campo Verde 61, 4th floor, Jardim Paulistano. **Money changers** There are many *câmbios* on or near Praça da República. Most travel agents on Av São Luís change TCs and cash at good rates, but very few are open on Sat; **Amoretur**, Praça da República 203, will change TCs; **Avencatur**, Av Nações Unidas 1394, Morumbi, changes TCs, euro, good rates; **Coraltur**, Praça da República 95; **Interpax**, Praça da República 177, loja 13, changes cash (many currencies) and TCs, Mon-Fri 0930-1800, Sat 0930-1300.

Cultural centres

Centro Brasileiro Britânico, R Ferriera de Araújo 741, Pinheiros, T30390567. **American Library**, União Cultural Brasil-Estados Unidos, R Col Oscar Porto 208. **Goethe-Instituto**, R Lisboa 974 (Mon-Thu 1400-2030). **Centro Cultural Fiesp**, Av Paulista 1313 (Tue-Sun 0900-1900), has foreign newspapers and magazines. See under Entertainment for

Alliance Française Theatre. If you are interested in cultural articles related to São Paulo and Brazil in general, check out the website of the **Instituto Cultural Itaú**, www.ici.org.br.

Embassies and consulates

Consulates Argentina, Av Paulista 1106, T2841355 (0900-1300, very easy to get a visa here); **Australia**, R Tenente Negrão 140, T38496281; **Austria**, R Augusta 2516, 10th floor, T2826223 (Mon-Thu 0930-1130); **Bolivia**, R Honduras 1447, T30811688 (0900-1300); **Canada**, Av Nações Unidas 12901, T55094343 (0900-1200, 1400-1700); **Denmark**, R Oscar Freire 379, T30613625, (Mon-Thu 0900-1700, Fri 0900-1400); **France**, Av Paulista 1842, 14th floor, T2879522 (0830-1200); **Germany**, Av Brigadeiro Faria Lima 2092, T38146644 (0800-1130); **Ireland**, Av Paulista 2006, 5th floor, T2876362 (1400-1700), T2842044; **Israel**, Av Brig Faria Lima 1713, T38157788; **Netherlands**, Av Brigadeiro Faria Lima 1779, T38130522 (0900-1200); **New Zealand**, Av Campinas 579, T2880700; **Norway and Sweden**, R Oscar Freire 379, 3rd floor, (Norway) T8833322, (Sweden) T30611700 (0900-1300); **Paraguay**, R Bandeira Paulista 600, 15th floor, T38490455 (0830-1600); **Peru**, R Votuverava 350, T38191793 (0900-1300); **South Africa**, Av Paulista 1754, T2850433; **Switzerland**, Av Paulista 1754, 4th floor, Caixa Postal 30588, T2534951; **UK**, Av Paulista 37, 17th floor, T2877722, consulad@uol.com.br; **Uruguay**, Av Santos 905, T2840998 (1000-1600); **US**, R Padre João Manuel 933, T30816511 (0800-1700); **Venezuela**, R Veneza 878, T38874583 (0900-1130).

Immigration

Federal Police, Marginal Tiete, open 1000-1600 for visa extensions.

Internet

Av Paulista 1499, conj 1001 (Metrô Trianon), 1100-2200, English spoken, 2nd-hand books; **Kiosknet**, Shopping Light, 4th floor, R Cel Xavier de Toledo 23, opposite Teatro Municipal, T31513645, US$2.50 per hr; **O Porão**, R Tamandaré 1066, near Vergueiro metro station; **Saraiva Megastore**, Shopping El Dorado, US$3.

Language courses

The official **Universidade de São Paulo (USP)** is situated in the Cidade Universitária (buses from main bus station), beyond Pinheiros. There are a number of architecturally interesting buildings plus the museums mentioned above. They have courses available to foreigners, including a popular Portuguese course, registry is through the Comissão de Cooperação Internacional, R do Anfiteatro 181, Bloco das Colméias 05508, Cidade Universitária, São Paulo. Other universities include the **Pontifical Catholic University (PUC)**, and the **Mackenzie University**. Both these are more central than the USP, Mackenzie in Higienopolis, just west of the centre, and PUC in Perdizes. Take a taxi to either. Both have noticeboards where you can leave a request for Portuguese teachers or language exchange which is easy to arrange for free. Any of the gringo pubs are good places to organize similar exchanges.

Laundry

Chuá Self Service, R Augusta 728, T2584953, limited self-service, not cheap; **Di-Lelles**, R Atenas 409, T72983928, pricey.

Medical services

Hospital das Clínicas, Av Dr Enéias de Carvalho Aguiar 255, Jardins, T30696000; **Hospital Samaritano**, R Cons Brotero 1468, Higenópolis, T8240022. Recommended. Both have *pronto-socorro* (emergency services). Contact your consulate for names of doctors and dentists who speak your language. **Emergency and ambulance**: T192. **Fire**: T193.

Post office

Correio Central, Praça do Correio, corner of Av São João and Prestes Máia, T8315222. Booth adjoining tourist office on Praça da República, weekdays only 1000-1200, 1300-1600, for letters and small packages only.

Telephone

Embratel, Av São Luís 50, and Av Ipiranga 344. For the international operator dial 000111, for international collect calls dial 000107. Red phone boxes are for national calls, blue ones for international phone calls.

The Coast of São Paulo

The coast of São Paulo state, referred to as the Litoral Norte or Costa Linha Verde (North of Santos) and the Litoral or Costa Sul (South of Santos) is very popular with Paulistanos for weekends away from the city. In either direction there are many resorts to choose from. The central point is the port of Santos, but even here, the beach is close at hand and it is a good place from which to start exploring, especially if you don't want to waste time with the traffic in the state capital. » For Sleeping, Eating and other listings, see pages 219-226.

History

The coast around Santos is one of the sites which has yielded evidence of the Sambaqui culture of around 5,000 BC (see page 679). The Tupinikin were the people who lived in this region when the Portuguese arrived, but the first European settlements at São Vicente and Santos were under constant attack from the Tamoio (allies of the French), who lived further north. For a long time, it was touch-and-go whether the Portuguese settlements would survive. The colony on São Vicente island was founded in 1532 by Martim Afonso de Sousa and the port of Santos was founded soon after. By the 1580s it was reported that there were 400 houses in São Vicente and Santos.

The French and the Tamoio did not succeed in driving the Portuguese out of their captaincy of São Vicente and Santos became one of the most important ports on the Atlantic coast. The ascent of the Serra do Mar to the Paulista plateau, so treacherous in the early days because of both its steepness and Indian attacks, did not deter the harbour's growth. Sugar was grown on the levels at the foot of the mountains and on the plateau. This was the port's main commodity for shipping, but there was also the trade with São Paulo and, when coffee was introduced to the region, Santos was its outlet.

Up to the end of the 19th century, Santos had an evil reputation for its proneness to yellow fever. "Formerly whole ships' crews were stricken down with fever and died, and the ships being left without the slightest protection, ran ashore, and their skeletons are in evidence at the port at the present day". So wrote Frederick Alcock in

São Paulo coast

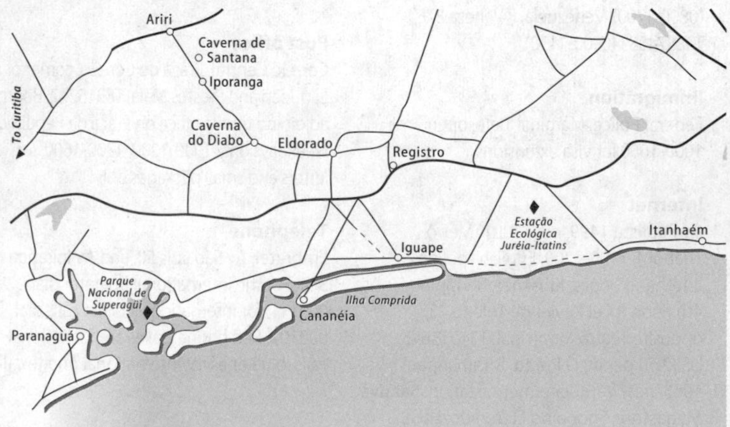

The railway up the hill

The British-built Santos a Jundiaí up the hill to São Paulo is one of the railway wonders of the world; beyond São Paulo it carries on 60 km to Jundiaí. Having passed through Cubatão on the coastal plain, it runs on toothed tracks up the escarpment, going through interesting hill scenery.

Today, RFFSA, the national railway company, runs a tourist train at weekends between São Paulo and Santos (see page 202 for the schedule). Today's timetable bears no relation to how the system operated in the line's heyday. Trains left São Paulo at 0600 in order to get the passengers to their businesses by 0800. At the top of the Serra, the engine was detached from the carriages which were attached to a wire rope. They were then allowed to go down the slope to the port by force of gravity, with another train coming up acting as a counterweight.

1907, who visited Santos "not without some slight feelings of fear". He was, in fact, pleasantly surprised by the place and, once measures been taken to eradicate the fever, Santos soon became a pleasure resort, In addition to its commercial activities.

The hinterland between the sea and mountains gained another reputation for horrors in the 20th century. A few kilometres inland from the city of Santos an important industrial area, including many chemical plants, built up round the steelworks, oil refinery and hydroelectric plant at Cubatão. At one time the pollution was so appalling that it was called 'The Valley of Death'. In the mid-1980s, it was claimed to be the most contaminated part of the planet, with so much toxic waste undermining the hills that the whole lot threatened to slip down into the sea. Such a tragedy has been averted and cleaning-up operations have taken place.

Santos → *Phone code: 013. Colour map 5, A6. Population: 418,000.*

Although better known for its busy commercial port and football team (a museum dedicated to Pelé has has long been planned), the island has a long seafront with

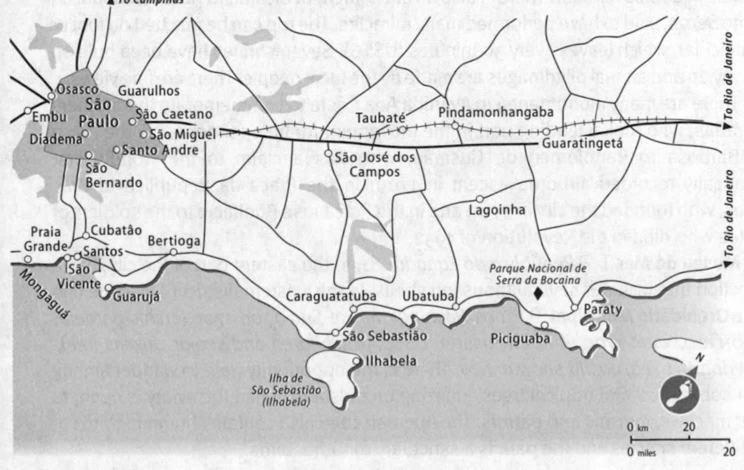

 popular beaches especially during the weekend and holidays. Less than an hour away from São Paulo and its international airport, Santos makes a manageable, friendly base. Gonzaga is the centre of the city's leisure industry with cinemas, bars and restaurants. The centre has some interesting churches and other sights such as the imposing Bolsa Official de Café as well as good views from the summit of Monte Serrat.

The scenery on the routes crossing the Serra do Mar is superb and the roadway includes many bridges and tunnels. From Rio the direct highway, the **Linha Verde** (see pages 164 and 208) is also wonderful for scenery.

Situated 72 km southeast of São Paulo and 5 km from the open sea, Santos is the most important Brazilian port. By sea it is approached along the winding Santos Channel, at the mouth of which is an old fort (1709). A free-port zone for Paraguay, 1,930 km by rail or road, has been established. The island upon which the city stands can be circumnavigated by small boats.

The centre of the city is on the north side of the island. Due south, on the Baía de Santos, is **Gonzaga**, where hotels line the beachfront and the city's entertainment takes place. Between these two areas, the eastern end of the island curves round within the Santos Channel. At the eastern tip, a ferry crosses the estuary to give access to the beaches of the sophisticated resort of Guarujá. The city has impressive modern buildings, wide, tree-lined avenues, and wealthy suburbs. There are **Tourist offices** at the rodoviária (limited information), Praía do Gonzaga on the seafront (in a disused tram, very helpful, lots of leaflets) and **Orquidário Municipal** ⓘ *T0800173887*, limited opening.

Security Although poverty is apparent the city is generally safe but it is wise to exercise caution at night and near the port.

Sights

The streets around **Praça Mauá** are very busy in the daytime, with plenty of cheap shops. In the centre, an interesting building is the **Bolsa Oficial de Café** ⓘ *R 15 de Novembro 95*, the coffee exchange, with a small coffee museum and café inside. Two restored churches in the centre are the 17th-century **Santo Antônio do Valongo**, which is by the railway station on Largo Monte Alegre, and the **Capela da Ordem Terceira de Nossa Senhora do Carmo** (1760), on Praça Barão do Rio Branco. A **Tourist Tram Line** ⓘ *Tue-Sun 1100-1700*, runs from Mauá Square.

It is easy to visit the centre on foot and the only real need to use buses or taxis is to get to Gonzaga or to visit nearby beaches.

Monte Serrat, just south of the city centre, has at its summit a semaphore station and look-out post which reports the arrival of all ships in Santos harbour. There is also an old church, dedicated to Nossa Senhora da Monte Serrat, said to have performed many miracles. The top can be reached on foot or by funicular, which leaves every 30 minutes (US$6). Seven shrines have been built on the way up and annual pilgrimages are made by the local people. There are fine views.

There are many monuments: in Avenida Ana Costa to commemorate the brothers Andradas, who took a leading part in the movement for Independence; in the Praça Rui Barbosa to Bartolomeu de Gusmão, who has a claim to the world's first historically recorded airborne ascent in 1709; in the Praça da República to Brás Cubas, who founded the city in 1534; and in the Praça José Bonifácio to the soldiers of Santos who died in the Revolution of 1932.

Museu do Mar ⓘ *R República do Equador 81*, in the eastern part of the city, has a collection that includes several thousand shells. In the western district of José Menino is the **Orquidário Municipal** ⓘ *Praça Washington, Tue-Sun 0900-1700 (orchid garden), 0800-1100, 1400-1700 (bird enclosure), US$0.50 (children and senior citizens free), flowering Oct-Feb, orchid show in Nov*. There is the opportunity here to wander among giant subtropical and tropical trees, amazing orchids and, when the aviary is open, to meet macaws, toucans and parrots. The open-air cage also contains hummingbirds of 20 different species and the park is a sanctuary for other birds.

Beaches

Santos' 8 km of beaches stretch round the Baía de Santos and lead into those of São Vicente at the western end. From east to west they are **Ponta da Praia**, below the sea wall and on the estuary, no good for bathing, but fine for watching the movements of the ships. Next come **Aparecida**, **Embaré**, **Boqueirão**, **Gonzaga** and **José Menino** (the original seaside resort for the merchants of Santos). São Vicente's beaches of **Itararé** and **Ilha Porchat** are on the island, while **Gonzaguinha** is on the mainland. The last beach is **Itaquitanduva**, which is in a military area, but may be visited with authorization. In all cases, check the cleanliness of the water before venturing in (a red flag means it is too polluted for bathing). See page 208 for Guarujá.

Excursions from Santos

The small island of **Ilha Porchat** is reached by a bridge at the far end of Santos/São Vicente bay. It has beautiful views over rocky precipices, of the high seas on one side and of the city and bay on the other. At the summit is **Terraço Chopp** ⓘ*Av Ary Barroso 274*, a restaurant which has live music most evenings; the views from here are wonderful. On summer evenings the queues to get in can last up to four hours, but in winter, even if it may be a little chilly at night, you won't have to wait.

Itatinga, a village 30 km from Santos in the Serra do Mar, offers the chance to see what is left of the Atlantic forest at close quarters and to trek through mangrove, sandbanks and hillside forest. The area is full of wildlife (lizards, toucans,

The Bandeirantes

Reviled in some quarters for their appalling treatment of Indians, revered in others for their determination and willingness to withstand extreme hardship in the pursuit of their goals, the bandeirantes are an indispensable element in the formation of Brazil.

The Portuguese knew that South America held great riches; their Spanish rivals were shipping vast quantities back to Europe from Peru. They also knew soon after setting up their colonies on the Atlantic side of the continent that Brazil was not readily yielding equivalent wealth. Legends proliferated of mountains of precious stones, golden lakes and other marvels, also of terrifying places, all in the mysterious interior. Regardless of the number of expeditions sent into the *sertão* which returned empty-handed (or failed to return at all), there was always the promise of silver, emeralds or other jewels to lure the adventurous beyond the coast.

The one thing that Brazil had in abundance was Indians. Throughout the colony there was a demand for slaves to work the plantations and farms and the indigenous population satisfied the need for labour. This was especially true in the early 17th century when Portugal temporarily lost its African possession of Angola, from which it sent many slaves to Brazil.

The men who settled in São Paulo, both the Europeans and those of mixed parentage, the mamelucos, proved themselves expert at enslaving Indians. Without official sanction, and certainly not blessed by the Jesuits, these adventurers formed themselves into expeditions which would leave São Paulo, often for years at a time, to capture slaves for the internal market. The Guaraní Indians who had been organized into reducciones by the Jesuits around the Río Paraguay were the top prize and there developed an intense rivalry between the bandeirantes and the Jesuits. The priests regarded the Paulistas as murderous and inhumane; the slavers felt they had some justification in attacking the

butterflies), and thick with vegetation (bromeliads, orchids, eucalyptus). Each trail is graded according to difficulty. You travel to the village of Itatinga by boat on a three-hour trip down the Estuário and the Rio Itapanhaú and then by street car. Or take the BR-101 (Santos-Rio) road, a three-minute crossing by boat and then 7½ km by street car. Access is only through one of the travel agencies officially permitted to lead groups: contact **Sictur** (the tourism department) ⓘ *Praça dos Expedicionários 10, 8th floor, T32224166.*

From here **Alto da Serra**, the summit of the forest-clad mountain range, there are magnificent views. The return journey can be done in under two hours by road.

The Litoral Norte

Guarujá → *Phone code: 013. Colour map 5, A6. Population: 230,000.*

This sophisticated resort becomes very crowded in summer as holidaymakers come to take advantage of its fine beaches, hotels, restaurants and spas. There is a strong undertow on nearly all the Guarujá beaches; the Praia de Pernambuco (also called Jequiti-Mar) is the safest. The beaches in town are mostly built-up and can be polluted, while several of those further away have condominium developments which make public access difficult. If you have a car, try São Pedro beach, passing Praia de Pernambuco and Praia do Perequê with a fishing village beside it, where missions because they were in Spanish territory and, in the 17th century, the entire western boundary of Brazil was in dispute.

This was one side of the coin. The other was that the bandeirantes were incredibly resourceful, trekking for thousands of kilometres, withstanding great hardships, travelling light, inspired not just by the desire to get rich, but also by a fierce patriotism. They certainly did show barbaric treatment to the Indians, but the enthusiasm that inspired the slave drives combined well with the desire to demystify the **sertão**, to uncover its riches. It was this which fuelled the prospecting expeditions after Angola had been recaptured in 1648. The bandeirantes trekked into Minas Gerais, Goiás and Mato Grosso looking for precious metals. Through their efforts, the Minas Gerais gold rush began. They were also enlisted by governors in the northeast to wage war on Indians and they were involved in the destruction of the **quilombo** at Palmares (see page 684).

The principal effect of the expansionist spirit of the bandeira movement was that the interior of Brazil was explored. In the bandeirantes' footsteps came settlers and cattle herders who took over the lands that had been emptied of their Indian population. Although Indians were exploited as labour and became a source of income for the Paulistas, they also intermarried with the Europeans. The mixed-race **mamelucos** and even Indians themselves took part in the **bandeiras**, hastening the miscegenation process which became so evident throughout Brazil. Portuguese control of territory was extended by the bandeirantes' journeys. In their later phase, these journeys also filled Portugal's coffers because much of the wealth derived from the discovery of gold was sent back to Europe.

Further reading John Hemming, *Red Gold* (chapters 12 and 13); and Richard M Morse (editor), *The Bandeirantes*.

excellent seafood restaurants line the seafront. It was formerly a private beach, now open to the public, but be there as early as possible because only 150 cars are allowed: a beautiful spot. **Tourist office** ⓘ *R Quintino Bocaiúva 248, T33877199*.

Bertioga→ *Phone code: 013. Colour map 5, A6. Population: 17,000.*

There are good seafood restaurants on the road (SP-061) between Guaraujá and Bertioga, the next major beach centre up the coast (one hour by bus). It, too, can be an overcrowded place in the summer. A ferry crosses the mouth of the Canal de Bertioga. The town is on the north bank of the canal and beyond is a long sweeping bay with seven beaches divided by a promontory, the Ponta da Selada. Going northeast, the beaches are **Praias de Bertioga** (Enseada, Vista Linda and Indaía), **Praia São Lourenço** (which has been developed as the Riviera de São Lourenço, with condos, hotels, green areas and sports facilities), **Praia Itaguaré**, **Praia Guaratuba** and **Praia Boracéia** (campsite, meals served). The hills behind Bertioga are covered in forest which is now being used for walking and appreciation of the Mata Atlântica by local agencies. **Tourist offices** ⓘ *Departamento de Esportes e Turismo Municipal, R Luiz Pereira de Campos 901, Vila Itapanhaú, T33171213 ext 2075*.

Two forts, São Felipe and São João, were built to protect the coast from attack by the Tamoio Indians in the 16th century. São João, in Bertioga, can be visited and part of it houses the **João Ramalho Museum**, which contains a variety of historical objects. There is a Festa da Primavera in October.

Camburi and Maresias → *Phone code: 012.*

Beyond Boracéia are a number of beaches, including Barra do Una, Praia da Baleia and **Camburi**. The latter is surrounded by the Mata Atlântica. The sea is clean and good for bathing and watersports, including surfing (see Surfing, page 66, for this and other recommendations), especially at the best of the beaches, Camburizinho (though you should avoid swimming in the river which is not clean). There are a number of good hotels and one excellent dining restaurant in Camburi. You can walk on the Estrada do Piavu into the Mata Atlântica to see streams, vegetation and wildlife (bathing in the streams is permitted, but use of shampoo and other chemicals is forbidden). About 5 km from Camburi is Praia Brava, 45 minutes' walk through the forest, camping is possible. The surf here is very heavy (hence the name).

The road carries on from Camburi, past beaches such as Boiçucanga to **Maresias**, which is beloved of well-to-do Paulistas who come here mostly to surf. It has some chic *pousadas* and restaurants and tends to be younger and less family orientated than Camburi.

São Sebastião → *Phone code: 012. Colour map 5, A6. Population: 59,000.*

From Maresias it is 21 km to São Sebastião, a built-up resort town surrounded by good beaches. The many small islands offshore have good snorkelling and scuba-diving (for Brazil – poor by Australian or Caribbean standards). The most beautiful is **Ilhabela** (see below), shrouded in forest and fringed with some of the country's very best beaches.

São Sebastião is on a narrow strait which separates the mainland from the Ilha de São Sebastião, popularly called Ilha Bela, Brazil's largest marine (as opposed to riverine) island. Since colonial times, this has been an important area. The island, which was called Ciribaí, island of peace, by the Indians, was reported by Amerigo Vespucci in 1502, who renamed it after the saint of the day of his discovery. São Sebastião was settled at the end of the 16th century. With good sugar-growing land on the mainland and the island it was both a port for sending the sugar back to Europe and another point of defence against the Tamoio. Gold was discovered in the vicinity in 1722 so this, too, and later coffee were shipped out. Slaves were also brought through here. The oil industry has subsequently taken advantage of the harbour by building a terminal here.

For **tourist information**, contact **Sectur** ⓘ *Av Dr Altino Arantes 174, T4521808*, who are friendly and helpful except regarding Ilhabela.

The natural attractions of the area include a large portion of the **Parque Estadual da Serra do Mar** on the mainland, with other areas under protection for their different ecosystems. Trails can be walked through the forests. There are also old sugar plantations. The **Centro de Biologia Marinha da Univesidade de São Paulo** is located here and, for divers, as well as the marine fauna, there are a large number of wrecks in the strait that can be explored.

In São Sebastião the colonial centre is under the aegis of the Patrimônio Histórico e Artístico. A **Museu de Arte Sacra** ⓘ *R Sebastião Neves 90, daily 1000-1700, free,* is in the 17th-century chapel of São Gonçalo in the town centre. The town's parish church on Praça Major João Fernandes was built in the early 17th-century and rebuilt in 1819. There is a **Museu do Naufrágio** ⓘ *free*, near the church exhibiting shipwrecks and natural history of the local area. Other colonial constructions are the **Cadeia Pública** (the prison) ⓘ *Praça Tobias de Aguiar*, now the military police HQ, and the **Casa Esperança** ⓘ *Av Altino Arantes 154*. There is an internet café on the beachfront.

The beaches within 2 or 3 km of São Sebastião harbour are polluted; others to the south and north are clean and inviting. Ilhabela tends to be expensive in season, when it is cheaper to stay in São Sebastião.

Ilhabela (Ilha de São Sebastião)→ *Phone code: 012. Colour map 5, A6. Population: 21,000 (100,000 high season).*

ⓘ Ferries leave regularly from São Sebastiao, opposite the island. It is very difficult to find space for a car on the ferry during summer weekends. Come during the week when the island feels deserted, and avoid the high season at all costs. You will need insect repellent as there are small biting flies on some of the beaches. The Secretaria de Turismo, R Bartolomeu de Gusmão 140, Pequeá, T4721091, www.ilhabela.sp.gov.br.

The island of São Sebastião, known popularly as Ilhabela since the 1940s, is of volcanic origin, roughly 390 sq km in area. The four highest peaks are **Morro de São Sebastião**, 1,379 m above sea-level, **Morro do Papagaio**, 1,309 m, **Ramalho**, 1,285 m, and **Pico Baepi**, 1,025 m. All are often obscured by mist. Rainfall on the island is heavy, about 3,000 mm a year. The slopes are densely wooded and 80% of the

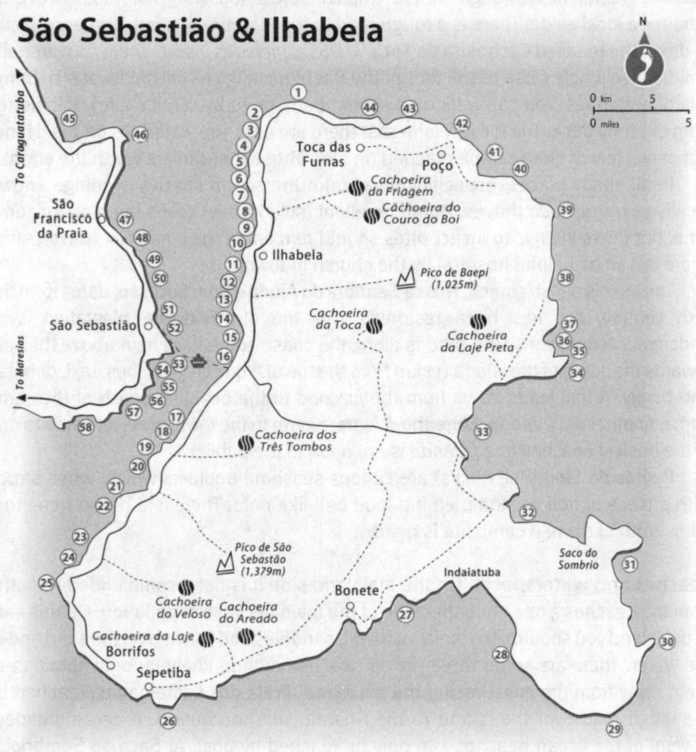

Beaches ○

Ponta das Canas **1**
Armação **2**
Pinto **3**
Ponta Azeda **4**
Pedra do Sino **5**
Arrozal **6**
Siriúba **7**
Viana **8**
Mercedes **9**
Saco do Indaiá **10**
Saco Grande **11**
Pequeá **12**
Engenho d'Água **13**
Itaguaçu **14**
Itaquanduba **15**
Perequê **16**
Cabras **17**
Pedra Miúda **18**
Portinho **19**
Feiticeira **20**
Julião **21**
Grande **22**
Curral **23**
Veloso **24**
Ponta da Sela **25**
Ponta da Sepetiba **26**
Enchovas **27**
Ponta do Diogo **28**
Ponta do Boi **29**
Ponta da Pirabura **30**
Saco Grande **31**
Figueira **32**
Baía dos Castelhanos **33**
Ponta da Cabeçuda **34**
Eustáquio **35**
Guanxuma **36**
Caveira **37**
Serraria **38**
Ponta Grossa **39**
Poço **40**
Ponta do Lobo **41**
Fome **42**
Jabaquara **43**
Pacuíba **44**
Enseada **45**
Cigarras **46**
Olaria **47**
Arrastão **48**
Pontal da Cruz **49**
Deserta **50**
Porto Grande **51**
Centro **52**
Preta **53**
Grande **54**
Pitangueiras **55**
Timbó **56**
Barraqueçaba **57**
Guaecá **58**

forest is protected by the **Parque Estadual de Ilhabela**. Many endangered Atlantic coast rainforest species (including some felines) live here. Birdwatching is good and the beaches are magnificent. The state park also encompasses the eight other islands In the archipelago, of which Ilhabela is the largest; only two other islands are inhabited, Vitória and Búzios.

Most of the flatter ground on Ilhabela is given over to sugar-cane. In the 19th-century illegal slave traders used the island. The only settled district lies on the coastal strip facing the mainland, the Atlantic side being practically uninhabited except by a few fisherfolk. The place abounds in tropical plants and flowers, and many fruits grow wild; their juice mixed with *cachaça* and sugar makes as delicious a cocktail as can be imagined.

A 50-km return journey on foot over the hump of the island down towards the Atlantic, sometimes through dense tropical forest following the old slave trail, requires a local guide. There is a rough road to the Atlantic side, but it is very difficult to drive. The terraced **Cachoeira da Toca** ⓘ *US$4, includes insect repellent*, waterfalls amid dense jungle close to the foot of the Baepi peak, give cool freshwater bathing; lots of butterflies. You can walk on a signed path, or go by car; it's a few kilometres from the ferry dock. The locals claim that there are over 300 waterfalls on the island, but only a few of them can be reached on foot. Those that can are worth the effort.

In all shady places, especially away from the sea, a species of midge known locally as *borrachudo* thrives. **Autan** repellent (sold locally) keeps them off for some time, but those allergic to insect bites should remain on the inhabited coastal strip. There is a small helpful hospital by the church in town.

The town's parish church, **Nossa Senhora da Ajuda e Bom Sucesso**, dates from the 17th century, but has been restored. Visit the old **Feiticeira** plantation, with underground dungeons. The road is along the coast, sometimes high above the sea, towards the south of the island (11 km from the town). You can go by bus, taxi, or horse and buggy. A trail leads down from the *fazenda* to the beautiful beach of the same name. Another old *fazenda*, **Engenho d'Água**, nearer to the town, gives its name to one of the busiest beaches (the *fazenda* is not open to the public).

Pedras do Sino (Bell Rocks) are curious seashore boulders which, when struck with a piece of iron or stone, emit a loud bell-like note. There is a beach here, too, 4 km north of town. A campsite is nearby.

Beaches and watersports On the mainland side it is not recommended to bathe from the beaches 3 or 4 km either side of the town because of pollution. On this side of the island you should also look out for oil, sandflies and jellyfish on the sand and in the water. There are some three dozen beaches around Ilhabela, only about 12 of them away from the coast facing the mainland. **Praia dos Castelhanos**, reached by the rough road over the island to the Atlantic side (no buses), is recommended. Several of the ocean beaches can only be reached by boat. At **Saco do Sombrio**, a cove on the Atlantic coast, English, Dutch and French pirates sheltered in the 16th and 17th centuries. Needless to say, this has led to legends of hidden treasure, but the most potent story about the place is that of the Englishman, Thomas Cavendish. In 1592 he sacked Santos and set it on fire. He then sailed to Saco do Sombrio where his crew mutinied, hanged Cavendish, sank their boats and settled on the island.

On the south coast is the fishing village of **Bonete**, which has 500 m of beach and can be reached either by boat (1½ hours), or by driving to Borrifos at the end of the road, then walking along a trail for three hours.

The island is considered the *Capital da Vela* (capital of sailing) because its 150 km of coastline offers all types of conditions. The sheltered waters of the strait are where many sailors learn their skills and the bays around the coast provide safe anchorages. There are, however, numerous tales of shipwrecks because of the unpredictable winds, sudden mists and strange forces playing havoc with compasses, but these provide plenty of adventure for divers. There are over 30 wrecks that can be dived, the most notable being the *Príncipe de Asturias*, a transatlantic liner that went down off the Ponta de Pirabura in 1916.

Caraguatatuba → *Phone code: 012. Population: 69,000.*

On the Santos-Rio road is São Francisco da Praia, opposite the northern end of Ilhabela, beyond which begin the beaches of Caraguatatuba. In all there are 17 good beaches to the northeast and southwest, most divided between two sweeping bays. As well as watersports, Caraguatatuba is known for hang-gliding and, like so many places that are denominated 'capital' of something, is called the **Capital do Vôo Livre** (capital of hang-gliding). It is a popular place at weekends and in the summer, with good hotels, restaurants, bars and campsites. For tourist information, contact the **Secretaria Municipal de Turismo** ⓘ *R Luiz Passos 50, T4208142, www.caraguatatuba.sp.gov.br.*

In common with other places on this coast, there are opportunities for walking in the forest behind the coastal strip. The road which goes inland, called the Rodovia dos Tamoios, climbs steeply into the densely wooded hills, with lots of hairpins. There are striking views of Caraguatatuba and the coast; one viewpoint is called O Mirante da Chegada, at Km 70. It takes about 25 minutes before the road levels out in the district of Paraibuna and crosses the high agricultural lands, running beside the bays of a huge artificial lake, the Represa de Paraibuna. The road joins the Dutra highway at São José dos Campos.

Further northeast from Caraguatatuba is **Lagoinha**, 34 km west of Ubatuba, with chalets and sailing boats for hire. There is exotic birdlife in the nearby forest and the ruins of an 18th-century *fazenda*, **Engenho Bom Retiro**. Boat trips can be made to beaches and islands.

Ubatuba → *Phone code: 012. Colour map 5, A6. Population: 67,000.*

This is one of the most beautiful stretches of the São Paulo coast and has been recognized as such by the local tourist industry for many years. In all, there are 72 beautiful beaches, some large, some small, some in coves, some on islands. Surfing is the pastime of which it is said to be capital, but a whole range of watersports is on offer, including sailing to and around the offshore islands. The **Tropic of Capricorn** runs through Ubatuba (through the beach of Itaguá to be precise).

The beaches are spread out over a wide area, so if you are staying in Ubatuba town, you need to use the buses which go to most of them. Either that, or hire a car. The area gets very crowded at carnival time as people from Rio come to escape the crowds in their city. Ubatuba, though, does celebrate Carnival itself.

The commercial centre of Ubatuba is at the northern end of the bay, by the estuary which the fishing boats enter and leave. A bridge crosses the estuary, giving access to the coast north of town. A small jetty with a lighthouse at the end protects the river mouth and this is a nice place to watch the boats come and go. The seafront, stretching south from the jetty, is built up along its length, but there are hardly any high-rise blocks. In the commercial centre are shops, banks, services, lots of restaurants (most serving pizza and fish), but few hotels. These are on the beaches north and south and can be reached from the Costamar bus terminal. The **tourist office** ⓘ *Av Iperoig opposite R Prof Thomaz Galhardo*, is on the seafront.

History

This part of the coast was a hotly contested area between the local indigenous population and the Portuguese. The Jesuits José Anchieta and Manuel Nóbrega came to the village of Iperoig, as it was called in 1563, to put a stop to the fighting; the former was even taken hostage by the locals during the negotiations. A cross on the

Praia do Cruzeiro (or Iperoig) in the centre commemorates the peace which the town proudly claims to be the first peace treaty on the American continent. The colonists eventually prevailed and the town of Vila Nova da Exaltação da Santa Cruz do Salvador de Ubatuba became an important port until Santos overtook it in the late 18th century. In the 20th century its development as a holiday resort was rapid, especially after 1948 when it became an Estância Balneária. The shortened name of Ubatuba derives from the Tupi-Guarani, meaning 'place of ubas', a type of tree used for making bows and canoes. Cariocas disparagingly refer to it as Uba 'chuva' – as it can rain heavily here at any time.

Sights

Ubatuba has a few historic buildings, such as the **Igreja da Matriz**, Praça da Matriz, which is 18th-19th century and has only one tower, the old 19th-century prison which now houses the small historical museum, **Cadeia Velha** on Praça Nóbrega, the 18th-century **Câmara Municipal** on Avenida Iperoig, and the **Sobrado do Porto**, the 19th-century customs house at Praça Anchieta 38, which contains **Fundart** (the Art and Culture Foundation). Mostly, though, it is a modern, functional town. In the surrounding countryside there are *fazendas* which are often incorporated into the trilhas ecológicas (nature trails) which are proliferating along the coast.

The **Projeto Tamar** ⓘ *R Antonio Athanasio da Silva 273, Itaguá, T4326202*, is a branch of the national project which studies and preserves marine turtles. The **Aquário de Ubatuba** ⓘ *R Guarani 859, T4321382, Fri-Wed 1000-2200*, has well-displayed Amazon and Pantanal species including caimans and piranhas.

There is a small airport from which stunt fliers take off to wheel and dive over the bay. In summer 10-minute panaromic flights and helicopter rides over Ubatuba are on offer (US$15).

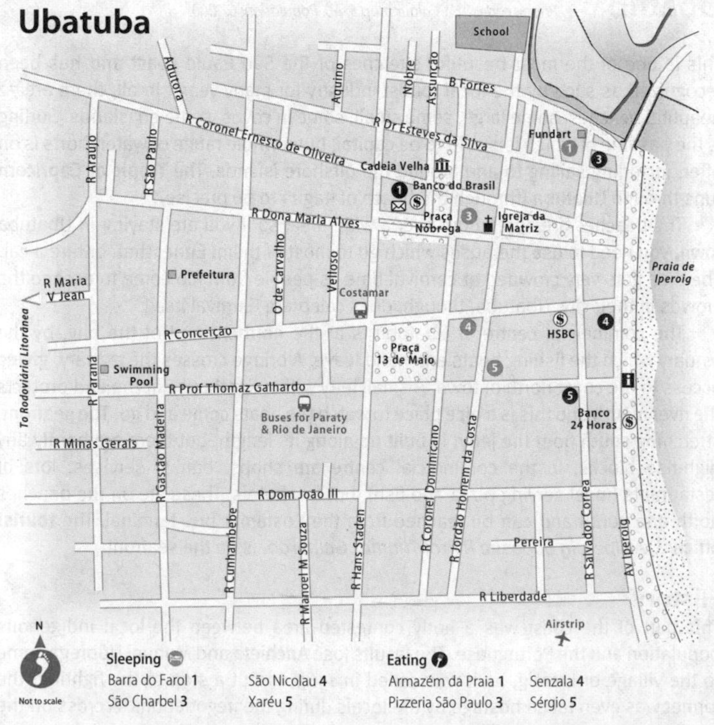

Beaches

The only beach where swimming is definitely not recommended is that part of the beach near the town's outflow between Praia do Cruzeiro and Praia Itaguá. The sand and water close to the jetty don't look too inviting either. The most popular are Praias Tenório, Grande and Toninhas (4½, 6 and 8 km south respectively). Condominiums, apartments, hotels and *pousadas* line these beaches on both sides of the coast road. Of the municipality's 72 beaches, those to the south are the more developed although the further you go from town in either direction, the less built-up the beaches are. Boogie boards can be rented at many of the beaches, or you can buy your own in town for around US$5.

Saco da Ribeira, 13 km south, is a natural harbour which has been made into a yacht marina. Schooners leave from here for excursions to **Ilha Anchieta** (or dos Porcos), a popular four-hour trip (US$10, for agencies, see below). On the island are beaches, trails and a prison, which was in commission from 1908-1952. The Costamar bus from Ubatuba to Saco da Ribeira (every 20-30 minutes, US$0.85) drops you at the turn-off by the Restaurante Pizzeria Malibu. It's a short walk to the docks and boatyards where an unmade road leads right, through the boatyards, to a track along the shore. It reaches the Praia da Ribeira which you can walk along to another track going round a headland. This leads to the beaches of **Flamengo, Flamenguinho** and **Sete Fontes**. It's a pleasant stroll (about one hour to Flamengo), but there is no shade and you need to take water. Note the sign before Flamengo on one of the private properties: "Propriedade particular. Cuidado c/o elefante!".

Parque Nacional Serra da Bocaina

ⓘ *Permission to visit must be obtained in advance from Ibama, ToXX12-31172183/88 in São José do Barreiro, the nearest town; there are hotels and trekking agencies here, including Vale dos Veados, Estr da Bocaina, Km 42, ToXX12-5771194, FoXX12-5771303, part of the Roteiros de Charme hotel group,* *see p47.*

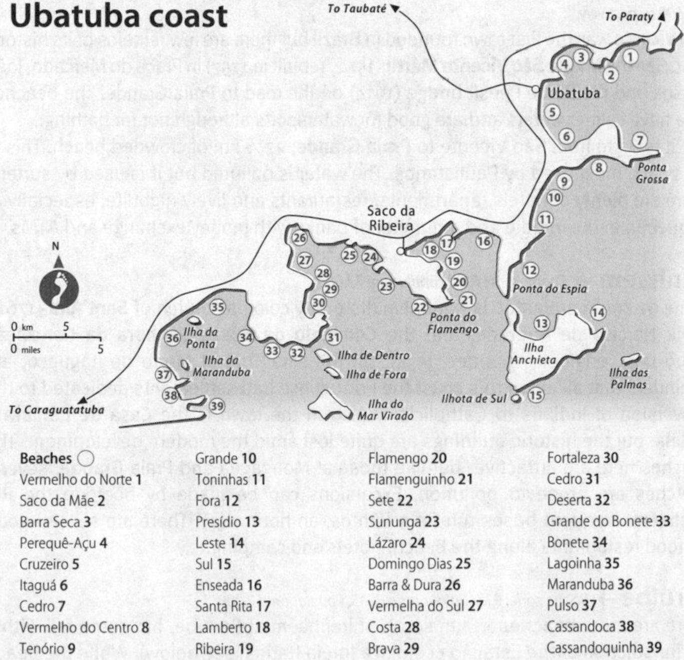

Straddling the border of São Paulo and Rio de Janeiro states is the Parque Nacional Serra da Bocaina, which rises from the coast to its highest point at **Pico do Tira** (or Chapéu) at 2,200 m, encompassing three strata of vegetation. Up to 1,000 m the forest is mainly made up of large trees such as *maçaranduba* (milk, or cow trees), *jatobá* (courbaril), cedar and *angelim* (angely). Between 1,000 and 2,000 m the predominant varieties are pines and myrtles. Higher than this, the landscape is more grassy and open, with bromeliads, orchids and lichens. The main river flowing through it is the Mambucaba, which cascades down the mountainsides in a series of waterfalls. Trails lead to some of the falls and an old gold trail leads through the park (a three or four-day hike).

All the remaining patches of Mata Atlântica along the Linha Verde provide habitat for some of Brazil's rarer endemic birds. A book such as Nigel Wheatley's *Where to watch birds in South America* can give far greater detail than this guide has space for. Otherwise, contact specialists locally and, where necessary, ask permission to birdwatch on private land.

The Litoral Sul

Unlike the Linha Verde, the Litoral Sul between Santos and Cananéia is not continuously developed. From São Vicente to Itanhaém, the whole coast is completely built-up with holiday developments. But beyond Itanhaém the road does not hug the shore, so that a large area has been left untouched. This zone and several others on the southern São Paulo coast add up to almost 80% of the region being under some form of environmental protection. An organization called **SOS Mata Atlântica** ⓘ *Rua Manoel da Nóbrega 456, São Paulo, CEP 04001-001, T011-88701195, smata@ax.apc.org*, aims to help preserve what is left of the coastal vegetation.

São Vicente and Praia Grande → *Phone code: 013. Population: 279,500 and 150,500 respectively.*

São Vicente was the first town founded in Brazil but there are few remains of its historic past. See the **Matriz São Vicente Mártir** (1542, rebuilt in 1757) in Praça do Mercado, João Pessoa and the Ponte Pênsil bridge (1914) on the road to Praia Grande. The beaches here have calmer waters and are good for watersports although not for bathing.

It is 8 km from São Vicente to **Praia Grande**, 22½ km of crowded beach. This is the beach most used by Paulistanos. The water is polluted but it is used by surfers. There are plenty of hotels, apartments, restaurants and lively nightlife, especially at Boqueirão in the middle and a number of banks with money exchange and ATMs.

Itanhaém → *Phone code: 013. Population: 72,000.*

Some 61 km from Santos is Itanhaém. Its pretty colonial church of **Sant'Ana** (1761), Praça Narciso de Andrade, and the **Convento da Nossa Senhora da Conceição** (1699-1713, originally founded 1554), on the small hill of Morro de Itaguaçu, are reminders that all along this coast the Portuguese had settlements dedicated to the conversion of Indians to Catholicism. Also in the town is the **Casa de Câmara e Cadeia**, but the historic buildings are quite lost amid the modern development. The beaches here are attractive, but like those at Mongaguá and Praia Grande, several stretches are prone to pollution. Excursions can be made by boat up the **Rio Itanhaém**. Frequent buses run from Santos, an hour away. There are several good seafood restaurants along the beach, hotels and camping.

Peruíbe → *Phone code: 013. Colour map 5, A5. Population: 52,000.*

There are more beaches 31 km south of Itanhaém at Peruíbe, but some fall within the jurisdiction of the Estação Ecológica Juréia-Itatins (see below). While the beach culture has been well developed here, with surfing, windsurfing, fishing and so on, a number of 'alternative' options have recently flourished. The climate is said to be unusually healthy owing to a high concentration of ozone in the air; this helps to filter out harmful ultraviolet rays from the sun. UFO watchers and other esoterics claim that it is a very mystical place. Local rivers have water and black mud which has been proven to contain medicinal properties. And the neighbouring ecological station is a major draw now that ecotourism has become big business in São Paulo state. Peruíbe's history dates back to 1530 when the village of Abarebebê was founded; about 9 km northeast of here, the ruins can be visited, with its church built of stone and shells.

For tourist information, contact the **Secretaria de Turismo** ⓘ *R Nilo Soares Ferreira 50, T4552070*. You may have to ask permission in the **Departamento da Cultura** ⓘ *Centro de Convenções, Av Sã João 545, T4552232*, to visit Abarebebê and other sites. Also at this address is the **Secretaria Estadual do Meio Ambiente** ⓘ *T4579243*, for information on the **Estação Ecológico Juréia-Itatins**. There is a **Feira do Artesanato** ⓘ *Av São João, Sat and Sun 1400-0100 (1400-2300 in winter)*. Buses connect the town with Santos (for São Paulo).

Estação Ecológico Juréia-Itatins

ⓘ *For permission to visit the ecological station, contact the Secretaria Estadual do Meio Ambiente, address above, or the Instituto Florestal (DRPE), R do Horto 931, CEP 02377, São Paulo, T011-9528555.*

Peruíbe marks the northernmost point of the Estação Ecológico Juréia-Itatins, 820 sq km of protected Mata Atlântica. The station was founded in 1986. The four main ecosystems are restinga, mangrove forest, Mata Atlântica and the vegetation at about 900 m on the Juréia range of mountains. Its wildlife includes many endangered species, including rare flowers and other plants. There are deer, jaguar, monkeys, dolphins, alligators and birds, including the yellow-headed woodpecker and toucans. Human occupation of the area has included sambaqui, builders, *fazendeiros* and present-day fishing communities who preserve an isolated way of life.

Tourism in the ecological station is very carefully monitored and only certain areas are open to the public. These are: the **Núcleo Itinguçu**, 18 km from Peruíbe, which contains the Cachoeira do Paraíso (Paradise Falls) and other pools and waterfalls; **Vila Barra do Una**, a fishing village with a 2-km beach, camping and places to eat, 25 km from Peruíbe; and **Canto da Praia da Juréia** at the extreme southern end, 38 km from Iguape, with 7 km of beach and all the coastal ecosystems. Hikers can walk the 4-km **Trilha do Arpoador** and the 5-km **Trilha do Imperador**, but both need prior reservation and numbers are limited; similarly the Despraiado mountain bike trail. Trips can be made, with authorization, up the **Rio Guaraú** (8 km from Peruíbe) and the **Rio Una do Prelado** (25 km from Peruíbe). Other places of interest are **Vila do Prelado**, which was a stop on the Imperial São Vicente-Iguape post route (electric light was only installed in 1995), and the **Casa da Farinha**, where manioc flour is made, 28 km from Iguape.

Iguape and Ilha Comprida → *Phone code: 013. Colour map 5, A5. Population: 28,000.*

At the southern end of the ecological station is the town of Iguape founded in 1538. In the early days of its existence, ownership of the town was disputed between Spain and Portugal because it was close to the line drawn by the Pope marking Spanish and Portuguese territory in the 'New World'. Typical of Portuguese architecture, the small **Museu Histórico e Arqueológico** ⓘ *R das Neves 45, Tue-Sun 0900-1730*, is housed in the 17th-century Casa da Oficina Real de Fundição. There is also a **Museu de Arte Sacra** ⓘ *Praça Rotary, Sat and Sun 0900-1200, 1330-1700*, in the former Igreja do Rosário. The main church, the **Basílica de Bom Jesus**, is a mid-19th-century construction. For **tourist information**, contact the **Prefeitura Municipal** ⓘ *R 15 de Novembro 272, T8411626, F8411620*.

Half a dozen beaches, but particularly yachting and fishing, bring tourists to the town. Excursions include the ruined *fazenda* of **Itaguá**. Handicraft specialities are items in wood and clay, basketware and musical instruments.

Opposite Iguape is the northern end of the **Ilha Comprida** with 86 km of beaches (some disappointing). This **Área de Proteção Ambiental** is not much higher than sea level and is divided from the mainland by the Canal do Mar Pequeno. The northern end is the busiest and on the island there are good restaurants, hotels and supermarket – fresh fish is excellent.

Caverns of the Vale do Ribeiro

The caves are southwest of the state capital, west of the BR-116, in one of the largest concentrations of caverns in the world. Among the best known is the 8-km **Caverna do Diabo** (Devil's Cave), or **Gruta da Tapagem** ⓘ *Mon-Fri 0800-1100, 1200-1700, Sat, Sun and holidays 0800-1700, US$2*. It has been described as huge 'as a cathedral' with well-lit formations in the 600 m that are open. It is 40 km from **Eldorado Paulista**.

Some 43 km from Caverna do Diabo is **Petar**, the Parque Estadual Turístico do Alto Ribeira. Here are three groups of caves: the Núcleo Santana, with the **Cavernas de Santana** (with 5.6 km of subterranean passages and three levels of galleries), Morro Preto and Água Suja, plus a 3.6-km ecological trail to the waterfalls in the Rio Bethary; and the Núcleo Ouro Grosso. This section of the park is 4 km from the town of **Iporanga**. Iporanga is the most convenient town for visiting all the caves; it is 64 km west of Eldorado Paulista, 42 km east of Apiaí, on the SP-165, 257 km southwest of São Paulo. The third Núcleo is Caboclos, near the town of Apiaí. Guided tours of Petar cost US$50 a day from the Associação Serrana Ambientalista, T015-5561188.

Registro → *Phone code: 013. Population: 49,000.*

A suitable stopping place for visiting the caves area is Registro on the BR-116, in the heart of the tea-growing region, populated mainly by Japanese-Brazilians. There are a number of cheap hotels around the corner from the rodoviária (including **D Brasília**, Rua Brasília) and banks with ATMs.

Cananéia and Ilha do Cardoso → *Phone code: 013. Colour map 5, A5. Population: 12,500.*

At the southern end of Ilha Comprida, across the channel, is Cananéia, 270 km from São Paulo. Another town with a long colonial history, it was one of Martim Afonso de Souza's landfalls, and is now a peaceful place of gently decaying colonial charm. The colonial centre, around Praça Martim Afonso de Souza and neighbouring streets, contains the 17th-century church of **São João Batista** and the **Museu Municipal**. On 15 August, there is the Festa de Nossa Senhora dos Navegantes, with a procession of boats. To the south are a number of good beaches and the waterways are popular with fisherfolk.

For tourist information, contact the **Departamento de Esportes e Turismo** ⓘ *Av Beira Mar 247, Cananéia, T8511473 ext 342*. A recommended guide ⓘ *Manoel Barroso, Av Independencia 65, T8511273*, speaks Portuguese only. Otherwise try the **Secretaria do Parque Estadual da Ilha do Cardoso** ⓘ *Av Prof Besnard*, near the port.

To reach the densely wooded **Ilha do Cardoso**, which is a Reserva Florestal e Biológica, take a ferry from the dock at Cananéia, four hours, three services daily (Rua Princesa Isabel, T8411122). Alternatively, drive 70 km along an unpaved road, impassable when wet, to **Ariri**, from where the island is 10 minutes by boat. The tiny village of Marujá, which has no electricity, has some very rustic *pousadas* and restaurants. Otherwise, the island is uninhabited. Camping is allowed at designated places. There are lots of idyllic beaches; best for surfing is Moretinho.

Sleeping

Santos *p205, map p207, phone code 013*

50% discounts often available in hotels during low season. There are many cheap hotels near the Orquidário Municipal a few blocks from the beach.

A Mendes Plaza, Av Floriano Peixoto 42, 1 block from beach in shopping street, T32894243, www.grupomendes.com.br. Big 1980s block with a/c rooms with TVs, a restaurant, sauna, massage and sports facilities. Afternoon tea served daily.

A Parque Balneário, Av Ana Costa 555, T32895700, www.parquebalneario.com.br. The best large hotel in town with a good restaurant, rooftop pool, convention centre and beach service.

B Atlântico, Av Pres Wilson 1, T32894500, www.atlantico-hotel.com.br. A/c rooms in a modest but well-kept hotel on the seafront. All have TVs. Sauna, bar, restaurant.

B Avenida Palace, Av Pres Wilson 10, T32893555, www.avenidapalace.com.br. On the seafront with rather simple rooms, but pleasant.

D Independência, Av Mcal Floriano Peixoto 206, T32376224. Friendly with small but bright airy rooms with a/c, radio and TV. On the seafront. Nice.

E Natal, Av Mcal Floriano Peixoto 104, T32842732. Clean and friendly with good breakfast.

E Pousada do Marquês, Av Floriano Peixoto 204, T32371951. Basic, small, family-run. Restaurant downstairs, shared bath. Recommended.

Guarujá *p208, phone code 013*

L Casa Grande Resort and Spa, Av Miguel Stéfano 1087, T/F33552300, www.casagrandehotel.com.br. Mock-colonial luxury on a pristine stretch of beach with a range of spa treatments. The hotel has a nightclub in the summer.

L Jequiti-Mar, 8 km beyond Guarujá on the road to Bertioga, T/F33533111. Extremely attractive holiday complex with private beaches (excellent swimming and boating), fine fishing grounds, and chalet accommodation, excellent restaurant, 2 nightclubs open each weekend and every night from Dec to Mar.

AL Delphin, Av Miguel Stéfano 1295, turn left in the centre of Guarujá and drive less than 1 km to the beginning of the long Praia da Enseada, T33862112, www.delphin hotel.com.br. A range of rooms overlooking the beach. Pool, good service and a reasonable restaurant.

B Pousada Mira Mar, R Antônio Marques

328, Tombo, T/F33541453. Standard simple beach *pousada* with breakfast included.

E **Guarujá**, R das Carmélias 10, Praia da Enseada, T33517779, IYHA youth hostel. Price per person.

Bertioga *p209, phone code 013*

B **Balsa**, Av Tomé de Souza 3268, T/F33171226. Simple but pleasant with good service and a restaurant.

B **Marazul 27**, Av Tomé de Souza 825, Enseada, T33171109. Simple hotel with a decent seafood restaurant.

Camburi and Maresias *p210, phone code 012*

A **Camburyzinho**, Estr Camburi 200 Km 41, Camburizinho, T38652625, www.pousada camburizinho.com.br. 30 or so smart rooms around a pool with a bar and beach service.

B **Piccolo Albergo**, R Nova Iguaçu 1979, Maresias, T34656227, www.piccolo albergo.com.br. 5 smart chalets in a forest setting near a waterfall. With sauna and a natural swimming pool.

B **Pousada das Praias**, Rua Piauí 70, Camburizinho, T38651474, www.pousada daspraias.com.br. Pleasant little beachside *pousada* with a pool and sauna.

São Sebastião *p210, phone code 012*

The city itself is not particularly desirable – head for Ilhabela and stay in São Sebastião only if you have to. There are a few cheap places near the main praça and rodoiviária.

B **Roma**, on the main praça, T4521016. Excellent service, simple but well-maintained rooms. Warmly recommended.

Camping

Camping do Barraqueçaba Bar de Mar de Lucas. Near the beach about 6 km south of São Sebastião, with hot showers, English spoken, cabins available. Recommended.

Ilhabela *p211, map p211, phone code 012*

There are a number of moderate and cheap hotels on the road to the left of the ferry.

LL-L **Maison Joly**, R Antonio Lisboa Alves 278, Morro do Cantagalo, T38961201, www.maisonjoly.com.br. Exquisite little *pousada* which is perfect for couples – wonderful view out over the bay, great restaurant and pool and each cabin tastefully decorated in its own style. Private, intimate, quiet. No children allowed.

AL-L **Barulho d'Agua**, Rua Manoel Pombo 250, Curral Km 14, T38941406, www.barulho dagua.com.br. Intimate little cabins set in rainforest next to a clear water river. Very romantic.

A **Ilhabela**, Av Pedro Paulo de Morais 151, Saco da Capela. T38961083, www.hotelilhabela.com.br. One of the larger *pousadas*, orientated to families and with a well-equipped, though small gym, pool, restaurant and bar and good breakfast. Recommended.

A **Porto Pousada Saco da Capela**, R Itapema 167, T38962255, www.sacodacapela.com.br. 18 carefully decorated cabins set in a rocky forest garden on a steep hill. Good pool and breakfast.

B **Pousada dos Hibiscos**, Av Pedro Paulo de Morais 714, T38961375, www.pousadados hibiscos.com.br. Little group of cabins set around a pool with a sauna, gym and bar. Nice atmosphere. Recommended.

B **Vila das Pedra**, R Antenor Custodio da Silva 46, Cocaia, T38962433, www.vila daspedras.com.br. 11 chalets in a forest garden. Tastefully decorated and with a very nice pool.

C **Canto Bravo**, Praia do Bonete, T97660478. Secluded on a deserted beach 1½ hrs' walk (or 20-min boat ride) from Ponta de Sepituba. Modest but elegantly decorated cabins and excellent simple breakfast and lunch (included in the price).

C-D **Tamara**, R Jacob Eduardo Toedtli 163, Itaquanduba, T38962543, www.pousada-tamara.com.br. 17 cabanas with a/c around a small pool.

E **Ilhabela**, Av Col José Vicente Faria Lima 1243, Perequê, T4728468, hostelling@ iconet.com.br. IYHA youth hostel. Price per person.

Camping

In addition to **Pedra do Sino**, there are campsites at **Perequê**, near the ferry dock, and at **Praia Grande**, a further 11 km south.

Caraguatatuba *p213, phone code 012*

B **Pé na Areia**, R Tsusuki Yoshimoto 615, town beach Km 10, T38842670, www.pena reia.com.br. A small group of well-appointed cabins with a pool, sauna, bike rental and beach services. Bright, clean and modern.

E **Recanto das Andorinhas**, R Eng João Fonseca 112, T4226181. Dorms and doubles a block behind the central bus terminal, 50 m from the beach.

Ubatuba *p213, map p214, phone code 012*

Very cheap accommodation is hard to come by and at all holiday times no hotel charges less than US$20.

Beach hotels

L **Recanto das Toninhas**, Praia das Toninhas, T38421410, www.toninhas.com.br, Part of Roteiros de Charme group (see p47). Elegant cabanas with sea views gathered around a very pretty pool with a full range of services and activities, including a sauna, restaurant, bar, tennis court and excursions.

AL **Refúgio do Corsário**, Baia Fortaleza, 25 km south of Ubatuba, T4439148, F4439158. A clean quiet hotel on the waterfront with full board and a range of activities including sailing and swimming. Very relaxing.

AL **Saveiros**, R Laranjeira 227, Praia do Lázaro, 14 km from town, T38420172, www.hotelsaveiros.com.br. Pretty little *pousada* with a pool and a decent restaurant, English spoken.

A **Solar das Águas Cantantes**, Estr Saco da Ribeira 253, Praia do Lázaro, Km 14, T4420178, www.ubatuba2000.com.br/solar. A mock-Portuguese colonial house replete with *azulejos* and set in a shady tropical garden. The restaurant is one of the best on the São Paulo coast and serves excellent seafood and Bahian dishes.

B-C **Rosa Penteado**, Av Beira-Mar 183, Praia de Picinguaba, T38338998, www.ubatubasite.com.br/atelierrosapenteado. 4 pretty beachside cabanas all decorated with paintings and objects made by the artist owner. The price includes a very good breakfast and dinner.

E **Maurício**, Av Abreu Sodré 607, north of town, near Praia do Perequê-Açu. Cheap rooms in a private house with a laundry service.

Ubatuba town

B **São Charbel**, Praça Nóbrega 280, T4321090, F4321080. Very helpful and comfortable, on busy main square, the advertised rooftop 'pool' is in reality a tiny plunge pool.

C **São Nicolau**, R Conceição 213, T4325007, F4323310. 3-min walk from the bus station, convenient for the town beach restaurants and services. Well run and looked after with a/c rooms with a TV and fridge and a good breakfast.

C **Xaréu**, R Jordão Homem da Costa 413, T4321525, F4323060. 3-min walk from the bus station, convenient for the town beach restaurants and services. Pretty rooms with wrought-iron balconies in a pleasant garden area. Good value, excellent breakfast. Recommended.

D **Barra do Farol**, R Dr Félix Guizard Filho 6, T4322019. Homely, motel-style rooms close to seafront.

E **Cora Coralina**, Rod Oswaldo Cruz Km 89, near the Horto Florestal, T011-2580388. Price per person. IYHA youth hostel, 0800-2300. Simple dorms and doubles. Friendly and helpful.

E **JS Brandão**, R Nestor Fonseca 173, Jardim Sumaré, near the Tropic of Capricorn sign south of town, T4322337. Price per person. IYHA youth hostel, 0700-2300. Pleasant staff, modest accommodation but clean and well kept.

Camping

Camping Clube do Brasil sites at Lagoinha (25 km from town), T4431536, and Praia Perequê-Açu, 2 km north, T4321682. There are about 8 other sites in the vicinity.

Peruíbe *p216, phone code 013*

A **Piero Al Mare**, R Indianópolis 20, Praia Orla dos Coqueiros, T4582603. Modest, plain rooms with breakfast and a restaurant.

B-C **Waldhaus**, R Gaviotas 1201, Praia do Guaraú, T4579170. Small hotel in a pleasant setting with friendly staff, a/c or fan-cooled rooms and a restaurant.

C-D **Vila Real**, Av Anchieta 6625, T4582797. Basic but well looked after and with good staff.

Iguape and Ilha Comprida *p218, phone code 013*

B **Silvi**, R Ana Cândida Sandoval Trigo 515, T/F8411421, silvihotel@virtualway.com.br. Simple, but pleasant and with friendly staff.

C **Solar Colonial Pousada**, Praça da Basilica

30, T8411591. A range of rooms in a converted 19th-century house.

D **Veleiro**, Av Beira Mar 579, T8952407. Modest but well maintained. Recommended.

Camping

There is a campsite at **Praia da Barra da Ribeira**, 20 km north, and wild camping is possible at **Praia de Juréia**, the gateway to the ecological station.

Caverns of the Vale do Ribeiro *p218, phone code 013*

C **Pousada das Cavernas**, Iporanga, T015-5561168 (or TXX011-5433082). Pleasant, simple with breakfast.

D **Pousada Rancho da Serra**, Iporanga, T015-5561168 (or TXX011-5882011). Friendly staff who give advice about caving.

E **Youth hostel**, near the Caverna do Diabo, Província de Tokushima, Parque Estadual da Caverna do Diabo, Km 43, SP-165, Eldorado Paulista, T0XX11-353077, 0800-1800.

Camping

Camping in **Petar** costs US$3 per person, 3 sites.

Cananéia and Ilha do Cardoso *p219, phone code 013*

B-C **Cananéia Glória**, Av Luís Wilson Barbosa, T8511377, F8511378. A range of chalets some with good views.

C **Villa São João Batista**, R Tristão Lobo 287, T8511587. Colonial-style 18th-century house, simple but very pleasant.

Eating

See also hotels in Sleeping, above.

Santos *p205, map p207, phone code 013*

TT **Dona Mineira**, R Djalma Dutra 1, Gonzago. Self-service, pleasant wooden terrace, homely interior on 2 floors, excellent food. Recommended.

TT **Mare Mansi**, in **Hotel Avenida Palace**, Av Presidente Wilson 9. Full menu, terrace overlooking beach. Seafaring theme, piped music, civilized.

TT **Restaurante Praia Gonzaga**, Av Mal Floriano Peixoto 104a, Gonzaga.

T **Point 44**, R Jorge Tibiriçá 44. Large, popular self service. Sports screen and live music from 2030, Tue-Sun. Self-service with *churrasco*, lunch only.

T **Shopping Miramar**, Av Mal Floriano Peixoto 44, With a number of fast-food outlets, including **Bob's**.

Camburi and Maresias *p210, phone code 012*

There are numerous cheap and mid-range restaurants with good food, bars and nightclubs in Camburi, Camburizinho and Maresias.

TTT **Manacá**, R do Manacá, T38651566, closed Mon and Wed in Nov and Mar. The best restaurant on the São Paulo coast and one of the best in the state, with French cooking techniques with Brazilian, Asian and seafood ingredients. Specialities include sole in orange and ginger sauce with puréed potato and wasabi. Very romantic setting – in a little tropical rainforest garden reached by a candlelit boardwalk. Come for dinner. Well worth a special trip.

Ilhabela *p211, map p211, phone code 012*

There are cheaper places in the main town, including a decent *padaria* (bakery) and some snack bars.

TTT **Pizzabela**, **Hotel Ilha Deck**, Av Alm Tamandaré 805, Itaguassu, T38961489. Paulistanos consider their pizza the best in the world. This is one of the few restaurants outside the city serving pizza, São Paulo-style. Expect lots of cheese. Nice surrounds.

TTT **Viana**, Av Leonardo Reale 1560, Praia do Viana, T38961089. The best restaurant on the island with excellent seafood and light Italian dishes. Good wine list. Book ahead. Pricey.

Ubatuba *p213, map p214, phone code 012*

There is a string of mid-range restaurants along the seafront on Av Iperoig, as far as the roundabout by the airport.

TTT **Giorgio**, Av Leovigildo Dias Vieira 248, Itaguá. Sophisticated Italian restaurant and bar.

For an explanation of the sleeping and eating price codes used in this guide, see the inside front cover. Other relevant information is provided in the Essentials chapter, pages 47 and 57.

Solar das Águas Cantantes, (see Sleeping, above). Very good seafood and Bahian restaurant in elegant surrounds.

Arabí, R Guarani 610, Itaguá. Popular, brightly lit, serving hot and cold Arabic food and desserts.

Pizzeria São Paulo, Praça da Paz de Iperoig 26. Undeniably chic gourmet pizzeria in beautifully restored building. Owned by a young lawyer who brings the authentic Italian ingredients for the gorgeous pizzas from São Paulo every weekend.

Senzala, Av Iperoig. Italian, established 30 years ago with a lovely atmosphere. Don't miss the seafood spaghetti. Recommended.

Armazém da Praia, R Cel Ernesto de Oliveira 149, opposite post office. Pretty, family-run self-service, open for lunch only.

Sérgio, R Prof Thomaz Galhardo 404. Serving ice-creams, pizzas and, at weekends, *feijoada*. Open for dinner weekends only.

Bars and clubs

Santos *p205, map p207, phone code 013*

Torto, Av Siquiera Campos 800, Boqueirão, Reggae, MPB. Rock Thu-Sun. **Bar do Três**, Av Washington Luiz 422, Gonzaga. Bar with live music. **Disco Friday**, Mendes Convention Center, Av Francisco Gilcério 206, T32287575. A/c complex with 6 bars and dancefloors. House and pop music. Minimum consumption US$10 for men, US$5 for women, plus US$2 entry. **Internetbar**, Av Mcal Floriano Peixoto 302, Pompéia. Popular, internet access R$5 per hr when eating or drinking.

Entertainment

Santos *p205, map p207, phone code 013*

Art galleries

Galeria de Arte Nélson Penteado de Andrade, Praça dos Expedicionários 10, Gonzaga, T32354245.

Cinemas

Av Ana Costa, Gonzaga. Mainstream films. **Cine Arte**, Posto 4, Av Vicente de Carvalho. Brazilian and foreign films.

Theatre

Teatro Municipal Brás Cubas, Av Sen Pinheiro Machado 48, Vila Mathias, T32336086.

Festivals and events

Santos *p205, map p207, phone code 013*

26 Jan Foundation of Santos.
Mar/Apr Good Fri.
Jun Corpus Christi; Festejos Juninos. Throughout the summer there are many cultural, educational and sporting events.
8 Sep Nossa Senhora de Monte Serrat.

Guarujá *p208, phone code 013*

Aug Procissão Marítima de Nossa Senhora dos Navegantes and a **Festival de Folclore**.

São Sebastião *p210, phone code 012*

20 Jan Festival of the patron saint, featuring *congadas*, a song and dance derived from slaves from the Congo.
Feb Carnival.
Jun Festas Juninas.
Aug Folklore festival.
Dec Mostrart, a demonstration of arts and craft.

Ilhabela *p211, phone code 012*

Feb Carnival.
May Ilhabela is rich in folklore and legends. Its version of the *congada* (see above and Music, p698) is famous, particularly at the Festival of São Benedito.
28 Jun São Pedro, with a maritime procession.
1st week of Jul Santa Verônica in Bonete.
Sep The town's anniversary.

There are sailing weeks and fishing tournaments throughout the year; dates change annually.

Ubatuba *p213, map p214, phone code 012*

End Jun São Pedro.
Jul Festa do Divino Espírito Santo.
Sep Ubatuba is known for its handicrafts (carved wood, basketware) and it holds an annual **Festa da Cultura Popular**.
28 Oct Ubatuba's anniversary.

Surfing championships are also held.

Peruíbe *p216, phone code 013*

18 Feb Founding of Peruíbe.
Jun Festival do Inverno.
Oct Mês das Missões.

Iguape and Ilha Comprida *p218, phone code 013*

Jan/Feb Summer festival in Iguape.
Feb Carnival on Ilha Comprida.
Mar/Apr Semana Santa.
Jun Corpus Christi.
Aug The month of the pilgrimage of Senhor Bom Jesus de Iguape.
3 Dec Iguape's anniversary.

Throughout the year there are other sporting and cultural events.

Activities and tours

Santos *p205, map p207, phone code 013*

Golf

Santos Golf Club, Av Pésio de Queiroz Filho, São Vicente. 9-hole course.

Guarujá *p208, phone code 013*

Golf

Guarujá Golf Club. 9-hole course.

Ubatuba *p213, map p214, phone code 012*

Tour operators

Agencies which run schooner trips to Ilha Anchieta and elsewhere: **Central de Passeios de Escuna**, Saco da Ribeira, T4411338; **Mykonos**, Av Leovigildo Dias Vieira 1052, Itaguá, T4322042, office also in Saco da Riberia; **Oceano Azul**, R Flamenguinho 277, Saco da Ribeira, T4420564.

Trekking

Guaynumby, T4322832, and **Terra Brasil**, T4351275. Trails are graded according to difficulty and last from 2 hrs to 2 days (to Pico do Corcovado). The **Guide Association**, T91413692, www.ubatuba.com.br/ecoturismo, have more information.

Transport

Santos *p205, map p207, phone code 013*

Bus

Local Within Santos US$.60. To São Vicente, US$0.90.

Long distance Rodoviária, Praça dos Andrades, T32192194. Buses arrive from São Paulo at the main bus station in the centre as well as stops at Ponta da Praia and José Menino which are both nearer to the main hotel district in Gonzaga. For most suburbs buses start from Praça Mauá, in the centre of the city. There are buses to **São Paulo** (50 mins, US$3.60) at intervals of approximately 15 mins, from the rodoviária near the city centre, José Menino or Ponta da Praia (opposite the ferry to Guarujá). (The 2 highways between São Paulo and Santos are sometimes seriously crowded, especially at rush hours and weekends.) To **Guarulhos/Cumbica Airport**, Expresso Brasileiro at 0600, 1330, 1830, return 0550, 0930, 1240, 1810, US$5, allow plenty of time as the bus goes through Guarulhos, 3 hrs. TransLitoral from Santos to **Congonhas airport** then to Guarulhos/Cumbica, 4 daily, US$7.25, 2 hrs. To **Rio** (**Normandy**), several daily, 7½ hrs, US$22.50, to Rio along the coast road is via São Sebastião (US$7.25, change buses if necessary), Caraguatatuba and Ubatuba.

Car

Plans for an airport have been put forward but for now the only access is by the Anchieta and Imigrantes highways from São Paulo and the coastal roads running north and south.

Taxi

All taxis have meters. The fare from Gonzaga to the bus station is about US$5. **Cooper Rádio táxi**, T32327177.

Train

Trains from São Paulo arrive at the station in the centre.

Guarujá *p208, phone code 013*

Ferry

The Guarujá vehicle ferry (every 10 mins, free for pedestrians) leaves from **Ponta da Praia**. The ferry is free from **Santos**, but back to Santos from Guarujá is US$2.80 on weekdays, US$4.20 Sat and Sun. On the other side proceed as far as **Enseada das Tartarugas** (Turtle Bay). During the season and weekends there is a long delay at the Ponta da Praia vehicle ferry; to avoid this take the ferry on foot and get the bus on the Guarujá side; motor boats also cross for US$0.50. A trolleybus runs from Praça Mauá in Santos to the ferry, then take one of the buses.

São Sebastião *p210, phone code 012*

Bus

2 buses a day from **Rio** with Normandy, 0830 and 2300 (plus 1630 on Fri and Sun), to Rio 0600 and 2330, heavily booked in advance, US$12.50 (US$5 from Paraty); 4 a day from **Santos**, 4 hrs, US$7.60; 4 **Litorânea** buses a day also from **São Paulo**, US$8.85, which run inland via São José dos Campos, unless you ask for the service via Bertioga, only 2 a day.

Ferry

Free ferry to **Ilhabela** for foot passengers, see below.

Ilhabela *p211, map p211, phone code 012*

Bus

A bus runs along the coastal strip facing the mainland. **Litorânea** buses from **São Paulo** connect with a service right through to Ilhabela town (office at R Dr Carvalho 136).

Ferry

At weekends and on holidays the 15-20-min ferry between **São Sebastião** and Perequê runs non-stop day and night. During the week it does not sail between 0130 and 0430. Passengers pay nothing; the fare for cars is US$7 weekdays, US$10 at weekends. Reservations for cars can be made in advance at Dersa, R Iaiá 126, Itaim-Bibi, São Paulo, T011-8206655 (this service costs extra); office in São Sebastião, Av São Sebastião, T4521576.

Caraguatatuba *p213, phone code 012*

Bus

There are direct buses to **Rio** (around 5 hrs), **Paraty** (3 hrs), **Santos** (2 hrs); change here for **São Paulo** (or go via São José dos Campos, which is quicker), and **Ubatuba** (45 mins).

Ubatuba *p213, map p214, phone code 012*

The road from São Sebastião is paved, so a journey from São Paulo along the coast is possible, 5 buses daily. Ubatuba is 70 km from Paraty (see p166).

Bus

There are 3 bus terminals: 1) **Rodoviária Costamar**, at R Hans Staden and R Conceição, which serves all local destinations; 2) **Rodoviária at R Prof** Thomaz Galhardo 513, for São José buses to **Paraty**, US$2.25, some **Normandy** services to **Rio de Janeiro**, US$9 and some Itapemirim buses; 3) **Rodoviária Litorânea**, the main bus station: go up Conceição for 8 blocks from Praça 13 de Maio, turn right on R Rio Grande do Sul, then left into R Dra Maria V Jean. Buses from here go to **São Paulo**, 3½ hrs, frequent, US$8, **São José dos Campos**, US$6, **Paraibuna**, US$5, **Caraguatatuba**, US$2.

Taxi

Taxis in town can be a rip-off, eg US$6 from the town centre to T Tenório.

Iguape and Ilha Comprida *p218, phone code 013*

Bus

To Iguape from **São Paulo**, **Santos**, or **Curitiba**, changing at Registro.

Ferry

A continuous ferry service runs from Iguape to Ilha Comprida (free but small charge for cars); buses run until 1900 from the ferry stop to the beaches. From Iguape it is possible to take a boat trip down the coast to **Cananéia** and **Ariri**. Tickets and information from **Dpto Hidroviário do Estado**, R Major Moutinho 198, Iguape, T8411122. It is a beautiful trip, passing between the island and the mainland.

Caverns of the Vale do Ribeiro *p218, phone code 013*

Bus

São Paulo-**Apiaí**, from Barra Funda rodoviária, US$22. If coming to Iporanga from Curitiba, change buses at Jacupiranga on the BR-116 for **Eldorado Paulista**.

Directory

Santos *p205, map p207, phone code 013*

Banks 1000-1730. ATMs in Santos are very unreliable and often out of order. Visa ATMs at **Banco do Brasil**, R 15 de Novembro 195, Centro and Av Ana Costa, Gonzaga. Many others. **Embassies and consulates**

Denmark, R Frei Gaspar 22, 10th floor, 106, T32196455 (1000-1100, 1500-1700); **France**, R General Câmara 12, sala 51, T32195161; **Germany**, R Frei Gaspar 22, 10th floor, 104,

T32195092; UK, R Tuiuti 58, 2nd floor, T32196622. **Immigration** Polícia Federal, Praça da República. For visa extensions. **Internet** Viva Shop, Shopping Parque Balneário. US$3 per hr. **Laundry** Av Mcal Floriano Peixoto 120, Gonzaga, self-service, wash and dry US$5. **Medical services** Ana Costa, R Pedro Américo 42, Campo Grande, T2229000; Santa Casa de Misericórdia, Av Dr Cláudio Luiz da Costa 50, Jabaquara, T2347575. **Post office** R Cidade de Toledo 41, Centro and at R Tolentino Filgueiras 70, Gonzaga. **Telephone** R Galeão Carvalhal 45, Gonzaga.

Guarujá *p208, phone code 013*

Banks Banco 24 Horas, in Pão de Açúcar supermarket, Av Dom Pedro I 195, Enseada. Bradesco, Av Dom Pedro I 1015, Praia da Enseada; **Medical services** Ana Costa, Via Santos Dumont 3651, T33868787.

Bertioga *p209, phone code 013*

Banks Bradesco, in Shopping Riviera, Av da Riviera 1256. **Medical services** Unidade Hospitalar Mista, Praça Vicente Molinari, T3171593.

Ilhabela *p211, map p211, phone code 012*

Banks Bradesco, Praça Col Julião M Negrão 29.

Ubatuba *p213, map p214, phone code 012*

Banks There is a Banco 24 Horas next to the tourist office and an HSBC ATM at 85 R Conceição. The branch of **Banco do Brasil** in Praça Nóbrega does not have ATMs. **Internet** Chat and Bar, upper floor of Ubatuba Shopping. US$3 per hr, Mon-Sat 1100-2000. **Post office** R Dona Maria Alves between Hans Staden and R Col Dominicano. **Telephone** On Galhardo, close to Sérgio restaurant.

Minas Gerais and Espírito Santo

Footprint features

Introduction

The inland state of Minas Gerais, or General Mines, was once described as having a heart of gold and a breast of iron. The state was founded solely to provide precious metals for the imperial coffers. As the gold mining camps grew and prospered they became towns of little cobbled streets crowned with opulent Manueline churches. Many are well preserved and these and the rugged forested hills around them are the principal reasons to visit.

Espírito Santo, immediately to the East of Minas, is less visited. But although its coastline is not as pretty as Bahia, immediately to its north, it is far less developed. Beaches here can be almost deserted but for the visiting turtles. The state's interior is rugged, swathed in coffee and eucalyptus and dotted with giant granite rocks far larger even than those to the south in Rio de Janeiro. The most famous and striking is Pedra Azul, which is on the main highway between Espírito Santo and Minas.

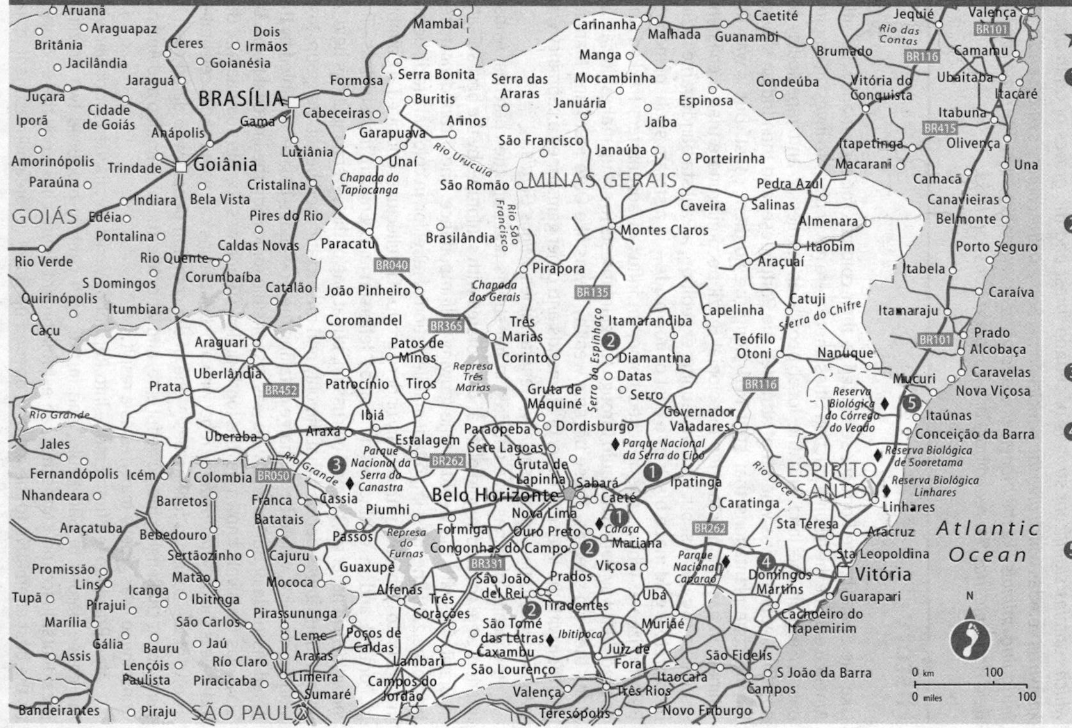

★ **Don't miss...**

1. **Parque Natural de Caraça or the Serra do Cipó** Hike through the reserves replete with wildlife including ultra-rare maned wolves and woolly spider monkeys, pages 236 and 237.
2. **Ouro Preto, Tirandentes or Diamantina** Meander through narrow cobbled streets in these enchanting colonial towns, pages 243, 253 and 266.
3. **Serra de Canastra** Explore rugged hills and stunning waterfalls, page 269.
4. **Pedra Azul** Enjoy watching the giant smooth-sided monolith change colour, from slate blue to fiery orange, as the day progresses, page 283.
5. **Beach towns** Relax on the little-visited beach towns of Espírito Santo's north coast and the turtle beaches and coastal national parks which surround them, page 284.

Minas Gerais

The state of Minas Gerais is a little larger than France and almost as mountainous. The south rises to over 2,700 m on the border of Itatiaia National Park in Rio, and in the east, to 2,890 m at the Pico da Bandeira in the Caparaó National Park. Both these areas of highland are part of the continuous chain of forest-clad mountains, studded with national parks, which form the escarpment cutting Minas Gerais off from the coastal lowlands of the states of Rio de Janeiro and Espírito Santo.

The foremost of the colonial towns are Tiradentes, Ouro Preto and Diamintina. Many of these have churches decorated with carvings by the country's most celebrated sculptor, Aleijandinho. The north of Minas is a dry and desolate region known as the sertão, *protected by the large national park Grande Sertão Veredas, which contains significant strands of* cerrado *forest and the groves of* buriti *palms known as* veredas *which give the park its name. Some of the country's rarest and most intriguing animals like the maned wolf and giant anteater live here. The state capital, Belo Horizonte, has few real attractions but good transport links.*

History

Like the Spanish, the Portuguese looked to their colonies for easy money. In Latin America outside the Jesuit reduction cities, there were never plans to invest in empire, only to exploit the land and the local people as ruthlessly and rapaciously as possible. At first it was wood that attracted the Portuguese, and then Indian slavery for the cane plantations that stretched along the northern coast. But it was the ultimate in easy money that led to colonial Brazil becoming more than a coastline empire. In 1693, whilst out on a marauding expedition, a Paulista bandeirante found *ouro preto* – gold made black by a coat of iron oxide – in a stream south of modern Belo Horizonte. When news reached home, an influx of adventurers trekked and hacked their way from São Paulo through the giant forests to set up makeshift camps along the gold streams. These became wealthy towns like Ouro Preto and Mariana and then with the later discovery of diamonds and other gemstones a captaincy was established and named, prosaically, General Mines: *Minas Gerais*.

The wealth of Minas was reflected in her streets and Baroque churches, whose interiors were covered in gold plate and decorated with sculptures by the best artisans in Brazil. And with the wealth came growing self-importance. The *Inconfidencia* (see box, page 248), the most important manifestation of rebellion in colonial Brazil, began in Ouro Preto in the late 18th century under a group of intellectuals educated at Coimbra in Portugal and in contact with Thomas Jefferson and English industrialists. The *Inconfidencia* never got beyond discussion, but at one of the several meetings held by its members, it was decided that the only non-aristocratic member of the group, José Joaquim da Silva, would be in charge of taking the Governor's palace, occupied by the hated Visconde of Barbacena, who was responsible for levying the imperial taxes. Da Silva was derisively known as 'the tooth puller' (Tiradentes) by his compatriots. But today he is the only *Inconfidente* rebel who most Brazilians can name and is celebrated as one of the country's folk heroes – one of the common people who dared even to think about challenging the powerful elite, and who, like Zumbi, Lampião and Antônio Conselheiro, was cruelly martyred as a result.

After Brazil lapsed from Empire into Republic, Minas Gerais vied for power with the coffee barons of São Paulo, and in the 20th century produced two Brazilian presidents. Juscelino Kubitschek, an establishment figure chosen by the electorate as the best alternative to the military, opened up Brazil to foreign investment in the

Famous Mineiras

If Mineiras were Europeans they would be Irish – less exuberant perhaps than Cariocas or Bahianas, staunchly Catholic, lyrical, literary, and given to reflection over a shared drink. The country's most highly respected author, **João Guimarães Rosa** is a Mineira. His great epic, *Grande Sertão: Veredas* is the *Finnegan's Wake* of the Portuguese language – a study of the roots of moral motivation set in the desert of Northern Minas and written as a stream of consciousness novel in a language partially invented by the author. **Sebastião Salgado**, whose transcendental studies of poverty, migrants and workers made him the most distinguished photographer of the late 20th century, is a Mineira. And Brazil's greatest serious song-writer, **Milton Nascimento**, whose 1970s work was a unique fusion of social protest, sophisticated jazz harmony and Afro-Brazilian and indigenous rhythms still plays impromptu gigs in the towns near his childhood home in the state's interior.

1960s. It was Kubitschek who founded Brasilia. Tancredo Neves also opposed the Brazilian military and to their disgust was elected to power in 1985. A few days before his inauguration he died in mysterious circumstances, supposedly from an intestinal complication. His last words were reportedly "I did not deserve this". He was replaced by José Sarney, a leading figure in the Brazilian landowning oligarchy.

Belo Horizonte

→*Phone code: 031. Colour map 4, B3. Population: 5 million.*

The capital of Minas Gerais is the third largest city in Brazil. Although moderately attractive it offers little in the way of sights beyond a handful of museums and parks. Most travellers who come here for more than a change of buses on the way to Ouro Preto or Tiradentes do so for language-teaching work. The bustling modern skyscraper-filled centre sits in a bowl circled by dramatic mountains which regularly trap pollution as the city strains under ever-burgeoning tides of rural migration. The city is pocked with hills which rise and fall in waves of red-tiled houses, tall apartment blocks and jacaranda- and ipe-lined streets. These are clogged with cars in the mornings and afternoons, a situation which has led the municipal government to introduce an efficient integrated public transport system linking the bus and metro networks, in imitation of Curitiba, in Paraná. ▸▸ *For Sleeping, Eating and other listings, see pages 238-242.*

Ins and outs

Getting there International flights land at Confins airport, 39 km from Belo Horizonte. Shuttle services from several cities including Rio and São Paulo arrive at Pampulha airport closer to the city. Interstate buses arrive at the rodoviária next to Praça Rio Branco at the northwest end of Avenida Afonso Pena. ▸▸ *See also Transport, page 241.*

Getting around The focus is on the large Parque Municipal in the heart of downtown Belo Horizonte and the broad main avenue of Afonso Pena. This is constantly full of pedestrians and traffic, except on Sunday morning when cars are banned and part of it becomes a huge open-air market. Daytime activity is concentrated on the main commercial district on Avenida Afonso Pena and around –

 the best area to eat in at lunchtime. At night activity shifts to Savassi, southwest of the centre which has a wealth of restaurants, bars and clubs.

The city has a good public transport system and some buses integrate with the regional, overground Metrô.

Best time to visit Central Minas enjoys an excellent climate (16-30°C) except for the rainy season (December to March); the average annual temperature in Belo Horizonte is 21°C.

Tourist information The municipal information office, **Belotur** ⓘ *R Pernambuco 284 Funciários, T32779797, www.pbh.gov.br/belotur*, is very helpful, with lots of useful information and maps. The monthly *Guía Turístico* for events, opening times, etc, is freely available. **Belotur** has offices also at the southwest corner of Parque Municipal, at Confins and Pampulha airports, and at the rodoviária. **Turminas** ⓘ *Praça Rio Branco 56, T32728573, www.turminas.mg.gov.br/intminas.html*, the tourism authority for the state of Minas Gerais, is also very helpful and its *Gerais Common Ways* booklet has a useful facts section. Other organizations include **Ibama** ⓘ *Av do Contorno 8121, Cidade*

Belo Horizonte orientation & Pampulha

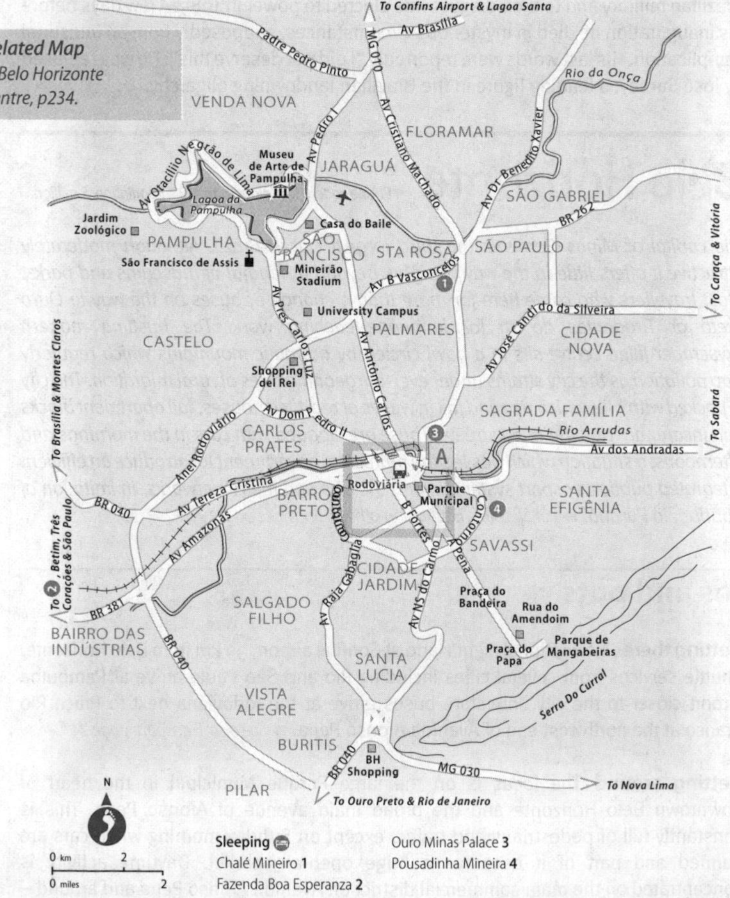

Jardim, CEP 30110-120, Belo Horizonte, T33372624, F33359955; **Instituto Estadual de Florestas** ⓘ *Maurício Luciano, T3307017*, for information on state parks, etc; and **Touring Club do Brasil** ⓘ *Av Brasil 1505, T2616868*.

Safety As in any large city, watch out for sneak thieves in the centre and at the bus station. The Parque Municipal is not too safe after dark, so it is best not to enter alone.

Sights

The **Parque Municipal** ⓘ *Tue-Sun 0600-1800*, is an oasis of green, right in the centre of the city. It has a small amusement park and playground and a tourist office in the southwest corner. The principal building in the park is the **Palácio das Artes**, Afonso Pena 1567, an arts complex with a cinema, theatre, gallery, library and an arts and crafts shop, the **Centro de Artesanato Mineiro** ⓘ *T32377234, Mon-Sat 1000-2200, Sun 1400-2200*, selling ceramics, soapstone carvings, sculpture and the like produced by Minas artists. On the stretch of Avenida Afonso Pena outside the Parque Municipal an **open-air market** ⓘ *0800-1430*, operates each Sunday. The avenue is transformed by thousands of coloured awnings covering stalls selling every conceivable type of local handicraft. It attracts thousands of shoppers.

Praça Sete de Setembro (usually called Praça Sete) is at the busy junction of Avenida Afonso Pena and Avenida Amazonas, midway between the Parque Municipal and the rodoviária. An obelisk commemorating Independence is the centre for political protests.

Six blocks up Avenida João Pinheiro from Avenida Afonso Pena is the **Praça da Liberdade**, which is surrounded by fine public buildings, some in eclectic, *fin-de-siècle* style, others more recent. These include the Secretaria da Fazenda, the Secretaria da Educação and the Casa Falci/Secretaria de Obras Públicas. At the end of the praça is the **Palácio da Liberdade** ⓘ *Sun only 0900-1800*. Among the new buildings are the Centro de Apoio Turístico Tancredo Neves (1991), which contains the offices of Turminas (see Tourist offices, above) and, not actually on the square, but visible from it, the Biblioteca Pública. The praça itself is very attractive, with trees, flowers, fountains which are lit at night and joggers and walkers making the most of the paths.

On the **Praça Carlos Chagas** are three fine modern buildings: the Legislative Assembly, a church and **Banco Central do Brasil**. At Rua da Bahia 1149 is a Gothic building near the Parque Municipal, which used to be the Museu da Mineralogia Professor Djalma Guimarães, remodelled as the Centro Cultural de Belo Horizonte.

As a modern city, Belo Horizonte has no churches to equal those of the colonial towns. In the centre are the **Catedral da Boa Viagem** ⓘ *R Sergipe 175* (completed 1932); **São José** ⓘ *R Tupis 164* (1906), the first church of the new city; and **Nossa Senhora de Lourdes** ⓘ *R da Bahia 1596* (begun 1923, consecrated 1958).

There are, however, a handful of moderately interesting museums. The **Museu Mineiro** ⓘ *Av João Pinheiro 342, T32691168, Tue-Fri 1000-1700, Sat and Sun 1000-1600*, houses religious and other art in the old Senate building, close to the centre. There is a section dedicated specifically to religious art, with six pictures attributed to Mestre Athayde (see under Ouro Preto), exhibitions of modern art, photographs and works by Naïve painters. See also the wood carvings by Geraldo Teles de Oliveira (GTO). The **Museu Histórico Abílio Carreto** ⓘ *Av Prudente de Morais 202, Cidade Jardim, T32778861, Tue, Wed, Fri, Sun 1000-1700, Thu 1000-1200*, is in an old *fazenda* which has been here since 1883, when Belo Horizonte was a village called Arraial do Curral d'el Rey. The fazenda now houses antique furniture and other most interesting historical exhibits. To get there, take bus 2902 from Avenida Afonso Pena. The **Jardim Botânico and Museu de História Natural** ⓘ *R Gustavo da Silveira 1035, Cidade Nova, T34615805, Tue-Fri 0800-1130, 1330-1700, Sat and Sun*

0900-1600, in the Instituto Agronómico, has interesting local ethnological, geological and archaeological exhibits and replica fossils. To get there, take bus 8001.

The **railway station**, with a museum on the second floor showing a model railway, is part of a complex which includes a number of buildings dating from the 1920s around the **Praça da Estação** (also called Praça Rui Barbosa). One of the earliest on the Praça is now the Centro Cultural da Universidade Federal de Minas Gerais.

Suburbs

Pampulha

Pampulha is the city's most interesting location outside the centre, with a series of buildings by Oscar Niemeyer gathered around an artificial lake alongside the city's prestigious university and the zoo, and which are set in gardens designed by Roberto Burle Marx. One of these buildings is the **Igreja São Francisco de Assis** ⓘ *Av Otacílio Negrão de Lima Km 12, T34419325, daily 0800-1800*, whose interlocking arches and modernist bell tower have become the city's most photographed landmark. Its exterior has beautiful blue and white tiles depicting St Francis' life by the painter Cândido Portinari, who also painted the altarpiece and the striking stations of the cross. The interior bronze panels are by Ceschiatti. The church dates from 1943.

On the opposite shore is the glass and marble **Museu de Arte de Pampulha**

Peter Lund and Lagoa Santa Man

Born in Copenhagen in 1801, Peter Wilhelm Lund came to be known as the father of Brazilian palaeontology. At the age of 24 he moved to Brazil for health reasons and settled in Nova Friburgo (now in Rio de Janeiro state). He collected material for the Danish Museum of Natural History, before sailing back to Hamburg in 1829. In 1833 he returned to Brazil and began to research the flora of Rio de Janeiro, São Paulo, Goiás and Mato Grosso, the results of which were published in *Observações respeito da vegetação dos campos do interior do Brasil, especialmente fito históricas* (1835). His explorations then led him to Lagoa Santa, Minas Gerais, where he lived from 1840 to 1880, the year he died. He turned his attention to palaeontology and the caves in the area; the discoveries he made there were of enormous importance to the understanding of early peoples in Brazil.

Lund found the fossils of humans who were dubbed Lagoa Santa Man. In the caves there were also the bones of mammals which, elsewhere on earth, had died out in the Pleistocene age (the first period of the Quaternary era, before the Neolithic age). Until it was surmised that these mammals lived longer in South America than in other regions and until carbon dating confirmed that Lagoa Santa Man was not more than about 10,000 years old, Lund's discoveries pre-dated by a long way any other humans found in Brazil. Regardless of the date of the human remains, the significance of Lagoa Santa Man lay in the fact that evidence of these people could be seen in a lasting form. Much of Brazilian palaeontology and archaeology was, and still is, hampered by the reliance of most early peoples on perishable materials (eg wood and natural fibres) for their houses and artefacts. Lagoa Santa Man also figured in the debate that raged after the publication of Charles Darwin's theories of evolution.

Near the town of Pedro Leopoldo, which is between Belo Horizonte and Sete Lagoas, is a village called Dr Lund. Beyond this village is a fazenda which offers accommodation, riding, fishing, swimming and other country pursuits: Hotel Fazenda Tarumã, T031- 3375379 Belo Horizonte, or T031-6611965, Pedro Leopoldo. For more details, contact Ametur in Belo Horizonte (see Tour operators).

(MAP) ⓘ *Av Octacílio Negrão de Lima 16585, T34434533, www.comartevirtual.com.br, Tue-Sun 0900-1900, free*, which has a fine collection of Mineira modern art and more than 900 works by national artists. The building was originally a casino, founded by Juscelino Kubitschek, and was the first project in the complex to be designed and landscaped. People would dance in the **Casa do Baile** ⓘ *Av Octacílio Negrão de Lima 751, T32777433, Tue-Sun 0900-1900, free*, on the opposite shore, and take a boat across the lake for some gambling, and then dance again in what is now the Auditório in the MAP (stand in the centre of the floor to hear the echo). With its snaking canopy leading up to the main dance hall, the Casa do Baile itself is a perfect example of Niemeyer's fascination with the curved line. There are wonderful panoramic views out over the lake from its numerous windows. The fourth building in the Pampulha architectural complex is the **Iate Tênis Clube**, the Yacht and Tennis Club. To get to the Lagoa da Pampulha, take bus No 2004 from Avenida Afonso Pena.

Just 700 m south of the lake is the **Mineirão** stadium, the second largest in Brazil after the Maracanã stadium in Rio, seating 92,000. Seats cost between US$3 and US$7.

DEPEL, Centro de Preparação Equestre da Lagoa ⓘ *Av Antônio Francisco Lisboa*

 481, T4410812, Tue-Sun 0800-1700, the Lake Riding School, is one of the largest equestrian centres in South America.

Mangabeiras

About 3 km south of the centre, the **Parque de Mangabeiras** ⓘ *Thu-Sun 0800-1800*, is on the Serra do Curral at between 1,000 m and 1,400 m above sea level. The recreation areas and public spaces were landscaped by Burle Marx in 1982. There are good views of the city, especially from the Mirante da Mata. Three forest trails have been laid out with picnic areas: the Roteiros do Sol (Sun Route), da Mata (Woods Route) and das Águas (Water Route). There are sports facilities and a café. To get there, take bus 2001 from Avenida Afonso Pena between Avenida Amazonas and Rua Tamóios.

The natural amphitheatre of **Praça do Papa** where the Pope spoke in 1980 is on the way up to Parque Mangabeiras. Just below, Rua Professor Otávio Magalhães is nicknamed **Rua do Amendoim** (Peanut Street). Its fame rests in an optical illusion that makes it appear that cars in neutral run up the slope, rather than down. The same happens with cans, etc, but it is difficult to find the exact spot without local knowledge.

Around Belo Horizonte

Lakes and grottoes

The **Gruta de Lapinha** ⓘ *Tue-Sun 0900-1700, US$2 entry to caves and small archaeological museum*, is only 36 km north of the city.

About 10 km before Lapinha is the town of **Lagoa Santa**, a weekend resort for Belo Horizonte. The sandy beach on the lake (close to the town centre and bus station) is used for fishing, sun bathing and boating (do not swim, the water is infected with schistosomiasis). Along the beach are bars and restaurants, with more in the nearby main praça, which also has two small hotels and an interesting modernistic church.

Within easy reach of Belo Horizonte are several of the 400 caves and grottoes for which the state is famous.

Some 80 km northwest of Belo Horizonte is the town of **Sete Lagoas**, near the **Gruta Rei do Mato** ⓘ *T7730888, 0800-1700*, where prehistoric inscriptions and cave paintings have been found. Sete Lagoas, which has hotels, can be reached by **Expresso Setelagoano** bus from Belo Horizonte in 1½ hours.

The best and most famous of the caves is the **Gruta de Maquiné** ⓘ *US$5*, with six chambers open to visitors. The caves are well lit, but hot at 26°C. The restaurants nearby greet potential customers with a combined history and menu leaflet. The nearby town of **Dordisburgo** has a **museum** ⓘ *Av Padre João 744, Tue-Sun 0800-1700*, to the writer João Guimarães Rosa.

Serra de Piedade, a high peak to the northeast of the city, offers spectacular views over the surrounding countryside. It is only accessible by car or special bus service ⓘ *T4995679*. There is a telescope on the hill, a small chapel and a *churrascaria*. From the peak are views of the small town of Caeté.

Parque Natural de Caraça

ⓘ *The park is open 0700-2100; if staying overnight you cannot leave after 2100; park entrance US$5 per vehicle.*

This is a remarkable reserve about 120 km east of Belo Horizonte. It can be visited in a day, but you will get much more out of your trip if you stay overnight.

Caraça has been preserved so well because the land belongs to a seminary. The seminary buildings and the church with its tall spire stand at about 1,220 m above sea level, surrounded on three sides by mountains which rise to 2,070 m at their highest (Pico do Sol). The name means 'big face', so called because of a hill which is said to resemble the face of a giant who is looking at the sky. To appreciate the setting, climb up to the Cruzeiro, a cross which is close to the seminary.

The **church** ⓘ *Sat, Sun and holidays 1300-1500 (or for hotel guests on request)*, built in Gothic style in 1880, has a museum. Inside is a painting of the Last Supper attributed to Mestre Athayde (see below); Judas Iscariot's eyes follow you (he is the one holding the purse). In the altar is an effigy of São Pio Martir. The stained-glass windows at the east end were a gift from France. Part of the seminary has been converted into a hotel, which is the only place to stay (see Sleeping, page 238).

The park extends from 720 m to 2,070 m. Its lower altitudes are covered in rich Atlantic forest while the heights are grassland and other mountain habitats. There are lakes, waterfalls and rivers. The rarest mammal is the maned wolf (the only wolf found in Brazil and endangered, partly because of loss of habitat, but also because of its insatiable appetite for chickens). Since the early 1980s, the monks have been leaving food for the wolves on the seminary steps in the evening; up to four may be seen. This is a popular tourist attraction, and the animals can be photographed. Another endangered mammal in the park is the southern masked titi monkey, of which family groups may be seen. Other primates include the tufted-eared marmoset and the brown capuchin monkey.

Birdlife includes various toucans, guans and hummingbirds (such as the Brazilian ruby and the white-throated hummingbird), various tanagers, cotingas, antbirds, woodpeckers and the long-trained and scissor-tailed nightjars. Some of the bird species are endemic, others rare and endangered.

The trails for viewing the different landscapes and the wildlife are marked at their beginning and are quite easy to follow. A guide is a good idea for seeing the birds and animals.

It is possible to stay in **Santa Bárbara** (**E Hotel Karaibe**; **E Santa Inés**), 25 km away on the road to Mariana and hitchhike to Caraça. Santa Bárbara is served by 11 buses a day from Belo Horizonte (fewer on Saturday and Sunday). There is also a bus service to Mariana, a beautiful route, via Catas Altas, which has an interesting church and a *pousada* belonging to the municipality of Santa Barbara. To get to the park itself turn off the BR-262 (towards Vitória) at Km 73 and go via Barão de Cocais to Caraça (120 km). There is no public transport to the seminary. Buses go as far as Barão de Cocais, from where a taxi is US$12. Book the taxi to return for you, or hitch (which may not be easy). The park entrance is 10 km before the seminary. The alternative is to hire a guide from Belo Horizonte, about US$75 (including guiding, transport and meals).

Parque Nacional da Serra do Cipó

ⓘ *For further details, contact Ibama in Belo Horizonte. T32916588, www.ibama.gov.br.*

The Serra do Cipó, some 120 km northeast of Belo Horizonte protects 33,400 sq km of important *cerrado* and gallery forest, habitats which provide a home for ultra-rare bird species like *cipo canastero* and grey-backed tachuri alongside endangered mammals. These include one of the world's more wimpy carnivores, the maned wolf; looking like a giant fox with overly long legs which hunts small grassland rodents with its feet. There are monkeys too – masked titi and brown capuchin and a number of endemic carnivorous plants. The walks which cut through the park pass through some of the most beautiful rugged grassland country in the state, leading to waterfalls and stands of tropical forest.

The national park can be reached via road MG-010. This road continues unpaved to Serro (see Colonial cities, page 242); buses run on this route. Agencies offer excursions from the city to the park. It is recommended to take a guide because the trails are unmarked; ask locally. The nearest accommodation is in the municipalities of Santana do Riacho, a town northwest of the park, or in Jaboticatubas.

Nova Lima → *Population: 52,500.*

Set in eucalyptus forests 27 km southeast of Belo, Nova Lima's houses are grouped round the gold mine of Morro Velho, the deepest mine in the Americas. The shaft has followed a rich vein of gold down to 2,591 m (not open to tourists). There are interesting carvings by Aleijadinho, recovered from elsewhere, in the modern parish church.

Sleeping

Belo Horizonte *p231, maps p232 and p234, phone code 031*

There are cheap options near the rodoviária and in R Curitiba, but many of these hotels are not used for sleeping in; you will have a more comfortable stay in one of the youth hostels.

You may only spend the night in the rodoviária if you have an onward ticket (police check at 2400).

L **Ouro Minas Palace**, Av Cristiano Machado 4001, T34294001 (toll free 0800-314000), www.ourominas.com.br. The most luxurious hotel in the city with palatial suites, including several for women only on the top floors, excellent service, a pool, sauna, gym with personal trainers and excellent business facilities. Not central but within easy reach of the centre and airports.

AL **Fazenda Boa Esperança**, in natural surroundings at about 900 m in the hills to the west of Belo Horizonte. It is part of the Roteiro de Charme group (www.roteirosdecharme.com.br), see p47.

AL **Grandarrell Minas**, R Espírito Santo 901, T32480000, www.grandarrell.com.br. One of the best business hotels in the centre, with a very large convention centre, full business facilities including DDI dialling and fax and email modems in the rooms, and a rooftop pool. Not much English spoken.

AL **Othon Palace**, Av Afonso Pena 1050, T32470000, www.hoteis-othon.com.br. A 1980s chain hotel with a rooftop pool, good service and an excellent location in the centre and opposite the Parque Municipal. Rooms on lower floors can be noisy.

A **Sol Meliá**, R da Bahia 1040, T/F2741344, www.solmeliabh.com.br. Well-renovated 1990s business hotel in the centre with a pool, sauna and respectable service.

B **Mercure**, Av Do Contorno 7315 (Santo Antonio), T32984100, www.accorhotels.com.br. The newest of the city's business hotels with a good pool, sauna, gym and rooms decked out in standard business attire. A few kilometres from the centre.

C **Ambassy**, R dos Caetés 633, near the rodoviária, T212200010, www.ambassy.com.br. A 2nd-grade business hotel tower between the centre and the bus station with a small convention centre. Some English spoken.

C-D **Esplanada**, Av Santos Dumont 304, T32735311. Close to the bus station. Shared bathrooms but a good restaurant and car parking.

D **Continental**, Av Paraná 241, T32017944. Central, quiet, but with small interior rooms newly renovated with modern fittings. Recommended.

D **São Salvador**, R Espírito Santo 227, T32227731. Centrally located and a good alternative to the **Continental**. Recommended.

Youth hostels

E **Chalé Mineiro**, R Santa Luzia 288, Santa Efigênia, T34671576. Price per person. Attractive, with a small pool, a shared kitchen, TV lounge and telephones. Towels and bed linen are extra.

E **Pousadinha Mineira**, R Araxá 514, Floresta, 15 mins from the rodoviária, T/F34231523. IYHA, cheaper for members, popular with Brazilians. Bedding and towels can be hired, breakfast extra on request, very helpful. Recommended.

Parque Natural de Caraça *p236, phone code 031*

AL-B **Santuário do Caraça**, for reservations, Caixa Postal 12, T35960000, Santa Bárbara, MG, T38372698. This on-site hotel has reasonable rooms; the restaurant serves good food from farms within the seminary's lands, lunch 1200-1330. No camping is permitted.

Parque Nacional da Serra do Cipó *p237, phone code 031*

AL-A **Cipó Veraneio**, Km 95, Jaboticatubas, MG-010, T36511000, www.cipoveraneiohotel.com.br. Smart but boxy little rooms in a mock-colonial hotel right on the banks of a mountain river in the Serra do Cipó. Sauna, games, walks and other organized activities.

L-AL **O Canto da Siriema**, 50 km from Belo Horizonte, municipality of Jaboticatubas, T34636955, or contact **Ametur** in Belo Horizonte (address under Tour operators). A *hotel fazenda* with full board, recreation, etc.

Camping

Camping Véu da Noiva, Km 101, Santana do Riacho, T32011166, www.guiaserradocipo.com.br/acm. Pretty little campsite in a forest grove near a waterfall and Swiss-style chalets (from D per person).

Eating

Belo Horizonte *p231, maps p232 and p234, phone code 031*

Look for lunchtime promotions at all restaurants in the centre.

Comida mineira is the local speciality; it is good, wholesome, meaty food, often self-served in big black earthenware pots sitting over a wood-fired oven. In restaurants you usually pay after you have made your selection. Chicken recipes include *frango ao molho pardo* (chicken in a blackbird blood sauce) which sounds foreboding and tastes delicious, alongside plates heavy with meat and various sausages, rice and plenty of vegetable, bean, potato and manioc side dishes.

TTT **Aurora**, R Expedicionário Mário Alves de Oliveira 421, São Luís, T34987567. One of the best restaurants in the city, in a garden setting next to the Lago da Pampulha. Imaginative menu with dishes fusing Mineira and Italian techniques and making use of unusual Brazilian fruits. Respectable wine list. Closed Mon and Tue.

TTT **Dona Derna**, R Tomé de Souza 1380, Savassi, T32236954. Traditional Italian home cooking with dining on the terrace and indoors. Very good homemade pasta. Decent wine list. Highly recommended.

TTT **Taste Vin**, R Curitiba 2105, Lourdes, T32925423. French food. Excellent soufflés and provençale seafood. The respectable wine list includes decent Brazilian options. Recommended.

TTT **Vecchio Sogno**, R Martim de Carvalho 75 and R Dias Adorno, Santo Agostinho, under the Assembléia Legislativo, T32925251. The best Italian in the city with an inventive menu fusing Italian and French cuisine with Brazilian ingredients. Excellent fish. Good wine list. Lunch only on Sun.

TTT **Xapuri**, R Mandacaru 260, Pampulha, T34966198. *Comida mineira*, great atmosphere, live music, very good food, expensive and a bit out of the way but recommended. Closed on Mon.

TT **Alpino**, Av Contorno 5761, Savassi, T32219015. Good value German food. Generous portions, lively and popular.

TT **Chico Mineiro**, R Alagoas 626, corner of Av Brasil, T32613237. *Comida mineira* including good local chicken specialities. Lunchtime only; until 1300 at weekends.

TT **Dona Lucinha**, R Sergipe 811, Savassi, T32615930 and at R Padre Odorico 38 (S Pedro), T32270562. A self-service restaurant with decent meat dishes and generous portions. Recommended. Lunchtime only on Sun.

TT **Pizzarela**, Av Olegário Maciel 2280, Lourdes, T32223000. Decent pizzas – almost up to São Paulo standard.

TT **Sushi Naka**, R Gonçalves Dias 92 Funcionários, T32872714. Excellent sushi, sashimi and soups. Close to the centre.

T **Flor de Líbano**, R Espírito Santo 234. Cheap and good.

T **Interior de Minas**, R Rio de Janeiro 1191, T2245549. *Comida mineira*, central, good for lunch, good value (also at Av Olegário Maciel 1781, Lourdes, T32925835).

T **Mala e Cuia**, a chain of restaurants serving good *comida mineira* at R Gonçalves Dias 874, Savassi, T32613059, Av Antônio Carlos 8305, Pampulha, T34412993, Av Raja Gabaglia 1617, São Bento, T3421421.

T **Mandala**, R Inconfidentes 1006, T32617056. Vegetarian.

Seriously cheap *comida mineira* is served in the restaurants around the rodoviária, *prato feito* US$1. There are many bars and restaurants around Praça Raúl Soares; more on R Rio de Janeiro.

Cafés

Blue Mountain, Av Cristóvão Colombo 536, Savassi, T32612296.

Café Belas Artes, R Gonçalves Dias 1581, Lourdes, in the cinema foyer at Unibanco Belas Artes Liberdade. Popular.

Café Belas Artes Nazaré, R Guajajaras 37, near Av Afonso Pena, in the foyer of the Unibanco Nazaré Liberdade cinema.
Café Três Corações, Praça Diego de Vasconcelos, Savassi. Coffees and snacks.
Casa Bonomi, R Cláudio Manoel 460, Funcionários, T32613460.
Koyote Street Bar, R Tomé de Souza 912. Street café.
Sabor e Saúde, Av João Pinheiro 232. Vegetarian and meat snacks and meals, also sells *pão integral*.
Tia Clara, R Antônio de Albuquerque 617. Tea room.

Bars and clubs

Belo Horizonte *p231, maps p232 and p234, phone code 031*

Bars Recommended are Alambique, Av Raja Gabaglia 3200, Chalé 1D, specializes in *cachaça*, with *mineira* appetizers, designed like a country house; **Americana**, R Pernambuco 1025; **Bar Nacional**, Av Contorno 1076, Barro Preto, good value; Heaven, Av Getúlio Vargas 809.

Clubs Recommended are Ao Bar, R Cláudio Manoel 572, Funcionários, T32617443; L'Apogée, R Antônio de Albuquerque 729, T32275133; Máscaras, R Santa Rita Durão 667, T32616050; Partenon, Rio Grande do Norte 1470, T32219856.

Entertainment

Belo Horizonte *p231, maps p232 and p234, phone code 031*

Cinema

Belo Horizonte is a good place to watch high-quality Brazilian and foreign films beside the usual Hollywood fare. There are many art cinemas and cineclubs in the centre such as the **Espaço Unibanco**, R Guajajaras 37.

Theatre

Belo Horizonte has at least a dozen theatres, including **Teatro da Cidade**, R da Bahia 1341, T32731050, **Teatro Alterosa**, Av Assis Chateaubriand 499, Floresta, T32376610, and **Teatro Marília**, Av Alfredo Balena 586, Centro, T322244445. The city prides itself on its theatre and dance companies (look out for the *Grupo Galpão*); don't expect to find many shows in any language other than Portuguese. The local press and tourist literature give details of shows and events.

Festivals and events

Belo Horizonte *p231, maps p232 and p234, phone code 031*

Maundy Thu; Corpus Christi; **15 Aug**, Assunção (Assumption); **8 Dec**, Conceição (Immaculate Conception).

Shopping

Belo Horizonte *p231, maps p232 and p234, phone code 031*

Bookshops

Acaiaca, R Tamóios 72. Good for dictionaries.
Daniel Vaitsman, R Espírito Santo 466, 17th floor, T2229071. English-language books.
Livraria Alfarrábio, R Tamóios 320, T32713603. Used foreign-language books.
Livraria Van Damme, R das Guajajaras 505, T32266492. National, Portuguese and local titles.

Gems and jewellery

Manoel Bernardes, Av Contorno 5417, Savassi, T32254200. Attractive jewellery. Very reasonable prices.

Market

Mercado Central, Av Augusto de Lima 744. Large, and clean, and open every day until 1800. Arts and crafts, miscellaneous produce and bric a brac. The Sun handicraft fair on Av Afonso Pena (see p233); hippies still sell their wares on **R Rio de Janeiro**, 600 block, each evening. A **flower market** is held at Av Bernardo Monteiro, near Av Brasil, every Fri 1200-2000. Also here on Sat is a **drinks and food market**.

Music

Cogumelo, Av Augusto de Lima 399, T2749915.

Activities and tours

Belo Horizonte *p231, maps p232 and p234, phone code 031*

Caving

Grupo Speleo, at the Universidade Federal de Minas Gerais, has the most experience in visiting out-of-the-way caves.

Ecotourism and adventure sports

Amo-Te, Associação Mineira dos Organizadores do Turismo Ecológico, R Monte Verde 125, lípio de Melo, T34775430, oversees ecotourism in the state of Minas Gerais. This includes trekking, riding, cycling, rafting, jeep tours, canyoning, visiting national parks, or *fazendas*. For companies which arrange these special interest tours, speak to Amo-Te first.

Horse riding

Tropa Serrana, T33448986, 99832356 (mob), tropaserrana@hotmail.com. Recommended.

Tour operators

Ametur, R Alvarengo Peixoto 295, loja 102, Lourdes, T/F32921976, has information on *fazendas* which welcome visitors and overnight guests.

Master Turismo (American Express representative), R da Bahia 2140, T33303655, www.masterturismo.com.br, at Sala VIP, Aeroporto de Confins and Av Afonso Pena 1967, T33303603. Very helpful.

Ouro Preto Turismo, Av Afonso Pena 4133, Grupo 109, Serra, T32215005. Recommended.

Revetur, R Espírito Santo 1892, 1st floor, Lourdes, T33372500. Recommended.

Transport

Belo Horizonte *p231, maps p232 and p234, phone code 031*

See also Ins and outs, p231.

Air

Tancredo Neves International Airport is at Confins, near Lagoa Santa, 39 km from Belo Horizonte. A taxi to the centre costs US$40, co-operative taxis have fixed rates to different parts of the city. Airport bus, either *executivo* from the exit, US$11, or comfortable normal bus (**Unir**) from the far end of the car park hourly, US$2, both go to the rodoviária. Getting to the airport, buses from the rodoviária, *executivo*, US$10.

Closer to the city, the domestic airport at **Pampulha**, has shuttle services to several cities including Rio and São Paulo. Transport from Pampulha airport is cheaper than from Confins. Blue bus 1202 to town leaves across the street from the airport, 25 mins, US$0.65, passing the rodoviária and the cheaper hotel district.

Airline offices American, R Guajajaras 557, T32733622, Confins, T36892670. **TAM**, Pampulha, T34435500. **United**, R Paraíba 1000, 10th floor, Funcionários, T32617777, Confins airport, T36892736.

Varig/RioSul/Nordeste, Av Olegário Maciel 2251, Lourdes, T32916444, Confins, T36892305, Pampulha airport, T34912466.

Vasp, Av Olegário Maciel 2221, T0800-998277, Confins, T36892411.

Bus

Local Red buses run on express routes and charge US$0.75; **yellow buses** have circular routes around the Contorno, US$0.50; **blue buses** run on diagonal routes charging US$0.65. Some buses link up with the regional, overground Metrô.

Long distance The rodoviária by Praça Rio Branco at the northwest end of Av Afonso Pena has toilets, post office, phones, left-luggage lockers (US$2, attended service 0700-2200), shops and is clean and well organized.

To **Rio** with **Cometa**, T32015611 and **Util**, T32017744, 6½ hrs, US$12.75 (ordinary), *leito*, US$25.50. To **Vitória** with **São Geraldo**, T2711911, US$14.50 and *leito* US$29. To **Brasília** with **Itapemirim**, T2919991, and **Penha**, T32711027, 10 hrs, 6 a day including 2 *leitos*, only 1 leaves in daylight (0800), US$19.25, *leito* US$38.50. To **São Paulo** with **Cometa** and **Gontijo**, T32016130, 10 hrs, US$15.60. To **Foz do Iguaçu**, US$42, 22 hrs. To **Salvador** with **Gontijo**, US$40, 24 hrs, at 1900 daily, and **São Geraldo** at 1800. **São Geraldo** also goes to **Porto Seguro**, 17 hrs, direct, via Nanuque and Eunápolis, US$33. To **Recife** with **Gontijo**, 2000, US$41. To **Fortaleza**, US$63. To **Natal**, US$66. To **Belém** with **Itapemirim** at 2030, US$72. To **Campo Grande** with **Gontijo** (at 1930) and **Motta**, 3 a day, T34640480, US$31-36, a good route to Bolivia, avoiding São Paulo. All major destinations served. For buses within Minas Gerais, see under each destination.

Car

Car hire: **Interlocadora**, R dos Timbiras 2229, T2754090; **Localiza**, Av Bernardo

Monteiro 1567, Pampulha and Confins airports, T2477957, or 0800-992000.

Taxi
Taxis are plentiful but hard to find at peak hours. **BH Táxi**, T32158081, **Coopertáxi**, T34212424.

Train
To **Vitória**, daily 0700, tickets sold at 0530, US$17.50 *executivo*, US$11.50 1st class, US$7.80 2nd class, 14 hrs.

Around Belo Horizonte *p236, phone code 031*

Lakes and grottoes
Buses (**Útil**) to the Gruta de Lapinha leave Belo Horizonte at 1015 and 1130 daily, returning 1600, also 1830 Mon only, 1¼ hrs, US$3.25 one-way. Half-hourly bus service Belo Horizonte-Lagoa Santa, US$2. Bus Lagoa Santa-Lapinha every 30 mins. The local bus stop for Lagoa Santa is 2 km downhill from the Lapinha caves. To Gruta de Maquiné, several buses daily (**Irmãos Teixeira**), 2¼ hrs, US$8.

Directory

Belo Horizonte *p231, maps p232 and p234, phone code 031*

Banks **Banco do Brasil**, R Rio de Janeiro 750, Av Amazonas 303. Cash is given against credit cards at **Banco Itaú**, Av João Pinheiro 195. Visa ATM at **Bradesco**, R da Bahia 947. **Citibank**, R Espírito Santo 871. **Master Turismo**, Av Afonso Pena 1967, T33303603. American Express representative. **Nascente Turismo**, Rio de Janeiro 1314, no commission. Changing TCs is difficult, but hotels will change them for guests at a poor rate. **Embassies and consulates** Austria, R José Américo Cançado Bahia 199, T33335363. **Denmark**, R Paraíba 1122, 5th floor, T32868626. **France**, R Pernambuco 712A, T32617805. **Germany**, R Timbiras 1200, 5th floor, T32131568. **Italy**, Av Afonso Pena 3130, 12th floor, T32814211. **Netherlands**, R Sergipe 1167, loja 5, T32275275. **UK**, R dos Inconfidentes 1075, sala 1302, Savassi, T32612072, F32610226, britcon.bhe@ terra.com.br. **USA**, R Timbiras 1200, 7th floor, T2131571. **Immigration** **Polícia Federal**, R Nascimento Gurgel 30, T2910005. For visa extensions. To get there take bus 7902 from the corner of R Curitiba and Av Amazonas and get off at the Hospital Madre Teresa. **Internet** Internet Café Club, R Fernandes Tourinho 385, Plaza Savassi, US$5 per hr. There are numerous others throughout the city. **Medical services** **Mater Dei**, R Gonçalves Dias 2700, T3399000. Recommended. **Post office** Av Afonso Pena 1270. Poste restante is behind the main office at R de Goiás 77. The branch on R da Bahia is less slow. **Telephone** Av Afonso Pena 1180, by the Correios, daily 0700-2200.

Colonial cities near Belo Horizonte

Streets of whitewashed 18th-century houses with deep blue or yellow window frames line steep and winding streets leading to lavishly decorated churches with Manueline façades and rich gilt interiors. Behind lies a backdrop of rainforest green and grey granite hills whose woods are still filled with tiny marmoset monkeys and flocks of canary-winged parakeets. The colonial gold mining towns of Southern Minas are the highlights of any visit to the state – islands of history and remnant forest in an otherwise dull agricultural landscape. Most lie south of Belo Horizonte and many people choose to visit them on the way to or from Rio. But they make a far more charming and restful base than Belo Horizonte and we would recommend spending time here and stopping either for a bus change or a quick night in the state capital on the way north or south. » *For Sleeping, Eating and other listings, see pages 260-266.*

Ins and outs

The cities fall into three groups: south of Belo Horizonte (Ouro Preto, Mariana Congonhas do Campo, São João del Rei and Tiradentes); east: (Sabará and Caeté);

and north (Diamantina and Serro). All of the southern towns are on the main Rio highway (Ouro Preto being the closest to the state capital and São João del Rei the furthest). The towns to the east are on the main highway to Espírito Santo. Those to the north are a longer journey from Belo Horizonte, off the inland route to Bahia.

The most famous of the towns is **Ouro Preto**. It can be visited in a day trip from Belo Horizonte, but a day is nothing like enough and Ouro Preto is a more interesting and pleasant place to stay than the capital. **Mariana** is easy to see in a day trip from Ouro Preto. The spectacular Aleijandinho church in **Congonhas do Campo**, further south, requires only a few hours to visit and is now reachable by a new highway. There is no need to stay overnight. **Tiradentes**, further south still, is the prettiest, best-preserved and most visited of all the cities but feels somewhat tourist twee. Nearby **São João del Rei** is more decrepit but more of a real city. They are linked at weekends by a 30-minute steam train ride and daily by frequent buses. **Sabará** and **Caeté**, to the east of the capital, can be visited as an easy day trip from Belo Horizonte or on the way to Espírito Santo. **Diamantina** and **Serro** are far to the north direction, on one of the routes to Bahia from Belo Horizonte and are easiest to see as a stopover en route to Bahia.

Ouro Preto → *Phone code: 031. Altitude: 1,000 m. Colour map 4, C3. Population: 67,000.*

Tourist information The **tourist office** ⓘ *Praça Tiradentes 41, T35593269, opens 0800*, has details of accommodation in *casas de família*, *repúblicas* and other places. It also has leaflets showing the opening times, which change frequently (very helpful but Portuguese only spoken). The **Secretaria de Turismo** ⓘ *Casa de Gonzaga, R Cláudio Manoel 61, T35593282*, produces information including hotel and restaurant lists, a map and lists of local sites. You can also check out the websites www.ouropretonaweb.kit.net and www.ouropreto.com.br (in Portuguese). Most of the churches now charge admission (conservation tax), between US$1.50 and US$5. In most churches and museums, bags and cameras are taken at the entrance and guarded in lockers (visitors keep their own key). The Aleijadinho museum publishes an Ouro Preto guide in English, French and Portuguese for $1.75. Also available is Lucia Machado de Almeida's *Passeio a Ouro Preto*, US$6 (in Portuguese, English and French). The tourist office and most churches and historic buildings open to the public have a selection of books for sale. A local guide from the **Associação de Guias de Turismo** (AGTOP) ⓘ *T35512655 at the tourist office, or 35511544 ext 269*, can be obtained through the tourist office (Cássio Antunes is recommended). Opposite the rodoviária is an office of the **Guiding Association** ⓘ *T35512504, or 5511544 ext 205*, which offers group tours of US$30 for one to 10 people, US$45 for more than 10. The guides also give advice to new arrivals. If taking a guide, check their accreditation. The map sold at either the tourist or the Guiding Association office costs US$2.50. Ouro Preto is also the name of a tour operator which offers selected trips around the town; see www.ouropretotour.com. » *For Transport information, see page 265.*

Sights

Ouro Preto, which is named after the black iron oxide-coated gold discovered here by Paulista adventurer Antônio Dias was one of the first of the Minas gold towns to be founded, and as the former state capital, became the wealthiest and most important. Although it now has a hinterland of ugly blocks of flats and crumbling *favelas* it preserves some of the most important colonial architecture in Brazil, remaining at its heart an 18th-century city of steep church-crowned hills, cobbled streets, *azulejos*, plazas and fountains. In homage to its historical importance Ouro Preto becomes the capital of Minas Gerais once again for one day only, every year on 24 June. The modern city bustles with young Brazilians

At least two days are needed to see everything. Photography is prohibited in all the churches and museums.

 studying and partying at the various local universities and has a thriving café and nightlife scene. Sadly the historic centre which was once closed to traffic is now thick with buses and cars and the toll is telling on some of the beautiful buildings.

The best place to start exploring the city is the central **Praça Tiradentes**, where you'll see a statue of the leader of the **Inconfidentes** (see box page 248). Another Inconfidente, the poet Tomás Antônio Gonzaga (whose house at Rua Cláudio Manoel 61 is close to São Francisco de Assis Church), was exiled to Africa. Most Brazilians know his poem based on his forbidden love affair with the girl he called Marília de Dirceu. Visitors are shown the bridge and decorative fountain where the lovers held their trysts (the house where she lived, on the Largo Marília de Dirceu, is now a school).

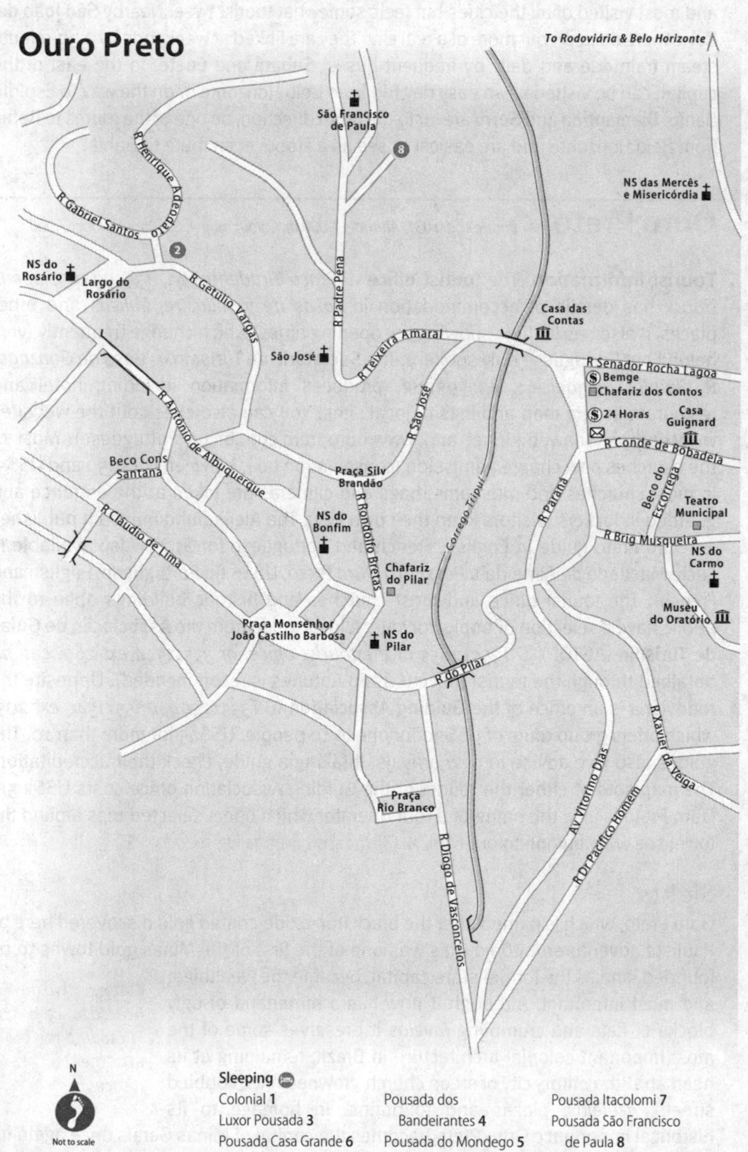

Sleeping

Colonial 1
Luxor Pousada 3
Pousada Casa Grande 6
Pousada dos Bandeirantes 4
Pousada do Mondego 5
Pousada Itacolomi 7
Pousada São Francisco de Paula 8

On the north side of the Praça Tiradentes (at No 20) is a famous Escola de Minas (School of Mining), founded in 1876, in the fortress-like Palácio dos Governadores (1741-1748); it has the interesting and not-to-be-missed **Museu de Mineralogia e das Pedras** ⓘ *Mon, Wed-Fri 1200-1645, Sat and Sun 0900-1300, US$1.50*. On the south side of the Praça, No 139, next to Carmo Church, is the **Museu da Inconfidência** ⓘ *T35511121, Mon-Fri 0800-1800, US$1.50*, a fine historical and art museum in the former Casa de Câmara e Cadeia, which has drawings by Aleijadinho and the Sala Manoel da Costa Athayde, in an annex. In the Casa Capitular of NS do Carmo is **Museu do Oratório** ⓘ *T35515369, daily 0930-1200, 1330-1730*, a collection of beautiful 18th- and 19th-century prayer icons and oratories including many made of egg and sea shell.

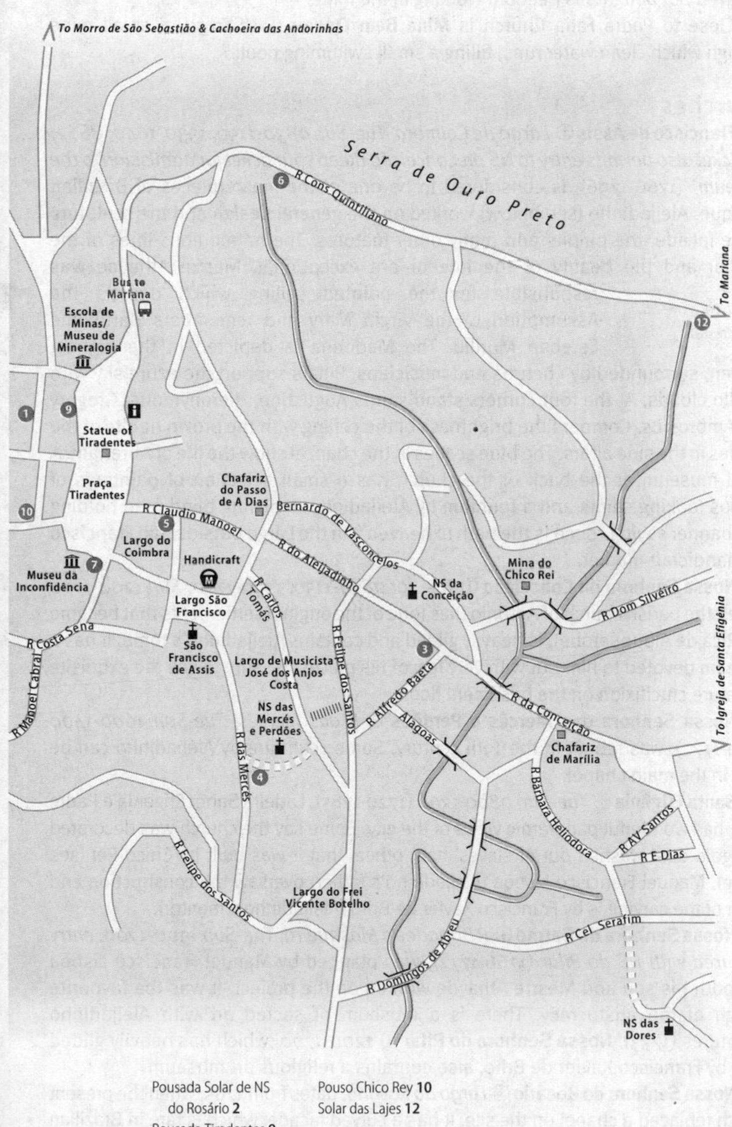

Casa das Contas ⓘ *R São José 12, T3551444, Tue-Sat 1230-1730, Sun and holidays 0900-1500, US$0.50* (1782-1784), is the Centro de Estudos do Ciclo de Ouro (Centre for Gold Cycle Studies) and a museum of money and finance, with manuscripts and coins; it also has a library. The **Casa Guignard** ⓘ *R Conde de Bobadela 110, T35515155, Tue-Fri 1200-1800, Sat, Sun and holidays 0900-1500, free*, displays the paintings of Alberto da Veiga Guignard. The **Teatro Municipal** ⓘ *R Brigadeiro Musqueiro, daily 1230-1800*, built in 1769, is the oldest functioning theatre in Latin America.

The **Mina do Chico Rei** ⓘ *R Dom Silvério, 0800-1700, US$1.50*, is not as impressive as some other mines in the area, but is 'fun to crawl about in'; restaurant attached. The Chico Rei is supposed to be an African king, called Francisco, who was enslaved but bought his freedom working in the mine.

Close to Padre Faria Church is **Mina Bem Querer** ⓘ *US$0.50*, a small mine through which clean water runs, filling a small swimming pool.

Churches

São Francisco de Assis ⓘ *Largo de Coimbra, Tue-Sun 0830-1150, 1330-1640, US$2; the ticket also permits entry to NS da Conceição (keep your ticket for admission to the museum)* (1766-1796), is considered to be one of the masterpieces of Brazilian Baroque. Aleijadinho (see below) worked on the general design and the sculpture of the façade, the pulpits and many other features. The harmonious lines of the exterior and the beauty of the interior are exceptional. Mestre Athayde was responsible for the painted ceiling which depicts the Assumption of the Virgin Mary and remembers Bartolomé Esteban Murillo. The Madonna is depicted in the highest heaven, surrounded by cherubs and musicians. Pillars support the azure sky with Murillo clouds. At the four corners stand saints Augustine, Hieronymous, Gregory and Ambrosius. Compare the brightness of the ceiling with the brown habits of the statues in the side altars. The blue scenes in the chancel show the life of Abraham. A small museum at the back of the church has a small selection of paintings of serious looking saints and a fountain by Aleijadinho depicting blind faith holding up a banner saying "such is the path to heaven". In the Largo outside São Francisco is a handicraft market.

These churches are all closed on Monday.

Nossa Senhora da Conceição ⓘ *Tue-Sat 0830-1130, 1330-1700, Sun 1200-1700* (1722), the parish church of Antônio Dias (one of the original settlements that became Vila Rica de Albuquerque), is heavily gilded and contains Aleijadinho's tomb. It has a **museum** devoted to him but with very few of his pieces. Be sure to see the exquisite miniature crucifixion on the basement floor.

Nossa Senhora das Mercês e Perdões ⓘ *R das Mercês, Tue-Sun 1000-1400* (1740-1772), was rebuilt in the 19th century. Some sculpture by Aleijadinho can be seen in the main chapel.

Santa Efigênia ⓘ *Tue-Sun 0800-1200* (1720-1785), Ladeira Santa Efigênia e Padre Faria, has wonderful panoramic views of the city. Some say the church was decorated with gold dust washed out of slaves' hair, others that it was built by Chico Rei (see above). Manuel Francisco Lisboa (Aleijadinho's father) oversaw the construction and much of the carving is by Francisco Xavier de Brito (Aleijadinho's mentor).

Nossa Senhora do Carmo ⓘ *R Brigadeiro Mosqueira, Tue-Sun 1300-1700, entry is shared with NS do Pilar* (1766-1772), was planned by Manuel Francisco Lisboa and both his son and Mestre Athayde worked on the project. It was the favourite church of the aristocracy. There is a museum of sacred art with Aleijadinho sculptures (1733). **Nossa Senhora do Pilar** ⓘ *1200-1700*, which has heavily gilded work by Francisco Xavier de Brito, also contains a religious art museum.

Nossa Senhora do Rosário ⓘ *Largo do Rosário*, dates from 1785, when the present church replaced a chapel on the site. It has a curved façade, which is rare in Brazilian Baroque. The interior is simpler than the exterior, but there are interesting side altars.

Nossa Senhora das Mercês e Misericórdia (1773-1793) is just north of the Praça Tiradentes; further west, on a neighbouring hill, is **São Francisco de Paula** ⓘ *0900-1700*, work on which started in 1804, making it the last colonial church in Ouro Preto. **São José**, Rua Teixeira Amaral, was begun in 1752, but not completed until 1811; some carving is by Aleijadinho.

There are a number of other churches and chapels. Also throughout the town are excellent examples of the public fountain (*chafariz*), oratories (*passos*) and stone bridges over the creeks and rivers.

Around Ouro Preto

The **Cachoeira das Andorinhas**, a waterfall north of town, is reached by taking a bus to Morro de Santana and then walking 25 minutes. To walk all the way takes 1½ hours. Near the waterfall it is possible to visit the **Zen Buddhist monastery** ⓘ *apply in advance to Mosteiro Zen Pico de Rajos, Morro de São Sebastião, Caixa Postal 101, 35400-000, Ouro Preto, ToXX31-9612484*. Excursions of 2½ hours are arranged at 0830 and 1430 visiting many cultural and ecological sites of interest.

The town is dominated by a huge cross, easily reached from the road to Mariana, which affords lovely views of the sunset; but don't go alone as it's in a poor district.

Parque Estadual de Itacolomi and the **Estação Ecológica do Tripuí** are protected areas close to the city. The former (a three-hour walk from the centre, cars prohibited) includes the peak of Itacolomi, which the first gold prospectors used as a landmark, the source of the Rio Doce as well as endangered wildlife and splendid views. Tripuí is in the valley where the first gold was found; it protects a rare flatworm, *Peripatus acacioi*. It can also be reached on foot, or the bus to Belo Horizonte will drop you near the entrance.

Minas de Passagem

ⓘ *Ouro Preto T5511068, Mariana T5571340, 0900-1800, entry US$7.50.*
Between Ouro Preto and Mariana is the Minas de Passagem gold mine, dating from 1719. A 20-minute guided tour visits the old mine workings and underground lake (take bathing suit). There is a waterfall, Cachoeira Serrinha, where swimming is possible, 30 minutes' walk from the bus stop to the mine. Initially you have to walk 100 m towards Mariana then ask for directions. Note that some signs say Mina de Ouro, omitting 'da Passagem'.

The nearest town to the Minas de Passagem is **Passagem de Mariana**. Where the bus stops at the edge of town is the *Pousada Solar dos Dois Sinos*, with a church behind it.

Mariana

Phone code: 031. Altitude: 697 m. Colour map 4, C3. Population: 47,000.

Mariana, another colonial mining city, is the oldest in Minas Gerais, founded a few years before Ouro Preto, on 16 July 1696 by *bandeirantes*. At first, when it was little more than a collection of huts, it was called Arraial de Nossa Senhora do Carmo. But by 1711 it had become the town of Vila de Nossa Senhora do Carmo, and by the mid-18th century it had grown to be the most important administrative centre in the newly created Capitania de São Paulo e Minas do Ouro. Its name was changed to Mariana in honour of the wife of Dom João V, Dona Maria Ana of Austria. It retains many fine colonial buildings, most of them constructed in the second half of the 18th century. The artist Mestre Athayde was born here, as was the Inconfidente Cláudio Manuel da Costa. The town was declared a national monument in 1945.

Tiradentes and the Inconfidência Mineira

In the last quarter of the 18th century, Vila Rica de Nossa Senhora do Pilar do Ouro Preto was a dynamic place. Gold had brought great wealth to the city and this was translated into fine religious and secular buildings. Much of the artistry that went into these constructions and their decoration was home-grown, such as the genius of O Aleijadinho. In conjunction with this flowering of the arts an intellectual society developed. And yet all this went on under the heavy hand of the Portuguese crown, which demanded its fifth share (the quinto), imposed punitive taxes and forbade local industries to operate. While the artists and artisans could not travel and had to seek inspiration in what was around them, the intellectuals were often from families who sent their young to Europe to further their education. So, when the gold yields began to decline and the Portuguese demands became even more exorbitant, some members of society began to look to Europe and North America for ways to free Minas Gerais from the crown.

One side of the argument was the view of the governor, the Visconde de Barbacena, who refused to admit that the mines were exhausted and that poverty was beginning to affect the community. As far as he was concerned, there was no gold because it was being smuggled out of the captaincy and there was no economic problem, just a large unpaid debt to the Portuguese crown. On the other side was the idea, as expressed by the French poet Parny, that Brazil was a paradise on earth, with everything except liberty. The Jesuit Antônio Vieira, who lived in the previous century, put it thus: "the cloud swells in Brazil and it rains on Portugal; the water is not picked up from the sea, but from the tears of the unfortunate and the sweat of the poor, and I do not know how their faith and constancy has lasted so long."

In the late 1780s a group of people began to have secret discussions on how to resolve the intolerable situation. It included the poets Cláudio Manuel da Costa, Tomás Gonzaga and Ignacio de Alvarenga, the doctors Domingos Vidal Barbosa and José Alvares Maciel, Padres Toledo and Rolim and the military officers Domingos de Abreu Vieira, Francisco de Paula Freire de Andrade and José de Resende Costa. Into this group came Joaquim José da Silva Xavier, a junior officer (*alferes*), who was

Unlike its more famous neighbour, Ouro Preto, in whose shadow the town tends to sit, Mariana has remained a working mining centre. For many years the **Companhia do Vale do Rio Doce** (CVRD), the state mining company, had major operations here and provided a great deal of assistance for the restoration of the colonial heritage. Since CVRD's concentration on its new investments at Carajás and subsequent privatization, there have been doubts about its commitment to mining in Mariana and consequently to the town.

The **tourist office** ⓘ *Praça Tancredo Neves, T35579044, www.mariana.mg.gov.br*, will help with guides and tours and offer a map and a free monthly booklet, *Mariana Agenda Cultural*, packed with local information including accommodation and eating. **Mariana Turismo** ⓘ *R Direita 31.* ▸▸ *For Transport information, see page 265.*

Sights

The historical centre of the town slopes gently uphill from the river and the Praça Tancredo Neves, where buses from Ouro Preto stop. The first street parallel with the Praça Tancredo Neves is Rua Direita, which is lined with beautiful, two-storey born at the Fazenda de Pombal near São João del Rei in about 1748. He was also a dentist and became known by the nickname Tiradentes – tooth-puller. Already dissatisfied with the way the army had treated him, by failing to promote him among other things, in 1788 he was suspended from active duty because of illness. The subsequent loss of pay roused him further. In trying to get reinstated he met Freire de Andrade and Alvares Maciel and later conversations prompted him to tell them of his idea of an uprising against the Portuguese. The Inconfidência grew out of these types of meeting, some planning action, others the future political and economic organization of a new, independent state.

The conspirators worked to gain support for their cause, but one soldier they approached, Coronel Joaquim Silverio dos Reis, used the information he had been given to betray the cause. The governor received reports from other sources and began to build up a picture of what was going on. Tiradentes was the first to be arrested, at the beginning of May 1789, in Rio de Janeiro. It seems that the plotters at this time still had no clear idea of what their ultimate aim was, nor of the importance of their attitudes. They never got the chance anyway because all were arrested soon after Tiradentes. They were imprisoned and kept incommunicado for two years while the case against them was prepared. Tiradentes was singled out as the most important member of the group and, under questioning, he did not disabuse his captors, taking full responsibility for everything. A defence for the Inconfidentes was prepared, but it almost totally ignored Tiradentes, as if he were being made a scapegoat. It made no difference, though, because the defence lost; 11 Inconfidentes were sentenced to death in November 1791. Soon afterwards the authorities in Brazil read out a surprising letter from the queen, Dona Maria I, commuting the death sentence for 10 of the conspirators to exile in Portugal or Africa. The 11th, Tiradentes, was not spared. On 21 April 1792 he was hanged and his body was quartered and his head cut off, the parts to be displayed as a warning against any similar attempts to undermine the crown. Even though Tiradentes would never have been freed, one of the astonishing things about the queen's letter was that it was dated 18 months before it was brought to light.

18th-century houses with tall colonial windows and balconies. The **Casa do Barão de Pontal** ⓘ *R Direita 54, Tue 1400-1700*, whose balconies are carved from soapstone, is unique in Minas Gerais. The ground floor of the building is a museum of furniture. The **Museu-Casa Afonso Guimarães** ⓘ *R Direita 35, free*, the former home of a symbolist poet: photographs and letters. The **Casa Setecentista** ⓘ *R Dieita 7*, another excellent example of 18th-century secular architecture, now belongs to the Patrimônio Histórico e Artístico Nacional. It has an enormous archive of documents from the colonial period, an exhibition hall and a multimedia centre.

Rua Direita leads to the Praça da Sé, on which stands the cathedral, **Basílica de Nossa Senhora da Assunção**. Before Vila de Nossa Senhora do Carmo became a town, a chapel, started in 1703, stood on this spot. In various stages it was expanded and remodelled until its completion in 1760. The portal and the lavabo in the sacristy are by Aleijadinho and the painting in the beautiful interior and side altars is by Manoel Rabello de Sousa. Also in the cathedral is a wooden German organ (1701), made by Arp Schnitger, which was a gift to the first diocese of the Capitania de Minas do Ouro in 1747. It was restored in 1984 after some 50 years of silence. Concerts are held in the cathedral including regular **organ concerts** ⓘ *Fri 1100 and Sun 1200, US$7.50*, see the local press for details.

Turning up Rua Frei Durão, on the right is the **Museu Arquidiocesano** ⓘ *R Frei Durão 49, Tue-Sun 0900-1200, 1300-1700, US$1.50*, which has fine church furniture, a gold and silver collection, Aleijadinho statues and an ivory cross. On the opposite side of the street is the **Casa da Intendência/Casa de Cultura** ⓘ *R Frei Durão 84, 0800-1130, 1330-1700*, which holds exhibitions and has a museum of music. The ceilings in the exhibition rooms are very fine; in other rooms there are *esteiro* (flattened bamboo) ceilings. The **Centro Cultural SESC Mariana** ⓘ *R Frei Durão 22*, has a theatre and occasional cinema presentations.

Praça Gomes Freire used to be where horses were tied up (there is an old drinking trough on one side) and where festivals were held. Now it has pleasant gardens. On the south side is the **Palácio Arquiepiscopal**, while on the north side is the **Casa do Conde de Assumar**, who was governor of the Capitania from 1717 to 1720; it later became the bishop's palace.

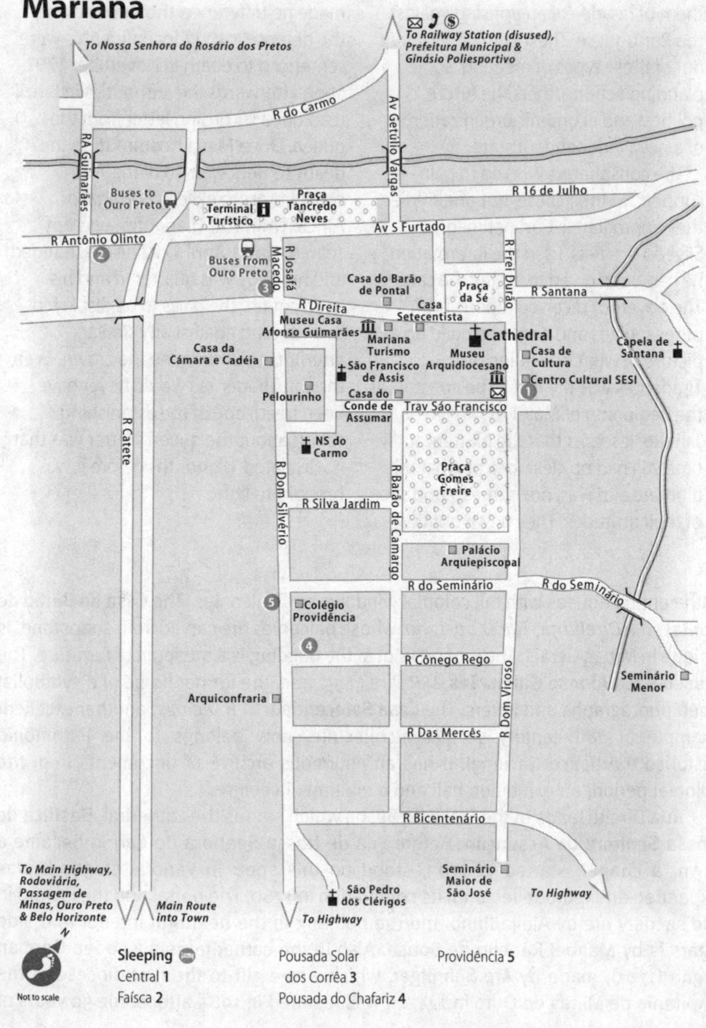

Praça Minas Gerais has one of the finest groups of colonial buildings in Brazil. In the middle is the **Pelourinho**, the stone Monument to Justice, at which slaves used to be beaten. The fine **São Francisco Church** ⓘ *daily 0800-1700* (1762-1794), has pulpits designed by Aleijadinho, paintings by Mestre Athayde, who is buried in tomb No 94, a fine sacristy and one side altar by Aleijadinho. The statue of São Roque is most important as he is the patron saint of the city (his day is 16 August). Among Athayde's paintings are the panels showing the life of St Francis on the ceiling of the right-hand chapel. The church is one of the most simple in Mariana, but in terms of art, one of the richest. There is a small exhibition of the restoration work funded by CVRD.

At right angles to São Francisco is **Nossa Senhora do Carmo** ⓘ *daily 1400-1700* (1784), with steatite carvings, Athayde paintings, and chinoiserie panelling. Its exterior is considered the most beautiful in Mariana by some. Unfortunately this church was damaged by fire in 1999. Across Rua Dom Silvério is the **Casa da Cámara e Cadéia** (1768), once the Prefeitura Municipal. It is a superb example of civic colonial construction.

On Rua Dom Silvério the **Colégio Providência** at No 61 was the first college for boarding students in Minas Gerais (part of it is now a hotel, see below). Also on this street is the **Igreja da Arquiconfraria** and, nearing the top of the hill, the **Chafariz de São Pedro**. On the Largo de São Pedro is the church of **São Pedro dos Clérigos**, founded by Manuel da Cruz, first bishop of the town (1764), one of the few elliptical churches in Minas Gerais. It is unadorned, although there is a painting by Athayde of *A Entrega do Menino Jesus a Santo Antônio*. The cedar altar was made by José Pedro Aroca. Look for the cockerel, carved in memory of the biblical verses about St Peter betraying Christ before the cock has crowed three times. Ask to see the view from the bell tower.

Capela de Santo Antônio, wonderfully simple and the oldest in town, is some distance from the centre on Rua Rosário Velho. Overlooking the city from the north, with a good viewpoint, is the church of **Nossa Senhora do Rosário** ⓘ *R do Rosário* (1752), with work by Athayde and showing Moorish influence.

Outside the centre, to the west, but within easy walking distance, is the **Seminário Menor**, now the Instituto de Ciencias Históricas e Sociais of the Federal University.

South of the river, Avenida Getúlio Vargas leads to the new **Prefeitura Municipal**. It passes the **Ginásio Poliesportivo** and, across the avenue, the **railway station**. This is a romantic building with a clock tower, but it is rapidly falling into disrepair. No trains run on the line any more.

Around Mariana

The small village of **Antônio Pereira**, 24 km north of Mariana, is where the Imperial topaz is mined. Tours can be made of an interesting cave with stalactites: pay local children a small fee to show you round. ▸▸ *For Transport information, see page 265.*

Congonhas do Campo

➔ *Phone code: 031. Altitude: 866 m. Colour map 4, C3. Population: 42,000.*

In the 18th century, Congonhas was a mining town. Today, in addition to the business brought by the tourists and pilgrims who come to the sanctuary, its industries include mining and handicrafts. There is little need to stay in Congonhas as the town's main sight – Aleijadinho's beautiful church and chapel-lined stairway – can be seen in a few hours between bus changes. Leave your bags at the information desk at the bus station. In town, the bus stops in Praça JK. You can walk up from Praça JK via Praça Dr Mário Rodrigues Pereira, cross the little bridge, then go up Ruas Bom Jesus and Aleijadinho to the Praça da Basílica. A bus marked Basílica runs every 30 minutes from the centre of the rodoviária to Bom Jesus, 5 km, US$0.45. A taxi from the rodoviária will cost US$5 1-way, US$10 return including the wait while you visit the sanctuary. **Fumcult** ⓘ *in the Romarias, T37311300 ext 114*, acts as the tourist office and is very helpful.

O Santuário de Bom Jesus de Matosinhos

ⓘ *Tue-Sun 0700-1900.*

The great pilgrimage church, and its Via Sacra dominate the town. The idea of building a sanctuary belonged to a prospector, Feliciano Mendes, who promised to erect a cross and chapel in thanks to Bom Jesus after he had been cured of a serious illness. The inspiration for his devotion came from two sources in Portugal, the cult of Bom Jesus at Braga (near where Mendes was born) and the church of Bom Jesus de Matozinhos, near Porto. Work began in 1757, funded by Mendes' own money and alms he raised. The church was finished in 1771, six years after Mendes' death, and the fame that the sanctuary had acquired led to its development by the most famous architects, artists and sculptors of the time as a Sacro Monte. This involved the construction of six linked chapels, or *pasos* (1802-1818), which lead up to a terrace and courtyard before the church.

There is a wide view of the country from the church terrace, below which are six small chapels set in an attractive sloping area with grass, cobblestones and palms. Each chapel shows scenes with life-size Passion figures carved by Aleijadinho and his pupils in cedar wood. In order of ascent they are: the chapel of the Last Supper, the chapel of the Mount of Olives, the chapel of the taking, or betrayal, of Christ, the chapel of the flagellation and the crowning with thorns, the chapel of Jesus carrying the Cross and the chapel of Christ being nailed to the Cross.

On the terrace stand the 12 prophets sculpted by Aleijadinho between 1800 and 1805 (thought of as his masterpieces). Carved in soapstone with a dramatic sense of movement, they constitute one of the finest works of art of their period in the world. Note how Aleijadinho adapted the biblical characters to his own cultural references. All the prophets are sculpted wearing leather boots, as all important men in his time would have done. Daniel, who entered the lion's den, is represented with the artist's own conception of a lion, never having seen one himself: a large, maned cat with a face rather like a Brazilian monkey. Similarly, the whale which accompanies Jonah is an idiosyncratic interpretation. Each statue has a prophetic text carved with it. The statues "combine in a kind of sacred ballet whose

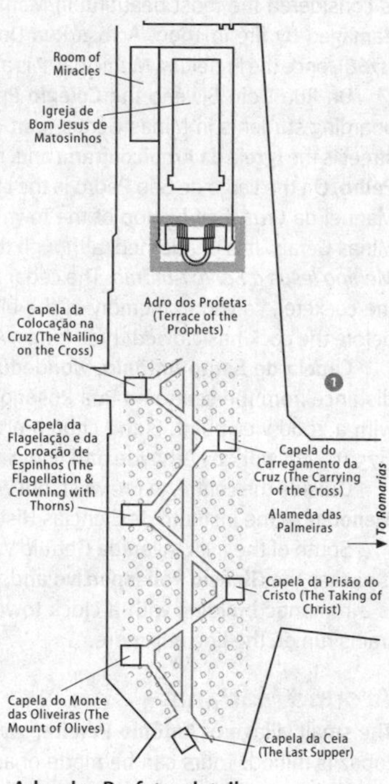

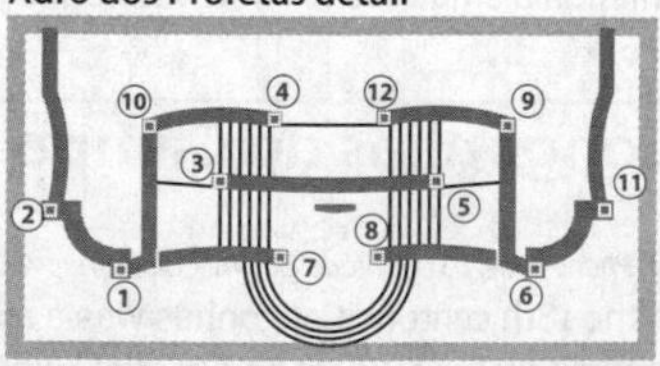

movements only seem uncoordinated; once these sculptures cease to be considered as isolated units, they take on full significance as part of a huge composition brought to life by an inspired genius." (*Iberian-American Baroque*, edited by Henri Stierlin, page 178.) The beauty of the whole is enhanced by the combination of church, Via Sacra and wide landscape over which the prophets seem to preside.

Inside the church, there are paintings by Athayde and the heads of four sainted popes (Gregory, Jerome, Ambrose and Augustine) sculpted by Aleijadinho for the reliquaries on the high altar. Other artists involved were João Nepomuceno Correia e Castro, who painted the scenes of the life and passion of Christ in the nave and around the high altar, João Antunes de Carvalho, who carved the high altar, and Jerônimo Félix and Manuel Coelho, who carved the crossing altars of Santo Antônio and São Francisco de Paula. Despite the ornate carving, the overall effect of the paintwork is almost muted and naturalistic, with much use of blues, greys and pinks. Lamps are suspended on chains from the mouths of black dragons.

To the left of the church, as you face it, the third door in the building alongside the church is the Room of Miracles, which contains photographs and thanks for miracles performed.

On the hill are a tourist kiosk, souvenir shops, the **Colonial Hotel** and **Cova do Daniel** restaurant. There are public toilets on the Alameda das Palmeiras. From the hotel the Alameda das Palmeiras sweeps round to the **Romarias**, a large, almost oval area surrounded by buildings. This was the lodging where the pilgrims stayed. It now contains the **Espaço Cultural**, the headquarters of the local tourist office (**Fumcult**), workshops, the museums of mineralogy and religious art, the **Memória da Cidade**, the **Estalagem** restaurant and a *lanchonete*. A winter festival is held here for one week in July.

Of the other churches in Congonhas do Campothe, the oldest is **Nossa Senhora do Rosário**, Praça do Rosário, built by slaves at the end of the 17th century. The **Igreja Matriz de Nossa Senhora da Conceição**, in Praça 7 de Setembro, dates from 1749; the portal is attributed to Aleijadinho, while parts of the interior are by Manuel Francisco Lisboa. There are also two 18th-century chapels, **Nossa Senhora da Ajuda**, in the district of Alto Maranhão, and the church at **Lobo Leite**, 10 km away.

Just past Lagoa Dourada is the turning (12 km) for Prados, a pleasant town known for its musical and handicrafts traditions. It maintains its historical church music (see under São João del Rei, below), but the chief tradition is leatherwork, especially saddles (some say this dates back to the time when mule trains had to be equipped – Prados was one of the earliest places to produce gold). The forge produces the ironwork (bits, etc) and another workshop produces the frames for the saddles. In this and other shops animals are carved in wood. Excellent leather clothing can also be found, good prices from **Mara e Café**, Rua Magalhães Gomes 90. Other crafts include crochet and sisal carpets.

Tiradentes → *Phone code: 032. Colour map 4, C3. Population: 6,000.*

Aside from Ouro Preto, Tiradentes is the most visited of the Minas colonial towns. Its winding, hilly streets lined with carefully restored Baroque Portuguese churches and neat whitewashed cottages trimmed in thick yellow and blue huddle around the Santo Antonio River beneath the rugged hills of the Serra de São José. Inside are art galleries, restaurants, souvenir shops and *pousadas*, all busy with tourists even during the week. Horse-drawn carriages clatter along the cobbles and at weekends a steam train puffs and chugs its way slowly below the mountains to São João del Rei towing Pullmans full of delighted children.

Tiradentes and São João del Rei make a good pair – lying within less than 30 minutes of each other by buses which leave every 30-40 minutes. Tiradentes is the more twee; São João is uglier but more of a real town. Use one as a base for visiting the other. Tiradentes has a far greater choice of accommodation. São João has better bus connections – to Rio, São Paulo, Belo Horizonte, Mariana and Ouro Preto. The **tourist office** ⓘ *R Resende Costa 71*, is in the Prefeitura.

Sights

Churches The **Igreja Matriz de Santo Antônio** ⓘ *daily 0900-1700, US$1 no photography*, first built in 1710 and enlarged in 1736, contains some of the finest gilded woodcarvings in the country. The main church is predominantly white and gold. Lamps hang from the beaks of golden eagles. The symbols on the panels painted on the ceiling of the nave are a mixture of Old Testament and medieval Christian symbolism (for instance the phoenix, and the pelican). A carved wooden balustrade separates the seating in the nave from richly carved side chapels and altars. The principal altar is also ornately decorated, as are the walls and ceiling around it. The church has a small but fine organ brought from Porto in the 1790s. The upper part of the reconstructed façade is said to follow a design by Aleijadinho. In front of the church, on the balustrade which overlooks the main street and the town, are also a cross and a sundial by him.

The charming **Nossa Senhora do Rosário** ⓘ *Wed-Mon 1200-1600, US$0.50*, on a small square on Rua Direita, has fine statuary and ornate gilded altars. On its painted ceiling colonnades rise to heaven; two monks stand on a hill and the Virgin and Child are in the sky. Other ceiling panels depicting the life of Christ are in poor shape. The church contains statues of black saints, including São Benedito, patron saint of cooks; in one of the statues he is holding a squash. The church dates from 1727, but building by the Irmandade dos Pretos Cativos (black slave brotherhood) began as early as 1708.

São João Evangelista ⓘ *Wed-Mon 0900-1700*, is on the Largo do Sol, a lovely open space. It is a simple church, built by the Irmandade dos Homens Pardos

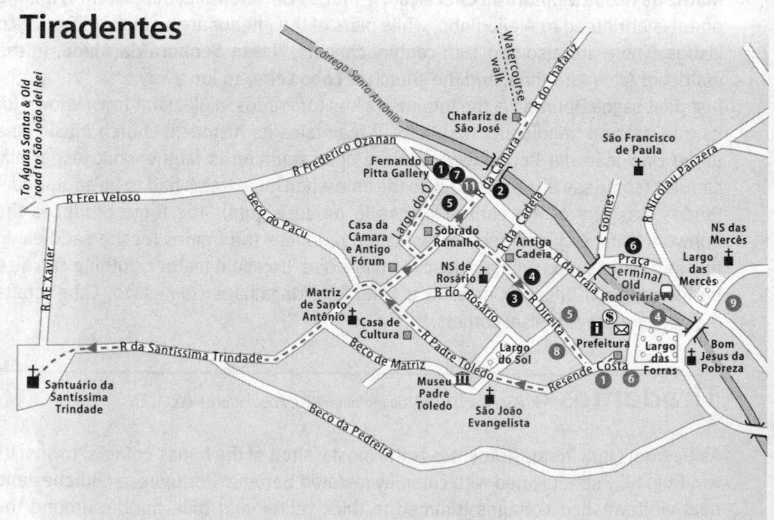

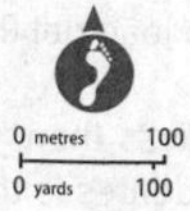

Sleeping
Ponto do Morro 1
Porão Colonial 2
Pousada do Alferes 3
Pousada Do Arco Iris 11
Pousada do Largo 4
Pousada do Laurito 5
Pousada Mãe d'Água 6
Pousada Maria Bonita 7
Pousada Três Portas 8
Pouso das Gerais 10
Solar da Ponte 9

Eating
Aluarte 1

(mulattos). It has paintings of the four Evangelists and a cornice painted in an elaborate pattern in pink, blue and beige.

The 18th-century **Nossa Senhora das Mercês** ⓘ *Largo das Mercês, Sun 0900-1700*, has an interesting painted ceiling and a notable statue of the Virgin.

There are other churches and chapels in the town, including the **Igreja de Bom Jesus da Pobreza**, on the Largo das Forras. **Santuário da Santíssima Trindade**, on the road which leads up behind the Igreja Matriz de Santo Antônio is well worth seeing. The chapel itself is 18th century while the Room of Miracles associated with the annual Trinity Sunday pilgrimage is modern. On the grassy Morro de São Francisco is the small chapel of **São Francisco de Paula** (mid-18th century).

Secular buildings and a suggested tour From the main praça, Largo das Forras, take Rua Resende Costa up to the Largo do Sol (Igreja São João Evangelista – see above). Beside the church is the **Museu Padre Toledo**, the house of this leader of the Inconfidência Mineira, which is now a museum protecting some handsome colonial furniture and a painted roof depicting the Five Senses. The **Casa de Cultura** in the row of 18th-century houses on Rua Padre Toledo, which leads from Largo do Sol to the Igreja Matriz de Santo Antônio, is protected by the same organization. From Santo Antônio, head down the Rua da Câmara, past the **Casa da Câmara e Antigo Fórum**. Here the road divides, the left-hand street, Jogo de Bola, leading to the Largo do Ó (which rejoins the main street), while Rua da Câmara goes to the crossroads with Rua Direita. At this junction is the **Sobrado Ramalho**, said to be the oldest building in Tiradentes. It is believed to be where the gold was melted down and has a lot of soapstone carving inside. It has been beautifully restored as a cultural centre.

There are five 18th-century churches in town, three of which are splendid examples of Brazilian colonial buildings.

Before taking Rua Direita back to Largo das Forras, you can carry straight on to the river and cross the bridge to the magnificent **Chafariz de São José** (the public fountain), installed in 1749. The water is brought by a stone aqueduct from springs in the forest at the foot of Serra São José. It is still used for drinking, clothes washing and watering animals.

Rua Direita has some interesting old buildings. Opposite the Praça Padre Lourival, on which stands Nossa Senhora do Rosário, is the **Antiga Cadeia** (18th-19th century) which now contains the **Museu de Arta Sacra**. Rua Direita meets the Largo das Forras at the **Prefeitura Municipal**, a two-storey building with an extra room under the roof. It now houses the tourist, post and phone offices.

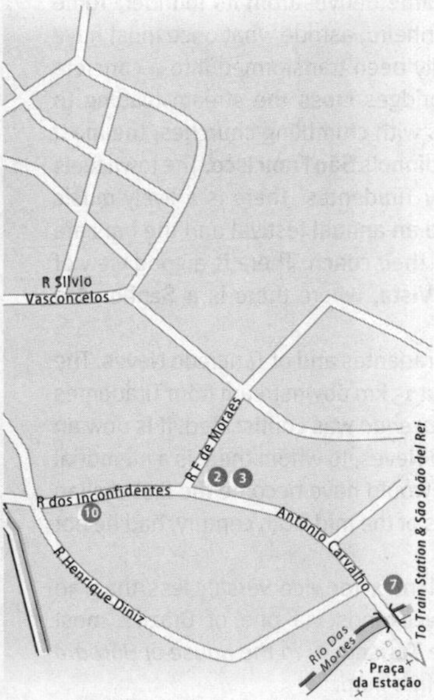

Bistrô Richard Rothe 3
Estalagem 2
Maria Luisa Casa de Chá 7
Quartier Latin 6
Quinto de Ouro 4
Virados do Largo 5
Walking tour

Excursions from Tiradentes

The **steam trains** ⓘ *Fri, Sat, Sun and holidays, 1000 and 1415 from São João del Rei, returning from Tiradentes at 1300 and 1700, US$8*, which run on the 76-cm gauge track between São João del Rei and Tiradentes (13 km) have been in continuous operation since 1881 – a testament to the durability of the rolling stock and locomotives made by the Baldwin Company of Philadelphia. The maximum speed is 20 km per hour. To get to the railway station from the centre of the village you have to cross the river and head out of town on the Rua dos Inconfidentes. Follow this road until it becomes the Rua Antônio Teixeira Carvalho, which carries on to the bridge over the Rio das Mortes. On the opposite bank is a small park and the station. The railway museum at the railway station in São João del Rei is described above.

A recommended walk from Tiradentes is to the protected forest on the **Serra de São José**. Easiest access is from behind the Chafariz, where a black door in the wall is opened at 0730 (Wednesday-Sunday). In just five minutes you are in the forest, following the watercourse, and monkeys and birds can be seen.

Alternatively, you can walk up into the **Serra** from behind the Mercês Church; ask for directions. It is recommended that you take a guide if you wish to walk along the top of the Serra.

There is a good one- or two-hour walk from Tiradentes to the **Balneário de Águas Santas** which involves crossing the Serra. At the Balneário is a swimming pool, also a lake and a *churrascaria*, **Senzala**. A map can be obtained from the **Solar da Ponte**, or ask locally for directions (taxi US$15). On the way you pass **Parque Frei Mariano Vellozo**, which contains the Cachoeira do Mangue falls. It is busy at weekends and can be reached by car on the old road to São João.

São João del Rei

→ *Phone code: 032. Colour map 4, C3. Population: 79,000.*

São João del Rei, whose apparently Spanish name derives from its founder, Tomé Portes del Rei, lies at the foot of the Serra do Lenheiro, astride what once must have been a winding little stream. This has now sadly been transformed into a concrete gutter with grass verges. Eighteenth-century bridges cross the stream leading to streets lined with colonial buildings and plazas with crumbling churches, the most interesting and best preserved of which is Aleijadinho's **São Francisco**. The town feels far less of a tourist museum piece than nearby Tiradentes. There is a lively music scene here – with two renowned orchestras and an annual festival and the bars are filled with locals rather than tourists waiting for their coach. There is a good view of the town and surroundings from **Alto da Boa Vista**, where there is a **Senhor dos Montes** (Statue of Christ).

São João del Rei is famous as the home of Tiradentes and of Tancredo Neves. The former was born in the Fazenda de Pombal, about 15 km downstream from Tiradentes on the Rio das Mortes. After his execution, the *fazenda* was confiscated. It is now an experimental station owned by Ibama. Tancredo Neves, to whom there is a memorial in the town (see also below), was the man who would have become the first civilian president of Brazil after the military dictatorships of the mid-20th century, had he not mysteriously died before taking office.

São João is a good base for visiting Tiradentes (or vice versa); less than 30 minutes away by bus or an hour away at weekends via one of Brazil's most memorable steam train rides. The **Secretaria de Turismo** ⓘ *in the house of Bárbara Heliodora, T333717833, 0900-1700*, provides a free map.

Sights

The Corrego do Lenheiro, a stream with steep grassy banks, runs through the centre of town. Across it are two fine, stone bridges, **A Ponte da Cadeia** (1798) and **A Ponte do**

Rosário (1800), as well as several other modern bridges. Both sides of the river have colonial monuments, which are interspersed with modern buildings. On the north side are many streets with pleasant houses, but in various states of repair. **Rua Santo Antônio** has many single-storey colonial houses which have been restored and painted. **Rua Santo Elias** has several buildings all in the same style. Behind the church of Nossa Senhora do Pilar (see below), the **Largo da Câmara** leads up to Mercês Church, which has quite a good view. Throughout the city you will see locked portals with colonial porticos. These are *passinhos*, shrines that are opened in Holy Week. They can be seen for instance on **Largo da Cruz** and **Largo do Rosário**.

Many streets and squares seem to have more than one name, which can be a little confusing, but as the town centre is not large, it is hard to get lost. One such street crosses the Ponte da Cadeia from Rua Passos; it has three names: Rua da Intendência, Manoel Anselmo and Artur Bernardes.

In their book *Iberian-American Baroque,* Stierlin and Bottineau describe the design for the façade of **São Francisco de Assis** ① *Praça Frei Orlando, Tue-Sun 0830-1700, US$1,* (1774), as Aleijadinho's highest achievement, "richly ornamented, yet, at the same time, simple and poetic in feeling". The towers are circular, the doorway intricately carved and the greenish stone frames the white paint to beautiful effect. Inside are two sculptures by Aleijadinho, and others of his school. The six side altars are in wood; restoration has removed the plaster from the altars, revealing fine

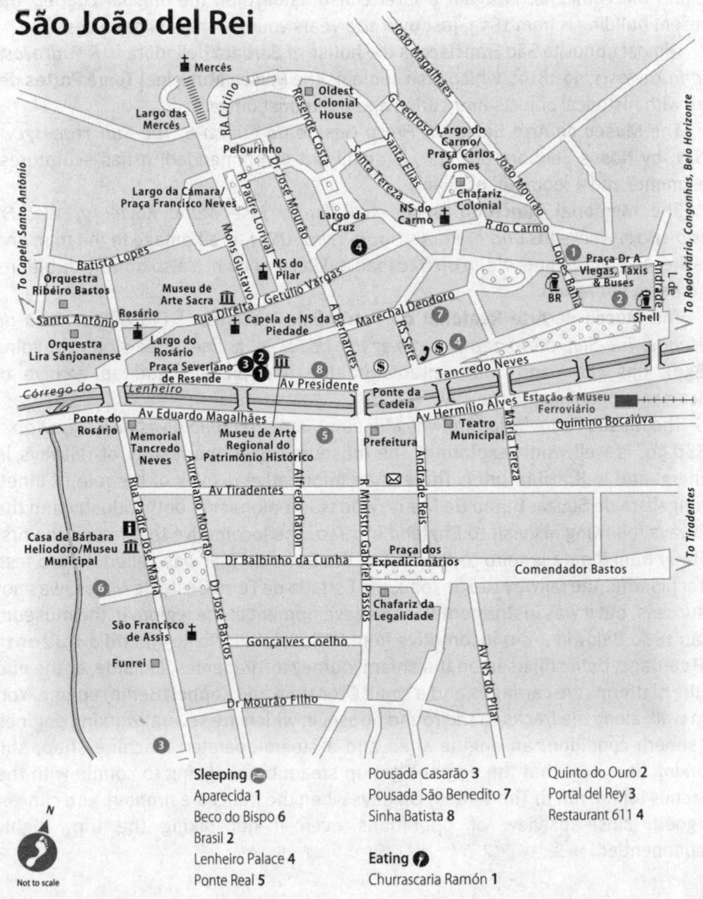

carving in sucupira wood. Their artistry is wonderful and the three pairs of altars mirror each other, each pair in a different style (note, for instance, the use of pillars and the different paintings which accompany each altar). The overall shape of the nave is elliptical, the gold altar has spiralling columns and an adoring St Francis kneels atop.

The **Basílica de Nossa Senhora do Pilar** ⓘ *R Getúlio Vargas (formerly R Direita), open afternoons*, the cathedral, was built in 1721, but has a 19th-century façade which replaced the 18th-century original. It has rich altars and a brightly painted ceiling (Madonna and Child in the middle, saints and bishops lining the sides). Note the androgynous gold heads and torsos within the eight columns set into the walls either side of the main altar. There is a profusion of cherubs and plants in the carving. This abundance and angelic innocence contrasts with the suffering of the Passion and the betrayal of the Last Supper (two pictures of which are before the altar), all common themes in Brazilian Baroque. In the sacristy are portraits of the Evangelists.

Nossa Senhora do Carmo ⓘ *Praça Dr Augusto Viegas (Largo do Carmo), open afternoons*, all in white and gold, has been very well restored. Construction commenced in 1733. The façade is outlined in lights at night.

There are three other churches in town: the **Igreja do Rosário** ⓘ *Largo do Rosário, open afternoons*, in its present form dates from 1753, but the first chapel on the site was put up in 1719. It is all white, except for silver angels. The **Igreja de Santo Antônio** ⓘ *R Santo Antônio*, is a chapel built in the 1760s. The **Igreja das Mercês**, on the hill behind the cathedral, is again a later construction than the original chapel. The present building is from 1853, just over 100 years younger than its predecessor.

Almost opposite São Francisco is the house of **Bárbara Heliodora** ⓘ *R Padre José Maria Xavier* (1759-1819), which also contains the **Museu Municipal Tomé Portes del Rei**, with historical objects and curios and the tourist office.

The **Museu de Arte Sacra** ⓘ *Praça Gastão da Cunha 8, Tue-Sun 1100-1700, US$1*, by Nossa Senhora do Pilar, is small but recommended; it has sculptures, vestments and a room full of silver.

The **Memorial Tancredo Neves** ⓘ *R Padre José Maria Xavier 7, Wed-Fri 1300-1800, weekends and holidays 0900-1700, US$1*, is a homage to the man and his life. An eight-minute video on São João del Rei is shown. It also holds exhibitions and has a bookshop.

The **Museu de Arte Regional do Patrimônio Histórico** ⓘ *Praça Severiano de Resende, Tue-Sun 0800-1200, 1330-1730, US$1*, in a fine three-storey building (1859), has 18th- and 19th-century furniture and pictures and an archive of documents pertaining to the city.

The **Museu Ferroviário** (Railway Museum) ⓘ *Av Hermílio Alves 366, T3718004, US$0.50*, is well worth exploring. The museum traces the history of railways in general and in Brazil in brief. There is an informative display of the role of Irineu Evangelista de Souza, Barão de Mauá, who was a pioneer of both industry and the railways following his visit to England in 1840. The locomotive that ran on the first railway from Rio de Janeiro to the foot of the Serra do Mar was called *A Baronesa* after his wife. The railway to São João, the Estrada de Ferro Oeste de Minas, was not a success, but it was instrumental in the development of the region. In the museum is an 1880 Baldwin 4-4-0 locomotive from Philadelphia (No 5055) and a 1912-1913 VIP carriage, both still used on the steam journey to Tiradentes. Outside, at the end of the platforms are carriages and a small Orenstein and Koppel (Berlin) engine. You can walk along the tracks to the round house, in which are several working engines in superb condition, an engine shed and a steam-operated machine shop, still working. It is here that the engines get up steam before going to couple with the coaches for the run to Tiradentes. On days when the trains are running, you can get a good, close-up view of operations even if not taking the trip. Highly recommended. ▸▸ *See page 256 for the train to Tiradentes.*

Sabará → *Phone code: 031. Colour map 4, B3. Population: 116,000.*

Some 23 km east of Belo Horizonte is the colonial gold-mining (and steel-making) town of Sabará. The town is strung along the narrow steep valleys of the Rio das Velhas and Rio Sabará. Since the late 17th century the Rio das Velhas was known as a gold-bearing river and a community soon grew up there. By 1702 it was the most populous in Minas Gerais. In 1711, the name Villa Real de Nossa Senhora da Conceição de Sabará was given to the parish and in 1838 it became the city of Sabará. There's a Secretaria de Turismo **tourist information office** ⓘ *R Pedro II 200, T6711522.*

The old churches and fountains, rambling cobbled streets and simple houses with carved doors are of great interest. From the bus terminus, walk up Rua Clemente Faria to Praça Santa Rita, where there's a large *chafariz* (fountain). The square adjoins Rua Dom Pedro II, which is lined with beautiful 18th-century buildings. They include the **Solar do Padre Correa** ⓘ *R Dom Pedro II 200* (1773), now the **Prefeitura**, a mansion with a rococo chapel and main reception room (*salão nobre*); the **Casa Azul** ⓘ *R Dom Pedro II 215* (also 1773), now the INSS building, with a chapel and a fine portal; and the **Teatro Municipal**, former Opera House, built in 1770 and the second oldest in Brazil. It has a superb interior, with three balconies, a carved wooden rail before the orchestra pit, wooden floors and *esteiro* (flattened, woven bamboo) ceilings.

At the top of Rua Dom Pedro II is the Praça Melo Viana, in the middle of which is **Nossa Senhora do Rosário dos Pretos** ⓘ *Tue-Sun 0800-1100, 1300-1700* (left unfinished at the time of the slaves' emancipation). Behind the façade of the unfinished building are the chancel, sacristy (both 1780) and the first chapel (1713). There is a museum of religious art in the church (same opening hours). To the right of the church is the **Chafariz do Rosário**. Also on the praça are the ornate Fórum Ministro Orozimbo Nonato and two schools. From the Praça Melo Viana, take Rua São Pedro to the church of **São Francisco** (1781); beyond the church is the **Chafariz Kaquende**.

In Rua da Intendência is the museum of 18th-century gold mining, the **Museu do Ouro** ⓘ *Tue-Sun 1200-1730, US$1.* It contains exhibits of gold extraction, plus religious items and colonial furniture. The building itself is a fine example of colonial architecture. Sources disagree as to its date of construction, but the general view is that it was before 1730. Originally the foundry, it became the Casa da Intendência in 1735. For most of the 19th century it was abandoned and became the gold museum in 1945.

Another fine example of civil colonial architecture is the **Casa Borba Gato** ⓘ *R Borba Gato 71*, so called because tradition has it that it belonged to the famous *bandeirante*, Manoel de Borba Gato, one of the first to settle on the Rio das Velhas, but exiled from the region after the murder of the king's representative, Rodrigo de Castel Blanco in 1682. The building currently belongs to the Museu do Ouro.

The church of **Nossa Senhora do Carmo** ⓘ *US$1, a leaflet about the town is given out* (1763-1774), with doorway, pulpits and choir loft by Aleijadinho and paintings by Athayde, is on Rua do Carmo. From the ceilings, painted blue and grey and gold, religious figures look down surrounding the Virgin and Child and the Chariot of Fire. In the chancel, the Ten Commandments in blue work have a distinctly Moorish air, what with the tents and the night-time scenes.

Similar in style externally is the **Capela de Nossa Senhora do Pilar**, which is beside the municipal cemetery and in front of a large building with blue gates and doors.

Nossa Senhora da Conceição ⓘ *Praça Getúlio Vargas, free* (1720), has a lot of visible woodwork and a beautiful floor. The carvings have a great deal of gilding, there are painted panels, and paintings by 23 Chinese artists brought from Macau. The clearest Chinese work is on the two red doors to the right and left of the chancel.

Nossa Senhora do Ó, built in 1717 and showing unmistakable Chinese influence (paintings in need of restoration), is 2 km from the centre of the town at the Largo Nossa Senhora do Ó. To get there, take the local bus marked 'Esplanada' or 'Boca Grande'.

If you walk up the **Morro da Cruz** hill from the **Hotel do Ouro** to a small chapel, the **Capela da Cruz**, or Senhor Bom Jesus, you can get a wonderful view of the whole region. Look for beautiful quartz crystals while you are up there.

Passeio a Sàbará, by Lúcia Machado de Almeida, with splendid illustrations by Guignard, is an excellent guide to the place.

Excursions from Sabará

Some 25 km from Sabará and 60 km from Belo Horizonte is **Caeté**. The town, originally called Vila Nova da Rainha, has several historical buildings and churches. On the Praça João Pinheiro are the **Prefeitura** and **Pelourinho** (both 1722), the **Igreja Matriz Nossa Senhora do Com Sucesso** ⓘ *daily 1300-1800* (1756, rebuilt 1790) and the **Chafariz da Matriz**. Also on the praça is the **tourist information office** ⓘ *in the Casa da Cultura, T6511855*. Other churches are **Nossa Senhora do Rosário** (1750-1768), with a ceiling attributed to Mestre Athayde, and **São Francisco de Assis**. The **Museu Regional** ⓘ *R Israel Pinheiro 176, Tue-Sun 1200-1700*, in the house of the Barão de Catas Altas, or Casa Setecentista, contains 18th- and 19th-century religious art and furniture. The house itself is a fine example of 18th-century civic architecture, with two floors and an interior patio.

From Caeté you can go to the **Serra da Piedade**; see page 236.

Sleeping

Ouro Preto *p243, map p244, phone code 031*

Prices indicated are for high season; many hotels will negotiate lower prices when things are quiet. Ask at the tourist office for reasonably priced accommodation in *casas de família*. Avoid touts who greet you off buses and charge higher prices than those advertised in hotels; it is difficult to get hotel rooms at weekends and holiday periods. Accommodation can be booked through www.ouropretotour.com; www.ouropreto.com.

A **Pousada do Mondego**, Largo de Coimbra 38, T35512040, F5513094. Beautifully kept colonial house in a fine location by São Francisco Church, room rates vary according to view, small restaurant, Scotch bar, popular with groups. Recommended (a Roteiro de Charme hotel, see p47), the hotel runs a *jardineira* bus tour of the city, 2 hrs, minimum 10 passengers, US$10 for non-guests.

A **Pousada Solar de NS do Rosário**, Av Getúlio Vargas 270, T35515200, www.hotelsolardorosario.com.br. Fully restored historic building with a highly recommended restaurant, bar, sauna, pool; all facilities in rooms.

B **Luxor Pousada**, R Dr Alfredo Baeta 16, Praça Antônio Dias, T35512244, www.luxorhoteis.com.br. Converted colonial mansion, no twin beds, comfortable and clean but spartan, good views, restaurant good but service slow.

C **Pousada Casa Grande**, R Conselheiro Quintiliano, 96, T/F35514314, www.hotelpousadacasagrande.com.br. Including breakfast, safe, good views. Recommended.

D **Colonial**, Trav Padre Camilo Veloso 26, close to Praça Tiradentes, T35513133, www.hotelcolonial.com.br. With new rooms and older rooms refurbished, pleasant.

D **Hospedária Antiga**, R Xavier da Veiga 1, T3552203. Spacious rooms in a restored colonial house. Recommended.

D **Pousada Itacolomi**, R Antônio Pereira 167, T35512891. Small but well kept with good rates for the 3-room apartments. Recommended. Next door to the Museu da Inconfidência.

D **Pousada Nello Nuno**, R Camilo de Brito 59, T35513375. The cheaper rooms have no bath. The friendly owner, Annamélia, speaks some French. Highly recommended.

D **Pousada Tiradentes**, Praça Tiradentes 70, T35512619. The rooms are spartan but well kept and moderately comfortable. Each has a TV, fridge. Conveniently located.

D Pouso Chico Rey, R Brig Musqueira 90, T35511274. A fascinating old house with Portuguese colonial furnishings, very small and utterly delightful, book in advance (room No 6 has been described as a 'dream').
D Solar das Lajes, R Conselheiro Quintiliano 604, T/F35513388, www.solardaslajes.com.br. A little way from the centre but with an excellent view and a pool. Well run.
E Pousada dos Bandeirantes, R das Mercês 167, T35511996. Behind the São Francisco de Assis Church and offering beautiful views.
E Pousada São Francisco de Paula, Padre JM Pen 202, next to the São Francisco de Paula Church, T35513456. One of the best views of any in the city; from the rooms or from a hammock in the garden. Services and facilities include the free use of a kitchen, multilingual staff, excursions. The hostel has 8 rustic rooms including a dormitory, which come with or without a simple breakfast, private or communal bathrooms. Full breakfasts and snacks are available, 100 m from the rodoviária. Recommended.

Youth hostels

E Hostel Ouro Preto, R Costa Sena, 30 Large de Coimbra, T35516705, www.hostel.org.br. Well-kept rooms with polished wooden floors and space for 12 in a colonial building next to the S Francisco de Assis Church right in the centre. Towels are extra.
F Brumas, R Pe José Marcos Pena 68, T35512944, www.brumasonline.hpg.com.br. 150 m downhill from rodoviária, just below São Francisco de Paula Church, T33357809. Dormitory, kitchen and laundry and superb views. Don't walk down from bus station after dark.
Student hostels Students may be able to stay, during holidays and weekends, at the self-governing student hostels, known as *repúblicas* (very welcoming, 'best if you like heavy metal music' and 'are prepared to enter into the spirit of the places'). The Prefeitura has a list of over 50 *repúblicas* with phone numbers, available at the **Secretaria de Turismo**. Many are closed between Christmas and Carnival.

Camping

Camping Clube do Brasil, Rodovia dos Inconfidentes, Km 91, 2 km north, T35511799. Quite expensive but very nice.

Mariana *p247, map p250, phone code 031*
Most of these hotels are housed in colonial buildings. Further details can be found on www.mariana.mg.gov.br.
C Faísca, R Antônio Olinto 48, T35571206. Up the street from the tourist office with both suites and rooms, breakfast included.
C Pousada Solar dos Corrêa, R Josefá Macedo 70 and R Direita, T/F35572080. A restored 18th-century townhouse with spacious a/c rooms.
D Pousada do Chafariz, R Cônego Rego 149, T35571492, www.pousadadochafariz.hpg.com.br. A converted colonial building with parking, breakfast and a family atmosphere. Recommended.
D Providência, R Dom Silvério 233, T35571444. Along the road that leads up to the Basílica; has use of the neighbouring school's pool when classes finish at noon.
D-E Central, R Frei Durão 8, T/F35571630. A charming but run-down colonial building on the Praça Gomes Freire. Recommended but avoid the downstairs rooms.

Congonhas do Campo *p251, map p252 phone code 031*
E Colonial, Praça da Basílica 76, opposite Bom Jesus, T37311834. Good and comfortable but noisy, breakfast extra (cheaper without bath), fascinating restaurant (**Cova do Daniel**) downstairs is full of colonial handicrafts and good local food.
E Freitas, R Marechal Floriano 69, T37311543. Basic, with breakfast, cheaper without bath.

Tiradentes *p253, map p254, phone code 032*
Prices are generally lower in the more expensive hotels between Sun and Thu. www.tiradentesturismo.com.br has general details and pictures of many of the *pousadas*.
A Solar da Ponte, Praça das Mercês, T33551255, www.roteirosdecharme/sol.htm. The atmosphere of a country house, run by John and Anna Maria Parsons, the price includes breakfast and afternoon tea, only 12 rooms, fresh flowers in rooms, bar, sauna, lovely gardens, swimming pool, light meals for residents only, for larger meals, the hotel recommends 5 local restaurants. Highly recommended (it is in the **Roteiros de Charme** group, see p47).

B **Pousada Mãe D'Água**, Largo das Forras 50, T33551206. One of the larger *pousadas*, with an outdoor pool set in a small garden, sauna, pool room and a/c rooms. Price includes breakfast.

B **Pousada Três Portas**, R Direita 280A, T33551444. Charming central hotel in a restored townhouse with 8 rooms and a suite. Facilities include a heated indoor pool, sauna and room service. Great for couples.

B-C **Pouso das Gerais**, R dos Inconfidentes 109, T33551234, www.pousodasgerais.hpg.com.br. Spotless, fresh fan-cooled rooms with parquet floors, desk, TV and marble basins in the bathrooms. Central, quiet, pool and breakfast included. Recommended.

C **Hotel Ponto do Morro**, Largo das Forras 2, T33551342. A central motel, just off the main square. Avoid the darker, lower rooms.

C **Porão Colonial**, R dos Inconfidentes 447, T3551251. Pleasant, though a little out of town. With a pool, sauna and parking.

C **Pousada Maria Bonita**, R Antônio Teixeira Carvalho 134, T/F33551227, www.idasbrasil.com.br. A motel with a pool and a garden full of gnomes leading down to the river. About 10 mins out of town, near the station. At the weekend the price includes breakfast, lunch and an evening snack.

C-D **Pousada do Arco Iris**, R Frederico Ozanan 340, T33551167. The best of a string of pousadas in houses on this stretch of road just out of town. Swimming pool, popular, family run, 5 rooms only. Price includes breakfast. Book ahead.

D **Pousada do Alferes**, R dos Inconfidentes 479, T33551303. Simple but central on the main shopping street close to the main square.

D **Pousada do Largo**, Largo das Forras 48, T/F33551219. With a pool, sauna and rooms with Brazilian TV.

D **Pousada do Laurito**, R Direita 187, T33551268. Central, cheap and good value. Very popular with international backpackers.

São João del Rei *p256, map p257, phone code 032*

B **Lenheiro Palace**, Av Pres Tancredo Neves 257, T/F33718155. Modern hotel with good facilities, parking, cheaper in low season, teahouse, breakfast.

C **Ponte Real**, Av Eduardo Magalhães 254, T/F33717000. Modern, comfortable, sizeable rooms, good restaurant.

C-D **Beco do Bispo**, Beco do Bispo 93, 2 mins west of the igreja São Francisco de Assis, T33718844, www.becodobispo.com.br. The best in town – well-kept, bright a/c rooms with firm sprung mattresses, hot showers, cable TV, a pool, convenient location and a very helpful English-speaking staff. Organize tours. Highly recommended.

D **Aparecida**, Praça Dr Antônio Viegas 13, T33712540. Unillustrious but centrally located – by the bus and taxi stop, with a restaurant and *lanchonete*.

D **Pousada Casarão**, Ribeiro Bastos 94, opposite São Francisco Church, T333717447. Housed in a delightful converted mansion house. The decent-sized rooms have firm beds. Also a games room with a pool table.

E **Brasil**, Av Pres Tancredo Neves 395, T33712804. In an old house full of character, on the opposite side of the river from the railway station, cheap. Recommended but basic, no breakfast.

E **Pousada São Benedito**, R Mcal Deodoro 254, T33717381. Price per person. Basic, with shared rooms and bathrooms.

E **Sinha Batista**, R Manock Anselmo 22, T33715550. The best of the cheaper options. With largish rooms in a colonial building conveniently located by the central canal.

Sabará *p259, phone code 031*

B **Del Rio**, R São Francisco 345, T6713040. Standard 3-star rooms. Reasonable service.

C **Solar das Sepúlvedas**, R da Intendência 371, behind the Museu do Ouro, T6712708. Grandiose, popular with Brazilian families and with a pool.

E **Hotel do Ouro**, R Santa Cruz 237, Morro da Cruz, T6715622. Rooms with en suite bathrooms, hot water, breakfast and a marvellous view, great value.

Eating

Ouro Preto *p243, map p244, phone code 031*

Try the local *licor de jaboticaba*.

TTT **Le Coq D'Or**, R Getúlio Vargas 270 (next to the Rosário church), T35515200. Brazilian French fusion cooking in a smart dining room with live music. One of the city's best.

TT **Adega**, R Teixeira Amaral 24, 1130-1530, T35514171. Vegetarian smorgasbord, US$5, all you can eat. Highly recommended.

Beijinho Doce, R Direita 134A. Café Gerais, 124 R Direita. Decent bacalhau and steaks, good cakes and lousy coffee. Delicious pastries and cakes, try the truffles.
Forno de Barro, Praça Tiradentes 54. Decent Mineira cooking in generous portions.
Pasteleria Lampião, Praça Tiradentes. Good views at the back (better at lunchtime than in the evening).
Taverna do Chafariz, R São José 167, T35512828. Good local food. Recommended.
Café e compania, R São José 187, T35510711, closes 2300. Very popular, *comida por kilo* at lunchtime, good salads and juices.
Deguste, R Coronel Alves 15, T35516363. Large portions. Small expense. Good value.
Vide Gula, R Sen Rocha Lagoa 79a, T35514493. Food by weight, good, friendly atmosphere. Recommended.

Mariana *p247, map p250, phone code 031*
Engenho Nôvo, Praça da Sé 26. Bar at night, English spoken by the owners and clients. Recommended.
Mangiare della Mamma, D Viçoso 27. Italian. Recommended.
Tambaú, R João Pinheiro 26. Regional food.
Panela de Pedra, in the Terminal Turístico serves food by weight at lunchtime.

Congonhas do Campo *p251, phone code 031*
Estalagem Romaria, 2 mins from **Hotel Colonial** in the Romarias. Good restaurant and pizzeria, reasonable prices.

Tiradentes *p253, map p254, phone code 032*
Bistrô Richard Rothe, R Direita 224, T33551775. French and Italian food served in the most beautiful setting in Tiradentes – the hillside garden of one of the largest colonial townhouses. The best for romantic dining.
Estalagem, R Min Gabriel Passos 280, T33551144. Excellent and generous traditional Mineira meat dishes.
Quartier Latin, R São Francisco de Paula 46, Praça da Rodoviária, T33551552. French-trained cordon bleu chef with a menu of French-inspired, Italian and good seafood. Salads are made from their own organic vegetables. Respectable wine list. Good and expensive.
Quinto de Ouro, R Direita 159. Mineira and international dishes. Recommended.
Virados do Largo, Largo do Ó, T33551111. The best Mineira restaurant in town together with **Estalagem**.
Aluarte, Largo do Ó 1, T33551608. Bar with live music in the evening, nice atmosphere, US$4 cover charge, garden, sells handicrafts. Recommended.
Maria Luisa Casa de Chá, Largo do Ó 1, diagonally opposite **Aluarte**, T33551502. Tea, cakes and sandwiches in an arty Bohemian atmosphere. Great for breakfast.

There are many other restaurants, snack bars and *lanchonetes* in town and it is a small enough place to wander around and see what takes your fancy.

São João del Rei *p256, map p257, phone code 032*
Churrascaria Ramón, Praça Severiano de Resende 52. One of the town's better *churrascarias* with generous portions and plenty of side dishes.
Quinto do Ouro, Praça Severiano de Rezende 04, T33717577. Tasty and well-prepared regional food at reasonable prices. Said to be the best Mineira cooking in town.
Portal del Rey, Praça Severiano de Rezende 134. *Comida por kilo*, Minas and Arabic food; good value.
Restaurant 611, R Getúlio Vargas 145, T33718793. Very cheap but excellent Mineira cooking – eat as much as you like for less than US$2. Plenty of choice too. Beloved of locals.

Sabará *p259, phone code 031*
Cê Que Sabe, R Mestre Caetano 56. Mineira and other Brazilian fare. Recommended.

Entertainment

São João del Rei *p256, map p257, phone code 032*

Music

São João del Rei has 2 famous orchestras which play Baroque music. In colonial days, the music master not only had to provide the music for Mass, but also had to compose new pieces for every festival. All the music has been kept and the **Riberio Bastos** and **Lira Sanjoanense** orchestras preserve the tradition. Both have their headquarters, rehearsing rooms and archives on R Santo Antônio (Nos 54 and 45 respectively). The Orquestra Ribeiro Bastos plays at Mass every Sun in São Francisco de Assis at 0915, as well as at many religious ceremonies throughout the year (for example Holy Week). The Orquestra Lira Sanjoanense plays at Mass in Nossa Senhora do Pilar at 1900 every Thu and on Sun in Nossa Senhora do Rosário at 0830 and Nossa Senhora das Mercês at 1000, as well as on other occasions. It is best to check at their offices for full details. (There are similar orchestras in Prados – see above – and Tiradentes, but the latter is not as well supported as those in São João.)

Festivals and events

Ouro Preto *p243, map p244, phone code 031*

Many shops close during Holy Week and on winter weekends.

Ouro Preto is famous for its **Holy Week** processions, which in fact begin on the Thu before Palm Sun and continue (but not every day) until Easter Sun. The most famous is that commemorating Christ's removal from the Cross, late on **Good Fri**. Attracting many Brazilians, Carnival here is also memorable. In **Jun**, **Corpus Christi** and the **Festas Juninas** are celebrated. Every **Jul** the city holds the **Festival do Inverno da Universidade Federal de Minas Gerais (UFMG)**, the Winter Festival, about 3 weeks of arts, courses, shows, concerts and exhibitions. On **8 Jul** is the anniversary of the city. **15 Aug** is **Nossa Senhora do Pilar**, patron saint of Ouro Preto. **12-18 Nov** is the **Semana de Aleijadinho**, a week-long arts festival.

Mariana *p247, map p250, phone code 031*

Carnival and **Holy Week** are celebrated in traditional style in the town. **29 Jun São Pedro**. In **Jul**, Mariana shares some events of the **Festival do Inverno da UFMG** with Ouro Preto.

São João del Rei *p256, map p257, phone code 032*

Apr, Semana Santa; **15-21 Apr,** Semana da Inconfidência. **May** or **Jun**, Corpus Christi. FUNREI, the university (on R Padre José Maria Xavier), holds **Inverno Cultural** in **Jul** each year. First 2 weeks of **Aug**, **Nossa Senhora da Boa Morte**, with Baroque music (*novena barroca*). Similarly, **12 Oct**, *Nossa Senhora do Pilar*, patron saint of the city. **8 Dec**, founding of the city.

Sabará *p259, phone code 032*

The patron saint of Sabará is Nossa Senhora da Conceição. There are many festivals throughout the year. The most significant are the **Folia de Reis**, **25 Dec-6 Jan**; in **Jun** are the **Festas Juninas** and a **Festival da Cachaça**; Nossa Senhora do Rosário, 2nd Sun in **Oct**.

Shopping

Ouro Preto *p243, map p244, phone code 031*

Gems and jewellery

Gems are not much cheaper from freelance sellers in Praça Tiradentes than from the shops. If buying gems on the street, ask for the seller's credentials.

Gemas de Minas, Conde de Bobadela 63. One of the city's better jewellers.

Videmaju, R Conselheiro Santana 175. The home of Vincente Júlio de Paula, a professor at the School of Mines who sells stones at very good prices.

Buy soapstone carvings at roadside stalls and bus stops rather than in the cities; they are much cheaper. Many artisans sell soapstone carvings, jewellery and semi-precious stones in the Largo de Coimbra in front of São Francisco de Assis Church.

Other

Also worth buying is traditional cookware in stone, copper or enamelled metal.

Tiradentes *p253, map p254, phone code 032*

Art galleries

Fernando Pitta, Beco da Chácara, T/F3551475. Produces fascinating painting, mixed media and sculpture, worth a visit.

Oscar Araripe, R da Câmara. Paints Tiradentes and other local scenes in bright colours, popular and commercial.

São João del Rei *p256, map p257, phone code 032*

The pewter factory, Av Leite de Castro 1150, T33718000, 10 mins' walk from the rodoviária, 0900-1800. Run by Englishman

John Somers and his son Gregory, is worth a visit for both its exhibitions and its shop. The nearby town of **Resende Costa** (30 km north) is known for its textile handicrafts.

Activities and tours

Ouro Preto *p243, map p244, phone code 031*
Yoga centre, Shiatsu and Kerala massage, down an alley between Nos 31 and 47 (Cine Teatro Vila Rica), Praça Alves de Brito, T35513337.

Tiradentes *p253, map p254, phone code 032*
For horse-riding treks, contact John Parsons at the **Solar da Ponte**, see p261.

Transport

Ouro Preto *p243, map p244, phone code 031*
Bus The rodoviária is at R Padre Rolim 661, T35511081. A 'Circular' bus runs from the rodoviária to Praça Tiradentes, US$0.40; it is a long walk to the centre. Taxis charge exorbitant rates.

There are 11 buses a day from **Belo Horizonte** (2 hrs, Pássaro Verde), US$3.75, taxi US$30. Day trips are possible; book your return journey to Belo Horizonte early if returning in the evening; buses get crowded. Bus to **Rio**, Útil at 0705, 1715 and 2000 (US$15, 12 hrs), and buses to **Brasília** at 1830 (12 hrs) and **Vítoria** at 2100 (8 hrs). There are also Útil buses to **Conselheiro Lafaiete**, 3-4 a day via Itabirito and direct services to **Congonhas do Campo** via the new Caminho de Ouro highway. Other Útil services to **Rio**, **Barbacena**, **Conselheiro Lafaiete** and **Congonhas** go via Belo Horizonte. Direct buses to **São Paulo**, 3 a day with Cristo Rei, 11 hrs, US$19.25. Gontijo go to Salvador via Belo Horizonte.

Mariana *p247, map p250, phone code 031*
Bus Buses run from the Escola de Minas near Praça Tiradentes in **Ouro Preto** every 30 mins, US$0.60, all passing Minas de Passagem (buses also leave from Ouro Preto rodoviária). Ouro Preto buses stop at the new rodoviária, out of town on the main road, then at the Posto Mariana, before heading back to the centre of Mariana at Praça Tancredo Neves. Many buses seem to go only to the *posto* above the town, but it's a long walk from the centre. A bus from the rodoviária to the centre via the *posto* and Minas de Passagem costs US$0.40. Buses from Mariana to Ouro Preto can be caught by the bridge at the end of R do Catete.
Bus from Belo Horizonte (via Ouro Preto), US$4.50, 2¼ hrs. Buses for **Santa Bárbara** (near Caraça) leave from the rodoviária.

Around Mariana *p251, phone code 031*
Bus 3 buses a day from **Mariana** to Antônio Pereira, Mon-Fri, 0800, 1200, 1445, plus 1100, 1750 and 2100 on Sat.

Congonhas do Campo *p251, phone code 031*
Bus The rodoviária is 1½ km outside town; bus to town centre US$0.40; for Basílica, see above. To/from **Belo Horizonte**, 1½ hrs, US$3, 8 times a day. To **São João del Rei**, 2 hrs, US$3.60, tickets are not sold until the bus comes in. To **Ouro Preto**, go via Belo Horizonte, Murtinho or Conselheiro Lafaiete. Whether going from Ouro Preto or Rio to Congonhas do Campo, there is no direct bus; you have to change at the town of **Conselheiro Lafaiete**. Frequent service Conselheiro Lafaiete-Congonhas do Campo, US$1.

Tiradentes *p253, map p254, phone code 032*
Bus Last bus back to **São João del Rei** is 1815, 2230 on Sun.
Taxi Around town there are pony-drawn taxis; ponies can be hired for US$5. A taxi to **São João del Rei** costs US$10. See Excursions, p256 for the **train** between the 2 towns.

São João del Rei *p256, map p257, phone code 032*
Bus The rodoviária, 2 km west of the centre, has a phone office, toilets, luggage store, *lanchonetes* and a tourist information office. Buses to **Rio**, 5 daily with **Paraibuna** (3 on Sat and Sun), 5 hrs, US$10-12. **Cristo Rei** to **São Paulo**, 8 hrs, 5 a day (also to Santos), and **Translavras**, 4 a day (also to Campinas), US$12.50. **Belo Horizonte**, 3½ hrs, US$6.60. To **Juiz de Fora**, US$5.40, at least 8 a day with **Transur**. Frequent service to **Tiradentes**

with Meier, 8 a day, 7 on Sat, Sun and holidays, US$0.65; on the return journey to São João, the bus stops outside the railway station before proceeding to the rodoviária.

Sabará *p259, phone code 032*
Bus Viação Cisne, from **Belo Horizonte**, US$0.75, 30 mins, from separate part of Belo Horizonte rodoviária from main departure hall.
Car There is a road, mostly unpaved, that runs from Sabará to Ravena on the BR-381 Belo Horizonte-Vitória highway which crosses the hills and is a pleasant drive.

Directory

Ouro Preto *p243, map p244, phone code 031*
Banks Banco 24 Horas, Praça Alves de Brito, next to Correios; **Banco do Brasil**, R São José 189, good rates, also for TCs; **Bradesco**, corner of Sen Rocha Lagoa and Padre Rolim, opposite the Escola de Minas. **Internet** Point, R Xavier da Veiga 501A, language school and cultural centre. **Post office** Praça Alves de Brito.

Tiradentes *p253, map p254, phone code 032*
Post office and telephone Combined office on Largo das Forras in the Prefeitura Municipal, R Resende Costa 71. It closes at 1200 for lunch.

São João del Rei *p256, map p257, phone code 032*
Banks Bradesco, Av Hermílio Alves 200, next to the Theatro Municipal, has an exchange, 1000-1600 and a Visa cash point.

Northern and Western Minas Gerais

The population thins out in Northern Minas and as it stretches into the sertão *backlands and the state of Bahia the landscape gets ever more arid. Water mostly comes from the river São Francisco, a blue streak cutting through the beiges and browns of the semi-desert. Few tourists, however, get further than the colonial mining town of Diamantina, recently declared a World Heritage site and every bit as pretty as its more famous contemporaries to the south. There are extensive tracts of beautiful* cerrado *forest towards the border with Goiás, parts of it protected by the Grande Sertão Veredas National Park.*

Western Minas is less visited still, yet there are some beautiful stretches of forest in the Serra da Canastra which can be visited on the way to or from Matto Gross or Goiás
▸▸ *For Sleeping, Eating and other listings, see pages 270-271.*

Diamantina → *Phone code: 038. Altitude: 1,120 m. Colour map 4, B3. Population: 48,000.*

This friendly, beautiful town is situated deep in the interior, amid barren mountains and was once the centre of an active diamond industry. Whilst not as grand as Ouro Preto, Dimantina is less spoilt, retaining many beautiful colonial buildings with carved overhanging roofs and brackets and many handsome churches (some of which are difficult to get into). It was recently awarded UNESCO World Heritage status. The **Tourist information office** ⓘ *Casa de Cultura in Praça Antônio Eulálio 53, 3rd floor, T35311636, F35311857*, is friendly and helpful and provides pamphlets and a reliable map, as well as information about church opening times. The office will arrange a free tour of churches with a guide who has access to keys (tip guide). One excellent guide is *Passeio a Diamantina*.

History

In 1720 diamonds were discovered at Arraial do Tijuco, the first settlement of gold prospectors who had come to the region. Within 14 years it had become important enough to be made the administrative capital of the Distrito de Diamantina. Since the Portuguese crown made the same impositions on diamond mining as on gold, there was a similar resentment among those people who saw no chance of improvement in their living conditions. One such was Padre José da Silva de Oliveira Rolim (Padre Rolim), who joined the Inconfidência Mineira. The town was one of the most wealthy in 18th-century Brazil and in 1838 it was elevated to the status of city and renamed Diamantina.

President Juscelino Kubitschek, the founder of Brasília, was born here. His house, Rua São Francisco 241, has been converted into a museum.

Sights

The oldest church in Diamantina is **Nossa Senhora do Rosário** ⓘ *Largo Dom Joaquim*, built by slaves in 1728. **Nossa Senhora do Carmo** ⓘ *R do Carmo*, dates from 1760-1765 and was built by João Fernandes de Oliveira (see below) for the Carmélite Third Order. It is the richest church in the town, with fine decorations and paintings and a pipe organ, covered in gold leaf, made locally. Apparently, the tower is at the back of the church to please Chica da Silva (see below), who did not like to hear the sound of the bells.

São Francisco de Assis ⓘ *R São Francisco*, just off Praça JK, was built between 1766 and the turn of the 19th century. It is notable for Its paintings. Other colonial churches are the **Capela Imperial do Amparo** (1758-1776), **Nossa Senhora das Mercês** (1778-1784) and **Nossa Senhora da Luz** (early 19th century), erected to fulfil the vow of a Portuguese lady, Dona Tereza de Jesus Perpétuo Corte Real, who survived the 1755 Lisbon earthquake.

The **Catedral Metropolitana de Santo Antônio** ⓘ *Praça Correia Rabelo*, was built in the 1930s in neo-colonial style to replace the original cathedral.

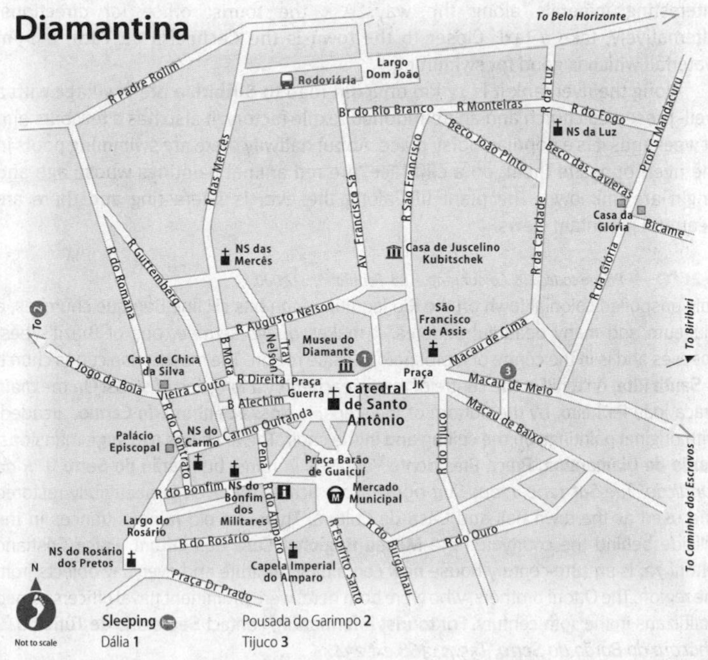

After repeated thefts, the diamonds of the **Museu do Eiamante** ⓘ *R Direita 14, US$1*, in the house of Padre Rolim, have been removed to the **Banco do Brasil**. The museum does house an important collection of the materials used in the diamond industry, plus other items from the 18th and 19th centuries. Diamonds are still sought (see traditional methods at **Guinda**, 7 km away). Other local industries are the making of Portuguese Arraiolos-style tapestry carpets by hand, at a cooperative in the centre, and etchings on leather.

At Rua Quitanda 48 is the **Biblioteca Antônio Torres**, also known as the **Casa Muxarabi**. This name derives from the enclosed balcony, of Moorish design, on one of the windows of this 18th-century house.

The **Casa de Chica da Silva** ⓘ *Praça Lobo Mesquita 266, free*, is the house of a woman who was a slave in the house of Padre Rolim's father. She became the mistress of João Fernandes de Oliveira, a diamond contractor. They had 14 children and lived in luxury until Fernandes returned to Portugal in 1772 when his last contract ended. Chica, who died on 15 February 1796, has become a folk heroine among Brazilian blacks.

Behind the 18th-century building which now houses the **Prefeitura Municipal** (originally the diamonds administration building, Praça Conselheiro Matta 11), is the **Mercado Municipal** or **dos Tropeiros** (muleteers) ⓘ *Praça Barão de Guaicuí*. It was built in 1835 as a residence and trading house before being expanded; it has wooden arches. The **Casa da Glória** ⓘ *R da Glória 297*, is in fact two houses on either side of the street connected by an enclosed bridge. Among its earlier inhabitants was the first bishop of Diamantina. It now contains the Instituto Eschwege de Geologia.

Excursions from Diamantina

Walk along the **Caminho dos Escravos**, the old road built by slaves between the mining area on Rio Jequitinhonha and Diamantina. A guide is essential and also cheap, ask at the Casa de Cultura (beware of snakes and thunderstorms).

About 9 km from town is the **Gruta de Salitre**, a big cave with a strange rock formation. There is no public transport, but it is a good walk and you can find some interesting minerals along the way. Ask the tourist office for directions. Alternatively, take a taxi. Closer to the town is the **Cachoeira da Toca**, a 15-m waterfall which is good for swimming.

Along the riverbank it is 12 km on a dirt road to **Biribiri**, a pretty village with a well- preserved church and an abandoned textile factory. It also has a few bars and at weekends it is a popular, noisy place. About halfway there are swimming pools in the river; opposite them, on a cliff face, are red animal paintings whose age and origin are unknown. The plant life along the river is interesting and there are beautiful mountain views.

Serro → *Phone code: 038. Colour map 4, B3. Population: 22,000.*

This unspoiled colonial town on the Rio Jequitinhonha has six fine Baroque churches, a museum and many beautiful squares. It makes *queijo serrano*, one of Brazil's best cheeses and is in the centre of a prosperous cattle region. The most conspicuous church is **Santa Rita**, on a hill in the centre of town, reached by a long line of steps. On the main Praça João Pinheiro, by the bottom of the steps, is **Nossa Senhora do Carmo**, arcaded, with original paintings on the ceiling and in the choir. The town has two large mansions. **Barão de Diamantina**, Praça Presidente Vargas is in ruins, but **Barão do Serro** ⓘ *R da Fundição, Tue-Sat 1200-1700, Sun 0900-1200*, across the river, is beautifully restored and used as the town hall and Casa de Cultura. There are old mine entrances in the hillside behind the courtyard. The **Museu Regional Casa dos Ottoni**, Praça Cristiano Ottoni 72, is an 18th-century house now containing furniture and everyday objects from the region. The Ottoni brothers, who were born here, were prominent naval officers turned politicians in the 19th century. For **tourist information**, contact **Secretaria de Turismo** ⓘ *Chácara do Barão do Serro, T35411368 ext 234*.

Just by the Serro turn-off is the town of **Datas**, whose spacious church (1832) decorated in red and blue, contains a wooden image of Christ with the crown of thorns.

Rio São Francisco

Passenger services on the river have been discontinued but masters of cargo boats in the port may permit passage. The regular stops are at **Januária** (famous for Brazil's reputed best *cachaça*) and **Bom Jesus da Lapa** in Bahia (a pilgrimage centre with a church built in a grotto inside a mountain, but a very poor town; there are hotels and a choice of bars on the river beach).

Pirapora → *Phone code: 038. Colour map 4, B3. Population: 50,000.*

North of Três Marlas is this terminus for boat journeys on the Rio São Francisco. The cutting down of trees, in part as fuel for the boats, and the low rainfall in recent years, has reduced the river's flow. The town itself is a tourist attraction because of the falls in the river which make for excellent fishing. The fishermen use punt-like canoes. The sandy river beaches are used for swimming. The riverboats' grotesque figureheads, *carrancas*, are from the workshops of **Lourdes Barroso** ⓘ *R Abaeté 390.*

São Francisco → *Phone code: 038. Colour map 4, A3. Population: 50,000.*

Between Pirapora and Januária is the colonial fishing town of São Francisco, with many attractive houses and a good handicraft market in the town hall. Of the two remaining wood-burning stern-wheel boats, allegedly built for Mississippi services in the 1860s and imported from the USA in 1922 to work on the Amazon, one, the *Gaiola*, was restored for services on the Rio São Francisco. The town is popular during Semana Santa, Festas Juninas and a carnival in July.

Western Minas Gerais and the Serra da Canastra

Araxá → *Phone code: 034. Altitude: 997 m. Population: 76,000.*

Situated in the Minas Triangle west of Belo Horizonte, Araxá has thorium and radioactive waters, sulphur and mud baths. The **Grande Hotel Araxá** (see Sleeping, below), where the springs and the ruins of the Hotel do Rádio are located, is 8 km from the town at Estâncio do Carreiro.

Parque Nacional da Serra da Canastra

ⓘ *Details on visiting the park can be obtained from Ibama, Av do Contorno 8121, Cidade Jardim, CEP 30110-120, Belo Horizonte, T32916588 ext 119/122, or from Caixa Postal 01, CEP 37928-000 São Roque de Minas, T031 34331195. All gates close at 1800.*

South of Araxá is the Serra da Canastra National Park, in which the Rio São Francisco rises. It is a cool region (temperatures in May and June average 18°C), comprising two ranges of hills, the Serra da Canastra and the Serra das Sete Voltas, with the Vale dos Cândidos between. The altitude ranges from 900 m to 1,496 m above sea level and the vegetation is mostly grassland, rising to high altitude plants on the uplands. Animals include the maned wolf, the great anteater, armadillos and deer. Birds that can be seen in the park are rheas, owls, seriema, king vulture and the diving duck. There are also other birds of prey, partridges and tinamous. Besides the source of the Rio São Francisco (6½ km from the São Roque park entrance), visitors can see the two parts of the **Dasca d'Anta waterfall**.

The park has a **visitor centre** just inside the park, at the São Roque de Minas entrance. There are three other entrances: Casca d'Anta, São João Batista and Sacramento. The park is best reached from Piumhi, on the MG-050, 267 km southwest of Belo Horizonte (this road heads for Ribeirão Preto in São Paulo). From Piumhi you go to São Roque de Minas (60 km).

Uberaba and around → *Phone code: 034. Colour map 4, B1. Population: 240,500.*

From Araxá, the BR-262 heads 120 km west to Uberaba, also in the Minas Triangle on the Rio da Prata, and 485 km from São Paulo. It is an important road junction on the direct highway between São Paulo and Brasília and serves a large cattle-raising district. At the beginning of April each year the Rural Society of the Minas Triangle holds a famous cattle and agricultural exhibition at Uberaba.

Between Uberaba and Ponte Alta (31 km east on the BR-262) is **Peirópolis**, which is an incredibly important palaeontological site, with dinosaur remains, including eggs. The **Centro de Pesquisas Paleontológicas – Museu do Einossauro** ⓘ *T9720023, weekdays 0800-1800, Sat and Sun 1100-1700*, is 23 km east of Uberaba, at Km 784.5.

Uberlândia → *Phone code: 034. Population: 439,000.*

About 100 km north of Uberaba is Uberlândia, founded in 1888 as São Pedro do Uberabinha. It is a fast-growing city with good communications by air and road. Several major bus routes (eg Campo Grande-Brasília) pass through here. There is a helpful tourist information kiosk in the rodoviária.

Sleeping

Diamantina *p266, map p267, phone code 038*

B **Pousada do Garimpo**, Av da Saudade 265, T/F35312523, pgarimpo@diamantina.uemg.br. Bland upmarket option with pool and sauna.

D **Dália**, Praça JK (Jota-Ka) 25, T35311477. Ordinary but reasonably well-maintained.

D **Tijuco**, R Macau do Melo 211, T/F35311022. Good food, undistinguished rooms.

E **JK**, opposite the rodoviária. With good breakfast, clean, friendly, hot showers.

E **Pensão Comercial**, Praça M Neves 30. Basic.

Camping

Wild camping is possible near the waterfall just outside town.

Serro *p268, phone code 038*

B **Pousada Vila do Príncipe**, R Antônio Honório Pires 38, T/F35411485. Very clean, in an old mansion containing its own museum, the artist Mestre Valentim is said to have been born in the slave quarters. There are other cheaper hotels.

Pirapora *p269, phone code 038*

C **Canoeiras**, Av Salmeron 3, T7411933. Used by river-tour parties.

C **Pirapora Palace**, Praça Melo Viana 61, 7 blocks west and 1 block south of rodoviária, T7413851. Ask for a room on the garden, safe.

E **Daila**, Praça JK 13. With breakfast but no bath.

E **Grande**, R da Quitanda 70. With bath but without breakfast.

São Francisco *p269, phone code 038*

B **Hotel Green Fish**, R Min Hermenegildo de Barros 560, T/F6311106.

Araxá *p269, phone code 034*

AL **Grande Hotel Araxá**, Estâncio do Barreiro. Has been completely renovated while maintaining its 1940s-50s style and gardens designed by Burle Marx. It is now run by the Tropical chain (Av Paulista 1765, 1 andar, 01311-200, São Paulo, T/F0XX11 32532003, or T0XX34 36628001 for the thermal resort.

B **Colombo**, Estâncio do Barreiro, T/F36624016. Pool, sports facilities.

B **Virgilius Palace**, R Dr Franklin de Castro 545, T/F36625000. Restaurant.

D **Imbiara**, Av Imbiara 356, T/F36612500.

Uberaba *p270, phone code 034*

B **Novotel**, Av Filomena Cartafina 150, 5 km from town, T33364288. Pool, restaurant.

B **Pousada São Francisco**, on BR-330, 7 km from town, T33145553. Horse riding available.

C **Karajá**, Av Fernando Costa 146, T33361000.

D **Porto Bello**, Av Barão do Rio Branco 1000, T/F33366701.

Uberlândia *p270, phone code 034*

A **Plaza Inn Master**, R da Bandeira 400, T32398000, F2398100. With restaurant.

B **Estância das Flores**, Km 166 BR-050, T32340120. Horse riding and fishing available.

E **Hotel Nacional**, Higino Guerra 273, opposite the rodoviária, T32354983. With view (cheaper without), shower and breakfast.

Eating

Diamantina *p266, map p267, phone code 038*

₶₶Capistrana, R Campos Carvalho 36, near Cathedral square. Mineira and other Brazilian dishes. Recommended.

₶₶O Garimpeiro, Pousada do Garimpeiro, Av Da Saudade 265, T35311044. One of the best in town with regional cooking and wonderful views. Lunch only on Mon.

Serro *p268, phone code 038*

₶₶Churrascaria Vila do Príncipe, Praça Dom Epaminondas 48. Large slabs of meat and ancillary salads and side dishes.

₶Itacolomi, Praça João Pinheiro 20. Cheap and ordinary but with decent portions.

Pirapora *p269, phone code 038*

₶₶₶Egnaldo, Av São Francisco, T37411501. The best restaurant in town – decent fish dishes. There are a number of per-kilo restaurants dotted around town serving huge portions and excellent *caipirinhas*.

Bars and clubs

Diamantina *p266, map p267, phone code 038*

Serestas (serenades) are sung on Fri and Sat nights. Many young people hang out in the bars in Beco da Mota. **Cavernas Bar**, Av Sílvio Felício dos Santos. Good for *pagode* on Sat and Sun from late afternoon. **Taverna de Gilmar** is recommended for a good mix of music, although it gets packed quickly.

Festivals and events

Diamantina *p266, map p267, phone code 038*

Carnival is said to be very good here and the town is trying to establish another festival in Sep, Semana Santa. **May-Jun**, Corpus Christi. **13 Jun** Santo Antônio. **50 days after Pentecost**, O Divino Espírito Santo, a major 5-day feast. **12 Sep**, O Dia das Serestas, the Day of the Serenades, for which the town is famous; this is the birthday of President Juscelino Kubitschek, who was born here. First half of **Oct**, Festa do Rosário.

Transport

Diamantina *p266, map p267, phone code 038*

Bus There are 6 buses a day to **Belo Horizonte**, via Curvelo, with Pássaro Verde, 2½ hrs to **Curvelo**, US$3, to **Belo Horizonte**, US$10, 5½ hrs. There are daily **Gontijo** buses at 1600 to **São Paulo**, 16-17 hrs, US$19.25, but uncomfortable journey; the journey ends at the Bresser terminal. It is better to go to Belo Horizonte and change buses there if you want to arrive at Tietê in São Paulo.

If en route to Bahia, take the **Gontijo** Belo Horizonte-Salvador bus to **Araçuaí** and change there, the fare is US$11.50 but you have to check an hr or so beforehand to see if there is space in the bus. The bus passes Diamantina at about 1330-1400, or 0200. It's a very bumpy ride through Couto de Magalhães de Minas and Virgem da Lapa. (At Araçuaí is E **Pousada Tropical**, opposite the rodoviária behind the policlínica, T37311765. With bath, clean and friendly.) From there you can take a bus to Itaobim (US$2.65, 2 hrs, **Rio Doce** company) then make an onward connection to Vitória da Conquista (US$5.50, 4 hrs, same company – see p281). The BR-116 passes interesting rock formations at Pedra Azul before crossing the border with Bahia.

Araxá *p269, phone code 034*

Bus From **Belo Horizonte**, Gontijo, US$12.65-23.50, depending on service. There is an airport.

Uberaba *p270, phone code 034*

Bus From **Belo Horizonte**, US$15 (*leito* US$30), 7 hrs.

Uberlândia *p270, phone code 034*

Air Airport 8 km from town, T2125192.

Airline offices Rio-Sul, T32361414. TAM, T32531000.

Bus To **Brasília**, 6 hrs, US$9; To **Belo Horizonte**, 9 hrs, US$15; To **São Paulo**, US$18.

Directory

Diamantina *p266, map p267, phone code 038*

Banks Banco do Brasil, Praça Cons Mata 23.

Eastern and Southern Minas Gerais

The border area between Minas and Espírito Santo is the most rugged area of the state, marked by the ridges and remnant forests of the Serra do Caparaó, which are home to some of the country's highest peaks, and still important as a centre of semi-precious stone processing and crystal carving. The two principal towns, Governador Valadares and Teófilo Otôni, are both on the BR-116 inland Rio-Salvador road, and both have good connections with Belo Horizonte. ▸▸ For Sleeping, Eating and other listings, see pages 277-280

Caratinga Biological Station

ⓘ *US$15 per person per day (payable only in reais). Tours can be arranged through Focus Tours (www.focustours.com; see Tour operators, page 23).*

You can visit the private Caratinga Biological Station, 880 ha of mountainous, inland Atlantic forest protected by a conscientious family and **Conservation International**. The reserve is home to four rare primates: half of the world's northern muriquis (*Brachyteles hypoxanthus*) – a sub-species of woolly spider monkeys which are the largest primates in the Americas and one of the most critically endangered); the brown (or black-capped) capuchin; the brown howler monkey and a sub-species of tufted eared marmoset; the buffy-headed marmoset. Also at the station are brown-throated three-toed sloths and one of the largest inventories of birds outside the Andean regions of the Amazon – 217 species at last count. The primates and many of the birds are easily seen.

December to March is the high season.

Rio Doce

ⓘ *T8223006, or phone the Instituto Estadual de Florestas T3307013. Access is by the roads BR-262 or 381, both of which you have to turn off onto dirt roads to get to the park.*

The **Parque Estadual do Rio Eoce** is 248 km east of Belo Horizonte in the municipalities of Dionísio, Timóteo and Marliéria. Between 230 m and 515 m above sea level and covering almost 36,000 ha, this is one of the largest tracts of Mata Atlântica in southeast Brazil. As well as forest there are a number of lakes, on which boat trips are possible, besides swimming and fishing. The park is home to a great many birds and animals. There is an information centre, a campsite 6 km into the park and trails have been laid out for hiking.

Parque Nacional Caparaó

ⓘ *Contact via Caixa Postal 17, alto Jequitibá, MG, CEP 36976-000, T255, via operator on 101-PS 1, Alto do Caparaó. Otherwise, information from Ibama, T2916588 ext 119/122.*

This is one of the most popular parks in Minas, with good walking through strands of Atlantic rainforest, *paramo* and to the summits of three of Brazil's highest peaks, **Pico da Bandeira** (2,890 m), **Pico do Cruzeiro** (2,861 m) and the **Pico do Cristal** (2,798 m). Wildlife is not as plentiful as it is in Caratinga as the park has lost much of its forest and its floral biodiversity, but there are nonetheless a number of Atlantic coast primates here, like the brown capuchins, together with a recovering bird population. From the park entrance (where a small fee has to be paid) it is 6 km on a poorly maintained road to the car park at the base of the waterfall. From the hotel (see Sleeping, page 277) jeeps (US$20 per jeep) run to the car park at 1,970 m (2½ hours' walk), then it's a three- to four-hour walk to the summit of the Pico da Bandeira, marked by yellow arrows; there are plenty of camping possibilities all the way up, the highest being at **Terreirão** (2,370 m). It is best to visit during the dry season (April-October), although it can be quite crowded in July and during Carnival.

Teófilo Otoni: towards Southern Bahia → *Phone code: 033. Population: 127,500.*

Situated 138 km from Governador Valadares, this is a popular buying spot for dealers of crystals and gemstones, with the best prices in the state. There are various hotels (see Sleeping page 277). Regular buses arrive from Belo Horizonte and travel on to Porto Seguro via **Nanuque**, where it is possible to break the Belo Horizonte-Salvador journey (**E Hotel Minas**, at the rodoviária, adequate, and others nearby).

Juiz de Fora → *Phone code: 032. Altitude: 695 m. Colour map 4, C3. Population: 424,500.*

Juiz de Fora, which sits in a deep valley between the Serra de Mar and Mantiqueira mountain chains is the commercial centre of Southern Minas and was one of the first cities in Brazil to industrialize. It has only a handful of sights of interest to tourists, but sitting as it does midway between Belo Horizonte and Rio de Janeiro, it makes an obvious stopover on the route between Minas and Rio states (it is 117 km south of Barbacena, 184 km north of Rio). There are reasonable hotels and restaurants here, a few museums and some respectable 20th-century architecture. The Parque Florestal de Ibitipoca, which protects the Atlantic coast forest is an hour or so away. Juiz de Fora is famous within Brazil for its love affair with Rio; to which its locals are said to look with longing eyes.

The city centre is very busy commercially and the streets are a maze of shopping galleries. The main thoroughfare through the clty centre is Avenida Barão do Rio Branco, broken by the Halfeld park and the major bus stop where it meets Rua Halfeld. Rua Halfeld is pedestrianized from Avenida Rio Branco to Avenida Getúlio Vargas and is the banking as well as the main shopping street in the centre. The **Banco do Brasil** has a building close to the junction of Rio Branco and Halfeld which

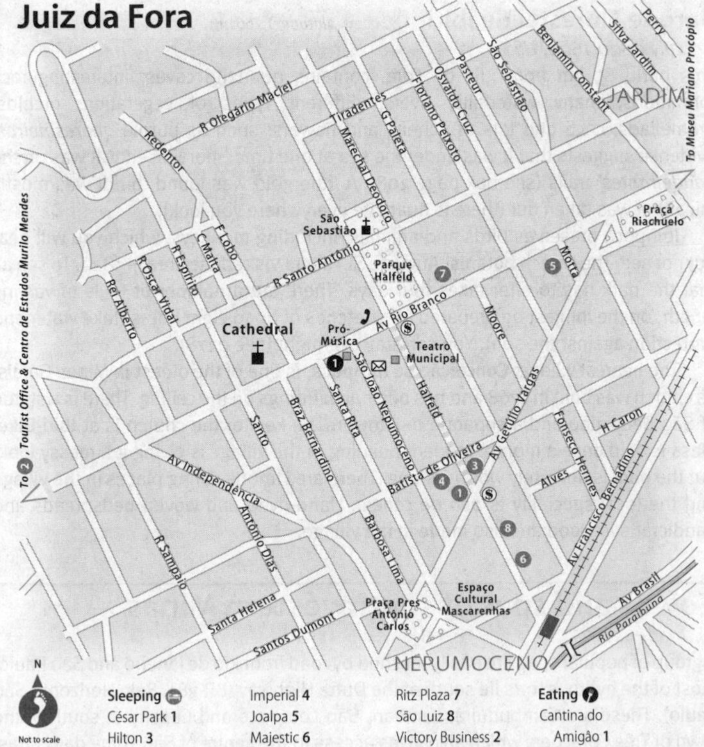

was designed by Oscar Niemeyer (there's another branch at the junction of Halfeld and Getúlio Vargas). On the same street is the **Teatro Municipal** ⓘ *R Halfeld 1179, T32155255*, opposite the Edifício São Joaquim. The **Praça da Estação** has some handsome *belle époque* architecture: the station hall, the hotels **Príncipe** and **Renascença** and the **Associação Comercial** building and a cultural centre, the **Espaço Cultural Mascarenhas** ⓘ *Av Getúlio Vargas 200, T32297208*. Look out for the Portinari mural of tiles in the foyer of **Edifício Clube Juiz de Fora**, on Rua Halfeld.

The **Centro de Estudos Murilo Mendes** ⓘ *Av Rio Branco 3372, T32133931, Mon-Fri 1300-1700*, is a small cultural centre which holds exhibitions, lectures, film shows, etc. It is part of the Universidade Federal de Juiz da Fora and is dedicated to the work of the poet, Murilo Mendes, with an exhibition on his links with famous painters (Picasso, Miró, Léger, Guignard, Portinari) and other poets (Cecília Meireles, Jorge de Lima). The **Museu Mariano Procópio** ⓘ *R Mariano Procópio, opposite the Mariano Procópio railway station, T32111145, Tue-Sun 1200-1800 (museum), 0800-1730 (grounds), US$1*, is in beautiful wooded grounds and has collections covering various stages of Brazilian history up to the New Republic. The room on Tiradentes, for example, has a huge painting by Pedro Américo de Figueiredo e Melo of his quartered body (1893). There are a great many objects and portraits from the Imperial period. It also houses some natural history, geology (including types of stones), paintings and sculpture. It is an enormous exhibition and a guide would be helpful to explain it all. In the grounds are a *cantina*, playground, lake, monkeys on an island and caged birds. To get back to the centre, take any bus going to Av Rio Branco (for example No 606).

Santos Dumont, 47 km north of Juiz de Fora, is a town named after the aviator (see page 151); some 17 km away is the **Fazenda Cabangu**, where he was born.

Parque Florestal de Ibitipoca → *Altitude: 1,760 m.*

ⓘ *Daily 0800-1600, US$2.*

This park, 85 km from Juiz de Fora, contains quartzite caves, interesting rock formations, many waterfalls, rivers, different types of vegetation, orchids, bromeliads, cacti and lots of lichens and flowers, such as purple *quaresmeiras*. Evidence suggests that it was under the sea at one time; more recently it was on the *bandeirantes*' trails (see box page 208). A little gold was found, but it was mostly mica that was taken out (there is quartzite everywhere you look).

Ibitipoca preserves birds and animals, including monkeys, which you will hear but not see. The French botanist Auguste St-Hilaire visited the area in 1822. To see all that the park has to offer takes four days. There are a number of trails of varying length; on the longest be prepared for stretches of up to eight hours (take water and protection against the sun). You can stay overnight (see p278).

The nearest village, **Conceição de Ibitipoca**, is one of the oldest in Minas Gerais. Its church was built in 1768 and has original paintings on the ceiling. There is a statue of São Sebastião and a separate bell tower. The key for the church is at **Ibiti-Bike**. Mass is said once a month. Modern building in the village is giving it a messy look, but the park is definitely worth visiting. There are various eating places in the village and the local speciality is *pão de canela*. Hand-dyed and woven bedspreads and handicrafts in wood are also made in the village.

Towns and spas of southwestern Minas

A group of popular spas are easily reached by road from Rio de Janeiro and São Paulo. Most of the hydro resorts lie south of the Dutra Highway (BR-381, Belo Horizonte-São Paulo). These are Cambuquirá, Lambari, São Lourenço and Caxambu, south of the town of Três Corações, which also gives access to the centre of São Tomé das Letras.

Further west and north, on the Minas/São Paulo border is the much larger resort of Poços de Caldas. Some 240 km southwest of Belo is the huge lake formed by the Furnas Dam. It can be seen from the BR-381 road to São Paulo.

Tres Corações → *Phone code: 035. Colour map 4, C2. Population: 64,000.*

The modern city of Tres Corações is a convenient place for making connections to the spas but is desperately uninteresting otherwise. It is the birthplace of Pelé, the legendary football star, to whom there is a statue in Praça Coronel José Martins.

The rodoviária is beside the old railway station where a steam engine is on show (the railway is used but there is no passenger traffic). At Avenida Getúlio Vargas 154 is the Casa de Cultura Godofredo Rangel (Departamento de Turismo e Cultura and Library). Praça Odilon, Rua de Andrade has a post office and **Banco do Brasil** (but no exchange facilities).

From Praça Martins, Avenida Julião Arbex leads steeply uphill to a statue of Christ on top of a chapel on Praça Monsenhor Fonseca.

São Tomé das Letras → *Phone code: 035. Colour map 4, C2. Population: 6,750.*

São Tomé das Letras, 35 km from Três Corações, is a beautiful hilltop town which is very popular at weekends. Once the streets were lined with houses made of local stone – giving the town a distinctive architectural identity. But its popularity as a tourist destination has seen many of these replaced or overshadowed by ugly concrete buildings and São Tomé is sadly beginning to lose its charm. At 1,291 m it is one of the five highest places in Brazil. The average maximum temperature is 26°C and the minimum is 14°C. The rainy season is October-March.

Rock paintings found in caves nearby have been dated to about 2000 BC. The inscriptions have lent the town a mystical reputation, attracting 'new age' visitors. Many believe it is a good vantage point for seeing UFOs (some claim the inscriptions are extraterrestrial in origin) and that there are places with special energies. The **Carimbado cave** is rich in myths and legends; its passages lead to an underground civilization; its powers form an energy source linked to Machu Picchu in Peru. Shangri-lá, which is a beautiful spot, is also called the **Vale do Maytréia**. The shops reflect this atmosphere andthe hotels are classified by UFOs instead of stars! Whatever you think of it, São Tomé is certainly an unusual place. There is a **tourist office** ⓘ *R José Cristiano Alves 4*.

The spas of Minas Gerais & São Paulo

History

A quarry town since the beginning of the 20th century, there is evidence of the industry everywhere you look. Settlement in colonial times dates from the mid- to late-18th century when the *bandeirantes* from São Paulo moved into this area, displacing the indigenous inhabitants. Even before the 20th-century 'alternative' arrivals, the hill acquired a legend: at the end of the 18th century, an escaped slave hid in a cave for a long time. A finely dressed man appeared, asking him why he was living there. On hearing the slave's story, the man gave him a message on a piece of paper which, on presentation to his master, would earn the slave forgiveness. The slave duly did as the man said and the master, impressed by the writing and the paper, went to the cave to seek the mysterious man for himself. He found no one, but instead a statue of São Thomé (St Thomas). The master therefore built a chapel at the site, which was replaced by the Igreja Matriz in 1784, now standing beside the cave. The inscriptions, in red, can just about be seen in the cave; they are the 'Letras' of the town's name.

Sights

The town is almost at the top of the hill. Behind it are rocky outcrops on which are the **Pyramid House**, the **Cruzeiro** (Cross, 1,430 m, with good 360° views), the **Pedra da Bruxa** and paths for walking or, in some parts, scrambling.

The bus stops at the main praça, where there is the frescoed 18th-century **Igreja Matriz** beside the fenced cave. A second church, the 18th-century **Igreja das Pedras** (Nossa Senhora do Rosário) is on a praça to the left as you enter town (Rua Ernestina Maria de Jesus Peixoto). It is constructed in the same style as many of the charming old-style buildings, with slabs of the local stone laid on top of each other without mortar.

Tours from São Tomé das Letras

In the surrounding hills are many caves: **Sobradinho**, 12 km; **Carimbado**, 5 km; **Gruta do Feijão**, a short walk from town; **Gruta da Bruxa**, 6 km. Seven waterfalls are also close by, including: **Cachoeira de Eubiose**, 4 km; **Véu de Noiva**, 12 km; **Paraíso**, near Véu de Noiva; **Vale das Borboletas da Lua**, 8 km; and **do Flávio**, 6 km. Also rapids such as **Shangri-lá**, 17 km, and **Vale dos Gnomos**, near the Vale das Borboletas. Some of these places make a good hike from the town, but you can also visit several in a day on an organized tour (car with four passengers): for example the waterfalls Flávio, Eubiose, Paraíso and Véu de Noiva, US$50; Shangri-lá, US$70; Vale das Borboletas, Gruta do Carimbado and Ladeira do Amendoim (a slope on which cars appear to run uphill when in neutral – like the one in Belo Horizonte), US$50 (T32371283 or enquire at **Néctar** shop on Rua José Cristiano Alves; tours run on weekends and holidays from the praça at 1000 and 1400 to waterfalls, caves, etc, T32371353 and ask for Jaime or Iraci).

Hydro resorts

Cambuquirá → *Phone code: 035. Altitude: 946 m. Population: 13,000.*

Some 20 km south of Três Corações by paved road, Cambuquirá's **Parque das Águas** is a hilly town with a pleasant atmosphere. Horse-drawn taxis ferry visitors around. Nearby *fazendas* sell *cachaça*.

Lambari → *Phone code: 035. Altitude: 900 m. Population: 19,000.*

This is another hilly town, 27 km south of Cambuquirá. The **Parque das Águas** ⓘ *daily 0600-1800*, has seven mineral springs and mineral water swimming pools on Praça Conselheiro João Lisboa. There are boat trips on the **Lago Guanabara** and to **Ilha dos Amores**. The resort has a casino.

São Lourenço → *Phone code: 035. Altitude: 850 m. Population: 35,000.*

São Lourenço, which is about 60 km southeast of Lambari, and is easily accessible from Rio de Janeiro (five or six hours by bus) or São Paulo (six or seven hours by bus) is useful as a junction but is fairly dull in its own right. There is a splendid park, tennis, boating, swimming, a flying field and fishing. Its rich mineral waters are used in the treatment of various medical complaints. The famous carbo-gaseous baths are unique in South America and can be found at **Parque das Águas** ⓘ *Praça Brasil, daily 0800-1700*. There is a grand ride through fine scenery to the **Pico de Buqueré** at 1,500 m.

Caxambu → *Phone code: 035. Altitude: 900 m. Population: 21,000.*

The waters at Caxambu, 31 km northeast of São Lourenço, are used for treating stomach, kidney and bladder diseases, and are said to restore fertility (the Parque das Águas is closed on Monday). The waters seemed to work for Princess Isabel, daughter of Dom Pedro II, who produced three sons after a visit. The little church of **Santa Isabel da Hungária** (1868) stands on a hill as a thanks offering. The surrounding mountains and forests are very beautiful and there is a view over the city from **Morro Caxambu**, 1,010 m.

Poços de Caldas → *Phone code: 035. Colour map 4, C2. Population: 124,000.*

The city is right on the São Paulo state border, some 150 km north of the hydro resorts around Lindóia. It is 272 km from São Paulo, 507 km from Rio and 510 km from Belo Horizonte. Sited at 1,180 m on the crater of an extinct volcano in a mountainous area, it has an excellent climate. The resort, a traditional honeymoon centre, has thermal establishments for the treatment of rheumatic, skin and intestinal diseases (you need a local doctor's certificate to use these facilities). Venetians from Murano settled here and established a crystal-glass industry.

Excursions from Poços de Caldas

These include the **Véu das Noivas** with its three waterfalls illuminated at night; the tall statue of **Cristo Redentor** at 1,678 m, which can be reached by cable car, hang gliders fly from here; **Pedra Batão**, an 80-m granite rock; and the Japanese teahouse at the **Recanto Japonês**. An arts and handicrafts fair is held every Saturday and Sunday in Praça Pedro Sanches.

Sleeping

Parque Nacional Caparaó *p272, phone code 032*

C Caparaó Parque, 2 km from the park entrance, 15 mins' walk from the town of Caparaó, T7412559. Nice.

E São Luiz, in Manhumirim. Good value, but Cids Bar, next door, Trav 16 do Março, has better food.

Camping

Ask locally where camping is permitted in the park.

Teófilo Otoni: towards Southern Bahia *p273, phone code 033*

There are several C-grade hotels.

D Pousada Tio Miro, R Dr Manoel Esteves 389, T35214343. Relaxed atmosphere. Recommended.

Juiz de Fora *p273, phone code 032*

AL Victory Business, Av Independencia 1850, T32491850, www.victorybusinesshotel.com.br. The best in town with a pool, sauna and bar and the most extensive business services in the city.

C César Park, Av Getúlio Vargas 181, T/F32154898, www.cesarparkhotel.com.br. Mock US chain hotel now looking a bit frayed but with a sauna and pool.

C-D Imperial, R Batista de Oliveira 605, T32157400. Faded but popular low-grade business hotel in the centre, **E** without bath.

C-D Joalpa, R Afonso Pinto da Motta 29, between Av Rio Branco and Av Getúlio Vargas, T32156055. Sauna, pool, parking, credit cards accepted.

C-D Ritz Plaza, Av Barão do Rio Branco 2000, T32157300. Sauna, pool, parking, takes all credit cards except Amex.

D São Luiz, R Halfeld 360, T32151155. Art deco lobby, winter garden, TV, fridge, parking, good, helpful.

E Hilton, Av Getúlio Vargas 483-99, near the junction with Batista de Oliveira, T32158112. Clean, polite and anonymous business hotel.

E Majestic, R Halfeld 284, T32155050. TV, cheaper without bath.

Many of the cheaper hotels on Av Getúlio Vargas are houses of dubious repute.

Parque Florestal de Ibitipoca *p274, phone code 032*

D Estrela da Serra, Conceição de Ibitipoca. Price per person, more expensive with TV and fridge, price includes breakfast and dinner; lunch costs US$10.

A 4-star hotel is under construction outside the village.

Camping

Ibiti-Lua, in the park itself, is a campsite for 50 tents, with toilets, showers, restaurant/bar and car park.

Tres Corações *p275, phone code 035*

C Cantina Calabreza, R Joaquim Bento de Carvalho 65, T/F32311183. Pool, sauna, has a reasonable restaurant (Italo-Brasileira), and a takeaway service.

E Avenida, Av Getúlio Vargas 55. Older than the Capri. Very basic, older and somewhat more decrepit than the **Capri**.

E Capri, Av Getúlio Vargas 111, not far from the bridge across the river, T32311427. With or without bath, simple but OK, TV in the more expensive rooms.

There are other, more basic hotels near the rodoviária.

São Tomé das Letras *p275, phone code 035*

There are lots of *pousadas* and rooms to let all over town. Streets are hard to follow because their names can change from one block to the next; numbering is also chaotic.

C-E Rancho Paraíso, about 8 km on the road to Sobradinho, T32371342. Basic lodging, campsite, restaurant, garden and trekking.

D Pousada Arco-Iris, R João Batista Neves 19, T/F32371212. Rooms and chalets, sauna, swimming pool.

E Fundação Harmonia, on the road to Sobradinho (4 km), Bairro do Canta Galo, São Tomé das Letras, CEP 37418-000, T32371280, or T0XX11-32043766 in São Paulo. Cheap and cheerful accommodation, price per person. The community emphasizes several disciplines and principles for a healthy lifestyle, for mind and body, 'new age', workshops, massage, excursions, vegetarian food (their shop is on the main praça).

E Hospedaria dos Sonhos I, R Gabriel Luiz Alves. Price per person. With bath, no TV, restaurant, shop, groups accommodated. Clean accommodation.

E Mahã Mantra, R Plínio Pedro Martins 48, T39895563. IYHA Youth hostel, open all year.

E Pousada Baraunas, R João Cristiano Alves 19, T33461330. Basic youth hostel with dorms and double. Price per person.

E Pousada Novo Horizonte, R João Cristiano Alves 10. Price per person. Simple rooms, friendly staff and information on local attractions.

E Sonhos II (do Gê), Trav Nhá Chica 8, T32371235. Price per person. Very nice, restaurant, swimming pool, sauna, television in rooms. Recommended.

Hydro resorts *p276, phone code 035*

As well as those listed there are many others in all price ranges.

B Emboabas, Av Jorge Amado 350, São Lourenço, T33324600. Standard plain town hotel with a restaurant.

B Parque Hotel, R Américo Werneck 46, Lambari, T32712000. Central, standard town hotel with plain rooms.

C Itaici, R Dr Jos dos Santos 320, Lambari, T/F32711366. Simple, anonymous but centrally located.

C Pousada Canto do Sabiá, about 3 km out of Caxambu, BR-354 towards Itamonte,

For an explanation of the sleeping and eating price codes used in this guide, see the inside front cover. Other relevant information is provided in the Essentials chapter, pages 47 and 57.

T33413499. This charming *pousada* has chalets and serves excellent breakfast.

D **Santos Dumont**, Av Virgílio de Melo Franco 400, Cambuquirá.

Camping

Fazenda Recanto das Carvalhos, BR-460 towards Pouso Alto, 10 km from Lambari, T33322098.

Poços de Caldas *p277, phone code 035*

There are some 80 hotels and pensions in town.

B **Novo Hotel Virgínia**, R Minas Gerais 506, T37222664. Simple standard town hotel with a/c and fan-cooled rooms.

B **Palace**, Praça Pedro Sanches, T37223636. Old fashioned but well run, with sulphur baths. Good.

There are many others in the **B** range, but very few under US$50 a night.

Eating

Juiz de Fora *p273, phone code 032*

Belas Artes, Galeria Tte Belfort Arantes 26, entrance at Halfeld 631. One of the better international restaurants in town.

Berttu's, R Santo Antônio 572. Very good, *mineira* and international food.

Brasão, Av Rio Branco 2262. Reasonable food in a plush dining room.

Le Beau Bistrot, R Delfim Moreira 22. A little mock French bar/restaurant, ordinary food.

Cantão Suíço, R Santa Rita 557/59. Good value self-service with an extensive choice.

Cantina do Amigão, R Santa Rita 552. Italian, good, including pizzas, T32152179 for home delivery. Others on same street and R São João Nepomuceno.

Tres Corações *p275, phone code 035*

Pizzeria Per Tutti, Av Getúlio Vargas, above Bemge.

Xodó Quinta da Bock, Av Getúlio Vargas, opposite the **Cantina Calabreza**, just up from Hotel Capri, open-air restaurant and beer place.

Pizzeria Jardins, Av Getúlio Vargas 363, beyond the praça. Cheap, good *executivo* menu and other dishes, popular, on 1st floor.

São Tomé das Letras *p275, phone code 035*

O Alquimista, R Capt Pedro Martins 7. The best in town, with a decent menu of Minas dishes. Closed Mar-Jun and Aug-Nov.

das Magas, R Camilo Rosa. A varied menu of Minas and pasta dishes. Good cheap lasagna.

Padarias Bom Dia, 1 opposite the bus stop on the main praça. Pleasant bakery with a range of cheap lunches and sandwiches.

Veranda Pôr-do-Sol, R Plínio Pedro Martins, comida caseira. Pizza. Brazilian home cooking including a range of Minas dishes and pizzas.

Ximama, Martins at the corner of G L Alves. Pizzas. Simple pizza restaurant with generous lashings of cheese on the toppings.

There are many other restaurants and bars

Poços de Caldas *p277, phone code 035*

There are plenty of restaurants and all the good hotels have dining rooms. Local specialities are smoked cheese, sausages, sweets and jams (try squash-and-coconut).

Bars and clubs

Juiz de Fora *p273, phone code 032*

Best nightclub is **Clube Noturno Vila das Tochas**, R Roberto Stiegert 4, Bairro São Pedro. American bar, crêperie, dance floor. **Bar do Bené**, Pres Costa de Silva 2305, Bairro São Pedro. Friendly. Prova Oral, R A Braga 210. Highly recommended bar with live music.

For lots of bars, restaurants, pizzerias and nightlife, visit the **Bairro São Mateus**, bounded by Av Independência, R São Mateus, R Padre Café, R Monsenhor Gomes Freire, with R Manoel Bernardino running down the middle.

Festivals and events

Poços de Caldas *p277, phone code 035*

Carnival; São Benedito **1-13 May**; the Festa UAI of popular *mineira* music and dance, foods and handicrafts is held in the 2nd half of **Aug**.

Activities and tours

Parque Florestal de Ibitipoca *p274, phonec code 032*

Tour operators

Serra do Ibitipoca, R Braz Bernardino 105, loja 212, Braz Shopping, Juiz de Fora T322163657. Organized tours from Juiz de Fora.

Transport

Parque Nacional Caparaó *p272, phone code 033*
Bus Caparaó National Park is 49 km by paved road from Manhuaçu on the Belo Horizonte-Vitória road (BR-262). Services from Belo Horizonte (twice a day with **Pássaro Verde**), Ouro Preto or Vitória to **Manhumirim**, 15 km south of Manhuaçu. From Manhumirim, take a bus direct to Caparaó, 0930, 1630, US$1, or to Presidente Soares (several, 7 km), then hitch 11 km to Caparaó.

Car Drive from the BR-262, go through Manhumirim, Presidente Soares and Caparaó village, then 1 km further to the **Hotel** Caparaó Parque.

Juiz de Fora *p273, phone code 032*
Air Flights arrive at the small but modern airport, Av Guadalajara, T32331315. Flights to **Belo Horizonte**, **Ipatinga** and **São Paulo**. Bus 520 on the hour to the centre.

Bus Local: town buses charge US$0.40. It is difficult to tell the routes because the route plaques are beside the back door entrance and cannot be seen as the bus approaches; you need to know the route numbers.
Long distance: the rodoviária is outside town on Av Brasil 4501, T32157696. Take bus 630 to town. Taxi to centre US$5. To/from **Rio**, many daily, **Útil**, US$5.50 *convencional*, US$6.75 *super* (a spectacular trip through mountains and tropical forest on an excellent, dualled highway); **Útil** to **Belo Horizonte**, frequent, US$9.15-11 (**Viaçao** Útil, T32153976, rodoviária, or in town R Henrique Surerus 22, T32156759, Mon-Fri 0800-1800, Sat 0800-1200). To **São João del Rei** via Barbacena, 6 hrs, US$5; to **Conselheiro Lafaiete** (for Congonhas do Campo), US$5.75. To **Petrópolis**, 7 a day, 2 hrs, US$4.25. Frota Nobre to **Teresópolis** and **Nova Friburgo** once a day, US$4.80 and US$7.35 respectively. To **Foz do Iguaçu** with Pluma, US$40, via Londrina, Maringá and Cascavel, Tue, Thu, Sun 0800.

Parque Florestal de Ibitipoca *p274, phone code 033*
Bus Frota Nobre from **Juiz da Fora** to Lima Duarte, 8 a day, US$2.10; bus Lima Duarte-**Ibitipoca** daily at 0700 and 1600.

Car By unpaved road it is 27 km from Lima Duarte to Conceição de Ibitipoca. The road is rough and difficult in the wet, but in the dry season especially, ordinary cars can make it. From Conceição it is a 3-km walk (or hitchhike) to the park.

Tres Corações *p275, phone code 035*
Bus There are 3 daily buses (2 on Sun) to **São Tomé das Letras**, US$1.65, 1½ hrs (the first 30 mins is on a paved road). To **Belo Horizonte**, Gardénia, 4 a day (3 on Sun), US$10.50, 5½ hrs, roadworks permitting. To **São Paulo**, Transul, 7 a day, US$8.10. Beltour runs buses to **Rio de Janeiro**; Cristo Rei to **Santos**.

São Tomé das Letras *p275, phone code 035*
Bus If going by bus, take the one that leaves Três Corações at dawn to see the mist in the valleys; schedule and fare are given under Três Corações, above.

Car If driving to the town, take care at the unsigned road junctions. After the pavement ends, at the next main junction, turn right.

Hydro resorts *p276, phone code 035*
Bus São Lourenço and Caxambu have frequent, numerous buses to **São Paulo**, **Rio** and **Belo Horizonte**. São Paulo-**Três** Corações bus (**Gardênia**) passes through Cambuquira, US$8.10. 4 buses a day from Bresser station in São Paulo to **Lambari**, US$8.10.

Poços de Caldas *p277, phone code 035*
Air Poços de Caldas has an airport.

Bus The rodoviária is 3 km from the centre. **Rio**, 8 hrs, US$13.25; **São Paulo**, 4½ hrs, US$7.25. A monorail runs down main avenue, Av Francisco Sales, to cable car station.

Directory

São Tomé das Letras *p275, phone code 035*
Bank Bemge in the main praça. **Post office** In the group of buildings at the top right of the praça, facing the Gruta São Tomé.

Espírito Santo

Sandwiched between Rio de Janeiro, Minas Gerais and Bahia, the coastal state of Espírito Santo is relatively little known, except by Mineiros heading for the coast for their holidays. It has many beaches, but they are overshadowed by those of its northern and southern neighbours. There are a number of nature reserves and turtle breeding grounds in Espírito Santo, and European immigration has given the towns a distinctive atmosphere. The state capital, Vitória, is also the main industrial and commercial centre. People here are known as Capixabas, after a former tribe.

The state has a hot, damp seaboard with a more-or-less straight, low coastline and long beaches open to the Atlantic. The south is mountainous and dotted with vast granite boulders even larger than Sugar Loaf. The most spectacular is Pedra Azul. The slopes are covered with pine plantations and remnants of Mata Atlântica rainforest. The coast is covered with restinga scrub and grassland. The north of the state is flat and dominated by vast eucalyptus plantations which run down to the long coastal sand dunes. » *For Sleeping, Eating and other listings, see pages 285-288.*

Background

Espírito Santo was one of the original captaincies created by the Portuguese In the 16th century, but their colony was very precarious in its early days. During the struggle for supremacy, the son of Mem de Sá (the governor in Bahia) was killed, but, as elsewhere, the invaders eventually prevailed, though not as successfully as in many of the other captaincies, as the Portuguese were only able to gain a foothold on the coastal plains. When the focus of attention moved to the mines in Minas Gerais in the 18th and subsequent centuries, the state became strategically important. Initially it was not on the gold exporting route, but after iron mining began, a trail from Belo Horizonte to Vitória was created. This remains one of the major economic corridors in the country.

Vitória → *Phone code: 027. Colour map 4, C5. Population: 266,000.*

The town of Vitória is beautifully set, its entrance second only to Rio's. Its beaches are as attractive, but smaller and the climate is less humid. Five bridges connect the island on which the town stands with the mainland.

Vitória dates from 1551 and takes its name from a battle won by the Portuguese over the local indigenous people. There are a few colonial remnants, but it is largely a modern city and port. The upper, older part of town, reached by steep streets and steps, is much less hectic than the lower harbour area which suffers dreadful traffic problems. A rail connection westwards to Minas Gerais, provides transport for export of iron ore, coffee and timber. Port installations at Vitória and nearby Ponta do Tubarão have led to some beach and air pollution in the area. **Tourist information** is available at **Cetur** ⓘ *Av Princesa Isabel 54, T3228888, at airport T3278855 and at the rodoviária*, where they are friendly and distribute a good free map. **Instituto Jones dos Santos Neves** ⓘ *Av Marechal Campos 310, 3rd floor, Edif Vitória Center, CEP 29040-090, T3222033 ext 2215*, also provide information.

Sights

On Avenida República is the huge **Parque Moscoso**, an oasis of quiet, with a lake, playground and tiny zoo. Other parks are the **Morro da Fonte Grande**, a state park with good views from the 312-m summit, and the **Parque dos Namorados**, 6 km from the centre at Praia do Canto. Two islands reached by bridge from Praia do Canto are **Ilha do Frade** and **Ilha do Boi**.

Colonial buildings still to be seen in the city are the **Capela de Santa Luzia**, Rua José Marcelino in the upper city (1551), now an art gallery; the church of **São Gonçalo**, Rua Francisco Araújo (1766) and the ruins of the **Convento São Francisco** (1591), also in the upper city. In the **Palácio do Governo**, or **Anchieta**, Praça João Climaco (upper city) is the tomb of Padre Anchieta, the 16th-century Jesuit missionary and one of the founders of São Paulo. The **Catedral Metropolitana** was built in 1918 and stands in Praça Dom Luís Scortegagna. The **Teatro Carlos Gomes**, on Praça Costa Pereira, often presents plays, also jazz and folk festivals.

Vila Velha, reached by a bridge across the bay, has an excellent beach, but is built up and noisy: take a bus from Vitória marked Vilha Velha. See the ruined, fortified monastery of **Nossa Senhora da Penha**, on a hill above Vila Velha; the views are superb. The Dutch attacked it in 1625 and 1640. There is also a pleasant ferry service to Vila Velha.

Beaches

Urban beaches such as **Camburi** can be affected by pollution (some parts of it are closed to bathers), but it is quite pleasant, with fair surf. South of the city is Vila Velha (see above), but for bigger waves go to **Barra do Jucu**, which is 10 km further south.

There is a hummingbird sanctuary at the **Museu Mello Leitâo** ⓘ *Av José Ruschi 4, T2591182, 0800-1200, 1300-1700*, a library including the works of the hummingbird and orchid scientist, Augusto Ruschi. Hummingbird feeders are hung outside the library. Also in the municipality is the **Dr Augusto Ruschi Biological Reserve** (formerly the Nova Lombardia National Biological Reserve), a forest rich in endemic bird species, including several endangered hummingbirds, Salvadori's antwren, cinnamon-vented Piha, russet-winged spadebill, Oustalet's tyrannulet, rufous-brown solitaire and hooded berryeater. Before visiting, permission must be obtained from **Ibama** ⓘ *Av Marechal Mascarenhas de Moraes 2487, Caixa Postal 762, Vitória ES, CEP 29000.*

Vitória

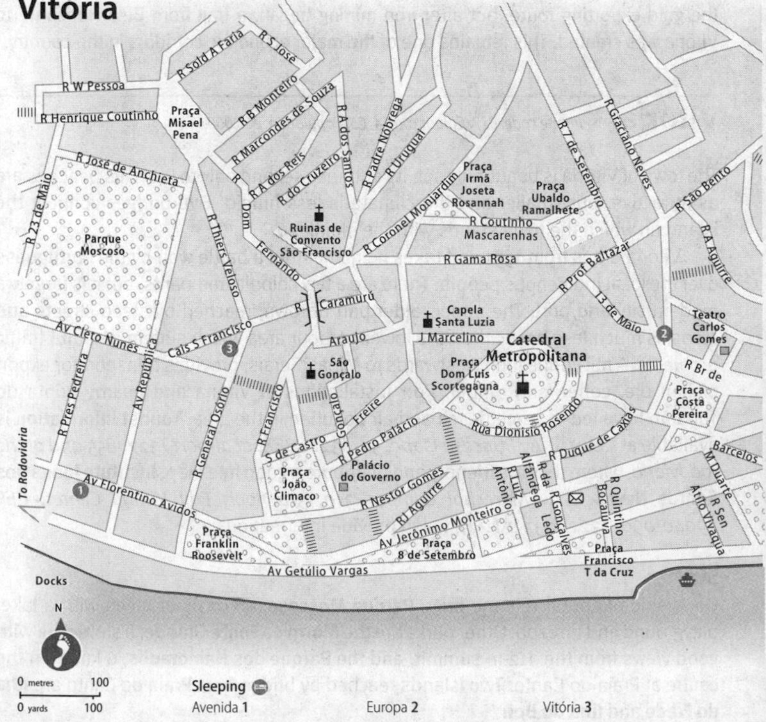

The coastal mountains

Mountains separate Vitoría from Minas. Once these were covered in lush Atlantic coastal rainforest, which now survives only in isolated patches; replaced by pine plantations and acres of coffee. The road to Minas is nonetheless picturesque, climbing steeply off the coastal plain and winding its way around the hills and through steep valleys. Many of the towns here were settled by Germans and Swiss; and their alpine heritage lives on in a curiously kitsch way – it never gets close to freezing here but the tourist chalets which dot the route are built with long sloping roofs which look like they could fend off a ton of snow. These are much beloved of Brazilians, who like to romanticize hills and a little cool air into the Alps. Some customs brought over in the 1840s by the first German and Swiss settlers, are loosely preserved in the villages of **Santa Leopoldina** and **Domingos Martins**, both around 45 km from Vitória, less than an hour by bus (two companies run to the former, approximately every three hours). Domingos Martins (also known as Campinho) has a Casa de Cultura with some items of German settlement. Santa Leopoldina has an interesting **museum** ⓘ *Tue-Sun 0900-1100, 1300-1800*, covering the settlers' first years in the area. **Santa Teresa**, which lies beyond them, is a favourite weekend retreat for people from Vitoría. It is linked to Santa Leopoldina by a dirt road.

Whilst these are moderately interesting, the only real reason to break the journey between Vitoría and Minas is to see **Pedra Azul** ⓘ *www.pedraazul.com.br*, a giant granite mountain which juts out of the nearby hills and changes colour from slate blue to deep orange as the day passes. Although surrounded by pine plantations it preserves a little indigenous forest around its flanks and the state park in which it sits is good for a day's light walking.

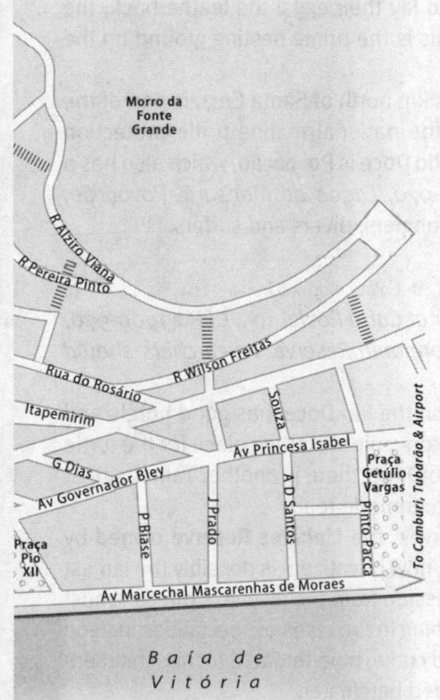

South of Vitória

Cachoeiro do Itapemirim is a busy city on both banks of the fast-flowing Rio Itapemirim. **Cachoeira Alta** with a natural swimming pool is 38 km away on the road to Castelo. The countryside south of Vitoría is flat and uninteresting, broken by fields of sugar cane and the occasional granite mountain which looms over the plain and whose flanks are covered in remnants of the forests which once swathed the entire coast. The beaches which dot the coast are less beautiful than those in the north of the state and considerably less beautiful than those in neighbouring Rio. Few stop to see them. The most popular are those at **Guarapari**, some 50 km south of Vitória on the coast road. The town gets very crowded at holiday times, especially mid-December to the end of February when Mineiros flood down from Belo Horizonte. The sand here is mildly radioactive but if the Casa de Cultura in town is to be believed it is a radiation which is good for the health. Plenty of Capixabas and Cariocas seem to believe so as they come here to cure everything from rheumatism to backache. There are many hotels and plenty of cheap seafood restaurants in town and by the beach. A little further south still is the far quieter village of **Ubu** and, 8 km beyond, **Anchieta** which has a small esturarine river much beloved of water birds. Boatmen from the Colônla da Pesca charge about US$20 for a short trip along the river. Close by is **Iriri**, a small village in a beautiful setting with two beaches, Santa Helena and Inhaúma. There are a few hotels. Five kilometres beyond is **Piúma**, a calm, little-visited place, renowned for its craftwork in shells, a skill which has been passed down through generations of craftsmen and women. The name derives from the Indian word *pium*, meaning mosquito. The resort town of Marataízes is the last before the border.

North of Vitória

Santa Cruz

The ES-010 road follows the coast from Vitória north to the mouth of the Rio Doce. It passes beaches such as Manguinhos and Jacaraípe and the town of Nova Almeida before reaching Santa Cruz, 60 km north of the state capital. The town, at the mouth of the Rio Piraquê-Açu, depends economically on cellulose factories, which have been the subject of an international outcry over child labour. It is a simple place, with few facilities. The coast around Santa Cruz, called **Aracruz**, has several good beaches, mostly undeveloped, which are tranquil and uncrowded.

Turtle beaches

The **Reserva Biológica Comboios** ⓘ *Contact Ibama, Av Marechal Mascarenhas 2487, Caixa Postal 762, CEP 29000, Vitória, or T2641452*, 44 km north of Santa Cruz, is designed to protect the marine turtles which frequent this coast. Three species use this long stretch of sand backed by *restinga* to lay their eggs: the leatherback, the green (*araunã*) and the *cabeçuda*, for which this is the prime nesting ground on the Brazilian seaboard.

Regência, at the mouth of the Rio Doce, 65 km north of Santa Cruz, is part of the reserve and has a regional base for **Tamar**, the national marine turtle protection project. On the north shore of the mouth of the Rio Doce is **Povoação**, which also has a **Tamar office** ⓘ *Caixa Postal 105, CEP 29900-970, Lagoa do Monsorá, Povoação, Linhares, ES*. Regência is popular with sailors, anglers, divers and surfers.

Linhares and Sooretama reserves → *Colour map 4, B5.*

ⓘ *For information on the turtles, contact Tamar at Caixa Postal 105, CEP 29900-970, Linhares, ES. For authorization to visit the Sooretama Reserve, researchers should phone T3740016.*

The town of **Linhares**, 143 km north of Vitória on the Rio Doce, has good hotels and restaurants but is otherwise deadly dull. It is a convenient starting place for the turtle beaches. Besides those at the mouth of the Rio Doce, there is another Tamar site at **Ipiranga**, which is 40 km east of Linhares by an unmade road.

Linhares is close to two other nature reserves: the **Linhares Reserve** owned by CVRD (the former state-owned mining company, now privatized) is possibly the largest remaining lowland tract of Atlantic forest; permission from the reserve's director must be obtained to visit. There is very good birdwatching in the reserve; specialities include red-billed curassow, minute hermit, rufous-sided crake, blue-throated (ochre-cheeked) parakeet, black-billed scythebill and black-headed berryeater.

The **Sooretama Biological Reserve**, some 45 km north of Linhares and 65 km south of Conceição da Barra, on the BR-101, protects tropical Atlantic rainforest and its fauna and birds (it contains several bird species not found in the Linhares Reserve). Much of the wildlife is rare and endangered. Both Sooretama and Linhares have orchids apparently not found anywhere else. Sooretama has been protected since 1969. With year-round tropical humidity, vegetation here is dense with ancient trees reaching over 40 m in height. Two rivers, the Barra Seca and the Cupido, cross the reserve and, together with Lagoa Macuco, provide marshlands which attract migratory birds as well as numerous resident flocks. The reserve is strictly monitored by Ibama and is not open to the public, but drivers and cyclists can cut across it by road.

São Mateus, 88 km north of Linhares, is another unillustrious but inoffensive inland town. It is 13 km from good beaches at Guriri, which is another **Tamar** base ⓘ *Caixa Postal 130.153, CEP 29930-000 São Mateus, T027-7611267.*

Conceição da Barra → *Phone code: 027. Colour map 4, B5. Population: 25,500.*

The most attractive beaches in Espírito Santo, however, are around Conceição da Barra, 261 km north of Vitória. It is an organized town which welcomes visitors. Many come in summer and for Carnival, otherwise it is quiet. Viewed from its small port, the sunsets are always spectacular. Corpus Christi (early June) is celebrated with an evening procession for which the road is decorated with coloured wood chips.

Itaúnas

Itaúnas, 27 km north of Conceição, is an interesting excursion (it has some *pousadas* and a small campsite). The small town has been swamped by sand, and has been moved to the opposite riverbank. There is now a fantastic landscape of 30-m high dunes, coastal swamp land (with numerous capybara) and deserted beaches. From time to time, winds shift the sand dunes enough to reveal the buried church tower. The theory is that the sudden encroachment of the sands in the 1970s was caused by massive deforestation of the surrounding area. The coast here, too, is a protected turtle breeding ground. (**Tamar** ⓘ *Caixa Postal 53, Conceição da Barra, T7621124.*) Buses run here three to four times a day from Conceição da Barra. The town is very popular with middle-class Mineiros and Paulistanos in high season who regard it as less spoilt than Trancoso and the other once laid-back resort towns of southern Bahia.

Meleiras beach, 3 km south, is accessible only on foot or by boat (one of a number of pleasant trips). It is 12 km long and offers fabulous diving and fishing. **Guaxindiba**, 3 km north, is partially developed, with hotels and restaurants, but the natural vegetation is still intact. It is possible to drive all the way along dirt roads into southern Bahia if you have a 4WD.

Sleeping

Vitória *p281, map p282, phone code 027*

AL Senac Ilha do Boi, R Bráulio Macedo 417, Ilha do Boi, T3450111, www.hotelilhadoboi.com.br. The most luxurious in town with its own marina, bay views and restaurant and pool.

A Best Western Porto do Sol, Av Dante Michelini 3957, Praia de Camburi, T33372244, F3372711. A beachside hotel built in the 1980s some 7 km from the centre, with a restaurant, pool, sauna and bar.

B Pousada da Praia, Av Saturnino de Brito 1500, Praia do Canto, T/F2250233. Ordinary little hotel near the beach with a pool.

C Avenida, Av Florentino Avidos 350, T2234317. Adequate though undistinguished a/c rooms and a decent breakfast. Recommended.

C Vitória, Cais de São Francisco 85, near Parque Moscoso. Basic hotel with a good restaurant, changes money. Recommended.

D Europa, 7 de Setembro, corner of Praça Costa Pereira. Noisy but cheap both as a hotel and restaurant. Advice on nearby veggie restaurants.

E Jardim da Penha, R Hugo Viola 135, take Universitário bus, get off at the first University stop, T3240738. Youth hostel.

E Praia da Costa, R São Paulo 1163, Praia da Costa, Vila Velha, T3293227. IYHA youth hostel.

E Príncipe Hotel, Av Dario Lourenço de Souza 120, Ilha do Príncipe, T3222799, F2233392. IYHA youth hostel.

There are a string of adequate but scruffy hotels opposite the rodoviária and plenty of others in the beach areas: **Camburi** to the north, **Vila Velha** to the south, both about 15 mins from city centre. Accommodation is very easy to find here except in the high season.

The coastal mountains *p283, phone code 027*

C Pousada Peterle, Estrada Pedra Azul, Domingos Martins, T32481171. Spacious mock-Swiss chalets set in a little garden with good views of the rock and a generous breakfast. No restaurant.

South of Vitória *p283, phone code 027*

There are plenty of hotels and *pousadas* near the various beaches. The most popular beach is **Castelhanos** and its extension **Guanabara**, which separate Anchieta from Ubu. Castelhanos has more beachside palapa restaurants. Gunanbara is quieter. Both have calm waters.

AL Flamboyant, Km 38 Rod do Sol, Guarapari, T/F2290066, www.hotelflamboyant.com.br. *Fazenda* hotel with fishing and horse riding. 5 days minimum stay.

A Best Western Porto do Sol, Av Beira Mar 1, Praia do Morro, Guarapari, T3611100, www.geocities.com/portadosol. Mediterranean-style village on a rocky point overlooking a calm beach, pool, sauna.

A Thanharu Praia, R Jovina Serafim dos Anjos, Praia de Castelhanos, between Anchieta and Ubu, T/F5361246, www.thanaru.com.br. Beachside hotel with a pool and sauna. Popular with families and on one of the livelier beaches.

A-B Praia Costa Azul, Iriri. Lodging in private houses is possible. A regular bus runs from Guarapari.

B Pontal de Ubu, R Gen Oziel 1, Praia de Ubu, T2613111, www.hotelpontaldeubu.com.br. Popular family hotel with a pool, saunas, bike rental and various organized activities.

B-C Pousada da Meméia, R Manuel Alves Abrantes, Iriri, T35341534, www.pousadamemeia.com.br. A range of rooms in a medium-sized *pousada* with a bar and sauna.

B-C Pousada Haras Monte Agha, R das Castanheiras, Piúma, T35201363. Fazenda hotel with horse riding.

C Costa Sul, R Getúlio Vargas 101, Guarapari. Basic, friendly, clean and good breakfast. Much beloved of Brazilians and mosquitoes.

C-D Alto da Praia, Av Estr Dos Cancelas 111, Alto da Praia, Marataízes, T35323630, www.altodapraia.com.br. Small *pousada* with a/c rooms and a pool.

C-D Coqueiros Praia, Av D Helvécio 1020, Praia dos Namorados, Iriri, T35341592. Small beachside *pousada* with a/c rooms and a play area for kids.

C-D Dona Judith, Av Lacerda de Aguiar 353, Marataízes, T5321436, F5321305. Basic but friendly.

C-D Pousada do Sol, Av das Ostras, Praia da Guanabara, between Anchieta and Ubu, T35361643, www.pousadadosol.com. Small *pousada* with a/c rooms and a pool near the beach. Good value.

E Youth hostel Simple IYHA hostel at Guarapari popular with students from Vitória.

Camping

Marataízes, Municipal site on Praia do Siri, 9 km south of Marataízes centre, T3252202.

Praia de Itapessu, R Antônio Guimarães s/n, quadra 40, Guarapari, T2610475, F2610448. Turn left out of the rodoviária, then right and right again, past **Pousada Lisboa**, 2 blocks, across a dual carriageway (Av Jones de Santos Neves), 1 block to the campground, US$10 with good breakfast. Recommended.

Santa Cruz *p284, phone code 027*

B Pousada dos Cocais, Praia de Sauê, T/F2501515. With a restaurant and a pool.

C Coqueiral Praia Park, Praia do Coqueiral, 6 km along the road to Barra do Riacho, T2501214. A/c rooms with TVs and a restaurant, pool, pretty location.

D Pousada das Pedras, Praia dos Padres, T2501716. Basic but friendly with plain rooms.

There are *pousadas* at Praia Formosa, 3 km south of town, and campsites at Barra do Sahy, Praia do Putiry and Formosa beaches.

Linhares and Sooretama reserves *p284, phone code 027*

B-D Reserva Natural da Vale do Rio Doce, BR 101 km 120, T33719797, www.cvrd.com.br/linhares. Beautiful location within the natural reserve. Great for birds and wildlife.

With a bar, sauna and simple but pleasant rooms.

B-D **Virgínia**, Av Gov Santos Neves 919, Linhares, T/F2641699. Modern building with a range of rooms at different prices. Good if you get stuck in town.

Conceição da Barra *p285, phone code 027*

There are plenty of beach hotels to choose from here and you will have no problem finding one after a short browse – as long as it is not high season.

C **Pousada Gandia**, Av Atlântica 1054, (Praia de Guaxindiba), T/F7621248. Small *pousada* with simple rooms, a pool, baby sitting services and helpful staff.

C **Praia da Barra**, Av Atlântica 350, T/F7621100, www.hotelpraiadabarra.com.br. Simple and friendly 50-room *pousada* with a/c or fan, a pool and sauna.

D **Caravelas**, Av Dr Mário Vello Silvares 83, 1 block from the beach, T7621188. Basic with shared bathrooms and a light breakfast. Recommended.

E **Pousada Pirámide**, next to rodoviária, T7621970. The owner Lisete Soares speaks English, good value, 100 m from beach. Recommended.

Camping

Camping Clube do Brasil, Rod Adolfo Serra, Km 16, T7621346. Site with full facilities.

Itaúnas *p285, phone code 027*

There are numerous attractive little *pousadas* on and around the town's grassy main square.

C **Pousada Bem Te Vi**, R Adolpho Pereira Duarte 41, T37625012, www.pousadabemtevi.com. One of the few *pousadas* in town with a pool, with a range of modern rooms organized around a courtyard; all with a/c or fans, TVs, fridges and breakfast.

C **Pousada Cambucá**, just off the Praça Principal, T37625004, www.portonet.com.br/cambuca. Wooden-floored rooms, some with balconies and a decent seafood restaurant.

C -D **Casa da Praia**, R Dercílio Fonseca, T37625028, www.casadapraiaitaunas.com.br. Simple *pousada* close to the beach.

Eating

Vitória *p281, map p282, phone code 027*

Moqueca capixaba, a seafood dish served in an earthenware pot is the local speciality. It is a variant of the *moqueca* which is typical of Bahia.

¥¥¥ **Lareira Portuguesa**, Av Saturnino de Brito 260, Praia do Canto, T3450329. Portuguese, expensive.

¥¥ **Mar e Terra**, opposite the rodoviária. Good food, live music at night.

¥¥ **Pirão**, R Joaquim Lírio 753, Praia do Canto. Regional food.

¥ **Lavacar**, Praia Camburi. One of many similar on this beach, which like the others serves food and has live music.

South of Vitória *p283, phone code 027*

¥ **Peixada do Garcia**, Av Magno Ribeiro Muqui, Guarapari. Respectable seafood.

¥ **Peixada do Menelau Garcia**, Av Mário Neves, Guarapari. More respectable seafood.

Conceição da Barra *p285, phone code 027*

There are plenty of simple seafood restaurants town and some basic *palapas* on the beach.

¥ **Tia Teresa**, R Dr Mário Vello Silvares 135. Brazilian food, self-service, good value.

Transport

Vitória *p281, map p282, phone code 027*

Air Eurico Salles airport at Goiaberas, 11 km from the city, T3270811. There are flights to **Belém**, **Belo Horizonte**, **Brasília**, **Guarapari**, **Maceió**, **Porto Alegre**, **Recife**, **Rio de Janeiro**, **Salvador** and **São Paulo**.

Airline offices Rio Sul/Nordeste, Av NS dos Navegantes 2091, conj 102, T2271588. TAM, Av Fernando Ferrari 3055, Goiaberas, T3270868. **Varig**, Av Jerônimo Monteiro 1000, loja 3, at airport T3270304. **Vasp**, R Desembargador Sampaio 40, T3241499, at airport, T3270236.

Bus The rodoviária is 15 mins' walk west of the centre. **Rio**, 8 hrs, US$15 (*leito* 25). **Belo Horizonte**, US$14.50 (*leito* 29). **Salvador**, 18 hrs, US$27; **Porto Seguro** direct 11 hrs with lots of stops, US$18 (also *leito* service); alternatively, take a bus to Eunápolis, then change to buses which run every hour.

Car hire Localiza, Praça do Aeroporto, T3270211; at the airport T0800-992000; **Vila Velha**, Av Carlos Lindemberg 2707, T2004466.

Hitchhiking To hitch to **Salvador**, take a bus to Serra, which is 13 km beyond Carapina, itself 20 km north of Vitória; alight where the bus turns off to Serra.

Train Daily passenger service to **Belo Horizonte**, 14 hrs, US$17.50 *executivo* (very comfortable), US$11.50 1st class, US$7.80 2nd.

South of Vitória *p283, phone code 027*
Bus There are regular buses to Gurarpari from Vitoría and onward from here to the other resorts down the coast. The Alvorada bus company has a separate rodoviária from Itapemirim/Penha, Sudeste, São Gerardo and others. They are close together, 15 mins' walk from the city centre or US$5 by taxi. Penha tickets are sold at R-Tur Turismo, in the centre at R Manoel Severo Simões and R Joaquim da Silva Lima where air tickets, free brochures, maps, and hotel addresses can also be obtained. To **Vitória**, 1 hr with Sudeste, US$2. To **Rio** with Itapemirim, 2 a day, US$12.

Linhares and Sooretama reserves *p284, phone code 027*
Bus Frequent buses from Vitoría. Most Bahia-bound buses stop at Linhares.

Itaúnas *p285, phone code 027*
Bus Bus from the *padaria* in Conceição da Barra at 0700, returns 1700.

Directory

Vitória *p281, map p282, phone code 027*
Banks American Express: Saytur, Av Des Santos Neves 1425, T3251899, F3251391. **Embassies and consulates** Denmark, R do Sol 141, Sala 210, T2224075, 0900-1300, 1500-1900. Spain, R Aristides Freire 22, Centro, T2232846. **Medical services** Santa Casa, R Dr Jones de Santos Neves 143, T3220074. **Post office** Av Jerônimo Monteiro, between R Gonçalves Ledo and R Quintino Bocaiúva. **Telephone** Palácio do Café, Praça Costa Pereira 52.

South of Vitória *p283, phone code 027*
Banks Banco 24 Horas, Praça do Coronado, Praia da Areia, Guarapari; **Banco do Brasil**, R Joaquim da Silva Lima 550, Guarapari; **Bradesco**, R Henrique Coutinho 901, Guarapari; **Banco do Brasil**, Av Lacerda de Aguiar 356, Marataízes.

Iguaçu Falls and the south

Footprint features

Introduction

Southern Brazil is famous first and foremost for one sight – Iguaçu. These are the world's mightiest and grandest waterfalls, surrounded on all sides by lush subtropical forest, stretching for almost 3 km, and falling in a thunderous two-tier curtain from a height almost twice that of Niagara. But although Iguaçu is undoubtedly the highlight, it would be a shame to rush in and out of Southern Brazil without seeing anything more. There are many other spectacularly beautiful natural sights – toy trains winding their way through jagged, verdant mountain ranges to some of the largest stretches of lowland coastal forest in South America; bays studded with islands, each of which is home to different and often unique fauna; the crumbling ruins of Jesuit monasteries and of course miles of glorious beaches.

The feel of the south is very different to the rest of Brazil; towns are more European and made up of settlers from the Ukraine, Germany and Italy. In Joinville and Blumenau an archaic Bavarian dialect is still widely spoken and there is an annual *bierfest*. Buses run on time, streets are relatively clean and many of the people don't talk much. Things change again in the border country with Argentina and Uruguay, which retains an insular and macho *gaúcho* culture which seems to have more in common with the pampas than Brazil.

★ Don't miss...

1. **The Serra da Graciosa** Cross Brazil's prettiest mountains in one of the most attractive railway lines in South America, page 296.
2. **Ilha do Mel and the Parque Nacional de Superagüi** Hang out at the laid-back beach in the midst of Brazil's largest stretch of coastal forest, page 299.
3. **Iguaçu** Join the sightseers at the largest waterfalls on the planet and one of its great natural wonders, page 300.
4. **Florianópolis** Take time out at this relaxed little city on an island fringed with the country's best surf beaches, page 322.
5. **Praia da Rosa** Watch the humpbacks and sperm whales, Brazil's best whalewatching site, especially between June and November, the calving season, page 332.
6. **The Serra Gaúcha** Enjoy mountain scenery, good hiking and twee villages, page 346.
7. **São Miguel das Missoes** Visit the hulking ruins of the Guaraní mission camps whose story inspired *The Mission*, page 350.

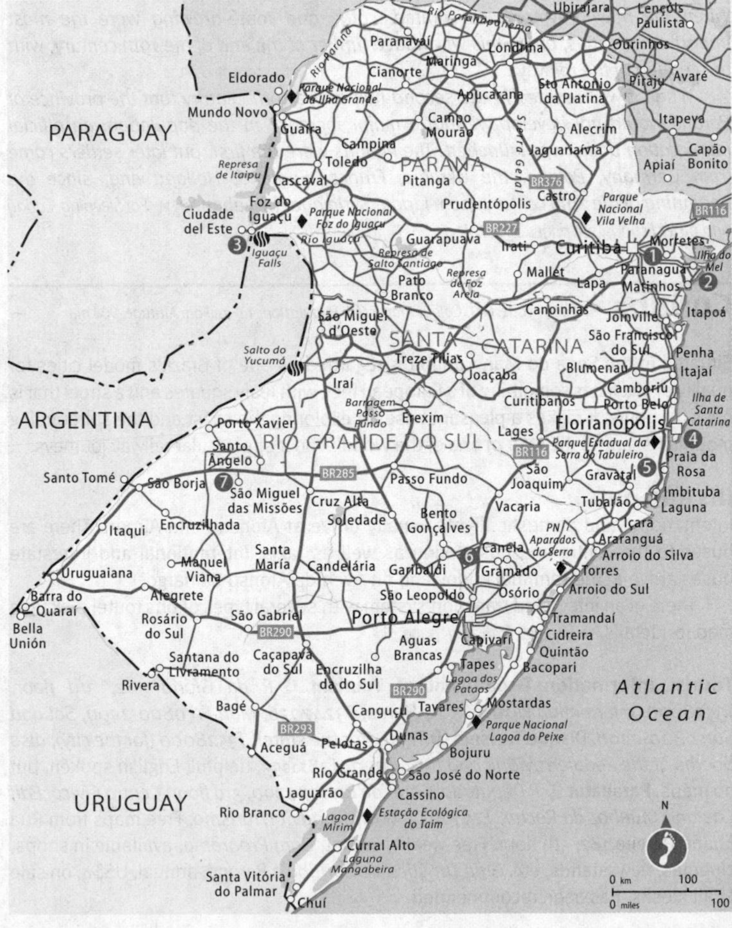

Paraná
→ *Population: 9.5 million.*

Paraná is most famous for the Iguaçu falls, the largest and most magnificent waterfalls in the Americas. No guidebook can do justice to the spectacle and they are a must on any itinerary to Brazil. Besides Iguaçu, Paraná has a great deal to offer those in search of pristine nature: the largest area of coastal rainforest in Brazil swathes the mountains of the northern coast; little beach-fringed islands, like Ilha do Mel, sit a short way offshore. Both are easily reached from the neat and tidy capital, Curitiba, on one of the continent's most impressive railway journeys. The interior of the state is pocked with villages and towns founded by the European settlers that flocked here at the end of the 19th century.

The area of what is now Paraná was neglected by the Portuguese until the beginning of the 17th century when gold was discovered. The region fell under the control of São Paulo, but there was no great success in the extraction of gold, partly because indigenous labour was unavailable to work the finds (they had all been sent elsewhere or had died of disease). As soon as the metal was discovered in Minas Gerais, the mines shut down in Paraná. Instead, the colonists turned to agriculture and cattle-raising and, in the 18th and 19th centuries, fazendeiros and drovers were the dominant people of Paraná. Until 1853, the area was controlled from São Paulo. When the new province was created, cattle and maté*-growing were the most important activities, but to this was added timber at the end of the 19th century, with the coming of the railways.*

When it was realized in the second half of the 19th century that the province of Paraná would not develop without a major increase in the population, an official immigration policy was launched. The Italians were the first, but later settlers came from Germany, Poland, the Ukraine, France, England, Holland and, since the beginning of the 20th century, from Japan, Syria and the Lebanon. ▸▸ *For Sleeping, Eating and other listings, see pages 309-321.*

Curitiba
→ *Phone code: 041. Colour map 5, A4. Population: 1.6 million. Altitude: 908 m.*

Situated in the Serra do Mar, Curitiba is regarded as one of Brazil's model cities for quality of life. It has something of a European feel, with leafy squares and a street that is open 24 hours. It makes a pleasant base for exploring the coast and the surrounding mountains, and is the start of one of the world's most spectacular railway journeys.

Ins and outs

International and domestic flights usually arrive at Afonso Pena Airport. There are buses to the centre and bus station as well as taxis. International and interstate buses arrive at the Terminal Rodoviário on Avenida Afonso Camargo.

There is an integrated transport system with several types of bus route; pick up a map for details. ▸▸ *See also Transport, page 317.*

Tourist information Department of Tourism ⓘ *R da Glória 362, 3rd floor, T3528000, information kiosk at R 24 Horas, T3247036, Mon-Fri 0800-2400, Sat and Sun 0800-2200.* **Disque Turismo** ⓘ *T1516 (for the state), T3528000 (for the city), also booths at the Rodoferroviária and the airport, T3811153*, helpful, English spoken, but no maps. **Paranatur** ⓘ *R Deputado Mário de Barros 1290, 3rd floor, Centro Cívico, Edif Caetano Munhoz da Rocha, T2546933, www.pr.gov.br/turismo.* Free maps from Rua Ebano Pereira 187, 5th floor. Free weekly leaflet, *Bom Programa*, available in shops, cinemas, newsstands, etc. *Guía Turística de Curitiba e Paraná*, annual, US$4, on sale at all kiosks, has been recommended.

Background

The state capital, Curitiba, which sits on a plateau above the Serra do Mar, was founded as Vila Nossa Senhora da Luz dos Pinhais on 29 March 1693 on the spot which is now Praça Tiradentes. For many years it was little more than a pit stop for cattle herders on their way between Rio Grande do Sul and the cities to the north. But in 1842 it was elevated to the rank of city and given the name of Curitiba, and in 1853 it was made the state capital.

After an influx of European immigrants in the 19th and 20th centuries, Curitiba rapidly expanded and is now one of the country's more progressive and carefully planned modern cities; said to be one of the three cleanest in Latin America. It has some attractive public architecture and a well-planned transport system, much of it paid for by the proceeds of the Itaipú hydroelectric plant. The new opera house, the greenhouse in the Botanical Garden and several of the larger 'tubo' bus stations (which cover the entire city) all share the same semi-circular arch-steel-tube- and-glass style.

In outlying areas, **Ruas da Cidadania**, 'citizenship streets', or malls, which throng with activity have been built next to bus stops to provide municipal services, shops, child care and leisure activities so that local people avoid the need to travel to the centre. The first and most famous of these was built at **Boqueirão**, but **Rua da Cidadania da Matriz**, next to the Praça Rui Barbosa transport terminal and inaugurated in 1997, is more central and has the added innovation of 20 computer terminals for free access to the internet.

Sights

A panoramic view can be had from the glass observation deck of the telecommunications tower, **Torre Mercês**, built by Telepar and so also called the **Telepar Tower** ⓘ *R Jacarezinho, on the corner with R Professor Lycio Veloso 191, T3228080, Tue-Fri 1230-2030, Sat, Sun and holidays 1030-2030, US$1.50*. The 110 m tower stands at an elevation of 95 m above sea level. There is a map of the city on the floor so that you can locate key sites.

The commercial centre is the busy Rua 15 de Novembro, part of which is a pedestrian area called **Rua das Flores**. Since urban planning first began in 1720, the Rua das Flores has been a place for street happenings and is now well decorated with flowers and trees, with benches, cafés and restaurants, cinemas and shops. The **Boca Maldita** is a particularly lively part and a good meeting place. Another pedestrian area behind the cathedral, near Largo da Ordem, with a flower clock and old buildings, is very beautiful in the evening when the old lamps are lit – nightlife is concentrated here. There is an art market on Saturday morning in the **Praça Rul Barbosa**, and an even better one on Sunday morning in **Praça Garibáldi**, beside the attractive Rosário church.

The **Centro Cívico** is at the end of Avenida Dr Cândido de Abreu, 2 km from the centre: a monumental group of buildings dominated by the **Palácio Iguaçu**, headquarters of the state and municipal governments. In a patio behind it is a relief map to scale of Paraná. The **Bosque de João Paulo II**, behind the Civic Centre on Rua Mateus Leme, was created in December 1980 after the Pope's visit to Curitiba. It also contains the **Memorial da Imigração Polonesa no Paraná** (Polish immigrants memorial). In contrast to the Civic Centre is the old municipal government building in French Art Nouveau style, now housing the **Museu Paranaense** ⓘ *Praça Generoso Marques*.

All that remains of the magnificent old **Palácio Avenida** ⓘ *Travessa Oliveira Belo 11, T3216249*, is the façade, which was retained during remodelling works in 1991. Nowadays it has a completely modern interior, with banks, offices, an auditorium for 250 people and various cultural activities. The **Solar do Barão** ⓘ *R Presidente Carlos Cavalcanti 533, T3221525*, is another old building, built in 1880-83 as a home for the Baron of Serro Azul. Today it is used as a centre for art and leisure, with concerts in the auditorium, exhibitions and courses. The **Teatro Paiol** ⓘ *south of the centre on R Coronel Zacarias next to Praça Guido Viaro, T3221525*, was built in 1906 as a depository for gunpowder, and its round construction has a defensive, military feel to it. It has been a theatre since 1971. In contrast, the **Teatro Guaíra** ① *R 15 de Novembro, T3222628*, has always been a theatre. First built in 1884 as the Teatro São Teodoro, the present building dates from 1953 and has three auditoria of different sizes.

The **Ópera de Arame** and the **Pedreira Paulo Leminski** lie north of the centre on the site of an old stone quarry. The pit has been transformed into a site of major cultural importance where open-air shows and concerts are held. It has a capacity to entertain up to 70,000 people and it was here that the tenor, José Carreras, gave his first performance in Brazil in March 1993, to celebrate Curitiba's 300th anniversary. The opera house itself is a beautiful tubular structure, circular, with a glass and metal dome, which radiates light when performances are held at night.

Another example of the use of tubular steel and glass is the arcade of **Rua 24 Horas**. The street's two clocks use the 24-hour system and the bars and cafés (all very similar) never close. The theme of light, glass and space is developed further in education. Attached to several schools are **Faroles de Saber**, lighthouses of knowledge, which are modular 5,000-book libraries with a lighthouse tower, a beacon on top and a guard.

Parks

The most popular public park is the **Passeio Público** ① *closed Mon*, in the heart of the city, with three lakes, each with an island, and a playground.

On the northeast edge of the city **Parque do Barigüi** (take bus 450 'São Braz' from Praça Tiradentes) contains an exhibition centre, amusement park, football, volleyball, *churrascarias*, a lake and lots of other entertainments. Near the shores of

Lagoa Bacacheri, on the northern edge of the city, is an unexpected **Egyptian temple** ⓘ *R Nicarágua 2453*. Visits can be arranged to the Brazilian centre of the Rosicrucians; take Santa Cândida bus to Estação Boa Vista, then walk.

About 4 km east of the rodoferroviário, the **Jardim Botânico Fanchette Rischbieter** has a fine glass house, again with domes, curves and lots of steel, inspired by Crystal Palace in London. The gardens are in the French style and there is also a **Museu Botánico** ⓘ *R Ostoja Roguski (Primeira Perimetral dos Bairros), T3218646*. It can be reached by the orange Expreso buses from Praça Rui Barbosa.

Other parks include: **Bosque João Carlos Hartley Gutierrez** ⓘ *R Jacarezinho between Vista Alegre and Mercês*, where there is a memorial to Chico Mendes; **Bosque de Portugal** ⓘ *R Osório Duque Estrada, corner with Rua Fagundes Varela*, with Portuguese architecture and some lovely hand-painted tiles; **Bosque Alemão**, between Ruas Franz Schubert, Nicollo Paganini and Francisco Schaffer, where there is an Oratório Bach, used for concerts, and tile murals depicting the Hansel and Gretel fairy tale. **Parque Tingüi** ⓘ *between Ruas Fredolin Wolf and José Valle*, named after an indigenous tribe who lived in the area, contains a **Memorial da Imigração Ucraniana**, in honour of one of the main sources of immigration to the city, and a replica of the church of São Miguel Arcanjo.

Churches

On Praça Tiradentes is the **Cathedral** ⓘ *R Barão do Serro Azul 31, T2221131*. It was originally a small wooden chapel, which was elevated to the Primeira Igreja Matriz in 1715, but improvements in the colonial style of construction led to cracks appearing and in 1875 it had to be demolished. The present cathedral, built in neo-Gothic style and inaugurated in 1893, was restored in 1993 and promoted to Catedral Basílica Menor de Curitiba.

The oldest church in Curitiba is the **Igreja de Ordem Terceira de São Francisco das Chagas**, built in 1737 in Largo da Ordem. Its most recent renovation was in 1978-80. In its annex is the **Museu de Arte Sacra** ⓘ *T2237545*. The **Igreja de Nossa Senhora do Rosário de São Benedito** was built in the Praça Garibáldi in 1737 by slaves and was the Igreja dos Pretos de São Benedito. It was demolished in 1931 and a new church was inaugurated in 1946. There is a mass for tourists, Missa do Turista, which is held on Sundays at 0800.

Museums

Museu Paranaense ⓘ *Praça Generoso Marques, T3231411, Tue-Fri 0930-1730, Sat-Mon 1300-1800, closed 1st Mon of each month*, was founded in 1876 by Agostinho Ermelino de Leão, although it has not always been at this location. The collection of exhibits includes documents, manuscripts, ethnological and historical material, stamps, works of art, photographs and archaeological pieces. The **Museu Niemeyer (Novo Museu)** ⓘ *R Mal, Hermes 999,*

 T3504400, www.novomuseu.org, Tue-Sun 1330-1830, which opened in late 2002, was designed by and is devoted to the famous Brazilian modernist architect who designed Brasília and was a disciple of Le Corbusier, alongside other Paranense artists. The stunning principal building is shaped like a giant eye. An underground passage lined with exhibits and photographs links it to a sculpture garden. **Museu de Arte Contemporânea** ⓘ *R Desembargador Westphalen 16, Praça Zacarias, T2225172, Tue-Fri 0900-1900, Sat and Sun 1400-1900*, displays Brazilian contemporary art in its many forms, with an emphasis on artists from Paraná. **Casa Andersen** ⓘ *R Mateus Leme 336, Mon-Fri 0900-1200, 1400-1800*, is the painter's house. **Museu de Arte do Paraná** ⓘ *T2343172*, in the Palácio São Francisco, was built in the 1920s for the Garmatter family and used in 1938-53 as the Governor's palace. The museum dates from 1987 and exhibits the work of many of Paraná's artists. **Museu da Imagem e do Som** ⓘ *R Barão do Rio Branco 395, T2329113*, was created with the aim of preserving audiovisual and photographic memories of Paraná. **Museo do Automóvel** ⓘ *Av Cândido Hartmann 2300, Sat 1400-1800, Sun 1000-1200, 1400-1800*, has a collection of cars dating from as early as 1910 to the McLaren of Emerson Fittipaldi. **Museu de História Natural** ⓘ *R Benedito Conceição 407, T3663133*, is a natural history museum with lots of zoology and scientific collections of things like spiders, insects and parasites, which also has details on endangered species in the state.

Curitiba to Paranaguá

When the first European ships arrived at Paraná in the mid-16th century, they would have been daunted at the prospect of conquering the lands of southern Brazil. From the sea, the thickly forested and steep crags of the **Serra da Graciosa** must have seemed an insurmountable wall fortifying the continent from the coast. But in a cruel twist of fate, it was native trails cutting through the mountains that led to inland Paraná being colonized. After the paths were discovered, the Portuguese forced African slaves to pave them with river stones. Miners and traders were soon dragging mules laden with gold, silver, textiles and *herva maté* up and down the mountains. As trade grew, the port at Paranaguá became the most important south of Santos and little towns of whitewashed churches and smart Portuguese buildings like Morretes and Antonina grew up along the trails. In 1885 the routes were busy enough to merit the construction of a railway, which wound its way around the slopes, across rushing rivers and through the forest to the sea. This remains the most spectacular railway journey in Brazil, cutting

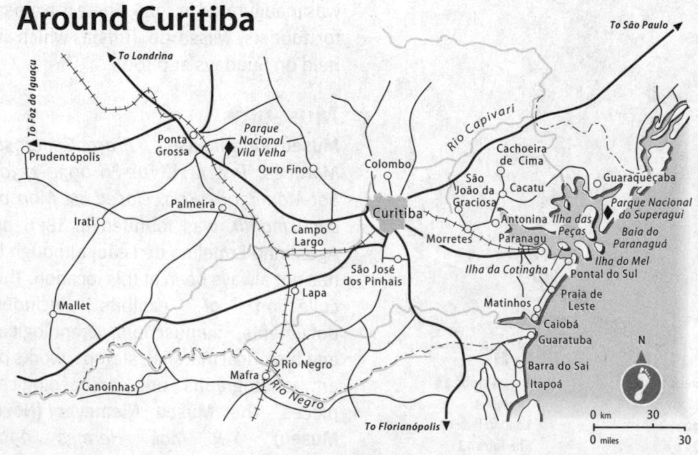

Sexual politics

The world-famous anti-impotency drug Viagra is big business in Brazil, but one wily mayor took it upon himself to distribute the pills free of charge in a desperate bid to boost his town's flagging population.

Elcio Berti, mayor of Bocaiuva do Sul in the southern state of Paraná, hoped to secure the city a bigger slice of federal cash, shared among municipalities according to their size. 'Enlarging the local population is the only way to get a larger chunk of the federal fund', the Brazilian daily newspaper *O Globo* quoted Berti as saying.

His plan was an improvement on an earlier attempt to increase the town's population, when he passed a municipal law banning the sale of condoms, a move quickly cancelled by a judge on the grounds of unconstitutionality.

through numerous tunnels, crossing dizzy viaducts (especially imported from Belgium), offering sudden views of deep gorges and high peaks and waterfalls before arriving at the sea in Paranaguá. Near Banhado station (Km 66) is the waterfall of **Véu da Noiva**, and from the station at Km 59 you can reach the Marumbl mountain range. The principal trail between Curitiba and Paranaguá is now a spectacular cobbled road which runs for 15 km through the mountains and the Marumbi National Park. There are fire grills, shelters and camping at the various rest stops. You can also hike the original trail which follows the road and passes the rest stops – trails leave from just outside Morretes railway station and are well signposted. Take food, water and plenty of insect repellent. »» *For information on the Curitiba to Paranaguá train, see Transport, page 317.*

Morretes → *Colour map 5, A5.*

Morretes, which was founded in 1721, is one of the prettiest colonial towns in southern Brazil. A parade of whitewashed Portuguese colonial buildings with painted window frames straddle the pebbly river and church spires stick up from a sea of red tiled roofs against the backdrop of the deep green forest-swathed hills. The Estrada da Graciosa road passses through Morretes and the train stops here too, for a lunch break. Most of the numerous restaurants serve the local speciality, *barreado* (meat stew cooked in a clay pot), originally a day in advance of *Carnaval* in order to allow women to escape from their domestic cooking chores and enjoy the party. There are a handful of *pousadas* too and a series of walks lead from the town into the mountains. The town is tiny and easily managed on foot and the tourist office is by the river.

Antonina, just 14 km from Morretes, is almost as picturesque and sits on the Bahia do Paranaguá. It can be reached by local bus from Morretes.

Paranaguá and around

→ *Phone code: 041. Colour map 5, A5. Population: 128,000.*

After the endless lorry parks and the messy dual carriageway leading into the town, the centre of Paranaguá, 268 km south of Santos, comes as a pleasant surprise, especially around the waterfront. Colonial buildings decay quietly in the heat and humidity, some are just façades encrusted with bromeliads; and fishermen get quietly drunk in little *botiquines*. There's not much to do in the town but stroll along the cobbles and while away the time in the interesting city museum, housed in a formidable 18th-century **Jesuit convent** ⓘ *R 15 Novembro 575, T4232511, www.proec.ufpr.br, 0800-1200, 1400-1800, R$2*, which showcases aspects of the city's interesting past.

Before it was Paranaguá, the region was an important centre of indigenous life. Colossal shell middens, called *sambaquis* (see Museu Arqueológico do Sambaqui, Joinville, page 330), some as high as a two-storey bulding, protecting regally adorned corpses, have been found on the surrounding estuaries. They date from between 7,000 and 2,000 years ago and were built by the ancestors of the tupinguin and carijo people who were here when the first Europeans arrived here. The Bay's outer islands were initially claimed and occupied by the Spanish (who thought they had reached the coast near Potosí in Bolivia, thousands of miles inland in the Andes, when they first saw the Serra da Graciosa). But in the late 16th century a *bandeira* expedition under Heiliodoro Eobano found gold in Paranaguá. The Portuguese began to realize the importance of the area, then beating the Spanish off the land and later fortifying the southern end of Ilha do Mel and establishing a port at Paranaguá.

The town makes much of its history but is more remarkable for what lies on its doorstep: the Ilha do Mel and the **Bahia do Paranaguá**, one of Latin America's biodiversity hotspots and the best place on the Brazilian coast to see rare rainforest flora and fauna. Mangrove and lowland subtropical forests, islands, rivers and rivulets here form the largest stretch of Atlantic coast rainforest in the country and protect critically endangered species like the black-faced lion tamarin, which was only discovered in 1990, and the red-tailed Amazon parrot (which despite its name is found only here), alongside a full gamut of South American spectaculars including jaguars. Most of the bay is protected by a series of national and state parks (see Superagüi, page 300), but it is possible to visit on an organized tour from Paranaguá (or with more difficulty from Guraquecaba on the northern side of the bay). The **BARCOPAR boatman's cooperative** ⓘ *T4228159*, reached through the tourist office on the waterfront, offer a range of excellent trips in large and small vessels ranging from two hours to two days and R$20 per person to R$200.

Other attractions are a 17th-century fountain, the church of **São Benedito**, and the shrine of **Nossa Senhora do Rocio**, 2 km from town.

Tourist offices ⓘ *outside the railway station, 1100-1700*, provides free maps, and at the docks in front of the pier where boats leave for Ilha do Mel ⓘ *T4226882, 0800-1900*, with boat schedules, toilet and left-luggage available.

Excursions from Paranaguá

Matinhos, 40 km south, is a medium-sized Mediterranean-style resort, invaded by surfers in October for the Paraná surf competition. Accommodation at **Praia e Sol** (**B**, Rua União 35, T4521922) has been recommended. There are four campsites and a few other cheap *pousadas* in the vicinity.

About 8 km south is **Caiobá**, at the mouth of a bay, the other side of which is **Guaratuba**, which is less built up than Caiobá. The ferry between the two towns is frequent and is a beautiful crossing (free for pedestrians, US$1.50 for cars). Both towns have a few hotels but most close in winter; there is also camping at Guaratuba. The Sol Nascente restaurant (Rua Vicente Machado 967) is superb.

Vila Velha

ⓘ *Opens at 0800, US$1, the entrance is also to the Furnas, so keep your ticket.*
On the road to Ponta Grossa is Vila Velha, now a state park, 97 km from Curitiba, 10 km from Ponta Grossa. The sandstone rocks have been weathered into most fantastic shapes, although many have been defaced by thoughtless tourists. The **Lagoa Dourada**, surrounded by forests, is close by. Nearby are the **Furnas**, three waterholes, the deepest of which has a lift (US$1 – not always working) that descends almost to the level of the lake. The park office is 300 m from the highway and the park a further 1½ km. You can camp in the church grounds or put your tent up in a disused campground which is now overgrown with no facilities.

Ilha do Mel → *Colour map 5, A5.*

Ilha do Mel is a weekend escape and holiday island popular with Paraná and Paulista surfers, twenty-something hippies and day-tripping families. There are no roads, no vehicles and limited electricity. Outside of Carnaval and New Year it is a laid-back little place. Bars pump out Bob Marley and Maranhão reggae; spaced-out surfers lounge around in hammocks; and barefooted couples dance *forró* on the wooden floors of simple beachside shacks. Much of the island is forested, its coastline is fringed with broad beaches and in the south broken by rocky headlands. Its location in the mouth of the Bahía de Paranaguá made it strategically important to the Portuguese in the 18th century. The lighthouse, **Farol das Conchas**, was built in 1872 to guide shipping into the bay. The **Gruta das Encantadas** is surrounded with myths and legends about mermaids, enchanting all who came near them.

The island divides into two sections connected by a spit of sand at the **Nova Brasília** jetty, the principal port of arrival. The rugged eastern half, where most of the facilities are to be found, is fringed with curving beaches and capped with a lighthouse. The flat, scrub forest-covered and balloon-shaped western half is predominantly an ecological protection area, its northern side, watched over by the **Fortaleza Nossa Senhora dos Prazeres**, a fort built in 1767 on the orders of King José I of Portugal, to defend what was one of the principal ports in the country. In 1850, a British warship captured three illegal slave trading ships, giving rise to a battle known as **Combate Cormorant**. The view from the 20th-century gun emplacements on the hill above the fort is the best on the island.

The best surf beaches are **Praia Grande** and **Praia de Fora**. Both are about 20 minutes' walk from the Nova Brasília jetty. **Fortaleza** and **Ponta do Bicho** on the north shore are more tranquil and are safe for swimming. They are about 45 minutes' walk

Ilha do Mel

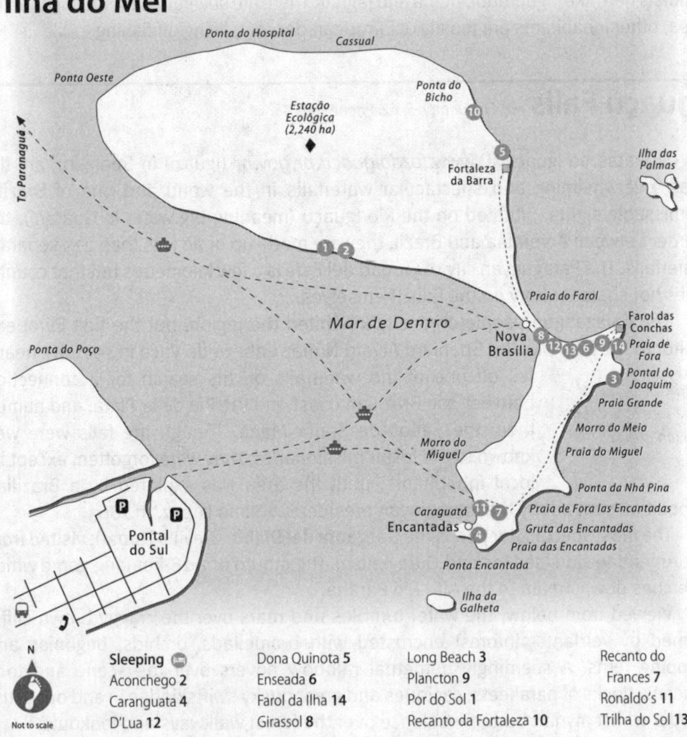

Sleeping
Aconchego 2
Caranguata 4
D'Lua 12
Dona Quinota 5
Enseada 6
Farol da Ilha 14
Girassol 8
Long Beach 3
Plancton 9
Por do Sol 1
Recanto da Fortaleza 10
Recanto do Frances 7
Ronaldo's 11
Trilha do Sol 13

 from the jetty or five minutes by boat. **Farol** and **Encantadas** are the liveliest and have the most accommodation, restaurants and nightlife. Encantadas is getting somewhat polluted nowadays, with the cesspits overflowing into open sewers in the wet.

Walking on Ilha do Mel A series of well-signposted trails lead throughout Ilha do Mel and its coast. The most walked are as follows: the **lighthouse trail from Farol beach** (20 minutes), which is paved but steep; the views are wonderful. The **Nova Brasília to Encantadas trail** (three hours) offers a series of beautiful views, paths through the forest and stretches of semi-deserted beach. However, once you reach the end of the trail, you will either have to return the same way or take a boat taxi around the rocks back to Nova Brasília. This involves clambering over rocks at the end of Praia Grande; take appropriate footwear. The **Nova Brasília to Fortaleza trail** takes 1½ hours. It is also possible to take a long day walking around the entire island (apart from the stretch between Encantadas and Nova Brasília which requires a boat taxi).

Superagüi National Park

The island of **Superagüi** and its neighbour, **Ilha das Peças** lie at the heart of the largest single stretch of Atlantic Coast rainforest in the country and are the focus for the Guaraqueçaba Environmental Protection Area which is part of the **Nature Conservancy's Parks in Peril Programme** ⓘ *http://parksinperil.org*. They also form a national park and UNESCO World Heritage Site. Access to the park and accommodation can be arranged through the village on Superagüi beach, just north of Ilha do Mel. Many endangered endemic plants and animals live in the park, including hundreds of endemic orchids, Atlantic rainforest specific animals like brown howler monkeys and large colonies of red-tailed Amazons (a parrot on the Red list of critically endangered species and which can be seen nowhere else but here). There are also rare neotropical animals here like jaguarundi, puma and jaguar. There are several Guarani villages in the area; other inhabitants are mostly of European descent, living off fishing.

Iguaçu Falls

→ *Colour map 5, A2. Phone code 45.*

As Cataratas do Iguaçu ⓘ *www.fozdoiguaçu.pr.gov.br* (Iguazú in Spanish), are the most overwhelming and spectacular waterfalls in the world and one of Brazil's unmissable sights. Situated on the Rio Iguaçu (meaning big water in Guaraní), the border between Argentina and Brazil, they are made up of no less than 275 separate waterfalls. The Paraguayan city of Ciudad del Este is a few kilometres but that country does not share territory on the falls themselves.

The Caiagangue people originally inhabited the region, but the first European visitor to the falls was the Spaniard Alvaro Núñez Cabeza de Vaca in 1541. He nearly fell off one of the waterfalls on his search for a connection between the Brazilian coast and the Río de la Plata, and named them the Saltos de Santa María. Though the falls were well known to the Jesuit missionaries, they were forgotten, except by local inhabitants, until the area was explored by a Brazilian expedition sent out by the Paraguayan president, Solano López, in 1863.

To get the most out of Iguaçu be sure to visit both the Brazilian and Argentinian side.

The most spectacular part is the **Garganta del Diablo** (Devil's Throat), visited from the Argentine side (see Ins and Outs below), the mouth of a 28-km-long gorge which stretches downstream to the Alto Río Paraná.

Viewed from below, the water tumbles and roars over the craggy brown cliffs, framed by verdant rainforest encrusted with bromeliads, orchids, begonias and dripping ferns. A seemingly perpetual rainbow hovers over the scene and toco toucans, flocks of parakeets, caciques and great dusky swifts dodge in and out of the vapour whilst myriad butterflies dance over the forest walkways and lookouts.

Ins and outs

Around 80% of the falls lie in Argentina, which offers the most spectacular views and the best infrastructure. There are national parks protecting extensive rainforest on both sides. Transport between the two parks is via the **Ponte Tancredo Neves**, as there is no crossing at the falls themselves. **Tourist facilities** on both sides are constantly being improved.

Between October and February Brazil is one hour ahead of Argentina and, from December, two hours ahead of Paraguay. The best time to visit is in summer when the water levels are highest.

The **Brazilian park** offers a superb panoramic view of the whole falls and is best visited in the morning (four hours is enough for the highlights) when the light is better for photography. The **Argentine park** (which requires at least half a day) is incredible value, and includes a railway trip in the entrance fee as well as offering closer views of the individual falls. To appreciate the forest with its wildlife and butterflies properly you need to spend a full day and get well away from the visitors areas. Both parks can, if necessary, be visited in a day, starting at about 0700, but, in the heat, the brisk pace needed for a rapid tour is exhausting for the non-athletic. Sunset from the Brazilian side is a worthwhile experience.

Busiest times are holiday periods and on Sunday, when helicopter tours over the falls from the Brazilian side are particularly popular. Both parks have visitor's centres, though the information provided by the Argentine centre is far superior to that in the Brazilian centre.

There are many advantages in staying in Foz and commuting to the Argentine side (a bigger choice of hotels and restaurants, for example). Whichever side you decide to stay on, most establishments will accept reais, pesos or dollars. Cross-border transport usually accepts guaraníes as well.

A useful guidebook is *Iguazú, The Laws of the Jungle* (in Spanish, *Iguazú, las leyes de la selva*), by Santiago G de la Vega, Contacto Silvestre Ediciones (1999), available from the visitor's centre.

Clothing In the rainy season, when water levels are high, waterproof coats or swimming costumes are advisable for some of the lower catwalks and for boat trips. Cameras should be carried in a plastic bag. Wear shoes with good soles, as the rocks can be very slippery in places.

Parque Nacional Foz do Iguaçu (Brazil)

The Brazilian National Park was founded in 1939 and designated a World Heritage Site by UNESCO in 1986. The park covers 185,262 ha on the Brazilian side and 67,000 ha on the Argentinian side, extending along the north bank of the Rio Iguaçu, then sweeping northwards to Santa Tereza do Oeste on the BR-277. The subtropical rainforest benefits from the added humidity in the proximity of the falls, creating an environment rich in vegetation and fauna. Given the massive popularity of the falls, the national parks on either side of the frontier are surprisingly little visited.

The Brazilian side of the falls is closed on Monday until 1300 for maintenance.

Fauna The parks on both sides of the falls are replete with wildlife and are a haven for birders. The most common mammals seen are coatis, which look like long-nosed racoons and squeakily demand food from visitors; do not be tempted as these small animals can be aggressive. There are other mammals here too, including jaguar, puma, ocelot and margay, which can occasionally be seen along the park roads just before and after dawn. They are wary of humans, although in 2003 a jaguar broke into the Parque das Aves (see page 306) and ate the zoo's prize caiman. Most frequently encountered are little and red brocket deer, white-eared opossum, *paca* (which look like a large dappled guinea pig) and a subspecies of the brown capuchin monkey.

Other mammals present include white-lipped peccary, bush dog and southern river otter. The endangered tegu lizard is common. Over 100 species of butterflies have been identified, among them the electric blue *morpho*, the poisonous red and black *heliconius* and species of *Papilionidae* and *Pieridae*.

The birdlife is especially rewarding for birdwatchers. Five members of the toucan family can be seen: toco and red-breasted toucans, chestnut-eared araçari, saffron and spot-billed toucanets. In the bamboo stands you may see spotted bamboo wren, grey-bellied spinetail, several antshrikes, short-tailed ant-thrush. In the forest you might see rufous-thighed kite, black-and-white hawk-eagle, black-fronted piping-guan, blue ground dove, dark-billed cuckoo, black-capped screech-owl, surucua trogon, rufous-winged antwren, black-crowned tityra, red-ruffed fruitcrow, white-winged swallow, plush-crested jay, cream-bellied gnatcatcher, black-goggled and magpie tanagers, green-chinned euphonia, black-throated and utlramarine grosbeaks, yellow-billed cardinal, red-crested finch. (Bird and mammal information supplied by Douglas Trent, **Focus Tours**; see Tours and tour operators, page 23.)

The falls ⓘ *All cars and public buses stop at the Visitors' Centre, where there are souvenir shops, a Banco do Brasil ATM and câmbio (1300-1700), a small café and car park. If possible, visit on a weekday when the walks are less crowded, daily 0800-1700. 10 reais – US$3 – car parking fee, payable only in Brazilian currency; transfer made to free park shuttle bus.*
First stop with the shuttle bus is **Macuco Safari**, US$33 (bookable through most agencies, which may charge a premium for transfers). The safari takes one hour 45 minutes, leaving every 15 minutes and is highly recommended (see box page 304).

Iguaçu Falls orientation

Second stop with the bus is the **Cataratas Trail** (starting from the hotel of the same name, non-residents can eat at the hotel, midday and evening buffets). This 1½-km paved walk runs part of the way down the cliff near the rim of the falls, giving a stupendous view of the whole Argentine side of the falls. It ends up almost under the powerful **Floriano Falls**; from here an elevator used to carry visitors to the top of the Floriano Falls but has not been functioning recently; a path adjacent to the elevator leads to Porto Canoa. A catwalk at the foot of the Floriano Falls gives a good view of the **Garganta do Diabo**.

Helicopter tours over the falls leave from the **Hotel das Cataratas**, ⓘ *US$60 per person, 10 minutes. Booked through any travel agency or direct with Helisul, T5231190*. Apart from disturbing visitors, the helicopters are also reported to present a threat to some bird species which are laying thinner-shelled eggs: the altitude has been increased, making the flight less attractive.

The **Porto Canoas** complex, with its snack bar, souvenir shops and terraces with views of the falls, was completed in 2000 after some controversy. Its restaurant serves a US$12 buffet. Highly recommended for a memorable meal. There are toilets here.

Parque Nacional Iguazú (Argentina)

Created in 1934, the park extends over an area of 67,620 ha, most of which is covered by the same subtropical rainforest as on the Brazilian side. It is crossed by Route 101, a dirt road which runs southeast to Bernardo de Yrigoyen on the Brazilian frontier. Buses operate along this route in dry weather, offering a view of the park.

Fauna You would have to be very lucky to see jaguars, tapirs, brown capuchin monkeys, collared anteaters and coatimundi. As in Brazil, very little of the fauna in the park can be seen around the falls; even on the nature trails described below you need to go in the early morning. Of the more than 400 species of birds, you are most likely to spot the following: black-crowned night heron, plumed kite, white-eyed parakeet, blue-winged parrolet, great dusky swift, scale-throated hermit, suruca trogon, Amazon kingfisher, toco toucan, tropical kingbird, boat-billed flycatcher, red-rumped cacique, and the colourful purple-throated euphonia.

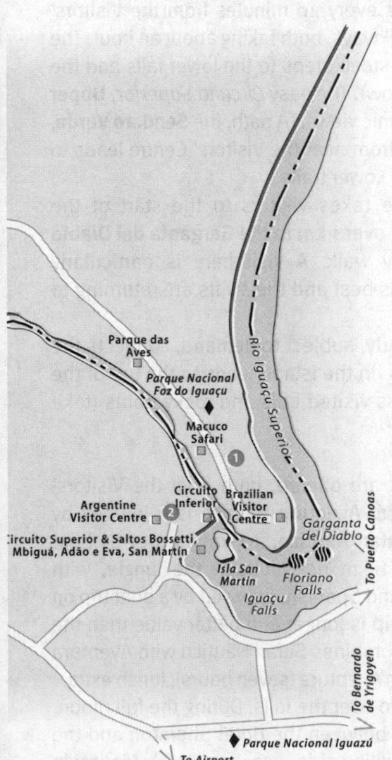

The falls ⓘ *The park is open 0800-1900 every day. Entry US$5, payable in pesos or dollars (but not reais). Guests at Hotel Sheraton should pay and get tickets stamped at the hotel to avoid paying again. The Visitors' Centre includes a museum of local fauna and an auditorium for periodic slide shows (on request, minimum 8 people), no commentary, only music; it also sells a good guide book on Argentine birds. Food and drinks are available in the park but are expensive, so it is best to take your own. There is also a Telecom kiosk at the bus stop.*

The Macuco Safari

Electric vehicles take visitors to the start of a short, steep trail (those with walking difficulties can be driven the whole way). After about 20 minutes' ride on the trailer, you get off and begin hiking your way down the side of the Iguaçu gorge to the Macuco Falls, which cascade into a deep dark plunge pool. Steps cut into the rock allow you to descend to the foot of the falls, but beware, they are slippery and steep (take stout walking shoes). The tour is taken at a relaxed pace and there is no pressure to rush back up those steps. After the falls, you descend to the banks of the river, where you take to water in inflatable rafts capable of carrying 20 people. The ride is bumpy, but make sure you look up at the steep sides of the gorge. As the boat comes up to the edge of the falls, there is a deafening roar from above as the boat begins to turn and the spray is so powerful you have to shut your eyes. You will get very wet. Plastic raincoats are sold at the launch site and plastic bags are provided for cameras if you ask. The view of the falls is unbeatable. Once back on dry land, you are whisked up to the top of the canyon by jeep to rejoin the trailer to the entrance. From here, a free shuttle bus transfers you through the park to the top of the falls.

Guides speak Portuguese, English and Spanish; take insect repellent. **Macuco Safari**, Rodovia das Cataratas Km 22, T5296263, macucosafari@foznet.com.br.

A free train service completed in 2001 leaves every 20 minutes from the Visitors' Centre, departing for the start of two sets of walkways, both taking about an hour. The *Circuito Inferior*, **Lower Trail**, leads down very steep steps to the lower falls and the start of the boat trip to Isla San Martin (see below). The easy *Circuito Superior*, **Upper Trail**, follows the top of the falls, giving panoramic views. (A path, the **Sendero Verde**, taking about 20 minutes from near the Visitors' Centre leads to the start of the Upper and Lower trails.)

The catwalks and platform get very crowded in mid-morning after tour buses arrive.

A second train route takes visitors to the start of the walkway which leads just over 1 km to the **Garganta del Diablo** (Devil's Throat), an easy walk. A visit here is particularly recommended in the evening when the light is best and the swifts are returning to roost on the cliffs, some behind the water.

Below the falls, a free ferry leaving regularly, subject to demand, connects the Lower Trail with **Isla San Martín**. A steep path on the island leads to the top of the hill, where there are trails to some of the less-visited falls and rocky pools (take bathing gear in summer).

Tours and activities A number of activities are offered, both from the Visitors' Centre and through agencies in Puerto Iguazú. **Aventura Náutica** is a journey by launch along the lower Río Iguazú, US$15. **Safari Náutico**, a 4-km journey by boat above the falls, US$15. **Gran Aventura**, an 8-km ride through the jungle, with commentary on the flora and fauna in English and Spanish, followed by a boat trip on the rapids to the Devil's Throat, US$33. This trip is longer and better value than the Macuco Safari on the Brazilian side. **Full Day** combines Safari Náutico with Aventura Náutica, US$30 (five hours), or US$45 with Gran Aventura (seven hours), lunch extra.

On clear nights the moon casts a blue halo over the falls. During the full moon, there are sometimes night-time walking tours between the **Hotel Sheraton** and the falls (as there are from the **Tropical** on the Brazilian side – see page 311). **Mountain bikes** and **boats** can also be hired at US$3 per hour. For serious **birdwatching** and

nature walks with an English-speaking guide, contact Daniel Samay (**Explorador** agency) or **Miguel Castelino** ⓘ *Aptdo Postal 22, Puerto Iguazú (3370), Misiones, T420157, FocusTours@aol.com*. Highly recommended.

Iguaçu Falls

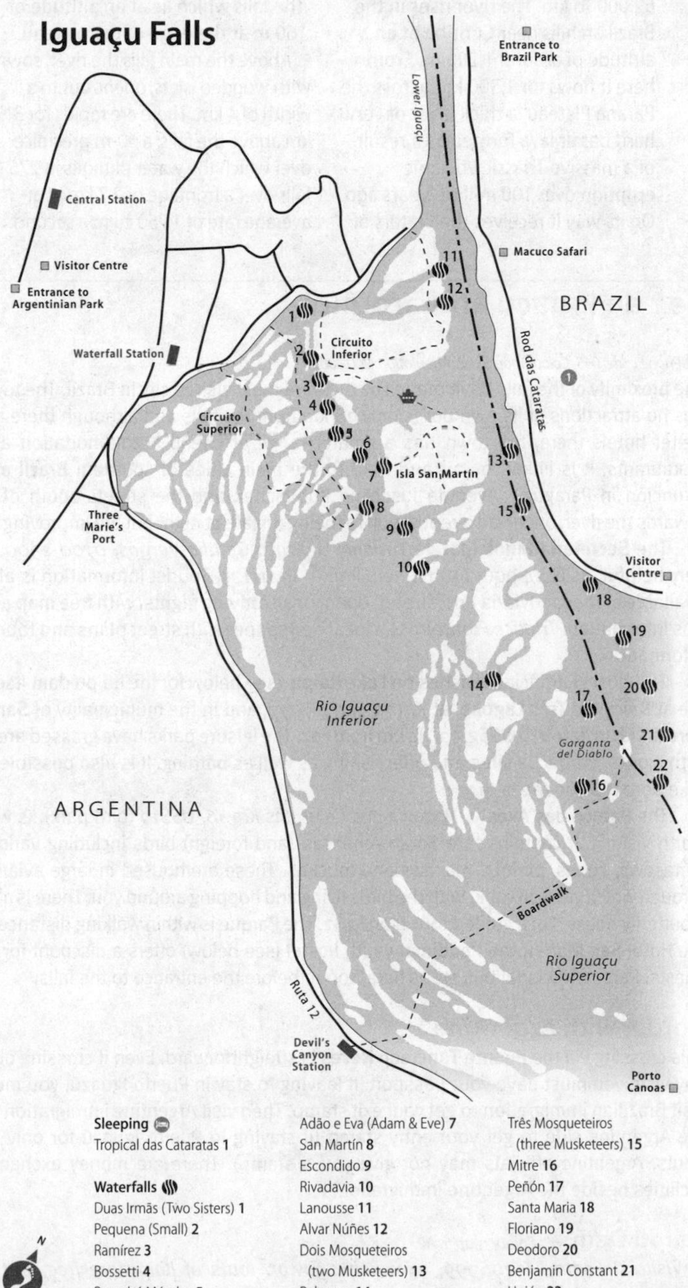

Sleeping
Tropical das Cataratas 1

Waterfalls
Duas Irmãs (Two Sisters) 1
Pequena (Small) 2
Ramírez 3
Bossetti 4
Bernabé Méndez 5
Mbiguá 6
Adão e Eva (Adam & Eve) 7
San Martín 8
Escondido 9
Rivadavia 10
Lanousse 11
Alvar Núñes 12
Dois Mosqueteiros (two Musketeers) 13
Belgrano 14
Três Mosqueteiros (three Musketeers) 15
Mitre 16
Peñón 17
Santa Maria 18
Floriano 19
Deodoro 20
Benjamin Constant 21
Unión 22

Water features

The Iguaçu river basin extends over 62,000 sq km. The river rises in the Brazilian hills near Curitiba at an altitude of around 1,200 m. From here it flows for 1,300 km across the Paraná Plateau, a thick layer of very hard basalt lava formed as a result of a massive Triassic volcanic eruption over 100 million years ago. On its way it receives the waters of about 30 rivers before reaching the falls which lie at an altitude of 160 m at the edge of the plateau.

Above the main falls the river, sown with wooded islets, opens out to a width of 4 km. There are rapids for 3½ km above the falls: a 60-m precipice over which the water plunges in 275 falls over a frontage of 2.7 km at an average rate of 1,750 cu m a second.

Foz do Iguaçu and around

→ *Phone code: 045. Colour map 5, A2. Population: 260,000.*

The proximity of the falls have made Foz the third most visited city in Brazil. The town has no attractions of its own but is only 28 km from the falls and although there are better hotels there, the town has a greater range of cheap accommodation and restaurants. It is linked by air and road to the main cities of southern Brazil and Asunción in Paraguay. Avenida Juscelino Kubitschek and the streets south of it, towards the river, once had a reputation for being unsafe at night but are improving.

The **Secretaria Municipal de Turismo** ⓘ *Praça Getulio Vargas, 0700-2300*, is very helpful, as is 24-hour tourist help line ⓘ *T5211125*. Tourist information is also available at the rodoviária and airport, open for all arriving flights, with free map and bus information. *Triplice Fronteira* is a local newspaper with street plans and tourist information.

The closest artificial beaches on **Lake Itaipu** (see below for the Itaipu dam itself) are at **Bairro de Três Lagoas**, at Km 723 on BR-277, and in the municipality of **Santa Terezinha do Itaipu** ⓘ *US$2.50*, 34 km from Foz. The leisure parks have grassed areas with kiosks, barbecue sites and offer fishing as well as bathing. It is also possible to take boat trips on the lake.

The **Parque das Aves** ⓘ *Rodovia das Cataratas Km 16, US$10* (bird park), is well worth visiting. It contains rare South American (and foreign) birds including various currasows, guans, parrots, macaws and toucans. These are housed in large aviaries through which you can walk, with the birds flying and hopping around you. There is also a butterfly house. For a guided tour T5298282. The Parque is within walking distance of the **Hotel San Martin**; the **Paudimar** youth hostel (see below) offers a discount for its guests. Parque Nacional bus stops here, 100 m before the entrance to the falls.

Border with Argentina

This crossing via the **Puente Tancredo Neves** is straightforward. Even if crossing on a day visit, you must have your passport. If leaving to stay in Puerto Iguazú, you must visit Brazilian immigration to get your exit stamp. Then visit Argentine immigration on the Argentine side to get your entry stamp (if staying in Puerto Iguazú for only 24 hours, Argentine officials may not give you a stamp). There are money exchange facilities beside the Argentine immigration.

Itaipu Dam → *Colour map 5, A2.*

ⓘ *Visitors' Centre, T5206999, www.itaipu.gov.br, tours of Itaipu are free, but in groups only, Mon-Sat at 0800, 0900, 1000, 1400, 1530 (closed between 1100 and 1400); 'technical' visits can be arranged.*

The Itaipu Dam, on the Río Paraná, is the site of the largest single power station in the world built jointly by Brazil and Paraguay. Construction of this massive scheme began in 1975 and it came into operation in 1984. The main dam is 8 km long, creating a lake which covers 1,400 sq km. The height of the main dam is equivalent to a 65-storey building, the amount of concrete used in its construction is 15 times more than that used for the Channel Tunnel between England and France. The 18 turbines have an installed capacity of 12,600,000 Kw and produce about 75 billion Kwh a year, providing 80% of Paraguay's electricity and 25% of Brazil's. The Paraguayan side may be visited from Ciudad del Este. Both governments are proud to trumpet the accolade, 'one of the seven wonders of the modern world' (the only one in South America), which was given to it by the American Society of Civil Engineering in *Popular Mechanics* in 1995. Whatever your views on the need for huge hydroelectric projects, it is worth visiting Itaipu to gain a greater understanding of the scale and impact of such constructions.

Be sure you know when the last bus departs from Puerto Iguazú for Foz (usually 2000) and remember that in summer Argentina is one hour ahead of Brazil.

The **Ecomuseu de Itaipu** ⓘ *Av Tancredo Neves, Km 11, T5205813, Tue-Sat 0900-1100, 1400-1700, Mon 1400-1700*, and **Iguaçu Environmental Education**

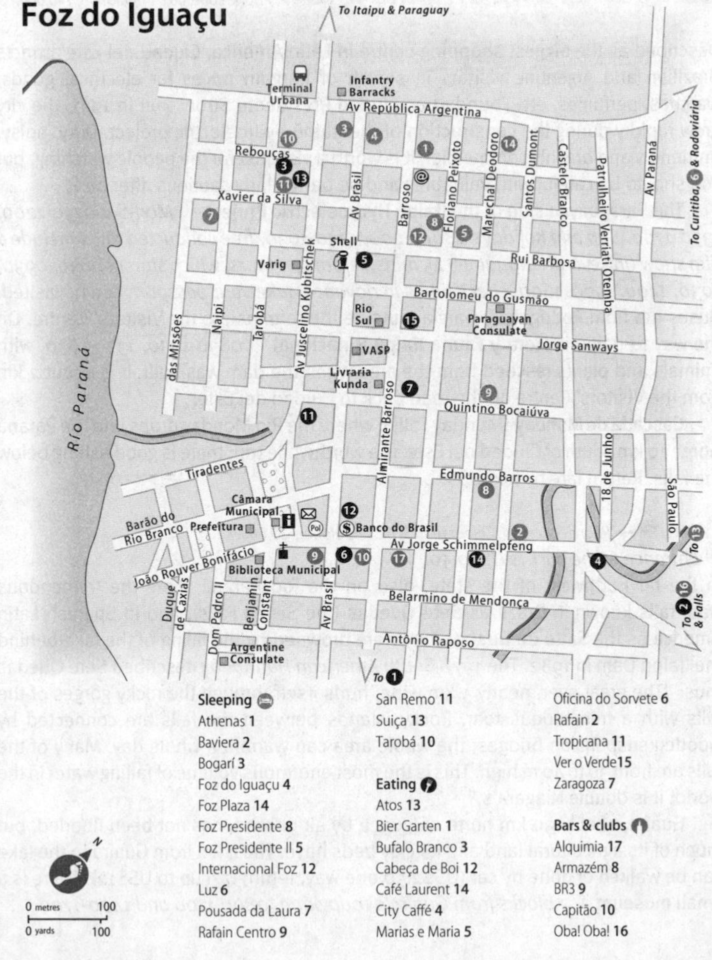

 Centre ⓘ *free with guide, recommended*, are geared to inform about the preservation of the local culture and environment, or that part of it which isn't underwater. A massive reforestation project is underway, and over 14 million seedlings have already been planted. Six biological refuges have been created on the lakeshore.

If it's sunny go in the morning as the sun is behind the dam in the afternoon and you will get poor photographs. The Visitors' Centre has a short video presentation (ask for the English version) with stunning photography and amazing technical information, apparently available in English but usually only in Portuguese. The spillways are capable of discharging the equivalent of 40 times the average flow of the Iguaçu Falls. If you are lucky, the spillways will be open. After the film and a brief visit to the souvenir shop where an English guidebook is available, a coach will take you to the dam itself. As it crosses the top, you get a stomach-churning view of the spillways and really begin to appreciate the scale of the project.

To get to Itaipu, the 'executive' bus and agency tours are an unnecessary expense. Buses No 110 or 120 from Terminal Urbana (stand 50 Batalhão) go every 13 minutes to the Public Relations office at the main entrance (US$0.40).

Ciudad del Este and around → *Phone code: 061. Population: 140,000.*

Described as the biggest shopping centre in Latin America, Ciudad del Este attracts Brazilian and Argentine visitors in search of bargain prices for electrical goods, watches, perfumes, etc. Founded as Ciudad Presidente Stroessner in 1957, the city grew rapidly during the construction of the Itaipú hydroelectric project. Dirty, noisy, unfriendly and brashly commercial, it is worth a visit just for the people watching, but you should be careful with valuables and be particularly cautious after dark.

The Paraguayan side of the **Itaipú Hydroelectric Project** ⓘ *Mon-Sat 0730-1200, 1330-1700, Sun and holidays 0800-1200, 1330-1630, free conducted tours include a film show (in several languages) 45 mins before bus tours, which start at 0830, 0930, 1030, 1400, 1500, 1600, check times in advance, take your passport*, can be visited. Buses run from Rodríguez y García, outside the terminal, to the Visitors' Centre. On the way to Itaipú is **Flora y Fauna Itaipú Binacional** ⓘ *0830-1030, 1330-1630*, with animals and plants rescued from the area when the dam was built. It is about 2 km from the Visitors' Centre on the road back to Cuidad del Este.

Cascada de Monday (Monday Falls), where the Río Monday drops into the Paraná Gorge 10 km south of Ciudad del Este, is a worthwhile trip; there is good fishing below the falls. Return fare by taxi US$20.

Guaíra → *Phone code: 044. Colour map 5, A2. Population: 29,000.*

ⓘ *Entrance to the park is US$0.50.*

In the far northwest of the state, also on the Rio Paraná, were the tremendous waterfalls known in Brazil as **Sete Quedas** (the Seven Falls), and in Spanish Latin America as the **Salto de Guaíra**; they were drowned by the filling of the lake behind the Itaipu Dam in 1982. The 1978 *South American Handbook* described Sete Quedas thus: "The great river, nearly 5 km wide, hurls itself through the rocky gorges of the falls with a tremendous roar. Rocky islands between the falls are connected by wooden suspension bridges; the whole area can warrant a whole day. Many of the falls are from 30 to 40 m high. This is the most enormous volume of falling water in the world; it is double Niagara's."

Guaíra, about 130 km north of Iguaçu by air or road, has not been flooded, but much of its agricultural land and its clay beds have. The 4 km from Guaíra to the lake can be walked or done by car (US$2.50 one way, return taxi up to US$12). There is a small **museum** ⓘ *3 blocks from Guaíra's rodoviária, 0800-1100 and 1400-1700*.

Shop till you drop

Though hardly on every traveller's list of destinations, Ciudad del Este is worth a visit if you are in the area. As you enter the city across the bridge from Brazil you see hunched figures struggling back into Brazil, dwarfed by the massive bags strapped on their backs. Nearing the border control, many bundle their bags over the side of the bridge, jump down on to the riverbank after them and clamber back up the slope with their valuables, undoubtedly worth more than the US$150 allowed duty-free by the law, but unchecked by the customs officers who watch the spectacle with disinterest.

The streets of the city itself are narrow and congested. On every side you are bombarded by street vendors trying to convince you to buy steak knives, hair clippers, massaging hair brushes, sweatshirts..., the list is endless and is accompanied by a cacophony of shouting in Spanish, Portuguese, Guaraní and English. To get a more distant view of the action, try the Fleur de Lys bar on the main street: it accepts almost any currency, offers a good range of drinks and snacks and allows you to watch Ciudad del Este in action down below.

Border with Paraguay

Immigration and transport There is an hourly passenger ferry service from Porto de Lanchas and Porto Guaíra to Salto del Guayra on the Paraguayan side, US$0.50, and an hourly car ferry from Porto Guaíra (US$4 for car with two people). The car ferry runs until 1830 (Brazilian time). Customs and immigration for documentation close at 1700. There is a time change when you cross the Paraná. The area is intensively patrolled for contraband and stolen cars, ensure that all documentation is in order.

Sleeping

Curitiba *p292, map p294, phone code 041*
General information: www.ondehospedar.com.br/pr/curitiba.php and www.cmoraes.com.br/webhotelshtml/curitiba.shtml. There are good hotels southeast of the centre in the vicinity of the rodoferroviária, but the cheaper ones are seedy and close to the wholesale market, which operates noisily throughout the night.

AL Bourbon & Tower, R Cândido Lopes 102, T3224001, www.bourbon.com.br. One of the better modern hotels in the centre with a mock old-fashioned charm engendered by wood panelling and fake period furniture. Rooms have jacuzzis. Business facilities.

AL Grand Hotel Rayon, R Visconde de Nacar, T30276006, www.rayon.com.br. Centrally located, staidly decorated, but much the best option for business travellers; with all the expected services alongside a pool, saunas, well-equipped gym and travel agency.

AL Slaviero Palace, R Sen Alencar Guimarães, T3227271, www.hotelslaviero.com.br. The best of the 2nd-grade business hotels in the centre. Anonymously decorated but with a business centre and airport transfer.

A Mercure, R Emiliano Perneta 747, T2341212, www.accorhotels.com.br. Standard 2nd-grade business hotel in the centre with a pool and business centre.

B Del Rey, R Ermelino de Leão 18, T/F3223242, www.hoteldelrey.com.br. Central, upmarket yet relaxed, large rooms, good restaurant, gym. Good value. Recommended.

B Deville Express, R Amintas de Barros 73, T3228558, www.deville.com.br. New hotel in the city centre with a bar, small modest restaurant. All rooms a/c with fridge.

B Slaviero Braz, Av Luis Xavier 67, T/F3222829, www.hotelslaviero.com.br. Refurbished hotel in a 1940s building preserved as '*Patrimonio Histórico*'. Business facilities.

C **King's**, Av Silva Jardim 264, T3228315, F3232383. Good apartment hotel, secure. Highly recommended.

C **Lumini**, R Gen. Carneiro, T/F2645244, www.hotellumini.com.br. Good apartment hotel in a quiet street. All rooms have a/c.

C **Nova Lisboa**, Av 7 de Setembro 1948, T2641944. With breakfast, bargain for cheaper rates without breakfast. Recommended.

C **O'Hara**, R 15 de Novembro 770, T2326044. Good location, fan, excellent breakfast, parking.

C **Paraty**, R Riachueto 30, T2231355, www.hotelparati.com.br. Central, apartments with kitchen, with breakfast, clean, spacious, good.

C **Piccolo**, R Dr Faivre 87, T/F2647553, www.hospedare.com.br. Small, central hotel built in the 1990s. All rooms en suíte with fridge.

C **San Juan Marcassa**, Av 7 de Setembro 2516, T3220505, www.sanjuanhoteis.com.br. Central apartment hotel with business facilties.

C **Tourist Universo**, Praça Gen Osório 63, T3220099, F2235420. On one of the city's most attractive squares, in centre. Very smart for price, with sauna and pool. Intimate and excellent value. Recommended.

D **Cervantes**, R Alfredo Bufrem 66, T2229593. Central, small, but cosy.

D **Estação Palace**, R Des Westphalen 126, T3229840, F3245307. Excellent for price, 24-hr room service and internet, rather stark but immaculate. Recommended.

E **Hostel Roma**, Rua Barao do Rio Branco 805, T2242117, www.hostelroma.com.br. Smart newly opened hostel with 110 beds in single sex dorms. All have private bathrooms. Breakfast included in the price. With TV room, fax, internet and a member's kitchen.

E **Casa do Estudante Luterano Universitario**, R Pr Cavalcanti, T3243313. Good youth hostel. ISIC student card required.

E **Casa dos Estudantes**, Parque Passeio Público, north side. Clean, well kept hostel but with a 4-night minimum stay. ISIC student cards required.

E **Inca**, R João Negrão 370, T2238563. Price per person. Breakfast OK, clean, friendly, safe, German spoken, good.

E **Lusitano**, R João Negrão 420, T3232232. Basic but clean hostel with noisy front rooms.

F **Pensão PP**, R Gen Carneiro 657, T2631169. Basic, no breakfast.

Camping

Camping Clube do Brasil, BR-116, Km 84, 16 km in the direction of São Paulo, T3586634.

Morretes *p297, phone code 041*

General information: www.morretes.com.br.

B **Pousada Graciosa**, Estrada da Graciosa Km 8 (Porto da Cima village), T4621807, www.morretes.com.br/pousadagraciosa. Much the best in the area; some 10 km north of Morretes with simple but comfortable wooden chalets set in rainforest. No children under 12.

C **Pousada Cidreira**, R Romulo Pereira 61, T4621604. Centrally located with characterless but clean tiled rooms, most with balconies and all with TV and en suites. Some rooms have space for 3. Breakfast included.

D **Hotel Nhundiaquara**, R General Carneiro 13, T4621228, F4621267. A smart whitewashed building beautifully set on the river whose exterior appearance belies the hotel's poor service, gloomy public areas and very ordinary rooms. With breakfast.

Paranaguá *p297, phone code 041*

General information: www.paranagua.pr.gov.br.

AL **Hotel Camboa**, R João Estevão (Ponta do Caju), T4232121, www.hotelcamboa.com.br. Family resort with tennis courts, large pool, saunas, trampolines, restaurant and a/c rooms. Out of town near the port. Book ahead.

AL **São Rafael**, R Julia Costa 185, T4232123, www.sanrafaelhotel.com.br. Business hotel with plain tiled rooms, a business centre, restaurants, pool and jacuzzis in the en suites.

D **Pousada Itibere**, R Princesa Isabel 24, T4232485. Very smart spartan rooms with polished wood floors, some with sea views. Friendly service from the elderly Portuguese owner. Shared bathrooms (sex segregated). 3 blocks east of the boat dock.

D **Hotel Ponderosa**, R Pricilenco Corea 68 at 15 Novembro, T4232464. Tiled rooms with en suites, 1 block from the sea, some with a view. A block east and north of the boat dock.

Camping

Arco Iris, Praia de Leste, on the beach, 29 km south of Paranaguá, T4582001.

Ilha do Mel *p299, map p299, phone code 041*
General information: www.ilhadomelonline.com; www.pousadasilhadomel.com.br. All rooms are fan cooled unless otherwise stated.

You can rent a fisherman's house on Encantadas – ask for **Valentim's Bar**, or for Luchiano. Behind the bar is **Cabanas Dona Maria**, shared showers, cold water; food available if you ask in advance. Many *pousadas* and houses with rooms to rent (shared kitchen and living room). Shop around, prices from about US$10 double, low season, mid-week.

B Long Beach, Praia Grande, T99064040, www.lbeach.cjb.net. The best on this beach with comfortable chalets for up to 6 with en suites. Very popular with surfers. Book.

C Caranguata, Encantadas, T4269097/9998 7770, http://martinetas.sites.uol.com.br. A/c en suites in wood with fridges and Monet prints on walls. Recently opened. Very close to jetty.

C Dona Quinota, Fortaleza, T4236176. Little blue and cream cottages with polished wood floors and en suites. Right on the beach. 3 km from Nova Brasília. Price includes breakfast and supper. **Dona Clara** next door is very similar in yellow instead of blue.

C Enseada, Farol, T/F4268040. 4 rooms with en suites, TVs and fridges. Charmingly decorated. Lots of rescued cats.

C Por do Sol, Nova Brasília, T4268009, www.pousadapordosol.com.br. Simple but elegant en suite rooms in grey tile and wood around a garden shaded by sombrero trees. A large deck with hammock-strewn cabanas sits next to the beach. Includes breakfast.

C Recanto do Frances, Encantadas, T3543904. French owned and full of character, with each chalet built in a different style to represent a different French city. 5 mins from Prainha or Encantadas. Good crêpe restaurant.

D Aconchego, Nova Brasília, T4268030, http://clubmatrix.com.br/aconchego. 10 scrupulously clean rooms in a house behind an expansive beachside deck strewn with hammocks. Public TV and breakfast areas. Charming. Includes breakfast.

D Girassol, T4268006, heliosilva@onda.com.br. Wooden rooms with en suites in a little bougainvillea and fruit tree garden. Very close to jetty. Includes breakfast.

D Plancton, Farol at Fora, T/F4268061. A range of wooden buildings in a humming-bird filled garden. Rooms for 5 split over 2 levels. Wood and slate-tiled en suites for couples. Clean, fresh. Italian food available in high season.

D Recanto da Fortaleza, Ponta do Bicho, T2754455, www.ilhadomelpousada.com.br. The best of the 2 next to the fort. Basic cabins with en suites and tiled floors. Free pick-up by boat from Nova Brasília (ring ahead), bike rental. Price includes breakfast and dinner.

D Ronaldo's, Encantadas, T4269019. Simple rooms with private bathrooms. Friendly owner.

E D'Lua, Farol, T4268031. Basic and hippy with a very friendly new-age owner, Jo.

E Farol da Ilha, Nova Brasília, T4268017. Plain wood and terracotta tiled dorms and double rooms in a garden. Surfboards for rent. Price includes generous breaksfast.

E Trilha do Sol, Farol, T4268025. Simple wooden rooms with en suites.

Camping

There are mini campsites with facilities at **Encantadas, Farol** and **Brasília**. Camping is possible on the more deserted beaches (good for surfing). If camping, watch out for the tide, watch possessions and beware of the *bicho de pé* which burrows into feet (remove with a needle and alcohol) and the *borrachudos* (discourage with **Autan** repellent).

Iguaçu Falls *p300, maps p302 and p305, phone code 045*

Brazil

The best hotels with the most modern facilities and the easiest access to Iguaçu are all near the falls. There is little here for budget travellers.

L Hotel Tropical das Cataratas, directly overlooking the falls, 28 km from Foz, T5217000, www.tropicalhotel.com.br. The only hotel within the park on the Brazilian side is a mock belle époque building with slightly frayed rooms, grand public areas and a poolside garden visited by numerous birds, butterflies, and at dawn, occassional small mammals. The hotel is right next to the falls offering by far the easiest access and the chance to beat the crowds. Special offer and discounts are available for those who fly with **Varig**. Non-residents can eat here or drink cocktails in the pool garden. The international food is adequate, as good as any in town, but hardly dazzling. (Non-resident evening diners will be in the park after it closes and must take a taxi back to town.)

AL Bourbon Iguassu Golf Resort, Av das Cataratas 6845, Km 8.5, T529999, www.iguassugolf.com.br. A golf resort purpose-built in the 1990s. Accommodation is in bungalows with polished wood floors and standard 5-star catalogue furniture. The course has 18 holes and the resort has a pool, tennis courts and saunas. Tours of the falls can be booked from here. Some English is spoken.

E Paudimar Campestre, Av das Cataratas Km 12.5, Remanso Grande, near airport, T/F5722430, www.paudimar.com.br. Youth hostel with spotless dorms (sex segregated), pool, communal kitchen, football pitch, IYHA camping and gardens visited by myriad birds and occasional small mammals. Highly recommended. For assistance, ask for owner, Gladis. From airport or town take Parque Nacional bus (0525-0040) and get out at Remanso Grande bus stop, by **Hotel San Juan**, then take the free shuttle bus (0700-1900) to the hostel, or 1,200 m walk from main road. Breakfast included. Tours arranged. There's a **Paudimar** desk at the rodoviária. Only IYHA members in high season when the hostel gets very busy.

Camping

Pretty cold and damp in winter. Camping is not permitted by the Hotel das Cataratas and falls. Sleeping in your car inside the park is also prohibited.

Argentina

AL Sheraton Internacional Iguazú Resort, Parque Nacional Iguazú, Argentina, T+54-3757491800, www.starwood.com. A 1970s wedge of concrete built on the opposite side of the falls from the **Tropical**. Views are spectacular, especially out over the pool from the room balconies on the upper storey. But the falls are a 20-min walk from the hotel rather than on the doorstep as they are at the **Tropical**. Well maintained, well run. Baby-sitting service available.

Camping

Camping Puerto Canoas, 600 m from Puerto Canoas; tables, but no other facilities, nearest drinking water at park entrance.

Foz do Iguaçu *p306, map p305, phone code 045*

Many hotels offer excursions to the falls. In a bid to get their commission, touts may tell you the hotel of your choice no longer exists, or offer you room rates below what is actually charged. In high season (eg Christmas-New Year) you will not find a room under US$15, but in low season there are many good deals.

L Internacional Foz, R Alm Barroso 2006, T5214100, www.internacionalfoz.com.br. The only 5-star hotel in the region with excellent business and conference facilities and spacious but very standard upmarket hotel rooms and services.

A Rafain Centro, Mcal Deodoro 984, T/F5231213, www.rafaincentro.com.br. The smart and upmarket communal areas and attractive pool area belie the rather well-worn rooms.

B Baviera, Av Jorge Schimmelpfeng 697, T5235995, www.hotelbavieraiguassu.com.br. A mock Bavarian folly with a chalet-style exterior. On the main road; central for bars and restaurants. The gloomy rooms look as if they haven't been renovated since the 1980s.

B Suiça, Av Felipe Wandscheer 3580, T5253232, www.hotelsuica.com.br. Old 70s hotel with dark tiled rooms and a pool. Helpful Swiss manager.

C Bogarí, Av Brasil 106, T/F5232243, www.bogarihotel.com.br. Restful atmosphere, large pool with pleasant walled terrace, central, in shopping street.

C Foz do Iguaçu, Av Brasil 97, T5234455, hotelfoz@purenet.com.br. Another gloomy 70s monstrosity with faded rooms. But good value, and with large breakfasts included in the price.

C Foz Plaza Hotel, R Marechal Deodoro 1819, T/F5231448, www.challengerhoteis.com.br. Serene and well-refurbished 1980s hotel with a restaurant and a bar, swimming pool, fitness centre, sauna and a games room.

C Foz Presidente, R Xavier da Silva 1000, T/F5724450, www.fozpresidentehoteis.com.br. Restaurant, pool, with breakfast, convenient for buses. Brighter and more modern than most of Foz's offerings. Recommended.

C Foz Presidente II, R Mcal Floriano Peixoto 1851, T5232318, www.fozpresidentehoteis.

com.br. Smaller and a little more expensive than its sister hotel (with whom it shares leisure areas), but also with pool, bar and restaurant.

D Luz, Av Costa e Silva Km 5, near rodoviária, T5223535, www.luzhotel.com.br. Well-kept but bog standard small 1980s hotel with a buffet restaurant. Rooms have a/c and Brazilian TV. Recommended.

D Tarobá, R Tarobá 1048, T5239722, www.hoteltaroba.com.br. Good value. Clean with plain tiled a/c rooms, a tiny indoor pool and helpful staff. Recommended.

E Pousada da Laura, R Naipi 671, T5723374. Secure and run by the enthusiastic Laura who speaks some Spanish, English, Italian and French. The hostel has a kitchen, laundry facilities and en suites and is a good place to meet other travellers. Good breakfasts too.

E Pousada Evelina Navarrete, R Irlan Kalichewski 171, Vila Yolanda, T/F5743817, pousada.evelina@foznet.com.br. Lots of tourist information, internet, well-maintained dorms, doubles and singles (some with a/c) and good breakfast. English, French, Italian, Polish and Spanish spoken. Helpful staff with lots of useful tourist information and organized walks. Near Av Cataratas on the way to the falls – take a bus to Parque Nacional from the bus station and ask to be let off after 3.5 km, near the Chemin Supermarket. R Irlan Kalichewski is down the hill, 3 blocks towards the city on the left. Warmly recommended.

F Athenas, R Almte Barroso 2215 on corner of Rebouças, T5742563. Good value, special rates for backpackers, some rooms with shared bath, fan, breakfast extra, beers sold.

F San Remo, R Xavier da Silva 563 at Taroba, T5231619, roberto_171@hotmail.com. Scrupulously clean though small rooms with TVs and writing desks. All-you-can-eat breakfast. Englsih, Spanish and Hebrew spoken. In-house travel agency.

Camping

E Pousada Internacional, R Manêncio Martins 21, 1.5 km from Foz town, T5233053, www.campinginternacional.com.br. US$10 per person (half with International Camping Card), pool, clean, though basic cabins. Park vehicle or put tent away from trees in winter in case of heavy rainstorms, The food here is poor and the refectory closes at 2300.

Ciudad del Este *p308, phone code 061*

Accommodation is generally expensive.

A Convair, Adrián Jara y García, T500342. Comfortable business-style hotel with cheaper rooms without bath.

A Executive, Adrián Jara y Curupayty, T500942/3. Similar to **Convair** and with a good breakfast – restaurant recommended.

A Residence de la Tour, Paraná Country Club, 5 km from centre, T60316. Slickly run, smart Swiss-owned hotel in pleasant gardens and with a very nice pool. Excellent restaurant (US$12-16 per person).

B Catedral, C A López 838, several blocks from commercial area, T500378. Big modern block with a pool, a/c rooms and breakfast.

B San Rafael, Abay y Adrián Jara, T68134. Large rooms a/c rooms and breakfast, German and English spoken.

C Itaipú, Rodríguez y Nanawa, T500371. Small a/c rooms in need of a little care, with breakfast.

C Munich, Fernández y Miranda, T500347. Standard town block with a/c rooms, parking and breakfast.

C-D El Cid, Recalde 425, T512221. Simple a/c or cheaper fan-cooled rooms. With breakfast.

D Austria (also known as **Viena**), Fernández 165, above restaurant, T500883. With good breakfast and a/c, Austrian family, good views from upper floors. Warmly recommended.

E Caribe, Emiliano Fernández, opposite Austria. A/c rooms with hot-water showers set in a nice garden, helpful owner. Recommended.

Guaíra *p308, phone code 044*

A Deville, R Paraguai 1205, T/F6421617. Standard blocky Brazilian hotel which is nonetheless the best in town. With a restaurant and pool.

C Palace Hotel, Rui Barbosa 1190, near the rodoviária, T6421325. Simple, reasonably well looked after and convenient for the bus station.

D Majestic, opposite rodoviária. Rooms with or without bath and with breakfast, good.

For an explanation of the sleeping and eating price codes used in this guide, see the inside front cover. Other relevant information is provided in the Essentials chapter, pages 47 and 57.

Eating

Curitiba *p292, map p294, phone code 041*

Hot sweet wine is sold on the streets in winter to help keep out the cold.

TT **Boulevard**, R Vol da Pátria 539 (centre), T2248244. The city's most celebrated restaurant serving a mix of French, Italian and Brazilian cooking to a smart crowd. Reasonable wine list. Closed on Sun.

T **Baviera**, Alameda Augusto Stellfeld, at Av Dr Murici (centre), T2321995. A Curitiba institution, established over 30 years and serving pizza in an intimate beer cellar setting. Also deliver. Open 1830-0100.

T **Durski**, R Jaime Reis, 254 (centre), T2257893. Good Eastern European food, including a locally celebrated and lavish banquet of pâtés, borcht, *platzki*, filled pasties and a variety of meat dishes.

T **Green Life**, R Carlos de Carvalho 271 (centre), T2238490. Vegetarian buffet restaurant open for lunch only.

T **Happy Rango**, Av Visconde de Nacar 1350, near R 24 horas. Brightly lit, basic corner joint selling fast food and pizzas, open 24 hrs.

T **Kisco**, 7 de Setembro near Tibagi. Good, huge *prato do dia*, friendly.

T **Mister Sheik**, Av Vicente Machado 534. Arabic fast food in pitta with salad, popular for deliveries. Recommended.

T **Saccy**, R São Franscisco 350, at Mateus Leme. Pizza, tapas and a popular bar with live music, see Bars and clubs, below.

T **Salmão**, R Emiliano Perneta 924, T2252244. Restaurant in historic house, delicious fish and pizza, often special promotions, live music every night, open until 0100. Short taxi ride from centre.

There are a couple of **lanchonetes** in the market which is close to the rodoferroviária. Also good meals in the bus station.

Morretes *p297, phone code 041*

T **Armazém Romanus**, R Visc do Rio Branco 141, T4621500. Family-run restaurant with the best menu and wine list in the region. Dishes from home-grown ingredients include excellent *barreado* and flambéed desserts.

T **Madalozo**, R Alm Frederico de Oliveira 16, overlooking the river, T4621410. Good *barreado* and generous salads at a cheap price.

T **Terra Nossa**, R XV Novembro 109, T4622174. *Barreado*, pasta pizzas and fish. Middle of the road but generous portions and a small wine list. From R$25 for a 2-person *prato da casa*.

Paranaguá *p297, phone code 041*

The choice here is poor.

TT **Danúbio Azul**, R XV Novembro 95, T4233255, www.restaurantedaxcnubioazul.com.br. The best in town – a range of fish and chicken dishes, pastas and pizzas; all in enormous quantities. 1 block back from the sea at the east end of town.

TT **Divina Gula**, R XV Novembro 165, T4222788 (until 1400 only). Seafood buffet and *feijoada* at weekends. 3 blocks east of the Ilha do Mel dock.

T **Restaurant Rosa**, R Praia 16, T4232162. Cheap but decent seafood including good risotto. A block west of the Ilha do Mel dock.

Ilha do Mel *p299, map p299, phone code 041*

Many *pousadas* also serve food – some only in season (Christmas-Carnaval). Many have live music or dancing (especially in high season). Things kick off after 2200.

TT **Fim da trilha**, Prainha (Fora de Encantadas), T4269017. Spanish seafood restaurant. One of the best on the island.

T **Colmeia**, Farol, T4268029. Snacks, crêpes and good cakes and puddings.

T **Mar e Sol**, Farol, T4268021, www.restaurantemaresol.com. Huge portions of fish, chicken all with chips and rice and a small selection of more adventurous dishes like bass in shrimp sauce.

T **Recanto do Frances**, Encantadas. French crêpes and Moroccon cou cous.

T **Toca do Abutre**, Farol. Live music and the usual huge portions of fish or chicken with rice, beans and chips.

T **Zorro**, Encantadas. One of several cheap fish, beans and rice seafront palapa-shaded restaurants. *Forró* dancing in the evenings.

Foz do Iguaçu *p306, map p305, phone code 045*

TTT **Bufalo Branco**, R Rebouças 530, T5239744, superb all-you-can-eat *churrasco*, includes *filet mignon*, salad bar and dessert. Sophisticated surroundings and attentive service. Highly recommended.

TTT **Cabeça de Boi**, Av Brasil 1325, T5232100.

Churrascaria with live music and a buffet, coffee and pastries also.

¥¥¥ **Rafain**, Av das Cataratas, Km 6.5, T5231177, closed Sun. Set price for excellent buffet with folkloric music and dancing (2100-2300) from throughout South America, touristy but very entertaining. Out of town, take a taxi or arrange with travel agency. Recommended.

¥¥¥ **Tropical das Cataratas**, the nearest dining to the falls themselves (see p311).

¥¥¥ **Zaragoza**, R Quintino Bocaiúva 882, T5743084. Large and upmarket, for Spanish dishes and seafood. Respectable wine list. Recommended.

¥¥ **Atos**, Av Juscelino Kubitschek 865, T5722785. Per kilo buffet with various meats, salads, sushi and puddings. Lunch only.

¥¥ **Bier Garten**, Almirante Barroso 550, a bustling pizzaria and *choperia*.

¥¥ **Tropicana**, Av Juscelino Kubitschek 228. All-you-can-eat pizza or *churrascaria* with a salad bar, good value.

¥ **Café Laurent**, Av Jorge Schimmelpfeng 550, T5746666, smart student café serving decent tea, coffee, cakes and pies.

¥ **City Caffé**, Av Jorge Schimmelpfeng 898. Stylish café open daily 0800-2330 for sandwiches, Arabic snacks and pastries.

¥ **Marias e Maria**, Av Brasil 50. Good *confeitaria*.

¥ **Oficina do Sorvete**, Av Jorge Schimmelpfeng, 244 daily 1100-0100. Excellent ice creams, a popular local hang-out.

¥ **Ver o Verde**, R. Almirante Barroso 1713, T5745647. Buffet vegetarian food with some white meat and fish. Great value. Lunch only.

Ciudad del Este *p308, phone code 061*

Most restaurants close on Sun. Cheaper restaurants can be found along García and in the market.

¥¥ **Coreio**, San Blas 125. Good Korean food.

¥¥ **Hotel Austria/Viena** (see above). Good Austrian food in large portions.

¥ **Mi Ranchero**, on Adrián Jara. Good food, service and prices, well known.

Bars and clubs

Curitiba *p292, map p294, phone code 041*

A cluster of bars at the square of **Largo da Ordem** have tables and chairs on the pavement, music which tends to be rock, and bar food: **Fire Fox**, Av Jaime Reis 46, flanked by **Tuba's** and **The Farm**. **London Pub**, São Francisco 350, São Francisco. Recommended. **Rua 24 Horas** is an indoor street with very similar, functional bars and cafés, open 24 hrs. **Saccy**, R São Franscisco, 350, corner with Mateus Leme, 12. Pizza, tapas and lively bar with live music.

Foz do Iguaçu *p306, map p305, phone code 045*

Bars, all doubling as restaurants, concentrated on **Av Jorge Schimmelpfeng** for 2 blocks from Av Brasil to R Mal Floriano Peixoto. Wed-Sun are best nights; crowd tends to be young. **Alquimia**, Av Jorge Schimmelpfeng 334, T5723154. Popular nightclub, attached, 2400-0500, US$3. **Armazém**, R Edmundo de Barros 446, intimate and sophisticated, attracts discerning locals, good atmosphere, mellow live music, US$1 cover. Recommended. **BR3**, Av Jorge Schimmelpfeng corner with Av Brasil. Modern, open until 2400. **Capitão Bar** Av Jorge Schimmelpfeng 288 and Almte Barroso, T5721512. Large, loud and popular, nightclub attached. **Oba! Oba!**, Av das Cataratas 3700, T5742255 (Antigo Castelinho). Live samba show Mon-Sat 2315-0015, very popular, US$9 for show and 1 drink. **Rafain**, Av das Cataratas Km 6.5. With floor show and food, see p315.

Entertainment

Curitiba *p292, map p294, phone code 041*

Best to look In the newspaper for music and what's on in the bars, clubs and theatres. *Gazeta do Povo* has an arts and what's on section called *Caderno G*.

Cinema

Shopping Center Água Verde, T2428741. **Shopping Crystal**, R Comendador Araújo 731, T3233061, and other places show films from all over the world. **Shopping Curitiba**, Praça Oswaldo Cruz 2698, T3261412. **Shopping Novo Batel**, T2222107. Tickets are usually US$4-5 Mon-Thu, US$6-8 at weekends.

Theatre

Teatro Guaíra, R 15 de Novembro, T3222628. Plays and revues (also has free events – get tickets early in the day). **Teatro Paiol**, in the old arsenal, R Col Zacarias, T3221525. **Ópera de Arame**, R João Gava, T2529637; **Opera house**. **Teatro Universitário de Curitiba** (TUC). **Teatro Novelas Curitibanas**, R Carlos Cavalcanti 1222, T2338552. **Teatro Fernanda Montenegro**, Shopping Novo Batel, T2244986.

Foz do Iguaçu *p306, map p305, phone code 045*

Casinos Organized tours to casinos (illegal in Brazil) over the border in Paraguay and Argentina take 3 hrs. **Gran Casino Itaipu**, Av 11 de Septembre, 816, Cuidad del Este, Paraguay, T/F512294, restaurant, piano bar. **Casino Iguazú**, Ruta 12 Km, 1640, Puerto Iguazú, Misiones, Argentina, T3757-498000. Weekdays 1800-0500, 24 hrs weekends, restaurant.
Cinema **Boulevard**, Av das Cataratas 1118, T5234245. Large complex open from 1700 and all day Sun. Also bowling, games rooms and bingo.

Festivals

Curitiba *p292, map p292, phone code 041*

Feb Ash Wed (half-day).
Mar/Apr Maundy Thu (half-day).
8 Sep Our Lady of Light.

Shopping

Curitiba *p292, phone code041*

Curitiba is a good place to buy clothes and shoes.
Bookshop **O Livro Técnico**, Shopping Itália, R João Negrão and Mcal Deodoro.
Jewellers **H Stern** jewellers at Mueller Shopping Centre.
Souvenirs and handicrafts Try **Lojas Leve Curitiba**, at several locations, R 24 Horas, Afonso Pena airport, Ópera de Arame, Jardim Botánico, Memorial de Curitiba. **Lojas de Artesanato**, Casa de Artesanato Centro, R Mateus Leme 22, T3524021. **Lojas de Artesanato 'Feito Aquí'**, Dr Muricy 950, International Airport and Shopping Mueller. **Feira de Arte e Artesanato**, Praça Garibáldi, Sun 0900-1400.

Foz do Iguaçu *p292, map p305, phone code 045*

Av Brasil is the main shopping street.
Bookshop **Kunda Livraria Universitária**, R Almte Barroso 1473, T5234606. Guides and maps of the area, books on the local wildlife, novels, etc in several languages, including French and English.
Souvenirs and handicrafts **Tres Fronteiras**, Rodovia das Cataratas, Km 11. Large shop on road to falls, frequent stop on tours. Chocolates, and huge selection of crafts and jewellery, some of it overpriced.

Ciudad del Este *p308*

Prices are decidedly high for North American and European visitors. The **leather market** is well worth a visit, be sure to bargain. Don't buy perfume at tempting prices on the street, it's only coloured water. Make sure that shops that package your goods pack what you actually bought. Also watch the exchange rates if you're a short-term visitor from Argentina or Brazil.

Activities and tours

Curitiba *p292, map p294, phone code 041*

Golf Graciosa Country Club, Av Munhoz da Rocha 1146. 9 holes.
Tour operators BMP Turismo (American Express), R Brig Franco 1845, T2247560.

Foz do Iguaçu *p306, map p305, phone code 045*

Tour operators
Beware of overcharging for tours by touts at the bus terminal. There are many travel agents on Av Brasil and in larger hotels. Most do not accept credit cards.
Acquatur, Av das Cataratas 3175, T/F5299554, www.acquaturturismo.com.br. Offer full range of tours in executive cars with bilingual guides and airport transfers.
Caribe Tur, international airport and **Hotel das Cataratas**, T5239959. Tours from the airport to the Argentine side and **Hotel das Cataratas**.
Falls Tur, R Xavier da Silva 563, T5744157, rdfallstur@hotmail.com. Backpacker-orientated tours of Iguaçu, the Itaipu Dam, abseiling, rappelling and longer excursions to the coast and Prudentopolis. English, Spanish and Hebrew spoken.

Recommended guides **Wilson Engel**, T5741367, friendly, flexible. **Ruth Campo Silva**, STTC Turismo, **Hotel Bourbon**, Rodovia das Cataratas, T5743849, F5743557 (American Express). **Chiderly Batismo Pequeno**, R Almte Barroso 505, Foz, T5743367.

Transport

Curitiba *p292, map p294, phone code 041*

Air

There are 2 airports: Afonso Pena, 21 km away for international and national flights, T3811515, and Bacacheri for military and commercial flights, T2562121. There are buses to the centre and bus station as well as taxis. Bus 208 goes to Afonso Pena airport every 25 mins, US$0.60, 30 mins from hotels Presidente and Araucária with a stop near the bus terminal.

Flights to **Campinas**, **Cascavel**, **Foz do Iguaçu**, **Joinville**, **Londrina**, **Maringá**, **Porto Alegre**, **Rio de Janeiro** and **São Paulo**.

Bus

Local There are several route types on the integrated transport system; pick up a map for full details. There are 25 transfer terminals along the exclusive busways and trunk routes, allowing integration between all the different routes. **Express** are red, often articulated, and connect the transfer terminals to the city centre, pre-paid access, they use the 'tubo' bus stops. **Feeder** orange conventional buses connect the terminals to the surrounding neighbourhoods. **Interdistrict** green conventional or articulated buses run on circular routes, connecting transfer terminals and city districts without passing through the centre. **Direct** or **speedy** silver grey buses use the 'tubo' stations (3 km apart on average), to link the main districts and connect the surrounding municipalities with Curitiba. **Conventional** yellow buses operate on the normal road network between the surrounding municipalities, the Integration Terminals and the city centre. **City circular** white minibuses, **Linha Turismo**, circle the major transport terminals and points of interest in the traditional city centre area. US$3.50 (multi-ticket booklets available), every 30 mins from 0900-1700, except on Mon. First leaves from R das Flores, narrow street in front of McDonald's. 3 stops allowed.

Short-distance bus services within the metropolitan region (up to 40 km) begin at Terminal Guadalupe at R João Negrão, T3218611. The Terminal Rodoviário/Estação Rodoferroviária is on Av Afonso Camargo, T3224344, for other cities in Paraná and other states. There are restaurants, banks, bookshops, shops, phones, post office, pharmacy, tourist agency, tourist office and other public services.

Longdistance Frequent buses to **São Paulo** (6 hrs, US$10.25-12.50) and **Rio de Janeiro** (12 hrs, US$25). To **Foz do Iguaçu**, 10 a day, 10 hrs, US$15; **Porto Alegre**, 10 hrs; **Florianópolis**, every 2 hrs, 4½ hrs, US$12; **Blumenau**, 4 hrs, US$6.50, 7 daily with Penha/Catarinense; good service to most destinations in Brazil. Pluma bus to **Buenos Aires** and to **Asunción**. TTL runs to **Montevideo**, 26 hrs, 0340 departure (semi-cama).

Car

Car hire Localiza, at the airport and Av Cândido de Abreu 336, T2530330. Interlocadora, at the airport, T3811370, F3324648.

Train

Rodoferroviária, Av Afonso Camargo, T3229585, T3234007 (Serra Verde Express). Passenger trains to **Paranaguá**, see below.

Curitiba to Paranaguá *p296*

Train There are 2 trains running from Curitiba to **Paranaguá**. The Litorina is a modern a/c railcar with on-board service and bilingual staff, which stops at the viewpoint at the Santuário da Nossa Senhora do Cadeado and Morretes. Hand-luggage only. Tickets can be bought 2 days in advance; departs Fri, Sat, Sun 0900, returns 1500, US$25 one-way tourist class. The **Trem Classe Turística** stops at Marumbi and Morretes, buy tickets 2 days in advance, departs 0800 daily except Mon, returns 1600, *turístico* US$100. The journey takes 4 hrs. Schedules change frequently; check times in advance. For information and reservations, Serra Verde Express, T3234007. Tickets sold at the rodoferroviária, Portão 8, Curitiba, 0800-1800. Sit on the left-hand side on the journey from Curitiba. On cloudy days there's little to see on the higher parts. The train is usually crowded on Sat and Sun. Many travellers recommend returning by bus (1½ hrs, buy ticket immediately on arrival, US$6.50), if you do not want to stay 4½ hrs. A tour bus meets the train and offers a tour of town and return to Curitiba.

Morretes *p297*

Bus From **Paranaguá** to Morretes at 1830, US$1, to Antonina, stopping en route at Morretes, 6 a day (US$1.50). 12 buses daily Morretes-Curitiba US$2; 11 buses a day Curitiba-Antonina.

Paranaguá *p297, phone code 041*

Bus All operated by Graciosa. To **Curitiba**, US$3, many, 1½ hrs (only the 1500 to Curitiba takes the old Graciosa road); direct to **Rio** at 1915, 15 hrs, US$23. 8 buses a day to **Guaratuba** (US$1, 2 hrs), **Caiobá** and **Matinhos**. The buses to Guaratuba go on the ferry, as do direct buses to Joinville, 0740, 1545.

Car hire Interlocadora, T4234425, F3324648.

Vila Velha *p298, phone code 041*

Bus Take a bus from **Curitiba** to the national park, not to the town 20 km away. Ask the bus driver where you should get off. **Princesa dos Campos** bus from Curitiba at 0730 and 0930, 1½ hrs, US$5.65 (return bus passes park entrance at 1600); it may be advisable to go to **Ponta Grossa** and return to Curitiba from there. Last bus from Vila Velha car park to Ponta Grossa at 1800. Bus from Vila Velha at 1310, 1610 and 1800, US$1, 4½ km to turn-off to Furnas (another 15-min walk) and Lagoa Dourada (it's not worth walking from Vila Velha to Furnas because it's mostly uphill along the main road). Allow all day if visiting all 3 sites (unless you hitch, or can time the buses well, it's a lot of walking).

Ilha do Mel *p299, map p299, phone code 041*

Ferry There are 2 routes to Ilha do Mel: by ferry from **Paranaguá** to **Encantadas** and **Nova Brasília**, at 0930 and 1500 (1 hr 40 mins, $4), boats with a capacity of 40, 60 or 80 passengers leave from R Gen Carneiro (R da Praia) in front of the tourist information kiosk; by ferry from **Pontal do Paraná** (Pontal do Sul), daily 0800-1800 (last boat from island to mainland) every hr at weekends, less frequently in the week. From **Paranaguá**, take the bus to Pontal do Sul (many daily, 1½ hrs, US$0.60), then wait for the ferry, US$2.50. There are souvenir and handicraft stalls at the ferry point. The last bus back to Paranaguá leaves at 2200.

Alternatively, go to the small harbour in Paranaguá and ask for a boat to Ilha do Mel, US$15 one-way (no shade). Make sure the ferry goes to your chosen destination (Nova Brasília or Encantadas are the most developed areas).

Superagüi *p300, phone code 041*

Boat From **Paranaguá**, Sat 1000 arriving 1400, return Sun 1530 (2 stops en route), US$6 one way. **Private boats** from Praia da Fortaleza on Ilha do Mel run if the weather is good. There is superb swimming from deserted beaches, but watch out for stinging jelly fish. Contact **Ibama** on the island, 2 km out of the village, for information. Commercially organized tours are available through IBAMA, T2520180, or BARCOPART.

Iguaçu Falls *p300, maps p302 and 305*

For transport between the Argentine and Brazilian sides see under Foz do Iguaçu and Border with Argentina, below. Motorists can park overnight in the national park, free.

Brazil

Bus Buses leave Foz do Iguaçu, from the Terminal Urbana on Av Juscelino Kubitschek, 1 block from the Infantry Barracks. The grey or red **Transbalan** service goes to the falls every 30 mins, 0530-2330, past the airport and **Hotel das Cataratas**. 40 mins, US$0.80 oneway, payable in reais only. Return buses 0800-1900. The bus terminates at the visitors' centre, where you must pay the entrance fee and transfer to the free park shuttle bus, which leaves every 5 mins or so from 0830-1900.

Car Private cars must be left in the Visitors' Centre car park.

Taxi Taxis charge US$7 one way or US$30 for return trip, including waiting (negotiate in advance). Many hotels organize tours to the falls: these have been recommended in preference to taxi rides.

Argentina

Bus Transportes El Práctico buses run every hr from Puerto Iguazú bus terminal, stopping at the national park entrance for the purchase of entry tickets and continuing to Puerto Canoas. Fares US$5 return to visitors' centre (cars US$3), a further US$0.50 to Puerto Canoas, payable in pesos, dollars, guaraníes or reais. First bus 0740, last 1940, last return 2000, journey time 30 mins. These buses are sometimes erratic, especially when it is wet, even though the times are clearly indicated.

Taxi There are fixed rates for taxis, US$15 one-way, up to 5 people. A tour from the bus terminal, taking in both sides of the falls, costs US$40.

Hitchhiking to the falls is difficult, but you can hitch up to the Posadas intersection at Km 11, then it is only a 7-km walk.

Foz do Iguaçu *p306, map p305, phone code 045*

Air

Iguaçu international airport, 18 km south of town near the falls. In arrivals is Banco do Brasil and Caribe Tur and *câmbio*, car rental offices, tourist office and an official taxi stand, US$8 to town centre (US$11 from town to airport). **Transbalan** (Parque Nacional) town bus for US$0.50, first at 0530, does not permit large amounts of luggage but backpacks OK. Many hotels run minibus services for a small charge. Daily flights to **Rio**, **São Paulo**, **Curitiba** and other Brazilian cities.

Airline offices Rio Sul, R Jorge Sanways 779, T5741680, freephone T0800-992994. TAM, R Rio Branco, 640 T5238500 (offers free transport to Ciudad del Este for its flights, all cross-border documentation dealt with). **Varig**, Av Juscelino Kubitschek 463, T5232111. **Vasp**, Av Brasil 845, T5232212.

Bus

For transport to the falls, see above under Parque Nacional Foz do Iguaçu. Long-distance terminal (rodoviária), Av Costa e Silva, 4 km from centre on road to Curitiba, T5223633; bus to centre, any bus that says 'Rodoviária', US$0.65. Book departures as soon as possible. As well as the tourist office, there is a **Cetreme** desk for tourists who have lost their documents, Guarda Municipal (police) and luggage store.

To **Curitiba**, Pluma, Sulamericana, 9-10 hrs, 3 daily, paved road, US$15; to **Guaíra** via Cascavel only, 5 hrs, US$10; to **Florianópolis**, Catarinense and **Reunidas**, US$28, 14 hrs; Reunidas to **Porto Alegre**, US$30; to **São Paulo**, 16 hrs, Pluma US$30, *executivo* 6 a day, plus 1 *leito*; to **Rio** 22 hrs, several daily, US$38. To **Asunción**, Pluma, RYSA (direct at 1430), US$11.

Car

Car hire Avis, airport, T5231510. **Localiza** at airport, T5296300, and Av Juscelino Kubitschek 2878, T5221608. **Unidas**, Av Santos Dumont, 1515, near airport, T/F3390880.

Taxi

Taxis are only good value for short distances when you are carrying all your luggage.

Border with Argentina *p306*

Bus To **Puerto Iguazú** run every 20 mins from the Terminal Urbana, crossing the frontier bridge; 30 mins' journey, **Três Fronteiras**, US$1.50, or 2 reais. If you have to get out of the bus to get your passport stamped at immigration, the bus waits. To get to the Argentine side of the falls without going into Puerto Iguazú, get off the bus from the frontier bridge at the first traffic lights and cross the road for the bus to the falls. To **Buenos Aires**, Pluma daily 1200, US$46. It is cheaper to go to **Posadas** via Paraguay.

Taxi Foz to the border, waiting for Brazilian immigration, US$10; Foz-Argentina US$35, US$45 to **Hotel Sheraton Iguazú**.

Ciudad del Este *p308, phone code 061*

Air

To **Asunción**, Arpa, 3 flights Mon-Sat, 1 on Sun. Also TAM daily en route to São Paulo.

Airline offices TAM, Edif SABA, Monseñor Rodríguez.

Bus

The terminal is on the southern outskirts. No 4 bus from the centre goes there, US$0.50 (taxi US$3.50). Many buses

(US$17.50 *rápido*, 4½ hrs, at night only; US$10 *común*, 6 hrs) to and from **Asunción**. Nuestra Señora and Rysa recommended. To **Encarnación** (for Posadas and Argentina), along a fully paved road, frequent, 3 hrs, US$7.50 (cheaper than via Foz do Iguaçu).

To Brazil International bus from outside the terminal to the new long-distance terminal (Rodoviária) outside Foz. Local buses from the terminal run along Av Adrián Jara and go to the city terminal (*terminal urbana*) in **Foz** every 15 mins, 0600-2000, US$0.65. Most buses do not wait at immigration, so disembark to get your exit stamp, walk across the bridge (10 mins) and obtain your entry stamp; keep your ticket and continue to Foz on the next bus free. Paraguayan taxis cross freely to Brazil (US$20), but it is cheaper to walk across the bridge and then take a taxi, bargain hard. You can pay in either currency.

To Argentina Direct buses to **Puerto Iguazú**, frequent service by several companies from outside the terminal, US$2, you need to get Argentine and Paraguayan stamps (not Brazilian); the bus does not wait so keep your ticket for the next bus.

Guaíra *p308, phone code 044*
Bus To **Campo Grande**, buy a ticket (US$25) at the Guaíra rodoviária, take a ferry from the Porto da Paragem at the end of Av Almte Tamandaré to Porto Ilha Grande in Mato Grosso do Sul, then bus to Mondo Novo, change bus there for Campo Grande. Morning and night bus, 12 hrs in all. There is a bus service between **Curitiba** and Guaíra, US$15, 10 hrs. To **São Paulo**, US$30, 16 hrs. Other destinations include **Iguaçu** (bumpy, but interesting), 5 hrs, but may be cancelled in the wet, US$10.

Directory

Curitiba *p292, map p294, phone code 041*
Banks Bradesco, R 15 de Novembro, Visa ATM. Plus or Cirrus associated credit cards can be used at **Citibank**, R Mcal Deodoro 711, or at Buenos Aires 305 near Shopping Curitiba. **Credicard**, R Saldanha Marinho 1439, Bigorrillo. Cash with MasterCard. **Diplomata**, R Pres Faria 145 in the arcade. **Transoceânica**, R Mcal Deodoro 532, English and German spoken. **Triangle Turismo Travel**, Praça Gen Osório 213. Cash and Tcs. **Cultural centres** **Instituto Goethe**, R Schaffenberg, near Military Museum, Mon-Thu 1500-1900, Library, Mon-Tue until 2130. **Sociedade Brasileira de Cultura Inglesa** (British Council), R Gen Carneiro 679, Caixa Postal 505. **Embassies and consulates** Austria, R Cândido Hartmann 570, Edif Champagnat, 28th floor, T3361166 (Mon-Fri 1000-1300). **Denmark**, R Prof Francisco Ribeiro 683, Caixa Postal 321, T8432211, F8431443. **Germany**, R Emiliano Perneta 297, 2nd floor, T2226920 (Mon-Fri 0800-1200). **Netherlands**, Av Candido de Abreu 469, conj 1606, T2547846. Consul Tony Bruinjé (1400-1700). **Switzerland**, Av Mcal F Peixoto 228, Edif Banrisul, conj 1104/5, T2237553. **UK**, R Pres Faria 51, 2nd floor, T3221202, consulado.britanico@mais.sul.com.br (Mon-Fri 0830-1200, 1400-1730). **Uruguay**, R Voluntários da Pátria 475, 18th floor. **Immigration** Federal police, Dr Muricy 814, T3622313. For visa extensions 1000-1600. **Internet** Digitando o Futuro, R 24 Horas. Open 24 hrs, free for 1 hr, government sponsored. Only 2 machines; T3506366 to book. **Monkey**, Av Vicente Machado 534, corner with R Brigadeiro. Cool, modern with lots of computers and internet games. Open daily until 2400. **Medical services** Emergency, T192 or T100. **Cajuru Hospital**, Av São José 300, T3621100. **Evangélico**, Av Augusto Stellfeld 1908, T3224141. Both deal with emergencies. **Post office** Main post office is at Mcal Deodoro 298. Branches at R 15 de Novembro and R Pres Faria. **Telephone** Galeria Minerva, R 15 de Novembro. **Information**, T102.

Morretes *p297, phone code 041*
Banks Banco do Brasil, does not officially change money, but friendly staff will sometimes do so. It has an ATM.

Paranaguá *p297*
Banks Banco do Brasil, Largo C Alcindino 27. **Bradesco**, R Faria Sobrinho 188. **Câmbio**, R Faria Sobrinho. For cash.

Foz do Iguaçu *p306, map p305, phone code 045*
Banks There are plenty of banks and travel agents on Av Brasil. **Banco do Brasil**, Av Brasil 1377 has ATM. High commission for TCs. **Bradesco**, Av Brasil 1202. Cash advance on

Visa. Banco 24 Horas at Oklahoma petrol station. HSBC, Av Brasil 1151, ATM. **Embassies and consulates** Argentina, Travessa Eduardo Bianchi 26, T5742969 (Mon-Fri 1000-1430). France, R Federico Engels 48, Villa Yolanda, T5743693. Paraguay, Bartolomeu de Gusmão 480, T5232898. **Internet** Boulevard, Av das Cataratas 1118, T5234245. Café Internet, R Rebouças 950, T/F5232122, US$1.50 per hr; also phone, fax and photocopying. Ask for fastest machine, Mon-Sat 0900-2300 and Sun afternoon. Café Pizzanet, R Rio Branco, 412, corner with Av Juscelino Kubitschek, US$2 per hr. Pizzeria, fax, phone, photocopier. Zipfoz.com, R Barão do Rio Branco 412, corner with Av Juscelino Kubitschek. Smart, a/c, US$1.50 per hr. **Laundry** Londres Lavanderia, R Reboucas, 711, only US$1.50 per kg, open Sat. **Medical services** There is a free 24-hr clinic on Av Paraná, 1525, opposite Lions Club, T5731134. Few buses: take taxi or walk (about 25 mins). **Post office** Praça Getúlio Vargas 72. **Telephone** Telepar on Edmundo de Barros.

Ciudad del Este *p308, phone code 061*
Banks Local banks open Mon-Fri 0730-1100. Dollars can be changed into reais in town. Banco Holandés Unido, cash on MasterCard, 5% commission. Several exchange houses: Cambio Guaraní, Monseñor Rodríguez, changes TCs for US$0.50. Branch on Friendship Bridge has good rates for many currencies, including dollars and reais. Tupi Cambios, Adrián Jara 351. Cambios Chaco, Adrián Jara y Curupayty. Casa de cambio rates are better than street rates. Money changers (not recommended) operate at the bus terminal, but not at the Brazilian end of the Friendship Bridge. **Embassies and consulates** Brazil, C Pampliega 337, corner of Pai Perez, T561500984, F56163283. **Telecommunications** Antelco, Alejo García and Pai Pérez, near the centre on the road to the bus terminal.

Guaíra *p308, phone code 044*
Embassies and consulates Brazil, Av Pres Stroessner 259, T/F546305. Paraguay, T6421505.

Santa Catarina

→ *Population: 5.5 million*

Santa Catarina is famous above all for its beaches, especially those around the cities of Florianópolis and Laguna. These are among the most beautiful in southern Brazil, and have the best surf in the country. The state is also famous for its beautiful people – supermodel Gisele Bundchen is from Santa Catarina. Like many Santa Catarenses she defies the stereotype and is tall, blonde and blue eyed. For this was an area which saw much northern European immigration in the 20th century. Immigrant communities still give a unique personality to a number of the state's towns and districts where German and Ukrainian are spoken as much as Portuguese. Every year one million people visit the Oktoberfest in Blumenau. The highlands, just in from the coast, are among the coldest in Brazil and are covered in remnant Aracauria pine forest, a tree related to the Chilean monkey puzzle. Except for the summer months of January and February, Santa Catarina's beaches are pleasant and uncrowded. The best months to visit are March, April and May before the water gets too cold for swimming.

As well as each region having its own climate and scenery, Santa Catarina also has a distinctive culture depending on its immigrants. The Portuguese from the Azores settled along the coast, the Germans moved along the Itajaí Valley, the Italians headed for the south and into Rio Grande do Sul, while in the north there are Ukrainians, Japanese, Africans, Hispanics and Indians. Each group maintains its traditions and festivals, its architecture, food and language or accent. The vast majority of people today can trace their family to these ethnic origins. ▸▸ *For Sleeping, Eating and other listings, see pages 334-340.*

Florianópolis → *Phone code: 048. Colour map 5, B5. Population: 345,000.*

Halfway along the coast of Santa Catarina is the state capital Florianópolis, founded in 1726 on the Ilha de Santa Catarina. The natural beauty of the island, beaches and bays make Florianópolis a magnet for holidaymakers in summer. The southern beaches are usually good for swimming, the east for surfing, but be careful of the undertow. 'Floripa' is accepted as a shortened version of Florianópolis, with the people known as 'Floripans', although they like to call themselves 'Ilhéus', or Islanders.

Florianópolis is a small city, quite hilly but easy and safe to walk around. To explore the island you need to use the good bus services; standard buses and more expensive yellow microbuses run to nearly every important point on the island. *See also Transport, page 339.*

The main **tourist information office** ⓘ *Mercado Público, 3rd booth along from R Arcipreste Paiva, T2445822, Mon-Fri 0800-1200, 1330-1800, Sat and Sun 0800-1200*. **Setur** ⓘ *Head Office, Portal Turístico de Florianópolis, mainland end of the bridge, Av Eng Max de Souza 236, Coqueiros, T2445822, Mon-Fri 0800-2000, Sat and Sun 0800-1800; at rodoviária, Av Paulo Fontes, T2232777; at airport Mon-Fri 0700-1800, Sat and Sun 0800-1800*, maps available, free (www.guiafloripa.com.br). **Santur** ⓘ *Edif ARS, R Felipe Schmidt 249, 9th floor, T2246300, www.ciasc.gov.br and www.sc.gov.br/santur*, are helpful. A good series of bilingual books on all of southern Brazil is published by **Mares do Sul** ⓘ *R Luiz Pasteur, Trindade, T/F3331544, www.maresdosul.com.br.*

Sights

The island is joined to the mainland by two bridges, one of which is **Ponte Hercílio Luz**, the longest steel suspension bridge in Brazil, now closed but beautifully lit up at night. The newer **Colombo Machado Salles** bridge has a pedestrian and cycleway beneath the roadway.

In the 1960s Florianópolis port was closed and the aspect of the city's southern shoreline was fundamentally changed, with land reclaimed from the bay. The two main remnants of the old port area are the late 19th-century **Alfândega** ⓘ *R Conselheiro Mafra, T2246082, Mon-Fri 0900-1900, Sat 0900-1200*, and **Mercado Público** ⓘ *R Conselheiro Mafra T2253200, Mon-Fri 0600-1830, Sat 0600-1300 (a few fish stalls open on Sun)*, fully restored and painted ochre. In the Alfândega is a handicraft market. The market is divided into stalls, some are bars and restaurants, others shops. The **Cathedral** ⓘ *Praça 15 de Novembro* (1773), was built on the site of the first chapel erected by the founder of the city, Francisco Dias Velho. Inside is a life-size sculpture in wood of the flight into Egypt, originally from the Austrian Tyrol. **Forte Santana** (1763) houses a **Museu de Armas Major Lara Ribas** ⓘ *beneath the Ponte Hercílio Luz, T2296263, Tue-Sun 0830-1200, 1400-1800, Mon 1400-1800, free*, with a collection of guns and other items, mostly post Second World War. There are four other museums. The **Museu Histórico** ⓘ *Praça 15 de Novembre, T2213504, Tue-Fri 1000-1800, Sat, Sun and holidays 1000-1600, US$1*, in the 18th-century Palácio Cruz e Souza, has a lavish interior with highly decorated ceilings and contains furniture, documents and objects belonging to governors of the state. The **Museu de Antropologia** ⓘ *T3318821, Mon-Fri 0900-1200, 1300-1700*, at the Trindade University Campus, has a collection of stone and other archaeological remains from the indigenous cultures of the coast. There is a look-out point at **Morro da Cruz** (take **Empresa Trindadense** bus, US$0.60, waits 15 minutes, or walk). On the north shore, outside the perimeter road, the mangroves of the **Mangue do Itacorubi** are being protected.

Ilha de Santa Catarina

The long, skinny island is scalloped by no less than 42 beaches; the only problem is choosing which one. The most popular are the surfers' beaches such as **Praia Mole,**

Joaquina or **Barra da Lagoa**. For peace and quiet, try **Campeche** or the southern beaches; for sport, the **Lagoa de Conceição** has jet skis and windsurfing. You can walk in the forest reserves, hang-glide or paraglide from the **Morro da Lagoa**, or sandboard in the dunes of **Joaquina**. Surfing is prohibited 30 April-30 July because of the migration of the island's largest fish, the *tainha*. Note that the temperature in the north can differ from the south by several degrees. Almost all the beaches are easily reached by public buses (US$1), which run hourly. You need to ask at the Terminal Interurbano and the Terminal Urbano, or get a schedule from the tourist office.

Lagoa da Conceição is worth visiting for its beaches, sand dunes, fishing and the church of Nossa Senhora da Conceição (1730). It also has a market every Wednesday

Florianópolis

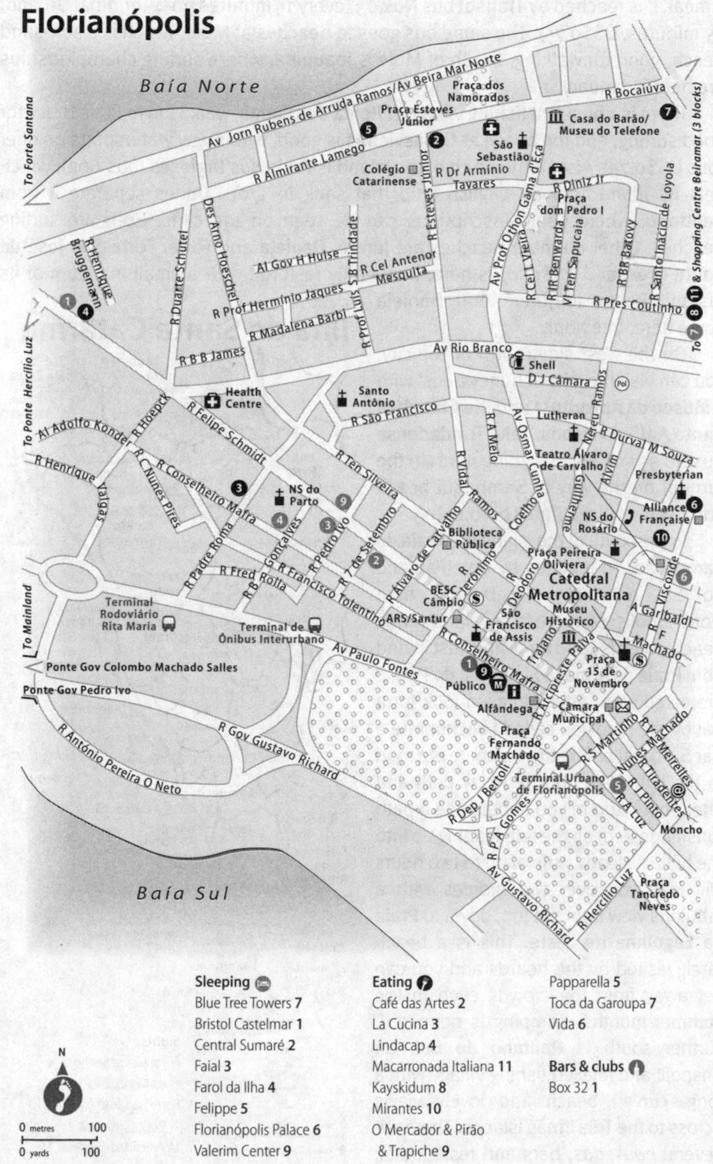

and Saturday. For tandem hang-gliding, contact **Lift Sul Vôo Livre** (T2320543). From the Centro da Lagoa on the bridge there are daily boat trips to Costa da Lagoa which run until about 1830, check when you buy your ticket, US$4 return. The service is used mostly by the local people who live around the lake and have no other form of public transport. The ride is spectacular and there is a charming restaurant to greet you at the end of a thirsty journey. A recommended meal is the local fish, *tainha*, with salad, chips and an abundance of rice.

Across the island at **Barra da Lagoa** is a pleasant fishing village and beach, lively in the summer season, with plenty of good restaurants. You can walk across the wooden suspension bridge to one overlooking the bay, a spectacular setting for a meal. It is reached by **Transol** bus No 403 (every 15 minutes from Terminal Urbano, 55 minutes, US$0.75). The same bus goes to beaches at **Mole**, which is a soft-sand beach, good for walking. South of Mole is **Joaquina**, where surfing championships are held in January.

There is a pleasant fishing village at **Ponta das Canas**, walk 1 km to Praia Brava for good surfing, and the beach at **Canasvieiras** is good, with many watersports on offer (bus US$0.75). Also in the north of the island is **Praia dos Ingleses** (bus 602), which gets its name from an English ship that sank in 1700. Dunes separate it from **Santinho**, where Carijó inscriptions can be seen on the cliffs. Both are surfing beaches. Other northern beaches are **Jureré**, **Daniela** and **Forte**. **Forte São José da Ponta Grossa** ⓘ *US$1.50*, is here, beautifully restored with a small museum of its history. Buses to Jureré and Daniela come here, one hour.

On the west side, north of the city, you can visit the 'city of honey bees' with a **Museo da Apicultura** and the **Church of Santo Antônio Lisboa**. Take **Trindadense** bus No 331 or any bus going north to the turn-off on the way to Sambaqui beach and fishing village (fare US$0.65).

In the south of the island are **Praia do Campeche**, 30 minutes by bus (Pantano do Sul or Costa de Dentro) from Florianópolis; offshore is an island with a beach which is good for diving. Just inland from **Praia da Armação** is **Lagoa do Peri**, a protected area. After Armação look for a bar by the roadside called **Lanchonette e Bar Surf**. Just before the bar there is a road to the left. Walk up a red clay path and after about 200 m you should see a path (unsignposted) on the left, leading up into the hills. A steady walk of up to two hours will lead you over two *montes* with a fabulous view from the top, down to **Praia da Lagoinha de Leste**. This is a beach rarely visited by the hoards and you can get away from the crowds even in the summer months. Camping is permitted. Further south is **Pantano do Sul**, an unspoilt and relaxed fishing village with a long, curved beach and lovely views across to the Três Irmãs islands. There are several *pousadas*, bars and restaurants,

though not much nightlife. For **Praia dos Naufragados**, take bus to Caieira da Barra do Sul and walk for an hour through fine forests. **Forte Nossa Senhora da Conceição** is on a small island just offshore. It can be seen from the lighthouse near Praia dos Naufragados or take a boat trip with Scuna Sul from Florianópolis.

Around Florianópolis

The BR-282 heads west from the capital to Lages (see page 334). About 12 km along are the hot springs at **Caldas da Imperatriz** (41°C) and **Águas Mornas** (39°C). The latter are open to the public Monday-Friday morning only. Both have good spa hotels (see page 334).

The **Parque Estadual da Serra do Tabuleiro**, just south of the BR-282, is the largest protected area in Santa Catarina, covering 87,405 ha, or nearly 1% of the state. Apart from its varied and luxuriant flora which is home to many birds and animals, it is also important to Florianópolis for its water supply. There is a small **reserve** ⓘ *daily 0800-1700*, near the park headquarters (near Paulo Lopes, Km 252, BR-101), where animals and birds previously in captivity are rehabilitated before returning to the wild.

North of Florianópolis

Porto Belo and around → *Phone code: 047. Colour map 5, B5. Population: 10,500.*

The coast north of Florianópolis is dotted with resorts. They include **Porto Belo** (www.portobelo.com.br), a fishing village on the north side of a peninsula settled in 1750 by Azores islanders, with a calm beach and a number of hotels and restaurants. Around the peninsula are wilder beaches reached by rough roads: **Bombas**, **Bombinhas** (both with the same sort of accommodation as Porto Belo), **Quatro Ilhas** (quieter, good surfing, 15 minutes' walk from Bombinhas), **Mariscal** and, on the southern side, **Zimbros** (or Cantinho). Many of the stunning beaches around Bombinhas are untouched, accessible only on foot or by boat. Its clear waters are marvellous for diving.

Porto Belo beaches

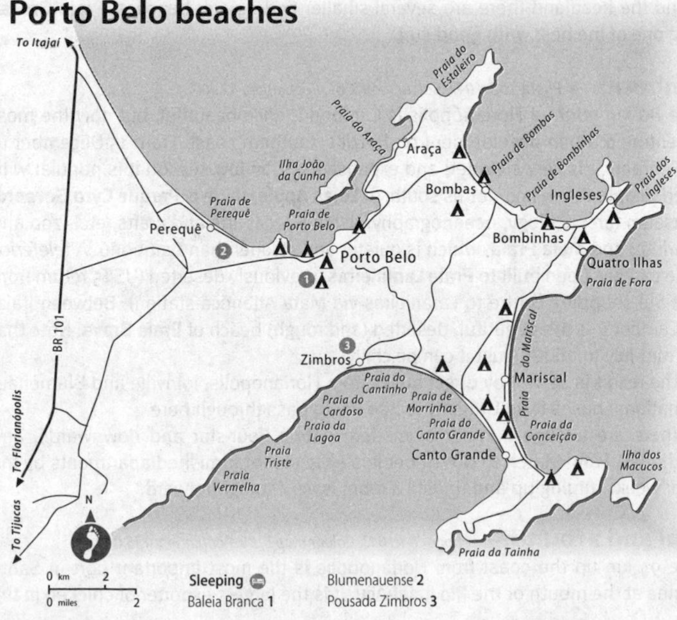

Italian crosses and saints

In 1889, Padre Jesuíta Luís Maria Rossi decided to commemorate the new century by erecting crosses on the highest hills above Nova Trento. Padre Alfredo Russel, a missionary, promised to put a statue of Nossa Senhora do Bom Socorro beside the highest cross, which eventually came to pass in 1901 on Morro da Cruz; a sanctuary was later built there.

Nova Trento's most famous inhabitant was Madre Paulina, who was beatified by the Pope in 1991. Born in Trento, Italy, in 1865, the young Amabile Visintainer emigrated to Brazil with her family in 1875 and they were given land in Nova Trenta. Amabile cared for the sick and her charitable works led her to a religious calling and the founding of the Sisters of the Immaculate Conception. She took the name of her Sister Pauline, leading a humble life until her death in 1942. Since then several miracles have been claimed in her name, which led to her beatification.

Southwest of Porto Belo, reached by turning off the BR-101 at Tijucas and going west for 30 km, is **Nova Trento**, a small town in a valley first colonized by Italians and still showing heavy Italian influence. The local cuisine includes cheese, salami and wine such as you might find in Italy; there are several Italian restaurants and wine producers where you can buy *vinho artesanal*. A good view down the Tijucas valley and as far as the sea (on a clear day), can be had from the **Morro da Cruz**, at 525 m.

West of Porto Belo is **Praia de Perequê**, with a handful of hotels on the long beautiful beach .

Itapema, 60 km from Florianópolis, is another former fishing village on a wide sweep of sandy beach now dominated by tourism. In high season the town accommodates around 300,000 visitors. The **Plaza Itapema Resert e Spa**, all-inclusive, is the best such establishment on this part of the coast (T3682222). Around the headland there are several smaller and quieter beaches, **Praia Grossa** being one of the best, with good surf.

Camboriú → *Phone code: 047. Colour map 5, B5. Population: 42,000.*

Some 80 km north of Florianópolis is Camboriú, once beautiful, but now the most concentrated urban development on Brazil's southern coast. From 15 December to late February it is very crowded and expensive and in low season it is popular with retired people. A few kilometres south, at **Lojas Apple**, there is **Parque Cyro Gevaerd**, a museum (archaeology, oceanography, fishing, local arts and crafts, etc), zoo and aquarium; and **Meia Praia**, which is quieter and cleaner than Camboriú. A *teleférico* (cable car) has been built to **Praia Laranjeiras**, previously deserted (US$5 return from Barra Sul shopping centre to Laranjeiras via Mata Atlântica station). Between Itajaí and Camboriú is the beautiful, deserted (and rough) beach of **Praia Brava**. Note that from mid-July to mid-August it can be chilly.

The resort is served by direct buses from Florianópolis, Joinville and Blumenau. International buses from Uruguay to São Paulo pass through here.

There are a huge number of modern hotels, four-star and downwards, and aparthotels. From March to November it is easy to rent furnished apartments by the day or week. Turning up and finding a room is very straightforward.

Itajaí and around → *Phone code: 047. Colour map 5, B5. Population: 135,000.*

Some 94 km up the coast from Florianópolis is the most important port in Santa Catarina at the mouth of the Rio Itajaí-Açu. It is the largest exporter of chicken in the country and the fourth largest container port. It has thriving fishing and shipbuilding industries and is the centre of a district largely colonized by Germans and Italians, although the town itself was founded by immigrants from the Azores.

Despite the port, tourism is heavily promoted and in summer the population triples. Itajaí celebrates a **Marejada Festival** in October in honour of Portugal and the sea. It is held in the Centro de Promoções Itajaí Tur, where there are musical and folkloric festivities, a pavilion for dancing and shows, and a pavilion for food (with lots of different ways of preparing *bacalhau* and masses of seafood). For **tourist information**, contact the **Centro de Promoções Itajaí Tur** ⓘ *T3481080*.

The local beaches are **Atalaia**, **Geremias** and **Cabeçudas** (within walking distance, quiet and small), but within the municipality there is also **Praia do Morcego** which is considered a health resort because of the high mineral content of the water. There is also a cave here, the **Caverna do Morcego**, about which there are many myths and legends.

About 50 km southwest of Itajaí is the **Caverna de Botuverá**, which you enter through a dripping tunnel which can flood in the wet season. The first gallery is like a cathedral, with stalactites and rock formations, one of which is called 'the organ', and the guide will play a sort of tune for you. There are several galleries, not all of which are fully explored. Pillars of 20 m have been found; each metre of rock taking 10,000 years to form. To get to Botuverá, take the road to Brusque off the BR-101, where there is tourist information and they can give you directions and other details.

Penha → *Population: 15,000.*

About 20 km north of Itajaí is Penha, another resort along the BR-101, with a broad, curved, sandy beach with rocky headlands at either end, offering smaller coves for swimming, surfing and fishing. The town was founded by Portuguese fishermen in the 18th century and fishing is still important as elsewhere along the coast. Tourism took off in the 1970s and during the high season the population rises to 100,000. Its major claim to fame is the **Beto Carrero World**, opened in 1991 on Praia de Armação, one of the largest theme parks in the world. Penha even offers themed shopping, at the **Shopping Temático** on Avenida Eugênio Krause, where you can visit different countries in different ages.

There are several **fiestas** and events in Penha, starting with a seafood festival in February, Carnival, the Festa do Divino (procession and crowning of the Emperor) in May or June, and the Festa de São João e São Pedro, 24-29 June (a tradition from the Azores). There are hotels, *pousadas* and camping.

Other resorts north of Itajaí include **Piçarras**, with sandy beaches interspersed with rocky headlands (ideal for fishing, several hotels), and **Barra Velha**, with a good, cheap hotel, **Hotel Mirante**, which has a restaurant, and two more expensive hotels.

Blumenau → *Phone code: 047. Colour map 5, B4. Population: 262,000.*

Blumenau is in a prosperous district settled mostly by Germans. A clean, orderly city with almost caricatured Germanic architecture, the German *enxaimel* design (exposed beams and brickwork) typifies some of the more famous buildings such as the **Mayor's Residence**, the **Molemann Shopping**, which resembles a medieval German castle, and the **Museum of the Colonial Family** ⓘ *Av Duque de Caxias 78, Mon-Fri 0800-1130, 1330-1730, Sat morning only. US$0.15* (1868), the German immigrant museum. Blumenau offers a charming alternative to the less-organized Brazilian way of life.

The first Germans to arrive were the philosopher Herman Bruno Otto Blumenau and 16 other German explorers, who sailed up the river in 1850. Work began to build schools, houses and the first plantations, and the city soon became a notable textile

Blumenau's Oktoberfest

In 1983, Blumenau suffered a great flood. After its destructive impact, the idea was born to introduce a German-style 'traditional' Oktoberfest beer-festival to motivate people to reconstruct the city. The festival celebrating German music, beer and the German way of life was started in 1984 here, and was expected to become the second largest in the world after Munich's (bands come from Germany for the event). It is the second largest street party in Brazil, after Carnival. It is set next to the São Francisco de Assis National Park and usually held in the first half of October. During the day the narrow streets are packed around the Molemann Centre, which is where many locals like to begin their festivities before the Oktoberfest Pavilion opens. The centre contains a mixture of bars, live music and, of course, Chopp. At 1900 the doors open and you will find four decorated pavilions, each holding different events from drinking competitions to the 'sausage Olympics', all accompanied by non-stop traditional German music. The cultural pavilion holds traditional dress and cake-making competitions, as well as getting the audience involved in the singing, which grows steadily worse as the evening rolls on. There is also a fun fair and folk dancing shows. Food around the stalls is German and half a litre of Chopp will cost you around US$2. Brazilian popular bands are slowly being introduced, much to the disapproval of the older inhabitants. Visitors report it is worth attending on weekday evenings but weekends are too crowded. It is repeated, but called a 'summer festival', in the three weeks preceding Carnival.

centre. Today, high-tech and electronics industries are replacing textiles as the town's economic mainstay. There is a helpful **tourist office** ⓘ *R 15 de Novembro, on the corner of R Ângelo Dias*.

The **German Evangelical Church**, and also the houses, now **museums** ⓘ *both 0800-1800*, of **Dr Bruno Otto Blumenau** and of **Fritz Müller** are all worth a visit. Müller, a collaborator of Darwin, bought the Blumenau estate in 1897 and founded the town.

Excursions from Blumenau

The **Parque Ecológico Spitzkopf** ⓘ *US$1.50*, is a pleasant day trip for hiking, with very nice trails through the forest, passing waterfalls, natural pools, up to the Spitzkopf Peak at 936 m, 5½ km from the entrance, from where you get a wonderful view of the region. If you are not up to hiking up hills, there are paths around the lower slopes which will take you half a day. Get the 'Garcia' bus from Avenida 7 de Septembro via Rua São Paulo to Terminal Garcia, then change to 'Progresso' until the end of the paved road, US$0.60 each bus. Then walk 1½ km to the park entrance, German spoken, small zoo and cabins to rent.

You can also visit Timbó and Pomerode (from the riverside road opposite the Prefeitura), by bus past rice fields and wooden houses set in beautiful gardens. At **Pomerode**, 33 km north of Blumenau, there is an interesting **zoo** ⓘ *R Hermann Weege 160*, founded in 1932 and the oldest in the state. It houses over 600 animals of different species. The tourist office can be contacted on T3872627. Next door to the Prefeitura Municipal is the **Associação dos Artistas e Artesãos de Pomerode**, where you can find exhibitions of local arts and crafts and a shop. The north German dialect of Plattdeutsch is still spoken here and there are several folkloric groups keeping alive the music and dance of their ancestors: *Alpino Germânico*,

Pomerano, Edelweiss and *Belgard*. Shooting and hunting is also traditional in the area and there are 16 **Clubes de Caça e Tiro** which are active at all festivities. The men compete for the title of **Rei do Tiro Municipal** in July and the women compete for the **Rainha do Tiro Municipal** in November. Other activities include parapenting (T3870803), a jeep club (T3872328), horse riding (T3872290) and swimming pools with water slides. The **Museu Pomerano** ⓘ *Rodovia SC 418, Km 3, T3870477*, tells the story of the colonial family. **Museu Ervin Kurt Theichmann** ⓘ *R 15 de Novembro 791, T3870282*, has sculptures. The **Confeitaria Torten Paradies** ⓘ *R 15 de Novembro 211*, serves excellent German cakes.

A half-day excursion to **Gaspar** (15 km) allows you to visit the cathedral, Igreja Matriz São Pedro Apóstolo, set high above the river (*Verde Vale* bus company from stop outside the huge supermarket on Rua 7 de Setembro in the centre, office at Rua Angêlo Dias 220, sala 207, Blumenau, T3266179, www.braznet.com.br/~verdetur/index.html). There are two water parks in Gaspar with water slides and other amusements: **Parque Aquático Cascanéia** ⓘ *R José Patrocínio dos Santos, T3390690*, with chalets, parking, restaurants, and **Cascata Carolina** ⓘ *Estrada Geral da Carolina-Belchior Alto, T3390779*, with water coming straight from the rocks.

Further west along the Rio Itajaí-Açu, around Ibirama, the river is good for whitewater rafting. You can take a break between rapids to bathe in the waterfalls.

Blumenau to Iguaçu

As an alternative to a direct bus, daily from Florianópolis and Itajaí to Iguaçu via Blumenau, you can travel through rich and interesting farming country in Santa Catarina and Rio Grande do Sul, stopping at the following places: **Joaçaba**, a town of German immigrants, in the centre of the Vale do Contestado (for information, T5223000); **Erexim**, which has a strong *gaúcho* influence; **Iraí**, a town with thermal springs, situated in an Italian immigrant area. The town is good for semi-precious stones. From any of these places you can go to Pato Branco and Cascavel and thence to Foz do Iguaçu.

Two hours from Joaçaba is **Treze Tílias**, a village where 19th-century Tyrolean dialect is still spoken and the immigrant culture is perfectly preserved. It was settled in 1933 by a group led by Andreas Thaler, who had been the Austrian Minister of Agriculture. Dairy farming is the main economic activity and children are taught German and Portuguese in school. The style of architecture has been lifted straight from the Alps and the city prides itself on being in the mountains, with all the associated romanticizing of European mountain life found in such resorts throughout Brazil. It may get a bit chilly but it never snows, so the long steep views are very Disney. The major festivity of the year is the four-day **Tirolerfest** in October, celebrating the customs of the Tirol, with food, sculpture and art. There's **tourist information** ⓘ *Praça Andreas Thaler 25, T/F5370176*, and buses run to and from Joaçaba and Blumenau.

São Francisco do Sul → *Phone code: 047. Population: 27,000.*

At the mouth of the Baia de Babitonga, São Francisco do Sul is the port for the town of Joinville, 45 km inland at the head of the Rio Cachoeira. It is the country's third oldest city (Binot Paulmier de Gonneville landed here in 1504), after Porto Seguro in Bahia and São Vicente in Rio de Janeiro. The colonial centre has over 150 historical sites and has been protected since 1987. An interesting **Museu Nacional do Mare** ⓘ *R Manual Lourenço de Andrade, T4441868, Tue-Fri 0900-1800, Sat and Sun 1100-1800, US$1*, reflects Brazil's seafaring history. The **cathedral**, Nossa Senhora da Graça (1719), still has its original walls made with sand, shells and whale oil. The **Museu Histórico de São Francisco do Sul** ⓘ *R Coronel Carvalho*, is in the 18th-century Cadeia Pública. There is a **tourist information** desk in the cinema behind the Prefeitura. Not far from the historical centre is the modern port. Petrobrás has an oil refinery here.

There are about 13 excellent **beaches** nearby, such as **Ubatuba**, **Enseada**, which has good nightlife, hotels, pensions and three campsites, **Prainha** (surf championships are held here) and **Cápri**. Quieter waters can be found at **Ingleses**, **Figueiras**, **Paulas** and **Calixtos** but, being in the bay, the sea is polluted. A ferry crosses the Baia de Babitonga from Bairro Laranjeiras, 8 km from the centre, to Estaleiro, 30 minutes. The historic town of **Vila da Glória** (6 km from Estaleiro) can be visited. See under Excursions from Joinville, below, for the *Príncipe de Joinville* boat trip. For schooner trips T9747266. Take mosquito repellent.

Joinville → *Phone code: 047. Colour map 5, B5. Population: 430,000.*

The state's largest city lies 2 km from the main coastal highway, BR-101, by which Curitiba and Florianópolis are less than two hours away. Joinville is known as the 'city of the princes' for its historical connections with royalty, although it is also nicknamed the 'city of flowers', and even 'Manchester Catarinense'. Although its industry does not spoil the character of the city and the large German population gives it a distinctly European feel, there is not much reason for visitors to stop here. **Tourist information** ⓘ *corner of Praça Nereu Ramos with R do Príncipe, T4331511, F4331491*, and at **Promotur** ⓘ *Centreventos, Av José Vieira 315, sala 20, T4232633, www.promotur.com.br, also www.joinville.sc.gov.br.*

Sights

The **Museu Nacional da Imigração e Colonização** ⓘ *R Rio Branco 229, Tue-Fri 0900-1800*, in the Palácio dos Príncipes, has a collection of objects and tools from the original German settlement and other items of historical interest. **Arquivo Histórico de Joinville** ⓘ *Av Hermann August Lepper 65, T4222154, Mon-Fri 0830-1200, 1330-2000*, houses a collection of documents dating from the town's foundation. There is also the **Museu de Fundição** ⓘ *R Helmuth Fallgatter 3345, T4320133, Mon-Fri 0800-1200, 1330-1700*, with around 800 items, including books, documents, photographs, old equipment and tools, minerals and artistic items. The interesting **Museu de Artes de Joinville** ⓘ *R 15 de Novembro 1400, Tue-Sun 0900-2100*, is in the old residence of Ottokar Doerfell. It promotes temporary exhibitions by local and other Brazilian artists. The **Casa da Cultura** ⓘ *R Dona Fransisca 800, Mon-Fri 0900-1800, Sat 0900-1300* (Galeria Municipal de Artes 'Vistor Kursansew'), also contains the School of Art 'Fritz Alt', the School of Music 'Vila Lobos' and the School of Ballet. **Casa Fritz Alt** ⓘ *R Aubé, Tue-Sun 0900-1200, 1400-1800*, is the home of the sculptor, exhibiting his works of art and personal possessions; several of his monuments are on display in the town.

The **Museu Arqueológico do Sambaqui** ⓘ *R Dona Francisca 600, T4330114, Tue-Sun 0900-1200, 1400-1800*, has a collection dating back to 5000 BC, with an exhibition devoted to the life of the indigenous people who built the sambaqui shell mounds along the south coast of Brazil (see page 298). There are also two archaeological reserves: **Sambaqui do Rio Comprido**, carbon dated to BC 2865, and **Sambaqui Morro do Ouro**.

The **Alameda Brustlein**, better known as the **Rua das Palmeiras**, is an impressive avenue of palm trees, leading to the **Palácio dos Príncipes**. The trees were planted in 1873 by Frederico Brustlein with seeds brought in 1867 by Louis Niemeyer. The **Railway Station** ⓘ *R Leite Ribeiro, T4222550*, dates from 1906 and is a fine example of the German style of architecture , and the **Mercado Municipal** ⓘ *Praça Hercílio Luz*, is in the *enxaimel* style. At the other end of the spectrum, the **Cathedral**, on Avenida Juscelino Kubitscheck with Rua do Príncipe, is futuristic with spectacular windows recounting the story of man. The **Cemitério dos Imigrantes** ⓘ *R 15 de Novembro 978, Mon-Fri 1400-1730*, is interesting; the attached **Casa da Memória do Imigrante** has information on the town's history, with audiovisual and documentary displays.

The **Parque Zoobotânico** ⓘ *R Pastor Guilherme Rau 462, T4331230, Tue-Sun 0900-1800*, 15 minutes' walk in the direction of Mirante, is a good zoo and park, with many local species of birds and animals and a children's park. From here it is another 25 minutes' walk to the **Mirante** for a beautiful view of the town and the bay. The tower on the top is at an altitude of 250 m and you can walk up a spiral staircase on the outside for a panoramic view. An **Orchid Farm** ⓘ *R Helmuth Fallgatter 2547, opposite the Terminal de Integração Tupy, Boa Vista, 0800-1200, 1330-1800*, is open to the public for sales or just to look around.

At **Expoville**, 4 km from the centre on BR-101 (continuation of 15 de Novembro), is an exhibition of Joinville's industry, although it is used for many other exhibitions and festivals as well. The new, multifunctional **Centreventos Cau Hansen** has been built to house sporting activities, shows, festivals, conferences and other events. It has the first Bolshoi Ballet School outside Moscow. The tiled mural around the entrance, by Juarez Machado, depicts a circus. There are some 600 industries in the manufacturing park, many of which are substantial exporters.

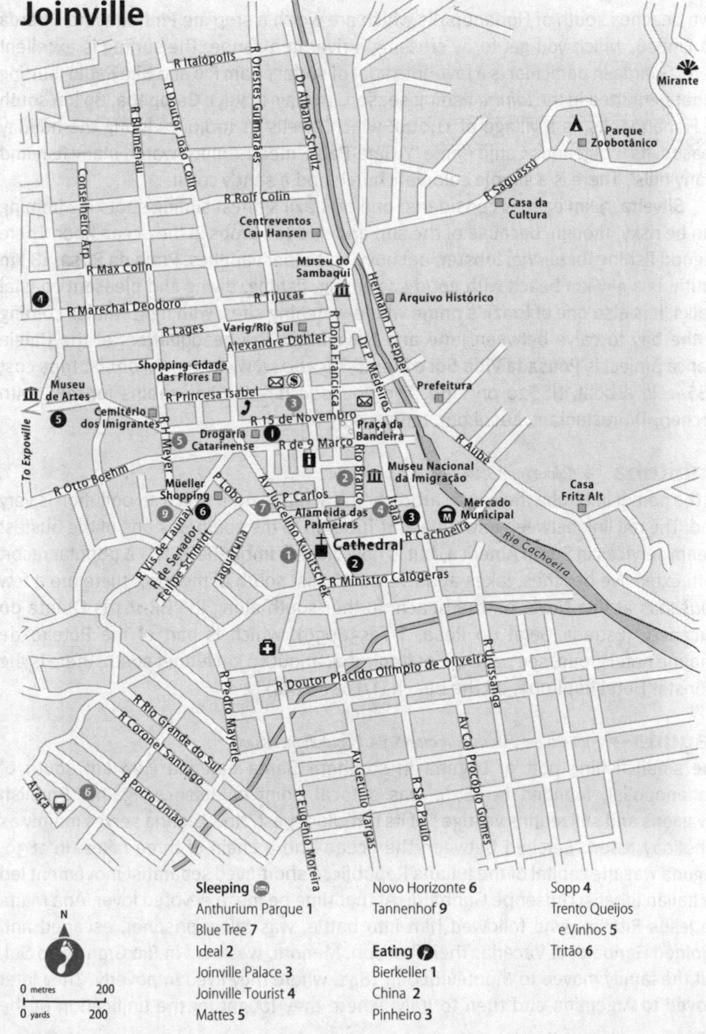

Excursions from Joinville

You can take a boat trip on the **Príncipe de Joinville III** ① *T4550824, US$10 per person*, at 1000 from Lagoa Saguaçú, Bairro Espinheiros (9 km from the centre), past several islands to São Francisco do Sul. Stops include the Museu Nacional do Mar, the port, lunch at a fish restaurant, Ilha da Rita and Ilha das Flores, getting back at 1600.

Four daily buses go to **Ubatuba** beach, a weekend resort (see above under São Francisco do Sul).

Guaratuba (see page 298) by bus, 1¼ hours, US$2 (connections to Paranaguá).

The **festival of São João** in June can be seen best in Santa Catarina at **Campo Alegre**, the first town on the road inland to Mafra. There are bonfires, a lot of (German) folk dancing, and large quantities of local specialities, *quentão* and *pinhões*. It is a beautiful climb on the road from the BR-101 to Campo Alegre.

South of Florianópolis

Two beaches south of Florianópolis which are worth a stop are **Pinheira** and **Guarda do Embaú**, which you get to by crossing a river in a canoe. The surfing is excellent here; Guarda in particular is a favourite spot of surfers from Rio and São Paulo (surfing is not permitted in the *tainha* fishing season, 15 May-15 July). **Garopaba**, 89 km south of Florianópolis, is a village of 11,000, which swells to 100,000 during the holiday season. Its indigenous Carijó name 'Y-Gara-Paba' means 'much water, many fish and many hills'. There is a simple colonial church and a sandy coast.

Silveira, 3 km east, is considered one of Brazil's finest surfing spots. Swimming can be risky, though, because of the surf and sudden drops in the ocean floor. There is good fishing for *tainha*, lobster, anchovy and other varieties. **Praia da Rosa**, 18 km south, is a 3½-km beach with good swimming, fishing, diving and pleasant coastal walks. It is also one of Brazil's prime whale-watching sites, with right whales coming to the bay to calve between June and November. The headquarters of the Baleia Franca project is **Pousada Vida Sol e Mar** ① *T3540041, www.vsmar.com.br*, trips cost US$42 in a boat, US$20 on land. The *pousada* (**L**) also has cabins for rent, with kitchen, TV, restaurant, sushi bar, tennis, surf school.

Imbituba → *Colour map 5, B4. Population: 33,000.*

At the port of Imbituba there is a carbo-chemical plant, from which air pollution is very bad. The rail link between Imbituba and Tubarão to the south was one of the busiest steam services in South America, but is now closed. Imbituba is now a popular resort with extensive beaches, lakes and lively surf. Just south of the town there are a few *pousadas* at **Vila Nova**; on the beach, further south along the BR-101 is **Quinta do Bucanero** (Estrada Geral do Rosa, T/F3556056), which is part of the Roteiro de Charme hotel group, see page 47; at **Itapirubá**, about 10 km further south, there is the four-star **Hotel Itapirubá**, on the beach (T/F6460294).

Laguna → *Phone code: 048. Colour map 5, B4. Population: 48,000.*

The small fishing port of Laguna in southern Santa Catarina (124 km south of Florianópolis), founded in 1676, was a focal point of defence against Spanish invasions and still retains vestiges of its turbulent past. Now Laguna serves mainly as a holiday resort, perched between the ocean and a chain of three lakes. In 1839, Laguna was the capital of the Juliana Republic, a short-lived separatist movement led by Italian idealist Guiseppe Garibáldi. At that time he met a devoted lover, Ana Maria de Jesus Ribeiro, who followed him into battle, was taken prisoner, escaped and rejoined Garibáldi at Vacaria. Their first son, Menotti, was born in Rio Grande do Sul, but the family moved to Montevideo in 1841, where they lived in poverty. They later moved to Argentina and then to Italy, where they fought for the unification of the peninsula. Ana Maria (or Anita) died near Ravenna in 1849 while they were fleeing to Switzerland from the Austrian army. She became a heroine in both Brazil and Italy and there are monuments to her in Rome, Ravenna, Porto Alegre, Belo Horizonte, Florianópolis, Juiz da Fora, Tubarão and Laguna. At Laguna is the **Anita Garibáldi Museum**, containing documents, furniture and her personal effects.

Laguna's beach, 2 km from the centre, is not very good, but 16 km away (by ferry and road) are beaches and dunes at **Cavo de Santa Marta**. Also from Laguna, take a **Lagunatur** or **Auto Viação São José** bus to **Farol** (four buses a day Monday-Friday, one on Saturday, US$1.50, beautiful ride). You have to cross the mouth of the Lagoa Santo Antônio by ferry (10 minutes) to get to Farol; look out for fishermen aided by dolphins (*botos*). Here is a fishing village with a lighthouse, the **Farol de Santa Marta**, the largest lighthouse in South America with the third largest view in the world. It was built by the French in 1890 of stone, sand and whale oil. Guided tours available (taxi, US$10, not including ferry toll). It may be possible to bargain with fishermen for a bed, or there are campsites at Santa Marta Pequena by the lighthouse, popular with surfers.

Gravatal and Tubarão → *Phone code: 048. Colour map 5, B4. Population: 83,500.*

Some 75 km north of Araranguá is the coalfield town of Tubarão. Inland from the main road are the coalfields of Criciúma and Içara, with good beaches nearby. Tubarão has a railway museum with a large collection of steam engines used in South America. Trips are run once a month to Urussaga (see below), April-October, and to Imbituba and Jaguaruna, November to March (T9761257). **Termas do Gravatal** can be visited from Tubarão for its mineral pools. It is a quiet and peaceful area and has a few pricey hotels near the springs.

North of Gravatal are the towns of **Armazém**, settled by Germans, where agriculture and livestock are the main economic activities, and **São Martinho**, wlth *enxaimel* architecture brought by German immigrants. West of Gravatal is **São Ludgero**, also colonized by Germans and a major producer of cheese and fruit. Along the same road and about 60 km inland from Tubarão is **Orleães**, first colonized in 1883 by Italians, followed by the Germans, Portuguese and Polish. Its museum has an original water-powered workshop and sawmill, complete with waterwheel. It dates from the original settlers, and is still in working order. To get there get off the bus at the junction about 3 km from the town. From here you can continue inland to the west through **Lauro Müller** and up into the mountains, or south to **Urussanga**, where the Italian influence is very strong, and down to Cruciúma and the coast.

Araranguá → *Phone code: 048 Population: 51,000*

Continuing down the coast on the BR-101, you come to Araranguá, 13 km from which is the beautiful beach of **Arroio do Silva**, with a range of moderate and cheap hotels and a lively seasonal nightlife scene. Also reached from here is another beach resort, **Morro dos Conventos**, with hotels and campsites.

Just before you get to the border with Rio Grande do Sul (but not on the BR-101) is **Praia Grande**, which has a hotel and a good, cheap *churrascaria* just off the praça (see page 348 for access to Parque Nacional de Aparados da Serra).

São Joaquim → *Phone code: 049. Colour map 5, B4. Population: 23,000.*

Buses from Tubarão go inland to Lauro Müller, then over the Serra do Rio do Rastro (beautiful views of the coast in clear weather, really spectacular). The road continues to São Joaquim. At 1,360 m, it is the highest town in Southern Brazil, with regular snowfalls in winter. About 11 km outside the town, on the way to Bom Jardim da Serra, is the **Parque Ecológico Vale da Neve** (Snow Valley). It is an easy hike and very beautiful, the entrance is on the main road, US$3, and there is a restaurant. The owner is American and an English-speaking guide will take you for a 1½-hour walk through the forest. From São Joaquim, northeast over Pericó to Urubici is unpaved. These roads go around the **Parque Nacional de São Joaquim** (33,500 ha) in the Serra Geral, with canyons containing subtropical vegetation, and araucaria forest at higher levels. There is no bus. For **tourist information** Ibama office ⓘ *T048-2226202*, and **Secretaria de Turismo de São Joaquim** ⓘ *T2330258*.

Lages and around

→ *Phone code: 049. Colour map 5, B4. Population: 160,000.*

West of Florianópolis, the area around Lages is particularly good for 'rural tourism', with lots of opportunities for hiking, horse riding, river bathing, working on a farm and other activities. The weather can get really cold in winter and even the waterfalls have been known to freeze. Many of the local *fazendas* are open for visitors and offer accommodation. This is *gaúcho* country and you will get *gaúcho* hospitality, culture and food.

Sleeping

Florianópolis *p322, map p323, phone code 048*

L **Blue Tree Towers**, R Bocaiúva 2304, next to Shopping Beira Mar, T2515555, www.bluetree.com.br. Very smart, well-equipped modern business hotel in this excellent upmarket chain. Good restaurant, pool, gym and sauna.

B **Bristol Castelmar**, R Felipe Schmidt 1260, T2253228, www.bristol-hotelaria.com.br. Standard 1980s B-grade business hotel with a restaurant, pool and sauna.

B **Faial**, R Felipe Schmidt 603, T2252766, www.hotelfaial.com.br. Comfortable and traditional with simple rooms and a good restaurant.

B **Florianópolis Palace**, R Artista Bittencourt 14, T2249633, www.floph.com.br. Once the best hotel in town; now a 1970s throwback but with a decent enough pool, sauna and large a/c rooms. Recommended.

C **Farol da Ilha**, R Bento Gonçalves 163, T2252766, www.hotelfaial.com.br. 1990s hotel with 35 a/c rooms owned by the Hotel Faial. Convenient for the bus station. Well kept.

C **Valerim Center**, R Felipe Schmidt 554, T2251100. Functional 2-star with large rooms, hot water and hard beds.

C-D **Central Sumaré**, R Felipe Schmidt 423, T2225359. Clean and friendly, good value but with some rooms which are significantly better than others. Look at several. Breakfast included. More expensive with bath.

D-F **Felippe**, R João Pinto 132, 1 block from 15 de Novembro, by Terminal Urbano, T2224122. Small rooms, some with no windows, breakfast is just a cup of coffee, dirty bathrooms, cheaper without bath.

E **Ilha de Santa Catarina**, R Duarte Schutel 227, T2253781, F2251692. Price per person, IYHA youth hostel, breakfast included, cooking facilities, clean, some traffic noise, very friendly, will store luggage. Recommended. Prices rise in Dec-Feb; more expensive for non-members. See under Canasvieiras, p334.

Camping

Camping Clube do Brasil, São João do Rio Vermelho, north of Lagoa da Conceição, 21 km out of town; also at **Lagoa da Conceição**, Praia da Armação, **Praia dos Ingleses**, **Praia Canasvieiras**. 'Wild' camping allowed at **Ponta de Sambaqui** and **Praias Brava**, **Aranhas**, **Galheta**, **Mole**, **Campeche**, **Campanhas** and **Naufragados**; 4 km south of Florianópolis, camping site with bar at **Praia do Sonho** on the mainland, beautiful, deserted beach with an island fort nearby. 'Camping Gaz' cartridges from **Riachuelo Supermercado**, on R Alvim and R São Jorge.

Ilha de Santa Catarina *p322, map p324, phone code 048*

L **Aguas Mornas Palace Hotel**, Águas Mornas, T2451315, at the springs. Well-maintained luxury spa with a range of treatments.

L **Lexus-Hotel**, RHG Pereira 745, Canasvieiras, T2660909, F2660919. Studio flats on the beach and with breakfast. Friendly.

L-A Porto Ingleses, R das Gaivotas 610, Praia dos Ingleses, T2691414, www.portoingleses.com.br. Small resort with a pool, play area for kids, restaurant and beach service. All accommodation has a/c and is spacious.

AL Plaza Caldas da Imperatriz, Caldas da Imperatriz, T2451333. Very well appointed with baths, swimming pools and a range of treatments.

A Cabañas Verde Limão, on the beach, Barra da Lagoa. Small cabins with bath, fan and fridge.

A Caldas da Imperatriz, Caldas da Imperatriz, T2451388. A grand, old-fashioned European spa built in 1850 under the auspices of Empress Teresa Cristina, originally with public baths. All meals are included in the price.

A Hotel Cris, Joaquina, T2325380. Very comfortable cabins and friendly staff. Recommended.

A Hotel São Sebastião da Praia, Av Campeche 1373, Praia de Campeche, T/F2374247, www.hotelsaosebastiao.com.br. Resort hotel on a splendid beach. Offers special monthly rate Apr-Oct, excellent value.

A Pousada 32, on beach, Barra da Lagoa, T/F2323665. Comfortable apartments with kitchens and helpful staff.

B Pousada dos Tucanos, Estr Geral da Costa de Dentro 2776, near Pântano do Sul, T2375084, Caixa Postal 5016. English, French, Spanish spoken, spacious bungalows in garden setting. Excellent organic food. Very highly recommended. Take bus to Pântano do Sul, walk 6 km or telephone and arrange to be picked up by German owner.

C Pousada Floripaz, Estrada Geral (across hanging bridge at bus station), Barra da Lagoa, T2323193. Safe, family-run and with helpful owners. Organize boat and car tours. Highly recommended. Book in advance.

D Compania Inglesa, R Dr João Becker 276, Praia dos Ingleses, T2691350, www.hotelciainglesa.com.br. Little beach hotel with a pool and friendly staff. Good for families.

D Pousada-Lanchonete Sem Nome, Praia do Moçambique, Barra da Lagoa. 4-bunk dorms with shared bathrooms, a kitchen and laundry. Recommended.

D Pousada Zilma, R Geral da Praia da Joaquina 279, Lagoa da Conceição, T2320161. Quiet, safe and simple with helpful staff. Recommended.

D Ricardo, R Manoel S de Oliveira 8, CEP 88062, Lagoa da Conceição, T2320107. Rents self-contained apartments or houses.

E Albergue da Juventude Canasvieiras, R Dr João de Oliveira 100, esq Av das Nações, Canasvieiras, T2662036, F2660220. IYHA youth hostel, 2 blocks from sea. Convenient, well run and with dorms and doubles. Opens in the summer only.

F Albergue do Pirata, Pântano do Sul, www.megasites.com.br/pirata. Doubles and dorms with breakfast in natural surroundings with lots of trails.

Camping

Camping da Barra, Barra da Lagoa, T2323199. Beautiful clean site, helpful owner.

Porto Belo and around *p325, map p325, phone code 047*

B Baleia Branca, Av Nena Trevisan 98, Porto Belo, T3694011, www.hotelbaleiabranca.com.br. 12 chalets in a garden with a pool, sauna and camping area.

B Porto Belo, R José Amâncio 246, Porto Belo T0XX47-3694483, F2431057. IYHA. Lots of apartments, mostly sleep 4-6, in **B** range, good value for a group.

B Pousada Zimbros, R da Praia 527, Zimbros, T3693225. Cheaper off season, on beach, sumptuous breakfast, restaurant. Highly recommended.

C-D Blumenauense, Av Sen Atílio Fontana, Praia do Perequê, T3694208. Simple rooms with en suites and breakfast; on the beach.

Camping

There are lots of campsites around the peninsula.

Itajaí and around *p326, phone code 047*

B-C Marambaia Cabeçudas, Praça Marcos Konder 46, Praia de Cabeçudas, 6 km out of town, www.maramabaiahotel.com.br. Modern resort hotel with a pool and gym. Comfortable though anonymous rooms.

C Grande, R Felipe Schmidt 198, T3480968, www.iai.matrix.com.br/grandehotel. Classic 1940s hotel now looking somewhat frayed.

Blumenau *p327, phone code 047*
C **Schroeder**, R 15 de Novembro 514, T3870933. A/c, TV, phone, fridge, pool.
D **Pousada Max**, R 15 de Novembro 257, T3870598. Apartment with satellite TV, fridge, a/c, parking.

Excursions from Blumenau *p328, phone code 047*
AL **Fazenda Park Hotel**, Estrada Geral do Gasparinho 2499, Gaspar, T3265696. A new hotel with a swimming pool, fishing, walking and riding.
D **Pousada Ecológoca Spitzkopf**, R Bruno Schreiber 3777, T3365422, bar but no restaurant, pool, heating, beautiful, clean, extremely quiet.

Joinville *p330, map p331, phone code 047*
A **Anthurium Parque**, R São José 226, T/F4336299, www.anthurium.com.br. In a colonial building, once home to a bishop, good value, English spoken, pool, sauna, part of the **Roteiro de Charme** hotel group, see page 47.
A **Blue Tree**, Av Juscelino Kubitschek 300, T4618000, www.bluetree.com.br. Excellent business hotel which opened in 2002. Very good service and business facilities and spick and span modern rooms. Sauna, gym and an excellent restaurant and bar.
A **Tannenhof**, R Visc de Taunay 340, T/F4338011, www.tannenhoff.com.br. 4-star, pool, gym, traffic noise, excellent breakfast, restaurant on 14th floor.
B **Joinville Tourist**, R 7 de Setembro 40, T4331288, www.touristhotel.com.br. Smart though anonymous 3-star with a pool, bar and restaurant.
B-C **Joinville Palace**, R do Príncipe 142, T4336111, www.joinvillepalacehotel.com.br. Simple a/c rooms with heating and TV. Visa accepted.
D **Ideal**, R Jerônimo Coelho 98, T4223660. Simple, well kept and convenient for the rodoviária Municipal.
D-E **Mattes**, 15 de Novembro 801, T4339886. Simple but with good service and facilities and a big breakfast.
E **Novo Horizonte**, at the bus station. Very basic fan-cooled rooms but clean.

South of Florianópolis *p332*
A **Morada do Bouganvilles**, Estr Geral do Morro, Praia da Rosa, T3556100, www.pousadabougainville.com.br. Chalets in a bougainvillea-filled garden with a small pool and a bar.
A **Quinta do Bucanero**, Estr Gerald a Rosa, Praia da Rosa, T3556056, www.bucanero.com.br. Tastefully decorated luxury resort with private access to the beach. Set in lush vegetation in a protected area and with a range of activities from horse riding to boat trips available. Closed Jun-Jul. No children.
B **Pousada da Lagoa**, R Rosalina de Aguiar Lentz 325, Garopaba, T/F2543201, www.pousadadalagoa.com.br. Comfortable countryside *pousada* with an outdoor pool, reasonable restaurant and bar and a series of trails running into the environs.
C **The Rosebud**, Estr Geral do Morro, Praia da Rosa, T3556101. Simple little *pousada* with breakfast.
E **Praia do Ferrugem**, Estr Gerals do Capão, Garopaba, T0XX48-2540035, IYHA youth hostel. Price per person.

Laguna *p332, phone code 048*
L-A **Laguna Tourist**, Av Castelo Branco, Praia do Gi, 4 km, T6470022, www.lagunatourist.com.br. 1970s resort with a view out over the bay from its hilltop setting. Popular with families and with many activities on offer.
C **Turismar**, Av Rio Grande do Sul 207, T6470024, F6470279. A simple 2-star with a view out over Mar Grosso beach.
D **Beiramar**, 100 m from **Recanto**, opposite Angeloni Supermarket, T6440260. No breakfast, clean, TV, rooms with view over lagoon.
D **Recanto**, Av Colombo 17, close to bus terminal. With breakfast. Modern but basic.

São Joaquim *p333, phone code 049*
B **Pousada Caminhos da Neve**, Av Irineu Bornhausen, T/F2330385. One of the smartest in town, with heated rooms.
C **Incomel Park**, Av Ivo Silveira 340, 1 km from centre towards Lages, T2330980, F2330281. Simple but with central heating, accepts Visa.
D **Nevada**, R Manuel Joaquim Pinto 213, T/F2330259. A cheap hotel with simple rooms and a restaurant serving surprisingly expensive meals.

E Maristela, R Manoel Joaquim Pinto 220, 5 mins' walk from rodoviária, T233007. French spoken, no heating so can be cold, friendly, helpful, good breakfast.

Lages and around *p334, phone code 049*
A Grande, R João de Castro 23, T/F2223522. Standard town 3-star.
D Rodeio, T2232011. One of 3 similar hotels near the rodoviária with rooms with or without bath and a good breakfast. In the same building there is a good *churrascaria*, open in the evening, US$7.50.

Fazendas near Lages
All on working farms. On average, prices include all meals.
A Fazenda Aza Verde, Antiga BR-2, Soroptimista 13, T2220277. Horses, fishing, boats, games room, heating, pool.
A Fazenda Ciclone, BR-116, Km 276, localidade Vigia, T2223382. Horses, fishing, table tennis, billiards, river beach.
A Fazenda do Barreiro, Rod SC 438, Km 43, T2223031. Games room, library, horses, pool, fishing, boats, TV.
A Fazenda Dourado Turismo Rural, Estr Lages-Morrinhos Km 14, T2222066/99822094. Simple but comfortable a/c chalets surrounding a grassy lawn and in the edge of Araucária pine forest. With restaurant, pool and live music at weekends.
A Fazenda Nossa Senhora de Lourdes, R Aristiliano Ramos 565, T2220798. Pool, games room, library, horses, fishing, good walking.
A Fazenda Rancho do Boqueirão, BR-282, Km 4, Saída São José do Cerrito, T2260354, F2260354. Heating, TV, library, games room, pool, horses, bicycles, good walking, fishing.
A Fazenda Refúgio do Lago, Rod SC 438, Km 10, Pedras Brancas, T2221416. Pool, games room, library, horses, shooting, fishing, boats, river beach.

Eating

Florianópolis *p322, map p323, phone code 048*
Take a walk along R Bocaiúva, east of R Almte Lamego, to find the whole street filled with Italian restaurants, barbecue places.
TTT Toca da Garoupa R Alves de Brito 178, just off R Bocaiúva. The city's best seafood restaurant.
TT La Cucina, R Padre Roma 291. Buffet lunch, Mon-Sat, pay by weight, good, vegetarian choices. Recommended.
TT Lindacap, R Felipe Schmidt 1162 (closed Mon, Sun lunch only). Fish, chicken and meat *pratos* as well as seafood, smart, good views. Recommended.
TT Macarronada Italiana, Av Beira Mar Norte 2458. Good, comfortable, upmarket Italian, with a decent pizzeria next door.
TT O Mercador, Box 33/4 Mercado Público. Excellent self-service specializing in fish and seafood, tables outside on cobbled street. Recommended.
TT Papparella, Almte Lamego 1416. Excellent and enormous pizzas thick with cheese.
TT Pirão, Mercado Público, upper floor on main square. Elegant rustic-style restaurant with an international menu and views over the market, open 1100-1430. Self service. Recommended.
TT Trapiche, Box 31, Mercado Público. Self-service fish and seafood, tables on pavement.
TT Vida, R Visc de Ouro Preto 298, next to Alliance Française. Decent vegetarian set meals and pay by weight.
T Café das Artes, at north end of R Esteves Junior 734. Nice café, excellent cakes.
T Cía Lanches, Ten Silveira e R Trajano, downstairs, and, in Edif Dias Velho, Av R Felipe Schmidt 303. A wide selection of juices and snacks.
T Kayskidum, Av Beira Mar Norte 2566. *Lanchonete* and crêperie, very popular.
T Mirantes, R Alvaro de Carvalho 246, Centro. Buffet self-service, good value. Recommended.

Ilha de Santa Catarina *p322, map p324*
TT-T Oliveira, R Henrique Veras, Lagoa da Conceiçao. Excellent if simple seafood in pleasant surrounds.
T Meu Cantinha, R Orlando Shaplin 89, Barra da Lagoa. Excellent simple seafood.

For an explanation of the sleeping and eating price codes used in this guide, see the inside front cover. Other relevant information is provided in the Essentials chapter, pages 47 and 57.

Joinville *p330, map 331, phone code 047*
TTT Pinheiro, R Rio Branco 299, T4551254. Well worth a visit for excellent fish and shrimp dishes.
TTT Tritão, R Visc de Taunay 902, T4334816. Very good seafood and a handful of other national dishes.
TT Bierkeller, R 15 de Novembro 497, T4221360. Respectable German cooking.
TT China, R Abdon Batista 131, opposite the cathedral, T4223323. Eat in or home delivery service for oriental food.
TT Sopp, R Mcal Deodoro 640, on corner with R Jaraguá, T4223637. German cooking with a sausage-heavy menu.
TT Trento Queijos e Vinhos, R 15 de Novembro 2973, T4531796. Traditional Italian with OK pastas and pizza.

The **Müeller Shopping** has a good food hall.

Bars and clubs

Florianópolis *p322, map p323, phone code 048*
To find out about events and theme nights check the Beiramar Shopping Centre for notices in shop windows, ask in surf shops or take a trip to the University of Santa Catarina in Trindade and check out the noticeboards. The newspaper *Diário Catarinense* gives details of bigger events, eg Oktoberfest.

The **Mercado Público** in the centre, which is alive with fish sellers and stalls during the day, has a different atmosphere at the end of the day when hard-working locals turn up to unwind. However, this area is not particularly safe at night and most bars and restaurants are closed by 2200. The stall, **Box 32**, is good for seafood and has a bar specializing in *cachaça*. **Restaurant Pirão** overlooks the market square with a quieter view and live Brazilian music on Tue, Thu and Fri. **Empórium**, Bocaiúva 79, is a shop by day and popular bar at night.

You may need a car to get to other clubs and bars such as **Café Matisse**, Av Irineu Bornhausen 5000, inside the Centro Integrade de Cultura, or the hot spots at the beaches. **Ilhéu**, Av Prof Gama d'Eça e R Jaime Câmara, US$5. Bar open until early hours, tables spill outside, very popular with locals, fills up quickly, venue for live music rather than a disco (tiny dancefloor). **Café Cancun**, Av Beira Mar Norte, T2251029. Wed-Sun from 2000, US$5, bars, restaurant, dancing, sophisticated.

Ilha de Santa Catarina *p322, map p324*
Throughout the summer the beaches open their bars day and night; during the rest of the year the beginning of the week is very quiet. The beach huts of **Praia Mole** invite people to party all night (bring a blanket), while the **Club Seven** (in the Boulevard) and **L'Equinox** bar (Joaquina) are more for clubbers who don't mind 'sand in their shoes'. **Seven** offers theme nights and is very popular with surfers. Any bars are worth visiting in the Lagoon area (around the Boulevard and Barra da Lagoa) where the great Brazilian phrase '*qualquer lugar é lugar*' fits perfectly. This means whichever place is the place to be, reflecting the laid-back Brazilian mood at the beach. Other clubs and bars generally require a car: **Latitude 27**, near Praia Mole, **Ilhéus** bar (Canasvieras) and the popular **Ibiza** nightclub in Jureré.

Entertainment

Florianópolis *p322, map p323*
Cinema The 3-screen cinema at **Shopping Centre Beiramar** has international films with subtitles. **Music** Free live music every Sat morning at the marketplace near the bus terminal.

Festivals

Florianópolis *p322, map p323*
Easter **Farra de Boi** (Festival of the Bull). It is only in the south that, controversially nowadays, the bull is killed on Easter Sun. The festival arouses fierce local pride and there is much celebration around this time.
Dec and Jan The whole island dances to the sound of the **Boi-de-Mamão**, a type of dance which incorporates the puppets of Bernunça, Maricota (the Goddess of Love, a puppet with long arms to embrace everyone) and Tião, the monkey. The Portuguese brought the tradition of the bull, which has great significance in Brazilian celebrations.

Joinville *p330, map p331*
Nov Annual flower festival, mostly orchids, disappointing, US$1.50 entry.
Oct Fenachopp, beer festival.
May Fenatiro, the annual festival for the 2,000 or so members of the local shooting clubs (shooting is a favourite local pastime).
Jul Joinville hosts one of the largest **dance festivals** in the world; around 4,000 dancers stay for 12 days and put on shows and displays, ranging from jazz and folklore to classical ballet, seen by some 30,000 spectators in a variety of locations.

Shopping

Florianópolis *p322, map p323*
Shopping Centre Beiramar is a famous shopping centre which attracts bus loads of eager shoppers from outside the state. There are many things on offer, from surfboards to fashion items. There are many smaller shopping malls dotted around the resorts. However, bargain hunters are better off bartering in the family-run businesses at the **Mercado Público**. Here, **Casa da Alfândega**, has a good selection of crafts and souvenirs.

Activities and tours

Florianópolis *p322, map p323, phone code 048*
Tour operators
Ilhatur Turismo e Cambio, R Jerónimo Coelho 185, T2246333, F2236921. Very popular boat trips can be made in the bay with Scuna Sul, T2221806, www.scunasul.com.br, from US$7.50.

Transport

Florianópolis *p322, map p323, phone code 048*
Air
International and domestic flights arrive at Hercílio Luz airport, Av Deomício Freitas, 12 km from town, T2360879. Take **Ribeiroense** bus 'Corredor Sudoeste' from Terminal Urbano.

Airline offices Aerolíneas Argentinas, R Tte Silveira 200, 8th floor, T2247835, F2227267. **Gol**, T0300-7892121, www.voegol.com.br **Nordeste/Rio Sul**, Jerônimo Coelho 185, sala 601, T2247008, airport T2361779. **TAM**, at airport, T2361812. **Varig**, Av R Branco 796, T2247266, F2222725. **Vasp**, Av Osmar Cunha 105, T2241122, F2242970.

Bus
Local There are 3 bus stations for routes on the island, or close by on the mainland: **Terminal de Ônibus Interurbano** between Av Paulo Fontes and R Francisco Tolentino, west of the Mercado Público; **Terminal Urbano** between Av Paulo Fontes and R Antônio Luz, east of Praça Fernando Machado; a terminal at **R Silva Jardim** and R José da Costa. Yellow microbuses (**Transporte Ejecutivo**), starting from the south end of Praça 15 de Novembro and other stops, charge US$0.75-1.45 depending on the destination. Similarly, normal bus fares vary according to destination, from US$0.65.

Long distance International and buses from other Brazilian cities arrive at the rodoviária **Rita Maia** on the island, at the east (island) end of the Ponte Colombo Machado Salles.

Regular daily buses to **Porto Alegre** (US$16, 7 hrs), **São Paulo**, 9 hrs (US$23.75, *leito* US$36.25), **Rio**, 20 hrs (US$31 *convencional*, US$42 executive, US$55 *leito*); to **Foz do Iguaçu** (US$22, continuing to **Asunción** US$30). To **São Joaquim** at 1145, 1945 with **Reunidos**, 1815 with **Nevatur**, 5-6 hrs, US$9.30; to **Laguna** US$5.25. No direct bus to Corumbá, change at Campo Grande.

International **Montevideo**, US$52, daily, by **TTL**. **Buenos Aires**, US$55, **Pluma**, buses very full in summer, book 1 week in advance.

Car
Car hire Auto Locadora Coelho, Felipe Schmidt 81, vehicles in good condition. **Localiza** at the airport, T2361244, and at Av Paulo Fontes 730, T2255558. **Interlocadora**, T2360179 at the airport, F2361370, rates from US$40 a day before supplements.

Porto Belo *p325*
Bus **Florianópolis** to Porto Belo, several daily with **Rainha**, US$3, fewer at weekends, more frequent buses to **Tijucas**, **Itapema** and **Itajaí**, all on the BR-101 with

connections. Buses run from Porto Belo to the beaches on the peninsula.

Blumenau *p327, phone code 047*
Bus Coletivos Volkmann (T3871321), **Blumenau-Pomerode**, daily US$0.75, 1 hr, check schedule at tourist office. There are also buses from Pomerode to **Jaraguá do Sul**, **Joinville**, **São Bento do Sul**, **Florianópolis**, **São Paulo**, **Curitiba** and other local places with Rex (T3870387), União, Reunidas and Penha/Itapemirim (T3870387).

São Francisco do Sul *p329*
Bus The bus terminal is 1½ km from centre. Direct bus (Penha) daily to **Curitiba** at 0730, US$6, 3½ hrs.

Joinville *p330, map p331, phone code 047*
Air Airport 5 km from city, T4671000.
Airline offices TAM, T4332033. Varig/Rio Sul, R Alexandre Dohler 277, T4332800.

Bus To **Blumenau**, US$3, 2¼ hrs. The rodoviária is 2½ km outside the town, south exit, T4332991 (regular bus service).

Car hire Localiza, R Blumenau 1728, T4339393, or at the airport T4671020; Interlocadora, R do Príncipe 839, T4227888; Olímpia, R 9 de Março 734, T4331755.

Laguna *p332*
Bus To **Porto Alegre**, 5½ hrs, with Santo Anjo Da Guarda; same company goes to **Florianópolis**, 2 hrs, US$5.25, 6 daily; to **Tubarão**, every hr with Alvorada, US$2.75, 50 mins.

São Joaquim *p333*
Bus To **Florianópolis** 0700 and 1700 via Bom Retiro (**Reunidos**) and 0800 via Tubarão (**Nevatur**), 5½ hrs, US$9. Several daily buses to **Criciúma**, **Tubarão**, **Cascavel** and **Foz do Iguaçu**.

Lages *p334*
Bus Bus station is 30 mins' walk southeast of the centre. Bus to the centre (Terminal Municipal), 'Rodoviária' runs Mon-Fri only, or 'Dom Pedro II' every 40 mins at weekends. To **Florianópolis**, 6-8 buses daily on the direct road (BR-282), 5 hrs, US$10; to **Caxias do Sul**, 3¾ hrs, US$5.60.

Directory

Florianópolis *p322, map p323, phone code 048*
Banks Banco do Brasil, Praça 15 de Novembro, exchange upstairs, 1000-1500, huge commission on cash or TCs. Lots of ATMs downstairs. HSBC, ATM, R Felipe Schmidt 376, corner with R Álvaro de Carvalho. Banco Estado de Santa Catarina (BESC), *câmbio*, R Felip, Schmidt e Jerônimo Coelho, 1000-1600, no commission on TCs. Lovetur, Av Osmar Cunha 15, Ed Ceisa and Centauro Turismo, same address. Açoriano Turismo, Jaime Câmara 106, T2243939, takes Amex. Money changers on R Felipe Schmidt outside BESC. ATM for MasterCard/Cirrus at Banco Itaú, Shopping Centre Beiramar (not in the centre, bus Expresso). **Embassies and consulates** Austria, R Luiz Delfino 66, Apto 501, T2225952 (Mon-Fri 1500-1700), phone in advance. **Chile**, R Alvaro de Carvalho 267, 6th floor, Edif Mapil, T2233383. **France**, Alliance Française, T2227589 (Fri 0900-1200). **Spain**, R Almte Alvim 24, Casa 9, T2221821, F2241018. **Uruguay**, R Prof Walter de Bona Castela 26, T2344645 (0800-1200, 1400-1800). **Internet** Moncho, Tiradentes 181. **Laundry** Lav e Lev, R Felipe Schmidt 706, opposite Valerim Plaza. **Post office** Praça 15 de Novembro 5. **Telephone** Praça Pereira Oliveira 20.

Joinville *p330, map p331, phone code 047*
Internet Biernet Bar, R Visconde de Taunay 456. **Medical services** 24-hr pharmacies: Drogaria Catarinense, Filial Boa Vista, in front of the Hospital Regional, T4372355, or Filial São João, Av Getúlio Vargas 1343, T4227691. Farmacia Catarinense, R 15 de Novembro 503, T4222318.

Rio Grande do Sul

Brazil's southernmost state stands out as utterly different from the rest of the country. A huge chunk of the population still retain the German or Italian appearance and values of their ancestors. This is gaúcho *(cowboy) country and the herders are regularly seen in traditional garb. In restaurants, steaks the size of Texas are order of the day. The capital, Porto Alegre, is the most industrialized and cosmopolitan city in the south and tops the country's urban quality of life rankings. Nearby, there are good beaches, interesting coastal national parks and the stunning scenery of the Serra Gaúcha. On the border with Santa Catarina is the remarkable Aparados da Serra National Park where it can snow. In the far west are the remains of Jesuit missions. Look out for local specialities such as* comida campeira, te colonial *and* quentão. ➤➤ *For Sleeping, Eating and other listings, see pages 353-362.*

The Great Escarpment, in places over 1,000 m high, runs down the coastal area as far as Porto Alegre providing escape from the summer swelter. From the south of Santa Catarina to the borders of Uruguay, the green hills of Rio Grande do Sul are fringed along the coast by sand bars and lagoons, making one of the world's longest beaches. In southern Rio Grande do Sul, south and west of the Rio Jacuí, there are great grasslands stretching as far as Uruguay to the south and over 800 km westwards to Argentina. This is the distinctive land of the *gaúcho*, or cowboy (pronounced ga-oo-shoo in Brazil), of the flat black hat, *bombachas* (baggy trousers), poncho and *ximarão* (*mate* without sugar, also spelt *chimarrão*), the indispensable drink of southern cattlemen. There are many millions of cattle, sheep and pigs, rice production is on the increase, and some 75% of all Brazilian wine comes from the state. The *gaúcho* culture has developed a sense of distance from the African-influenced society further north. Many people will tell you they have more in common with Uruguayans or Argentines than Brazilians – apart from when it comes to football.

! A favourite all-purpose gaúcho exclamation, which means nothing but is used all the time, is 'Tchê'!

A lot of people from this region are strikingly beautiful: tall, with light brown skin and hair and intensely green eyes. Folk dances, unchanged since early settlers brought them from Europe, are still practised, both privately and for the benefit of tourists.

Since 1999, the state government has implemented a radical consultative scheme whereby people in all 497 municipalities jointly decide school, road and other infrastructure spending. The Participatory Budget, pioneered for over a dozen years in Porto Alegre, is widely supported and has attracted international acclaim. For more info log onto www.estado.rs.gov.br. The state tourism website is: www.turismo.rs.gov.br.

Porto Alegre → *Phone code: 051. Colour map 5, B3. Population: 1,361,000.*

Sited at the meeting of five rivers and freshened by over a million trees, Porto Alegre is one of Brazil's more pleasant cities. Culturally rich, ethnically diverse and progressive, it is the capital of the southern frontier and the hub of trade with Argentina and Uruguay. It is a good base for exploring the rest of Rio Grande do Sul's natural beauty and historical sites.

The capital of Rio Grande do Sul is where cowboy culture meets the bright lights. Though it is the biggest commercial centre south of São Paulo, it is friendly and manageable on foot. Get a map out in downtown Porto Alegre and someone will try to help you (get a map out in downtown São Paulo and they will probably try to rob you).

Ins and outs

Getting there International and domestic flights arrive at Salgado Filho airport. There are regular buses to the rodoviária and a Metrô service to the city centre. International and Interstate buses arrive at the terminal at Largo Vespasiano Júlio Veppo, on Avenida Mauá with Garibáldi. ▶▶ *See also Transport, page 358.*

Getting around First-class minibuses (*Lotação*), painted in a distinctive orange, blue and white pattern, stop on request. Safer and pleasanter than normal buses, fare about US$0.60. The Trensurb Metrô runs from the southern terminal at the

Porto Alegre

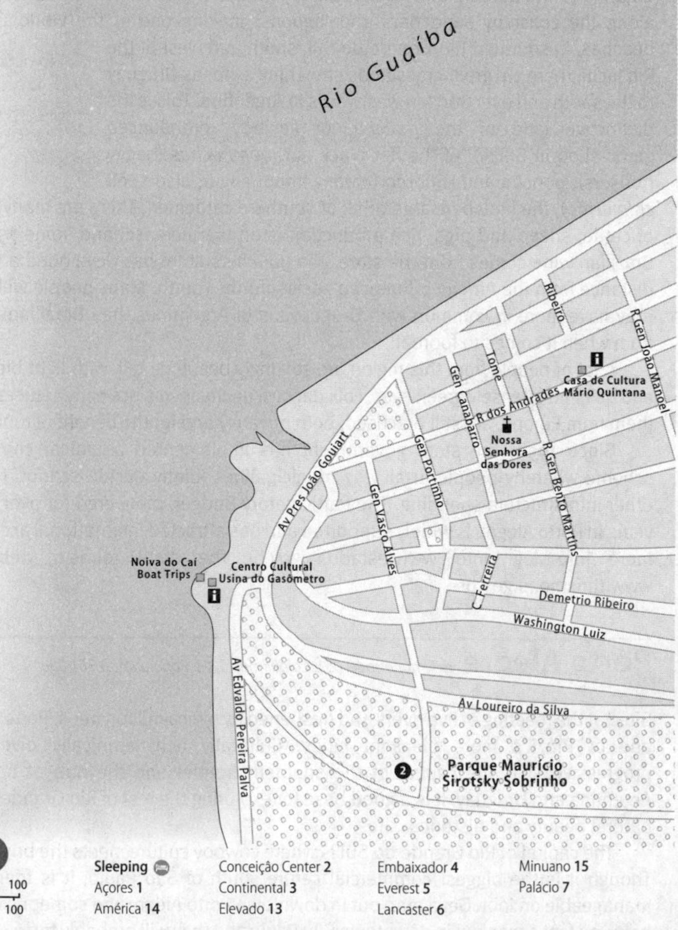

Mercado Público (station beside the market), going as far north as Sapucaia do Sul. The second station serves the rodoviária and the fifth the airport (10 minutes), 0500-2300, single journey US$0.40.

Tourist information ⓘ *T0800-517686, www.portoalegre.rs.gov.br/turismo*. **Central de Informações Turísticas** ⓘ *R Vasco da Gama 253, Bom Fim, T3115289, daily 0900-2100*. **Setur** ⓘ *Borges de Medeiros 1501, 10th floor, T32285400; also at Salgado Filho airport (friendly); interstate bus station (very helpful)*, free city maps; **Casa de Cultura Mário Quintana** ⓘ *Tue-Fri 0900-2100, Sat and Sun 1200-2100*; **Usina do**

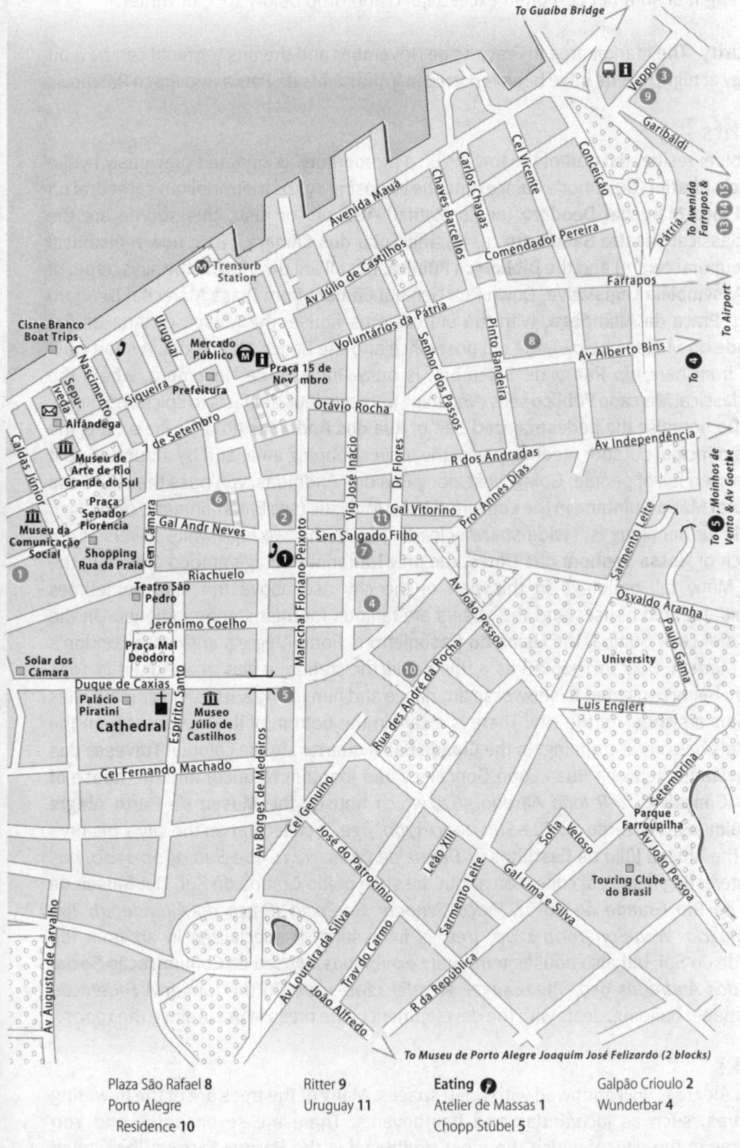

Plaza São Rafael **8**
Porto Alegre Residence **10**
Ritter **9**
Uruguay **11**

Eating
Atelier de Massas **1**
Chopp Stübel **5**
Galpão Crioulo **2**
Wunderbar **4**

 Gasômetro ⓘ *daily 1000-1800*; **Mercado Público** ⓘ *Mon-Sat 0900-1600*. **Guided walks** ⓘ *Sun from Praça da Alfândega, Sat from Praça da Matriz, T0800-517686, 1500 or 1600, free, or contact the tourist office, or in the Mercado Público.*

Maps Army maps (1:50,000) of Rio Grande's trekking regions (Canela, Parque Nacional de Aparados da Serra) are available at **Junta Servicio Militar** ⓘ *Prefeitura Municipal, R Prof E Castro 850, T32233611*. Note these maps are not available in rural areas.

Climate Standing on a series of hills and valleys on the banks of Lake Guaíba, Porto Alegre has a temperate climate through most of the year, though the temperature at the height of summer can often exceed 40°C and drop below 10°C in winter.

Security The market area in Praça 15 de Novembro and the bus terminal can be a bit dodgy at night; thefts have been reported in Voluntários da Pátria and Praça Parcão.

Sights

The older residential part of the town is on a promontory, dominated previously by the **Palácio Piratini** (Governor's Palace) and the imposing 1920s metropolitan **cathedral** on the **Praça Marechal Deodoro** (or da Matriz). Also on, or near, this square are the neoclassical **Theatro São Pedro** (1858), the **Solar dos Câmara** (1818, now a historical and cultural centre) and the **Biblioteca Pública**, but all are dwarfed by the skyscraper of the **Assembléia Legislativa**. Down Rua General Câmara from Praça Marechal Deodoro is the **Praça da Alfândega**, with the old customs house, the Museu de Arte de Rio Grande do Sul (see below), the old post office and the Banco Meridional. A short walk east from here, up Rua 7 de Setembro, is busy Praça 15 de Novembro, where the neoclassical **Mercado Público** sells everything from religious artefacts to spice and meat.

Do not miss the pedestrianized part of **Rua dos Andradas** (Rua da Praia). It is the city's principal outdoor meeting place, the main shopping area, and by around 1600 it is jammed full of people. Going west along Rua dos Andradas, you pass the pink **Casa Cultural Mário Quintana** in the converted Hotel Majestic (see Entertainment, page 357). A little further along is a wide stairway leading up to the two high white towers of the church of **Nossa Senhora das Dores,** the only National Heritage graded church in the city. Many tall buildings in this part of the city rise above the fine, sometimes dilapidated, old houses and the streets are famous for their steep gradients. On the banks of Lake Guaíba, the **Usina do Gasômetro** is Porto Alegre's answer to London's Tate Modern. Built in 1926-28 as a thermoelectric station, it was abandoned in 1974 before being converted to showcase art, dance and film in 1992. Its 117-m chimney has become a symbol for the city. There is a café in the bottom of it. The sunset from the centre's balcony is stunning. In the **Cidade Baixa** quarter are the colonial **Travessa dos Venezianos** (between Ruas Lopo Gonçalves and Joaquim Nabuco) and the **house of Lopo Gonçalves** ⓘ *R João Alfredo 582*, which houses the **Museu de Porto Alegre Joaquim José Felizardo** ⓘ *Tue-Sun 0900-1700, free*, a collection on the city's history.

The **Museu Júlio de Castilhos** ⓘ *Duque de Caxias 1231, Tue-Sun 0900-1700*, has an interesting historical collection about the state of Rio Grande do Sul. The **Museu de Arte do Rio Grande do Sul** ⓘ *Praça Senador Florêncio (Praça da Alfândega), Tue 1000-2100, Wed-Sun 1000-1700, free*, is interesting. It specializes in art from Rio Grande do Sul, but also houses temporary exhibitions. **Museu de Comunicação Social** ⓘ *R dos Andradas 959, T32244252, Mon-Fri 1200-1900*, in the former *A Federação* newspaper building, deals with the development of the press in Brazil since the 1920s.

Parks

Porto Alegre is well endowed with open spaces. Many of the trees are of the flowering varieties, such as jacarandas and flamboyants. There are seven parks and 700 squares in the city, of which the most traditional is the **Parque Farroupilha** (called

Parque Redenção), a fine park near the city centre. It has a triangular area of 33 ha between Avenida Osvaldo Aranha, Avenida José Bonifácio and Avenida João Pessoa, and contains a lake, minizoo, amusement park, bicycle hire, the Araújo Viana auditorium and a monument to the *Expedicionário*. On Sundays there is a *feira* of antiques, handicrafts and all sorts at the José Bonifácio end, where locals walk, talk and drink *chimarrão*, the traditional *gaúcho* drink. **Parque Moinhos de Vento** is popular for jogging and you can see lots of fit people around who train in the gym of the same name nearby. There is a replica of a windmill in the middle of the park, but there used to be plenty of working mills, which gave the *bairro* its name. The riverside drive, Avenida Edvaldo Pereira Paiva, around Parque Maurício Sirotsky Sobrinho, is closed to traffic on Sunday, for cycling, skating, jogging and strolling. **Marinho do Brasil** is another large park between the centre and the *zona sul*, where there are lots of sporting activities. The **Jardim Botânico**, the **Botanic Garden**, is on Rua Salvador França 1427, zona leste (Bairro Jardim Botânico, bus 40 from Praça 15 de Novembro).

The 5-km-wide **Lake Guaíba** lends itself to every form of boating and there are several sailing clubs. Two boats run trips around the islands in the estuary: **Cisne Branco** ⓘ *T32245222, several sailings on Sun, fewer mid-week, 1 hr, US$5*, from Cais do Porto, near Museu de Arte de Rio Grande do Sul; and **Noiva do Caí** ⓘ *T2117662, several on Sun, fewer mid-week, 1 hr, US$1.90, check winter schedules*, from the Usina do Gasômetro. Jet-skiers jump the wake of the tour boats. **Ipanema beach**, on the southern banks of the river, has spectacular sunsets. You can see a good view of the city, with glorious sunsets, from the **Morro de Santa Teresa** (take bus 95 from the top end of Rua Salgado Filho, marked 'Morro de Santa Teresa TV' or just 'TV').

Cervejaria Brahma ⓘ *Av Cristovão Colombo 545*, offers tours of its brewery (but not December-March).

Beaches around Porto Alegre

Tramandaí to Torres → *Phone code: 051. Population: 31,000.*

The main beach resorts of the area are to the east and north of the city. Heading east along the BR-290, 112 km from Porto Alegre is **Osório**, a pleasant lakeside town with a few hotels. From here it is 18 km southeast to the rather polluted and crowded beach resort of **Tramandaí**. The beaches here are very popular, with lots of hotels, bars, restaurant, and other standard seaside amenities. Extensive dunes and lakes in the region provide an interesting variety of wildlife and sporting opportunities. The beach resorts become less polluted the further north you travel, and the water is clean by the time you reach Torres (see below).

The BR-101 heads north, just inland of the coast from Osório to Florianópolis and beyond. A series of lakes separates the road from the coastal belt and the beach resorts, but there is another road running all along the coast from Tramandaí to Torres and the border with Santa Catarina. Between the two towns are the resorts (heading south to north) of **Atlântida do Sul**, **Capão da Canoa**, **Arroio Teixeira** and **Arroio do Sal** (**Casa da Sogra** serves good food). At **Capão da Canoa** there is surfing at Atlântida beach, while the **Lagoa dos Quadros**, inland, is used for windsurfing, sailing, waterskiing and jet-skiing.

Torres → *Phone code: 051. Colour map 5, B4. Population: 30,900.*

Torres is a well developed resort, with a number of beaches, several high class hotels, a wide range of restaurants, professional surfing competitions and entertainment. There is a lively club scene during the holidays. There is no lack of cheap accommodation, but from Christmas to Carnaval rooms are hard to find. Torres holds a ballooning festival in April. There is an annual Independence day celebration, when a cavalcade of horses arrives in town on 16 September from Uruguay.

Torres gets its name from the three huge rocks, or towers, on the town beach, Praia Grande. Some 2 km long, the beach is safe for swimming and there is surf near the breakwater. Fishing boats can be hired for a trip to **Ilha dos Lobos**, a rocky island 2 km out to sea, where sea lions spend the winter months. Dolphins visit Praia dos Molhes, north of the town, year round and whales en route to Santa Catarina can occasionally be seen in July. On the edge of Rio Mampituba, which marks the state boundary, this beach is good for net fishing and has restaurants. About 2 km south of Torres, past rocky little Prainha, is **Cal** (**Pradise Dunas** campsite, December-February only), popular with surfers. A further 2 km south, passing the Praia da Guarita leisure development, is **Itapeva**, with a campsite open year round. The water here is calm, OK for swimming and there is good dune trekking in the **Parque da Guarita**. There are bars and cafés and a **tourist information office** ⓘ *R Rio Branco 315, Torres, T6641219/ 6261937.*

Tramandaí to São José do Norte → *Phone code 051.*

A paved road runs south from Tramandaí (mostly prohibited to trucks) along the coast to **Quintão**, giving access to many beaches. One such beach is **Cidreira**, 26 km south of Tramandaí. It is not very crowded and has **Hotel Farol** on the main street. Bus from Porto Alegre US$3.40. A track continues to charming **Mostardas**, thence along the peninsula on the seaward side of the Lagoa dos Patos to São José do Norte, opposite Rio Grande (see Excursions from Rio Grande, page 349). There is accommodation in **Palmares do Sul** (across the peninsula from Quintão) and Mostardas. The latter also has a Banco do Brasil and good pizza (Rua Luís Araújo 941 (closed Monday). About 30 km south of Mostardas is **Tavares**, with a barely passable hotel (**F**) in the praça. Mostardas makes a good base for visiting the **Lagoa do Peixe National Park**, one of South America's top spots for migrating birds. Flamingos and albatrosses are among the visitors. There is free access to the park, which has no infrastructure. From Mostardas you can hop off the bus (1045 daily) which passes through the northern end of the park on its way to the beach (where there are basic hotels and restaurants). The main lake (which has the highest bird concentration) is about 20 km from both Mostardas and Tavares. **Park information** ⓘ *Praça Luís Martins 30, Mostardas, T6731464.*

Porto Alegre coast

The Serra Gaúcha

Some of the Serra Gaúcha's most stunningly beautiful scenery is around the towns of Gramado and Canela, 130 km north of Porto Alegre. There is a distinctly Swiss/Bavarian flavour to many of the buildings in both towns. In spring and summer the flowers are a delight, and in winter there are frequent snow showers.

This is excellent walking and climbing country among hills, woods, lakes and waterfalls. The area is developing as an adventure tourism centre. The Rio Paranhana at Três Coroas is well known for canoeists, especially for slalom. It is 25 km south of Gramado. In both towns it is difficult to get rooms in the summer/Christmas. Local crafts include knitted woollens, leather, wickerwork and chocolate.

Gramado

→ *Phone code: 054. Colour map 5, B4. Population: 28,600.*

At 850 m above sea level, Gramado provides a summer escape from the 40°C heat of the plains. The town lies on the edge of a plateau with fantastic views. It is clean and full of Alpine-style buildings making it feel either Swiss or like Disneyworld, depending on your point of view. Gramado lives almost entirely by tourism. Its main street, Avenida Borges de Medeiros, is full of kitsch artisan shops and fashion boutiques. In the summer, thousands of hydrangeas (*hortênsias*) bloom. Among its parks are **Parque Knorr** and **Lago Negro**, and **Minimundo** ⓘ *T2861334, Tue-Sun 1300-1700*, a collection of miniature models such as European castles. About 1½ km along Avenida das Hortênsias heading towards Canela is the **Prawer Chocolate Factory** ⓘ *Av das Hortênsias 4100, T2861580, www.prawer.com.br, Mon-Fri 0830-1130 and 1330-1700*, which offers free tours of the truffle-making process and free tasting. Opposite is the incongruous but good **Hollywood Dream Car Automobile Museum** ⓘ *Av das Hortênsias 4151, T2864515, 0900-1900, US$2.10*, which has an excellent collection of American gas guzzlers dating back to a 1929 Ford Model A and Harley-Davidson motorbikes from 1926. For a good walk or bike ride into the valley, take the dirt road Turismo Rural 28, *Um Mergulho no Vale* (A Dive into the Valley), which starts at Avenida das Hortênsias immediately before Prawer Chocolate Factory. Each August, Gramado holds a festival of Latin American cinema. There are two **tourist information offices** ⓘ *Av das Hortênsias (Pórtico), T2861418, and Praça Maj Nicoletti/Av Borges de Medeiros 1674, T2861475, www.gramadosite.com.br.*

Canela and around

→ *Phone code: 054. Colour map 5, B4. Population: 33,600.*

A few kilometres along the plateau rim, Canela has been spared the plastic makeover of its neighbour. The painted wooden buildings provide a certain downtown charm. Canela is surrounded by good parks and is developing as a centre of adventure tourism, with rafting, abseiling, trekking, etc on offer. There's a **tourist information office** ⓘ *Laga da Fama 227, T2822200, www.canela.com.br.*

About 7 km from Canela is the **Parque Estadual do Caracol** ⓘ *T2783035, 0830-1800, US$1.75*, which has a spectacular 130-m high waterfall. Emerging from thick forest, Rio Caracol tumbles like dry ice from an overhanging elliptical escarpment. East-facing, photos are best before noon. A 927-step metal staircase ("equivalent to a 45-storey building") leads to the plunge pool. If on bike, there is an 18-km circular route continuing on to Park Ferradura (along a 4-km spur) where there is a good view into the canyon of the Rio Cai. From the Ferradura junction, turn right to continue to the national forest **Floresta Nacional** ⓘ *T2822608, 0800-1700, free*, run by IBAMA (the Brazilian Environment Ministry) with woodland walks. From here, the dirt road continues round to Canela. Another good hike or bike option is the 4-km dirt track southeast of Canela past Parque das Sequóias to Morro Pelado. At over 600 m, there are spectacular views from the rim edge.

Maps Army 1:50,000 maps exist but are only available from military posts in Caxias do Sul and Porto Alegre. The urban department in Canela's Prefeitura Municipal, R Dona Carlinda, and the environmental lodge in Parque Estadual do Caracol have copies available for viewing only.

Parque Nacional de Aparados da Serra

ⓘ Aparados da Serra, Wed-Sun 0900-1700, US$2.10 plus US$1.75 for a car, T2511262; Serra Geral is open all year, daily, free. It has no infrastructure but does have a campground. The best time to visit is May to Aug. Rain is heaviest in Sep. For further information, contact Ibama, R Miguel Teixeira 126, Cidade Baixa, Caixa Postal 280, Porto Alegre, CEP90050-250, T32252144, www.ibama.gov.br, or tourist information at the Centro Cultural Cambará do Sul, R Adail Valim 39, T2511320, daily 0800-1200, 1330-1800. For guides in Cambará do Sul visit the Centro Cultural, R Adail Valim 39, T2511320 (which also has a 1:50,000 scale trekking map on view), or T2511265 and in Praia Grande ToXX48-5320330. Some of the hotels in Cambará run trips into the park (see page 354).

Some 88 km from São Francisco de Paula (138 km east of Canela, 117 km north of Porto Alegre) are the spectacular **Parque Nacional de Aparados da Serra** and **Parque Nacional da Serra Geral**. Formed 115-130 million years ago when the American and African plates were separating, the parks lie in a 250-km mountain range. Aparados da Serra's major attraction is the canyon Itaimbezinho, 7.8 km long and 720 m deep. Here, two waterfalls cascade 350 m into a stone circle at the bottom. For experienced hikers (and with a guide) there is a difficult path to the bottom of Itaimbezinho. Other easier hikes follow the upper rim of the canyon. You can then hike 20 km to Praia Grande in Santa Catarina (see page 333). **Parque Nacional da Serra Geral** was opened in 1992. Its main attractions are the **Malacara** and **Fortaleza** canyons, the latter 1,170 m deep. From the top there are spectacular views to the coast. As well as the canyons, the parks and surrounding region have several bird specialities. Red-legged seriema, a large conspicuous bird, can be seen on the way to the park, and there are two fox species.

The nearest town to the park is **Cambará do Sul** (bus from São Francisco de Paula at 0945 and 1700, 1 hour 15 minutes, US$2 and one direct bus per day from Porto Alegre). From here it is 18 km, unpaved, to the park entrance at Guarita Gralha Azul . There's a bus or it's possible to hitchhike. Gralha Azul is 20 km by unpaved road from Praia Grande. There is a snack bar but no accommodation and camping is banned. From Cambará do Sul to the Fortaleza canyon is 23 km on an unmade road.

South of Porto Alegre

Pelotas → *Phone code: 053. Colour map 5, C3. Population: 323,200.*

Pelotas, Rio Grande do Sul's second largest city, was founded in the early 19th century and grew rich on the *charque* (dried beef) trade. On the BR-116, 271 km south of Porto Alegre, it lies on the banks of Rio São Gonçalo which connects the Lagoa dos Patos with the Lagoa Mirim. Its heyday was 1860-90 and its early colonial architecture, among the usual flat-fronted buildings, enhances the city's air of being stuck in a time warp. It is sleepy yet prosperous, with much typically Brazilian charm. It has an array of shops, good for browsing, in the pedestrianized town centre, and pleasant parks with plenty of green. There is a 19th-century cathedral, **São Francisco de Paula**, and, as testament to British settlers of the time, the Anglican church **Igreja Episcopal do Redentor**, a couple of blocks from the main square on Rua XV de Novembro. The tree-lined Avenida Bento Gonçalves offers a pleasant escape from the summer heat. There's no official tourist information centre but **Terrasul** ⓘ *R Gen Neto 627, T2279973*, has local maps and can organize good value city and regional tours. Recommended. Also **Cispella Viagens** ⓘ *R Andrade Neves 1991, T2255944*. Pelotas is famous for its cakes and sweets; preserved fruits from the many small confectioners are worth trying.

Excursions from Pelotas

Within a radius of 60 km (about an hour's drive), there are numerous excursions to the farms of settlers of German descent in the hilly countryside (for example Cerrito Alegre and Quilombo), where you can find simple and clean accommodation, with cheap, good and plentiful food.

The **Lagoa dos Patos** is very shallow; at low tide it is possible to walk 1 km out from the shore. During heavy rain, saltwater entering the lake brings with it large numbers of crabs which are a local delicacy. Fishermen are generally happy to take tourists out on sightseeing or fishing trips for a small fee (best to go in a group). **Praia do Laranjal** is full of locals' beach houses and there are several friendly bars. **Barro Douro** is very green with no beach, but is the site of a big local festival for *Iemanjá* on 1-2 February, which is well worth visiting, campsite, *Ze3* buses (or taxi US$30) from Pelotas.

South of Pelotas, on the BR-471, is the **Taim Water Reserve** ⓘ *information from Ibama in Porto Alegre, ToXX51-2267211, www.ibama.gov.br*, on the Lagoa Mirim. The road cuts the reserve in two and capibaras, killed by passing traffic, are sadly a common sight along the route. Many protected species, including black-necked swans and the *quero-quero* bird, migrate to the Taim for the breeding season. There are no facilities. Visitors should stay in Rio Grande, 80 km away, or in Pelotas. About 5 km from Taim there is an **ecological station** with a small museum of regional animals; there is some accommodation for scientists or other interested visitors.

Rio Grande → *Phone code: 053. Colour map 5, C3. Population: 186,500.*

At the entrance to the Lagoa dos Patos, 274 km south of Porto Alegre, is Rio Grande, founded in 1737. The city lies on a low, sandy peninsula, 16 km from the Atlantic Ocean. Today it is the distribution centre for the southern part of Rio Grande do Sul, with significant cattle and meat industries.

During the latter half of the 19th century, Rio Grande was an important centre. It has lost much of its importance but is still notable for the charm of its old buildings. The **Catedral de São Pedro** dates from 1755-75. The **Museu Oceanográfico** ⓘ *2 km from centre on Av Perimetral, T2313496, daily 0900-1100, 1400-1700*, has an interesting collection of 125,000 molluscs. To get there take bus 59 or walk along waterfront. At Praça Tamandaré is a small zoo. There is a **tourist information kiosk** ⓘ *junction of R Duque de Caxias and R Gen Becaler*.

Excursions from Rio Grande

Cassino is a popular seaside town with hotels and shops, 24 km from Rio Grande via a good road. There are several beaches within easy reach of Cassino, but they have no facilities. A wrecked ship remains on the shore where it was thrown by a storm in 1975; unfortunately the road is used as a roadway. Travelling south, the beaches in order are **Querência** (5 km), **Stela Maris** (9 km), **Netuno** (10 km), all with surf.

The breakwater (the Barra), 5 km south of Cassino, through which all vessels entering and leaving Rio Grande must pass, is a tourist attraction. Barra-Rio Grande buses, from the east side of Praça Ferreira, pass the Superporto. Very good fishing. The coastline is low and straight, lacking the bays to the north of Porto Alegre. One attraction is railway flat-cars powered by sail (agree on the price in advance); the railway was built for the construction of the breakwater.

Across the inlet from Rio Grande, the little-visited settlement of **São José do Norte** makes a pleasant trip (see Tramandaí to São José do Norte, page 346). Founded in 1725 and still mostly intact, the village depends on agriculture and crab fishing. There are only three hotels, a good campsite, **Caturritas**, T2381476, in pine forests 5 km from the town, and several long beaches. Ferries (departing every half-hour, 30 minutes) link São José with Rio Grande; there are also three car ferries daily, T2321500. **Tourist information** ⓘ *R General Osório 127*.

Western Rio Grande do Sul

Passo Fundo → *Phone code: 054. Colour map 5, B3. Population: 168,500.*

Northwest of Porto Alegre by 328 km is Passo Fundo, regarded as 'the most *gaúcho* city in Rio Grande do Sul', so much so that the town's square boasts a statue of a *maté* gourd and bombilla. There is an international *rodeio* in December. The town has several hotels (**A-B**).

Santo Ângelo and the Jesuit Missions → *Phone code: 055. Colour map 5, B2. Population: 76,700.*

West of here are the **Sete Povos das Missões Orientais**. Santo Ângelo is a pleasant town with the best infrastructure for visiting the missions. It has a missionary **museum** in the main square where there is also a **cathedral** with a hideous fresco of missionaries indoctrinating the indigenous population. The only considerable Jesuit remains in Brazilian territory are the very dramatic ones at **São Miguel das Missões**, some 50 km from Santo Ângelo. At São Miguel, now a World Heritage Site, there is a church, 1735-45, and small **museum** ⓘ *0900-1800*. A *son et lumière* show in Portuguese is held daily, in winter at 2000, and later in summer, although all times rather depend on how many people there are. The show ends too late to return to Santo Ângelo and there are one or two options for accommodation (see Sleeping, page 355). It is difficult to find a good place to eat in the evening; you could try a snack bar for hamburgers. *Gaúcho* festivals are often held some Sunday afternoons, in a field near the Mission (follow the music).

Porto Xavier and the Argentine missions

You can continue into Argentina to see the mission ruins at San Ignacio Miní and Posadas by getting a bus from Santo Ângelo (0615, 1300 or 1930) to the quiet border town of **Porto Xavier** (four hours, US$4), on the Rio Uruguay. Buses also to Porto Xavier, from Porto Alegre (one daily), and Santa Maria.

Border crossing The Policia Federal post for the entry and exit stamps is about 100 m north of the ferry in a white building, friendly. Take the **ferry** ⓘ *Mon to Fri 0800-1145, 1400-1745, Sat 0900-0945, 1500-1545, closed Sun, US$1*, to Puerto Javier, on the Argentine side of Rio Uruguay. From there, there are frequent **buses** to Posadas and, via connections at Alem and Santa Ana, to Iguaçu Falls.

Salto do Yucumâ

Between November and April, the Rio Uruguay overflows along its east bank for over 1,800 m, making the world's longest waterfall. The 12 m-high Salto do Yucumâ is in the 17,000-ha Parque do Turvo. Its isolation (530 km northwest of Porto Alegre on the Argentine border) means few tourists visit. Accordingly it is a wildlife haven with over 220 bird species (including 10 under threat in Brazil) and 34 mammal species (12 threatened). The nearest town, **Derrumbadas**, 4 km from the park and has an **information point** ⓘ *T35511558, ext 228*. Lemon extract production is an important local industry.

Uruguaiana and the border with Argentina

→ *Phone code: 055. Colour map 5, B1. Population: 127,000.*

It is also possible to cross the border through Uruguaiana, a cattle centre 772 km from Porto Alegre, and its twin Argentine town of Paso de los Libres the in the extreme west. A 1,400-m bridge over the Rio Uruguai links the two cities.

Border crossing Brazilian immigration and customs are at the end of the bridge, 5 blocks from the main *praça*. Buses connect the bus stations and centres of each city every 30 mins. If you have to disembark for visa formalities, a following bus will pick

The legend of Negrinho do Pastoreio

There used to be a cruel landowner in Rio Grande do Sul; greedy and evil-tempered, he treated the many slaves on his *estância* very badly. Delimited only by natural boundaries, his property was enormous. Animals could roam more or less as they wished, but in those days it was normal to assign a slave to shepherd duties, keeping the livestock within reach of the farm.

The slave assigned to the task on this property was known as Negrinho. One day he lost an animal. Furious, the boss beat him until he bled, then tied him to a plank of wood and sent him out to find the animal. Barely able to walk, Negrinho searched all day. When night fell, he was sent out again. To light his way, his boss gave him a candle-end and an armful of cinders from the fire, still smoking.

Returning at dawn without the lost animal, Negrinho was tied once more to a plank. He was tied so tightly that he died – or he seemed dead. The boss sent his broken little body away, with instructions that it should be stuffed into the centre of a live ant hill.

Next day, the boss took a party to look at the ant hill. When they opened it up, there was Negrinho the shepherd, safe and well, with the lost animal by his side.

To this day, Negrinho do Pastoreio is the patron 'saint' of lost things. All he charges for his service is the stub of a candle, or some smoke. The most widespread of *gaúcho* legends, the story is valued as a reminder of a shameful era in the region's history.

you up without extra charge. There are bus services to **Porto Alegre**. **Planalto** buses run from Uruguaiana via Barra do Quaraí/Bella Unión (US$4.50) to Salto and Paysandú in Uruguay. Exchange and information in the same building. Exchange rates are better in the town than at the border. There are a number of cheap and mid-range hotels in town. Taxi or bus across the bridge about US$3.50.

The crossing furthest west is **Barra do Quaraí** to **Bella Unión**, via the Barra del Cuaraim bridge. This is near the confluence of the Rios Uruguai and Quaraí. Bella Unión has three hotels and a campsite in the Parque Fructuoso Rivera (T0642-2261). **Brazilian Consulate** ⓘ *C Lirio Moraes 62, T/F7392054*; buses to Salto and Montevideo.

Some 30 km east is another crossing from **Quaraí** to **Artigas**, in a cattle-raising and agricultural area. **Brazilian consulate** ⓘ *C Lecueder 432, T86422504, F86424504*. Artigas has hotels, a youth hostel and campsites. Buses run to Salto and Montevideo.

There are two further crossings at **Aceguá**, 60 km south of Bagé, 59 km north of the Uruguayan town of Melo, and further east, **Jaguarão/Rio Branco**. The 1½-km-long Mauá bridge across the Rio Jaguarão joins these two towns. The police post for passport checks is 3 km before the bridge; customs are at the bridge.

Santana do Livramento and the border with Uruguay

→ *Phone code: 055. Colour map 5, C2. Population: 91,100.*

The southern interior of the state is the region of the real *gaúcho*. Principal towns of this area include Santana do Livramento. Its twin Uruguayan city is Rivera (see below). All you need do is cross the main street, but by public transport this is not a straightforward route between Brazil and Uruguay. For motorists there are three customs offices in Santana do Livramento; about 30 minutes is needed for formalities. For road traffic, Chuy is better than Río Branco or Aceguá.

Border crossing Before crossing into Uruguay, you must visit Brazilian Polícia Federal to get an exit stamp; if not, the Uruguayan authorities will send you back. **Brazilian**

consulates are at **Melo** ⓘ *R Del Pilar 786, T0462-2136*, and at **Río Branco** ⓘ *Lavalleja and Palomeque*. Exchange rates are usually better at Melo than at the border.

Uruguayan immigration is in the new Complejo Turístico at Sarandí y Viera, 14 blocks, 2 km, from the border (take bus along Agraciada). There is also a tourist office. **NB** You must have a Brazilian exit stamp to enter Uruguay and a Uruguayan exit stamp to enter Brazil.

Uruguayan customs Luggage is inspected when boarding buses out of Rivera; there are also three checkpoints on the road out of town.

Chuí and the border with Uruguay → *Phone code: 053. Colour map 5, C2.*

On the Brazilian side of the border is Chuí, a tranquil town, whilst on the Uruguayan side is Chuy. The BR-471 from Porto Alegre and Pelotas skirts the town and carries straight through to Uruguay, where it becomes Ruta 9. Each country's immigration is outside the town (see below); if you are staying in town you can walk anywhere as long as you do not go beyond the immigration posts. The main street is Avenida Internacional: on the Brazilian side it is called Avenida Uruguaí and on the Uruguayan side Avenida Brasil. Each side carries two-way traffic. On the Brazilian side the shops are mainly clothes, shoes and household goods, while the Uruguayan side has duty-free shops and a casino. São Miguel fort, built by the Portuguese in 1737, now reconstructed with period artefacts, is worth a visit. A lighthouse 10 km west marks the Barro do Chuí inlet, which has uncrowded beaches and is visited by sea lions.

From October to February, Brazil is one hour ahead of Uruguay (GMT-2; Uruguay GMT-3).

The Uruguayan town of **Chuy** is 340 km from Montevideo. On the Uruguyan side, on a promontory overlooking Laguna Merín and the *gaúcho* landscape of southern Brazil, stands the restored fortress of **San Miguel** ⓘ *closed Mon, US$0.20, bus from Chuy US$0.45*, dating from 1752 and surrounded by a moat. It is set in a park in which many plants and animals are kept. Tours (US$10 from Chuy) end for the season after 31 March. Nearby, **Parador San Miguel** is excellent, beautiful rooms, fine food and service.

Brazilian immigration Immigration is about 2½ km from the border, on BR-471, the road to Pelotas. All buses, except those originating in Pelotas, stop at customs on both sides of the border; if coming from Pelotas, you must ask the bus to stop for exit formalities. International buses, for example **TTL** from Porto Alegre, make the crossing straightforward: the company holds passports; hand over your visitor's card on leaving Brazil and get a Uruguayan one on entry. Have luggage available for inspection. Make sure you get your stamp or you will have trouble leaving Brazil.

Uruguayan immigration Uruguayan passport control is 2½ km before the border on the road into Chuy, US$2.50 by taxi, officials are friendly and co-operative. If travelling by bus, make sure the driver knows you want to stop at Uruguayan immigration, it will not do so automatically. If you stay overnight in Chuy you cannot get your exit stamp in advance. You may only do so immediately prior to leaving the country.

Entering Brazil From Uruguay, on the Uruguayan side, the bus will stop if asked, and wait while you get your exit stamp (with bus conductor's help); on the Brazilian side, the appropriate form is completed by the rodoviária staff when you purchase your ticket into Brazil. The bus stops at Polícia Federal (BR-471) and the conductor completes formalities while you sit on the bus. Customs officials may ask you to open your luggage for inspection. Also, if entering by car, fill up with petrol in Brazil, where fuel is cheaper.

Entering Uruguay To enter Uruguay, you must have a Brazilian exit stamp and a Uruguayan entry stamp, otherwise you will not be permitted to proceed. Those requiring a visa must have a medical examination before a visa can be issued in Chuí, cost about US$20 and US$10 respectively.

Sleeping

Porto Alegre *p341, map p342, phone code 051*

Hotels in the area around R Garibáldi and Voluntários da Patria between Av Farrapos and rodoviária are overpriced and used many times a day.

L **Plaza São Rafael**, Av Alberto Bins 514, T32227000, www.plazahoteis.com.br. Newly refurbished 1970s luxury hotel with excellent service and business facilties including laptop computer rental and 2 free internet lines in each room. Gym and sauna. Less anonymous than the city's US chain hotels (there is a Sheraton in town).

AL **Continental**, Lg Vespasiano Júlio Veppo 77, T32112344, www.hoteiscontinental.com.br. Reasonable business hotel with a pool, gym and with good weekend discount rates. Recommended.

AL **Everest**, R Duque de Caxias 1357, T32159500, www.everest.com.br. Modest 4-star with a business centre and good views.

A **Porto Alegre Residence**, R Des André da Rocha 131, T32258644, F32240366. Large rooms. Recommended.

B **Açores**, R dos Andradas 885, T32217588, F32251007. Centrally located but with cramped rooms. Friendly staff and weekend discounts.

B **Embaixador**, R Jerônimo Coelho 354, T32156600, www.embaixador.com.br. Comfortable 4-star with an unexciting restaurant, gym and sauna. Weekend discounts.

B **Ritter**, Lg Vespasiano Júlio Veppo 55, opposite rodoviária, T32284044, www.ritterhoteis.com.br. 4-star and 3-star wings, English, French, German spoken, bar, small pool, sauna. Fine restaurant, good service. Recommended.

C **Conceição Center**, Av Sen Salgado Filho 201, T32257774, www.hoteisconceicao.bom.br. Simple but respectable town hotel with plain but well kept a/c rooms with fridges. With a cheaper (D) sister hotel (see website).

C **Lancaster**, Trav Acelino de Carvalho 67, T32244737, F32244630. Centrally located quiet and with a/c rooms and a restaurant.

D **Elevado**, Av Farrapos 65, T/F32245250, www.hotelelevado.com.br. Big rooms, noisy at front, microwave and coffee, good value.

D **Palácio**, Av Vigário José Inácio 644, T32253467. Centrally located and with hot water, family and a safe. Recommended.

E **América**, Av Farrapos 119, T/F32260062, www.hotelamerica.com.br. Bright, friendly, large rooms with sofas, quiet rooms at back, garage. Highly recommended.

E **Minuano**, Av Farrapos 31, T/F32263062. Small but immaculate rooms and parking.

E **Uruguay**, Dr Flores 371. Simple fan-cooled rooms. Recommended.

Camping

Praia do Guarujá, 16 km out on Av Guaíba.

Beaches around Porto Alegre *p345, map p346, phone code 051*

A **Solar da Barra**, R Plínio Kroeff 465, Mampituba, near Torres, T6641811, F6641090. 2 pools, 1 of which is thermal, sauna, children's playground. Low-season discounts.

B **Beira-Mar**, Av Emancipação 521, Tramandaí beach, T6611234, F6611133. Pleasant but simple hotel with a thermal pool and sports facilities.

B **Napoli**, Av Paraguassu 3159, Capão da Canoa, T/F6652231. Simple beach *pousada* (C low season).

B-C **Pousada Brisa do Mar**, R Júlio de Castilhos and R Borges de Medeiros, Torres, T6642019. With a good breakfast. Recommended.

C **Alvorada**, Arroio Teixeira on the beach, T6221242. Good facilities, café, only open Dec-Mar.

C **Ibiama**, R Dr Mário Santo Dani 1161, Osório beach, T/F6632822. Simple rooms and breakfast.

C **Kolman**, R Sepé 1800, Capão da Canoa, T6252022, T6252021. Standard family beach hotel with a pool.

D **Hotel Costa Azul**, Av José Bonifácio 382, Torres, T/F6643291. Friendly and close to rodoviária, with breakfast.

D **São Jorge**, F Amaral 19, Tramandaí beach, T6611154. Quiet, simple and recommended.

E **São Domingos**, R Júlio de Castilhos 875, Torres, T6641865, F6641022. IYHA youth hostel, clean, closed out of season. Price per person.

E **Tramandaí**, R Belém 701, Tramandaí beach, T2283802, F2265380. IYHA youth hostel with dorms and doubles. Price per person.

Camping

Pinguela Parque, BR-101, 22 km, Osório beach, T6288080.
Marina Park, RS-389, 7 km, Capão da Canoa, T3016150.
Praia de Itapeva, 5 km, Torres T6055112.

Tramandaí to São José do Norte *p346, phone code 051*

D **Hotel Farol**, on the main street, Cidreira. With bath.
E **Hotel Mostardense**, R Bento Conçalves 200, Mostardas, T6731368. Good.

Gramado *p347, phone code 054*

AL **Serra Azul**, R Garibáldi 152, T2861082, F2863374. 2 pools, one of which is thermal, sauna, massage, tennis.
A **Estalagem St Hubertus**, R da Carriere 974, Lago Negro, T/F2861273. Part of the Roteiro de Charme hotel group, see p47.
A **Gramado Parque**, R Leopoldo Rosenfeldt 818, T/F2862588. Bungalows, good breakfast, reasonable laundry service.
A **Ritta Höppner**, R Pedro Candiago 305, T2861334, F2863129. Cabins with TV and fridge. Very good value, friendly, good breakfasts. German owners, pool and miniature trains in grounds, closed in May.
B **Chalets do Vale**, R Arthur Reinheimer 161 (off Av das Hortênsias at about 4700), T2864151, chaletsdovale@ via-rs.net. 3 high-quality homely chalets in lovely wood setting, 2 double beds, kitchen, TV. Good deal for groups of 4 or families. Recommended.
B **Pequeno Bosque**, R Piratini 486, located in wood close to Véu da Noiva waterfall, T2861527, F2861771. Simple but pleasant and with a good breakfast.
B **Pousada Zermatt**, R da Fé 187, Bavária, T/F2862426. Simple and plain accommodation but recommended.
C **Luiz**, Sen Salgado Filho 432, T2861026. Pleasant rooms, friendly service and a good breakfast.
C **Pousada Pertuti**, Av Borges de Medeiros 3571, T2862513. Good breakfast, use of kitchen, friendly. Recommended.
D **Brisa Pousada**, R Tristão de Oliveira 252, T2866788. Another good cheap option.
D **Dinda**, R Augusto Zatti 160, T2861588. Basic but one of the cheapest in town.
E **Albergue Internacional de Gramado**, Av das Hortênsias 3880, T2951020. 50 dormitory beds in new, cosy hostel.

Canela and around *p347, phone code 054*

AL **Laje de Pedra**, Av Pres Kennedy Km 3, T2824300, F2824400. Restaurant, pool, thermal pool, sauna, tennis.
A **Vila Suzana Parque**, R Col Theobaldo Fleck 15, T2822020, F2821793. Chalets, heated pool, attractive.
C **Canela**, Av Osvaldo Aranha, 223, T2822774. Breakfast, English-speaking staff. Recommended.
C **Pousada das Sequóias**, R Godofrede Raymundo 1747, T2821373, www.sequoias.cjb.net. Pretty forest cabins and decent service and breakfast.
D **Central**, Av Júlio de Castilhos 146. Safe, simple fan-cooled rooms. Recommended.
D **Pousada Schermer**, Travessa Romeu 30, T2821746. Basic backpacker accommodation but very friendly, well kept and highly recommended.
E **Pousada do Viajante**, R Ernesto Urbani 132, behind rodoviária, T2822017. Youth hostel offering dorms and doubles with kitchen facilities. Recommended.

Camping

Camping Clube do Brasil, 1 km from waterfall in Parque do Caracol, 1 km off main road (signposted), take bus for Parque Estadual do Caracol, 8 km from Canela, T282431. Excellent honey and chocolate for sale here. Highly recommended.
Sesi, R Francisco Bertolucci 504, 2½ km outside Canela, T/F2821311. Cabins also available, restaurant, clean. Recommended.

Parque Nacional de Aparados da Serra *p348, phone code 054*

L **Parador Casa da Montanha**, Estrada Parque Nacional, T5045302, reservations T99739320, www.paradorcasadamontanha.com.br. 7 cabins up a precarious dirt road, all with stunning views. Very beautiful. Full board included in the price and optional excursions into the park on horseback or foot. Minimum stay 2 days.

D **Itaimbeleza**, next to the rodovíaria. Very simple fan-cooled rooms and advice on getting into the park.

Pelotas *p348, phone code 053*

A **Manta**, R Gen Neto 1131, T2252411, www.hoteismanta.com.br. Blocky 1970s hotel with a pool, restaurant and bar. The best in town though somewhat frayed.
D **Aleppo Hotel**, R Gen Osório 708, T/F2253950. Bright, clean and big rooms and breakfast. Recommended.
D **Motel Mediterâneo**, Av Presidente João Goulont 5473, T2714746. About 150 m from rodoviária. Recommended if arriving late.

Rio Grande *p349, phone code 053*

A **Atlântico Rio Grande**, R Duque de Caxias 55, T/F2313833. Standard town hotel with a/c rooms. Good value. Recommended.
B **Europa**, R Gen Neto 165, main square, T/F2313933. Conveniently located in the centre of town with a range of a/c rooms.
D **Paris**, R Mcal Floriano Peixoto 112. In an old colonial building. Charming. Recommended.

Excursions from Rio Grande *p349, phone code 053*

A **Atlântico**, Av Rio Grande 387, Cassino, T2361350. Clean, refurbished and with special rates for students.
B **Marysol**, Av Atlântica 700, Cassino, T2361240. Friendly, simple *pousada* near the beach.

Santo Ângelo and the Jesuit Missions *p350, phone code 055*

A **Maerkli**, Av Brasil 1000, Santo Ângelo, T/F3122127. Pleasant but basic 1980s hotel.
C **Hotel Barichello**, Av Borges do Canto 1567, São Miguel das Missões, T33811272. Nice, clean and quiet. It also has a restaurant, Churrasco, for lunch.
D-E **Hotel Nova Esperança**, Trav Centenario 463, Santo Ângelo, T33121173, behind bus station. Simple, reasonably well maintained but with no breakfast.
E **Comércio**, Av Brasil 1178, Santo Ângelo, T33122542. A bit run down but good for the price, clean, friendly.
E **Pousada das Missões**, next to the ruins, São Miguel das Missões, T33811030, pousada.missoes@terra.com.br. Very good youth hostel.

Porto Xavier and the Argentine missions *p350*

D **Rotta**, Av Mal Fl Peixoto 757, near the *praça*, T3541014. Plain rooms with or without a/c, and/or TV, bath, breakfast, good restaurant closed Sat and Sun evening; good cheap, **pizzeria** on the terrace on the main square. Recommended. The hotel is about 5 mins' walk from the ferry at the end of the main street.

Salto do Yucumâ *p350, phone code 55*

There are several cheap hotels in the area.
C-D **Hotel Imperial**, Av Jn Castilhos 544, Três Passos, 28 km from park, T35222135. Standard small town hotel with breakfast included.
F **Hotel Iucuma**, R Tapulas 271, T35511120 or F **Hotel Avenida**, beside petrol station, T35511859, both in Tenente Portela, 16 km from park.

Chuí and the border with Uruguay *p352, phone code 053*

Brazil

B **Turis Firper**, Av Samuel Prilliac 629, Chuí, T2651398, F2651068. Basic with a/c rooms, TV and bar.
E **Bianca**, Chile 1620, Chuí, T2651500. Very simple but adequate for short stays. All rooms have a bath.
E **San Francisco**, Av Colômbia and R Chile. Very simple rooms with a bath and an equally simple restaurant.

Uruguay

B **Nuevo Hotel Plaza**, Gral Artigas y Arachanes, Chuy, T/F0474-2309. On the plaza, central, helpful and with breakfast, TV and a restaurant, **El Mesón de la Plaza**.
B-C **Alerces**, Laguna de Castillos 578, Chuy, T0474-2260. Simple rooms with heaters, bath, TV, breakfast.
D **Madrugada**, C S Priliac y India Muerta, Chuy, T0474-2346. Very simple but well looked after and quiet.

Camping

Barra del Chuy campsite, Ruta 9 Km 331, turn right 13 km, T2425. Good bathing, many birds. **Cabañas** for up to 4 persons cost US$20 daily or less, depending on amenities. From Chuy, buses run here every 2 hrs.

Eating

Porto Alegre *p341, map p342, phone code 051*
Gaúcho cooking features large quantities of meat, while German cuisine is also a strong influence. Regional farm (*campeiro*) food, now a dying art, uses plenty of rice, vegetables, and interesting sauces. Vegetarians might try some of the *campeiro* soups and casseroles and growing number of alternative or natural restaurants, otherwise stick to Italian restaurants or *churrascaria* salad bars.

Apart from the many good restaurants, much of the tastiest food can be found in street stalls and cheap *lancherias*; the Central Market along the Praça is lined with them.

TTT **Portoalgrense**, Av Pará 913, São Geraldo, T33432767, closed Sun. The best carnivore restaurant in the city with excellent beef steak and a respectable wine list.

TTT **Galpão Crioulo**, Av Loureiro da Silva (Parque da Harmonia aka Maurício Sirotsky Sobrinho, Cidade Baixa), T32268194. Good *churrascaria* with a show and dancing, 1130-1600, 1900-0100.

TT **Atelier de Massas**, R Riachuelo 1482, T32251125. Lunch and dinner, closed Sun. Fantastic pastas and 8-cm thick steaks, excellent value. Highly recommended.

TT **Chopp Stübel**, R Quintino Bocaiúva 940, Moinhos de Vento, T33328895. Open 1800-0030, closed Sun. One of the best in the city for reasonably priced German food. Recommended.

TT **Le Bon Gourmet**, Av Alberto Bins 514 (in **Plaza São Rafael** hotel), 1900-2300, closed Sun. Steaks, pasta and fine fish dishes. The 24-hr **514 Bar** is at the back of hotel lobby.

TT **Wunderbar**, R Marquês do Herval 598, Moinhos de Vento, T32224967. Popular and very friendly German restaurant and bar which is always very busy. Open 1830 until the last diner leaves (about 0100). Recommended.

T **Coqueiros**, R João Alfredo 208, T32271833. 1130-1430, 1930-2400, closed Sun and Mon evenings. Cheap and cheerful *churrrascaria*. Meat salty and a bit overdone.

T **Ilha Natural**, R Gen Câmara 60, T32244738. Self-service, cheap, lunch only Mon-Fri.

T **Nova Vida Restaurant Alternativo**, Av Borges de Medeiros 1010, 1100-1500, closed Sun. Good lasagne and salads. Also at Demetrio Ribeiro 1182.

T **Restaurant Majestic and Café Dos Cataventos**, Casa de Cultura Mário Quintana, R dos Andrades 736. 2 snack and *almoco* restaurants – the latter in the courtyard and the other on the roof. Both serve good drinks, snacks and meals. Fantastic rooftop sunsets.

Gramado *p347, phone code 054*
There's no lack of choice of decent, if a bit pricey, restaurants along Av Borges de Medeiros.

TT **Churrascaria Patrão Velho**, Av das Hortênsias 4759, T2860823. Very good barbecued meat and side dishes. Recommended.

TT **Gasthof Edelweiss**, R da Carriere 1119, T2861861. Some of the best German food in town.

T **Lancheria Tissot**, Av Borges de Medeiros 3283. Tasty, inexpensive snacks and meals in family-run snack bar.

Canela *p347, phone code 054*

TT **Bifão & Cia**, Av Osvaldo Aranha 301, T2829156. Reasonable *churrascaria* with huge slabs of meat and side dishes.

T **Café Canela**, Praça Joã Correa 7, T2823304. Good meat and cheese dishes.

T **Parati Lanches**, Praça Joã Correa 97. Traditional watering hole with pool tables, 0800-2400.

Rio Grande *p349, phone code 053*

TT **Blue Café**, R Luís Loréa 314. Expresso machine and good cake, 0830-1930 (2300 Fri, jazz/blues music).

T **Barrillada Don Lauro**, R Luís Loréa 369, T2332037. Uruguayan steak in nice restaurant.

T **Rio's**, R Val Porto 393, T2311180. Vast but good *churrascaria*.

Pelotas *p348, phone code 053*

TTT **El Paisano**, R Mcal Deodoro 1093, T2271507. Legendary Uruguayan steak and style, closed Mon, opening hours vary seasonally.

TT **Lobão**, Av Bento Gonçalves 3460, T2256197. Standard barbecue *churrascaria*, plenty of side dishes.

T **Mama Pizza**, R Gen Osório 720. Good affordable pizza run by **Hotel Manta**.

Chuí and the border with Uruguay
p352, phone code 053
Most restaurants are on Av Brasil.
Parrillada Jesús, at the corner of L Olivera, Chuí. A good bet.
Parrillada/Pizzería Javier, Arachanes 589, Chuí. Reasonable food.
Los Leños, Av Gral Artigas, Chuí. For meat and pizzas.

Bars and clubs

Porto Alegre *p341, map p342, phone code 051*
There are many classy bars, cafés and bistros in the pleasant **Moinhos de Vento**, the city's richest suburb. Try the roads (like R Padre Chagas) around Moinhos de Vento shopping centre (a US$2 taxi ride from downtown).

On weekend nights, thousands spill out of the huge beer bars and clubs along Av Goethe between R Vasco de Gama and R Dona Laura in Rio Branco (a US$2 taxi ride from the centre).
Bar do Beto, Av Venâncio Aires 876, Cidade Baixa, T33320063. 1700-0300, serves food too.
Bar do Goethe, R 24 de Outubro 112, Moinhos de Vento, T2222043, www.compuserve.com.br/bardogoethe/. Bar hosting reunion each Tue 2030 for foreign-language speakers.
Bar do Nito, Av Cel Lucas de Oliveira 105, Moinhos de Vento, T33334600. Popular music bar.
Cía Sandwiches, Getúlio Vargas 1430, T32337414. 1800-0200, beer, sandwiches and music.
Cult, R Gen Lima e Silva 806, Cidade Baixa, T32216299. Open 1900-late, restaurant too.
Doce Vício, R Vieira de Castro 32. 3 floors with games room, bar and restaurant, Tue-Sun 1830-0230.
Dr Jekyll, Travessa do Carmo 76, Cidade Baixa, T32269404. Nightclubs open from 2200, closed Sun.
Fly, R Gonçalvo de Carvalho 189. Predominantly male, attractive gay bar with art exhibition, sophisticated, Wed-Mon 2100-0200.
João de Barro, R da República 546, Cidade Baixa. Good jazz.
Kripton, R Mariante 606, Rio Branco, T33316651. Bar with popular music.
Ossip, Av Republica 677 (corner with João Afredo). Pleasant wine bar.
Restaurant Majestic, R dos Andradas 736. Don't miss a sunset drink here, on the roof of Casa de Cultura Mário Quintana.
Sargeant Peppers, Dona Laura 329, T33313258. Bar with live music Thu-Sat, closed Mon.
Teatro de Elis, Av Protásio Alves 1670, Petrópolis, T32863475. Nightclub.
Trivial, R Dona Laura 78, Rio Branco, T33467046, www.trivialbar.com.br. Bar open from 2100.
Wanda Bar, R Comendador Coruja 169, Floresta, T32244755. Gay nightclub, open from 2030.

Entertainment

Porto Alegre *p341, map p342, phone code 051*
Art galleries Casa de Cultura Mário Quintana, R dos Andradas 736, T32217147. A centre for the arts, exhibitions, theatre etc, Mon-Fri 0900-2100, Sat and Sun 1200-2100.
Usina do Gasômetro, Av Pres João Goulart 551, T32271387. Tue-Sun 1000-2200. Spunky displays by young artists.
Theatre São Pedro, Praça Mcal Deodoro, T32275100. Free noon and late afternoon concerts Sat, Sun, art gallery, café.

Festivals

Porto Alegre *p341, map p342, phone code 051*
2 Feb The main event is the festival of Nossa Senhora dos Navegantes (*Iemanjá*), whose image is taken by boat from the central quay in the port to the industrial district of Navegantes.
Sep Semana Farroupilha celebrates *gaúcho* traditions with parades in traditional style, its main day being 20 Sep. The Carnival parade takes place in Av A do Carvalho, renamed Av Carlos Alberto Barcelos (or Roxo) for these 3 days only, after a famous carnival designer.

Shopping

Porto Alegre *p341, map p342, phone code 051*
Bookshops
Idiomas, Galeria Central Park, R Mostardeiro 333, Mon-Fri 0900-1200, 1400-1830, Sat

0930-1230, closed Sun.

Livraria Londres, Av Osvaldo Aranha 1182. Used books in English, French and Spanish and old *Life* magazines.

Prosa i Verso, Galeria Av Center, R Mostardeiro 120, T32222409. 0930-1800, closed Sun.

Saraiva Megastore, in Shopping Praia de Belas.

Siciliano, R dos Andradas 1273 and other branches. Each year a **Feira do Livro** is held in Praça da Alfândega, Oct-Nov.

Jewellers

H Stern jewellers at Shopping Center Iguatemi and international airport.

Markets

There is a street market (leather goods, basketware, etc) in the streets around the Central Post Office. Good leather goods are sold on the streets. Sun morning handicraft and bric-a-brac market (plus sideshows) Av José Bonifácio (next to Parque Farroupilha). There is a very good food market.

Shopping centre

The **Praia de Belas shopping centre**, among the largest in Latin America, is a US$1.50 taxi ride from town.

Activities and tours

Porto Alegre *p341, map p342, phone code 051*

Gyms Academia do Parcão, 24 de Outubro 684. Weights and aerobics.

Golf Porto Alegre Country Club, Av Líbero Badaró 524, Bela Vista, 18 holes, closed to non-members. Several 9-hole courses in nearby towns.

Swimming Forbidden from the beaches near or in the city because of pollution, except for **Praia do Lami**, in the south of the city, which has been cleaned up. Beaches in Belém Novo and Ipanema are OK too.

Tour operators Klift Tur, R Mcal Floriano 270, T32113255, F2287959. American Express. One of several tour companies offering trips to Foz do Iguaçu and Ciudad del Este, overnight journey each way (12 hrs in Paraguay). 3-day trips with 1 night's hotel accommodation, US$30 including sightseeing (time at the falls may be limited).

See also Turismo section in *Zero Hora* classifieds (Tue) for tour companies' advertisements.

Beaches around Porto Alegre *p345, map p346, phone code 051*

Tour operators Marcelo and Saraia Müller, Blue Beach Tur, Av Silva Jardim 257, Torres T/F6643096, bluebeach@terra.com.br. Boat trips up Rio Mampitumba, abseiling, trekking, and visits to Parque Nacional Aparados da Serra/ Geral. Recommended.

Flamingo Turismo Náutico, run trips during summer to Ilha dos Lobos, departing from Rio Mampitumba estuary.

Canela and around *p347, phone code 054*

Tour operators Atitude, Av Osvaldo Aranha 391, T2826305, www.atitude.tur.br. Rafting, waterfall abseiling, and trips to Aparados da Serra National Park. Recommended.

JM Turismo, Av Osvaldo Aranha 1038, T2821542, www.jmrafting.com.br. Class 3 and 4 rapids.

Santo Ângelo and the Jesuit Missions *p350, phone code 055*

Caminho das Missões, R Marguês do Herval 1061, T33129632, www.caminhodasmissoes.com.br. 3-, 5- and 7-day hikes ('pilgrimages' – 80, 130 and 180 km respectively) between the various ruins. US$77-150. Open to all beliefs.

Transport

Porto Alegre *p341, map p342, phone code 051*

See also Ins and outs, p.

Air

The international airport is on Av dos Estados, 8 km from the city, T33421082. A regular bus runs from the rodoviária, as well as a Metrô service from the centre.

Bus

The rodoviária is on Lg Vespasiano Júlio Veppo, an easy walk from the city centre, T32868230, www.rodoviaria-poa.com.br (with links to bus companies running intermunicipal, interstate and international services which have timetable, fare and availability information). There are good facilities, including a post office and long-distance telephone service until 2100. There are 2 sections to the terminal; the ticket offices for interstate and international destinations are together in 1 block, beside the municipal tourist office (very helpful). The intermunicipal (state) ticket offices are in another block; for travel information within the state, ask at the very helpful booth on the station concourse.

To **Rio**, US$60, 24 hrs (**Itapemirim** www.itapemirim.com.br); **São Paulo** (Itapemirim), US$29.80 (*leito* 51), 18 hrs; **Brasília** (Itapemirim), US$60, 34 hrs; **Uruguaiana** (Pluma, www.pluma.com.br), US$17.50, 8 hrs; **Florianópolis**, US$16, 7 hrs with Santo Anjo (take an *executivo* rather than a *convencional*, which is a much slower service); **Curitiba** (Itapemirim), from US$21 *convencional* to US$17.50 (*leito* 28.50), coastal and *serra* routes, 12 hrs; **Rio Grande**, US$9, every 2 hrs from 0600, 4 hrs. **Foz do Iguaçu**, *convencional* US$26, 15 hrs, *executivo* US$30, 13 hrs (*leito* once a week 41). Many other destinations. To **Cascavel** (Paraná) for connections to Campo Grande, Cuiabá and Porto Velho: 4 daily with Unesul, US$27, 12 hrs. To **Jaguarão** on Uruguayan border at 2400, US$10, 6 hrs.

International buses Take your passport and tourist card when purchasing international bus tickets.

To **Montevideo**, with TTL *executivo* daily 2030 US$43 (*leito* Fri only at 2100, US$43), alternatively take bus to border town of Chuí at 1200 and 2330 daily, US$12.60, 7 hrs, then bus to Montevideo (US$13). To **Asunción** with Unesul at 1900, Tue, Fri, 18 hrs via **Foz do Iguaçu**, US$18. **Santiago**, Pluma 0705, Tue and Fri, US$79.

There are bus services to **Buenos Aires** (Pluma), US$54, 19 hrs (depending on border) with Pluma, 1805 daily, route is Uruguaiana, Paso de los Libres, Entre Ríos and Zárate. For **Misiones** (Argentina), take 2100 bus (not Sat) to Porto Xavier on the Río Uruguay, 11 hrs, US$15, get exit stamp at police station, take a boat across to San Javier, US$2, go to Argentine immigration at the port, then take a bus to Posadas (may have to change in Leandro N Além).

Car

Good roads radiate from Porto Alegre, and Highway BR-116 is paved to Curitiba (746 km). To the south it is paved (mostly in good condition), to Chuí on the Uruguayan frontier, 512 km. In summer visibility can be very poor at night owing to mist, unfenced cows are a further hazard. The paved coastal road to Curitiba via Itajaí (BR-101), of which the first 100 km is the 4-lane Estrada General Osório highway, is much better than the BR-116 via Caxias and Lajes. The road to Uruguaiana is entirely paved but bumpy.

Car hire Allocar, R 25 de Julho 102, T33371717, www.allocar.com.br. Bazzoni, T33252913, www.bazzoni.com.br. Hello Rent a Car, T33422422, www.hellocar.com.br. At airport and delivers to hotels. Milhas, R Pereira Franco 400, T33372223. Pontual, Av Pernanbuco 1700, São Geraldo, T33422282.

Beaches around Porto Alegre *p345, map p346, phone code 051*

Bus Porto Alegre-**Tramandaí**, 5 a day, US$3.50. **Osório-Mostardas**/Tavares, 1600 daily, US$4.40. Porto Alegre-**Torres**, 9 a day, US$6; **Tramandaí** 1300, 1700 daily, **Osório** 0630, 1100, 1300, 1830.

Tramandaí to São José do Norte *p346, phone code 051*

Bus There are 3 buses a week from Mostardas and Tavares to **São José do Norte** (130 km) via Bojuru (leaving Mostardas 0630 and Tavares 0700 Sun, Wed, Fri, 5 hrs, US$4.50). If travelling northwards from São José do Norte, the bus leaves 0800, Tue, Thu, Sat. There is also a daily bus from both Tavares and São José do Norte to **Bojuru**, where there is a basic hotel. The road south of Tavares is called the Estrada do Inferno. Car drivers should carry a shovel and rope. 4WD only after rains.

Taxi For local transport from Mostardas, try José Carlos Martins Cassola, T6731186, or Itamar Velho Sessin, T6731431.

Gramado *p347, phone code 054*

Bus Bus service to **Canela**, 10 mins, runs every 20 mins. Several daily buses from **Porto Alegre** US$3.85.

Canela and around *p347, phone code 054*
Bus Parque Estadual do Caracol, from outside Parati Lanches, Praça Joã Correa, 0800, 1200, 1730, US$0.30 (returning at 1220, 1800). Several daily Canela-**Caxlas do Sul**, 2 hrs, US$2. Every 2 hrs to São Francisco de Paula, US$1.10. (Take 0800 for connection to Cambará for Parque Nacional de Aparados da Serra.) From **Florianópolis**, it is quickest to go via Porto Alegre. Porto Alegre-Canela US$4.15.

Bike Bike hire from **Pousada das Sequóias** or **Pousada Casa Rosa**, R Gov Flores da Cunha 150, T2822400.

Pelotas *p348, phone code 053*
Air Mon-Fri flight to **Porto Alegre** (1530, US$60).

Bus Rodoviária is far out of town, with a bus every 15 mins to the centre. Frequent daily buses to **Porto Alegre**, 244 km (US$7.50, 3-4 hrs, paved road); **Rio Grande** (US$1.80, 1 hr); **Chuí** (5 daily, US$6.15). TTL bus services (Montevideo-Porto Alegre) depart at 2400 daily, US$35. Bus service to **Buenos Aires** via Uruguaiana (0710, 2030, US$18). From Bagé, where there is a police post, the Uruguayan company **Núñez** runs buses 3 times a week to **Melo**, via Aceguá. Good direct road northwest to Iguaçu via **São Sepé**, **Santa Maria** and **São Miguel** mission ruins. **Santa Maria** (5 daily, US$8.80, 4 hrs) and **Santa Ângelo** (0805 daily, US$16, 8 hrs).

Taxi Radio Taxi Princesa, T2258466. Recommended.

Rio Grande *p349, phone code 054*
Boat Boat trip across mouth of Lagoa dos Patos, to pleasant village of **São José do Norte**, every hr from Porto Velho.

Bus **Pelotas**, every half hr, 60 mins, 56 km, US$1.75); **Bagé**, 280 km, 0700 and 1400; **Santa Vitória**, 220 km; **Porto Alegre**, 5 a day, US$10, 4 hrs; **Itajaí**, 14 hrs, US$15. All buses to these destinations go through Pelotas. Road to Uruguayan border at **Chuí** is paved, but the surface is poor (5 hrs by bus, at 0700 and 1430). Bus tickets to **Punta del Este** or **Montevideo** (daily 2330) at rodoviária or **Benfica Turismo**, Av Silva Paes 373, T2321807.

Santo Ângelo and the Jesuit Missions *p350, phone code 055*
Bus **Porto Alegre**-Santo Ângelo, 5 *convencional* daily, 6 hrs, US$15, and *executivo* at 1830, US$19.50. **São Miguel**, 0715, 1100, 1530, 1700 (Sat 1000, 1330, Sun 0930, 1830), 1 hr, US$2. **Foz do Iguaçu**, via Cascavel, 1930, 13 hrs, US$21.

Santana do Livramento and the border with Uruguay *p351*
Bus The rodoviária is at Gen Salgado Filho and Gen Vasco Alves. To **Porto Alegre**, 2 daily, 7 hrs, US$20; 3 daily to **Urugaiana** (4 hrs, US$10), services also to **São Paulo** and other destinations.

Salto do Yucumâ *p350, phone code 55*
Bus There are 4 buses daily from **Três Passos** to Santo Ângelo. 2 daily **Tenente Portela**-Santo Ângelo.

Chuí *p352, phone code 053*
Rodoviária on R Venezuela. Buses run from Chuí to **Pelotas** (6-7 daily, US$6.60, 4 hrs), **Rio Grande** (0700, 1400, 5 hrs, US$6.10) and **Porto Alegre** (1200, 2400, 7¾ hrs, US$13); also from Chuí to **Santa Vitória do Palmar** nearby, US$0.60, where there are a few hotels and rather quicker bus services to the main cities.

Chuí and the border with Uruguay *p352, phone code 053*
Bus To **Montevideo** (COT, Cynsa, both on Av Brasil between Olivera and Artigas, or Rutas del Sol, on L Oliveria), US$13, 5 hrs.

Directory

Porto Alegre *p341, map p342, phone code 051*
Banks Lloyds Bank, R Gen Câmara 249. 1000-1630. **Banco do Brasil**, Uruguai 185, 9th floor. 1000-1500, good rates for TCs. **Bradesco**, Praça Sen Florência. Visa machine. **Citibank**, R7 de Setembro 722, T32208619. Exchange on Av Borges de Medeiros, good rate, cash only. **Platino Turismo**, R dos Andrades and Av Borges de Medeiros (only one to change TCs, Amex, but 6 less than cash). **Exprinter**, Sen Salgado Filho 247 (best for cash).

MasterCard, cash against card, R 7 de Setembro 722, 8th floor, Centro. For other addresses consult tourist bureau brochure. **Cultural centres** Sociedade Brasileira da Cultura Inglesa, Praça Mauricio Cardoso 49, Moinhos de Vento. Instituto Goethe, 24 de Outubro 122. Mon-Fri 0930-1230, 1430-2100, occasional concerts, bar recommended for German *Apfelkuchen*. See also Casa de Cultura Mário Quintana and Usina do Gasômetro p357. **Embassles and consulates** Argentina, R Coronel Bordini 1033, Moinhos de Vento, T/F33211360. 0900-1600. Germany, R Prof Annes Dias 112, 11th floor, T32249255, F32264909 (0830-1130). Italy, Praça Marechal Deodoro 134, T32282055 (0900-1200). Japan, Av João Obino 467, Alto Petrópolis, T33341299, F33341742 (0900-1230, 1500-1700). Portugal, R Prof Annes Dias 112, 10th floor, T/F32245767 (0900-1500). Spain, R Eng Ildefonso Simões Lopez 85, Três Figueiras, T33381300, F33381444 (0830-1330). Sweden, Av Viena 279, São Geraldo, T32222322, F32222463 (1400-1745). UK, R Itapeva 110, Sala 505, Edif Montreal, Bairro Passo D'Areia, T/F33410720 (0900-1200, 1430-1800). USA, R Riachuelo 1257, 2nd floor, T32263344 (1400-1700). Uruguay, Av Cristóvão Colombo 2999, Higienópolis, T33256200, F33256200 (0900-1500). **Internet** .Com Cyber Café, R da Praia Shopping, S17, R dos Andradas 1001, T32864244, www.com-cybercafe.co.br. US$3 per hr. Ciber Café, Câncio Gomes e C Colombo 778, T33463098. 0900-2300. Livraria Saraiva Megastore, Shopping Praia de Belas, T32316868, www.livrariasaraiva. Com.br. Mon-Sat 1000-2200. PC2 Publicidad Café, Duque de Caxias 1464, T32276853, pc2.com@terra.com.br. US$2 per hr. Portonet, R Maracheal Floriano 185, T32274696. 0900-2100, US$2.50 per hr. **Language courses** Portuguese and Spanish, Matilde Dias, R Pedro Chaves Barcelos 37, Apdo 104, T33318235, malilde@estadao.com.br. US$9 per hr. **Laundry** Several along Av Andre da Rocha including Lavandería Lav-Dem, No 225. US$1.50 per kg wash and dry. **Post office** R Siqueria Campos 1100, Centro. Mon-Fri 0800-1700, Sat 0800-1200. UPS, T3434972 (Alvaro). **Telephones** R Siqueira de Campos 1245 and upstairs at rodoviária.

Beaches around Porto Alegre *p345, map p346, phone code 051*

Banks Banco do Brasil, 15 de Novembro 236, Torres and at the Torres rodoviária.

Gramado *p347, phone code 054*

Banks Banco do Brasil, R Garibáldi corner Madre Verónica. **Internet** Cyber, Av Borges de Medeiros 2016, T2869559. 1300-2300, US$2.80 per hr.

Canela *p347, phone code 054*

Banks Banco do Brasil, Av Julio de Castilhos 465. **Internet** Posto Telefõnico, Av Júlio de Castilhos 349, Sala 5, T2823305, 0800-2100, Sat 0900-2000, Sun 1000-1200, 1400-1800.

Pelotas *p348, phone code 053*

Banks Banco do Brasil, corner R Gen Osório and R Lobo da Costa. Also at R Anchieta 2122. Will change TCs. It is difficult to change money at weekends.

Rio Grande *p349, phone code 053*

Embassies and consulates Denmark, R Mcal Floriano 122, T2337600 (0800-1200, 1330-1800). UK, R Riachuelo 201, T2337700, F3211530 (0800-1200, 1330-1730). **Telephone** R Gen Neto 227.

Santo Ângelo and the Jesult Missions *p350, phone code 055*

Banks Banco do Brasil charges a commission of US$15 for TCs. Good rates for cash at the garage with red doors opposite Hotel Maerkli on Av Brasil.

Santana do Livramento and the border with Uruguay *p351*

Banks Banco do Brasil, Av Sarandí. Best rates for Amex TCs at Val de Marne.

Chuí and the border with Uruguay *p352, phone code 053*

Brazil

Banks Cambios on the Uruguayan side, see below. Banco do Brasil, Av Uruguaí, 3 blocks west of post office. Change all remaining Uruguayan pesos into reais before leaving Uruguay, not even black marketeers in Brazil want them. **Post office** Av Uruguaí, between Colômbia and Argentina. **Telephone** Corner of R Chile and Av Argentina.

Banks Several cambios on Av Brasil, eg Cambio Gales, Gral Artigas y Brasil, Mon-Fri 0830-1200, 1330-1800, Sat 0830-1200; in World Trade Center 1000-2200. Also Los Aces and Val, either side of Gales. All change TCs at US$1 per cheque and 1 commission and give similar rates, without commission, for cash (pesos, dollars and reais). On Sun, try the casino, or look for someone on the street outside the *cambios*. Brazilian currency can be bought here. Banco de la República Oriental Uruguay, Gral Artigas, changes TCs. **Embassies and consulates** Brazil, A Fossati, T0474-2049. **Telephone** Antel, S Priliac, between C L Olivera and C Gen Artigas, 0700-2300.

Bahia

Footprint features

Introduction

White-sand beaches backed by coconut palms, steep winding streets lined with pastel-paint houses; ornate Baroque churches; Afro-Brazilian ceremonies; gymnastic martial art ballet, the rhythm of the *berimbau*, the aroma of coconut milk and spices… Bahia conjures up almost as many exotic images, sounds and smells as Rio de Janeiro. And it has an even stronger claim to be the heart of Brazil. The state capital Salvador was the country's first city for far longer than any other, and it still lays claim to being the country's cultural centre.

Brazil's most famous novelist was a Bahian, many of its greatest musicians are Bahians; its best cooking, by far, is from Bahia. Bahia gave Brazil and the world samba, *capoeira*, carnival and *candomblé*; and it has many of the best beaches. Bahia's beautiful coast stretches far to the north and south of Salvador and is dotted with resorts along its length – laid-back little places like Itacaré, Morro do São Paulo and Trancoso and larger, more hedonistic party towns like Porto Seguro and Arraial de Ajuda. Inland, in the wild semi-desert of the Sertão is one of Brazil's best hiking destinations, the Chapada Diamantina, whose towering escarpments are cut by clearwater rivers and dotted with plunging waterfalls.

★ Don't miss...

1. **Salvador** Brace yourself for Brazil's most vibrant city, with its riotous carnival celebrations and beautiful historic city centre, page 366.
2. **Morro do São Paulo** Wind down on this *Bounty* bar advert tropical island with coconut palm beaches, a relaxed atmosphere and a young crowd, page 399.
3. **Itacaré** Enjoy Southern Bahia's up and coming beach destination: great restaurants, chic little hotels, Atlantic coast rainforest and tens of kilometres of white sand and coconut palms, page 400.
4. **Porto Seguro** Let your hair down at Bahia's nightlife capital: just south, Arraial de Ajuda, is a little quieter and cheaper, but with the same intense beach bar and nightlife scene, page 402.
5. **Trancoso** Lie back and enjoy the endless stretches of beautiful sand and a smattering of cool little bars and restaurants on the pretty colonial square, page 405.
6. **Praia do Forte** Discover pristine turtle-nesting beaches near Salvador's sophisticated little beach resort getaway with lively nightlife, page 407.
7. **Chapada Diamantina** Hike over cable top mountains, through canyons and along gorges, page 420.

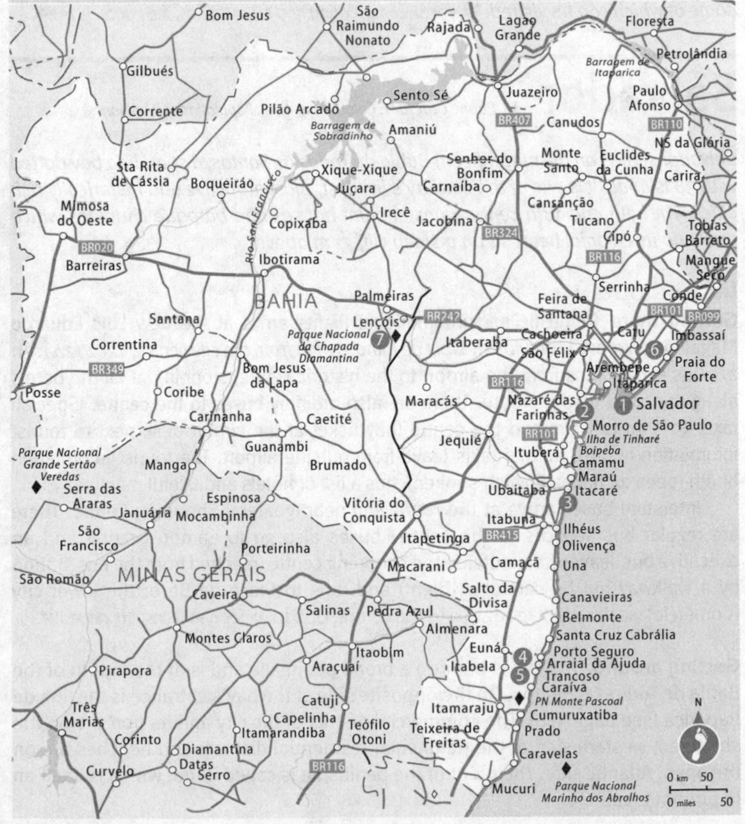

Salvador and the Recôncavo

The capital of the State of Bahia, Salvador de Bahia, is often just called Bahia. Salvador is a definite highlight of Brazil, where many Brazilians choose to spend their holidays (and Carnival, now that Rio's has become so commercialized). It would be quite easy to spend a whole vacation here without leaving this heady mix of colonial buildings, beautiful beaches, African culture and pulsating musical rhythms.

The Recôncavo is Brazil's largest bay and is dotted with islands, many of them private and home to some of the Northeast's wealthy, others weekend resorts for people from Salvador. The best known is Itaparica, a long thin island lined with palms, with a pretty colonial capital and some reasonable beaches. Many buses run from here to the south and taking the ferry across from Salvador and then road transport from Itaparica is the quickest way of getting to southern Bahia. The area around the bay and immediately south of Salvador is known as the Recôncavo Baiano. This was one of the chief centres of sugar and tobacco cultivation in the 16th century and there is some fine colonial architecture here. Most impressive is Cachoeira, *which is also famous for its numerous festivals. There are other small fishing villages on the bay which are worth exploring, such as Bom Jesus dos Pobres, and dotted throughout the countryside are the decaying ruins of once-productive sugar refineries* (engenhos), *some of which can be visited.* ▸▸ *For Sleeping, Eating and other listings, see pages 381-398.*

Salvador

→ *Phone code: 071. Colour map 4, A6. Population: 3.2 million.*

Salvador stands on the magnificent Bahia de Todos os Santos, a sparkling bay dotted with 38 islands. It is one of the country's liveliest, most attractive and historically rich cities. The 17th and 18th century pastel-paint houses and baroque churches which make-up its colonial heart sit on a steep cliff 71 m above.

Ins and outs

Getting there Domestic and international flights arrive at the new **Luís Eduardo Magalhães Airport** ⓘ *previously Dois de Julho, 32 km from the city centre, T2041244*. An a/c bus service runs from the airport to the historic centre, stopping at all the hotels along the coast road en route. There are also ordinary buses to the centre. 'Special' taxis go both to Barra and the centre (buy ticket at the airport desk next to tourist information booth). Normal taxis leave from outside airport. The tourist information booth (open 24 hours, English spoken), has a list of hotels and useful map.

Interstate buses arrive at the *rodoviária* near Iguatemi Shopping Centre. There are regular bus services to the centre; buses also go to Campo Grande and an executive bus leaves from outside the shopping centre (reached from the bus station by a walkway but be careful at night) and runs to Praça da Sé or the lower city (Comércio) via the coast road. Taxi to the centre, US$10. ▸▸ *See also Transport, page 394..*

Getting around The city is built on a broad peninsula and is at the mouth of the Bahia de Todos Os Santos. On the opposite side of the bay's entrance is the Ilha de Itaparica (see page 378). The commercial district of the city and its port are on the sheltered, western side of the peninsula; residential districts and beaches are on the open, Atlantic side. The point of the peninsula is called Barra, which is itself an important area.

The Bahians

Bahia is perceived in the south of the country as being a place where life moves at a different pace. The word *preguiça* (laziness) will inevitably creep into a conversation with paulistas and cariocas when the topic is Salvador. This slightly malicious accusation from the southerners cannot take away the great infectious joy for life, so obvious in Bahians.

Bahians have a great propensity for partying; there is even a popular carnival song that says that every day is party day in Bahia. The cycle of massive street festivals throughout the year is evidence of this.

There is no doubt that Bahians have a different slant on time keeping. For instance, the clock in the main bus station is officially seven minutes fast as Bahians will almost always be late. The weekend and carnival are among the few events that start early: the former on Thursday night, the latter four days before anywhere else in the country. If you want someone to turn up for an appointment on time you will need to emphasize that you are expecting them at 'horário britónico'. Another popular saying is that it takes nine months to leave the womb, so why hurry now! While this laid-back attitude can be frustrating, Bahians are very open, warm, hospitable, endearing people to spend time with, willing to try to understand, either in words or gestures. People still have time to talk to one another in this town.

The centre of the city is divided into two levels, the **Cidade Alta** (Upper City) where the Historic Centre lies, and the **Cidade Baixa** (Lower City) which is the commercial and docks district. The two levels are connected by a series of steep hills called *ladeiras*. The easiest way to go from one level to the other is by the *Lacerda* lift, which connects Praça Municipal (Tomé de Sousa) in the Upper City with Praça Cairu and the famous Mercado Modelo (take care with belongings). There is also the Plano Inclinado Gonçalves, a funicular railway that leaves from behind the Cathedral going down to Comércio, the commercial district.

Most visitors limit themselves to the centre, Barra, the Atlantic suburbs and the Itapagipe peninsula, which is north of the centre. The roads and avenues between these areas are straightforward to follow and are well served by public transport. Other parts of the city are not as easy to get around, but are of less interest to most visitors. If going to these areas, a taxi may be advisable until you know your way around.

Tourist information **Bahiatursa** ⓘ *R das Laranjeiras 12, Historic Centre, T3212133, daily 0830-2200; Rodoviária, T4503871*, good, English spoken; **airport** ⓘ *T2041244, daily 0800-2245*, friendly; **Mercado Modelo** ⓘ *T2410242, Mon-Sat 0900-1800*; **Sac Shopping Centre** ⓘ *Av Centenario 2992, T2644566*. Useful information (often only available in Portuguese) includes *BahiaCultural*, the month's programme of events and leaflets with maps of themed points of interest. **Bahiatursa** has lists of hotels and accommodation in private homes. Clear map of historic centre available. The offices also have details of travel throughout the State of Bahia as well as noticeboards for messages. **Emtursa** ⓘ *airport, T3772262, Mon-Sat 0800-2200*, is helpful and has good maps. A useful website for culture, tourism and history is www.bahiabeat.com.br.

T131-06000030 for tourist information in English.

Maps Available from **Departamento de Geografia e Estadística** ⓘ *Av Estados Unidos (opposite Banco do Brasil, Lower City*; also from news-stands including the airport bookshop, US$1.50.

 Climate It rains somewhat all the year, but the main rainy season is between May and September. The climate is pleasant and the sun is never far away. Temperatures range from 25°C to 32°C, never falling below 19°C in winter.

Safety Tourist Police ⓘ *R Gregório de Matos 16, T2422885*. **Delegacia de Proteção ao Turista** ⓘ *R Gregório de Matos 1, T2423504*. Be very careful of your money and valuables at all times and in all districts. At night, buses and the area around and in the lifts are unsafe. The civil police are sympathetic and helpful and more resources have been put into policing the areas of Pelourinho and the old part of the city and also Barra, which are well lit at night. Police are little in evidence after 2300, however. Be cautious of pickpockets any time after dark.

History

On 1 November 1501, All Saints' Day, the navigator Amérigo Vespucci sailed into the bay. As the first European to see it, he named it after the day of his arrival. When Martim Afonso was sent by the Portuguese crown to set up a permanent colony in Brazil, he decided against the Bahia de Todos Os Santos in favour of São Vicente in

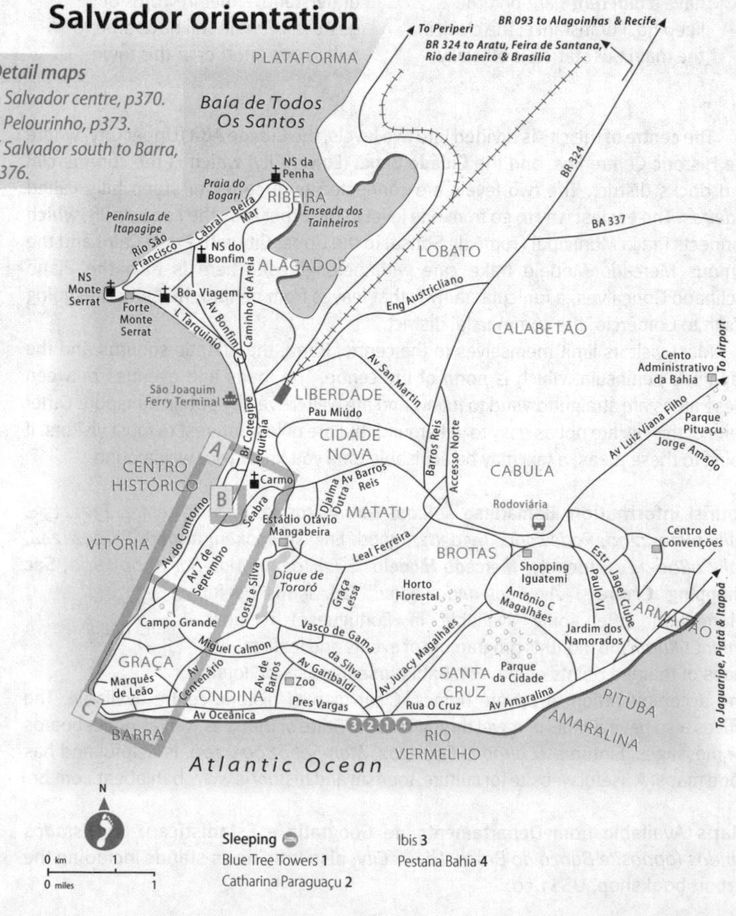

Ochente!

The rest of Brazil tends to find the northeastern accent funny: in common with the poorest and oldest regions of many countries, it retains outmoded structures, expressions and pronunciations which, language historians claim, recall the Portuguese spoken by the earliest settlers. It is an attractive accent, with rising cadence that lends a sing-song quality to the language (considered downmarket in Southerners), and is easy for visitors to manage, since it is spoken comparatively slowly and clearly.

The minute you arrive in the northeast, you are likely to hear the local all-purpose exclamation: 'Ochente!', probably at maximum decibels. Meaning everything from 'You don't say!' to the unprintable, it's a particularly satisfying yell, capable of a thousand inflections, and is almost impossible not to adopt. The short version, 'Oshh!', is reserved for situations where hushed tones are required, as in 'She didn't!'

present-day São Paulo, even though the bay was one of the finest anchorages on the coast and a favourite port of call for French, Spanish and Portuguese ships and a known export point for *pau brasil*.

This strategic importance was finally recognized and it was chosen as the place from which the new colony of Brazil was to be governed when the first Governor General, Tomé de Sousa, arrived on 23 March 1549, to build a fortified city to protect Portugal's interest from constant threats of Dutch and French invasion. Salvador was formally founded on 1 November 1549 and remained the capital of Brazil until 1763. One short-lived disruption in the city's growth was its capture by the Dutch in 1624. The Portuguese, with the help of Spain, recaptured it a year later.

On the strength of the export of sugar and the import of African slaves to work the plantations, Salvador became a wealthy city. By the 18th century, it was the most important city in the Portuguese Empire after Lisbon, ideally situated in a safe, sheltered harbour along the trade routes of the 'New World'. Its fortunes were further boosted by the discovery of diamonds in the interior, but this could not compensate for the eventual decline in the sugar industry, which led to the loss of capital status and the rise of Rio de Janeiro as Brazil's principal city. Until the introduction of 20th-century industries such as tourism and petrochemicals, the local economy could not rival the gold and coffee booms of the Southeast, but the city always played an influential part in the political and cultural life of the country.

African presence

The city's first wealth came from the cultivation of sugar cane and tobacco, the plantations' workforce coming from the west coast of Africa. For three centuries, Salvador was the site of a thriving slave trade. Even today, Salvador is described as the most African city in the Western hemisphere and the University of Bahia boasts the only choir in the Yoruba language in the Americas. The influence permeates the city: food sold on the street is the same as in Senegal and Nigeria, Bahian music is fused with pulsating African polyrhythms, men and women nonchalantly carry enormous loads on their heads, fishermen paddle dug-out canoes in the bay, and the pace of life is a little slower than elsewhere.

Modern Salvador

Salvador today is a city of 15 forts, 166 Catholic churches, 1,000 *candomblé* temples and a fascinating mixture of old and modern, rich and poor, African and European,

Salvador centre

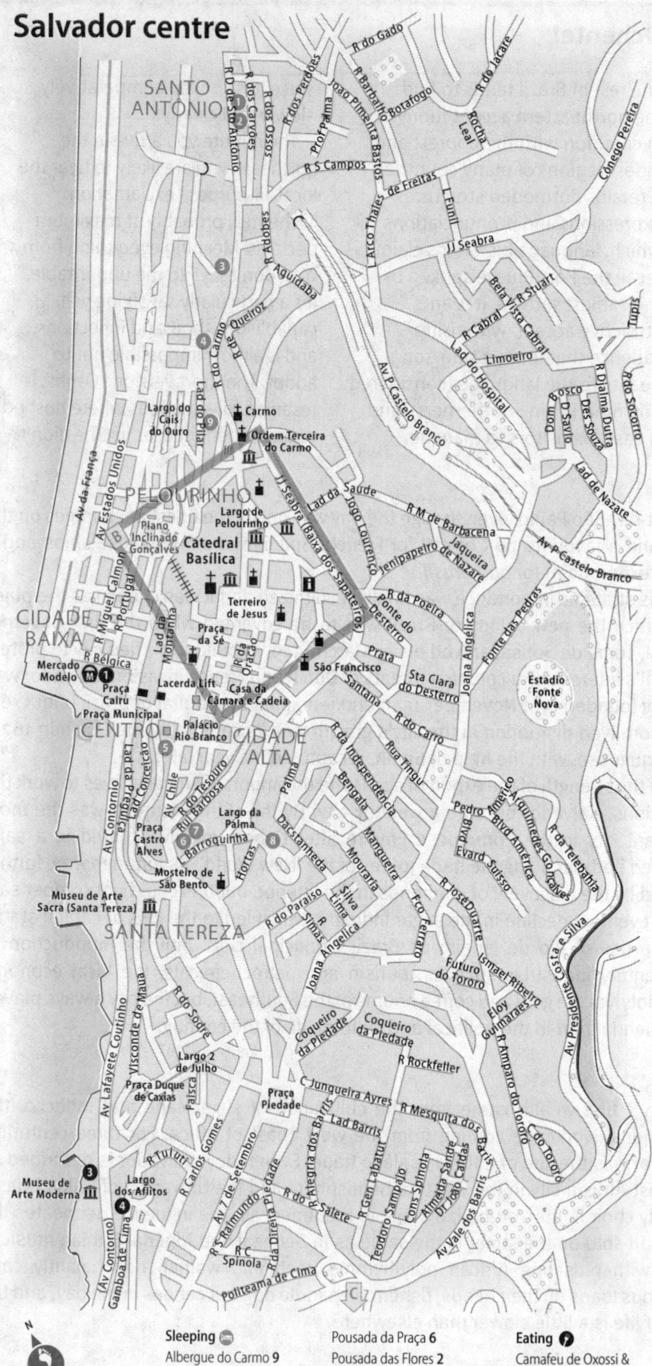

Sleeping

Albergue do Carmo 9
Palace 5
Paris 7
Portas Velhas 8
Pousada da Praça 6
Pousada das Flores 2
Pousada do Boqueirão 3
Pousada Redfish 1
Pousada Villa Carmo 4

Eating

Camafeu de Oxossi & Maria de São Pedro 1
Chez Bernard 4
Solar do Unhão 3

Sand Captains

In his earlier works, Bahia's most famous son, the internationally renowned author Jorge Amado (see page 401), campaigned for the oppressed. One of his own favourites is the novel *Capitães de areia* (*Sand Captains*), which is about the daily life of a group of abandoned street children in Salvador. The problem of street children still exists in Salvador and their treatment at the hands of the authorities and vigilante groups sometimes makes international headlines.

The *Projeto Axé* (pronounced ash-ay, Yoruba for 'life source') was set up as a means of reading out to children and adolescents living on their wits in the streets of Salvador.

Using a team of highly professional educators and sociologists, the project won the trust of the children who had hitherto seen any approach from adults as being potentially threatening. Once initial contact had been made, the children would gain confidence and seek further contact with the project where they would be offered the opportunity to take part in activities such as *capoeira*, dance, percussion and circus skills. A number of local companies offer them work experience and training programmes monitored by the project. There is a paper recycling unit and a clothes manufacturing unit, where all stages, from design to the final finished product, are taught. Goods such as T-shirts and paper products can be purchased in the project's store in Rua Francisco Muniz Barreto das Laranjeiras. All proceeds go to the project. There is a visitor centre in Rua Professor Lemos Brito in Barra, where there is more information in English.

The Projeto Axé is a shining example of a major social problem being dealt with in a non-patronizing way, laying real foundations in the future instead of the sands of the past.

religious and profane. It is still a major port, exporting tropical fruit, cocoa, sisal, soya beans and petrochemical products. Its most important industry, though, is tourism; after Rio it is the second largest tourist attraction in the country, being very popular with Brazilian tourists who see Bahia as an exotic destination. Local government has done much to improve the fortunes of this once run-down, poor and dirty city, and most visitors feel that the richness of its culture is compensation enough for any problems they may encounter.

Major investments are being made in infrastructure and public health areas. A new comprehensive sewage system has been installed throughout the city, with a view to improving living conditions and dealing with pollution.

The once-forgotten Lower City, Ribeira and the Itapagipe Peninsula districts have received major facelifts. Bahia has become more industrialized, with major investments being made by multinational firms in the automotive and petrochemical industries, principally in the Camaçari complex, 40 km from the city. The Bahian economy is currently the fastest growing in the country.

Centro Histórico

Most of the interesting sights are concentrated in the Upper City (see Getting around, page 366), particularly the Centro Histórico. From Praça Municipal to the Carmo area, 2 km north along the cliff, the Centro Histórico is a national monument and protected by UNESCO. It was in this area that the Portuguese built their fortified city and where today stand some of the most important examples of colonial architecture in the Americas. The historic centre has undergone a massive restoration programme. The colonial houses have been painted in pastel colours. Many of the bars have live music which spills out onto the street on every corner. Patios have been created in the open areas behind the houses, with open-air cafés and bars. Artist ateliers, antique and handicraft stores have brought new artistic blood to what was once the bohemian part of the city. Many popular traditional restaurants and bars from other parts of Salvador have opened new branches in the area.

Praça Municipal and Praça da Sé

Dominating the Praça Municipal is the old Casa de Câmara e Cadeia or **Paço Municipal** (Council Chamber – 1660), while alongside is the **Paláclo Rio Branco** (1918), once the Governor's Palace and now the headquarters of Bahiatursa, the state tourist board. Leaving it with its panoramic view of the bay, Rua Misericôrdia goes north passing the **Santa Casa Misericôrdia** (1695) ⓘ *see the high altar and painted tiles, open by arrangement 0800-1700, T3227666* to **Praça da Sé**. This *praça*, with its mimosa and flamboyant trees, has a statue of Salvador's founder, Thomé da Souza and good views of the bay. On the platform is the Cruz Caido, by the sculptor Mario Cravo. It is dedicated to the old Igreja da Se, which was pulled down in 1933 and whose remaining foundations have been uncovered. One of the viewing pits displays the remains of slaves and mariners who were buried in the churches' grounds in the 16th century.

Terreiro de Jesus

Terreiro de Jesus is a picturesque *praça* named after the church which dominates it. Built in 1692, the **church of the Jesuits** became the property of the Holy See in 1759 when the Jesuits were expelled from all Portuguese territories. The façade is one of the earliest examples of baroque in Brazil, an architectural style which was to dominate the churches built in the 17th and 18th centuries. Inside, the vast vaulted ceiling and 12 side altars in baroque and rococo frame the main altar completely leafed in gold. The tiles in blue, white and yellow in a tapestry pattern are also from Portugal. It houses the tomb of Mem de Sá. The church is now the **Catedral Basílica** ⓘ *daily 0900-1100, 1400-1700*. Across the square is the church of **São Pedro dos Clérigos** ⓘ *Sun 0800-0930*, which is beautifully renovated. Alongside is the church of the **Ordem Terceira de São Domingos** ⓘ *Mon-Fri 0800-1200, 1400-1700, US$0.25*, which has a beautiful painted wooden ceiling.

The **Museu Afro-Brasileiro** ⓘ *Mon-Fri 0900-1700, US$1*, is in the former Faculty of Medicine building on the Terreiro de Jesus. Its interesting displays (all in Portuguese) compare African and Bahian Orixás (deities) celebrations; there are some beautiful murals and carvings. In the basement of the same building, the **Museu Arqueológico e Etnográfico** ⓘ *Mon-Fri 0900-1700, US$0.40*, houses archaeological discoveries from Bahia, such as stone tools, clay urns, an exhibition on Indians from the Alto Rio Xingu area, including artefacts, tools, photos. Recommended. The **Memorial de Medicina** (Museum of Medicine) is in the same complex.

São Francisco

Facing Terreiro de Jesus is Praça Anchieta and the church of **São Francisco** ⓘ *0830–1700, cloisters US$0.20, church free*. Its simple façade belies the treasure inside. The entrance leads to a sanctuary with a spectacular painting on the wooden ceiling by local artist José Joaquim da Rocha (1777). The main body of the church is the most exuberant example of baroque in the country. The cedar wood carving and later gold leaf was completed after 28 years in 1748. The cloisters of the monastery are surrounded by a series of blue and white tiles from Portugal. Next door is the church of the **Ordem Terceira de São Francisco** ⓘ *0800-1200 and 1300-1700, US$0.20*, (Franciscan Third Order – 1703), with its façade intricately carved in sandstone. Inside is a quite remarkable Chapter House, with striking images of the Order's most celebrated saints.

Largo do Pelourinho

Rua Alfredo Brito, a charming, narrow cobbled street lined with fine colonial houses painted in different pastel shades, leads to the Largo do Pelourinho (Praça José Alencar). Considered the finest complex of colonial architecture in Latin America, it was once the site of a slave market and a pillory where slaves were publicly punished and ridiculed. After complete renovation in 1993, new galleries, boutiques and restaurants have opened, and at night the Largo is lively, especially on Tuesday (see

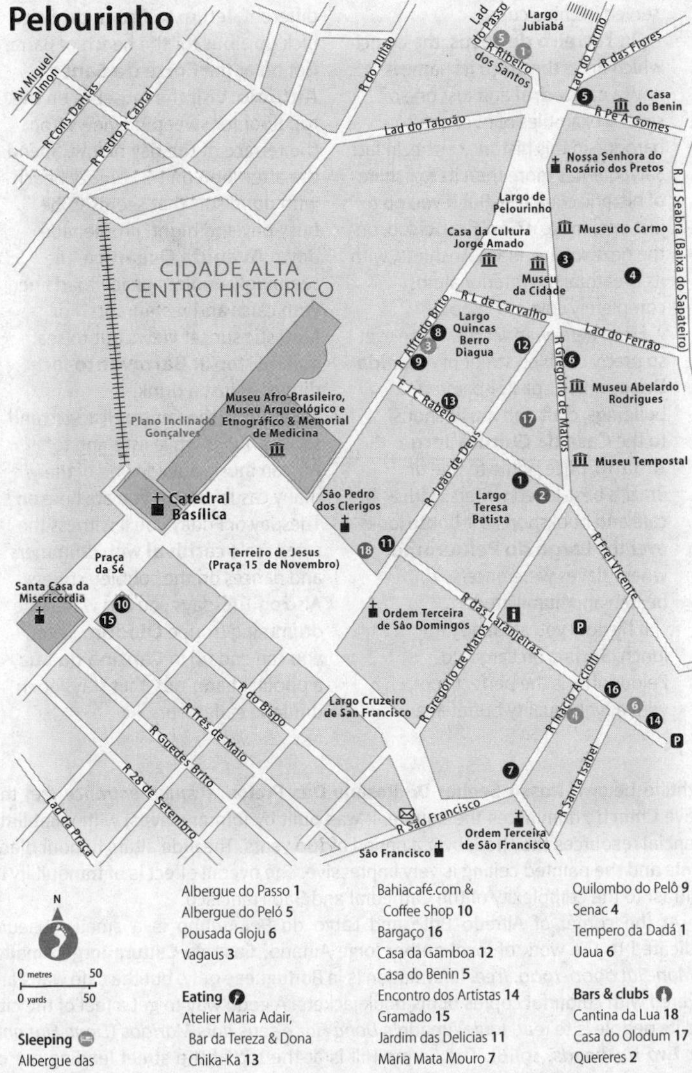

24 hours in Salvador

Start the day in Terreiro de Jesus, a lovely square at the heart of the historic centre. If you need breakfast, **Bahiacafe.com**, around the corner at Praça da Se 20, is a funky, Belgian-run café with excellent food and atmosphere. Or, for just a caffeine hit, the Cuban-style **Coffee Shop** a couple of doors along has great coffee and tea served in china cups.

On **Terreiro de Jesus**, the church which gives the *praça* its name is now a **cathedral** and just one of several examples of over-the-top baroque in this historic centre. In fact, Salvador has more than its fair share of historic churches. But if you go to just one, make it **São Francisco**, on the next square, Praça Anchieta, with its breathtaking interior almost completely covered in gold.

From here, wander down the ever so pretty cobbled street of **Avenida Brito**, with its pastel-painted buildings, craft and music shops, to the **Casa da Cultura Jorge Amado**, once home to one of Brazil's best-loved writers, with a café and bookshop. The house looks over the **Largo do Pelourinho**, where slaves were once sold, beaten and humiliated.

If by now you are ready for lunch, **Senac**, on Largo do Pelourinho, is the perfect spot, with a high-quality buffet at a really good price because all the food is prepared by catering students.

Walk back up João de Deus, parallel to Avenida Brito, an equally charming street with more small shops. You may want to stay and mooch around this area for a while; there always seems to be something to look at in the streets around here.

For something completely different, return to **Praça da Se** to pick up a bus for the beach of Barra. Get off at the **Forte de Santo Antônio**. Visit the museum on the top floor for sweeping views from the terrace of the bay below. Spend the afternoon on this breezy beach with good surf that seems to be busy day and night. Promenade down **Avenida Oceânica**, the seemingly endless beach road lined with cafés and restaurants. For fantastic sunset views out to sea, make a stop at **Barravento** for dinner or just a drink.

Return to the Centro Histórico and sip *caiprinhas* while listening to African music outside one of the many casual bars. If you are here on Tuesday or Friday you'll witness the small scale **carnival** with drummers and dances on the cobbled streets. Also on Tuesdays you can watch the drumming troupe **Olodum**. Later, you can end up in **Cantina da Lua**, a popular hang-out that stays open until the early hours.

Nightlife below). **Nosso Senhor Do Rosário Dos Pretos** ⓘ *small entrance fee*, the 'Slave Church', dominates the square. It was built by former slaves, with what little financial resources they had, over a period of 100 years. The side altars honour black saints and the painted ceiling is very impressive. The overall effect is of tranquillity in contrast to the complexity of the Cathedral and São Francisco.

At the corner of Alfredo Brito and Largo do Pelourinho is a small museum dedicated to the work of local author Jorge Amado, **Casa da Cultura Jorge Amado** ⓘ *Mon-Sat 0900-1900, free*. Information is in Portuguese only, but the café walls are covered with colourful copies of his book jackets. A good way to get a feel of the city and its people is to read Jorge Amado's *Dona Flor e seus dois Maridos* (*Dona Flor and Her Two Husbands*, 1966). The Carmo Hill is at the top of the street leading out of Largo do Pelourinho. The **Carmo church** ⓘ *Mon-Sat 0800-1130, 1400-1730, Sun*

66 99 The drops of blood are made from whale oil, ox blood, banana resin and 2,000 rubies...

1000-1200, US$0.30, (Carmelite Third Order, 1709) houses one of the sacred art treasures of the city, a sculpture of Christ made in 1730 by a slave who had no formal training, Francisco Xavier das Chagas, known as O Cabra. The drops of blood are made from whale oil, ox blood, banana resin and 2,000 rubies. **Museu do Carmo** ⓘ *Mon-Sat 0800-1200, 1400-1800, Sun 0800-1200, US$0.10*, in the Convento do Carmo, has a collection of icons and colonial furniture.

The **Museu Abelardo Rodrigues** ⓘ *Solar Ferrão, Pelourinho, Tue-Sun 1300-1900, US$0.40*, is a religious art museum, with objects from the 17th, 18th and 19th centuries, mainly from Bahia, Pernambuco and Maranhão.

The **Museu da Cidade** ⓘ *Largo do Pelourinho, Tue-Fri 0930-1830, Sat 1300-1700, Sun 0930-1300, free*, has exhibitions of arts and crafts and old photographs. From the higher floors of the museum you can get a good view of the Pelourinho.

Below Nossa Senhora do Rosario dos Pretos, **Casa do Benin** ⓘ *Mon-Fri 1000-1800*, shows African crafts, photos, a video show on Benin and Angola.

South of the centre

The modern city which is dotted with skyscrapers sits to the south of the old centre towards the mouth of the bay. Rua Chile leads to **Praça Castro Alves**, with its monument to the man who started the campaign which finally led to the Abolition of Slavery in 1888. Two streets lead out of this square, Avenida 7 de Setembro, busy with shops and street vendors selling everything imaginable, and, parallel to it, Rua Carlos Gomes. **São Bento** church ⓘ *Av 7 de Setembro, Mon-Sat 0630-1230, 1600-1900, Sun 0700-1130, 1700-1900 Sun*, was rebuilt after 1624, but with fine 17th-century furniture.

Museu de Arte Sacra ⓘ *R do Sodré 276 (off R Carlos Gomes), Mon-Fri 1130-1730, US$1.50*, is in the 17th-century monastery and church of Santa Tereza, at the bottom of the steep Ladeira de Santa Tereza. Many of the 400 carvings are from Europe, but a number are local. Among the reliquaries of silver and gold is one of gilded wood by Aleijadinho (see page 708). The collection of treasures which used to be in the Casa de Calmon, Avenida Joana Angêlica 198, are well worth a visit. Opposite is **Tempostal** ⓘ *R do Sodré 276, Tue-Fri 0900-1830, Sat and Sun 0900-1800*, a private museum of postcards whose proprietor is Antônio Marcelino do Nascimento.

Further south, the **Museu de Arte Moderna** ⓘ *T3290660, Tue-Fri 1300-2100, Sat 1500-2100, Sun 1400-1900*, converted from an old estate house and outbuildings off Avenida Contorno, is only open for special exhibitions. But it has a good restaurant (**Solar do Unhão**), and the buildings are worth seeing for themselves (take a taxi there as access is dangerous).

Heading towards Porta da Barra, the **Museu de Arte da Bahia** ⓘ *Av 7 de Setembro 2340, Vitória, Tue-Fri 1400-1900, Sat and Sun 1430-1900, US$1.20*, has interesting paintings of Brazilian artists from the 18th to the early 20th century.

Museu Carlos Costa Pinto ⓘ *Av 7 de Setembro 2490, Vitória, www.guasar.com.br/mccp/mccp.htm, Mon and Wed-Fri 1430-1900, Sat and Sun 1500-1800, US$2*, is a modern house with collections of crystal, porcelain, silver, furniture, etc. It also has the only collection of *balangandãs* (slave charms and jewellery) and is highly recommended.

Salvador south to Barra

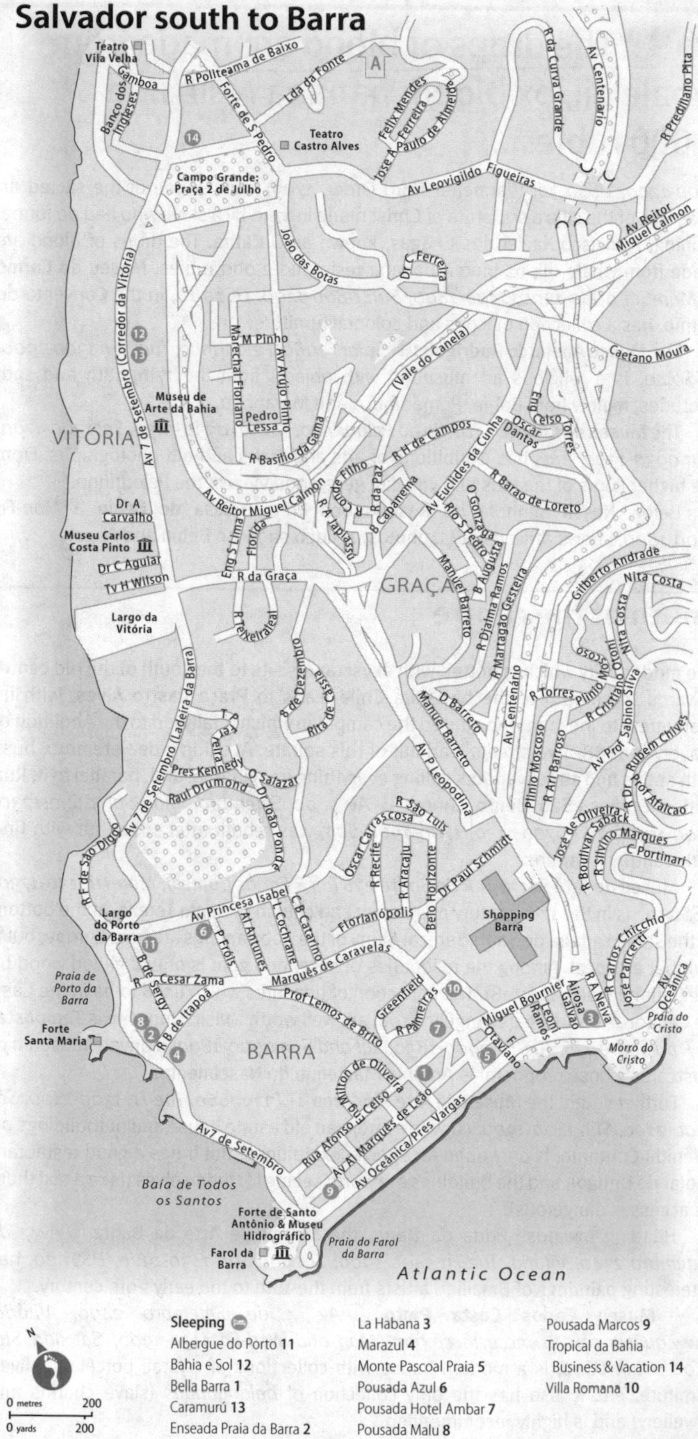

Sleeping

- Albergue do Porto **11**
- Bahia e Sol **12**
- Bella Barra **1**
- Caramurú **13**
- Enseada Praia da Barra **2**
- La Habana **3**
- Marazul **4**
- Monte Pascoal Praia **5**
- Pousada Azul **6**
- Pousada Hotel Ambar **7**
- Pousada Malu **8**
- Pousada Marcos **9**
- Tropical da Bahia
- Business & Vacation **14**
- Villa Romana **10**

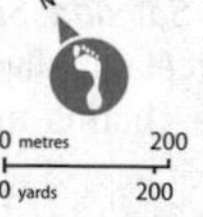

Candomblé

The pulse of the city is *candomblé*, a religion brought over by slaves from West Africa and syncretized with Catholicism and indigenous belief systems (see Religion, page 695). The pantheon of deities (*orixás*) worshipped in temples (*terreiros*) which can be elaborate, decorated halls, or simply someone's front room with tiny altars to the *orixá*. Ceremonies are divided into two distinct parts. The first is when the *orixás* are invoked through different rhythms, songs and dances. Once the dancers have been possessed by the *orixá*, they are led off in a trance-like state to be changed into sacred, often very elaborate costumes, and come back to the ceremonial area in a triumphant procession in which each one dances separately for their deity. Overseeing the proceedings are *mães* or *pães de santo*, priestesses or priests.

Candomblé ceremonies may be seen by tourists, usually on Sundays and religious holidays. The ceremonies can be very repetitive and usually last several hours, although you are not under pressure to remain for the duration. Appropriate, modest attire should be worn; visitors should not go in shorts, sleeveless vests or T-shirts. White clothing is preferred, black should not be worn especially if it is combined with red. Men and women are separated during the ceremonies, women always on the left, men on the right. No photography or sound recording is allowed. Most temples are closed during Lent, although each one has its own calendar. Bahiatursa often has information about forthcoming ceremonies, but accurate information on authentic festivals is not always easy to come by.

Porto da Barra

The best inner-city beaches are in this area, which is busy at night with people playing football and volleyball and swimming. Many sidewalk restaurants and bars are open along the strip from Porto da Barra, as far as the Cristo at the end of the Farol da Barra beach. **Forte de Santo Antônio** is right at the mouth of the bay where Bahia de Todos Os Santos and the South Atlantic Ocean meet. On the upper floors, the **Museu Hidrográfico** ⓘ *Tue-Sat 1300-1800, US$1*, has fine views of the bay and coast and is recommended.

Atlantic beach suburbs

The promenade leads away from the Forte de Santo Antônio and its famous lighthouse, following the coast to the beach suburbs of **Ondina**, **Amaralina** and **Pituba**. Confusingly the road is called both Avenida Oceânica and Avenida Presidente Vargas, but with different numbering. Beyond Pituba are the best ocean beaches at **Jaguaripe**, **Piatã** and **Itapoã** (take any bus from Praça da Sé marked Aeroporto or Itapoã, about one hour). En route the bus passes small fishing colonies at Amaralina and Pituba, where *jangadas* (small rafts peculiar to the northeast) can be seen. Near Itapoã is the **Lagoa do Abaeté**, a deep freshwater lake surrounded by brilliant, white sands. This is where local women traditionally come to wash their clothes and then lay them out to dry in the sun. The road leading up from the lake offers a panoramic view of the city in the distance and the white sands and freshwater less than 1 km from the sea and its golden beaches.

Avoid the more distant beaches out of season, when they are empty. There have been reports of armed muggings on the sand dunes surrounding Lagoa do Abaeté. Don't visit them alone.

Near the lighthouse at **Itapoã** are two campsites on the beach. A little beyond them are the magnificent ocean beaches of **Stella Maris** and **Flamengo**, both quiet during the week but very busy at the weekends. Beware of strong undertow.

North of the centre

Bonfim and Itapagipe

See the famous church of **Nosso Senhor do Bonfim** ⓘ *Mon 0630-0800, Tue-Sun 0600-1200, 1400-2000*, on the Itapagipe Peninsula in the suburbs north of the centre, whose construction began in 1745. It draws extraordinary numbers of supplicants (particularly on Friday and Sunday), making ex-voto offerings to the image of the Crucified Lord set over the high altar. The processions over the water to the church on the third Sunday in January are particularly interesting. Also on the Itapagipe peninsula is a colonial fort on **Monte Serrat** point, and at Ribeira the church of **Nossa Senhora da Penha** (1743). The beach here has many restaurants, but the sea is polluted (bus from Praça da Sé or Avenida França).

Excursions from Salvador

From the lower city, the **Trem do Leste** (train) leaves Calçada for a 40-minute journey through the bayside suburbs of Lobato, **Plataforma** (canoes and motor boats for Ribeira on the Itapagipe peninsula), **Escada** (17th-century church), Praia Grande, Periperi and Paripe (take a bus for the 17th-century church at **São Tomé de Paripe**). The train runs Monday-Friday only; the same trip can be made by bus, less picturesquely, but much more comfortably. About 36 km from the city is the **Museu do Recôncavo** (**Museu do Vanderlei do Pinho**) ⓘ *near the town of São Francisco do Conde, 7 km from the main highway, Tue, Thu and Sun 0900-1700*, in the old Freguesia Mill (1552), in which you can find artefacts and pictures going back three centuries of the economic and social life of this region. The Casa Grande e Senzala (the home of the landowner and the combined dwelling and working area of the slaves) is still intact. It is a peaceful way to spend an afternoon, but difficult to get to by public transport.

Itaparica and other bay islands

→ Phone code: 071. Colour map 4, A6.

Across the bay from Salvador lies the island of Itaparica, 29 km long and 12 km wide. The town of Itaparica is very picturesque, with a fair beach in the town, and well worth a visit. Take a bus or kombi by the coast road (Beira Mar) which passes through the villages of Manguinhos, Amoureiras and Ponta de Areia. The beach at Ponta de Areia is one of the best on the island and is always very popular. There are many *barracas* on the beach, the most lively is **Barraca Pai Xango**.

In Itaparica there are many fine residential buildings from the 19th century, plus the church of **São**

Lourenço, one of the oldest in Brazil, a delightful walk through the old town. During the summer months the streets are ablaze with the blossoms of the beautiful flamboyant trees. There are many *pousadas* in **Mar Grande** and at the nearby beaches of **Ilhota** and **Gamboa** (both to the left as you disembark from the ferry). The beaches at Mar Grande are fair but can be dirty at times.

From **Bom Despacho** there are many buses to other towns such as Nazaré das Farinhas, Valença (see below) and also **Jaguaribe**, a small, picturesque colonial port. Both of these towns are on the mainland connected by a bridge on the southwest side of the island; turn off between Mar Grande and Cacha Pregos (bus company is Viazul). There are good beaches on the mainland, but a boat is needed to reach these (US$12).

Small boats cross the 25 km between Salvador and the **Ilha da Maré** between 0900 and 1100 (US$1.70), docking at the island's villages of Itamoaba, Praia Grande and Santana. The boat returns next day from Santana between 0400-0500. The departure point is near the naval base; take a 'Base Naval/São Tomé' bus from the foot of the Lacerda Lift; follow a path that leads off from the left-hand side of the naval base gate. Santana is a centre for lace-making, Praia Grande for basket-weaving. None of the villages has a hotel, but there are restaurants and bars and camping is possible.

From São Tomé de Paripe, near the naval base at Aratu, irregular boats go to **Ilha dos Frades**, sparsely populated, no electricity, one *pousada*. The beach is busy at lunchtimes with trips from Salvador, but otherwise is quiet, with good snorkelling.

Nazaré das Farinhas → *Phone code: 075 Population: 25,000*

On the mainland some 60 km inland from Itaparica, Nazaré das Farinhas is reached over a bridge by bus from **Bom Despacho**. This 18th-century town is celebrated for its market, which specializes in the local ceramic figures, or *caxixis*. There is a large market in Holy Week, particularly on Holy Thursday and Good Friday. About 12 km from Nazaré (taxi US$4.25, also buses) is the village of **Maragojipinha**, which specializes in making the ceramic figures. Bus from Salvador, 1530, takes five hours.

The Recôncavo

This fertile region south of Salvador was once an important area for the cultivation of tobacco and cacão. It retains many attractive colonial towns.

Ins and outs Leaving Salvador on the Feira road, fork left at Km 33 on the BR-324 to visit the **Museu do Recôncavo Vanderlei de Pinho** (see page 378). Further west, round the bay, is **São Francisco do Conde,** 54 km from Salvador, with a church and convent of 1636 and the ruins of Don Pedro II's agricultural school, said to be the first in Latin America.

Santo Amaro da Purificação and around

→ *Phone code: 075. Colour map 4, A6. Population: 59,000.*

Some 73 km from Salvador, Santo Amaro da Purificação is an old and sadly decaying sugar centre. It is noted for its churches (which are often closed because of robberies), the municipal palace (1769), fine main *praça* and ruined mansions including **Araújo Pinto**, former residence of the Barão de Cotegipe. It is also the birthplace of the singers Caetano Veloso and his sister Maria Bethânia. Other attractions include the splendid beaches of the bay, the falls of Vitória and the grotto of Bom Jesus dos Pobres. The festivals of **Santo Amaro,** 24 January to 2 February, and **Nossa Senhora da Purificação** on 2 February itself, are interesting. There is also the **Bembé do Mercado** festival on 13 May. Craftwork is sold on the town's main bridge. There are no good hotels or restaurants.

Sisters of Good Death

The Sisterhood of the Boa Morte (Good Death) was formed nearly two centuries ago in the *senzalas* (slave quarters), where slaves would gather to discuss abolition and pray for those killed in the struggle for emancipation. Once freed, ex-slaves would often form religious associations under the mantle of the Catholic church. The real purpose of these associations, however, was to free other slaves from captivity, help them to survive in the free world and preserve the traditions handed down orally from generation to generation. To this day they continue the tradition of only admitting women of African descent. Each August they parade through the streets of Cachoeira with the image of Nossa Senhora da Boa Morte. The sisterhood worships *iyás*, the female spirits of the dead. The sisters were expelled from the Catholic Church for refusing to surrender their statue of Nossa Senhora to the Vatican. At one point they were reduced to only 25 members, but the sisterhood has managed to survive through the support of African American solidarity groups from Bahia and the USA, and through the promotion of the ceremony as a tourist attraction by the state government. The sisters are a living document of the African Diaspora in the Americas.

The first procession takes place on the Friday after 15 August, on the Feast of the Assumption of the Virgin Mary, and is followed by a banquet. On the Saturday, after prayers, a funeral procession takes place, accompanied by a local brass band. On the Friday and Saturday, ceremonies begin at 1800. The following morning, after a night's vigil and a ceremony in the Casa da Irmandade at 1000, the sisters and novices parade through the town in their finery with the miraculously reborn Nossa Senhora carried aloft. Then the celebrations begin as the sisters dance Samba de Roda, a spinning samba danced in beautifully coloured skirts which create a kaleidoscope effect as the sisters twirl to the music. This form of samba originated in Cachoeira and is seldom seen anywhere else. During the festival weekend there are also displays of *capoeira* and top Brazilian reggae stars often play to honour the sisterhood and the town.

About 3 km beyond Santo Amaro on BR-420, turn right onto the BA-878 for **Bom Jesus dos Pobres**, a small, traditional fishing village with a 300-year history. There is one good hotel (see Sleeping, page 385). To get there, take a bus from Salvador rodoviária (four a day, Camurjipe, US$3).

Cachoeira → *Phone code: 075. Colour map 4, A6.*

At 116 km from Salvador, and only 4 km from the BR-101 coastal road, are the towns of Cachoeira (Bahia's 'Ouro Preto') and **São Félix**, on either side of the Rio Paraguaçu below the Cachoeira dam. In Cachoeira there's a **tourist office** ⓘ *Casa de Ana Néri*.

History

Set deep in the heart of some of the oldest farmland in Brazil, Cachoeira was once a thriving riverport that provided a vital supply link with the farming hinterland and Salvador to the east. The region was the centre of the sugar and tobacco booms which played such an important role in the early wealth of the colony. The majestic *saveiro*, a gaff-rigged boat, traditionally transported this produce down the Rio Paraguaçu to Salvador across the bay. These boats can still be seen on the river at Cachoeira. The town was twice capital of Bahia: once in 1624-25 during the Dutch invasion, and once in 1822-23 while Salvador was still held by the Portuguese.

With the introduction of roads and the decline of river transport and steam, the town stopped in its tracks and thus maintains its special charm. As in Salvador, *candomblé* plays a very important part in town life (see box page 377). Easy access by river from Salvador allowed the more traditional *candomblé* temples to move in times of religious repression. Cachoeira was the birthplace of Ana Néri, known as 'Mother of the Brazilians', who organized nursing services during the Paraguayan War (1865-70).

Sights

Cachoeira's main buildings are the **Casa da Câmara e Cadeia** (1698-1712), the **Santa Casa de Misericórdia** (1734 – the hospital; someone may let you see the church), the 16th-century **Ajuda** chapel (now containing a fine collection of vestments) and the Convent of the **Ordem Terceira do Carmo**, whose church has a heavily gilded interior. Other churches are the **Matriz**, with 5-m high *azulejos*, and **Nossa Senhora da Conceição do Monte**. There are beautiful lace cloths on the church altars. All churches are either restored or in the process of restoration.

The **Museu Hansen Bahia** ⓘ *R Ana Néri*, houses fine engravings by the German artist who made the Recôncavo his home in the 1950s (recommended). There is a great woodcarving tradition in Cachoeira and many of its artists can be seen at work in their studios. Best are **Louco Filho, Fory**, both in Rua Ana Néri, **Doidão** in front of the Igreja Matriz, and **J Gonçalves** on the main *praça*. A 300-m **railway bridge** built by the British in the 19th century spans the Rio Paraguaçu to São Felix, where the **Danneman cigar factory** can be visited to see hand-rolling in progress. A trail starting near the **Pousada do Convento** leads to some freshwater bathing pools above Cachoeira. There are beautiful views from above São Félix.

Excursions from Cachoeira

About 6 km from Cachoeira, on the higher ground of the Planalto Baiano, is the small town of **Belém** (the turning is at Km 2.5 on the road to Santo Amaro), a healthy spot where people from Salvador have summer homes. **Maragojipe**, a tobacco exporting port with a population of 39,000, is 22 km southeast of Cachoeira along a dirt road (BA-123); it can also be reached by boat from Salvador. See the old houses and the church of São Bartolomeu, with its museum. The main festival is **São Bartolomeu**, in August. Good ceramic craftwork is sold in the town. The tobacco centre of **Cruz das Almas** can also be visited, although transport is poor.

Sleeping

Salvador *p366, maps p368, 370 and 373, phone code 071*
The Centro Histórico is the ideal place to stay; the Pelourinho if you're on a tight budget and Santo Antônio if you are looking for reasonably priced hotels with real charm and character. Barra also has some cheap options but is increasingly seedy. Business visitors will find the best hotels in Rio Vermelho, overlooking the ocean and a 10-min taxi ride from the centre.

Self-contained a/c apartments with kitchens and hotel services can be rented by the day. Standards are generally high.

Centro Histórico *p371, map p 370*
AL-B Portas Velhas, Largo da Palma 6, Santana, T3248400, www.acasadasportasvelhas.com.br. Newly opened and New York-owned themed boutique hotel in the square made famous by Jorge Amado's *Dona Flor and Her Two Husbands*. Small but tastefully decorated a/c rooms, 1 larger suite and a good restaurant.

The smartest in the city centre.

Self-contained a/c apartments with kitchens and hotel services can be rented by the day. Standards are generally high.

Accommodation in the city tends to get very full over Carnaval and New Year, when prices go up.

B **Palace**, R Chile 20, T3221155, palace@e–net.com.br. One of the few upper-range hotels in the centre, very traditional and a little past its best; though there are plans to renovate it and turn it into a luxury hotel.

C **Imperial**, Av 7 de Setembro 751, Rosário, T/F3293127. Faded a/c rooms, helpful staff, breakfast. Recommended.

C **Pousada da Praça**, Rui Barbosa 5, T3210642, gifc@zaz.com.br. Simple, pretty colonial house in quiet street with good security. Big breakfast, rooms with and without bath. Warmly recommended.

D **Paris**, Rui Barbosa 13, T3213922. Fan cooled and more expensive a/c rooms, shared bathrooms and breakfast. Recommended.

E-F **Albergue das Laranjeiras**, R Inácio Accioli 13, T/F3211366, www.alaranj.com.br. IYHA hostel in a beautiful colonial building in the heart of the historic centre. Can be noisy. Café downstairs, English spoken. Good for meeting other travellers. Warmly recommended.

E-F **Albergue do Carmo**, R do Carmo 06, 3 mins' walk north of the Pelourinho, T3263750, albergue@bol.com.br. Spruce dormitories, lockers, sea view, luggage rooms, kitchen, English-speaking staff, computers with free internet access. Recommended.

E-F **Albergue do Peló**, R Ribeiro dos Santos 5, T/F2428061. Very basic IYHA hostel with laundry facilities.

E-F **Albergue do Passo**, R Ladeira do Passo 3, T3261951, F3513285. Clean, safe, friendly, with breakfast and with group rates available, English, French and Spanish spoken. Highly recommended.

E-F **Pousada Gloju**, R das Laranjeiras 34, T3218249. No breakfast but stunning views of Pelourinho, clean rooms, en suite bathrooms, warm showers.

E-F **Vagaus**, R Alfredo Brito 25, Pelourinho, T3216398, vagaus@elitenet.com.br. Independent youth hostel, all rooms collective with breakfast, internet access available. Recommended.

South of the centre *p375, map p376*

Campo Grande/Vitória is a quiet, upmarket residential area, between Barra and the city centre, convenient for museums.

L **Tropical Hotel da Bahia Business and Vacation**, Praça 2 de Julho 2, Campo Grande, T2552000, www.tropicalhotel.com.br. A designated 1950s business hotel in need of some renovation. Good service, pool, sauna, business facilities and a discount for **Varig** customers. Convenient city centre location.

A **Bahia e Sol**, Av 7 de Setembro 2009, T3388800, F3367776. Comfortable and safe family-run hotel with frigobar in rooms. Good breakfast and restaurant, bureau de change, but no pool. Recommended.

D **Caramurú**, Av 7 de Setembro 2125, Vitória, T3369951. Cosy hotel with a lounge area, terrace, breakfast and parking. Recommended.

Porto da Barra *p377, map p376*

This was once the focal point of nightlife in Salvador, but has fallen from grace in recent years and grown somewhat seedy. Unless you are desperate to be by a beach, and not the cleanest beach at that, it makes more sense to stay in the Centro Histórico. Taxis are recommended after dark. Care should be taken on Sun when the beaches are very busy. Most hotels are very close to the beach.

A **Bahia Flat**, Av Oceânica 235, Barra, T3394140, dflat@terra.com.br. Apartment hotel on the beach and with a pool and sauna. English spoken.

A **Marazul**, Av 7 de Setembro 3937, Barra, T2648200, www.marazulhotel.com.br. Blocky 1970s 4-star with a pool near Farol and Porto da Barra beaches; discounts for longer stays.

A **Monte Pascoal Praia**, Av Oceânica, Farol beach, T2034000, www.montepascoal.com.br. Newly renovated 1970s hotel with a pool, sauna, gym, restaurant and decent service.

B **La Habana**, Av Oceânica 84, T3315432. Newly renovated seafront hotel with 9 a/c rooms.

B **Pousada Hotel Ambar**, R Afonso Celso 485, T3321507. Pleasantly decorated little family run *pousada* owned by a Franco-Brazilian couple. Excellent breakfast, convenient, English spoken. Recommended.

B-C **Villa Romana**, R Lemos Brito 14, T3366522, www.villaromana.com.br. 1960s hotel wIth basic a/c rooms and a pool. In a good location. Recommended.

C **Enseada Praia da Barra**, R Barão de Itapoã 60, Porto da Barra, T2359213. Breakfast, safe, money exchange, accepts credit cards, laundry bills high, otherwise good value, near beach.
C **Pousada Malu**, 7 de Setembro 3801, T2644461. Small and welcoming, with breakfast, cooking and laundry facilities.
D **Bella Barra**, R Afonso Celso 439, T2378401, F2354131. One of the less tawdry low-end options, with some a/c rooms.
E **Carmen Simões**, R 8 de Dezembro 326 and **Gorette**, R 8 de Dezembro 522, Apt 002, Edif Ricardo das Neves, Graça, T2643016, gorete@e-net.com.br. Rooms to let in private apartments.
E-F **Albergue do Porto**, R Barão de Sergy 197, Barra, T2646600, albergue@e-net.com.br. YHA hostel in a beautiful turn-of-the-20th-century house 1 block from beach, and a short bus ride or 20 mins on foot from historic centre. Good breakfast, English spoken and double a/c rooms with baths available alongside dorms. Other facilities include, kitchen, laundry, safe, TV lounge, games room and a internet. Highly recommended.
E-F **Pousada Azul**, R Praguer Fróis 97, Barra, T2649798, pousada@provider.com.br. Youth hostel-style, near the beach, with airport transfers.
E-F **Pousada Marcos**, Av Oceânica 281, Barra, T2355117. Great location near the lighthouse. Always busy and especially popular with Israeli travellers.

Atlantic beach suburbs *p377, map p376*

L **Catussaba**, R Alameida da Praia, Itapoã, 25 km from the city, T3748000, www.catussaba.com.br. Elegant resort hotel with a mock-colonial interior and beautiful gardens which lead out to the beach. Beware of ocean currents when swimming. Convenient for the airport. Recommended.
L **Ondina Apart Hotel**, Av Oceânica 2400, Ondina beach, T2038000. 5-star, self-contained apartments, on the beach some 8 km from the centre. Highly recommended.
A **Sol Bahia Atlântico**, R Manoel Antônio Galvão 1075, Patamares, 17 km from the city (next to one of the best beaches in Salvador), T2060500, www.solbahia.com.br. Modern family hotel set high on the hill with great views of the coastline with a pool, restaurant and sauna and 200 or so a/c rooms. The hotel's private tram connects the higher and lower parts of the resort and there is free transport to the beach (around ½ km away).
A **Villa Farol**, R das 7 casas 10, Praia do Pedra do Sol, Itapoã, T3742107, www.geocities.com/villafarol. Welcoming Swiss-run *pousada* with 5 rooms, a pool and a good restaurant, 1 block from beach. Highly recommended. Closed in June.
D **Pousada Glória**, R do Retiro 46, T/F3751503. Basic *pousada* a stroll from the beach. No breakfast.
D-E **Casa Grande**, R Minas Gerais, 122, Pituba, T2480527, F2400074. IYHA hostel on a beach some 15 km from the centre with laundry and cooking facilities.

North of the centre *p378, map p370*

Santo Antônio is a quiet district just 5 mins' walk northeast of Pelourinho and Carmo which has attracted Europeans in recent years; many have set up carefully designed *pousadas* in beautifully restored buildings. A number have magnificent views of the bay. Most are mid-range, but there are cheaper options too.
B **Pousada Redfish**, R Direita do Santo Antônio, T/F2438473, www.hotelredfish.com. English-owned stylish little boutique. Some rooms have terraces and open-air showers. Recommended. The owners have recently opened a larger and equally chic sister hostel just down the street at R Ladeira do Boqueirão 1, T2410639.
B **Pousada das Flores**, R Direita de Santo Antônio 442, T/F2431836, www.pflores.com.br. A beautiful old house decorated in colonial style and owned by a Brazilian/French couple. Great breakfast. Recommended.
B **Pousada do Boqueirão**, R Direita do Santo Antônio 48, T2412262, www.pousadaboqueirao.com.br. The most stylish of all the *pousadas* in Salvador; lovingly renovated by the Italian interior-designer owner and with a variety of different themed rooms. Wonderful views, good service and excellent food. Several languages spoken. Highly recommended.
B **Pousada Villa Carmo**, R do Carmo 58, T/F2413924. Very comfortable, rooms with fan or a/c in an Italian/Brazilian-owned colonial house. Several languages spoken.
B-C **Pousada Baluarte**, R Baluarte, 13, T3270367. 5 rooms in an arty little *pousada*. The owners are very friendly and attentive. Rooms with a fan are cheaper.

Elsewhere

Near the bus station

B Portal da Cidade, Av Antônio Carlos Magalhães 4230, T3710099. Next to rodoviária with a/c and a pool.

Rio Vermelho

This modern suburban area which has long been the home of Salvador's well-to-do artists and musicians (Carlinhos Brown lives here), has a handful of decent restaurants, some good bars and a far safer feel than the Pelourinho, which is a 10-min taxi or 20-min bus ride away. It is particularly suited to business visitors and families.

LL Pestana Bahia, R Fonte de Boi 216, T4538000, www.pestanahotels.com.br. Newly revamped tower with wonderful views out over the ocean, a pool, gym, restaurant, sauna and very good business facilities. Online discounts available. With restaurant and bar.

LL-L Blue Tree Towers, R Monte Conselho 505, T3302233, www.bluetree.com.br. Smart new business hotel in this excellent Brazilian chain. Very good service and decent facilities including pool, tennis courts and a respectable restaurant.

A-B Catharina Paraguaçu, R João Gomes 128, Rio Vermelho, T2471488, www.hotelcatharinaparaguacu.com.br. Small colonial-style hotel with attractive courtyards and a range of decent rooms, some of which, however are distinctly better than others. Very good service. Recommended.

C Ibis, R Fonte do Boi 215, T3308300, www.accorhotels.com.br. Blocky new hotel in this budget business chain. Safe, a/c and great seaviews from the upper floors. Great value.

Apartments and pensionatos

At Carnaval it is a good idea to rent a flat or stay in a shared room in a private house (*pensionatao*) as other accommodation can be hard to come by and hotels and hostels are heaving. *Pensionatos* usually charge between US$5 and US$35 per person. Be careful with your belongings as not all householders are honest.

The tourist office has a list of estate agents for flat rental (eg José Mendez, T2371394/6) or you can find flats through **Bahia Online** (T3285891), www.bahia-online.net, who are good for flats, but whose hotel recommendations appear less than disinterested and less than impartial.

Houses or rooms can be rented from **Pierre Marbacher**, R Carlos Coqueijo 68A, Itapoã, T2495754 (Caixa Postal 7458, 41600 Salvador), who is Swiss, owns a beach bar at Rua K and speaks English.

Camping

Sea bathing is dangerous near the campsites.

Camping Clube do Brasil, R Visconde do Rosario 409, Rosario, T2420482.

Camping de Pituaçu, Av Prof Pinto de Aguiar, Jardim Pituaçu, T2317143.

Ecológica, R Alameida da Praia, near the lighthouse at Itapoã, take bus from Praça da Sé direct to Itapoã, or to Campo Grande or Barra, change there for Itapoã, about 1 hr, then 30 mins' walk, T3743506. Bar, restaurant, hot showers. Highly recommended.

Igloo Inn, Terminal Turistico de Buraquinho, Praia Lauro de Freitas, T3792854.

Itaparica and other bay islands *p378, map p378, phone code 071*

Itaparica

LL-L Club Med, Praia da Conceição, Km 13, T6817141, www.clubmed.com.br. An old-fashioned grand resort with all manner of facilities (even including a theatre), and 20 different sporting activities including wind-surfing, horse riding, canoeing and archery.

A Pousada Arco Iris, Estrada da Gamboa 102, Mar Grande beach, T8331130. Magnificent, though dishevelled 19th-century building romantically set in a garden of mango trees. Decent restaurant with slow service, a pool and unkempt but shady camping facilities available in the owners' adjacent property.

B Quinta Pitanga, Itaparica town, T8311554. Beautifully decorated beachfront property lovingly run by owner Jim Valkus. 3 suites, 2 singles and an excellent restaurant open to non-guests.

C Pousada Babalú, Cacha Pregos beach, T8371193. Spacious bungalows with a frigobar, fan, good breakfast.

C Pé na Praia, Praia das Amoureiras, T8311389. Good simple *pousada* with spacious rooms and friendly owners who speak both English and French.

D Icarai, Praca da Piedade, Itaparica town, T8311110. An unpretentious, simple *pousada* in a convenient location.

D Lagoa e Mar, R Parque das Dunas, 01-40, Mar Grande beach, T/F8231573. Spacious bungalows, 200 m from the sea, swimming pool and a generous breakfast.
D Pousada Cacha Pregos, next to the supermarket, Cacha Pregos beach, T8371013. Plain rooms with a fan, en suite bath but no breakfast.
D Pousada Casarão da Ilha, near the church in the main *praça*, Mar Grande beach, T8331106. Spacious a/c rooms, pool and a great view of Salvador across the bay.
D Pousada Estrela do Mar, Av NS das Candeias 170, Mar Grande beach, T8331108. Modest but well-kept a/c or fan-cooled rooms.
D Pousada Scórpio, R Aquárius, Mar Grande beach, T8231036. Simple rooms around a little swimming pool. Reasonable breakfast and a weekend restaurant.
D Pousada Sonho do Verão, R São Bento 2, Mar Grande beach. Chalets and apartments with cooking facilities, French and English spoken. Bike and horse rental (US$3/5 per hr).
D Pousada Zimbo Tropical, Aratuba beach, Estrada de Cacha Pregos, Km 3, R Yemanjá, T/F8381148. French/Brazilian run, simple, good breakfast, optional evening meals.
D Zula, R Monsenhor Flaviano 3, Itaparica town, near the fort, T/F8313119, taiike@hotmail.com. Modest but friendly guesthouse whose manager, Enrique speaks English and Spanish. Price includes breakfast and there are laundry facilities and internet available.
E Pousada Samambaia, Av NS das Candeias 61, Mar Grande Beach. A simple *pousada* with plain rooms and a good breakfast, French spoken.
E Hotel Village Sonho Nosso, Estrada Praia Cacha Pregos, Km 9 Cacha Pregos, T8371040. Very clean huts on one of the island's cleanest beaches. The good service includes pick-up, from anywhere on the island. Bom Despacho Kombis stop a 5-min walk from the front door.

Santo Amaro da Purificação and around *p379, phone code 075*

A Água Viva, T075-6991178, reservations T071-3591132, on the beachfront, with chalets or apartments, a/c or fan, good breakfast and restaurant, on one of the oldest farms in the region, good beach. Recommended.

Cachoeira *p380, phone code 075*

B Pousada do Convento de Cachoeira, R Inocência Boaventura, T7251716. 26 rooms in a newly restored 18th-century convent; with a convention centre in the former convent church. Decent restaurant.
D Pousada Paraguaçu, Av Salvador Pinto 1, São Félix, T7252550. A pretty riverside *pousada*, with spartan rooms and breakfast.
D Santo Antônio, near the rodoviária, T7251402. Basic but safe and with laundry facilities. Recommended.
E-F Pousada Tia Rosa, near Casa Ana Neri, T7251692. Very basic and simple but with a reasonable breakfast.
E-F Youth hostel, Av Parnamirim 417, T2684844.

Eating

Salvador *p366, map p368, 370 and 373, phone code 071*

Centro Histórico *p371, map 370*

TTT Bargaço, R das Laranjeiras 26, T2426546. Traditional Bahian seafood restaurant. Open daily except Tue.
TTT Casa do Benin, Praça José Alencar 29. Afro-Bahian restaurant, great surroundings, try the shrimp in the cashew nut sauce, open Tue-Sun 1200-1600, 1900-2300.
TTT Maria Mata Mouro, R Inácio Acciolli 8, T3213929. International menu, excellent service, relaxing atmosphere, a quiet corner in bustling Pelourinho. Closed Sun night.
TTT Pizzeria Micheluccio, R Alfredo Brito 31, T3230078. Best pizzas in Pelourinho, open daily 1200 till late. Does not accept Visa. Recommended.
TTT Uaua, R Gregorio de Matos, 36, T3213089. Elegant, colonial restaurant and bar, typical Bahian cuisine. Open 1130-0200.
TT Jardim das Delicias, R João de Deus, 12, T3211449. An elegant restaurant and antiques shop with an enchanting tropical garden. Incredibly reasonable for its setting. Classical or live music. Warmly recommended.
TT Quilombo do Pelô, R Alfredo Brito 13, T3224371. Rustic Jamaican restaurant, daily 1100-2400, good food with relaxed, if not erratic service. One of the few places offering vegetarian options.
TT Senac, Praça José Alencar 8, Largo do Pelourinho. State-run catering school, a

Bahian cuisine

Bahian cooking is spiced and peppery. The main dish is *moqueca*, seafood cooked in a sauce made from coconut milk, tomatoes, red and green peppers, fresh coriander and *dendê* (palm oil). It is traditionally cooked in a wok-like earthenware dish and served piping hot at the table. Served with *moqueca* is *farofa* (manioc flour) and a hot pepper sauce which you add at your discretion – it's usually extremely hot so try a few drops before venturing further. The *dendê* is somewhat heavy and those with delicate stomachs are advised to try the *ensopado*, a sauce with the same ingredients as the *moqueca*, but without the palm oil.

Nearly every street corner has a Bahiana selling a wide variety of local snacks, the most famous of which is the *acarajé*, a kidney bean dumpling fried in palm oil which has its origins in West Africa. To this the Bahiana adds *vatapá*, a dried shrimp and coconut milk paté (also delicious on its own), fresh salad and hot sauce (pimenta). For those who prefer not to eat the palm oil, the *abará* is a good substitute. *Abará* is steamed and wrapped in banana leaves. Seek local advice on which are the most hygienic stalls to eat from.

Recommended Bahianas are Chica, at Ondina beach (in the street behind the Bahia Praia Hotel) and in Rio Vermelho, *Dinha* (who serves acarajé until midnight, extremely popular) and Regina at Largo da Santana (very lively in the late afternoon), and Cira in Largo da Mariquita. Bahians usually eat *acarajé* or *abará* with a chilled beer on the way home from work or the beach at sunset. Another popular dish with African origins is *xin-xin de galinha*, chicken on the bone cooked in *dendê*, with dried shrimp, garlic and squash.

selection of 40 local dishes, buffet, lunch 1130-1530, dinner 1830-2130, all you can eat for US$16, inconsistent quality but very popular, folkloric show Thu-Sat 2030, US$5.

ǂ **Bahiacafe.com**, Praça da Sé, 20. Funky, Belgian-run internet café. Good breakfast menu, excellent food, English spoken. Highly recommended.

ǂ **Coffee Shop**, Praça da Sé. Cuban-style café serving sandwiches; main attraction is excellent coffee, and tea served in china cups. Doubles as cigar shop. Recommended.

ǂ **Gramado**, Praça da Sé. One of few food-by-weight restaurants in area. Basic, lunch only.

South of the centre *p375, map p376*

ǂǂǂ **Chez Bernard**, R Gamboa de Cima, 11. French cuisine, open Mon-Sat.

ǂǂǂ **Solar Do Unhão**, Av Contorno, T3295551, www.solardounhao.com.br. Beautiful former sugar mill, on the edge of the bay offering lunch, dinner and the best folklore show in town.

ǂǂ **Baby Beef**, Av AC Magalhães, Iguatemi. The best *churrascaria* in Salvador. Great value. Excellent service. Daily 1200-1500, 1900-2300.

ǂǂ **Beni-Gan**, Praça A Fernandes 29, Garcia. One of the city's better Japanese restaurants. Intimate atmosphere, Tue-Sun 1900-2400.

ǂǂ **Ristorante d'Italia**, Av 7 de Setembro, 1238, Campo Grande. Award-winning Italian with an expansive menu, generous portions and occasional live music. Closed Sun night.

ǂǂ-ǂ **Camafeu de Oxossi** and **Maria de São Pedro**. 2 good restaurants on upper floor of Mercado Modelo, Praça Cairu, at the bottom of the Lacerda Lift. Both serve Bahian dishes, have a great atmosphere and views out over the bay. Daily 1130-2000, Sat lunchtime is particularly busy.

ǂ **Nosso Cantinho**, Av 7 de Setembro s/n near **Hotel Madrid**. Good-value snack and juice bar.

ǂ **Kentefrio**, Av 7 de Setembro 379. Excellent, scrupulously clean snack bar with counter service only, closed Sun.

ǂ **Grão de Bico**, Av 7 de Setembro 737. Cheap but decent vegetarian.

Porto da Barra *p377, map p376*
There are a number of reasonable restaurants and snack bars near the lighthouse at the mouth of the bay in the Farol da Barra area.

TTT **Frutos do Mar**, R Marquês de Leão 415. The best Bahian restaurant in the area.

TT **Caranguejo do Farol**, Av Oceânica 231. Raised above the road and serving crab dishes (a local speciality) to a vibrant young crowd. You might have to wait for a table.

TT **Baitakão**, Av Oceânica 11. Very popular restaurant serving burgers.

TT **Ban Zai**, Av 7 de Setembro 3244, Ladeira da Barra, T3364338, by the yacht club. A well-liked Sushi bar open Tue-Sun.

TT **Micheluccio**, Av Oceânica 10. Very popular pizza restaurant.

TT **Mon Filet**, R Afonso Celso 152. Reasonable steak and pasta. Open 1830-2400.

TT **Yan Ping**, on R Airova Galvão, T2456393. Good Chinese, daily 1100-2400, reasonably priced, very generous portions, clean.

T **Mediterrânio**, R Marques de Leão 262. A cheap and cheerful pay-by-weight, open at lunchtimes daily.

T **R A Porteira**, Afonso Celso 287, 2 blocks back from the seafront, T2355656. Pay-by-weight Bahian and general northeastern Brazilian food. Open for lunch only.

North of the centre *p378, map 370*

TT **Atelier Maria Adair**, R J Castro Rabelo 2. Specializing in coffees and cocktails, owner Maria is a well-known artist whose highly original work is on display. Recommended.

TT **Axego**, R do Carmo 36. Good views.

TT **Casa da Gamboa**, R João de Deus 32, 1st floor. 1200-1500 and 1900-2400, closed Mon; also at R Newton Prado 51 (Gamboa de Cima). Beautifully located in old colonial house overlooking the bay, good reputation, open Mon-Sat 1200-1500 and 1900-2300.

TT **Casa da Roça**, R Luís Viana 27. Pizzas, *caipirinhas* and live music at weekend.

TT **Tempero da Dadá**, R Frei Vicente 5. Open Wed-Mon 1130 till late. Excellent Bahian cuisine, owners Dadá and Paulo are genial hosts, their restaurant extremely popular. Across the street is **Quereres**, a restaurant and bar with good live music.

T **Bar da Tereza**, R J Castro Rabelo 16. Open daily 0900-2330. Good wholemeal snacks and juices. Recommended.

T **Carvalho**, R Conselheiro Cunha Lopez 33, Centro, T7413249. By-weight food with decent fish and Bahian cooking. Recommended.

T **Dona Chika-Ka**, R J Castro Rabelo 10. Open 1100-1500 and 1900-0200. Good local dishes. The open gates beside the restaurant lead to a square, Largo de Quincas Berro d'Água (known locally as Quadra 2M), which has many similar bars and restaurants including **Quincas Berro D'Agua**, T3215472, which serves upmarket Bahian cooking.

T **Encontro dos Artistas**, R das Laranjeiras 15, T3211721, Ribeiro do Santos 10. Passo – Pelourinho. Cheap Bahian and general Brazilian dishes.

Elsewhere

Rio Vermelho

TT **Casa da Dinha**, R João Gomes 25, just west of the **Catharina Paraguaçu Hotel** and a few yards from the Largo de Santana, T330525. One of the best mid-range Bahian restaurants in the city with a varied menu.

Itaparica and other bay islands *p378, map p378, phone code 071*

TTT **Philippe's Bar and Restaurant**, Largo de São Bento, Mar Grande, Itaparica. With French and local cuisine and a menu in English and French.

T **Rafael**, in the main *praça*, Mar Grande, Itaparica. Basic with pizzas and snacks.

There are many Bahianas selling *acarajé* in the late afternoon and early evening, in the main *praça* and by the pier at Mar Grande.

Cachoeira *p380, phone code 075*

TT **Do Nair**, R 13 de Maio. Delicious food and occasional live music.

T **Cabana do Pai Thomaz**, 25 de Junho 12. Excellent Bahian food, good value, also a hotel, **C**, with private bath and breakfast.

T **Xang-hai**, São Félix, good, cheap food, try the local dish, *maniçoba* (meat, manioc and peppers). Warmly recommended.

Bars and clubs

Salvador *p366, maps p368, 370 and 373, phone code 071*

Centro Histórico *p371, map 370*
Nightlife is concentrated on and around the Pelourinho where there is always a free live street band on Tue and at weekends. The

Moqueca de peixe

There are as many recipes for this marinaded fish dish, as there are cooks in Brazil. Named after the main Indian method of barbecuing fish wrapped in banana leaves, developed in the great plantation houses of the sugar zone, the dish is now cooked on top of the stove in a pan. Many cooks add coconut milk, giving the sauce a Caribbean flavour typical of the Northeast. In this recipe, the fish flavour is fresh and sharp, balanced by coconut rice.

To serve 6

Marinade ingredients

1 kg fillets of mixed, fresh white fish
1 chopped medium onion
50 ml *dendê* (palm) oil or olive oil
2 fresh hot chillis, seeded and chopped
2 large peeled tomatoes, chopped
1 crushed clove of garlic
A handful of fresh coriander leaves
3 tbsp lime juice
Salt

Method

Crush the marinade ingredients to a purée in a mortar, or use a blender. Cut the fish into 5-cm pieces, mix with the purée in a non-metallic bowl and leave for one hour. Transfer to a saucepan. Add 75 ml water and half the oil. Cover and simmer until the fish is cooked (about 10 minutes). One minute before serving, add the rest of the oil and turn up the heat. Serve with hot pepper, lime sauce and coconut rice.

Pelourinho area is also good for a bar browse; though be wary after 2300. There are many bars on the **Largo de Quincas Berro d'Água**, especially along **R Alfredo do Brito**. **R João de Deus** and its environs are dotted with simple pavement bars with plastic tables.

The most famous music from Salvador are the *maracatú* drum orchestras like **Olodum** and **Ilê Aiyê**, whose 40-piece drum orchestras can be heard frequently around the Pelourinho (Olodum played on Paul Simon's *Rhythm of the Saints* album). Both groups have their own venues and play in the individual parades or *blocos* at carnival. See box, p392, for times and venues of the *bloco* rehearsals. There is live music all year round but the best time to hear the most frenetic performers – particularly the *axê* stars – is during carnival.

Bahia Cafe, Quartel dos Aflitos (at the far end of the square). An expansive bar with good bay views. Very popular.

Bar do Reggae and Praça do Reggae, Ladeiro do Pelourinho, by the NS dos Rosarios dos Pretos church. Live reggae bands every Tue and more frequently closer to carnival.

Cailleur, R Gregório de Matos 17, open daily from 0930. Good café, great chocolate and bar service until 0100.

Cantina da Lua, Praça Quinze de Novembro 2, Terreiro De Jesus, T3224041. Open daily, popular and a good spot on the square with outdoor seating, but gets crowded and the food isn't good.

Casa do Olodum, R das Laranjeiras, T3215010, www2.uol.com.br/olodum. Olodum's headquarters where they perform live every Tue and Sun at 1930 to packed crowds.

Ilê Aiyê, R do Curuzu 197, Liberdade, Barra, T2561013. Ilê Aiyê's headquarters. Details of live performances can be obtained from here.

NR, R Gregorio de Matos 15. A great after-hours' bar with live music (which is not always so great). There's a US$0.50 charge if you sit down.

Quereres, R Frei Vicente 7, T 3211616. Lively little club in a colonial house playing Brazilian samba funk, hip hop and *axê*. Busy on Tue and Fri.

Vila Velha, Passeio Publico, Gamboa da Cima, T3361384. A historically important music venue where many of the *tropicalistas* first played. Nowadays it has an eclectic programme of modern dance, theatre and live music.

Porto da Barra *p377, map p373*
Barra nightlife, which can be unpleasantly seedy, is concentrated around the **Farol da Barra** (lighthouse) and **R Marquês de Leão**, which is busy with pavement bars. Like the Pelourinho the whole area is good for a browse, but be wary of pickpockets.
Mordomia Drinks, Ladeira da Barra. Enter through a narrow entrance to an open-air bar with a spectacular view of the bay, very popular.
Habeas Copos, R Marquês de Leão 172. A popular and traditional street-side bar which is a Salvador institution.

Elsewhere

The district of **Rio Vermelho** was once the bohemian section of town and it still has good live music and exciting bar nightlife. There are a number of lively bars around the **Largo de Santana** a block west of Hotel Catharina Paraguaçu.
Café Calypso, Travessa Prudente Moraes 59, Rio Vermelho, T3346446. Live Brazilian rock music on Tue and Fri.
Café Cancun, Otavia Mangabeira 6000, Aeroclube Plaza, Boca do Rio, T4610603. The city's premier dance club for Bahian 20 to 40-something middle classes. Kicks off after 2300. Busiest on Wed, *forró* night.
Fashion Club, Av Octávio Mangabeira, 2471, Jd dos Namorados, T3460012. Similar to **Café Cancun** but with a predominantly 20-something crowd. Busy on Thu.
Havana Music Bar, R Cardeal da Silva 117, Rio Vermelho, T2375107. Live bands (mostly rock) Wed-Sat. Best after 2230.
Korunn, R Ceará 1240, Pituba, T2484208. Lively dance club with a bohemian crowd. Very popular Thu-Sat.
Pimentinha, Boca do Rio. One of the few clubs to be lively on a Mon.
Rock In Rio Café, Aeroclube Plaza Show, s/n, Boca do Rio, T4610300. Dance club with a young crowd and an emphasis on rock and MPB. Busiest at the weekends.
Teatro Sesi Rio Vermelho, R Borges dos Reis 9, Rio Vermelho, T3340668. The best place in the city to see contemporary Salvador bands live.

Cachoeira *p380*

Casa do Licor, R 13 Maio 25. Interesting bohemian bar with a range of bizarre drinks. Try the banana-flavoured spirit.

Entertainment

Salvador *p366, maps p368, p370 and p373, phone code 071*

The **Fundação Cultural do Estado da Bahia** edits *BahiaCultural*, a monthly brochure listing the main cultural events for the month. These can be found in most hotels and **Bahiatursa** information centres. Local newspapers *A Tarde* and *Correio da Bahia* have good cultural sections listing all events in the city.

Cinema

The main shopping malls at Barra, Iguatemi, Itaigara and Brotas, and **Cineart** in Politeama (Centro), run more mainstream movies. The impressive Casa do Comércio building near Iguatemi houses the **Teatro do SESC** with a mixed programme of theatre, cinema and music Wed-Sun.

Theatre and classical music

Theatro Castro Alves, Largo 2 de Julho, Campo Grande, T3398000. The city's most distinguished performance space and the home of the Bahian Symphony Orchestra and the Castro Alves Ballet Company. The theatre also hosts occasional performances by more cerebral MPB artists and contemporary performers like Hermeto Pascoal or Egberto Gismonti.
Sala de Coro, Largo 2 de Julho, Campo Grande, T3398000. The repertory theatre for Castro Alves; showing more experimental productions.
Teatro Vila Velha, Passeio Publico, T3361384. Márcio Meirelles, the theatre's director, works extensively with **Grupo Teatro Olodum**; although performed in Portuguese, productions here are very visual and well worth investigating.
Instituto Cultural Brasil-Alemanha (ICBA), Corredor de Vitória. Germano-Brazilian co-productions and art cinema showings.
Associação Cultural Brasil Estados Unidos (ACBEU), Corredor de Vitória. US cultural shows and cinema.
Teatro XVIII, R Frei Vicente, T3320018. Experimental theatre in Portuguese.
Teatro Gregorio de Matos, Praça Castro Alves, T3222646. Programmes dedicated to showcasing new productions and writers. Also see Vila Velha, p389.

Music in Bahia

Walking the streets of the old town on busy nights is like surfing the wavebands of your radio. A short walk from one bar and you hear the music coming from the next. Grupo Cultural Olodum began life in 1980 as a carnival option for the inhabitants of Pelourinho, then a much neglected area. Every Tuesday night **Banda Olodum**, a drumming troupe made famous by their innovative powerhouse percussion and involvement with Paul Simon, Michael Jackson and Branford Marsalis, rehearse in the Largo Teresa Batista (starts 1930, US$10) in front of packed crowds. They also rehearse free of charge in the Largo do Pelourinho on Sunday, T3215010.

Ilê Aiyê is just as much revered for its socio-political profile as its musicality; it still maintains its original pure percussion format. Established in Liberdade, the largest suburb of the city, Ilê Aiyê is a thriving cultural group dedicated to preserving African tradition, which under the guidance of its president Vovô is deeply committed to the fight against racism. Rehearsals take place mid-week at Boca do Rio and on Saturday nights on the street in front of their headquarters at Ladeira do Curuzu in Liberdade. You don't need to understand the words to be moved by the sheer joy in the air.

Araketu hails from the sprawling Periperi suburb in the Lower City. Once a purely percussion band, Araketu has travelled widely and borrowed on various musical forms (samba, *candomblé*, soukous etc) to become a major carnival attraction and one of the most successful bands in Bahia. Rehearsals take place on Wednesday nights on Avenida Contorno. These get very full and it is best to buy tickets in advance from Avenida Oceânica 683, Barra Centro Comercial, Sala 06, T2476784.

Neguinho do Samba was the musical director of Olodum until he founded **Didá**, an all-woman drumming group similar to Olodum. They rehearse on Friday nights in the Praça Teresa Batista, Pelourinho (starts 2000, US$10).

Festivals and events

Salvador *p366, maps p368, p370 and p373, phone code 071*

6 Jan Epiphany. Public holiday with many free concerts and events. Beautiful masses in many of the historic churches.

Jan Festa do Nosso Senhor do Bonfim; Always on the 2nd Sun after Epiphany. On the preceding Thu there is a colourful parade at the church with many penitents and a ceremonial washing of the church itself. Great for pictures.

Feb Carnival, see box p392.

2 Feb Pescadores do Rio Vermelho. Boat processions with gifts for Yemanjá, Goddess of the Sea accompanied by African Brazilian music.

Mar/Apr Holy Week. The week before Easter sees many colourful processions around the old churches in the upper city.

Cachoeira *p380*

24 Jun São João, 'Carnival of the Interior'. Celebrations include dangerous games with fireworks, well attended by tourists.

Mid-Aug Nossa Sehora da Boa Morte, see box, p380.

4 Dec A famous candomblé ceremony at the Fonte de Santa Bárbara.

Shopping

Salvador *p366, maps p368, p370 and p373, phone code 071*

Arts, crafts and cigars

Instituto Mauá, R Gregorio de Matos 27, Pelourinho, open Tue-Sat 0900-1800, Sun 1000-1600. Good-quality items, better value and quality than the Mercado Modelo.

Loja de Artesanato do SESC, Largo Pelourinho, T3215502, Mon-Fri 0900-1800 (closed for lunch), Sat 0900-1300.

Faithful to their traditions are **Filhos de Gandhi**, the original African drumming group and the largest, formed by striking stevedores during the 1949 carnival. The hypnotic shuffling cadence of Filhos de Gandhi's *afoxé* rhythm is one of the most emotive of Bahia's carnival.

Carlinhos Brown is a local hero. From humble beginnings he has become one of the most influential musical composers in Brazil today, mixing great lyrics, innovative rhythms and a powerful stage presence. He played percussion with many Bahian musicians, until he formed his own percussion group, **Timbalada**. His first album, *Alfagamabetizado*, is perhaps the most successful fusion album in Brazilian music. Ever faithful to his background in the poor Candeal district, he has invested heavily in his old neighbourhood, both socially and culturally. He has created the Candy All Square, a centre for popular culture where the Timbalada rehearsals take place every Sunday night (1830, US$10) from September to March. Not to be missed.

During the winter (July-September), ring the *blocos* to confirm that free rehearsals will take place.

Artists and bands using electronic instruments and who tend to play in the *trios eléctricos* draw heavily on the rich rhythms of the drumming groups, creating a new musical genre known as *Axé*. The most popular of such acts is **Daniela Mercury**, following the steps to international stardom of Caetano Veloso, Maria Bethânia, João Gilberto and Gilberto Gil. Other newer, interesting acts are **Margareth Menezes**, who has travelled extensively with David Byrne. **Gerónimo** was one of the first singer/songwriters to use the wealth of rhythms of the Candomblé in his music and his song '*E d'Oxum*' is something of an anthem for the city. All of the above have albums released and you can find their records easily in most record stores. See Shopping, page 390. Also try Billbox in the Shopping Barra on the third floor.

Oficina de Investigação Musical, Alfredo Brito 24, T3222386, Mon-Fri 0800-1200 and 1300-1600. Handmade traditional percussion instruments (and percussion lessons – US$15 per hr).

Artesanato Santa Bárbara, R Alfredo Brito 7, Pelourinho. Excellent handmade lace products.

Atelier Portal da Cor, Ladeira do Carmo 31, Pelourinho, T2429466. A gallery run by a co-operative of artists, Totonho, Calixto, Raimundo Santos, Jô, good prices. Recommended.

Casa do Índio, Ladeira do Carmo 27, Pelourinho. Indigenous artefacts and art.

FIEB-SESI, Av Tiradentes 299, Bonfim; Av Borges dos Reis 9, Rio Vermelho; Av 7 de Setembro 261, Mercês. Some of the best artisan products in the city ranging from textiles and ceramics to musical instruments.

Rosa do Prado, R Inacio Aciolly 5, Pelourinho. Cigar shop packed with every kind of Brazilian '*charuto*' imaginable.

Bookshops

Livraria Brandão, R Ruy Barbosa 104, Centre, T2435383. Second-hand English, French, Spanish and German books.

Graúna, Av 7 de Setembro 1448, and R Barão de Itapoã 175, Porto da Barra. Many English titles.

Livraria Planeta, Carlos Gomes 42, loja 1. Sells used English books.

Jewellery

Scala, Praça da Sé, T/F3218891. Handmade jewellery using locally mined gems (eg aquamarine, amethyst and emerald), workshop at back.

Casa Moreira, Ladeira da Praça, just south of Praça da Sé. Exquisite jewellery and antiques. Most very expensive, but some affordable charms.

Carnival in Bahia

The **pre-Carnival festive season** begins towards the end of November with São Nicodemo de Cachimbo (penultimate Sunday of November), then comes Santa Bárbara (4 December), then the Festa da Conceição da Praia, centred on the church of that name (normally open 0700-1130) at the base of the Lacerda Lift. (8 December is the last night – not for those who don't like crowds!) The last week of December is the Festa da Boa Viagem in the lower city; the beach will be packed all night on 31 December. On 1 January is the beautiful boat procession of Nosso Senhor dos Navegantes from Conceição da Praia to the church of Boa Viagem, on the beach of that name in the lower city. The leading boat, which carries the image of Christ and the archbishop, was built in 1892. You can follow in a sailing boat for about US$1; go early (0900) to the dock by the Mercado Modelo. A later festival is São Lázaro on the last Sunday in January.

Carnival officially starts on Thursday night at 2000 when the keys of the city are given to the Carnival King 'Rei Momo'. The unofficial opening though is on Wednesday with the Lavagem do Porto da Barra, when throngs of people dance on the beach. Later on in the evening is the Baile dos Atrizes, starting at around 2300 and going on until dawn, very bohemian, good fun. Check with Bahiatursa for details on venue, time etc (see under Rio for carnival dates).

Carnival in Bahia is the largest in the world and encourages active participation. It is said that there are 1½ million people dancing on the streets at any one time.

There are two distinct musical formats. The **Afro Blocos** are large drum-based troupes (some with up to 200 drummers) who play on the streets, accompanied by singers atop mobile sound trucks. The first of these groups was the Filhos de Gandhi (founded in 1949), whose participation is one of the highlights of Carnival. Their 6,000 members dance through the streets on the Sunday and Tuesday of Carnival dressed in their traditional costumes, a river of white and blue in an ocean of multicoloured carnival revellers. The best known of the recent *Afro Blocos* are Ilê Aiye, Olodum, Muzenza and Malê Debalê. They all operate throughout the year in cultural, social and political areas. Not all of them are receptive to foreigners among their numbers for Carnival. The basis of the rhythm is the enormous *surdo* (deaf) drum with its bumbum bumbum bum anchor beat, while the smaller *repique*, played with light twigs, provides a crack-like overlay. Ilê Aiye take to the streets around 2100 on Saturday night and their departure from their headquarters at Ladeira do Curuzu in the Liberdade district is not to be missed. The best way to get there is to take a taxi to Curuzu via Largo do Tanque, thereby avoiding traffic jams. The ride is a little longer but much quicker. A good landmark is the Paes Mendonça supermarket on the corner of the street, from where the *bloco* leaves. From there it's a short walk to the departure point.

Markets

The **Mercado Modelo**, at Praça Cairu, lower city, Sat 0800-1900, Sun 0800-1200. Live music and dancing, especially Sat. Expect to be asked for money if you take photos. Many tourist items such as woodcarvings, silver-plated fruit, leather goods, local musical instruments. Lace items for sale are often not handmade (despite labels), are heavily marked up, and are much better bought at their place of origin (eg Ilha de Maré, Pontal da Barra and Marechal Deodoro, see p434). **Cosme e Damião**, 1st floor. High-quality musical instruments.

The enormous **trios eléctricos**, 12-m sound trucks with powerful sound systems that defy most decibel counters, are the second format. These trucks, each with its town band of up to 10 musicians, play songs influenced by the *Afro blocos* and move at a snail's pace through the streets, drawing huge crowds. Each **Afro Bloco** and **bloco de trio** has its own costume and its own security personnel, who cordon off the area around the sound truck. The **bloco** members can thus dance in comfort and safety.

The traditional Carnival route is from Campo Grande (by the Tropical Hotel da Bahia) to Praça Castro Alves near the old town. The **blocos** go along Avenida 7 de Setembro and return to Campo Grande via the parallel Rua Carlos Gomes. Many of the trios no longer go through the Praça Castro Alves, once the epicentre of Carnival. The best night at Praça Castro Alves is Tuesday (the last night of Carnival), when the famous 'Encontro dos Trios' (Meeting of the Trios) takes place. Trios jostle for position in the square and play in rotation until the dawn (or later!) on Ash Wednesday. It is not uncommon for major stars from the Bahian (and Brazilian) music world to make surprise appearances.

There are grandstand seats at Campo Grande throughout the event. Day tickets for these are available the week leading up to Carnival. Check with Bahiatursa for information on where the tickets are sold. Tickets are US$10 (or up to US$30 on the black market on the day). The *blocos* are judged as they pass the grandstand and are at their most frenetic at this point. There is little or no shade from the sun so bring a hat and lots of water. Best days are Sunday to Tuesday. For those wishing to go it alone, just find a friendly barraca in the shade and watch the *blocos* go by. Avoid the Largo da Piedade and Relógio de São Pedro on Avenida 7 de Setembro: the street narrows here, creating human traffic jams.

The other major centre for Carnival is Barra to Ondina. The **blocos alternativos** ply this route. These are nearly always *trios eléctricos*, connected with the more traditional *blocos* who have expanded to this now very popular district. Not to be mIssed here is Timbalada, the drumming group formed by the internationally renowned percussionist Carlinhos Brown (see box, page 390).

Recommended

Blocos Traditional Route (Campo Grande): Mel, T2454333, Sunday, Monday, Tuesday; Cameleão, T3366100, Sunday, Monday, Tuesday; Pinel, T3360489, Sunday, Monday, Tuesday; Internacionais, T2450800, Sunday, Monday, Tuesday; Cheiro de Amor, T3366060, Sunday, Monday, Tuesday. **Afro Blocos**: Araketu: T2370151, Sunday, Monday, Tuesday; Ilê Aiye, T3884969, Saturday, Monday; Olodum, T3215010, Friday, Sunday. **Blocos alternativos**: Timbalada, T2456999, Thursday, Friday, Saturday; Nana Banana, T2451000, Friday, Saturday; Melomania, T2454570, Friday, Saturday.

Prices range from US$180 to US$450. The quality of the *bloco* often depends on the act that plays on the *trio*. See box, page 390.

Feira de São Joaquim, 5 km from Mercado Modelo along the seafront, daily 0800-1900, Sun 0800-1200. The largest and least touristy market in the city selling mainly foodstuffs and a few artisan products. Very smelly.
Feira de Artesanjato, Santa Maria fort, Wed 1700-2100. Arts and crafts in the fort at the far end of Porto da Barra beach.

Music and carnival souvenirs

Boutique Olodum, on Praça José Alencar, Pelourinho. Olodum CDs, music, T-shirts and musical instruments.
Ilê Aiyê, on R Francisco Muniz Barreto 16,

Pelourinho. Ilê Aiyê CDs, music, T-shirts and musical instruments.

Modaxé, R Francisco Muniz Barreto s/n, Pelourinho. Clothes manufactured by street children under the auspices of the Projeto Axé, expensive, but the trendiest T-shirts in town.

Brazilian Sound, R Francisco Muniz Barreto 18, Pelourinho. Brazilian and Bahia CDs.

Flashpoint, Shopping Iguatemi. One of the best general music and CD shops in the city.

Photography

Gil Filmes, R Chile 7. Reasonably priced slide film – though still far more than back home.

Shopping centres

These are the most comfortable places to shop in Salvador – havens of a/c cool in the heat of the Bahian summer offering a chance to rest over an ice-cold beer, to lunch and to shop for essentials like Havaianas, bikinis, CDs and beach wraps along with comestibles like batteries, supermarket food and suntan cream. **Barra** and **Iguatemi** are the largest and best stocked.

Activities and tours

Salvador *p366, maps p368, p370 and p373, phone code 071*

Football

Otávio Mangabeira Stadium, Trav Joaquim Maurício, Nazaré, T/F2423322. 90,000-seat stadium which is home to the **Esporte Clube Bahia** and **Vitória** football clubs. 10 mins away from the Pelourinho, and the Barroquinha terminal.

Tours and tour operators

Bus tours are available from several companies, including **LR Turismo**, T2640999, who also offer boat trips, **Itaparica Turismo**, T2483433, **Tours Bahia**, T3223676, and **Alameda Turismo**, T2482977, who run a city tour for US$15 per person.

Tatur Turismo, Av Tancredo Neves 274, Centro Empresarial Iguatemi, Bloco B, Sala 228, Iguatemi, Salvador, T4507216, www.tatur.com.br. Excellent private tours of the city and the entire state as well as general travel agency services including flight booking and accommodation. Can organize entire packages prior to arrival, in Bahia or Brazil as a whole. Good English, reliable. Owned by Conor O'Sullivan from Cork.

Itaparica and other bay islands *p378, map p378, phone code 071*

Tour operators

Small boats for **trips around the bay** can be hired privately at the small port by the Mercado Modelo, Salvador, called Rampa do Mercado. A pleasant trip out to the mouth of the bay should take 1½ hrs as you sail along the bottom of the cliff. When arranging to hire any boat, ensure that the boat is licensed by the Port Authority (Capitânia dos Portos) and that lifejackets are on board. The **Companhia de Navegação Bahiana**, T3217100, sails 5 times a week to **Maragojipe** on the Rio Paraguaçu to the west (see p381). The trip across the bay and up the valley of the river takes 3 hrs. There are some very beautiful views along the way with 2 stops. A good trip would be to continue to Cachoeira by bus from Maragojipe and return to Salvador the following day. Departures from Salvador from the Terminal Turístico in front of the Mercado Modelo, Mon-Thu 1430 (1530 in summer). Fri departure is at 1130. Departures from Maragojipe Mon-Thu 0500 and Fri 0830, US$4.50.

Steve Lafferty, R do Sodré 45, apt 301, T2410994. A US yachtsman who comes highly recommended for enjoyable sailing trips around Salvador, for up to 4 people.

Recôncavo *p379, phone code 075*

Guides Claudio, T9826080. Local tour guide, doesn't speak much English, but is friendly and knowledgeable.

Transport

Salvador *p366, maps p368, p370 and p373, phone code 071*

See also Ins and outs, p366.

Air

Domestic and international flights arrive at the new **Luís Eduardo Magalhães Airport** (previously Dois de Julho), 32 km from the city centre, T2041244. An a/c bus service leaves every 30-40 mins 0500-2200 weekdays and 0600-2200 weekends from the airport to the historic centre, US$1.20. This service stops at all the hotels along the coast road en route (a long way round if you are going to the centre). Also ordinary buses,

Capoeira

Capoeira is a sport developed from the traditional foot-fighting technique introduced from Angola by African slaves. It comprises a series of choreographed fight moves accompanied by drum, tambourine and berimbau. There are several schools of *capoeira* fighting; some more acrobatic than others. You can also see the experts outside the Mercado Modelo on most days, around 1100-1300, and at Campo Grande and Forte de Santo Antônio on Sunday afternoons (they often expect a contribution; negotiate a price before taking pictures or demands may be exorbitant).

If you want to attempt *capoeira*, the best school Is Academia de Mestre Bimba, Rua das Laranjeiras, T3220639, open 0900-1200, 1500-2100, basic course US$25 for 20 hours. Other schools are Filhos de Bimba, R Durval Fraga, 6, Nordeste, T3457329 and Escola de Mestre Pastinha, Rua Castro Rabelo, T321 6251. Classes on Monday, Wednesday and Friday 1900-2100, Saturday-Sunday 1500-1700. Classes are held in the evening (if you want to get the most out of it, knowledge of Portuguese is essential). There are two more schools in Forte de Santo Antônio behind Pelourinho. Exhibitions take place in the Largo do Pelourinho, very picturesque, in the upper city (US$2).

US$0.50. 'Special' taxis to both Barra and centre (buy ticket at the airport desk next to tourist information booth), US$23; normal taxis (from outside airport), US$18, bus-taxi service, US$10. ATM machines are hidden around the corner on the ground floor to the right as you arrive. The tourist information booth (open 24 hrs, English spoken), has a list of hotels and useful map.

A/c buses leave from Praça da Sé via the coast road between 0630 and 2100, US$2, 1¼ hrs (1 hr from Barra). Ordinary buses 'Aeroporto' from same stop US$0.50. Official airport taxis booked through the booths in arrivals are far more expensive than the standard city taxis who wait outside the terminal. Expect to pay around US$20 to the centre.

International flights to **Amsterdam**, **London**, **Paris** and **Rome**. Domestic flights to **Aracaju**, **Barreiras**, **Belo Horizonte**, **Brasília**, **Ilhéus**, **Maceió**, **Paulo Afonso**, **Petrolina**, **Porto Seguro**, **Recife**, **Rio de Janeiro**, **São Paulo** and **Vitória da Conquista**.

Airline offices Aerolineas Argentinas, R da Belgica 10, Loja D, T3410217. **Air France**, Edif Regente Feijo, R Portugal 17, T3516631. **Alitalia**, Av Tancredo Neves 3343, Sala 503, T3415831. **American Airlines**, Trav Marques de Leão 13, T2454077. **British Airways**, T0800-996926. **KLM**, Av Tancredo Neves 3323, Pituba, T3410217. **Lufthansa**, Av Tancredo Neves 805, Sala 601, Iguatemi, T3415100. **Nordeste/Rio-Sul**, R Almte das Espatodias 100, Caminho das Arvores, T0800-992004. **TAM**, Praça Gago Coutinho, T0800-123100. **TAP**, Edif Ilheus, sala 401, Av Estados Unidos 137, T2436122. **Transbrasil**, R Almte Marques de Leão 465, Barra, T0800-151151. **Varig**, R Carlos Gomes 6, T0800-997000. **Vasp**, R Chile 27, T0800-998277.

Bus

Local US$0.70, a/c *executivos* US$1.40, US$1.5 or US$3 depending on the route. On buses and at the ticket sellers' booths, watch your change and beware pickpockets (one scam used by thieves is to descend from bus while you are climbing aboard). Take a 'Barra' bus from Praça da Sé for the nearest ocean beaches. The Aeroporto *frescão* (last 2130) leaves from R Chile, passing Barra, Ondina, Rio Vermelho, Amaralina, Pituba, Costa Azul, Armação, Boca do Rio, Jaguaripe, Patamares, Piatã and Itapoã, before turning inland to the airport. The glass-sided Jardineira bus goes to Flamengo beach (30 km from the city), following the coastal route; it passes all the best beaches; sit on the right-hand side for best views. It leaves from the Praça da Sé daily 0730-1930, every 40 mins, US$1.50. For beaches beyond Itapoã, take the *frescão* to Stella Maris and Flamengo beaches. These follow the same route as the Jardineira.

Long distance The rodoviária is 5 km from the city with regular bus services, US$0.70, take bus RI or RII, 'Centro-Rodoviária-Circular', get on in the Lower City at the foot of the Lacerda Lift (the journey can take up to 1 hr especially at peak periods). A quicker executive bus from Praça da Sé or Praça da Inglaterra (in front of McDonald's), Comércio, runs to Iguatemi Shopping Centre, US$1.50, weekdays only, from where there is a walkway to the rodoviária (take care in the dark, or a taxi, US$10). There are frequent services to the majority of destinations; a large panel in the main hall of the bus terminal lists destinations and the relevant ticket office.

To **Belém**, US$48 *comercial* with Itapemirim. To **Recife**, US$18-25, 13 hrs, 2 a day and 1 *leito*, **Itapemerim**, T3580037. To **Rio**, 28 hrs, US$45.50, *leito* US$91, **Itapemirim**, good stops, clean toilets, recommended. To **São Paulo,** 30 hrs, US$51, *leito* US$64 (0815 with **Viação Nacional**, 2 in afternoon with **São Geraldo**, T3580188). To **Fortaleza**, 19 hrs, US$33 at 0900 with **Itapemerim**. To **Ilhéus**, 7 hrs, **Aguia Branca**, T3587044, *comercial* US$14.50, *leito* US$29, several. To **Lençóis** at 2200, 8 hrs, US$12 with **Real Expresso**, T3581591. To **Belo Horizonte**, **Gontijo**, T3587448, at 1700, US$40 *comercial*, US$50 *executivo*, **São Geraldo** at 1800. There are daily bus services to **Brasília** along the fully paved BR-242, via Barreiras, 3 daily, 23 hrs, **Paraíso**, T3581591, US$27.

Car

Car hire **Avis**, Av 7 de Setembro 1796, T2370155, also at airport, T3772276, T0800-118066. **Budget**, Av Pres Vargas 409, T2373396. **Hertz**, R Baependi, T2458364. **Interlocadora**, T3772550 (airport), T3774144 (centre). **Localiza**, T0800-992000 (airport) Oceânica 3869, T3321999, and Av Otávia Mangabeira 29, T3368377. **Unidas**, Av Oceânica 2456, Ondina, T3360717. If renting a car check whether credit card or cash is cheapest.

Hitchhiking

Take a 'Cidade Industrial' bus from rodoviária at the port; it goes on to the highway.

Taxis

Meters start at US$0.50 for the 'flagdown' and around US$0.10 per 100 m. They charge US$10 per hr within city limits, and 'agreed' rates outside. **Taxi Barra-Centro,** US$3 daytime; US$4 at night. Watch the meter, especially at night; the night-time charge should be 30% higher than daytime charges. **Teletaxi** (24-hr service), T3219988.

Itaparica and other bay islands *p378, map p378, phone code 071*

Ferry

The island is reached from the mainland by several ferry services. The main passenger ferry leaves for **Bom Despacho** from São Joaquim (buses for Calçada, Ribeira stop across the road from the ferry terminal; the 'Sabino Silva-Ribeira' bus passes in front of the Shopping Barra). The first ferry from **Salvador** leaves at 0540 and, depending on demand, then at intervals of 45 mins until 2230. Returning to Salvador, the first ferry is at 0515 and the last one at 2300. During the summer months the ferries are much more frequent. Enquiries at the **Companhia de Navegação Bahiana** (CNB), T3217100 from 0800 to 1700. A one-way ticket for foot passengers on Mon-Fri is US$1, Sat-Sun US$1.20. There is also a catamaran service which departs for **Bom Despacho** twice daily, US$3.

Mar Grande can be reached by a smaller ferry (*lancha*) from the Terminal Marítimo, in front of the Mercado Modelo in Salvador. The ferries leave every 45 mins and the crossing takes 50 mins, US$1.80 return.

Road

From **Bom Despacho** there are many buses, kombis and taxis to all parts of the island. The best beaches are at Ponta de Areia, Mar Grande (US$1 by kombi), Berlinque, Aratuba and Cacha Pregos. Kombis and taxis can be rented for trips around the island but be prepared to bargain, US$30 for a half-day tour.

Recôncavo *p379, phone code 075*

Bus

From **Salvador** (**Camurjipe**) every hr or so from 0530. To **Feira Santana**, 2 hrs, US$3.

Directory

Salvador *p366, maps p368, p370 and p373, phone code 071*

Banks Selected branches of major banks have ATMs (which accept Visa and Cirrus cards) and exchange facilities. Don't change money on the street (see below), especially in the Upper City where higher rates are usually offered. Changing at banks (open 1000-1600) can be bureaucratic and time-consuming. **Citibank**, R Miguel Calmon 555, Comércio, centre, changes TCs. Branch at R Almte Marquês de Leão 71, Barra, has ATM. **Banco Econômico**, R Miguel Calmon 285, Comércio is the American Express representative (also in Ondina, under Ondina Apart Hotel). Visa ATM at **Banco do Brasil**, Av Estados Unidos 561, Comércio, in the shopping centre opposite the rodoviária (also a *câmbio* here), very high commission on TCs, at the airport on the 1st floor (open Mon-Fri 0830-1530, 1600-2100 and Sat, Sun and holidays 0900-1600); branches in Barra, R Miguel Bournier 4, in Shopping Barra and in Ondina. MasterCard at **Credicard**, 1st floor, Citibank building, R Miguel Calmon 555, Comércio. **Figueiredo**, opposite Grande Hotel da Barra on Ladeira da Barra, will exchange cash at good rates. **Shopping Tour** in Barra Shopping centre changes US dollars, as will other tour agencies. If stuck, all the big hotels will exchange, but at poor rates.

Cultural centres Cultura Inglesa, R Plínio Moscoso 357, Jardim Apipema. **Associação Cultural Brasil-Estados Unidos**, Av 7 de Setembro 1883, has a library and reading room with recent US magazines, open to all, free use of internet for 30 mins. **German** Goethe Institut, Av 7 de Setembro 1809, also with a library and reading room. **Embassies and consulates** Austria, R Jardim Armacao, T3714611. **Belgium**, Av Trancredo Neves 274A, sala 301, Iguatemi, T6232454. **Denmark**, Av 7 de Setembro 3959, Barra, T3369861 (Mon-Fri 0900-1200, 1400-1700). **France**, R Francisco Gonçalves 1, sala 805, Comércio, T2410168 (Mon/Tue/Thu 1430-1700). **Germany**, R Lucaia 281, floor 2, Rio Vermelho, T3347106 (Mon-Fri 0900-1200). **Holland**, Av Santa Luzia, 1136 Edif, Porto Empresarial Sala 302, T3410410 (Mon-Fri 0800-1200). **Italy**, Av 7 de Setembro 1238, Centro, T3295338 (Mon, Wed, Fri 1500-1800). **Norway**, Av Estados Unidos, 14, floor 8, T3268500 (Mon-Fri 0900-1200, 1400-1600). **Portugal**, Largo Carmo, 4, Sto Antonio, T2411633. **Spain**, R Mcal Floriano 21, Canela, T3361937 (Mon-Fri 0900-1400). **Sweden**, Av EUA 357, Edif Joaquim Barreto, sala 501, Comércio, T2424833. **Switzerland**, Av Tancredo Neves 3343, 5th floor, sala 506b, T3415827. **UK**, Av Estados Unidos 4, 18B, Comércio, T2437399 (Mon-Thu, 0900-1100, 1400-1600, Fri 0900-1100). **USA**, R Pernam buco, 51 Pituba, T3451545 (Mon-Fri), 0900-1130, 1430-1630. **Immigration Polícia Federal**, Av O Pontes 339, Aterro de Água de Meninos, Lower City, T3196082. Open 1000-1600. For extensions of entry permits show an outward ticket or sufficient funds for your stay, visa extension US$15.

Internet There are numerous internet cafés throughout the touristy parts of the city.

Language courses Casa do Brasil, R Milton de Oliveira 231, Barra, T2645866, www.casadobrazil.com.br. Portuguese for foreigners. **Superlearning Idiomas**, Av 7 de Setembro 3402, Ladeira da Barra, T3372824, www.allways.com.br/spl. **Diálogo**, R Dr João Pondé 240, Barra, T2640007, www.dialogo-brazilstudy.com, with optional dance, *capoeira* and cooking classes and accommodation arranged with host families. **Laundry** Kit Lavaderia, Av Amaralina 829, Amaralina. **Laundromat**, R Oswaldo Cruz, Rio Vermelho. **Lav e Lev**, Av Manoel Dantas da Silva 2364, loja 7. **Unilave**, Av Magalhães Neto 18, Pituba. **Medical services** Clinic, Barão de Loreto 21, Graça. **Delegação Federal de Saúde**, R Padre Feijó, Canela. Free yellow fever vaccinations.

Cachoeira *p380, phone code 075*
Banks Bradesco, in the main square, ATM accepts Visa credit but not debit cards, Mon-Fri 0830-1700. **Post office** in the main square, Mon-Fri 0900-1700.

The Coast of Bahia

This seemingly endless stretch of coast has one magnificent beach after another. Porto Seguro, some 12 hours from Salvador, is the major resort town and has a notoriously hedonistic party scene. Things get a little quieter in Arraial de Ajuda, but only a little, and more upmarket in Trancoso further to the south where Leonardo Di Caprio has bought up property in one of the super luxurious condominiums. Morro de São Paulo, on the island of Tinharé, offers beautiful beaches and lively nightlife. Those seeking seclusion should head for Itacaré, the latest discovery on the Bahian coast, where the coconut-shaded white sand is relatively peaceful. . . for the time being.

Heading north from Salvador airport, the coast road (BA-099), or Estrada de Coco (Coconut Highway), passes many coconut plantations and 50 km of beautiful beaches. From south to north the best known are Ipitanga (famous for its reefs), Buraquinho, Jauá, Arembepe, Guarajuba, Itacimirim, Castelo Garcia D'Ávila (where there is a 16th-century fort) and Forte. North of the smart mini-resort town of Praia do Forte, the road is called the Linha Verde (Green Line) as it runs along another beautiful stretch of coast. Buses serve most of these destinations. ▸▸ *For Sleeping, Eating and other listings, see pages 408-420.*

The southern coast

Valença → *Phone code: 075. Colour map 4, A5.*

Although Valença has a few colonial buildings and two moderately interesting churches, it is at heart an ugly town. The best reason to come here is to take a boat to or from Tinharé, taking an hour or two perhaps to stroll around the dirty market and visit the church of **Nossa Senhora do Amparo**, from where there are good views out over the town, the estuary and the surrounding mangroves. Valença is in the middle of an area producing black pepper, cloves and *piaçava* (used in making brushes and mats) but it markets itself as the prawn capital of Brazil and smells the part. Other industries include the building and repair of fishing boats (*saveiros*).

The city has a little airport 15 km from the centre with flights to Salvador. There are frequent buses between Valença and Salvador. The fastest go via the island of Itaparica (two to three hours including the ferry). Avoid touts at the rodoviária; it's better to visit the friendly **tourist office** ⓘ *at the port, T6413311, www.valencabahia.com.br*, who have both maps and transport information. Boats to Tinharé leave at least once a day.

Tinharé → *Phone code: 075. Colour map 4, A5. Population: 78,000.*

Depending on whom you ask, Tinharé is either a single large island separated from the mainland by the estuary of the Rio Una and mangrove swamps, or a mini archipelago divided by estuaries, mangroves and an impossibly turquoise sea. The beaches here are some of the best within easy access of Salvador.

The main town here, **Morro de São Paulo**, is situated on the headland at the northernmost tip of Tinharé, which is lush with patches of fern-filled forest and coconut palms. The town is dominated by a lighthouse and the ruins of a colonial fort (1630), built as a defence against European raiders. This did not stop the Dutch and French using the waters around the island as hiding places for attacks on the Portuguese.

The town has a landing place on the sheltered landward side, dominated by the old gateway of the fortress. From the lighthouse a path leads to a ruined lookout with cannon, which has panoramic views. Dolphins can be seen in August. **Fonte de Ceu** waterfall is reached by walking along the beach to **Gamboa**, then inland. Watch the tide; it is best to take a guide. Alternatively, take a boat back to Morro (US$0.50-1). All roads are unmade and no motor vehicles are allowed on the island. The beaches are good and you can swim or watch fish in the saltwater pools that appear at low tide. Fish can be bought from the fishermen in summer, or borrow a pole and catch your own at sunset. On 7 September there is a big fiesta with live music on the beach.

The fort is a good place to watch the sun set.

Morro is expensive between December and March and gets very crowded during public holidays. This influx of tourists means it is not the paradise it once was; beware of drugs and theft at the busiest times. There is a port tax of US$1 payable at the *prefeitura* on leaving the island, which is resented by many.

Ilha de Boipeba → *Colour map 4, A5.*

Ilha de Boipeba, a few hours from Morro, is a similar but far quieter island and with less infrastructure. Accommodation is split between the little town where the riverboat ferry arrives, the adjacent beach, **Boca da Barra**, which is more idyllic and the fishing village of **Moreré** half an hour's boat ride to the south (high tlde only). With just a few simple restaurants and a football field on the beach overlooking a beautiful turquoise bay, life here is tranquil even by Bahian standards. Expect to pay at least US$20 for a boat ride to Moreré. Walking along the beaches will take about two hours. Have your camera at the ready, bring sunscreen and go at low tide as there is a river to ford.

Ituberá and Camamu → *Phone code: 073. Colour map 4, A5.*

These two towns which have yet to be overrun by seasonal visitors are the first stops south on the bus route from Valença. Neither have good beaches but both have access to good beaches by boat. Ituberá is a tiny town sitting on a deep inlet – the most beautiful beach in the area, **Barra do Carvalho**, is two hours away by boat; Camamu sits in a maze of mangroves some 30 km further south. It is the jumping-off point for the peninsula of Maraú; the next stretch of the Bahian coast in line for beach resort development. The town has a handful of pretty colonial buildings, including the 17th-century church of **Nossa Senhora da Assunção**.

Barra Grande and the Peninsula de Maraú → *Phone code: 073.*

This long thin peninsula stretches north from the town of Maraú near Itacaré (see below) towards the southern extremity of the island of Tinharé and is fringed with beautiful beaches along its entire ocean length. Access is difficult to many of these beaches if you don't have a car (and possible without a 4WD only when the weather is dry) but there are some which are reachable on foot from the little fishing village of **Barra Grande** at the tip of the peninsula. Tractors run from the village to more remote beaches further south.

Boats run between Camamu and Barra several times a day between October and March and once a day in the morning all year round (two to three hours, US$4). There are plenty of *pousadas* in Barra (www.barragrande.net), see Sleeping, page 410.

Itacaré → *Phone code: 073.*

This picturesque fishing village sits in the midst of remnant Atlantic Coast rainforest at the mouth of the Rio de Contas. Some of Bahia's best beaches stretch north and south. A few are calm and crystal clear, the majority are washed by moderately powerful waves which are great for surfing. There are plenty of beaches within walking distance of town.

Itacaré is the latest discovery on the Brazilian tourist circuit and is rapidly becoming a sophisticated resort town for the discerning São Paulo middle classes; it is very busy with Brazilian tourists in high season. Come off season, speaking some Portuguese if you can, and take time to find your own way to smaller places barely mentioned in any travel guidebook.

Much of the accommodation here is tasteful, blending in with the natural landscape, and there are many excellent restaurants and lively if still low-key nightlife. The town has yet to be discovered by the *Condé Nast Traveller* reading international set. *Pousadas* are concentrated on and around Praia da Concha, the first beach south of the town centre. More deserted beaches lie along dirt roads to the south and north. To explore the area to the full you will need a car.

There's a **tourist office** ⓘ *Secretaria de Turismo de Itacaré, T2512134, www.itacare.com.br. Bahia Alegria, T2513461,* and **Itacaré Ecoturismo** organize abseiling trips and the like.

Ilhéus and around → *Phone code: 073. Colour map 4, A5. Population: 242,500.*

Everyone is happy to point out that Ilhéus is the birthplace of Jorge Amado (1912) and the setting of one of his most famous novels, *Gabriela, cravo e canela* (*Gabriela, Clove and Cinnamon*, 1958; see box, page 401). Amado also chronicled life on the region's cocoa plantations in two novels, *Cacau* (1933) and the much better-known *Terras do Sem Fim* (*The Violent Lands*, 1942). A later novel, *São Jorge dos Ilhéus* (1944), continues the story. Ilhéus's history stretches back to the earliest days of Portuguese colonization, when it was one of the captaincies created by King João III in 1534. Today the port, which sits at the mouth of the Rio Cachoeira, serves a district that produces 65% of all Brazilian cocoa. Shipping lines call regularly. A bridge links the north bank of the river with Pontal, where the airport is located. The beaches south of the town are splendid and increasingly deserted the further away you go, but the central city beach is polluted. There are good views of the city from the Convento de Nossa Senhora da Piedade. Most tourists stay a day or so before heading north towards Itacaré or south towards Porto Seguro.

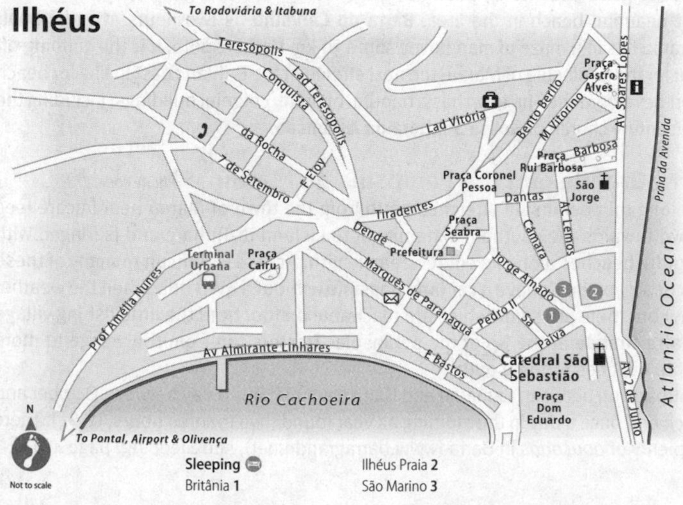

Jorge Amado

Amado is, both among Brazilians and foreigners reading Brazilian fiction, by far the most popular writer of the 20th century. Born in 1912 on a cocoa plantation outside Ilhéus, he had a very adventurous youth, and had direct experience of the endemic violence surrounding land claims that he was later to dramatize in such novels as *Terras do sem-fim* (*The Violent Land*) (1943). He was always committed to the left, though his position has softened somewhat in later years, accompanying changes in his fiction. In the early period (1931-1952), it showed first in an interest in the rural and urban poor: in such novels as *Jubiabá* (1935), about the self-education of a black man, and *Capitães da areia* (1937), one of his best, centred on a gang of street children, he began to show interest in the power of *candomblé* (Afro-Brazilian religion) as a political consciousness-raiser. He became a Federal deputy for the Communist Party in 1946: in 1948, after the party was banned, he went into exile in Europe, and was something of a propagandist for Soviet Communism, receiving the Stalin Peace Prize in 1951. The fiction he wrote at this time (for example *Seara vermelha* [*Red Harvest*]) is by common consent his worst.

In 1953 he returned to Brazil, and in 1958 published the novel which gave his career a new lease of life, *Gabriela, cravo e canela* (*Gabriela, Clove and Cinnamon*). To achieve this, he abandoned politics for comedy and myth: Ilhéus in the 1920s, its harbour about to be opened so that it can export its cocoa, is presented to us in a colourful array of characters, at the centre of whom are Nacib, an Arab immigrant and shopkeeper, and spicy Gabriela, a girl from the interior whose cooking and sexual prowess keep him in her thrall. It is a modern, optimistic version of Alencar's *Iracema* (see page 704): immigrant meets native girl, and has to adjust to her culture, while in the background, the (export) economy is opening up. *Gabriela* was a phenomenal success, selling 100,000 copies in just over a year. In part, Amado had tuned into the optimism of the years of the Kubitschek presidency which led to the foundation of Brasília.

Sex, comedy and cookery proved a potent combination. Other novels since *Gabriela* have been equally successful with the public: *Dona Flor e seus dois maridos* (1966), about a cookery teacher whose respectable second marriage is haunted by the ghost of her bohemian first husband (it actually provides the reader with recipes); *Tenda dos milagres* (*The Tent of Miracles*) (1969) about racial discrimination, and others there is no space to deal with here, many of them set in the city of Salvador (Bahia). Amado has been attacked by critics as being unconsciously anti-feminist and even racist (his Blacks do tend to be stereotypically good-hearted, with a perpetual smile on their faces). Perhaps this is to miss the point: essentially, he is a popular novelist in the tradition of Scott, Dumas and hundreds of others, predecessors of television soap operas, and he has often been successfully adapted to that medium.

The church of **São Jorge** ⓘ *Praça Rui Barbosa* (1556), the city's oldest, has a small museum. The cathedral of **São Sebastião** ⓘ *Praça Dom Eduardo, near the seashore*, is a huge, early 20th-century building. In Alto da Vitória is the 17th-century **Nossa Senhora da Vitória,** built to celebrate a victory over the Dutch. Ask in travel agencies for trips to Rio de Engenho to visit the church of Santana (see above). The house where **Jorge Amado** grew up and wrote his first novel is at Rua Jorge Amado 21. It is now a small **museum** ⓘ *0900-1600, US$0.50*. The **tourist information office** ⓘ *on the beach opposite Praça Castro Alves*, is a few minutes' walk from the cathedral, friendly, maps US$2, recommended.

North of Ilhéus, two good beaches are Marciano, with reefs offshore and good surfing, and Barra, 1 km further north at the mouth of the Rio Almada. South of the river, the beaches at **Pontal** can be reached by 'Barreira' bus; alight just after the **Hotel Jardim Atlântico**. Between Ilhéus and Olivença are a number of fine beaches, for example **Cururupe**, **Batuba** (good surfing) and Cai n'Água in **Olivença** itself (also a surfers' beach). The **Balneário de Tororomba**, on the Rio Batuba, 19 km from Ilhéus, has hot mineral baths. São Jorge or Canavieiras buses go there and frequent buses also go to Olivença.

Buses run every 30 minutes to **Itabuna** (32 km), the trading centre of the rich cocoa zone (also many lumber mills). **Ceplac installations** ⓘ *Km 8, on the Itabuna-Ilhéus road, T2143000, Mon-Fri 0830-1230*, show the whole processing of cocoa. Tours of cocoa plantations can be arranged through the **Ilhéus Praia** hotel. Also at Km 8, the Projeto Mico-Leão Baiano at the **Reserva Biológica del Una** ⓘ *T6331121, US$15, book in advance to visit*, was founded to protect the *mico-leão da cara dourada* (golden-faced tamarin). This is the wettest part of Bahia (most notably in October). Jeeps leave from the rodoviária. Buses from Salvador take 6½ hours (US$12). The paved BA-415 links Itabuna to Vitória da Conquista (275 km) on the BR-116.

Beyond Ilhéus, the paved coastal road continues south through Olivença and Una, near the **Reserva Biologica de Una**, ending at **Canavieiras**, a picturesque town which benefited from the cocoa boom. It has several fine beaches. A rough road continues from there to Port Seguro.

Porto Seguro

→ *Phone code: 073. Colour map 4, B5. Population: 96,000.*

Pedro Álvares Cabral is credited with being the first European to lay eyes on Brazil, sighting land at Monte Pascoal south of Porto Seguro in 1500. The sea here was too open to offer a safe harbour, so Cabral sailed his fleet north, entering the mouth of the Rio Burnahém to find the harbour he later called 'Porto Seguro' (safe port). On the road between Porto Seguro and Santa Cruz Cabrália a cross marks the spot where the first mass was celebrated. A tourist village, **Coroa Vermelha**, has sprouted at the site of Cabral's first landfall, 20 minutes by bus to the north of Porto Seguro. It has souvenir shops selling Pataxó-Tupi Indian items, beach bars, hotels and rental houses; all rather uncoordinated.

There are borrachudos, little flies that bite feet and ankles in the heat of the day; coconut oil keeps them off. At night mosquitoes can be a problem (but there is no malaria, dengue or yellow fever).

Today, the old town of Porto Seguro is a popular holiday resort with many charter companies flying in directly from Rio de Janeiro and São Paulo. It is now Bahia's second most popular tourist destination. But while many visit Bahia's beaches to escape the hustle and bustle, those who come to Port Seguro are in search of it. Don't expect peace and quiet, unspoilt coastline or pretty colonial buildings here.

From the roundabout at the entrance to Porto Seguro take a wide, steep, unmarked path uphill to the **Cidade Histórica** (historical city), three churches – **Nossa Senhora da Misericórdia** (1530), **Nossa Senhora do Rosário** (1534) and **Nossa Senhora da Pena** (1718) – the former jail and the stone monument marking the landfall of Gonçalo Coelho, a small, peaceful place with lovely gardens and panoramic views.

Guided tours of the area can be arranged with **BPS** ⓘ *at the Shopping Centre, T2882373*. **Companhia do Mar** ⓘ *Praça dos Pataxós, T2882981*, does daily trips by

Jorge Amado's books are held to be archetypically Bahian; evocative of this landscape of red-tiled roofs, whitewashed churches and coconut palms swaying next to an impossibly aquamarine sea.

schooner to coral reefs off the coast. The most popular is to Recife de Fora, with good snorkelling (it leaves daily at 1000, returns at 1630, about US$18, US$3 extra for snorkelling gear). Dugout canoes fish on the Rio Burnahém and trips can be taken by canoe to explore the mangroves. The **tourist office** ① *T2884124, turismo@portonet.com.br*, can be contacted for further information on tours.

The best **beaches** are north of the town along the road to Santa Cruz de Cabrália (known as Avenida Beira Mar – BR-367). The most popular beaches are **Itacimirim, Curuípe, Mundaí** and **Taperapuã**. Regular buses (**Expresso Brasileiro**) run along this busy road from Praça dos Pataxós, with many stops on the seafront in the town. Porto Belo and Santa Cruz Cabrália buses go to the beaches frequently from the port. There

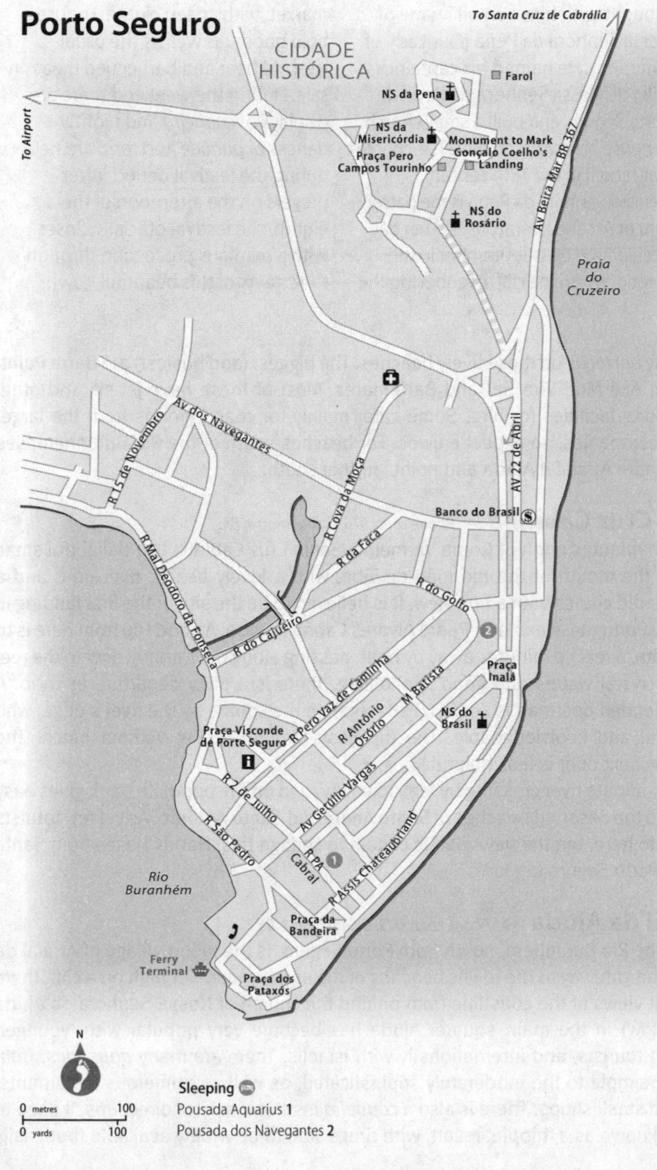

The Festival of Nossa Senhora da Pena

The cult of Nossa Senhora da Pena began in Leiria, Portugal, a century after the reconquest of the country from the Moors. It arrived in Porto Seguro in 1535 when a Portuguese noble, Donatário Pero do Campo Tourinho (a recipient of one of Brazil's 16th-century *capitanias*), brought with him a small image of Nossa Senhora da Pena (Our Lady of Suffering). He named his captaincy 'Villa de Nossa Senhora da Pena de Porto Seguro' and built a small church to house his favourite saint. The church was rebuilt in the 18th century.

Nossa Senhora da Pena is the patron saint of Art and Literature and her day is celebrated on 8 September in the historic city on the cliff, overlooking the beach hotels of the modern resort of Porto Seguro. Devotees of the cult called *romeiros* travel great distances to her shrine and the surrounding area becomes a huge campsite of tents, caravans and tour buses.

The festival resembles a cross between a Brazilian street party and market, with cheap clothes, household goods, as well as the usual ice-cold beer and barbecued meat on sale. During the weekend there are displays of *capoeira* and nightly dances of *pagôde* and *forró* are held during the festival period. After prayers on the afternoon of the eighth, the festival officially closes with a religious procession through the streets of this beautiful town.

are many *barracas* on these lively beaches. The biggest (and busiest) are **Barra Point, Toá Toa, Axé Moi, Vira Sol** and **Barramares.** Most of these have jet-ski and other watersports facilities for hire. Some cater mainly for coach groups from the larger charter companies, so expect crowds. For beaches south of the Rio Buranhém, see below under Arraial d'Ajuda and points further south.

Santa Cruz Cabrália → *Phone code: 073. Colour map 4, B5.*

About 10 minutes north of Coroa Vermelha, Santa Cruz Cabrália is a delightful small town at the mouth of the Rio João de Tiba, with a lovely beach, river port, and a 450-year-old church with a fine view. It is believed to be the site of the first landing in Brazil by Portuguese explorer Pedro Álvares Cabral in 1500. A good trip from here is to **Coroa Alta**, a reef 50 minutes away by boat, passing along the tranquil river to the reef and its crystal waters and good snorkelling. There is a daily departure at 1000. A recommended boatman is Zezé (T/F2821152) on the square by the river's edge, who is helpful and knowledgeable. The trip costs around US$15 without lunch. The company next door is less helpful.

A 15-minute river crossing by ferry to a new road on the opposite bank gives easy access to the deserted beaches of **Santo André** and **Santo Antônio**. As yet few tourists make it to here, but the new road is certain to change this. Hourly buses from Santa Cruz to Porto Seguro (23 km).

Arraial da Ajuda → *Phone code: 073. Colour map 4, B5.*

Across the Rio Buranhém, south from Porto Seguro, is the resort village of Arraial da Ajuda, the gateway to the idyllic beaches of the south coast. Set high on a cliff, there are great views of the coastline from behind the church of Nossa Senhora da Ajuda (see below) in the main square. Ajuda has become very popular with 'younger' Brazilian tourists, and internationally with Israelis. There are many *pousadas*, from the very simple to the moderately sophisticated, as well as numerous restaurants, bars and small shops. There is also a *capoeira* institute; ask for directions. It used to be well known as a 'hippie' resort, with drugs said to be widely available (but easily avoided), but there is nothing laid back about the town now – it has become far larger in scale and more rave orientated. Parties are held almost every night, on the beach or in the main street, called the *Broadway*. At Brazilian holiday times (especially New Year and Carnival) it is very crowded – almost to bursting point.

The beaches, several protected by a coral reef, are splendid. The nearest is 15 minutes' walk away. During daylight hours those closest to town (take Rua da Praia out of town to the south) are extremely busy; excellent *barracas* sell good seafood, chilled drinks, and play plenty of music. The best beaches are **Mucugê**, **Pitinga** (*'bronzeamento irrestrito'* or nude sunbathing) and **Taipé**.

Each August there is a pilgrimage to the shrine of **Nossa Senhora da Ajuda** (1549). In the church is an interesting room full of ex-voto offerings. There are good views from behind the church. Legend has it that a spring miraculously appeared during mass, aiding the construction of the Jesuit church. The spring can be seen at the foot of the steep hill leading up to the town.

Trancoso → *Phone code: 073. Colour map 4, B5.*

This once sleepy little village 15km south of Arraial is rapidly developing as southern Bahia state's chicest resort after Itacaré. Expensive São Paulo boutiques fill the tiny shopping centre and there are a range of smart little boutique *pousadas* and a handful of restaurants offering more than fish, rice, beans and chips. Leonardo Di Caprio is rumoured to have bought a number of properties in the exclusive condominiums to the south of town; *forró* star Elba Ramalho lives here; and Gisele Bundchen is a frequent visitor. This has inevitably pushed prices up and up. Despite its new-found status, Trancoso remains a simple little town, with life concentrated on the long grassy main square, crowned with the little whitewashed 17th-century church of São João Batista which looks down over the top of the cliff to the numerous beaches stretching away to the north and south. The most famous, **Praia dos Nativos**, is also the closest to town and is lined with numerous *barraca* beach bars which have begun to host rave parties during the summer months. **Coquieros** across the little river to the north is quieter. **Espelho**, a 40-to 60-minute drive along the dirt road to Caraiva, is one of the state's most beautiful, with a glassy bay fringed with white sand and rocks. Like any of the Bahian resorts, Trancoso can be packed out at this time. Be sure to book ahead. Cheap rooms tend to be in the upper city with more luxurious accommodation lining the road that runs to and along the coast.

The town divides into the upper area focused on the main square (or *quadrado*), a square kilometre of grass with a football pitch, watched over by pretty pastel coloured colonial houses. Behind it lies the new part of town with its tiny shopping area of upmarket boutiques. The beach is about 10 minutes' walk from both across the river, along a road lined with the best of the *pousadas*, many of them set in their own private gardens. The newly paved road between Porto Seguro, Ajuda and Trancoso is regularly run by buses – at

 least every hour in high season ($2 to Porto Seguro, US$1.20 to Arraial). Various tour operators around the main square sell kombi, bus (and air) tickets for destinations throughout Bahia and organize day trips. It is possible to walk to Arraial along the beach via the village of **Rio da Barra**. Allow three hours. A dirt road behind the beach follows the same route. There are internet cafés on the main square but no bank.

Caraíva → *Phone code: 073. Colour map 4, B5.*

This incredibly peaceful, atmospheric fishing town, 65 km south of Porto Seguro, is on the banks of the Rio Caraíva. There are no wheeled vehicles (the streets are sand), no electricity nor hot water, so the marvellous beaches here make a real escape from Trancoso and Porto Seguro. Despite difficulty getting there, it is increasingly popular.

There are plenty of cheap *pousadas* and restaurants along the rustic sandy streets. Most bars have live *forró* in the summer. Caraíva can only be reached by canoe across the river. Access roads are poor and almost impossible after heavy rain. There are services several times a day from Trancoso, which is the easiest point of departure.The **Aguia Azul** bus company runs there from Porto Seguro at 1500 daily. If arriving by bus from the south, change to **Aguia Azul** bus in Itabela (departs at 1500), or take a taxi, about 50 km. Good walks are north to **Praia do Satu** (Sr Satu provides an endless supply of coconut milk), or 6 km south to a rather sad **Pataxó** indigenous village (watch the tides as you may get cut off). Horses can be hired from **Pousada Lagoa** or **Pizzeria Barra Velha.** Boats can be hired for US$40 per day from **Zé Pará** to Caruípe beach, for snorkelling at Pedra de Tatuaçu reef and Corombau (take your own mask and fins) or for diving (best December-February). **Prainha** river beach, about 30 minutes away, and mangrove swamps can also be visited by canoe or launch. The high season is December-February and July; the wettest months are April-June and November. Use flip-flops for walking the sand streets and take a torch. There are no medical facilities and only rudimentary policing.

Parque Nacional de Monte Pascoal

ⓘ *Caixa Postal 076, CEP 45830-000 Itamaraju, T2812419.*

The National Park was set up in 1961 to preserve the flora, fauna and birdlife of the coastal area in which Europeans made landfall in Brazil. A Pataxó reservation is located at Corombau village, on the ocean shore of the park, where a small luxury resort has been built. Corombau can be reached by schooner from Porto Seguro. From Caraíva there is a river crossing by boats which are always on hand. Buses run from Itamaraju 16 km to the south, at 0600, Friday-Monday only.

Cumuruxatiba and Prado → *Phone code: 073. Colour map 4, B5.*

From Itamaraju (93 km south of Eunápolis) are the coastal towns of Curumuxatiba (www.cumuru.com.br) and Prado (www.acampe.com.br/prado). The latter has some 16th-century buildings and beautiful beaches both north and south. It is 214 km south of Porto Seguro via Eunápolis.

Caravelas → *Phone code: 073. Colour map 4, B5.*

Further south still, 107 km from Itamaruju, is this charming little town, rapidly developing for tourism, which was a major trading town in the 17th and 18th centuries. Caravelas is in the mangroves; the beaches are about 10 km away at **Barra de Caravelas** (hourly buses), a fishing village. There is a helpful tourist information at *Ibama Centro de Visitantes*, Barão do Rio Branco 281.

Parque Nacional Marinho dos Abrolhos

ⓘ *Permission from Parque Nacional Marinho dos Abrolhos, Praia do Kitombo, Caravelas, Bahia 45900, T2971111, or Ibama, Av Juracy Magalhães Junior 608, CEP 40295-140, Salvador, T071-2407322.*

The Parque Nacional Marinho dos Abrolhos is 70 km east of Caravelas. Abrolhos is an abbreviation of *Abre os olhos*, 'Open your eyes', from Amérigo Vespucci's exclamation when he first sighted the reef in 1503. Established in 1983, the park consists of five small islands (**Redonda**, **Siriba**, **Guarita**, **Sueste**, **Santa Bárbara**), which are volcanic in origin, and several coral reefs. Darwin visited them in 1830 and Jacques Cousteau studied the marine environment here. The islands and surrounding reefs are home to goats, birds, whales, fish, turtles and giant fire corals. The warm current and shallow waters (8-15 m in depth) make a rich undersea life (with 160 species of fish) and good snorkelling. The park is best visited October-March, when underwater visibility reaches 30 m. The waters are warmest and calmest at this time too. Humpback whales breed and give birth here from July to December. Diving is best December-February.

The archipelago is administered by **Ibama** and a navy detachment mans a lighthouse on Santa Bárbara, which is the only island that may be visited. Visitors are not allowed to spend the night on the islands, but may stay overnight on schooners.

The northern coast

The **Linha Verde** runs for 142 km to the Sergipe state border; the road is more scenic than the BR-101, especially near Conde. There are very few hotels or *pousadas* in the more remote villages. Among the most picturesque are **Subaúma** (*pousada*) and **Baixio**; the latter, where the Rio Inhambupe meets the sea, is very beautiful.

Arembepe → *Phone code: 071. Colour map 4, A6.*

Some 45 km north of Salvador, this former fishing village is now a quiet resort. There is an 'alternative' village of palm huts, 30 minutes' walk along the beach, behind the sand dunes, with a café and swimming. The best beaches are 2 km north of town. A popular music festival is held the weekend after Carnaval.

Praia do Forte → *Phone code: 071. Colour map 4, A6.*

About 80 km north of Salvador, is this pleasant mini resort town much beloved of wealthy people from Salvador. Praia may no longer be a fishing village but it still feels low key. Aside from the town's main street Alameda do Sol, most of the streets are sand. Much of the area around the town is protected, with remnant coastal restinga forest, a small area of marshland and **Tamar**-managed turtle nesting beaches nearby. The marshland is home to a large number of birds, caymans and other animals. Birdwatching trips on the *pantanal* are rewarding and can be organized through the town's large scale 'eco' resort.

The **Tamar Project** ⓘ *Caixa Postal 2219, Rio Vermelho, Salvador, Bahia CEP 40210-990, T8761045, F8761067*, was set up to preserve the sea turtles that lay their eggs in the area. Praia do Forte is the headquarters of the **national turtle preservation programme** and is funded by the Worldwide Fund for Nature. There is a visitor's centre at the project (US$1.50 to visit the turtle sanctuary). Praia do Forte is also ideal for windsurfing and sailing, owing to constant fresh Atlantic breezes.

Praia do Forte takes its name from the castle built by a Portuguese settler, Garcia D'Ávila, in 1556, to warn the city to the south of enemy invasion. Garcia D'Ávila was given a huge area of land, from Praia do Forte to Maranhão, on which he made the first farm in Brazil. He brought the first head of cattle to the country, cleared the virgin Atlantic forest and brought the first coconut and mango trees to Brazil.

Imbassaí → *Phone code: 071. Colour map 4, A6.*

About 14 km from Praia do Forte is the simple village of Imbassaí, which has a beach at the mouth of the Rio Barroso. Other nearby beaches are **Praia de Santo Antônio**, 4 km away, with sand dunes and a small fishing village, and **Porto Sauípe**, 22 km north, which has recently been transformed into an ugly and old fashioned mega resort modelled on those which infected southern Spain in the 1980s. It caters almost exclusively to the worst kind of national and international package tourism.

Sítio do Conde → *Phone code: 075. Colour map 2, C5.*

Situated on the coast, 6 km from Conde, Sítio do Conde is a site for **Projeto Tamar** (the national project that studies and preserves marine turtles). The beaches are not very good but it's an ideal base to explore other beaches at **Barra do Itariri**, 12 km south, at the mouth of a river, which has fine sunsets. The road passes unspoilt beaches; the best are **Corre Nu** and **Jacaré**. You can also go to **Seribinha**, 13 km north of Sítio do Conde. The road goes along the beach through coconut groves and mangroves; at Seribinha are beach huts serving cool drinks or food.

Mangue Seco → *Phone code: 075. Colour map 2, C5.*

The last stop on the Linha Verde is Mangue Seco. A steep hill rising behind the village to tall white sand dunes offers a superb view of the coastline. The encroaching dunes have caused the mangrove to dry up. The town was immortalized in Jorge Amado's book *Tieta*.

Access from Sergipe is by boat or canoe on the Rio Real from Pontal (10-minute crossing). Buses run between Pontal and Estancia twice a day. The ferry across the river usually leaves before 1000 in the morning. A private launch will cost US$10, but it is usually possible to find someone to share the ride and cost.

Sleeping

Valença *p398, phone code 075*

A **Portal Rio Una**, R Maestro Barrinha, T/F7415050, www.portalhoteis.tur.br. Resort hotel by the riverside with a pool, tennis courts and organized activities.

B **do Porto**, Av Maçônica 50, T7413066. Clean, helpful, safe, good breakfast and a reasonable restaurant.

B **Guabim**, Praça da Independência, T7413408. Modest but well looked after with singles, doubles and triples.

D **Valença**, R Dr H Guedes Melo 15, T7411807. Simple hotel with plain but well-kept rooms and a good breakfast. Recommended.

Tinharé *p398, phone code 075*

In **Morro de São Paulo**, there are many cheap *pousadas* and rooms to rent near the fountain (Fonte Grande), but this part of town is very hot at night.

There are 4 **beaches** next to Morro town, which are quieter the further from town you go. The 1st and 2nd beaches, **Primeira** and **Segunda Praia** are designated party areas, with throbbing bars and many beachside shacks selling food and drinks well into the night. There are only *pousadas* and a few restaurants on the final 2 beaches. To reach the beaches turn right at the end of the main street; there is only one trail out of town. You'll have to walk as there are no cars on the island – porters can be hired to wheel your luggage to the hotel in a barrow.

A **Pousada Catavento**, 4th beach, T/F4831052,www.cataventopraiahotel.com.br. One of the most luxurious of the hotels on the Island with well-appointed mock colonial rooms arranged around a beautiful sculpted swimming pool, a decent restaurant and good service. Feels more secluded than any others.

A **Pousada Fazenda Caeira**, 3rd beach, T4411042, www.fazendacaeira.com.br. Very spacious and airy chalets in a large coconut grove overlooking the sea. Good breakfasts, a well-stocked library and a games room with snooker and board games.

A **Pousada Vistabella**, 1st beach, T073-7831001. Good rooms, those to the front have good views and are cooler and all have fans and hammocks. The owner Petruska is extremely welcoming, Recommended.

A-C **Fazenda Vila Guaiamú**, 3rd beach, T4831035, www.vilaguaiamu.com.br. 7 tastefully decorated chalets of various sizes and styles set in their own tropical gardens and visited by marmosets, tanagers and rare cotingas. The hotel has a spa service with wonderful massage and the Italian photographer owner runs an ecotourism project protecting a rare species of crab which live in the river that runs through the *fazenda*. Guided rainforest walks available. Excellent food. The best for nature lovers. Highly recommended.

B **Pousada Colibri**, near the fountain, Morro de São Paulo, which stays cool, has only 6 apartments and pleasant sea views. Helmut, the owner, speaks English and German.

B **Pousada Farol do Morro**, 1st beach, T4831036, www.faroldomorro.com.br. Little huts running up the hill all with a sea view and served by a private funicular railway. The pool sits perched on the edge of the hill.

C **Pousada Gaúcho**, near the fountain, with a huge breakfast and shared bathrooms.

C **Pousada Ilha da Saudade**, 1st beach, T4831015, www.ilhadasaudade.com.br. Elegant hillside *pousada* with a beautiful pool with a view, a small gym and deluxe suites with jacuzzis. Restaurant, bar and good breakfast.

C **Pousada Ilha do Sol**, 1st beach. Modest but scrupulously clean little *pousada* with good views. Recommended.

D **Pousada Aradhia**, 3rd beach. Rooms with balconies and an ocean view. Recommended.

D **Pousada Oxum**, 2nd beach. Newly renovated and very popular but this beach can be noisy.

E **Pousada Govinda**, 3rd Beach. Simple rooms, a good breakfast and other meals available, English and Spanish spoken. Recommended.

Ilha de Boipeba *p399*

Accommodation is split between the little town where the riverboat ferry arrives, the adjacent beach, Boca da Barra, which is more idyllic and the fishing village of Moreré ½-hr boat ride to the south (high tide only).

A **Pousada Tassimirim**, T99812378 (R Com Madureira 40, 45400-000, Valença), Tassimirim Beach (½-hr walk south of town). A coconut grove shading bungalows, bar, restaurant and pool . The price includes breakfast and dinner. Secluded and very tranquil.

A-B **Vila Sereia**, Boca da Barra beach, T6356045. Elegantly simple duplex wooden chalets overlooking the beach. Breakfast served on your own private veranda. Very romantic.

A-C **Santa Clara**, Boca da Barra beach, T6536085, www.santaclaraboipeba.com. Californian-owned *pousada* with the island's best restaurant and large, tastefully decorated duplex cabanas. Very good value room for 4 at D per person. Superlative therapeutic massages available. Both are highly recommended.

C-D **Horizonte Azul**, Boca da Barra beach, T6536080. Pretty little *pousada* next door to Santa Clara, with a range of chalets set in a hillside garden visited by hundreds of rare birds from the nearby Atlantic coast rainforest. Very friendly owners who speak English and good French. Highly recommended. Very simple and with lunch available.

D **Cheiro do Mar**, Moreré town, just north of the Pousada Moreré. Hillside cabins, the best of which has a breathtaking view. Ask for Fatima or João.

D **Mar e Coco**, Moreré, T6536013. 1 or 2 very simple rooms with a Bahian family and a wonderful seafood restaurant. 5 mins north of town. The restaurant **Paraiso** next door is as good and also rents a room (**D**). Ask for Gentil or Angelica.

D Pousada Luar das Águas, T99811012. Simple and good value.

D Pousada Moreré, Moreré town, T99871513. Simple fan-cooled rooms, some of which are a little musty. Good restaurant which doubles up as the town's only bar. The owner is the island's *prefeito*.

Ituberá and Camamu *p399, phone code 073*

C Rio Acaraí, Praça Dr Francisco Xavier, T2552315, www.hotelrioacarai.com.br. Ugly modern *pousada* with a pool and restaurant.

D Tropical, Av Hildebrando Araújo Góes 270, Ituberá, T2562233. Standard, simple, small town *pousada* with a/c rooms, a restaurant, bar and pool.

E Green House, next to the rodovíaria, T2552178. Very basic and friendly with breakfast and a simple restaurant.

Barra Grande and the Peninsula de Maraú *p399, phone code 073*

LL Kiaroa, Praia Taipus de Fora, T2586215, www.kiaroa.com.br. One of the country's most luxurious resorts, sitting on a glorious beach, with a range of beautifully appointed rooms and excellent restaurant, pampering and various organized activities.

AL-A Lagoa do Cassange, Praia do Cassange, T2582166, www.maris.com.br. Family resort with a pool, restaurant and 14 individual chalets overlooking the beach.

AL-A Taipú de Fora, Praia Taipus de Fora, T2252276, www.taipudefora.com.br. Small upscale mini-resort with a good range of activities including diving and kayaking.

D Meu Sossego, R Dr Chiquinho 17, Barra town, T2586012, www.meusossego.com. 19 plain a/c rooms with fridges.

Itacaré *p400, phone code 073*

The area is becoming very popular and prices are going up all the time. Book well ahead in high season.

LL Txai Resort, Praia de Itacarezinho, T6346956, www.txai.com.br. The most exclusive and luxurious resort in Bahia; on a deserted beach with very spacious and tastefully appointed bungalows overlooking a long, deep blue pool shaded by its own stand of palms. Excellent spa and a full range of activities including diving and horse riding.

AL-A Sage Point, Praia de Tiririca, T2512030, www.pousadasagepoint.com.br. Oceanfront *pousada* with smart wooden chalets in a tropical garden overlooking the sea, each with their own hammock-strewn terraces. Some are a little small but all have wonderful views. The Cuban owner, Ana, speaks English and can organize trips to nearby beaches.

AL-A Vila de Ocaporan, T2512470, www.viladeocaporan.com.br. Brightly coloured, spacious chalets gathered around a charming little pool in a hammock-filled garden. Between the town and Praia da Concha. Good Bahian restaurant.

A-B Art Jungle, T99962167. 6 tree houses in a modern sculpture garden in the middle of forest. All have views out to the sea and to the Rio de Contas. A favourite with celebrities – Sean Penn, Jade Jagger and Gisele Bundchen all come here.

B-C Pousada da Lua, Praia da Concha, T2512209, www.itacare.com.br/pousadadalua. A handful of little chalets in forest filled with marmosets and parakeets. Great breakfast.

C Pousada Litoral, R de Souza 81, 1 block from where buses stop. The owner João Cravo speaks English and can organize tours to remote beaches and hire fishing boats. Recommended.

Ilhéus and around *p400, map p400, phone code 073*

There are plenty of cheap hotels in Ilheus near the municipal rodoviária in centre; not all are desirable (check for hot pillows!).

AL Hotel Jardim Atlântico, Pontal, near Ilheus, T6322222. Sports facilities, restaurant, bar, etc.

A Hotel Barravento, on Malhado beach, R NS das Graças 276, Ilheus, T/F6343223. Ask for the penthouse – there is usually no extra charge, includes breakfast and refrigerator.

A Ilhéus Praia, Praça Dom Eduardo (on beach), Ilheus, T6342533. With a pool and helpful staff. Recommended.

A Pontal Praia, Av Lomanto Júnior 1358, Praia do Pontal, Ilheus, T/F6343033. A little outside city but with frequent buses passing. Unpretentious family hotel with a/c rooms and a swimming pool.

A **Tarik Plaza**, Av Aziz Maron, Itabuna, T2148800, www.tarikplaza.com.br. The best in town; modern with a pool and fairly good restaurant.
B **Pousada Sol Atlântico**, Av Lomanto Júnior 1450, Pontal, T2318059. Rooms with views over bay, fan, TVs and balconies.
B **São Marino**, 28 de Junho 29, Ilheus, T2316511 and at 28 de Junho 16.
C **Britânia**, Ilheus, T6341722. Cheap and fairly cheerful with breakfast.
D **Hotel Atlântico Sul**, R Bento Berilo 224, Ilheus Centro, T2314668. Good value with a bar/restaurant. Recommended.
D **JG**, Jardim Grapiúna, Itabuna, T/F2112858, www.bahiaclick.com.br/jg. Basic hotel with plain a/c and fan-cooled rooms and a pool.
E **Fazenda Tororomba**, R Luiz Eduardo Magalhães s/n, Olivença centre, near Ilheus, T2691139. Youth hostel.

Camping

Estância das Fontes, 19 km on road south to Olivença, T2122505. Cheap, shady. Recommended.

Porto Seguro *p402, map p400, phone code 073*

Prices rise steeply Dec-Feb and Jul. Off-season rates can drop by 50%, negotiate the rate for stays of more than 3 nights. Room capacity is greater than that of Salvador. Outside Dec-Feb, rooms with bath and hot water can be rented for about US$150 per month.

A **Estalagem Porto Seguro**, R Mcal Deodoro 66, T2882095, F2883692. In an old colonial house with a tranquil atmosphere, a/c, TV, pool, good breakfast.
A **Pousada Alegrete**, Av dos Navegantes 567, T/F2881738. Simple rooms and very friendly and helpful staff. Recommended.
A **Pousada Casa Azul**, 15 de Novembro 11, T/F2882180. TV, a/c, good pool and garden, quiet part of town.
A **Pousada Gaivota**, Av dos Navegantes 333, Centro, T/F2882826. A/c rooms in a hotel with, pool, sauna, parking facilities.
A **Pousada Imperador**, Estrada do Aeroporto, T2882759, F2882900. Modest 4-star with views out over the city, especially from the pool deck.
A **Vela Branca**, R Dr Antonio Ricaldi (Cidade Alta), T2882318, www.velabranca.com.br. Luxury resort with a wonderful view out over the water. Beautiful pool, tennis courts, sauna and spacious a/c rooms.
B-D **Pousada dos Raizes**, Praça dos Pataxós 196, T/F2884717. Well-kept unpretentious city hotel with helpful staff. Cheaper without breakfast. Recommended.
B **Pousada Las Palmas**, Praça Antônio Carlos Magalhães 102, T/F2882643. A/c rooms with TVs in a little hotel with no pool, but highly recommended.
C **Pousada Alcantara**, R das Papagaias 70, T/F2881657. Centrally located with fan-cooled rooms only. Well looked after.
C **Pousada Coral**, R Assis Chateaubriand 74, T/F2882630. A/c rooms with a TV in a dull building in a good location.
C **Pousada da Orla**, Av Portugal 404, T/F2881131. Fan-cooled simple rooms and a good breakfast. Great location. Highly recommended.
C **Pousada dos Navegantes**, Av 22 de Abril 212, T2882390, www.portonet.com.br/navegantes. A/c rooms with en suites and TVs crowding over a little pool.
C **Pousada Jandaias**, R das Jandaias 112, T2882611, F2882738. Fan-cooled rooms and a great breakfast, tranquil. Recommended.
D **Estalagem da Ivonne**, R Mcal Deodoro 298, T2881515. Basic hotel with some a/c rooms.
D **Maracaia**, Coroa Vermelha, on road to Santa Cruz Cabrália, T8721155, F8721156. IYHA hostel. Price per person.
D **Porto Seguro**, R Cova da Moça 720, T/F2881742. IYHA hostel. Price per person.
D **Pousada Aquarius**, R Pedro Álvares Cabral 174, T/F2882738. No breakfast but clean, family run, friendly and central.
E **Porto Brasília**, Praça Antônio Carlos Magalhães 234. Fans, mosquito nets, with breakfast.
F **Pousada Casa Grande**, Av dos Navegantes 107, Centro, T2882003. Comfortable, very simple with helpful multilingual staff and a hearty breakfast.

Camping

Camping da Gringa, Praia do Cruzeiro, T2882076. Laundry, café, pool, excellent, US$5 per night.
Camping do Sítio, R da Vala. Mosquitoes can be a problem here.
Camping dos Marajas, Av Getúlio Vargas, central.

Camping Mundaí Praia, T8792287. US$8 per night.
Tabapiri Country, BR-367, Km 61.5, next to the rodoviária on the road leading to the Cidade Histórica, T2882269.

Santa Cruz Cabrália *p404, phone code 073*
A-B **Baía Cabrália**, R Sidrack de Carvalho 141, in the centre, T/F2821111, www.baiacabralia.com.br. Medium-size family resort with a large pool, sauna and gym.
B-C **Victor Hugo**, Villa de Santo André, km 3, Santa Cruz Cabrália,T6714064, www.portonet.com.br/victorhugo. Smart, tastefully decorated little *pousada* right on the beach. Rooms are plain and scrupulously clean, with whitewashed walls and dark wood floors.
C **Pousada do Mineiro**, T2821042. A/c rooms around a pool and with a sauna, friendly staff and a *churrascaria* barbecue. Recommended.
C **Tribo da Praia**, Av Beira de Santo André, T2821620. *Pousada* with a helpful American owner.

Arraial da Ajuda *p404, phone code 073*
At busy times such as New Year's Eve and Carnival, don't expect to find anything under US$15 per person in a shared room, for a minimum stay of 5-7 days. D-grade hotels tend to be at the uppermost end of that range.

Note We have received warnings about Pousada da Anginha and would advise travellers to avoid staying there. For more information contact the Porto Seguro Delegacia de Proteçao ao turista.
A **Pousada Pitinga**, Praia Pitinga, T5751067, www.pousadapitinga.com.br. Wooden chalets in a coconut filled rainforest garden on a hill overlooking the sea. Tranquil atmosphere, great food and a pool, member of the Roteiros de Charme group, see p47. Recommended.
A-C **Pousada Canto d'Alvorada**, on road to Ajuda, T8751218, www.cantodalvorada.com.br. Cheaper out of season. Pretty, Swiss-run *pousada* a little out of town with 7 cabins, a restaurant, pool, sauana and laundry facilities.
B **Ivy Marey**, near the centre on road to beach, T8751106. Franco Brazilian *pousada*, tasteful y decorated, 4 rooms and 2 bungalows.
B **Pousada do Robalo**, T8751053/1528, F8751078. Welcoming *pousada* with a nice pool set in pleasant garden surroundings.
B **Sole Mio**, T8751115, just off the beach road leading from the ferry to Arraial. French owners, English spoken, laid-back with 4 chalets and an excellent pizzeria.
C **Pousada Erva Doce**, Estrada do Mucugê 200, T8751113. Well-appointed chalets and a decent restaurant. Highly recommended.
C **Pousada Mar Aberto**, Estrada do Mucugê 554, T/F8751153, Pretty little *pousada* set in lush gardens very near Mucugê beach, 400 m from the centre.
C **Pousada Tubarão**, R Bela Vista, beyond the church on the right, T8751086. With sweeping views of the sea, a cool sea breeze and a reasonable restaurant.
C-E **O Cantinho**, Praça São Bras, T5751131, www.arraialnet.com.br/pousadacantinho. Terraces of smart a/c and fan-cooled rooms around a fruit tree garden courtyard. Excellent breakfast, pleasant public areas and off-season discounts.
D **Pousada Corujão**, T/F8751508. Basic bungalows on the way to the beach with cooking facilities, a laundry, restaurant and book exchange.
D **Pousada do Mel**, Praça São Bras, T8751309. Simple but clean and with a good breakfast. Recommended.
D **Pousada Flamboyant**, Estrada Mucugê 89, T8751025. Rooms arranged around a little courtyard. Good breakfast and a pool.
E-F **Daunbailó**, Estrada do Mucugê 125, T5751194, linobeto@yahoo.com. Very simple backpacker orientated *pousada* with tiny but well-kept rooms, some with a/c.
E-F **Good's**, Estrada do Mucugê 69, T5751998, www.arraialdajudahostel.com.br. Price per person. Backpacker hostel with IYHA discount, snack bar, internet and book exchange. Very good location.

Camping
Generally, Arraial da Ajuda is better for camping than Porto Seguro.
Praia, on Mucugê beach. Good position and facilities.
Chão do Arraial, 5 mins from Mucugê beach. Shady, good snack bar, also hires tents. Recommended.

Trancoso *p405, phone code 073*

As well as the *pousadas*, there are many houses to rent; contact Clea at **Restaurant Abacaxi** on the main square on the right.

A **Caipim Santo**, to the left of the main square, T6681122. Pleasant *pousada* with one of the better restaurants in Trancoso. Recommended.

A **Pousada Brasília**, Estrada do Arraial, T6681128. Party *pousada* popular with young and well-to-do Paulistanos. Not for seekers of tranquility.

A-B **Mata N'ativa**, Estrada Velha do Arraial (next to the river on the way to the beach), T6681830, www.matanativapousada.com.br. The best in town, with a series of elegant cabins gathered in a lovingly maintained orchid and heliconia garden by the riverside. Owners Daniel and Daniela are very hospitable. Good English, Spanish and Italian.

B **Pousada Calypso**, Parque Municipal, T6681113, www.pousadacalypso.com.br. Comfortable, spacious rooms, a library and sitting area and helpful staff who speak German and English. Recommended.

C **Gulab Mahal**, on the main square. Mock oriental and set in a little tropical garden. Vast breakfast. Highly recommended.

C **Pousada do Bosque**, Estrada Velha do Arraial (on the way to the beach). Simple *pousada* in a garden and with camping facilities. English, German and Spanish spoken. Decent breakfast.

D **Luana Pousa**, in the *invasão* (the newer part of Trancoso), further along on the left from Quarto Crescente. With well-ventilated modest rooms. Recommended.

D **Pousada Quarto Crescente**, About 500 m inland, away from main square, in the *invasão*, with cooking facilities, laundry and helpful owners who speak English, German, Dutch and Spanish. Highly recommended.

E **Pousada Beira Mar**. Very simple rooms with bath and an equally simple restaurant serving *prato feito*.

Caraiva *p406, phone code 073*

D **Pousada da Barra**, at the far end of the village. Simple rooms with breakfast included.

D **Pousada da Canoa**, attached to Bar do Pará, by the river. Simple fan-cooled rooms and a restaurant serving the best fish in the village, US$7-8 (try *sashimi* or *moqueca*).

D **Pousada da Terra**, far end of the village near the indigenous reserve. Simple rooms with breakfast. Recommended.

D **Pousada Lagoa**, T/F99656662. Chalets and bungalows under cashew trees, good restaurant, own generator; the owner, Hermínia, speaks English, is very helpful and can arrange local trips and excursions.

Cumuruxatiba and Prado *p406, phone code 073*

C **Casa de Maria**, R Seis, Novo Prado, Prado, T2981424, www.casademaria.com.br. Simple beachside *pousada* with a pool, claims that it serves the best breakfast in southern Bahia.

C-D **Novo Prado**, Praia Novo Prado, Prado, T2981455, www.novoprado.com.br. Pleasant beach hotel with a pool, sauna and a range of a/c and fan-cooled rooms.

D **Pousada Guainamby**, R Bela Vista, CEP 45983, Cumuruxatiba. German and Brazlllan owned with small, clean, comfortable chalets and good views out over the long beach, a good breakfast and a restaurant with fish and Italian meals. Recommended.

E **Praia de Cumuruxatiba**, Av Beira Mar s/n, Cumuruxatiba, T8731020, F8731004. Basic beachside hostel.

Caravelas *p406, phone code 073*

A **Marina Porto Abrolhos**, R da Baleia, T6741082, www.marinaportoabrolhos.com.br. Luxurious beachfront family resort with 34 apartments, a pool, sauna and a range of activities.

C **Pousada Caravelense**, 50 m from the rodoviária, T2971182. Plain rooms with a TV, fridge, a good breakfast and an excellent restaurant. Recommended.

D **Shangri-la**, Barão do Rio Branco 216. Simple rooms with en suites and breakfast.

E **Pousada Jaquita**, Barra de Caravelas. Basic with the use of a kitchen, big breakfast, bath, airy rooms. The owner, Secka, speaks English. There are some food shops nearby as well as restaurants and bars.

Arembepe *p407, phone code 071*

B-C **Arembepe Refúgio Ecológico**, Estrada Aldeia Hippie, T6241031, www.aldeiaarembepe.com.br. 11 well-appointed a/c chalets around a pool in a protected area next to the **Tamar** turtle beach project. Very peaceful.

C-D Gipsy, R Eduardo Pinto, Km 3, T6243266, www.gipsy.com.br\. 40-room hotel with a/c rooms and a pool.

Praia do Forte *p407, phone code 071*
Prices rise steeply in the summer season. It can be difficult to find cheap accommodation.
LL-AL Praia do Forte EcoResort, Av do Farol, T6764000, reservas@pfr.com.br. Large-scale family resort set in tropical gardens on the beach and with programmes to visit the nearby protected areas. Rooms are spacious, well appointed and comfortable and service, which includes a spa and entertainment, is excellent. Beautiful pool.
AL Pousada Solar da Lagoa, R do Forte, T6761271. Smart chalets with room enough for 4, a decent pool and excellent service. The price is for full board.
A Pousada Praia do Forte, Av do Farol, T6761116, www.pousadapraiadoforte.com.br. Chalets in peaceful setting, in ideal position on beach. Recommended.
A-B Sobrado da Vila, Av do Sol, T/F6761152, www.sobradodavila.com.br. The best *pousada* in the village itself with a range of individually decorated rooms with balconies and a good-value restaurant. Very convenient for the restaurants.
B Ogum Marinho, Av Alameda do Sol, T6761165, www.ogummarinho.com.br. A/c or cheaper fan-cooled rooms in a mock colonial house with a nice little courtyard garden. Good restaurant and service.
B-C Pousada João Sol, R da Corvina, T6761054, www.pousadajoaosol.com.br. 6 well-appointed and newly refurbished chalets. The owner speaks English, Spanish and German. Great breakfast.
C Pousada Tatuapara, Praça dos Artistas, T6761015. Spacious and well-maintained, fan-cooled rooms with a fridge. Good breakfast.
D Tia Helena, just east of the Praça dos Artistas. Helena, the motherly proprietor, provides an excellent meal and enormous breakfast. The rooms are simple but well kept and the price reduced for 3-day stays.
D Albergue da Juventude, Praia do Forte, R da Aurora 3, T6761094, praiadoforte@albergue.com.br. Smart youth hostel with decent rooms with en suites, a large breakfast, Private bathroom, fan, breakfast, kitchen and shop, more expensive for non-IYHA members.

Imbassaí *p407, phone code 071*
B Pousada Caminho do Mar, T/F8322499. Bungalows with a/c, restaurant, German-run.
B Pousada Imbassaí, T/F8761313. A/c chalets and apartments.
C Pousada Lagoa da Pedra, T2485914. Chalets set in large grounds, some English spoken, friendly.
D Pousada Anzol de Ouro, T3224422. Modest fan-cooled chalets around a simple pool.

Sítio do Conde *p408, phone code 075*
A Hotel Praia do Conde, T4291129, in Salvador T071-3212542. Smart a/c chalets with en suites around a pool.
C Pousada Oasis, T4212397. Very simple, plain accommodation either fan-cooled or a/c rooms. With breakfast.

Mangue Seco *p408, phone code 075*
There are plenty of small cheap places in Mangue Seco along the seafront from the jetty, none with addresses or phone numbers (the village is tiny). There are simple restaurants around the main square next to the church. The beach has a handful of *barracas* serving cheap fish.
B-C Asa Branca, T4459054, www.infonet.com.br/asabranca. The plushest in town with a range of simple a/c rooms in terraces overlooking a rectangular pool. Good restaurant.

Eating

Tinharé *p398, phone code 075*
There are plenty of restaurants in Morro de São Paulo town and on the 2nd and 3rd beaches. Most of them are OK though somewhat overpriced. For cheap eats stay in a *pousada* that includes breakfast in its daily rate, stock up at the supermarket and buy seafood snacks at the *barracas* on the 2nd beach.
TT **Belladonna**, Morro town. Decent Italian restaurant with live music and a good meeting point. The owner Guido speaks Italian, English and French. Evenings only.
TT **Bianco e Nero**, Morro town. Reasonably good pizza, pasta and grilled food.

ΨΨ **Chez Max**, Morro town, 3rd beach. Simple but decent seafood in a pretty restaurant overlooking the sea.

ΨΨ **Fazenda Vila Guaiamú** (see p409), Morro town. Excellent seafood restaurant which must be booked in advance for non-guests.

ΨΨ **Piscina**, Morro town, 4th beach, T4831072. One of Morro's few good, as opposed to adequate, seafood restaurants.

Ψ **Comida Natural**, Morro town, on the main street. Good breakfasts, pay-by-weight lunches and juices.

Ilha de Boipeba *p399*

Boipeba has cheap eats in the town and surpirisingly good food at the Pousada Santa Clara and the rustic restaurants in Moreré.

ΨΨ **Santa Clara** (see p409), Boipeba. San Francisco panache in rustic but elegantly decorated tropical surrounds. Come for dinner. Highly recommended.

Ψ **Mar e Coco** (see p409), Boipeba. Very fresh seafood in idyllic surroundings; shaded by coconuts and next to a gently lapping bath-warm sea.

Barra Grande and the Peninsula de Maraú *p399*

ΨΨ **Tapera**, Barra, in the town serves good seafood.

Itacaré *p400, phone code 073*

There are plenty of restaurants in Itacaré, most of them on R **Lodônio Almeida**. Menus here are increasingly chic and often include a respectable wine list.

ΨΨΨ **Casa Sapucaia**, R Lodônio Almeida, T2513091. Sophisticated Bahian food with an international twist from 2 ex-round-the-world sailors. Try the delicious king prawn caramelized with ginger.

ΨΨΨ **Dedo de Moça**, R Plinio Soares (next to the São Miguel Church), T2513391. One of Bahia's best restaurants. Chef Vagner Aguiar trained at São Paulo's award-winning **Laurent** restaurant (see p193), and cooks dishes which combine Brazilian ingredients with French and Oriental techniques. Offerings include tempura with pear rice cooked in port wine and served and lightly caramelized with balsamic vinegar.

ΨΨΨ **O Casarão Amarelo**, Praia da Coroinha, T99960599. Swiss-owned and run restaurant in one of the most beautiful colonial buildings in the town. International menu which is good in parts. The fish is reliable.

ΨΨ **Boca de Forno**, R Lodônio Almeida 134, T2512174. The busiest restaurant in Itacaré, serving good wood-fired pizzas in tastefully decorated surroundings to a well-dressed post-beach crowd.

Ψ **O Restaurante**, R Pedro Longo 150, T2512012. One of the few restaurants with a *prato feto*, alongside a mixed seafood menu.

Ilhéus and around *p400, map p421, phone code 073*

Specialities include the local drink, *coquinho*, coconut filled with *cachaça*, which is only for the strongest heads. There are cheap eats from the various seafood stalls on the *praça* and near the cathedral.

ΨΨΨ **Vesúvio**, Praça Dom Eduardo, T6344724. Next to the cathedral, made famous by Amado's novel (see p401), now Swiss-owned, very good but pricey.

ΨΨ **Os Velhos Marinheiros**, Av 2 de Julho. Decent seafood and juices on the waterfront. Recommended.

Ψ **Come Bem**, near Praça Cairu. Cheap but good Bahian food.

Ψ **Nogar**, Av Bahia 377. Close to the sea. Decent pizzas and pasta.

Porto Seguro *p402, map p400, phone code 073*

ΨΨΨ **Cruz de Malta**, R Getúlio Vargas 358. Good seafood in pleasant surrounds.

ΨΨ **Anti-Caro**, R Assis Chateaubriand 26. Good food in a working antique shop, great atmosphere.

ΨΨ **Les Agapornis**, Av dos Navegantes 180. Wide selection of crêpes and pizzas.

ΨΨ **Prima Dona**, No 247. Decent pasta, pizza and other Italian dishes.

ΨΨ **Tres Vintens**, Av Portugal 246. Good imaginative seafood dishes. Recommended.

ΨΨ **Vida Verde**, R Dois de Julho 92, T2882766. Reasonable vegetarian food, one of few that serve it. Mon-Sat 1100-2100.

Ψ **da Japonêsa**, Praça Pataxós 38. Excellent value with a varied Brazilian and Japanese menu, open 0800-2300. Recommended.

Ψ **Pau Brasil**, Praça dos Pataxós. Simple café with good breakfast.

Ψ **Ponto do Encontro**, Praça Pataxós 106. Good simple food, the owners also rent rooms, open 0800-2400.

Ỷ **Preto Velho**, Praça da Bandeira. Good value for à la carte or self-service.

Arraial da Ajuda *p404, phone code 073*

Food in Arraial is pricey and restaurants tend to look better than the dishes they serve.

ỸỸỸ **Don Fabrizio**, Estrada do Mucugê 402, T5751123. The best Italian in town, in an upmarket open air-restaurant with live music and reasonable wine.

ỸỸỸ **Manguti**, Estrada do Mucugê, 5752270, www.manguti.com.br. Reputedly the best in town, though the food looks like mutton dressed up as lamb. Meat, pasta, fish served as comfort food alongside other Brazilian dishes. Very popular and informal.

ỸỸ **Pizzaria do Arraial**, Praça São Bras s/n. Basic pizzeria and pay-by-weight restaurant.

ỸỸ **Nipo**, Estrada do Mucugê 250, T5753033. Reasonably priced but decent Japanese with hotel delivery.

Ỷ **Mineirissima**, Estrada do Mucugê, T5753790. Good value pay-by-weight with very filling Minas Gerais food and *moquecas*. Opens until late but menu service only after 1800.

Ỷ **Paulinho Pescador**, Estrada do Mucugê. Excellent seafood, also chicken and meat, one price (US$5), English spoken, good service. *Bobó de camarão* highly recommended. Very popular, there are often queues for tables. Open 1200-2200.

Recommended *barracas* are **Tem Q Dá** and **Agito** on Mucugê beach, as well as **Barraca de Pitinga** and **Barraca do Genésio** on Pitinga.

Trancoso *p405, phone code 073*

Food in Trancoso is expensive. Those on a tight budget should shop at the supermarket between the main square and the new part of town. There are numerous fish restaurants in the *barracas* on the beach. None are cheap. Elba Ramalho, when in town, gigs at her restaurant, **Para Raio**.

ỸỸỸ **Cacao**, on the main square, T6681266. One of the best in town with a varied international and Brazilian menu. Pleasant surrounds.

ỸỸ **Laila**, in the new shopping area just before the main square. Elegant little restaurant serving good Moroocan and Lebanese food.

ỸỸ-Ỷ **Silvana e Cia** in the historical centre. Respectable Bahian food at a fair price.

Ỷ **Portinha**, on the main square. The only place serving food at a reasonable price. Excellent pay-by-weight options and good if overpriced juices.

Arembepe *p407, phone code 071*

ỸỸ **Mar Aberto**, Lg de São Francisco 43, T8241257. Good seafood with a French twist.

Praia do Forte *p407, phone code 071*

ỸỸỸ **Sabor da Vila**, Alameda do Sol, T6761156. International menu with good Bahian cooking and seafood.

ỸỸ **Bar Da Souza**, Av do Sol (on the right as you enter the village). Excellent seafood and live music at weekends. Recommended. Reasonably priced.

ỸỸ **O Europeu**, Alameda do Sol, T6760232. English-owned and run restaurant with the most adventurous menu in town. Great risotto, steak, salads and esserts. Highly recommended. The owner William is affable and knowledgeable about the area.

Ỷ **Cafe Tango**, Praça das Artistas. Pleasant open-air tea and coffee bar with great pastries and cakes.

Ỷ **La Crêperie**, Alameda do Sol. Excellent savoury and sweet crêpes, Tue-Sun, good music. The owner, Kleber, is very friendly.

Ỷ **Pizzeria Le Gaston**, Alameda do Sol. Good pizza, pasta and home-made ice cream, open daily.

Ỷ **Tutti-Frutti**, recommended ice cream parlour.

Bars and clubs

Tinharé *p398, phone code 075*

There is always plenty going on in Morro. The liveliest bars are **87** and **Jamaica**; both on the 2nd beach. These tend to get going after 2300 when the restaurants in town empty.

Ilha de Boipeba *p399*

Nightlife on Boipeba is limited to watching the stars or having a beer at the reggae bar in town.

Itacaré *p400*

The liveliest bars of the moment are **Toca do Calango, Praça dos Cachorros** and **Mar e Mel** on the Praia das Conchas. The **Casarão Amarelo** restaurant becomes a dance club after 2300 on weekends. There is frequent extemporaneous *forró* and other live music all over the city and most restaurants and bars have some kind of music between Oct and Apr.

Porto Seguro *p402, map p400*
Porto Seguro is famous for the *lambada,*see Music p698).
A good bar for live music is **Porto Prego** on R Pedro Álvares Cabral, small cover charge. **Sotton Bar**, Praça de Bandeira, is lively, as are **Pronto Socorro do Choppe, Doce Letal 50** and **Studio Video Bar**. There are bars and street cafés on Av Portugal.

Arraial da Ajuda *p404*
The *lambada* is danced at the **Jatobar** bar (summer only), by the church on the main square (opens 2300 – *pensão* at the back is cheap, clean and friendly). **Limelight** has raves all year round. Many top Brazilian bands play at the beach clubs at **Praia do Parracho** during the summer, entry is about US$20. Entry to other beach parties is about US$10.

Festivals and events

Ilhéus and around *p400, map p421*
17-20 Jan Festa de São Sebastião.
Feb Shrove Tue, Carnival.
23 Apr Festa de São Jorge.
28 Jun Foundation day.
Oct Festa do Cacau.

Shopping

Praia do Forte *p407*
Afro-Bahia, Alameda do Sol. A range of funky T-shirts.
Boutique Ogum Marinho, Alameda do Sol. Quirky woodcarvings by local artists.
Kennedy Bahia, Alameda do Sol. Gallery run by a family of Irish-Brazilian artists. Recommended.
Vivire, Alameda do Sol. High-quality swimwear from a Bahian brand.

Activities and tours

Porto Seguro *p402, map p400, phone code 073*
Diving
Portomar Ltda, R Dois de Julho 178. Equipment hire, also arranges diving and snorkelling trips to the coral reefs offshore, professional instructors.

Tour operators
Brazil Travel, Av 22 de Abril 200, T/F2881824 and braziltravel@braziltravel.tur.br. Dutch-run travel agency, all types of trips organized. English, German, Dutch, French and Spanish spoken.

Several agencies at the airport, including **Grou Turismo**, T2884155, **Soletur**, T2881736, and **Viagens Costa**, T2885288.

Arraial da Ajuda *p404, phone code 073*
Eco Calicute, T99795452, www.calicute.com.br. Not 'eco' at all; as usual in Brazil the word translates as mucking about in nature, in this case with a 4WD, glider, quad bike, horse or scuba gear. Don't expect guides to know anything about wildlife or show any interest in it.

Trancoso *p405, phone code 073*
Joáçio, T6681270, or ask at the **Bouganvillea** restaurant on the main square, runs good day trips to Espelho Beach, Caraíva and other beaches and forested areas in the area. Expect to pay US$10-15 per person depending on group size and distance.

Caravelas *p406, phone code 073*
Teresa and **Ernesto** (from Austria) organize boat trips (US$40 per day), jeep and horse hire (turn left between the bridge and the small supermarket). 'Alternative' beach holidays (organic vegetarian food, yoga, meditation, other activities) with Beky and Eno on the unspoilt island of Coçumba, recommended, contact **Abrolhos Turismo**, Praça Dr Imbassahi 8, T2971149, also rent diving gear and arrange boat trips.

Praia do Forte *p407, phone code 071*
Odara Turismo, in the **EcoResort Hotel**, T6761080, F6761018, run imaginative tours to surrounding areas and outlying villages and beaches using 4WD vehicles, very friendly and informative, recommended; owners, Norbert and Papy, speak English and German.

Transport

Valença *p398, phone code 075*
Air The airport is at Praia Guaibim, T3539227, 20-mins' taxi from town. Flights mainly go to Salvador.

Bus Long-distance buses run from the new rodoviária, Av Maçônica, T7411280, while the old one is for local buses.

Many buses a day to/from **Salvador**, 5 hrs, US$6, several companies, including **Aguia Branca**, T4504400. São Jorge to **Itabuna**, 5 hrs, US$5, very slow. For the shortest route to Valença, take the ferry from São Joaquim to Bom Despacho on Itaparica island, from where it is 130 km to Valença via Nazaré das Farinhas (see p379). To/from **Bom Despacho** on **Itaparica**, **Camarujipe** and **Águia Branca** companies, 16 a day, 1 hr 45 mins, US$3.60.

Tinharé *p398, phone code 075*

Air There are direct flights between **Salvador** and the 3rd beach at Morro de São Paulo several times daily. These cost US$50 one way. Times vary seasonally and from year to year but are usually as follows: **Sal-Morro** (0815, 1430, 1500), **Morro-Sal** (0900, 1015, 1315, 1715). For further details ask your hotel to contact **Addey** T071-3771993, www.addey.com.br, or drop into the airport office next to the landing strip on Morro.

Ferry

From **Salvador**, several companies operate a catamaran (1½ hrs) from the Terminal Marítimo in front of the Mercado Modelo to Morro de São Paulo. Times vary according to the season and weather but there are usually several a day every 2 hrs or so between 0800 and 1400; check with the tourist office or **Catamarã Gamboa do Morro**, T99756395. Part of the trip is on the open sea, which can be rough. There are also various water taxis.

Boats leave every day from **Valença** for Gamboa (1½ hrs) and Morro de São Paulo (1½ hrs) from the main bridge in Valença 5 times a day (signalled by a loud whistle). The fare is US$2.50. The *lancha rápida* takes 25 mins and costs US$8. Only buses leaving between 0530 and 1100 from Salvador to Valença connect with ferries. If not stopping in Valença, get out of the bus by the main bridge in town, don't wait until you get to the rodoviária, which is a long way from the ferry. Private boat hire can be arranged if you miss the ferry schedule. A responsible local boatman is **Jario**, T7411681; he can be contacted to meet travellers arriving at the rodoviária for transfer to the Morro. He also offers excursions to other islands, especially Boipeba. Overnight excursions to the village are possible. There is a regular boat from Valença to Boipeba on weekdays 1000-1230 depending on tide, return 1500-1700, 3-4 hrs.

Ilha de Boipeba *p399, phone code 075*

Boat Day trips leave daily from **Morro** at 0900 in front of the Fazenda Caiera and travel around most of Boipeba. They can leave you on Boipeba but you must pay the full tour fare (around US$15). All the *pousadas* will book these. Toyotas leave for Boipeba from behind the 2nd beach every morning (around US$10); usually at around 0800 and return at midday. Contact **Zé Balacha** T91480343 or book through your *pousada* in Morro or Boipeba.

Itacaré *p400*

Bus The rodoviária is a few mins' walk from town. Porters are on hand with barrows to help with luggage.

Frequent buses to **Ilhéus** (the nearest town with an airport), 45 mins, US$7 along the newly paved road. To **Salvador**, change at Ubaitaba (3 hrs, US$3), Ubaitaba-Salvador, 6 hrs, US$12, several daily.

Ilhéus and around *p400, map p421*

Bus The rodoviária is 4 km from the centre on R Itabuna, but the Itabuna-Olivença bus goes through the centre of Ilhéus.

Several buses run daily to **Salvador**, 7 hrs, US$14.40 (*leito* US$29, **Expresso São Jorge**), 0620 bus goes via Itaparica, leaving passengers at Bom Despacho ferry station on the island – thence 50-min ferry to Salvador. To **Itacaré**, 4 hrs, US$5. To **Eunápolis**, 5 hrs, US$5.40, this bus also leaves from the central bus terminal. Other destinations also served; local buses leave from Praça Cairu.

Taxi Insist that taxi drivers have meters and price charts.

Porto Seguro *p402, map p400, phone code 073*

At Brazilian holiday times, all transport north or south should be booked well in advance.

Air Flights to Belo Horizonte, Rio de Janeiro, Salvador and São Paulo. Taxi to airport US$7. Airport, T2881877.

Bus The rodoviária has reliable luggage store and lounge on 3rd floor, on the road to Eunápolis, 2 km from the centre, regular bus service (30 mins) through the city to the old rodoviária near the port. Local buses US$0.30. Taxis charge US$5 from the rodoviária to the town or ferry (negotiate at quiet times).

To **Salvador** (Águia Branca), daily, 12 hrs, US$22.25. To **Vitória**, daily, 11 hrs, US$18. **Ilhéus**, daily 0730, 5½ hrs, US$11. To **Eunápolis**, 1 hr, US$2. For **Rio** direct buses (São Geraldo), leaving at 1745, US$35 (*leito* 70), 18 hrs, from Rio direct at 1600 (very cold a/c, take warm clothes), or take 1800 for Ilhéus and change at Eunápolis. To **Belo Horizonte**, daily, direct, US$33 (São Geraldo). To **São Paulo** direct, 1045, 25 hrs, not advisable, very slow, much better to go to Rio then take Rio-São Paulo express. Other services via Eunápolis (those going north avoid Salvador) or Itabuna (5 hrs, US$9).

Car hire Several companies located at the airport, including Localiza, T2881488 (and R Cova da Moça 620, T2881488) and Nacional, T2884291.

Cycle Oficina de Bicicleta, Av Getúlio Vargas e R São Pedro, about US$10 for 24 hrs, also at Praça de Bandeira and at 2 de Julho 242.

Arraial da Ajuda *p404*

Ferry Rio Buranhém from Porto Seguro takes 15 mins to the south bank, US$0.60 for foot passengers, US$3.60 for cars, every 30 mins day and night. It is then a further 5 km to Arraial da Ajuda, US$0.50 by bus, kombis charge US$0.75 per person, taxis US$5.

Caravelas *p406*

Air There are flights from **Belo Horizonte**, **São Paulo** and **Salvador**. Another option is to fly to Porto Seguro.

Bus Caravelas is well connected, with buses to **Texeira de Freitas** (4 a day), **Salvador**, **Nanuque** and **Prado**.

Train There are rail connections to **Minas Gerais**.

Parque Nacional Marinho dos Abrolhos *p406*

Air 3-day, 2-night packages from São Paulo cost around US$700, including return flights.

Boat The journey to the islands takes 1-6 hrs, depending on the boat. Mestre Onofrio Frio in Alcobaça, Bahia, T2932195, is authorized by the Navy to take tourists. Tours also available from Abrolhos Turismo, see above, Caravelas (about US$170 for a slow 2½-day tour by *saveiro*). 1-day tours can be made in a faster boat (US$100) from Abrolhos or the Marina Porto Abrolhos.

Arembepe *p407*

Bus From Terminal Francês, **Salvador**, every 2 hrs, 1½ hrs, US$2, last bus back at 1700. Buses also run from **Itapoã**.

Praia do Forte *p407*

Bus From **Salvador** Santa Maria/Catuense leaves 5 times daily from the rodoviária, 1½ hrs, US$2. Estancia and Sergipe – 45 daily (US$5). It is easy to flag down buses from the crossroads on the main highway out of town. Take a kombi (every 15 mins, US$0.25) into town from there. Taxis are a rip-off.

Sítio do Conde *p408*

Bus From **Salvador** to Conde with São Luís, T071-3584582, 3 a day, 4 on Fri, US$7.25.

Directory

Valença *p398*

Banks There is a Bradesco and Banco do Brasil in town which have ATMs and change money.

Ilhéus and around *p400, map p421, phone code 073*

Banks Empresa de Cambio e Turismo, T6343900, will change money.

Porto Seguro *p402, map p400, phone code 073*

Banks Agência do Descobrimento, Av Getúlio Vargas, also arranges flight tickets and house rental. Banco do Brasil, Av Beira Mar, 1000-1500, changes TCs and US$ cash, also Visa ATMs. Also at airport. Bradesco, Av Getulio Vargas, Visa ATMs. Deltur, in the new shopping centre, near Banco do Brasil.

Laundry New Porto, Shopping Av, daily 0900-2230, priced per item. **Post office** In the mini-shopping on the corner of R das Jandaias and Av dos Navegantes. **Telephone** Shopping Av, daily 0700-2300, corner of Av dos Navegantes and Av Beira Mar, also at Praça dos Pataxós, beside ferry terminal. Daily 0700-2200, cheap rates after 2000, receives and holds faxes, F2883915.

Arraial da Ajuda *p404, phone code 073*
Banks There is a Banco do Brasil with a cambio and ATM in the small shopping centre on Estrada do Mucugê. Several bars on Broadway change US$ cash, but rates are poor. **Internet** Dotted throughout town. **Post office** Praça São Bras. **Telephone** Telemar on the main square. Daily 0800-2200, number for receiving faxes is F8751309, US$1.

Caravelas *p406*
Banks The Banco do Brasil, Praça Dr Imbassahi, does not change money but has an ATM.

Chapada Diamantina and the Sertão

→ *Colour map 4, A5.*

The beautiful Chapada Diamantina National Park comprises a series of escarpments swathed in tropical forest, dripping with numerous waterfalls and dotted with dramatic caverns. It is one of the highlights of inland Bahia. Although little of the forest is original, there is still much wildlife here, including jaguar and maned wolf, and the area is good for birdwatching. Various trails cut through the park offering walks of a few hours to a few days. The road from Salvador to the Chapada passes through Feira de Santana, famous for its Micareta, an extremely popular out-of-season carnival, before arriving at Lençóis. This small colonial town, once a main centre for diamond prospectors, is the most convenient base for exploring the national park.

The harsh beauty of the Sertão and its hospitable people are the reward for those wanting to get off the beaten track. The region has been scarred by droughts and a violent history of bandits, rebellions and religious leaders. Euclides da Cunha and Canudos are good places to start to explore this history. The Raso da Catarina, once a hiding place for Lampião, and the impressive Paulo Afonso waterfalls, can both be visited from the town of Paulo Afonso located on the Rio São Francisco. This important river continues through the Sertão, linking agricultural settlements such as Juazeiro, Ibotirama and Bom Jesus de Lapa before entering northern Minas Gerais. ▸▸ *For Sleeping, Eating and other listings, see pages 424-426.*

Parque Nacional da Chapada Diamantina

Palmeiras

ⓘ *Information, T075-3322175, or Ibama, Av Juracy Magalhães Junior 608, CEP 40295-140, Salvador, T071-2407322.*

About 50 km from Lençóis is this headquarters of the Parque Nacional da Chapada Diamantina (founded 1985), which contains 1,500 sq km of mountainous country. There is an abundance of endemic plants, waterfalls, large caves (take care, and a strong torch, there are no signs and caves can be hard to find without a guide), rivers with natural swimming pools and good walking tours. The park forms part of the Brazilian shield, like the Guayana Highlands, a geological remnant of when the world comprised only one land mass.

The trails in the park are often not on specially marked routes, and can involve a lot of clambering over rocks and stepping stones. A reasonable level of physical fitness is advisable. Walking boots are preferable but good training shoes are adequate. Avoid using new shoes, which give less grip on rocks. The most essential item for any trek is a flashlight with strong beam. Some of the walking may be after nightfall, but guides take trouble to avoid this. Carry mosquito repellent as there are a lot of them around in the encampment areas. (For guides and tours, see Lençois tour operators, page 426).

For overnight trips it is highly advisable to bring a sleeping bag and/or a blanket and a roll-up mattress as nights in the 'winter' months can be cold. Sometimes, guides can arrange these. A tent is useful but optional; many camps are beside reasonably hospitable caves. Matches and paper for kindling camp fires, as well as a first aid kit, are necessary.

Lençóis → *Phone code: 075. Colour map 4, A5. Population: 9,000.*

This historical monument and a colonial gem was founded in 1844 to exploit the diamonds in the region; the tents assembled by the prospectors who first arrived there looked like sheets, *lençóis* in Portuguese, when seen from the hills, hence the name. While there are still some *garimpeiros* (gold prospectors) left, it is not precious metals that draws most visitors, but the cool climate, the relaxed atmosphere and the

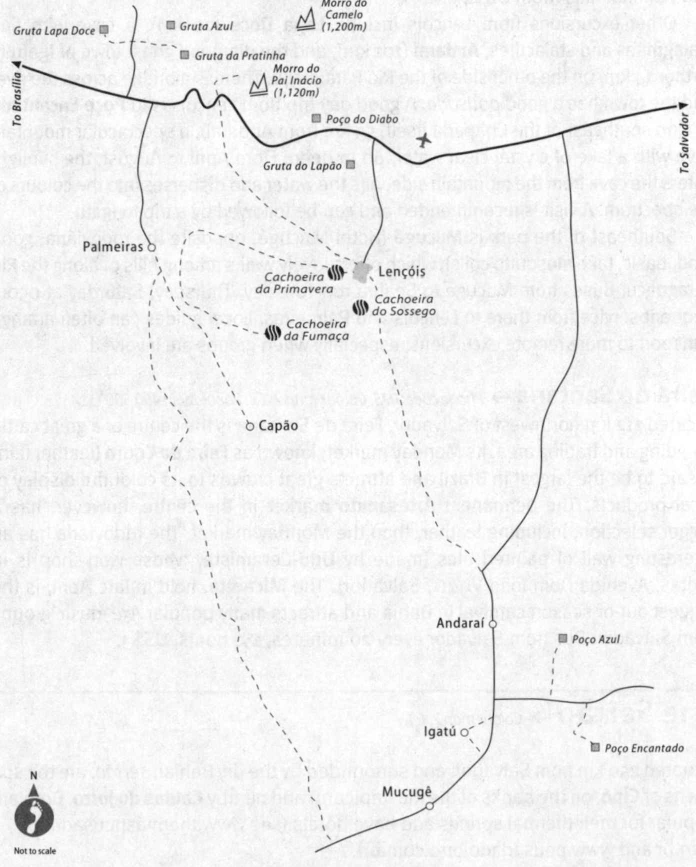

wonderful trekking in the hills of the Chapada Diamantina. This is also a good place for buying handicrafts. **Tourist information** ⓘ *Sectur, Praça Oscar Maciel, T3341327*, is next to the church across the river from town.

Around Lençóis

Near Lençóis, visit the **Serrano** with its wonderful natural pools in the riverbed, which give a great hydromassage. A little further away is the **Salão de Areia**, where the coloured sands for the bottle paintings come from. **Ribeirão do Meio** is a 45-minute walk from town; here locals bathe in the river and slide down a long natural watershute into a big pool (it is best to be shown the way it is done and to take something to slide in). **Gruta do Lapão**, three hours from Lençóis, guide essential, is in quartz rock and therefore has no stalagmites (some light rock climbing is required). **Cachoeira da Primavera**, two pretty waterfalls close to town, is recommended. **Cachoeira Sossego**, two hours from town, a waterfall where you can swim in the pool is recommended.

Morro de Pai Inácio, 30 km from Lençóis, has the best view of the Chapada, recommended at sunset (bus from Lençois at 0815, 30 minutes, US$1). In the park is the **Cachoeira da Fumaça** (Smoke Waterfall, also called **Glass**), 384 m, the highest in Brazil. To see it, go by car to the village of **Capão** and walk 2½ hours. The view is astonishing; the updraft of the air currents often makes the water flow back up, creating the 'smoke' effect. Olivia Taylor at the **Pousada dos Duendes** offers a three-day trek seeing the falls from top and bottom, the village of Capão and Capivara and Palmital falls (from US$45).

Other excursions from Lençois include **Lapa Doce** (70 km), a cave with fine stalagmites and stalactites, **Andaraí** (101 km), and the diamond ghost town of **Igatu** (a further 14 km) on the other side of the Rio Paraguaçu. There is a bridge across the river and the town has a good *pousada*. A good day trip from Lençóis is to **Poço Encantado** (23 km southeast of the Chapada itself, 55 km from Andaraí), a spectacular mountain cave with a lake of crystal-clear water, 60 m deep. From April to August, the sunlight enters the cave from the mountain side, hits the water and disperses into the colours of the spectrum. A visit is recommended and can be followed by a trip to Igatu.

Southeast of the park is **Mucugé** (**Hotel Mucugé**, opposite the rodoviária, good food, basic, take mosquito coils), which offers lovely walks among hills or along the Rio Paraguaçu. Buses from Mucugé to Seabra run Tuesday, Thursday, Saturday at 0500, frequent service from there to Lençóis and Palmeiras. Local guides can often arrange transport to more remote excursions, especially when groups are involved.

Feira de Santana → *Phone code: 075. Colour map 2, C4. Population: 450,500.*

Located 112 km northwest of Salvador, Feira de Santana is the centre of a great cattle breeding and trading area. Its Monday market, known as **Feira do Couro** (leather fair), is said to be the largest in Brazil and attracts great crowds to its colourful display of local products. The permanent **Artesanato market** in the centre, however, has a bigger selection, including leather, than the Monday market. The rodoviária has an interesting wall of painted tiles (made by **Udo-Ceramista**, whose workshop is in Brotas, Avenida Dom João VI 411, Salvador). The **Micareta**, held in late April, is the biggest out-of-season carnival in Bahia and attracts many popular *Axé* music groups from Salvador. Bus from Salvador every 20 minutes, 1½ hours, US$3.

The Sertão → *Colour map 2, C4.*

Situated 250 km from Salvador, and surrounded by the dry Bahian *sertão*, are the spa towns of **Cipó**, on the banks of the Rio Itapicuru, and nearby **Caldas do Jorro**. Both are popular for their thermal springs and have hotels (see www.thermaspousadahpg.com.br and www.pousadadojorro.com.br).

Euclides da Cunha and Monte Santo → *Phone code: 075.*

North of Feira da Santana, at Km 225 on the BR-116 road to Fortaleza, is Euclides da Cunha, a good base for exploring the Canudos area. The bus station is on the BR-116, T2711365.

About 38 km west is the famous hill shrine of **Monte Santo in the Sertão**, reached by 3½ km of steps cut into the rocks of the Serra do Picaraça. It takes about 45 minutes' walk each way, so set out early. This is the scene of pilgrimages and great religious devotion during Holy Week. The shrine was built by an Italian who had a vision of the cross on the mountain in 1765. One block north of the bottom of the stairs is the **Museu do Sertão**, with pictures from the 1897 Canudos rebellion.

Canudos → *Phone code: 075.*

Canudos itself is 100 km away. Religious rebels, led by Antônio Conselheiro, defeated three expeditions sent against them in 1897 before being overwhelmed. The Rio Vaza Barris, which runs through Canudos, has been dammed, and the town has been moved to **Nova Canudos** by the dam. Part of the old town is still located 10 km west in the **Parque Estadual de Canudos**, created in 1997. For **tourist information**, contact the **Prefeitura** ⓘ *T8942165*. There are direct buses to Canudos from Salvador.

Paulo Afonso and Parque Nacional de Paulo Afonso

→ *Phone code: 075. Colour map 2, C5. Population: 94,000.*

Part of the northern border of Bahia is formed by the Rio São Francisco. From Salvador, the paved BR-110 runs 471 km north to the river at Paulo Afonso. The town was founded in 1913 during the construction of the dam and is some distance from the falls in the Parque Nacional de Paulo Afonso. Handicrafts (embroidery, fabrics) are available from **Núcleo de Produção Artesanal** ⓘ *Av Apolônio Sales 1059*. Nearby is the **Raso da Catarina** ⓘ *T2813347*, a series of trails in the *caatinga* which was used as a hideout by the bandit Lampião; guides and a 4WD vehicle are recommended due to the heat and lack of shade. For tourist information and excursions, contact **InfoTur** ⓘ *Av Apolonio Sales s/n, T28127757*.

About 25 km northwest of Paulo Afonso is the Parque Nacional de Paulo Afonso. The **Falls of Paulo Afonso** ⓘ *in a security area with admission from 0800-1100 only by car or taxi, accompanied by a guide from the tourist information office, T2821717, 2 hrs, US$6 per car*, once one of the great cataracts of the world but now exploited for hydroelectric power, are 270 km from the mouth of the São Francisco river, which drains a valley three times the size of Great Britain. There are 2,575 km of river above the falls to its source in Minas Gerais. The 19th-century British linguist and explorer, Sir Richard Burton, took an expedition down the river and negotiated some of its treacherous rapids. Below the falls is a deep, rock gorge through which the water rushes. The national park is an oasis of trees and the lake amid a desert of brown scrub and cactus. The best time to visit the falls is in the rainy season (January-February); only then does much water pass over them, as almost all the flow now goes through the power plant. The best view is from the northern (Alagoas) bank.

The Rio São Francisco is navigable above the falls from above the twin towns (linked by a bridge) of Juazeiro, in Bahia, and Petrolina, in Pernambuco, thriving towns compared to many on the upper São Francisco. Navigation is possible as far as **Pirapora** in Minas Gerais, linked by road to the Belo Horizonte-Brasília highway (see page 269).

Juazeiro → *Phone code: 074. Colour map 2, C4. Population: 172,500.*

Juazeiro is located at an important crossroads where the BR-407 meets the Rio São Francisco. For information on river transport, T075-8112465. On the opposite bank in Pernambuco is Petrolina (see page 453). The local economy revolves around agriculture and its exportation. There is a market on Friday and Saturday and simple hotels in town (www.juazeiro.ba.gov.br). The bus from Canudos (five hours) gets crowded; buy ticket early to ensure a seat. The second half of the route is unpaved.

Xique-Xique and Ibotirama → *Phone code: 074. Colour map 2, C2.*

The next major town upriver is Xique-Xique, an agricultural town 587 km from Salvador. The remains of what may be a pre-Neanderthal man have been found in the nearby **Grotto of the Cosmos**, whose cave paintings suggest that it could well have been used as an observatory.

The next town upriver, **Ibotirama**, 650 km from Salvador on the BR-242, is famous for its fishing, especially for *surubim* and *pocomã*. There are a few moderately priced hotels with restaurants.

Bom Jesus de Lapa → *Phone code: 077. Colour map 4, A4.*

An important stop on the Rio São Francisco and 148 km from Ibotirama on the BR-242 is **Bom Jesus de Lapa**. The **Igreja Nossa Senhora da Soledad** is situated within a grotto near to Praça da Bandeira. This sanctuary, discovered by a monk in the 17th century, is the centre of a *romaria* between July and September that brings thousands of visitors to the town. There are a few places to stay and a bank in town. The airport is at Av Manuel Novais, T4814519.

Sleeping

Lençois *p421, phone code 075*

A **Portal de Lencois**, R Chacara Grota, at the top of the town,T3341233, www.portalhoteis.tur.br. 15 smart chalets in a mini-resort on the edge of the park, with a pool, sauna, restaurant, bar and play area for kids. Activities and walks organized.

A-B **Pousada de Lençóis**, R Altinha Alves 747, T/F3341102, www.hoteldelencois.com.br. Plain, dark wood and white-tiled rooms with terracota roofs organized in mock colonial terraces and set in a grassy garden on the edge of the park. Good breakfast, pool and a restaurant.

B **Canto das Águas**, Av Senhor dos Passos, T/F3341154, www.lencois.com.br. Medium-size riverside hotel with modest a/c or fan-cooled rooms, a pool and efficient service. The best rooms are in the new wing. Others can be musty.

C **Aguas Claras**, R P Benjamin, T3341471 (100 m from the rodoviaria). Simple *pousada* with plain but well-looked-after rooms; some with a fridge.

C **Fazenda Guaxo**, Rodoviária Ba 850, s/n, T3341356. Simple and tranquil mock ranch house hotel a little outside the town.

C **O Casarão**, Av 7 de Setembro 83, T3341198. Modest *pousada* with a/c or fan-cooled rooms with a fridge. Recommended.

C-D **Estalagem de Alcino**, R Gen Vieira de Morais 139, T3341171. An enchanting and beautifully restored period house with a range of rooms furnished with 19th-century antiques. Most have shared bathrooms. The superb breakfast is served in the little hummingbird-filled garden. Highly recommended.

C-D **Pousalegre**, R Boa Vista 95, T3341124. Dormitories only with hot shared showers, a tasty breakfast and a good vegetarian restaurant.

D **Casa da Geleia**, R Gen Viveiros 187, T3341151. 6 smart chalets set in a huge garden at the entrance to the town, English spoken, good breakfast (Ze Carlos is a keen birdwatcher and an authority on the region, Lia makes excellent jams).

D **Casa de Hélia**, R da Muritiba, T3341143. Attractive and welcoming little guesthouse. English spoken. Good facilities, legendary breakfast. Recommended.

D **Tradição**, R José Florêncio, T3341137. Plain rooms with TV, breakfast, fridge and mosquito nets. Friendly service.

E **Pousada dos Duendes**, R do Pires, T/F3341229. English-run *pousada* with rooms with shared showers and breakfast. Their tour agency (Saturno on R Miguel Calmon) arranges tours and treks from 1 to 11 days and more.

House rental

There are mostly very simple houses to rent

throughout Lençois. **Juanita** on R do Rosário rents rooms with access to washing and cooking facilities, US$3.50 per person. **Claudia and Isabel**, R da Baderna 95, T3341229, rent houses all over the town; both for around US$4 per person without breakfast.

Camping

Alquimia, at the entrance to Lençóis, T3341213.

Camping Lumiar, near Rosário church in the town centre, T3341241, and with a popular restaurant. Friendly, recommended.

Around Lençois *p422, phone code 075*

C **Candombá**, Capão, good breakfast, excellent food, home-grown vegetables, run by Claude and Suzana (Claude speaks French and English and guides in the region), F3322176, or through **Tatur Turismo** in Salvador (T4507216, www.tatur.com.br).

D **Pousada Verde**, at entrance to Capão. Very good breakfast. Recommended.

E **Pouso Riacho do Ou**, Capão. Simple and friendly. Recommended.

E **Tatu Feliz**, Capão. Very basic with no breakfast but adequate.

Feira de Santana *p422, phone code 075*

There are several cheap hotels in Praça da Matriz and near the rodoviária (quite near the centre).

A **Feira Palace**, Av Maria Quitéria 1572, T2215011, www.feirapalacehotel.com.br. Blocky 1970s hotel in need of renovation, but the best in town; with a restaurant and pool.

B-C **Acalanto**, R Torres 77, T6253612, www.hotelalacanto.com.br. Modern, standard, small-town hotel with around 50 modest rooms with en suites.

D **Paládio**, Av Getúlio Vargas 294, T6238899. Far less grand than its name but nonetheless well kept and less than 10 years old.

Euclides da Cunha and Monte Santo *p423, phone code 075*

B **do Conselheiro**, Av Mcal Juarez Tvora 187, Euclides, T271814. Standard town hotel with breakfast in the price.

C **Grapiuna**, Praça Monsenhor Berenguer 401, Euclides, T2751157. Basic rooms with a/c and cheaper options without bath. Recommended.

Canudos *p423, phone code 075*

E **Brasil**, Nova Canudos. Very simple rooms with en suites and fans. Cheaper without breakfast.

Paulo Afonso and Parque Nacional de Paulo Afonso *p423, phone code 075*

B **Belvedere**, Av Apolônio Sales 457, Paulo Afonso, T2813314. Plain rooms with a/, pool.

B **Grande Hotel de Paulo Afonso**, T2811914, F2811915. Parque Nacional Paulo Afonso, at the falls. A/c rooms and a pool. There are simple rooms in the adjacent guesthouse (reservations recommended).

B **Palace**, Av Apolônio Sales (next door to Belvedere), Paulo Afonso, T2814521. The best in town with a/c rooms and a pool.

Xique-Xique and Ibotirama *p424, phone code 074*

B **Carranca Grande**, Xique-Xique, Km 1, BA-052, T/F6611674. Standard blocky hotel with a pool and restaurant.

Eating

Lençois *p421, phone code 075*

ŦŦ **A Picanha da Praça**, on main *praça*. The best steaks in town.

ŦŦ **Artistas da Massa**, R Miguel Calmon. Reasonable pasta and pizza, with a sprinkling of other Italian dishes.

ŦŦ **Raizes Arte Culinaria**, R das Pedras 79. Tasty regional dishes and good service.

Ŧ **Goody**, R da Rodaviária. Very simple dishes in generous portions.

Ŧ **Lanchonette Zacão**, Main *praça*. Natural yoghurts, juices and *bolinhos de queijo*, fried balls of dough filled with melted cheese. Recommended.

Feira de Santana *p422*

ŦŦ **Panela de Barro**, R Sen Quintino 259. Good Bahian food.

Bars and clubs

Lençois *p421, phone code 075*

Bar Lençóis on the main *praça*. Good *cachaça* and *caipirinhas*. Recommended.

Clube Sete, R das Pedras. Little dance club open Fri and Sat nights.

Doce Barbaros, R das Pedras, 21. Lively little bar almost any night of the week.

Shopping

Lençois *p421, phone code 075*
Artesanato Areias Coloridas, R das Pedras, owned by Taurino, is the best place for local sand paintings made in bottles. These are inexpensive and fascinating to see being made. For ceramic work, the most original is **Jota**, who has a workshop which can be visited. Take the steps to the left of the school near the **Pousada Lençóis**. The market on Mon and Fri mornings is recommended. There are *artesanato* stalls in the main square, open every evening.

Activities and tours

Lençois *p421, phone code 075*

Tour operators

Cirtur, R da Baderna 41, T3341133, cirtur@neth.com.br. Lentur, Av 7 de Setembro 10, T/F3341271. Speak to Paulo, daily 0730-1200, 1500-2200, who organizes day trips to nearby caves and to see the sunset at Morro do Pai Inácio.

Pé de Trilha Turismo Aventura, Praça 7 de Setembro, T3341124. Guiding, trekking, rent camping equipment, etc, can make reservations for most of the *pousadas* in the Chapada Diamantina, represented in Salvador by **Tatur Turismo** (see p394).

Guides

There are many guides offering their services at most *pousadas* (about US$20-30 per trip); most of them are very young. The following are recommended:

Roy Funch, T/F3341305, royfunch@ligbr.com.br. The ex-director of the Chapada Diamantina National Park is an excellent guide and has written a visitors' guide to the park, which has just been published in English. (It is recommended as the best for information on the geography and trails of the Chapada.) Highly recommended. He can be booked through www.elabrasil.com from the USA or UK.

Trajano, contact via Casa da Helia, T3341143. Speaks and is a good-humoured guide for treks to the bottom of the Cachoeira da Fumaça.

Edmilson (known locally as Mil), R Domingos B Souza 70, T3341319. Knows the region extremely well and is very knowledgeable and reliable.

Luiz Krug, contact via **Pousada de Lençois**, T3341102. An independent guide specializing in geology and speleology (caving). He speaks English.

Índio, contact at **Pousada Diangela**, R dos Minheiros 60, Centro Histórico. Reliable, goes off the beaten track.

Ereas, R Jose Florencio 60, T3341155. The only specialist birding guide in the town.

Transport

Lençois *p421, phone code 075*
Air Airport, Km 209, BR-242, 20km from town, T6256497.

Bus Real Expresso from **Salvador** 3 times daily, US$17, *comercial*. Book in advance, especially at weekends and holidays. **Feira de Santana**, returns at 0900, 2100. Buses also from Recife, Ibotirama, Barreiras or Brasília, 16 hrs, US$33 (take irregular bus to Seabra, then 2 a day to Brasília).

Paulo Afonso and Parque Nacional de Paulo Afonso *p423*
Air The airport is 4 km from town and has flights to Recife and Salvador – see www.varig.com.br.

Bus The bus station, Av Apolônio Sales, has connections to Maceió, Recife and Salvador.

Directory

Lençois *p421, phone code 075*
Banks There are several banks with ATMs and money changing facilities in town, including a **Banco do Brasil** and a **Bradesco**.

Feira de Santana *p422, phone code 075*
Banks Banco 24 Horas, Av Senhor dos Passos 1332. **Banco do Brasil**, Av Getúlio Vargas 897.

Recife and the northeast coast

Footprint features

Introduction

The coast between Bahia and Pernambuco is overlooked by most travellers. But there is no good reason why it should be. Aracaju and Maceió, the capitals of Sergipe and Alagoas, are both laid-back, pleasant little cities surrounded by miles of gentle, sweeping beaches backed by coconut palms and washed by a bottle green sea. Maceió was the site of the most successful African rebellion in the Americas, the Quilombo das Palmares, led by the warrior Zumbi. Pernambuco, the state to the north of Alagoas, was the seat of Dutch Brazil for some 20 years and the ancestors of these denizens still inhabit the region, giving it the reputation of being the most reserved state in the northeast. But Porto de Galinhos, the state's favourite resort town with a vibrant nightlife scene, certainly doesn't seem that way; nor does Recife and its neighbouring city Olinda, which have the most creative music scene in the northeast and are famous for their wild carnival. Olinda is replete with pretty brightly painted houses and Portuguese baroque churches. Pernambuco is separated from Natal by another state which is unjustly overlooked, Paraíba, famous throughout Brazil for its São João festival and with some fascinating archaeological sites in its interior.

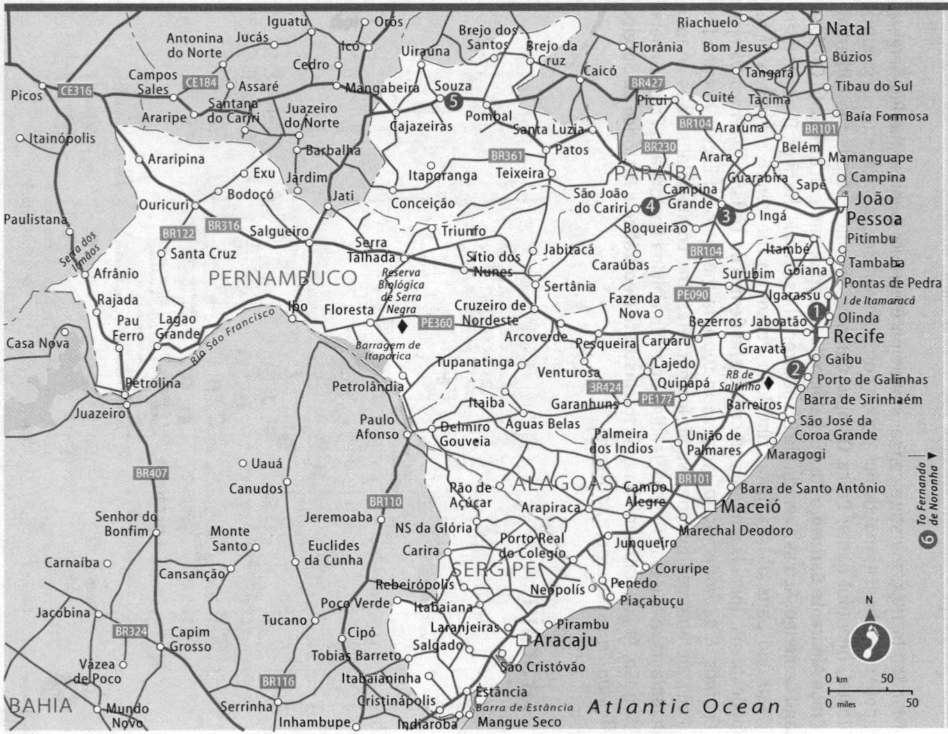

★ Don't miss...

1. **Olinda** Wander the streets of this World Heritage site, with its fine colonial buildings or come in time for the most popular carnival north of Salvador, page 446.
2. **Porto de Galinhas** Indulge yourself at the most vibrant resort on the coast with great beaches and natural low-tide swimming pools, page 449.
3. **The São João celebrations in Campina Grande, Paraíba** Let your hair down at the biggest *forró* party in Brazil, page 462.
4. **Cariri** Wonder at the haunting, mystical landscape of hollowed-out boulders strewn across a giant rocky plain in the middle of the Sertão, page 472.
5. **Souza** Follow in the footsteps of dinosaurs at one of a handful of places in the world where their imprints have been preserved in fossilized mud, page 473.
6. **Fernando de Noronha** Explore the archipelago of rugged islands set in crystal-clear waters and said by middle-class Brazilians to have the most beautiful beaches in the country, page 479.

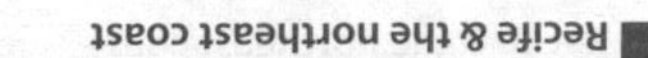

Sergipe and Alagoas

The state of Sergipe has beautiful beaches around its capital Aracaju, as well as some interesting towns such as colonial São Cristóvão and Imperial Laranjeiras, making it worth at least a short stop en route along the coastal highway between Salvador and Recife. Most of the population of Sergipe lives near the coast. The Rio São Francisco forms the border with Alagoas to the north, whilst the Rio Real defines the southern border with Bahia. The area of sertão *is quite small in this state compared with other parts of the northeast.*

The state of Alagoas has a pleasant capital, Maceió, with many beaches. There is also the interesting river culture of Penedo at the mouth of the important Rio São Francisco, which flows from Minas Gerais through the arid interior to meet the Atlantic Ocean. It is one of the poorest and least-developed states; most people live near the coastal strip and in the capital. » *For Sleeping, Eating and other listings, see pages 436-440.*

Aracaju → *Phone code: 079. Colour map 2, C5. Population: 462,600.*

Founded in 1855, the state capital stands on the south bank of the Rio Sergipe, about 10 km from its mouth and 327 km north of Salvador. In the centre is a group of linked, beautiful parks: **Praça Olímpio Campos**, in which stands the cathedral, **Praça Almirante Barroso**, with the Palácio do Governo, and praças **Fausto Cardoso** and **Camerino**. Across Avenida Rio Branco from these two is the river. The streets are clean and parts of Laranjeiras and João Pessoa in the centre are reserved for pedestrians. There is a handicraft centre, the **Centro do Turismo** ⓘ *Praça Olímpio Campos, R 24 Horas, 0900-1300, 1400-1900*, in the restored Escola Normal; the stalls are arranged by type (wood, leather, etc). The commercial area is on ruas Itabaianinha and João Pessoa, leading up to Rua Divina Pastora and Praça General Valadão. At Rua Itabaianinha 41 is the **Instituto Geográfico e Histórico de Sergipe** ⓘ *Mon-Fri 0800-1200, 1400-1700*.

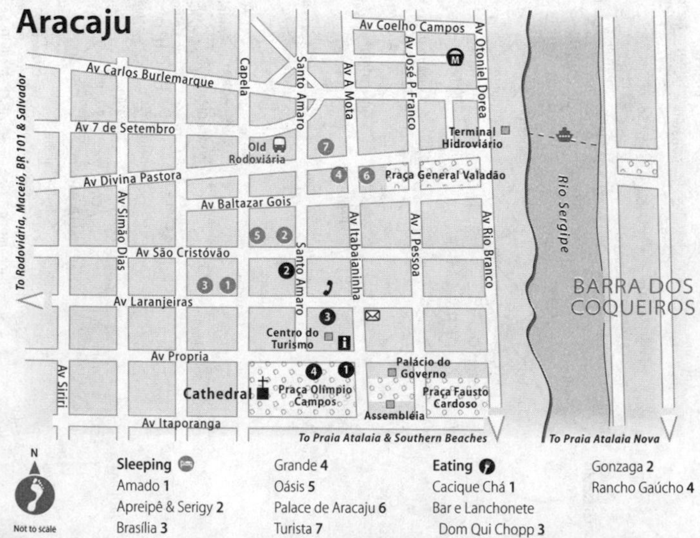

Tourist offices The **Bureau de Informações Turísticas de Sergipe** ⓘ *R 24 Horas, T2245168*, is very friendly, helpful, and has abundant leaflets. **Emsetur** ⓘ *Trav Baltazar Gois 86, Edif Estado de Sergipe, 11th-13th floors, T3171950, www.prodase.com.br/emsetur, weekdays 0700-1300* In the centre, go to **Aracatur** ⓘ *R Maruim 100, Sala 10, T2241226, F2243537*, which has leaflets and maps such as *Aracaju no bolso* and *Onde?*, helpful, English spoken.

Beaches

A 16-km road leads to the fine **Atalaia** beach (although there are oil-drilling rigs offshore). Beaches continue south down the coast along the Rodovia Presidente José Sarney. This long stretch of sand is between the mouths of the rios Sergipe and Vaza Barris; the further you go from the Sergipe, the cleaner the water. There is an even better beach, **Nova Atalaia**, on Ilha de Santa Luzia across the river. It is 30 km long and is easily reached by boat from the Hidroviária (ferry station), which is across Avenida Rio Branco from Praça General Valadão. Boats cross the river to **Barra dos Coqueiros** every 15 minutes. Services are more frequent at weekends, when it is very lively. The river at Barra dos Coqueiros is busy with fishing and pleasure craft.

Excursions from Arcaju

About 23 km northwest from Aracaju is **Laranjeiras**, a small pleasant town with a ruined church on a hill. It is reached by the São Pedro bus, from the old rodoviária in the centre of Aracaju, 30-60 minutes. It has several churches from the Imperial period, when it was an important sugar producer, although the town was originally founded in 1605. The 19th-century **Capela de Sant'Aninha** has a wooden altar inlaid with gold. There are three museums: **Museu Afro-Brasileiro** ⓘ *R José do Prado Franco 70, Tue-Fri 1000-1700, Sat and Sun 1300-1700*; **Museu Sacro** ⓘ *Praça Dr H Diniz Gonçalves, Tue-Sun 1000-1700*; and the **Centro de Cultura** ⓘ *João Ribeiro*. The town's main festival is **São Benedito** in the first week of January.

Some 70 km west of Aracaju is **Itabaiana**, which has a famous gold market on Saturday. There are a few hotels (**D**) in the centre.

São Cristóvão → *Phone code: 079. Colour map 2, C5. Population: 65,000.*

This is the old state capital of Sergipe, situated 17 km southwest of Aracaju on the road to Salvador. It was founded in 1590 by Cristóvão de Barros and is the fourth oldest town in Brazil. Built on top of a hill, its colonial centre is unspoiled, the majority of buildings painted white with green shutters and woodwork.

The **Museu de Arte Sacra e Histórico de Sergipe** ⓘ *Tue-Fri 1000-1700, Sat and Sun 1300-1700*, in the **Convento de São Francisco** contains religious and other objects from the 17th-19th centuries. Also worth visiting (and keeping the same hours) is the **Museu de Sergipe** in the former **Palácio do Governo**; both are on Praça de São Francisco. On the same square are the churches of **Misericórdia** (1627) and the **Orfanato Imaculada Conceição** (1646, permission to visit required from the Sisters), and the **Convento de São Francisco**.

On Praça Senhor dos Passos are the churches of **Senhor dos Passos** and **Terceira Ordem do Carmo** (both 1739), while on the Praça Getúlio Vargas (formerly Praça Matriz) is the 17th-century **Igreja Matriz Nossa Senhora da Vitória** ⓘ *all are open Tue-Fri 1000-1700, Sat-Sun 1500-1700*. Also worth seeing is the old **Assembléia Legislativa** ⓘ *R Coronel Erundino Prado*.

Estância → *Phone code: 079. Population: 57,000.*

Estância is 247 km north of Salvador, on the BR-101, almost midway between the Sergipe-Bahia border and Aracaju. It is one of the oldest towns in Brazil. Its colonial buildings are decorated with Portuguese tiles (none are open to the public). Its heyday was at the turn of the 20th century and it was one of the earliest places to get electricity and telephones. Estância is also called Cidade Jardim because of its parks. The month-long festival of São João in June is a major event.

Maceió → *Phone code: 082. Colour map 2, C6. Population: 780,000.*

The capital of the state of Alagoas is a friendly city with a low crime rate. It is mainly a sugar port, although there are also tobacco exports and a major petrochemical plant. A lighthouse (*farol*) stands in a residential area of town, about 1 km from the sea. The commercial centre stretches along the seafront to the main dock and climbs the hills behind.

Ins and outs

Getting there Flights arrive at Campos dos Palmares airport, 20 km from the centre. Taxis to the centre charge about US$20. Interstate buses arrive at the rodoviária, 5 km from the centre. Luggage store is available. Take bus marked 'Ouro Preto p/centro' (taxi quicker, US$7) to Pajuçara. ▸▸ *See also Transport, page 439.*

Getting around The commercial centre is easy to walk around but you need to take a bus to the main hotel and beach area of the city at Pajuçara. Frequent buses, confusingly marked, serve all parts of the city. Bus stops are not marked; it is best to ask where people look as if they are waiting. The ferroviária is in the centre, Rua Barão de Anádia 121. Train services are suburban.

Sights

Two of the city's old buildings, the **Palácio do Governo**, which also houses **Fundação Pierre Chalita** (Alagoan painting and religious art) and the church of **Bom Jesus dos Mártires** (1870 – covered in tiles), are particularly interesting. Both are on the Praça dos Martírios (or Floriano Peixoto). The **cathedral**, Nossa Senhora dos Prazeres (1840) is on Praça Dom Pedro II.

The **Instituto Histórico e Geográfico** ⓘ *R João Pessoa 382, T2237797*, has a good small collection of indigenous and Afro-Brazilian artefacts.

Lagoa do Mundaú, a lagoon, whose entrance is 2 km south at **Pontal da Barra**, limits the city to the south and west: excellent shrimp and fish are sold at its small restaurants and handicraft stalls; it's a nice place for a drink at sundown. Boats make excursions in the lagoon's channels (T2317334).

Beaches

Beaches fronting the old city, between the Salgema terminal and the modern port area (Trapiche, Sobral), are too polluted for swimming. Beyond the city's main dock, the beachfront districts begin; within the city, the beaches are more exclusive the further from the centre you go. The first, going north, is **Pajuçara** where there is a nightly craft market. At weekends there are wandering musicians and entertainers and patrols by the cavalry on magnificent Manga Larga Marchador horses. There are periodic *candomblé* and *axé* nights and rituals to the goddess Iemanjá. Next is Ponta Verde, then Jatiúca, Cruz das Almas, Jacarecica (9 km from the centre), Guaxuma (12 km), Garça Torta (14 km), Riacho Doce (16 km), Pratagi (17 km) and Ipioca (23 km). Jatiúca, Cruz das Almas and Jacarecica are all good for surfing. The beaches, some of the finest and most popular in Brazil, have a protecting coral reef 1 km or so out. Bathing is much better three days before and after a full or new moon, because tides are higher and the water is more spectacular. ▸▸ *For beaches beyond the city, see Excursions from Maceió below.*

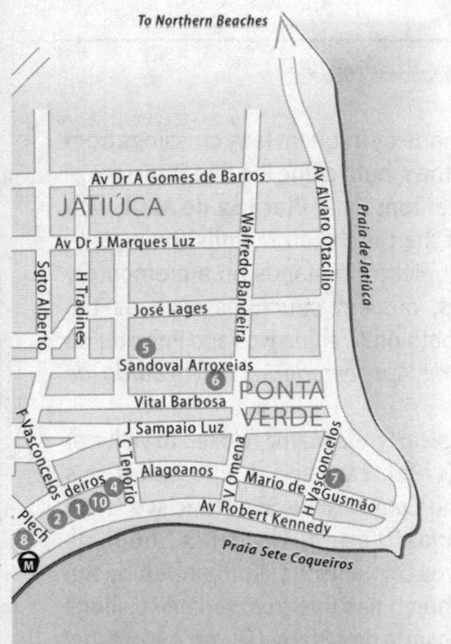

There is a natural swimming pool 2 km off Pajuçara beach (**Piscina Natural de Pajuçara**), at low tide you can stand on the sand and rock reef (beware of sunburn). You must check the tides, there is no point going at high tide. *Jangadas* cost US$5 per person per day (or about US$20 to have a *jangada* to yourself). On Sunday or local holidays in the high season it is overcrowded. At weekends lots of *jangadas* anchor at the reef, selling food and drink.

For tourist information, **Ematur** ⓘ *Av da Paz 2014, Centro, T2219465, F2218987*, also at the airport and rodoviária. Helpful, has good maps and leaflets. The municipal tourist authority is **Emturma** ⓘ *R Saldanha da Gama 71, Farol, T2234016*; information post on Pajuçara beach, opposite **Hotel Solara**.

Excursions from Maceió

Marechal Deodoro

About 22 km south, by bus past Praia do Francês, is the attractive colonial town and former capital of Alagoas, Marechal Deodoro, which overlooks the Lagoa Manguaba.

Schistosomiasis is present in the lagoon.

The 17th-century **Convento de São Francisco**, Praça João XXIII, has a fine church (Santa Maria Magdalena) with a superb baroque wooden altarpiece, which has been badly damaged by termites. You can climb the church's tower for views. Adjoining it is the **Museu de Arte Sacra**. ⓘ *Mon-Fri, 0900-1300, US$0.30, guided tours available, payment at your discretion.* Also open to visitors is the **Igreja Matriz de Nossa Senhora da Conceição** (1783).

The town is the birthplace of Marechal Deodoro da Fonseca, founder of the Republic; the modest **house** ⓘ *R Marechal Deodoro, Mon-Sat 0800-1700, Sun 0800-1200, free,* where he was born is close to the waterfront. The *Restaurant São Roque* is simple but good and good local lacework can be bought.

On a day's excursion, it is easy to visit the town, then spend some time at beautiful **Praia do Francês**. The northern half of the beach is protected by a reef, the southern half is open to the surf. Along the beach there are many *barracas* and bars selling drinks and seafood; try *agulhas fritas*.

Further out from Maceió is the beach of **Barra de São Miguel**, entirely protected by the reef. It gets crowded at weekends. You can make excursions to other beaches. Several good, cheap *barracas* serve food and drink (**da Amizade**, recommended). Carnival here has a good reputation. The **Village Barra Hotel** ⓘ *R Sen Arnon de Mello, T2721207* (**A**), has a pool, restaurant and runs excursions. The **Pousada da Barra is good.**

Penedo → *Phone code: 082. Colour map 2, C5. Population: 57,000.*

A more interesting crossing into Alagoas can be made by frequent ferry crossings from **Neópolis** in Sergipe, to Penedo some 35 km from the mouth of the Rio São Francisco.

Penedo is a charming town, with a nice waterfront park, **Praça 12 de Abril**, with stone walkways and walls. Originally the site of the Dutch Fort Maurits (built 1637, razed to the ground by the Portuguese), the colonial town stands on a promontory above the river. Among the colonial buildings, modern structures such as the **Associação Comercial** and **Hotel São Francisco,** both on Avenida Floriano Peixoto, do not sit easily. There's a **tourist office** ⓘ *Casa da Aposentadoria, Praça Barão de Penedo, T5512827, ext 23.*

On the Praça Barão de Penedo is the neoclassical Igreja Matriz (closed to visitors) and the 18th-century **Casa da Aposentadoria** (1782). East and a little below this square is the Praça Rui Barbosa, on which are the **Convento de São Francisco** (1783 and later) and the church of **Santa Maria dos Anjos** ⓘ *free guided tours* (1660). As you enter, the altar on the right depicts God's eyes on the world, surrounded by the three races (indigenous, black and white). The church has fine *trompe-l'oeil* ceilings (1784). The convent is still in use. The church of **Rosário dos Pretos** ⓘ *Praça Marechal Deodoro* (1775-1816), is open to visitors as are **Nossa Senhora da Corrente** ⓘ *Praça 12 de Abril* (1764), and **São Gonçalo Garcia** ⓘ *Av Floriano Peixoto, Mon-Fri 0800-1200, 1400-1700* (1758-70). On the same street is the pink **Teatro 7 de Setembro** ⓘ *Av Floriano Peixoto 81, Mon-Fri 0800-1200, 1400-1730, Sat am only* (1884). Between it and the old covered market are fruit and vegetable stalls.

The **Casa de Penedo** ⓘ *R João Pessoa 126, T5512516, Tue-Sun 0800-1800* (signs point the way up the hill from Floriano Peixoto), displays photographs and books on, or by, local figures.

The slave state of Palmares

From the introduction of African slaves to northeast Brazil, fujões (runaways) would disappear into the interior and set up villages or mocambos. Between the 1630s and the end of 17th century the *mocambos* prospered – especially during times of crisis such as the Dutch invasion in 1630 – and together formed quilombos, free territories which accepted not only runaway slaves but also freed ones and whites who had fallen out with the re-established Portuguese colony. The most famous of these *quilombos*, established in what is now the state of Alagoas, was called Palmares after the large number of palm trees in the area. It consisted of 30,000 people living in several *mocambos* in an area of 17,000 square miles (44,000 sq km). According to reports from Bartholomeus Lintz, the leader of a Dutch expedition in 1640, the largest settlement in Palmares had 220 buildings, a church, four smithies and a meeting house.

The political and social structures were very similar to those found in West Africa, and although Catholicism was practised, so was polyandry, mainly due to the lack of women in the republic. The leader of Palmares was one Ganga-Zumba who was revered like a king. But it appears he was killed by his followers in 1680 after making some concessions to the Portuguese two years earlier; he was succeeded by the republic's brave military commander, Zumbi. The existence of Palmares was a constant thorn in the side of Portuguese domination of Brazil and dozens of attempts were made to destroy it. However, Zumbi managed to defend the republic until it was finally smashed by the Portuguese with bandeirante help in 1695. Zumbi was killed and his decaptitated head was put on display in Recife to discourage other potential runaways and prove that he was not immortal as his followers believed. He is still remembered every year on 20 November, Brazil's Black Conciousness Day. He has also become a popular theme at Carnival time.

The site of the Palmares Republic is situated on the Serra da Barriga, close to modern União do Palmares in Alagoas state, reached by driving north out of Maceió on the BR-101, turning left after Messias and driving for 40 km along a paved road. There is one hotel, Parque Hotel dos Quilombos, T2811135, on the BR-104 towards Recife, TV, a/c, fridge, restaurant.

Very few of the long two-masted sailing vessels that used to cruise on the river can be seen now, although there are plenty of smaller craft. **Beaches** in Sergipe (for example, Arambipe) or Alagoas (for example, Peba) can be reached by boat; the latter also by road. Either side of the river mouth are turtle nesting grounds which are protected. For information contact the **Fundação Pró-Tamar** ⓘ *Reserva Biológica de Santa Isabel, CEP 49190-000, Pirambu, SE, T079-2761201, F2761217.*

North of Maceió

There are many interesting stopping points along the coast between Maceió and Recife. At **Paripueira**, 40 minutes' bus ride from Maceió (rodoviária), the beach is busy only during high season. As at Pajuçara (see page 433), low tide leaves lots of natural swimming pools.

Barra de Santo Antônio

Some 45 km north is this busy fishing village, with a palm-fringed beach on a narrow peninsula, a canoe ride away. The beaches nearby are beautiful: to the south, near the village of Santa Luzia, are Tabuba and Sonho Verde. To the north is Carro Quebrado, from which you can take a buggy to Pedra do Cebola, or further to Prala do Morro, just before the mouth of the Rio Camaragibe.

Beyond Barra do Camaragibe, a coastal road, unpaved in parts, runs to the Pernambuco border and São José da Coroa Grande. The main highway, BR-101, heads inland from Maceió before crossing the state border to Palmares.

Sleeping

Aracaju *p430, map p430, phone code 079*

A **Apreipê**, R São Cristóvão 418, T2111880. Centrally located with restaurant. Rooms include a/c, phone and fridge.

A **Palace de Aracaju**, Praça Gen Valadão, T2245000. Centrally located 3-star hotel with a/c, TV and fridge in the rooms. The hotel includes a pool, restaurant and parking facilities.

A **Grande**, R Itabaianinha 371, T/F2111383. Centrally located with restaurant. A/c, TV, and fridge in the rooms.

A **Serigy**, R Santo Amaro 269, T2111088. A comfortable hotel with the same management and facilities as the Aperipê.

B **Brasília**, R Laranjeiras 580, T2248022. Modest hotel but good value and with a good breakfast. Recommended.

B **Oásis**, R São Cristóvão 466, T2242125. Good breakfast, hot water, fair, a bit tatty.

C **Amado**, R Laranjeiras 532. A/c rooms, cheaper with a fan and laundry facilities.

D **Turista**, R Divina Pastora 411. Noisy, mosquitoes, no hot water or breakfast but at least it's friendly.

Laranjeiras *p431, phone code 079*

B **Pousada Vale dos Outeiros**, Av José do Prado Franco 124, Laranjeiras, T2811027. One of several hotels in town, this one with 10 a/c rooms and a restaurant. Recommended.

São Cristóvão *p431, phone code 079*

There are no hotels, but families rent rooms near the rodoviária at the bottom of the hill.

Estância *p431, phone code 079*

There are a number of cheap, very simple hotels around the Praça Barão do Rio Branco.

C **Jardim**, Praça Joaquim Galazans 202, T5221638. A modern hotel with a/c. They serve a huge buffet breakfast. Recommended.

C **Turismo Estanciano**, Praça Barão do Rio Branco 176, T5221404. A modest and very standard blocky town hotel with fan and a/c rooms, some with en suites.

D **Magnus**, T5222453. Breakfast. Rooms include TV and fridge.

D **Praia Abais**, T7510020. Breakfast, TV, pool.

D **Sawana**, T9851570. With own restaurant.

Maceió *p432, map p432, phone code 082*

There are many hotels on Praia Pajuçara, mostly along Av Dr Antônio Gouveia and R Jangadeiros Alagoanos. It can be hard to find a room during the Dec-Mar holiday season, when prices go up.

L **Matsubara**, on Cruz das Almas beach, Av Brig Eduardo Gomes 1551, T2353000, www.matsubarahotel.com. Resort hotel with a large pool, tennis courts and organized games. Recommended.

L **Tambaqui Praia**, R Eng Mário de Gusmão 176, Ponta Verde beach, T2310202. Rooms with a/c, TV, phone and there is a restaurant.

AL **Enseada**, Av A Gouveia 171, T2314726, www.enseada.com.br. 1980s business hotel on the waterfront with a pool and restaurant. Recommended.

AL **Sete Coqueiros**, Av A Gouveia 1335, T2318583, www.setecoqueiros.com.br. 3-star hotel with a/c, rooms with TVs and a phone. There is a pool and a popular restaurant.

A **Velamar**, Av A Gouveia 1359 (next door to the Coqueiros), T3275488, www.hotelvelamar.com.br. A/c rooms with a TV, fridge, and safes in rooms.

B **Buongiorno**, Av A Gouveia 1437, T2317577, F2312168. Rooms have a/c and fridge. The English-speaking owner is very helpful.

C **Amazona**, Av A Gouveia 1095. Modest and ordinary town hotel with a great breakfast.

C **Baleia Azul**, Av Sandoval Arroxeias 822, Ponta Verde beach, 3274040, www.hotelbaleiaazul.com.br. Plain rooms with a/c, fridge and TV.

C **Casa Grande da Praia**, Av A Gouveia 1528, T2313332. A/c and TV available but cheaper without. Recommended.

C **Costa Verde**, Av A Gouveia 429, T2314745. A good family atmosphere here. Rooms have bath and fan. English, German spoken. The rooms on 1st floor are the best.

C **Hospedaria de Turismo Costa Azul**, Av João Davino and Manoel Gonçalves Filho 280, not close to town centre, T2316281. Rooms with a shower and fan and discounts for stays over a week. English spoken.

C **Pousada Bela Vista**, Av Eng Mário de Gusmão 1260, Ponta Verde beach, T2318337. Well situated, excellent breakfast, a/c, TV. Recommended.

C **Pousada Cavalo Marinho**, R da Praia 55, Riacho Doce (15 km from the town centre), facing the sea, T/F2351247. Friendly *pousada* popular with twenty-something surfers with bike canoes and body-board rental. Rooms have hot showers. German and English spoken, tropical breakfasts, Swiss owner. Very highly recommended. There are some bars and restaurants nearby.

C **Pousada Shangri-La**, Antônio de Mendonça 1089, T2313773. Simple hotel with friendly staff, a/c rooms with optional safes.

D **Mandacaru**, Almte Maranenhas 85, 2 corners from the beach. Safe with simple rooms with fans, but good value.

D **Pousada Saveiro**, No 805. Clean, simple, good value. Rooms available with a/c, bath and TV but it's cheaper without a/c.

D **Sol de Verão**, R Eng Mário do Gusmão 153, Ponta Verde beach. Small rooms without baths and some lager and more expensive a/c options with en suites.

E **Nossa Casa**, R Pref Abdon Arroxelas 327, Ponta Verde, T2312246. IYHA youth hostel. Reservations required Dec-Feb, Jul and Aug.

E **Pajuçara**, R Quintino Bocaiúva 63, Pajuçara, T2310631. Youth hostel. Reservations required Dec-Feb, Jul and Aug.

E **Stella Maris**, Av Des Valente de Lima 209, Mangabeiras, T3252217. Reservations required Dec-Feb, Jul and Aug.

Camping

Camping Clube do Brasil site on Jacarecica beach, T2353600. A 15-min taxi drive from the town centre.

Camping Pajuçara, Largo da Vitória 211, T2317561. Clean, safe, food for sale. Recommended.

Marechal Deodoro *p434, phone code 082*

B **Pousada Bougainville e Restaurant Chez Patrick**, R Sargaço 3 T2601251. A very nice *pousada* with a/c, rooms with TVs, a pool, seafood and international cooking.

C **O Pescador**, 40 m from Praia do Francês, T2316959. Restaurant, beach huts, chalets with fridge, TV.

Penedo *p434, phone code 082*

A **São Francisco**, Av Floriano Peixoto, T5512273, F5512274. A/c provided except in standard rooms. TV and fridge also available. Recommended except for poor restaurant.

B **Pousada Colonial**, Praça 12 de Abril 21, T5512355, F5513099. A spacious *pousada* with a good cheap restaurant. The front rooms have a view of Rio São Francisco, the *luxo* rooms and suites have phone, TV and fridge and the suites a/c.

D **Turista**, R Siqueira Campos 143, T5512237. Simple rooms with a bath, fan and hot water. Recommended.

Barra de Santo Antônio *p436*

This is a tiny place with no visible addresses. Locals will point you to *pousadas* but it is a struggle to get lost.

D **São Geraldo**. Very simple but very clean, and with a restaurant.

D-E **Pousada Buongiorno**, T2317577, F2312168 (in Maceió). 6 modest rooms to rent in a farmhouse, bathrooms but no electricity, many fruit trees.

Eating

Aracaju *p430, map p430, phone code 079*

TTT **O Miguel**, Av António Alves 340, Atalaia Velha, T2431444. Much the best restaurant in the city, serving regional food, which is heavy on meat and includes carne de sol – a type of jerky cooked in to a stew.

TT **Cacique Chá**, in the cathedral square. Good bar and restaurant. Lively at weekends.

ŸŸ **Rancho Gaúcho**, Praça Olímpio Campos 692. Reasonable and very friendly *churrascaria*.
ŸŸ-Ÿ **Cantinha da Bahia**, Av Oceânica 180. Recommended for fresh crab and other seafood.
Ÿ **Bar e Lanchonete Dom Qui Chopp**, opposite Telemar on Rua Laranjeiras. Very popular simple snack bar serving beer and drinks.
Ÿ **Gonzaga**, R Santo Amaro 181. Lunch only, good value, very popular, excellent traditional dishes.

São Cristóvão *p431, phone code 079*
Ÿ **Senzala do Preto Velho**, R Messias Prado 84. Recommended for Northeastern specialities.

Maceió *p432, map p432, phone code 082*
There are many good bars and restaurants in Pajuçara and Av Antônio Gouveia. The beaches for 5 km, from the beginning of Pajuçara to Cruz das Almas in the north, are lined with *barracas* (thatched bars) providing music, snacks and meals until midnight (later at weekends). Vendors on the beach sell beer and food during the day; clean and safe. There are many other bars and *barracas* at Ponto da Barra, on the lagoon side of the city. Local specialities include oysters, *pitu*, a crayfish (now becoming scarce), and *sururu*, a kind of cockle. Local ice-cream, Shups, is recommended.
ŸŸŸ **Ao Lagostão**, Av Duque de Caxias 1348. Seafood and a fixed price menu.
Ÿ **Nativa**, Osvaldo Sarmento 56. Similar to O Natural but with good views.
Ÿ **O Natural**, R Libertadora Alagoana (R da Praia) 112. Reasonable vegetarian restaurant with a choice of hot and cold dishes.
Ÿ **Pizzeria Sorrisa**, Av Alagoana and J Pessoa Imperador. Very cheap and popular with good pizzas and Italian food.

Barra de Santo Antônio *p436, phone code 082*
ŸŸ **Estrela Azul**, more expensive, good, popular with tourists.
Ÿ **Peixada da Rita**, try prawns with coconut sauce. Recommended for local seafood.

Bars and clubs

Aracaju *p430, map p430, phone code 079*
Augustu's, T2432274. Nightclub, closed Mon.
Espaço Ernes, Av Tancredo Neves 225, T2319138. Venue for live shows.
Gonzagao, Av Heraclito Rollemberg. Live shows.

Maceió *p432, map p432, phone code 082*
The bars here are relaxed and varied and there are nightclubs to suit most tastes. are 3 popular *barracas* are:
Bar Lampião (or **Tropical**) and **Ipaneminha**, Pajuçara. Brazilian pop.
Fellini, Ponta Verde. Good blues and jazz.
Calabar, in Pajuçara, for *forró* and *lambada*.
Lambadão at Cruz das Almas. Excellent *lambada*, weekends only.
Bar Chapéu de Couro, José Carneiro 338, Ponto da Barra. A popular music bar for young people

Entertainment

Aracaju *p430, map p430, phone code 079*
Cinema 10-screen **Cinemark**, in Shopping Jardins.

Maceió *p432, map p 432, phone code 082*
Cinema **Cinema São Luiz**, R do Comércio, in the centre. **Arte 1 and 2**, Pajuçara and Iguatemi shopping centres.
Theatre **Teatro Deodoro**, Praça Mcal Deodoro, in the centre.

Festivals and events

Aracaju *p430, map p430, phone code 079*
1 Jan Bom de Jesus dos Navegantes, procession on the river.
1st weekend in Jan Santos Reis (Three Kings).
Jun Festas Juninas.
8 Dec Both Catholic (Nossa Senhora da Conceição) and Umbanda (*Iemenjá*) religious festivals.

São Cristóvão *p431, phone code 079*
Mar Senhor dos Passos is held 15 days after Carnival.

For an explanation of the sleeping and eating price codes used in this guide, see the inside front cover. Other relevant information is provided in the Essentials chapter, pages 47 and 57.

8 Sep Nossa Senhora de Vitória, the patron saint's day.
Oct/Nov The town holds a Festival de Arte (the date varies).

Maceió *p432, map p432, phone code 082*
27 Aug Nossa Senhora dos Prazeres.
16 Sep Freedom of Alagoas.
8 Dec Nossa Senhora da Conceição.
15 Dec Maceiofest, a great street party with *trios elêctricos*.
24 Dec Christmas Eve.
31 Dec New Year's Eve, half-day.

Shopping

Aracaju *p430, map p430, phone code 079*
The *artesanato* is interesting: pottery figures and lace particularly. See **Centro de Turismo**, p430. A fair is held in Praça Tobias Barreto every Sun afternoon. The municipal market is a block north of the Hidroviária.

Penedo *p434, phone code 082*
Daily market on streets off Av Floriano Peixoto, good hammocks. Ceramics for sale outside Bompreço supermarket, on Av Duque de Caxias.

Activities and tours

Maceió *p432, map p432, phone code 082*
Aeroturismo, R Barão de Penedo 61, T3262020, F2214546, American Express representative.

Transport

Aracaju *p430, map p430, phone code 079*
Air Santa Maria airport, 11 km from the centre, on Av Sen Júlio César Leite, Atalaia, T2431388. Flights to Maceió, Rio de Janeiro and Salvador.

Airline offices Vasp, T2432535.

Bus Local: Look for route plates on the side of buses and at bus stations in town. The old bus terminal in town is at Santo Amaro and Divina Pastora, Praça João XXIII. Buses from here to **Laranjeiras** and **São Cristóvão** (45 mins, US$1.25).

Long distance Interstate buses arrive at the rodoviária, 4 km from the centre, linked by local buses from the adjacent terminal (buy a ticket before going on to the platform). Bus 004 'T Rod/L Batista' goes to the centre, US$0.50. Buses go from Praça João XXIII, the terminal near the Hidroviária and from Capela at the top of Praça Olímpio Campos.

To **Salvador**, 6-7 hrs, 11 a day with Bonfim, US$11, executive service at 1245, US$14, saves 1 hr. To **Maceió**, US$9 with Bonfim. Many coastal destinations served; also **Vitória** (US$26.50), **Rio** (US$51), **São Paulo**, **Belo Horizonte** (US$35). To **Estância**, US$2, 1½ hrs. To **Recife**, 7 hrs, US$12-14, 1200 and 2400

São Cristóvão *p431, phone code 079*
Bus São Pedro buses depart from the old rodoviária in the centre of **Aracaju**, see above.

Train A tourist train runs between **Aracaju** and São Cristóvão each Sat and Sun, 0900, 3½ hrs, T2113003 to check it is running – a minimum of 15 passengers is needed.

Estância *p431, phone code 079*
Bus Many buses stop at the rodoviária, on the main road. Bus from **Salvador** 4 hrs, US$12-14.

Maceió *p432, map p432, phone code 079*
See also Ins and outs, p432.
Air Airport, BR-101, 20 km north, T3221300. Flights to Aracaju, Recife, Rio de Janeiro, Salvador and São Paulo. Taxi about US$25. Buses to airport from near Hotel Beiriz, R João Pessoa 290 or in front of the Ferroviária, signed 'Rio Largo'; alight at Tabuleiro dos Martins, then 7-8 mins' walk to the airport, bus fare US$0.75.

Bus Local: the 'Ponte Verde/Jacintinho' bus runs via Pajuçara from the centre to the rodoviária, also take 'Circular' bus (25 mins Pajuçara to rodoviária). Taxis from town go to all the northern beaches (for example 30 mins to Riacho Doce), but buses run as far as Ipioca. The Jangadeiras bus marked 'Jacarecica-Center, via Praias' runs past all the beaches as far as **Jacarecica**. From there you can change to 'Riacho Doce-Trapiche', 'Ipioca' or 'Mirante' buses for Riacho Doce and Ipioca. These last 3 can also be caught in the centre on the seafront avenue below the Praça Sinimbu (US$0.50 to Riacho Doce). To return take any of these options, or take a bus marked 'Shopping Center' and change there for 'Jardim Vaticana' bus, which goes through Pajuçara.

Bus and kombi: to **Marechal Deodoro**, **Praia do Francês** and **Barra de São Miguel** leave from R Barão de Anádia, outside the *ferroviária*, opposite **Lojas Americanas**: bus US$0.75, kombi US$1 to Marechal Deodoro, 30 mins, calling at Praia do Francês in each direction. Last bus back from Praia do Francês to Maceió at 1800.

Long distance The rodoviária is on a hill with good views. Bus to **Recife**, 10 a day, 3½ hrs express (more scenic coastal route, 5 hrs), US$9. To **Aracaju**, US$9, 5 hrs (potholed road). To **Salvador**, 10 hrs, 4 a day, US$20 (*rápido* costs more).

Car hire Localiza, Av Alvaro Otacilio 6445, Jatiuca, T3256565/6553. Rotacar, R Quintino Bocaiuva 123, Pajucara, T3273388.

Penedo *p434, phone code 082*

Bus **Salvador**, 451 km (US$12-14, 6 hrs, by daily bus at 0600, book in advance), at same time for **Aracaju** (US$6); buses south are more frequent from Neópolis, 6 a day (0630-1800) to Aracaju, 2 hrs, US$3.60. **Maceió**, 115 km, 5 buses a day in either direction, US$5.40-6.60, 3-4 hrs. The rodoviária is on Av Duque de Caxias, behind Bompreço.

Ferry Frequent launches for foot passengers and bicycles across the river to **Neópolis**, 25 mins, US$0.50. The dock in Penedo is on Av Duque de Caxias, below Bompreço. The ferry makes 3 stops in Neópolis, the 2nd is closest to the rodoviária (which is near the **Clube Vila Nova**, opposite the Texaco station). There is also a half-hourly car ferry (US$3, take care when driving on and off).

Directory

Aracaju *p430, map p430, phone code 079*

Banks Visa ATMs at Shopping centres, Banco do Brasil, Praça Gen Valadão and Bradesco in the city centre. MasterCard ATMs at Banco 24 hours, Av Francisco Porto and Av Geraldo Sobral, in the city centre close to the Shell gas station. **Embassies and consulates** France, T2248610. Italy, T2433814. Portugal, T2226662. **Medical services** Clinica São Domingos Savio, T2111344, casualty department. São Lucas, R Col Stanley Silveira 33, São José, T2111738. Dental emergencies: Pronto Odonto, Av Barão de Maruim, T2222927. **Post office** Laranjeiras and Itabaianinha. **Telephone** Laranjeiras 296, national and international calls until 2200, also at rodoviária.

Maceió *p432, map p432, phone code 082*

Banks Open 1000-1500. Good rates at Banespa. Cash against MasterCard at Banorte, R de Comércio, 306, Centro. **Embassies and consulates** France, T2352830. Portugal, T3364564. Spain, T2412516. **Laundry** Lave-Sim, R Jangadas Alagoanas 962, Pajuçara. Washouse, R Jangadas Alagoanas 698, Pajuçara. **Medical services** Unimed, Av Antonio Brandao 395, Farol, T2211177, used to be São Sebastião hospital. Pediatria 24 horas, R Durval Guimaraes 519, Ponta Verde, T2317742/7702. Dentist: Pronto Socorro Odontologico de Maceio, Av Pio XV11, Jatiuca, T3257534. **Post office** R João Pessoa 57, Centro, 0700-2200. **Telephones** R do Comércio 508, almost opposite Bandepe. There is a small post on Pajuçara beach, opposite the Othon hotel. Also at the rodoviária.

Penedo *p434, phone code 082*

Banks Open 0830-1300. Banco do Nordeste do Brasil, on Av Floriano Peixoto. Banco do Brasil and Bradesco on Av Duque de Caxias, opposite Bompreço supermarket. Restaurant e Bar Lulu, Praça 12 de Abril, will change cash if conditions suit the owner, fair rates. **Post office** Av Floriano Peixoto, opposite Hotel Imperial. **Telephone** On Barão de Penedo.

Pernambuco

Once producer of all the world's sugar, today the state of Pernambuco offers a variety of attractions from beaches, traditional culture, colonial cities and museums. Recife, the state capital, is the main industrial and commercial centre, while Olinda has colonial elegance and imposing churches. Towns such as Caruaru in the agreste, *the region between the coast and the* sertão, *have distinctive regional fairs selling clay, straw and leather handicrafts. Pernambuco is saturated with music, from the rustic forms of* forró *to the urban mixes of* maracatu *with modern pop which spawned bands that have influenced mainstream Brazilian muslc and fortified Northeastern pride. Carnival here is distinctive, a mixture of Latino party atmosphere and African cultural processions, all set to the backdrop of breathtaking colonial architecture.* *▸▸ For Sleeping, Eating and other listings, see pages 453-466.*

Recife → *Phone code: 081. Colour map 2, B6. Population: 1.2 million.*

Recife is a major city and the gateway to the Northeast. It is a popular tourist destination thanks to its beaches, historical monuments and its close neighbour Olinda. Spending carnival here is a good option.

Ins and outs

Getting there International and domestic flights arrive at Guararapes airport in the hotel district of Boa Viagem (airport taxis US$5 to the seafront) and 12 km from the city. Bus to airport, No 52, US$0.40. There is a bank desk before customs which gives much the same rate for dollars as the moneychangers in the lobby.

Unlike just about every other city, Recife's airport is central and its bus station is in the suburbs. Long-distance buses arrive at the Terminal Integrado dos Passageiros, or TIP (pronounced 'chippy'), 12 km outside the city. There is a 30-min Metrô connection to the central railway station. The train to the centre is much quicker than the bus. *▸▸ For more information, see Transport, page 463.*

Getting around The city centre consists of three sections: Recife proper, Santo Antônio and São José, and Boa Vista and Santo Amaro. The first two are on islands formed by the rivers Capibaribe, Beberibe and Pina, while the third is made Into an island by the Canal Tacaruna, which separates it from the mainland. The centre is always very busy by day; the crowds and the narrow streets, especially in the Santo Antônio district, can make it a confusing city to walk around. Recife has the main dock area, with commercial buildings associated with it. South of the centre is the residential and beach district of Boa Viagem, reached by bridge across the Bacia do Pina. Olinda, the old capital, is only 7 km to the north (see page 446).

Tourist offices **Empetur main office** ⓘ *Centro de Convenções, Complexo Rodoviário de Salgadinho, T34278000, F32419601, between Recife and Olinda, www.empetur.gove.br* Branches at **airport** ⓘ *T32242361 24 hrs*, cannot book hotels, helpful but few leaflets, English spoken, and **Boa Viagem** ⓘ *T34633621*, English spoken, very helpful. **Secretaria de Turismo do Recife** ⓘ *T32247198*. Maps are available at tourist offices or can be bought at newspaper stands in the city. The newspapers, *Diário de Pernambuco* and *Jornal do Comercio* publish a sketch map of the city as well as opening hours for museums, art galleries, churches, etc.

Sights

About 285 km north of Maceió and 839 km north of Salvador, Recife was founded on reclaimed land by the Dutch prince Maurice of Nassau in 1637 after his troops had burnt Olinda, the original capital. **Forte do Brum** ⓘ *Tue-Fri 0900-1600, Sat and Sun 1400-1600, donation optional*, built by the Dutch in 1629, is an army museum. **Forte das Cinco Pontas**, built by the Dutch in 1630, was altered by the Portuguese in 1677. The two forts controlled access to the port at the northern and southern entrances respectively. Within Forte das Cinco Pontas is the **Museu da Cidade do Recife** ⓘ *Mon-Fri 0900-1800, Sat and Sun 1300-1700, US$0.50 donation preferred*, which houses a cartographic history of the settlement of Recife.

The first Brazilian printing press was installed in 1706 and Recife claims to publish the oldest daily newspaper in South America, *Diário de Pernambuco*, founded 1825 (but now accessible on the internet). The distinctive lilac building is on the Praça da Independência.

The artists' and intellectuals' quarter is based on the **Pátio de São Pedro** ⓘ *For more information, T34262728*, the square round São Pedro dos Clérigos. Sporadic folk music and poetry shows are given in the square during the evening from Wednesday to Sunday , and there are atmospheric bars and restaurants. It is an excellent shopping centre for typical northeastern craftware; clay figurines are cheapest in Recife.

Not far away off Avenida Guararapes, two blocks from the central post office, is the **Praça do Sebo**, where the city's second-hand booksellers concentrate; this **Mercado de Livros Usados** is off the Rua da Roda, behind the Edifício Santo Albino, near the corner of Avenida Guararapes and Rua Dantas Barreto. You can also visit the city **markets** in the São José and Santa Rita sections.

The former municipal prison has now been made into the **Casa da Cultura** ⓘ *Mon-Sat 0900-1900, Sun 0900-1400 (dances 1700 Mon, Wed and Fri, T32842850 to check in advance)*, with many cells converted into art or souvenir shops and with areas for exhibitions and shows (also public conveniences). Local dances such as the *ciranda*, *forró* and *bumba-meu-boi* are held as tourist attractions.

Among other cultural centres are Recife's three traditional theatres: **Santa Isabel** ⓘ *Praça da República, open to visitors Mon-Fri 1300-1700*, built in 1850; the restored and beautiful **Parque** ⓘ *R do Hospício 81, Boa Vista, Mon-Fri* 0800-1200, 1400-1800, and **Apolo** ⓘ *R do Apolo 121, 0800-1200, 1400-1700.*

Churches

The best are **Santo Antônio do Convento de São Francisco** ⓘ *R do Imperador* (1606), which has beautiful Portuguese tiles, and adjoining it the finest sight of all, the **Capela Dourada** ⓘ *US$0.25, no flash photography, entry through the Museu Franciscano de Arta Sacra, Mon-Fri 0800-1130 and 1400-1700, Sat 0800-1130; US$1*, or Golden Chapel.

São Pedro dos Clérigos ⓘ *daily 0800-1130 and 1400-1600*, in São José district (1782) should be seen for its façade, its fine wood sculpture and a splendid *trompe-l'oeil* ceiling. **Nossa Senhora da Conceição dos Militares** ⓘ *R Nova 309, Mon-Fri 0800-1700* (1771), has a grand ceiling and a large 18th-century primitive mural of the battle of Guararapes. There is a museum next door.

The churches are often closed to visitors on Sunday because of services; many are in need of repair.

Other important churches to be seen are **Santo Antônio** ⓘ *Praça da Independência, daily 0800-1200 and Mon-Fri 1400-1800, Sat 1700-1900* (1753-91), rebuilt in 1864; **Nossa Senhora do Carmo** ⓘ *Praça do Carmo Mon-Fri 0800-1200, 1400-1900, Sat and Sun 0700-1200* (1663); **Madre de Deus** ⓘ *Tue-Fri 0800-1200, 1400-1600* (1715), in the street of that name in the district of Recife, with a splendid high altar, and sacristy; the **Divino Espírito Santo** ⓘ *Mon-Fri 0800-1630, Sat 0800-1400, Sun 1000-1200* (1689), the original church of the Jesuits, Praça 17 in Santo Antônio district.

About 14 km south of the city, a little beyond Boa Viagem and the airport, on Guararapes Hill, is the historic church of **Nossa Senhora dos Prazeres** ⓘ *Tue-Fri 0800-1200 and 1400-1700, Sat 0800-1200 Sat, closed to tourists on Sun*. It was

Recife orientation

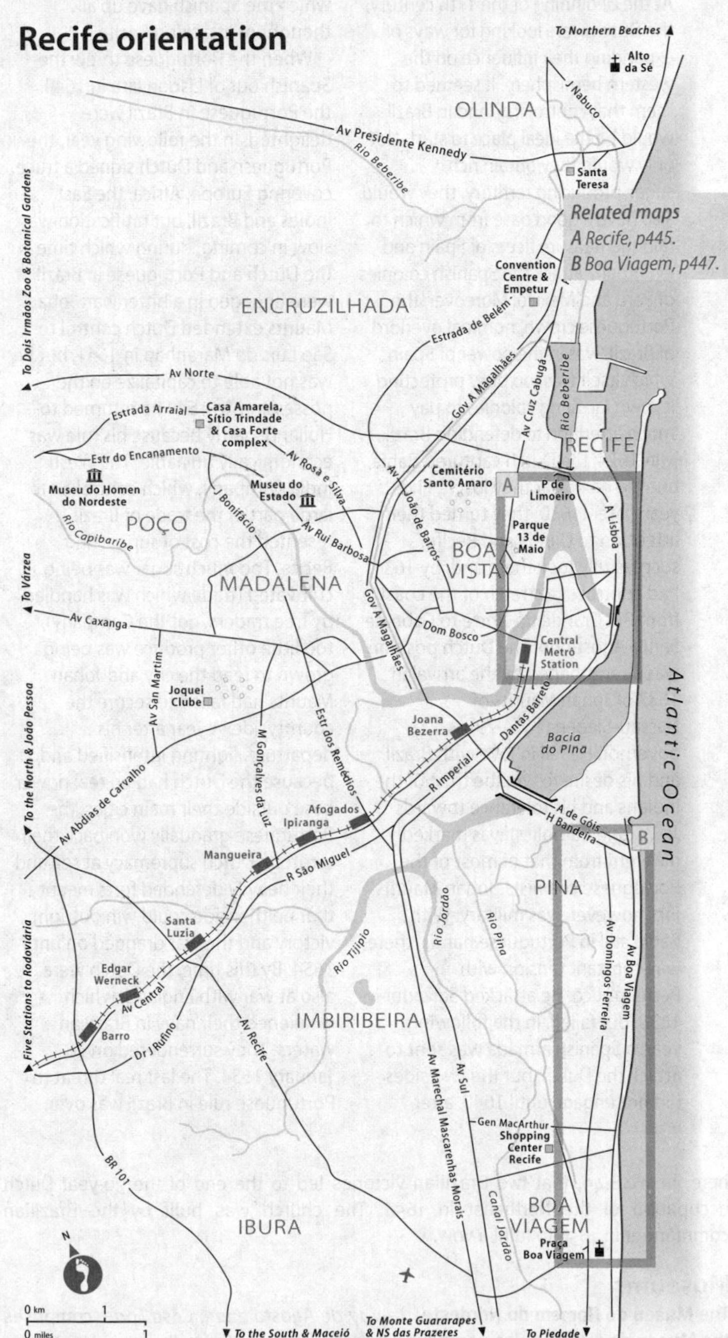

The Dutch in Brazil

At the beginning of the 17th century, the Dutch were looking for ways of expanding their influence on the western hemisphere. It seemed to them that controlling land in Brazil would be the ideal place to start. Not only would they obtain rich, sugar-producing territory, they would also have a good base from which to raid the treasure fleets of Spain and eventually attack the Spanish colonies of Peru and Mexico. Moreover, the Portuguese crown, nominal overlord of Brazil, was in the power of Spain, which itself was too busy protecting its own far-flung colonies to pay much attention to defending Brazil.

In 1624, the Dutch captured Bahia, but the next year they lost it. Five years later (1630) they turned their attention to Olinda and Recife, successfully took them and, by 1634, had control of a stretch of the coast from Rio Grande do Norte to Cabo de Santo Agostinho. The Dutch position was strengthened by the arrival in 1637 of Johan Maurits of Nassau-Siegen (1604-79) as governor. He fell in love with Brazil, and his desire to win the trust of the Indians and his tolerance towards Jews (and Catholics) was markedly different from that of most of the Portuguese colonists. Johan Maurits' job, however, was military. With Bahia still in Portuguese hands, there was constant tension with Pernambuco. He attacked Salvador in 1638, but failed. In the following year, a Spanish armada was sent to attack the Dutch, but the two sides did not engage until 1640, after which the Spanish gave up all thought of attacking Recife.

When the Portuguese threw the Spanish out of Lisbon late in 1640, the Portuguese in Brazil were delighted. In the following year, the Portuguese and Dutch signed a truce, covering Europe, Africa, the East Indies and Brazil, but ratification was slow in coming, during which time the Dutch and Portuguese in Brazil were engaged in a bitter war. Johan Maurits extended Dutch control to São Luís do Maranhão in 1641, but he was not able to capitalize on the possession. In 1644 he returned to Holland, partly because his rule was economically unviable. The West India Company, which controlled a large part of the trade of Brazil, resented the cost of supporting Recife. Too much sugar was being cultivated (trade which was handled by free traders, not the Company), too little other produce was being grown to feed the city and Johan Maurits had failed to secure the countryside. A year after his departure, fighting intensified and, because the Dutch had no real power base outside their main cities, the Portuguese gradually won back their territory. Dutch supremacy at sea and their heavily defended forts meant that neither side could win outright victory and the war dragged on until 1654. By this time, the Dutch were also at war with England, which weakened their navy in Brazilian waters. They surrendered on 26 January 1654. The last real threat to Portuguese rule in Brazil was over.

here, in 1648-49, that two Brazilian victories led to the end of the 30-year Dutch occupation of the Northeast in 1654. The church was built by the Brazilian commander in 1656 to fulfil a vow.

Museums

The **Museu do Homem do Nordeste** ① *Av 17 de Agosto 2223, Casa Forte*, comprises the **Museu de Arte Popular**, containing ceramic figurines (including some by Mestre

Alino and Zé Caboclo); the **Museu do Açúcar**, on the history and technology of sugar production, with models of colonial mills, collections of antique sugar bowls and much else; the **Museu de Antropologia**, the **Nabuco Museum** ⓘ *Av 17 de Agosto 1865*, and the modern museum of popular remedies, **Farmacopéia Popular** ⓘ *T34415500 Tue-Fri 1100-1700, Sat and Sun 1300-1700, US$1*. To get to the museum complex, you

Recife

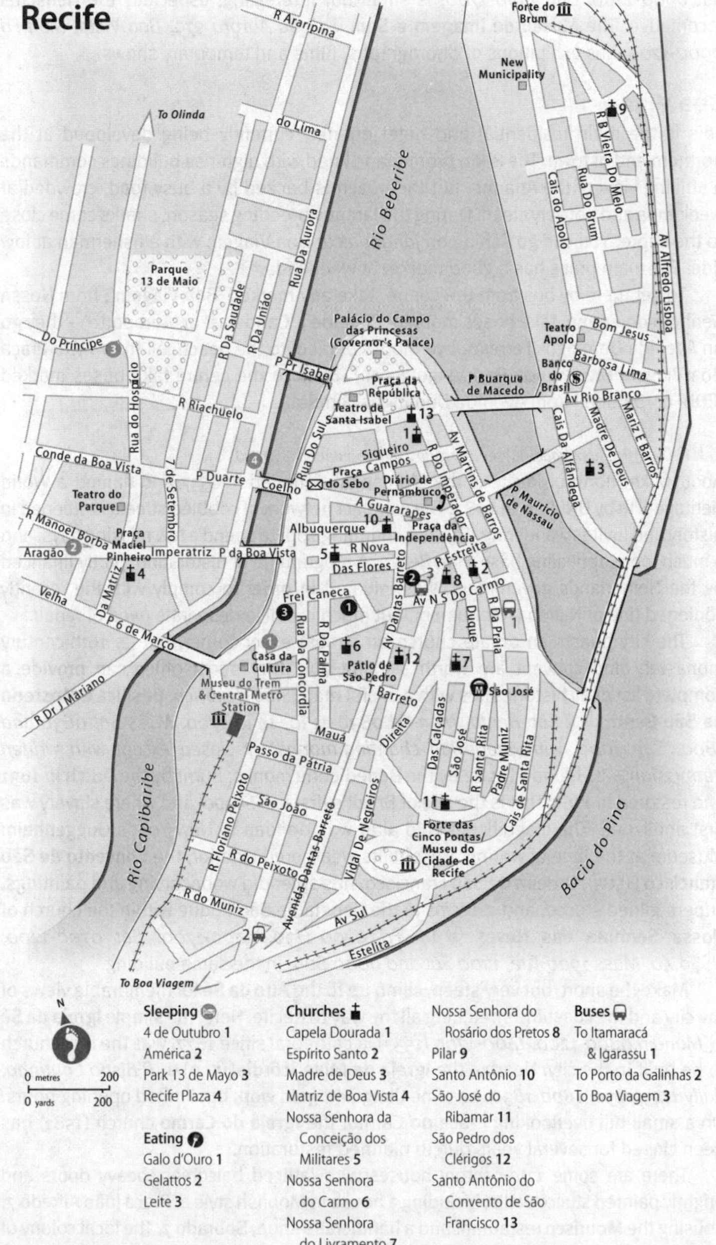

Sleeping
4 de Outubro 1
América 2
Park 13 de Mayo 3
Recife Plaza 4

Eating
Galo d'Ouro 1
Gelattos 2
Leite 3

Churches
Capela Dourada 1
Espírito Santo 2
Madre de Deus 3
Matriz de Boa Vista 4
Nossa Senhora da Conceição dos Militares 5
Nossa Senhora do Carmo 6
Nossa Senhora do Livramento 7
Nossa Senhora do Rosário dos Pretos 8
Pilar 9
Santo Antônio 10
São José do Ribamar 11
São Pedro dos Clérigos 12
Santo Antônio do Convento de São Francisco 13

Buses
To Itamaracá & Igarassu 1
To Porto da Galinhas 2
To Boa Viagem 3

 can take the 'Dois Irmãos' bus (check that it's the correct one, with 'Rui Barbosa' posted in window, as there are two) from outside the Banorte building near the post office on Guararapes, but it is much easier to take a taxi.

The **Museu do Estado** ⓘ *Av Rui Barbosa 960, Graças, Tue-Fri 0900-1700, Sat and Sun 1400-1700*, has excellent paintings by the 19th-century landscape painter, Teles Júnior. **Museu do Trem** ⓘ *Praça Visconde de Mauá, Tue-Fri 0900-1200, 1400-1700, Sat 0900-1200, Sun 1400-1700*, is small but interesting, especially the Henschel locomotive. The **Museu de Imagem e Som** ⓘ *R da Aurora 379, Boa Vista, Mon-Fri 0900-1700*, has exhibitions of photographs, films and temporary shows.

Boa Viagem

This is the main residential and hotel quarter, currently being developed at the northern end of town. The 8-km promenade lined with high-rise buildings commands a striking view of the Atlantic, but the beach is backed by a busy road, crowded at weekends and not very clean. During the January breeding season, sharks come close to the shore. You can go fishing on *jangadas* at Boa Viagem with a fisherman at low tide. The main praça has a good market at weekends.

To get there by bus from the centre, take any marked 'Boa Viagem'; from Nossa Senhora do Carmo, take buses marked 'Piedade', 'Candeias' or 'Aeroporto' – they go on Avenida Domingos Ferreira, two blocks parallel to the beach, all the way to Praça Boa Viagem (at Avenida Boa Viagem 500). Back to the centre take buses marked 'CDU' or 'Setubal' from Avenida Domingos Ferreira.

Olinda → *Phone code: 081. Colour map 2, B6. Population: 350,000.*

About 7 km north of Recife is the old capital, founded in 1537 and named a World Heritage Site by UNESCO in 1982. The compact network of cobbled streets is steeped in history and invites wandering. This is a charming spot to spend a few relaxing days, and a much more appealing base than Recife. A programme of restoration, partly financed by the Netherlands government, was initiated in order to comply with the recently conferred title of National Monument, but much is still in desperate need of repair.

The city boasts an ornate church on almost every corner, but its 16th-century monastery and convent are worth seeking out. The tourist office can provide a complete list of all historic sites with a useful map, *Sítio Histórico*. **Basilica e Mosterio de São Bento** ⓘ *R São Bento, Mon-Fri 0830-1130, 1430-1700, Mass Sat 0630 and 1800; Sun 1000, with Gregorian chanting.monastery closed except with written permission*, was founded 1582 by the Benedictine monks, burnt by the Dutch in 1631 and restored in 1761. This is the site of Brazil's first law school and where slavery was first abolished. The magnificent gold altar was on loan to New York's Guggenheim Museum at the time of writing. Despite its weathered exterior, the **Convento de São Francisco** (1585), Ladeira de São Francisco, has splendid woodcarving and paintings, superb gilded stucco, and *azulejos* in the Capela de São Roque within the church of **Nossa Senhora das Neves** ⓘ *Tue-Fri 0700-1130, 1400-1700, Sat 0700-1200, US$0.40. Mass 1900 Tue, 1700 Sat and 0800 Sun*, in the same building.

Make the short, but very steep, climb up to the **Alto da Sé** for memorable views of the city and the coastline stretching all the way to Recife. Here, the simple **Igreja da Sé** ⓘ *Mon-Fri 0800-1200, 1400-1700* (1537), a cathedral since 1677, was the first church to be built in the city. Nearby, the **Igreja da Misericórdia**(1540) ⓘ *R Bispo Coutinho, daily 1145-1230, 1800-1830*, has fine tiling and gold work but limited opening hours. On a small hill overlooking Praça do Carmo, the **Igreja do Carmo** church (1581) has been closed for several years due to planned restoration.

There are some 17th-century houses with latticed balconies, heavy doors and brightly painted stucco walls, including a house in Moorish style at Praça João Alfredo 7, housing the **Mourisco** restaurant and a handicrafts shop, **Sobrado 7**. The local colony of artists means excellent examples of regional art (mainly woodcarving and terracotta

Boa Viagem

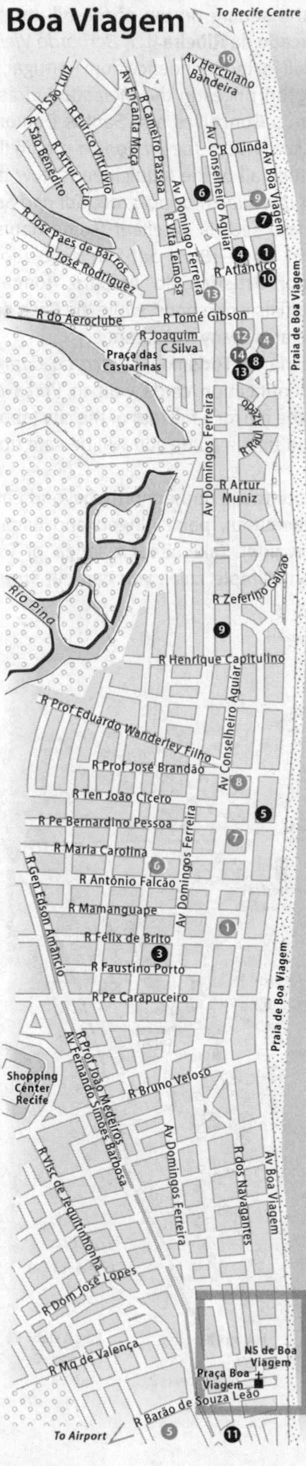

To Recife Centre
Av Herculano Bandeira
R São Luiz
R Eurico Vitrúvio
R São Benedito
R Artur Lício
Av Encanta Moça
R Carneiro Passoa
Av Conselheiro Aguiar
R Olinda
Av Boa Viagem
Av Domingo Ferreira
R Vita Teimosa
R Josepaes de Barros
R José Rodriguez
R Atlântico
Praia de Boa Viagem
R do Aeroclube
R Tomé Gibson
R Joaquim C Silva
Praça das Casuarinas
R Raul Azedo
Av Domingos Ferreira
R Artur Muniz
R Zeferino Galvão
Rio Pina
R Henrique Capitulino
R Prof Eduardo Wanderley Filho
Av Conselheiro Aguiar
Atlantic Ocean
R Prof José Brandão
R Ten João Cicero
R Pe Bernardino Pessoa
R Maria Carolina
R Gen Edson Amâncio
R Antônio Falcão
Av Domingos Ferreira
R Mamanguape
R Félix de Brito
R Faustino Porto
R Pe Carapuceiro
Praia de Boa Viagem
Shopping Center Recife
R Prof João Medeiros
Av Fernando Simões Barbosa
R Bruno Veloso
R Visc de Jequitinhonha
Av Domingos Ferreira
R dos Navegantes
Av Boa Viagem
R Dom José Lopes
R Mq de Valença
NS de Boa Viagem
Praça Boa Viagem
R Barão de Souza Leão
To Airport

Boa Viagem detail

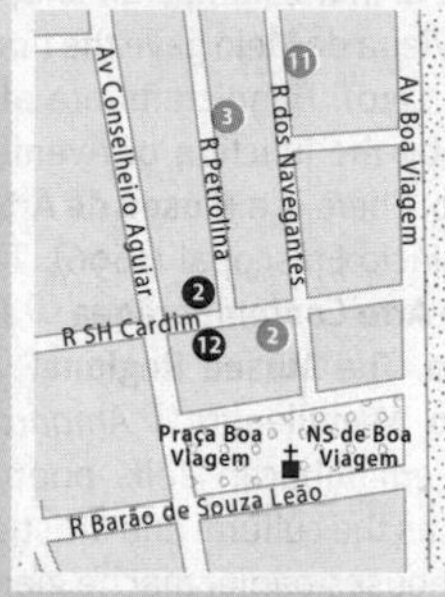

Av Conselheiro Aguiar
R Petrolina
R dos Navegantes
Av Boa Viagem
R SH Cardim
Praça Boa Viagem
NS de Boa Viagem
R Barão de Souza Leão

N
0 metres 200
0 yards 200

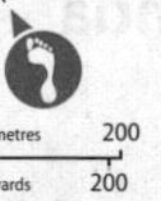

Sleeping
Aconchego **1**
Albergue do Mar **2**
Coqueiral **3**
Do Sol **4**
Mar **5**
Maracatus do Recife **6**
Navegantes Praia **7**
Pousada da Julieta **8**
Pousada da Praia **9**
Praia **10**
Recife Monte **11**
Uzi Mar **12**
Uzi Praia **13**

Eating
Bargaço **1**
Chica Pitanga **2**
Churrascaria Porcão **3**
Dunkin' Donuts **4**
Ilha da Kosta **5**
La Capannina **6**
La Maison **7**
Parraxaxa **8**
Peng **9**
Real eza **10**
Romana **11**
Tempero Verde **12**
Tio Dadá **13**

Bars & clubs
Balthazar **14**

 figurines) may be bought in the Alto da Sé, the square on top of the hill by the cathedral, or in the handicraft shops at the **Mercado da Ribeira** ⓘ *R Bernardo Vieira de Melo* (Vieira de Melo gave the first recorded call for Independence from Portugal, in Olinda in 1710). Handicrafts are also sold at good prices in the Mercado Eufrásio Barbosa, by the junction of Avenida Segismundo Gonçalves and Santos Dumont, Varadouro. There is a **Museu de Arte Sacra** ⓘ *Alto da Sé 7, Tue-Fri 0900-1300*, in the former Palácio Episcopal (1696). The 18th-century jail of the Inquisition is now the **Museu de Arte Contemporânea** ⓘ *R 13 de Maio 157, Tue-Fri 0900-1700, Sat and Sun 1400-1700*. The **Museu Regional** ⓘ *R do Amparo 128*, is excellent (same hours). **Museu do Mamulengo** ⓘ *Amparo 59, Mon-Fri 0900-1800, Sat-Sun 1100-1800*, houses Pernambucan folk puppetry. **Corredor Artístico do Amparo**, formally identified as the cultural and artistic zone, has artists workshops, while the **Casa dos Bonecos** houses papier mache giants; there are also many restaurants.

For **tourist information** go tho the **Secretaria de Turismo** ⓘ *Praça do Carmo, T34299279, daily 0900-2100*. **Guides** with identification cards wait in Praça do Carmo. They are former street children and half the fee for a full tour of the city (about US$12) goes to a home for street children. If you take a guide you will be safe from mugging which does, unfortunately, occur.

The **beaches** close to Olinda are polluted, but those further north, beyond Casa Caiada – at **Janga**, and **Pau Amarelo** – are beautiful, palm fringed and usually deserted (although the latter can be dirty at low tide). Take either a 'Janga' or 'Pau Amarela' bus, Varodouro bus to return. At many simple cafés you can eat *sururu*

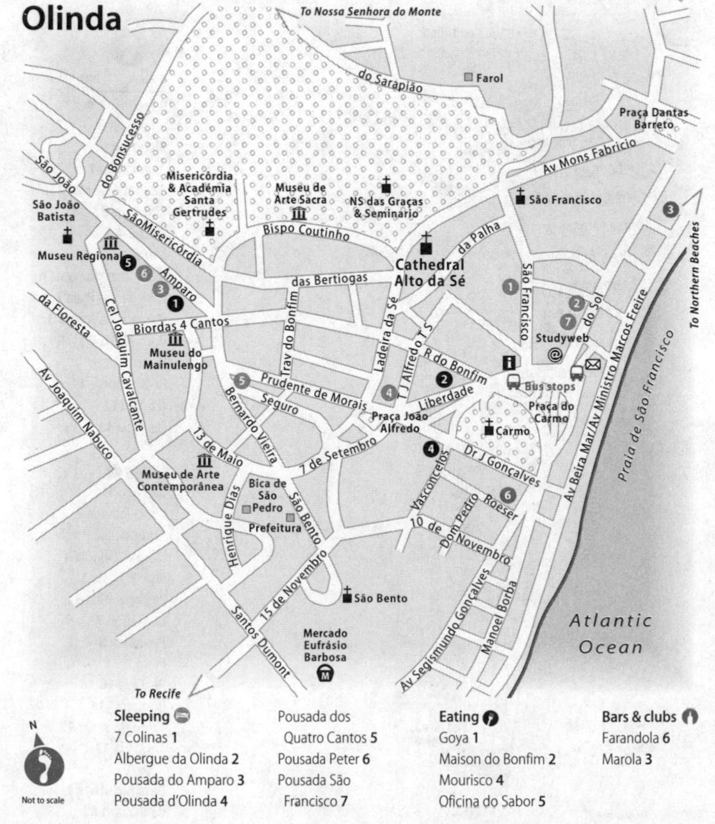

(clam stew in coconut sauce), *agulha frita* (fried needle-fish), *miúdo de galinha* (chicken giblets in gravy), *casquinha de carangueijo* (seasoned crabmeat) and *farinha de dendê* (served in crabshells). Visit the Dutch fort on Pau Amarelo beach where there is a small craft fair on Saturday nights.

Biological reserves

Pernambuco's two reserves are **Saltinho**, in the south of the state, which preserves some of the last vestiges of Atlantic Forest in the Northeast, and **Serra Negra**, in the centre of the state, which has some of the last remaining forest at higher altitude in the interior. For information contact **Ibama** ⓘ *Av 17 de Agosto 1057, Casa Forte, CEP 52060-590, T4415033, F4411380, Recife.*

The southern coast

About 30 km south of Recife, beyond Cabo, is the beautiful and quiet **Gaibu** beach, with scenic Cabo de Santo Agostinho on the point 5 km east of town. It has a ruined fort. In 1996 surfing in this area was banned owing to the danger of shark attacks. To get there, take bus 'Centro do Cabo' from the airport, then frequent buses – 20 minutes – from Cabo. There are places to stay and cheap restaurants. About 1 km on foot from Gaibu is Praia Calhetas, which is very nice. Itapuama beach is even more empty, both reached by bus from Cabo. Cabo, Pernambuco's main industrial city, has interesting churches and forts and a Museu da Abolição, and at nearby Suape there are many 17th-century buildings and a biological reserve.

Porto de Galinhas → *Phone code: 081.*

Brazilians rave about Porto Galinhas, with its sand streets and beautiful beach. But because of a reef close to the shore, swimming is only possible at high tide (take heed of local warnings) and a rash of recently built upmarket resorts is changing its rustic atmosphere. The name means 'port of chickens' because slaves were smuggled here in chicken crates. For **tourist information** ⓘ *T35521480*; otherwise you can contact Roberto ⓘ *T35521514*, for information and assistance on all aspects of Porto Galinhas' attractions. He can also give lifts to Recife and Olinda. Alternatively, Sylvie, a well-known local French guide, speaks five languages and knows the area well.

Barra do Sirinhaém

Further south (80 km from Recife) are the beaches of Barra do Sirinhaém, with some tourist development and three hotels, including **Dos Cataventos** (**D**). Fishermen make trips to offshore island (good views).

The northern coast

Igarassu → *Phone code: 081. Colour map 2, B6. Population: 77,500.*

Some 39 km north of Recife on the road to João Pessoa, Igarassu has the first church built in Brazil, **SS Cosme e Damião** (1535), the **Livramento** church nearby, and the convent of **Santo Antônio** with a small museum next door. The church of **Sagrado Coração** is said to have housed Brazil's first orphanage. Much of the town, which was founded in 1535, has been declared a National Monument; it is an attractive place, with a number of colonial houses and Brazil's first Masonic hall.

Itamaracá → *Phone code: 081. Population: 14,000.*

North of Igarassu you pass through coconut plantations to Itapissuma, where there is a bridge to **Itamaracá** island. According to the locals, this is where Adam and Eve

Chico Science and Mangue Beat

If Bahia produced Brazil's musical innovations in the late 1980s and early 1990s, more recent steps forward have been taken by Pernambucans. It is again a case of outside influences mixing well with Brazilian rhythmic flair. As in Bahia, where Olodum took reggae and added it to 'afoxe' rhythms, a local band called Science and Nação Zumbi took Pernambucan popular music forms including maracatu, baião and ciranda, and welded them to modern dance forms such as hip-hop, electro and jungle. The fusion became known as Mangue-Beat, best translated as 'Mangroove', after a 1991 manifesto written by a local DJ, Renato Lins, summed up the local music scene and the local mangrove swamps with the same word: stagnant.

Chico Science was killed in February 1997, casting a shadow over the carnival of that year, but, in 1999, Nacão Zumbi returned with a reshuffled line-up to prove, with devastating new material, that their intention was always to carry on Chico's work. Although there are also innovative and exciting rock bands like Eddie, River Raid and Supersoniques, the so-called 'Mangue -Beat' sees to it that talent scouts from Rio and Sao Paulo-based record companies still descend on Pernambuco regularly, in the hope of finding new stars. And they have been successful. Two of Brazil's most internationally famous new acts are Nação Zumbi alumni: DJ Dolores, who won Radio 3's Club Global World Music award in 2004, and percussionist Otto.

Three major festivals take place each year which showcase new bands. February sees Carnival's Rec-Beat in Recife take over the Rua da Moeda in the renovated old town. In April, the Pro-Rock festival is to be found at the Pernambuco State Convention Centre between Recife and Olinda – Sepultura played in 1999 – and in July each year, Pe-No-Rock takes place at the Circo Maluco Beleza in the Aflitos district of Recife. At least there aren't any awkward dance steps to learn.

spent their holidays (so does everyone else on Sunday now). It has the old Dutch **Forte Orange**, built in 1631; an interesting penal settlement with gift shops, built round the 1747 sugar estate buildings of Engenho São João, which still have much of the old machinery; charming villages and colonial churches, and fine, wide beaches. At one of them, **Praia do Forte Orange**, Ibama has a centre for the study and preservation of manatees: **Centro Nacional de Conservação e Manejo de Sirênios or Peixe-boi**ⓘ *Tue-Sun 1000-1600*.

There are pleasant trips by *jangada* from Praia do Forte Orange to **Ilha Coroa do Avião**, a recently formed sandy island (developing wildlife and migratory birds – for which there is a research station) with rustic beach bars. **Praias do Sossego** and **da Enseada** have some bars but are quiet and relatively undiscovered. The crossing is 3 km north of Itamaracá town, recommended for sun worshippers.

Further north again, two hours from Recife by bus, is **Pontas de Pedra**, an old fishing village, nice beach, fishing and diving expeditions, lots of bars.

Goiana → *Phone code: 081. Population: 67,250.*

Situated on the Recife-João Pessoa road and founded in 1570, Goiana is an important town for ceramics. The **Carmelite church** and monastery, founded 1719, is impressive but poorly restored. **Matriz Nossa Senhora do Rosário dos Brancos** (17th century), on Rua Direita, is only open for 1800 mass. Also worth a visit are the

Convento da Soledade ⓘ *R da Soledade* (1735); **Nossa Senhora do Amparo dos Homens Pardos** ⓘ *R do Amparo* (1681), with a sacred art museum; and **dos Milagres da Misericórdia** ⓘ *R da Misericórdia* (1723).

Visit the workshop of **Zé do Carmo** ⓘ *R Padre Batalha 100*, opposite the **Buraco da Giá** restaurant (excellent seafood; owner has a tame crab which will offer you a drink).

At the Pernambuco-Paraíba border, a 27-km dirt road goes to the fishing village of **Pitimbu**, with *jangadas*, lobster fishing, surf fishing, and lobster-pot making. No tourist facilities but camping is possible; food from **Bar do Jangadeiro**. Bus from Goiana, US$1.

West of Recife

Gravatá → *Phone code: 081. Colour map 2, B6. Population: 62,000.*

Some 82 km west of Recife, by the paved BR-232 road that passes through the Serra dos Russos, is Gravatá, known as the Switzerland of Pernambuco for its scenery and good hill climate. On one of its hills is a replica of the Cristo Redentor of Rio de Janeiro. The former prison on Rua Cleto Campelo has become a **Casa da Cultura and Historical Centre** ⓘ *Mon-Fri*. There's a **Secretaria de Turismo** ⓘ *R Cleto Campelo, Mon-Fri*.

Bezerros → *Colour map 2, B6. Population: 52,000*

About 15 km further west on the BR-232 is Bezerros, on the Rio Ipojuca. It has some old houses, fine praças and churches. Some, like the **Igreja de Nossa Senhora dos Homens Pretos**, **São José** and the **Capela de Nossa Senhora**, date from the 19th century. The former railway station has been converted into the **Estação da Cultura**, with shows and other cultural performances. The city's main attraction is handicrafts, which are found in the district of **Encruzilhada de São João**; items in leather, clay, wood, papier maché and much more. The best known artist and poet is J Borges (born 1935), whose work has been exhibited internationally. Most typical are the Papangu masks, made of painted papier maché. The masks are used at carnival, as interior decoration, even as key-holders. Wooden toys are also popular. About 10 km from the centre of Bezerros, near the village of Serra Negra, a small ecotourism park, **Serra Negra ecological tourism trail**, has been set up. Trails lead to caves and springs; the flora is typical of the *agreste*.

Carnival here is famed throughout Brazil and is known as **Folia do Papangu**. The Papangu characters wear masks that resemble a cross between a bear and a devil and are covered from head to foot in a costume like a bear skin (a variant is an all-covering white tunic). Other celebrations in the year are **São João** in June, and Christmas.

For tourist information contact the **Departamento de Turismo** ⓘ *Praça Duque de Caxias 88, Centro, CEP 55660-000, T3281286, F37281316*. **Associação dos Artesãos de Bezerros**, the Artisans' Association, is at the same address.

Caruaru → *Phone code: 081. Altitude: 554 m. Colour map 2, B6. Population: 254,000.*

Situated 134 km west of Recife, the paved road there passes through rolling hills, with sugar cane and large cattle *fazendas*, before climbing an escarpment. As the road gets higher, the countryside becomes drier, browner and rockier. Caruaru itself is a busy, modern town, one of the most prosperous in the *agreste* in Pernambuco. It is also culturally very lively, with excellent local and theatre and folklore groups.

Worth a visit are the **Espaço Cultural Tancredo Neves** (known as the Forro Village), which has an exhibition space, **Museu do Barro e da Cerâmica**, which does contain works by Vitalino and other clay sculptors and **Museu da Fábrica de Caroá**, with an art gallery, music school and headquarters of the municipal tourist office. **Casa da Cultura José Condé**, in Parque 18 de Maio, contains the **Museu José Condé** and a **museum of Forró**, as well as an art gallery, the municipal library and a theatre.

The little clay figures (*figurinhas* or *bonecas de barro*) originated by Mestre Vitalino (1909-63), and very typical of the Northeast, are the local speciality; most of the local potters live at **Alto da Moura**, 6 km away, and you can visit a house – **Casa Museu Mestre Vitalino** – once owned by Vitalino, with personal objects and photographs, but no examples of his work. Unesco has recognized the area as the largest centre of figurative art in the Americas. There is a bus, 30 minutes, bumpy, US$0.50.

Fazenda Nova and Nova Jerusalém

During Easter Week each year, various agencies run package tours to the little country town of Fazenda Nova, 23 km from Caruaru. Just outside the town is Nova Jerusalém, where, from the day before Palm Sunday up to Easter Saturday, an annual passion play, suggested by Oberammergau, is enacted. The site is one third the size of the historic quarter of Jerusalem, with nine stages on which scenes of the Passion are presented; 50 actors and 500 extras re-enact the story. The latest sound and lighting effects are used as the audience moves from one stage to another while the story unfolds. Performances begin at 1800, lasting about three hours. There is also a sculpture park, where gigantic figures carved from blocks of stone represent motifs of *Nordeste* culture.

Garanhuns → *Phone code: 081. Colour map 2, C5. Population: 110,000.*

Good roads via Caruaru or Palmares run to the city of Garanhuns, 209 km southwest of Recife. Its claims to be the best holiday resort in the Northeast are attributed to its cool climate – it stands at 890 m, and has an average temperature of 21°C – its mineral waters and its beautiful landscapes and parks.

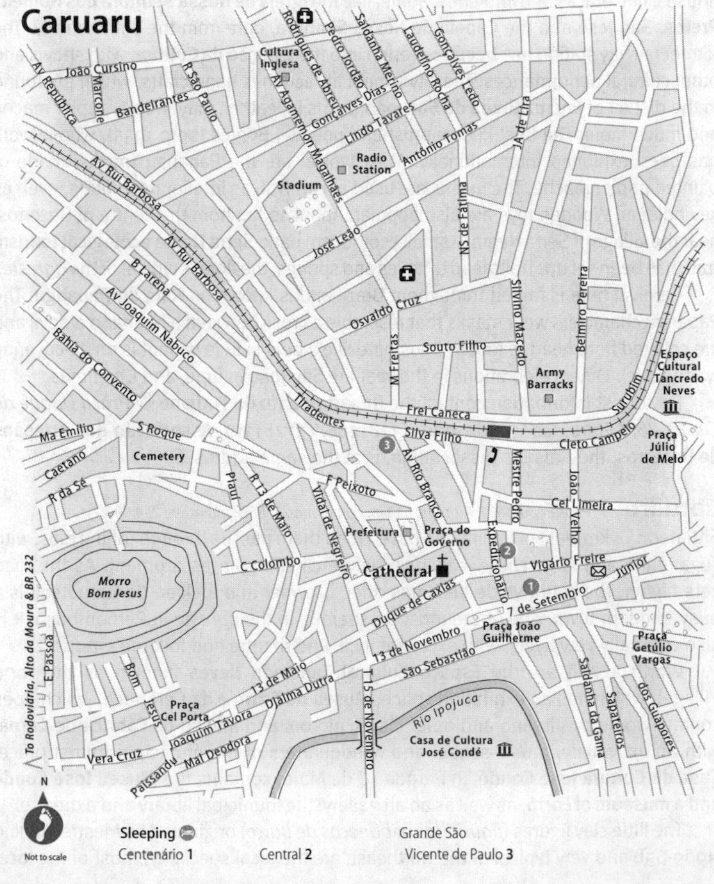

West to Triúnfo → *Phone code: 081. Colour map 2, B5.Population: 15,000.*

About 126 km west of Caruaru (bus 2½ hours, US$6) is **Arcoverde**, a market town in the *sertão*, with a market every Saturday; it is cool at night. There are various hotels (**C-D**). About 200 km west of Arcoverde, via Serra Talhada, is this delightful small town in the Serra de Borborema. It has a good climate and a great variety of crops, flowers and fruits. There is a sugar mill, **Engenho Boa Esperança**, that can be visited, and waterfalls, for example at **Cachoeira do Pingas**, 6 km away (signposted); if there has been no rain the waterfalls may be dry, so ask before setting off. You can also see the convent of **São Boaventura**, and the **Museu do Cangaço**, which has exhibits on the lives and relics of the traditional bandits of the *Nordeste*.

The Sertão

Beyond Serra Talhada the BR-232 continues to Salgueiro, where it meets the BR-116 heading north to Fortaleza. The BR-232 becomes the BR-316 and heads northwest to Araripina before entering Piauí. This part of Pernambuco was the haunt of the bandit Lampião until his death in 1938. Even today the area is still quite lawless and buses are often escorted by armed police. Also cultivation of marijuana in the area between Salgueiro and Floresta means that visitors are not generally welcome.

Petrolina → *Phone code: 081. Population: 173,500.*

Located on the Rio São Francisco which forms the southern border of Pernambuco, Petrolina is best visited from Juazeiro in Bahia (see page 423). Like Pirapora, Petrolina is famous for the production of *carrancas* (boat figureheads, mostly grotesque) of wood or ceramic. Petrolina has its own airport and close to this is the small **Museu do Sertão**, with relics of rural life in the Northeast and the age of the *coronéis* and the bandit Lampião (see page 492).

Sleeping

Recife *p441, phone code 081*

For Olinda hotels, see p454.

Boa Viagem is the main tourist district and the best area to stay. All hotels listed in this area are within 1-2 blocks of the beach, although none in any price range have much character. There is not much reason to be in the city centre, and accommodation here is of a pretty low standard. Hotels in the Santa Rita area are not recommended either, as this area is dangerous at night. Many hotels sell 5-day Carnival packages (at high prices), which you must take regardless of the length of time you wish to stay, although you may find regular-priced accommodation at Boa Viagem. Shop around.

During Carnival and for longer stays at other times, private individuals rent rooms and houses in Recife and Olinda; listings can be found in the classified ads of *Diário de Pernambuco*. This accommodation is generally cheaper, safer and quieter than hotels.

Recife - Centro *p442, map p445, phone code 081*

A Recife Plaza, R da Aurora 225, T32311200, Boa Vista, overlooking the Rio Capibaribe. Fairly comfortable business hotel with a fine restaurant (very popular at lunchtime).

B 4 de Outubro, R Floriano Peixoto 141, Santo Antônio, T32244900, F34242598. 4 standards of room, all with hot water, TV, phone and a/c.

C Hotel Park 13 de Mayo, T32317627 (not the same as **Hotel Parque** nearby, both opposite park), R do Hospicio. Modest hotel with plain rooms but safe.

D América, Praça Maciel Pinheiro 48, Boa Vista, T2211300. Bog-standard town 2-star, with a/c (cheaper without), front rooms pleasanter, quiet.

D Interlaine, R do Hospício 186, T4232941. Very simple but with pleasant staff and reasonable rooms. Good value, in the town centre.

Recife - Boa Viagem *p446, map p447, phone code 081*
The main beachfront road is Av Boa Viagem; hotels here tend to be more expensive.

AL **Mar**, near the beach at R Barão de Souza Leão 451, T4624444, F4624445. Enormous, anonymous and rather dated.

A **Recife Monte**, on the corner of R Petrolina and R dos Navegantes 363, T34657422, F34658406. Very smart and good value for category, caters to business travellers.

B **Aconchego**, Félix de Brito 382, T33262989, aconchego@novaera.com.br. Motel-style rooms around pleasant pool area, a/c, sitting room. English-speaking owner, will collect you from the airport.

B **Do Sol**, Av Boa Viagem 978, T34656722, reservas@hsol.com.br. Decent, if rather bland with business facilities.

B **Praia**, Av Boa Viagem 9, T/F4653722. Large modern block with bar, restaurant and decent-sized pool.

B **Setúbal**, R Setúbal 932, T33414116. Helpful standard town hotel with good breakfast and fairly comfortable rooms.

C **Casa da Praia**, Av Beira Mar 1168, Praia de Piedade, T34611414. On a quiet street, with garden, good breakfast, owner speaks French. Recommended.

C **Coqueiral**, R Petrolina, 43, T33265881. Dutch-owned (Dutch, English, French spoken). Small and homely rooms with a/c and a pretty breakfast room. Recommended.

C **Praia Mar**, Av Boa Viagem 1660, T34653759. Intimate and safe. Recommended.

C **Uzi Praia**, Av Conselheiro Aguiar 942, T/F34669662. Plain rooms with a/c and a cosy, sister hotel across the road.

D **Albergue Mandacaru**, R Maria Carolina 75, T3261964. Youth hostel. Stores luggage, English and German spoken, good breakfast. Recommended.

D **Navegantes Praia**, R dos Navegantes, 1997, T33269609, F33262710. One block from beach. Basic but has a/c, TV and room service. Good value.

D **Pousada da Julieta**, R Prof José Brandao 135, T33267860, hjulieta@elogica.com.br. Friendly and clean. One block from beach, very good value. Recommended.

D **Pousada da Praia**, Alcides Carneiro Leal 66, T33267085. A/c available, TV, safe, a/c, rooms vary (some tiny), very helpful, popular with Israelis. Roof-top breakfast room.

E **Maracatus do Recife**, R Maria Carolina 185, T33261221, alberguemaracatus@yahoo.com. IYHA hostel. Simple, safe, cooking facilities. Has a pool. Mosquitoes can be a problem, membership not needed, good breakfast.

E **Albergue do Mar**, R dos Navegantes 81, T33262196. Youth hostel with good breakfast and atmosphere.

Camping

Paraíso Camping Clube, Av Dantas Barreto 512, loja 503, T32243094. Can give information on camping throughout the state. There is no camping within the city.

Olinda *p446, map p448, phone code 081*
Prices at least triple during Carnival when 5-night packages are sold. Rooms at regular prices can often be found in Boa Viagem during this time. In the historic centre, accommodation is mostly in converted mansions that are full of character. If you can afford it, staying in one of these *pousadas* is the ideal way to absorb Olinda's Colonial charm. All of the following, and even most of the cheaper hotels outside the old city, have a pool.

AL **Pousada do Amparo**, R do Amparo 199, T34391749, www.pousadoamparo.com.br. Undoubtably Olinda's best hotel. Gorgeous, 18th-century house, full of atmosphere. Very individual rooms with a/c, fridge, and some with jacuzzi. Flower-filled garden, sauna, good view. Very helpful service, English spoken. Delightfully romantic restaurant, in the **Roteiros de Charme** group (see p47). Highly recommended.

AL **7 Colinas**, Ladeira de Sao Francisco 307, T/F34396055, 7colinas@hotel7colinas.com.br. Spacious, new hotel in beautiful grounds with large swimming pool. An oasis with full facilities.

B **Oh! Linda Pousada**, Av Ministro Marcos Freire 349, Bairro Novo, T34392116. Outside the historic centre. Plain rooms, breakfast and dreadful puns. Recommended.

B-C **Pousada dos Quatro Cantos**, R

For an explanation of the sleeping and eating price codes used in this guide, see the inside front cover. Other relevant information is provided in the Essentials chapter, pages 47 and 57.

Prudente de Morais 441, T34290220, F34291845, www.pousada4cantos.com.br. Converted mansion with original furniture; full of character, yet homely. Garden, terraces and simple restaurant open til 2100. Highly recommended.
C **Cinco Sóis**, Av Ministro Marcos Freire 633, Bairro Novo, outside the historic centre, T/F34291347. A/c, fridge, hot shower, parking.
C **Pousada São Francisco**, R do Sol 127, T34292109. Outside the historic centre. Comfortable, a/c with very pleasant pool area. Recommended, modest restaurant.
C-D **Pousada Peter**, R do Amparo 215, T/F34392171, www.pousadapeter.com.br. A/c rooms with a bath, clean, small pool, German owner, family atmosphere, good value. Rooms can viewed and booked on website.
C-E **Albergue da Olinda**, R do Sol 233, T34291592. Youth hostel with motel-style rooms with bath (more expensive), as well as communal bunk, rooms, laundry facilities and TV room. Large seating area with hammocks around pool. Highly recommended.
C-E **Pousada d'Olinda**, P João Alfredo 178, T/F34942559. Nice pool area,sociable. Discount of 10% for owners of **Footprint Handbooks**, 2 communal rooms with good view (cheaper), restaurant, English, French, German and Spanish spoken. Warmly recommended.
D **São Pedro**, Praça Conselheiro João Alfredo 168, outside the historic centre, T34292935. Cosy,with helpful staff. Laundry available. Danish run, English spoken. Recommended.
E **Jangada**, R 15 de Novembro 98, T34294747. Very basic but an option for those on a tight budget.
D **Cheiro do Mar**, Av Min Marcos Freire 95, T34290101. IYHA hostel, more expensive for non-members, very good small hostel with some double rooms (room No 1 is noisy from the disco), cooking facilities, ask driver of 'Rio Doce/Piedade' or 'Bairra de Jangada/Casa Caiada' bus (see below) to drop you at Albergue de Juventude on the sea front.

Camping

Olinda Camping, R Bom Sucesso 262, Amparo, T34291365. US$5 per person, space for 30 tents, 5 trailers, small huts for rent, quiet, well-shaded, town buses pass outside. Recommended.

The Southern Coast *p449, phone code 081*

C **Pousada Águas Marinhas**, Belgian-Brazilian owned, beautiful garden and location, highly recommended.
C **Pousada Beto Qualhado, Oliver y Daniel**, Av Laura Cavalcante 20. German, very relaxed.

Porto de Galinhas *p449, phone code 081*

A **Solar Porto de Galinhas**, T/F35521211 or T33250772. A beautiful place situated on the beach with good facilities.
B **Pousada Beira Mar**, Av Beira Mar 12, T/F35521052, www.pousadabeiramar.com.br. A pleasant, comfortable *pousada* on the beach.
B **Pousada Som das Ondas**, in Ipojuca, T/F35521454, somdasondas@ somdasondas.com.br. Close to beach, with a pleasant pool area and hammocks. Run by Jean-Marc, 5 European languages spoken.
C **Maracatú**, half a block from beach, pleasantly cool, with nice rooms including bath and TV.
C **Morada Azul**, Loteamento Recanto Porto de Galinhas, Lote 5, Ipojuca, T35521143, www.moradaazul.com.br. 12 flats with kitchens and en suites bathrooms and 4 simple rooms with en suites in a modern building close to the beach; the price includes a good breakfast.
D **Meninão**, above the bakery. Includes breakfast and dinner.
E **Pousada do Dona Benedita**, in the street where the bus stops. Very basic but clean.

Igarassu *p449, phone code 081*

Camping

Engenho Monjope, 5 km before Igarassu coming from Recife, T35430528, US$5. A **Camping Clube do Brasil** site on an old sugar estate, now a historical monument (bus US$1, alight at the 'Camping' sign and walk 5-10 mins).

Itamaracá *p449, phone code 081*

B **Casa da Praia**, Av da Forte Orange, T35441255. With breakfast, pool, minibar, breakfast and optional dinner.

C Pousada Itamaracá, R Fernando Lopes 205/210, T35441152. Some mins from the beach, but has a pool.
C Pousada Jaguaribe, R Rios 355 (close to bus terminal) near the beach. Fans and mosquito nets in all rooms, kitchen, laundry facilities, swimming pool.

Gravatá *p451, phone code 081*
L Casa Grande Gravatá, BR-232 Km 82, T34653011, F35330812. A very comfortable 4-star hotel. The restaurant serves regional food and an excellent breakfast.There is a swimming pool with waterslides and splendid gardens.Sauna and hydromassage available. English-speaking owner,
A Portal de Gravatá, BR-232 Km 82, T32270345, F35330610. Comfortable 3-star hotel. Rooms include a/c, TV, phone.The restaurant serves regional food and a good breakfast. There is a pool, large garden and bar.
C-D da Serra, BR-232 Km 77, T35330014. The 1st hotel in Gravatá, 2-star with a/c, TV, phone, swimming pool, bar and garden, English-speaking owner.
C-D Petur-Hotel Centro Gravatá, BR-232 Km 77, T35330016, F35330075. Unexciting small 2-star with a swimming pool but no restaurant. The a/c rooms have TVs, phone

Caruaru *p451, map p430, phone code 081*
A large number of cheap *hospedarias* can be found around the central square, Praça Getúlio Vargas.
A Grande Hotel São Vicente de Paulo, Av Rio Branco 365, T37215011, F37215290. A good, centrally located hotel with a/c, laundry, garage, bar, restaurant, pool, TV. It also houses the local cinema.
C Centenário, 7 de Setembro 84, T37224011, F37211033. Also has more expensive suites and a pool. The breakfast is good. As the hotel is in the town centre it can be noisy, but otherwise recommended.
C Central, R Vigario Freire 71, T37215880. Suites or rooms, all with a/c, TV, good breakfast, in the centre. Recommended.

Fazenda Nova and Nova Jerusalém *p452, phone code 081*
E Grande, Av Poeta Carlos Penha Filho, T7321137. Very basic but the best in town nonetheless.

Garanhuns *p452, phone code 081*
C D'Nyl, Praça Dom Moura 302, T/F37610998. Telephone, TV, minibar, breakfast included, also serves optional dinner.
C Village, Av Santo Antônio 149A, T37613624. In the town centre 15 mins' walk from the rodoviária. The rooms all have en suites and are cheaper with fans rather than a/c.
D Diplomata, R Dr José Mariano 194. Phone, shower, TV, minibar, breakfast included.

Camping
Camping Treze, BR-432, Km 105.

West to Triúnfo *p453, phone code 081*
C Fazenda Calugi, Estr Santa Tereza, T38461183. Farm hotel with a few organized activities, good food, a pool and modest accommodation. Recommended.
D Lar Santa Elizabeth, opposite church on hill near rodoviária, T38461236. The sisters offer lodging and profits support social work. Good, clean accommodation with bath, fan, balcony and patio.
D Pousada Baixa Verde, R Manoel Paiva dos Santos 114, T/F38461103. Simple but tidy and well-kept rooms and a good breakfast.

Petrolina *p453, phone code 081*
Choices here are poor; avoid the Central Hotel at all costs.
C Hotel Neuman, Av Souza Filho 444, T9610595. Overpriced with pokey little a/c rooms all with en suites.
D Pousada da Carranca, BR-122, Km 4, T9613421. Pleasant and fairly well looked after but a little inconvenient for the town.

Eating

Recife *p441, phone code 081*
There are many good restaurants, at all prices, in the city, and along the beach at Boa Viagem. Many of the restaurants in the city centre cater to office workers and are closed evenings and weekends. Be careful of eating the local small crabs, known as *guaiamum*; they live in the mangrove swamps which take the drainage from Recife's *mocambos* (shanty towns).

Coconut rice with shellfish

Use condensed or dried coconut milk, or the solid concentrate available from Asian grocers. Make it up, according to the instructions, to a milky (not creamy) consistency. Quantity serves 6-8.

Ingredients:
350 g long-grain rice
50 ml olive oil
1 finely chopped medium onion
350 ml coconut milk
1 tomato, peeled, seeded and chopped
1 tbsp lime or lemon juice
2 handfuls fresh coriander, chopped
24 clams or mussels (fresh, canned or preserved in water)
Water to make the fish juice up to 350 ml

Method:
In a heavy saucepan, sauté the onion with the oil over a medium heat. When it is soft and transparent, add the rice. Stir for a few minutes until the rice is coated with oil, but not brown. Add the coconut milk with the fish water, the tomato, and some salt if needed. Bring to the boil, then reduce the heat and simmer until the rice is tender and the liquid all absorbed (about 30 minutes). Pour the lime juice over the shellfish. Five minutes before the rice has finished cooking, stir in the shellfish and herbs.

Recife - Centro *p442, map p445, phone code 081*

There are many cheap *lanchonetes* in the city, catering to office workers, they tend to close in evening.

Leite (lunches only), Praça Joaquim Nabuco 147/53 near Casa de Cultura, Centro. Old and famous, good service, smart (another branch in Boa Viagem, at Prof José Brandão 409).

Casa de Tia. Gamboa do Carmo, 136. Lunch only, must arrive by 1215, try *cosido*, a meat and vegetable stew, enough for 2.

Galo D'Ouro, Gamboa do Carmo 83. Well established, international food.

Lisboa á Noite, R Geraldo Pires 503. Good, reasonable prices, open Sun evenings (unlike many).

O Vegetal, R Cleto Campelo and Av Guararapes (2nd floor) behind Central Post Office. Lunch only, closed Sat-Sun. Reasonable veggie restaurant wth a range of pre-prepared dishes.

Tivoli, R Matias de Albuquerque, Santo Antônio. Lunches downstairs, a/c restaurant upstairs, good value.

Buraquinho, Pátio de São Pedro. Lunch only, all dishes good, generous servings of *caipirinha*, friendly.

Casa dos Frios, da Palma 57, loja 5. Delicatessen/sandwich bar, salads, pastries.

Gelattos, Av Dantas Barreto, 230. Great *sucos* (try the delicious *guarana do amazonas* with nuts), hamburgers and sandwiches. Pay at counter. Recommended.

Recife - Boa Viagem *p446, map p447, phone code 081*

Restaurants on the main beach road of Av Boa Viagem are, like the hotels here, pricier. Venture a block or 2 inland for cheaper deals.

Bargaço, Av Boa Viagem 670. Typical northeastern menu specializing in seafood dishes. Sophisticated with small bar.

La Maison, Av Boa Viagem, 618, T33251158. Fondue restaurant in low-lit basement with illicit feel. Appropriately cheesey and good fun, with rosé wine and peach melba on menu.

Chica Pitanga, R Petrolina, 19, T34652224. Upmarket, excellent food by weight. Be prepared to queue. Recommended.

Churrascaria Porcão, Av Eng Domingos Ferreira 4215. Good for meat- and salad-eaters alike, very popular.

Ilha da Kosta, R Pe Bernardino Pessoa, 50, T34662222. Self-service seafood, sushi, pizza and Brazilian cuisine. Nothing special, but open 1100 to last client and all afternoon.

La Capannina, Av Cons Aguiar 538, T34659420. Italian pizzas, salad, pasta and sweet and savoury crêpes. Delivers. Recommended.

ƳƳ **Parraxaxa**, R Baltazar Pereira, 32, T91080242. Rustic-style, award-winning buffet of northeastern cuisine, including breakfast. Recommended.

Ƴ **Gibi**, Av Cons Aguiar, 542. Basic but popular hamburger joint.

Ƴ **Peng**, Av Domingos Ferreira, 1957. Self-service, some Chinese dishes. Bargain, rather than gourmet food, in area with few other restaurants.

Ƴ **Real eza**, Av Boa Viagem, on corner with Av Atlântico. Beachfront location, hamburgers, snacks and pizza.

Ƴ **Romana**, R Setubal, 225. Deli/bakery with a few tables and chairs. Sells pastries, coffee, yoghurt for breakfast and snacks.

Ƴ **Tempero Verde**, R SH, Cardim, opposite Chica Pitanga. Where the locals go for a bargain meal of beans, meat and salad, US1.50. Simple, self-service, pavement tables.

Ƴ **TioDadá**, R Baltazar Pereira, 100. Loud, TV screens, good-value portions of beef.

There are many a/c cheapies in the Shopping Center Recife, 1000-2200, T34646000.

Cafés

Cafe Cordel, R Domingos José Martins. Northeastern dishes, cordel literature, regional books (some in English), good CD collection with requests accepted.

Savoy, Av Guararapes, open since 1944 and a haunt of Pernambucan intellectuals, Simone de Beauvoir and Jean Paul Sartre once ate here according to a book written on the bar, poetry all over the walls.

Olinda *p446, map p448, phone code 081*

In Olinda try *tapioca*, a local dish made of manioc with coconut or cheese. The traditional Olinda drinks, *pau do índio* (which contains 32 herbs) and *retetel* are both manufactured on R do Amparo.

ƳƳƳ **Oficina do Sabor**, R do Amparo 355, T34293331. Probably the city's best restaurant, consistently wins awards. Pleasant terrace overlooking city, food served in hollowed-out pumpkins and lots of vegetarian options.

ƳƳƳ **Goya**, R do Amparo 157, T34394875. Regional food, particularly seafood, beautifully presented.

ƳƳ **Maison do Bonfim**, R do Bonfim 115, T34291674. Serene, fan-cooled, rustic-style restaurant. French cuisine, such as chicken chasseur and escargots, as well as Brazilian and Italian food.

ƳƳ **Samburá**, Av Min Marcos Freire 1551. With terrace, try *caldeirada* and *pitu* (crayfish), also lobster in coconut sauce or daily fish dishes, very good.

Ƴ **Grande Pequim**, Av Min Marcos Freire 1463, Bairro Novo. Good Chinese food.

Ƴ **Mourisco**, Praça João Alfredo. Excellent, good-value food by weight in lovely, part-covered garden. Delicious deserts. A real find. Warmly recommended.

Ƴ **Mama Luise** and **Gibi**, Av Min Marcos Freire, and **Leque Moleque**, Av Sigismundo Gonçalves 537. A few of several *lanchonetes* and fast-food options along the seafront.

Itamaracá *p449, phone code 081*

ƳƳƳ **Vila Velha** (Call T9712962, ask for Newton Bezerra, dealer for artist Luis Jasmim. Those with a car and above-budget means should have lunch and a swim at this charming villa. Pay a visit, and any purchase comes with an offer of lunch included in the deal), allow all afternoon.

Goiana *p450, phone code 081*

See also under Sleeping, above.

ƳƳ **Buraco da Giá**, R Padre Batalha. Excellent for seafood. The owner has a tame crab which will offer you a drink!

Gravatá *p451, phone code 081*

There are many good restaurants with regional and international food; fondue is very good in Gravatá.

ƳƳƳ **Faisão Dourado**, BR-232 Km 82. An old and famous hotel with Swiss architecture.There is good service with international and regional food, T35330054, open Sat and Sun.

ƳƳƳ **Taverna Suíça** , BR-232 Km 78, T35330299. Old, Swiss style, good service, international food (fondue a speciality), good wine list, English, French and Italian spoken by the owner.

Ƴ **Picanha da Serra**, R 15 de Novembro 1472, T9629960. Good service, regional food, good value. Closed Mon.

Caruaru *p451, map p452, phone code 081*
Alto da Moura is a real tourist spot and gets very busy.

ΨΨ-Ψ **Costela do Baiano**, close to Igreja do Rosário. Very good value northeastern cooking with good seafood.

ΨΨ-Ψ **Catracho's**, close to the São Sebastião hospital. Has a Caribbean feel and the Honduran owner mixes great cocktails.

Ψ **A Massa**, R Vidal de Negreiros. The best of a number of cheap lunch restaurants in the centre near Banco do Brasil. With respectable pizzas and pasta.

Bars and clubs

Recife *p441, map p445, phone code 081*
Most bars (often called 'pubs', but nothing like the English version) stay open until dawn. The historic centre of **Recife Antigo** has been restored and is now an excellent spot for nightlife.

The **Graças** district, west of Boa Vista, on the Rio Capibaribe, is popular for bars and evening entertainment. Discotheques here tend to be expensive and sophisticated. Best times are around midnight on Fri or Sat, take a taxi.

The Pina zone, north of the beginning of Boa Viagem, is one of the city's major hang-out areas with lively bars, music and dancing.

Try to visit a northeastern *forró* where couples dance to typical music, very lively especially on Fri and Sat, several good ones at Candeias.

London Pub, R do Bom Jesus 207, is one of several good bars on this street, the result of a scheme to renovate the dock area.

Calypso Club, R do Bom Jesus, US$5, has live local bands playing anything from traditional music to rock.

Downtown Pub, R Vigário Tenório, disco, live music, US$5 and **Fashion Club**, Av Fernando Simões Barbosa, 266, Boa Viagem (in front of Shopping Centre Recife), T33274040, US$8. Techno and rock bands. These are the 2 most popular nightclubs (both enormous, open 2300 to dawn).

Capibar, Aflitos, on River Capibaribe. Recommended bar.

Shoparia, 2 doors from Maxime restaurant, good beer and atmosphere, live rock music after 2200.

Baltazar, R Baltazar Pereira 130, Boa Viagem, T33270475. Live music nightly, bar snacks, large and popular. Open 1600 to early hours.

Papillon Bar, Av Beira Mar, 20, Riedade, T33417298. *Forró* Wed-Sat.

Olinda *p446, map p448, phone code 081*
Beginning at dusk, but best after 2100, the Alto da Sé becomes the scene of a small street fair, with arts, crafts, makeshift bars and barbecue stands, and impromptu traditional music; even more animated at Carnival. Every Fri night bands of wandering musicians walk the streets serenading passers-by. Each Sun from 1 Jan to Carnival there is a mini Carnival in the streets of the city, with music and dancing.

Cantinho da Sé, Ladeira da Sé 305, T34398815. Lively, good view of Recife, food served.

Farandola, R Dom Pedro Roeser, 190, tucked away behind Igreja do Carmo church. Mellow bar with festival theme and 'big-top' -style roof. Live mellow music nightly, plans for a circus next door. Drinks are cheap; try *bate bate de maracuja* (smooth blend of *cachaça*, passionfruit juice and honey) or *raspa raspa* fruit syrup. Warmly recommended.

Marola, Tr Av Dantas Barreto 66, T34292499. Funky wooden *barraca* on rocky shoreline specializing in seafood. Great *caiprifrutas* (frozen fruit drink with vodka – try the cashew). Can get crowded. Recommended.

Pernambucanamente, Av Min Marcos Freire 734, Bairro Novo, T34291977. Live, local music every night.

Itamaracá *p449, phone code 081*
Bar da Lia, R do Jaguaribe, close to the Forte Orange, weekends feature *cirandas* danced at the bar, led by the well-known singer, Dona Lia, and her band. Also serves food.

Entertainment

Recife *p441, map p445, phone code 081*
Look out for *Agenda Cultural*, a free booklet available from tourist offices, and some shops and theatres, which details the cultural events for the month, in Portuguese only.

Football Recife's 3 clubs are Sport, Santa Cruz and Nautico. **Sport** play at Ilha do Retiro, T32271213, take Torrões bus from Central Post Office on Av Guararapes. **Santa Cruz** play at Arruda, T34416811, take Casa

Carnival in Pernambuco

Carnival in Pernambuco encompasses trios eléctricos and samba schools as well as having its own distinctive dances and rhythms such as Maracatu and Frevo. Avenida Guararapes in Recife, Pina near Boa Viagem, Largo do Amparão and Mercado Eufrásio Barbosa (Varadouro) in Olinda are the main centres for the festivities.

There is a pre-carnavalesca week which starts with the 'Bloco da Parceria' in Boa Viagem bringing top Axé music acts from Bahia and the 'Virgens de Bairro Novo' in Olinda which features men in drag. These are followed by Carnival balls such as Baile dos Artistas (popular with the gay community) and the Bal Masque held at the Portuguese club, Rua Governador Agamenon Magalhães, T2315400. On the following Saturday morning the bloco Galo da Madrugada with close on a million participants officially opens carnival (wild and lively), see the local press for routes and times. The groups taking part are *maracatu, caboclinhos, troças, tribos de índios, blocos, ursos, caboclos de lança, escolas de samba* and *frevo*. Usually they start from Rua Conde da Boa Vista and progress along Rua do Hospício, Rua da Imperatriz, Ponte da Boa Vista, Praça da Independência, Rua 1° de Março and Rua do Imperador. This is followed by the main days Sunday to Tuesday. During Carnival (and on a smaller scale throughout the year) the Casa de Cultura has frevo demonstrations where visitors can learn some steps of this unique dance of Pernambuco (check press for details of Frevioca truck and frevo orchestras during Carnival in the Pátio de São Pedro). The best place to see the groups is from the balconies of Hotel do Parque or Recife Palace Hotel. Seats in the stands and boxes can be booked up to a fortnight in advance at the central post office in Avenida Guararapes.

The Maracatu groups dance at the doors of all the churches they pass; they usually go to the Church of Nossa Senhora do Rosário dos Pretos, patron saint of the slaves (Rua Estreita do Rosário, Santo Antônio), before proceeding into the downtown areas. A small car at the head bears the figure of some animal and is followed by the king and queen under a large, showy umbrella. The bahianas, who wear snowy-white embroidered skirts, dance in single file on either side of the king and queen. Next comes the dama do passo carrying a small doll, or calunga. After the dama comes the tirador de loas who chants to the group which replies in chorus, and last comes a band of local percussion instruments.

Still flourishing is the dance performance of the *caboclinhos*. The groups wear traditional indigenous garb: bright feathers round their waists and ankles, colourful cockades, bead and animal teeth necklaces, a dazzle of medals on their red tunics. The dancers beat out the rhythm with bows and arrows; others of the group play primitive musical instruments, but the dance is the thing: spinning, leaping, and stooping with almost mathematical precision. Further information from Casa da Carnaval, office of Fundação da Cultura de Recife, Pátio de São Pedro, lojas 10-11. Galo da Madrugada, Rua da Concórdia, Santo Antônio, T2242899.

The Prefeitura and Secretaria de Turismo has published three booklets on História Junina, História de Carnaval and História do Folclore, all by Claudia Lina, which provide a good introduction to these topics.

Amarela bus from Central Post Office. **Nautico** play at Aflitos, T34238900, take Água Fria or Aflitos bus. Local derbies are sometimes full beyond safe capacities. Avoid 'Arquibancada' tickets for Santa Cruz-Sport games. For games at Arruda, dress down.

Horse-racing Pernambucan Jockey Club, T32274961.

Theatre Shows in the Recife/Olinda Convention Center, US$10, traditional dances in full costume.

Festivals and events

Recife *p441, map p445, phone code 081*
For Carnival, see box on p460.
1 Jan, *Universal Brotherhood*. **12-15 Mar**, parades to mark the city's foundation.
Mid-Apr Pro-Rock Festival, a week-long celebration of rock, hip-hop and manguebeat at Centro de Convenções, Complexo de Salgadinho and other venues. Check *Diário de Pernambuco* or *Jornal de Comércio* for details.
Jun Festejos Juninos, see box, p460.
11-16 Jul Nossa Senhora do Carmo, patron saint of the city.
Aug Mes do Folclore.
Oct Recifolia, a repetition of the carnival over a whole weekend; dates differ each year.
1-8 Dec Festival of Lemanjá, with typical foods and drinks, celebrations and offerings to the goddess.
8 Dec Nossa Senhora da Conceição.

Olinda *p446, map p448, phone code 081*
Carnival thousands of people dance through the narrow streets of the old city to the sound of the *frevo*, the brash energetic music which normally accompanies a lively dance performed with umbrellas. The local people decorate them with streamers and straw dolls, and form themselves into costumed groups (*blocos*) which you can join as they pass (take only essentials). Among the best-known *blocos*, which carry life-size dolls, are **O homem da meia-noite** (Midnight Man), **A Corda** (a pun on 'the rope' and 'acorda' – wake up!), which parades in the early hours, **Pitombeira** and **Elefantes**. Olinda's carnival continues on Ash Wed, but is much more low-key, *a quarta-feira do batata* (Potato Wednesday, named after a waiter who claimed his right to celebrate carnival after being on duty during the official celebrations). The streets are very crowded with people dancing and drinking non-stop. The local cocktail, *capeta* (guaraná powder, sweet skimmed milk and vodka) is designed to keep you going.
12-15 Mar Foundation Day, 3 days of music and dancing, night-time only.

Gravatá *p451, phone code 081*
Mar/Apr Semana Santa (Holy Week) sees dancing, music and a *vaquejada* (rodeo) at Km 78 on the BR-232, Haras da Serra.
Jun Feast of São João is celebrated with fireworks, music, dancing and local food throughout the city.
Oct **Strawberry festival** of the Northeast, with more typical food, drink, music and dancing.
17 Dec-2 Jan Festas Natalinas.

Caruaru *p451, map p452, phone code 081*
Mar/Apr Semana Santa, Holy Week, with lots of folklore and handicraft events.
18-22 May City's anniversary.
13 Jun Santo Antônio.
24 Jun São João, a particularly huge *forró* festival, part of Caruaru's **Festas Juninas**. The whole town lights up with dancing, traditional foods, parties like the *Sapadrilha*, when the women dress as men, and the *Gaydrilha*, where the men dress as women, and there is even a *Trem do Forró* which runs from Recife to Caruaru, rocking the whole way to the rhythms.
Sep **Micaru**, a street carnival; also in Sep, **Vaquejada**, a Brazilian cross between rodeo and bull fighting), biggest in the Northeast

Shopping

Recife *p441, map p445, phone code 081*
Bookshops Livraria Brandão, R da Matriz 22 (used English books and some French and German), and bookstalls on the R do Infante Dom Henrique. **Livro 7**, a huge emporium with a very impressive stock, R Sete de Setembro 329. **Saraiva**, R Sete de Setembro 280, best selection of Brazilian literature in

São João and the Festas Juninas

As well as the Brazilian equivalent to Valentine's Day falling on 12 June, the days of Santo Antônio (13 June), São João (24 June), São Pedro and São Paulo (29 June), form the nuclei of a month-long celebration whose roots go back to the Portuguese colony. In addtion to these Catholic traditions are Indian and African elements in the celebrations. Potential visitors to Brazil with a fear of fireworks should take note: this is when the streets of northeastern cities fill with stalls offering their bangers, catherine wheels and rockets.

The annual cycle begins in fact on São José's day, 19 March, historically the first day of planting maize; the harvest in June then forms a central part of the celebrations. The region's many maize-based recipes such as *pamonha* and *canjica* are traditionally eaten and washed down with a drink known as *quentão*, pinga heated with cloves and cinnamon.

During the festivals the *forró* is danced. This dance, now popular throughout the Northeast, is believed to have originated when the British builders of the local railways held parties that were for all. This is just one aspect of the festivities which makes Pernambuco's **festejos juninos** distinct from those that are celebrated all over Brazil.

The cities of Caruaru, Pernambuco and Campina Grande, Paraíba have built up a reputation for staging the wildest parties, with a million people descending on Campina Grande, which has the largest São Joao celebrations in the world. The central square in the Paraíba town becomes a giant arena filled with stalls, shows and half a dozen stages showcasing the hottest *forró* acts in Brazil. The arena is so packed with people dancing that you can barely move. The town itself turns into a giant museum in honour of the *sertão*. Caruaru, in neighbouring Pernambuco, builds and annual **Forró Village**, a full mock-up of a Sertão town complete with a bank and a post office, which are fully functional throughout the festivities. The 'Forró trains', with live *forró* trios entertaining the passengers, leave for Caruaru from Recife's central station.

The festival will always be the best setting to hear the music of *forró* king, Luiz Gonzaga, who died in 1989 but whose classic São João song, *Olha pro Céu* (Look to the Sky), is sung to this day. Gonzaga tells of falling for a girl at a São João party and, in the song, he tells her to look to the sky... purely for her to admire the fireworks, of course.

the city. **Sintese**, Riachuelo 202. **Almanque Livros**, Largo do Varadouro 418, loja 58, bohemian atmosphere, sells food and drink. **Sodiler** at Guararapes airport has books in English, newspapers, magazines; also in the **Shopping Center Recife**. **Livraria do Nordeste**, between cells 118 and 119, Ralo Leste, Casa da Cultura, for books in Portuguese on the Northeast. **Livraria Nordeste**, R Imperatriz 43, Boa Vista. **Melquísidec Pastor de Nascimento**, at R Bispo Cardoso Aires, 215. A great local character, 2nd-hand bookseller; also has a stall at Praça do Sebo (see p442).

Markets The permanent craft market is in the Casa da Cultura (see above); prices for ceramic figurines are lower than Caruaru (see below). **Mercado São José** (1875) for local products and handicrafts. **Hippy fair** at Praça Boa Viagem, on the sea front, life-sized wooden statues of saints, weekends only. Sat craft fair at **Sítio Trindade**, Casa Amarela, during the feast days of 12-29 Jun, fireworks, music, dancing, local food. On 23 Apr, here and in the Pátio de São Pedro, one can see the *xangô* dance. Herbal remedies, barks and spices at Afogados market. **Cais de Alfândega**, Recife Barrio, market of local artisans work, 1st weekend of every month. **Domingo na Rua**, Sun market in Recife Barrio, stalls of local *artesanato* and performances.

Shopping malls **Shopping Center Recife** between Boa Viagem and the airport, one of the largest malls in South America, www.shopping-recife.com.br. **Shopping Tacaruna**, in Santo Amaro, buses to/from Olinda pass.

Bezerros *p451*

The city's main attraction is handicrafts, which are found in the district of **Encruzilhada de São João**; items in leather, clay, wood, papier maché and much more.

Caruaru *p451, map p452, phone code 081*

Caruaru is most famous for its markets which, combined, are responsible for about 70% of the city's income. The **Feira da Sulanca** is basically a clothes market supplied mostly by local manufacture, but also on sale are jewellery, souvenirs, food, flowers and anything else that can go for a good price. There's one area where they sell electronic goods (this is called the *Feira de Paraguaí*, or the illegal import market). The most important day is Mon. There is also the **Feira Livre** or **do Troca-Troca** (free, or barter market). On the same site, Parque 18 de Maio, is the **Feira do Artesanato**, leather goods, ceramics, hammocks and basketware, all the popular crafts of the region; it is tourist orientated but it is on a grand scale and is open daily 0800-1800.

Activities and tours

Recife *p441, map p445, phone code 081*

Diving

Offshore are some 20 wrecks, including the remains of Portuguese galleons; the fauna is very rich.

Mergulhe Coma, T35522355, T91026809 (mob), atlanticdivingasr@ hotmail.com. English-speaking instructors for PADI courses.

Seagate, T34261657, www.seagaterecife.com.br. Daily departures and night dives.

Golf

Caxangá Golf Clube, Av Caxangá 5362, T32711422. 9 holes.

Sailing

Recife Yacht Club, T34652002.

Itamaraca Yacht Club, T32212648.

Tour operators

Jacaré e Cobra de Água Eco-Group, T34473452, 9687360 (mob), www.truenet.com.br. Regular excursions in Pernambuco.

Souto Costa Viagens e Turismo Ltda, R Felix de Brito Melo 666, T34655000, and Aeroporto de Guararapes (American Express representative).

Student Travel Bureau (STB), R Padre Bernardino Pessoa 266, T34654522, F34652636, stbmaster@ stb.com.br. ISIC accepted, discounts on international flights but not domestic Brazilian flights.

Trilhas, T32226864, recommended for ecologically oriented excursions.

Olinda *p446, map p448, phone code 081*

Tour operators

Victor Turismo, **Felitur**, Rua Getulio Vargas 1411, Bairro Novo, T/F4391477.

Viagens Sob O Sol, Prudente de Moraes 424, T/F4293303, T9718102 (mob), English spoken, transport offered to all parts and car hire.

Victor Turismo, Av Santos Domont, 20, Loja 06, T34941467. Day and night trips to Recife.

Porto de Galinhas *p449, phone code 081*

Diving

Porto Point Diving, Praça Principal de Porto de Galinhas, T5521111. For diving and canoeing trips, as well as excursions to Santo Aleixo island.

AICA Diving, Nossa Senhora do Ó, T/F5521290 or T9684876 (mob), run by Mida and Miguel. For diving and canoeing trips, as well as excursions to Santo Aleixo island.

Transport

Recife *p441, map p445, phone code 081*

Air

Guararapes airport, conveniently located in the hotel distict of Boa Viagem, 12 km from the city centre. International flights to Lisbon and Milan. Domestic flights to Brasília, Campina Grande, Fernando de Noronha, Fortaleza, João Pessoa, Juazeiro do Norte, Maceió, Natal, Paulo Afonso, Petrolina, Rio de Janeiro, Salvador and São Paulo.

Airline offices BRA, T34217060, Gol, T34644793. TAM, reservations T3425011, at airport, T34624466. TAP Air Portugal, Av Conselheiro de Aguiar 1472, Boa Viagem T34658800, at airport T33410654. Nordeste/RioSul, Av Domingos Ferreira 801, loja 103-5, T4656799 (RioSul T34656799), at airport, T3413187. Trip, 34644610. United, R Progreso 465/802, T34232444. Varig, R Conselheiro de Aguiar 456, Boa Viagem, T34644440, R J E Favre 719, T33392998, at airport T33414411, cargo T34658989. Vasp, R da Palma 254, Santo Antônio, T34213088, R Dr Nilo Dornelas Câmara 90, Boa Viagem, T34213611, F33253434, at airport, T33417742.

Bus

Local City buses cost US$0.30-0.60; they are clearly marked and run frequently until about 2230. Many central bus stops have boards showing routes. On buses, especially at night, look out for landmarks as street names are written small and are hard to see. Integrated bus-metrô (see Trains below) routes and tickets (US$1) are explained in a leaflet issued by CBTU Metrorec, T32515256. Trolleybuses run in the city centre. Taxis are plentiful; fares double on Sun, after 2100 and during holidays.

Long distance Rodoviária, mainly for long-distance buses, is 12 km outside the city at São Lourenço da Mata, T34521999. There is a 30-min Metrô connection from the central railway station, entrance through Museu do Trem, opposite the Casa da Cultura, 2 lines leave the city, take train marked 'Rodoviária'. From Boa Viagem a taxi all the way costs US$20, or go to Central Metrô station and change there. Bus US$, 1 hr, from the centre or from Boa Viagem. Bus tickets are sold at Cais de Santa Rita (opposite EMTU).

To **Salvador**, daily 1930, 12 hrs, US$18-25, 4 a day (all at night) (1 *leito*, 70). To **Fortaleza**, 12 hrs, US$20 *convencional*, US$30 *executivo*. To **Natal**, 4 hrs, US$9. To **Rio**, daily 2100, 44 hrs, US$58-65. To **São Paulo**, daily 1630, 50 hrs, US$60-70. To **Santos**, daily 1430, 52 hrs, US$60. To **Foz do Iguaçu**, Fri and Sun 1030, 55 hrs, US$90. To **Curitiba**, Fri and Sun, 52 hrs, US$76. To **Brasília**, daily 2130, 39 hrs, US$49-60. To **Belo Horizonte**, daily 2115, 34 hrs, US$41. To **São Luís**, 28 hrs, *Progresso* at 1430 and 1945, US$75. To **Belém**, 34 hrs (*Boa Esperança* bus recommended). To **João Pessoa**, every 30 mins, US$2.50. To **Caruaru**, every hr, 3 hrs, US$3. To **Maceió**, US$9, 3½ hrs (express), 6 hrs (slow), either by the main road or by the coast road daily via 'Litoral'. Buses to the nearby destinations of **Igarassu** (every 15 mins) and **Itamaracá** (every 30 mins) leave from Av Martins de Barros, in front of Grande Hotel. To **Olinda**, see below; those to the beaches beyond Olinda from Av Dantas behind the post office. To **Cabo** (every 20 mins) and beaches south of Recife from Cais de Santa Rita.

Car

Car hire Budget, T33412505. 24 hrs, just outside Guararapes airport. **Localiza**, Av Visconde de Jequitinhonha 1145, T33410287, and at Guararapes airport, T33412082, freephone, T0800-992000. **Hertz**, T4623552.

Train

Commuter services, known as the **Metrô** but not underground, leave from the central station; they have been extended to serve the rodoviária (frequent trains, 0500-2300, US$0.40 single). If going to Boa Viagem from the rodoviária, get off the Metrô at Central station (Joanna Bezerra station is unsafe) and take a bus or taxi (US$8) from there.

Olinda *p446, map p448, phone code 081*

Bus

From **Recife** take any bus marked 'Rio Doce', No 981, which has a circular route around the city and beaches, or No 33 from Av Nossa Senhora do Carmo, US$0.60, or 'Jardim Atlântico' from the central post office at Siqueira Campos; from Boa Viagem, take bus marked 'Piedade/Rio Doce' or 'Barra de Jangada/Casa Caiada' (US$0.60, 30 mins). Change to either of these buses from the airport to Olinda: take 'Aeroporto' bus to Av Domingos Ferreira, Boa Viagem, and ask to be let off; and from the Recife rodoviária: take the Metrô to Central station (Joana Bezerra is unsafe) and then change. In all cases, a light in Praça do Carmo.

Taxi
Taxi drivers between Olinda and Recife often try to put their meters on rate 2 (only meant for Sun, holidays and after 2100), but should change it to rate 1 when queried. (taxi to Boa Viagem US$8, US$12 at night).

Itamaracá *p449, phone code 081*
Bus From **Recife** (Av Martins de Barros opposite Grande Hotel, US$1.10, very crowded) and **Igarassu.**

Igarassu *p449, phone code 081*
Bus Igarassu buses leave from Cais de Santa Rita, **Recife**, 45 mins, US$1.

Gravatá *p451, phone code 081*
Bus To **Recife** and **Caruaru** run every hour; the rodoviária is at Km 80 on the BR-232, T35330691.

Caruaru *p451, map p452, phone code 081*
Bus The rodoviária is 4 km from the town; buses from **Recife** stop in the town centre. Alight here and look for the Livraria Estudantil on the corner of Vigário Freire and R Anna de Albuquerque Galvão. Go down Galvão, turn right on R 15 de Novembro to the 1st junction, 13 de Maio; turn left, cross the river to the Feira do Artesanato. Bus from the centre, at the same place as Recife bus stop, to rodoviária, US$0.40. Many buses from TIP in **Recife**, 2 hrs express, US$3. Bus to **Maceió**, 0700, 5 hrs, US$9. Bus to **Fazenda Nova** 1030, 1 hr, US$2, returns for Caruaru 1330.

West to Triúnfo *p453, phone code 081*
2 Progresso buses daily to and from **Recife** (10 hrs). It is quicker to take a bus from Recife to Serra Talhada, then a colectivo to Triunfo (US$2). In Truinfo colectivos leave from the lakeside. To Triúnfo from **Caruaru**, 1 bus per day, 0830, US$10.

Directory

Recife *p441, map p445, phone code 081*
Banks
1000-1600, hours for exchange vary between 1000 and 1400, sometimes later. Banco do Brasil, R Barão da Souza Leão 440, Boa Viagem, Av Dantas Barreto, 541, Santo Antonio, exchange and credit/debit cards, TCs. Bandepe, Av Dantas Barreto 1110, Santo Antonio. MasterCard ATMs. Bradesco, Av Cons Aguiar 3236, Boa Viagem, T34653033. Av Conde de Boa Vista, Boa Vista, R da Concordia 148, Santo Antônio, 24-hr VISA ATMs, but no exchange. Citibank, Av Marquês de Olinda 126, T32161144, takes MasterCard. Av Cons Aguiar, 2024, ATM. Lloyds Bank, R AL Monte 96/1002. MasterCard, Av Conselheiro Aguiar 3924, Boa Viagem, cash against card.

Money changers Anacor, Shopping Center Recife, loja 52, also at Shopping Tacaruna, loja 173. Monaco, Praça Joaquim Nabuco, cambio, TCs and cash, all major currencies, no commission but poor rates. Norte Cambio Turismo, Av Boa Viagem 5000, also at Shopping Guararapes, Av Barreto de Menezes.

Cultural centres
British Council, Av Domingos Ferreira 4150, Boa Viagem, T34657744, www.britcoun.org/br. 0800-1500, reading room with current British newspapers, very helpful. Alliance Française, R Amaro Bezerra 466, Derby, T32220918.

Embassies and consulates
Denmark, Av Marques de Olinda 85, Edif Alberto Fonseca 2nd floor, T32240311, F32240997 (0800-1200, 1400-1800). France, Av Conselheiro Aguiar 2333, 6th floor, T34653290. Germany, Av Dantas Barreto 191, Edif Santo Antônio, 4th floor, T34253288. Japan, R Pe Carapuceiro, 733, 14th floor, T33277264. Netherlands, Av Conselheiro Aguiar 1313/3, Boa Viagem, T33268096. Spain, R Sirinhaem, 105, 2nd floor, T34650607. Sweden, Av Conde de Boa Vista 1450, T32312581. Switzerland, Av Conselheiro Aguiar 4880, loja 32, Boa Viagem, T33263144. UK, Av Eng Domingos Ferreira 4150, Boa Viagem, T34657744 (0800-1130). USA, R Gonçalves Maia 163, Boa Vista, T34212441, F32311906.

Internet
Shopping Centre Recife, Boa Viagem. Also, lidernet, Shopping Boa Vista, city centre. popul@r.net, R Barao de Souza Leao, near junction with Av Boa Viagem, daily 0900-2100.

Laundry
AcquaClean, Domingos Ferreira, 4023, Boa Viagem, T34660858, Mon-Fri 0630-1900, Sat 0800-1600.

Medical services
Dengue has been resurgent in Recife. Previous sufferers should have good insurance as a 2nd infection can lead to the haemorhagic form, requiring hospitalization. Hospital Santa Joana, R Joaquim Nabuco 200, Graças, T34213666. Unicordis, Av Conselheiro Aguiar 1980, Boa Viagem, T33265237 and Av Conselheiro Rosa de Silva 258, Aflitos, T34211000, equipped for cardiac emergencies. Unimed, Av Bernardo Vieira de Melo 1496, Guararapes, T34621955, general medical treatment, general practitioners.

Dentist Artur Queroz, R Aldemar da Costa Almeida, 140, T34613835, T99657446 (mob), 24 hrs.

Post office
Poste Restante at Central Correios, Av Guararapes 250, next to Rio Capibaribe. 0900-1700, outgoing mail leaves at 1500 each day. Also has a philately centre. Another on R 24 de Maio 59. Poste Restante also with American Express representative Souto Costa, R Félix Brito de Melo 666, T4655000, and at Av Conselheiro Aguiar, Boa Viagem.

Security
Opportunistic theft is unfortunately common in the streets of Recife and Olinda (especially on the streets up to Alto da Sé). Keep hold of bags and cameras, and do not wear a watch. Prostitution is reportedly common in Boa Viagem, so choose nightclubs with care. Tourist Police, T33269603.

Telephones
Embratel, Av Gov Agamenon Magalhães, 1114, Parque Amorim. Also at Praça da Independencia. International calls at phone centres on Av Cons Aguiar, Boa Viagem, Av Herculano Bandeira, 231, Pina and Av Conde da Boa Vista, 0800-1800, phone cards sold, faulty cards replaced. The news-stand on the corner of Av Guararapes and Dantas Barreto is an official vending point. Also at R Diario de Pernambuco 38 and airport, 2nd floor.

Olinda *p446, map p448, phone code 081*
Banks There are no facilities to change TCs, or ATMS, is the old city. Banco do Brasil, R Getulio Vargas 1470. Bandepe, Av Getulio Vargas, MasterCard ATMs. Bradesco, R Getulio Vargas 729, Visa ATMs. **Internet** Studyo Web, Praça do Carmo, US$1.20, 30 mins, a/c. Olind@.com, 15, Av Beira Mar, $US1.50, 30 mins. **Laundry** Cooplav, Estr dos Bultrins, cost per weight of laundry, easily visible from main road, take Bultrins bus from Olinda. **Medical** services Prontolinda, R José Augusto Moreira 1191, T4321700, general, but also equipped for cardiac emergencies. **Post office** Praça do Carmo, open 0900-1700. **Security** Olinda has been severely afflicted by rapidly worsening poverty, the effects of which are perhaps more noticeable in this attractive and comparatively prosperous area. Please exercise caution, and sympathy. **Telephone** Private booths and international phones in Praça do Carmo across the road from the bus stop, Mon-Sat 0900-1800.

Gravatá *p451, phone code 081*
Banks Banco do Brasil, in the centre of town, 1000-1600, very helpful, English-speaking manager, T5330388.

Caruaru *p451, map p452, phone code 081*
Banks Banca Terceiro Mundo, a magazine stall which exchanges dollars, in front of the new Cathedral, will tell you what's going on. **Cultural centres** Cultura Inglesa, Av Agamenon Magalhães 634, Maurício de Nassau, CEP 55000-000, T37214749, cultura@netstage.com.br, will help any visitors with information.

Paraíba

Travellers who once used to bypass Paraíba are now beginning to discover that there are many reasons to stop here. The beaches are some of Brazil's best, and least spoilt; some of the most important archaeological sites in the Americas sit in the haunting, rugged landscapes of its interior and the state capital João Pessoa is a tranquil and restful place with some attractive colonial architecture and a laid-back but lively night scene. Every June Campina Grande, an attractive and prosperous city on the edge of the Sertão hosts one of the countries biggest festivals, a Festa do São João, with great live music and up to a million people dancing forró into the small hours.

The Portuguese did not gain a foothold on this part of the northeast coast until the very end of the 16th century. Their fort became the city of Filipéia, which grew to become the third largest in Brazil. This was later re-named Parahyba and then Joao Pessoa, in honour of the once state governor who refused to form alliances with other powerful politicians during the 1930s run for the vice-presidency. This led to his assassination, an event which swept his running mate, the fascist, Getúlio Vargas to power. Pessoa's '*nego*' ('I refuse') is written on the state's flag.

The dense tropical forest which once covered the coastal strip now only survives in patches, one of which is within the city of João Pessoa; forming one of the largest areas of wilderness within any city in the world. The seaboard is marked for much of its length by offshore reefs. Inland from the coastal plain the Zona da Mata is an abrupt line of hills and plateaus, a transitional region between the moist coast and the much drier interior. Most people live in this zone, especially in and around the state capital and a couple of other industrial centres.

João Pessoa → *Phone code: 083. Colour map 2, B6. Population: 598,000.*

It is a two hour bus ride through sugar plantations on a good road from Recife (126 km) to João Pessoa, the state capital, on the Rio Paraíba. It retains a small town atmosphere.

Founded in 1585 as Nossa Senhora das Neves, it became Friederikstaadt during the Dutch occupation (1634-54) and was only given its current name in 1930 in memory of a governor who was killed in Recife.

The well-preserved **Centro Histórico** has several churches and monasteries which are worth seeing. The São Francisco Cultural Centre (Praça São Francisco 221), one of the most important baroque structures in Brazil, includes the beautiful 16th-century church of **São Francisco** and the Convento de Santo Antônio, which houses the **Museu Sacro e de Arte Popular** ⓘ *Tue-Sat 0800-1100, Tue-Sun 1400-1700, T2212840*, with a magnificent collection of colonial and popular artefacts. This is also the best point to see the sun set over the forest.

Other tourist points include the **Casa da Pólvora**, an old gunpowder store which has become the city museum, and **Museu Fotográfico Walfredo Rodríguez** ⓘ *Ladeira de São Francisco, Mon-Fri 0800-1200 and 1330-1700*. The **Teatro Santa Rosa** at Praça Pedro Américo, Varadouro, was built in 1886 with a wooden ceiling and walls. ⓘ *T2184382, Mon-Fri 0800-1200 and 1330-1800*. The **Espaço Cultural José Lins de Rego** ⓘ *R Abdias Gomes de Almeida 800, Tambauzinho, T2116222*, a cultural centre named after the novelist (see Literature, page 703), includes an art gallery, history and science museums, several theatres, cinema and a planetarium. The **Fundação José Américo de Almeida** ⓘ *Av Cabo Branco 3336, Cabo Branco*, should be visited by those interested in modern literature and politics; it is in the former house of the novelist and sociologist.

 João Pessoa prides itself in being a green city and is called **Cidade Verde.** Its parks include the 17-ha **Parque Arruda Câmara,** also known as Bica, located north of the centre in the neighbourhood of Roger; it has walking trails, an 18th-century fountain, an aviary and a small zoo. **Parque Solon de Lucena** or **Lagoa** is a lake surrounded by impressive palms in the centre of town, the city's main avenues and bus lines go around it. **Mata** or **Manancial do Bouraquinho** is a 471-ha nature reserve

Joâo Pessoa orientation

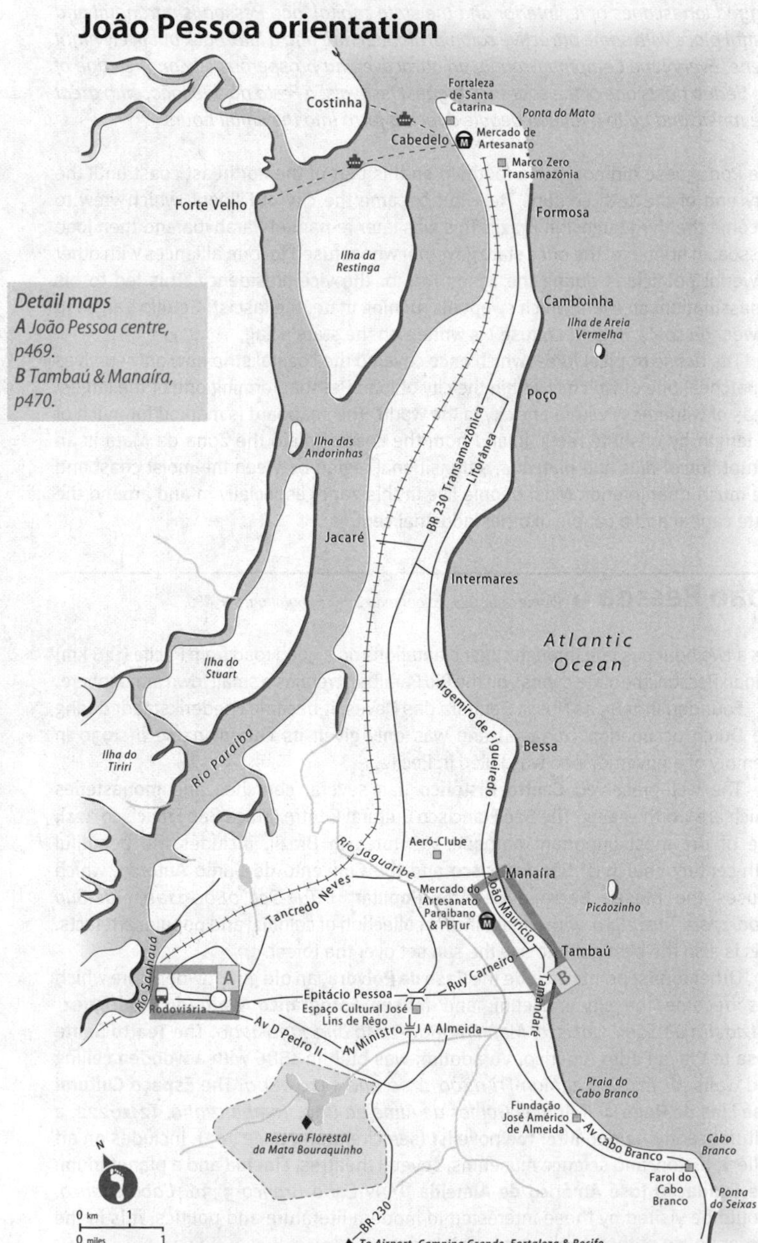

of native *mata atlântica*, one of the largest urban forest reserves in Brazil. It is located south of the centre and administered by **Ibama** ⓘ *T2442725*, which organizes guided walks; access is otherwise restricted.

João Pessoa's urban beaches

The beachfront stretches for some 30 km from Ponta do Seixas (south) to Cabedelo (north); the ocean is turquoise green and there is a backdrop of lush coastal vegetation. By the more populated urban areas the water is polluted, but there are also parts away from town which are reasonably clean, some spots are calm and suitable for swimming while others are best for surfing. About 7 km from the city centre, following Avenida Presidente Epitáceo Pessoa, is the beach of **Tambaú**, which has many hotels, restaurants and the state tourism centre and is for all intents and purposes the centre of the city. The pier by **Hotel Tambaú** affords nice views (bus No 510 'Tambaú' from outside the rodoviária or the city centre, alight at **Hotel Tropical Tambaú**). South of Tambaú are **Praia de Cabo Branco** and **Praia do Seixas** and to the north are the beaches of **Manaíra**, **Bessa**, **Intermares, Poço** and **Camboinha**, before reaching the port of **Cabedelo**.

There's a tourist office, **PBTUR** ⓘ *Centro Turístico Almte Tamandaré 100, Tambaú, T2148279 or T0800-2819229, and others at the rodoviária and airport* ⓘ *T2186655 and T2534010, all open 0800-1900*. They provide useful information, pamphlets and maps. At least one member of staff in the Tambaú centre speaks good English and some French.

Excursions from João Pessoa

About 14 km from the centre, south down the coast, is the **Cabo Branco** lighthouse at Ponta do Seixas, the most easterly point of continental Brazil and South America (34° 46' 36" W) and thus the first place in the Americas where the sun rises; there is a panoramic view from the clifftop. **Cabo Branco** is much better for swimming than Tambaú. Take bus 507 'Cabo Branco' from outside the rodoviária to the end of the

line; hike up to the lighthouse. At low tide you can walk from Tambaú to Ponta do Seixas in about two hours.

The port of **Cabedelo**, on a peninsula between the Rio Paraíba and the Atlantic Ocean, is 18 km north by road or rail. Here, Km 0 marks the beginning of the **Transamazônica highway**. At the tip of the peninsula are the impressive, but somewhat run-down walls of the 17th-century **Fortress of Santa Catarina**, amid oil storage tanks and the commercial port. The **Mercado de Artesanato** is at Praça Getúlio Vergas, Centro.

The estuary of the Rio Paraíba has several islands; there is a regular boat service between Cabedelo and the fishing villages of **Costinha** and **Forte Velho** on the north bank; Costinha had a whaling station until the early 1980s.

The beaches between João Pessoa and Cabedelo have many bars and restaurants and are very popular with the locals on summer weekends (Bar do Sumé, Rua Beira Mar 171, Praia Ponta do Mato, Cabedelo, has good fish and seafood). Take bus marked Cabedelo-Poço for the beach as most Cabedelo buses go inland along the Transamazônica; taxi Tambaú-Cabedelo US$24.

At Km 3 of the Transamazônica, about 12 km from João Pessoa, is the access to **Jacaré**, a nice beach on the Rio Paraíba (take Cabedelo bus and walk 1½ km or take the train and walk 1 km, taxi from Tambaú US$10). There are several bars along the riverfront where people congregate to watch the lovely sunset to the sounds of Ravel's *Bolero*. Here you can hire a boat along the river to visit the mangroves or ride in an ultralight aircraft (Flaviano Gouveia, T9821604, US$19 for eight-minute ride or US$115 for an hour). Brian Ingram, originally from Kent, England, runs **Sea Tech** (PO Box 42, João Pessoa, 56001-970, T2451476, F2452302), a boatyard and frequent port of call for international yachtspeople plying the Brazilian coast.

From Tambaú tour boats leave for **Picãozinho**, a group of coral reefs about 700 m from the coast which at low tide

Tambaú & Manaíra

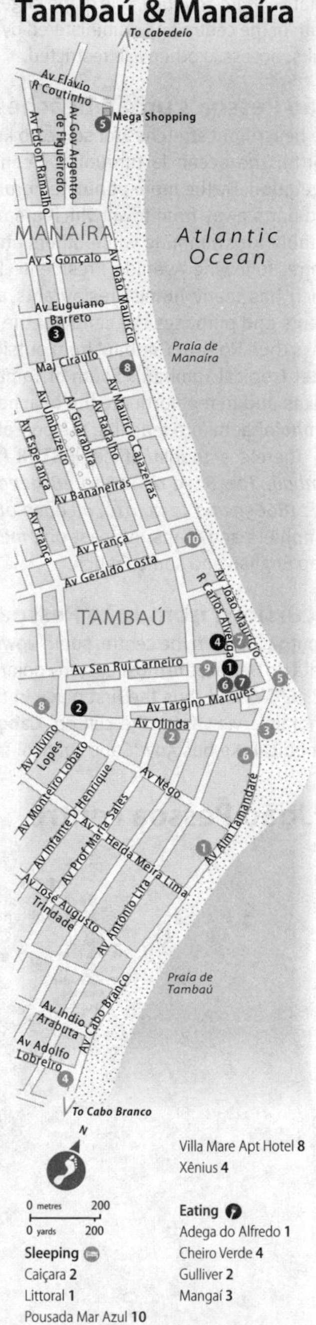

Sleeping
Caiçara 2
Littoral 1
Pousada Mar Azul 10
Royal Praia 5
Solar Filipéia 9
Tambía Praia 7
Tropical Tambaú 3
Victory Business Flat 6
Villa Mare Apt Hotel 8
Xênius 4

Eating
Adega do Alfredo 1
Cheiro Verde 4
Gulliver 2
Mangaí 3

Bars & clubs
Fashion Club 5
Incognito 6
Mr Caipira 8
Zodiaco 7

turn into pools of crystalline water, suitable for snorkelling (US$20 per person). Further north, across from Praia de Camboinha (boats leave from here), is **Areia Vermelha**, a large sandbank surrounded by corals. This becomes exposed at low tide, around the time of the full and new moon, and is a popular bathing spot (US$20 per person tour, US$5 per person transport in a *jangada*). Floating bars are set up at both locations, travel agencies arrange trips.

The Paraíba Coast

The Paraíba coastline has 117 km of beautiful beaches and coves, surrounded by cliffs and coconut groves. These are among the least developed of the Northeast.

Tambaba → *Colour map 2, B6.*

The best known beach of the state is Tambaba, the only official nudist beach of the Northeast and one of only two in Brazil. It is located 49 km south of João Pessoa in a lovely setting: the green ocean, warm water, natural pools for swimming formed by the rocks, cliffs up to 20 m high full of caves, palms and lush vegetation. Two coves make up this famous beach: in the first bathing-suits are optional, while the second one is only for nudists. Strict rules of conduct are enforced, unaccompanied men are not allowed in this area and any inappropriate behaviour is reason enough to be asked to leave. The only infrastructure is one bar (meals available).

Between Jacumã and Tambaba are several nice beaches such as **Tabatinga**, which has many summer homes built on the cliffs, and **Coqueirinho**, surrounded by nice vegetation, good for bathing, surfing and exploring caves. There are plenty of cheap and mid-range *pousadas* at both and a very good seafood restaurant at Coquerinho, Canyon de Coqueirinho on the beach. Near the border with Pernambuco is the 10-km long beach of **Pitimbu**, see page 451.

Campina

The nicest beaches of northern Paraíba are in the vicinity of the fishing village of **Campina**; although there is little infrastructure in this area, the shore is worth a visit. Access is via a turnoff to the east at Km 73.5 of the BR-101, 42 km north of João Pessoa. It is 28 km along a dirt road (PB-025) to Praia Campina, with a wide beach of fine sand, palms and hills in the background. Nearly 3 km south is **Praia do Oiteiro**, in which the white sand stands out in contrast with the multicoloured cliffs and calm blue ocean. About 2 km north of Campina is **Barra do Mamanguape**, where Ibama runs a preservation centre for marine manatee.

Some 85 km from João Pessoa is **Baia da Traição**, a fishing village and access point for a number of beaches. Its name refers to a massacre of 500 residents of a sugar plantation in the 16th century. There is a reserve near town where wood and string crafts are made by the local indigenous people. An annual festival, **Festa do Toré** (an Indian dance), takes place on 19 April. Inho, a fisherman, offers tours by sea to the less accessible beaches in the area (US$15 per person). **Barra de Camaratuba**, about 17 km north of Baia da Traição, is a popular surfing beach.

The Sertão

The Transamazônica runs due west of João Pessoa as the BR-230, along the axis of the state of Paraíba and through the heart of the *sertão*.

Campina Grande → *Phone code: 083. Colour map 2, B6. Population: 340,500.*

Located in the Serra da Borborema at 551 m above sea level and 130 km west of João

 Pessoa, the second city in Paraíba has a very pleasant climate. Known as the *porta do sertão*, it is an important centre for light industry and an outlet for goods from most of the Northeast. In the 1920s it was one of the most important cotton producing areas in the world; a decline in this industry brought a decrease in prosperity in the 1940s and 1950s and the diversification of industry to areas such as sisal and leather. The city's two universities have been instrumental in technological development and reactivation of the local economy.

Avenida Floriano Peixoto is the main street running east-west through the entire city, with Praça da Bandeira at its centre. The **Museu de Arte Assis Chateaubriand** ⓘ *Parque do Açude Novo, T3413300, Mon-Fri 0900-1200, Mon-Sun 1400-2200*, has a collection of paintings and etchings by Brazilian artists and temporary exhibits. **Museu Histórico de Campina Grande** ⓘ *Av Floriano Peixoto 825, Centro, daily 0800-1130, 1300-1645*, is the city museum housed in a 19th-century building, with a photo and artefact collection reflecting the cycles of prosperity and poverty in the region. **Museu da História e Tecnologia do Algodão** ⓘ *Centro Nacional de Produção do Algodão, Oswaldo Cruz 1143, Centenário, Mon-Fri 0730-1130, 1330-1730, Sat-Sun 0800-1200, T3413608*, has machines and related equipment used in the cotton industry in the 16th and 17th centuries. **Museu Regional de São João** ⓘ *Largo da Estação Velha, Centro, T3412000, daily 0800-1300*, houses an interesting collection of objects and photographs pertaining to the June celebrations.

The **Teatro Municipal Severino Cabral** ⓘ *Av Floreano Peixoto*, is a modern theatre where there are regular performances. The main parks in town are: the **Parque do Açude Novo** (Evaldo Cruz), a green area with playgrounds, fountains and restaurants; the nearby **Parque do Povo** with its *forródromo*, where the main festivities of the city take place; and the **Açude Velho**, a park around a dam south of the centre. The **Mercado Central**, where a large roof has been built over several blocks of old buildings, has regional crafts and produce; interesting and worth a visit. The **tourist offices** are **PBTUR** ⓘ *T156 for information*, and **DEMTUR** ⓘ *T3413993, Municipal*.

Excursions from Campina Grande

Some 35 km east of Campina Grande, off the road to João Pessoa, is Ingá, site of the **Pedra de Itacoatiara** archaeological centre, where inscriptions dated as 10,000 years old were found on a boulder 25 m long and 3 m high; a small museum at the site has fossils of a giant sloth and a tyrannosaurus. During the June festivities there is a train service to Itacoatiara.

The **Boqueirão** dam on the Rio Paraíba, 70 km southeast of town, is where locals flock on holidays for watersports; there is a hotel-*fazenda* (T3911233).

The Sertão proper begins near **Cariri** an hour or so from Campina Grande. This is an area of fascinating **rock formations** – with giant weather worn boulders sitting on top of gently curved expanses of rock that look out over a plain of low bushes and stunted trees. Although the vegetation is quite different the landscape itself, the arid conditions and the size of the trees recalls the outback; and the rocks themselves have been compared to the Devil's Marbles. The most spectacular of all the formations sit in the private grounds of *fazenda* **Pae Mateus**. Like various other sites in Paraíba and Rio Grande do Norte, boulders here are covered in important pre-Colombian rock art, some of which has controversially been dated as pre-Clovis; making it older than recent datings for the first waves of American population coming from over the Bering Strait. A famous local holy man lived inside one of the giant hollowed out stones and the views from his former home at sunset are particularly spell binding. The *fazenda* itself is a very pleasant place to stay and there is rich, though depleted wildlife in the area and good birding. Very good tours can be organized with Manary (see page 498), who provide fascinating information about the archaeological sites but have no knowledge at all of the fauna in the region. The *fazenda*'s guides are informative about life in the Sertão and the use of medicinal plants, but again as ever in Brazil, knowledge of birds and animals is poor.

To the north, 46 km of Campina Grande, is **Areial**, main town of the **Brejo Paraibano**, a scenic region of green hills and valleys, with a pleasant climate, where colonial sugar *fazendas* have been transformed into hotels like **Bruxaxá** (**A**, Floriano Peixoto, T3622423, with a pool and restaurant). About 10 km north from Campina Grande is **Lagoa Seca**, where figures in wood and sacking are made and there is a **Museu do Índio**.

Patos → *Colour map2, B5. Population: 84,500.*

West of Campina Grande the landscape turns to vast, flat expanses, flanked by rolling hills and interesting rock formations; very scenic when green, but a sad sight during the prolongued *sertão* droughts. Situated 174 km from Campina Grande is Patos, centre of a cattle ranching and cotton growing area, and an access point for the Serra do Teixeira 28 km away, which includes Pico do Jabre, the highest point in the state, at 1,130 m above sea level. There are various hotels and restaurants in Patos.

Souza → *Phone code: 081. Colour map 2, B5. Population: 59,000.*

Northwest of Patos by 130 km is this pleasant *sertão* town, with hot temperatures year-round, which is gaining fame for the nearby dinosaur tracks and prehistoric rock carvings. The **Igreja do Rosário** at the Praça Matriz has paintings dating to the Dutch occupation of the area. It currently functions as a school. About 3 km from the centre, atop a hill, is a statue to Frei Damião, an important religious leader of the northeast who died in 1997. Frei Damião was an Italian friar who came to Brazil in the 1930s and stayed to become an inspiration for the faith of its most recent generation of dispossessed. He is seen as belonging to the same tradition as O Conselheiro and Padre Cícero.

Fossilized dinosaur prints, of as many as 90 different species which inhabited the area between 110 and 80 million years ago, are found in a number of sites in the Souza region. These were extensively studied by the Italian Palaeontologist Giussepe Leonardi in the 1970s and 1980s. The **Vale dos Dinossauros**, on the sedimentary river bed of the Rio do Peixe, is one of the closest sites to Souza; it has some impressive Iguanodontus prints; access is 4 km from town along the road north to Uiraúna; the best time to visit is the dry season, July to October. The area has no infrastructure and is best visited with someone to guide you. (Contact Robson Marques of the **Movisaurio Association** R João Rocha 7, Souza, PB 58800-610, T5221065, he worked with Leonardi and is very knowledgeable); otherwise contact the Prefeitura Municipal. Tours can be organized through **Manary in Natal** (see page 498), these can be combined with visits to Cariri.

Cajazeiras → *Colour map 2, B5. Population: 51,000.*

Some 37 km west of Souza, the Transamazônica (BR-230) reaches Cajazeiras, centre of a cotton growing area, with an impressive looking tower on the main church and various hotels. This is an access point for the **Brejo das Freiras** thermal, mineral baths 32 km to the north, an oasis with natural springs in the middle of the *sertão*, Estância Termal Brejo das Freiras.

From Cajazeiras it is 17 km to the Ceará border; the Transamazônica continues west across the *sertãos* of Ceará and Piauí and on to Maranhão, Tocantins and Pará. Southwest of Cajazeiras it is 118 km to Juazeiro do Norte, an important pilgrimage centre, see p514.

Sleeping

João Pessoa centre *p467, map p469, phone code 083*

The town's main attractions are its beaches, where most tourists stay. Hotels in the centre are poorer and tend to cater to business clients. The centre is dead after dark and it is difficult to find a restaurant. Cheaper hotels can be found near the rodoviária; look carefully first, some are quite sleazy. The most convenient beach and the focus of nightlife and restaurants is **Tambaú**. There are good restaurants and a few hotels in **Manaíra**, to the north of Tambaú. There are also a few in the southern beach suburb of **Cabo Branco**. But this is quieter and has fewer eating and nightlife options.

C-B **Hotel JR**, R João Ramalho de Andrade, T2416262, www.bomguia.com.br/jr. 1990s business hotel with basic facilities and a restaurant. The largest and most comfortable in the centre.

C-D **Guarany**, R Almeida Barreto 181 and 13 de Maio, T/F2415005, guarany@bomguia.com.br/guarany (cheaper without a/c and TV, cheaper still in low season). A pleasant, safe, extremely good-value establishment with its own self-service restaurant. Recommended.

D **Aurora**, Praça João Pessoa 51, T2413238, A/c or cheaper fan-cooled rooms, on an attractive square.

D **Ouro Preto**, Idaleto 162, T2215882, Varadouro near rodoviária. Very simple rooms with baths and a fan.

João Pessoa urban beaches *p469, map p468, phone code 083*

Accommodation can also be found in the outer beaches such as Camboinha and Seixas, and in Cabedelo.

L **Littoral**, Av Cabo Branco 2172, T2471100, F2471166. A full luxury service. Low-season discounts available.

AL **Caiçara**, Av Olinda 235, T/F2472040, www.hotcaicarara.com.br. A slick, business-orientated place with a pleasant restaurant attached.

AL **Tropical Tambaú**, Av Alm Tamandaré 229, T2473660, www.tropicalhotel.com.br. An enormous round building on the seafront which looks like a rocket-launching station and has motel-style rooms around its perimeter. Comfortable and with good service. Recommended.

AL **Xênius**, Av Cabo Branco 1262, T2263535, www.xeniushotel.com.br. Popular standard 4 star with a pool, good restaurant and well-kept but standard a/c rooms (low-season reductions).

A-B **Royal Praia**, Coração de Jesus, T21063000, www.royalhotel.com.br. Comfortable a/c rooms with fridges, pool.

A-B **Victory Business Flat**, Av Tamandaré 310, T2473011, www.victoryflat.com.br. Furnished apartments with a pool and sauna. Cheaper in low season.

B **Pouso das Águas**, Av Cabo Branco 2348, Cabo Branco. A homely atmosphere with landscaped areas and a pool.

B **Tambía Praia** , R Carlos Alverga 36, T2474101, www.tambiahotel.hpg.com.br. Centrally located and 1 block from the beach. Intimate, with balconies and sea view. Recommended.

B **Villa Mare Apartment Hotel**, Av Négo 707, T2262142, www.pbnet.com.br/openline/george. Comfortable apartments for 2 or 3 people with full amenities per night or from US$400-500 per month. Helpful staff. Recommended.

B-C **Pousada Casa Rosada**, Av Cabo Branco 1710, Cabo Branco. T2472470. Well-kept rooms with bath and fans run by a friendly family. Cheaper with shared bath.

C **Pousada Casa Grande**, R Infante Dom Henrique 750, Manaíra, T2262071, www.holandahhoteisezdir.net. Well-kept, simple rooms with en suites and friendly staff in a discreet small family hotel 2 blocks from the beach.

C-D **Solar Filipéia**, Av Incognito Coracão de Jesus 153, www.solarfilipeia.com.br. Brand new, very smart hotel with large, bright rooms with bathrooms in tile and black marble and excellent service. A real bargain.

E **Pousada Mar Azul**, Av João Maurício 315, T2262660. Very clean large rooms, the best are on the upper level, right on the ocean-front road. Some have a/c and private bathrooms, others have fans. Well kept, safe and a real bargain.

Youth hostels

Hostel Manaíra, R Major Ciraulo 380, Manaíra, T2471962, www.manairahostel.br2.net. Friendly, new hostel close to the beach, with a pool, internet, barbecue, cable TV and breakfast. A real bargain.

Camping

Camping Clube do Brasil, Praia de Seixas, 13 km from the centre, T2472181.

Tambaba *p471, phone code 083*

B **Chalé Suiço**, R Chalé Suiço 120, Tabatinga, T9812046. Small, shared bath, restaurant, upstairs rooms with balconies towards the ocean.

B **Pousada Corais de Carapebus**, Av Beira Mar, Carapebus, T2901179, a few kilometres south of Jacumã. With bath, pool, restaurant and a nice breeze since it is located on a cliff across from the ocean.

B **Vivenda Ocean**, R Sidine C Dore 254, Carapebus, T2266017. Chalets for 5 plus restaurant.

C **Vallhalla**, R Niterói, Jacumã, T2901015. Away from the beach with nice views. Rooms are simple with a fan as the only extra. It's Swedish run and the restaurant has a varied menu.

Camping

Camping is possible in Tambaba with permission from the guards, also in Coqueirinho, no infrastructure in either.

Campina *p471, phone code 083*

C **Pousada Ponto do Sol**, Dom Pedro II 537, Baia da Traição, T2961050. Rooms withbaths, fridges and a restaurant.

On the same street are the simpler *pousadas* **Alvorada** and **2001**, T2961043. Several others in town.

C **Pousada Porto das Ondas**, Barra de Camaratuba, T2472054. Bath, fan, restaurant.

Campina Grande *p471, phone code 083*

Many hotels are clustered around Praça da Bandeira.

A **Ouro Branco**, João Lourenço Porto 20, T3412929, F3225788. Cheaper rooms are available with discounts for cash.

A **Serrano**, Tavares Cavalcante 27, T3413131, F3210635. Luxury standard with pool and restaurant. You can get discounts for cash.

B **Mahatma Gandi**, Floriano Peixoto 338, T/F3215275. With bath, a/c (cheaper with fan), fridge.

B **Souto Maior**, Floriano Peixoto 289, T3218043, F3212154. Rooms include bath a/c and fridge.

C **Regente**, Barão do Abiaí 80, T3213843, F3213843. With bath, a/c or fan), fridge.

C-D **Pérola**, Floriano Peixoto 258, T3415319. With bath, a/c (cheaper with fan), parking and a very good breakfast.

D **Avenida**, Floriano Peixoto 378, T3411249. With fan, good value, cheaper with shared bath.

D-E **Eliu's**, Maciel Pinheiro 31B, 1st floor, T3214115. Clean, friendly, a/c and bath (cheaper with fan; cheaper still without bath), good value. Breakfast not provided.

D **Verona**, 13 de Maio 232, T3411926. With bath, fan, good value, friendly service.

E **Aurora**, 7 de Setembro 120, T3214874. Shared bath, very basic and run down.

Excursions from Campina Grande

p472, phone code 081

Fazenda Pae Mateus, Souza

B **Gadelha Palace**, Trav Luciana Rocha 2, Cariri, T5211416. With bath, a/c, fridge, pool and restaurant.

B **Santa Terezinha**, R Col Zé Vicente 101, Cariri, T5211412. With fan and bath so overpriced for what you get.

C **Dormitório Sertanejo I**, R Col Zé Vicente, Cariri. Rooms nice and clean with bath and fan.No breakfast, but good value. Recommended.

E **Dormitório Aguiar**, R João Gualberto, Cariri. Very basic.

Cajazeiras *p473, phone code 081*

A **Estância Termal Brejo das Freiras**, São João do Rio do Peixe, T5221515. Rooms or chalets with bath, a/c, fridge. There is a pool and restaurant.

C **Regente**, in centre, 15 mins' walk from rodoviária, a/c available but cheaper without. TV, bath.

E **Cacique**, near rodoviária, cheaper without a/c.

Eating

João Pessoa *p467, map p469, phone code 083*

There are few eating options in the city centre. Locals eat at the stalls in Parque Solon de Lucena next to the lake, where there are a couple of siple restaurants.

João Pessoa's urban beaches *p469*

Every evening on the beachfront stalls are set up selling all kinds of snacks and barbecued meats. At Cabo Branco there are many straw huts on the beach serving cheap eats and seafood.

TTT **Adega do Alfredo**, Coração de Jesus. Very popular traditional Portuguese restaurant in the heart of the club and bar area.

TTT **Gulliver**, Av Olinda 590, Tambaú. Fashionable French/Brazilian restaurant frequented by João Pessoa's upper middle classes.

TT **Mangaí**, Av General Édson Ramalho 696, Manaíra, T2261615. This is one of the best restaurants in the Northeast to sample the region's cooking. There are almost 100 different hot dishes to chose from, sitting in copper tureens over a traditional wood-fired stove some 20 m long. The open-sided dining area is very welcoming and spacious. Very good Italian too with a charming atmosphere.

TT **Cheiro Verde**, R Carlos Alverga 43. Self service, well established, regional food.

TT **Sapore d'Italia**, Av Cabo Branco 1584, Standard Italian fare including pizza.

Campina Grande *p471, phone code 083*

R 13 de Maio by Rui Barbosa in the centre has several good restaurants. There are many bars near Parque do Povo, busy at weekends.

TT **A Cabana do Possidônio**, 13 de Maio 207 T3413384. A varied menu of regional and international dishes.

TT **La Nostra Casa**, R 13 de Maio 175, T3225196. Modest but friendly pasta and pizza restaurant.

T **Carne & Massa**, R 13 de Maio 214, T3228677. Regional cooking including *carne de sol* together with pasta and a range of desserts.

T **Lanchonette Casa das Frutas**, Marquês de Herval 54. Good-value meals, fruit juices and snacks.

T **La Suissa**, Dep João Tavares 663. Good savory and sweet snacks.

T **Manoel da Carne de Sol**, Félix de Araújo 263. T3212877. One of the city's best-value regional restaurants including an excellent *carne de sol* lunch with runner beans, *farofa* manioc flour and vegetables.

T **Vila Antiga**, R 13 de Maio 164, T3414718. A popular pay by weight restaurant with a broad range of regional dishes, pastas, salads and desserts.

Souza *p473, phone code 081*

There are several restaurants on R Col Zé Vicente.

T **Diagonal**, Getúlio Vargas 2. Ordinary but reasonale pizzeria.

Bars and clubs

João Pessoa *p467, map p469, phone code 083*

There are many open bars on and across from the beach in Tambaú and Cabo Branco; the area known as Feirinha de Tambaú, on Av Tamandaré by the Tambaú Hotel and nearby streets, sees much movement even on weekend nights, with R Coração do Jesus being the epicentre. There are numerous little bars and *forró* places here and this is the place for a night-time browse. Other beachfront neighbourhoods also have popular bars.

Fashion Club, Mega Shopping, Manaíra. Still the most popular nightclub in the city – with a twenty-something crowd and mostly techno and MPB. Large beachfront *baracca* restaurant with live music at weekends. Not as popular as it once was.

Incognito, R Coração do Jesus. A very popular and lively closed bar and dance club. There are many others here including KS.

Zodiaco, Incognito Coração do Jesus 144. One of several nightclubs in the area attracting a lively young crowd especially at the weekends.

Mr Caipira, Av João Maurício 1533, Manaíra, T2467597. Live acoustic music, Brazilian barbecued food and standards like *feijoada* and a smart thirty-something crowd. On the seafront road.

Festivals and events

João Pessoa *p467, map p469, phone code 083*

Feb Pre-carnival celebrations in João Pessoa are renowned: the *bloco* **Acorde Miramar** opens the celebrations the Tue before Carnival and on Wed, known as **Quarta Feira de Fogo**, thousands join the **Muriçocas de Miramar**, forming a *bloco* second only to Recife's **Galo da Madrugada** with as many as 300,000 people taking part in the celebrations.

5 Aug The street celebrations for the patroness of the city, **Nossa Senhora das Neves**, take place for 10 days to the rhythm of *frevo*.

Campina Grande *p471, phone code 083*

Apr Micarande, the out-of-season Salvador-style carnival.

Jun-Jul Campina Grande boasts the largest **São João** celebrations in Brazil; from the beginning of Jun into the 1st week of Jul the city attracts many visitors; there are bonfires and *quadrilhas* (square dance groups) in every neighbourhood; *forró* and invited artists at the Parque do Povo; *quentão*, *pomonha* and *canjica* are consumed everywhere.

Aug The annual **Congresso de Violeiros**, which gathers singers and guitarists from all of the Nordeste.

Shopping

João Pessoa *p467, map p469, phone code 083*

Regional crafts, including lace-work, embroidery and ceramics, are best bought at **Terra do Sol**, R Coração do Jesus 145, T2261940, www.terradosol.art.br, which has very elegant, high-quality bedspreads, hammocks, bath robes, tablecloths, etc, some of which are made from the newly created natural beige cotton. The shop also sells a range of work by Paraíba artists and artisans. Cheaper arts and crafts can be bought at: **Mercado de Artesanato**, Centro de Turismo, Almte Tamandaré 100, Tambaú. Daily 0800-1800; **Mercados de Artesanato Paraibano**, Av Rui Carneiro, Tambaú. Daily 0900-1700; **Bosque dos Sonhos**, by the Cabo Branco lighthouse. Weekends only.

Activities and tours

João Pessoa *p467, map p469, phone code 083*

Roger Turismo, Av Tamandaré 229, T2471856. Half-day city tours (US$6), day trips to Tambaba (US$8) and Recife/Oldina (US$12). A large agency with some English-speaking guides and a range of other tours.

Cliotur, Av Alm Tamandaré 310, Sala 2, T2474460. Also offer trips to the Sertão and light adventure activities.

Transport

João Pessoa *p467, map p469, phone code 083*

Air Domestic flights arrive at Presidente Castro Pinto airport, 11 km from centre, T2321200. Flights to São Paulo, Brasília, Recife and Rio de Janeiro. Taxi to centre costs US$8, to Tambaú US$12. **Gol** will fly from São Paulo or Rio to Recife, then offering free bus transport to João Pessoa.

Airline offices BRA, Av Almirante Barroso 651, T2226222. **TAM**, at airport, T2472400, Av Senador Rui Carneiro 512, T2472400. Varig, Av Getúlio Vargas 183, Centro, T2478383, freephone T0800-997000. Vasp, Parque Solon de Lucena 530, Centro, T2141500, F2223879, at airport, T2472400. Gol, www.vooegol.com.br, and at the airport.

Bus All city buses stop at the rodoviária and most go by the Lagoa (Parque Solon de Lucena). Take No 510 for Tambaú, No 507 for Cabo Branco.

Bus Rodoviária is at R Francisco Londres, Varadouro, 10 mins from the centre, T2219611. Luggage store and PBTUR information booth, helpful. Taxi to the centre US$1.50, to Tambaú US$5.

Buses to **Recife** with Boa Vista or Bonfim, every 30 mins, US$2.50, 2 hrs. To **Natal** with Nordeste, every 2 hrs, US$8 *convencional*, US$7.50 *executivo*, 3 hrs. To **Fortaleza** with Nordeste, 2 daily, 10 hrs, US$18. To **Campina Grande** with Real, every 30 mins, US$4, 2 hrs. To **Juazeiro do Norte** with Transparaíba, 2 daily, US$14, 10 hrs. To **Salvador** with Progresso, 4 weekly, US$30, 14 hrs. To **Brasília** via Campina Grande, with Planalto, 2 weekly, US$57, 48 hrs. To **Rio de Janeiro** with São

Geraldo, daily, US$67*convencional*, US$80 *executivo*, 42 hrs. To **São Paulo** with Itapemirim, daily, US$73 *convencional*, US$76 *executivo*, 47 hrs. To **Belém** with Guanabara, daily, US$46, 36 hrs.

Car hire Avis, Av Nossa Senhora dos Navegantes, 402, T2473050. Localiza, Av Epitácio Pessoa 4910, T2474030, and at the airport, T0800-992000. Tempo, Almte Tamandaré 100, at the Centro de Turismo, T2470002.
Train Ferroviária at Av Sanhauá, Varadouro, T2214257. Regional service west to Bayeux and Santa Rita and Cabedelo to the north.

Tambaba *p471, phone code 083*
Access to Jacumã is via the BR-101, 20 km south from João Pessoa to where the PB-018 goes 3 km east to Conde and continues 11 km to the beach of Jacumã; from here a dirt road goes 12 km south to Tambaba. There are hourly buses from the João Pessoa rodoviária (0530-1900) to Jacumã; in the summer, dune buggies can be hired at Jacumã to go to Tambaba. Buggy from João Pessoa to Tambaba US$25 per person return (leave 0930, return 1730). Day trip in a taxi US$95.

Campina Grande *p471, phone code 083*
Air Airport João Suassuna, 7 km south of centre on the road to Caruaru, T3311149. Daily flights to Recife with Nordeste. Taxi to airport US$7. City bus Distrito Industrial from Praça Clementino Procópio, behind Cine Capitólio.

Bus Rodoviária is at Av Argemiro de Figuereido, a 20-min ride from the centre, T3215780. To **João Pessoa**, with Real, every 30 mins, US$3, 2 hrs. To **Souza** with Transparaíba, 6 daily, US$7, 6 hrs. To **Juazeiro do Norte** with Transparaíba, 2 daily, US$10, 9 hrs. To **Natal** with Nordeste, 0800 daily, US$6, 18 hrs. To **Rio** with Itapemirim, 1600 daily, US$65, 42 hrs. To **Brasília** with Planalto, 2 weekly, US$55, 46 hrs.

Car hire On R Tavares Cavalcante are Intermezzo, No 27, T3214790, F3210835. Kelly's, No 301, T/F3224539. Localiza, R Dr Severino Cruz 625, T3414034, and at the airport, T3314594.

Souza *p473, phone code 081*
Bus The rodoviária is 1 km from the centre, there are no city buses, walk (hot), take a moto-taxi (US$1) or a taxi (US$5). To **Campina Grande** with Transparaíba, 6 daily, US$7, 6 hrs. To **João Pessoa** with Transparaíba, 6 daily, US$10, 8 hrs. To **Juazeiro do Norte** with Transparaíba or Boa Esperança, 4 daily, US$4, 3½ hrs. To **Mossoró**, RN, with Jardinense, 4 daily, US$6, 4½ hrs.

Directory

João Pessoa *p467, map p469, phone code 083*
Banks Banco 24 horas , Av Almirante Tamandaré, 100, in front of Centro de Turismo, Tambaú, ATM for Cirrus, Visa and MasterCard. Banco do Brasil, Praça 1817, 3rd floor, Centro, Isidro Gomes 14, Tambaú, behind Centro de Turismo, helpful but poor rates. HSBC, R Peregrino de Carvalho, 162, Centre, ATM for cirrus and visa. Mondeo Tour, Av Négo 46, Tambaú, T2263100. 0900-1730, cash and TCs. PB Câmbio Turismo, Visconde de Pelotas 54C, Centro, T2214676, Mon-Fri 1030-1630, cash and TCs. **Internet** Cyberpointy Cafe, Av Almirante Tamandaré, 100, in Centro Turístico Tambaú, daily 0800-2100, US1.60 per hr. **Post office** Main office is at Praça Pedro Américo, Varadouro; central office is at Parque Solon de Lucena 375; also by the beach at Av Rui Carneiro, behind the Centro de Turismo. **Telephones** Calling stations at: Visconde de Pelotas and Miguel Couto, Centro; Centro de Turismo, Tambaú; Av Epitácio Pessoa 1487, Bairro dos Estados; rodoviária and Airport.

Campina Grande *p471, phone code 083*
Banks Banco do Brl, 7 de Setembro 52, cash and TCs at poor rates. Mondeo Tour, R Índios Cariris 308, T/F3216965, cash at good rates and TCs, Mon-Fri 1000-1600. **Post office** R Marquês do Herval, Praça da Bandeira. **Telephone**: Floriano Peixoto 410 by Praça da Bandeira, in the industrial district and at the rodoviária.

Fernando de Noronha

→ Phone code: 081.

This small archipelago, 345 km off the northeast coast, is legendary among Brazilian tourists for its beautiful beaches, wonderful snorkelling and diving, its untouched natural beauty and fascinating wildlife. It is frequently voted the number one luxury destination in Brazil by the country's travel magazines. It was declared a Marine National Park in 1988.

The islands were discovered in 1503 by Amérigo Vespucci and were for a time a pirate lair. In 1738 the Portuguese built the Forte dos Remédios (later used as a prison), and a church to strengthen their claim to the islands. Remains of the early fortifications still exist. One of the more famous prisoners in the 20th century was Luis Carlos Prestes, who led the famous long march, the Prestes Column, in 1925-27.

Vila dos Remédios, near the north coast, is where most people live and socialize. At the northeast end is Baía de Santo Antônio, which has a jetty. Some of the beaches on this side are Conceição, Boldró, Americano, Bode, Baía dos Porcos (a beautiful cove at the beginning of the marine park) and Baía do Sancho. Beyond is the Baía dos Golfinhos, with a lookout point for watching the spinner dolphins in the bay. On the south, or windward side, there are fewer beaches (for example Praia do Leão, Baía do Sueste, Atalaia), higher cliffs and the whole coastline and offshore islands are part of the marine park. As with dive sites, Ibama restricts bathing in low-tide pools and other sensitive areas to protect the environment.

Ibama has imposed rigorous rules to prevent damage to the nature reserve and everything, from development to cultivation of food crops to fishing, is strictly administered, if not forbidden. Many locals are now dependent on tourism and most food Is brought from the mainland; prices are about double. Entry to the island has been limited to 100 tourists per day because of the serious problems of energy and water supply. A maximum of 420 tourists is allowed on the island at any one time. Moreover, there is a tax of US$13, payable per day for the first week of your stay. In the

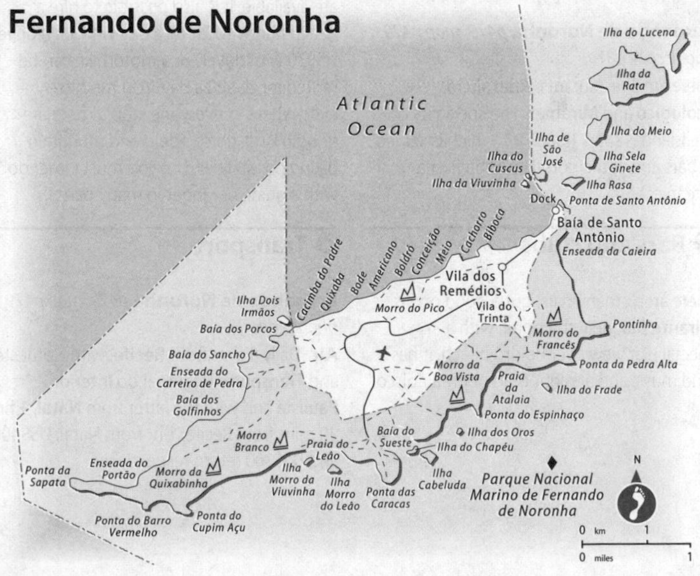

second week the tax increases each day. Take sufficient *reais* as dollars are heavily discounted. For information, contact the **park office** ① *Paranamar-FN, T6191210.*

The rains are from February to July; the island turns green and the seawater becomes lovely and clear. The dry season is August to March, but the sun shines all year round. The time is one hour later than Brazilian Standard Time. Take repellent with you as it is not available for the many mosquitoes.

Sleeping

Fernando de Noronha *p479, map p479, phone code 081*

L **Pousada Esmeralda**, T/F36191355. The only establishment classified as a hotel, rates are full board but it is none too comfortable. Its location used to be an airbase. Packages from mainland travel agents usually place visitors in the **Esmeralda**.

B **Estrela do Mar**, T36191366. With breakfast, excursions arranged. Independent travellers can go much cheaper as many local families rent out rooms with full board, from US$50 per person per day. The best known is that of Suzanna and Rocha, T36191227, rooms with fan and bathroom. Vanilda across the street has been highly recommended. There are plenty of others and the home owners have an association, **Associação das Hospedarias Domiciliares de Fernando de Noronha**, T36191142 for information.

Eating

Fernando de Noronha *p479, map p479, phone code 081*

There are 3 restaurants, **Anatalício**, **Ecológico** and **Miramar**. The speciality of the island is shark (*tubarão*), which is served in bars and at the port (Noronha Pesca Oceânica).

Bars and clubs

There aren't many bars, but a good one is **Mirante Bar**, near the hotel, with a spectacular view over Boldró beach, it has loud music and at night is an open-air disco.

Activities and tours

Fernando de Noronha *p479, map p479, phone code 081*

Watersports

Scuba-diving is organized by **Atlantis Divers**, T6191371, Águas Claras, T36191225, in the hotel grounds, and Noronha Divers, T36191112. Diving costs between US$50-75 and equipment rental from US$50. This is the mecca for Brazilian divers with a great variety of sites to explore and fish to see. Further details will be found under Adventure sports, p61. Enquire in advance whether it is possible to swim with the dolphins at the Baía dos Golfinhos. If it is not allowed they can be seen from the beach. Similarly, sharks and turtles can be seen without entering the water. For details on the turtles, contact Fundação Pró-Tamar, Caixa Postal 50, CEP 53990-000, Fernando de Noronha, T36191269, F6191386.

Tour operators

Boat trips and jeep tours around the island are available; it is also possible to hire a beach buggy (US$100 a day without a driver, US$30 with driver) or a motorbike can be rented for US$80 a day. You can hitch everywhere as everyone stops. There are good hiking, horse riding and mountain biking possibilities, but you must either go with a guide or ranger in many parts.

Transport

Fernando de Noronha *p479, map p479, phone code 081*

Air Daily flights from **Recife**, with Nordeste and **Transporte Regional do Interior Paulista** and with the latter from **Natal**, 1 hr 20 mins from Recife, 1 hr from Natal, US$400 and US$300 return respectively.

Fortaleza & the north coast

Footprint features

Introduction

Bahia may have the prettiest stretch of coastline in Brazil but the north of the northeast has the most dramatic. Broken, striated cliffs and dramatic dunes tower above the pretty beaches of Pipa, Natal, Genipabu, Areia Branca and Jericoacoara, plunging into the sea and glowing deep yellow or fiery red in the setting sun. As the coast stretches north they give way to the wetland wilderness of the Delta do Parnaíba, the largest delta in the western hemisphere and exceeded in size only by the deltas of the Ganges, Mekong and Nile. The river Parnaíba spreads like an outstretched palm to divide the land into myriad islands, a maze of narrow channels and an infinity of lakes. All these are ecological sanctuaries. Beyond lies the coastal Sahara of the Lençóis Maranhenses – a grand erg of dunes pocked with perched freshwater lakes. There are an unprecedented three Ramsar sites along the Maranhão coast and off its shore is the largest bank of coral in Atlantic South America, the Parque Estadual Marinho do Parcel Manoel Luís, which is only beginning to open up to diving. The state capital, São Luís is covered in blue and white Portuguese *azulejos* and filled with decaying baroque churches. Together with neighbouring Alcântara, it is the only town of interest on the coast. São Luís is one of two World Heritage sites in the region, the other being the Parque Nacional da Serra da Capivara in Piauí, whose bizarre honeycomb domes tower over canyons covered in what may be the oldest rock painting ever to be found in the Americas.

★ Don't miss...

❶ **Pipa** Sit back and relax in this laid-back little resort town which attracts an interesting arty crowd and has some great hotels and restaurants, page 488.

❷ **Areia Branca** Explore this bleak, biblical landscape of plunging cliffs, shifting seas of pink and lemon yellow dunes and seemingly endless beaches, page 489.

❸ **Parque Nacional de Sete Cidades and Parque Nacional Serra da Capivara** Seek out the 50,000 BC rock art at two of the most important archaeological sites in the Americas and perhaps the cradle of its civilizations, page 530.

❹ **São Luís** Vies with Salvador and Olinda for the title of the most beautiful coastal city in the north east, page 532.

❺ **Alcântara** An unlikely fusion of pretty little colonial town with some of the finest buildings in the north east and rocket launching station, page 534.

❻ **The Lençóis Maranhenses** A disorientating sea of shifting dunes dotted with lakes, page 535.

❼ **The Delta do Parnaíba** One of Brazil and the world's great wildlife locations overflowing with birds, mammals and reptiles and with miles of unspoilt coast washed by a warm tropical sea, page 535.

Rio Grande do Norte

This state is famous for its beaches and their dunes, especially around Natal. The coastline begins to change here, becoming gradually drier and less green, as it shifts from running north-south to east-west. The vast sugar cane plantations and a few remaining strands of mata atlântica *(coastal forest) are replaced by the dry* caatinga *vegetation and* caju *orchards. The people are called 'Potiguares', after an Indian tribe that once resided in the state.*

History

Like its neighbour to the south, Rio Grande do Norte was not taken into Portuguese possession until the end of the 16th century, but here the impediment was French and Indian resistance. Only after the construction of the Forte dos Reis Magos and a year-long struggle did the Portuguese prevail in 1599. The Dutch domination during from 1630 to 1650 saw the expansion of salt production, sugar cane and cattle rearing.

In the late 17th and early 18th centuries there was a rebellion by Indians against enslavement, the Confederação dos Cariris, but it was put down by troops led by *bandeirantes* (see page 208). In the mid-18th century, the Portuguese crown banned the export of salt and dried beef, which decimated the economy; it did not recover until Brazilian Independence removed the prohibition. Throughout its history drought has been a determining factor in Rio Grande do Norte's fortunes. ▸▸ *For Sleeping, Eating and other listings, see pages 491-500.*

Natal → *Phone code: 084. Colour map 2, B6. Population: 713,000.*

The state capital, located on a peninsula between the Rio Potengi and the Atlantic Ocean is pleasant enough but has few sights of touristic interest. Most head for the beaches to the north and south. During World War II, the city was, somewhat bizarrely, the second largest US base outside the United States. As the most easterly point in the Americas, it was used for African airborne operations and housed 8,000 American pilots.

Ins and outs

Getting there Flights arrive at Augusto Severo airport, 15 km south from centre. Taxi US$25 to centre, US$20 to Ponta Negra. Buses run every 30 minutes to the old rodoviária near the centre, US$0.65. Interstate buses arrive at the rodoviária, 6 km southwest of the centre. Buses from the south pass Ponta Negra first, where you can ask to be let off. The city buses 'Cidade de Esperança Avenida 9', 'Areia Preta via Petrópolis' or 'Via Tirol' to centre. Taxi US$6 to centre, US$10 to Ponta Negra. ▸▸ *See also Transport, page 498.*

Getting around Unlike most Brazilian buses, in Natal you get on the bus at the front and get off at the back. The old rodoviária on Avenida Junqueira Aires, by Praça Augusto Severo, Ribeira, is a central point where many bus lines converge. Buses to some of the beaches near Natal also leave from here.

Tourist offices **Secretaria Estadual de Turismo (SETUR)** ⓘ *Av Alfonso Pena, 1155, Tirol, T2322500*. There are information booths at **Centro de Turismo** ⓘ *Av Pres Café Filho s/n, Praia dos Artistas, T2116149, daily 0800-2100*; **Cajueiro de Pirangi,** *Parnamirim, T2382347 (see Excursions, below)*, **rodoviária** ⓘ *T2054377* and **airport** ⓘ *T6431811. For information T1516 or 2194216*. **SETUR** publishes a list of prices for tourist services such as tours, taxi fares, food and drinks.

Sights

No one comes to Natal for sightseeing, but the city is not without culture. The oldest part is the **Ribeira** along the riverfront where a process of renovation has been started. This can be seen on Rua Chile and in public buildings restored in vivid art-deco fashion, such as the **Teatro Alberto Maranhão** ⓘ *Praça Agusto Severo, T/F2229935* (built 1898-1904) and the **Prefeitura** ⓘ *R Quintino Bocaiuva, Cidade Alta*. The **Cidade**

Natal

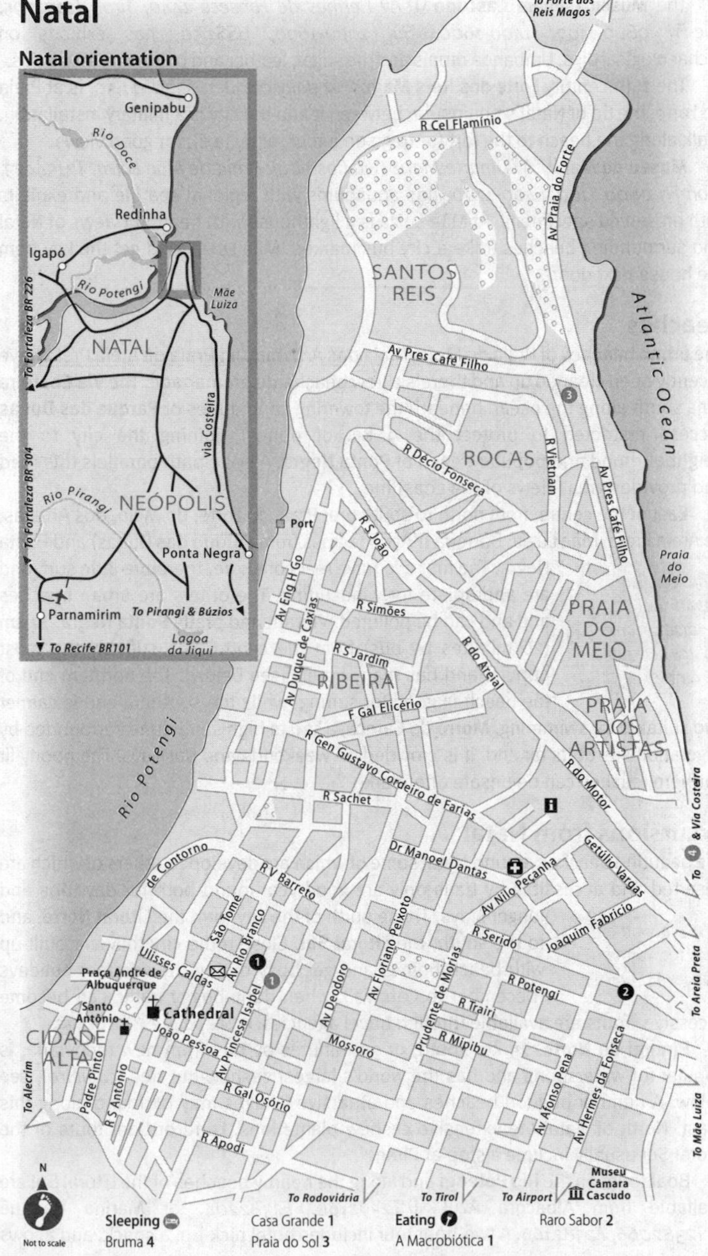

 Alta, or Centro, is the main commercial centre and Avenida Rio Branco its principal artery. The main square is made up by the adjoining **praças**: **João Maria**, **André de Albuquerque, João Tibúrcio** and **7 de Setembro**. At Praça André de Albuquerque is the old cathedral (inaugurated 1599, restored 1996). The modern cathedral is on Avenida Deodoro, Cidade Alta. The church of **Santo Antônio** ⓘ *R Santo Antônio 683, Cidade Alta, Tue-Fri 0800-1700, Sat 0800-1400*, dates from 1766, and has a fine, carved wooden altar and a sacred art museum.

The **Museu Câmara Cascudo** ⓘ *Av Hermes de Fonseca 1440, Tirol, T2122795, Tue-Fri 0800-1100, 1400-1600, Sat 1000-1600, US$1.50*, has exhibits on archaeological digs, Umbanda rituals and the sugar, leather and petroleum industries.

The 16th-century **Forte dos Reis Magos** ⓘ *daily 0800-1645, US$1.50*, is at Praia do Forte, the tip of Natal's peninsula; between it and the city is a military installation. Walk along the beach to the fort (or to go on a tour, or by taxi), for good views.

Museu do Mar ⓘ *Av Dinarte Mariz (Via Costeira), Praia de Mãe Luiza, T2154433, Mon-Fri 0800-1100, 1400-1700*, has aquariums with regional sea life and exhibits with preserved specimens. At Mãe Luiza is a lighthouse with beautiful views of Natal and surrounding beaches (take a city bus marked 'Mãe Luiza' and get the key from the house next door).

Beaches

The urban beaches of Praia do Meio, Praia dos Artistas and Praia de Areia Preta have recently been cleaned up and there's a new beachside promenade. The **Via Costeira** runs south along the ocean beneath the towering sand dunes of **Parque das Dunas** (access restricted to protect the 9 km of dunes), joining the city to the neighbourhood and popular beach of **Ponta Negra**. A cycle path parallels this road and provides great views of the coastline.

East of the centre, from north to south are: Praia do Forte, do Meio, dos Artistas, de Areia Preta, Mãe Luzia, Barreira d'Água (across from Parque das Dunas) and Ponta Negra. The first two have reefs offshore, therefore little surf, and are appropiate for windsurfing. The others are urban beaches and and can be polluted. Vibrant and pretty **Ponta Negra**, 12 km (20 minutes by bus) from the centre, is justifiably the most popular and has many hotels (see below). The northern end of the beach is good for surfing, while the southern end is calmer and suitable for swimming. **Morro do Careca**, a 120 m high sand dune surrounded by vegetation sits at its far end. It is crowded on weekends and holidays. The poorly lit northern reaches can be unsafe after dark.

Natal has excellent beaches with lively nightlife; many people prefer to stay here rather than the centre.

Excursions from Natal

The beautiful beaches around Natal some of which are developed others of which are deserted and accessible by trails only are good year-round both for day trips and longer stays. Those north of the city form the **Litoral Norte**, and to the south, the **Litoral Sul**. Close tothe city they are built-up with beach homes and get busy during the summer holidays (December to Carnival), when dune-buggy traffic can become excessive. Tours are available through travel agencies. » *See page 498 for details.*

See also the Southern Coast and the Northern Coast, pages 487 and 489.

Pirangi do Norte, 25 km south, or 30 minutes by bus from new rodoviária, is popular for watersports and has the world's largest cashew-nut tree (*cajueiro*), see below. A number of good beaches and attractive villages may be found along this coast. North of Natal are extensive cashew plantations. Land or boat tours of the Litoral Sul usually include a stop at Pirangi.

Boat tours on the **Rio Potengi** and along the nearby beaches of the Litoral Sul are available from **Albacora Azul** ⓘ *T2392160, F2382204*, or **Marina Badauê** ⓘ *T2382066, F2382166*. A two-hour tour includes hotel pick-up, a snack, and allows time for a swim, US$15 per person. Boat trips to **Barra do Cunhaú**, 86 km south of Natal, go through mangroves, visit an island and a salt mine (**Passeio Ecológico Cunhaú** ① *T2111123*); see beaches below. **Fishing** for marlin, possible just 11 km from shore, is said by some to be the best in Brazil.

Ultralight flights over the Rio Potengi and sand dunes and beaches north of Natal are available for US$29 per person including hotel pick-up (**Ultraleve** ① *T9827348*.

The **Centro de Lançamento da Barreira do Inferno** ① *T2114799, visits by appointment on Wed from 1400*, the launching centre for Brazil's space programme, is located 11 km south of Natal on the road to Pirangi.

The southern coast

Rota do Sol

The Rota do Sol/Litoral Sul (RN-063) follows the coastline for some 55 km and is the access to beaches south of Ponta Negra (bus from Natal: Campos, in summer every 30 minutes, from both rodoviárias, US$1 to Pirangi, one hour; US$1.50 to Tabatinga, 1¼ hours). **Praia do Cotovelo**, 21 km from Natal, offers a view of the Barreira do Inferno rocket-launching centre to the north. At its southern end it has some cliffs and coconut palms where camping is possible.

Pirangi do Norte, 25 km from Natal, has calm waters, is popular for watersports and offshore bathing (500 m out) when natural pools form between the reefs. Nearby is the world's largest cashew-nut tree (*cajueiro*); branches springing from a single trunk cover an area of some 7,300 sq m. From Natal (Viação Campos), US$0.60, five times a day from 0630 to 1815, three on Sunday, 0730, 0930, 1645; the snack bar by the tree has schedules of buses back to Natal. Pirangi has a lively Carnival. Lacemakers here offer good bargains for clothing and tableware.

Búzios, 35 km from Natal, has a pleasant setting with vegetation-covered dunes and coconut palms, the water is mostly calm and clear; making it good for bathing.

Barra de Tabatinga, 45 km from Natal, is surrounded by cliffs used for parasailing. Waves are strong here, making it a popular surfing beach. A new 'shark park' complete with resident biologist is its latest attraction.

Camurupim and **Barreta**, 46 and 55 km from Natal respectively, have reefs near the shore, where bathing pools form at low tide; this area has many restaurants specializing in shrimp dishes. Beyond Barreta is the long, pristine beach of **Malenbar** or **Guaraíra**, access walking or by 10-minute boat ride accross the Rio Tibau to the south end. Buggy tour from Natal US$100.

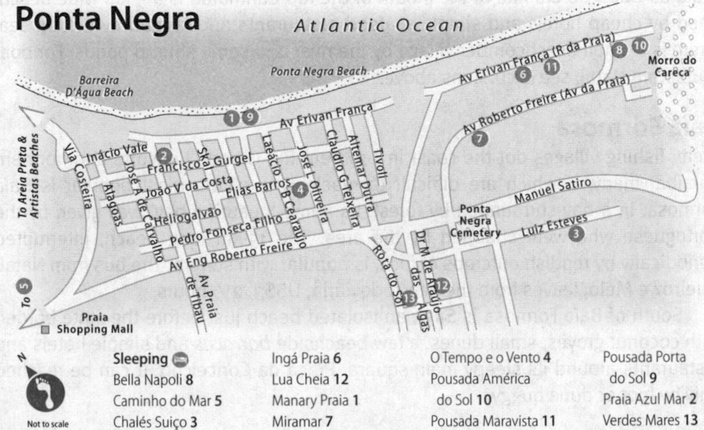

Tibau do Sul and around → *Colour map 2, B6. Population 6,124.*

Long curves of white sand backed by multicoloured sandstone cliffs and sweeping dunes, black tea lagoons, bays filled with dolphins and fragments of Atlantic forest alive with rare birds make this one of the most popular stretches of coast in the northeast. Thankfully it is still relaxed and feels small scale (outside the peak of the high season). Several species of turtles, including giant leatherbacks, still nest here, although before the growth in beach buggy tourism they did so in far greater numbers.The best place to stay along the coast is Pipa, a lively little town with good *pousadas* and restaurants.

Tibau do Sul is a little fishing town with cobbled streets sitting high on a cliff between surf beaches and the manatee-filled Lago de Guaraíra. Boat trips can be arranged from here – to the *lago* or to see dolphins in the calm waters offshore. Although most tourists head straight for Pipa which is more developed, the beach *barracas* in Tibau are lively at night with Forró and MPB, Natal's finest restaurant lies here and there are a handful of decent *pousadas* in town.

A series of wide crescents of white sand, separated by rocky headlands and backed by high cliffs crowned with coconut groves and remnant coastal forest stretch south from Tibau to **Pipa**. This is one of Natal's most enchanting little tourist towns, whose mix of local fishermen and settlers from all over Brazil has formed an interesting and eclectic alternative community. *Pousadas* and restaurants here are excellent in all price ranges and the nightlife is lively. The town is ever more popular but only during Carnival and New Year do the numbers of people become overwhelming. Although the town beach is somewhat developed there are plenty of others around Pipa. **Praia dos Golfinhos** to the south and **Madeiro** beyond it have only a few hotels and **Praia do Amor** to the north is secluded by cliffs and has reasonable surf. Access to the shore is down the steps built by the few clifftop hotels or by walking along the beach from Pipa at low tide. There are ocean boat tours to see the dolphins from US$5 per person and around the mangrove-lined **Lagoa Guaraíra** at Tibau which is particularly beautiful at sunset.

Just north of town, on a 70-m high dune, is the **Santuário Ecológico de Pipa** ⓘ *0800-1600, US$3*, a 60-ha park created in 1986 to conserve the *mata atlântica* forest; there are several trails and lookouts over the cliffs which afford an excellent view of the ocean and dolphins. Although larger animals like cats and howler monkeys are long gone, this is one of the few areas in the state where important indicator bird species like guans can be found.

Praia da Barra de Cunhaú

Praia da Barra de Cunhaú at the mouth of the Rio Curimataú is a 5-km wide beach, lined by cheap hotels and simple seafood restaurants and lapped by a calm sea. There is a small beachcomber village by the river and some shrimp ponds. For boat tours from Natal, see Excursions above.

Baía Formosa

Pretty fishing villages dot the coast in southern Rio Grande do Norte and northern Paraíba, many of which are difficult to reach. One of the most popular is Baía Formosa, in a bay surrounded by forest. Its name 'beautiful bay' was given by the Portuguese who were charmed by the area. The 15-km long beach, interrupted periodically by reddish outcrops of rock, is popular with surfers. The bus from Natal, **Queiroz e Melo**, leaves from the new rodoviária, US$3, 2½ hours.

South of Baía Formosa is **Sagi**, an isolated beach just before the state border, with coconut groves, small dunes, a few beachside *barracas* and simple hotels and restaurants around its sleepy main square, Praça da Conceição. It can be reached only by foot or dune buggy.

Genipabu and the northern coast

The coast north of Natal is known for its many impressive, light-coloured sand dunes, some reaching a staggering 50 m in height. Genipabu, a weekend resort for the Natal middle classes, is the most famous of these and is only a very short bus ride from the city. The country beyond is well off the tourist trail, with vast long beaches backed by multicoloured sand dunes and salt lakes. It is dramatic terrain, so much so that it has been used as the backdrop to numerous Biblical films. Three crosses sit over the cliffs at Areia Branca, left there by one of the most recent productions, *Maria, A Mãe do Filho de Deus*. Fixed dunes are protected and should not be disturbed, but shifting dunes can be visited by buggy, camel or horse.

Redinha → *Colour map 2, B6.*

A 25-minute ferry crossing on the Rio Potengi, or a 16-km drive along the *Rota do Sol/Litoral Norte*, takes you from Natal to Redinha, an urban beach, with ocean and river bathing, and buggies to hire. The local delicacy is fried fish with tapioca, served at the market. About 5 km north of Redinha on a point is **Santa Rita**. From its high dunes there is a great view of the nearby coastline.

Genipabu and around

The best-known beach in the state, Genipabu is 30 km north of Natal. Its major attractions are very scenic dunes and the **Lagoa de Genipabu**, a lake surrounded by cashew trees and dunes where tables are set up on a shoal in the water and drinks served. There are also many bars and restaurants on the sea shore. Buggy rental from **Associação dos Bugueiros** ⓘ *T2252077, US$25 for dune tour*; ultralight flights are also available.

North of Genipabu, across the Rio Ceará Mirim, are several beaches with coconut groves and dunes. They have fishing villages combined with summer homes owned by people from Natal; access is via the town of Extremoz. One of these beaches, **Pitangui**, 35 km from Natal, is 6 km long and has a cristaline lake where colourful schools of fish can be seen in the water. **Jacumã**, 49 km from Natal, has a small waterfall and inland Lagoa de Jacumã, a lake surrounded by dunes where sand skiing is practised.

Muriú, 44 km from Natal, is known for its lovely green ocean where numerous small boats and *jangadas* anchor, the beach has nice palms (buggy tour from Natal, including shifting dunes US$100). About 5 km to the north is **Prainha** or **Coqueiro**, a beautiful cove with many coconut palms and strong waves.

Lovely beaches continue along the state's coastline; as you get further away from Natal the beaches are more distant from the main highways and access is more difficult. Some 83 km north of Natal, by **Touros**, centre of a coconut and lobster producing region, the coastline veers east-west.

The far north → *Phone code: 084.*

As the coast turns west in northern Rio Grande do Norte, the terrain gets bleaker and more dramatic. Rather than sheltering little coves, long vast beaches stretch in seemingly interminable long broad curves. Behind them are pink, brown and red cliffs, or large expanses of dunes. Highlights are the sleepy little village of **Galinhos**, with its sand streets and beautiful gentle beach washed by a calm sea, and the **Costa Branca** near the little fishing towns of **Areia Branca**, **Ponta do Mel** and **Rosadao**, where vast pink and white dunes converge behind magnificent long beaches.

There are buses to Areia Branca and the other little towns along the northern coast from Mossoró (see below). Galinhos sits on a long broad sandspit and has ocean- and coast-facing beaches. Access is by ferry from the little village of Guamaré which is connected to Mossoró by bus or to Natal via the small town of Jandaíra.

Mossoró mix-up

It could not have been any hotter. The shimmer off the black ribbon of asphalt, known as highway BR-304, conjured up many a mirage but no relief. We were taking a bus on the long haul from Fortaleza to Recife and drinking water was in short supply. The air-conditioning had failed and everybody's patience wore thin.

"Dez minutos", grumbled the driver as we lurched into the Mossoró rodoviária, still in a haze. Bathrooms ... a line-up ... a shop for *água mineral* ... *tem não*? ... another shop ... Oh my God, the bus has gone! We could see it pulling away, but our sprint and acrobatics attracted no-one's attention. Still well in sight, it accelerated along the endless BR with all our gear on board. At the crowded Recife bus terminus it would quickly disappear.

What do we do now? A taxi, "Follow that bus!", and so we did, but the *fusca* (VW Beetle) was no match for the motor coach on the open highway. In an hour that seemed an eternity we managed to overtake it, only because it had made another stop along the way. The bleary-eyed bus driver didn't even seem surprised to see us. We breathed a transient sigh of relief until the taxi driver presented us with the bill.

How much was an hour-long break-neck chase worth? How much was our luggage worth? Regardless, we didn't have enough at hand. The bus driver wanted to be on his way, the taxi driver wanted his money (or we were going back with him to visit the Mossoró jail) and we were feeling increasingly desperate when someone came forward, sweat dripping from his brow. "These *estrangeiros* are lost. We've passed the hat among the passengers and collected enough to pay for the cab. Let's get going!"

It would be many years before we understood the complex meaning of o *jeitinho brasileiro*, 'the Brazilian way' (out of any predicament), but we had certainly experienced it that day outside Mossoró, where the heat of the climate was only matched by the warmth of the people.

Mossoró → *Phone code: 084. Colour map 2, B5. Population: 206,000.*

About halfway between Natal (277 km) and Fortaleza (262 km) is the second city of Rio Grande do Norte, commercial centre for the largest salt and land-based petroleum-producing region in the country. The area also produces natural gas, cashew nuts, carnauba wax, fruits and minerals. With an average of 30°C, temperatures are high all year round.

The **Hotel Thermas Mossoró** ⓘ *0700-2300, US$14 per person, see Sleeping, below*, a resort with a hot, mineral water pool system, 10 pools, each on a terrace, with temperatures ranging from 54°C at the top to 30°C at the bottom, water-slide, spa, sports facilities, restaurant, is open to the public. While drilling for thermal water here in 1979 oil was struck, and this first derek in the area is still working and can be seen at the hotel.

The **Museu Histórico Lauro da Escossia** ⓘ Praça Antônio Gomes 514, Centro, Tue-Fri 0700-1800, Sat 0800-1100, 1400-1700, Sun 0800-1100, free, has a small but interesting display, with the highlights of the region's history and an extensive photo collection relating to the *Cangaço* (see page 492). The Escola Superior de Agricultura de Mossoró (ESAM), which concentrates on agricultural and veterinary studies specific to semi-desert areas, runs a park, **Parque Zoobotânico Onélio Porto** ⓘ *T3215755*, with species of the Sertão.

Excursions from Mossoró

The main beach resort for Mossoró is **Tibau**, 44 km to the north, just on the Ceará border, set in a lovely palm-fringed bay. A village of 5,000 inhabitants, its population swells to 35,000 during the peak vacation period between December and Carnival. The town is particularly lively in January during Mossoró's *Fest Verão* and during Carnival. The beach here is wide, with good waves and is popular for surfing. Beach homes continue to the east at **Praia das Manoelas**, beyond which there is buggy access to several beaches with good fishing. Ricardo Lopes, **Alibi Turismo**, ⓘ *T3262398*, offers tours in this area and has very good photographs of the region. The local handicraft is coloured sand arrangements in bottles. The bus from Mossoró leaves from near **Hotel Zenilândia** (0630 and 1330, returns 1130 and 1630, US$1.60, 40 minutes).

Grossos, 46 km to the north, is an Antarctic landscape in the tropical heat. As the centre of the important salt-mining industry, white salt dunes extend into the horizon against the blue sky and turquoise ocean. They are very scenic and worth a visit. Official tours can be hired at **Hotel Thermas** or arranged with the different companies' headquarters in Mossoró (for example, **Salina Maranhão** ⓘ *T3211290, Mon-Sat*); just walking around can be very interesting. Bus from Mossoró weekdays 0630 and 1330, US$1.50, leaves from near **Hotel Zenilândia**.

From Grossos a ferry crosses the Rio Mossoró (every 30 minutes, Monday-Friday 0730-1630, Saturday until 1700, Sunday until 1730, US$5 car, US$1 per person) to **Areia Branca**, the main port for salt exports and access to the Costa Branca, 42 km of beaches to the east. The area remains undeveloped for the time being, with pleasant coves and some fishermen's villages, but tourist development may not be far off. There are several places to stay in Areia Blanca.

The Sertão → *Population: 11,000.*

The interior of Rio Grande do Norte, like that of its neighbours, is a combination of semi-desert *sertão*, with hilly areas covered in green vegetation and with pleasant temperatures between 16°C and 25°C. The state is rich in archaeological sites, and numerous caves with primitive paintings have been found.

In the mountainous south-central region of the state is **Acari**, with an 18th-century church of Nossa Senhora da Guia. It is the access point for the Serra do Bico de Arara and is 221 km from Natal and 224 km from Mossoró. South of town, in the **Seridó** area, are multicoloured cave paintings where human remains dating back 11,000 years have been discovered.

In the centre of the state, on the east shore of the Armando Rua Gonçalves dam, is **São Rafael**. The town is surrounded by granite mountains on top of which are natural waterholes of up to 3 m deep, containing countless fossils of giant fauna of the Pleistocene period. There are also rock paintings and engravings in boulders in this area.

Some 76 km southwest of Mossoró is **Apodi**, a town with colonial mansions, where people live from agriculture, ceramics and lime extraction. About 10 km from town is **Lajedo de Soledade**, a limestone shelf, 1 km wide and 2 km long which has been weathered into canyons, grottos and interesting formations. Paintings of animals and geometric figures, dated between 3,000 and 5,000 years, have been found in the caves. On the BR-405, Km 76, is *Passeio Hotel*, T3332031 (one-star). In Apodi is *Pousada Chapado*, Rua Dep Dauto Cunha 30, Apodi, T3332049, with air conditioning, fridge and a restaurant serving regional food.

Sleeping

Natal *p484, map p485, phone code 084*
The **Via Costeira** is a strip of enormous, upmarket beachfront hotels, which are very isolated, with no restaurants or shops within easy walking distance. **Ponta Negra** is the ideal place to stay, with its attractive beach and concentration of restaurants. In Ponta Negra the most popular hotels are those

Lampião

Were they subversives, common criminals or heroes? The debate rages on about the armed band led by Virgulino Ferreira da Silva, better known as Lampião. He is regarded by some as a Robin Hood of the Northeast, stealing from the coroneis (wealthy landowners with almost feudal powers) and urban gentry, to give to the ubiquitous poor of the Sertão. Others look on Lampião and his followers as nothing more than common criminals; looting, raping and killing as they terrorized towns in the Northeast during the 1920s and 1930s. This was the *Cangaço*, the reign of banditry, which inspired so much fear and fascination throughout Brazil and attracted worldwide attention.

The controversial religious leaders of the Sertão were also involved. Lampião claimed the spiritual protection of Padre Cícero and the legacy of the Cangaço retains an unusual religious dimension. The tomb of Jararaca, for example, one of Lampião's lieutenants who was captured during the band's unsuccessful 1927 siege of Mossoró, and supposedly buried alive, is attributed miraculous powers and has become a site of pilgrimage. Yet Jararaca is reputed to have been a ruthless killer.

There was even a middle eastern connection. Several early cinemato-graphers from the US, Germany and France tried to film Lampião and his band, but only Lebanese-born Benjamin Abrahão was sufficiently taken into his confidence to do so. Abrahão spent almost seven months recording the day-to-day life of the *cangaceiros*. His footage was considered so subversive that he was subsequently murdered under mysterious circumstances and his film confiscated by the government of Getúlio Vargas. It languished in an official vault for 20 years, much of it destroyed by time and the elements.

Today the Sociedade Brasileira de Estudos do Cangaço is one of the organizations which collects data, anecdotes and artefacts from this important episode in the region's and the nation's history. It also carries on the unresolved debate as to whether the *cangaceiros* were really heroes or villains.

right on the beach, on Av Erivan França facing the sea and R Francisco Gurgel behind that street. The latter is quieter. Economical hotels are easier to find in the city proper but very few people stay here and what they save by doing so is often spent on public transport to the beaches.

The distinction between **Praia do Meio** and Praia dos Artistas is often blurred. Most hotels here are on the beachfront **Av Pres Café Filho**, the numbering of which is illogical.

LL Manary Praia, R Francisco Gurgel 9067, Ponta Negra, T/F2192900, www.manary.com.br. The best and most tranquil hotel facing the beach and the only one with a trace of style. The rooms, which are decorated in hard wood and pastel colours, have ample bathrooms and secluded private terraces. Good food. A member of the Roteiro de Charme group, see p47.

L Maine, Av Salgado Filho 1741, Lagoa Nova, T2065774, F2065707. A business-orientated 4-star with reasonable service and a restaurant.

L Ocean Palace, Km 11, near Ponta Negra, T2194144, F2193081. Luxury hotel, rooms and facilities of suitable standard, generally well designed with lovely ocean front pool and terrace; service very Brazilian.

AL Praia Azul Mar, R Franscisco Gurgel 92, Ponta Negra, T2193555, www.praiaazulmarhotel.com.br. Pleasant package holiday hotel for Europeans, with a/c rooms and a pool.

AL-A Imirá Plaza, Via Costeira 4077, T2114104, F2115722, cheaper in low season. On the beach and with a pool and tennis court. Recommended.

AL-C Porto Mirim, Av Pres Café Filho 68, Praia do Meio, T2024200. Big luxury hotel with a rooftop pool and deck. Cheaper off season.

A-B Hotel e Pousada O Tempo e o Vento, R Elias Barros 66, Ponta Negra, T/F2192526, www.digicom.br/otempoeovento. A/c , rooms with a fridge and cheaper with fan around a pool, The *luxo* rooms are very comfortable. Cheaper in low season. Recommended.

A-C Chalés Suíço, R Luiz Esteves 2272, Ponta Negra, T2363090. Simple a/c furnished cabins for up to 5 people, cheaper in low season.

A Praia do Sol, Av Pres Café Filho 750, Praia do Meio, T2114562, F2226571. Quiet a/c rooms opposite beach. Recommended.

B Bruma, Av Pres Café Filho 1176, T/F2114308, www.hotelbruma@zaz.com.br. Slick and intimate with beachfront balconies a pool and terrace. Recommended.

B Caminho do Mar, R Des HH Gomes 365, Ponta Negra, T2193363. Simple plain rooms and breakfast a short walk from the beach.

B Casa Grande, R Princesa Isabel 529, Centro, T2110555. Built around a family home and popular with business visitors. A/c, cheaper without bathroom. Good breakfast, pleasant, excellent value with off-season discounts. Recommended.

B Ingá Praia, Av Erivan França 17, Ponta Negra, T2193436, www.ingapraiahotel.com.br. A pink cube on the beach with comfortable, well-looked-after rooms and a rooftop terrace. Recommended.

B Miramar, Av da Praia 3398, Ponta Negra, T2362079. Well maintained, family-run *pousada*. Engish spoken.

B Oassis Swiss, R Joaquim Fabrício 291, Casa 08, Petrópolis, T/F2022455. Swiss-owned hotel with, a/c and fan cooled rooms cheaper with fan (a pool, massive breakfasts and off season discounts. Exceptional value.

B Pousada Esperança, Av Capt Mor Gouveia 418, near the rodoviária, T2051955. Rooms with or without a/c and bathrooms. Basic but respectable.

C Pousada América do Sol, R Erivan França 35, Ponta Negra, T2192245, www.pousadaamericadosol.com.br. Very simple a/c rooms with pokey bathrooms and TVs. Good breakfast in a terrace overlooking the beach and substantial off-season reductions.

C Pousada Porta do Sol, R Erivan França 9057, Ponta Negra, T2362555, F2052208. Basic rooms with a TV, fridge, fan and an excellent breakfast, pool, beachfront, good value. Recommended.

C-D Bella Napoli, Av Erivan França 3188, Ponta Negra, T2192666, www.pousadabellanapoli.com.br. Poky little a/c rooms with a fridge, in a hotel above the restaurant of the same name. In need of renovation but it's right on the beach. Cheaper in low season.

D Beira Mar, Av Pres Café Filho, Praia do Meio, T2021470. Motel-style, beach front a/c rooms, with breakfast, and a small pool. Good value, popular. Recommended.

D Bom Jesús, Av Rio Branco 384, Centro. Simple, popular cheapie, reasonable breakfast.

D Cidade do Sol, Piancó 31, near the rodoviária, T2051893. Very basic rooms with or without baths or a/c.

D Fenícia, Av Rio Branco 586, Centro, T2114378. Fan-cooled and more expensive a/c rooms with breakfast. English spoken, low-season discount.

D Le Bateau, Praia de Areia Preta, on beachfront. Simple but helpful and with a good breakfast, English and French spoken.

D Lua Cheia, R Dr Manoel Augusto Bezerra de Araújo 500, Ponta Negra, T2363696, www.luacheia.com.br. One of the best youth hostels in Brazil; in a 'castle' with a 'medieval' **Taverna Pub** in basement (see Bars and clubs below). IYHA, price (per person) includes breakfast. Highly recommended.

D Pousada Maravista, R da Praia 223, Ponta Negra, T2364677, marilymar@hotmail.com. Plain and simple but with a good breakfast, English spoken, TV, fridge.

D Verdes Mares, R das Algas 2166, Conj Algamar, Ponta Negra, T2362872, F2362872. IYHA youth hostel, price (per person) includes breakfast, discount in low season.

E Meu Canto, R Manoel Dantas 424 Petrópolis, T2113954. Youth hostel with rooms and dorms and friendly staff. Highly recommended.

E Pousada Beth Shalom, R Patos 45, near the rodoviária, T2051141. Little fan-cooled rooms and friendly service.

E Pousada Marina, Av Pte Café Filho 860, Praia do Meio, T2021677, www.hotelpousadamarina.com.br. Plain and simple, with a/c, TV and fridge.

E Pousada Ponta do Morcego, R Valentin de Almeida 10, Praia dos Artistas, T2022367. Dorm-style rooms and a handful of others. Basic. Price per person.

E Pousada Porto Seguro, Av Pres Café Filho 1174, Ponta Negra, T94121039. Very lively, with a beachfront terrace and small but decent rooms. Good value. Recommended.

Camping

Sítio do Jiqui, Pirangi, T2172603. Camping Clube do Brasil. Expensive.

Vale das Cascatas, Via Costeira Km 8.5, Ponta Negra beach. Little shade, swimming pool, leisure facilities.

Rota do Sol *p487, phone code 084*

A Cotovelo Apart-hotel, R Estrela D'Alva 34, Praia do Cotovelo, T2372051. Rooms with kitchenettes around a pool.

A Colinas Chalés, Estr de Pirangi, Praia do Cotovelo, T2372168. Cabins with a fridge. Restaurant and a pool.

A-B Chalés de Pirangi, R Sebastião 56, Pirangi do Norte, T2382241. Standard apartment hotel with a/c rooms and en suites.

B Barreira do Sol, Estr para Búzios, Pirangi do Sul (across the river), T2382230. Modest rooms with en suites, most with a/c.

B Portal do Kutuvelo, Estr para Búzios, Praia do Cotovelo, T2372121. Reasonable plain rooms with attached kitchen, pool.

B Pousada Esquina do Sol, R Dom Bosco and Av Dep Márcio Marinho, Pirangi do Norte, T2382078, F2115637. Rooms and cabins for 4. Breakfast not included.

B Pousada Vista do Atlântico, R do Cajueiro 141, Pirangi do Norte, T23820778. In the town itself but in walking distance of the beach. The upstairs rooms are better ventilated and have good views.

B Varandas de Búzios, Estr Principal, Búzios, T2392121. Cabins with a fridge around pool. Reasonablerestaurant.

Tibau do Sul and around *p488, phone code 084*

In Pipa more than 30 *pousadas* and many private homes offer accommodation.

LL-A Sombra e Água Fresca, Praia do Amor, T2462144, www.sombraeaguafresca.com.br. (cheaper in low season). Tastefully decorated though small chalet rooms and vast luxury suites with separate sitting and dining areas. All with magnificent views.

LL-A Toca da Coruja, Praia da Pipa, T2462225, www.tocadacoruja.com.br. One of the best small luxury hotels in Brazil with a range of chalets set in forested gardens and decorated with North East Brazilian antiques and art. Beautiful pool and an excellent restaurant. A member of the **Roteiros de Charme** group, see p47.

AL Village Natureza, Estr para Pipa Km 5, T/F5022325. A/c Chalets overlooking the sea and Madeiro beach, a pool, nice grounds, lovely views.

AL Ponta do Madeiro, R da Praia, Estr para Pipa Km 3, T/F2464220, www.pontadomadeiro.com.br. Very comfortable spacious a/c chalets, beautiful pool with bar and spectacular views over the Praia do Madeiro. Excellent service and a good restaurant. Highly recommended.

A Marinas Tibau Sul, Tibau do Sul, T/F5022323. Cabins for 4, pool, restaurant, watersports, horse riding and a boat dock.

A-B Mirante de Pipa, Rua do Mirante 1, Praia da Pipa, T2462251, www.mirantedepipa.com.br. Fan-cooled chalets with a veranda set in a forested garden. Wonderful views.

C A Conchego, R do Ceu s/n, Praia da Pipa, T94197181, www.pipa.com/aconchego. Family-run *pousada* with simple chalets with red-tiled roofs and terraces in a cashew and palm tree-filled garden. Good breakfast, tranquil and central.

D Pousada da Pipa, Praia da Pipa, T2462217. Small rooms decorated with a personal touch. The best are upstairs and have a large shared terrace with glazed terracotta tiles, sitting areas and hammocks. Large breakfast.

D Vera-My house, Praia da Pipa, T2462295. Good value, friendly and well maintained though simple. Rooms with a bath, US$5 per person in dormitory, use of kitchen, no breakfast. Recommended.

Camping

Espaço Verde, behind restaurant, T9885145, US$3 per person. Sandy lots with some shade.

Praia da Barra de Cunhaú *p488, phone code 084*

A Caribe Sul, T5022624. Modest beach hotel, a/c rooms with baths, also pool and restaurant.

C Mirante, T2412313. Unpretentious beachside chalets and a restaurant.

Baía Formosa *p488, phone code 084*
B **Pousada Sonho Meu**, R Dr Manuel Francisco de Melo 143, T9821704. Well-kept a/c rooms with baths and fridges, and a simple restaurant.

Redinha *p489, phone code 084*
A **Atlântico Norte**, Av Litorânea, Redinha Nova, T2242002, F2242001. Comfortable a/c rooms with fridge looking over a pleasant pool.

Genipabu and around *p489, phone code 084*
A **Genipabu**, Estr de Genipabu, s/n, 2 km from beach,T2252063, www.genipabu.com.br. A very relaxing spa hotel on a hillside outside of town with wonderful views out over the beaches and sea. Smart and very well-kept a/c rooms with en suites. Treatments include Ayurvedic massage, reiki, yoga, body wraps and facials. Attractive pool and a sauna.
A **Pousada Sinos do Vento**, Praia das Garças, Touros, 6 km from town, T2632453, www.sinosdovento.com.br. Attractive beachside *pousada* with accommodation in 14 spacious chalets on a deserted stretch of beach and surrounded by forested gardens. Offers a range of activities including horse riding, bike rental and buggy tours.
B **do Gostoso**, Praia Ponta de Santo Cristo, 27 km west of town, T2214399. Pleasant, modern chalets and a simple restaurant.
B **Mar-Azul**, on the beach, Genipabu, T2252065. One of many modest beachside hotels with pleasant rooms all with bath and fridge.
B **Pousada Villa do Sol**, Enseada do Genipabu, Km 4, T2252132, www.villa dosol.com.br 20 attractive a/c chalets, the best of which are the 5 newest, with views over the river. Decent pool and restaurant and good service.
C **Pousada do Coruja**, R Principal 100, Genipabu, T2252592. Simple but adequate rooms with a fan; in the town.
C **Pousada Marruá**, Av Beira Mar 438, Pitangui, T2022404. Simple but reasonably well maintained and friendly.
C **Bangalôs Muriú**, Muriú, T/F2193731. Modest furnished chalets and breaksfast.
C **Tabuão**, R Principal, Genipabu, T2252134. Modest furnished bungalows in the main town and no breakfast.
D **Aldeia**, R Principal, Estr de Genipabu, T/F2252011, www.hotelaldeia.hpg.com.br. 5 comfortable and nicely decorated bungalows with room for as many as 4 people, a pool and a decent restaurant.
E **Pousada Porta Alberta**, on beach, Genipabu. Basic but with a good breakfast and friendly service.

The far north *p489, phone code 084*
Galinhos town is very sleepy and *pousadas* often close up for a few days whilst their owners go away. There are at least 7 in town so it is always possible to find a room; either on the ocean or the coastal side.
D **Pousada e Restaurante Brasil Aventura**, Galinhos, T5520085. One of several very simple beachfront *pousadas* with a fish restaurant. Plain but well kept and popular with backpackers.

Mossoró *p490, phone code 084*
L **Hotel Thermas Mossoró**, Av Lauro Monte 2001, by entrance to town from Fortaleza, T3181200, F3182344. Luxurious resort, a/c, fridge, friendly management (see p490).
A **Imperial**, R Santos Dumont 47, Centro, T3216351, F3173524. A/c, fridge, modern, very clean, restaurant.
B **Ouro Negro**, Av do Contorno, on BR-304, near rodoviária, T/F3172070. A/c rooms with bath, fridge, modern, restaurant, parking, pool.
B-C **Scala**, R Dionísio Filgueira 220 (across from market), T3213034. Simple a/c rooms with bath. Cheaper with fan.
D-E **Zenilândia**, Praça Souza Machado 89, Centro, T3212949. Basic town hotel with plain, fan-cooled rooms with a en suites or with shared bath, breakfast not included.

Excursions from Mossoró *p491, phone code 084*
There plenty of *pousadas* in **Tibau** and many restaurants and bars along the beach. Although there are some *pousadas* in Areia Branca, it isn't a good base for the beaches. **Ponta do Mel**, which is flanked by 2 magnificent beaches is better and it has a couple of very basic *pousadas* in the town.
A **Pousada Costa Branca**, Ponta do Mel, Costa Branca, T3327062, www.costabranca. com.br. The best hotel between Genipabu and Ceará with a range of cabins on a bluff with magnificent views out over an endless stretch of beach. Organized tours to the

dunes to the south which are among the most spectacular in the state. Good restaurant, service and pool, and Lord Byron tribute bar with live music.

B Dunas Praia, Praia das Manoelas, Tibau, T3262304. Friendly staff, a restaurant and a series of chalets all with a fridge.

B Leiria Mar, Tibau, T3262541. Plain a/c rooms with a fridge around a pool. Reasonable restaurant.

D Panorama, Tibau. Very basic rooms with a bath and more expensive options with fans.

The Sertão *p491, phone code 084*

C Pousada do Gargallheiras, Açude Marechal Dutra, about 5 km from Acari, with a restaurant.

D Conceição Palace Hotel, R Otávio Lamartine 432, Jardim do Seridó, Some 27 km south of Acari, T4722249. A simple option.

Eating

Natal *p484, map p485, phone code 084*

Prawns feature heavily on menus here as Natal is the largest exporter of prawns in Brazil.

TTT **Chaplin**, Av Pres Café Filho 27, Praia dos Artistas. Traditional seafood restaurant withseaviews. Part of a leisure complex with a bar, English pub and a nightclub.

TTT **Doux France**, R Otâvio Lamartine, Petrópolis. Authentic French cuisine, outdoor seating.

TTT **Estação Trem de Minas**, Av Pres Café Filho, 197, Praia dos Artistas, T2022099. Charming rustic style, distinctly upmarket. 40 brands of *cachaça* live music nightly, terrace and cocktails. Self-service lunch and dinner.

TTT **Manary**, Manary Praia Hotel, R Francisco Gurgel (see p492), Ponta Negra. The best seafood restaurant in the city in a poolside restaurant overlooking Ponta Negra beach.

TTT **Raro Sabor**, R Seridó 722, Petrópolis, T2021857. Exclusive bistro with Russian caviar on menu.

TTT **Roschti**, Av Erivan França, Ponta Negra, T2194406. A relaxed beachfront bistro and more formal upstairs dining room serving international cuisine.

TTT **Sobre Ondas**, Av Erivan França 14, Ponta Negra, T2194222. Average seafood and international dishes in an intimate beachfront setting with an underwater theme.

TT **A Macrobiótica**, Princesa Isabel 524, Centro. Vegetarian restaurant and shop. Lunch only.

TT **Atlântico**, Av Erivan França 27, Ponta Negra, T2192762. Relaxed, warm service, semi-open air, beachfront. Portuguese-owned, Italian and Portugese dishes, fish and *carne do sol*. Recommended.

TT **Barraca do Caranguejo**, Av Erivan França 1180, Ponta Negra, T2195069. Live music nightly from 2100 and 8 prawn dishes for US$8.

TT **Bob's**, Av Sen Salgado Filho, 2234, Hamburger chain, daily 1000-2200.

TT **Camarões**, Av Eng Roberto Freire, 2610, Ponta Negra. Also at Natal Shopping Centre. Touristy, but very good seafood.

TT **Camarões Express**, Av Sen Salgado Filho, 2234, Centro. Express prawns in 15 styles. Open for lunch only at weekends.

TT **Carne de Sol Benigna Lira**, R Dr José Augusto Bezerra de Medeiros 09, Praia do Meio. Traditional setting, regional cuisine.

TT **Cipó Brasil**, Av Erivan 3, Ponta Negra, T0800-284051. Funky little Playa del Carmen-style bar with a jungle theme, 4 levels, sand floors, lantern-lit, very atmospheric. Average food (pizzas and crêpes), good for cocktails, live music nightly after 2100.

TT **Fiorentina**, Augusto Bezerra de Medeiros 529, delivery T2020020. An Italian pizzeria with a huge range of seafood, try the lobster with spaghetti. Friendly service, 10% tax. Warmly recommended.

TT **Peixada da Comadre**, R Dr José Augusto Bezerra de Medeiros 4, Praia dos Artistas. Lively seafood restaurant with popular prawn dishes.

TT **Ponta Negra Grill**, Av Erivan 20, Ponta Negra, T2193714. A large, lively restaurant with live music and several terraces, popular, lively and overlooking the beach. Steaks, seafood and cocktails.

TT **Saint Antoine**, R Santo Antônio 651, Cidade Alta, Centro. Mediocre self-service by kg.

TT-T **Farol Bar**, Av Sílvio Pedrosa 105 (at the end of Via Costeira on Praia Areia Preta). Famous dried meat dishes – a local speciality.

T **Beach baraccas** for snacks and fast food.

T **Ponta Negra Mall**, Ponta Negra, stalls sell sandwiches and snacks.

Tibau do Sul and around *p488, phone code 084*

There are many restaurants and bars along Pipa's main street, **Av Baía dos Golfinhos**.

TTT **Al Buchetto**, Av Baía dos Golfinhos 837, Pipa, T2462318. Decent, Italian-made pasta and a lively atmosphere.

ΨΨΨ **Camamo Beijupirá**, Tibau do Sul, T2464195. One of the best restaurants in Brazil with a eclectic mix of fusion dishes like prawns with slices of leek in a spicy cashew sauce with raisins and ginger, served with fervent enthusiasm by owner Tadeu Lubambo. Excellent wine list.

ΨΨΨ **Toca da Coruja**, Praia da Pipa (see p494). Superlative and beautifully presented regional food in a tropical garden setting. Intimate and romantic. Highly recommended.

ΨΨΨ **Vivendo**, Av Baía dos Golfinhos, Pipa. One of the town's best seafood restaurants and a good place to watch the passers by.

Ψ **Casa de Taipe and Shirley My House**, Av Baía dos Golfinhos 1126 and 1213, Praia da Pipa. Very cheap but decent self-service restaurants, the latter owned by the sister of 'Vera' of **Vera My House**.

Ψ **São Sebastião**, R do Ceu, Pipa. Vegetarian and wholefood. Good value. Good juices.

Ψ **Sopa de Patrick/Chez Lisa**, Av Baía dos Golfinhos s/n, Praia da Pipa. Generous portions of various delicious soups – in a little shack beyond the main square.

Ψ **Tatoo Batata**, R do Ceu, Pipa, T94197181. Enormous baked potatoes with fillings like cheese and sweet corn. Salads and juices too. Friendly owner. Next to **A Conchego** *pousada*.

Mossoró *p490, phone code 084*

ΨΨ **Churrascaria A Gauchinha**, R Bezerra Mendes 99, Centro. Reasonable *churrascaria* meat grill which is closed Sun.

ΨΨ **O Severino**, R Felipe Camarão 2975 (road to Apodi, by airport). Modest restaurant serving north eastern and regional specialities.

Bars and clubs

Natal *p484, map p485, phone code 084*

Dance is an important pastime in Natal. Although there are a handful of respectable clubs, Ponta Negra beach is now somewhat seedy, although the municipal authorities are coming down very hard on the sex industry and its clients, and are installing video cameras all along the beach. However, **Alto Punta Negra** is very lively and has live music and a range of bars and clubs openuntil dawn. In an area in the centre known as **Riberia**, there are a few popular bar/nightclubs in restored historic buildings in R Chile.

Baraonda, Av Erivan França, 44, Ponta Negra, T94813748. Live music nightly except Tue, including *forró* and MPB from 2300 until late.

Budda Pub, Av Engenheiro Roberto Freire (an annex of the Tiberius). A little bar with good bar food and a laid-back atmosphere.

Taverna Pub, R Dr Manoel, Araújo, 500, Alta Ponta Negra, T2363696. Medieval-style pub in youth hostel basement. Eclectic (rock, Brazilian pop, jazz, etc.) live music Tue-Sun from 2200, best night Wed. Recommended. **Tapiocaria Salsa Bar** and the **Calderão da Bruxa** and a cluster of small venues in front of the Taverna are very popular with tourists and locals.

Centro de Turismo (see Shopping below) has *Forró com Turista*, a chance for visitors to learn this fun dance, Thu at 2200; there are many other enjoyable venues where visitors are encouraged to join in.

Blackout B52, R Chile 25, T2211282. Lively venue with a 1940s theme. The best night is 'Black Monday'. There is live rock, blues and MPB on other nights. The crowd is 20s and early 30s.

Amiça, Av Engenheiro Roberto Freire s/n. New club with techno and house popular with locals and tourists.

Novakapital, Av Presidente Café Filho, 872, Praia dos Artistas, T2027111. With *forró*, live music, especially rock and foam parties, US$4, from midnight.

Chaplin, Av Presidente Café Filho, 27, Praia dos Artistas, T2021188. 6 different zones with everything from MPB and *forró* to techno and progressive house.

Tibau do Sul and around *p488*

Tibau do Sul has various beach *barracas*. There is always something going on in Pipa, whatever the night and whatever the month.

Carvalho do Fogo, Tibau do Sul, has forró until dawn every Wed.

The Reggae Bar, just off Av Baía dos Golfinhos in Pipa centre, which has live reggae bands; usually on Tue.

Aruman, Av Baía dos Golfinhos s/n, Pipa, has good cocktails and a trendy crowd.

The Blue Bar, Av Baía dos Golfinhos s/n, Pipa, which has live *pagodé* and samba on Wed.

Calangos, Baía dos Golfinhos s/n (at the southern end of Pipa), is a club with famous name DJs, like Patife, techno and MPB from Thu to Sun.

Mossoró *p490*
Cheiro Nordestino, R Wenceslau Braz 817, São José. Drinks and snacks, pleasant atmosphere, live music on weekends.
Acapulco's, R Chico Linhares, quadra 7. Snacks and drinks, open Wed-Sun.

Festivals and events

Natal *p484, map p485*
Jan Festa de Nossa Senhora dos Navegantes, when numerous vessels go to sea from Praia da Redinha, north of town.
Mid-Oct Country show, **Festa do Boi**, bus marked Parnamirim to the exhibition centre, it gives a good insight into rural life.
Mid-Dec Carnatal, the Salvador-style out-of- season carnival, a lively 4-day music festival with dancing in the streets.

Mossoró *p490*
Jan Fest Verão – much movement during the local *Carnaval fora de época*.
3-13 Dec Santa Luzia, 10 days of fairs and celebrations closed by a large procession.

Shopping

Natal *p484, map p485, phone code 084*
Centro de Turismo, R Aderbal de Figueiredo, 980, off R Gen Cordeiro, Petrópolis, T2122267. A converted prison with a wide variety of handicraft shops, art gallery, antique shop and tourist information booth, offers good view of the Rio Potengi and the sea, Sun-Wed 0900-1900, Thu 2200.
Centro Municipal de Artesanato, Av Pres Café Filho, Praia dos Artistas. Daily 1000-2200. Sand-in-bottle pictures are very common in Natal and there are plenty here alongside other touristy items.
Natal Shopping, Av Senador Salgado Filho, 2234, between Ponta Negra and Via Costeira. Large mall with restaurants, ATMS, cinemas and 140 shops. Free shuttle bus service to major hotels.

Tibau do Sul and around *p488*
Pipa is a good place for raw cotton and costume jewellery made from tropical seeds.
The Bookshop (next to the reggae bar), run by a wonderfully knowledgable Brazilian eccentric, Cyntia, rents out books from Oscar Wilde to Dostoyevsky.

Activities and tours

Natal *p484, map p485, phone code 084*

Alternative therapies

Marta Sena, T99662868, martageorgia@yahoo.com.br. Ayurvedic massage, reiki etc. Well trained and experienced.

Buggy tours

Buggy tours are by far the most popular, US$35-90, depending on the destination.
Nataltur, Av Deodoro 424, Centro, T2110117, F2116325.
Marsol Turismo, Av Senador Salgado Filho, 141, T2063308.
China's Turismo, R Mossoro 574, T2221564, American Express representative.

City tours

A city tour costs US$15; if it includes the northern beaches US$20-25; including southern beaches US$30-35.

Tour operators

Manary Ecotours, R Francisco Gurgel 9067, Ponta Negra, T/F2192900, manary@digi.com.br. Excellent tours to some of the most interesting sights in the northeastern interior like Souza, Cariri and the Serra da Capivara.

Transport

Natal *p484, map p485, phone code 084*
See also Ins and outs, p484.
Air Aeroporto Augusto Severo, Parnamirim, T6441000. Flights to Belém, Brasília, Fernando de Noronha, Fortaleza, Recife, Rio de Janeiro, Salvador and São Paulo.

Airline offices BRA, Av Prudente de Morais, 507, Centro, T2211155, at airport, T6432068. **FLY**, Av Prudente de Morais, 3857, T2069070, at airport, T6432124. **Nordeste**, at airport, T2726814. **TAM**, Av Campos Sales, 500, Tirol, T2012020, at airport, T6431624, F2722624, freephone 0800 123100. **Transbrasil**, Av Deodoro 429, Petrópolis, T2211805, F2216025, at airportT6431135, freephone 0800 151151. **Trip**, T2341717, freephone 08002747. **Varig**, R Mossoro, 598, Centro, T2019339, F2211531, at airport,T7431100, freephone 0800 997000. **Vasp**, R João Pessoa 220, Centro, T2214453, F2213548, at airport, T6431441.

Bus Rodoviária, Av Capitão Mor Gouveia 1237, Cidade da Esperança, T2054377. Regional tickets are sold on street level, interstate on the 2nd floor.

To **Recife** with Napoles, 5 daily, US$6.60 *convencional*, US$9 *executivo*, 4 hrs. With Nordeste to **Mossoró**, US$6 *convencional*, US$10 *executivo*, 4 hrs. To **Aracati**, US$7.50, 5½ hrs. To **Fortaleza**, US$11 *convencional*, US$15.50 *executivo*, US$25 *leito*, 8 hrs. To **João Pessoa**, every 2 hrs, US$4 *convencional*, US$5 *executivo*, 3 hrs. With São Geraldo to **Maceió**, buses both direct and via Recife, US$14 *convencional*, US$20 *executivo*, 10 hrs. To **Salvador**, US$32.50 *executivo*, 20 hrs. To **Rio de Janeiro**, US$69.65. To **São Paulo**, US$66 *convencional*, US$84 *executivo*, 46-49 hrs. With Boa Esperança to **Teresina**, US$26 *convencional*, US$31.25 *executivo*, 17-20 hrs. To **Belém**, US$45, 32 hrs.

Car hire Hertz, airport, T6431660. Dudu Locadora, Av Rio Branco 420, Centro, T2117000, F2214694. Buggy Mille, Av Praia de Ponta Negra 8848, T2363373, F2362382. Localiza, Av Nascimento de Castro 1792, T2065296, or at airport, T0800-992000. Avis, at airport, T644 2500.

Taxi Taxis are expensive compared to other cities (eg 4 times the price of Recife); US$8 for 10-min journey.

Tibau do Sul and around *p488, phone cod e084*

Bike Rentals from Blue Planet, Pipa. US$5 ½ day, US$10 full day.

Buggy Rentals, US$50 south to **Barra de Cunhaú**, US$100. Buggy tour **Natal**-Pipa US$115.

Bus From **Natal**, Queiroz e Melo, from new rodoviária, 0800 and 1515, to Tibau do Sul, US$3, 2 hrs. To Pipa, US$4, 2¼ hrs, return from Pipa 0500, 1600. Minivans also do this run and are easiest to catch from the beach. Buses to or from **Paraíba** pass through Goianinha on the insterstate road. Frequent combis connect **Goaninha** with Pipa (30 mins, $1.50). Combis connect Pipa and Tibau until around 2300.

Taxi After hours taxi – Carlos, T99770006 (basic English).

Redinha *p489*

Ferry There is a frequent ferry service for Redinha from **Cais Tavares de Lira**, Ribeira, weekdays 0530-1900, weekend and holidays 0800-1830, US$0.50 per person, US$3 for car.

Bus Regular bus service from the old rodoviária, last bus back starting at **Genipabu** at 1830.

Mossoró *p490, phone code 084*

Bus The rodoviária is at Av do Contorno (BR-304); bus to centre 'Boa Vista' or 'Circular', US$0.50, taxi US$6. With Nordeste to **Natal**, US$6 *convencional*, US$10 *executivo*, 4 hrs. To **Fortaleza**, US$5, 4 daily, 4 hrs. To **Aracati**, US$2.50, 2 hrs, not all buses bound for Fortaleza will let you off at Aracati, enquire before. Guanabara to Recife. São Geraldo for main cities in the south. Several regional carriers for points in the interior.

Car hire Yes, Av Pres Dutra 2020, Alto de São Manoel, T3214526.

Directory

Natal *p484, map p485, phone code 084*

Banks Banco 24 horas, Natal Shopping, Cirrus, Visa, MasterCard and Plus. Banco do Brasil, Seafront ATM, Ponta Negra for Cirrus, Visa, MasterCard and Plus. Also, Av Rio Branco 510, Cidade Alta, US$ cash and TCs at poor rates, cash advances against Visa, Mon-Fri 1000-1600. Banespa, Av Rio Branco 704, Cidade Alta, US$ cash and TCs at dolar turismo rate, Mon-Fri 1000-1430. Sunset Câmbio, Av Hermes da Fonseca 628, Tirol, T2122552, cash and TCs, 0900-1700. Dunas Câmbio, Av Roberto Freire 1776, Loja B-11, Capim Macio (east of Parque das Dunas), T2193840, cash and TCs, 0900-1700.

Embassies and consulates Canada, Av Roberto Freire 2951, Bloco 01, Loja 09-CCAB Sul, Ponta Negra, T2192197. Germany, R Gov Sílvio Pedrosa 308, Areia Preta, T2223596. Italy, R Auta de Souza 275, Centro, T2226674. Spain, R Amintas Barros 4200, Lagoa Nova, T2065610.

Internet Sobre Ondas, Ponta Negra (also bar and restaurant, see above), 0900-2400, 10 centavos 1 min. **Post office** R Princesa Isabel 711, Centro; Av Rio Branco 538, Centro, Av Engenheiro Hildegrando de Góis 22, Ribeira, Av Praia de Ponta Negra 8920,

Ponta Negra. **Poste restante** is in Ribeira, near the old rodoviária, at Av Rio Branco and Av General Gustavo Cordeiro de Farias, hard to find. **Security** Tourist police (Delegacia do Turista): T2363288, 24 hrs. **Telephone** R Princesa Isabel 687 and R João Pessoa, Centro; Av Roberto Freire 3100, Ponta Negra, Shopping Cidade Jardim, Av Roberto Freire, Ponta Negra; and rodoviária.

Mossoró *p490*

Banks Banco do Brasil, Praça Dix-Sept Rosado. **Post office** Praça Rafael Fernandes. **Telephone** Av Dix-Sept Rosado 56, Centro, national and international calls, 0730-1130, 1330-1730.

Ceará

The state which has been dubbed terra da luz *(land of light) is known for its 573 km of coastline, with glorious beaches, scenic dunes and almost constant sunshine. The sophisticated city of Fortaleza is still home to traditional* jangadas, *while inland is the harsh* sertão *and several sites of natural and cultural interest such as Juazeiro de Norte.*

It was only during the period of Dutch rule that efforts were made to populate the interior of Ceará. Many Portuguese, fleeing the Dutch, moved into the sertão *to raise cattle. Beef and leather came to typify the region. The Cearenses participated in the republican movements that flared up in the Northeast in the early 19th century, but real development did not begin until the second half of that century. Ceará was one of the foremost provinces in the drive to abolish slavery. It remains largely underdeveloped.*

The ocean is warm with average temperatures of 29°C and a constant breeze makes the temperature pleasant. Most rain falls between March and July and locals refer to this period as winter. Europeans will find it warm and sunny with sporadic rainy days. One third of the coast is east of Fortaleza in the Litoral Leste or Costa Sol Nascente (Sunrise Coast), which has a fair concentration of towns and fishing villages. Two thirds of the coastline is west of Fortaleza in the Litoral Oeste or Costa Sol Poente (Sunset Coast), which has some beautiful undeveloped stretches. *▸▸ For Sleeping, Eating and other listings, see pages 516-529.*

Fortaleza

→ *Phone code: 085 (088 outside metropolitan Fortaleza, but numbers beginning with 3 must be prefixed with 085). Colour map 2, A5. Population: 2.1 million.*

The fifth largest city in Brazil and capital of the State of Ceará is a busy metropolis with many high-rise buildings, an important clothes manufacturing industry, lots of hotels and restaurants and a lively nightlife. Fishermen's jangadas *still dot the turquoise ocean across from the beach and transatlantic cruise ships call in for refuelling. The midday sun is oppressive, tempered somewhat by a constant breeze, evening temperatures can be more pleasant, especially by the sea.*

Ins and outs

Getting there International and domestic flights arrive at Pinto Martins airport, 6 km south of the centre. Bus No 404 runs from the airport to Praça José de Alencar in the centre, US$0.70. **Expresso Guanabara** minibus runs to the rodoviária and Beira Mar (US$1.00), also No 066 Papicu to Parangaba and No 027 Papicu to Siqueira. Taxis charge around US$6 minimum to centre, Avenida Beira Mar or Praia do Futuro, US$7-10 at night depending on destination. Use **Cooperativa Taxi Comum** or **Taxi Especial Credenciado.** Interstate buses arrive at the rodoviária, 6 km south from the centre (mo luggage store, only lockers). *▸▸ See also Transport, page 525.*

Getting around The city is spread out, its main attractions are in the centre and along the seashore, transport from one to the other can take a long time. The city bus system is efficient if a little rough. Fare US$0.70; vans also charge US$0.70. The cheapest way to get to know the city is to take the **Circular 1** (anti-clockwise) or **Circular 2** (clockwise) buses which pass Avenida Beira Mar, the Aldeota district, the University (UFC) and the city centre and cathedral; fare US$0.90. Alternatively, take the new **Top Bus** of **Expresso Guanabara**, an air-conditioned minibus starting at Avenida Abolição (US$1.50, T0800-991992).

Tourist offices **Secretaria do Turismo** (Setur) ⓘ *Centro Administrativo Virgílio Távora, Cambeba, T4883858/3900, www.turismo.ce.gov.br, freephone 0800 991516*, is the main office of the state tourism agency;there are also several **information booths** ⓘ *Centro de Turismo in ex-municipal prison, T4887411, Mon-Sat 0700-1800, Sun 0700-1200*, helpful, has maps (sometimes) and information about beach tours; ⓘ *Rodoviária, T2564080 daily 0600-2100; airport, T4771667 (24 hrs); and Museu de Fortaleza, old lighthouse, Mucuripe, T2631115, 0700-1730*. **Posta Telefônica Beira Mar** ⓘ *Av Beira Mar almost opposite Praiano Palace*, provides information, sells Redenção tickets to Jericoacoara, and has a good range of postcards, as we'll as clothes and papers and magazines. **Tourist police** ⓘ *R Silva Paulet 505, Aldeota, T4338171*.

Security Generally, though, the city is safe for visitors. However, tourists should avoid the following areas: Serviluz *favela* between the old lighthouse (Avenida Vicente de Castro), Mucuripe and Praia do Futuro; the *favela* behind the railway station; the Passeio Público at night; Avenida Abolição at its eastern (Nossa Senhora da Saúde church) and western ends.

Sights

Walking through the centre of Fortaleza, it is hard to ignore the city's history, which dates back to the 17th century. Pedestrian walkways radiate from the **Praça do Ferreira**, the heart of the commercial centre, and the whole area is dotted with shady green squares. The **Fortaleza Nossa Senhora da Assumpção** ⓘ *Av Alberto Nepomuceno, T2551600 in advance for permission to visit, daily 0800-1100, 1400-1700*, originally built in 1649 by the Dutch, gave the city its name. Near the fort, on Rua Dr João Moreira, is the 19th-century **Passeio Público** or Praça dos Mártires, a park with old trees and statues of Greek deities. West of here a neoclassical former prison (1866) houses a fine tourist centre, the **Centro de Turismo do Estado**(Emcetur), ⓘ *Av Senador Pompeu 350, near the waterfront, T0800-991516, closed Sun*, with museums, theatre and craft shops. It houses the renovated **Museu de Arte e Cultura Populares** and the **Museu de Minerais** ⓘ *T2123566, both museums in late 2003, no schedule for reopening*. Further west along Rua Dr João Moreira, at **Praça Castro Carreira**, (commonly known as Praça da Estação), is the nicely refurbished train station, **Estação João Felipe** (1880).

The **Teatro José de Alencar** ⓘ *on the praça of the same name, T2291989, Mon-Fri 0800-1700, hourly tours, some English speaking guides, US$1, Wed free*, was inaugurated in 1910. It is a magnificent iron structure imported from Scotland and decorated in neoclassical and art nouveau styles, and is worth visiting. It also houses a library and art gallery. The **Praça dos Leões** or **Praça General Tibúrcio** on Rua Conde D'Eu has bronze lions imported from France. Around it stand the 18th-century **Palácio da Luz** ⓘ *T2315699*, former seat of the state government; the **Igreja Nossa Senhora do Rosário**, built by slaves in the 18th century; and the former provincial legislature, dating from 1871, which houses the **Museu do Ceará** ⓘ *R São Paulo, next to Praça dos Leões, T2511502, Tue-Fri 0830-1730, Sat 0830-1400, US$0.80*. The museum has displays on history and anthropology. To get there, take bus marked 'Dom Luís'. The new **cathedral** ⓘ *Praça da Sé*, completed in 1978, in Gothic style but built in concrete, with beautiful stained-glass windows, stands beside the new semi-circular **Mercado Central**.

There are several worthwhile museums to visit in and around Fortaleza. The **Museu do Maracatu** ⓘ *Rufino de Alencar 231*, at Teatro São José, has costumes of this ritual dance of African origin. The **Museu Artur Ramos** ⓘ *Av Perimetral, Messejana, 15 km from the centre, T2291898, Tue-Sun 0800-1200, 1400-1700, Mon 1400-1730*, in the Casa de José de Alencar, displays artefacts of African and indigenous origin collected by the anthropologist Artur Ramos, as well as documents from the writer José de Alencar, see below.

The new and exciting **Centro Dragão do Mar de Arte e Cultura** ⓘ *R Dragão do Mar 81, Praia de Iracema, T4888600, www.dragaodomar.org.br, Tue-Thu 1000-1730, Fri-Sun 1400-2130, US$0.75 for entry to each museum/gallery, free on Sun*, hosts music concerts, dance, and art and photography exhibitions. It has various entrances, from Ruas Almirante Barroso, Boris and from junction of Monsenhor Tabosa, Dom Manuel and Castelo Branco. This last one leads directly to three museums: on street level, the **Memorial da Cultura Cearense**, with changing exhibitions; on the next floor down is an art and cultural exhibit; in the basement is an excellent audio-visual museum of **El Vaqueiro**. Also at street level is the **Livraria Livro Técnico.** There is a planetarium with a whispering gallery underneath. The centre also houses the **Museu de Arte Contemporânea do Ceará**. This area is very lively at night (see Entertainment below).

Beaches

Those urban beaches between Barra do Ceará (west) and Ponta do Mucuripe (east) are considered polluted and not suitable for swimming. There are a number of minibus day tours to beaches, $US4 and Jericoacoara, US$15; minibuses gather along seafront, also agency **CPVTUR** ⓘ *Av Monsenhor Tabosa 1001*.

Eastern beaches Just east of the centre is **Praia de Iracema**, one of the older beach suburbs, with some original turn-of-the-century houses. It is not much of a sunbathing beach as there is little shade or facilities and swimming is unsafe, but don't miss it at night. Of its many bars and restaurants, the **Estoril**, housed in one of the earliest buildings, has become a landmark. At the shore Ponte Metálica or Ponte dos Ingleses is a good place to see the sunset and view dolphins.

East of Iracema, the **Avenida Beira Mar** (Avenida Presidente Kennedy) connects Praia do Meireles (divided into Praia do Ideal, dos Diários and do Meireles proper) with Volta da Jurema and Praia do Mucuripe; it is lined with high-rise buildings and most luxury hotels are located here. A *calçado*, or walkway, following the palm-lined shore becomes a night-time playground as locals promenade on foot, roller skates, skate boards and bicycles (children ride mini-motorbikes, scooters or the 'happiness' train with its real life *Disney* characters). Take in the spectacle sipping a *agua de coco* or *caipirinha* on the beachfrontwhere there are volleyball courts, bars, open-air shows and a crafts fair in front of the **Imperial Othon Palace Hotel.**

Fortaleza has 25 km of beaches, many of which are the scene of the city's nightlife.

Praia do Mucuripe, 5 km from the centre, is Fortaleza's main fishing centre, where *jangadas* (rafts with triangular sails) bring in the catch; there are many restaurants serving *peixada* and other fish specialities. The symbol of this beach is the statue of Iracema, the main character of the romance by José de Alencar (see Literature section, page 703); from the monument there is a good view of Mucuripe's port and bay. At Mucuripe Point is a lighthouse built by slaves in 1846, which houses the **Museu de Fortaleza** (now sadly run down and not a safe area, according to the tourist office). There is a lookout at the new lighthouse, good for viewing the *jangadas* which come in, in the late afternoon, and the sunset.

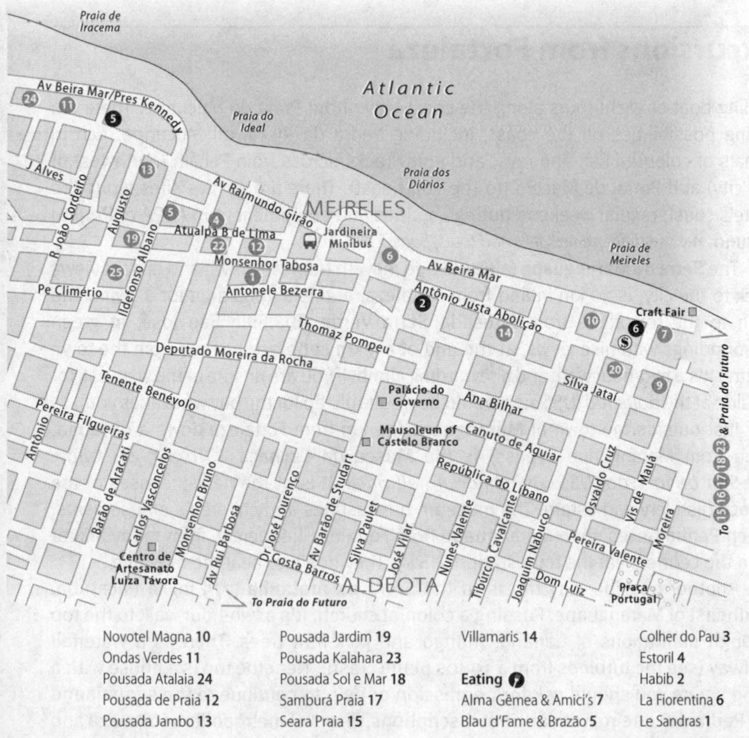

Praia do Futuro, 8 km southeast of the centre, is the most popular bathing beach. It is 8 km long, with strong waves, sand dunes and freshwater showers, but no natural shade. Many vendors and straw shacks serve local dishes. On Thursday nights it becomes the centre for the city's nightlife, with people enjoying live music, *forró* and crab. The south end of the beach is known as Caça e Pesca; water here is polluted because of the outflow of the Rio Cocó. Praia do Futuro has few hotels or buildings because the salt-spray corrosion is among the strongest in the world.

Buses to Praia do Futuro, marked 'Caça e Pesca', pass all southeast beaches en route.

At **Praia de Sabiaguaba**, 20 km southeast of the centre, is a small fishing village known for its seafood; the area has mangroves and is good for fishing.

Some 29 km southeast of the centre is **Praia Porto das Dunas**, a pleasant beach popular for watersports including surfing. Buggies and ultralight tours can be arranged. The main attraction is **Beach Park** ⓘ *US$20*, the largest water park in South America, with pools, water toboggans, sports fields, restaurants.

Western beaches Northwest of the centre is **Praia Barra do Ceará**, 8 km, where the Rio Ceará flows into the sea (take a Grande Circular 1 bus). Here are the ruins of the 1603 Forte de Nossa Senhora dos Prazeres, the first Portuguese settlement in the area, partially covered by dunes; with beautiful sunsets. The palm-fringed beaches west of the Rio Ceará are cleaner but have strong waves. A bridge across this river has been built, making the area more accessible and open to development, as at **Praia de Icaraí**, 22 km to the northwest, and **Tabuba**, 5 km further north.

Beyond Tabuba, **Cumbuco** is a lively beach (it can be dirty in high season) with palm trees and bars. For the active, there are buggies, horse riding and *jangadas* as well as dunes which you can slide (known locally as *skibunda*) down into a freshwater lake (**Lagoa de Parnamirim**). A buggy tour, US$7 per person, is recommended.

Excursions from Fortaleza

Sailing boat or yacht tours along the coast leave from Praia do Mucuripe. There are diving possibilities off the coast, including Pedra da Risca, off Mucuripe, rich in shoals of colourful fish and rays, and shipwrecks across from Pecém (northwest of the city) and Portal de Maceió (to the southeast). There are 14 dive sites along the state's coast; regular weekend outings, guides and equipment from **ASPA** or **Projeto Netuno.** » *For details see Activities and tours, page 524.*

The **Serra de Maranguape** (altitude 890 m) with tropical growth and distant views back to the city, is 30 km inland from Fortaleza, and is a good area for a swim. The path to the top starts from **Pousada Serra Verde** (**B**), Sítio São José, in green surroundings with nice views, at the end of a 5-km cobblestone road from the town centre. It's a two-hour walk and a rewarding climb. If you are unsure of the way, ask for a guide at the *pousada* (US$2.75 would be a suitable tip for the boy who takes you).

Just outside the town of **Maranguape** (30 km from Fortaleza down a dirt road, 4 km from Maranguape bypass) is the **Museu da Cachaça** ⓘ *Toxx85-341 0407, Tue-Sun 0830-1700, US$1.85, children half price*. It is at the neat premises of the **Ypióca** distillery and estate. The museum has tastings and children's amusements. Green **Penha** buses go to Maranguape from Fortaleza frequently, from rodoviária or from the centre, near the train station, US$3. They don't go near the museum

Another possible day trip is to the **Serra da Aratanha** (775 m) in Pacatuba, southeast of Maranguape. Passing a colonial church, it's a two-hour walk to the top through plantations of banana, mango and jack-fruit trees. There is a waterfall halfway (see the turbines from a 1980s plane crash). Near the top is a house with a pond where you should ask for permission or help to continue to the summit and the Pedra de Letreiro, with ancient inscriptions, views of metropolitan Fortaleza and a colony of vultures. Bus from rodoviária one hour, US$2. The town is said to be haunted by ghosts from the time of the slave trade.

Those interested in crafts should visit **Aquiraz**, 31 km southeast of Fortaleza, and the nearby beaches of **Prainha** (6 km north) and **Iguape** (18 km south), where craftspeople can be seen using the techniques of *bilro* and *labirinto* with amazing speed, to create beautiful lacework. There are several hotels and restaurants in all these locations.

The coast east of Fortaleza

The most prominent feature of the Eastern Coast is the impressive coloured-sand cliffs. There are also freshwater springs near the shore, along with palm groves and mangroves. Lobster fishing is one of the main activities.

Aquiraz and around → *Phone code: 085. Colour map 2, A5. Population: 61,000.*

The first capital of Ceará conserves several colonial buildings and has a religious art museum. Some 31 km east of Fortaleza, it is also the access point for the following beaches:

Prainha, 6 km east, a fishing village and weekend resort with a 10-km long beach and dunes. The beach is clean and largely empty and the waves are good for surfing. You can see *jangadas* coming in daily in the late afternoon. The village is known for its lacework; the women using the *bilro* and *labirinto* techniques at the **Centro de Rendeiras**. In some of the small restaurants it is possible to see displays of the *carimbó*, one of the North Brazilian dances. Just south of Prainha is **Praia do Presídio** with calm surf, dunes, palms and *cajueiros* (cashew trees).

About 18 km southeast of Aquiraz is **Praia Iguape**, another fishing and lacework village. The beach is a large, elbow-shaped sandbank, very scenic especially at Ponta do Iguape. Nearby are high sand dunes where skiing is popular. There is a lookout at Morro do Enxerga Tudo; trips on *jangadas* one hour for US$8.50. Lacework is sold at the **Centro de Rendeiras**. Locals are descendants of Dutch, Portuguese and Indians, some traditions such as the *coco-de-praia* folk dance are still practised. About 3 km south of Igape is **Praia Barro Preto**, a wide, tranquil beach, with sand dunes, palms and lagoons.

Cascavel, 62 km southeast of Fortaleza, has a Saturday crafts fair by the market. It is the access point for the beaches of Caponga and Águas Belas, where traditional fishing villages coexist with fancy weekend homes and hotels.

Caponga, 15 km northeast of Cascavel, has a wide, 2-km-long beach lined with palms. *Jangadas* set sail in the early morning; arrangements can be made to accompany fishermen on overnight trips, 90-minute ride by beach, US$14 for up to five people. There is a fish market and crafts sales (ceramics, embroidery and lacework) on the beach.

A 30-minute walk south along the white-sand beach leads to **Águas Belas**, on the mouth of the Rio Mal Cozinhado, offering a combination of fresh and saltwater bathing (access also by road, 15 km from Cascavel, 4 km from Caponga). The scenery here, and 5 km further east at Barra Nova, changes with the variations of the tide. A walk north along the beach for 6 km takes you to the undeveloped Praia do Batoque, which is surrounded by cliffs and dunes.

It is possible to hike along much of the eastern coast. From Prainha to Águas Belas, for example, is seven hours (take plenty of water and sun protection). Where rivers have to be crossed, there is usually a boatman. Fishing villages have accommodation or hammock space.

Morro Branco and Praia das Fontes → *Phone code: 085.*

Beberibe, 78 km from Fortaleza, is the access point for Morro Branco and Praia das Fontes, some of the better known beaches of the east coast.

About 4 km from Beberibe is Morro Branco, with a spectacular beach, coloured craggy cliffs and beautiful views. *Jangadas* leave the beach at 0500, returning at 1400-1500, lobster is the main catch in this area. The coloured sands of the dunes are bottled into beautiful designs and sold along with other crafts such as lacework, embroidery and straw goods. *Jangadas* may be hired for sailing (one hour for up to six people US$30). Beach buggies (full day US$100) and taxis are also for hire. There are summer homes along the beach which can get very crowded at holiday times.

South of Morro Branco and 6 km from Beberibe is Praia das Fontes, which also has coloured cliffs with freshwater springs; there is a fishing village and at the south end a lagoon. Near the shore is a cave, known as **Mãe de Água**, visible during low tide. Buggies and ultralight aircraft can be hired on the beach. A luxury resort complex has been built here, making the area expensive.

South of Praia das Fontes are several less developed beaches including **Praia Uruaú** or **Marambaia**, about 6 km from Praia das Fontes along the beach or 21 km by road from Beberibe, via Sucatinga on a loose sand road. The beach is at the base of coloured dunes; there is a fishing village with some accommodation. Just inland is Lagoa do Uruaú, the largest in the state and a popular place for watersports. A buggy from Morro Branco costs US$45 for four.

About 50 km southeast of Beberibe is **Fortim**, access point to **Pontal de Maceió**, a reddish sand point on the mouth of the Rio Jaguaribe, from where there is a good view of a large section of the eastern coast. In the winter the river is high and shrimp is fished, while in the summer it dries up, forming islands and freshwater beaches; boats go to the islands from Fortim. There's a fishing village about 1 km from the ocean with bars, restaurants and small *pousadas*.

Community tourism Some 120 km east of Fortaleza, in the district of Beberibe, is **Prainha do Canto Verde**, a small fishing village on a vast beach, which has an award-winning community tourism project. There are guesthouses (eg **Dona Mirtes, E** with breakfast, will negotiate other meals), houses for rent (eg **Casa Cangulo,** or **Vila Marésia**), restaurants (good food at **Sol e Mar**), a handicraft cooperative, *jangada* and catamaran cruises, fishing and walking trails. Each November there is a **Regata Ecológica**, with *jangadas* from up and down the coast competing (for the regatta, Christmas and Semana Santa, add 30% to prices). This is a simple place, which lives by artesanal fishing (ie no big boats or industrial techniques) and has built up its tourism infrastructure without any help from outside investors (they have been fighting the speculators since 1979). It's a very friendly place and foreigners are welcome to get to know how the fisher folk live; knowledge of Portuguese is essential. For **information** ⓘ *www.fortalnet.com.br/~fishnet, contact René Schärer, Toxx88-4131426, fishnet@uol.com.br (Swiss, also speaks English), or Lagomar, Toxx85 96088222; the tourism coordinator is Antônio Aires*. To get to Prainha do Canto Verde, take a São Benedito bus to Aracati or Canoa Quebrada, buy a ticket to Quatro Bocas and ask to be let off at Lagoa da Poeira, two hours from Fortaleza. If you haven't booked a transfer in advance, Márcio at the **Pantanal** restaurant at the bus stop will take you, US$2.75.

Aracati → *Phone code: 088. Population: 62,000.*

Situated on the shores of the Rio Jaguaribe, Aracati is the access point to the southeastern-most beaches of Ceará. The city is best known for its Carnival, the liveliest in the state, and for its colonial architecture, including several 18th-century churches and mansions with Portuguese tile façades. There is a religious art museum (closed lunch time and Sunday afternoon) a Saturday morning crafts fair on Avenida Coronel Alexandrino, and a number of simple *pousadas* on the same street (**B-E**).

Community tourism **Ponta Grossa**, about 30 km southeast, is near Icapuí, the last municipality before Rio Grande do Norte (access from Mossoró), from where you then head to Redonda. Ponta Grossa is down a sand road just before Redonda. Both Ponta Grossa and Redonda are very pretty places, nestled at the foot of the cliffs, but Ponta Grossa has its own community tourism development. The fishing community here has many inhabitants of Dutch origin, following a shipwreck in the 19th century (many have fair hair). One of the main attractions of Ponta Grossa is that, offshore, is one of the few places visited by manatees (*peixe boi marinho*). You can try to spot them from the cliffs. Beach trips go from Canoa Quebrada to Ponta Grossa for lunch, but if you want to stay here, you need to speak Portuguese. Cabins for rent are under construction and there are restaurants/bars. For **information** ⓘ *tourism coordinator Eliabe, Toxx88-432 5001, or 9964 5846*. To the south are the beaches of Redonda and Barreiras, good for surfing, with a hotel.

For further information on community tourism and the preservation of traditional ways of life in Ceará, contact **Instituto Terramar** ⓘ *R Pinho Pessoa 86, Joaquim Távora, Fortaleza, oxx85-226 4154, or Toxx85-8804 0999, ask for Esther Neuhaus, www.terramar.org.br.*

Canoa Quebrada → *Phone code: 088. Colour map 2, A5.*

Canoa Quebrada stands on a sand dune 10 km from Aracati. An isolated fishing village until 1982, when a road was built, it is now a very popular resort known for its easygoing party atmosphere (there have been reports of drug problems here), many bars, restaurants and *forró* establishments. The village is also famous for its *labirinto* lacework and coloured sand sculpture, for sand-skiing on its dunes and for its beaches. Fishermen have their homes in Esteves, a separate village also on top of the cliff; they still live off the sea and rides on *jangadas* can be arranged at the beach. To avoid biting insects (*bicho do pé*) it is best to wear shoes or sandals. There is nowhere to change money except **Banco do Brasil** in Aracati. In the second half of July the **Canoarte** festival takes place, which includes a *jangada* regatta and music festival.

Excursions from Canoa Quebrada

South of Canoa Quebrada, **Majorlândia** is a very nice village, with many-coloured sand dunes (used in bottle pictures and cord crafts) and a wide beach with strong waves, good for surfing. The arrival of the fishing fleet in the evening is an important daily event; lobster is the main catch. It is a popular weekend destination with beach homes for rent and Carnival here is quite lively. There are plenty of *pousadas* at all levels and the town is easy to find your way around. You will have no trouble finding a room outside of the Christmas or Carnaval breaks. About 5 km south along the beach is the village of **Quixaba** on a beach surrounded by coloured cliffs, with reefs offshore and good fishing (**Pousada Lúcia**, T4211576). At low tide you can reach Lagoa do Mato, some 4 km south. Between Canoa Quebrada and Majorlândia is **Porto Canoa**, a resort town (opened 1996), fashioned after the Greek islands. It includes beach homes and apartments, shopping areas, restaurants and hotels, and there are facilities for watersports, horse riding, ultralight flights, buggy and *jangada* outings.

Buggy rentals are available at Canoa Quebrada beach; a popular destination going through the dunes is **Lagoa do Mato**, about 12 km southeast, a pristine beach, surrounded by dunes, cliffs and palms (buggy US$30 for four). There is a hotel with a restaurant. **Ponta Grossa,** about 30 km southeast, is another beautiful beach, where there is a natural lookout on the cliffs (buggy US$75 for four, four hours). The fishing community here has many inhabitants of Dutch origin, following a shipwreck in the 19th century. To the south are the beaches of **Redonda** and **Barreiras,** good for surfing, with a handful of hotels.

The coast west of Fortaleza

The coast northwest of Fortaleza has many wide beaches, near fixed or shifting dunes, surrounded by swathes of coconut groves. The main roads are some distance from the shore, making access to the beaches somewhat more difficult than on the eastern coast. This means the fishing villages retain a traditional lifestyle and responsible travel is especially important.

Pecém and Taíba → *Phone code: 085. Population: 5,500 (Pecém).*

Some 58 km northwest of Fortaleza, **Pecém** is a village set by a cove with a wide beach, dunes, inland lagoons. There is a strong surf, here and in Taíba, a 14-km long beach to the north (19 km by road), and surfing and fishing championships. By Taíba, a long point filled with palms extends into the sea. Nearby is **Siupé**, a village that maintains colonial characteristics, where embroidered hammocks, a trademark of Ceará, are made.

There are a few simple *pousadas* in each, 11 daily buses from Fortaleza to Pecém and four daily buses to Siupé. (The town's calling centre: T3441064 and T3401328; 3-digit numbers indicated are extensions on these central lines.)

Paracuru and Lagoinha → *Phone code: 085. Population: 28,000 (Paracuru).*

Some 106 km northwest of Fortaleza is Paracuru, a fishing port which has the most important Carnival in the northwest coast, including street dancing and parades, decorated boat parades, sports championships and a beauty contest. It has some lovely deserted white-sand beaches with good bathing and surfing, and the people are very friendly. There are several *pousadas* in the centre. Restaurant **Ronco do Mar** has good fish dishes. **Boca do Poço** bar has *forró* at weekends. There are eight buses daily from Fortaleza rodoviária, US$3; For **information** ⓘ *T2724483 (in Fortaleza).*

Lagoinha's calling centre: T3631232. 3-digit numbers indicated are extensions on this central line.

West of Paracuru and 12 km from the town of Paraipaba, is **Lagoinha**, a very scenic beach with hills, dunes and palms by the shore; a fishing village is on one of the hills. Nearby are some small but pleasant waterfalls and 3 km west of town **Lagoa da Barra**, a lake surrounded by dunes. Local legend says that one of the hills, **Morro do Cascudo**, has hidden treasure, left by French pirates.

There are six daily buses from Fortaleza with **Brasileiro**, three hours, US$2.60 and plenty of cheap seafood restaurants.

Fleixeiras → *Phone code: 085. Colour map 2, A4.*

Further northwest, some 135 km from Fortaleza, is **Trairi**, access point to a series of beaches which conserve a natural beauty and, until the mid-1990s, were untouched by tourism. North of Trairi, 15 km by road, is Fleixeiras, where at low-tide pools, good for snorkelling, form near the beach. There are strong waves for surfing and wind for windsurfing as well as dunes by the wide beach. In the village there is a *jangada* repair shop, a good place to learn about these crafts, and a workshop where lacework and embroidered clothing and linen are made.

About 5 km west is **Imboaca**, a scenic beach with interesting rock formations and shifting dunes. Further west, at the mouth of the Rio Mundaú, is **Mundaú**, another beautiful area, with beach, palms, dunes and an old working lighthouse. Take a raft across to the spit and walk for hours on deserted sands; see the centre of wind-eroded dunes; take a boat from the quay up the river to see the mangroves. Access roads from Imboaca and Cana to the south are often impassable because of shifting dunes; at low tide it is possible to reach it along the beach from Fleixeiras. A fishing village is near the beach; there are some *pousadas* and restaurants. From

Fortaleza to Fleixeiras there are three buses daily (US$3.85, information T2724128).

You can cross the Rio Mundaú and walk 8 km to **Baleia**, a developing beach resort with plenty of *pousadas* (**C Maresia**, Swiss-run; **C Som das Águas**, OK). There is one daily bus from Fortaleza, 1300, five hours, US$10). For another 40 km there are beautiful dune landscapes and fishing villages, how Canoa Quebrada and Jericocoara must have been 30 years ago. **Icaraí de Amontada** is in a windy bay, good windsurfing, simple accommodation (**D**). There is one daily bus from Fortaleza, 0900, six 'horrible' hours, US$12.

The sleepy fishing village of **Almofala**, 230 km from Fortaleza, is home of the Tremembés Indians who live off the sea and some agriculture. There is electricity and one rather rough *pousada*, just beyond the church. Locals rent hammock space and cook meals. Bathing is better elsewhere, but the area is surrounded by dunes and is excellent for hiking along the coast to explore beaches and lobster-fishing communities. There is an Ibama turtle sanctuary, part of the Tamar Project, on the beach beyond the village. In Almofala, the church, with much of the town, was covered by shifting sands and remained covered for 50 years, reappearing in the 1940s; it has since been restored. Itarema, 10 km from Almofala, has wild, sweeping sand flats on the river estuary. It's worth a stroll here and staying overnight (**E Portal da Barra**, Toxx88-667 1358, Praia da Barra, just beyond Itarema town (also known as **Mulheres de Areia**). From Fortaleza there are buses with Redenção at 0700 and 1730, US$6.65.

Jijoca → *Phone code: 088. Colour map 2, A4.*

Jijoca de Jericoacoara (also spelt 'Gijoca'), is near the south shore of scenic **Lagoa Paraíso** (or Lagoa Jijoca) , the second largest in the state. –There are nice *pousadas* on its shore. It is excellent for windsurfing as it has a 'comfortable' wind, very good for beginners and those gaining experience (Jericoacoara is for 'professionals'). There is also good kite surfing. Note that the low season, August to November, is the windy season. From town the lake is 1 km along the shore when the lake is low, or 3 km along the road with high water, taxi (pick-up truck) US$5. Jijoca is one of the access points for Jericoacoara, one of the most famous beaches of Ceará and all Brazil.

Jericoacoara → *Phone code: 088. Colour map 2, A4.*

Nestled in the dunes is the fishing community of Jericoacoara, or Jerí as the locals call it. It is popular with both Brazilian and international travellers. Despite the large influx of visitors, it remains a tranquil and safe town. Visitors are rewarded with towering sand dunes, deserted beaches with little shade, cactus-covered cliffs rising from the sea, interesting rock formations and a pleasant atmosphere. Watching the sunset from the top of the large dune just west of town, followed by a display of *capoeira* on the beach, is a tradition among visitors. There is nightly *forró* in high season; Wednesday and Saturday at other times.

Jericoacoara is ostensibly part of an environmental protection area which includes a large coconut grove, lakes, dunes and hills covered in *caatinga* vegetation, but the relentless buggy-based tourism and proliferation of *pousadas*, together with local authorities who are very amenable to persuasion from business has seen this beautiful area become a little spoilt in recent years. Too much building has led to pollution and buggy tourism has disturbed both the dunes and the flora and fauna in the area. A youth group publishes *Força Jovem Jericoacoara*, a monthly newspaper with information for visitors and general issues of environmental protection in the area. There are several possibilities for walks, horse riding (US$2-3 per hour). Buggy trips on the dunes are on offer but you can see them equally well on foot and discourage the destruction of the dunes. Take water and sun protection, it gets very hot and there is no shade; several hotels offer tours.

Excursions from Jericoacoara

Going west along the beach takes you through a succession of sand dunes and coconut groves; the views are beautiful. In 2 km you reach the beach of **Mangue Seco**, and 2 km beyond an arm of the ocean which separates it from **Guriú** (bridge across), where there is a village atop a fixed dune. Some of the best scenery in the area is by **Nova Tatajuba** (see below), about 35 km west of Jerí. It is reached by land from Camocim, or along the beach by dune-buggy including a river crossing on a barge (US$20 per person, minimum four) or by sea, three hours (US$100); there are basic *pousadas*, see Sleeping, page 520.

A 45-minute walk to the east takes you to the **Pedra Furada**, a stone arch sculpted by the sea, one of the symbols of Jerí, accessible only at low tide (check the tide tables at the Casa do Turismo). In the same direction, but just inland, is **Serrote**, a large hill with a lighthouse on top; it is well worth walking up for the magnificent views.

About 15 km east along the shore (43 km by road via Jijoca and Caiçara) is **Praia do Preá**, with light sand and blue ocean. At low tide you can visit the **Pedra da Seréia** (a little towards Jeri), a rock with natural swimming pools on top.

Some 10 km beyond Praia do Preá (62 km by road) is the beach of **Barrinha**, with access to the picturesque **Lagoa Azul**.

About 10 km inland through the dunes (20 km along the road), to **Lagoa Paraíso** or **Jijoca**, is a turquoise, freshwater lake, great for bathing (buggy US$10 per person) – see above.

Cruz

Some 40 km east of Jijoca is Cruz, an obligatory stop if travelling by bus from Sobral to Jericoacoara. It is a pleasant small town, surrounded by a *carnauba* palm forest (used in making brooms). At the south end is a large wooden cross dating from 1825, nearby is a statue to São Francisco. There is a lively market on Sunday when, at dawn, *pau d'arara* trucks, mule carts and bicycles converge on the town. There are two very basic hotels.

Camocim → *Phone code: 088. Colour map 2, A4. Population: 51,500.*

This regional centre (www.camocimnet.com.br) with some industry is an important fishing port and crafts centre. It has a pleasant Beira Mar on the Rio Coreaú, facing the dunes on the eastern shore and looking out to where the river meets the sea. Fishing boats and *pousadas* line the Beira Mar (the main activity is 0700 to 0730). There is a handicraft shop just past the ferry (*balsa*). This is car ferry, for one vehicle at a time, taking 8 minutes to cross, running all daylight hours, US$3.75 per car. The *balsa, Salmão 1*, is opposite the **Pousada Ponta Porã** (T9955 3465). On the other side, buggies run to Jericoacoara in 1½ hours, via Nova Tatajuba. The front is rather tatty, desperately awaiting the investment that should come when (if) a new international airport is built – a contentious issue with conservationists – or Parnaíba is expanded (the Parnaíba Delta is only 1½ hours away by road).

Beyond, along Avenida Beira Mar is the **Boa Vista Resort** (**LL**, www.boavistaresort.com.br) and the **Camocim Park Hotel** (T0xx88-621 1180, www.camocimparkhotel.com.br) with the **Acqua water park**. Just before this hotel, an unmade road to the left, goes inland to **Lago Seco**, 3 km, a pretty freshwater lake with an Italian restaurant, **Marelago**, *barracas* and pedalos for hire. It's very busy at weekends, but quiet mid-week. The coast road ends at lighthouse, but tracks go on to unspoilt beaches like **Maceió**, 28 km west. By the lighthouse is **Praia do Farol** with a *barraca* and shaded tables, otherwise there is no shade on the coast.

Nova Tatajuba, 40 km east, access requires a vehicle with good traction to cross the beach and dunes. Nova Tatajuba has magnificent scenery, it is on the west margin of the outflow of Lagoa Grande; the beach is wide, dunes follow the shore, the ocean is clear and calm and there is a fishing village with a few basic *pousadas*. The town was built to replace old Tatajuba, which was buried by the shifting sands. Tatajuba is part of the **Instituto Terramar** project to protect its environment and fishing community from tourism speculation (see above under Eastern beaches, Community tourism). For transport see Jericoacoara, page 527.

Western Ceará

Mark Greenwood (resident in Fortaleza) writes: At **Itapajé**, some 130 km west of Fortaleza, there is good adventurous walking. One hike is to a working sugar mill (*engenho*) over a large, humpback mountain overlooking town to the north (up to two hours to get there). The path starts at the bottom end of town below the mountain; ask at shops for the right direction. Go up to the right of the hump, a steep, hot climb. As you reach the rock, there are herb gardens. Proceed through a village, then banana groves until you reach a school with the mill next door. The friendly owner will explain everything. Another walk is to the **Pedra do Frade** (*Ita pajé* in Tupi), a monk-shaped rock; ask in the **Pousada Doce Lar** for details. There is a US$1.85 charge to go up to the base of the rock at the end of the climb (an office in town arranges this). In town, lots of cloth handicrafts (*bordados*) are sold.

Sobral → *Phone code: 088. Colour map 2, A4. Population: 145,000.*

Sobral, 238 km west of Fortaleza (four hours by bus, US$5), is the principal town in western Ceará and the access point to beaches in the west of the state. The city has a handful of well-preserved colonial buildings including the **Catedral da Sé**, **Teatro São João** and a mansion on the **Praça da Sé**. There is a **Museu Diocesano** ⓘ *Praça São João*, a Cristo Redentor Statue and a monument to the 1919 solar eclipse. Near town is the **Parque Ecológico Lagoa da Fazenda**.

Chapada de Ibiapaba

In the Chapada de Ibiapaba, an area of tablelands, caves, rock formations, rivers and waterfalls, is **Tianguá**. The town is surrounded by waterfalls; 3 km to the north is Cachoeira de São Gonçalo, a good place for bathing; 5 km from town are natural pools at the meeting place of seven waterfalls. About 16 km from town on the edge of the BR-222 is Cana Verde, a 30-m high waterfall surrounded by monoliths and thick vegetation.

Some 30 km north of Tianguá is **Viçosa do Ceará**, a colonial town also within the Chapada, known for its ceramics, hang-gliding, food and drink. The Igreja de Nossa Senhora das Vitórias, a stone church on top of the 820-m high Morro do Céu, is reached walking up 360 steps. There is an excellent view of the town, the surrounding highlands and the *sertão* beyond. Near the town are interesting rock formations such as the 100-m wide **Pedra de Itagurussu** with a natural spring. There is good walking in the area. Basic walking maps are available at the **Secretaria de Turismo** near the old theatre on the street to the right of the Praça on which the church stands. Ask about visiting the community which makes sun-baked earthenware pots. **Expresso Serrana** bus from Fortaleza, six hours, US$8.40, five a day via Sobral.

Parque Nacional Ubajara → *Colour map 2, A4.*

At 340 km from Fortaleza, 18 km south of Tianguá, and at 840 m is **Ubajara** ⓘ *T634 1300 ext 231 for tourist information, www.ubajara.ce.gov.br*, with an interesting Sunday morning market selling produce of the *sertão*. Three kilometres from town is Parque Nacional Ubajara, with 563 ha of native highland and *caatinga* brush. It is the smallest of Brazil's national parks. The park's main attraction is the **Ubajara cave** on the side of an escarpment. Fifteen chambers totalling 1,120 m have been mapped, of which 360 are open to visitors. Access is along a 6-km footpath and steps (two to three hours, take water) or with a **cablecar** ① *T634 1219, 0900-1430, last up at 1500, US$1.50, locals US$0.15 (they use it as a means of transport)*, which descends the cliff to the cave entrance. Lighting has been installed in nine caverns of the complex. An **Ibama** guide leads visitors in the cave, which is completely dry and home to 14 types of bat. At one point the lights are turned out to appreciate total blackness. Several rock formations look like animals: horse's head, jacaré, snake. There's an **Ibama office** ① *park entrance, 5 km from the caves, Toxx85-634 1388, www.ibama.gov.br*, and a bar by the entrance serving juices, snacks, *refrigerantes*, etc. In the national park there is a new easy walkway through the woods with stunning views at the end. Start either to the left of the park entrance or opposite the snack bar near the cable car platform. The locals' route, and another good trail through *caatinga*, is from Araticum, 8 km, which is 7 km by bus from Ubajara.

The views of the sertão from the upper cablecar platform are superb.

South from Ubajara

The Chapada de Ibiapaba continues south from Ubajara for some 70 km. Other towns along the highlands are: **Ibiapina**, with the nearby Cachoeira da Ladeira, reached by a steep trail, a good place for bathing; **São Benedito**, known for its straw and ceramic crafts and a working *engenho* sugar mill; and **Carnaubal**, with waterfalls and a bathing resort.

Ipu, 80 km south of Ubajara, is a town at the foot of the Serra de Ibiapaba, on the edge of the Sertão. It's an interesting transition as you descend from the green Serra, with its sugar cane, tall *babaçu* palms and cattle, down the escarpment to the Sertão. Ipu's main claim to fame is the **Bica do Ipu** (180-m), a waterfall plunging off the sheer edge of the Serra into a pool,said to be the site of the legendary love affair between the Indian, Iracema, and the founder of Fortaleza. You can cool off under the fall and there are basic facilities and a few places to stay around town

If driving, you can cross the Sertão on good roads via **Varjota** (33 km), on the large lake of the **Açude de Araras**, **Santa Quitéria** (a further 41 km) to **Canindé** (111 km on CE-257).

Monsenhor Tabosa, in the centre of the state, has the highest peak in Ceará. The area around the mountain, called **Cabeço Branco**, has been made into an environmental protection area, with *caatinga* and patches of *mata atlântica*. This remote town is very friendly, with three hotels: **dos Viajantes** and **São Sebastião**, both contactable through the phone exchange (ToXX88- 8261150), and **Pousada Gaia**, just behind the cemetery on the road out to Santa Quitéria (ToXX88-6961904), ask for Márcia or Honório Júnior. Honório will draw rough walking maps and, if asked, can arrange for the *forró* band to play. It can get very wet in the rainy season (around March). The easiest way to get there is by car or **Horizonte** bus on the CE032 from Canindé, but there are roads from Nova Russas, south of Ipu, and the BR-020 from Boa Viagem (which is very rough).

Continuing south, the greenery of the Chapada de Ibiapaba eventually gives way to the dry **Sertão dos Inhamuns**. One of the main towns in this area is **Crateús**, about 210 km south of Sobral, a remote town with rich folkloric traditions seen during festivals in August (**Mergulho Folclórico**) and September (**Festival de Repentistas**); nearby are archaeological sites with rock inscriptions. There is a regular bus service on the paved road to Fortaleza (347 km). Bus service from Crateús over a very bad road to Teresina, every two days.

South of Fortaleza

Serra de Baturité → *Phone code: 085. Colour map 2, A5. Population: 32,000. Altitude: 171 m.*

The town of **Baturité** is surrounded by the hills and waterfalls of the **Maciço de**

Baturité, an irregular massif with beautiful scenery. Baturité is more in the foothills, than the Serra proper. It has some colonial buildings and a historical museum. It is home of the **Pingo de Ouro** distillery which can be visited and there are hotels and restaurants. You can also stay in the **Jesuit Seminary** ⓘ *T3470362 in advance*, where a few monks still work in the local community and tend the cloister garden (**E** per person full board per day (US$11.10), including morning and afternoon coffee with local fruits, ask for 'Jesuitas' if taking a taxi, or walk up). Baturité is the largest town in the area. Another historical town is Redenção. Northwest of Baturité, at 365 m above sea level is Guaramiranga (16 km on a very twisty road through lush vegetation and fruit trees; lots of birdsong). Several *pousadas* line the road on the way up. Guaramiranga is the centre of a fruit and flower growing area and it is packed with visitors at weekends (if you want to stay overnight you must book in advance). At Carnival (February) it holds a **Festival de Jazz & Blues**. Carnival music is forbidden! And if you want to stay in town for it, you must book in November. It also holds a **Festival Nordestino de Teatro** in September in the Teatro Municipal Rachel de Queiroz. This theatre is in the centre of town and around it are a number of eating places, eg **Café com Flores, Taberna Portuguesa, O Alemão, Confrari** (pastas and fondues). For **information** ⓘ *secultguaramiranga@hotmail.com*.

In the area is a remnant of native forest, now a nature reserve. About 7 km further north is **Pacoti**, with large botanical gardens (*horto forestal*), trails and several waterfalls; good for a dip and for viewing the highland flora. On the main road to Pacoti, turn left at Forquilha to climb **Pico Alto** (1,115 m above sea level, previously thought to be the highest peak in Ceará – see Monsenhor Tabosa, below), which offers special views and sunsets. You can go up by car, or if you leave early in the morning you may be able to catch a lift with the school bus. Between Baturitá and Guaramiranga is a turning west to Mulungu and Aratuba, a town in the south of the Serra.

Canindé → *Colour map 2, A4.*

The pilgrimage centre of Canindé, 108 km southwest of Fortaleza, is located in the Sertão Central of Ceará. A large modern church stands on a hill; it has carved baptistry doors and many *ex votos*. It receives hundreds of thousands of pilgrims from all over the northeast between 26 September and 4 October; devotees of São Francisco das Chagas, '*O pobrezinho de Asis*', many of them dressed like Franciscan priests. The pilgrims flock to town on foot, by bus and mostly on *pau de arara* trucks. It is reputed to be second in the world, after Assisi, as a pilgrimage centre for Saint Francis. There is a regional museum with artefacts representative of northeast culture and several restaurants. There is a daily bus service from Fortaleza rodoviária with **Viação Nova Esperança**, three hours, and interesting dry-land vegetation along route. From Canindé south to the Sertão Central (Quixadá), CE-456 is under repair – mostly not too bad, but some short rough bits (95 km).

Quixadá → *Phone code: 088. Population: 64,500.*

Quixadá is on the **Serra do Estevão**, with its rocky outcrops and dry hills representative of the central *sertão*. It is one of the top hang-gliding sites in the world and is also good for climbing and trekking. The town has a dam, **Açude de Cedro**, built by ex-slaves during the empire by order of Dom Pedro II, following the terrible drought of 1877-79. The scenery around the dam has interesting rock formations including the **Galhina Choca** (broody hen). There are restaurants and bars at the start of the dam, which you can walk across. There are two-hour trails to the **Galhina Choca** (take an ATEC guide – see below) and climbing and abseiling on the rocks by the dam, too. The reservoir was only 8% full in 2003; the last time it was to capacity was 1989. In town there is a historical museum.

Nossa Senhora Inmaculada Rainha do Sertão is a pilgrimage centre 10 km from town, halfway up the highest peak in the region, **Pico do Urucum**, or Serra Preta, at

 600 m. The views are tremendous. It's a modern sanctuary (inaugurated 1995) holding over 800 worshippers, decorated with the flags and images of the patron saints of every Latin American country and Italy. The main festival is 11 February, so all February is *super lotado*. Strangely, the chief hang-gliding ramp is just below the church; there is also climbing and abseiling on the PIco.

About 21 km from town is **Gruta do Pajé**, a complex of religious buildings dating from the early 1900s (see Sleeping, page 516).

Quixeramobim is an important regional centre and the geographical centre of Ceará, 20 minutes from Quixadá. The town centre is pleasant and is being completely refurbished. It has a lovely old market building. There is a **Memorial de Antônio Conselheiro** (of Canudos), who was born here in 1830 and lived in the town until, shamed by his first wife's adultery, he left for a wandering life before becoming the religious figure famous in history, novels, etc. The Memorial has some sculptures, high-relief pictures and a tiny remnant of railway. Nearby is an old iron railway bridge, another 'postcard' of the town. Nearby are **archaeological sites** ⓘ *contact Sr Simão, R Mons Salviano Pinio 233, T6380000*, with ancient inscriptions on boulders. The regional dam has been used for irrigation with good results. In August it has an important musical event, the **Festival de Violas e Violeiros**, drawing participants from far and near, and in September the **Grande Vaquejada de Quixeramobim** (a typical *sertão* rodeo). Another festival is the **Festa de Santo Antônio**, 12-15 June.

Vale do Jaguaribe

Because of the Rio Jaguaribe, 20% of the agricultural land of the state is concentrated in the east, in the region known as the Vale do Jaguaribe. Using irrigation, the *sertão* becomes quite fertile, with rice and beans as the main crops here. Among the towns are **Morada Nova**, 161 km from Fortaleza, and **Limoeiro do Norte**, 201 km from Fortaleza; just south of Limoeiro is **Tabuleiro do Norte**, where an important religious pilgrimage takes place in honour of Nossa Senhora da Saúde, 11-15 August. Festivities include processions, musical shows and much *forró*. The area is rich in crafts made with *carnauba* palm thatch, including fine basketry and hats. The town of **Jaguaruana**, 185 km from Fortaleza, is an important producer of hammocks. A deeply rooted tradition in this area is the *vaquejada* (rodeo), accompanied by country *violeiros* (guitar music) and regional food.

South of the Vale do Jaguaribe is the area known as the **Sertões do Salgado**, in the Rio Salgado valley. The most prominent feature here is the **Orós** dam, with a capacity of 2.1 billion cubic meters; the reservoir has 300 islands and is used for watersports. Some of the towns in the area are **Orós** (403 km from Fortaleza), **Icó** (372 km from Fortaleza) and **Iguatu** (378 km from Fortaleza), all historical cities with well preserved colonial structures. **Lavras de Mangabeira** (432 km from Fortaleza), is surrounded by rocks, caves and a canyon formed by the Rio Salgado, 4 km from town.

Juazeiro do Norte

→ *Phone code: 088. Colour map 2, B4. Population: 200,000.*

The south of the state is known as the **Cariri region**, the name of an indigenous group which lived in the interior and resisted Portuguese colonization for a long time. The main centre in this area is Juazeiro do Norte, the second city in Ceará. Along with its two satellites, Crato and Barbalha, 10 km to the west and south respectively, they form an oasis of green in the dry *sertão*.

Juazeiro do Norte was the home of Padre Cícero Romão Batista, a controversial and very popular priest who advocated the interests of the city and its most dispossessed inhabitants from the 1870s to the 1930s. Even before his death, Padre Cícero had become a legend and Juazeiro do Norte an important pilgrimage site, drawing the faithful from throughout the northeast and increasingly nationwide. Today it is the most important pilgrimage centre of the region; there are six main annual pilgrimages but visitors arrive all year round. Religious tourism is the principal source of income in this otherwise poor area; prices rise during pilgrimages and there are many beggars at all times. Another cultural manifestation seen throughout the Cariri region is the *bandas cabaçais ou de pífaros*, musical groups which participate in all celebrations. As well as playing instruments, they dance, imitating animals, and perform games or fights.

On Praça do Cinquentenário the **Memorial Padre Cícero** ⓘ *Mon-Fri 0730-1130, 1330-1730, Sat-Sun 0800-1200, free*, is a museum featuring photographs and religious artefacts; a good selection of books is on sale. Nearby is the **Chapel of Nossa Senhora do Perpétuo Socorro**, which houses Padre Cícero's tomb. A 27-m high statue to him stands in the Logradouro do Horto, a park overlooking the town; either take the pilgrim trail up the hill (one hour, start early because of the heat) or take the Horto city bus. Also worth seeing is the **Church of Nossa Senhora das Dores** with the adjacent pilgrimage grounds, roughly fashioned after St Peter's Square in Rome.

Excursions from Juazeiro do Norte

The **Chapada do Araripe**, a tableland about 850 m high, is south of Juazeiro do Norte and extends from east to west for 220 km. The area is believed to have been uplifted and numerous fossilized plants and animals including giant sloths have been found. It has one of the main native forest reserves in the state, the **Floresta Nacional do Araripe**, 20 km from Crato, with grottos, palaeontological sites, springs and cloud forest with ferns and orchids. Some 22 km south of Juazeiro do Norte, within the Chapada, is **Balneário do Caldas**, a pool fed with natural springwater (0700-1700), access through Barbalha.

In the area of **Jardim**, 34 km south of Barbalha, there are several natural springs, while by **Missão Velha**, 22 km east of Barbalha, are the rapids on the Rio Salgado and a nice waterfall. Another access to the Chapada is through **Santana do Cariri**, 60 km west of Juazeiro do Norte. Its main attraction is the **Nascente dos Azedos**, a natural spring good for bathing. There is also a palaeontology museum and one basic hotel. Transport is with Pernambucana, daily at 1430, returning 0600, US$2.50, two hours.

Crato is an older city which lost its limelight in the region, owing to the increased importance of Juazeiro do Norte. It has several nice *praças* and a small **Museu de Fósseis** ⓘ *Praça da Sé 105, Mon-Fri 0800-1200, 1400-1800, free*, housing an impressive collection of fossils from the Cretaceous period gathered in the Chapada do Araripe.

Sleeping

Fortaleza *p500, map p502, phone code 085/088*
Most hotels offer reduced prices in the low season. There is a wide range of accommodation and places to eat at all the beaches closer to the city and Cumbuco.

LL Ceasar Park, Av Beira Mar 3980, Mucuripe, T2631133, F2631444. Anonymous luxury 5-star a long way from the centre of beach activity but with all expected facilities, Brazilian, French and Japanese restaurants and a heliport.

L Imperial Othon Palace, Av Beira Mar 2500, Meireles, T2429177, F2427777. 5-star, beach- front location (recommended *feijoada* on Sat).

L Marina Park, Av Pres C Branco 400, Jacarecanga, T2525253, www.marinapark.com.br. Huge 5-star luxury leisure complex with all facilities, modern mooring for yachts at reasonable prices and day rates available for non-residents. Like the Caesar Park this is an all-inclusive resort a long way from the main attractions.

L Seara Praia, Av Beira Mar 3080, Meireles, T2429555, www.hotelseara.com.br. Smart, comfortable 4-star with a pool, fitness centre, cyber café and restaurant with French cuisine. 30% discounts off season.

AL Novotel Magna, Av Beira Mar 2380, Meireles, T2449122, F2612793. Standard chain business 4-star with anonymous but comfortable rooms, a pool and restaurant.

A Esplanada Praia, Av Beira Mar 200, Meireles, T2481000, www.esplanadapraia@secrel.com.br. Enormous, spacious, beachfront, somewhat isolated location, caters to business visitors.

A Samburá Praia, Av Beira Mar 4530, Meireles, T2631999, www.sambura.com.br. Good value 1980s hotel with a pool and fading a/c rooms which is cheaper than most others on the beach.

A Colonial Praia, R Barão de Aracati 145, Iracema, T4559600, www.colonialpraia.com.br. A somewhat faded 1970s 4-star with a big pool and set in pleasant grounds. (10 mins' walk from Av Beira Mar).

A Pousada Jardim, Ildefonso Albano 950, Aldeota, T2269711, www.hoteljardim.com.br. Simple hotel , near Iracema beach with no sign outside, a nice garden, organized excursions and many languages spoken. 20% discount for owners of the *Footprint Brazil Handbook*. Warmly recommended.

B Nordeste Palace, R Assunção 99 in centre, T2211999, F2211999. Slightly faded but large a/c rooms. Good value.

B Ondas Verdes, Av Beira Mar 934, Iracema, T2190871. A range of different, simple fan cooled rooms with TVs. Recommended.

C Abrolhos Praia, Av Abolição, 2030, Meireles, T/F2481217, abrolhos@rotaceara.com.br. Pleasant, simple hotel 1 block from beach withinternet access.

C Alfa Residence, Av Monsenhor Tabosa 1320, Meireles, T2482020, F2483417. 11 plain simple a/c apartments with TV, fridge, sauna and pool. The hotel also has apartments in 3 nearby blocks.

C Nossa Pousada, Av Abolição 2600, Meireles, T2614699. Faded 1970s rooms with shared bathrooms in a hotel near the beach. Helpful staff and a good-value self-service restaurant.

C Pousada Icaraí, Praia Icaraí, just before town on curve in road, T0xx85-3182000. A good out-of-town base with beautiful gardens, lots of budgerigars flying free, pools, restaurant, near beach and bus to Fortaleza. English/Brazilian owners, ask for Fiona.

C Pousada da Praia, Av Monsenhor Tabosa 1315, Iracema, 2 blocks from beach, T2485935. Faded and occasionally musty a/c rooms with fridges.

C Pousada Jambo, R Antonia Augusto 141, T2193873, T9929481 (mob). A variety of rooms, some with kitchens at no extra cost and a small pool in a tranquil and easy-to-miss Swiss-run *pousada* with no sign in a quiet street. Fan-cooled rooms are cheaper. Very friendly and changes cash and traveller's cheques. Warmly recommended.

C Pousada Sol e Mar, Av Beira Mar 3052, T2425636. Basic, family-run *pousada* above a restaurant. Good value for beachfront location.

C Villamaris, Av Abolição, 2026, Meireles, T2483834, www.hotelvillamaris.com.br. Cosy hotel with security guard, TV, fridge and asmall rooftop pool, 1 block from beach.

C-E Pousada Atalaia, Av Beira Mar 814, Iracema, T/F219 0658, www.albergueda juventudeatalaia.com.br. HI hostel. Cheaper in dormitory, a/c, fan, TV, good breakfast, prices fall in low season.

D Caxambu, Gen Bezerril 22, T2262301. A/c rooms in a little hotel in a central location opposite the cathedral. Smart for the category and good value. Cheaper in the low season.

D Ibis Praia, Atualpa Barbosa de Lima 660, Iracema, T2192121, www.accorhotels.com.br. A very good-value renovated beach hotel with a/c rooms with fridges a restaurant and a pool.

D Dom Luís, R Ildefonso Albano, 245, T/F2191321. Friendly *pousada* with a small terrace/garden and bar, simple a/c rooms and a laundry service in a quiet street. Recommended.

D Passeio, R Dr João Moreira 221,T2269640, F2536165. Pleasant but simple a/c or fan-cooled rooms with high ceilings off a series of long gloomy passageways. Opposite a once lovely and now decidedly tawdry park near the Centro Turismo.

D Pousada Kalahara, R Raimundo Esteves 41, Praia do Futuro, T2623144, near beach. Big rooms, pool, friendly. Recommended.

D Universo, R Senador Pompeu 1152. One of several similar hotels along this street, with simple rooms, some with mosquito nets and rooms with 3 beds. Smokers not welcome.

F Albergue Praia de Iracema, Av Almirante Barroso 998, T219 3267, www.aldeota.com/albergue. Price per person. Hostel with dormitories, a shared kitchen and various other services. Pleasant but very busy.

Camping

Fortaleza Camping Club, R Pedro Paulo Moreira 505, Parque Manibura, Água Fria, 10 km, T2732544. Many trees for shade, US$7 per person.

Barra Encantada, Praia do Barro Preto, 42 km southeast, T2441916 (office Av Barão de Studart 2360, s 1607). US$9 per person, Camping Club members US$4 per person, see East Coast below.

Fazenda Lago das Dunas, Uruaú (115 km southeast), T2442929. US$4 per person for Camping Club members, US$9 per person others, also rents rooms, see Beberibe, East Coast below.

Aquiraz and around *p505, phone code 085*

In Águas Belas, there are simpler rooms available in private houses.

L New Life, Alto da Prainha, Prainha, T3621314. Weight reduction centre, with fridge, pool, restaurant.

A Aquiraz Praia e Escola de Hotelaria, Estr da Prainha, Km 5, T3621006. Pleasant and comfortable rooms with baths, fridges and a/c arranged around a pool. The hotel has a reasonable restaurant.

A Marina Barro Preto, R Francisco das Chagas 10, Barro Preto, T3701166. With bath, fridge, pool, restaurant.

A Village Barra Mar, Caponga, T334 8088, www.barramar.com. A pleasant beach hotel set in a tropical garden with a range of a/c chalets, all with a fridge, a restaurant and a pool.

B Chalés Barra Encantada, R Francisco das Chagas 13, Barro Preto, T3701466. Cabins for up to 6, fridge, pool, restaurant, large camping area with palms, US$9 per person, Camping Club members US$4 per person.

B Da Prainha, R Berlim, Alto da Prainha, T3621122. Standard a/c rooms with a bath. The rooms on the top floor have more air, nice views.

B Do Sol, Praia do Presídio, T3701222. Large rooms with bath, a/c, a couple of chalets, pool, restaurant.

B Iguape Hotel de Turismo, R 8, Praia do Presídio, T3701444. Cabins, pool with springwater, restaurant.

B Jangadeiro Praia, Praia do Presídio, T2546466, or 0xx85-3616039, www.hoteljangadeiro.com.br. With bath, fridge, restaurant, pool, nice lawns down to the beach.

B Prainha Solar, R Principal, Prainha, T3621355, F3621366. Plain rooms with fridge, restaurant, pool. Comfortable.

B Recanto da Fantasia, R Francisco das Chagas, Barro Preto, T2394943. Well-equipped cabins for up to 4, no breakfast.

B Sol Leste, R São Pedro, Iguape, T/F3701233. With bath, fridge, pool, restaurant, sports fields. Other hotels and *pousadas* also available.
C Coqueiral, R Laureano de Paula Santana 537, Caponga, T3351073. Chalets with a bath and small terraces strewn with hammocks.
C Fateixa, R Laureano de Paula Santana 555, Caponga, T3351122. One of several similar *pousadas* on this street, with a selection of chalets in a bougainvillea garden with en suites and a pool.
C Le Paradis, Águas Belas, T3351050, F3351289. Simple rooms with attached bathrooms in a hotel with a pool and restaurant.
C Mon Kapitan, R Pedro Moita on the square, Caponga, T3351031. Large rooms with attached bathrooms, very helpful staff and a good restaurant.
C Praia Águas Belas, Águas Belas, T3351060. A range of rooms, some in individual cabins, all with baths and a/c. The restaurant has a reasonable restaurant and a pool.
D Versailles, R J Irineu Araujo, Caponga, 1.5 km from the beach, T3351071. Rooms with tiny en suites. Breakfast is extra.

Morro Branco and Praia das Fontes *p505, phone code 085*
B Recanto Praiano, Morro Branco, T2247118. Peaceful little *pousada* with a good breakfast. Recommended.
C Pousada Sereia, on the beach, Morro Branco, T3301144. Lovely simple *pousada* with an excellent breakfast and friendly staff. Highly recommended.
D Rosalias', Morro Branco, T3301131. Very simple and somewhat run down but only 50 m from bus stop, and with a shared kitchen.

Praia das Fontes *p505, phone code 085*
L Praia das Fontes, Av A Teixeira 1, Praia das Fontes, T3381179, www.oasispraiadasfontes.com.br. Luxurious resort, watersports, horse rental, tennis courts and a simple spa. Recommended.
B Das Falésias, Av Assis Moreira 314, Praia das Fontes, T3381018, www.hotelfalesias.com.br. Pleasant German-owned cliffside *pousada* with a pool and well-kept rooms.

Camping
Lago das Dunas, access 9 km south of Beberibe on CE-004, then east from Sucatinga 5 km on a poor dirt road; large area with grass and palms for shade, pool, restaurant, sports fields, it is 1 km through dunes to Praia Marambala or Uruaú, US$4 per person **Camping Club** members, US$9 per person non members; also rents rooms with shared bath (US$45 room for 4, US$55 room for 6).

Canoa Quebrada *p507, phone code 088*
Town's calling centre: T4211748, 3-digit numbers indicated below are extensions on these central lines. Villagers will let you sling your hammock or will put you up cheaply. Verónica is recommended, European books exchanged. Sr Miguel rents good clean houses for US$10 a day.
A Tranqüilândia, T4217012, www.tranquilandia.it. 9 a/c chalets around a pool in a tropical garden. Decent restaurant.
B Pousada Latitude, R Dragão do Mar, T323. A/c, fridge, cheaper with fan, restaurant.
B Pousada Lua Estrela, R Nascer do Sol 106, T421 7040, www.pousadaluaestrela.com.br. IYHA affiliated smart hostel with fan-cooled rooms with fridges and hot showers. Great sea views.
C Pousada Alternativa, R Francisco Caraço. Rooms with or without bath. Centrally located and recommended.
C Pousada Oásis do Rei, R Nascer do Sol 112, T4217081 www.oasisdorei.com. Simple rooms in a pousada with a pool. All have a fan and fridge and are set in a little tropical garden. Recommended.
C Pousada Via Láctea, off the main street (so quieter). Beautiful view of beach some 50 m away. Some rooms with hot shower, fridge, fan, good breakfast, safe parking, horse and buggy tours, English spoken. Highly recommended.
C Tenda do Cumbe, at end of the road on cliff, T4211761. Thatched huts in a hotel with a restaurant. Warmly recommended.
D Beco's, R José Melancia 2300. Simple rooms with a bath all with little terraces slung with hammocks and organized around a pleasant inner courtyard.

Paracuru and Lagoinha *p508, phone code 085*
C O Milton, T102. Plain cabins on the beach and with an outdoor restaurant.
D Ondas do Mar, T146. Pleasant cabins with

a bath and with porches hung with hammocks. Reasonable restaurant.

C **Monalisa**, T126. Large, plain fan-cooled rooms with attached bathrooms.

Fleixeras *p508, phone code 085*

Fleixeras T511184, Mundaú T3511210; 3-digit numbers indicated are extensions on this central line.

A-C **Mundaú Dunas**, Mundaú, T351901. Exceptional value, with well-kept rooms with fridges around a pool. Reasonable restaurant. Cheaper in the low season.

A **Solar das Fleixeiras**, Fleixeras, T136. Beach hotel with standard rooms with en suites, a pool and restaurant.

B **Sombra dos Coqueiros**, Mundaú, T200. Rooms with a bath and a modest restaurant.

C **Da Célia**, R São Pedro, Fleixeras, T105. Plain a/c rooms with en suites and no breakfast.

D **Brisa do Mar**, Mundaú. Small rooms with en suite bathrooms. Breakfast is extra.

E **Casa de Retiro Estrela do Mar**, Mundaú, T3511220, ext 154. A Priest's retreat home, must reserve ahead, rooms with hammocks, some with bath, use of kitchen.

Jijoca de Jericoacoara *p509, phone code 088*

B **Jardim do Paraíso**, Córrego do Urubu, on the lakeshore T/F669 1195, www.jericoacoara.tur.br/pousadachezloran. Small, with bath, restaurant, windsurfing equipment.

B-C **Pousada do Paulo**, Córrego do Urubu s/n, on the lakeshore.T0xx88-669 1181, www.jericoacoara.tur.br/pousadadopaulo. Has a windsurf school, US$18.50 for beginner's course, US$20 equipment hire per hour, US$50 per day, longer rates negotiatiable. It's also a good place to stay (prices depends on season and cabin, lovely location with lake views, garden, beach, hammocks and various sizes of cabin, all very nice, some with TV and a/c; excellent restaurant, bar.

C **Capitão Tomaz**, on the lakeshore. Rooms and chalets, sports equipment, boat trips.

D **Pousada dos Corsos**, T6691144. The best of several cheapies in the town owned by a Corsican and with excellent Corsican food.

Jericoacoara *p509, phone code 088*

There are crowds at weekends mid-Dec to mid-Feb, in Jul and during Brazilian holidays. Many places full in low season, too. 4-5-day packages for Reveillon are available, but prices rise steeply.

LL-L **Recanto do Barão**, R do Forró 433, T669 2149, www.recantodobarao.com. 21 rooms mostly for 3 to 5 (ie families, groups), nicely decorated with hibiscus theme, lots of hammocks, a/c, TV, fridge, hot shower, big rooms, upper balcony for sunset, pool, Land Rover tours. Good reputation.

A **Avalon**, R Principal, T669 2066, www.jericoacoara.tur.br/avalon/index.html. Nice rooms with a fan and a pleasant restaurant.

A **Casa do Turismo**, R das Dunas, T669 2000, www.jericoacoara.com, or www.casadoturismo.com. Comfortable, well-maintained rooms, all a/c, hot shower and TV. Information, tours, horse rental, **Redenção** bus tickets (only place selling them, 1030-1400 and 1730-2200), windsurf school, kite surf, sandboard rental, telephone calls, post office, exchange.

A **Hippopotamus**, R do Forró, T268 2722. Hotel with a decent pool, with a range of a/c rooms all with hot water and a restaurant.

B **Matusa**, T0xx85-246 7354, www.matusa.com.br. Standard package hotel a/c rooms with a TV, fridge and hot shower in a hotel with a pool.

C **Casa Nostra**, R das Dunas, T669 2035, www.jericoacoara.tur.br/casanostra/index.html. Decent rooms, good breakfast and the option to pay with US$ or German marks. Money change, Italian spoken. Recommended.

C **Isalana Praia**, R Principal, T6601334, www.jericoacoara.tur.br/isalanapraiahotel/index.html. A/c rooms with minibars, TVs, and very helpful staff: ask for Will Louzada.

C **Pousada Papagaio**, Beco do Forró, T669 2142, www.jericoacoara.tur.br/pousadapapagaio/index.html. Plain rooms with en suites and organized tours. Recommended.

C **Pousada Renata**, T669 2061, www.jericoacoara.tur.br/pousadadarenata. Owned by the sister of Fernanda at **Pousada do Paulo** at Jijoca. Pleasant, simple rooms with patios strung with hammocks, breakfast, English, Italian and German spoken. They also own the **Pousada do Serrote**, 100 m from Praia da Malhada, same phone, and 9961 5522 (mob), www.jericoacoara.tur.br/pousadadoserrote.

D **Calanda**, R das Dunas, T669 2285,

www.jericoacoara.tur.br/calanda. Plain rooms with en suite bathrooms, solar-heated water and good service from the Swiss owners and their staff. Good views, good breakfast, a full moon party each month and German, English and Spanish spoken. Warmly recommended.

D Pousada do Véio, R Principal. T6692015, www.jericoacoara.tur.br/pousadadoveio. Popular *pousada* with a/c rooms or fan-cooled rooms, all with baths and hot water.

E Pousada Tirol, R São Francisco 202, T669 2006, www.jericoacoara-tirol.com. IYHA-affiliated hostel with dorms with hot water showers and doubles (**C**-**D** in low season). Very friendly and popular with party loving travellers. Very busy cyber café, US$3 per hr – 10 mins free use for all guests.

Excursions from Jericoacoara *p510, phone code 088*

D Pousada Azul do Mar, Praia do Preá, T0xx88-660 3062, with bath, electricity, good food and, if you are lucky, kite surfing.

Cruz *p510, phone code 088*

F Hotel Magalhães, R Teixeira Pinto 390. Very basic, shared bath, friendly, meals available.

F Hospedaria, R 6 de Abril 314. Very basic simple little pousada with tiny rooms.

Western Ceará *p511, phone code 088*

D Pousada Doce Lar, R Felipe Sampaio 181, Centro, Itapajé, T0xx85-346 1432. Ask for a room with a mountain view, clean, comfortable, no restaurant. Eat in restaurants close by.

Quixadá *p513, phone code 088*

C Casa de Reposo São José, Gruta do Pajé, 21 km from Quixadá, today a popular hotel run by nuns (T4120927, with bath).

C Pedra dos Ventos, Near Juatama between Quixadá and Quixeramobim, T0xx85-257 4464/99884684, www.pedradosventos.com.br. Cheaper with fan, all rooms with TV, hot water, fridge. Great views (even at night) as it is built high up a rock. Good breakfast, pool, 3 trails of 30 mins each, can help with adventure sports. You need a car to get there although the Redenção bus passes the turn-off.

D Hotel Fazenda Magé, Km 3 Antiga Estrada de Baturité, CEP 63.900.000, T0xx88-412 0467, nemesio@quixadanet.com.br. With breakfast in the *fazenda*, all facilities, cold water, cheaper singles with fan. Down a track is the restaurant which has tables under an overhanging rock, open Sat, Sun and once a month at full moon, has hammocks. The rock has a viewpoint, climbing and abseiling routes, equipment hire US$5.55, plus US$7.40 for instructor.

C Hotel Fazenda Parelhas, Km 133 Rodovia do Algodão, a short distance out of Quixeramobim, just off the Quixadá road, T0xx88-402 2847/9946 7640, aceterbr@yahoo.com.br Ricardo Porto is the owner and set this place up as the first *turismo rural* place in Ceará in 1998. Price includes breakfast, full board is US$7.50 extra. Chalets with a/c TV, fridge and cold water. It's a working sheep and goat farm in the *caatinga*, offering horse rides of 1½ and 3 hrs, or 30 km to Serra do Caboclo, also pony and trap rides and river bathing.

Serra de Baturité *p512, phone code 085*

A Estância Vale das Flores, Sítio São Francisco, Pacoti, T3251233. Chalets and rooms, price includes lunch, fridge, restaurant, pool, sauna, lake, horses.

B-C Hofbräuhaus, Estrada de Aratuba, Chapada de Lameirão, Mulungu, CEP 62754-000, T0xx85-221 6170, www.hofbrauhaus-brasil.com. Run by Wolfgang Helmut Rühle, who has restaurants in Guaramiranga (O Alemão), Pacoti and 2 in Fortaleza, speaks German, English, Portuguese (and maybe more). This is an exceptional place in that every room is designed in a different style (Spanish, Arabic, Japanese, etc) with all comfort, homely, very clean and smart, rooms with veranda cost a little more and prices are cheaper Mon-Thu (a bargain). The restaurant is German and Cearense. All vegetables and herbs (for all the restaurants) are grown on the property, also has a snail farm for its house speciality. Lots of flowers and grapes, 350-km views over the Sertão, mini-disco, small business centre, completely safe. A real surprise!

B Remanso Hotel da Serra, 5 km north of Guaramiranga, T3251222. Bath, restaurant, pool, lake, sports fields.

B Senac Hotel Escola de Guaramiranga, in Guaramiranga, T/F3211106, escola_hotel aria@ce.senac.br. Bath, fridge, hot water, restaurant, pool, atop a hill in an 8-hut estate which includes forest, orchards and an old convent, it doubles as a tourism school. Lots of events held here, so it is often full. It's 500 m outside town up a road from the main street, past Parque das Trilhas.

Parque Nacional Ubajara *p511, phone code 085*

B-C Pousada da Neblina, Estrada do Teleférico, near the park. 2 km from town, T/F634 1270. In beautiful cloudforest, swimming pool, with breakfast (cheaper without) and private shower restaurant open 1100-2000. Meals recommended. Campground (US$15 per tent).

C Le Village, on Ibiapina road 4 km south from Ubajara town, T634 1364. Restaurant, pool, sauna, good value.

C Pousada Gruta da Ubajara, almost opposite, close to park entrance, rustic, restaurant. Recommended.

D Paraíso, in the centre, Ubajara, T634 1728. Reckoned to be the best in town.

D Pousada da Neuza, R Juvêncio Luís Pereira 370, Ubajara, T634 1261. Small restaurant.

D Sítio do Alemão, take Estrada do Teleférico 2 km from town, after the **Pousada da Neblina** turn right, signposted, 1 km to Sítio Santana, in the coffee plantation of Herbert Klein (Caixa Postal 33, Ubajara, CE, CEP 62350-000, T0xx88-9961 4645), on which, down a path, there are 3 small chalets, with full facilities, and 2 older ones with shared bath (**E**), view from breakfast/hammock area to Sertão, excursions, bicycle hire offered, if chalets are full Klein may accommodate visitors at the house. No meals other than breakfast but **Casa das Delícias** in Ubajara will send lasagne if necessary – it's owned by Klein's partner. Warmly recommended.

Sobral *p511, phone code 088*

A Beira Rio, R Conselheiro Rodrigues 400 across from the rodoviária, T6131040. A/c (cheaper with fan), fridge.

A Visconde, Av Lúcia Saboia 473, 10 mins from the rodoviária, T6114222, F6114197. Friendly, a/c, cheaper with fan, good breakfast.

B Cisne, Trav do Xerez 215, T/F6110171. A/c, cheaper with fan, friendly.

B Vitória, Praça Gen Tibúrcio 120, T6131566. Bath, a/c, cheaper with fan, some rooms without bath (**C**), restaurant.

D Francinet's, R Col Joaquim Ribeiro 294. With fan, bath, cheaper with shared bath.

Chapada de Ibiapaba *p511, phone code 088*

A Serra Grande, about 2 km from town, BR-222 Km 311, T6711818, F6711477. All amenities, good.

C Complexo de Lazer Rio's, Viçosa do Ceará, Km 4.5 on the road from Tianguá, T0xx88-632 1510/1099. Swiss-style chalets, water park, good local food in the restaurant.

South from Ubajara *p512, phone code 088*

B Pousada de Inhuçu, R Gonçalo de Freitas 454, São Benedito, T6261173, pool, restaurant.

D Crateús Palace Hotel, Crateús, very reasonable and clean, with breakfast, good restaurant. **Churrascaria Pequena Cabana** is at the back of the hotel.

E Bar e Churrascaria Pousada da Bica, Ipu, T0xx88-683 2236, serves very good, cheap *comida caseira* lunch and has rooms, with breakfast included.

E Hotel Ipu, in upper town, basic, friendly.

A *pousada* is being built at the *SAT posta* on the exit to Varjota and Sobral; it also has a *churrascaria.*

Juazeiro do Norte *p514, map p515, phone code 088*

You can expect prices to be higher during pilgrimages. There are many basic hotels and hospedarias for pilgrims on R São José and around Nossa Senhora das Dores Basilica.

A Verde Vales Lazer, Av P A Castelo, 3 km from town on the road to Barbalha, T/F5712544. Pool, restaurant.

B Panorama, Santo Agostinho 58, T5213100, F5123110. Pool, restaurant, good value.

C Municipal, São Francisco 220, Praça Padre Cícero, T5122899. Comfortable large rooms, good value, cheaper with fan. Recommended.

C-D Plaza, Padre Cícero 148, T5110493. With bath, a/c, cheaper with fan and cheaper still with shared bath.

C-D Viana Palace, São Pedro 746, T5112585, F5112476. With bath, a/c, fridge, cheaper with fan.

D Aristocrata, São Francisco 402, T5111889. With bath, fan, cheaper without bath, basic, family run, restaurant.

D Maceió, São José 208, T5112930. With bath, fan, cheaper with shared bath. restaurant.

D-E **Pousada Cariri**, São José 218, T5122079. With bath, cheaper without breakfast, basic, friendly, family run, good restaurant.

Excursions from Juazeiro do Norte

p515, phone code 088

A **Hotel das Fontes**, Balneário do Caldas, T5321060, with bath, fridge, restaurant.

B-D **Crato**, R Bárbara de Alencar 668 near Praça Cristo Rei, Crato, T5212824. A friendly hotel with bath, a/c, cheaper with fan and restaurant.

There are 2 other simpler hotels in town.

Eating

Fortaleza *p500, map p502, phone code 085/088*

Iracema and **Dragão do Mar** are good areas for a restaurant browse, with plenty of variety. The junction of Tabajaras and Tremembés has a good choice of smarter a/c places.

There are several good fish restaurants at **Praia de Mucuripe**, where the boats come ashore between 1300 and 1500. **R J Ibiapina**, at the Mucuripe end of Meireles, 1 block behind beach, has pizzerias, fast-food restaurants and sushi bars.

In the city centre there are several options around and in the railway station.

TTT-TT **La Fiorentina**, Osvaldo Cruz 8, corner of Av Beira Mar, Meireles. Unpretentious restaurant with good service and a range of seafood, pasta and other Italian dishes.

TTT-TT **Le Sandras**, Av Santos Dumont 938, Aldeota, T254 4282. A recently opened restaurant in a brightly painted old building with cool yellow interiors and a French-trained chef. The food is *novo cearanse* and Mediterranean with a lunchtime buffet.

TT **Alma Gêmea**, R Dragão do Mar 30. Bar and restaurant with a good atmosphere by the cultural centre.

TT **Amici's**, R Dragão do Mar 80. Pasta, pizza and lively atmosphere in music-filled street, evenings only. One of the most celebrated restaurants in this area.

TT **Colher do Pau**, R Tabajaras 412, Iracema. Opens daily at 1830. Sertaneja and seafood in a restaurant with indoor and outdoor seating and live music. Recommended.

TT **Estoril**, R dos Tabajaras 397, Iracema. Regional and general Brazilian cooking and a cookery school.

T **Alivita**, Barão do Rio Branco 1486, Centro. Good for fish and vegetarian options, lunch only, Mon-Fri.

T **Blau d'Fame**, R João Cordeiro 41, Iracema. Decent self-service, serving lunch much later than others, especially on Sat.

T **Brazão**, R João Cordeiro corner of Av R Girão, Iracema, next to **Blau d'Fame**. Dull food, but the only place open 24 hrs.

T **Churrascaria Picanha de Veras**, R Carlos Vasconcelos 660, Aldeota. A cheap *churrascaria* with a range of cuts and decent chicken.

T **Fonte de Saúde**, R Pedro 339, Centro. Excellent vegetarian food, sold by weight, and a wide range of fruit juices.

T **Habib**, Av Abolição, corner with Av Barão de Studart, Meireles. Middle Eastern fast food in sanitized surrounds in this very popular chain restaurant.

T **Ideal**, Av Abolição e José Vilar, Meireles. Open 0530-2030. A little bakery serving lunches and a small supermarket and deli.

Cafés

La Habanera, Praça da Igreja in Iracema, Av Beira Mar e Ararius. A delightful café decorated with photos of Fidel and Che and decked out with whicker chairs and marble tables. Cuban cigars available.

Santa Clara Café Orgânico, R Dragão do Mar 81, at end of red girder walkway (or upstairs depending which way you go), www.santaclara.com.br. Delicious organic coffees, juices, cold drinks, sandwiches and sweets.

Jericoacoara *p509, phone code 088*

There are several restaurants serving vegetarian and fish dishes.

TT **Carcará**, R do Forró, T6692013. Restaurant and bar, northeastern specialities, seafood and pastas, said to be the best in town.

TT **Espaço Aberto**, R Principal, T6692063. Meat dishes, delicious seafood, salads, pleasant atmosphere. Recommended.

TT **Naturalmente**. On the beach. Nice atmosphere, wonderful crêpes. Recommended.

TT **Pizzaria Banana**, R Principal 26, T6692282. The best of many pizzerias on this street with plenty of choice of other dishes from pasta to salads and snacks.

TT **Taverna**, R Principal. Cantina and

restaurant with lovely pasta and pizza, crêpes and espresso coffee. Drinks.

ŸŸ Tudo na Brasa, R Principal. Recommended *churrascaria*.

Ÿ Tempero da Terra, R São Francisco. Restaurant and *lanchonete*, *comida caseira*, meat and fish dishes, nothing fancy, but well cooked and tasty.

Quixadá *p513*

ŸŸ-Ÿ Churrascaria Drinks, Quixeramobim, by the BR *posta* on the Quixadá road. One of the best in the city.

Sobral *p511*

ŸŸ Casa Grande o Louro, R Tabelo Idelfonso Cavalcante 611. Good meat.

ŸŸ Hotel Vitória, good lunch buffet. Recommended.

Ÿ Churrascaria Gaúcho, Av Dom José, meat.

Ÿ Chico 1000 and **2000**, varied menu.

Ÿ Lataro, self-service.

Juazeiro do Norte *p514, map p515*

Several restaurants around Praça Padre Cícero, more economical ones on R São José.

ŸŸ Cheiro Verde, S Cândido 72, varied menu. Several restaurants around Praça Padre Cícero, more economical ones on R São José;

ŸŸ Pousada, R São José, good food.

Bars and clubs

Fortaleza *p500, map p502, phone code 085/088*

Fortaleza is renowned for its nightlife and prides itself with having the liveliest Mon night in the country.

Some of the best areas for entertainment, with many bars and restaurants are: the Av Beira Mar, Praia de Iracema, the hill above Praia de Mucuripe and Av Dom Luís. The streets around Centro Cultural Dragão do Mar on R Dragão do Mar are lively every night of the week. Brightly painted, historic buildings house restaurants where musicians play to customers on their terraces and the pavements are dotted with cocktail carts. The cultural centre hosts free concerts some nights, pick up a copy of the month's events. **Caros Amigos**, R Dragão do Mar, 22, T226657. Live music at 2030: Tue, Brazilian instrumental; Wed, jazz; Thu, samba; Sun, Beatles covers, $US1. **Restaurant e Crêperie Café Crème**, R Dragão do Mar 92, live music on Tue. Clubs include **Armazém**, Av Almirante Barroso, 444, T2194322, techno, free entry; Fri and Sat US$4. **Ritzy&Cafe**, mix of retro music, US$2. Some recommended bars: **Mucuripe Club**, on Av Beira Mar, popular. **Espaço Cultural Diogo Fontenelle**, R Gustavo Sampaio 151, art gallery and bar with live music.

Forró is the most popular dance and there is a tradition to visit certain establishments on specific nights. **Mon** *Forró* is danced at the **Pirata Bar**, US$5, open-air theme bar, from 2300, and other establishments along R dos Tabajaras and its surroundings, at Praia de Iracema. **Tue** Live retro 70s and 80s music at **Boate Oásis**, Av Santos Dumont 6061, Aldeota. **Wed** Regional music and samba-reggae at **Clube do Vaqueiro**, city bypass, Km 14, by BR-116 south and E-020, at 2230. **Thu** Live music, shows and crab specialities at the beach shacks in Praia do Futuro. **Fri** Singers and bands play regional music at **Parque do Vaqueiro**, BR-020, Km 10, past city bypass. **Sat** *Forró* at **Parque Valeu Boi**, R Trezópolis, Cajueiro Torto, **Forró Três Amores**, Estrado Tapuio, Euzébio and **Cantinho do Céu**, CE-04, Km 8. **Sun** *Forró* and *música sertaneja* at **Cajueiro Drinks**, BR-116, Km 20, Euzébio.

Jericoacoara *p509*

There are frequent parties to which visitors are welcome. About once a week in high season there is a folk dance show which includes *capoeira*. *Forró* nightly in high season at R do Forró, Wed and Sat in low season, starts about 2200. Action moves to the bars when *forró* has stopped about 0200. **Bar Barriga da Lua** and **Pizza Reggae**, opposite *forró*. After *forró*, **Padaria Santo Antônio** opens, selling special breads, coconut, banana, cheese, 0230-0700.

Entertainment

Fortaleza *p500, map p502, phone code 085/088*

Cinema For information about cinema programming, T139. **Theatre** In the centre are **Teatro José de Alencar**, Praça José de Alencar (see Sights p501), and **Teatro São José**, R Rufino de Alencar 363, T2315447, both with shows all year.

Festivals and events

Fortaleza *p500, map p502*
6 Jan Epiphany.
Feb Ash Wed.
19 Mar São José.
Jul Last Sun in Jul is the **Regata Dragão do Mar**, Praia de Mucuripe, with traditional *jangada* (raft) races.
Jul During the last week of Jul is the out-of-season Salvador-style carnival, **Fortal**, takes place along Av Almte Barroso, Av Raimundo Giro and Av Beira Mar. In Caucaia, 12 km to the southeast, a *vaquejada*, traditional rodeo and country fair, takes place during the last weekend of Jul.
15 Aug, the local Umbanda *terreiros* (churches) celebrate the **Festival of Iemanjá** on Praia do Futuro, taking over the entire beach from noon till dusk, when offerings are cast into the surf. Well worth attending (members of the public may 'pegar um passo' – enter into an inspired religious trance – at the hands of a *pai-de-santo*). Beware of pickpockets and purse-snatchers.
Mid-Oct **Ceará Music**, a 4-day festival of Brazilian music, rock and pop, is held in Marina Park.
Dec **Christmas Eve** and **New Year's Eve**, half-day.

Juazeiro do Norte *p514*
6 Jan Reis Magos (Epiphany).
2 Feb Candeias (Candelmas), Nossa Senhora da Luz.
24 Mar Padre Cícero's birth.
20 Jul Padre Cícero's death.
10-15 Sep Nossa Senhora das Dores, the city's patron saint.
1-2 Nov Finados, the city receives some 600,000 visitors for the All Saints' Day pilgrimages.

Shopping

Fortaleza *p500, map p502*
Bookshops **Livraria Livro Técnico**, see Dragão do Mar, above, has several branches, on Dom Luis, Praça Ferreira, Shopping Norte and at UFC university. **Siciliano**, bookstore and coffee shop in new part of **Iguatemi** shopping mall, with just a bookstore in the old part. **Livraria Nobel** bookstore and coffee shop in Del Paseo shopping centre in Aldeota.

Handicrafts Fortaleza has an excellent selection of locally manufactured textiles, which are among the cheapest in Brazil, and a wide selection of regional handicrafts. The local craft specialities are lace (mostly hand-made) and embroidered textile goods; also hammocks (US$15 to over US$100), fine *alto-relievo* wood carvings of Northeast scenes, basketware, leatherwork and clay figures (*bonecas de barro*). Bargaining is OK at the **Mercado Central** near Praça da Sé (closed Sun) and the **Emcetur Centro de Turismo** in the old prison (more expensive). Leather, lacework and cashew nuts at the Mercado Central are excellent.
Crafts are also available in shops near the market (eg *Itaparica*, R Conde D'Eu 434, sells hammocks and textiles), while shops on R Dr João Moreira 400 block sell clothes. Every night (1800-2300), there are stalls along the beach at Praia Meireiles, lively, fair prices. Crafts also available in the commercial area along Av Monsenhor Tabosa. **Ceart**, Av Monsenhor Tabosa 777, is a big outlet and a school which teaches people how to set up a business. Clothes boutiques along Monsenhor Tabosa are closer to the centre, between Sen Almino and João Cordeiro.

Shopping centres The biggest is **Iguatemi**, south of Meireles on the way to the Centro de Convenções; it also has modern cinemas. Others are **Aldeota** and **Del Paseo** in Aldeota, near Praça Portugal.

Activities and tours

Fortaleza *p500, map p502, phone code 085/088*
Diving
ASPA (**Atividades Subaquáticas e Pesquisas Ambientais**), R Eduardo Garcia 23, s 13, Aldeota, T2682966. See Manta Diving, below. Diving trips (see Excursions above), lessons and equipment rental.
Projeto Netuno, R do Mirante 165, Mucuripe, T264 4114, www.pnetuno.com.br

Golf
The *Ceará Golf Club* has 9 holes.

Surfing

Surfing is popular on a number of Ceará beaches, including those by the towns of Paracurú and Pecém, to the west of Fortaleza, and Porto das Dunas to the east.

Tour operators

Many operators offer city and beach tours. Others offer adventure trips further afield, most common being off-road trips along the beaches from Natal in the east to the Lençois Maranhenses in the west.

Ceará Saveiro, Av Beira Mar 4293, T2631085. *Saveiro* (schooner) and yacht trips, daily 1000-1200 and 1600-1800 from Praia de Mucuripe.

Dunnas Expedições, Av Desembargador Moreira 2001, Sl 1104, Aldeota, T0xx85-264 2514, www.dunnas.com.br Off-road tours with a fleet of white Land Rover Defenders, experienced, environmentally and culturally aware, very helpful and professional staff. Recommended.

Martur, Av Beira Mar 4260, T2631203. Sailing boat and schooner trips, from Mucuripe, same schedule as **Ceará Saveiro.**

Sunny Tour, Av Prof A Nunes Freire 4097, Dionísio Torres, T0xx85-9986 5689, also has a bus-cum-stand on Av Beira Mar near the craft fair. Offers beach tours (eg 3 in 1 day, 6 in 4 days, trips to Jericoacoara).

Trekking

The Fortaleza chapter of the **Trekking Club do Brasil** has walks once a month to different natural areas, visitors are welcome to join, US$20 for transport and T-shirt, T2122456.

Windsurfing

Due to constant trade winds, a number of Ceará beaches are excellent for windsurfing.

Bio Board, Av Beira Mar 914, T2198585, www.bioboard.com.br. Looks after equipment for you, windsurf school, **Açaizeiro Café** with *açai*, juices, sandwiches upstairs (Mon-Fri 1000-2000, Sat till 1900, Sun till 1800), also **Manta Diving** and travel agency – next to **Ondas Verdes**. Equipment can be rented at some of the more popular beaches such as Porto das Dunas and in the city from **Windclub**, Av Beira Mar 2120, Praia dos Diários, T9825449. Lessons also available.

Jericoacoara *p509, phone code 088*

Clube dos Ventos, R das Dunas, T6210211, www.clubedosventos.com. Same owner as **Casa de Turismo**, equipment hire US$18 per hr, US$44 per day for experienced, US$13 and US$31 for beginners, US$270 deposit (R$700). Basic course US$55.55, 3 hrs and up. Kite surfing at Preá and Lagoa Jijoca.

Jeri Off Road, T0xx88-669 2022, T99614167 (mob), www.jeri.tur.br. João Gaúcho runs adventure trips in the area. Recommended, but popular. They also have a travel agency run by Paula Salles.

Quixadá *p513, phone code 088*

Assossiação de Montanhismo e Escalada de Quixadá, Secretário, Henrique Cavalcante, T0xx88-9956 4722. 4 members, 14 climbers; climbing up to grade 7. Henrique can help with every type of adventure sport, trekking, orienteering and historical information.

Assossiação de Turismo Ecológico (ATEC), guides for US$11.10 a day, city tour prices depend on group size.

Sertão & Pedras, T4125995, www.quixadanet.com.br/sertaopedras. Acadêmia de Aventuras. **Hang-gliding**: Paulo Rocha (delta wing), T0xx88-9251 1955; Paragliding: Sívio, T0xx85-9979 6027; Climbing, Kido, T0xx88-9956 7127.

Transport

Fortaleza *p500, map p502, phone code 085/088*

See also Ins and outs, p500.

Air

Aeroporto Pinto Martins, Praça Eduardo Gomes, 6 km south of centre. Airport has a tourist office, T4771667, car hire, food hall upstairs, small internet facility at US$3 per hr, **Laselva** bookstore and **Banco do Brasil** (changes cash, US$20 commission on TCs, 1100-1500). Regular international flights from Lisbon and Milan. Domestic flights to most major cities, as well as Juazeiro do Norte.

Airline offices BRA, T4771470. Fly, Av Mons Taboso 1069, T219 7171. **Varig**, Av Santos Dumont 2727, Aldeota, T2668000, F2440500, freephone 0800 997000. Vasp, Av Santos Dumont 3060, sala 803, Aldeota, T2543434, F2723046, freephone T0800

998266. TAM, Av Santos Dumont 2849, Aldeota, T2610916. **TAF (Transportes Aéreos Fortaleza)**, T2727474, flights to Juazeiro do Norte and other places in the interior, 0900-1630.

Bus

Rodoviária at Av Borges de Melo 1630, Fátima, 6 km south from centre, T2562100, info T2564080 or 24-hr Disque Turismo. Many city buses (US$0.65) including 'Aguanambi' 1 or 2 which go from Av Gen Sampaio, 'Barra de Fátima-Rodoviária' from Praça Coração de Jesus, 'Circular' for Av Beira Mar and the beaches, and 'Siqueira Mucuripe' from Av Abolição. Taxi to Praia de Iracema, or Av Abolição US$5. No luggage store, only lockers. Opposite the rodoviária is **Hotel Amuarama**, which has a bar and restaurant; there's also a *lanchonete*.

Nordeste, T2562342: To **Mossoró**, 10 a day, US$8.75, **Natal**, 8 daily, US$17.75, *semi-leito*, US$25.15 *executivo*, US$40 *leito*, 7½ hrs. **João Pessoa**, 2 daily, US$26.35 *semi-leito*, US$36 *leito*, 10 hrs. **Boa Esperança**, T2565006, stops at Fortaleza on its Belém-Natal route only. **Itapemirim** to **Salvador**, US$57.40, 1900, 23 hrs. Guanabara, T2560214, to **Recife**, 5 daily, US$29 *executivo*, US$41.50 *leito*, 12 hrs, book early for weekend travel. **Guanabara** to **Teresina**, several daily, US$20.35, *leito* US$35.55, 10 hrs; to **Parnaíba** US$18.15; to **Belém**, 2 daily, US$49 *executivo*, 23 hrs. **Piripiri**, for Parque Nacional de Sete Cidades, US$15.20, 9 hrs, a good stop en route to Belém, also Guanabara, who go to **São Luís**, 3 daily, US$33.35, 18 hrs. Other long-distance companies: Transbrasiliana, T2561306, Açailândia, T2568525, Eucatur/União Cascavel, T2564889, Pantanal to Palmas, Gontijo to São Paulo, São Gonçalo to **Belo Horizonte**.

In Ceará: **Guanabara** to **Sobral** US$5.55, **Ubajara** 0800, 1800, return 0800, 1600, 6 hrs, US$8.15. Also **Ipu Brasília** to Sobral US$9.25, and to **Camocim** 1120, 1530. To **Majorlândia**, US$4, **Campina Grande**, US$22.20, 13 hrs.

To **Juazeiro do Norte**, **Rio Grande/Rápido Juazeiro**, T2543600, 5 a day from 1230-2145, 8-9 hrs, US$36.55, *leito* US$73. **Redenção** to **Quixadá**, many daily, US$4, also **Redentora**, 0600,1200 via Baturité. **Redenção** to **Almofala** 0700, 1730, US$6.65, **Cruz** 0900, 1030, 1630, 1830, US$6.40. **Redenção** to **Gijoca** and **Jeri** from rodoviária 0900, 1830 Gijoca, US$7.60, 1030, 1830 Jeri US$10. Tickets are also sold at the **Posta Telefônica** Beira Mar, on Beira Mar almost opposite Praiano Palace (see Tourist offices).

Buses to beaches For eastern beaches near Fortaleza (Prainha, Iguape, Barro Preto, Batoque) and towns such as Aquiraz, Eusêbio or Pacajus, you must take **São Benedito** buses, T2722544, from rodoviária: to **Beberibe** 10 a day US$2, **Cascavel** US$1.10, **Morro Branco** 0745, 1000, 1515, 1750, US$2.25, **Canoa Quebrada** 0830, 1100, 1340, 1540 (plus 1730 on Sun) US$4.25, **Aracati** 0630, 0830, 1100, 1340, 1540, 1900 last back at 1800, US$3.90.

Driving When driving outside the city, have a good map and be prepared to ask directions frequently as road signs are non-existent or are placed after junctions.

Car hire Many car hire places on Av Monsenhor Taboso, eg Shop, No 1181, T2197788, **Reta**, No 1171, T2195555, **Amazônia**, No 1055, T2190800, and many more at the junction with Ildefonso Albano. **Brasil Rent a Car**, Av Abolição 2300, T0xx85-242 0868, www.brasillocadora.com.br Localiza, Av Abolição 2236, T0800-992020. There are also many buggy rental shops.

Trains

Station at Praça da Estação (Castro Carreira) in the centre, T2114255. Commuter services only.

The coast east of Fortaleza *p505, phone code 088*

Bus Daily bus service from Fortaleza rodoviária to **Prainha**, 11 daily, US$1; **Iguape**, hourly between 0600 and 1900, US$1.10. To **Caponga**: direct bus from Fortaleza rodoviária (4 a day, US$1.30) or take a bus from Fortaleza to Cascavel (80 mins) then a bus from Cascavel (20 mins); bus information in Caponga T334 1485. For bus information in Fortaleza, **São Benedito**, T272 2544, at rodoviária: to **Beberibe**, 10 a day, US$2; **Cascavel**, US$1.10; **Morro Branco**, 0745, 1000, 1515, 1750, US$2.25; **Canoa Quebrada**, 0830, 1100, 1340, 1540 (plus

1730 Sun), US$4.25; **Aracati**, 0630, 0830, 1100, 1340, 1540, 1900, last back at 1800, US$3.90. Natal-Aracati bus via Mossoró, 6 hrs, US$7.50; from Mossoró (90 km) US$2.50, 2 hrs; Fortaleza-Aracati (142 km), besides *São Benedito*, *Guanabara* or *Nordeste* many daily, US$4, 2 hrs; Aracati-Canoa Quebrada from Gen Pompeu e João Paulo, US$0.60; taxi US$3.60.

Jijoca *p509*
A *jardineira* (open-sided 4WD truck) does the 23 km, 1½ hrs, trip from Jijoca to Jericoacoara. A rough but very pretty ride through sand dunes and hills, sadly criss-crossed by vehicle tracks which have damaged the fragile *caatinga* vegetation (4WD and high clearance are necessary on this road).

Jericoacoara *p509, phone code 088*
Buggy Tours cost US$44.45 for a buggy to all the sites. **Associação de Bugueiros**, ABJ, R Principal, *barraca* near Ibama. If seeking a *bugueiro* who speaks English, Spanish, Italian and French, ask for Alvaro, the school teacher, who is Uruguayan.

Bus **Redenção** buses from Fortaleza to **Jijoca** and **Jericoacoara** from the rodoviária 0900, 1700 and the Av Beira Mar at the Posta Telefônica opposite Praiano Palace Hotel 30 mins later. The day bus goes via Jijoca and the night bus via Preá. The journey takes 6 hrs and costs US$10 one way. Always check times of the **Redençao** buses from Fortaleza as they change with the season. The night bus requires an overnight stop in Preá; make your own way to Jeri next day. A *jardineira* (open-sided 4WD truck) meets the **Redenção** bus from Fortaleza, at Jijoca (included in the **Redenção** price). Buses return from Jeri at 1400 (via Preá) and 2230 (via Jijoca); the *jardineira* leaves from Casa do Turismo (see p519 for ticket sale times). Hotels and tour operators run 2- or 3-day tours to Jeri from Fortaleza. If not on Redenção or a tour, 'guides' will besiege new arrivals in Jijoca with offers of buggies, or guiding cars through the tracks and dunes to Jeri for US$5.55. If you don't want to do this, ask if a pick-up is going: try Francisco Nascimento, O Chicão, at **Posta do Dê**, or T6691356, US$3.70 per person up front, 22 km, 30 mins (but some only charge US$1.50 per person). In a buggy it's US$16.65 per buggy.

If coming from **Belém** or other points north and west, go via Sobral (from Belém US$28.25, 20 hrs), where you change for Cruz, 40 km east of Jijoca, a small pleasant town with basic hotels (there is only one bus a day Sobral-Cruz, US$7.25, 3-4 hrs, but **Redenção** runs to **Cruz** from Fortaleza 0900, 1030, 1630, 1830, US$6.40. Either continue to Jijoca the next day (Cruz-Jijoca, daily about 1400, US$1.25, meets *jardineira* for Jeri, Cruz-Jericoacoara, US$2.20) or take an *horário* pick-up Cruz-Jijoca.

An alternative from the west, especially if going through Parnaíba, is by buggy or *jardineira* from **Camocim**, which is 1½ hrs by road from Parnaíba. They leave 0900-1030. You can break the journey from Camocim to Jericoacoara at villages such as Nova Tatajuba (see below), or **Guriú** where hammock space can be found. There is good birdwatching here. The village musician sings his own songs in the bar. Walk 4 hrs, or take a boat across the bay to Jericoacoara.The journey along the beach has beautiful scenery. In Jericoacoara ask around for buggy or *jardineira* rides to Camocim, about US$11-15 per person. Inland, there is an unmade road from Jijoca through cashew plantations to Granja (61 km), on the CE-364, which heads north 21 km to Camocim. If driving, ask the way frequently.

Motorcycle If on a motorcycle, it is not possible to ride from Jijoca to Jericoacoara (unless you are an expert in desert conditions). Safe parking for bikes in Jijoca is not a problem.

Cruz *p510*
Bus The bus to **Jijoca** goes through about 1400, US$2 or US$3.50 to **Jericoacoara**, wait for the bus by 1330.

Chapada de Ibiapaba *p511*
Bus From **Fortaleza** US$8, from **Belém** US$30.

Serra de Baturité *p512, phone code 085*
Bus Baturité rodoviária is beyond town on the way out to Guaramiranga. **Redentora** bus from **Fortaleza** rodoviária (T2562729) to Baturité, 4 a day (plus 1300 on Sat), 3 hrs. To **Guaramiranga** Mon-Fri 0830, daily 1030,

1700, also to **Araturba**. Also Pinheiro to Guaramiranga and Aratuba, T2563729.

Quixadá *p513*

Bus Redenção bus from **Fortaleza** rodoviária to Quixadá, many daily, 3 hrs, US$4, also Redentora, 0600, 1200 via Baturité. Redenção to **Quixeramobim**, 4 hrs, US$7.

Juazeiro do Norte *p514, map p515, phone code 085/088*

Air Airport is 7 km from the centre along Av Virgílio Távora, T5112118. Flights to **Fortaleza**, **Petrolina** and **Recife**. Taxi from centre US$5.75, motorcycle taxi US$3; taxi from rodoviária US$8.40.

Airline offices TAF (Táxi Aéreo Fortaleza), T5110699.

Bus Rodoviária, Av Dalmiro Gouveia, on the road to Crato, T5112868. Taxi from the centre US$3, motorcycle taxi US$0.60. To **Fortaleza** with Rio Negro, 2 daily, US$13.50 *convencional*, US$17.50 *executivo*, 8 hrs. To **Picos** with Boa Esperança, 2 daily, US$5.75, 5 hrs. To **Teresina** with Boa Esperança, Progresso or Aparecida, 3 daily, US$11-12, 11 hrs. To **São Luís** with Progresso, US$20, 16 hrs. To **Belém** with Boa Esperança, 1 daily (often full), US$30, 25 hrs. To **Campina Grande** with Transparaiba, 2 daily, US$9, 9 hrs. To **João Pessoa** with Braga, 1 daily, US$12, 10 hrs. To **Recife** with Braga, 1 daily, US$14, 11 hrs. To **Salvador** with Itapermirim, 2 weekly, US$17.50, 14 hrs. To **São Paulo** with Itapemirim, 1 daily, US$63, 40 hrs.

Car hire Unidas, Av Padre Cícero, Km 2 on road to Crato, T5711226, F5711855. **IBM**, Santo Agostinho 58, T5110542. **Localiza**, Airport and Av Padre Cícero Km 03, No 3375, T5712668.

Directory

Fortaleza *p500, map p502, phone code 085/088*

Banks Banco do Nordeste, R Major Facundo 372, a/c, helpful, recommended. TCs exchanged and cash with Visa at **Banco do Brasil**, R Barão do Rio Branco 1500, also on Av Abolição (high commission on TCs). ATM for Cirrus, Visa and MasterCard outside cinema at Centro Cultural Dragão do Mar. Also at Av Antonio Sales and Iguatemi Shopping. **Banco Mercantil do Brasil**, R Mayor Facundo 484, Centro, Praça do Ferreira, cash against MasterCard. Exchange at **Tropical Viagens**, R Barão do Rio Branco 1233, T2213344, English spoken. **Libratur**, Av Abolição 2194, T2483355, Mon-Fri 0900-1800, Sat 0800-1200; also has kiosk outside Othon hotel on Av Beira Mar which is open every day till 2300. Recommended. More *câmbios* on Av Mons Tabosa: eg **TourStar**, No 1587, **Sdoc**, No 1073, T2197993.
Embassies and consulates Belgium, R Eduardo Garcia 909, Aldeota, T2612451, nattur@secrel.com.br. **France**, R Bóris 90, Centro, T2542822. **Germany**, R Dr Lourenço 2244, Meireles, T2462833, gja435@sec.secrel.com.br. **Italy**, Rua E 80, Parque Wáshington Soares, T2732606. **Netherlands**, Av Pe Antônio Tomás 386, T4612331. **Sweden and Norway**, R Leonardo Mota 501, Aldeota, T2420888, marcos@emitrade.com.br. **Switzerland**, R Dona Leopoldina 697, Centro, T2269444. **UK**, c/o Grupo Edson Queiroz, Praça da Imprensa s/n, Aldeota, T4668888, annette@edsonqueiroz.com.br. **US**, Nogueira Acioli 891, Centro, T252 1539. **Internet** Many internet cafés around the city. **Beira Mar Internet Café**, Av Beira Mar 2120A, Meireles, 0800-0200, US$2.60 per hr (discounts with receipt from Habib's), also international phones, coffee. Outside Av Shopping, Av Dom Luís 300, US$2.50 per hr. Abrolhos Praia, Av Abolição 2030, Meireles, part of hotel of same name, US$1.25 per hr, Mon-Fri 0800-2000, Sat 0800-1400. **Cyber Net**, Av Beira Mar 3120 in small mall, smart, US$2.20 per hr. **Ligue.com**, Osvaldo Cruz in Beiramar Trade Center. **Cearápontocom**, Av Beira Mar e R dos Ararius, across from La Habanera. US$3 per hr, popular, cafés around it.
Internet Express, R Barão de Aracati opposite **Colonial Praia**, opens 0800. Via Veneto Flat, Av Abolição 2324, has **C@fé Digital**, US$2.25 per hr, open Sun evening. 2 doors from Pousada Casa Nossa is **Falô**, Av Abolição 2600 block, daily 0800-2000, US$1.50 per hr, also phones. Others in Pôlo Comercial at Av Mons Tabosa e Ildefonso Albano.
Laundry Laundromat, Av Abolição 3038, Meireles. **Medical services** Instituto Dr José Frota (IJF), R Barão do Rio Branco 1866, T2555000, recommended public hospital.

Post office Main branch at R Senador Alencar 38, Centro; Av Monsenhor Tabosa 1109 and 1581, Iracema; at train station; opposite rodoviária. Parcels must be taken to Receita Federal office at Barão de Aracati 909, Aldeota (take 'Dom Luiz' bus). **Telephone** International calls from **Emcetur** hut on Iracema beach and from **Telemar** offices: R Floriano Peixoto 99, corner of R João Moreira, Centro; R José Vilar 375, Aldeota; Av Beira Mar 736, Iracema; Av Beira Mar 3821, Meireles; Av César Cals 1297, Praia do Futuro; at rodoviária and airport.

Jijoca *p509*
Banks Banco do Brasil does not change foreign currency in Jijoca.

Juazeiro do Norte *p514, map p515*
Banks Banco do Brasil, R São Francisco, near Praça Pradre Cícero, poor rates, Mon-Fri 1100-1600. No *câmbios* in town. **Post office** R Conceição 354 and at rodoviária. **Telephone** R São Pedro 204, half a block from Praça Padre Cícero and at rodoviária.

Piauí and Maranhão

Piauí is possibly the poorest state in Brazil. Its population is about 2.7 million, but many leave to seek work elsewhere. The economy is almost completely dependent upon agriculture and livestock, both of which in turn depend on how much rain, if any, falls.

Maranhão state is about the size of Italy, with flat and low-lying land and highlands to the south. The Atlantic coastline – a mass of sandbanks and creeks and sandy islands on one of which stands São Luís – is 480 km long. The colonial centre of São Luís, with its use of ceramic tiles as exterior decoration, has been restored and is now part of UNESCO's list of sites of worldwide cultural importance. The coast to the east, stretching to the Parnaíba delta, contains an area of sand dunes and freshwater lakes, the Lençóis Maranhenses, which deserves a visit for its beauty and remoteness. The area around Carolina, south of Imperatriz, is renowned for its mountain scenery and spectacular waterfalls. As for culture, the Bumba-Meu-Boi is typical of the region and the African influence harks back to the days when slaves were imported into the city, which is also considered Brazil's reggae capital. ▸▸ *For Sleeping, Eating and other listings, see pages 537-542.*

History

The history of Piauí springs from cattle farmers who moved into the interior from Bahia at the beginning in the 17th century. Until the early 19th century, though, the state was under the control of neighbouring Maranhão. At Independence, there was bitter fighting between the Portuguese supporters of the colony and the Brazilians who sought their freedom.

Initially, the Portuguese did not show much interest in this part of the Northeast, so the French were the first to bring in colonists. By the end of the 16th century, the Portuguese took over, but this was interrupted by a brief period of Dutch dominance in the early 1640s. The Companhia Geral do Comércio do Maranhão e Grão-Pará, 1685-1777, was the major influence in the area, but after its demise, there was unrest until Maranhão finally bowed to the Independence movement.

Teresina ➔ *Phone code: 086. Colour map 2, A3. Population: 716,000.*

About 435 km up the Rio Parnaíba is the Piauí state capital. There are paved road and rail connections (freight only) with the neighbouring state capitals. The city itself is reputed to be the hottest after Manaus, with temperatures up to 42°C.

The **Palácio de Karnak** ⓘ *just west of Praça Frei Serafim, Mon-Fri 1530-1730*, the old Governor's Palace, contains lithographs of the Middle East in 1839 by David

 Roberts RA. Also see the **Museu do Piauí** ① *Praça Marechal Deodoro, Tue-Fri 0800-1730, Sat-Sun 0800-1200, US$0.60*,which has displays on the history of the state (in Portuguese) and an impressive and extensive collection of fossils.

There is an interesting open market by the Praça Marechal Deodoro and the river is picturesque, with washing laid out to dry along its banks. The market is a good place to buy hammocks, but bargain hard. Every morning along the river bank there is the **troca-troca**, where people buy, sell and swap. An undercover complex, **Mercado Central do Artesanato** ① *R Paissandu 1276, Praça Dom Pedro II, Mon-Fri 0800-2200*, has also been built. Most of the year the river is low, leaving sandbanks known as *coroas* (crowns).

For tourist information there are several options: **Piemtur tourist offices** ① *R Álvaro Mendes 2003, Caixa Postal 36, and at R Magalhães Filho (next to 55 N, English spoken); also at R Acre, Convention Centre, T2217100, and kiosks at the rodoviária and airport.* The **Singtur** (Sindicato dos Guías de Turismo de Piauí) **office** ① *R Paissandu 1276, T2212175, has information booths at the Centro de Artesanato, Praça Dom Pedro II (helpful, friendly), the Encontro das Águas, Poty Velho and on the shores of the Rio Poty.* Another office is **Ana Turismo** ① *R Álvaro Mendes 1961, Centro, T/F2233970.*

Parque Nacional de Sete Cidades → *Colour map 2, A3.*

① *Ibama, Av Homero Castelo Branco 2240, Teresina, CEP 64048-400, T2321142. , entrance US$3.*

Some 190 km northeast of Teresina, this interesting park has strange eroded rock formations which from the ground look like a medley of weird monuments. The inscriptions on some of the rocks have never been deciphered; one theory suggests links with the Phoenicians, and the Argentine Professor Jacques de Mahieu considers

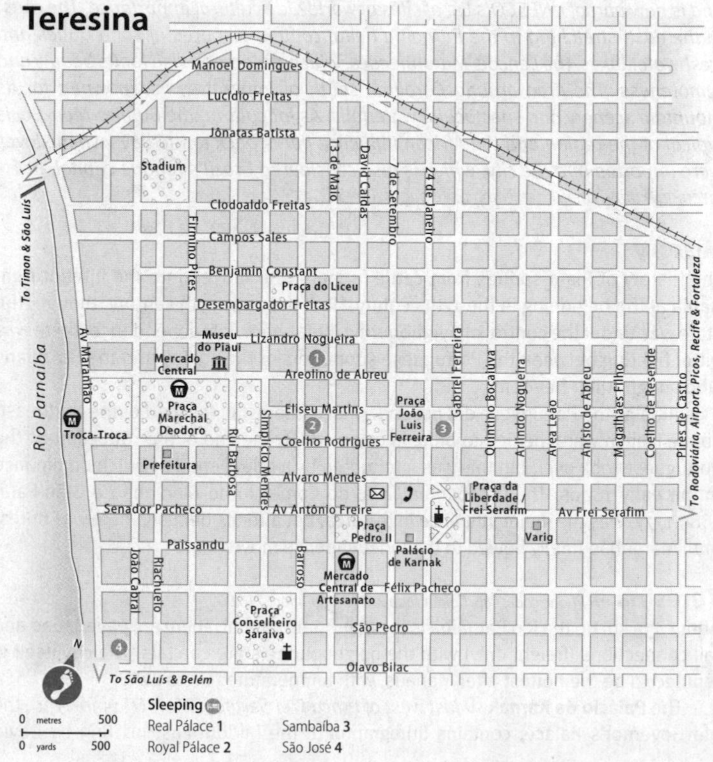

Cabeça-de-Cuia

Crispim was a fisherman who lived at the confluence of the rivers Poti and Parnaíba, in Teresina. One day, returning home after a hard day's fishing with no catch whatsoever, he discovered that there was no food in the house. Infuriated, he grabbed a large bone which was lying nearby and beat his mother to death. Her dying curse was that Crispim should live out his days as a hideous monster with an enormous head.

A young and single man, Crispim was driven to despair by his now terrifying appearance. He drowned himself in the Parnaíba. Legend has it that Crispim will be restored to life, and his good looks, when he has managed to eat seven virgins named Maria. Young laundresses, when they go to the river, are still afraid of him.

Cabeça-de-Cuia means 'head of a gourd'. Carvings of this strange figure are a common sight in Teresina.

them to be Nordic runes left by the Vikings. Within the 20 sq km of the park, there is plenty of birdlife and iguanas, which descend from their trees in the afternoon. If hiking in the park, beware of rattlesnakes. **Ibama** provides a free bus. A small booklet with sketch map is available from Ibama, but is not really good enough for walking. Local food is limited and monotonous, so bring a few delicacies, and especially fruit. Some 50 km away, **Pedro Segundo** is a good place to buy opals.

Parnaíba and around → *Phone code: 086. Colour map 2, A3. Population: 133,000.*

Between the states of Maranhão and Piauí runs the Rio Parnaíba. Near the river mouth is the anchorage of Luís Correia, where ships unload for final delivery by tugs and lighters at Parnaíba, 15 km upriver, the collection and distribution centre for the trade of Piauí (tropical products and cattle). Parnaíba is partly encircled by shifting sands in white dunes up to 30 m high. The town is a relaxed, friendly place. If crossing the delta, buy all provisions here. There is a regular connection here to **Tutóia**, for boats across the Parnaíba delta; a tour in the delta costs US$20 per person. For tourist information, there's **Piemtur** ⓘ *T3211532*, and **Secretaria de Turismo e Meio Ambiente** ⓘ *T3231715*, both at Porto das Barcas.

There are beaches at **Luís Correia**, 14 km from Parnaíba, with radioactive sands. About 18 km from Parnaíba is **Pedra do Sal**, with dark blue lagoons and palm trees. At **Lagoa de Portinho**, 12 km from Parnaíba, there are bungalows, a bar and restaurant, and it is possible to camp; canoes for hire. **Praia do Coqueiro** is a small fishing village with natural pools formed at low tide. Seafood is good at **Alô Brasil** and **Bar da Cota.**

Southern Piauí

In **Oeiras**, the old capital of Piauí, the state government is restoring some of the old buildings, such as the bishop's palace and the church of Nossa Senhora da Vitória.

Parque Nacional Serra da Capivara → *Colour map 2, B3.*

ⓘ *The main organization is the Fundação do Homem Americano (Fumdham), R Abdias Neves 551, CEP 64770-000, São Raimundo Nonato, Piauí, T5821612/1389, F5821656, which has a museum for scientists. For further information on the park and reservations in local hotels, contact Dr Niéde Guidon, Fumdham Parque Nacional, at the address above.*

About 500 km south of Teresina is this 130,000-ha park, on the UNESCO World Heritage list. Some 30,000 prehistoric rock paintings on limestone have been found, dating to between 6,000 and 12,000 years ago. The paintings are of daily life, festivities and celebrations, as well as hunting and sex scenes. Excavations by Brazilian and French archaeologists have uncovered fossilized remains of extinct animals such as the sabre-toothed tiger, giant sloths larger than elephants and armadillos the size of a car.

The BR-407 is reported unsafe near the border with Pernambuco due to robberies of vehicles travelling this route.

Nearly 400 archaeological sites have been identified in the park since research began in 1970. About 22 of those sites have been set up to receive tourists. Roads and all-weather paths allow visitors to view the site with ease. Specially trained guides are available. The area is good for hiking in the *caatinga*, with its canyons and mesas. It is also possible to see much of the *caatinga* wildlife, in particular the birds.

Much investment has gone into the park, not just for visitors' facilities, but also in educating the local population about protecting the paintings and establishing a beekeeping project to provide income in times of drought. The **Museu do Homen Americano** ⓘ *Centro Cultural Sérgio Motta, Bairro Campestre, São Raimundo Nonato, Piaui, T89-5821612, www.fumdham.org.br*, has a fascinating collection of artefacts found in the Serra. These are well displayed (though the information in English is poor). The museum is in the town of São Raimundo Nonato, some 35 km from the park.

Hyacinth Site

In the far southwest of the state, near **São Gonçalo do Piauí**, is one of the best places for seeing hyacinth macaws. The Hyacinth Site is on private land, 20 km from São Gonçalo, in a region of *cerrado* with red sandstone cliffs where the macaws nest. This used to be an area in which the illegal bird trade flourished, but the local people now guard the site, which is supported by the **Kaytee Avian Foundation** (USA) and others. Many other *cerrado* birds may be seen, together with black-and-gold howlers and, less commonly, maned wolves and giant anteaters. Accommodation is in very simple huts with mosquito nets, sand floors and shared bathrooms. Meals are served at the site. Access is via the airport at Barreiras in Western Bahia, 340 km south, five or six hours' drive away. Tours are only possible through **Focus Tours**, see Essentials page 26.

São Luís

→ *Colour map 2, A2. Phone code: 098. Population: 870,000.*

The capital and port of Maranhão state, founded in 1612 by the French and named after St Louis of France, stands upon São Luís island between the bays of São Marcos and São José. The urban area extends to São Francisco island, connected with São Luís by three bridges. The historic centre is being restored with UNESCO support and the splendid results (eg the part known as the *Reviver*) rival the Pelourinho in Salvador. An old slaving port, the city has retained much African culture. It is in a region of heavy tropical rains, but the surrounding deep forest has been cut down to be replaced by *babaçu* palms, the nuts and oils of which are the state's most important products.

Sights

The old part of the city, on very hilly ground with many steep streets, is still almost pure colonial. The damp climate stimulated the use of ceramic tiles for exterior walls, and São Luís shows a greater variety of such tiles than anywhere else in Brazil; in Portuguese, French and Dutch styles. The commercial quarter (Rua Portugal, also called Rua Trapiche) is still much as it was in the 17th century; the best shopping area is Rua de Santana near Praça João Lisboa. For tourist information, there's **Fumtur** ⓘ *Praça Benedito Leite, T2225281, and at the airport*, and **Maratur** ⓘ *Praça João Lisboa 66, opposite the post office, T2312000, maratur@geplan.ma.gov.br*.

The **Palácio dos Leões** ⓘ *Av Dom Pedro II, Mon, Wed and Fri 1500-1800*, the Governor's Palace, has beautiful floors of dark wood (*jacarandá*) and light (*cerejeira*). There are marvellous views from the terrace. The restored **Fortaleza de Santo Antônio**, built originally by the French in 1614, is on the bank of the Rio Anil at Ponta d'Areia.

The **Fábrica Canhamo** ⓘ *R São Pantaleão 1232, Madre de Deus, near Praia Grande, T2322187, Mon-Fri 0900-1900*, is a restored factory and houses an arts and crafts centre. The **Centro da Creatividade Odylo Costa Filho** ⓘ *R da Alfândego 200, Praia Grande T2314058, Mon-Fri 0800-2200*, is an arts centre with theatre, cinema, music, etc, with a bar and café; a good meeting place.

The best colonial churches in town are the **cathedral** ⓘ *Praça Dom Pedro II* (1629), and the churches of **Carmo** ⓘ *Praça João Lisboa* (1627), **São João Batista** ⓘ *Largo São João* (1665), **Nossa Senhora do Rosário** ⓘ *R do Egito 1717*, and the 18th-century **Santana** ⓘ *R de Santana*. On Largo do Desterro is the church of **São José do Desterro**, which was finished in 1863, but has much older parts.

As for museums in São Luís, the **Cafua das Mercês** ⓘ *R Jacinto Maia 43*, is a museum housed in the old slave market, in a small building opposite the Quartel Militar. It is a space devoted to the history of African culture in Maranhao. The various exhibits include pieces of African art, musical instruments and ritual objects, alongside displays about Afro-Brazilian history and life. Information is in Portuguese. It is well worth the effort to find it. ⓘ *Mon-Fri 1330-1700*. Also worth a visit is the **Casa dos Negros** next door. The **Museu Histórico e Artístico do Estado** ⓘ *R do Sol 302*, in a fine early 19th-century mansion (complete with slave quarters). Also on the Rua do Sol is the **Teatro Artur Azevedo** (1816). **Museu de Artes Visuais** ⓘ *Av Portugal 289, Mon-Fri 0800-1300, 1600-1800*, shows ceramics and post-war art.

São Luís

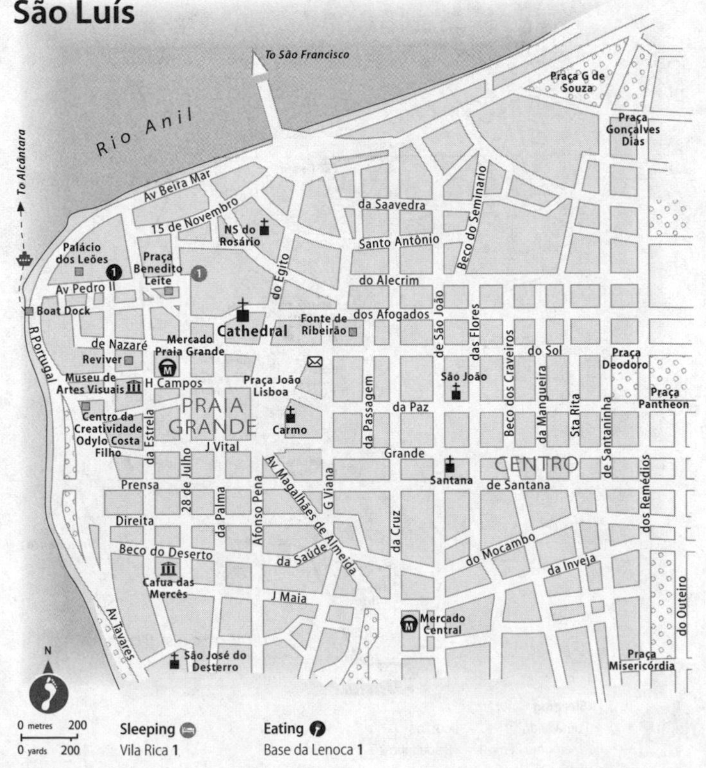

Calhau is a huge beach, 10 km away. **Ponta D'Areia** is nearer to São Luís but more crowded. **Raposa**, a fishing village built on stilts, is a good place to buy handicrafts. There are a few places to stay on Avenida Principal. It is an hour's bus ride with **Viação Santa Maria**, every 30 minutes from the Mercado Central, São Luís. Another fishing village is **São José de Ribamar**, whose church dedicated to the patron saint is a centre for *romeiros* in September; many bars on the seafront serve local specialities such as fried stonefish. It is a 30-minute bus ride with **Maranhense** from in the market, São Luís.

Alcântara ➔ *Phone code: 098. Colour map 2, A2. Population: 22,000.*

Some 22 km away by boat is Alcântara, the former state capital, on the mainland bay of São Marcos. Construction of the city began at the beginning of the 17th century and it is now a historical monument. There are many old churches, such as the ruined **Matriz de São Matias** (1648) and colonial mansions, including the **Casa** and **Segunda Casa do Imperador**, and the old cotton barons' mansions with their blue, Portuguese-tiled façades. In the Praça da Matriz is the **Pelourinho** ⓘ *0900-1330, US$0.75* (1648), the traditional pillory, and a small museum. You can also see the **Forte de São Sebastião** (1663), now in ruins, and the **Fonte de Miritítiua** (1747).

Canoe trips go to **Ilha do Livramento,** where there are good beaches and walking around the coast (can be muddy after rain). Watch out for mosquitoes after dark. A rocket-launching site has been built nearby!

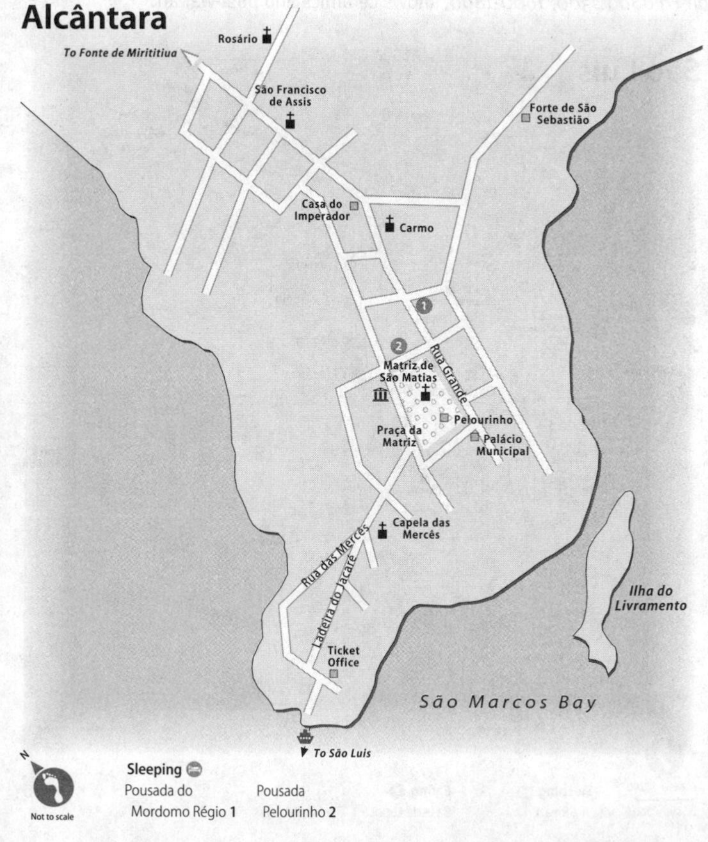

Parque Nacional Lençóis Maranhenses

→ *Phone code: 098 Colour map 2, A3.*

To the east of São Luís, on the Atlantic Coast, is the Parque Nacional Lençóis Maranhenses, 155,000 ha of beaches, lakes and dunes, with very little vegetation and largely unstudied wildlife.

Despite its remoteness, Lençóis Maranhenses (which means 'sheets of Maranhão') is not too difficult to visit. Travellers with a few days to spare are rewarded as much by the amazing panorama of watery dunes, reaching from horizon to horizon, as by deserted beaches, boat rides on the aptly named **Rio Preguiça** (Lazy River) and tiny, quiet hamlets where strangers are still a novelty. Interest in the region among Brazilian holidaymakers – and developers – is growing fast, so explorers would be well advised to go there soon.

A strange landscape of shifting white dunes, stretching about 140 km along the coast between **Tutóia** and Primeira Cruz, west of **Barreirinhas**, has created a unique and delicate ecosystem which has been protected since 1981. The sand, which extends from the coast up to 50 km inland, is advancing by as much as 200 m a year in some places. Dumped by the sea and blown by the wind, it forms ridges 50 m high in long flowing patterns which change constantly. The best time to visit is during the rainy season (June-September), when the dune valleys fill with water. Reflections of the sky make the water appear vivid blue, providing a spectacular contrast against the brilliant white sand.

Barely visited until recently, Lençóis Maranhenses provides a refuge for severely endangered species: giant turtles come here to lay their eggs; among the mammals are *paca*, some deer and sea cow; and there are almost-extinct varieties of fish such as the *camurupim*, which likes both salt and freshwater. The dunes are a breeding ground for migratory birds and recent studies have shown the sparse vegetation to include grasses unknown elsewhere. Excavations were begun in 1995 on the supposed site of a Jesuit settlement which, according to persistent local rumour, was buried intact by a sandstorm.

Traversing Lençóis Maranhenses

The area to the west of Rio Preguiça is the park proper. The dunes east of the river form a 'protected area' which is easier to travel through, and has several small, friendly settlements.

Along the coast from Barreirinhas to Tutóia in either direction, allow about three days on foot. Camping is permitted, but you must take all supplies with you including water, since some dune lakes are salty. Because of the hot and sandy conditions, this is a punitive trek, only for the very hardy. Do not try the treacherous hike inland across the dunes. By horse: contact Ibama, see below. Allow two days by jeep, staying overnight at Paulino Neves (US$20). From Tutóia, José Neves Rodrigues, known as 'O Anjo' (the Angel), does the trip for around US$40 per passenger. By boat: a regular river-boat service plies between Tutóia and Paulino Neves/Rio Novo; another from there goes to Barreirinhas (both four hours, US$10). It is also possible to hire a speedboat, or get a ride from a fisherman. A very bad road passing inland links Tutóia and Barreirinhas: hardy drivers could stop at Rio Novo and explore the dunes from there.

The Parnaíba delta

The extensive Parnaíba delta, its 70 islets variously covered in forest, palms or dunes, is the only seawater delta in the Americas: river and saltwater flow side by side through its channels. Catch a boat on the riverside in Parnaíba, hook up your hammock, and pass a few desultory hours watching herons nesting in the trees, fishermen asleep in their rowing boats and admiring the daily crab harvest. » *See below for Ilha do Caju.*

When you arrive at the delta mouth you have the choice between stopping at Ilha do Caju, which gets its name from the hundreds of cashew trees that grow there (www.ilhadocaju.com.br), or continuing to **Tutóia**, where millions of birds populate freshwater lakes, formed by rain collecting between massive white dunes. Both are protected areas of outstanding natural beauty. Good food and accommodation are available on the island and in Tutóia, but many people in this region live as they have done for generations, in adobe houses, on a diet of fish cooked in baked-earth ovens. Illiteracy is the norm. Travel is by jeep or, more commonly, by horse. There is no mains electricity and the nearest shopping is at Parnaíba.

Crossing the Parnaíba delta, which separates Piauí from Maranhão, is possible by boat, arriving in Tutóia; an interesting trip through swamps sheltering many birds. Trucks from Tutóia go to Barreirinhas, gateway to the **Parque Nacional dos Lençóis Maranhenses**, a vast protected area of sand dunes with rare birds and other wildlife.

Ilha do Caju → *Population: 70.*

Virtually unchanged for four centuries, Ilha do Caju has an astonishing variety of terrain, with lakes, forest, marshes and an expanse of white dunes to the northwest. Much of the water, including the sea, is salobre – a mixture of fresh and salty. Swimming is from a vast, shimmering beach, through alternating currents of sea and river water, a heartily recommend experience.

There are lakes, caused by flooding, in which trees killed by the brine content stand, bleached and knotted, an unnerving image of lifelessness surrounded by vigorous vegetation. Another lake is full of nesting herons and peregrines, which take off in clouds of flashing green feathers as you pass. Tiny, long-legged *cafézinho* birds hop from leaf to leaf on the water lilies. Walking in the forest that surrounds the lake, myriad butterflies hover around your head. Many of the islanders still live in rustic adobe houses where the stove is made of baked earth. The whole island is environmentally protected and no chemical pesticides are used.

Caxias → *Population: 149,500.*

The main road from Teresina passes through the Maranhense town of Caxias, a battle site during the Balaiada rebellion in 1838. It has a good *churrascaria*, **Selva do Braz**, Avenida Central 601, with live music in the evening. About 3 km from the town on the Buriti Bravo road is a spring for medicinal bathing, with a restaurant serving regional food.

Southern Maranhão

Imperatriz → *Phone code: 098. Colour map 2, A1. Population: 295,000.*

On the Eastern bank of the Rio Tocantins, at Maranhão's western border with Tocantins, is Imperatriz, a city serving a large cattle region. Founded in 1851, the **Igreja de Santa Tereza D'Ávila** ⓘ *R 15 de Novembro*, is dedicated to the city's patron saint. River beaches appear between July and October when the river is low.

Carolina → *Phone code: 098. Population: 26,000.*

South of Imperatriz, also on the Rio Toncantins, Carolina is set in an area of spectacular waterfalls and mountain scenery. Near to the **Cachoeira da Prata**, on the Rio Farinha, is **Morro das Figuras**, which has rock inscriptions. Access is by unmade road from the BR-230, requiring a 4WD. Some 35 km south of Carolina, on the road to Estreito, is **Cachoeria de Pedra Caída**. For tourist information, **Secretaria de Turismo**, ⓘ *R Duque de Caxias 522, T7311613, Mon-Fri 0800-1300*.

Sleeping

Teresina *p529, map p530, phone code 086*

L **Rio Poty**, Av Mcal Castelo Branco 555, Ilhota, T2231500, F2226671. 5-star. Recommended.

A **Real Pálace**, R Lizandro Nogueira 1208, T2212768, F2217740. A/c, pool, restaurant.

A **São José**, João Cabral 340, T2232176, F2232223. Reasonable restaurant.

B **Royal Pálace**, R 13 de Maio 233N, T/F2217707. A/c, restaurant.

B **Sambaíba**, R Gabriel Ferreira 230-N, T2226711. 2-star, central, good.

D **Fortaleza**, Felix Pacheco 1101, Praça Saraiva, T2222984. Fan, basic. Recommended.

D **Santa Terezinha**, Av Getúlio Vargas 2885, opposite rodoviária, T2195918. With a/c or fan, clean, friendly. Many other cheap hotels and *dormitórios* around Praça Saraiva.

D **Grande**, Firmino Pires 73. Very friendly and clean. Many cheap ones in R São Pedro and in R Alvaro Mendes.

D **Glória**, at 823 (clean, best), blocks 800 and 900 on each street.

Parque Nacional de Sete Cidades *p530, phone code 086*

Piripiri, 26 km from the park, is a cheap place to break the Belém-Fortaleza journey. As well as those listed, there are other options near bus offices and behind the church.

B **Hotel Sete Cidades**, Km 63 on BR-222, 6 km from the park entrance, T086-2762222. Chalets with private bath, swimming pool, good restaurant and bicycle or horse transport; also has a free pick-up to the park (and a most unpleasant zoo).

E **Ibama hostel**, in the park, T3431342. Price per person. Rooms with bath, pleasant, good restaurant, natural pool nearby, camping. Recommended.

E **Novo Hotel Central**, town centre, Piripiri. With fan, bath, breakfast and safe parking, friendly. Recommended.

Parnaíba and around *p531, phone code 086*

L **Cívico**, Av Gov Chagas Rodrigues 474, Parnaíba, T3222470, F3222028. Restaurant, pool, good breakfast. Recommended.

A **Pousada dos Ventos**, Av São Sebastião 2586, Universidade, Parnaíba, T3222177, F3224880. Pool. Recommended.

A **Rio Poty Praia**, Av dos Magistrados 2350, Luís Correia, T/F3671277, bar, restaurant, pool.

D **Rodoviária**, and other basic hotels in the centre of Parnaíba.

São Luís *p532, map p533, phone code 098*

AL **La Ravadière**, Av Mcal Castelo Branco 375, São Francisco, T2352255, F2352217. Pool, restaurant, sauna.

AL-A **Praia Mar**, Av São Marcos, Ponta d'Areia, on the beach, T2352328.

B **Deodoro**, R de Santaninha 535, T2315811. A/c, parking, good.

B **Ponta D'Areia**, Av dos Holandeses, Ponta D'Areia, T2353232, F2272892. Pool.

B **Pousada Colonial**, R Afonso Pena 112, T2322834. In a beautiful restored, tiled house. Recommended.

B **São Marcos**, R da Saúde 178, T2323768, F2317777. Restored colonial house, a/c, family-run. Recommended.

B **Vila Rica**, Praça Dom Pedro II 299, T2323535, www.hotelvilarica.com.br Central, pool, business centre with internet connection. Recommended.

C **Lord**, R de Nazaré 258, facing Praça Benedito Leite, T/F2214655. A/c, comfortable, good value, good breakfast. Recommended.

D **Hotel Casa Grande**, R Isaac Martins 94, Centro, T2322432. Clean, basic, single, double or triple rooms. Recommended.

D **Pousada Solar dos Nobres**, R 13 de Maio 82, Centro, T2325705. Bright, welcoming, superb breakfast, very good.

D **Pousada Turismo Jansen Müller**, R Jansen Müller 270, T2310997. With breakfast and bath.

E-F **Dois Continentes**, R 28 de Julho 129, Praia Grande, T/F222 6286. Family run youth hostel.

E-F **Solar das Pedras**, R da Palma 127, T/F2326694. Youth hostel.

G **Pousada Ilha Bela**, R Formosa. Safe.

Many cheap hotels can be found in R das Palmas, very central, and R Formosa.

Excursions from São Luís *p534, phone code 098*

In **Raposa**, there are a few places to stay on Av Principal.

C **Hotel Sol e Mar**, Av Gonçalves Dias 320, São José de Ribamar, with a restaurant.

Alcântara *p534, map p534, phone code 098*
B **Pousada dos Guarás**, Praia da Baronesa, T3371339. Bungalows with bath, good restaurant, canoe hire.
C **Pousada do Mordomo Régio**, R Grande 134, T3371197. TV, fridge, good restaurant.
D **Pousada Pelourinho**, Praça da Matriz 55, T3371257. Breakfast, good restaurant, shared bathroom. Recommended.
E **Pousada da Josefa**, R Direita, T3371109. Restaurant. Ask for hammock space or rooms in private houses, friendly but no great comfort, provide your own mineral water.

Parque Nacional Lençóis Maranhenses *p535, phone code 098*
There are *pousadas* and restaurants at Rio Novo and Paulino Neves, in Tutóia.
C **Tutóia Palace Hotel**, Av Paulino Neves 1100, Tutóia, T4791247. Crumbling mock colonial hotel in garish pink with 12 fading rooms, 5 of which have a/c.
D **Pousada Em-Bar-Cação**, R Magalhães de Almeida 1064, T4791219, on the beach. Breakfast US$3, friendly, good food and *tiquira*, a drink made of manioc.
D **Pousada do Baiano**, R Col Godinho, Barreirinhas, T3491110. Many others.
D **Pousada Lins**, Av Joaquim Soeiro de Carvalho, Barreirinhas, T3491203. Restaurant, good, but shop around before taking their tours.

The Parnaíba delta *p535, phone code 086*
AL **Pousada Ecológica Ilha do Caju**, contact address: Av Presidente Vargas 235, Centro, 64-200-200, Parnaíba, Piauí, T3222380, F3211308, helpful, welcoming staff; the owner, Ingrid, and senior staff speak English. Children must be aged 12 or over.
The *pousada* is an attractive converted farmhouse with thatched guesthouses in the grounds; each has its own hammock outside, but inside there is a huge bed, handmade by the same craftsmen who made much of the *pousada's* highly individual furniture.

Imperatriz *p536, phone code 098*
There are many cheap hotels near the rodoviária.
A **Posseidon**, R Paraíba 740, T7232323. Central, best, pool. Recommended.
A **Imperatriz Park**, BR-010, Km 1347, opposite rodoviária, T7232950. Pool.

Carolina *p536, phone code 098*
Pousada Pedra Caída, BR-010 Km 30, T7311318. Chalets with fan, restaurant, natural pool and 3 waterfalls.
Pousada do Rio Lages, BR-230 Km 2, T7311499. Chalets with a/c. **Cafuné**, BR-230 Km 2. Local food.

Eating

Teresina *p529, map p530, phone code 086*
There are many places for all budgets in Praça Dom Pedro II.
TTT **Camarão do Elias**, Av Pedro Almeida 457, T2325025. Best restaurant in the city, with fish and prawn dishes. Try the Fish of the day in caper and lemon sauce.
TT Pesqueirinho, R Domingos Jorge Velho 6889, in Poty Velho district, T2252268. Excellent fish restaurant on the river bank.
T **Sabores Rotisserie**, R Simplício Mendes 78, Centro. By the kg, good quality and variety.

Parnaíba and around *p531*
T **Recanto Gaúcho**, Trav Costa Fernandes, next to university, *churrasco*.
T **Renatinho**, Av das Nações Unidas, Beira Rio. Crab and seafood.
T **Sorveteria Araújo**, R Pires Ferreira 615. Good ice-cream from local fruits.

São Luís *p532, map p532*
Bases are good for home cooking in simple surroundings, although most are found away from the centre and beaches.Typical dishes are *arroz de cuxá* and *torta de camarão*. Desserts and liquors are made from local fruits. Try the local soft drink called *Jesús* or *Jenève*.
TT **Base do Edilson**, R Joao Damasceno 21, Ponta do Farol. Excellent for prawns.
TT **Base do Germano**, Av Venceslau Brás, Camboa. Excellent *caldeirada de camarão* (shrimp stew).
T **Beiruth 2**, Av Mcal Castelo Branco 751B. Recommended.
T **Naturalista Alimentos**, R do Sol 517. Very good, natural food shops and restaurants, open till 1900.
T **Base da Lenoca**, Av Dom Pedro II 181. Good view, big portions.

Senac, R Nazaré 242, next to hotel **Lord**. Tourism school restaurant, good food in a beautifully restored mansion.
Tia Maria, Av Nina Rodrigues 1, Ponta d'Areia. Recommended for fried fish with *castanha* and *caju*.

Alcântara *p534, map p534*
Bar do Lobato, Praça da Matriz. Pleasant with good, simple food, fried shrimps highly recommended.

Imperatriz *p536*
Fogão Mineiro, Av Getúlio Vargas 2234. Minas Gerais wood oven cooking with a range of heavy, meaty dishes and side vegetables like squash.
Rafaello Grill, in Imperatriz Shopping, Av Dorgival Pinheiro Sousa 1400. Self-service. Modest *churrascaria* with a reasonable choice of side dishes.

Bars and clubs

Teresina *p529, map p530*
Centro Cultural Porto das Barcas, a pleasant shopping and entertainment complex with several good restaurants and a large open-air bar on the riverside.

São Luís *p532, map p533*
Antigamente, Praia Grande, live music Thu-Sat.
Poeme-Sei, R João Gualberto 52, Praia Grande, is a bar/gallery open in the evening, good atmosphere, no food.
Senac (see Eating, above). Piano bar Thu-Sat.
Tombo da Ladeira, Praia Grande, good for reggae on Wed.
Coqueiro Bar, Av dos Holandeses, Praia da Ponta D'Areia. Reggae on Thu.
Extravagance, Av Conselheiro Hilton Rodrigues, Calhau. A good nightclub.

Imperatriz *p536*
Fly Back Disco Club, Beira Rio, north of the ferry crossing. Two dance floors, one fast, one slow (for couples only), good.

Entertainment

São Luís *p532, map p533, phone code 098*
Cinema **Colossal**, Av Mcal Castelo Branco 92, São Francisco. **Passeio**, R Oswaldo Cruz 806. **Theatre** **Teatro Artur Azevedo**, see Sights above. **Teatro Viriato Correa**, Av Getúlio Vargas, Monte Castelo, T2189019.

Festivals and events

Teresina *p529, map p530*
Feb/Mar Teresina is proud of its **Carnival**, which is then followed by **Micarina**, a local carnival in Mar.
Jul/Aug Much music and dancing at the **Bumba-meu-Boi**, a Teresina dance festival, **Festidanças**, and a convention of **itinerant** guitarists.

São Luís *p532, map p533*
24 Jun (São João) is the **Bumba-Meu-Boi**, see box, above. For several days before the festival street bands parade, particularly in front of the São João and São Benedito churches. There are dances somewhere in the city almost every night in Jun.
Aug São Benedito, at the Rosário church.
Oct Festival with dancing, at Vila Palmeira suburb (take bus of same name).

Alcântara *p534*
Festa do Divino, at Pentecost (Whitsun).
29 Jun São Pedro
early **Aug**, **São Benedito**.

Shopping

Teresina *p529, map p530*
Crafts Teresina is an excellent and cheap source of northeastern *artesanato*, for which Piauí is renowned throughout Brazil. Panels of carved and painted hardwood, either representing stylized country scenes or of religious significance, are a good buy, as are clay or wooden models of traditional rural characters. Many of these eccentric figures come from the region's rich fund of myths and legends. Hammocks, straw and basket ware are also varied, interesting and well made here. Other local handicrafts include leather and clothes.
Supermarket Praça Mcal Deodoro 937, clean, good, fresh food.

Parnaíba and around *p531*
Crafts **Artesanato de Parnaíba**, R Dom Pedro II 1140 and **Cooperativa Artesanal Mista de Parnaíba**, R Alcenor Candeira, for local handicrafts.

Bumba-Meu-Boi

Throughout the month of June the streets of São Luís are alive to the sound of tambores and dancers recreating the legend of Catirina, Pai Francisco and his master's bull. Although this mixture of African, indigenous and Portuguese traditions exists throughout the North it is in Maranhão that it is most developed with around 100 groups in São Luís alone. Here there are various styles called *sotaques*, which have different costumes, dances, instruments and *toadas*. These are **Boi de Matraca da Ilha** and **Boi de Pindaré**, both accompanied by small percussion instruments called *matracas*, **Boi de Zabumba** marked by the use of a type of drum, and **Boi de Orquestra** accompanied by string and wind instruments. Although there are presentations throughout June the highpoints are the 24th (São João) and the 29th (São Pedro) with the closing ceremony lasting throughout the 30th (São Marçal), particularly in the *bairro* João Paulo. The shows take place in an *arraial*, which are found all over the city, with the ones at **Projeto Reviver** and **Ceprama** being more geared towards tourists (however be aware that a livelier more authentic atmosphere is to be found elsewhere in other *bairros*, such as Madre Deus). The **Centro de Cultura Popular Domingos Vieira Filho** at Rua do Giz 221, Praia Grande is the place to learn more about these variations as well as many other local festivals and traditions such as **Tambor de Crioula or Cacuriá**, both sensual dances derived from Africa. A good location to see these dances and *capoeira* practised is *Labouarte*, Rua Jansen Muller, Centro (Cacuriá de Dona Tetê is particularly recommended with participation encouraged).

São Luís *p532, map p533*

Crafts **Ceprama**, R de São Pantaleão 1232, Madre Deus, handicraft shops in an old colonial house.

Activities and tours

São Luís *p532, map p533, phone code 098*

Sport centres

Parque do Bom Menino, Av Jaime Tavares, has a running track and sports courts.

Vida e Sade, R Rio Branco 174. Gym.

São Francisco, Av Mcal Castelo Branco 120. Gym.

Tour operators

Taguatur, R do Sol 141, loja 15, T2320906, F2321814.

Babaçu Viagens, Av Dom Pedro II 258, lojas A/B/C, T/F2314747, good.

Parque Nacional Lençóis Maranhenses *p535, phone code 098*

Tour operators

Ribamar at Ibama, Av Jaime Tavares 25, São Luís, T2223066/3006, is helpful on walks and horse rides along lesser routes; other **Ibama** address, Av Alexandre Mowa 25, Centro, T2313010, F2314332.

Agencies in São Luís are **Nasaturismo**, T2354429; **Baluz Turismo**, T2226658; **Jaguarema**, T2224764; **Sunset Turismo** at the airport; **Maratur**, T2211231. At Barreirinhas, **Pousada Lins** (see p538); **Parna Lençóis Maranhenses**, director Sr Edson; **Pocof Barreirinhas**, director José de Ribamar Santos Silva, both at R Cazuza Ramos 3, T3491155.

Transport

Teresina *p529, map p530*

Air Flights to Fortaleza, Brasília, Rio de Janeiro, São Paulo, Goiânia, São Luís. Outside the airport, buses run straight into town and to the rodoviária.

Bus The bus trip to **Fortaleza** is scenic and takes 9 hrs (US$13.50). There are direct buses to **Belém** (13 hrs, US$23.40), **Recife** (16 hrs, US$27) and **São Luís** (7 hrs, US$12).

Parque Nacional de Sete Cidades *p530*
Bus A free bus service leaves the Praça da Bandeira in Piripiri (in front of Telemar office), at 0700, passing Hotel Fazenda Sete Cidades at 0800, reaching the park 10 mins later; return at 1630, or hitchhike.
Taxi From Piripiri, US$15, or from Piracuruca, US$20. Bus Teresina-Piripiri and return, throughout the day 2½ hrs, US$4. Bus São Luís-Piripiri, 1200, 1630, 2130, 10 hrs, US$15. Several daily buses Piripiri-Fortaleza, 9 hrs, US$11. Bus Piripiri-Ubajara marked 'São Benedito', or 'Crateús', 2½ hrs; US$4, first at 0700 (a beautiful trip).

Parque Nacional Serra da Capivara *p531*
Car Access is from São Raimundo Nonato on the BR-324, or from Petrolina in Pernambuco (the nearest airport, 290 km away).

Taxi From Petrolina airport will cost about US$200 one way, or there are buses.

São Luís *p532, map p533, phone code 098*
Air Marechal Cunha Machado airport, 15 km from centre, Av Santos Dumont, T2451688. Flights to Belém, Fortaleza, Imperatriz, Parnaíba and Teresina. **São Cristovão** buses to city until midnight, US$0.75. Taxi to city US$12.50.

Airline offices TAM, T2440461. **Transbrasil**, Praça João Lisboa 432, T2321414. **Varig/Nordeste**, Av Dom Pedro II 267, T2315066. **Vasp**, R do Sol 43, T2314422.

Bus Rodoviária is 12 km from the centre on the airport road, 'Rodoviária via Alemanha' bus to centre (Praça João Lisboa), US$0.50. To **Fortaleza**, US$270, 4 a day, 18 hrs. To **Belém**, 13 hrs, US$20, **Transbrasiliana** at 1900 and 2000 (no *leito*). Also to **Recife**, US$45, 25 hrs, all other major cities and local towns.

Ferry These cross the bay daily from Porto do Itaqui to Porto do Cujupe. T2228431 for times. US$3 foot passenger, US$15 car.

Trains 3 trains a week on the Carajás railway to **Parauapebas**, 13½ hrs, 890 km, leave São Luís 0800, Mon, Wed, Fri, return 0800, Tue, Thu, Sat (crowded, take your own food). For the station take 'Vila Nova' or 'Anjo da Guarda' bus.

Alcântara *p534, map p534, phone code 098*
Boat Lancha Diamantina leaves São Luís dock at about 0700 and 0930, returning from Alcântara about 0815 and 1615: check time and buy the ticket at the *hidroviária*, west end of R Portugal, T2320692, the day before as departure depends on the tides. The journey takes 90 mins, return US$15. The sea can be very rough between Sep and Dec. Old wooden boats, the *Newton Bello* and *Mensageiro da Fé*, leave São Luís at 0630 and 1600, returning at 0730 (1½ hrs, US$5 return). There are sometimes catamaran tours bookable through tour operators in São Luís, meals not included.

Parque Nacional Lençóis Maranhenses *p535, phone code 098*
Boat Excursions from/to Barreirinhas: regular boat service between Barreirinhas and Atins (7 hrs return, US$5): boat along Rio Preguiça, 4 hrs then 1 hr's walk to the dunes, US$12. Highly recommended.

Speedboats charge about US$100 for 5 people, from Claúdio, T5491183, or Sr Carlos, T3491203. They also have a Kombi, US$150 for up to 15 people.
Bus Parnaíba-Tutóia: bus, 4 hrs, US$6; river boat up the Parnaíba delta, 8 hrs, US$6. Recommended. Private boat hire is also possible. São Luís-Barreirinhas: bus, 8 hrs on an awful road, US$12; private tour buses, US$24, are more comfortable but cannot improve the road, organized bus tours cost US$72.50; plane (single propeller), 1 hr, US$75. Recommended. A fabulous experience, giving panoramic views of the dunes, pilot Amirton, T2252882. Agencies charge about US$200 for a tour with flight.

Other The only forms of transport that can get across the dunes right into the park are a jeep or a horse, both about US$15. It is a 2- to 3-hr walk from Barreirinhas to the park; you will need at least another 2 hrs in the dunes. At Mandacuru, a popular stop on tours of the area, the lighthouse gives an impressive view.

Imperatriz *p536, phone code 098*
Air Airport, T7224666. Flights to Altamira, Araguaína, Belém, Brasília and São Luís. **Air taxi**: Heringer, at airport, T7223009. **Airline offices** Penta, R Luís Domingues 1420, T7231073. TAM, R Ceará 678, T7223148. Varig/RioSul, R Luís Domingues 1471, T7232155.

Bus Bus station, R Lias Barros, Nova Carolina, T7311195. Lying on the BR-010 **Belém-Brasília** highway, Imperatriz has bus connections with both cities; there is a slow, crowded bus service to **Teresina**. To get to **Marabá** on the Transamazônica, you can either take a **Transbrasiliana** bus direct, 7-10 hrs (starting on the Belém highway, the bus then turns west along a poorer road, passing finally through destroyed forest, new *fazendas* and unplanned cities), or a faster route, involving taking a ferry across the river in the early morning (0600-0700) to catch a pick-up on the other side, takes about 5 hrs, but is more expensive. To get to the ferry across the river, go along R Luís Domingues, which runs parallel to Av Getúlio Vargas.

Car hire Interlocadora, Av Dorgival Pinheiro de Souza 990, T7223050. **Localiza**, BR-010, Setor rodoviária, T7214507, and at airport, T7218611.

Train Station, T7232260. Trains to Pará and other towns in Maranhão.

Directory

Teresina *p529, map p530, phone code 086*
Banks Banks with ATMs **Banco do Brasil** and **Unibanco**, Av Nossa Senhora de Fátima, in front of Caixa Econômica Federal. **Itaú**, in same avenue at P Center Shopping. Bradesco, Av Frei Serafim, at corner of 1 de Maio. **Mirante Câmbio**, Av Frei Serafim 2150, T2233633. **Alda Tur**, R A de Abreu 1226.

Parnaíba and around *p531, phone code 086*
Banks Banco do Brasil, Praça da Graça 340. Bradesco, Av Pres Getúlio Vargas 403. **Medical services** Pró-Médica, Av Pres Vargas 799, T3223645. 24-hr emergency ward. **Post office** Praça da Graça. **Telephone** Av Pres Getúlio Vargas 390.

São Luís *p532, map p533, phone code 098*
Banks Banco do Brasil, Praça Deodoro, for TCs and Visa ATMs. HSBC, off Praça João Lisboa. Accepts MasterCard/Cirrus/Maestro. Agetur, R do Sol 33A. **Embassies and consulates** Denmark, Av Colares Moreira 444, Monumental Shopping, Sala 220, T2357033. **France**, R Santo Antônio 259, T2314459. **Germany**, Praça Gonçalves Dias 301, T2327766. **Italy**, R do Genipapeiro, Jardim São Francisco, T2270270. **Spain**, Praça Duque de Caxias 3, João Paulo, T2232846. USA, Av Daniel de La Touche, Jardim Buriti, T2481769. **Internet** HCG, R Paparaúbas 11, São Francisco. **Language courses** Senhora Amin Castro, T2271527, for Portuguese lessons. Recommended. **Laundry** Nova China, R da Paz 518. **Libraries** Arquivo Público, R de Nazaré 218, rare documents on local history. **Medical services** Clínica São Marcelo, R do Passeio 546, English-speaking doctor. Hospital Monte Sinai, R Rio Branco 156, T2323260, 24 hrs. **Post office** Praça João Lisboa 292. **Telephone** Embratel, Av Dom Pedro II 190.

Alcântara *p534, map p534*
Banks Banco do Estado do Maranhão, R Grande 76, exchanges US$ cash and TCs. **Post office** R Direita off Praça da Matriz. **Telephone** Telemar, R Grande, daily 0700-2200.

Imperatriz *p536, phone code 098*
Banks Banco do Brasil, Av Getúlio Vargas 1935. **Medical services** Santa Mônica, R Piauí, T7223415, 24 hrs emergency ward. **Security** The town can be quite a rough place and it is wise to exercise caution, especially at night. **Telephone** R Rio Grande do Norte 740, a side street off Av Getúlio Vargas, near Hotel Posseidon, 0630-2400.

Carolina *p536, phone code 098*
Banks Banco do Brasil, A Mascarenhas 159. **Medical services** FNS, R Benedito Leite 57, T7311271. **Telephone** Av E Barros, 0730-2230.

The Amazon

Footprint features

Introduction

The Amazon is a region of great geographical diversity. To the north, along the border with Venezuela, are the forests and savannahs of the Guiana shield, the ancient heart of the South American continent covered in a forest which grows like a giant filigree over white sand and recycles 99.9% of all its water and nutrients. Giant boulders the size of mountains break intermittently through the canopy. To the east lie the expansive Amazon savannahs, which stretch across Roraima and southern Venezuela into the Rupununi of Guyana. The world's largest table-top mountains tower over them, their brows heavy with perpetual thunder cloud. Further south the Amazon pours out into the ocean leaving an island of silt the size of Denmark in its wake and turning the Atlantic fresh for 100 miles offshore. The forest gets thicker and more vibrant and the mud on which it grows is as red and sticky as blood. To the east it is gentler and more fertile; filled with life around the magical Rio Javarí, where the trees seem permanently full of parrots, macaws and monkeys and where grey and pink dolphins surface from the deep, languid brown. In the south the trees are broken by the squares of giant fields which cut into the green with greedy geometric order, and the Amazon exists as mere segments.

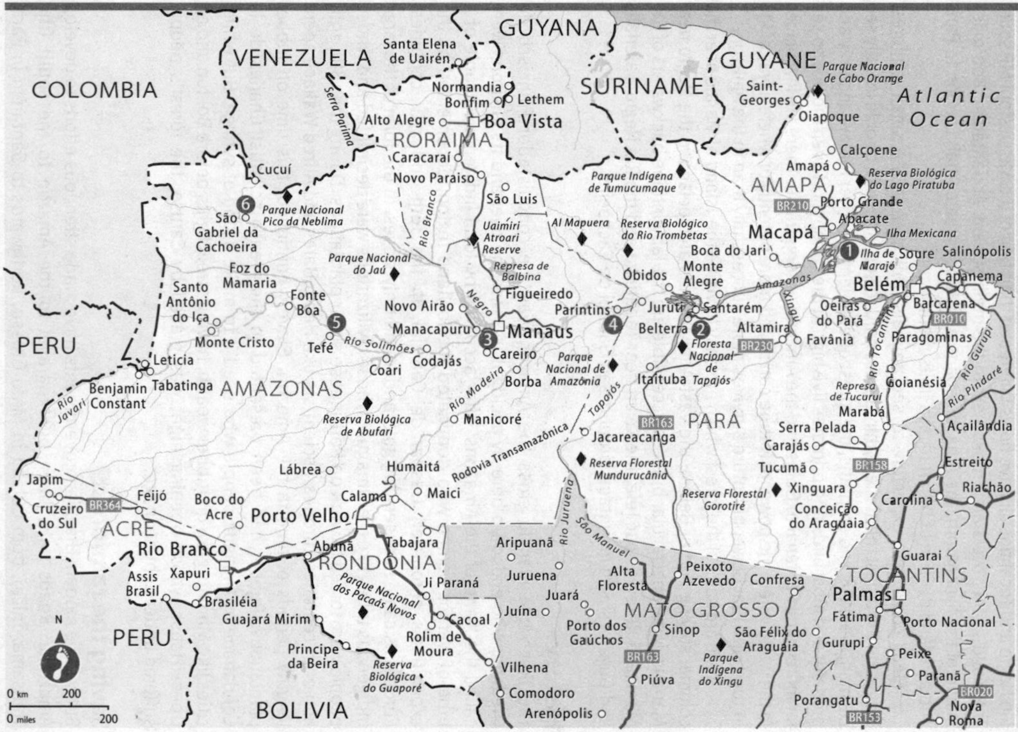

★ Don't miss...

1. **Ilha de Marajó** Primeval forests filled with escaped buffalo, on a country-sized island in the mouth of the Amazon, page 559.
2. **Alter do Chão, Santarem** White sand, blue water and pink dolphins at a river junction as wide as the distance between London and Paris, page 572.
3. **The meeting of the waters** Where the coffee with milk Amazon flows alongside the black tea Negro for kilometres without mixing, page 578.
4. **Boi Bumba festival in Parintins** Brazil's largest and most colourful after Carnaval. And just as wild, page 582.
5. **Mamirauá wetland reserve near Tefé** One of the best spots in the Amazon for wildlife, page 582.
6. **São Gabriel da Cachoeira** A tiny town filled with glorious white-sand beaches nestled under a vast rock on the edge of the Rio Negro, page 586.

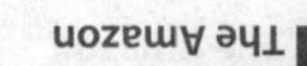

The Amazon

Many who visit the Amazon imagine it as a single river. It is not; it is many. Before there were mountains to the west, the Amazon flowed into the Pacific. But the crash of continental plates which produced the Andes some 15 million years ago cut the river off from its ocean and the ancient Amazon became a vast inland sea. Over millions of years this sea eroded the ancient sandstone of the Guiana Shield which hemmed it in at the east until it burst through in the Piocene, spilling into the Atlantic. The sea left behind a vast filigree of veins which today make up the Amazon river system, populated by prehistoric air breathing fish and unique freshwater species like Amazon stingray, whose closest relatives still live in the Pacific. A third of the world's fresh running water flows through this system along a rainbow of tributaries whose colours range from vodka clear and tea black to coffee with milk and opaque aquamarine sprinkled with brilliant pink blind dolphins. Many dwarf the world's other rivers. The Madeira, Tapajos, Rio Negro and Tocantins all have flows far greater than that of the Mississippi Missouri. The world's other rivers are brooks next to the main stream. At Santarem, 800 miles inland of the river mouth, the Amazon spans a distance greater than London to Paris and an island the size of Denmark sits in its mouth.

Many come here expecting to see animals. But even in the small rainforest lodges on the tiniest tributaries, animals are hard to see. Although people usually see cayman, monkeys and dolphins, the forest offers plenty of cover for lowland prey and predator and most birds and primates live high in the canopy. Yet even those who see far more in the Pantanal or Goiás find the Amazon unforgettable. There are few places in the world where the power of Nature can be felt more potently or where a way of life in tune with that power of Nature survives more successfully than in the Amazon.

There are parts of the forest which are easy to visit – the island of Marajó near the colonial slaving port of Belém; the vast Analvilhanas archipelago in the Negro near Manaus. More spectacular but less accessible are the labyrinthine backwaters of the Mamirauá Reserve near Tefé, the Javari near Tabatinga and the Rio Negro waterfalls and Guyana shield mountains around São Gabriel da Cachoeira.

History

The first white man to cross the Amazon was the conquistador Francisco de Orellana, who ended up here by accident in 1541. The river and its environs were called the 'Land of the Amazons' after accounts by local indigenous people of a tribe of warrior women who dominated the lowland region, documented by the expedition's chronicler, Gaspar de Carvajal. In the 16th and 17th centuries, Europeans came here seeking gold and found only slaves, in the form of the large indigenous tribes like the Omagua, whose civilizations were decimated and whose people were forced to work on Portuguese sugar plantations. During the 18th, 19th and 20th centuries European scientists like Henry Bates and Alfred Wallace spent lengthy periods of time in the Amazon. Slavery continued, this time on rubber plantations. Rubber had been presented to the French scientist Charles de la Condamine by Omagua people who used it to make a kind of syringe. But whilst cities like Manaus grew on rubber wealth, having street lights before Boston and an Opera House whose opening night was graced by Caruso, the forest's people suffered under debt peonage.

Saving the rainforest?

Successive modern Brazilian governments have made strenuous efforts to develop Amazônia. Roads have been built parallel to the Amazon to the south (the Transamazônica), from Cuiabá in Mato Grosso, northwards to Santarém in Pará,

“” ...colours range from vodka clear and tea black to coffee with milk and opaque aquamarine sprinkled with brilliant pink blind dolphins.

and northeast from Porto Velho through Humaitá to the river bank opposite Manaus. Unsuccessful attempts were made to establish agricultural settlements along these roads; major energy and mining projects for bauxite and iron ore are bringing rapid change.

More environmental damage has been caused to the region by gold prospectors (*garimpeiros*), especially by their indiscriminate use of mercury, than by organized mining carried out by large state and private companies using modern extraction methods. The most important cause of destruction, however, has been large-scale deforestation to make way for soya plantations,cattle ranching and to provide hardwoods for the Asian markets.

It is estimated that 600,000 sq km, an area the size of France, has now been shed of its forest cover, with more destruction occurring in the last three decades than in the last four centuries. To make a more regional comparison, an area the size of the state of Sergipe is lost every year to the chainsaw and match. A lot of the destruction occurred in the 1980s. It slowed down in the early 1990s, but with the recovery of the Brazilian economy and very dry weather in the mid-1990s the destruction sped up again.

Areas like the Xingu forests now sit islands of soya and beef cattle pasture, protected only because they belon to indigenous people. For Brazil's Indians and their colleagues like the Vilas Boas brothers and British explorer and co-founder of Survival, John Hemming have done more than any other national or international group to preserve the forest. Some maps, for instance, show a road north of the Amazon, marked Perimetro (or Perimetral) Norte; this road does not exist, never has and probably never will, thanks to the courageous and spirited campaigns of the people of the Upper Rio Negro.

There is a gradually growing awareness of the importance of the country's indigenous people among Brazilians. A recent survey by one of the country's largest magazines showed that the overwhelming majority of Brazilians believed that these indigenous people were good custodians of the forest. Brazilians also seem increasingly aware that their northern hinterland is a unique treasure and requires some form of protection, anz some encouraging moves have been made. At the end of 1997 the **Amanã Sustainable Development Reserve** (SDR) was set up, linking two other reserves to form the world's largest protected rainforest area. The Amanã SDR surrounds Lake Amanã north of Tefé and covers 23,500 sq km. It is sandwiched between the Jaú National Park to the east and the Mamirauá SDR to the west, forming a 640-km long corridor. It is hoped that whole ecosystems will be preserved and that local inhabitants will be able to find sustainable work in the reserve's management.

But there is a long way to go. Lula has been stringently criticized by the confederation of Amazon Indians for his policy towards them and has failed to demark a key reserve in Roraima, preferring to cut a deal with local politicians for political support. And deforestation in 2003 was at an all time high thanks to his failure to curb illegal deforestation by soya and cattle ranchers. Ecotourism, although far more primitive in Brazil than in Peru or Bolivia greatly contributes to a positive view of the value of forest among local people.

Anyone interested in indigenous peoples and the Amazonian development programme and its ecological, social, economic and political effects should read John

A voice from the Amazon

Humanity finds itself at a critical point. Can Science solve the mounting problems which confront us in every corner of globe?

Soon after human beings lost themselves to the blind, unconscious forces of systematic self-interest and greed, we, the Indians found ourselves robbed both of what lay buried beneath our lands of our lands themselves.

Thankfully, through the power of memory our history has been preserved, continues, and is passed on from generation to generation. Thankfully, the memory of Indians cannot be blotted out so easily.

We Indians have the power to see the truth behind history. Just as we have cures for those abounding problems which then, as now are the consequence of systematic self-interest and greed.

The United Nations have not succeeded in bringing peace to our world. This is because wars do not begin with nations. They begin inside each and every one of us. What we must do, and with urgency, is to re-integrate humankind with its spiritual leaders and with them bring about a cure in the interior life and the repayment of our interior debts.

In much of the world tourism continues a destructive path without thinking of the consequences of its actions for future generations. But whilst this is happening there are many individual tourists who after speaking with true spiritual masters and shamans find truth and a solution to eternal problems.

Manoel Fernandes Moura, head of FIUPAM an organization seeking to unite indigenous spiritual leaders from around the world and based in Tabatinga in the Amazon is one of the leading indigenous rights' campaigners of his generation. He was instrumental in helping to halt the Calha Norte northern perimeter road project in Roraima and Amazonas states. Moura is the seventh son of seven generations of shamans. FIUPAM, fiupam@yahoo.co.uk; T/F97-4124484.

Hemming's *Die If You Must*; Richard Bourne's masterly *Assault on the Amazon* (London, Gollancz, 1978); *Dreams of Amazonia*, by Roger D Stone (Penguin, 1986); or *Amazon*, by Brian Kelly and Mark London (Harcourt Brace Jovanovich, New York, 1983). *The Fate of the Forest*, by Suzanne Hecht and Alexander Cockburn (Penguin, 1991), has also been recommended.

Geography and climate

Brazilian Amazônia, much of it still covered with tropical forest, is 56% of the national area. Its jungle is the world's largest and densest rain forest, with more diverse plants and animals than any other jungle in the world. It has only 8% of Brazil's population, and most of this is concentrated around Belém (in Pará), and in Manaus, 1,600 km up the river. The population is sparse because other areas are easier to develop.

The rainfall is heavy, but varies throughout the region; close to the Andes, up to 4,000 mm fall annually, at Manaus it's under 2,000 mm. Rains occur throughout the year, but the wettest season is between December and May; the driest month is October. The humidity can be extremely high and the temperature averages 26°C. There can be cold snaps in December in the western reaches of the Amazon basin. The soil, as in all tropical forest, is poor.

River transport

Although air services are widespread throughout the region and road transport is gradually increasing, rivers remain the arteries of Amazônia for the transport of both passengers and merchandise. The two great ports of the region are Belém, at the mouth of the Amazon, and Manaus at the confluence of the Rio Negro and Rio Solimões. Manaus is the hub of river transport, with regular shipping services east to Santarém and Belém along the lower Amazon, south to Porto Velho along the Rio Madeira, west to Tabatinga (the border with Colombia and Peru) along the Rio Solimões, northwest to São Gabriel da Cachoeira along the Rio Negro, and more sporadically north to Caracaraí (for Boa Vista) along the Rio Branco. There is also a regular service connecting Belém and Macapá (on the northern shore of the Amazon delta), Santarém and Macapá, as well as Santarém and Itaituba, south along the Rio Tapajós. All of the above services call at intermediate ports and virtually every village has some form of river boat service.

The size and quality of vessels varies greatly, with the largest and most comfortable ships generally operating on the Manaus-Belém route. Hygiene, food and service are reasonable on most vessels, but overcrowding can be a problem. Most boats have some sort of rooftop bar serving expensive drinks and snacks.

Types of tickets

Many of the larger ships offer air-conditioned berths with bunkbeds and, for a higher price, 'suites', with a private bathroom (in some cases, this may also mean a double bed instead of the standard bunkbed). The cheapest way to travel is 'hammock class'; on some routes first class (upper deck) and second class (lower deck) hammock space is available, but on many routes this distinction does not apply. Although the idea of swinging in a hammock may sound romantic, the reality is you will probably be squeezed in with other passengers, possibly next to the toilets, have difficulty sleeping due to noise and end up with an aching back.

River boat travel is no substitute for visiting the jungle. Except for a few birds and the occasional dolphin, little wildlife is seen. However, it does offer an insight into the vastness of Amazônia and a chance to meet some of its people, making a very pleasant experience.

Choosing a river boat

The vessels operate on a particular route and their schedules are frequently changing; it is generally not possible to book far in advance. Extensive local inquiry and some flexibility in your schedule are indispensable for river travel. Agencies on shore can inform you of the arrival and departure dates for several different ships, as well as the official (highest) prices for each; they are sometimes amenable to bargaining. Whenever possible, however, see the vessel yourself (it may mean a journey out of town) and have a chat with the captain or business manager to confirm departure date and time, length of voyage, ports of call, price, etc. Inspect cleanliness in the kitchen, toilets and showers. All boats are cleaned up when in port, but if a vessel is reasonably clean upon arrival then chances are that it has been kept that way throughout the voyage. You can generally arrange to sleep on board a day or two before departure and after arrival, but be sure to secure your belongings carefully when in port. If you take a berth, lock it and keep the key even if you will not be moving in right away. If you are travelling hammock class, board ship at least six to eight hours before sailing in order to secure a good spot (away from the toilets and the engine and check for leaks in the deck above you). Be firm but considerate of your neighbours as they will be your intimate companions for the duration of the voyage. Always keep your gear locked. Take some light warm clothing, it can get very chilly at night.

Refer to the appropriate city sections for details of port facilities in each.

The Amazon and the Theory of Evolution

Whilst the Spanish and Portuguese came to the Amazon to plunder, pillage and enslave, the Europeans who proceeded them in the 18th and 19th centuries were more interested in beetles and botany than gold. Among the first was the Frenchman Charles Marie de la Condamine, who came to the Andes in the mid-1700s to ascertain whether the Earth was orange shaped or a perfect sphere and narrowly escaped being stoned by a superstitious mob in Cuenca, Ecuador. He fled for Cayenne and in doing so was obliged to cross the Amazon, producing the first accurate map of the basin along the way and bringing rubber back to Europe. La Condamine inspired other Enlightenment scientists to follow him. The greatest was Alexander von Humboldt, today known for the Humboldt current which he did not discover and the Humboldt River which he never saw, but in his time considred the pre-eminent scientist in Europe. During his stay on the upper Rio Negro, this great German collected some 12,000 specimens and survived shocks by electric eels, *curaré* poison and bathing with piranhas. He captured and dissected a 7-m cayman and established the region as the pre-eminent in the world for the study of natural sciences. The English followed him – "Henry Bates, Richard Spruce and in 1848 Alfred Russel Wallace who wrote; I'd be an Indian here, and live content, To fish and hunt, and paddle my canoe, And see my children grow, like wild young fawns, In health of body and peace of mind, Rich without wealth, and happy without gold!"

The seemingly infinite variety of plants and animals in the Amazon had Wallace reflecting: how had all this variety come about, so alike in design yet so changeable in detail? "Places not more than fifty or a hundred miles apart have a species of insects and birds at the one which are not found at the other. There must be some boundary which the determines the range of each species; some external peculiarity to mark the line which each one does not pass." Charles Darwin had had the same thought two years earlier after his return from Brazil and whilst reading an essay by Thomas Malthus on population. In his essay the economist argued that the realization of a happy society will always be hindered by its tendencies to expand more quickly than its means of subsistence. If this is true of animals, thought Darwin then they must compete to survive and Nature must act as a selective force, killing off the weak and species must evolve each from another, through this process. Darwin was terrified by the implications of his thought and did not commit it to paper for six years, then sealing it and handing it to his wife with instructions to publish it after his death.

Wallace was younger and less timid. Whilst in a high fever on a field trip in Indonesia he was pondering over the thoughts which had haunted him since his days on the Amazon and he too recalled the same essays by Malthus. The same thought which had struck Darwin, flashed into his on mind: 'I saw at once that the ever-present variability of all living things would furnish the material from which, by the mere weeding out of those less adapted to the actual conditions, the fittest alone would survive the race.' Wallace wrote to Darwin, who was at that time the most famous natural scientist in Britain, explaining his theory and asking for his advice. Darwin's hand was forced and after papers written by both scientists were presented at the Linnean Society on the same day the Theory of Evolution was born.

Compare fares for different ships and remember that prices may fluctuate with supply and demand. As a general rule of thumb they will be about one-third of the prevailing ome-way airfare, including all meals, but not drinks. Most ships sail in the evening and the first night's supper may not be provided. Empty cabins are sometimes offered to foreigners at reduced rates once boats have embarked. Payment is usually in advance. Insist on a signed ticket indicating date, vessel, class of passage, and berth number if applicable.

All ships carry cargo as well as passengers, and the amount of cargo will affect the length of the voyage because of weight (especially when travelling upstream) and loading/unloading at intermediate ports. All but the smallest boats will transport vehicles, but these are often damaged by rough handling. Insist on the use of proper ramps and check for adequate clearance. Vehicles can also be transported aboard cargo barges. These are usually cheaper and passengers may be allowed to accompany their car, but check about food, sanitation, where you will sleep (usually in a hammock slung beneath a truck), and adequate shade.

The following are the major shipping routes in Amazônia, giving a selection of vessels and indicating intermediate ports, average trip durations and fares. Prices vary depending on the vessel; generally it is not a good idea to go with the cheapest fare you are quoted. Not all ships stop at all intermediate ports. There are many other routes and vessels providing extensive local service. All fares shown are one-way only and include all meals unless otherwise stated. Prices for berths and suites are for two people, hammock space is per person. Information is generally identical for the respective reverse voyages (except Belém-Manaus, Manaus-Belém).

A hammock is essential on all but the most expensive boats; it is often too hot to lie down in a cabin during the day. Light cotton hammocks seem to be the best solution. Buy a wide one on which you can lie diagonally; lying straight along it leaves you hump-backed. A climbing carabiner clip is useful for fastening hammocks to runner bars of boats. It is also useful for securing baggage, making it harder to steal.
» *For details of routes in Amazônia, see page 594.*

Practicalities

Health

There is a danger of malaria in Amazônia. Mosquito nets are not required when in motion as boats travel away from the banks and are too fast for mosquitoes to settle, though repellent is a boon for night stops. From April to October, when the river is high, the mosquitoes can be repelled by Super Repelex spray or K13. A yellow fever inoculation is strongly advised; it is compulsory in some areas and may be administered on the spot with a pressurized needle gun. The larger ships must have an infirmary and carry a health officer. Drinking water is generally taken on in port (ie city tap water), but taking your own mineral water is a good idea. » *See also Essentials, page 68.*

Food

This is ample but monotonous, better food is sometimes available to cabin passengers. Meal times can be chaotic. Fresh fruit is a welcome addition; also take plain biscuits, tea bags, seasonings, sauces and jam. Fresh coffee is available; most boats have a bar of sorts. Plates and cutlery may not be provided. Bring your own plastic mug as drinks are served in plastic beakers which are jettisoned into the river. A strong fishing line and a variety of hooks can be an asset for supplementing one's diet; with some meat for bait, piranhas are the easiest fish to catch. Negotiate with the cook over cooking your fish. The sight of you fishing will bring a small crowd of new friends, assistants, and lots of advice – some of it useful.

 Local specialities Inevitably fish dishes are very common, including many fish with indigenous names, eg *matrinchã*, *jaraqui*, *pacu*, *tucunaré* and *tambaqui*, which are worth trying, *pirarucu* is another much proferred local delicacy though due to overfishing this it is in danger of becoming extinct. Shrimp and crab dishes (more expensive) are also available. Specialities of Pará include duck, often served in a yellow soup made from the juice of the root of the manioc (*tucupí*) with a green vegetable (*jambu*); this dish is the famous *pato no tucupi*, highly recommended. Also *tacaca* (shrimps served in *tucupí*), *vatapá* (shrimps served in a thick sauce, highly filling, simpler than the variety found in Salvador), *maniçoba* (made with the poisonous leaves of the bitter cassava, simmered for eight days to render it safe – tasty). *Caldeirada*, a fish and vegetable soup, served with *pirão* (manioc puree), is a speciality of Amazonas. There is also an enormous variety of tropical and jungle fruits, many unique to the region. Try them fresh, or in ice creams or juices. Avoid food from street vendors.

Banks

Exchange Facilities are sparse in Amazônia: banks and exchange can be found in Belém, Macapá, Santarém and Manaus. Small amounts of US dollars cash can usually be exchanged in many other towns, but some boat captains will not take US dollars.

Amapá and Pará

Sometimes called the Brazilian Guyana, the isolated border state of Amapá, once exploited for its natural resources, is now making efforts towards sustainable development. Located near the European Union territory of Guyane with its cheap air link to Paris, it is another good port of entry into northern Brazil. Tourist infrastructure outside the capital Macapá is negligible, but for the adventurous there are opportunities for ecotourism such as the Cabo Orange National Park. The state, a quarter the size of France, has a population of just under half a million.

South of Amapá, the state of Pará has many places of ecological interest, such as the fluvial island of Marajó in the Amazon Delta and the Amazônia National Park on the River Tapajós. There is excellent sport fishing and local cuisine based around the many varieties of local fish and fruits. The capital, Belém, is a good place to begin or end a journey on the River Amazon, while Santarém with its nearby river beaches is a quiet spot to spend a few days while changing boats. The more isolated parts of the state are linked by air as road travel can be difficult during the rainy season from December to May. ▸▸ *For Sleeping, Eating and other listings, see pages 562-569.*

Macapá

→ *Phone code: 096. Colour map 1, A5. Population: 284,000.*

The capital of Amapá is a pleasant city on the banks of the northern channel of the Amazon Delta. It has an impressive fortress as well as a monument to the equator that divides the city. There is a museum detailing the research being carried out in the rainforest and nearby Curiaú, a village originally formed by escaped slaves.

The town was founded around the first Forte de São José do Macapá, built in 1688. In 1751 more settlers from the Azores arrived to defend the region from Dutch, English and French invasions and the aldea became a Vila in 1758. Many slaves were later brought from Africa for the construction of the Fortaleza.

Ins and outs

Flights arrive at the airport close to the city. There are also international connections from Cayenne and Paramaribo. The centre is a short taxi ride from the airport. There are also buses. Boats from Belém and Santarém arrive at nearby Porto Santana, which is linked to Macapá by bus or taxi. Buses from Oiapoque pass through the centre of Macapá after a long and uncomfortable journey over mainly unsurfaced roads. This journey can take longer during the rainy season from Jan-May. ▸▸ *See also Transport, page 566.*

There is an air taxi service to some towns. Towns are linked by trucks, community minibuses and the main bus companies leaving from the new rodoviária on the BR-156 around 3 km north of the centre. The centre and the waterfront are easily explored on foot. Buses to other parts of the city leave from a bus station near the Fortaleza.

Tourist offices Detur ⓘ *Av Raimundo Álvares da Costa 18, Centro, CEP 68906-020, T2230627, www.detur.ap.gov.br and branch at airport.* **Ibama** ⓘ *R Hamilton Silva 1570, Santa Rita, CEP 68906-440, Macapá, T/F2141100.*

Sights

Each brick of the **Fortaleza de São José do Macapá**, built between 1764 and 1782, was brought from Portugal as ballast. Fifty iron cannons still remain and there is a museum. The Fortaleza is used for concerts, exhibits and colourful festivities on the anniversary of the city's founding on 4 February. **São José Cathedral**, inaugurated by the Jesuits in 1761, is the city's oldest landmark. The **Centro de Cultura Negra** ⓘ *R General Rondon*, has a museum and holds frequent events. The **Museu do Desenvolvimento Sustentável** ⓘ *Av Feliciano Coelho 1509, Tue-Fri 0830-1200, 1500-1800, Mon and Sat 1500-1800*, exhibits research on sustainable development and traditional community life in Amazônia. The museum shop sells arts and crafts.

The riverfront has been landscaped with trees, lawns and paths and is a very pleasant place for an evening stroll. The **Complexo Beira Rio** has food and drink kiosks and a nice lively atmosphere. The recently rebuilt pier (*trapiche*) is a lovely spot for savouring the cool of the evening breeze, or watching the sunrise over the Amazon.

There is a monument to the equator, **Marco Zero** (take Fazendinha bus from Avenlda Mendonça Furtado). The equator also divides the nearby enormous (capacity 9,000) football stadium in half, aptly named O Zerão. The Sambódromo is located nearby. South of here are the **Botanical Gardens** ⓘ *Rodovia Juscelino Kubitschek, Km 12, Tue-Sun 0900-1700.*

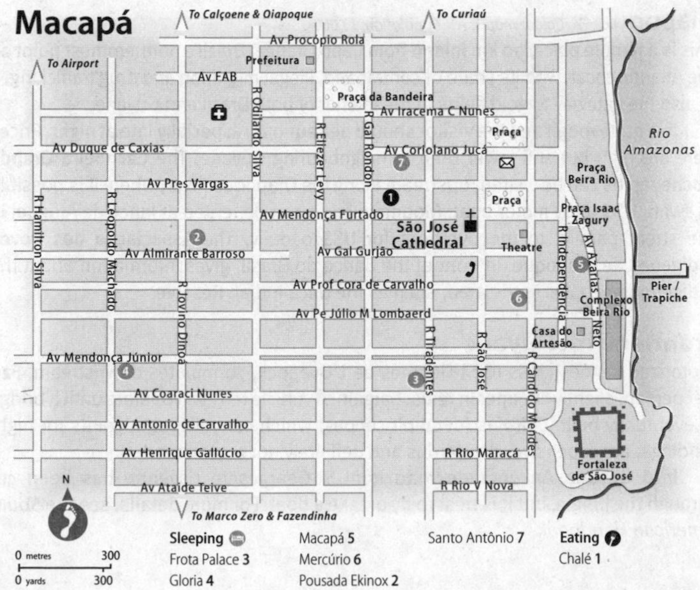

Excursions from Macapá

Some 16 km from the centre, **Fazendinha** is a popular local beach, which is very busy on Sunday, with many seafood restaurants. **Curiaú**, 8 km from Macapá, is inhabited by the descendants of African slaves who have maintained many of the customs of their ancestors. They are analogous to the Bush Negroes of Suriname, but apparently the only such village in Brazil. Popular at weekends for dancing and swimming, the surrounding area is an environmental reserve with many water buffalo.

North of Macapá

Only the first section of the road north to the Guyane border (BR-156) is paved. Although precarious in places, it is open throughout the year with buses and pick-ups operating even in the wet season. At all times, however, take food and water for the journey as services are scarce. Gasoline and diesel (not alcohol) are available along the road, but drivers should take extra fuel from Macapá.

North of Macapá the road divides at **Porto Grande**, and a branch heads northwest to Serra do Navio where manganese extraction has now ended (Hotel Serra do Navio and several bars and restaurants). The BR-156 continues north, passing the turn-offs for two jungle hotels (see Sleeping). The road goes to **Ferreira Gomes** on the shores of the Rio Araguari, where the pavement ends. Further on is **Amapá**, formerly the territorial capital and location of a Second World War American airbase. There are a few hotels. Beyond Amapá is **Calçoene**, with a government-owned hotel which serves expensive food in an adjoining canteen; very cheap sleeping space is also advertized in a café on the Oiapoque road. North of Calçoene a road branches west to **Lourenço**, whose gold fields continue to produce even after various decades of prospecting. The main road continues north across the Rio Caciporé and on to the border with French Guyane at Oiapoque, on the river of the same name. About 7 km to the west is Clevelândia do Norte, a military outpost and the end of the road in Brazil.

December to June is the wet season; the rest of the year is hot and dry. Malaria is rampant in the interior, especially in the areas mined by gold prospectors.

Oiapoque → *Colour map 1, A5. Population: 13,000.*

This is a remote place, 90 km inland from Cabo Orange, Brazil's northernmost point on the Atlantic coast, with its share of contraband, illegal migration and drug trafficking. It is also the gateway to gold fields in the interior of both Brazil and Guyane.

It is quite rough and the visitor should be cautious, especially late at night. Prices here are high but still lower than in neighbouring Guyane. The **Cachoeira Grande Roche** rapids can be visited, upstream along the Oiapoque River, where it is possible to swim, US$30 by motor boat. Mountain bikes can be rented at Jance de Aluguel in the street parallel to the riverfront for US$10 daily. The **Associação dos Povos Indígenas de Oiapoque**, in front of the Banco do Brasil, gives information about the indigenous peoples in the area, such as the Uaçá Indian Reserve.

Frontier with Guyane

Motorized canoes cross to St-Georges de L'Oyapock, 10 minutes downstream, F20 per person, slightly cheaper in reais, bargain. A vehicle ferry will operate until a bridge is eventually built. *Catraias* (decrepit canoes) which carry illegal migrants for night landings, are expensive, dangerous and definitely not recommended.

Into Guyane An unmade road from St-Georges to Cayenne has been cut through the jungle, but it is best to fly or take a boat. For more details, see the *South American Handbook*.

Daniel Ludwig and the Jari Project

In the 1960s, the American billionaire and supertanker magnate, Daniel K Ludwig, investigated the possibilities of converting an area of Amazon rainforest into a large-scale, commercially viable plantation, producing wood for pulp and timber. His experts had convinced him that a tree called Gmelina arborea (originally from Burma and India) would grow in sufficient volume, and fast enough in an equatorial climate, to fulfil Ludwig's dream of supplying the world's wood pulp needs before the end of the 20th century. Politically and, apparently, agriculturally, conditions favoured Brazil, so Ludwig bought four million acres of land (at only US$1 per acre) on the northern shore of the Amazon and the east and west banks of the Rio Jari, which forms the border between Amapá and Pará. As two lengthy articles by Dr Jerry A Shields in the South American Explorer magazine in January and April 1993 show, the project was beset with difficulties and delays, not least the failure of the Gmelina to grow quickly enough in the rainforest soil. Controversy surrounded every aspect of Jari, environmental, political/ nationalistic, social and economic, and Ludwig had to sink an enormous amount of money into the land that he had cleared of jungle. Parallel with the forestry project were agricultural schemes (for example, huge rice paddies), kaolin production and bauxite mining. Ludwig himself ran out of enthusiasm in 1981, when he put Jari up for sale. The Brazilian government, which had initially encouraged the project, had to garner funds from a wide variety of public and private sources to buy Ludwig out and cover Jari's debts. By 1993 the pulp plant was operating profitably, but whether it could be called a success is a matter of debate. Loren McIntyre, in the June 1993 issue of the South American Explorer, in which he updated Shields' report and questioned some of his conclusions, was not pessimistic about the future. Daniel Ludwig himself died in 1992, aged 95.

Belém → *Phone code: 091. Colour map 1, A6. Population: 1.3 million.*

Belém do Pará is the great port of the Amazon. The city has much of cultural interest, a fascinating market, and is the starting point for boat trips into the Amazon. With mean temperatures of 26°C, it is hot, but frequent showers freshen the streets.

Ins and outs

Getting there Val-de-Cans airport is 12 km from the city. Buses take 40 minutes to the centre and charge US$0.50. Taxis charge US$10. Belém can be reached from Cayenne, Miami and Paramaribo as well as from Brasília, Rio de Janeiro and other cities in Brazil by air. There are road connections from São Luís and the northeastern coast as well as a three-day bus link from São Paulo via Brasília. The rodoviária for interstate buses is 3 km from the centre; bus US$0.50, taxi US$5-7 to the centre. Boats arrive at the port from Macapá, Manaus and Santarém as well as other parts of the Amazon region and delta. ▸▸ *See also Transport, page 567.*

Getting around The city centre is easily explored on foot. City buses and taxis run to all the sites of interest and transport hubs away from the centre.

Tourist offices **Belemtur** ⓘ *Av Gov José Malcher 592, T2420900, F2413194, belemtur@cinbesa.com.br, also at airport T2116151.* **Paratur** ⓘ *Praça Waldemar*

Henrique on the waterfront, T2232130, F2236198, by the handicraft shop, helpful, many languages spoken, has a good map of Belém in many languages (but some references are incorrect), town guidebook, US$2.75. **Ibama**ⓘ *Av Conselheiro Furtado 1303, Batista Campos, CEP 66035-350, T2412621, F2231299.*

Safety Belém has its share of crime and is prone to gang violence. Take sensible precautions especially at night.

History

Established because of its strategic position in 1616, Belém soon became the centre for slaving expeditions into the Amazon Basin. The Portuguese of Pará, together with those of Maranhão, treated the Indians abominably. Being remote from the longer-established colonies, and having stronger links with distant Portugal itself, both places were relatively lawless. In 1655, the Jesuits, under Antônio Vieira, attempted to lessen the abuses, while enticing the Indians to 'descend' to the *aldeias* around Belém. This eventually led to further misery when smallpox spread from the south, striking the Pará *aldeias* in the 1660s.

Soon after Brazil's Independence, the Revolta da Cabanagem, a rebellion by the poor blacks, Indians and mixed-race *cabanos* (who lived in *cabanas*), was led against the Portuguese-born class that dominated the economy. The movement came to an end in 1840 when the *cabanos* finally surrendered, but the worst years of violence were 1835-36. Some estimates say 30,000 were killed. The state's strategic location once again became important during the Second World War, when Belém was used as an airbase by the Americans to hunt German submarines in the Atlantic.

Sights

There are some fine squares and restored historic buildings set along broad avenues. Belém used to be called the 'City of Mango Trees' and there are still many such trees

remaining. The largest square is the **Praça da República**, where there are free afternoon concerts; the main business and shopping area is along the wide Avenida Presidente Vargas, leading to the river and the narrow streets which parallel it.

The neoclassical, recently restored, **Teatro da Paz** ⓘ *Tue-Fri 0900-1800, tours cost US$1.50* (1874), is one of the largest theatres in the country and worth a visit. It stages performances by national and international stars and also gives free concert and theatre shows.

The **cathedral** ⓘ *Praça Frei Caetano Brandão, Mon 1500-1800, Tue-Fri 0800-1100, 1530-1800* (1748), is another neoclassical building which contains several remarkable paintings. The cathedral stands directly opposite the restored 18th-century **Santo Aleixandre** church, which is noted for its wood carving.

The 17th-century **Mercês** church (1640), near the market, is the oldest church in Belém. It forms part of an architectural group known as the Mercedário, the rest of which was heavily damaged by fire in 1978 and has now been restored.

The **Basílica of Nossa Senhora de Nazaré** ⓘ *Praça Justo Chermont, Av Magalhães Barata, Mon-Sat 0500-1130, 1400-2000, Sun 0545-1130, 1430-2000* (1909), built from rubber wealth in romanesque style, is an absolute must for its beautiful marble and stained-glass windows. A museum at the Basílica describes the Círio de Nazaré religious festival (see below).

The **Palácio Lauro Sodré** and **Museu do Estado do Pará** ⓘ *Praça Dom Pedro II, T2253853, Mon-Fri 0900-1800, Sat 1000-1800*, is a gracious 18th-century Italianate

Belém

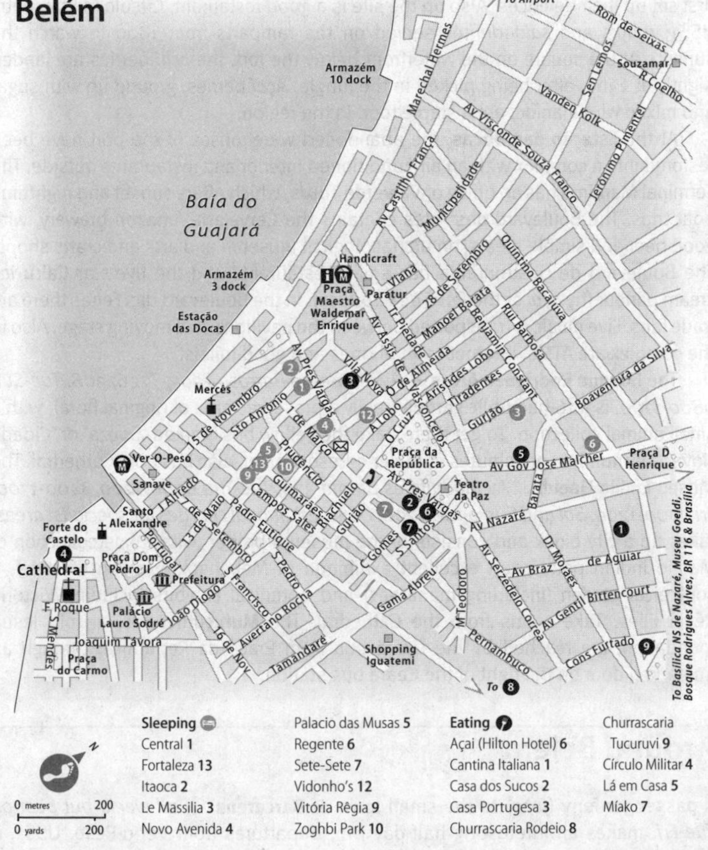

Sleeping
Central 1
Fortaleza 13
Itaoca 2
Le Massilia 3
Novo Avenida 4
Palacio das Musas 5
Regente 6
Sete-Sete 7
Vidonho's 12
Vitória Rêgia 9
Zoghbi Park 10

Eating
Açaí (Hilton Hotel) 6
Cantina Italiana 1
Casa dos Sucos 2
Casa Portugesa 3
Churrascaria Rodeio 8
Churrascaria Tucuruvi 9
Círculo Militar 4
Lá em Casa 5
Miako 7

building. It contains Brazil's largest framed painting, 'The Conquest of Amazônia', by Domenico de Angelis. The building was the work of the Italian architect Antonio Landi who also designed the Cathedral and was the administrative seat of the colonial government. During the rubber boom many new decorative features were added. Also on Praça Dom Pedro II is the **Palácio Antônio Lemos**, which houses the **Museu de Arte de Belém** as well as the **Prefeitura** ⓘ *Tue-Fri 0900-1200, 1400-1800, Sat and Sun 0900-1300*. It was originally built as the Palácio Municipal between 1868 and 1883, and is a fine example of the Imperial neoclassical style. In the downstairs rooms there are old views of Belém; upstairs the historic rooms, beautifully renovated, contain furniture, paintings, etc, which are all well explained.

The Belém market, known as **Ver-o-Peso**, was the Portuguese Posto Fiscal, where goods were weighed to gauge taxes due, hence the name: 'see the weight'. It now has lots of gift shops selling charms for the local African-derived religion, *umbanda* and interesting medicinal herb and natural perfume stalls. You can see giant river fish being unloaded around 0530, with frenzied wholesale buying for the next hour; a new dock for the fishing boats was built just upriver from the market in 1997. The area around the market swarms with people, including many armed thieves and pickpockets.

One of the most varied and colourful markets in South America.

In the old town, too, is the **Forte do Castelo** ⓘ *Praça Frei Caetano Brandão 117, T2230041, daily 0800-2300*, which was rebuilt in 1878. The fort overlooks the confluence of the Rio Guamá and the Baía do Guajara and was where the Portuguese first set up their defences. Also on the site is a good restaurant, Círculo Militar (entry US$1; drinks and *salgadinhos* served on the ramparts from 1800 to watch the sunset). At the square on the waterfront below the fort, the *açaí* berries are landed nightly at 2300, after being picked in the jungle. *Açaí* berries, ground up with sugar and mixed with manioc, are a staple food in the region.

At the **Estação das Docas**, the abandoned warehouses of the port have been restored into a complex with an air-conditioned interior and restaurants outside. The Terminal Marítimo has an office of **Valverde Tours**, which offers sunset and nighttime boat trips. The Boulevard das Artes contains the **Cervejaria Amazon** brewery, with good beer and simple meals, an archaeological museum and arts and crafts shops. The Boulevard de Gastronomia has smart restaurants and the five-star **Cairu** ice cream parlour (try *açaí* or the *Pavê de Capuaçu*). In the Boulevard das Feiras there are trade fairs. Live music is transported between the pavilions on a moving stage. Also in the complex are ATMs, internet café, phones and good toilets.

The **Bosque Rodrigues Alves** ⓘ *Av Almirante Barroso 2305, T2262308, Tue-Sun 0800-1700*, is a 16-ha public garden (really a preserved area of original flora), with a small animal collection. To get there, take the yellow bus marked 'Souza' or 'Cidade Nova' (any number) 30 minutes from Ver-o-Peso market, also bus from Cathedral. The **Museu Emílio Goeldi** ⓘ *Av Magalhães Barata 376, Tue-Thu 0900-1200, 1400-1700, Fri 0900-1200, Sat and Sun 0900-1700, US$1, additional charges for specialist areas*, takes up a city block and consists of the museum proper (with a fine collection of Marajó Indian pottery, an excellent exhibition of Mebengokre Indian lifestyle), a zoological garden (including manatees) and botanical exhibits including Victoria Régia lilies. Take a bus from the Cathedral. The **Murucutu** ruins, an old Jesuit foundation, are reached by the Ceará bus from Praça da República, through an unmarked door on the right of the Ceará bus station.

Around Belém

A passenger ferry (*foca*) to the small town of **Barcarena** ⓘ *all week, but best on Tue-Fri*, makes an interesting half-day trip, departures from Ver-o-Peso, US$1. A return trip on the ferry from Ver-o-Peso to **Icaoraci** provides a good view of the river. Several restaurants here serve excellent seafood; you can eat shrimp and drink coconut water and appreciate the breeze coming off the river. Icaoraci is 20 km east of the city and is well known as a centre of ceramic production. The pottery is in Marajóara and Tapajonica style. Take the bus from Avenida Presidente Vargas to Icoaraci (one hour). Artisans are friendly and helpful, will accept commissions and send purchases overseas.

The nearest beach is at **Outeiro** (35 km) on an island near Icoaraci, about an hour by bus and ferry (the bus may be caught near the Maloca, an Indian-style hut near the docks which serves as a nightclub). A bus from Icoaraci to Outeiro takes 30 minutes. Further north is the island of **Mosqueiro** (86 km), accessible by bridge and an excellent highway, with many beautiful sandy beaches and jungle inland. It is popular at weekends when traffic can be heavy (also July) and the beaches can get crowded and polluted. Buses from Belém to Mosqueiro run every hour from rodoviária (US$1.50, 80 minutes). There is also a ferry from Porto do Sal, on the street between Forte de Castelo and the cathedral. It takes about two hours. There are many hotels and weekend villas at the villages of Mosqueiro and Vila, which are recommended, but these may be full weekends and July.

Ilha de Marajó → *Colour map 1, A5. Take plenty of insect repellent.*

This is the world's largest river island, a claim disputed by the Bananal, which is partly flooded in the rainy season January-June. It provides a suitable habitat for large numbers of water buffalo, which are said to have swum ashore after a shipwreck; many are now farmed; try the cheese and milk. Marajó is also home to numerous bird species, including thousands of roseate spoonbills and for black cayman, river turtles and other wildlife. It has many good beaches. The island is full in the July holiday season and was the site of the pre-Columbian Marajóaras culture, celebrated for its ceramics.

The capital of the island is **Soure**. There are fine beaches: **Araruna**, 2 km away; take supplies and supplement with coconuts and crabs, beautiful walks along the shore; **do Pesqueiro** (bus from Praça da Matriz, 1030, returns 1600, eat at **Maloca**, good, cheap, big, deserted beach, 13 km away); and **Caju-Una** (15 km).

A ferry from Belém sails at weekends (four hours, US$5). Small craft await passengers from the **Enasa** boats, for **Salvaterra** village (good beaches and bars: seafood), US$12, 10 minutes. There is a ferry to Porto do Cámara (three hours). Then take a bus to Salvaterra and a ferry to Soure. There is a taxi-plane service to Soure. The **Banco do Brasil** has an ATM. Changing money is only possible at very poor rates.

Ponta de Pedras

Boats leave Belém, near Porto do Sal, most days for the five-hour crossing to Ponta de Pedras. Seats are US$3.60, two-berth cabins US$38. In Ponta de Pedras is **Hotel Ponta de Pedras** (**D**) which serves good meals. Bicycles can be hired at US$1 per hour to explore beaches and the interior of the island. Fishing boats make the eight-hour trip to Cachoeira do Arari (one hotel, **D**), where there is a fascinating **Marajó museum**. A 10-hour boat trip from Ponta de Pedras goes to the **Arari lake** where there are two villages: **Jenipapo** and **Santa Cruz**, which is less primitive, but less interesting; a hammock and a mosquito net are essential. There is a direct boat service to Belém twice a week.

Salinópolis → *Colour map 1, A6. Population: 33,500.*

Some 223 km away, at the extreme end of the eastern part of the Amazon Delta, this seaside resort has many small places where you can eat and drink at night by the waterfront and a fine sandy beach nearby (buses and cars drive on to the beach). The water is murky. It is a peaceful place mid-week but very busy at weekends and in high season and is best during the holiday month of July. **Atalaia**, an island opposite

Roads to nowhere

In the early 1970s, Brazil's military rulers became increasingly unnerved by what they saw as foreign designs upon the resources of the Amazon basin. This real or imaginary fear of invasion was not only directed against the rich, developed countries, but also Brazil's neighbours who the Brazilians felt were slowly encroaching upon the country's borders. In the early 1960s, Peru's President Fernando Belaunde Terry had proposed the construction of the Carretera Marginal in order to link Peru's jungle with the rest of the country. Under the slogan of 'Integrar para não entregar' (takeover not handover), the Brazilian military announced the construction of the Transamazônica Highway. The road was originally designed to link João Pessoa, Paraíba, with Acre, thence to link up with the Peruvian road system to complete a road route across South America to the Pacific and open up Brazilian products to Asian markets. The Transamazônica itself would be 5,400 km, and would integrate Amazônia from east to west and unify it with the rest of the nation. In addition, it would give opportunities for people from the northeast to resettle in areas not affected by drought and to become economically active in small agricultural schemes. In the often-quoted words of President Emílio Garrastazu Médici, it would move 'Homens sem terra para terras sem homens' (men without land to land without men). All along the highway, purpose-built 'agrovilas' would offer Brazil's poor a new life. The project was proposed in 1970; huge financial investment failed to make the project work. Not only did fewer than anticipated north-easterners take up the offer, but those that did found that the Amazonian soils did not permit the type of rewards that they had been led to expect. The colonizers also found that social infrastructure did not meet their needs and the road itself began to deteriorate as the

Salinópolis, is pleasant and can be reached by taxi (US$6) or with a fisherman. Salinópolis is four hours from Belém by bus on a good road, US$6.

The agreeable town of **Capanema** is a good place to stop if you prefer not to stay in Belém en route to São Luís.

The little riverside village of **Tomé-Açu**, south of Belém on the Rio Acará-Mirim, affords a view of life on a smaller river than the Amazon; three buses a day from Belém, US$8. Hotel Las Vegas owner, Fernando, is very friendly. Boat back to Belém on Sunday at 1100, arriving 1800, US$5.

South of Belém

Marabá and around

→ *Phone code: 094. Colour map 1, B5. Population: 170,000. Altitude: 84 m.*

Near Marabá are beaches on the Tocantins and Itacaiúnas rivers, which are best visited June-October. With the filling of the Tucuruí dam, the town has been moved; even so, it suffers from flooding. There is a bridge across the Tocantins at Marabá. There are essentially three parts of the town: **Marabá Velha** (also called Marabá Pioneira), **Marabá Nova** and **Cidade Nova**. The distance between Marabá Nova and Velha is about 2½ km. A good travel agent is **IBR Travel** on the main street of Marabá Velha. **Banco do Brasil** will not cash traveller's cheques; the parallel market operates in larger stores; for example, **Supermercado Bato Logo**.

whole project wound down. By the late 1980s, a Movement for Survival along the Transamazônica had been set up by the farmers.

Another road which was intended to promote development in the Amazon region was the BR-364, from Cuiabá to Acre state. The government in the mid-1970s hoped that it would reinvigorate settlement in the Amazon, in a way that the Transamazônica had failed to do. Like the latter, the BR-364 was supposed to encourage small landholders to follow the building of the main highway and its feeder roads, but in Rondônia the main colonizers were cattle ranchers and land speculators who speeded up the process of deforestation and land conflicts with the traditional cultivators, forest farmers and indigenous people.

A third road in the Amazon which has come to grief, even more so than the other two, is the BR-319 from Manaus to Humaitá on the Transamazônica. Planned in 1960 and opened to traffic in 1975, the road has become a route from nothing to nowhere. The people living along it have been deserted, the only maintenance being the occasional team from Embratel who come to look at the telephone lines which follow the road. Initially there were farms, hotels, petrol stations and restaurants along the BR-319. Most have now gone. Access to health clinics and schools is all but impossible and the only public transport on the southern part of the road is a once-weekly truck. The only people to benefit are the shipping owners who take the traffic, which would have used the road, on barges along the Rio Madeira. The journalist Giuliano Cedroni tried to take the BR-319 in the late-1990s. He and his companions made it through, but not without a tow from the weekly truck after their jeep broke down. One inhabitant of the region pleaded with him, "Tell the people down there [in the south] what is happening in the north. This here is not a life."

The **Serra Pelada** gold mines made famous by Sebastião Salgado whose images made them look like the circles of Hell are now worked by heavy machinery. This massive excavation was the scene of much human misery and also some fabulous fortunes. To get there, take a bus to Km 6 and change for the Serra Pelada bus, US$6, three hours, last bus back 1400. About 11 km before the town is a police post: search for weapons and alcohol (forbidden); second search at the airport 2 km from the mine.

Carajás

Companhia Vale Rio Doce (CVRD) ⓘ *ToXX91-3275300, or enquire in Marabá, São Luís, São Paulo or Rio: Avenida Graça Aranha 26, 16° andar, Centro, Rio 20030000 – attention Dr Hugo Mourão (hotel bookings handled here too)*, operates the very impressive iron mine at Carajás, which looks like a giant red hole in a green jungle. The ore is almost pure iron oxide and is therefore extremely profitable. It is ground, washed and shipped to São Luís by trains up to 2 km long, without further treatment or chemical processing. Apart from iron, other metals like manganese are also mined by the CRVD in the area. A city has built up around Carajás, but most of it is within CVRD bounds. To get into Carajás (the Núcleo and to visit the mine) and to pass the checkpoint 35 km from the project, you must have a permit, available from CVRD. You need to apply in advance and have a good reason for visiting. There is accommodation in **Parauapebas** built as a temporary settlement for the Carajás construction workers, and now a town in its own right.

Macapá *p552, map p553, phone code 096*
A **Atalanta**, Av Coaracy Nunes 1148, T/F2231612, www.atlantahotel.com.br. Blocky 80s hotel with a laundry service, bar and restaurant.
A **Frota Palace**, R Tiradentes 1104, T2233999, F2237011. Reasonable town hotel with free airport pick-up.
A **Macapá**, Av Francisco Azarias Neto 17, on waterfront, T2171350, www.hotelmacapa.kit.net. Business hotel with a pool, tennis courts, sauna, restaurant and a convention centre.
A **Marabaixo**, R Cândido Mendes 340, T2237853, F2232157. Standard apartment hotel with meals available.
A **Pousada Ekinox**, R Jovino Dinoá 1693, T2230086, www.ekinox.com.br. One of the best in town with a library. Helpful, French-speaking staff, excellent restaurant. Recommended.
B **Gloria**, Leopoldo Machado 2085, T2220984. Basic town hotel with some a/c rooms.
B **Mara**, R São José 2390, T2220859, F2234905. A/c rooms with a TV and fridge, good value.
C-D **Santo Antônio**, Av Coriolano Jucá 485, T2220244. Conveniently located near the main praça. Cheaper accommodation in dormitory.
D **Mercúrio**, R Cândido Mendes 1300, 2nd floor, T2231699. Basic but close to Praça São José (where bus from Porto Santana stops).

North of Macapá *p554, phone code 096*
B **Pontal das Pedras**, Km 109, North of Porto Grande, T2512781. Jungle hotels, restaurant, fishing, boat trips, ecological trail, popular at weekends, recommended.
B **Recanto Ecológico Sonho Meu**, Km 108, North of Porto Grande, T2341298. Similar jungle hotel.
C **Hotel Amapá**, Amapá, T4211108.
D **Government-owned hotel**, Calçoene, by the bus stop. Serves expensive food in an adjoining canteen.

Belém *p555, map p557, phone code 091*
Hotels in the city are not up to much. All hotels are fully booked during Círio (see box p566. There are many cheap hotels close to waterfront (none too safe) and several others near the rodoviária (generally OK)
A **Itaoca**, Av Pres Vargas 132, T2413434, www.pousadadosguaras.com.br. A charming new hotel which can be noisy.
A **Regente**, Av Gov José Malcher 485, T2411222, hregente@libnet.com.br. A modest but comfortable hotel serving good breakfast and with some English-speaking staff.
B **Le Massilia**, R Henrique Gurjão 236, T2247147. Ordinary town hotel with a reasonable French restaurant.
C **Novo Avenida**, Av Pres Vargas 404,T/F2238893, avenida@hotelnovoavenida.com.br. Centrally located and on busy street, with a/c rooms and cheaper fan-cooled rooms with a fridge. Very well looked after. Recommended.
C **Vidonho's**, R Ó de Almeida 476, T2421444, F2247499. A series of a/c rooms with a fridge tucked away in a side street. Good breakfast
C **Zoghbi Park**, R Padre Prudêncio 220, T/F2411800, www.zoghbi.com.br. Smart though slightly frayed business hotel with a small pool and a restaurant. Recommended.
D **Sete-Sete**, Trav 1 de Março 673, T2227730, F2242346. Modest but clean, comfortable and safe and in a quiet street. With breakfast. Recommended.
D-E **Central**, Av Pres Vargas 290, T2424800. Faded art deco hotel on a busy street with comfortable (but often noisy) rooms and a reasonable restaurant. Some a/c rooms without bath in the cheaper price range.
D-E **Vitória Rêgia**, Trav Frutuoso Guimarães 260, T/F2122077. Basic hotel with a/c and fan-cooled rooms with a fridge (cheaper without).
E **Fortaleza**, Trav Frutuoso Guimarães 276, T2121055. Very basic and only for those on the tightest of budgets.
E **Palacio das Musas**, Trav Frutuoso Guimarães 275, T2128422. Large clean rooms with shared bathrooms.

Around Belém *p558, phone code 091*
B **Farol**, on Praia Farol, Mosqueiro, T7711219. 1920s architecture in good repair, small restaurant, rooms face beach, good views.

Camping
Camping is easy on Mosqueiro.

Oiapoque *p554, phone code 091*
C **Tránsito**, Av Joaquim Caetano da Silva, on the riverfront. Clean, with breakfast, fridge, TV, restaurant.
D-E **Kayama**, Av Joaquim Caetano da Silva 760, T5211256. A/c and bath, cheaper with fan, good, international calls.
D-E **Pousada Central**, Av Coaracy Nunes, T5211466. 1 street back from the river. A/c, bath, cheaper with fan and shared bath.
F **Sonho Meu**, R Honório Silva 731, T5211217, basic. Other cheap hotels along the waterfront are mainly used by Brazilians waiting to cross to Guyane.

Ilha de Marajó *p559, phone code 091*
A **Pousada dos Guarãs**, Av Beira Mar, Salvaterra, T/F37651133, www.pousadadosguaras.com.br. Well-equipped little resort hotel on the beach with an extensive tour programme.
B **Hotel Ilha do Marajó**, 2a Travessa 10, T7411315 (Belém 2413218), hiMarajó@interconect.com.br. Simple hotel popular with weekenders from Belém. Freindly staff.
C **Soure**, R 3 Centro. Basic hotel with a/c rooms.
C **Waldeck**, Trav 12, T7411414. Basic but friendly but with only 4 rooms.
E **Pensão** at 2a R 575 (**Bar Guarani**). Simple but well-run and recommended.

Salinópolis *p559, phone code 091*
Most of the basic hotels in the tiny nearby town of Capanema are pretty dilapidated.
A **Atalaia**, on Atalaia island, 15 km from Salinópolis, T/F4641122. A simple *pousada* in a pleasant setting. Reserve in advance for the weekend, take a taxi.
A **Solar**, Av Beira Mar, Salinópolis, T8231823. The best in town with smart rooms, all with en suites and a good restaurant.
A **Joana d'Arc**, Av João Pessoa 555, Salinópolis, T/F8231422. Modest but well looked after and with a generous breakfast.
B **Diolindina**, Av Pres Médici 424, Capanema, T8211667. Small clean a/c rooms with fridge and bath. The price includes breakfast and safe parking. Recommended. There are good restaurants and supermarket a opposite.

Marabá and around *p560*
There are various sliglhtly seedy cheap hotels near the rodoviária.
A **Del Príncipe**, Av Marechal Rondon 95, Cidade Nova, T3241175. A/c rooms with a TV and a fridge in modest hotel with a restaurant and games room.
A **Vale do Tocantins**, Folha 29, Cidade Nova, 7 km, T3222321, F3221841. Modern, characterless and with a restaurant, travel agency.
B **Dallas**, Nova Marabá. Well run and convenient for the rodoviária (immediately next door). Recommended.
B **Plaza**, Folha 32, Quadra 10, Lote 06, T3223543, F3221610. Fan-cooled rooms in a quiet and friendly hostel serving a very good breakfast. Some English spoken. Recommended.

Eating

Macapá *p552, map p553, phone code 096*
TTT **Chalé**, Av Pres Vargas 499, T2221970. Good Brazilian cooking and nice atmosphere.
TTT **Le Chateau**, Av 13 de Setembro 2022, corner of Barão de Mauá, T2422481. Small and intimate French restaurant but a long way from the centre.
TT **Cantino Bahiano**, Av Beira-Rio 1, South of the Fortaleza, T2234153. Respectable seafood restaurant.
TT **Martinho's Peixaria**, Av Beira-Rio 810. Good fish restaurant.
TT **Soho**, Av Capt Pedro Baião, 2201. Standard Chinese – to take away or eat in.
TT **Zero Grau**, R Leopoldo Machado 2405. One of the better pizzerias.
T **Bom Paladar Kilo's**, Av Pres Vargas 456. Pay-by-weight buffet with excellent ice cream made from local fruits; try *cupuaçu*.

Belém *p555, map p557, phone code 091*
All the major hotels have upmarket restaurants.There are numerous outdoor snack bars serving full meals at a far cheaper price than the restaurants. But view them with care.
TTT **Açaí**, Hilton Hotel, Av Pres Vargas 882, T2426500. Decent regional cooking; come for lunch or dinner daily, or brunch on Sun.
TTT **Círculo Militar**, Praça Ferreira Cantão, (in the grounds of Forte do Castelo), T2234374. Belém's best Brazilian cooking with a

comprehensive menu - try the *filetena brasa*. The restaurant has a fine view out over the river.

₸₸₸ **Lá em Casa**, Av Gov José Malcher 247, T2231212. Respectable local cooking; especially the *menu paraense*. Fashionable crowd.

₸₸ **Cantina Italiana**, Trav Benjamin Constant 1401, T2252033. Excellent Italian, with hotel delivery.

₸₸ **Casa Portuguesa**, R Sen Manoel Barata 897, T2424871. Decent traditional Portuguese dishes including delicious *bacalhau* (cod).

₸₸ **Churrascaria Rodeio**, Rodovia Augusto Montenegro Km 4, T2482004. Excellent barbecued meat with a salad bar and reasonable prices.

₸₸ **Churrascaria Tucuruvi**, Trav Benjamin Constant 1843, Nazaré. Good-value barbecued meat restaurant and generous portions.

₸₸ **Germania**, R Aristides Lobo 604. Mock German restaurant with Bavarian dishes.

₸₸ **Miako**, Trav 1 de Março 766, behind Praça de República, T2422355. Very good Japanese, oriental and international food.

₸₸ **Okada**, R Boaventura da Silva 1522, past R Alcindo Cacela, T2463242. Japanese dishes and barbecued meat. Very good prawns – *camarão à milanesa com salada*.

₸₸ **Pizzeria Napolitano**, Praça Justo Chermont 12, T2225177. Cheese-heavy pizzas and other Italian dishes.

₸ **Casa dos Sucos**, Av Pres Vargas, Praça da República. 41 types of juice (including Amazonian fruits) and delicious chocolate cake (vegetarian restaurant upstairs, recommended for lunches).

₸ **Charlotte**, Av Gentil Bittencourt 730, at Trav Quintino Bocaiúva. Outdoor snack bar serving the best *salgadinhos* (savoury pasties) in the city and good desserts.

₸ **Doce Vida Salgado**, Trav 1 de Março 217. One of many buffet-style restaurants in the *Comércio* district (there are many on the R Santo Antônio pedestrian mall). Like most, open for lunch only.

₸ **Nectar**, Av Gentil Bittencourt, Trav Padre Eutíquio 248, pedestrian zone. Good vegetarian open at lunch only.

₸ **Sabor Paranse**, R 13 de Maio, 450. Food by weight at lunchtimes only.

₸ **Tempero**, R Ò de Almeida, 348. Self-service. A real bargain with Brazilian and Middle-Eastern dishes. Warmly recommended.

Around Belém *p558, phone code 091*

₸₸ **Hotel Ilha Bela**, Av 16 de Novembro 409, Mosqueiro. Recommended for fish, no evening meals.

₸₸ **Marésia**, Praia Chapeu Virado, Mosqueiro. Highly recommended.

₸ **Sorveteria Delícia**, Av 16 de Novembro, serves good local fruit ice creams and the owner buys dollars.

Oiapoque *p554, phone code 091*

₸₸₸ **Restaurant Paladar Drinks**, 1 block up from the river, expensive.

₸₸ **Pantanal Bar**, next to the monument at riverfront, has dancing at weekends.

Ilha de Marajó *p559, phone code 091*

There are a number of cheap places to eat in Soure but few restaurants of any distinction.

₸ **Canecão**, Praça da Matriz. Soure. Sandwiches and standard beans, rice and cheap meals. Recommended.

Salinópolis *p559, phone code 091*

₸ **Bife de Ouro**, Av Dr Miguel Santa Brígida, opposite filling station. Simple, but with excellent fish and shrimp. Always crowded for lunch.

₸ **Gringo Louco**, further out than Atalaia, 15 km (take taxi or hitch), at Cuiarana beach, (follow signs). The US owner serves good, unusual dishes, and some 'wild' drinks known as 'bombs', popular.

Marabá and around *p560*

There are a few good *churrascarias* around the central praça.

₸₸ **Bambu**, Pedro Cameiro 111, Cidade Nova, 3 km. Mainly fish, clean, good value, 1100-1500, 1800-2300.

₸₸ **Lanchonete Domino**, opposite the rodoviária. Recommended.

For an explanation of the sleeping and eating price codes used in this guide, see the inside front cover. Other relevant information is provided in the Essentials chapter, pages 47 and 57.

Bars and clubs

Macapá *p552, map p553, phone code 096*
The food and drink kiosks in **Complexo Beira Rio** have live music most evenings.
Rithimus, R Odilardo Silva 1489, T2222354. Good for the frenetic local rhythm *brega*, which sounds like *forró* on speed.

Belém *p555, map p557, phone code 091*
There are many dance venues around **Av Doca de Souza Franco**, (often just called 'Doca'), Thu is the best night. The **Reduto** district is becoming the most fashionable nightlife area in the city.
African Bar, Praça Waldemar Henrique 2. Rock or samba at weekends only.
Baixo Reduto, R Quintino Bocaiúva, Reduto, T2426282. Live Blues on Wed; MPB, Thu; rock, Fri and jazz, Sat.
Bar Teatro Bora Bora, R Bernal do Couto 38, T2415848. Restaurant, bar and nightclub wih MPB and Pagode. Open from 2100 until late Thu-Sun.
Colarinho Branco Chopperia, Av Visconde de Souza Franco, 80, near the river. Tue-Sun, 1800 to last customer. Excellent draught beer and live MPB. Very popular.
Escapóle, Rodovia Augusto Montenegro 400. Huge dance hall with various styles of music from live bands and DJs. Open Wed-Sat from 2200 (take a radio taxi for safety), no a/c, dress informally.
Olê Olá, Av Tavares Bastos, 1234, T2432340. Live music and a DJ driven dance floor. Thu-Sun only, 2230 to last customer.

Entertainment

Macapá *p552, map p553, phone code 096*

Art galleries
Cândido Portinari, corner of R Cândido Mendes and Av Raimundo Álvares da Costa. Exhibits of local art.

Cinemas
In **Macapá Shopping**, R Leopoldo Machado 2334.

Theatre
Teatro das Bacabeiras, R Cândido Mendes. Concerts, poetry and plays.

Belém *p555, map p557, phone code 091*

Art galleries
Debret, R Arcipreste Manoel Theodoro 630, Batista Campos, T2224046. Contemporary painting and sculpture, also has library specializing in art and philosophy.
Casa das 11 Janelas (1768), Praça Frei Caetano Brandão, T2191105, cultural performances and art exhibitions, panoramic view.

Cinema
Olímpia, Av Pres Vargas 918, T2231882. In existence for over 80 years and was the first cinema in Belém.

Theatre
Margarida Schiwwazappa, Av Gentil Bittencourt 650, T2222923.

Festivals and Events

Macapá *p552, map p553, phone code 096*
Apr/May Marabaixo is the traditional music and dance festival held for 40 days after Easter.
Jun The Sambódromo has parades of Escolas de Samba at Carnival and Quadrilhas during **São João** in Jun.
14 Aug Festa de São Joaquim held in Curiaú.

Belém *p555, map p557, phone code 091*
Apr **Maundy Thu**, half-day; **Good Fri**, all shops closed, all churches open and there are processions.
9 Jun Corpus Christi.
15 Aug Accession of Pará to Independent Brazil.
7 Sep Independence Day, commemorated on the day with a military parade, and with a students' parade on the preceding Sun (morning).
Oct Círio (see box, p566); 30 Oct, half-day.
2 Nov All Souls' Day.
8 Dec, Immaculate Conception.
24 Dec Christmas Eve, half-day.

Shopping

Macapá *p552, map p553, phone code 096*
Macapá and Porto Santana were declared a customs-free zone in 1992. There are now many cheap imported goods available from

The Festival of Candles

Círio, the Festival of Candles in October, is based on the legend of the Nossa Senhora de Nazaré, whose image was found on the site of her Basílica around 1700. On the second Sunday in October, a procession carries a copy of the Virgin's image from the Basílica to the cathedral. On the Monday, two weeks later, the image is returned to its usual resting place. There is a Círio museum in the crypt of the Basílica, enter at the right side of the church; free entry. The festival, which is 'cheio de coração' (full of heart), has attracted many major Brazilian artists and musicians. It has developed into a massive national festival and is highly recommended. The biggest carnival performers attend, along with important rock groups and an increasing contingent of international artists. The non-religious element of the festival is known as Carnabelém. For dates check with Paratur, T2233130.

shops in the centre. In the handicraft complex **Casa do Artesão**, Av Azárias Neto, Mon-Sat 0800-1900, craftsmen produce their wares onsite. A feature is pottery decorated with local manganese ore, also woodcarvings and leatherwork.

Belém *p555, map p557, phone code 091*

Shopping Iguatemi, Trav Padre Eutique 1078.

Parfumaria Orion, Trav Frutuoso Guimarães 268. Has a wide variety of perfumes and essences from Amazonian plants, much cheaper than tourist shops.

Complexo São Brás on Praça Lauro Sodré. Has a handicraft market and folkloric shows in a building dating from 1911.

Belém is a good place to buy hammocks, look in the street parallel to the river, 1 block inland from Ver-o-Peso. Bookshop with English titles in the arcade on Av Pres Vargas.

Activities and tours

Macapá *p552, map p553, phone code 096*

Tour operators

Amapá Turismo, in Hotel Macapá, T2232667.

Fénix, R Cãndido Mendes 374, T/F2238200, and R Jovino Dinoá 1489, T2235353.

Belém *p555, map p557, phone code 091*

Sport

Amazônia Sport & Ação, Av 25 de Setembro, 2345, T226 8442. Extreme sports, diving, rock-climbing.

Iate Clube do Pará, Av Bernardo Sayão, 3324, T2297599. Swimming pools, gym and sports courts.

Tour operators

City tours (3 hrs) and river tours are offered by most companies.

Amazon Star, R Henrique Gurjão 236, T/F2126244, T9827911 (mob), amazstar@interconect.com.br. French run, good half-day boat tour with jungle walk, as well as tours to Marajó.

Angel, in Hilton Hotel, T2242111, angel@datanetbbs.com.br. Tours and events, issues ISIC and IYHA cards.

Gran-Para, Av Pres Vargas 676, T2123233, F2415531. Good for airline bookings.

Transport

Macapá *p552, map p553, phone code 096*

See also Ins and outs, p552

Air

Airport, R Hildemar Maia, 4 km from centre, T2232323. International flights to Cayenne and Paramaribo. Domestic flights to Belém, Belo Horizonte, Boa Vista, Brasília, Breves, Manaus, Oiapoque, Rio de Janeiro, Santarém and São Paulo. Air taxi service with Rio Norte.

Airline offices META, Av Mendonça Júnior 18, T2234628. **Penta**, Av Mendonça Júnior 13D, T2235226. **Rio Norte**, at airport, T2220033. **TAM**, at airport, T2232688. **Varig**, R Cândido Mendes 1039, T2234612. **Vasp**, R Independência 146, T2241016.

Boat

To **Belém**, **Atlântica**, fast catamaran 8 hrs, 3 times a week, US$30, reservations at **Martinica**, Jovino Dinoá 2010, T2235777, F2223569. Slower but slightly cheaper boats are **Bom Jesus**, **Comandante Solon**, **São Francisco de Paulo**, **Silja e Souza** of Souzamar, Cláudio Lúcio Monteiro 1375, Santana, T2811946, car ferry with **Silnave**, T2234011. Purchase tickets from offices 2 days in advance (Agencia Sonave, R São José 2145, T2239090, sells tickets for all boats). Also smaller boats to **Breves** as well as a regular direct service to **Santarém** (see River transport, p549).

Bus

New rodoviária on BR-156, north of Macapá. **Estrela de Ouro**, office on the main square, in front of the cathedral, leaves daily at 2000, and **Cattani**, office on Nunes between São José and Cándido Mendes, leaves daily at 0630 to **Amapá** (US$20), **Calçoene** (US$25, 7 hrs) and **Oiapoque** (12 hrs – dry season – with several rest stops, 14-24 hrs in rainy season, US$35). The Oiapoque bus does not go into Amapá or Calçoene and it is therefore very inconvenient to break the trip at these places.

Pick-up trucks run daily to various locations throughout Amapá, crowded on narrow benches in the back, or pay more to ride in the cab. Despite posted schedules, they leave when full. To **Oiapoque** at 0800, 10-12 hrs, US$35 cab, US$15 in back, to **Lourenço** at 0900.

Car

Car hire Localiza, R Independência 30, T2232799, and airport T2242336. **Sila Rent a Car**, Av Procópio Rola 1346, T2241443.

Train

Limited services from Porto Santana to Serra do Navio.

Oiapoque *p554, phone code 091*

Air Flights to **Macapá** 3 times a week.

Boat Occasional cargo vessels to Belém or Macapá (Porto Santana).

Bus Estrela de Ouro leaves for **Macapá** from the waterfront, daily at 1000, 12 hrs (dry season), 14-24 hrs (wet season), US$35, also **Cattani**. Pick-up trucks depart from the same area when full, US$35 in cab, US$15 in the back.

Belém *p555, map p557, phone code 091*

See also Ins and outs, p555

Air

International Airport, T2106272. International flights to Cayenne, Miami and Paramaribo. Domestic flights to Altamira, Brasília, Breves, Carajás, Fortaleza, Imperatriz, Macapá, Manaus, Marabá, Monte Dourado, Rio de Janeiro, Santarém, São Luís and São Paulo. Bus 'Perpétuo Socorro-Telégrafo' or 'Icoaraci', every 15 mins from the Prefeitura, Praça Felipe Patroni, to the airport, 40 mins, US$0.50. Taxi to airport, US$10 (ordinary taxis are cheaper than Coop taxis, buy ticket in advance in Departures side of airport). ATMs in the terminal.

Airline offices Penta, Av Sen Lemos 4700, T2447777. **Surinam Airways**, R Gaspar Viana 488, T2127144, F2247879. English spoken, helpful with information and documentation. **Taba**, Av Dr Freitas 1191, international airport, T2574000. **Varig**, Av Pres Vargas 768, T2243344, airport T2570481. **Vasp**, Av Pres Vargas 345, T2122496, airport T2570944.

Boat

River services to **Santarém**, **Manaus**, and intermediate ports (see River transport, p549 and Routes in Amazônia, p594). The larger ships berth at **Portobrás/Docas do Pará** (the main commercial port), either at Armazém (warehouse) No 3 at the foot of Av Pres Vargas, or at Armazém No 10, a few blocks further north (entrance on Av Marechal Hermes, corner of Av Visconde de Souza Franco). The guards will sometimes ask to see your ticket before letting you into the port area, but tell them you are going to speak with a ship's captain. Ignore the touts who approach you. Smaller vessels (sometimes cheaper, usually not as clean, comfortable or safe) sail from small docks along the **Estrada Nova** (not a safe part of town). Take a **Cremação** bus from Ver-o-Peso.

To **Macapá** (Porto Santana) daily service. **Silja e Souza** of Souzamar, Trav Dom Romualdo Seixas, corner of R Jerônimo Pimentel,

T2220719, and **Comandante Solon** of Sanave (Serviço Amapaense de Navegação, Av Castilho Franca 234, opposite Ver-o-Peso, T2227810). Via Breves, **ENAL**, T2245210. There are 2 desks selling tickets for private boats in the rodoviária; some hotels (eg **Fortaleza**) recommend agents for tickets. Purchase tickets from offices 2 days in advance. Smaller boats to Macapá also sail from Estrada Nova.

Bus

The **rodoviária** is at the end of Av Gov José Malcher, 3 km from the centre, take **Aeroclube**, Cidade Novo, No 20 bus, or **Arsenal** or **Canudos** buses, US$0.50, or taxi, US$5 (day), US$7 (night) (at rodoviária you are given a ticket with the taxi's number on it, threaten to go to the authorities if the driver tries to overcharge). It has a good snack bar and showers (US$0.10) and 2 agencies with information and tickets for riverboats.

Regular bus services to all major cities. Transbrasiliana go direct to **Marabá**, US$20 (16 hrs). To **Santarém**, via Marabá once a week (US$45, more expensive than by boat and can take longer, goes only in dry season). To **São Luís**, 2 a day, US$20, 13 hrs, interesting journey through marshlands. To **Fortaleza**, US$35-40 (24 hrs), several companies. To **Salvador**, US$50.

Car

Car hire Avis, R Antonio Barreto, 1653, T2302000, also at airport, freephone 0800 558066. **Localiza**, Av Pedro Álvares Cabral, 200, T2122700, and at airport, T2571541.

Hitchhiking

Going south, take bus to Capanema, 3½ hrs, US$2.30, walk 500 m from the rodoviária to BR-316 where trucks stop at the gas station.

Marabá and around *p560, phone code 091*

Air

Airport in Cidade Nova, 3 km. There are no direct flights to Altamira or Santarém, only via Belém with **Brasil Central** or **Varig**. **Brasil Central** flies to several local destinations, eg São Luís, Imperatriz.

Airline offices TAM, T3243644. Varig, T3221965.

Boat

Trips to **Belém** (24 hrs) and **Santarém** (18 hrs).

Bus

Rodoviária in Nova Marabá, 4 km on PA-150, T3211892. Buses leave daily for **Belém** (654 km, paved, US$20), for **Santarém** (34 hrs) and many daily for **Imperatriz** (7-10 hrs, US$10, there is also a pick-up to the bank of the Tocantins opposite Imperatriz, 5 hrs, but more expensive); buses can be caught going south at Tocantinópolis, opposite Porto Franco on the Belém-Brasília road. Also a bus can be taken to **Araguaína**, 12½ hrs, US$20; bus Marabá-Goiânia (change at Araguaína). Bus to **Santa Inês** (Maranhão, on the Belém-Teresina road), 19 hrs, US$55. **Transbrasiliana** bus to **Altamira** daily, 1300 (if road is passable), 15 hrs, US$30. There are direct buses to **Rio** and **São Paulo**. On these bus trips take plenty of food and drink as local supplies are expensive. From the rodoviária to the railway station for trains on the São Luís- Parauapebas line (see below), take a *colectivo* bus US$0.75 from opposite the rodoviária to Km 6 (a kind of suburb of Marabá), then another *colectivo* bus, US$0.75, to the Estação Ferrovia. The *colectivos* are not frequent but are crowded. Alternatively taxis, which can be shared, cost US$15 from the railway station to town.

Directory

Macapá *p552, map p553, phone code 096*

Banks Banco do Brasil, R Independência 250, and **Bradesco**, R Cândido Mendes 1316, have Plus ATMs for VISA withdrawals. For *câmbios* (cash only), **Casa Francesa**, R Independência 232. **Monopólio**, Av Isaac Alcoubre 80. Both US$ and euro can be exchanged here. Best to buy euro in Belém if heading for Guyane as *câmbios* in Macapá are reluctant to sell them and they are more expensive and hard to obtain at the border. **Embassies and consulates** France, at Pousada Ekinox (see Sleeping, above). Visas are not issued for non-Brazilians. **Hospitals** Geral, Av FAB, T2126127. **Hospital São Camila & São Luiz**, R Marcelo Candia 742, T2231514. **Internet** @llnet in Macapá Shopping. **Post office** Av Corialano Jucá. **Telephone** R São José 2050. Open 0730-2200.

Oiapoque *p554, phone code 091*

Banks It is possible to exchange US dollars and reais to euro, but dollar rates are low and TCs are not accepted anywhere. Banco do Brasil, Av Barão do Rio Branco, open 1000-1500, reais to euro and Visa facilities. Visa users can also withdraw reais at Bradesco, exchanging these to euro. Gold merchants, like Casa Francesa on the riverfront and a *câmbio* in the market, will sell reais for US$ or euro. Rates are even worse in St-Georges. Best to buy euro In Belém, or abroad. **Immigration** Polícia Federal for Brazilian exit stamp is on the road to Calçoene, about 500 m from the river. **Post office** Av Barão do Rio Branco, open 0900-1200, 1400-1700.

Belém *p555, map p557, phone code 091*

Banks Banks open 0900-1630, but foreign exchange only until 1300. Banco do Brasil, Av Pres Vargas, near Hotel Central, good rates, ATMs and other Brazilian banks (open 0900-1630, but foreign exchange only until 1300). HSBC, Av Pres Vargas near Praça da República has MasterCard Cirrus and Amex ATMs. Banco de Amazônia (Basa), on Pres Vargas, gives good rates for TCs (Amex or Citicorp only), but does not change cash. Itaú, R Boaventura 580, good TCs and cash rates. In early 2002 the local authorities closed all Casas de câmbio, so money could only be changed at banks during the week. At weekends hotels will only exchange for their guests, while restaurants may change money, but at poor rates. **Embassies and consulates** Denmark (Consul Arne Hvidbo), R Senador Barata 704, sala 1503, T2411588 (PO Box 826). Finland and Sweden, Av Senador Lemos 529, Umarizal, T2220148. France, www.ambafrance.org.br. Germany, www.alemanha.org.br. Italy, www.embitalia.org.br. UK, Edif Palladium Centre, room 410, Av Gov José Malcher 815, T2200274. USA,www.embaixada.americana.org.br. Venezuela, opposite French Consulate, R Pres Pernambuco 270, T2226396 (Venezuelan visa takes 3 hrs, costs US$30 for most nationalities, but we are told that it is better to get a visa at Manaus; latest reports indicate that a yellow fever vaccination certificate is not required but it is best to check in advance – see also medical services, below). **Internet** Amazon, 2nd floor of Estação das Docas. InterBelém, Av Jose Malcher 189, US$1 per hr, helpful South African owner, English spoken. Convert, Shopping Iguatemi, 3rd floor, US$1.40 per hr. **Language schools** Unipop, Av Sen Lemos 557, T2249074. Portuguese course for foreigners. **Laundry** Lav e Lev, R Dr Moraes 576. Lavanderia Paraense, Trav. Dom Pedro, 1104, T2220057, dry and steam cleaning. **Libraries** UFPA, Av Augusto Correa 1, T2111140, university library with many titles on Amazônia. **Medical services** Health A yellow fever certificate or inoculation is mandatory. It is best to get a yellow fever vaccination at home (always have your certificate handy) and avoid the risk of recycled needles. Medications for malaria prophylaxis are not sold in Belém pharmacies. You can theoretically get them through the public health service, but this is hopelessly complicated. Such drugs are sometimes available at pharmacies in smaller centres, eg Santarém and Macapá. Bring an adequate supply from home. Clínica de Medicina Preventativa, Av Bras de Aguiar 410 (T2221434), will give injections, English spoken, open 0730-1200, 1430-1900 (Sat 0800-1100). Hospital da Ordem Terceira, Trav Frei Gil de Vila Nova 59, T2122777, doctors speak some English, free consultation. Surgery Mon 1300-1900, Tue-Thu 0700-1100, 24 hrs for emergencies. The British consul has a list of English-speaking doctors. **Police** for reporting crimes, R Santo Antônio and Trav Frei Gil de Vila Nova. **Post office** Av Pres Vargas 498. Also handles telegrams and fax. **Telephone** Telemar, Av Pres Vargas.

Marabá and around *p560, phone code 091*

Banks Banco do Brasil, Praça Duque de Caxias 966. **Hospitals** Celina Gonçalves, T3221031.

The Amazon River and Amazonas

The mighty Amazon system is a staggering 6,577 km long, around half of which (3,165 km) is in Brazilian territory. Ships of up to 5,000 tons regularly negotiate the waterway as far as Iquitos in Peru, 3,646 km away.

Amazonas is the largest state in Brazil (1.6 million sq km), but with a population of only about 2.8 million. Half of the inhabitants live in the capital, Manaus, with the rest spread out amongst remote communities mainly linked by air and river only.

Manaus, the state capital, is the main departure point in Brazil for Amazon rainforest tours and stays in forest lodges. The Anavilhanas islands, the world's largest river archipelago, are a few hours away from the city, up the Rio Negro. These verdant islands set in a pitch black river are a spectacular (and almost mosquito free) sight. Animals here are not as easy to see as in Tefé or on the Rio Javari. The Negro is a black-water river because the surrounding forest grows on sandy soil, whose nutrient deficiency results in fewer floral species, less diversity and consequently fewer animals. The region's indigenous influence can be felt in the Festa da Boi, Brazil's largest festival after Carnaval, and New Year, held on Parintins Island, as well as in many other festivals throughout the year. Although the tribe after whom the capital city was named have long been decimated, there are still strong indigenous nations on the Upper Rio Negro and upper Amazon. Visiting them is difficult. » For Sleeping, Eating and other listings, see pages 587-599.

Along the Transamazônica

The Transamazônica, an almost impassable dirt road filled with pot holes and infringing forest throughout its 5,000 km, connects Brazil's eastern and western extremities. And for no good reason. Millions of dollars were spent on this road whilst others of real economic importance in the east of the country were crumbling. Together with other grandiose and unnecessary schemes like the Amazon dams, the Transamazônica was a major contributor to the country's national debt.

Driving the road is a real adventure. Do not leave without a 4WD and winch. Some sections are often totally impassable throughout the rainy season (for example, Santarém to the Belém-Brasília Highway). Others have scheduled bus services, but as conditions are constantly changing, detailed local inquiry is essential before heading out. The journey along the Transamazônica can be dangerous and it is essential to know some Portuguese. Also ensure that you have sufficient reais.

There are flights to Carajás from Belém, Marabá and Tucuruí and trains to **Marabá**, (leaves at 19302 hrs, US$4) and to **São Luís**, see page 541. Buses run to cities as far away as Rio and São Paulo.

Altamira → *Colour map 1, B5. Population: 77,500*

The Transamazônica crosses the Rio Xingu at Favânia, 41 km east of Altamira, a busy, booming Amazônian town with many gold dealers. A road is being paved 46 km north to the fishing village of Vitória on the lower Xingu, from which boats go to Belém; a good place to watch the *garimpeiros* working below the last rapids. There are no organized trips but a boat can be hired, US$25 per day, for a trip up the Xingu, which is highly recommended. Many animals can be seen. The area is an Assurine Indian reservation and it is not permited to enter villages; buy food in Altamira.

Itaituba → *Colour map 1, B4.*

This *garimpeiro town* is the jumping-off place for the **Amazônia National Park**. See Father Paul Zoderer, who may help to arrange a visit, at the church on the waterfront – nearest **Ibama information** ⓘ *Av Marechal Rondon, CEP 681811-970, Itaituba, T5181530.*

Malaria is present in Itaituba.

There is accommodation in a series of hotels (B-D) on and around the main praça. **Varig** fly here and there are buses to Marabá, (about 34 hours, US$45), Santarém via Rurópolis (11 hours, US$20) and Jacarèacanga and Humaitá.

Santarém → *Phone code: 093. Colour map 1, B4. Population: 262,500.*

The third largest city on the Brazilian Amazon is nonetheless small enough to walk around. It was founded in 1661 as the Jesuit mission of Tapajós; the name was changed to Santarém in 1758. There was once a fort here, and attractive colonial squares overlooking the waterfront still remain. Standing at the confluence of the Rio Tapajós with the Amazon, on the southern bank, Santarém is halfway (two or three days by boat) between Belém and Manaus and most visitors breeze in and out on a stopover by boat or air.

The yellow Amazon water swirls alongside the green-blue Tapajós at the **meeting of the waters** in front of the market square, which is nearly as impressive as that of the Negro and Solimões near Manaus. A small **Museu dos Tapajós** in the old city hall on the waterfront, now the **Centro Cultural João Fora**, downriver from where the boats dock, has a collection of ancient Tapajós ceramics, as well as various 19th-century artefacts and publications. The unloading of the fish catch between 0500 and 0700 on the waterfront is interesting. There are good beaches nearby on the Rio Tapajós. **Prainha**, a small beach, is between town and the port, by a park with many mango trees (Floresta-Prainha bus from centre). On the outskirts of town is Maracanã, with sandy bays (when the Tapajos is low) and some trees for shade (Maracanã bus from centre, 20 minutes). The **tourist office, Comtur** ⓘ *R Floriano Peixoto 434 T/F5232434*, has good information available in English.

Around Santarém

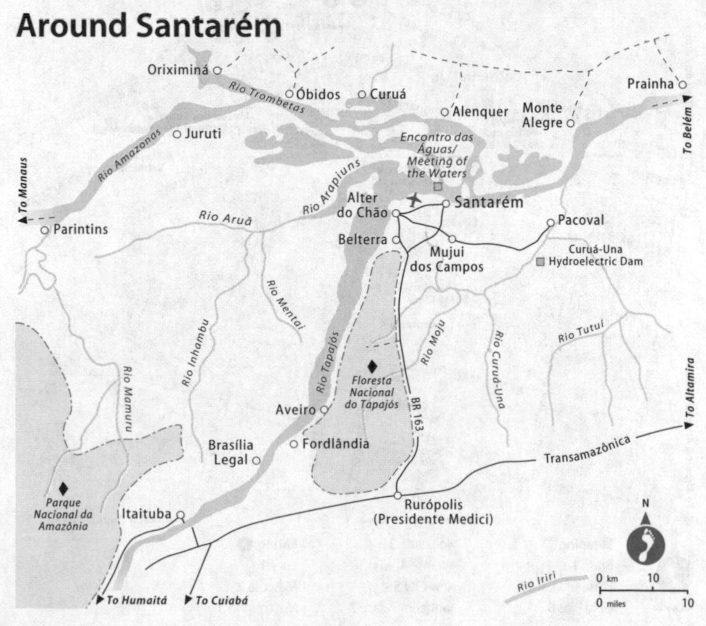

Alter do Chão → *Colour map1, B4.*

Alter do Chão is a friendly village on the Rio Tapajós, at the outlet of Lago Verde, 34 km west. Of particular interest is the **Centro do Preservação da Arte Indígena** ⓘ *R Dom Macedo Costa, T5271110*, which has a substantial collection of artefacts from tribes of Amazônia and Mato Grosso. There is good swimming in the Tapajós from the beautiful, clean beach. Close to Alter do Chão (30 minutes by boat), the conjunction of the Rio Tapajós with the Aruã and the Arapiuns creates an island surrounded by clean rivers of differing colours, each teeming with life. The forested island, already popular, is being developed as an ecopark, **Parque Ecoturístico Arapiuns**, with accommodation for visitors. Monkeys and birds inhabit the woodlands, protected more for commercial reasons than any other. For information, contact **Paratur** ⓘ *T2232130, in Belém.*

Floresta Nacional do Tapajós → *Colour map1, B4.*

ⓘ *Ibama, ToXX91-2245899, or Av Tapajos 2267, Aldeia CEP 68040-000, Santarém, T523-2964, F5235185.*

At Km 123, south of Santarém on BR 163, there is a section of the Floresta Nacional do Tapajós National Forest which has a vehicle track running due west through it. It is beautiful rainforest which can be entered with permission from Ibama if accompanied by one of their guides. It is well worth a visit if only to see the butterflies.

Belterra and Fordlândia → *Phone code 093. Colour map1, B4.*

Fordlândia, 300 km south of Santarém, was Henry Ford's first rubber plantation. He founded it in 1926 in an attempt to provide a cheaper source of rubber for his Ford Motor Company than the British and Dutch controlled plantations in Malaya. There is **Hotel Zebu**, in old Vila Americana (turn right from the dock, then left up the hill), one restaurant, two bars and three shops on the town square. A little pebble beach is north of the town.

Monte Alegre

Monte Alegre is the site of archaeological discoveries, which have threatened to alter radically views of the spread of civilization in South America. Dr Anna C Roosevelt, of the Field Museum of Natural History, Chicago, found in the early 1990s pottery fragments in a cave which, according to radio-carbon dating, appear to be from 7000 to 8000 BC. This predates by some 3,000 years what was thought to be the earliest ceramic ware in South America (from Colombia and Ecuador). Subsequent artefacts discovered here, however, have radio-carbon dates of 15000 BC, which calls for a significant rethink of the original idea that people moved from the Andes into the Amazon Basin. If nothing else, these finds suggest that the story of the people of the Americas is more diverse than hitherto understood. The cave which Dr Roosevelt excavated is called Caverna da Pedra Pintada. Also in the area are pictographs, with large designs of human and animal figures and geometrical shapes. Trips can be arranged.

We are grateful to Philip W Hummer, who sent us a description of a tour to the region, led by Dr Anna Roosevelt.

Closer to Santarém, 37 km south on a dirt road, is Belterra, where Henry Ford established his second rubber plantation. In the highlands overlooking the Rio Tapajós, it is much closer to Santarém than his first project, which was turned into a research station. At Belterra, Ford built a well laid-out new town, where the houses resemble the cottages of Michigan summer resorts, many with white paint and green trim. The town centre has a large central plaza that includes a bandstand, the church of Santo Antônio (c1951), a Baptist church and a large educational and sports complex. A major hospital, which at one time was staffed by physicians from North America, is now closed.

Ford's project, the first modern attempt to invest in the Amazon, was unsuccessful. It was difficult to grow the hevea rubber tree, where it was unprotected from the heavy rains and harsh sun in plantation conditions. Boats could only come this far upriver in the rainy season and there were a series of disputes between the American bosses and the local employees. Ford sold up in 1945 and the rubber plantation is now run down.

Óbidos → *Phone code: 093. Colour map1, A4. Population: 46,500.*

Óbidos is located at the narrowest and deepest point on the river, where millions of years ago the Amazon squeezed through the gap in the Guyana and Brazilian Highlands to meet the Atlantic. It was a strategic point in the Portuguese expansion of the Amazon. The **Forte Pauxi** (1697) is a reminder of this fact (Praça Coracy Nunes). Today, Óbidos is a picturesque and clean city with many beautiful, tiled buildings and some pleasant parks. Worth seeing are the **Prefeitura Municipal** ① *T5471194*, the cuartel and the **Museu Integrado de Ôbidus** ① *R Justo Chermont 607, Mon-Fri 0700-1100, 1330-1730*. There is also a **Museu Contextual**, a system of plaques with detailed explanations of historical buildings througout town. Boating and fishing trips can be made and there is a popular beach at **Igarapé de Curuçambá** (buses go there). It is five hours by boat upriver from Santarém (110 km). A poor road runs east to Alenquer, Monte Alegre and Prainha and west to Oriximiná, impassable in the wet season. The small airport has flights to Manaus, Santarém and Parintins.

Manaus → *Phone code: 092. Colour map 1, B3. Population: 1.4 million.*

Manaus, was at one time an isolated urban island in the jungle, before becoming one of the wealthiest cities in South America during the rubber boom. It is now the most important port of entry for visiting the Amazon, with river islands and tranquil waterways less than a day away. Most people come to arrange a jungle trip, but, thanks to a major restoration programme, there is much of architectural and cultural interest, so try to spend a day or two in the Manaus itself.

The city sprawls over a series of eroded and gently sloping hills divided by numerous creeks (igarapés). It is the collecting point for the produce of a vast area which includes parts of Peru, Bolivia and Colombia. Though 1,600 km from the sea, Manaus is only 32 m above sea level.

Ins and outs

Getting there The road from Porto Velho is very difficult and often impassable, making river or air travel essential. The road north to Boa Vista has been paved,

Manaus orientation

Related maps
A Manaus centre, p577.

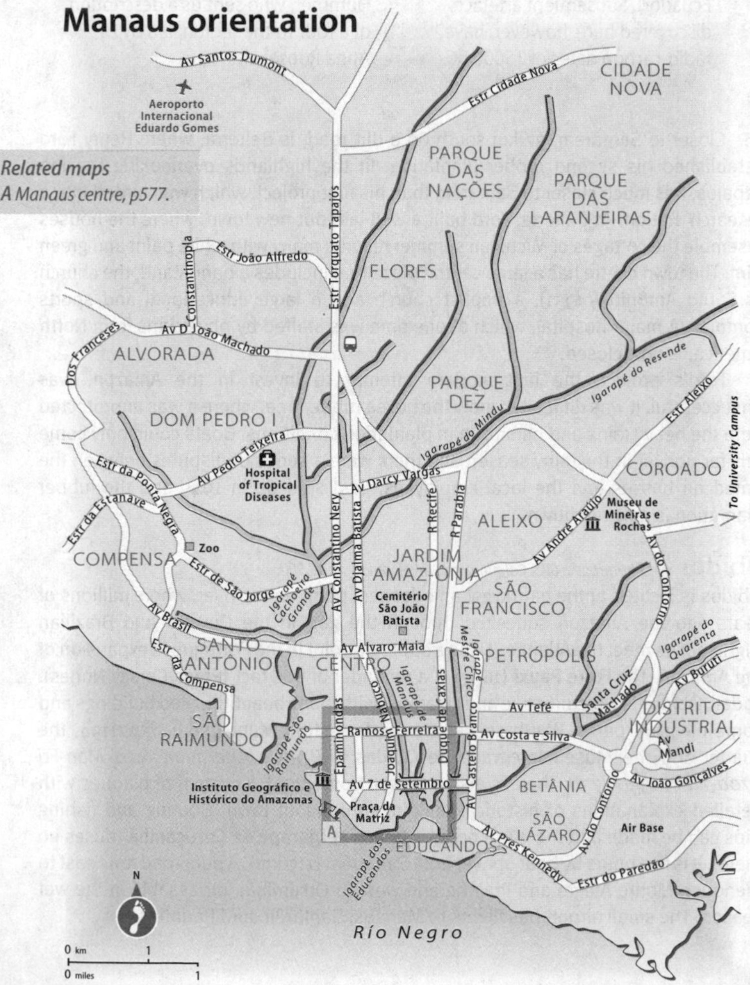

bringing the frontiers of Venezuela and Guyana within easy reach. There is good air and boat access. From the airport, which is 9 km from the city, a taxi to the centre costs US$16, fixed rate. Local buses to the city cost US$0.60, but there are none between 2330 and 0500. Manaus rodoviária is 5 km from the centre at the intersection of Avenida Constantino Nery and Rua Recife. The only long-distance route arriving here is that from Boa Vista and the Venezuelan border. Boat passengers arrive at the floating dock in the centre, with direct access to the main artery of Av Ed Ribeiro, a couple of blocks south from the Praça da Matriz. *See also Transport, page 596.*

Getting around The city centre is easily explored on foot. Buses serve the entire urban area and there are taxis. Other towns in the state are best visited by air or boat, especially during the December to June wet season when road travel is next to impossible.

Tourist offices ⓘ *Av Eduardo Ribeiro, 666, near Teatro Amazonas, T2311998, Mon-Fri 0800-1800, Sat 0800-1300*. Limited English and information. **Secretaria de Estado da Cultura e Turismo** ⓘ *Av 7 de Setembro 1546, Vila Ninita, behind Centro Cultural Pálacio Rio Negro, T6332850, F2339973, Mon-Fri 0730-1700*. There is a **tourist office at the airport** ⓘ *daily 0700-2300, T6521120*. Town map from **Amazon Explorers**, or from news kiosks. *Guide Book of Manaus*, US$3, in English, useful, available from **Selvatur**. Weekend editions of *A Crítica*, newspaper, list local entertainments and events.

Security Manaus is a friendly, if busy city and a good deal safer than the big cities of southern Brazil. As in any city, the usual precautions against opportunist crime should be taken (see Essentials chapter). Bars along Rua Joaquim Nabuco are particularly unsafe due to drugging of drinks. This and the port area are not places to hang around after dark. A tourist police force, **Politur**, has been created in an effort to assist visitors.

Sights

Today, Manaus is building fast, with 20-storey modern buildings rising above the traditional flat, red-tiled roofs. It is an important base for scientific research in the Amazon, carried out by **Insitituto Nacional de Pesquisas Amazonas** (INPA). Under recent municipal administrations the city, including the Zona Franca, old commercial district, port area and nearby markets, has been kept relatively clean and orderly and new markets have been built. An impressive initiative in 2001 saw the start of a significant restoration programme in which historic buildings have been given a new lease of life and theatres, cultural spaces and libraries have been created.

Manaus time is one hour behind Brazilian standard time (two hours during October-March when the rest of Brazil is on summer time).

Dominating the centre is a **cathedral** on Praça Osvaldo Cruz, built in simple Jesuit style and very plain inside and out. Originally constructed in 1695 in wood and straw, it was burnt down in 1850 and rebuilt in neoclassical style. Nearby is the main shopping and business area, the tree-lined **Avenida Eduardo Ribeiro**, crossed by Avenida 7 de Setembro and bordered by ficus trees.

The star attraction and not to be missed is the opera house, **Teatro Amazonas** ⓘ *on Praça São Sebastião, Mon-Sat 0900-1600, 20-min guided tour US$7, students US$2.50, recommended (around same price to attend a concert), information on programmes, T6221880*. Extraordinarily opulent, it was completed in 1896 during the great rubber boom and has been restored four times since then. It took 15 years to build because most of the materials were imported from Europe according to the fashion of the time. The driveway was paved in rubber to prevent the sound of carriage wheels spoiling performances and there is a wonderfully over-the-top ballroom. The designs on the backdrop inside the theatre and the black and white paving in the praça (copied throughout Brazil) at the front of the building represent

24 hours in Manaus

→ Start the day with an energy bomb of fresh juice and *guarana* from one of the many *suco* stalls in the **Zona Franca**. Wander down to the buzzing **waterfront** (not safe at night) and watch the boats at the huge floating dock. This is a great area for street food; try the delicious fried banana.

→ Take time to admire the 100-year-old **Customs House** before buying Amazonian handicrafts and magic potions for anything from happiness to fertility from **Mercado Municipal Adolfo Lisboa**. Lots of shops around the market offer bargain-priced goods. (Morning is the best time to come, as after lunch traders start to pack up.) This is also a good area for a bargain lunch, but if you want to splurge, tuck into the all-you-can-eat Brazilian buffet at the *churrascaria Búfalo*, a local institution.

→ After lunch, take a bus or taxi to the Botanic Gardens, **Instituto Nacional de Pesquisas Amazonas**. At this centre for Amazonian scientific research in the Amazon, you can see local wildlife and a large number of birds. From here, it's a short taxi ride to the **Museu de Ciências Naturais da Amazônia** (Natural Science Museum).

→ Soak up some early evening (starts 1800) culture at the **Teatro da Instalação**. This funky performance space hosts music and dance, both traditional and modern. If that leaves you wanting more, make your way to the **Teatro Amazonas** where there are ballet, theatre and opera performances several times a week, and Brazilian music on Monday nights between June and December.

→ For serious nightlife, you need to make a trip to **Ponta Negra** beach. This is where the city's best restaurants are found. Tuck into one of the local fish specialities such as *tambaqui* and then take your pick from everything from old-school samba to heavy techno. Look at listings magazines as nights change frequently. Most of the clubs here stay open all night, so you may as well continue until morning (taxis back to town are expensive) and have a swim in the river when the sun comes up.

the meeting of the waters. There are ballet, theatre and opera performances several times a week and popular Brazilian music on Monday nights, June-December, which is free. **Igreja São Sebastião** (1888), on the same square, is worth a look inside to see its unusual altar of two giant ivory hands holding a water lily of Brazil wood.

On the waterfront, the **Mercado Adolfo Lisboa** ⓘ *R dos Barés, 46* was built in 1882 as a miniature copy of the now-demolished Parisian Les Halles. The wrought ironwork, which forms much of the structure, was imported from Europe and is said to have been designed by Eiffel.

The remarkable **harbour installations**, completed in 1902, were designed and built by a Scottish engineer to cope with the Rio Negro's annual rise and fall of up to 14 m. The large passenger ship floating dock is connected to street level by a 150 m-long floating ramp, at the end of which, on the harbour wall, can be seen the high water mark for each year since it was built. When the water is high, the roadway floats on a series of large iron tanks measuring 2½ m in diameter. The large yellow **Alfândega** (Customs House) ⓘ *R Marquês de Santa Cruz, Mon-Fri 0800-1300*, stands at the entrance to the city when arriving by boat. It was entirely prefabricated in England, and the tower once acted as lighthouse.

The **Biblioteca Pública** (Public Library) ⓘ *R Barroso 57, Mon-Fri 0730-1730, T2340588*, inaugurated in 1871, is part of the city's architectural heritage. Featuring an ornate European cast-iron staircase, it is well stocked with 19th-century newspapers, rare books and old photographs, and worth a visit.

The very small **Museu Tiradentes** ⓘ *Praça da Polícia, Mon 1400-1800, Tue-Fri 0800-1200 and 1400-1800, T2347422*, is run by the military police and holds selected historical items and old photographs.

There is a curious little church, **Igreja do Pobre Diabo**, at the corner of Avenidas Borba and Ipixuna in the suburb of Cachoeirinha. It is only 4 m wide by 5 m long, and was built by a local trader, the 'poor devil' of the name. To get there, take Circular 7 de Setembro Cachoeirinha bus from the cathedral to Hospital Militar.

The **Instituto Geográfico e Histórico do Amazonas** ⓘ *R Bernardo Ramos 117 (near Prefeitura), T2327077, Mon-Fri 0800-1200, US$0.20*, is located in a fascinating older district of central Manaus. It houses a museum and library of over 10,000 books, which thoroughly document Amazonian life through the ages.

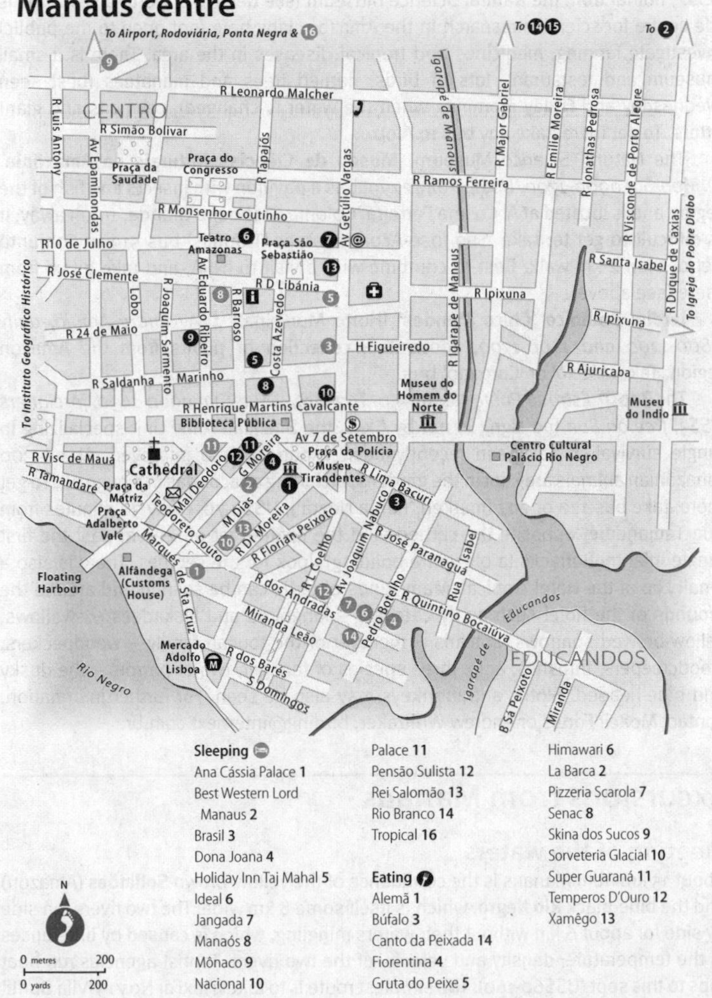

The **Centro Cultural Pálacio Rio Negro** ⓘ *Av 7 de Setembro, T2324450, Tue-Fri 1000-1700, Sat and Sun 1600-2100,* was the residence of a German rubber merchant until 1917 and later the state government palace. It now holds various cultural events, including exhibitions, shows and films; there is also a café.

The **Museu do Índio** ⓘ *R Duque de Caxias (near Av 7 Setembro), T2341422, Mon-Fri 0830-1200 and 1400-1700, Sat 0800-1130, US$3,* is managed by the Salesian missionaries, but is rather run down. It has an interesting collection that includes handicrafts, ceramics, clothing, utensils and ritual objects from the various Indian tribes of the upper Rio Negro and an excellent craft shop.

The **Museu do Homem do Norte** ⓘ *Av 7 de Setembro 1385 (near Av Joaquim Nabuco), T2325373, Mon-Thu 0900-1200, 1300-1700, Fri 1300-1700, US$1,* is an interesting review of the way of life of the Amazonian population, or 'men of the north', although it has deteriorated in recent years. Social, cultural and economic aspects are displayed with photographs, models and other pieces.

Botanic Gardens ⓘ *Instituto Nacional de Pesquisas Amazonas (INPA), Estrada do Aleixo at Km 3, T6433377, Mon-Fri 0900-1100, 1400-1630, Sat and Sun 0900-1600, US$2,* not far from the Natural Science Museum (see below), is worth a visit. This is the centre for scientific research in the Amazon; labs here (not open to the public) investigate farming, medicines and tropical diseases in the area. There is a small museum and restaurant, lots of birds, named trees and manatees (best seen Wednesday and Friday mornings when the water is changed), caymans and giant otters. To get there, take any bus to Aleixo.

The Natural Science Museum, **Museu de Ciências Naturais da Amazônia** ⓘ *Mon-Sat 0900-1700, US$4, T6442799,* has a pavilion with insects and fish of the region and is located at Al Cosme Ferreira, Colonia Cachoeira Grande, 15 km away. It is difficult to get to; take 'São José-Acoariquarape/Tropolis' bus 519 to Conjunto Petro, then 2-km walk. Best to combine with a visit to INPA, and take a taxi from there (see above).

Jardim Botânico 'Chico Mendes' (Horto Municipal) ⓘ *Av André Araujo, daily 0800-1200 and 1400-1700,* contains a collection of plants from the Amazon region. Take 'Aleixo' or 'Coroado' bus.

The **Zoo** ⓘ *Estrada Ponta Negra 750, T6252044, Tue-Sun 0900-1630, foreigners US$3, free on Sun* (no sign), is run by CIGS, the Brazilian Army Unit specializing in jungle survival. It has been recently been expanded and improved. About 300 Amazonian animals are kept in the gardens, including anacondas in a huge pit. To get there, take bus 120 or 207 (marked 'Ponta Negra'), US$0.70, every 30 minutes from Rua Tamandaré, opposite the cathedral in the centre, get off 400 m past the first Jungle Infantry Barracks (a big white building), look for the sentries. There is also a small zoo at the Hotel Tropical. Many kinds of birds can be seen in and around the grounds of the hotel such as fly catchers – kingbirds and kiskadees – swallows, yellow-browed sparrows, aracaris – member of the toucan family – woodpeckers, woodcreepers, thrushes, anis, three species of tanager, two of parrots – the dusky and blue-headed. Sloths and monkeys may also be seen. For further information, contact Moacir Fortes or Andrew Whittaker, birding@internext.com.br.

Excursions from Manaus

Meeting of the waters

About 15 km from Manaus is the confluence of the yellow-brown **Solimões** (Amazon) and the blue-black **Rio Negro**, which is itself some 8 km wide. The two rivers run side by side for about 6 km without their waters mingling, which is caused by differences in the temperature, density and velocity of the two rivers. Tourist agencies run boat trips to this spot (US$60-160). The simplest route is to take a taxi or No 713 'Vila Buriti' bus to the Careiro ferry dock, and take the car ferry across. The ferry, which is very basic with no shelter on deck and no cabins, departs at 0700 returning 1000, and 1500 returning 1800 (approximately). Small private launches cross, a 40-minute journey costing about US$10-15 per seat, ask for the engine to be shut off at the confluence. You should see dolphins especially in the early morning. Alternatively, hire a motorized canoe from near the market (US$15 approximately; allow three to four hours to experience the meeting properly). A 2-km walk along the Porto Velho road from the Careiro ferry terminal will lead to a point from which Victoria Regia water lilies can be seen in April-September in ponds, some way from the road. ▸▸ *See also Amazon tours, page 579.*

Manacapuru → *Colour map 1, B3.*

This typical Amazon small market town is situated on the Solimões west of Manaus. It has three basic hotels and **Il Maccarone** pizzeria (Avenida Eduardo Ribeiro 1000). It is 84 km on AM-070 by bus, four daily, US$5, two hours including ferry crossing.

Araça

This village on the Rio Mamori has plenty of wildlife close at hand. Canoes can be hired. It is three hours by No 11 bus from the rodoviária in the direction of Castanho; the journey includes the ferry at the confluence of the Negro and Solimões (fare to Araça US$1.50, bus leaves 0600 and 1100). Three buses a day return to Manaus.

Arquipélago de Anavilhanas

This is the second largest river archipelago in the world. It is located in the Rio Negro, some 100 km upstream from Manaus, near the town of Novo Airão. There are hundreds of islands, covered in thick vegetation. When the river is low, white sand beaches are revealed, as well as the roots and trunks of the trees. Tour companies arrange visits to the archipelago (US$195-285, one day).

Amazon tours

Choosing a tour

There are two types of tours: those based at jungle lodges and riverboat trips. Whatever you choose, bear in mind that the Amazon is a broad experience and not about one particular aspect. Most tours, whether luxury or budget, combine river outings on motorized canoes with piranha fishing, cayman spotting, visiting local families and short treks in the jungle. Specialist tours include fishing trips and those aimed specifically at seeing how the people in the jungle, *caboclos*, live.

Make sure to ascertain in advance the exact itinerary and that the price includes everything (even drinks and tips). Check that guides are knowledgeable, speak a language you understand, and will accompany you themselves. Insist that there will be no killing of anything rare, or even disruption of wildlife (many guides drag caymans out of the water which has negative long term effects). Ensure that others in your party share your expectations and are going for the same length of time. A shorter tour may be better than a long, poor one. Advance booking on the internet is likely to secure you a good guide (who usually work for several companies and may get booked up). Packaged tours, booked overseas, are usually of the same price and quality as those negotiated locally.

> *If using a camera, remember to bring a fast film as light is dim.*

Those used to the quality of wildlife information supplied by rainforest tour operators in Costa Rica, Peru, Ecuador or Bolivia will be disappointed with the lack of proper professional wildlife knowledge and ecotourism services on offer by Manaus's operators. They have simply not done their market research and remain unaware of the standards expected by wildlife tourists. However if you are looking for a taste of the forest, spectacular rainforest landscapes, well-run lodges and light adventure Manaus is a good place from which to take a rainforest tour. And there are a number of adventurous options on offer to the young and fit. Serious wildlife enthusiasts and birders looking to visit the Brazilian Amazon should head for the Mamirauá near Tefé or if they do not require specialist guides, Tabatinga/Leticia or Alta Floresta.

There are many hustlers at the airport and on the street (particularly around the hotels and bars on Joaquim Nabuco and Miranda Leão), and even at hotel receptions. It is not wise to go on a tour with the first friendly face you meet; all go-betweens earn a commission so recommendations cannot be taken at face value and employing freelance guides not attached to a company is potentially dangerous. Make enquiries and check credentials personally. **Secretaria de Estado da Cultura e Turismo** (see Directory above) are not allowed by law to recommend guides, but can provide you with a list of legally registered companies. Unfortunately, disreputable operations are rarely dealt with in any satisfactory manner, and most continue to operate. Book direct with the company itself and ask for a detailed, written contract if you have any doubts.

Tour duration and itinerary

» *See also Routes in Amazônia, page 594.*

Bill Potter, resident in Manaus, writes: "opposite Manaus, near the junction of the Rio Negro and the Rio Solimões, lies the **Lago de Janauri**, a small nature reserve. This is where all the day or half-day trippers are taken, usually combined with a visit to the 'meeting of the waters'. Although many people express disappointment with this area because so little is seen and/or there are so many 'tourist-trash' shops, for those with only a short time it is worth a visit. You will see some birds and, with luck, dolphins. In the shops and bars there are often captive parrots and snakes. The area

Around Manaus

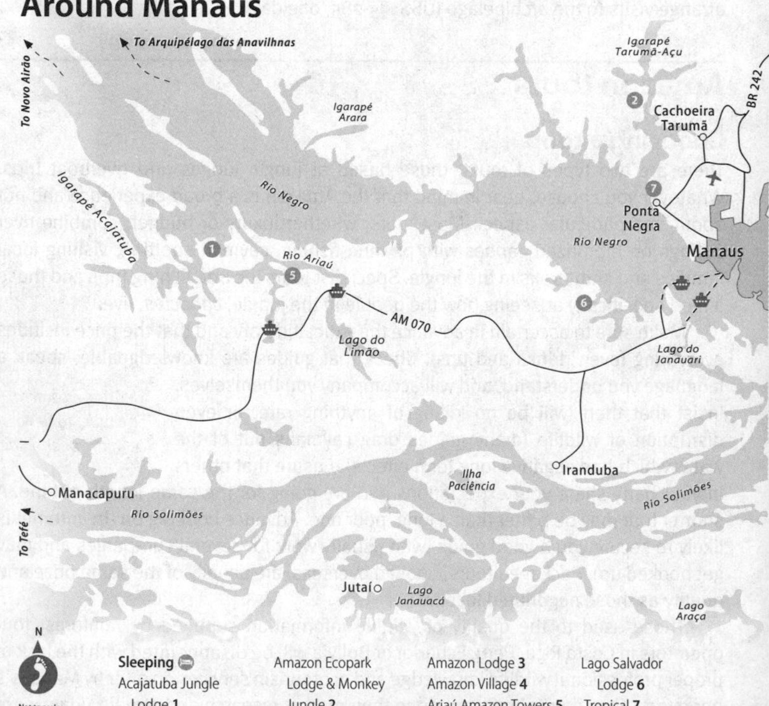

Sleeping
Acajatuba Jungle Lodge **1**
Amazon Ecopark Lodge & Monkey Jungle **2**
Amazon Lodge **3**
Amazon Village **4**
Ariaú Amazon Towers **5**
Lago Salvador Lodge **6**
Tropical **7**

is set up to receive large numbers of tourists, which ecologists agree relieves pressure on other parts of the river. Boats for day trippers leave the harbour constantly throughout the day, but are best booked at one of the larger operators such as **Amazon Explorers** or **Selvatur**. Remember that in the dry season, one-day tours may not offer much to see if the river is low."

Those with more time can take the longer cruises and will see various ecological environments. To see virgin rainforest, a five-day trip by boat is needed. Most tour operators run trips on both the Rio Solimões and the Rio Negro. The Rio Negro is considered easier to navigate, more pristine, generally calmer and with fewer biting insects. But there is a far lower speicies diversity. On the Rio Solimões there is a higher species count and diversity but more insects. The river is flooded for six months of the year offering great opportunities for exploring the varzea forest through flooded tracts known as igapós and through seasonal creeks called igarapés. .

Another alternative is to go upriver to one of the forest lodges. From here you can take short trips into the forest or along the river channels. Flights over the jungle give a spectacular impression of the extent of the forest.

Taking a transport boat from Manaus is not a substitute for a tour as they rarely get near to the banks and are only interested in getting from A to B as quickly as possible.

Generally, between April and September excursions are only by boat; in the period October-March, the Victoria Regia lilies virtually disappear. Fishing is best between September and March (no flooding).

Prices vary but usually include lodging, guide, transport, meals (but not drinks) and activities. The recommended companies charge within the following ranges (per person): one day, US$60-95; three days, for example to Anavilhanas Archipelago, US$195-285. Most tours or lodge stays will involve daytime canoe activity looking for birds, light treks to caboclo (literally peasant) communities for lunch, piranha fishing (these fish are very common) and night time cayman spotting with a halogen lamp to reflect the eye shine. Longer, specialized (eg fishing tours), or more luxurious excursions will cost significantly more. Most river trips incorporate the meeting of the waters on the first day, so there is no need to make a separate excursion.

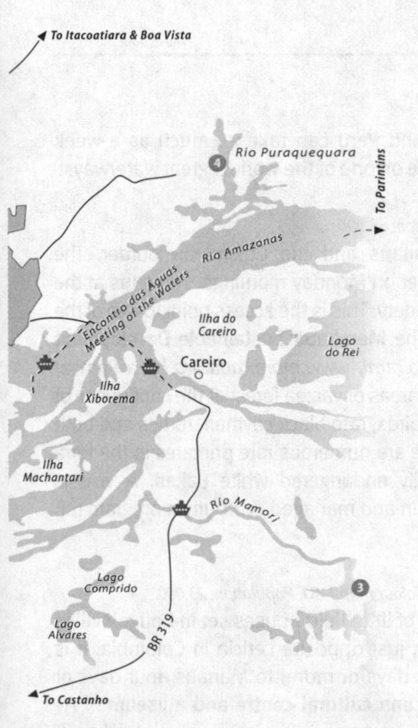

What to take

Leave luggage with your tour operator or hotel in Manaus and only take what is necessary for your trip. Long sleeves, long trousers, walking boots and insect repellent are advisable for treks in the jungle where insects are voracious. A hat offers protection from the sun on boat trips. Bottled water and other drinks are expensive in the jungle, so you may want to take your own supplies and a sturdier water bottle. A hammock mosquito net is useful for treks and a bed mosquito net is a good idea for the cheaper lodges where the provided net may have holes.

The Amazon River beyond Manaus

Parintins → *Phone code: 092. Colour map 1, B4. Population: 90,000.*

Downstream, just before the Amazonas-Pará border, between Manaus and Santarém, is Parintins, a town on the Ilha Tupinambana. Boat trips can be taken to river beaches in the dry season and to nearby lakes. In colonial times, this was the eventual resting point of a group of coastal indigenous Brazilians who made an astonishing trek through thousands of miles of dense forest to escape the ravages of the Portuguese slave trade. But they didn't escape it for long. Within a generation they had been found by slavers from Belém who took all the women and children and murdred all the men. Ironically the island is now the site of one of the countries most important and most spectacular festivals; Boi Bumba, which celebrates the triumph of the indigenous and *caboclo* poor over a tyrannical landowner, or as they are called in Brazil, *coronel*.

The **Festa do Boi Bumba** draws tens of thousands of visitors to Parintins on the last three days of June each year. But since the town has only two small hotels, finding a room can be a challenge. Everyone sleeps in hammocks on the boats that bring them to the festival from Manaus and Santarém (a large vessel will charge about US$130 per person, including breakfast, for the duration). The Festa do Boi de Parintins consists of lots of wild folkloric dancing, but its main element is the competition between two rival groups, the **Caprichoso** (whose colour is blue) and the **Garantido** (red), in the *bumbódromo*, built in 1988 to hold 35,000 spectators. There are about 2,500 competitors, but many more participants. During the festival, Mãe Catirina, Pai Francisco and Cunhãporanga (the beautiful woman) are major characters in this particular *boi-bumbá* drama. A preview of the festival is held in the **Hotel Tropical** in Manaus in the middle of June. Parintins' other main festival is the **Pastorinhas**, from 24 December-6 January.

Up the Rio Solimões

The river route from Manaus to Colombia and Peru can take as much as a week upriver. This journey will let you experience life on one of the world's great waterways.

Tefé → *Phone code: 097. Colour map 1, B2. Population: 65,000.*

Tefé is approximately halfway between Manaus and the Colombian border. The waterfront has a light sand beach and a market on Monday mornings. The nuns at the Franciscan convent sell handicrafts and embroidery. This is the access point to one of the world's most important waterfowl reserves, the **Mamirauá Sustainable Development Reserve** ⓘ *T3434160, www.cnpq.br/mamiraua.html, www.mamiraua.org.br*, a Ramsar site set up with British support to protect huge areas of varzea forest at the confluence of the Solimões and Japurá rivers. Thousands of birds, rare black cayman, turtles and both species of Amazon dolphin live here and there are numerous rare primates in the terra firme forest surrounds, including the critically endangered white uakari. A visit is unforgettable. There is an excellent, properly run and managed ecotourism program run here. This must be arranged in advance.

Benjamin Constant → *Phone code: 097. Colour map 1, B1. Population: 23,000.*

This tiny town with a big sawmill and a series of little tield houses set in bougainvillea gardens sits on the on the frontier with Peru, just opposite Leticia in Colombia. It is served by boat services from Manaus, seven days or more; to Manaus, four days or more and Iquitos. There is an interesting **Ticuna cultural centre and museum** ⓘ Av Castelo Branco 396, T4155624, with displayed artefacts, information panels and a gift shop. The music is haunting but sadly not for sale. Ticuna people run the museum.

Tabatinga → *Phone code: 097. Colour map 1, B1. Population: 38,000.*

Tabatinga is theoretically 4 km from Leticia in Colombia but in reality it is the scruffy half of the same town – a long street buzzing with mopeds, a port and some untidy houses in between. There is an important Ticuna centre here, and the town is the headquarters of one of the countries most important Indian NGOs, FIUPAM (see page 548. But there is little for tourists, who are better off staying in Leticia.

Border crossing No visas or entry stamps are required to pass between Tabatinga and Leticia, but immigration and customs in and out of Tabatinga by air can be very rigorous. The Port Captain here is reported as very helpful and speaking good English. The port area is called Marco. A good hammock will cost US$15 in Tabatinga (try Esplanada Teocides) or Benjamin Constant. A mosquito net for a hammock is essential if sailing upstream from Tabatinga; much less so downstream. There are regular boats for Manaus and to Benjamin Constant across the water. The best way to get to Leticia is to walk or take a cab or minibus (US$0.60). Airport to Tabatinga by minibus, US$1. Flights to Manaus (three times a week with **Varig**) via Tefé. Banco do Brasil, Av da Amizade, has a visa cash point and changes TCs at poor rate. It is easier to get Peruvian money for reais in Leticia. For Internet: Infocenter, Av Amizade 1581.

Leticia → *Phone code: 9859. Colour map 1, B1. Population: 27,000.*

This riverside city is clean and modern, though run down, and is rapidly merging into one town with neighbouring Marco in Brazil. Leticia is a good place to buy typical Amazon Indian products and tourist services are better than in Tabatinga or Benjamin Constant. The best time to visit the area is in July or August, the early months of the dry season. At weekends, accommodation may be difficult to find. There is a **tourist office** ⓘ *C 10, No 9-86. MA (Ministerio del Medio Ambiente), Cra 11, No 12-05*, for general information on national parks.

The **museum** ⓘ *Cra 11 y Calle 9*, set up by **Banco de la República**, covers local ethnography and archaeology, in a beautiful building with a library and a terrace overlooking the Amazon. There is a small **Amazonian zoo** ⓘ *US$1*, and botanical garden on the road to the airport, within walking distance of town (20 minutes).

Border with Colombia and Peru

It is advisable to check all requirements and procedures before arriving at this multiple border. As no foreign boat is allowed to dock at the Brazilian, Colombian and Peruvian ports, travellers should enquire carefully about embarkation/disembarkation points and where to go through immigration formalities. If waiting for transport, the best place for accommodation, exchange and other facilities is Leticia, Colombia. Travel between Colombia and Brazil and Peru is given below. Travel from/into Colombia is given under Leticia (see below).

Brazil

Brazilian immigration Entry and exit stamps are given at the Polícia Federal, 10 minutes' walk from the Tabatinga docks, opposite **Café dos Navegantes** (walk through the docks and follow the road to its end, turn right at this T-junction for one block to a white building). Monday-Friday 0800-1200, 1400-1800; also at the airport, Wednesday and Saturday only. Proof of US$500 or an onward ticket may be asked for. There are no facilities in Benjamin Constant, but it is possible to buy supplies for boat journeys. One-week transit in Tabatinga is permitted. In this area, carry your passport at all times. If coming from Peru, you must have a Peruvian exit stamp and a yellow fever certificate.

The **Colombian consulate** is near the border on the road from Tabatinga to Leticia, opposite **Restaurant El Canto de las Peixadas** (0800-1400). Tourist cards are issued on presentation of two passport photos.

Transport Travel between Tabatinga and Leticia is very informal. Taxis between the the towns charge US$5 (more if you want to stop at immigration offices, exchange houses etc. Beware of taxi drivers who want to rush you expensively over the border before it 'closes'), or US$0.80 in a colectivo (more after 1800). It is not advisable to walk the muddy path between Tabatinga and Leticia; robbery occurs here. » *For boats to/from Manaus, see River transport, page 549, Routes in Amazônia, page 594 and Boats, page 597.*

Boats from Manaus-Benjamin Constant, boats normally go on to Tabatinga and start from there when going to Manaus. They usually wait one or two days in both Tabatinga and Benjamin Constant before returning to Manaus; you can stay on board. Tabatinga and Leticia are 1½-2 hrs from Benjamin Constant (ferry/*recreio* US$2; 25 minutes by speedboat, US$4 per person, cheaper if more passengers).

Colombia

Colombian immigration DAS ⓘ *C 9, No 8-32, T27189, Leticia*, and at the airport. Exit stamps to leave Colombia by air or overland are given only at the airport. If flying into Leticia prior to leaving for Brazil or Peru, get an exit stamp while at the airport. Check both offices for entry stamps before flying into Colombia.

Entering Colombia To enter Colombia you must have a tourist card to obtain an entry stamp, even if you are passing through Leticia en route between Brazil and Peru (the Colombian consul in Manaus may tell you otherwise; try to get a tourist card elsewhere). The Colombian Consular Office in Tabatinga issues tourist cards;

Amazon border area with Colombia & Peru

24-hour transit stamps can be obtained at the DAS office. If visiting Leticia without intending to go anywhere else in Colombia, you may be allowed to enter without immigration or customs formalities (but travellers' cheques cannot be changed without an entry stamp).

Consulates Brazilian ⓘ *C 11, No 10-70, T27531, 1000-1600, Mon-Fri*, efficient, helpful; onward ticket and two black-and-white photos needed for visa (photographer nearby); allow 36 hours. **Peruvian** ⓘ *Cra 11, No 6-80, T27204, F27825, open 0830-1430*; no entry or exit permits are given here.

Peru

Peruvian immigration Entry/exit formalities take place at Santa Rosa. Every boat leaving Peru stops here. There is also an immigration office in Iquitos (Malecón Tarapacá 382), where procedures for leaving can be checked. **Exchange** is available at Islandia (see below).

Consulates In Iquitos there are consulates for **Brazil** ⓘ *C Sargento Lores 363, T005194-232081*, and **Colombia** ⓘ *C Putumayo 247, T231461*.

Transport Boats sail from Iquitos to a mud bank called **Islandia**, on the Peruvian side of a narrow creek, a few metres from the Brazilian port of Benjamin Constant. The journey time is a minimum of two days upstream, eight to 36 hours downstream, depending on the speed of the boat. In ordinary boats, fares range from US$30-40 per person, depending on standard of accommodation, food extra. Speedboats charge US$75 per person, three a week run by **Amazon Tours and Cruises**. Passengers leaving Peru must visit immigration at Santa Rosa when the boat stops there. For entry into Brazil, formalities are done in Tabatinga; for Colombia, in Leticia. Boats to Peru leave from Islandia, calling at Santa Rosa (two to three days upstream to Iquitos). **Amazon Tours and Cruises** also operate a luxury service between Iquitos and Tabatinga leaving Sunday, returning from Tabatinga on Wednesday, US$695 per person in the **Río Amazonas**. Also M/V **Arca** US$495 per person, return journey Wednesday to Saturday.

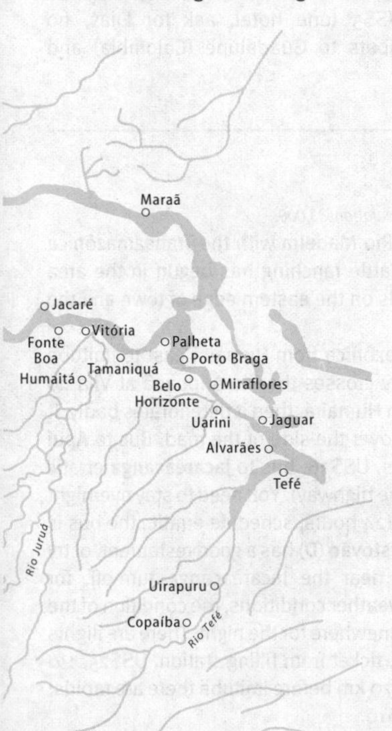

Up the Rio Negro

It is possible to get a public passenger boat (from Sao Raimundo port on the outskirts of Manaus) up the Rio Negro; see River transport, page 549 and Routes in Amazônia, page 594. There are hardly any villages of more than a few houses, but these places are important in terms of communications and food resources. It is vital to be self-sufficient in food and cash and to be able to speak Portuguese or have a Brazilian guide. **Nova Airão**, on the west bank of the Negro, is an overnight, eight-hour boat trip upstream. It has a large boat-building centre at the south end, and a fish and vegetable market at the north end. Ice and bread can also be purchased here. It has a telephone, from which international calls can usually be made. There is road access and a bus service from Manaus.

It's two days from Nova Airão to the **Parque Nacional Jaú**. The only way to get here is with a tour; there is no transport or facilities. Permits are necessary; contact the **Ibama office**ⓘ *R Ministro João Gonçalves de Souza, BR-319, Km 01, Distrito Industrial, Caixa Postal 185, Manaus, CEP 69900, T2373718/3710, F2375177.*

Moura is about five days upstream from Manaus. It has basic medical facilities and the military base has an airstrip (only usable September to December) and telecommunications. About a day further upstream is **Carvoeira**, almost opposite the mouth of the Rio Branco. There is a vibrant festival in the first week of August. More than a day beyond is **Barcelos**, with a daily air service, except Sundays (**Hotel Oasis**, German spoken; **Macedo**), the centre for bass fishing on the Amazon.

São Gabriel da Cachoeira → *Colour map 1, A2.*

A great distance further upstream is São Gabriel da Cachoeira, from where you can continue to Venezuela. It is a nice place, with beautiful white beaches and, in the river, rapids for 112 km. There is a daily air service, except Sundays. São Gabriel is near the **Pico da Neblina National Park**. Pico da Neblina is the highest mountain in Brazil (3,014 m). Contact the **Ibama** office in Manaus for more information and details of guides and trips to indigenous villages (not very traditional any more), see above. In São Gabriel there are two banks but no exchange facilities and the **Vaupes** hotel (E). Cargo boats ply **Cucuí** at the border between Brazil, Colombia and Venezuela. Also twice-weekly bus, US$5 (one hotel, ask for Elias, no restaurants). From Cucuí there are daily boats to Guadalupe (Colombia) and infrequent boats to Santa Lucía (Venezuela).

! The upper Rio Negro can be a rough area due to gold prospecting and drug running. Obtain local information and exercise caution when travelling in this region.

South on the Rio Madeira

Humaitá → *Phone code: 097. Colour map 1, B3. Population: 33,000.*

Humaitá is situated at the crossroads of the Rio Madeira with the Transamazônica highway and the BR-319 north to Manaus. Cattle ranching has begun in the area around the town. There are several basic hotels on the eastern edge of town and the Soltur rodoviária in the centre.

There is very little traffic on the Transamazônica from Humaitá east to Itaituba (1,025 km); local drivers may give lifts. A ferry crosses the Rio Aripuanã at Vila do Carmo. The road is good for about 350 km from Humaitá, then it deteriorates badly. It is hilly, narrow, and the jungle usually grows over the side of the road. Bus to **Apuí** (**Hotel Goaino**, basic), 458 km, about 12 hours, US$36, bus to **Jacarèacanga** erratic service, another 222 km (the town is 8 km off the highway). You need to stay overnight and catch the Transbrasiliana bus to Itaituba (24 hours, schedule erratic, the bus is replaced occasionally by a truck). **Hotel São Cristóvão** (**D**) has a good restaurant, or try the filling station, on the Transamazônica near the Jacarèacanga turn-off, for hammock space. Travel times depend on the weather conditions, the condition of the bus, and whether the driver decides to stop somewhere for the night. There are flights from Jacarèacanga to Itaituba. Boat, not daily, ticket from filling station, US$25, 1½ days, very basic, hammock space only. About 70 km before Itaituba there are rapids; the rest of the journey is done by pick-up, US$10.

Sleeping

Altamira *p570, phone code 091*
B **Alta Palace**, Av Tancredo Neves 3093, T5152057. Simple with a Bar/restaurant, a/c rooms and reasonable service.
C **Lisboa**, Lindolfo Aranha 405, T5151825. A/c rooms with a TV. Good value.

Alter do Chão *p572, phone code 091*
B **Pousada Tupaiulândia**, R Pedro Teixera 300, next to telephone office opposite bus stop, T5271157. Unprepossessing but adequate, with plain and boxy a/c rooms and very helpful, friendly staff. Good breakfast.
D **Alter do Chão**, R Lauro Sodré 74, T5271215. Simple with a reasonable restaurant and a little orchid garden.
D **Tia Marilda**, Trav Agostinho Lobato, T5271144. A/c and cheaper fan-cooled rooms.

Santarém *p571, map p572, phone code 091*
All hotels, except **Amazon Park**, are in the compact grid of streets in the heart of the city near the waterfront
A **Amazon Park**, Av Mendonça Furtado 4120, T5232800, amazon@stm.interconect.com.br. Large 1970s hotel 4 km from centre, with a swimming pool and friendly, competent staff.
C **Brasil Grande Hotel**, Trav 15 de Agosto 213, T5225660. Family-run, with a restaurant.
C **New City**, Trav Francisco Corrêa 200, T5233149. Standard town hotel with plain a/c rooms and an airport pick-up service. River trips can be organized from here.
C-D **Santarém Palace**, Rui Barbosa 726, T5232820, F5221779. 1980s hotel with 44 comfortable but simple a/c rooms with a TV and fridge.
D **Brasil**, Trav dos Mártires 30, T5235177. Pleasan family run and with fan-cooled rooms with shared bathrooms, breakfast and a small restaurant.
D **Mirante**, Trav Francisco Correa 115, T5233054, freephone 0800-7073054, www.mirantehotel.com. One of the new and cleaner cheapies, with a/c rooms all with fridges, TVs, and some with a balcony and individual safes. Internet facilities available. Recommended.
D-F **Horizonte**, Trav Senador Lemos, 737, T5225437, horizontehotel@bol.com.br. Plain, simple but well kept rooms with a/c or a fan.
E **Grão Rios**, in a little alley off Av. Tapajós between Travess dos Máritires and 15 de Agosto. Well-kept a/c rooms some with a river view.

Belterra and Fordlândia *p572, phone code 093*
E **Hotel Seringueira**, Belterra. 8 simple fan-cooled rooms and a pleasant restaurant.

Óbidos *p573, phone code 093*
C **Braz Bello**, R Corrêia Pinto, on top of the hill. Rooms with shared bathrooms; clean and with optional full board.
C-D **Pousada Brasil**, R Correia Pinto. Basic with fan-cooled rooms with en suites or shared bathrooms.

Manaus *p574, map p577, phone code 092*
Although the area around Av Joaquim Nabuco and R dos Andradas has lots of cheap (pretty grubby) hotels, this is a low-key red-light district and not particularly safe at night. A much better option is the nearby Zona Franca, which is convenient for shops, banks, restaurants and the port area.
L **Holiday Inn Taj Mahal**, Av Getúlio Vargas 741, Centre, T6331010, F2330068, tajmahal@internext.com.br. A large, well-run business and airline crew hotel near the opera house in the centre. Facilities include a tour agency, revolving restaurant and a spa.
L **Tropical**, Av Coronel Teixeira 1320, Ponta Negra. T6595000, www.tropicalhotel.com.br. A lavish 5-star hotel 20 km outside city in a semi-forested parkland setting next to the river. The hotel has a private beach, tennis court and a large pool with a wave machine. There are several restaurants including a decent *churrascaria*. The river dock is a departure point for many river cruises. Take minibus from R José Paranaguá in front of Petrobras building at corner of Dr Moreira, US$5 return, 0830, 0930, 1130 to hotel, 1200, 1400, 1500, 1800 to town, or take Ponta Negra bus, US$0.70, then walk. A taxi to the centre costs around US$20. The hotel charges a 12% service tax and offers substantial discounts for those arriving on **Varig** flights.
A **Ana Cássia Palace**, R dos Andradas 14, Centre, T6223637,

hacassia@internext.com.br. Gloriously faded, large rooms, some with great views of the port. The hotel has a reasonable restaurant and a pool.

A **Best Western Lord Manaus**, R Marcílio Dias 217, T6222844, bwmanaus@internext.com.br. Conveniently located in heart of Zona Franca, with a bar, restaurant and comfortable, anonymous rooms. Orientated to business.

A **Manaós**, Av Eduardo Ribeiro, 881, T6335744, hotelmanaos@brasilcomercial.com. A reasonable standard town centre 3-star conveniently located near the Teatro Amazonas.

A **Mônaco**, R Silva Ramos 20, T6226446, monaco@internext.com.br. Good-value 3-star whose upper rooms have a good view. Those on the lower floors are noisy and there is a rooftop restaurant/bar where a delicious breakfast is served.

B **Brasil**, Av Getúlio Vargas, 657, T2336575, hotel-brasil@ internext.com.br. A friendly, mid-market option close to centre.

D **Palace**, Av 7 de Septembro 593, T6224522. Recently restored, simple, traditional rooms with high ceilings; some with wrought-iron balconies. Excellent location on square overlooking cathedral. Highly recommended.

D **Rei Salomão**, R Dr Moreira 119, T2347374. In commercial centre, very clean, modern, quiet, a/c, restaurant. Excellent value. Recommended.

E **Rio Branco**, R dos Andradas 484, T/F2334019. Basic, laundry facilities, a/c.

E-F **Ideal**, R dos Andradas 491, T/F2339423. A/c, cheaper with fan.

E-F **Pensão Sulista**, Av Joaquim Nabuco 347, T2345814. Run-down, a/c, cheaper with fan and shared bathroom.

F **Dona Joana**, R dos Andradas 553, T2337553. A/c, fridge, TV. Newly decorated, homely, good value, the hotel is safe although the area is not.

F **Jangada**, R dos Andradas 473,T6220264. Basic, clean, a bargain. A/c and TV. Recommended.

Camping

There are no campsites in or near Manaus; it is difficult to find a good, safe place to camp wild.

Amazon tours

Lodges

Most of the lodges around Manaus do not accord to proper ecotouristic practice. In Brazil ecotourism is a very loose word and by and large neither the environment nor the local communities receive very much from Manaus 'ecotourism'. Only a handful of people have benefited from a boom which has seen the total number of beds rise from just 6 in 1979 to over 1000 today. Only 27% of labour derives from local communities and very few of the lodges are locally owned.There are several lodges within a few hours' boat or car journey from Manaus. Most emphasize comfort (although electricity and hot water is limited) rather than a real jungle experience, and you are more likely to enjoy a nice buffet in pleasant company than come face to face with rare fauna. Nevertheless the lodges are good if time is limited and you want a brief taste of the Amazon rainforest. 2 days is enough to experience the highlights (one day will be taken up with travel). Tour operators for reservations are also listed below.

L **Acajatuba Jungle Lodge**, Lago Acajatuba, 4 hrs up the Rio Negro from Manaus, contact office at R Dr Almino 36, Centro, Manaus, T/F2337642, www.acajatuba.com.br. 40 apartments with showers, a bar and a restaurant. About as comfortable as a damp forest can get.

L **Ariaú Amazon Towers**, Rio Ariaú, 2 km from Archipélago de Anavilhanas, 60 km and 2 hrs by boat from Manaus on a side channel of the Rio Negro. Contact **River Jungle Hotel**, R Silva Ramos 20, Centro, Manaus, T6225000, F2335615, www.ariautowers.com.br, or www.ariau.tur.br in Rio T/F021-2348779, in USA, Jill A Siegel, 17 Schenck Av 2C, Great Neck, NY 11021, T/F718-5230041, 1-800-4707636 (access 21), jsananda@aol.com. More of a theme park than a lodge, with almost pet animals, and scant regard for the proper disposal of rubbish. 271 rooms in complex of towers connected by walkways and a private riverbeach. Between Sep-Mar there are trips to the Anavilhanas islands in groups of 10-20. Rates per person: US$280 for 2-days/1-night, US$400, 3 nights/4 days.

L **Amazon Ecopark Lodge**, Igarapé do Tarumã, 20 km from Manaus, 15 mins by boat, T2332559, F2340027. 60 apartments with showers and a bar and restaurant. Nearby is the **Amazon Monkey Jungle**, an ecological park where many monkey species are treated and rehabilitated in natural surroundings. The **Living Rainforest Foundation** which administers the **Ecopark**, also offers educational jungle trips and overnight camps (bring your own food), entrance US$15.

L **Amazon Village**, Lago do Puraquequara, 60 km, 2 hrs by boat, from Manaus, T6331444, F6333217. A comfortable lodge on dry land, with nice cabins, 32 apartments with cold shower, restaurant. Recommended.

AL **Cristalino Jungle Lodge**, (Administration, Av Perimetral Oeste, 2001, Cep: 78580-000, Alta Floresta, T66-5127100), www.cristalinolodge.com.br. A beautifully situated and well-run lodge in an area of outstanding beauty. Trips from the lodge include canoe and snorkel trips on clear water rivers, the usual gammut of cayman spotting, piranha fishing and more adventuorus options such as rapelling and canyoning. The birdwatching here is superb and the lodge has a lookout with a view over the canopy. Accommodation is rustic and about as comfortable as you can get in the Amazon.

A **Amazon Lodge**, T6563878, F6566101, a floating lodge on Lago do Juma, 80 km from Manaus, 30 mins by Careiro ferry, then 1½ hrs by bus, then 2 hrs by boat. 12 basic apartments with cold shower, restaurant, good excursions. Highly recommended.

A **Boa Vida Jungle Resort**, 53 km from Manaus by route AM-10, direction Itacoatiara, T2345722, F2322482. 7 apartments and 6 chalets, shower, fridge, bar, restaurant, fishing, boating.

A **Lago Salvador Lodge**, Lago Salvador, 30 km from Manaus, 40 mins by boat from the Hotel Tropical, Manaus. T6595119, F6584221. 12 apartments with cold showers and a bar and restaurant.

A **Pousada dos Guanavenas** on Ilha de Silves, 300 km from Manaus on the road to Itacoatiara, then by boat along the Rio Urubu. Views of Lago Canacari, T6561500, F2381211, www.guanavenas.com.br. An overly large lodge with 44 a/c rooms and 26 bungalows, fridge, electric showers, contact **Guanavenas** Turismo, Av Constantino Nery 2486, Flores.

A **Rainforest Lodge**, on the banks of Lago Januacá, 4 hrs from Manaus. T2339182. 14 bungalows with fans, pool, restaurant, snack bar.

B **Aldeia dos Lagos Lodge**, Silves Project, T/F 5282124, www.viverde.com.br/aldeia_i.html. A community-based ecotourism project with WWF support. Located in a system of lakes with high environmental diversity. Rates from US$ 368.00 for 4 days/3nights.

A **Juma**, Lago da Juma, T (11) 30881937, www.jumalodge.com.br. Newly refurbished lodge in a beautiful location, with a burgeoning interest in birdwatching and proper wildlife tours.

Tefé *p582, phone code 097*

D **Anilce**, Praça Santa Teresa 294. Clean, a/c, do not leave valuables in your room, very helpful.

E **Hotel Panorama**, Recommended and with a good restaurant.

Benjamin Constant *p582, phone code 092*

There are a number of very cheap and very simple *pousadas* in town.

B **Benjamin Constant**, R Getulio Vargas 36, beside the ferry, T4155638. All rooms have a/c, some with hot water and TV. Good restaurant, arranges tours, postal address Apdo Aéreo 219, Leticia, Colombia.

Tabatinga *p583, phone code 092*

C **Pousada do Sol**, General Sampaio, T4123355. Simple rooms but in a hotel with a sauna and a pool. Friendly owners.

D-E **Travellers Jungle Home**, R Marechal Rondon, 86. A little hostel and tour operator with Brazilian and French owners and a pet snake.

Leticia *p583, phone code 9819*

AL **Anaconda**, Cra 11, No 7-34, T27119. The plushest in town with large a/c rooms, hot water a restaurant, good terrace and swimming pool.

B **Colonial**, Cra 10, No 7-08, T27164. A/c or fans, swimming pool, cafetería, noisy.

C-D **Residencias Fernando**, Cra 9, No 8-80, T27362. Simple but well apointed andclean. Recommended.

D **Residencias Marina**, Cra 9 No 9-29, T26014. TV, Standard cheap hotel rooms, some with a/c, cold water, good breakfast and meals at attached restaurant.

D **Residencias La Manigua**, C 8, No 9-22, T27121. Friendly staff and modest but well-maintained rooms.

E **Residencia Internacional**, Av Internacional, between centre and Brazilian border. Basic rooms with attached bathrooms and fans. Hard beds.

F **Residencias Colombia**, Calle 10 at C 8. Very basic rooms with a shared bathroom. Good value.

Eating

Altamira *p570, phone code 091*

There are a few *churrascarias* in the market.

ΨΨ **Restaurante Casa Grande**, R Anchieta, centre. Has good meat on a spit. Cheap, 1130-1430, 1930-2330.

ΨΨ **Restaurante Esquina**, next to hotel Lisboa. Good snacks and *sucos*, closed Sun. Recommended.

Alter do Chão *p572, phone code 091*

Ψ **Lago Verde**, Praça 7 de Setembro, good fresh fish, try *calderada de tucunaré*.

Santarém *p571, map p572, phone code 091*

As with other small towns in the interior of Brazil, most restaurants in Santarém serve basic café-style food, lunches (consisting of rice, beans, chips and a choice of beef, chicken or fish) and juices. The best choice is to be found along the waterfront in the centre.

ΨΨ **Mascote**, Praça do Pescador 10, T5232844. Open 1000-2330. Fish-orientated restaurant with a bar and ice cream parlour. Avoid *piraracu*.

ΨΨ **Mascotinho**, Praça Manoel de Jesus Moraes, on riverfront. Bar and pizzeria attracting a lively crowd at sunset. Great river view.

ΨΨ **Santo Antonio**, Av Tapajós 2061, T5232356. Barbecued meat and fish.

Ψ **Lucy**, Praça do Pescador. Good juices and pastries. Recommended.

Óbidos *p573*

There are plenty of fish restaurants near the waterfront and in the upper town. Most are cheap.

Manaus *p574, map p577, phone code 092*

Many restaurants close on Sun nights and Mon.

ΨΨΨ **Himawari**, R 10 de Julho 618, T233 2208. Swish, sushi and Japanese food restaurant with attentive service, opposite **Teatro Amazonas**, open Sun night, when many restaurants close. Recommended.

ΨΨΨ **La Barca**, R Recife 684, T6423040. Very swanky and popular, with a wide variety of fish dishes. Often has live music.

ΨΨΨ **Restaurant Tarumã** in **Hotel Tropical** (see p587). The best restaurant in town, formal and open for dinner only.

ΨΨ **Búfalo**, *churrascaria*, Av Joaquim Nabuco 628. The best *churrascaria* in Manaus, with a US$7, all you can eat Brazilian barbecue.

ΨΨ **Canto da Peixada**, R Emílio Moreira 1677 (Praça 14 de Janeiro), T2343021. Superb fish dishes, lively atmosphere, unpretentious, close to centre, take a taxi.

ΨΨ **Fiorentina**, R José Paranaguá 44, Praça da Polícia. Fan-cooled, traditional Italian with cheesy vegetarian dishes and even cheesier piped music. Average food but one of best options in centre, beware the mugs of wine! Great *feijoada* on Sat, half-price on Sun.

ΨΨ **Peixaria Moronguetá**, dinner cruise at the 'meeting of the waters'. Regional food, catering for big groups and with a transfer daily from R Jaith Chaves 30, CEASA, T6153362.

ΨΨ **Pizzeria Scarola**, R 10 de Julho,739, corner with Av Getúlio Vargas, T2326503. Standard Brazilian menu and pizza delivery, popular.

ΨΨ **Restaurante Natalia**, Av Epaminondas, downtown. With a garden and live Pagode music and dancing on Fri nights.

ΨΨ **São Francisco**, Blvd Rio Negro 195, 30 mins' walk from centre (or bus 705), in Educandos suburb. Good fish dishes in huge portions.

Ψ **Alemã**, R José Paranaguá, Praça da Polícia. Food by weight with great pastries, hamburgers, juices, sandwiches.

Ψ **Brasil**, next to hotel of same name, see above. Food by weight, juice and sandwich kiosk outside hotel.

Ψ **Casa do Guaraná**, R Marcílio Dias. Marvellous juices mixed with *guaraná*.

Ψ **Gruta do Peixe**, R Saldanha Marinho 609, T2348508. Self-service and *pratos* in attractive basement, lunch only. Recommended.

Ұ **O Naturalista**, R 7 de Setembro 752, 2nd floor. The best pay-by-weight vegetarian; lunch only.

Ұ **La Veneza**, Av Getúlio Vargas 257. Food by weight, lunch only.

Ұ **Senac**, R Saldanha Marinho 644, T6332277. Cookery school with a self-service restaurant. Open daily, lunch only. Highly recommended.

Ұ **Skina dos Sucos**, Eduardo Ribeiro e 24 de Maio. Regional fruit juices and snacks.

Ұ **Sorveteria Glacial**, Av Getúlio Vargas 161, and other locations. Recommended for unusual ice creams like *açai* and *cupuaçu*.

Ұ **Super Guaraná**, R Guilherme Moreira 395. *Guaraná* with juice, hamburgers, pies.

Ұ **Temperos D'Ouro**, G Moreira. Self-service, lunch only.

Ұ **Xamêgo**, Av Getúlio Vargas, corner with R 10 de Julio. Basic self-service, popular with locals.

Tefé *p582, phone code 097*

ҰҰ Ұ **Au Bec d'Or** by the port. With simple but very tasty French cuisine using Amazon ingredients.

Leticia *p583, phone code 9819*

There are plenty of cheap lunchtime *almuerzo* restaurants serving cheap dishes of the day in the centre of town. Fried banana and meat, fish and fruit is sold at the market near the harbour and there are many cheap café/bars overlooking the market on the river bank. Take your own drinking water or beer.

Ұ **Sancho Panza**, Cra 10, No 8-72. Good-value meat dishes, big portions, Brazilian beer.

Bars and clubs

Manaus *p574, map p577, phone code 092*

Boiart's, R José Clemente 500, next to Teatro Amazonas, T6376807. Touristy, popular disco with jungle theme and shows. Cachoeirinha has a number of bars offering music and dancing, liveliest at weekends.

Tucano nightclub in the **Hotel Tropical**, T6595000, attracts Manaus's wealthy citizens on Thu-Sat, as does its bingo club. Nearby Ponta Negra beach becomes extremely lively late on weekend nights and during holidays, with outdoor concerts and samba in the summer season.

Studio 5, R Contorno, Distrito Industrial, T2378333, disco, part of leisure complex with several cinema screens.

Entertainment

Santarém *p571, map p572, phone code 091*

Cinema Av Rui Barbosa 183.

Manaus *p574, map p577, phone code 092*

Performing Arts

For **Teatro Amazonas** and **Centro Cultural Pálacio Rio Negro**, see above.

Teatro da Instalação, R Frei José dos Inocentes, T/F2344096. Performance space in recently restored historic buildings with free music and dance (everything from ballet to jazz), Mon-Fri May-Dec at 1800. Charge for performances Sat and Sun. Recommended.

Cinema

In R 10 de Julho and 8 screens at Amazonas shopping centre, bus Cidade Nova 5, or 204, 207, 208, 307. Most foreign films are shown with original soundtrack and Portuguese sub-titles. Afternoon performances are recommended as long queues often form in the evenings.

In Praça da Saudade, R Ramos Ferreira, there is a Sun **funfair** from 1700; try prawns and *calaloo* dipped in *tacaca* sauce. A 'train' circling the old town with loud music and cartoon characters is good fun for children.

Festivals

Alter do Chão *p572, phone code 091*

2nd week in Sep Festa do Çairé, religious processions and folkloric events. Recommended.

Santarém *p571, map p572, phone code 091*

22 Jun Foundation of the city.

29 Jun São Pedro, with processions of boats on the river and boi-bumbá dance dramas.

8 Dec, Nossa Senhora da Conceição (the city's patron saint).

Manaus *p574, map p577, phone code 092*

6 Jan Epiphany.

Feb Carnival in Manaus has spectacular parades in a sambadrome modelled on Rio's, but with 3 times the capacity. Tourists may purchase grandstand seats, but admission at ground level is free (don't take valuables), with every samba school member guaranteed entrance. Carnival dates vary – 5 days of Carnival, culminating in the parade of the Samba Schools.

Third week in Apr Week of the Indians, Indian handicraft.

Jun **Festival do Amazonas**, a celebration of all the cultural aspects of Amazonas life, indigenous, Portuguese and from the northeast, especially dancing; **Festival Marquesiano** also in **Jun**; mostly typical dances from those regions of the world which have sent immigrants to Amazonas, performed by the students of the Colégio Marquês de Santa Cruz.

29 Jun São Pedro, boat processions on the Rio Negro.

Sep **Festival de Verão do Parque Dez**, 2nd fortnight, festival with music, fashion shows, beauty contests, local foods, etc, Centro Social Urbano do Parque Dez; **Festival da Bondade**, last week, stalls from neighbouring states and countries offering food, handicrafts, music and dancing, SESI, Estr do Aleixo, Km 5.

Oct **Festival Universitário de Música** (FUM), the most traditional festival of music in Amazonas, organized by the university students, on the University Campus.

8 Dec: Procissão de Nossa Senhora da Conceicão, from the Igreja Matriz through the city centre and returning to Igreja Matriz for a solemn mass.

Shopping

Santarém *p571, map p572, phone code 091*

Muiraquitã, R Lameira Bittencourt 131. Good for ceramics, wood carvings and baskets.

Manaus *p574, map p577, phone code 092*

All shops close at 1400 on Sat and all day Sun. Since Manaus is a free port, the whole area a few blocks off the river front is full of electronics shops. This area, known as the **Zona Franca**, is the commercial centre, where the shops, banks and hotels are concentrated.

Bookshops

Livraria Nacional, R 24 de Maio, 415. Stocks some French books. **Usados CDs e Livros**, Av Getúlio Vargas 766. Selection of used books, English, German, French and Spanish. **Valer**, R Ramos Ferreira 1195. A few English classics stocked, best bookshop in city.

Markets and souvenirs

Mercado Adolfo Lisboa (see p576), Mon-Sat 0500-1800, Sun and holidays 0500-1200. Go early in the morning when it is full of good-quality regional produce, food and handicrafts, look out for *guaraná* powder or sticks, scales of *pirarucu* fish (used for manicure), and its tongue used for rasping *guaraná*.

See the 2 markets near the docks, best in the early morning. In the Praça do Congresso, Av E Ribeiro, there is a very good Sun craftmarket. Ponta Negra beach boasts a small 'hippy' market, very lively at weekends. There is a good supermarket at the corner of Av Joaquim Nabuco and R Sete de Setembro. **Artesanato da Amazônia**, R José Clemente, 500, loja A, opposite Teatro Amazonas, has a good, reasonably priced, selection of regional products. The **Central Artesanato**, R Recife, near Detran, has local craft work. The souvenir shop at the INPA has some interesting Amazonian products on sale. **Selva Amazônica**, Mercado Municipal. For wood carvings and bark fabric. For hammocks, try the shops in R dos Andradas.

Photographic

Photo Nascimento,1194, Av 7 de Setembro, repairs, slide and black and white film. 1-hr film processing at **Studio Universal**, R 24 de Maio 146, cheap, good quality.

Activities and tours

Santarém *p571, map p572, phone code 091*

Tour operators

Amazon Tours, Trav Turiano Meira 1084, T5221928, T9751981 (mob), www.amazonriver.com. Owner Steve Alexander is very friendly and helpful and has lots of tips on what to do, he also organizes excursions for groups to Bosque Santa Lúcia with ecological trails, recommended.

Coruá-Una Turismo, R Dr Hugo Mendonça, 600, T5181014, F5232670, offers various tours, Pierre d'Arcy speaks French, recommended.

Gil Serique, Praça do Pescador 131, T5225174, English-speaking guide, recommended.

Santarém Tur, R Adriano Pimental 44, T5224847, www.santaremtur.com.br. Branch in **Amazon Park Hotel** (see Sleeping, above), friendly, helpful foreign-owned company with individual and group tours (US$50 per person per day for a group of 5), to Tapajós National Forest, Maiça Lake and Fordlandia. Recommended.

Manaus *p574, map p577, phone code 092*

Swimming

At Ponta Negra beach, 13 km from the centre (Soltur bus, US$0.70), though the beach virtually disappears beneath the water in Apr-Aug. Good swimming at waterfalls on the Rio Tarumã, where lunch is available, shade, crowded at weekends; take Tarumã bus from R Tamandaré or R Frei J dos Inocentes, 30 mins, US$0.70 (very few on weekdays), getting off at the police checkpoint on the road to Itacoatiara. There is also superb swimming in the natural pools and under falls of clear water in the little streams which rush through the woods, but take locals' advice on swimming in the river; electric eels and various other kinds of unpleasant fish, apart from the notorious *piranhas*, abound, and industrial pollution of the river is growing. Every Sun, boats leave from the port in front of the market to beaches along Rio Negro, US$2, leaving when full and returning at the end of the day. This is a real locals' day out, with loud music and food stalls on the sand.

Tour operators

Espaço Verde Turismo, R Costa Azevedo, 240, T6334522, rogerio-evtur@internext.com.br. Opposite Teatro Amazonas. River boat tours, one day US$30, including lunch; flights; trips to lodges. English spoken, helpful.

Swallows and Amazons, R Quintino Bocaiuva 189, Suite 13, T/F6221246, www.swallowsandamazonstours.com.

For flights, car hire, etc, tour agencies attached to 2 of largest hotels in city: Best Western Lord Manaus and Holiday Inn Taj Mahal. See below for advice on choosing a jungle tour.

Amazon tours *p579, phone code 092*

Amazon Explorers, R Nhamundá 21, Praça NS Auxiliadora, T6333319, www.amazonexplorers.com.br. Day tour including 'meeting of the waters', Lago do Janauari, rubber collecting and lunch has been highly recommended by most users (US$60), boat *Amazon Explorer* available for hire at about US$230 per day.

Amazonas Indian Turismo, R dos Andradas 311, T/F6335578 offers a different, authentic experience, staying with local river people, for around US$60 per day.

Amazon Travel Service, Av Joaquim Nabuco 1626, sala 201/203, Centro, T6222788, atstur@amazonet.com.br

Fontur, in Tropical Hotel, Estr da Ponta Negra, Km 18, T6583052, www.fontur.com.br.

Heliconia, R Col Salgado 63, Aparecida, T2345915, www.heliconia-amazon.com. Run by French researcher Thérèse Aubreton.

Iguana Turismo, R 10 de Julho 667, T6636507 or T91329367, www.amazonbrasil.com.br, iguanatours@hotmail.com. Provide an extensive range of trips over various lengths.

Good facilities including river-boat and campsite in the forest. They have another office at the airport in Manaus.

Selvatur, Praça Adalberto Vale 17, T6222577, www.selvatur.com.br. Rio Negro trip, 0800-1500, with lunch at *Janaurylândia* floating hotel.

Swallows and Amazons, R Quintino Bocaiúva 189, andar 1, Sala 13, opposite Best Western Lord Manaus hotel, T/F6221246, www.swallowsandamazonstours.com.

Guides

Guides sometimes work individually as well as for various tour agencies, and the best ones will normally be booked up well in advance. Some will only accompany longer expeditions and often subcontract shorter trips. It is generally safer to book guides through agencies.

Leticia *p583, phone code 9819*

Amazon Jungle trips, Av Internacional, 6-25, T27377. Lodge-based tours offering a variety of adventure options.

Anaconda Tours, Hotel Anaconda, T27119. Tours to Amacayacu, Isla de los Micos and Sacambu Lodge. Elvis Cuevas, Av Internacional, 6-06, T27780. An independent guide with trips to Amacayacu and indigenous communities nearby.

Transport

Routes in Amazônia

Belém-Manaus via Breves, Almeirim, Prainha, Monte Alegre, Curua-Uná, Santarém, Alenquer, Óbidos, Juruti and Parintins on the lower Amazon. 5 days upriver, 4 days downriver, including 18-hr stop in Santarém, suite US$350 upriver, US$250 down, double berth US$180 upriver, US$150 down, hammock space US$75 upriver, US$65 down. Vehicles: small car US$250, combi US$320 usually including driver, other passengers extra, 4WD US$450 with 2 passengers; motorcycle US$80. **Nélio Correa** is best on this route. **Defard Vieira**, very good and clean, US$75. **São Francisco** is largest, new and modern, but toilets smelly. **Cisne Branco** of similar quality. **Cidade de Bairreirinha** is the newest on the route, a/c berths. **Lider II** has good food and pleasant atmosphere. **Santarém** is clean, well organized and recommended. **João Pessoa Lopes** is also recommended. The Belém-Manaus route is very busy. Try to get a cabin if you can.

Belém-Santarém same intermediate stops as above. 2½ days upriver, 1½ days downriver, fares suite US$150, berth US$135, hammock US$45 upriver, US$38 down. All vessels sailing Belém-Manaus will call in Santarém.

Santarém-Manaus same intermediate stops as above. 2 days upriver, 1½ days downriver, fares berth US$85, hammock US$30. All vessels sailing Belém-Manaus will call in Santarém and there are others operating only the Santarém-Manaus route, including: **Cidade de Terezinha III** and **IV**, good. **Miranda Dias**, family-run and friendly. Speedboats (*lanchas*) are sometimes available on this route, 16 hrs sitting, no hammock space, US$35.

Belém-Macapá (Porto Santana)
Non-stop, 8 hrs on fast catamaran, **Atlântica**, US$30, 3 days a week, or 24 hrs on large ships, double berth US$110, hammock space US$30 per person, meals not included but can be purchased onboard (expensive), vehicle US$90, driver not included. **Silja e Souza** (Wed) is best. **Comandante Solon** (Sat) is state run, slightly cheaper, crowded and not as nice. Same voyage via Breves, 36-48 hrs on smaller river boats, hammock space US$25 per person including meals. **ENAL** (Sat); **Macamazônia** (every day except Thu), slower and more basic; **Bartolomeu I** of Enavi, food and sanitary conditions OK, 30 hrs; **Rodrigues Alves** has been recommended. **Golfinho do Mar** is said to be the fastest.

Macapá (Porto Santana)-Santarém
Via Vida Nova, Boca do Jari, Almeirim, Prainha, and Monte Alegre on the lower Amazon (does not call in Belém), 2 days upriver, 1½ days downriver, berth US$130, hammock US$40. Boats include **Viageiro V** (nice), **São Francisco de Paula**.

Santarém-Itaituba Along the Rio Tapajós, 24 hrs (bus service on this route is making this river trip less common).

Manaus-Porto Velho Via Borba, Manicoré, and Humaitá on the Rio Madeira. 4 days upriver, 3½ days downriver (up to 7 days when the river is low), double berth US$180, hammock space US$65 per person. Recommended boats are **Almirante Moreira II**, clean, friendly owner; **Lord Scania**, friendly; **Ana Maria VIII**, modern. The **Eclipse II** is a very nice boat which sails Manaus-Manicoré (2 days, US$80 double berth, US$20 hammock). Many passengers go only as far as Humaitá and take a bus from there to Porto Velho, much faster.

Manaus-Tefé via Codajás and Coari, 24 to 36 hrs, double berth US$70, 1st-class hammock space US$20 per person, 2nd-class hammock space US$20 per person. **Capitão Nunes** is good. **Jean Filho** also OK. Note that it is difficult to continue west from Tefé to Tabatinga without first returning to Manaus.

Manaus-Tabatinga Via Fonte Boa, Foz do Mamaria, Tonantins, Santo Antônio do Içá, Amataura, Monte Cristo, São Paulo de Olivença and Benjamin Constant along the Rio Solimões. Up to 8 days upriver (depending on cargo), 3 days downriver, double berth US$220, hammock space US$65 per person (can be cheaper downriver). When going from Peru into Brazil, there is a thorough police check some 5 hrs into Brazil. **Voyagers**, **Voyagers II** and **III** (T2363782) recommended; **Almirante Monteiro**, **Avelino Leal** and **Capitão Nunes VIII** all acceptable; **Dom Manoel**, cheaper, acceptable but overcrowded.

Manaus-Caracaraí (for Boa Vista)
Along the Rio Branco, 4 days upriver, 2 days downriver, many sandbars, impassable during the dry season. Now that the BR-174 (Manaus-Boa Vista) has been paved, it is almost impossible to get a passage on a boat. The only tourist boat is erratic.

Manaus-São Gabriel da Cachoeira
Via Novo Airão, Moura, Carvoeiro, Barcelos, and Santa Isabel do Rio Negro along the Rio Negro. Berth US$180, hammock US$60, most locals prefer to travel by road. Boats on this route: **Almirante Martins I** and **II**, **Capricho de Deus**, **Manoel Rodrigues**, **Tanaka Netto** departing from São Raimundo dock, north of main port.

Alter do Chão *p572, phone code 091*
Bus Tickets and information from the bus company kiosk opposite **Pousada Tupaiulândia**. From Santarém: bus stop on Av São Sebastião, in front of Colégio Santa Clara, US$1, about 1 hr.

Santarém *p571, map p572, phone code 091*
The port is in right in the centre of town; a taxi to any of the hotels in this area is around $US2.
Air
15 km from town, T5231021. Internal flights only, to Alta Floresta, Almerim, Altamira, Belém, Boavista, Breves, Cuiabá, Imperatriz,

Itaituba, Macapá, Manaus, Marabá, Monte Dourado, Óbidos, Oiapoque, Oriximiná, Parantins, Porto de Moz, Porto Trombetas, Rurópolis, Sinop and Urucu. Buses run to the centre or waterfront. From the centre the bus leaves in front of the cinema in Rui Barbosa every 80 mins from 0550 to 1910, or taxis (US$8 to waterfront). The hotels **Amazon Park, New City** and **Rio Dourado** have free buses for guests; you may be able to take these.

Airline offices Fly, Av Monsenhor Tabosa, 1069, T2197171. **META**, R Siquiera Campos 162, T5226222. **Penta**, Trav 15 de Novembro 183, T5232532. **TAVAJ**, R Floriano Peixoto, 95, T5237666. **Varig/Nordeste**, Av Rui Barbosa, 790, T5232488. **Vasp**, freephone 0800 998277.

Bus

Rodoviária, T5223392, is on the outskirts, take 'Rodagem' bus from the waterfront near the market, US$0.35. Santarém to **Itaituba**, US$11, 11 hrs, 2 a day. To **Marabá** on the Rio Tocantins (via Rurópolis US$7.50, 6 hrs, and **Altamira** US$23, 28 hrs), 36 hrs (if lucky; can be up to 6 days), US$41, with **Transbrasiliana**. Also to **Imperatriz**, via Marabá; office on Av Getúlio Vargas and at the rodoviária. Enquire at the rodoviária for other destinations. (Beware of vehicles that offer a lift, which frequently turn out to be taxis.) Road travel during the rainy season is always difficult, often impossible.

Boats

Shipping services to **Manaus**, **Belém**, **Macapá**, **Itaituba**, and intermediate ports (see River transport, p549 and Routes in Amazonia and Tours, p594). Boats to Belém and Manaus dock at the Cais do Porto, 1 km west, take 'Floresta-Prainha', 'Circular' or 'Circular Externo' bus; taxi US$4. Boats to other destinations, including Macapá, dock by the waterfront by the centre of town. Local service to **Óbidos**, US$10, 4 hrs, **Oriximiná** US$12.50, **Alenquer**, and **Monte Alegre** (US$10, 5-8 hrs).

Belterra and Fordlândia *p572, phone code 093*

There is a 1 hr time difference between Santarém and Belterra, so if you take the 1230 bus you'll miss the 1530 return bus. Bus from **Santarém** to Belterra (from Trav Silvino Pinto between Rui Barbosa and São Sebastião), 1000 and 1230, Mon-Sat, return 1300 and 1530, US$4, about 2 hrs. Boats from Santarém to Itaituba stop at Fordlândia if you ask (leave Santarém 1800, arrive 0500-0600, US$12 for 1st-class hammock space); ask the captain to stop for you on return journey, about 2300. The alternative is to take a tour with a Santarém travel agent.

Manaus *p574, map p577, phone code 092*

See also Ins and outs, p574.

Air

Modern Eduardo Gomes airport is 9 km from the city, T6521120. There are international flights to Guayaquil, La Paz, Mexico City, Miami, Orlando, Santa Cruz and Quito. To the Guyanas, a connection must be made in Belém. Domestic flights to Belém, Boa Vista, Brasília, Cruzeiro do Sul, Macapá, Parantins, Porto Velho, Rio Branco, Rio de Janeiro, Santarém, São Paulo, Tabatinga, Tefé and Trombetas.

Make reservations as early as possible, flights may be full. Do not rely on travel agency waiting lists; go to the airport 15 hrs early and get on the airport waiting list. Domestic airport tax US$7.

Taxi fare to airport US$7.25, fixed rate, or take bus marked 'Aeroporto Internacional' from Marquês de Santa Cruz at Praça Adalberto Vale, near the cathedral, US$0.70, or from Ed Garagem on Av Getúlio Vargas every 30 mins. No buses 2200-0700. Taxi drivers often tell arrivals that no bus to town is available, be warned! It is sometimes possible to use the more regular, faster service run by the **Hotel Tropical**; many tour agencies offer free transfers without obligation. Check all connections on arrival. Allow plenty of time at Manaus airport, formalities are very slow especially if you have purchased duty-free goods. The restaurant serves good à la carte and buffet food throughout the day. Many flights depart in the middle of the night and while there are many snack bars there is nowhere to rest. Local flights leave from Terminal 2. Check in advance which terminal you leave from.

Airline offices American Airlines, Av Eduardo Ribeiro 664, T6333363. **Lloyd Aéreo Boliviano**, Av 7 de Setembro 993, 1st floor, T6334200. **TAM**, Av Tarumã, 433, T2331828.

TAVAJ, R Rui Barbosa, 200B, freephone 0800 927070. **Transbrasil**, R Guilherme Moreira 150, T6221705. **Varig**, R Marcílio Dias 284, T6214500. **Vasp**, Av 7 de Setembro 993, T6223470.

Boat

See also River transport, p549 and Routes in Amazônia, p594.

To Santarém, Belém, Porto Velho, Tefé, Tabatinga (for Colombia and Peru), São Gabriel da Cachoeira, and intermediate ports. Almost all vessels now berth at the first (downstream) of the floating docks, which is open to the public 24 hrs a day. Bookings can be made up to 2 weeks in advance at the ticket sales area by the port's pedestrian entrance (bear left on entry). The names and itineraries of departing vessels are displayed here as well as on the docked boats themselves. Touts will engulf you when you arrive at the pedestrian entry; be calm, patient and friendly. Travellers still recommend buying tickets from the captain on the boat itself. The port is relatively clean, well organized, and has a pleasant atmosphere.

ENASA (the state shipping company) sells tickets for private boats at its office in town (prices tend to be high here), T6333280. Local boats and some cargo barges still berth by the concrete retaining wall between the market and Montecristi. Boats for São Gabriel da Cachoeira, Novo Airão, and Caracaraí go from São Raimundo, up river from the main port. Take bus 101 'São Raimundo', 112 'Santo Antônio' or 110, 40 mins; there are 2 docking areas separated by a hill, the São Raimundo *balsa*, where the ferry to Novo Airão, on the Rio Negro, leaves every afternoon (US$10); and the Porto Beira Mar de São Raimundo, where the São Gabriel da Cachoeira boats dock (most departures Fri).

From **Manaus-São Paulo** it is cheaper to go by boat Manaus-Porto Velho, then bus to São Paulo, than to fly direct or go by boat to Belém then bus. Departures to the less important destinations are not always known at the Capitânia do Porto, Av Santa Cruz 265, Manaus. Be careful of people who wander around boats after they've arrived at a port; they are almost certainly looking for something to steal.

Immigration For those arriving by boat who have not already had their passports stamped (eg from Leticia), the immigration office is on the first of the floating docks next to the tourist office. Take the dock entrance opposite the cathedral, bear right, after 50 m left, pass through a warehouse to a group of buildings on a T section.

Bus

Local All city bus routes start below the cathedral in front of the port entrance; just ask someone for the destination you want, also find some info on local buses at the site www.embarque.com.br.

Long distance Rodoviária is 5 km out of town at the intersection of Av Constantino Nery and R Recife; take a local bus from centre, US$0.70, marked 'Aeroporto Internacional' or 'Cidade Nova' (or taxi, US$5).

Car

The road north from Manaus to Boa Vista (770 km) is described on p601.

The Catire Highway (BR-319), from Manaus to Porto Velho (868 km), has been officially closed since 1990. Several bridges are out and there is no repair in sight. The alternative for drivers is to ship a car down river on a barge, others have to travel by boat (see below).

To **Itacoatiara**, 285 km east on the Amazon, with Brazil-nut and jute processing plants (bus service 8 a day, 4 hrs); now paved route AM-010, 266 km, through Rio Preto da Eva.

Car hire Localiza, R Major Gabriel 1558, T2334141, and airport, T6521176.

Hitchhiking

Common, but not recommended for women travelling alone. To hitch, take a Tarumã bus to the customs building and hitch from there, or try at 'posta 5', 2 km beyond the rodoviária.

Parintins *p582, phone code 092*

Boat Boats call on the Belém-Manaus route: 60 hrs from Belém, minimum 10, maximum 26 from Manaus (depending on boat and if going up or down river). There are irregular sailings from Óbidos (ask at the port), 12-15 hrs. A boat from Santarém takes 20 hrs. There is also a small airport with flights to Manaus (1¼ hrs), Óbidos and Santarém (1 hr 20 mins).

Tefé *p582, phone code 097*
Air The Airport has a connection to Manaus with Varig. If travelling on to Tabatinga, note that Manaus-Tabatinga boats do not usually stop at Tefé. You must hire a canoe to take you out to the main channel and try to flag down the approaching ship.

Leticia *p583, phone code 9819*
Air The airport is 1½ km from town, taxi US$1.60; small terminal, few facilities. Expect to be searched before leaving Leticia airport, and on arrival in Bogotá from Leticia. To Bogotá, Mon and Fri, SAM (Tabatinga airport if Leticia's is closed).

Directory

Santarém *p571, map p572, phone code 091*
Banks Banco do Brasil, Av Rui Barbosa 794, exchanges TCs and cash, also withdrawals on Visa. It is very difficult to change dollars and impossible to change TCs. **Internet** Tapajos On Line, Mendonça Furtado 2454, US$3.50 per hr. **Laundry** Storil, Trav Turiano Meira 167, 1st floor. **Post office** Praça da Bandeira 81. **Medical services** Hospital São Raimundo Nonato, Av Mendonça Furtado 1993, T5231176. **Telephone** Posto Trin, R Siquiera Campos 511. Mon-Sat 0700-1900, Sun 0700-2100.

Manaus *p574, map p577, phone code 092*
Banks Banco do Brasil, Guia Moreira, and airport changes US$ cash, 8% commission, both with ATMs for Visa, Cirrus, MasterCard and Plus. Most offices shut at 1500; foreign exchange operations 0900-1200 only, or even as early as 1100. Bradesco, Av 7 de Setembro 895/293, for Visa ATM. Credicard, Av Getúlio Vargas 222 for Diner's cash advances. Cash at main hotels; Câmbio Cortez, 7 de Setembro 1199, converts TCs into US$ cash, good rates, no commission. Do not change money on the streets. HSBC, R Dr Moreira,226. ATM for Visa, Cirrus, MasterCard and Plus. **Embassies and consulates** Most open in the morning only. Austria, R 5, Qd E No 4, Jardim Primeravera II, T6421939, F6421582. Belgium, Conj Murici, Qd D No 13, Parque 10, T2361452. Bolivia, Av Efigênio Sales 2226, Qd B No 20, T2369988. Colombia, R 24 de Maio 220, Rio Negro Center, T2346777, check whether a Colombian tourist card can be obtained at the border. Denmark, Estr da Refinaria, T6151555, also handles Norway. France, Av Joaquim Nabuco 1846, T2342947. Finland, R Marcílio Dias, 131, T6226686. Germany, R 24 Maio 220, Edif Rio Negro Centre, sala 812, T2349045, 1000-1200. Italy, R Belo Horizonte 240, Adrianópolis, T6114877. Japan, R Fortaleza 460, T2322000. Netherlands, R Miranda Leão 41, T6221366. Peru, R A, Casa 1, Conj Aristocrático, Chapada, T2363012. Portugal, R Terezina 193, T2345777. Spain, Al Cosme Ferreira 1225, Aleixo, T6443800. UK, R Paraquê 240, T2377869. USA, R Recife 1010, Adrianópolis, T6334907, will supply letters of introduction for US citizens. Venezuela, R Ferreira Pena 179, T2336004, F2330481 (0800-1200), everyone entering Venezuela overland needs a visa. The requirements are 1 passport photo, an onward ticket and the fee, usually US$30 (check in advance for changes to these regulations – it is reported that a yellow fever certificate is not needed). Takes 24 hrs. **Immigration** To extend or replace a Brazilian visa, take bus from Praça Adalberto Vale to Kissia Dom Pedro for Polícia Federal post, people in shorts not admitted. **Internet** Free internet access available from all public libraries in city, eg. recently created Biblioteca Arthur Reis, Av 7 de Setembro, 444, open 0800-1200 and 1400-1700, with virtual Amazon library and English books. Amazon Cyber Cafe, Av Getúlio Vargas, 626, corner with R 10 de Julho, US$1.50 per hr. Discover Internet, R Marcílio Dias, 304, next to Praça da Polícia, cabins in back of shop with Internet 'phones and scanners, US$1.50 per hr. **Laundry** Lavanderia Amazonas, Costa Azevedo 63, near *Teatro Amazonas*. US$0.40 per item, closed Sat afternoon and Sun. Lavanderia Central, R Quintino Bocaiúva 602. Lavalux, R Mundurucus 77, fast service washes. Lavlev, Av Sen A Maia 1108. One of few self-service laundries is opposite the cemetery, open Sun, a taxi ride away. **Medical services** Clinica Sao Lucas, R Alexandre Amorin 470, T6223678, reasonably priced, some English spoken, good service, take a taxi. Hospital Tropical, Av Pedro Teixeira (D Pedro I) 25, T6561441. Centre for tropical medicine, not for general complaints, treatment free, some doctors speak a little English. Take buses 201 or 214 from Av 7 de Setembro in the city centre. Pronto Soccoro 28 de Agosto, R Recife, free for emergencies. **Post office** Main office including poste restante

on Mcal Deodoro. On the 1st floor is the philatelic counter where stamps are sold, avoiding the long queues downstairs. Staff don't speak English but are used to dealing with tourists. For airfreight and shipping, Alfândega, Av Marquês Santa Cruz (corner of Marechal Deodoro), Sala 106. For airfreight and seamail, Correio Internacional, R Monsenhor Coutinho e Av Eduardo Ribeiro (bring your own packaging). UPS office, T2329849 (Custódio). **Telephone** International calls can be made from local boxes with an international card. Also at Telemar, Av Getúlio Vargas 950.

Leticia *p583, phone code 9819*
Banks Banco de Bogotá, will cash TCs, has ATM on Cirrus network, good rates for Brazilian reais. Apart from at this bank, TCs are hard to change, impossibe at weekends. Banco Ganadero, Cra 11, has a visa cashpoint.There are street money changers, plenty of *câmbios*, and banks for exchange. Shop around. **Post office** Avianca office, Cra 11, No 7-58. **Telephone** Cra 11/C 9, near Parque Santander.

Roraima

This extreme northern state is little visited by travellers, except those making the journey between Manaus and the borders with Venezuela and Guyana. The state's population is now only 325,000 in an area nearly twice the size of England. Land grants in the 1970s to encourage agricultural development caused the population to grow quickly from only 25,000 in 1960. Then, in the late 1980s a gold rush in the northwest of Roraima drew prospectors from all over the country. The mining took place on the Yanomami Indian Reserve, causing much disruption to their traditional way of life. Further tragedy came in January 1998 when forest fires spread across the state, causing massive destruction until extinguished by rains in March.

The forest cover gives way to grasslands in the northeast and there is a pronounced dry season. The Várzea (flood plain) along the main rivers irrigates the southeast of the state. Cattle ranching is important as is rice cultivation on the flood plain of the Rio Branco. Other crops are maize, beans, manioc and banana. Some gold mining still continues but at a reduced level. ▸▸ *For Sleeping, Eating and other listings, see pages 603-605.*

Boa Vista → *Colour map 1, A3. Phone code: 095. Population: 200,000.*

The capital of the extreme northern State of Roraima, 759 km north of Manaus, has a modern functional plan, which often means long hot treks from one place to another. It has an interesting modern **cathedral** and a badly kept **museum** of local indigenous culture. There is swimming in the Rio Branco, 15 minutes from the town centre (too polluted in Boa Vista), reachable by bus only when the river is low. Under heavy international pressure, the Brazilian government expelled some 40,000 gold prospectors (*garimpeiros*) from the Yanomami Reserve in the west of the state in the early 1990s. The economic consequences were very severe for Boa Vista, which went from boom to bust. An increase in cattle ranching in the area has not taken up the slack. There's a **tourist office** ⓘ *R Col Pinto 241, Centro, T6231230, F6231831*. Also at rodoviária ⓘ *T6231238* and the airport. Travellers can seek information (and free hammock space) from **Klaus** ⓘ *T9963 7915/9111*, or ask for Lula at **Guri Auto Elétrica** ⓘ *R das Mil Flores 738*, near rodoviária.Economic hardship has caused an increase in crime, sometimes violent.

Mount Roraima, after which the territory is named, is possibly the original of Sir Arthur Conan Doyle's 'Lost World'.

The Rio Branco

The yellow Rio Branco is better for fishing than the Rio Negro and there is more wildlife to see. However, biting insects and their associated diseases are more prevalent outside the wet season. About two days up the Rio Branco from Manaus, on the way to Caracaraí, is **Santa Maria de Boiaçu**, a village with a military airstrip (in use in July and August), very basic medical facilities and an indirect radio link with Manaus. Three small shops sell basic necessities (frequently closed), and there are several tiny, but lively, churches.

Caracaraí

A paved road connects this busy port, with modern installations, to Manaus. A new bridge crosses the river for traffic on the Manaus-Boa Vista road (see below). The river banks are closer, so there is more to see than on the Amazon and stops in the tiny riverside settlements are fascinating.

From Caracaraí to Boa Vista costs US$9, 3 hrs. The Perimetral Norte road marked on some maps from Caracaraí east to Macapá and west to the Colombian frontier does not yet exist; it runs only about 240 km west and 125 km east from Caracaraí, acting at present as a penetration road. Passengers are rarely allowed on boats now that the Manaus-Boa Vista has been paved.There is basic accommodation here. The hotels near the bus station are dirty, the best are in town opposite the fuel tanks and the pharmacy (*drogaria*) changes cash US$.

The massacre of the Yanomami

In the 1980s after gold was discovered in Roraima's Parima hills, peasant farmers disposed from their lands by wealthy northeastern landowners began to pour into to the territory of the last remaining isolated tribe in the Americas, the Yanomami. Many were supported by local businessmen who saw them as the vanguard of a new territorial expansion who would clear the way for their more organised mining and cattle ranching activities along the proposed Calha Norte road. Prospectors arrived at the rate of 200 a day and the population of the state more than doubled in a four year period. Prostitution, gun-running and shanty town bars boomed, Boa Vista airport became the busiest in South America and the state became almost lawless. The Yanomami were at first traded with, then enlisted into prostitution. Their game was killed by the miners and hundreds died from introduced disease or starvation. Many were reduced to begging at mining camps whilst those who opposed the miners were massacred, most notoriously at Haximú. Indian 'hunts' were common; Boa Vista taxi drivers reputedly used to offer visitors the opportunity to 'shoot a wild Indian.' the atrocities were reported outside Brazil by journalists like the BBC's Jan Rocha, Brazilian embassies around the word were picketed, Survival (www.survival-international.org) organised a protest at the United Nations and a surprised Brazil, used to being loved or ignored internationally was shamed into action. Miners were kicked out of the Yanomami lands by the army, only to return a year or so later. And after some five cumbersome years of legal process a handful of garimpeiros were imprisoned. Miraculously, thanks to the hard work and courage of Yanomami leaders like Davi Kopenawa the tribe's culture remained and remains largely intact. But gold prospecting continues to this day alongside widespread forest fire clearance for cattle ranches and the increasing inward migration promoted by the Roraima government eager to fill its 'millions of hectares of fertile land'. And in an ominous statement in 2001 the Ministry of Defence said that the park set up to protect the Yanomami by President Collor had been an 'error' committed to impress foreigners, which would be 'corrected.'

To Venezuela and Guyana

The road which connects Manaus and Boa Vista (ferry crosses the Rio Branco at Caracaraí as long as there is traffic) is fully paved and regularly maintained. There are service stations with toilets, camping, etc, every 150-180 km (all petrol is low octane). At Km 100 is Presidente Figueiredo, with many waterfalls and a famous cave with bats, as well as shops and a restaurant. About 100 km further on is a service station at the entrance to the **Uaimiri Atroari Indian Reserve,** which straddles the road for about 120 km. Private cars and trucks are not allowed to enter the Indian Reserve between sunset and sunrise, but buses are exempt from this regulation. However, nobody is allowed to stop within the reserve at any time. At the northern entrance to the reserve there are toilets and a spot to hang your hammock (usually crowded with truckers overnight). At Km 327 is the village of **Vila Colina** where **Restaurante Paulista** is clean with good food, and you can use the shower and hang your hammock. At Km 359 there is a monument to mark the **equator**. At Km 434 is the clean and pleasant **Restaurant Goaio.** Just south of Km 500 is **Bar Restaurante D'Jonas,** a good place to eat; you can also camp or sling a hammock. Beyond here, large tracts of forest have been destroyed for settlement, but already many homes have been abandoned.

Boa Vista has road connections with the Venezuelan frontier at **Santa Elena de Uairén**, 237 km away. The road is paved, but the only gasoline available is 110 km south of Santa Elena. Boa Vista is also linked to Bonfim for the Guyanese border at **Lethem**. Both roads are open all year.

Border with Venezuela

Immigration and customs Border searches are thorough and frequent at this border crossing. Ensure in advance that you have the right papers, including a yellow fever certificate, for entering Brazil before arriving at this frontier. Officials may give only two months' stay and car drivers may be asked to purchase an unnecessary permit. Ask to see the legal documentation. Everyone who crosses the border must have a visa for Venezuela. Current procedure is to take filled out visa form, onward ticket, a passport photo and deposit slip from **Banco do Brasil** (US$30) to the Venezuelan consulate in Boa Vista. Be prepared to wait an hour, but it may be possible to get a visa at the border; check requirements in advance. There is also a Venezuelan consulate in Manaus which issues 1-year, multiple entry visas (see page 598).

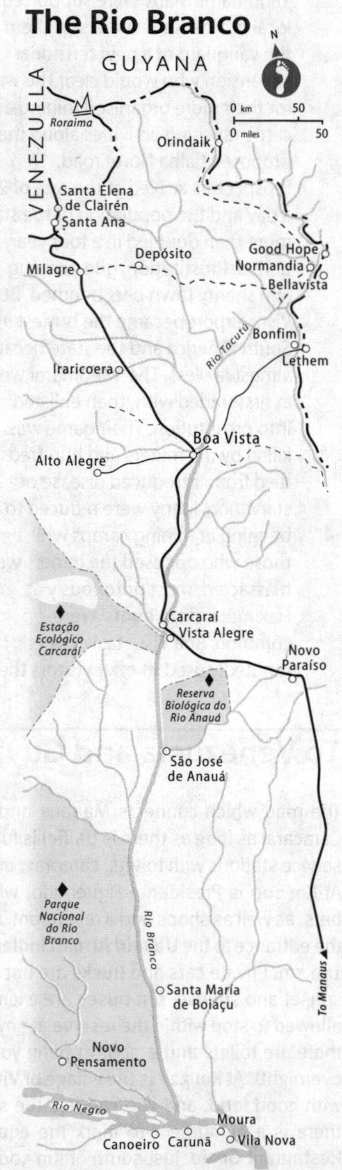

Santa Elena de Uairén

Santa Elena de Uairén is the gateway to the Venezuelan Guiana Highlands for those entering the country from Brazil. It is a growing, pleasant frontier town, 10-12 hours by bus from Ciudad Bolívar, itself nine hours from Caracas. The road is paved all the way and there are also flights. The landscape is beautiful, an ancient land of flat-topped mountains and waterfalls. The road skirts the Parque Nacional Canaima, in which is the highest fall in the world, Salto Angel (Angel Falls). Not far north of Santa Elena is the route to Mount Roraima.

In Santa Elena are plenty of hotels and places to eat, money changing facilities, a phone office with international connections and tour companies for trips into the Gran Sabana – as the region is known. The bus station is on Calle Mcal Sucre. Buses south to Ciudad Bolívar are run by several companies throughout the day, earliest at 0700, last at 1930 (10-12 hours). The Brazilian consulate is near the bus terminal opposite the Corpoven gas station (open 0800-1200, 1400-1800). Full details on this region, and the rest of the country, can be found in the *Venezuela Handbook*.

Border with Guyana

The main border crossing between Brazil and Guyana is from Bonfim, 125 km (all paved) northeast of Boa Vista, to Lethem. The towns are separated by the Rio Tacutu, which is crossed by small boats for foot passengers. Vehicles cross by ferry on demand, US$4, or drive across in the dry season. The river crossing is 2½ km from Bonfim, about 1½ km north of Lethem. A bridge is under construction. Formalities are generally lax on both sides of the border, but it is important to observe them as people not having the correct papers may have problems further into either country.

There is another border crossing at Laramonta from where it is a hard, but rewarding, walk to the Guyanese town of Orinduik.

Brazilian immigration At Polícia Federal (closed for lunch): from the rodoviária in Bonfim take a taxi, otherwise it's a long, dusty walk to the police checkpoint. Obtain an exit stamp at the Polícia Federal, then take the path to the river which leads to the right (going straight on also leads to the river, but not to the crossing point). After 10-15 mins you reach the canoes which go to Guyana. Once across, keep to the right, on the road to the airport. For immigration formalities, do not go to the Guyanese police, but to a building on the road to **Cacique** guesthouse. Ask directions. The office is someone's front room.

Brazilian customs At Ministério da Fazenda checkpoint, before entering Bonfim; jeeps from here charge US$1 to immigration.

Sleeping

Boa Vista *p599, map p600, phone code 095*
Accommodation is generally expensive
B **Aipana Plaza**, Praça Centro Cívico 53, T2244800, aipana@technet.com.br. Modern, a/c, good service, best food in town, buffet.
C **Eusébio's**, R Cecília Brasil 1107, T623 0300, F623 9131. Run-down but with a swimming pool, free transport and a range of a/c rooms and agood restaurant, to rodoviária or airport.
C **Itamaraty**, Av NS da Consolata 1957, T/F2249757, itamaraty@osite.com.br. Blocky and basic with a/c rooms and parking.
C **Roraima**, Av Cecília Brasil e Benjamin Constant, T2249843. Simple, plain a/c rooms. Recommended. Good restaurant opposite.
C **Uiramutam Palace**, Av Capt Ene Garcez 427, T/F2249912. Simple but with good service, a/c rooms a restaurant and apool.
D **Três Nações**, Av Ville Roy 1885, T/F2243439. Very basic but not dirty and convenient for the bus station. Some rooms have a/c.
E **Imperial**, Av Benjamin Constant 433, T2245592. A/c and cheaper fan-cooled rooms. Welcoming staff and safe motorcycle parking. Recommended.

Camping
Rio Caaumé, 3 km north of town. Unofficial, pleasant site with small bar and clean river.

Border with Venezuela *p602*
On the Brazilian side there is one basic hotel and many far better options in Santa Elena de Uairén (see the *South American Handbook*).

Border with Guyana *p603*
Electricity is officially turned off between 2200 and 0700; take a torch or candles.
D **Bonfim**, owned by Mr Myers, who speaks English and is very helpful, fan, shower. There is a café at the rodoviária, opposite the church, whose owner speaks English and gives information.

Eating

Boa Vista *p599, map p600*
Most restaurants and even delivery services close at night, except for pizzerias.
TT **Ver O Rio**, R Floriano Peixoto 116. The best for fish dishes.

🍴🍴 **Café Pigalle**, R Cecília Brasil, just off central praça, next to **Eusébio's**. Good food, drinks and atmosphere, open late.

🍴🍴 **Churrascaria La Carreta**, R Pedro Rodrigues 185, 500 m from **Eusébio's**. Good, US$3 buffet, nice atmosphere. Recommended.

🍴 **Vila Rica**, R Ville Roy, near the rodoviária. Good cheap lunch with the usual rice, beans, chips and meat/chicken or fish.

Border with Guyana *p603*

🍴 **Restaurante Internacional**, opposite the rodoviária, on other side from church.

Another restaurant, a bit further from the rodoviária, serves good food.

Activities and tours

Boa Vista *p599, map p600, phone code 095*

Guides

Boat trips on Rio Branco and surrounding waterways (jungle, beaches, Indian reservations), **Acqua**, R Floriano Peixoto 505, T2246576, guide **Elieser Rufino** is recommended.

Transport

Boa Vista *p599, map p600, phone code 095*

Air

International airport is 4 km from the centre. Taxi to rodoviária, US$9, to centre US$12. Bus 'Aeroporto' to/from the centre is US$0.40, 45 mins' walk. No left luggage, information or exchange facilities at the airport. Flights to Belém, Brasília, Macapá, Manaus, Santarém and São Paulo. Confirm flights before reaching Boa Vista as they are often fully booked. Aircraft maintenance, baggage checking and handling are unreliable. Air taxis with **Rondônia**, Praça Santos Dumond, T2245068.

Airline offices Penta, T2246849. META, Praça Santos Dumond 100, T2247677. **Varig**, T2242269.

Bus

Local The local bus terminal is on Av Amazonas, by R Cecília Brasil, near the central praça.

Long distance Rodoviária, Av das Guianas, 3 km out of town at the end of Av Ville Roy, T2240606. Taxi to centre, US$5, bus US$0.45, 10 mins. Note that it is difficult to get a taxi or bus to the rodoviária in time for early morning departures; as it's a 25-min walk, book a taxi the previous evening. To **Manaus**, with **União Cascavel**, US$32.50, 18 hrs, 4 a day each way, can be very crowded, advisable to book. To **Caracaraí** US$9, 3 hrs. Amatur to **Bonfim**, daily 0730, 1430, 1700, 2 hrs, US$3.70.

Car

Car hire Localiza, Av Benjamin Constant 291E, T/F2245222 and **Yes**, Av Maj Williams 538, T/F2243723.

Hitchhiking

to **Santa Elena**, Venezuela is not easy; either wait at the bridge and police checkpoint on the road to the border, or try to find a Venezuelan driver on the square. Hitching from Boa Vista to **Manaus** is fairly easy on the many trucks travelling south; try from the service station near the rodoviária. You may have to change trucks at Caracaraí. At the ferry crossing over the Rio Branco there is usually a long queue of waiting hikers; try to arrange a lift on the ferry. Truck drivers ask for approximately half the bus fare to take passengers in the cab, which is a bargain; it's much cheaper or free in the back. The view from the truck is usually better than from the bus and you can see the virgin forest of the Indian Reserve in daylight. Take some food and water.

Taxis

Radio taxis with **Tupã**, R Monte Castelo 318, T2249150.

Border with Guyana *p603*

Bus Boa Vista-Bonfim 3 a day, US$3.70. Weekly jeep Boa Vista-Laramonta US$30.

Boat To cross the river, take a canoe (see above) US$0.25 (no boats at night).

Border with Venezuela *p602*

Bus Buses leave Boa Vista rodoviária at 0730, 1000 and 1400 for Santa Elena de Uairén, stopping at all checkpoints, US$7.50, 3½-6 hrs, take water. Buses from Santa Elena to Boa Vista leave at 0830, 1200, 1500 and 1600. It is possible to share a taxi.

Directory

Boa Vista *p599, map p600, phone code 095*
Banks US$ and Guyanese notes can be changed in Boa Vista. TCs and cash in **Banco do Brasil**, Av Glycon Paiva 56, 1000-1300 (minimum US$200). There is no official exchange agency and the local rates for bolívares are low: the **Banco do Brasil** will not change bolívares. **Bradesco**, Jaime Brasil e Getúlioi Vargas. Visa ATM. Best rate for dollars, **Casa Pedro José**, R Araújo Filho 287, T2244277, also changes TCs and bolívares. **Timbo's** (gold and jewellery shop), on the corner of R Cecília Brasil e Av Getúlio Vargas, will change money. **Embassies and consulates** Venezuela, Av Benjamin Constant 525E, Boa Vista, T2242182, Mon-Fri 0830-1300, but may close earlier. **Medical services** Geral, Av Brig Eduardo Gomes, T6232068. Yellow fever inoculations are free at a clinic near the hospital.

Border with Guyana *p603*
Banks Reais can be changed into Guyanese dollars in Boa Vista. There are no exchange facilities in Lethem, but reais are accepted in town. **Embassies and consulates** Guyana, there is no consul in Boa Vista, so if you need a visa for Guyana, you must get it in São Paulo or Brasília.

Rondônia and Acre

Rondônia is a state peopled by immigrants from other parts of Brazil. Foreigners are welcomed without question or curiosity and there is no regional accent. A local academic described the state as "a land where nobody has a name and everyone can have a dream". Most visitors tend to arrive via the BR-364 from Cuiabá or the Rio Madeira from Manaus.

The intriguing state of Acre, rich in natural beauty, history and the seringueiro culture, is still very much off the beaten track. The area is beginning to develop its considerable potential for adventure tourism and historians, as links are opened up with neighbouring Peru and Bolivia. ▸▸ *For Sleeping, Eating and other listings, see pages 613-616.*

Background

Rondônia When the Portuguese first arrived in Rondônia, they thought the land they had found was an enormous island. The Madeira, Guaporé and Amazon rivers do almost form a circle, but the Guaporé was thought, erroneously, to link with the Rio Paraguay on the southwestern side. A group of Tupinambá Indians, who fled from the Portuguese colonists on the Atlantic coast, migrated up the Rio São Francisco to the Madeira, settling eventually on the Ilha de Tupinambaranas near the river's mouth. It was probably their accounts of the rivers in this region which encouraged the idea that the Amazon and Río de la Plata systems were linked, making Brazil an island.

Slave and gold hunters in the 18th century used the Guaporé and Madeira rivers for their expeditions. As a frontier area between Portuguese and Spanish colonization, the rivers were scenes of tension between the opposing powers, as well as of conflicts between Indians and slave-traders, and *bandeirantes* and Jesuits.

Rondônia became a state in 1981 after the central government's push to open up the unpopulated, undeveloped far west brought roads and settlers to the region. The destructive effects of this are well-documented. The BR-364 highway, one of those roads prompted by plans for exaggerated growth, led to widespread deforestation and erosion of the way of life of many indigenous groups. Ironically, the name given to the state was that of the founder of the **Indian Protection Service (SPI)** in 1910, **Colonel Cândido Mariano da Silva Rondon**. Rondon was part Indian and the policies which he incorporated into the SPI included respect for the Indians' institutions, guarantee of permanent ownership by the Indians of their land, the right to exclusive

The River of Doubt

In 1913, Colonel Rondon invited the former US president Theodore Roosevelt to accompany him on one of his surveys. Together they explored the Rio da Dúvida – the River of Doubt – in 1914, following it to the Rio Aripuanã, thence to the Madeira. On the expedition they suffered great difficulties on the river itself, and Roosevelt contracted a fever which incapacitated him on the voyage and from which he never fully recovered. Rondon rechristened the Rio da Dúvida the Rio Roosevelt. The former president's account is told in *Through the Brazilian Wilderness* (London: John Murray, 1914), which contains photographs of the expedition; *Missão Rondon, notes on the project of the Mato Grosso ao Amazonas telegraph*, by Coronel Cãndido Mariano da Silva Rondon, 1907-15, with photos, includes an account of the Roosevelt-Rondon expedition, Sam Moses, 'Down the River of Doubt' (*Travelers' Tales Brazil*, pages 351-9), gives an account, written in 1993, of an expedition in Roosevelt's footsteps, highlighting the effects of the late 20th-century mahogany trade on the Cinta Larga tribe who live on the Rio Roosevelt.

use of natural resources on their land, and protection of the Indians against rapid change once contact between indigenous and 'civilized' worlds had been made. The pressures of contact between Indians and the people who subsequently encroached on their world – ranchers, gold-prospectors, rubber-tappers, Brazil-nut gatherers and so on – made the SPI's task very difficult.

Rondônia falls within the same climatic zone as the rest of western Amazônia, with average temperatures of 24-26°C and between 2,000 and 3,000 mm of rain a year. The wettest months are November-April, the driest June-August. Acre is slightly drier, with 1,500-2,000 mm of rain a year. Rondônia can be subject to the phenomenon known as the *friagem*, a sudden drop in temperature, to about 6°C, as a result of low pressure over the Amazon Basin attracting polar air from the South Atlantic. The cold weather can last for a week or more and occurs in the winter months. It is said to be an effect of El Niño, the changing patterns in ocean currents in the Pacific at Christmas time.

Acre In the mid-19th century, what is now Acre was disputed land between Brazil and Bolivia. The Treaty of Ayacucho, 1866, gave the territory to Bolivia but allowed the Bolivians to use the Brazilian Amazon river system to transport their goods, rather than traverse the Andes to the Pacific Ocean. The onset of the rubber boom in the 1880s upset this arrangement because many of the landowners who were exporting rubber from Acre and down the Rio Madeira were Brazilian. They resented the fact that the Bolivian government had nominal control, exacting duties, but had signed economic rights over to North American interests. Many *Nordestinos* also migrated to this western frontier at the time in search of fortune. In 1899 the Brazilians rebelled. Four years later the Bolivian government yielded the territory to Brazil under the Treaty of Petrópolis and the American company received US$2 mn compensation. The other concession which the Brazilians made was the construction of the Madeira-Mamoré railway to allow Bolivian goods to be transported east. In 1913, Rio Branco became capital of the new Território Federal do Acre, which attained statehood in 1962.

Acre has a population of only 500,000, but as its land is much more productive than its neighbour, Rondônio, there was a flood of immigrants in the 1990s. The future of Acre's forests depend largely on whether any effort is made to improve the lot of the landless of the south, who constitute the majority of the migrants into the far northwest.

Porto Velho
→ *Phone code: 069. Colour map 1, B2. Population: 330,000.*

Porto Velho stands on a high bluff overlooking a curve of the Rio Madeira, one of the Amazon's main tributaries. The city has seen the rubber, gold and timber booms come and go. Service and IT industries are now major employers. Today the city is a large sprawl of streets, laid out in blocks stretching 8 km into the interior. The lack of town planning means that many of the best shops, hotels and banks are now a fair distance from the old centre near the river.

Ins and outs

Getting there Domestic flights arrive at the airport, 8 km west of town. Taxi to downtown US$15. Interstate buses from Rio Branco and Cuiabá arrive at the rodoviária on Jorge Teixeira. » *See also Transport, page 616.*

Getting around Urban bus services are good. Consider hiring a car if you're going to stay for some time. Be patient as local residents get confused themselves by directions. Taxis in town are cheap and plentiful, Radio Taxi Marmoré, T2247070. Find your favourite driver and stick with him, all have mobile phones and work with partners to give prompt 24-hour service.

Tourist offices Funcetur, Av 7 de Setembro, above Museu Estadual, T2211881, F2211831, seplan@ronet.com.br, very helpful, publishes free annual events list *Calendario do Porto Velho*. **Departamento de Turismo** ⓘ *R Padre Chiquinho 670, Esplanada das Secretarias, CEP 78904-060, T2211499, F2252827*. **Fundação Cultural do Estado de Rondônia** (Funcer) is at the same address. Street maps are hard to find. For a free map go to the **Teleron Office** ⓘ *Av Pres Dutra 3023, 0600-2300*, and ask for the *Guia de Porto Velho* which includes a map and city services listings.

Security The city is relatively safe for tourists despite rising crime and unemployment. Caution is advised in the evenings and at all times near the railway station and port.

Sights

At the top of the hill on Praça João Nicoletti is the **cathedral**, built in 1930, with beautiful stained-glass windows; the **Prefeitura** (town hall) is across the street. The principal commercial street is Avenida 7 de Setembro, which runs from the railway station and market hall to the upper level of the city, near the rodoviária. The centre is hot and noisy, but not without its charm, and the port and old railway installations are interesting. As well as the **Museu Ferroviário**, there is a **Museu Geológico** ⓘ *both are open 0800-1800*, at the old railway yards, known as Praça Madeira-Mamoré. Also here is the **Casa do Artesão** (see Shopping below) and a promenade with riverside bars, a wonderful place to watch the sunset.

! Malaria is common. The drinking water is contaminated with mercury from gold panning.

A neoclassical **Casa do Governo** faces Praça Getúlio Vargas, while Praça Marechal Rondon is spacious and modern. There are several popular viewpoints overlooking the river and railway yards. **Mirante I** (with restaurant) is at the end of Rua Carlos Gomes; **Mirante II** (with a bar and ice cream parlour) is at the end of Rua Dom Pedro II and **Mirante III** (with restaurant) is at the end of Benjamin Constant.

It is possible to visit the **cemetery**, where many people who died during the construction of the railway are buried. It's about 2 or 3 km from the railway station, but it is best to go with a local guide, as the cemetery is located in a poorer part of town and can be difficult to find. It is an eerie place, with many of the tombstones overgrown, some of which have been tampered with by practitioners of 'macumba', and there are rumoured to be ghosts.

Parque National Municipal de Porto Velho ⓘ *Av Rio Madeira s/n, 10 km, T2212769, Thu-Sun with volunteer guides*, is a small zoo with 12 km of marked trails.

Excursions from Porto Velho

The **Cachoeira de Santo Antônio**, rapids on the Rio Madeira 7 km upriver from Porto Velho, is a popular destination for a swim during the dry season. In the rainy season the rapids may be underwater and swimming is dangerous. Access is by boat, taking a tour from Porto Cai N'Água, one hour; or by city bus No 102, **Triângulo** (every 50 minutes from the city bus terminus or from the bus stop on Rua Rogério Weber, across from Praça Marechal Rondon). Gold dredges may be seen working near Porto Velho, ask around if interested.

The **Banho do Souza** is a bar, restaurant and swimming area, 36 km out of town on the BR-364. A coolbox of beers and soft drinks is left by your table and you pay for what you've drunk at the end of the afternoon, swimming is free.

Along the BR-364

The **Marechal Rondon Highway**, BR-364, runs 1,550 km from Porto Velho to Cuiabá in Mato Grosso. The paving of this road has led to the development of farms and towns along it. Cattle ranches can be seen all along the road, with least population density in the south between Pimenta Bueno and Vilhena.

Pousada Ecológica Rancho Grande (contact Caixa Postal 361, Ariquemes, Rondônia 78914, T/F5354301, pousada@ariquemes.com.br) is a working *fazenda* about 250 km south of Porto Velho with millions of rare butterflies, about 450 bird species and numerous mammals al of which can be seen on the 20 km of trails. Owner Harald Schmitz speaks English, German and Spanish. Highly recommended, especially for butterfly lovers. Reservations and tours can also be arranged through **Focus Tours**, see Tours operators, page 26. The **Bradesco** changes money and has an ATM.

Ji Paraná → *Phone code: 069. Colour map 1, B3. Population: 95,500.*

On the shores of the Rio Machado, 376 km from Porto Velho and half way to Cuiabá is this pleasant town with a small riverside promenade, and several bars which are lively at night. There is swimming in the river, beware of the current, and a telegraph museum on Avenida Marechal Rondon.

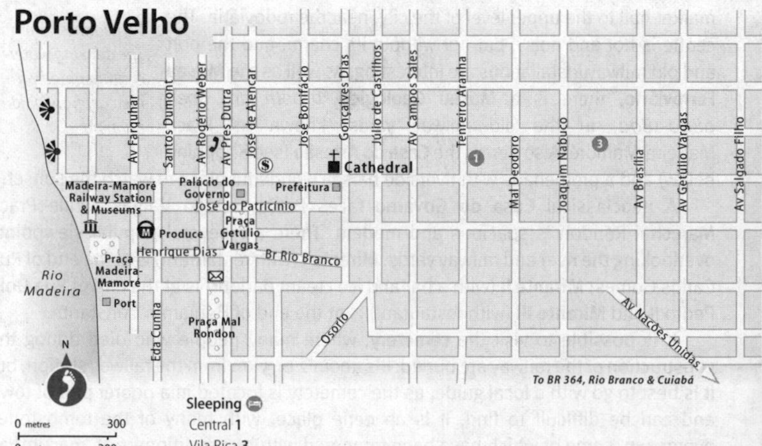

Pacaás Novos National Park and the Guaporé Biological Reserve → *Colour map 1, B2 and B3.*

Pacaás Novos protects some 765,800 ha of cerrado, rainforest and tropical savannah and lies west of the BR-364.. The fauna includes all the spectacular mammals like jaguar, brocket deer, puma, tapir and peccary alongside maned wolf. The average annual temperature is 23°C, but this can fall as low as 5°C when the cold front known as the *friagem* blows up from the South Pole. Details from **Ibama** ⓘ *Av Jorge Teixeira 3477, CEP 78904-320, T2232599/3597, Porto Velho, T2392002/2031, F2218021, or Rua João Batista Rios, CEP 78958-000 Pacaás Novas-RO.* Also enquire here about the **Jaru Biological Reserve** in the east of the state.

On the Rio Guaporé is the **Guaporé Biological Reserve** ⓘ *Av Limoeira, CEP 78971, Guaporé-RO, T6512239,* in which is the Forte Príncipe da Beira, begun in 1777 as a defence of the border with Bolivia. The fort, which is being restored, can be reached from Costa Marques (20 km by road), which is some 345 km by unpaved road west of **Rolim de Moura**. This unplanned town, 40 km west of Pimenta Bueno, relies on agriculture, livestock and a small furniture industry and has a few basic busnisess hotels and simple guest houses which are easy to find and which do not require reservations.

Guajará Mirim → *Phone code: 069. Colour map 1, C2. Population: 39,000.*

From Porto Velho, the paved BR-364 continues 220 km southwest to Abunã (with a few cheap hotels), where the BR-425 branches south to Guajará Mirim. About 9 km east of Abunã is a ferry crossing over the Rio Madeira, where it receives the waters of the Rio Abunã. The BR-425 is a fair road, partly paved, which uses the former rail bridges in poor condition. It is sometimes closed March-May. Across the Mamoré from Guajará Mirim is the Bolivian town of **Guayaramerín**, which is connected by road to Riberalta, from where there are air services to other Bolivian cities.

Guajará Mirim is a charming town. The **Museu Municipal** ⓘ *T5413362, 0500-1200, 1400-1800,* at the old Guajará Mirim railway station beside the ferry landing is interesting and diverse, and recommended. An ancient stern wheeler plies on the Guaporé; 26-day, 1,250-km trips (return) can be made on the Guaporé from Guajará Mirim to Vila Bela in Mato Grosso, the fare includes food.

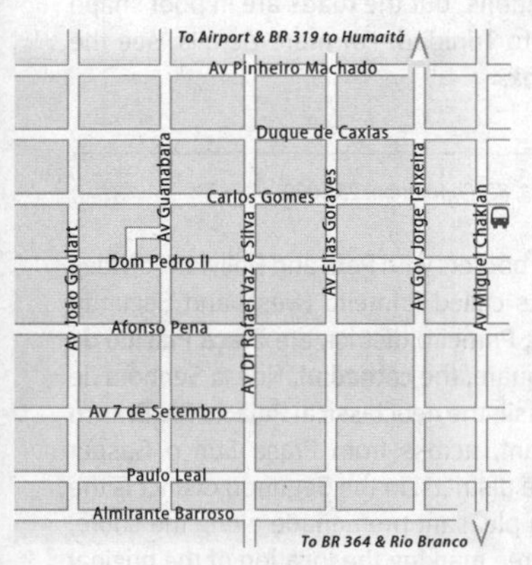

Border with Bolivia

Immigration Brazilian exit/entry stamps from **Polícia Federal** ⓘ *Av Pres Dutra 70, corner of Av Quintino Bocaiúva, T5414021.*

Transport Speedboat across the Rio Mamoré (border), US$1.65, 5-minute crossing, operates all day, tickets at the waterside; ferry crossing for vehicles, T5413811, Monday-Saturday 0800-1200, Monday-Friday 1400-1600, 20-minute crossing.

Guayaramerín

The Bolivian town of Guayaramerín is a cheerful, prosperous little town, on the bank of the Río Mamoré. It has an important **Zona Libre**. There are flights to

Chico Mendes – the first eco-martyr

The most famous *seringueiro* (rubber- tapper) was Francisco (Chico) Alves Mendes, born in 1944. Chico's father had come to Acre from northeast Brazil as a *soldado da borracha*, engaged in providing rubber for the Allies during the Second World War. Chico learnt the trade of his father, became a leader of the Xapuri Rural Workers' Union and was a founder member of the CNS. He was instrumental in setting up a number of 'extractive reserves', parcels of land preserved for sustainable exploitation by those that lived there. He was shot dead on 22 December 1988 by cattle ranchers, to whose land-grabbing Mendes was in open opposition. He was by no means the only *seringueiro* who had been killed in such circumstances (he was the 90th rubber-tapper to be killed in 1988 alone), but his murder was the culmination of a decade of *fazendeiro-seringueiro* confrontation. Over 4,000 people attended his funeral; the world's media latched onto the story and Chico Mendes became the first globally recognized eco-martyr. He was honoured by the United Nations for his efforts in stopping the destruction of the rainforest. The universal outcry at his assassination led to the arrest, trial and imprisonment of his killers, members of the family of Darly Alves da Silva, a rare event in the history of Amazon land disputes. His death inspired changes in government policy over environmental protection, greater involvement of rubber-tappers and other forest workers in local organizations and the development of extractive reserves, first promoted in 1985 as protected areas for the *seringueiros*. Father Andre Ficarelli, assistant to the Bishop of Acre, said that Mendes' murder was like "the lancing of a tumour, exposing all the corruption and problems which the government [chose] to ignore". To others it was an opportunity to portray the whole affair in Hollywood-style melodrama; there was fierce competition for the film rights of Mendes' life story.

Trinidad, La Paz, Cobija, Cochabamba and Santa Cruz, as well as buses to La Paz, Santa Cruz, Trinidad, Cobija and other destinations, but the roads are in poor shape and appalling in the wet season. Boats sail to Trinidad. For more details, see the *Bolivia Handbook* or *South American Handbook*.

Rio Branco → *Phone code: 068. Colour map 1, B2. Population: 253,000.*

Time is one hour behind Porto Velho and Manaus time therefore two hours behind Brazilian Standard Time.

The Rio Acre is navigable upstream as far as the borders with Peru and Bolivia. It divides Rio Branco, the state capital, into two districts called Primeiro (west) and Segundo (east), on either side of the river. In the central, Primeiro district, are **Praça Plácido de Castro**, the shady main square; the **cathedral**, Nossa Senhora de Nazaré, along Avenida Brasil; the neoclassical **Palácio Rio Branco** on Rua Benjamin Constant, across from Praça Eurico Gaspar Dutra. Two bridges link the districts. In the Segundo district is the **Calçadão da Gameleira**, a pleasant promenade along the shore, with plaques and an old tree marking the location of the original settlement. The airport and rodoviária are in the Segundo district. The **tourist office** ⓘ *Secretaria de Indústria e ComércioAv Getúlio Vargas 659, Centro, or Departamento de Turismo, BR-364, Km 05, Distrito Industrial, T2243997 for either office.*

There are several large parks in the city: the **Horto Forestal**, popular with joggers, in Vila Ivonete (Primeiro), 3 km north of the centre ('Conjunto Procon' or 'Vila Ivonete' city-buses), has native Amazonian trees, a small lake, walking paths and picnic areas; the **Parque Zoo-Botânico**, on the UFAC campus (Primeiro), is 5 km from the centre, along BR-364.

Museu da Borracha (Rubber Museum) ⓘ *Av Ceará 1177, Mon-Fri 0900-1700*, is in a lovely old house with a tiled façade. It has information about the rubber boom, archaeological artefacts, a section about Acreano Indians, documents and memorabilia from the annexation and a display about the Santo Daime doctrine (see Excursions below), recommended. **Casa do Seringueiro** ⓘ *Av Brasil 216, on the corner of Avenida Getúlio Vargas, Mon-Fri 0700-1200, 1400-1700*, has a good exhibit on rubber tappers and on **Chico Mendes** in particular; the Sala Hélio Melo has a display of Melo's paintings, mainly on the theme of the forest.

Security Despite improved air and road links, Rio Branco remains at the 'end of the line', a frontier outpost whose depressed economy, high unemployment and prevalent drug-running make the city unsafe at night, and some caution is advised at all hours.

Excursions from Rio Branco

About 8 km southeast of town, upriver along the Rio Acre, is **Lago do Amapá**, a U-shaped lake good for boating and watersports; access is by river or by land via route AC-40. About 2 km beyond along the AC-40 is **Praia do Amapá**, a bathing beach on the Rio Acre; an annual arts festival is held here in September. Excursions can be made to **rubber plantations** and rubber extraction areas in native forest (*seringais nativos*).

Some 13 km from Rio Branco is **Colônia Cinco Mil** (access along AC-10), a religious centre of the followers of the Santo Daime doctrine: its members, many originally from outside Acre and Brazil, live a communal life, working in agriculture

The legend of the rubber tree

Once upon a time, an Amazonian Indian called Maitá was unfairly accused of theft. As a punishment, the chief of his tribe condemned him to a very peculiar and cruel task: to empty a small lake by using a wicker basket. The work was of course extremely unproductive, as the water always flowed through the holes of the basket. Maitá soon realized that he would have to work for the rest of his life and still never empty the lake.

Knowing that Maitá was innocent, a forest fairy approached the poor Indian and asked him to follow her. They walked in the jungle until they reached a very large tree. There, she showed Maitá how to make some cuts in the tree and as he did, he noticed that a milk-like liquid started to flow. The tree was a rubber tree and the liquid was natural latex. Then the fairy told him to spread the sticky liquid over the basket and wait for a while. As the liquid started to dry, he realized that a thin layer of a water resistant material (rubber) was covering all the holes. On returning to the lake, he was very pleased to see that he had no problem in scooping out large amounts of the lake's water. He gratefully thanked the fairy and finished his task in a few days.

As in all good fairy tales, there was a happy ending. The chief discovered he had made a mistake and apologized to Maitá on his return to the tribe. A big party was held to celebrate Maitá's return and, most of all, an important secret had been revealed: the secret of the rubber tree.

and producing crafts made of latex. The religion centers around the use of *ayahuasca*, a hallucinogenic potion adopted from local Indians. Visitors are usually welcome, but enquire beforehand.

Cruzeiro do Sul → *Colour map 1, B1. Population: 65,000.*

From Rio Branco, the BR-364 continues west (in principle) to Cruzeiro do Sul and Japim, with a view to reaching the Peruvian frontier further west when completed. It is very difficult to get from Rio Branco to Cruzeiro do Sul by road because there is no bus service, but the occasional truck goes mainly in the dry season. The road is frequently impassable; it is open, on average, 20 days a year.

Cruzeiro do Sul is an isolated Amazonian town on the Rio Juruá in western Acre. Cheap excursions can be made on the river, for example to the village of Rodrigues Alves, two to three hours, return by boat or by road, 15 km. In the jungle one can see rubber-tapping, and collecting the latex into *borrachas*. Money changing is very difficult in Cruzeiro do Sul. There are a few basic boxy hotels in town (near the cathedral and facing the river) many offer full board. Flights connect the town with Rio Branco (Varig) and Pucallpa in Peru. In the wet there are sporadic boats to Manaus.

Border with Bolivia and Peru

The BR-317 from Rio Branco heads south and later southwest, parallel to the Rio Acre; it is paved as far as **Xapuri**. Here is the Fundação Chico Mendes, one very basic lodging and two restaurants. The road continues to **Brasiléia** opposite the Bolivian town of Cobija on the Rio Acre. In Brasiléia are a handful of hotels and restaurants; Polícia Federal give entry/exit stamps. There are three buses daily to/from Rio Branco, five hours in the wet, US$10. It is possible to stay in **Epitaciolândia** (**Hotel Kanda, D**, five minutes' walk from the police post) and cross the border into Bolivia early in the morning. There are two official crossings between Cobija and Brasiléia. One is by ferry to Cobija's boat wharf, just off Calle Bolívar, at the west end of town.

The other is via the international bridge, east of the ferry. The former is often quicker, and certainly cheaper (US$0.35), as taxis are expensive (US$12). All visitors must carry a yellow fever certificate.

The road ends at Assis Brasil, where the Peruvian, Bolivian and Brazilian frontiers meet. Across the Rio Acre are Iñapari (Peru), where the border crossing is difficult, even out of the wet season, and Bolpebra, Bolivia. A bus service operates only in the dry season beyond Brasiléia to Assis Brasil, access in the wet season is by river. In **Assis Brasil** there is one basic but clean hotel, **E**).

Security Despite improved air and road links, Rio Branco remains at the 'end of the line', a frontier outpost whose depressed economy, high unemployment and drug-running make the city unsafe at night, and caution is advised at all hours.

Rio Branco restaurants, some shops, a bank which does not change US dollars. The hotel owner may be persuaded to oblige. You get between Iñapari and Assis Brasil by wading across the river. **Note** There is no Polícia Federal in the village, get entry/exit stamps in Brasiléia. Take small denomination bills or Peruvian soles as there is nowhere to change money on the Peruvian side.

Cobija is roughly 500 km northwest of La Paz and there are air and road connections. The town is popular with Brazilians and Peruvians for duty-free shopping. For more details, see the *Bolivia Handbook* or the *South American Handbook*.

Sleeping

Porto Velho *p607, map p608, phone code 069*

AL Vila Rica, Av Carlos Gomes 1616, T/F2243433, www.hotelvilarica.com.br. Tower block hotel with a, restaurant, pool and sauna. Beloved of visiting minor dignitaries.

A Rondon Palace, Av Gov Jorge Teixeira, 491,corner R Jacy Paraná, away from the centre, T/F2242718. Business-orientated hotel with a restaurant, pool andtravel agency.

B Central, R Tenreiro Aranha 2472, T2242099, www.enter-net.com.br/hcentral Clean and friendly hotel with a/c rooms withTVs and fridges and agood breakfast. Highly recommended.

C Vitória Palace, R Duque de Caxias 745, T219232. A/c and cheaper fan-cooled rooms. Basic, clean and friendly.

D Líder, Av Carlos Gomes near rodoviária. Honest and welcoming but only reasonably clean. Rooms are fan cooled.

E Tía Carmen, Av Campos Sales 2995, T2217910. Very friendly and with simple well kept rooms. The snack bar in front of the hotel serves good cakes. Highly recommended.

Ji Paraná *p608, phone code 069*

Bus The bus station, R dos Mineiros, T4222233, has services to **Porto Velho**, US$16.25, 16 hrs. To **Cuiabá**, 15 hrs. There are a number of hotels in town, which is tiny and easy to negotiate. Reservations are not necessary.

Guajará Mirim *p609, phone code 069*

A Pakaas Palafitas Lodge, Km 18 Estrada do Palheta, T/F 5413058, www.pakaas.com.br. 28 bungalows smart bungalows in a beautiful natural setting out of town. $60 per day per person.

C Jamaica, Av Leopoldo de Matos 755, T/F5413721. A/c rooms with fridges and parking spaces. Simple but the best hotel in town.

C Lima Palace, Av 15 de Novembro 1613, T5413421, F5412122. Very similar to the Jamaica but with slightly scruffier rooms.

D Chile, Av Q Bocaiúva. Basic but well run. Includes breakfast, good value.

D Mamoré, R Mascarenhas de Moraes 1105, T5413753. Clean, friendly and popular with backpackers.

Rio Branco *p610, map p611, phone code 068*

There are few economical hotels in the centre, but a reasonable selection by the rodoviária.

A Pinheiro Palace, R Rui Barbosa 91, 1° distrito (west bank), T2247191, pinheiro@mdnet.com.br. Business orientated hotel with a pool. Recommended.

B Rio Branco, R Rui Barbosa 193, by Praça Plácido de Castro, 1° distrito, T2241785, F2242681. Simple but well-looked-after hotel with a/c rooms all with fridges and Tvs.

B-D Rodoviária, R Palmeiral 268, Cidade Nova by the rodoviária, T2244434. Convenient and with a range of plain a/c rooms with fridge and TV and cheaper options with shared baths and fans. Good value.

C Inácio Palace, R Rui Barbosa 72, 1° distrito (west bank), T2246397. The budget sister hotel to the **Pinheiro Palace** (same email) with a/c rooms and a modest restaurant.

C Triângulo, R Floriano Peixoto 727, 1° distrito (west bank), T2249265, F2244117. Simple a/c rooms with a TV and fridge.

C-D Albemar, R Franco Ribeiro 99, 1° distrito (west bank), T2241938. Well-kept a/c rooms with a fridge and TV and a good breakfast. Recommended.

D-F Nacional, R Palmeiral 496, 2° distrito in Cidade Nova, T2244822. Cheaper fan-cooled rooms and options with a shared bath.

Eating

Porto Velho *p607, map p608, phone code 069*

Avoid eating too much fish because of mercury contamination. There are a number of good restaurants around the intersection of Dom Pedro II and Av Joaquim Nabuco and plenty of snack bars and *padarias* throughout the city for those on a budget.

TTT Carovela do Madeira, R José Camacho 104. The city's business lunch venue. Reasonable international menu. A/c surrounds.

TT Almanara, R José de Alencar 2624. Good authentic Lebanese food, popular but not cheap. Recommended.

TT Bella Italia, Av Joaquim Nabuco 2205. Pasta, pizza and other basic Italian fare alongside Brazilian home cooking.

T Bar do Dico, Av Joaquim Nabuco 955. The best fish in town and lively in the evenings.

T Natal, Av Carlos Gomes 2783. Standard *churrascaria* with decent side dishes.

T Ponto Certo, Av Rio Madeira 45. Excellent view of river and the best *churrascaria* cuts in town, closed Mon.

Rio Branco *p610, map p611, phone code 068*

There are boats on the river serving cheap but good local food. The local delicacy is *tacacá*: a soup served piping hot in a gourd (*cuia*), made from manioc starch (*goma*), (cooked *jambu* leaves which numb the mouth and tongue), shrimp, spices and hot pepper sauce.

TT Kaxinawa, Av Brasil at the corner of Praça Plácido de Castro. The best in town for Acreano regional food.

TT Pizzeria Tutti Frutti, Av Ceará 1132, across from the Museu da Borracha. Expensive pizzas and exotic ice cream.

T Churrascaria Triângulo, R Floriano Peixoto 727. As much charcoal-grilled meat as you can eat. Recommended.

T Remanso do Tucunaré, R José de Melo 481, Bairro Bosque. Excellent river fish – though avoid the *piraracu*.

T Anexos, R Franco Ribeiro 99, next door to Albemar Hotel. Popular with young people and families for meals and drinks.

T Sorveteria Arte Sabor, Trav Santa Inés 28, corner Aviario, 1° distrito, 15 mins' walk from the centre. Excellent home-made ice cream, many jungle fruit flavours. Highly recommended.

Bars and clubs

Porto Velho *p607, map p608, phone code 069*

Tom Brasil club at Peixe Noturnos, near airport (taxi US$15 essential to book return fare). Every Sun night from 2200, US$3 entry for men.

Maria Fumaça collective, T2244385. Organizes regular raves, concerts and *festas* around town. Check radio and newspapers for details.

Mirantes I (see above), lively bar and a popular meeting place, excellent bar snacks and live acoustic music.

Shopping

Porto Velho *p607, map p608, phone code 069*

Indian handicrafts

At Casa do Índio, R Rui Barbosa 1407 and Casa do Artesão, Praça Madeira-Mamoré, behind the railway station.Thu-Sun 0800-1800. Hammocks are more expensive than in Manaus.

Markets

There is a clean fruit and vegetable market at the corner of R Henrique Dias and Av

Farquhar and a dry goods market 3 blocks to the south, near the port. On Sun there is a general market off Av Rogério Weber near port, excellent bargains but no souvenirs. Watch out for pickpockets.

Rio Branco *p610, map p611, phone code 068*
Arts and crafts
Fair in Praça do Seringueiro on Sun evenings. Market in 1° distrito, off R Epaminondas Jácome.

Activities and tours

Porto Velho *p607, map p608, phone code 069*
Tour operators
Ecoporé, R Rafael Vaz e Silva 3335, Bairro Liberdade, T2215021, carol@ronet.com.br. For ecotourism projects in rubber tappers' communities on the Brazil/Bolivia border, US$50 per person per day, full details from Carol Doria, who speaks English.

Guajará Mirim *p609, phone code 069*
Tour operators
Alfatur, Av 15 de Novembro 106, T/F5412853.

Rio Branco *p610, map p611, phone code 068*
Tour operators
Nilce's Tour, R Quintino Bocaiúva 20, T/F2232611, for airline tickets, helpful, 15 mins' walk from the centre.
Serra's Tur, R Silvestre Coelho 372, T2244629.
Inácio's Tur, R Rui Barbosa 91, at **Hotel** Pinheiro, T2249626.

Transport

Porto Velho *p607, map p608, phone code 069*
See also Ins and outs, p607
Air
Airport, 8 km west of town, T2251755. Flights to Brasília, Manaus and Rio Branco. Take bus marked 'Aeroporto' (last one between 2400 and 0100).

Airline offices TAM, R J Castilho 530, T2242180. **Tavaj**, T2252999. **Varig**, Av Campos Sales 2666, T2242262, F2242278, English spoken. **Vasp**, R Tenheiro Aranha 2326, T2244566.

Boat
See River transport, p549. Passenger service from **Porto Cai N'Água** (which means 'fall in the water', watch out or you might!), for best prices buy directly at the boat, avoid touts on the shore. The Rio Madeira is fairly narrow, so the banks can be seen and there are several 'meetings of waters'.

Shipping a car **São Matheus Ltda**, Av Terminal dos Milagros 400, Balsa, takes vehicles on pontoons, meals, showers, toilets, cooking and sleeping in your car is permitted. 6 days a week a boat leaves at 1800 for **Manaus** from Manicoré, at the confluence of the Rios Madeira and Manicoré, 2 nights and 1 day's journey, food included; boats from Porto Velho to Manicoré on Mon, Wed and Sat (1800, arrives 0200, but you can sleep on the boat), connecting with Manicoré-Manaus boats (a recommended boat is **Orlandina**).

Bus
Rodoviária is on Jorge Teixeira between Carlos Gomes and Dom Pedro II. From town take 'Presidente Roosevelt' bus No 301 (if on Av 7 de Setembro, the bus turns at Av Mcal Deodoro); 'Aeroporto' and 'Hospital Base' (No 400) also go to rodoviária. Health and other controls at the Rondônia-Mato Grosso border are strict. To break up a long trip is much more expensive than doing it all in one stretch.

Bus to **Humaitá**, US$5, 3 hrs. To **São Paulo**, 60-plus hrs, US$75. To **Cuiabá**, 23 hrs, US$45, expensive food and drink is available en route. To **Guajará-Mirim**, see below. To **Rio Branco**, **Viação Rondônia**, 5 daily, 8 hrs, US$12.50. Daily bus with **Eucatur** from **Cascavel** (Paraná, connections for Foz do Iguaçu) via Maringá, Presidente Prudente, Campo Grande and Cuiabá to Porto Velho (Porto Velho-Campo Grande 36 hrs, US$60). To **Cáceres** for the Pantanal, 18 hrs, US$30.

Car
Cuiabá (BR-364 – Marechal Rondon Highway) is 1,550 km, fully paved; see below and p663; Rio Branco, 554 km, BR-364, poorly paved; north to Humaitá (205 km) on the Madeira river, BR-319, paved, connecting with the Transamazônica, BR-230 (frequently closed, ascertain conditions before

travelling). The BR-319 north from Humaitá to Manaus is closed indefinitely. Road journeys are best done in the dry season, the 2nd half of the year.

Car hire LeMans, Av Nações Unidas 1200, T2242012. **Silva Car**, R Almte Barroso 1528, T2211423/6040. **Ximenes**, Av Carlos Gomes 1055, T2245766.

Guajará Mirim *p609*

Bus From **Porto Velho**, 5½ hrs or more depending on season, 8 a day with **Viação Rondônia**, US$18. Taxi from Porto Velho rodoviária, US$25 per person for 4-5, 3 hrs, leaves when full.

Rio Branco *p610, map p611, phone code 068*

Air

The airport is on AC-40, Km 1.2, in the 2° distrito, T2246833. Taxi from the airport to the centre US$20 flat rate, but going to the airport the meter is used, which usually comes to less. By bus, take 'Norte-Sul' or 'Vila Acre'. Flights to Porto Velho, Manaus, Brasília, São Paulo, Cuiabá and Campo Grande; once a week to Cruzeiro do Sul.

Airline offices Varig, T2111000.

Bus

Rodoviária on Av Uirapuru, Cidade Nova, 2° distrito (east bank), T2241182. City bus 'Norte-Sul' to the centre. To **Porto Velho**, **Viação Rondônia**, 5 daily, 8 hrs, US$12.50. To **Guajará Mirim**, daily with **Rondônia** at 1130 and 2200, 5-6 hrs, US$10; or take **Inácio's Tur** shopping trip, 3 per week.

Car

Car hire Car rentals with nationwide agencies are higher in Acre than other states. **Locabem**, Rodovia AC-40, Km 0, 2° distrito, T2233000, F2245222. **Localiza**, R Rio Grande do Sul 310, T2247746, airport T2248478. **Unidas**, T2245044.

Directory

Porto Velho *p607, map p608, phone code 069*

Banks Open in the morning only. **Banco do Brasil**, Dom Pedro II 607 and Av José de Alencar, cash and TCs with 2 commission, minimum commission US$10, minimum amount exchanged US$200. **Marco Aurélio Câmbio**, R José de Alencar 3353, T2232551, very quick, efficient, good rates for US$ cash, Mon-Fri 0900-1500. **Parmetal** (gold merchants), R Joaquim Nabuco 2265, T2211566, cash only, good rates, open Mon-Fri 0730-1800, Sat 0730-1300. Local radio news and papers publish exchange rates. Exchange is difficult elsewhere in Rondônia. **Laundry** Lavanderia Marmoré, Pinheiro Machado 1455B. **Medical Services** Hospital Central, R Júlio de Castilho 149, T/F2244389, 24 hr emergencies. **Dentist** at Carlos Gomes 2577; 24-hr clinic opposite. **Post office** Av Pres Dutra 2701, corner of Av 7 de Setembro. **Telephones** Av Pres Dutra 3023 and Dom Pedro II, daily 0600-2300.

Guajará Mirim *p609*

Banks Banco do Brasil, foreign exchange in the morning only. **Loja Nogueira**, Av Pres Dutra, corner Leopoldo de Matos, cash only. There is no market in Brazil for bolivianos. **Embassies and consulates** Bolivia, Av C Marquês 495, T5412862, visas are given here. **Medical services** Regional, Av Mcal Deodoro, T5412651. **Post office** Av Pres Dutra. **Telephone** Av B Ménzies 751.

Rio Branco *p610, map p611, phone code 068*

Hospitals Santa Casa, R Alvorada 178, T2246297. **Post office** On the corner of R Epaminondas Jácome and Av Getúlio Vargas. **Telephone** Av Brasil between Mcal Deodoro and Av Getúlio Vargas, long delays for international calls.

Goiás, Brasília & the Pantanal

Footprint features

Introduction

The wetlands and forest islands of the Pantanal, which covers southern Mato Grosso and almost all of Mato Grosso do Sul, are top of the destination list for enthusiasts of South American wildlife. Not only do almost all of the continent's big animals live here, they live here in large numbers. And there is nowhere on Earth where you will see so many different birds. Sunsets are a spectacular deep orange all year round and in the early summer the landscape is flecked with flashes of brilliant pink and lilac from flowering *ipê* and jacaranda trees.

Goiás, to the north of the Pantanal, is yet to be discovered by travellers. How it has stayed secret for so long is a mystery. If you include Brasília – Oscar Niemeyer and Lucio Costa's vision of Order and Progress in concrete and stone – it has the largest number of UNESCO World Heritage sites of any state in South America. Its scenery is wonderful: timeless colonial villages surrounded by table-top mountains dripping with waterfalls and swathed in a forest of medicinal plants; and its people are friendly and welcoming. Come before soya eats up all the forests and it turns into a vast agricultural plain.

Tocantins state which sits above Goiás is less visited still and is virgin territory for travellers. Like Goiás it is covered in *cerrado* forests and soya which give way to the Jalapão deserts in the east. Its border with Mato Grosso and Goiás is marked by the Ilha do Bananal – one of the world's largest river islands and a Ramsar wetland area as important for wildlife as the Pantanal. Much of the island is an indigenous reserve and those areas that are not are gradually being destroyed by settlers.

★ Don't miss...

1. **Brasília** Love or hate the country's purpose-built monument to a positivist future yet to materialize, page 621.
2. **Cidade de Goiás** Visit the best-preserved and least-visited colonial town in Brasil, page 629.
3. **Goiás Cerrado** Explore the World Heritage sites of Emas National Park – the best place in South America to see maned wolf – and the subtly beautiful Chapada dos Veadeiros table-top mountains; so vast and wild that an uncontacted tribe is rumoured to live somewhere within them, page 631.
4. **Southern Pantanal** Set off on a camping and trekking trip from Corumbá; wake up to the raucous calls of metre-long macaws and see a wealth of wildlife from giant anteaters to capybaras, page 647.
5. **Transpantaneira** Stay in a Pantanal ranch house on the Transpantaneira near Cuiabá; we saw a jaguar when we were there last, page 652.
6. **Ilha do Bananal** Visit one of the world's largest river islands, home to large groups of indigenous people and a Ramsar-listed wetland, page 669.

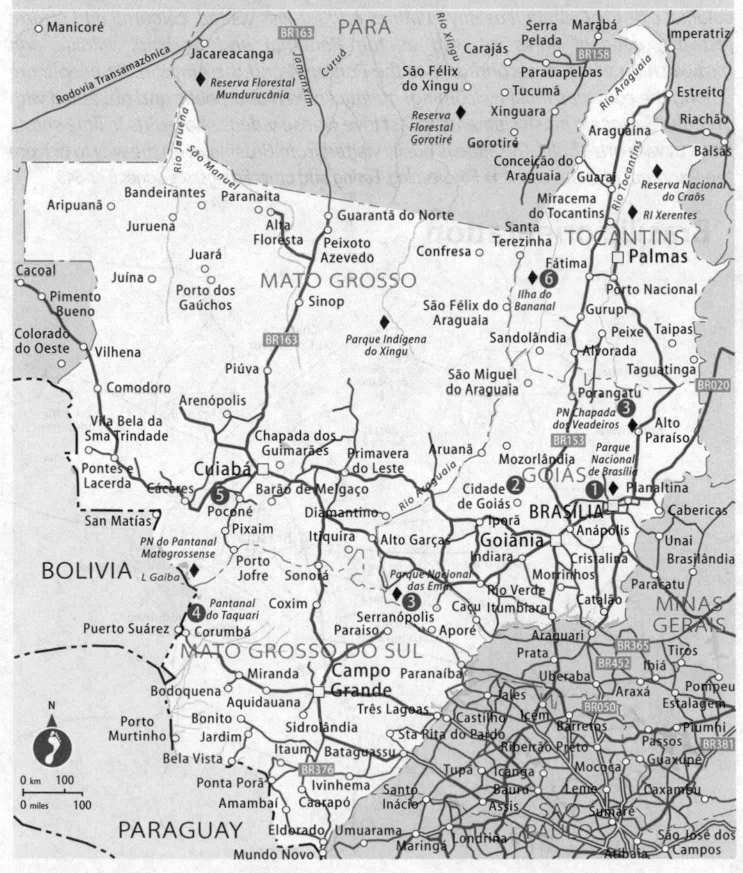

Brasília and the Goiás

This planned and impersonal capital city, sitting like a monument to the jet age in a vast plain and increasingly surrounded by the favela *and chaos of the real Brazil, may seem very un-Brazilian to those who are new to the country. This is after all a nation internationally famous for its relaxed attitude to time. But it also has 'Order and Progress' written proudly on its flag, in homage to the ideas of Comte. And the grandiose schemes of many of its 20th-century leaders have long been influenced by a desire to propel the country immediately and impetuously into a Positivist vision of the future. Brazil's capital was intended by its conceivers Lúcio Costa and Oscar Niemeyer and their then President Juscelino Kubitschek as a statement of that future in concrete; an attempt perhaps to make real the cliché repeated by every other Brazilian leader that this is 'the country of the future'. Although many of the remarkable buildings like the dome and saucer of the Congresso Nacional would alone make a visit here worthwhile, Brasília is every bit as Brazilian as Rio Carnaval and Pelé and a visit here is a must for those interested in the psychology of the country. The climate is mild and the humidity refreshingly low, but trying in dry weather. The noon sun beats hard, but summer brings heavy rains and the air is usually cool by night.*

For first-time Brazil visitors Goiás is rarely on the itinerary. But those who know it well often consider it their favourite state in the country. There is so much here – colonial cities as beautiful as any in Minas and far less visited, colourful and bizarre festivals, national parks as wild as the Pantanal and trekking, wildlife and birdwatching which is second only to the Pantanal and the Amazon. Its people are among the country's most welcoming: quietly spoken and poetic and obsessed with dreadful Sertanejo music; laments to lost love whose videos show girls in little shorts intercut with prize bulls. The state is easily visited from Brasília or on the way to or from the Pantanal and the coast. » *For Sleeping, Eating and other listings, see pages 633-643.*

Brasília orientation

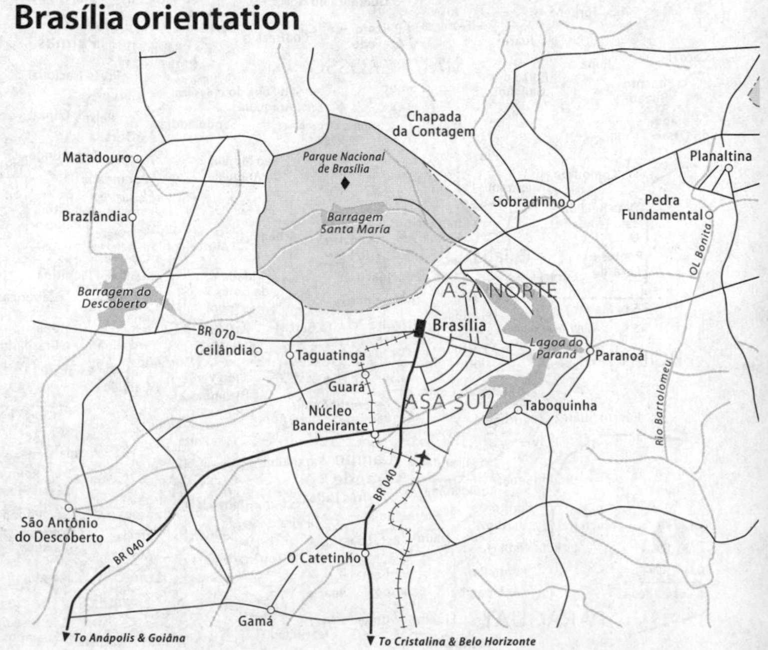

Brasília ➔ *Phone code: 061. Colour map 4, A2. Population: 2.1 million.*

Ins and outs

Getting there Flights arrive at the **international airport** ⓘ *T3649000*. Taxi to centre US$10, meter rate two is used to or from the airport. Left-luggage facilities at airport (locker tokens, US$0.50). Interstate buses arrive at the **rodoferroviária** ⓘ *T3632281*, beside the railway station. Bus No 131 between rodoviária, the municipal terminal in the city centre, and rodoferroviária, US$1.25. Both bus stations have large luggage lockers.

Getting around A good and cheap way of seeing Brasília is by taking bus rides from the municipal rodoviária at the centre: the destinations are clearly marked. The circular bus routes Nos 106, 108 and 131 go round the city's perimeter. If you go around the lake by bus, you must change at the Paranoá dam; to or from Paranoá Norte take bus 101, 'Rodoviária', and to and from Sul, bus 100, bypassing the airport. It is worth telephoning addresses away from the centre to ask how to get there. An urban railway, Metrô, to the southwest suburbs, has recently been completed, but is very limited. ➧ *See also Transport, page 642.*

There is some gang violence in the city, so caution is advised at night.

Tourist offices Adetur ⓘ *Centro de Convenções 3rd floor, T3255700, F2255706, open to public 0800-1200 and 1300-1800*, some English spoken, helpful, good map of Brasília; there's a **small stand at rodoferroviária** ⓘ *daily 0800-2000*, friendly but not very knowledgeable. **Airport tourist office** ⓘ *T3255730, daily 0800-2000*, will book hotels, limited English and information, no maps of the city. **Adetur** publishes a book called *Brasília, Coração Brasileiro*, which is full of practical information. **Embratur** ⓘ *Setor Comercial Norte, Quadra 02, bloco G, CEP 70710-500, T2249100, webmaster@embratur.gov.br*, office at airport. **Touring Club do Brasil** ⓘ *on Eixo*, has maps (members only). The information office in the centre of Praça dos Tres Poderes has a colourful map and lots of useful text information. The staff are friendly and have interesting information about Brasília and other places in Goiás – only Portuguese spoken.

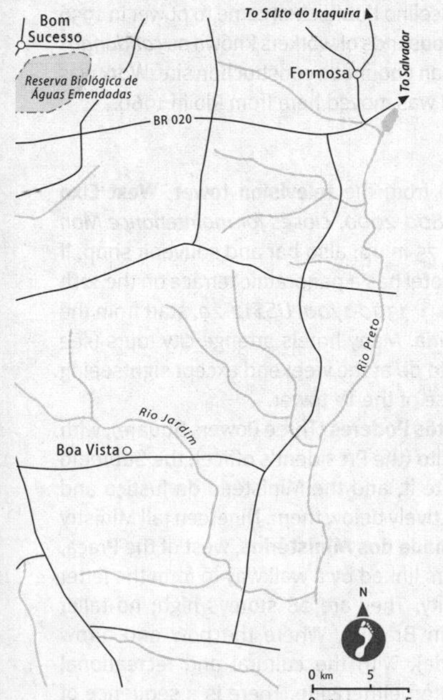

Maps Infomaps ⓘ www.infomaps.com.br, publish a comprehensive map of the city showing attractions and principal hotels. It is available from **Arte Capital** shops in the Airport, **Patio Brasil Shopping**, the lobby of the **Blue Tree Park** hotel and **Matriz** in the Asa Norte as well as the larger newsagents.

Design and orientation A competition for the best general plan was won by Professor Lúcio Costa, who laid out the city in the shape of a bent bow and arrow. It is also described as a bird or aeroplane in flight. The official name for central Brasília is the **Plano Piloto**.

The **Eixo Monumental** divides the city into **Asa Norte** and **Asa Sul** (north and south wings) and the **Eixo**

 Rodoviário divides it east and west. Buildings are numbered according to their relation to them. For example, 116 Sul and 116 Norte are at the extreme opposite ends of the city. The 100s and 300s lie west of the Eixo and the 200s and 400s to the east; Quadras 302, 102, 202 and 402 are nearest the centre, and 316, 116, 216 and 416 mark the end of the Plano Piloto.

Residential areas are made up of large six-storey apartment blocks, called the 'Super-Quadras'. Each Super-Quadra houses 3,000 people and has a primary school and playgroup. Each group of four Super-Quadras should have a library, police station, club, supermarket and secondary school. All Quadras are separated by feeder roads, along which are the local shops. There are also a number of schools, parks and cinemas in the spaces between the Quadras (especially in Asa Sul), though not as systematically as was originally envisaged. On the outer side of the 300s and extending the length of the city is the **Avenida W3**, and on the outer side of the 400s is the **Avenida L2**, both of these being similarly divided into north and south according to the part of the city they are in.

Asa Norte is growing very fast, with standards of architecture and urbanization that promise to make it more attractive than Asa Sul in the near future. The main shopping areas, with more cinemas, restaurants and other facilities, are situated on either side of the old bus station (rodoviária). There are now several parks, or at least green areas. The private residential areas are west of the Super-Quadras, and on the other side of the lake.

At right angles to these residential areas is the 'arrow', the 8-km long, 250-m wide Eixo Monumental. The main north-south road (Eixo Rodoviário), in which fast-moving traffic is segregated, follows the curve of the bow; the radial road is along the line of the arrow – intersections are avoided by means of underpasses and cloverleaves. Motor and pedestrian traffic is segregated in the residential areas.

History

Plans for the capital have a long history. In 1810, Chancelor Veloso de Oliveira, suggested moving the capital inland to protect against potential invasions. The city was finally created from scratch after President Juscelino Kubitschek came to power in 1956 and personally oversaw the project. Tens of thousands of workers known as *candangos* were recruited to transform the savannah into an enormous construction site. Work was completed in just three years, and the capital was moved here from Rio in 1960.

Sights

A good initial view of the city may be had from the **television tower, West Eixo Monumental** ⓘ *Mon 1400-2000, Tue-Sun 0800-2000, closes for maintenance Mon mornings*. It has a free observation platform 75 m up; also bar and souvenir shop. If the TV tower is closed, the nearby **Alvorada** hotel has a panoramic terrace on the 12th floor (lift to 11th only); ask at reception. **Tours** ⓘ *1300-1700, US$12-20*, start from the downtown hotel area and municipal rodoviária. Many hotels arrange city tours (see also Tour operators, page 641). There's little to do at the weekend except sightseeing (car needed) or visiting the market at the base of the TV tower.

At the 'tip of the arrow' is the **Praça dos Três Poderes** (Three Powers Square), with the Congress buildings, the Palácio do Planalto (the President's office), the Supremo Tribunal Federal opposite it, and the Ministério da Justiça and Palácio Itamaraty respectively below them. Nineteen tall Ministry buildings line the **Esplanada dos Ministérios**, west of the Praça, culminating in two towers linked by a walkway to form the letter H, representing Humanity. They are 28 storeys high; no taller buildings are allowed in Brasília. Where the bow and arrow intersect is the city bus terminal (rodoviária), with the cultural and recreational centres and commercial and financial areas on either side. There is a sequence of

Some buildings are open 1000-1400 Saturday and Sunday, with guided tours in English; well worth going.

Oscar Niemeyer and Brasília

Oscar Niemeyer Soares Filho (born 1907 in Rio de Janeiro) was educated at the Escola Nacional de Belas Artes and in 1936 joined the group of architects charged with developing Le Corbusier's project for the Ministry of Education and Health building in Rio de Janeiro. His first international project was the Brazilian pavilion at the New York International Fair in 1939 in partnership with Lúcio Costa. In the 1940s he was one of the main designers of Pampulha (see under Belo Horizonte) and in 1947 he worked on the United Nations headquarters in New York. This was the period in which he affirmed his style, integrating architecture with painting and sculpture. He transformed utilitarian constructions with the lightness of his designs, his freedom of invention and the use of complex, curved surfaces. Throughout the 1950s he was commissioned to design a wide variety of national and international projects, but it was the years 1956-1959 that stamped his signature on the architectural world. This was when he worked on Brasília, specifically the Palácio da Alvorada, the Ministries, the Praça dos Três Poderes, the Cathedral, University and, in 1967, the Palácio dos Arcos e da Justiça. After Brasília, Niemeyer continued to work at home and abroad; among his more famous later projects were the Sambódromo in Rio (1984) and the Memorial da América Latina in São Paulo (1989). The Royal Institute of British Architects awarded him the prestigious Royal Gold Medal for Architecture in 1998.

Many of Brazil's most famous architects, sculptors and designers were involved in Brasília. The city was built during Juscelino Kubitschek's term as president, 1955-1960, and was unparalleled in scale and architectural importance in Latin America at that time. Niemeyer was appointed chief architecture and technical adviser to Novacap, the government authority that oversaw the new capital. But while it is common knowledge who the famous names were, it is also worth noting that tens of thousands of workers were involved in bringing the plan to reality. Most of them came from the Northeast. The city has been honoured not just for its architecture, but also for being the first purpose-built capital of the 20th century. In 1987 it was named a Unesco World Cultural Heritage Site, the first contemporary city to gain such United Nation protection .

Niemeyer himself has said "The modern city lacks harmony and a sense of occasion. Brasília will never lack these." And it is true that the principal buildings, and the overall plan itself, are strikingly powerful. The whole enterprise is deeply rooted in the 20th century, not just in its design, but also in the idea that it is a city you jet into and out of. If you arrive by road (which most people do not), the experience is even more extra-ordinary. After hours and hours in the bus, travelling across the unpopulated central plateau, you come to this collection of remarkable buildings and sculptures in the middle of nowhere. The vastness of the landscape demands a grand city and yet, for all its harmony, it is almost as if not even Brasília can compete with the sky and the horizon.

Niemeyer is still working in his late nineties. His mostly recently opened grand building is the Niemeyer museum in Curitiba which opened in 2002. It sits like a giant black eye on a pedestal in one of the city's parks – fully living up to Niemeyer's pro-clamation that "the most important element in any work of art is to surprise, to startle." And Niemeyer is not done there. There are further state buildings due to open in Brasília over the next few years.

zones westward along the shaft of the arrow; a hotel centre, a radio city, an area for fairs and circuses, a centre for sports, the **Praça Municipal** (with the municipal offices in the Palácio do Buriti) and, lastly (where the nock of the arrow would be), the combined new bus and railway station (rodoferroviária) with the industrial area nearby. Other than the Santuário Dom Bosco and the JK bridge, the most impressive buildings are all by Oscar Niemeyer (see box, page 623).

The **Palácio da Alvorada**, the President's official residence (not very palatial and not open to visitors), is on the lakeshore. The 80-km drive along the road, round the lake to the dam, is attractive and there are spectacular falls below the dam in the rainy season. Between the Praça dos Três Poderes and the lake are sites for various recreations, including golf, fishing and sailing, and an acoustic shell for shows in the open air. Some 395 ha between the lake and the northern residential area (Asa Norte) are reserved for the **Universidade de Brasília**, founded in 1961. South of the university area, the Avenida das Nações runs from the Palácio da Alvorada along the lake to join the road from the airport to the centre. Along it are found all the principal embassies. Also in this scenic area is the attractive vice-presidential residence, the **Palácio do Jaburu**, not open to visitors.

Official buildings

Congresso Nacional ⓘ *Praça dos Três Poderes, Mon-Fri 0930-1200, 1430-1630, take your passport, guides free of charge (guides in English 1400-1600)*. Visitors may attend debates when Congress is in session (Friday morning). The building also has excellent city views from the 10th floor in Annex 3. The **Palácio do Planalto** ⓘ *Praça dos Três Poderes, ½-hr tours Sun only 0930-1330*. The guard is changed ceremonially at the Palácio do Planalto on Fridays at 1730; the President attends if he is available. Opposite sits the Supremo Tribunal Federal, which has hallmark Niemeyer marble columns, and between the two, beneath the *praça*, is the **Espaço Lucio Costa** ⓘ *Tue-Sun 0900-1800, free*, with a scale model of the city. The **Museu Histórico de Brasília** ⓘ *Praça dos Três Poderes, Tue-Sun and holidays 0900-1800*, is really a hollow monument, with tablets,

Town clothes (not shorts) should be worn when visiting these buildings

Brasília: Plano Piloto

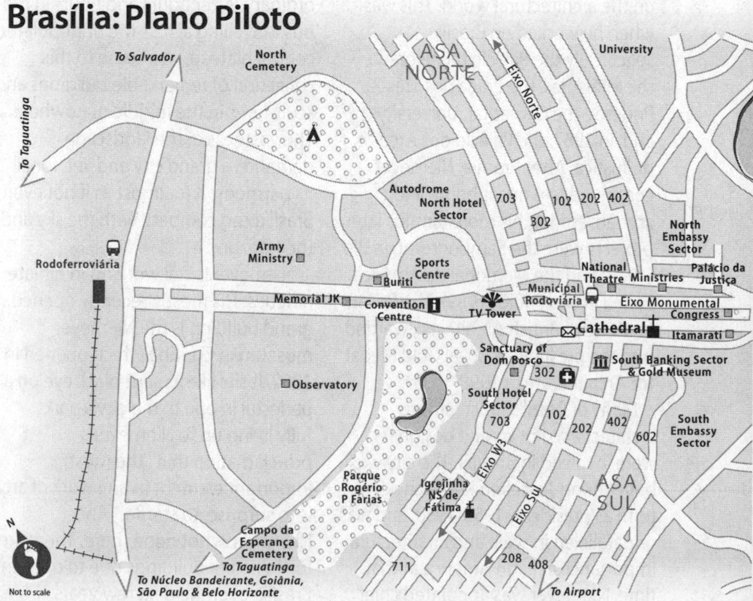

photos and videos telling the story of the city. The sculpture *Os Candangos* in front of the Planalto is something of a symbol of the city. By Bruno Giorgi, it pays homage to the *candangos*, or pioneer workers who built Brasília on empty ground. The marvellous building of the Ministry of Foreign Affairs, the **Itamarati**, has modern paintings and furniture and beautiful water gardens. Niemeyer is well into his nineties now but is still working. One of his most recent buildings, the **Procuradaria Geral da Republica** ⓘ *guided visits Mon, Wed, Fri 1500-1700, free*, comprising two glass cylinders, one suspended from a concrete cog, opened in 2002 and two more important public buildings and a major church are due to open in the next couple of years. Opposite the Itamarati is the **Palácio da Justiça** ⓘ *Mon-Fri 0900-1200, 1500-1700*, with artificial cascades between its concrete columns.

Churches, memorials, military buildings and sculptures

The **Catedral Metropolitana** ⓘ *Esplanada dos Ministérios, T2244073, 0800-1930*, is a spectacular circular building in the shape of the crown of thorns, designed by Oscar Niemeyer. The three aluminium angels, suspended from the airy, domed, stained-glass ceiling, are by the sculptor Alfredo Ceschiatti, who also made the four life-sized bronze apostles outside. The **baptistry** ⓘ *Sun only*, a concrete representation of the Host beside the cathedral, is connected to the main building by a tunnel. The outdoor carillon was a gift from the Spanish government; the bells are named after Columbus's ships.

South of the TV tower is the **Santuário Dom Bosco** ⓘ *Av W3 Sul, Quadra 702, T2236542, 0800-1800*, a modernist cube with tall Gothic arches filled with stained glass which shades from light to dark blue and indigo as it ascends. It is particularly beautiful in the late afternoon when shafts of light penetrate the building. The trunk of the enormous cross hanging over the altar was carved from a single piece of tropical cedar.

The **Templo da Boa Vontade** ⓘ *Setor Garagem Sul 915, lotes 75/76, T2451070, open 24 hrs*, is a seven-faced pyramid dedicated to all philosophies and religions topped by one of the world's largest rock crystals. To get there, take bus 151 from outside the Centro do Convenções or on Eixo Sul to Centro Médico.

About 15 km out along the Belo Horizonte road is the small wooden house, designed by Niemeyer, erected in only 10 days and known as **O Catetinho**. President Kubitschek stayed here in the late 1950s during his visits to the city when it was under construction; it is open to visitors and houses memorabilia and some of JK's furniture and personal items. A permanent memorial to Juscelino Kubitschek, the **Memorial JK** ⓘ *Tue-Sun 0900-1800, US$0.50, with toilets and lanchonete*, contains his tomb and his car, together with a lecture hall and exhibits. The **Quartel-General do Exército**, Brazilian Army headquarters designed by Oscar Niemeyer, is interesting too. The **Panteão Tancredo Neves** is a 'temple of freedom and democracy', built 1985-1986 by Niemeyer. It includes an

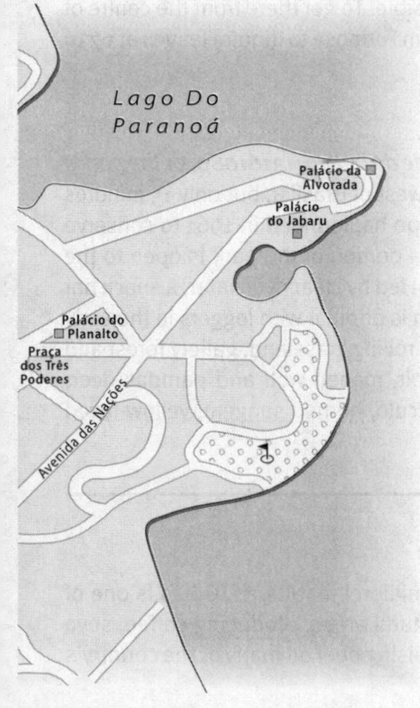

 impressive homage to Tiradentes (see box, page 248). **Espaço Lúcio Costa** contains a model of Plano Piloto, sketches and autographs of the designer's concepts and gives the ideological background to the planning of Brasília. The **Monumental Parade Stand** has unique and mysterious acoustic characteristics (the complex is north of the Eixo Monumental, between the 'Memorial JK' and the rodoferroviária). There are remarkable stained-glass panels, each representing a state of the Federation, on the ground floor of the Caixa Econômica Federal.

Brasília is famous for its wealth of **modern sculpture**. Examples are *Cultura* (on the University campus), *Meteoro* (above the Itamarati water-mirror), both by Bruno Giorgi; *A Justiça* (in front of Supremo Tribunal Federal), the four evangelists in front of the cathedral and *As Banhistas* (The Water Nymphs, above the Alvorada water-mirror) – all by Alfredo Scesciatte; *Rito dos Ritmos* (Alvorada gardens), by Maria Martins; and the beautiful *Sereia* (Mermaid), in front of the Navy Ministry on the Esplanada dos Ministérios. A statue of Juscelino Kubitschek stands above the 'Memorial JK'. A short distance west of here is a huge wooden cross marking the site of the first mass said in Brasília (3 May 1957), at the city's highest point.

Around Brasília

Some 40 km northeast of the Plano Piloto via Saída Norte is **Planaltina**, originally a settlement on the colonial pack route from the mines of Goiás and Cuiabá to the coast. The old part still contains many colonial buildings. There are two good *churrascarias* on the main street and it is a good place for a rural Sunday lunch. About 5 km outside Planaltina is the Pedra Fundamental, the foundation stone laid by President Epitácio Pessoa in 1922 to mark the site that was originally chosen for the new capital.

Also outside Planaltina, at Km 30 on the BR-020, lies **Águas Emendadas**. From the same point spring two streams that flow in opposite directions to form part of the two great river systems, the Amazon and the Plate. Permission from the biological institute in Brasília is required to visit. At Km 70 is **Formosa**. Some 20 km north of the town is the **Itiquira waterfall** (158 m high). From the top are spectacular views and the pools at the bottom offer good bathing, but it gets crowded at weekends. There are four smaller falls in the area and camping is possible. To get there from the centre of Formosa, follow the signs or ask. The only bus from Formosa to Itiquira leaves at 0730 and returns at 1700.

Parque Nacional de Brasília

ⓘ *Contact Ibama, SAIN, Av L/4 Lote 04/08, Ed Sede do Ibama, T3161080, or the park's office, Via Epia SMU, T2333251, F2335543*. Northwest of Brasília, but only 15 minutes by car from the centre, is this park of some 28,000 ha, founded in 1961 to conserve the flora and fauna of the Federal Capital. Only a portion of the park is open to the public without a permit. There is a swimming pool fed by clear riverwater, a snack bar and a series of trails through gallery forest, which is popular with joggers in the early morning and at weekends. The rest of the park is rolling grassland, gallery forest and *cerrado* vegetation. Large mammals include tapir, maned wolf and pampas deer; birdwatching is good (above all for Brasília tapaculo, horned sungem, yellow-faced parrot and least nighthawk).

Goiás

With an area of 364,714 sq km and some four million inhabitants, Goiás is one of Brazil's most rapidly developing frontier agricultural areas, producing coffee, soya and rice, most of Brazil's tin and tungsten, and raising beef on many of the country's largest cattle ranches.

Goiânia → *Phone code: 062. Colour map 4, A1. Population: 1.1 million.*

Just off the BR-060, 209 km southwest of Brasília, is the second of Brazil's planned state capitals, after Belo Horizonte. Goiânia was founded in 1933 and replaced Goiás Velho as capital four years later.

The state capital is famous for its street cafés and is a good place to stop between Brasília and the rest of the Centro-Oeste. Tourism is not as developed here as in other parts of the country, but the city is pleasant and there are some interesting sights within easy reach.

It is a spacious city, with many green spaces and well-lit main avenues, ornamented with plants, radiating out from the central **Praça Cívica**, on which stand the Government Palace and main Post Office.

Goiânia has more parks and gardens than any other of Brazil's large cities and many are filled with interesting forest and *cerrado* plants, as well as marmosets and remarkably large numbers of birds.

About 1½ km out along the Avenida Araguaia (which runs diagonally northeast from the *praça*) is the shady **Parque Mutirama**, with recreational and entertainment facilities and a **planetarium** ⓘ *sessions Sun 1530 and 1630*. More tranquil is the

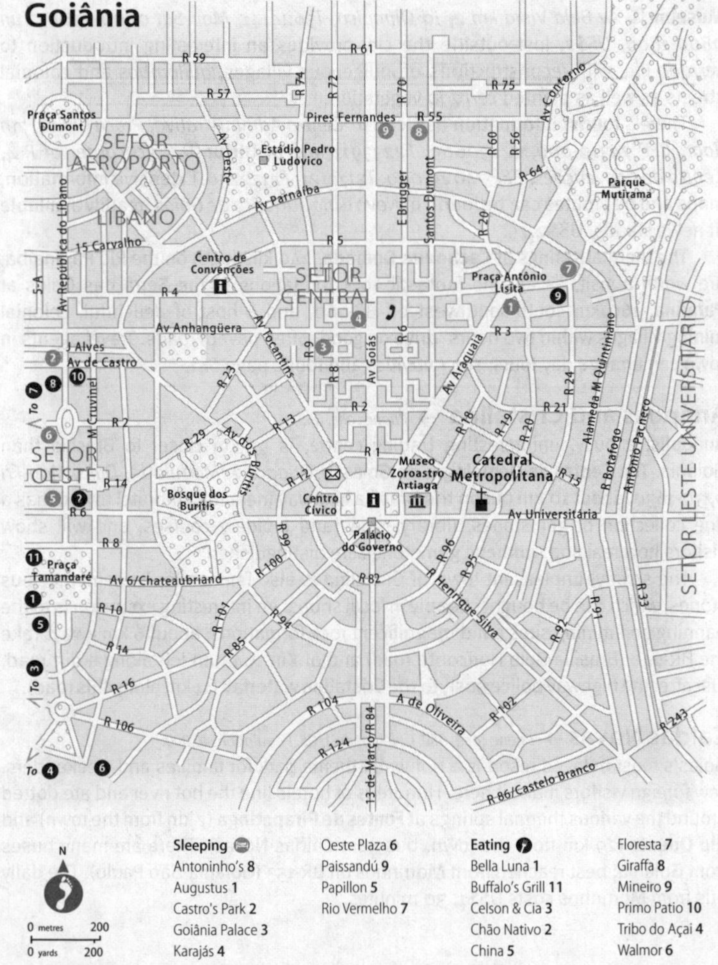

 Bosque dos Buritis ⓘ *1 km west of the Praça Cívica along R 10*, which has shaded walks in *buriti*-filled tropical gardens and a turtle-filled pond. The **Parque Zoólogico** ⓘ *Av Anhangüera, Tue-Sun 0700-1800*, 1 km west of the **Castro's Park** hotel is set in large gardens and is a good place to while away an afternoon.

The **Museu Zoroastro Artiaga** ⓘ *Praça Cívica 13, T2014676*, has a small but interesting collection of indigenous and historical objects, fossils and religious items as well as cases depicting Indian and early settler life in Goiás. The museum was twice the size before it was cherry picked by local politicians for their private collections. **Museu Antropológico do UFG** ⓘ *Praça Universitária, Mon-Fri 0900-1700*, 1 km east of Praça Cívica, houses wide-ranging ethnographic displays on the Indians of the Centre West. **Museu de Ornitologia** ⓘ *Av Pará 395, Sétor Campinas, Tue-Sun 0900-1900*, has more than 8,000 stuffed birds and animals from many countries. The **Museu de Arte de Goiânia** ⓘ *R 1 605, T5241190, Mon-Fri 0800-1700, Sat 0800-1300, free*, in the Bosque dos Buritis gardens, has a room showcasing the work of a number of local artists including Siron Franco, who is of national reknown. The **Casa do Indio** is a centre for indigenous arts and craft production and an important meeting place for indigenous peoples like the Xavantes. The shop there sells a variety of handicrafts. The **Memorial do Cerrado Museum** ⓘ *Av Bela Vista km 2, Jd Olímpico, T5624141, Mon-Sat 0800-2200, Sun 0800-1800, US$2*, just outside the city provides an interesting introduction to *cerrado* life, with reconstructions of indigenous villages, *quilombos* and colonial streets as well as planted *cerrado* vegetation.

There's **tourist information** at **Sictur** ⓘ *Centro Administrativo, Praça Cívica, 7th floor, CEP 74319-000, T2230669, F2233911* and at **Dirtur** ⓘ *R 30 corner of R 4, Centro de Convenções, CEP 74025-020, T2171121, F2172256*. Extensive information, maps and bus routes can be found in *Novo Guia Turístico de Goiás*, readily available at news stands, US$2.25.

The thermal springs at **Cachoeira Dourada**, 240 km south on the Rio Paranaíba, are worth a visit, as are the fantastic rock formations of the Serra das Galés at **Paraúna**, 160 km south-southwest off BR-060, and a host of delightful, colonial mining villages within two hours' drive on good (often paved) roads. Travel agents in town can arrange day tours, see Avtivities and tours, page 641.

Anápolis and Cristalina → *Phone code: 062.*

Anápolis, a busy, uninteresting trading centre, is 57 km closer to Brasília than Goiânia. The **Centro de Gemologia de Goiás** ⓘ *Quadra 2, Módulo 13, Daia, Mon-Fri 0730-1630*, about 10 km out on the Brasília highway (near the Embratel tower), has a fine collection of gemstones, library, sales and lapidary courses, and will show visitors how real and synthetic gemstones are distinguished.

The scruffy, unpleasant town of Cristalina is also famous for its semi-precious stones, which can be bought cheaply in local shops. An interesting excursion is to the panning and mining sites amid magnificent rock formations, about 6 km away. Take the BR-040 (Brasília-Belo Horizonte road) and at Km 104 turn left along a dirt road, just after the highway police post, to the **Cristalina waterfall** (11 km along this road).

Caldas Novas → *Phone code: 062. Colour map 1, C5. Population: 40,000.*

Goiás's most beloved resort is a hot water theme park for families and weekenders. Few foreign visitors make it here. Hundreds of hotels line the hot river and are dotted around the various thermal springs at **Fontes de Pirapetinga** (7 km from the town) and **Rio Quente** (29 km from the town, bus from Caldas Novas). There are many buses from Goiânia; best reached from Morrinhos on BR-153 (Goiânia-São Paulo). The daily bus from Morrinhos costs US$1, 30 minutes.

Cidade de Goiás (Goiás Velho)

→ *Phone code: 062. Colour map 1, C5. Population: 30,000.*

This delightful town nestled in the midst of *cerrado*-covered ridges is one of Central Brazil's hidden beauties. Cobbled streets lined with Portuguese whitewash and brilliant yellow and blue façades gather around a little river watched over by a collection of elegantly simple baroque churches. Horses and old VWs clatter along the heavy stone flags and the local residents go about their day to day business as they always have done, treating visitors like guests or curiosities rather than tourists. All this may change – Cidade de Goiás was recently awarded UNESCO World Heritage status.

The town was founded in 1727 as Vila Boa and like its Minas counterparts became rich on gold, before becoming the capital of Goiás state, which it remained until just before the Second World War. But while towns like Ouro Preto and Tiradentes lavished their churches in gilt, Goiás chose modesty, erecting simple façades whose more classical lines stand strong against the intense blue of the sky. Interiors too were plain – simple panelling that beautifully offset both the richly painted wooden ceilings and the virtuoso sculpture of the 'Goiás Aleijandinho' by Veiga Valle.

Ins and outs

Cidade de Goiás is well connected by bus to Goiânia, about 130 km away, but there are few services to anywhere else. The **tourist office** ⓘ *daily 0900-1700*, is housed in the Quintal do Vinte, a former barracks on the largest of the town's squares, the Praça Brasil Caiado (also called the Largo do Chafariz). No English is spoken. The Museu Casa de Cora Coralina is a better source of information.

Sights

The most interesting streets in the colonial part of town spread out from the two principal plazas Praça Brasil Caiado and immediately below it towards the river Praça do Coreto. The former is dominated by a lavish baroque fountain which once supplied all the town's water. The best of the churches and museums are in the small cobbled town centre which radiates out from the two central plazas and spreads a little way along the riverbank. It is easily navigable on foot. The oldest church, **São Francisco de Paula** ⓘ *Praça Zacheu Alves de Castro (1761)*, sits on a platform overlooking the the market and the Rio Vermelho. It has a beautiful 19th-century painted ceiling by André Antônio da Conceição, depicting the life of St Francis. **Nossa Senhora da Abadia** ⓘ *R Abadia s/n*, has a similarly understated but impressive painted ceiling, while the other 18th-century churches like **Nossa Senhora do Carmo** ⓘ *R do Carmo*, on the riverside, and **Santa Bárbara** ⓘ *R Passo da Pátria*, are almost Protestant in their simplicity. The latter sits on a hill a kilometre or so east of the town from where there are wonderful sunset views.

Churches are usually open in the mornings and closed on Monday.

Cidade de Goiás has a handful of interesting small museums. The **Museu das Bandeiras** ⓘ *Praça Brasil Caiado/Largo do Chafariz, T3711087, Tue-Fri 0900-1700, Sat 1200-1700, Sun 0900-1300, US$1*, was once the centre of local government. Its rooms, which remain furnished with period pieces, sit over a small but forbidding dungeon. The old governor's palace, the **Palacio Conde dos Arcos** ⓘ *Praça do Coreto, T3711200, Tue-Sat 0800-1700, Sun 0900-1300, US$1*, which sits in the square below Praça Brasil Caiado, has a display of 19th-century furniture and plaques describing the town's life in colonial times. Across the way the **Museu de Artes Sacras** ⓘ *Praça do Coreto, T3711200, Tue-Sat 0800-1700, Sun 0900-1300, US$1*, houses some clanky 18th-century church silverware and a series of painted wooden statues by one of Brazil's most important religious sculptors, Jose Joaquim da Veiga Valle. Veiga Valle was entirely self taught with little knowledge or access to the Latin American baroque style which he was later seen to represent. Look out for the double 'V' signatures in the patterns of the fingers and the uncannily realistic stained-glass eyes. A stroll from the Praça do Coreto, downhill and across the river, will bring you to the **Museu Casa de Cora Coralina** ⓘ *R do Candido 20, T3711990, Tue-Sun 0900-1700, US$1*, the former home of Goiás's most respected writer, with a collection of her belongings and a restful and beautifully kept walled riverside garden at the back. The staff here are extememly helpful and knowledgable about the city, though they speak no English. The 18th-century **Mercado Municipal**, next to the old rodoviária, 500 m west of the central Praça do Coreto, is a wonderful spot for cheap lunches, breakfasts and photography. All manner of interesting characters gather here and the small stall shops sell everything from shanks of beef to Catholic kitsch.

Pirenópolis → *Phone code: 062. Colour map 1, grid C5. Population: 23,000. Altitude: 770 m.*

This lovely colonial silver mining town, 165 km due west of Brasília, sits in the midst of rugged hills dripping with waterfalls and covered in rapidly disappearing but still pristine *cerrado*. Like Cidade de Goiás it was founded by *bandeirantes* in search of gold and then by small-scale cattle ranchers. Its centre remains well preserved and only a little less pretty than Cidade de Goiás, leading it to be declared a National Heritage Site in 1989. Pirenópolis's proximity to Brasília has made it a favourite weekend playground for the capital's middle classes who congregate in the lively restaurants and bars which line the northern end of Rua do Rosario. But the town's home-grown culture still thrives; one of Central Brazil's most unusual and vibrant festival takes place here every May/June (see Festivals and events, page 640) and on weekends the Praça Central fills to the brim with *peões* in stetsons and spurs blasting out *sertanejo* music from their souped-up cars. Pirenópolis is a great place to pass a few days or even weeks. The surrounding countryside offers good walking and light adventure activities and there are plenty of well-organized small operators offering a range of treks and tours; though as elsewhere in Brazil, little English is spoken.

Pirenópolis is Brazil's unofficial silver capital and is a good place to stock up on presents.

Tourist information is available at the **Centro de Atendimento ao Turista** ⓘ *R do Bonfim, Centro Historico, T3312729*, but they don't speak much English.

Sights

The **Igreja Matriz Nossa Senhora do Rosário**, which is finally undergoing restoration after being gutted by a fire in 2002, is the oldest church in the state (1728). The fire destroyed one of the most beautiful painted interiors in Goiás and plans to replicate this are not included in the restoration. **Nosso Senhor de Bonfim** (1750-1754), which houses an impressive life-size crucifix from Bahia, was transported here on the backs of 260 slaves. The more subtly beautiful image of Our Lady is Portuguese. The church of **Nossa Senhora do Carmo** ⓘ *daily 1300-1700*, serves as a museum of religious art. Another displays regional historical items, the **Museu Família Pompeu** ⓘ *R Nova 33, Tue-Fri 1300-1700, Sat 1300-1500, Sun 0900-1200*. Pirenópolis was the birthplace of José Joaquim da Veiga Valle, though many of whose works are in the Arte Sagrada museum in Goiás Velho (see page 629). Here you will find the best collection of pictures and documents devoted to the history of the city (in Portuguese only). The tiny, privately owned **Museu das Cavalhadas** ⓘ *R Direita 37, Fri and Sat 0800-1700 (officially, but sporadic in practice), US$1*, has a collection of masks and costumes from the Festa do Divino. **Fazenda Babilônia** ⓘ *Sat and Sun only 0800-1700; US$2*, 25 km southwest by paved road, is a fine example of an 18th-century sugar *fazenda*, now a small museum with the original mill (no public transport).

Around Pirenópolis

So far the *cerrado* and hills around the town are resisiting the onslaught of soya and there are still opportunities to get out into the midst of some genuine wild country. There are plenty of walks and adventure activities on offer, birding is good and there is a reasonably healthy population of maned wolf and the various South American cats, including jaguar. The landscape is rugged, with many waterfalls and canyons. Guides are essential as many of the attractions are well off the beaten track.

Santuário de Vida Silvestre Vagafogo ⓘ *T3358490, visits through Drena, see page 641*, is the labour of love of Evandro Engel Ayer who bought an area of the *cerrado* intending to start a farm. After falling in love with the plants and animals living here he instead decided to create a wildlife reserve. There is good birding here, with various rare species, a species list and a library of birding books. Animals seen here include ocelot, brown capuchin and a rare subspecies of tufted-eared marmoset. Evandro is very knowledgable and helpful, speaks good English and serves one of the best light lunches in Goiás.

The **Mosterio Buddhisto** ⓘ *information through Drena, see p641*, a simple Zen monastery near a series of beautiful waterfalls in the heart of pristine *cerrado* forest. Day visits can be arranged with light walks or longer term retreats. This is particularly magical at sunset.

Chapada dos Veadeiros → *Colour map 1, C6.*

ⓘ *Entry to the park without a guide is not permitted and visits to the surrounding countryside without one not recommended – it is easy to get lost and guides are not expensive.*

These table-top mountains, drained by countless fast-flowing rivers which rush through deep gorges and plummet over spectacular waterfalls, are less famous than Diamantina or Guimarães but are less spoilt and more subtly beautiful. The national park, which protects only a fraction of their area, is almost twice the size of Diamantina and eight times the size of Guimarães. And unlike both those areas, its forests have never been felled. It was designated a World Heritage site by UNESCO in 2001. At present trips within the park itself are limited to day visits only; but there are plans to change this. Walks of as long as nine days can be easily organized at a good price within the wilderness areas in the park's environs, together with a range of adventure activities from canyoning to rappelling. There is plenty of accommodation in Alto Paraíso and São Jorge and transport to and from Brasília is straightforward.

Like most of wild Goiás, the Chapada is covered in *cerrado* forest – a habitat of such floral diversity that it has recently been declared a biological hot spot by **Conservation International.** Kew Gardens arrange plant tours here (see **Trivium**, page 24). Rare mammals including jaguar, maned wolf, puma, tapir, ocelot and giant anteater are abundant and, although no one has yet compiled a serious bird list, spectaculars and rarities include red-shouldered macaw, coal-crested finch, helmeted manakin and various key indicator species like rusty-margined guan and bare-face currasow; king vultures are abundant.

The park is reached by paved state highway 118 to Alto Paraíso de Goiás, then a newly paved road around 40 km west to São Jorge (1 km from the park entrance). Alto Paraíso is best for visits to the eastern sections of the Chapada, São Jorge for the park itself.

Alto Paraíso and São Jorge

This ramshackle town filled with crystal shops has become famous over the years as a centre for alternative therapies. Judging only by appearance many of these seem superficial and hippy dippy. But there are some serious practitioners here doing excellent work, and at a fraction of the price of those in other parts of the world. The town has a few artisan shops worth a browse and is the best point to stock up on provisions like insect repellent and film before a trek.

The tiny village of São Jorge with its three dirt streets is smaller and prettier than Alto Paraíso but has fewer restaurants and tour services.

There are numerous hostels and hotels in both towns. The best tour companies are in Alto Paraíso where there is a small **tourist booth** on the main street (no English).

Parque Nacional das Emas

In the far southwest of the state, covering the watershed of the Araguaia, Taquari and Formoso rivers, is the small Emas National Park, just off the main BR-364 route between Brasília and Cuiabá (112 km beyond Jataí). The national park was recently named as one of UNESCO's World Heritage sites.

Douglas Trent of **Focus Tours** writes: "The near 132,868 ha of undulating grasslands and 'campo sujo' *cerrado* forests host the world's largest concentration of termite mounds. They provide a surreal setting for large numbers of pampas deer, giant anteater and greater rhea, or *ema* in Portuguese. Maned wolves are frequently seen roaming the grasses in search of tinamou and other prey. The park holds the greatest concentration of blue-and-yellow macaws outside Amazônia, and blue-winged, red-shouldered and red-bellied macaws can also be seen. There are many other animals and birds. A pair of bare-faced currasow, white-woodpeckers, streamer-tailed tyrants and other showy birds visit the park headquarters daily.

"Along with the grasslands, the park supports a vast marsh on one side and rich gallery forests on the other. The crystal clear waters of the Rio Formosa pass right by the headquarters and meander through the park. Many have compared this park with the African savannahs. As many of the interesting mammals are nocturnal, a spotlight is a must."

The most convenient base for visiting the park is **Chapada do Ceu** (www.chapadadoceu.gov.go.br), about 30 minutes to the east. This newly created soya town has some decent hotels and tour operators to take visitors to the park. At present sleeping in Emas at the research centre is not permitted but there are plans to change this. Four-day, three-night visits to the park can be arranged through agencies and tour operators (for example, **Walker Tur** in Pirenópolis, www.walker.tur.br, or **Focus Tours**, see page 23).

Serranópolis

This little town is close to some remnant *cerrado* forest that clings to a series of small table-top mountains in the flat sea of soya which is gradually taking over Goiás. Important cave paintings have been found here; these are now carefully protected and can be reached via a series of well maintained trails.There are a few simple hotels in town and two excellent forest *pousadas* here – carefully designed, wonderfully peaceful and great for birdwatching or just plain relaxing.

Aruanã and the Rio Araguaia → *Colour map 3, A5.*

Brazilians are firmly convinced that the 2,630-km-long Rio Araguaia is richer in fish than any other in the world, and a visit to the 220-km stretch between Aruanã and the Ilha do Bananal during the fishing season is quite an experience. As the receding waters in May reveal sparkling white beaches, thousands of Brazilian and international enthusiasts pour into the area, intent on getting the best camping spots. As many as 400 tent cities spring up, and vast quantities of fish are hauled in before the phenomenon winds down in September, when the rivers begin to rise again and flood the surrounding plains. Without Brazilian contacts, the best way of experiencing this annual event is with one of the specialist tour operators.

Health Yellow-fever vaccination is recommended for the region; *borrachudas*, tiny biting insects, are an unavoidable fact of life in Central Brazil in June and July; repellent helps a little.

The Araguaia is most readily accessible from Aruanã, a port 180 km northwest of Goiás Velho by paved highway, which sees little excitement outside the winter fishing season when its comfortable hotels are booked up for months. Boats can be rented to visit some of the beautiful lakes and beaches nearby. Buses from the rodoviária serve Araguapaz, Britânia and Goiânia. Brazilian Canoeing Championships are also held along the river.

Sleeping

Brasília *p620, map p624, phone code 061*
The best area is the northern hotel zone which has shops and restaurants nearby. Prices usually include breakfast. Weekend discounts of 30% are often available but must be requested. The best area for cheap accommodation is around W3 703 and 704 in the Asa Sul where residential houses have been turned into hostels. The quietest are northwest of the main Av W3 Sul. Beware of bus station touts. The tourist office has a list of *pensões*.

Southern hotel zone

L Nacional, Quadra 1 bloco A, T3217575, hotelnacional@hotelnacional.com.br. Cavernous, frayed old-fashioned and a city landmark with many tour agencies located outside.

A Alvorada, Quadra 4 bloco A, T3321122, www.alvoradahotel.com.br. Another relic with good view from roof terrace.

Northern hotel zone

Moderately priced hotels are mostly found in this sector only.

L Blue Tree Park, Trecho 1, lt 1-B, Bl C (Lago Norte), T4247000, www.bluetree.com.br. The city's newest, most luxurious business hotel, with rooms in a giant red horseshoe overlooking the lake, an enormous pool and excellent, comprehensive business facilities.

L Kubitschek Plaza, Quadra 2, bloco E, T3293333, www.kubitschek.com.br. Popular business hotel with modern rooms and excellent facilties; broadband in rooms, a pool, sauna and gym. Sister hotel, the **Manhattan Plaza**, manhattan.com.br, next door is very similar.

A-B Aristus, Quadra 2 bloco O, T3288675, www.aristushotel.com.br. Newly painted and delightfully dated 1970s block with simple a/c rooms and breakfast.

B Casablanca, Quadra 3 bloco A, T3288586, www.casablancaBrasília.com.br. Another 70s delight; more intimate than most in the area, but some noisy rooms.

B El Pilar, Quadra 3 bloco F, T3285915, F3289088. Plain, freshly painted, fan-cooled rooms with tiled floors and en suites. Avoid those below street level as they collect car fumes.

C Mirage, Quadra 2 bloco N, T/F3287150. Simple rooms with a fan but good value for the area.

C-E Pousada dom Bosco, 703 Sul, bloco N, Casa 34, T2269639. The best of the cheapies, with simple but neat rooms, some spacious and airy, some small and windowless. Owner Getúlio Valente will pick up from airport or bus station if you phone ahead and offers a range of other rooms around the city as well as cheap city tours (Portuguese only.)

D Cury's Solar, Av W3 Sul, HIGS 707, bloco I, casa 15, T4436252, www.conectanet.com.br/curyssolar. Cramped but helpful and safe, around 30 mins from the centre (Eixo Monumental) along W3 Sul. Recommended.

D Pousada Asa Sul, W3 Sul 704, bloco M, T2246775, www.pousadaasasul.tripud.com. Simple but relatively clean rooms, some windowless.

D Pousada da Nilza, W3 Sul 703, bloco A, T2255786. Pokey and a little musty but popular with travellers.

D Teresa Tasso, SQN312-'K'-505, T2734844/99726057, tc@spwinternet.com.br. Accommodation in an apartment in the Asa

Sul (sleeps 5, kitchen, bath, laundry facilities). Excellent value. Teresa gives city tours for US$15-20 per person for 3-4 hrs, and will collect you at the airport/bus station if you phone ahead (bus to flat from centre, 5 mins). Speaks English, Italian, Spanish and French.

E **Pousada do Sol**, 703 Sul, bloco K, Casa 3, T2249703/99696636. A range of simple rooms, some without windows, some for as many as 5 people. Family run.

Camping

The city's main site is 2 km out of the centre, by the Centro Esportivo, near the motor-racing track, with room for 3,100 campers, mixed reports. Take bus 109 (infrequent) from municipal rodoviária.

Associação Brasileira de Camping (Edif Márcia, 12th floor, Setor Comercial Sul, T2258768) has 2 sites: at Km 19 on the **Belo Horizonte Rd** and 125 km northeast of Brasília at Sobradinho.

Camping Clube do Brasil has a site at **Itiquira** waterfall, 100 km northeast of the city, near Formosa; information from Edif Maristela, room 1214, Setor Comercial Sul, T2236561.

Goiânia *p627, map p627, phone code 062*

The best hotels are 1 km from the centre in the Setor Oeste which has many restaurants and bars. Most hotels in the centre are frayed 1970s blocks.

L **Castro's Park**, Av República do Líbano 1520, Setor Oeste, T2124428, www.castrospark.com.br. A 5-star housed in a tower a few blocks from the centre with gym and swimming pool. The best for business. Plenty of restaurants and bars nearby.

AL **Papillon**, Av República do Líbano 1824, T2191500, www.papillonhotel.com.br. A tower in the new centre with modern tiled rooms and suites, a pool, gym, sauna, business facilities and 24-hr room service. Very popular, book ahead.

B **Oeste Plaza**, R 2 No 389 Setor Oeste, T2245012. Well maintained modern tower with small a/c rooms with tiled floors and en suites. Those on the higher floors have good views. Very small pool and gym and modest meeting room.

C **Augustus**, Praça Antônio Lisita 702, T2241022, www.augustus-hotel.com.br. Blocky B-grade 1970s business hotel with rather gloomy apartment rooms, a pool, sauna and gym. Conveniently located for the centre. Official rates higher but these are not adhered to.

D **Karajás**, Av Goiás and R 3 No 860, T2249666, www.hotelkarajas.com.br. Good value 1980s hotel rooms in a once-luxury hotel now fallen somewhat from grace. Convenient for the centre..

D **Rio Vermelho**, R 4 No 26, T2132555, www.hotelriovermelho.com.br. Simple hotel in a quiet street with lots of cheap restaurants. The cheapest rooms are fan cooled. With breakfast. Close to the centre

D-F **Goiânia Palace**, Av Anhangüera 5195, T2244874, Goiâniapalace@terra.com.br. Art deco building with a range of rooms from simple fan-cooled doubles to suites. Good breakfast. Friendly and well located.

F **Antoninho's**, R 68 No 41, T2231815. Very basic but clean and well-looked-after rooms, only a few have windows. Friendly, safe and with good breakfasts.

F **Paissandú**, Av Goiás 1290 at R 55, T2244925. Very simple fan-cooled or a/c rooms 8 blocks north of the centre. With breakfast.

Camping

Itanhangá municipal site, Av Princesa Carolina, Km 13, T2921145. Attractive wooded location, reasonable facilities.

Anápolis and Cristalina *p628, phone code 062*

AL **Estância Park**, in parkland setting 6 km northeast of Anápolis, T3181200, F3181300. Pool, tennis court and an unpleasant mini-zoo, but the best in town.

C **Hotel Goyás**, at R da Saudade 41, Cristalina. With fan and fridge.

D **Serra Dourada**, Av Brasil 375, Anápolis, T3240051. One of many cheap hotels around the rodoviária (Av Brasil-Norte). Restaurant, parking, fans, good value.

Caldas Novas *p628, phone code 062*

L-AL **Hotel Turismo and Pousada do Rio Quente**, T4521122, F4521177 (São Paulo T011-8525733, F2825281; Brasília T061-2247166). 4-star complex at Rio Quente. Breakfast and lunch, transportation to main pools and recreation facilities

included in price; other extras paid for with hotel's own currency, good hotel, accommodation in main buildings or chalets (the **Turismo** has a private airstrip).
B **Serra Dourada**, Av Correia Neto 574, T4531300. Recommended.
D **Imperial**, near rodoviária. Clean, friendly.

Camping

At Esplanada, and **Camping Clube do Brasil** site on the Ipameri Rd, 5 km from the centre.

Cidade de Goiás *p629, phone code 062*

AL-B **Vila Boa**, Av Dr Deusdete Ferreira de Moura, 1 km southeast on the Morro do Chapéu do Padre, T3711000. The best option, though out of town. Inconvenient for the centre but with a pool, bar, restaurant and good views.
B **Casa do Ponte**, R Moretti Foggia s/n, T3714467. An art deco building next to the bridge across the Rio Vermelho with small well-maintained a/c rooms with en suites and parquet floors. The best overlook the river.
C-D **Pousada do Ipê**, R Cel Guedes de Amorim 22, T3712065. Cloisters of rooms gathered around a courtyard dominated by a huge mango tree. The annex has a swimming pool and bar area. Breakfast is included.
C-D **Pousada do Vovô Jura**, R Sta Barbara 38, T3711746. A colonial house set in a little garden with views out over the river and Serra.
D-E **Pousada do Sol**, R Americano do Brasil, T3711717. Well-maintained, plain, fan-cooled rooms with lino floors. Friendly and central.
E **Pousada do Sonho**, R 15 Novembro 22, T3721224. A simple residential house with plain rooms with shared bathrooms. Good breakfast. Convenient.
E **Pousada Reyes**, R 15 Novembro 41, T3711565. A simple cheapie next to the *Sonho* offering similar rooms to **Pousada do Sonho** but shoddier service.

Camping

Attractive, well-run **Cachoeira Grande** campground, 7 km along the BR-070 to Jussara (near the tiny airport), with bathing place and snack bar. More basic site (**Chafariz da Carioca**) in town by the river.

Pirenópolis *p630, phone code 062*

There are plenty of rooms in town, although all are filled during Festa do Divino, even the campsites; it's better to book ahead or visit from Brasília at this time.
A-B **Hotel Fazenda Quinta da Santa Bárbara**, at R do Bonfim 1, T/F33111877. In garden setting near the centre. Popular with weekenders. Reasonable restaurant.
B **Pousada das Cavalhadas**, Praça da Matriz, T3311261. Central with plain rooms. Can be noisy at weekends.
C **Dona Geni**, R Pireneus 29, T3311128. A/c rooms in a little colonial house with a tree-filled garden opposite the post office. Friendly.
C **Pouso do Sô Vigario**, R Nova 25, T3311206, www.pousadaspirenopolis.com.br. Small rooms but pleasant public spaces decorated with objets d'art and posters from European painting exhibitions. Good location. Decent breakfast in a little garden next to the pool.
C **Rex**, Praça da Matriz, T3311121. 5 rooms, all with fridges and TVs arranged around a courtyard. Good breakfast and location.

Camping

Balneário Bonsuccesso, Estrada Bonsucesso Km 4, T3211217. **Cabanas Estrada Corumbá**, Km 1, T3313424. Also has rustic chalets with TVs and pool.

Alto Paraíso and São Jorge *p631, phone code 061*

Prices in São Jorge often go up 30% at weekends.
AL **Casa das Flores**, T99760603, São Jorge, www.pousadacasadasflores.com.br. Elegant little *pousada* with tastefully decorated rooms (lit only by candlelight), sauna, pool and great breakfast in the decent attached restaurant. The best in town, but overpriced.
A-B **Camelot**, on the main road just north of Alto Paraíso, T4461448, www.pousadacamelot.com.br. Delightfully kitsch mock-Arthurian castle with proper hot showers and comfortable a/c rooms with satellite TV.
A-B **Portal da Chapada**, 9 km along the road from Alto Paraíso to São Jorge, T4461820, www.portaldachapada.com.br. The best choice for birdwatchers – with cabins in the midst of the *cerrado*. Comfortable with a/c.
B **Casa Rosa**, R Gumersindo 233, Alto Paraíso, T4461319, www.pousadacasarosa.com.br. Range of well-looked-after a/c rooms, the best in chalets near the pool.

B Trilha Violeta, São Jorge, T4551088, www.trilhavioleta.com.br. Fan-cooled violet rooms with private bathrooms around a bougainvillea-filled garden. Reasonable restaurant. Friendly.

B-C Aquas de Março, São Jorge, T3472082, www.chapadadosveadeiros.com.br. Simple duplex rooms decorated with paintings by local artist, Moacir. Pleasant garden, saunas, *oforo* baths and decent breakfast.

D-E Pousada do Sol, R Gumersindo 2911, Alto Paraíso, T4461201. Small and simple, with a range of rooms, the best with balconies and fridges.

D-E Pousada Rubi, R Coleto Paulino, Alto Paraíso, T4461200. Simple rooms with Brazilian TV and fridge. Good breakfast.

E Casa Grande, São Jorge, T96235515, www.pousadacasagrande.com.br. Simple but well-looked-after rooms and a good breakfast.

Camping

Tatoo, at the top of São Jorge, tattoo@travessia.tur.br. Powered sites from only US$3. Decent wood-fired pizzas and a small bar. English spoken. Very friendly and helpful.

Parque Nacional das Emas *p632, phone code 438*

A Fazenda Santa Amélia, EstradaSerranópolis, Chapada do Ceu, T6341380. A working *fazenda* with a range of wildlife tours in the property's remnant *cerrado* forest (none in Emas except with special arrangement). Comfortable chalets, a pool and full board in the price.

D Paraná, Av Indiaiá, Chapada do Ceu, T6341227. Simple, clean and well run with fan-cooled rooms.

E Rafael, Av Indiaiá, Chapada do Ceu, T6341247. Very simple and clean with fan-cooled rooms and shared bathrooms.

Serranópolis *p632, phone code 062*

A-B Guardião do Cerrado, about 15 km south of Serranópolis at Km70 off BR184– take a taxi from the town. A magical forest *pousada* with a ring of beautifully appointed chalets all decorated individually, many with Xavantes indigenous art and tasteful photographs. Great food and walks and much wildlife. Currasows and maned wolf visit the camp for breakfast each morning.

B-A Araras, T6681054, www.pousadadasararas.com. Tasteful little chalets in an armadillo-filled garden next to a clearwater river with a natural swimming area. Trails lead to the various archaeological sites.

Aruanã and the Rio Araguaia *p632, phone code 062*

A Araguaia, Praça Couto Magalhães 53, Aruanã (opposite the docks), T3761251. Very similar to the **Sonhado** and also with a pool and restaurant.

A Recanto Sonhado, Aruanã, on the river at the end of Av Altamiro Caio Pacheco (2 km), T3761230. Simple but well-run hotel with a pool and self-service restaurant. The price, includes lunch (reservations can be made through T062-2417913 in Goiânia).

Camping

The official campground is a 20-min boat ride away from Aruanã on Ilha Redonda, but open (and full) only in Jul.

Eating

Brasília *p620, map p624, phone code 061*

The Southern Hotel Sector has more restaurants than the north. At weekends, few restaurants in central Brasília are open. There is plenty of choice of restaurants in all brackets in the **Pier 21** entertainment mall on the lakeshore. Other cheaper options are along R 405/406.

Snack bars serving *prato feito* or *comercial* (cheap set meals) can be found all over the city, especially on **Av W3** and in the **Setor Comercial Sul**. Other good bets are the **Conjunto Nacional** and the **Conjunto Venâncio**, 2 shopping/office complexes on either side of the municipal rodoviária. Tropical fruit flavour ice cream can be found in various parlours, eg **Av W3 Norte 302**. Freshly made fruit juices are available in all bars.

Asa Sul

There are good mid-range options on and around Av Anhaguera between Tocantins and Goiás; but by far the best choice is on and around **Praça Tamandaré** and **Av República Líbano**. For cheap bars/restaurants, try around Praça Tamandaré and on R 68 in the centre. There are many cheap places on Av W3 Sul, eg at Blocos 502 and 506.

ΨΨΨ **La Chaumière**, Av W3 Sul, Quadra 408, bloco A, loja 13, T2427599, lunch only Sun. The city's favourite French cooking in classical surroundings.

ΨΨΨ **Le Français**, Av W3 Sul, Quadra 404, bloco B, loja 27, T2254583. French food served in bistro atmosphere, classic and modern dishes, 40-bottle wine list.

ΨΨΨ **O Convento**, SHIS, Ql 9, conjunto 9, casa 4, T2481211, www.oconvento.com.br. The best for regional and Brazilian cuisine in a mock farmhouse dining room decorated with antiques and arts and crafts.

ΨΨΨ **Porcão**, Sector de Clubes Sul, Trecho 2, cj 35, rest. 3, T2232002, www.porcao.com.br. Upmarket chain restaurant specializing in *churrasco*, piano bar, large veranda.

ΨΨΨ **Kosui**, SCES, Trecho 4, lote 1B, Academia de Tênis, T3166900. Best of the city's Japanese food, from Tokyo-born chef Ryozo Koniya. Great Japanese banquet.

ΨΨ **China Food**, Comércio local Sul 402, bloco C, loja 13, T4435959. Reliable Chinese with a good lunchtime buffet and deliveries.

ΨΨ **Jera Pasta e Grill**, SCLS 305, bloco D, loja 1, Lago Sul, T2441493. Modest location next to a sandwich shop but good pasta and grilled dishes.

ΨΨ **O Espanhol**, Av W3 Sul, Quadra 404, bloco C, loja 07, T2242002. Open daily. Host to the city's annual Spanish festival and serving respectable seafood.

ΨΨ **Vercelli**, SCLS 410, bloco D, loja 34, T4430100, www.vercelli.com.br. Lunch only. Pizzas, pastas and a great deal more on a huge menu.

Ψ **Cedro do Líbano**, SCS, Quadra 06, bloco A, loja 218, Edifício Carioca, T3222285. Self-service, some Arabic dishes, friendly, closes 2200. Recommended.

Ψ **Centro Venâncio 2000**, at the beginning of Av W3 Sul. Has several budget options, including *salada mista*, lunch only.

Ψ **Naturama**, SCLS 102, bloco B, loja 9, T2255125. Vegetarian and wholefood dishes. Lunchtime only.

Asa Norte

All of the large hotels in this area have upmarket restaurants, most catering to business visitors.

ΨΨΨ **Trattoria da Rosario**, SHIS Ql 17, Bloco H, Loja 215, Lago Sul, Fashion Park, T2481672, closed Mon, lunch only on Sun. Northern Italian food from chef Rosario Tessier. Excellent Uruguayan lamb.

ΨΨΨ **Universal Diner**, SCLS 210, Bloco B, loja 30, T4432089 (lunch only on Sun), www.universaldiner.com.br. One of the city's best contemporary restaurants with strongly Asian influences from New York-trained chef Mara Alcamim.

ΨΨ **Boa Saúde**, Av W3 Norte Quadra 702, Edif Brasília Rádio Center. Sun-Fri 0800-2000. Respectable vegetarian with a range of salads, quiches and pies.

ΨΨ **Bom Demais**, Av W3 Norte, Quadra 706. Comfortable, serving fish, beef and rice etc, live music at weekends (cover charge US$0.50).

ΨΨ **Churrascaria do Lago**, SHTN, Conj 1-A, by Palácio da Alvorada, T2239266. One of the city's best meat-off-the-spit restaurants. Popular with diplomats.

ΨΨ **El Hadj**, in **Hotel Torre Palace**, Setor Hoteleiro Norte, Quadra 4 bloco A, T3285554. ReasonableArabic food in a crusty 1970s hotel.

Ψ **Conjunto Nacional**, SDN, Cj A. Enormous mall and food court with 50 restaurants.

Ψ **Habib's**, SCN Quadra 4, T3274400. Arabic food and pizzas at bargain prices at this upmarket chain restaurant. Recommended. The municipal rodoviária provides the best coffee and *pasteis* in town (bottom departure level).

Goiânia *p627, map p627, phone code 062*

Goiânian cooking is like that of neighbouring Minas – meat heavy, with huge portions of accompanying vegetable dishes and of course beans and rice. Local specialities include *arroz com piqui*, rice with a cruel *cerrado* fruit and practical joke of evolution whose outer flesh is soft and sweet but which if bitten even a little hard leaves the mouth full of sharp spines which have to be surgically removed.

The city has a good range of restaurants and bars, especially around **Praça Tamandaré** and **Av República Líbano** in the Setor Oeste where there are options in all price brackets.

Street stands (*pamonharías*) sell *pamonha* snacks, tasty pastries made with green corn, sweet, savoury, or *picante*/spicy; all are served hot and have cheese in the middle, some include sausage.

TTT **Bella Luna**, R 10 704 (Praça Tamandaré), T2143562, some of the best Italian food in Goiânia, including excellent pizza, pasta and northern Italian seafood dishes.

TTT **Celson & Cia**, R 15 539 at C 22, T2153043, www.celsonecia.com.br. Very popular Goiás and Mineira meat restaurant with a good cold buffet. Evenings only except weekends.

TTT **Chão Nativo**, Av República Líbano 1809 (opposite hotel **Papillon**), T2235396. The city's most famous Goiânian restaurant also serving local and Mineira food. Lively after 2000 and lunchtime on weekends.

TT **China**, R 7 623 (Praça Tamandaré), T2151122. Chinese and Japanese food in a/c surroundings. Respectable chop suey and *yakisoba*.

TT **Tribo do Açai**, R 36 590, T2816971. Buzzing little fruit juice bar with excellent buffet salads and health food. Just round the corner from Shopping Bougainville.

TT **Walmor**, R 3 1062 at r 25-B, T2155555, www.churrasciariadowalmor.com.br. Large portions of some of Brazil's best steaks served in an attractive open-air dining area. Best after 2000.

TT-T **Floresta**, R 2 at R 9, T2249560. Lively corner bar with grilled steaks, Brazilian standards (X with rice and beans) and snacks in cheap category. Open until late. Good draft lager.

T **Buffalo's Grill**, Praça Tamandaré, T2153935. Pizzas, grilled meat and chicken, sandwiches and crêpes. Open 24 hrs. See also Giraffas.

T **Giraffa**, Av República Líbano 1592, T2251969. Fast food joint with some more sumptuous set plates – steak/chicken, rice, beans and chips.

T **Mineiro**, R 4 53 (opposite hotel Rio Vermelho), T2249113. Cheap, good Mineira per kilo buffet with lots of choice and some veggie options. One of several on this block.

T **Primo Patio**, Av República Líbano (opposite Castro's Plaza), T2133366, Pizza, pasta and grilled steak and chicken (with the inevitable rice, beans and chips).

Anápolis and Cristalina *p628, phone code 062*

TT **Restaurante Caiçara**, 14 de Julho 905, T3243740. Good *churrasco*.

Cidade de Goiás *p629, phone code 062*

For the best very cheap options head for the **Mercado Municipal** between the São Francisco church and the river.

TT **Dali**, R 13 de Maio 26, T3721640. Riverside restaurant with a little patio offering a broad range of international and local dishes.

TT **Flor do Ipê**, Praça da Boa Vista 32 (end of the road leading from the centre across the bridge, T3721133. The best in town for Goiânian food, with an enormous variety on offer, a lovely garden setting and river and Serra views. Highly recommended.

T **Beco do Sertão**, R 13 de Maio 17, T3712459. Good value lunchtime buffet near the river with regional and international standards like pasta.

T **Degus't Fun Pizzaria**, R Quinta Bocaiuva, (next to Praça do Coreto), T3712800. Pizza, casseroles, soups and very friendly service from a mother and daughter team.

Pirenópolis *p630, phone code 062*

There are plenty of options along **R do Rosário**, serving a surprising range of international food including some vegetarian and Asian options. Many have live music at night (and an undisclosed cover charge – be sure to ask). There are cheaper options near the Igreja Bonfim in the upper part of town.

TT **Chiquinha**, R do Rosário 19, T3313052. Local cuisine (heavy on meat).

T **O Cafeteria**, R do Rosário 38, T99727953. Light food and about the cheapest option here.

Alto Paraíso and São Jorge *p631, phone code 061*

TT-T **Oca Lila**, Av João Bernades Rabelo 449, T4461773. Decent pizza and sandwiches, live music at the weekend, nice atmosphere.

T **Jatô**, R Coleto Paulino 522, T4461339. Self-service with some veggie options. Thu-Sun only.

T **Pizza 2000**, Av Ari Valadão 659, T4461814. The centre of the town's early evening social life. Respectable pizzas.

Aruanã and the Rio Araguaia *p632, phone code 062*

Restaurants in town rather poor, but try

T **Columbia**, R João Artiaga 221, opposite Municipal Stadium, T3761298. Clean, good menu.

Bars and clubs

Brasília *p620, map p624, phone code 061*
Arena Café, CA 7, bloco F1, loja 33, T4681141, www.cafearena.hpg.com.br. Popular gay bar with DJs from Thu to Sat.
Bar Brasília, SHC/S CR, Quadra 506, bloco A, loja 15, parte A, T4434323. Little *boteco* with 50s decor, draught beer and wooden tables. Lively after 1900, especially Fri.
Bier Fass, SHIS Quadra 5, bloco E, loja 52/53, T2481519, www.bierfass.com.br. Cavernous bar/restaurant with live music Tue-Sun and 20/30s crowd. Happy hour from 1800.
Café Cancún, Shopping Liberty Mall, SCN, Quadra 3, bloco D, loja 52, T3271566. Tacky Mexican restaurant by day and teen and 20-something beautiful people club after dark.
Clube de Choro, SDC, Quadra 3, bloco G, T3270494, www.clubedechoro.com.br. (Wed-Sat). One of the best clubs in the country devoted to the music which gave rise to samba. Top names from all over Brazil as well as the city itself. Great atmosphere. Tickets sold 9 days in advance.
Frei Caneca, Brasília Shopping, SCN, Quadra 5, bloco A, lojas 82s/94s, T3270202. Similar to Café Cancún. Dreadful 'flashback' night on Thu. Most interesting at weekends.
Gates Pub, Av W3 Sul 403, T2254576, www.gatespub.com.br. Great for *forró* dancing and live music with a young middle-class crowd.
UK Brasil Pub, SCLS 411, bloco B, loja 28, T3465214. Some of the best live bands in the city play here. Guinness, sandwiches, all ages.

Goiânia *p627, map p627, phone code 062*
Goiânia is surprisingly lively, with some of the best nightlife in central Brazil. This is especially true around the various festivals and carnaval. There is an active gay scene and plenty of choices of clubs and bars. Most locals tend to drink in the restaurants, many of which double up as bars before heading to a club at around 2300.
It's, the city's current favourite with a range of different music on different nights – from techno and hip hop to MPB.
Pulse, R9 1087, T2156133, www.pulse.com.br. Crowded little club with a small sound system and rather tired decoration. Sweaty and packed on Sat.
Tribo do Açai, see p638.
Café Cancún, Shopping Flamboyant and Av Jamel Cecilio 3, T5462035, www.cafecancun.com.br. With a lively *forró* night on Wed and a mix of club music on others.

Pirenópolis *p630, phone code 062*
Bars along **R do Rosário** cater for those from Brasília and the children of the hippies who migrated here in the 1970s. Locals hang out near the **Igreja Bonfim** – where there are 2 spit-and-sawdust bars and many booming car stereos.

Entertainment

Brasília *p620, map p624, phone code 061*
Information about entertainment, etc is available in 2 daily papers, **Jornal de Brasília** and **Correio Brasiliense**. Any student card (provided it has a photograph) will get you into the cinema/theatre/concert hall for ½ price. Ask for '*uma meia*' at the box office.
Pier 21, SCSS, Trecho 2, Cj 32/33. An enormous complex with 13 cinema screens, nightclubs, restaurants, video bars and children's theme park.

Cinema
There are 15 cinemas in the Plano Piloto; for programme details, T139, entrance is ½ price on Wed.

Music
Concerts are given at the **Escola Parque** (Quadras 507-508 Sul), the **Ginásio Presidente Médici** (Eixo Monumental, near TV tower), the **Escola de Música** (Av L2 Sul, Quadra 602) and the outdoor **Concha Acústica** (edge of lake in the Northern hotel zone).

Theatre
There are 3 auditoria of the **Teatro Nacional**, Setor Cultural Norte, Via N 2, next to the bus station, T3256109, foyer open 0900-2000, box office open at 1400: the **Sala Villa-Lobos** (1,300 seats), the **Sala Martins Pena** (450), and the **Sala Padre José Maurício** (120); the building is in the shape of an Aztec pyramid.

The Federal District authorities have 2 theatres, the **Galpão** and **Galpãozinho**, between Quadra 308 Sul and Av W3 Sul.

Other

Planetarium, Setor de Divulgaoção Cultural, T3256245. West Eixo Monumental next to the TV tower, being restored at time of writing.

❁ Festivals and events

Brasília *p620, map p624, phone code 061*
Feb Ash Wed.
Apr Maundy Thu (half-day).
8 Dec, Immaculate Conception.
24 Dec Christmas Eve.

Cidade de Goiás *p629, phone code 062*
Feb Carnaval is joyous and still little known to outsiders.
Apr The streets of Cidade de Goiás blaze with torches during the solemn **Fogaréu processions of Holy Week**, when hooded figures re-enact Christ's descent from the cross and burial.

Pirenópolis *p630, phone code 062*
May/Jun Festa do Divino Espírito Santo, held 45 days after Easter (Pentecost), is one of Brazil's most famous and extraordinary folkloric/religious celebrations. It lasts 3 days, with medieval costumes, tournaments, dances and mock battles between Moors and Christians, a tradition held annually since 1819. The city throbs with life over this period and there are numerous and frequent extemporaneous *forró* and *sertanejo* parties.

○ Shopping

Brasília *p620, map p624, phone code 061*
The best **shopping centres** are Shopping Brasília below the southern hotel zone and Patio Brasília below the northern hotel zone. Both have a wide range of boutiques and fast food restaurants. Others include the vast **Conjunto Nacional** on the north side of the rodoviária, the **Conjunto Venâncio** on the south side, the **Centro Venâncio 2000** at the beginning of Av W3 Sul, the **Centro Venâncio 3000** in the Setor Comercial Norte, **Parkshopping** and the **Carrefour** hypermarket just off the exit to Guará, 12 km from the centre.

For fine **jewellery**, H Stern has branches in the Nacional and Carlton hotels and at the Conjunto Nacional and Parkshopping. The embassy sector is good for low-priced, high quality menswear. For handicrafts from all the Brazilian states try **Galeria dos Estados** (which runs underneath the *eixo* from Setor Comercial Sul to Setor Bancário Sul, 10 mins' walk from municipal rodoviária, south along Eixo Rodoviário Sul); for **Amerindian handicrafts**, **Artíndia** SRTVS, Quadra 702, also in the rodoviária and at the airport. There is a **feira hippy** at the base of the TV tower Sat, Sun and holidays selling leather goods, woodcarvings, jewellery and bronzes. English books (good selection) at **Livraria Sodiler** in Conjunto Nacional and at the airport.

Goiânia *p627, map p627, phone code 062*
Ceramic, sisal and wooden handicrafts from **Centro Estadual do Artesanato**, Praça do Trabalhador (0800-1800); **Sun handicrafts markets** at the Praça Cívica (morning) and Praça do Sol (afternoon). The latter starts after 1530, until 2100, known as the **Honey Fair** as all types of honey are sold; also good for a Sun snack, with many sweets and tarts sold along the street. See also Casa do Indio, p628.

Cidade de Goiás *p629, phone code 062*
There are little artisan shops springing up all over the town.
Vovó Joaníca, Praça Brasil Caiado 1 (near the Sacred Art Museum). Ceramic pieces, knitwear and other nikc-nakcs.
Frutos da Terra, R Dom Cândido Penso 30 (next to the Cora Coralina Museum). Broad range of items from bags and belts to leather sandals and ceramics. Most is made in the town.
Baumann Artesania, R Boa Vista 30 (near Ipê restaurant), T3713760, bamboo door hangings, lampshades and pieces of naturally sculpted wood.

Pirenópolis *p630, phone code 062*
There are many **jewellery** and **arts and crafts** shops. 2 of the best jewellers are **CRISTIANO** who has travelled extensively in South America, as is reflected in his designs. Ask Rodrigo Edson Santos, R do Rosario 3, T3313804.

Activities and tours

Brasília *p620, map p624, phone code 061*

Tour operators

Many tour operators have their offices in the shopping arcade of the **Hotel Nacional**.

Buriti Turismo, SCLS 402, bloco A, lojas 27/33, Asa Sul, T2252686, American Express representative.

Presmic Turismo, SHS Q 1 Bloco A, loja, 35, T2255515. Full, half-day and night-time city tours (0845, 1400 and 1930 respectively). 3 to 4-hr city tours with English commentary can also be booked on arrival at the airport – a convenient way of getting to your hotel if you have heavy baggage. Some tours criticized as too short, others that the guides speak poor English, and for night-time tours, the floodlighting is inadequate on many buildings.

Toscana, SCLS 413, Bloco D, loja 22/24, T2429233. Recommended as cheap and good.

Goiânia *p627, map p627, phone code 062*

Sport

Many sporting facilities throughout Goiânia, visitors welcome. For sunbathing, swimming and waterskiing go to the **Jaó Club**, T2612122, on reservoir near the city.

Tour operators

Turisplan Turismo, R 8 No 388, T2241941. Can arrange tours to Paraúna and mining villages. They also sells regular bus tickets.

Cidade de Goiás *p629, phone code 062*

Wildlife and adventure tours

Serra Dourada Aventura, Praça Brasil Caiado (opposite the tourist office), T3714262, www.serradouradaecotur.com. Hikes in the surrounding forest and within the state park, visits to waterfalls, kayaking and canyoning.

Frans and Susana Leeuweenberg (through Serra Dourada, above), birding and wildlife trips in the surrounding area (or anywhere in Goiás – with advance warning) from a husband and wife team of biologists who have been working hard to protect the *cerrado* for many years. English, French and Dutch spoken. Highly recommended.

Around Pirenopolis *p631, phone code 062*

Tour operators

Drena, R do Carmo 11 (across the bridge and up the hill, on the left), T3313336. A range of walks and adventure activities as well as visits to the Vagafogo private reserve and the Mosteiro Buddhisto. Good value, well organized and well run but little English spoken.

Chapada dos Veadeiros *p631, phone code 062*

Tour operators

Alternativas, T4461000, www.alternativas.tur.br. Light adventure activities and treks.

Alpatour, R dos Nascentes, T4461820, www.altoparaiso.com. Van-based tours to the principal sights. Suitable for all ages.

Chapada Ecotours, T4461345, www.transchapada.com.br. Light adventure and visits to the major sights.

Travessia, T4461595, www.travessia.tur.br. Treks of several days to over a week and rappelling and canyoning from one of the most respected instructors, Ion David.

Alto Paraíso and São Jorge *p631, phone code 061*

Massage and treatments

Atash, R do Segredo 37, Alto Paraíso, T4461028. Ayurvedic and classical Thai massage and breathing meditation from a long-experienced practitioner. From US$40.

Sílvia Luz, Alto Paraíso, T2731397, T99569685, silvialuz@brturbo.com. One of the best Ayurvedic and Reiki practitioners in the country. Also works wlth Tulná and Shiatsu. Highly recommended. From US$40.

Parque Nacional das Emas *p632*

Contact the tourist office in the Prefeitura Municipal, Chapada do Ceu, for a list of authorized tour operators. Interest is growing but visits to Emas are still in the early stages.

Aruanã and the Rio Araguaia *p632, phone code 62*

Boats

Boats US$25 per hr, and guides can be hired in **Aruanã**, **Britânia**, **Barra do Garças** or **Porto Luís Alves**, where guide Vandeir will arrange boat trips to see wildlife; take food and water. Interesting walks in surrounding jungle with Joel, ask at the hotel.

Tour operators

KR International Travel, R Mexico 8th floor, S 801, Rio de Janeiro, T021-2101238, ex-Peace Corps manager, good for info on the Centre-West region.

Transworld, R 3 No 546, Goiânia, T2244340, F2121047. One-week group trips in a 'botel' out of Aruanã to Bananal).

Transport

Brasília *p620, map p624, phone code 061*

See also Ins and outs, p621.

Air

Airport, 12 km from centre, T3549000. Bus 102 or 118 to airport, regular, US$0.65, 30 mins. Taxi is US$10 after bargaining, worth it. Left-luggage facilities at airport (tokens for lockers, US$0.50).

Flights to Araguaína, Barreiras, Belém, Belo Horizonte, Carajás, Cuiabá, Fortaleza, Goiânia, Ilhéus, Imperatriz, Macapá, Manaus, Marabá, Palmas, Porto Velho, Recife, Rio Branco, Rio de Janeiro, Salvador, São Paulo, Teresina and Uberaba.

Airline offices BRA, SHS Quadra 1, bloco A, loja 71/72, in front of Hotel Nacional, T3217070. GOL, airport, T3649370, premium rate number, T0300-7892121. Rio-Sul/ Nordeste, SCLN 306, bloco B, loja 24, T2422590; airport T3659020. TAM/Brasil Central, SHN Hotel Nacional, Gallery Store, 36/37, T3251300; airport, T3651000. Varig, SCN Quadra 4, bloco B, T3291240; airport, T3649219. Vasp, SCLN 304, bloco E, lojas 80/100, T3290404; airport, T3653037.

Bus

The bus terminal (rodoviária), T3274631 (rodoferroviária, bus and train station T3632281, next door), from which long-distance buses leave, has post office (Mon-Fri 0800-1700, Sat 0800-1200), telephone and telegram facilities and showers (US$0.50). Taxi to Northern hotel zone (Setor Hoteleiro Norte), US$9. Bus 131 between rodoviária, the municipal terminal, and rodoferroviária, US$1.25.

To **Rio**, 17 hrs, 6 *comuns* (US$32) and 3 *leitos* (about US$64) daily. To **São Paulo**, 16 hrs, 7 *comuns* (about US$30) and 2 *leitos* (about US$60) daily (**Rápido Federal** recommended). To **Belo Horizonte**, 12 hrs, 9 *comuns* (US$20) and 2 *leitos* (US$40) daily. To **Belém**, 36 hrs, 4 daily (US$55, **Trans Brasília**, T2337589, buses poorly maintained, but no alternative). To **Recife**, 40 hrs, US$49-60. To **Salvador**, 24 hrs, 3 daily (US$27). To **Campo Grande**, **São Luís**, 15 hrs, 1915, US$30, or **Viação Motta** via São Paulo 0930, 1930, or 1820 direct. To **Corumbá**, US$46. To **Cuiabá**, 17½ hrs (US$30) daily at 1200 with *São Luís*. **Mato Grosso**, generally Goiânia seems to be the better place for Mato Grosso destinations. **Barra do Garças**, 0830 and 2000, takes 9 hrs with **Araguarina**, T2337598, US$13.20 return. All major destinations served. Bus tickets for major companies are sold in a subsidiary office in Taguatinga, Centro Oeste, C8, Lotes 1 and 2, Loja 1; and at the city rodoviária.

Car

Car hire All large companies are represented at the airport and the Car Rental Sector. **Avis**, airport, T/F3652780. **Interlocadora**, airport, T3652511 and **Localiza**, Setor Locadoras, T3651616, also at airport, T0800-992000. **Unidas**, T3653343, and at airport, T3651412.

Goiânia *p627, map p627, phone code 062*

Air

Santa Genoveva, 6 km northeast off Rua 57, T2071288. Flights to Brasília, Campinas, São Paulo, Uberaba and Uberlândia. Several car hire firms at the airport. Taxi from centre US$6.

Airline offices Varig, Av Goiás 285, T2245059. **Vasp**, R 3 No 569, T2246389.

Bus

Rodoviária on R 44 No 399 in the Norte Ferroviário sector, about a 40-min walk to downtown (T2248466). Buses 'Rodoviária-Centro' (No 404) and 'Vila União-Centro' (No 163) leave from stop on city side of terminal, US$0.80; No 163 goes on to the Praça Tamandaré.

To **Brasília**, 207 km, at least 15 departures a day, 2½ hrs, US$5, and **São Paulo**, 900 km via Barretos, US$25, 14½ hrs, *leito* services at night. To **Goiás Velho**, 136 km, hourly from 0500, 2½ hrs, US$5. **Pirenópolis**, 0700 and 1700, 2 hrs, US$5. **Campo Grande**, 935 km, 4 services daily, 18 hrs, US$30. To **Cuiabá** (Mato Grosso), 916 km on BR-158/070 via Barra do Garças, or 928 km on BR-060/364 via Jataí (both routes paved, most buses use the latter route), 4 buses a day, US$25, 15-16 hrs, continuing to Porto Velho (**Rondônia**) and Rio Branco (**Acre**) – a very trying journey indeed.

Car

Car hire Millenium, T96127842 (24 hrs), Siga, T2078388.

Anápolis and Cristalina *p628, phone code 062*

Road At Anápolis, the BR-153 (Brasília-Belém) turns north and begins the long haul (1,964 km) through Tocantins, Maranhão and Pará to Belém, a bumpy, monotonous trip of 35 hrs or more, US$55.

Cidade de Goiás *p629, phone code 062*

Bus The rodoviária is 2 km out of town. Regular bus services to Goiânia (2½ hrs), Aruanã, Barra do Garças and Jussara. All buses stop at the old bus station (rodoviária velha) next to the Mercado Municipal. Ask to get out here.

Pirenópolis *p630, phone code 062*

Bus Frequent buses to Brasília (2½ hrs).

Chapada dos Veadeiros *p631, phone code 62*

Bus Brasília-Alto Paraíso-São Jorge leave at 1100 (3-4hrs), returning 0900.

Parque Nacional das Emas *p632*

Bus One bus a day passes from **Serranópolis** to Chapada do Ceu, leaving at 0800. To get to Chapada Do Ceu from Campo Grande, go via Costa Rica or Chapada do Sul.

Directory

Brasília *p620, map p624, phone code 061*

Banks Foreign currency (but not always Amex cheques) can be exchanged at branches of **Banco Regional de Brasília** and **Banco do Brasil**, Setor Bancário Sul, latter also at airport (ATM, bank open weekends and holidays), charge US$20 commission for TCs. **American Express**, Buriti Turismo, CLS 402 Bloco A, Lojas 27/33, T2252686. **Diners Club**, Av W3 Norte 502. **MasterCard**, for cash against a card, SCRN 502, Bl B, lojas 30 e 31, Asa Norte. Good exchange rates at Hotel Nacional and from hotels with 'exchange-turismo' sign. **HSBC**, SCRS 502, bloco A, lojas 7/12, ATM.

Cultural centres British Council, Setor C Sul, Quadra 01, bloco H, 8th floor, Morro Vermelho Building, T3236080. **Cultura Inglesa**, SEPS 709/908 Conj B, T2433065. **American Library**, Casa Thomas Jefferson, Av W4 Sul, Quadra 706, T2436588. **Aliança Francesa**, Sul Entrequadra 707-907, bloco A, T2427500. **Instituto Cultural Goethe**, Edif Dom Bosco, Setor Garagem Sul 902, lote 73, bloco C, T2246773. Mon-Fri, 0800-1200, also Mon, Wed, Thu 1600-2000.

Embassies and consulates Australia, Caixa Postal 11-1256, SHIS QI-09, Conj 16, Casa 1, T2485569. **Austria**, SES, Av das Nações 40, T2433111. **Canada**, SES, Av das Nações 16, T3212171. **Denmark**, Av das Nações 26, T4438188 (0900-1200, 1400-1700). **Germany**, SES, Av das Nações 25, T4437330. **Guyana**, SDS, Edif Venâncio III, 4th floor, sala 410/404, T2249229. **Netherlands**, SES, Av das Nações 5, T3214769. **South Africa**, SES, Av das Nações, lote 06, T3129503. **Sweden**, Av das Nações 29, Caixa Postal 07-0419, T2431444. **Switzerland**, SES, Av das Nações 41, T4435500. **UK**, SES, Quadra 801, Conjunto K (with British Commonwealth Chamber of Commerce), or Av das Nações, Caixa Postal 070586, T2252710. **USA**, SES, Av das Nações 3, T3217272. **Venezuela**, SES, Av das Nações 13, T2239325.

InternetCafé.Com.Tato, CLS 505, bloco C, loja 17, Asa Sul, open daily. **Liverpool Coffee Shop**, CLS 108, R da Igreijinha.

Laundry Lavanderia Laundromat, CLN 104, bloco C, loja 106, Asa Norte. Self-service.

Post office Poste restante, Central Correio, 70001; SBN-Cj 03, BL-A, Edif Sede da ECT, the central office is in the Setor Hoteleiro Sul, between *Hotels Nacional* and *St Paul*. Another post office is in Ed Brasília Rádio, Av 3 Norte.

Goiânia *p627, map p627, phone code 062*

Banks National banks in the centre and along Av Rep Líbano. Travel agents will exchange cash, poor rates for Tcs.

Immigration Immigration office: R 235, Setor Universitário.

Parque Nacional das Emas *p632*

Banks There is a Banco do Brasil with a Visa ATM in Chapada do Ceu.

Mato Grosso do Sul and the Pantanal

Mato Grosso do Sul and its namesake and neighbour are dominated by the world's largest wetland, the Pantanal. This gently sloping area of savannah, forest, cerrado *and swamp roughly half the size of France slopes gently between Cuiabá in the north and the Bolivian border in the south. Its seasonal flooding and draining are accompanied by a spawn-and-migration lifecylce of millions of fish. These are preyed upon by enormous numbers of birds and cayman, which in turn feed upon predators like jaguar. Whilst wildlife can be difficult to see in the closed forests of the Amazon it parades in front of tourists here. Herds of grazing capybara, troops of coati, anacondas as thick as a rugby player's thigh, giant anteaters, rheas and wild pigs are seen by almost every visitor. The best points of access for the Pantanal in Mato Grosso do Sul are Corumba in the extreme southwest and the capital, Campo Grande.* » *For Sleeping, Eating and other listings, see pages 653-663.*

Mato Grosso do Sul

Campo Grande → *Phone code: 067. Colour map 3, C3. Population: 665,000.*

A major gateway to the Pantanal, Campo Grande is a pleasant, modern city on a grid system, with wide avenues. It was founded in 1899 and became the state capital in 1979. Because of the *terra roxa* (red earth), it is called the 'Cidade Morena'.

In the centre is a shady park, the **Praça República**, commonly called the Praça do Rádio after the Rádio Clube on one of its corners. Three blocks west is **Praça Ari Coelho**. Linking the two squares, and running through the city east to west, is the broad Avenida Afonso Pena; much of its central reservation is planted with yellow *ypé* trees. Their blossom covers the avenue, and much of the city besides, in spring. City tours are generally expensive and there are few obvious sights.

The **Parque dos Poderes**, a long way from the centre, covers several hectares. As well as the Palácio do Governo and state secretariats, there is a small zoo for rehabilitating animals from the Pantanal (phone the Secretaria do Meio Ambiente to visit), lovely trees and cycling and jogging tracks.

Maps and books are for sale at the municipal **Centro de Informação Turística e Cultural** ⓘ *Av Noroeste 5140, corner of Afonso Pena, T3245830, Tue-Sat 0800-1900, Sun 0900-1200*. Housed in Pensão Pimentel, a beautiful mansion built in 1913, also has a database about services in the city and cultural information. There's a **tourist information kiosk** ⓘ *T3633116, open 24 hrs*, at the airport.

Museu Dom Bosco ⓘ *R Barão do Rio Branco, T3833994, Mon-Sat 0800-1700, Sun 1200-1700, US$0.50*, 1843, is superb. Its exhibits come from the five indigenous groups with which the Salesian missionaries have had contact since the 20th century; all have explanatory texts. There are also collections of shells, stuffed birds, butterflies and mammals from the Pantanal, as well as a 'monstrous' display showing two-headed calves, etc. Each collection is highly recommended.

Museu do Arte Contemporâneo ⓘ *Marechal Rondón and Av Calógeras, Mon-Fri 1300-1800, free*, displays modern art from the region.

Coxim → *Phone code: 067. Population: 28,500.*

Coxim, 242 km north of Campo Grande on the BR-163 and halfway between Campo Grande and Rondonópolis, provides access to the Pantanal. It sits in a green bowl, on the shores of the Rio Taquari. The area has great potential for tourism, but there are no official tours to the Pantanal from here. However, it is a great place if you charter your own boat. There are a few hotels in town including some cheap options.

Campo Grande to São Paulo

The Campo Grande to São Paulo journey can be broken at **Três Lagoas**, 9½ hours from São Paulo (motorway) and six hours from Campo Grande by paved highway BR-262. About 16 km east of Três Lagoas is the massive **Jupiá Dam** ⓘ *T5212753, weekends and holidays only 0800-1800*, on the Rio Paraná, which can be visited with prior permission. Further north are other hydroelectric dams, most impressive of which is at **Ilha Solteira** (50 km, several hotels and good fish restaurants on São Paulo state side); guided tours at 1000 and 1500 weekends and holidays. Swimming is excellent at **Praia Catarina**, with bars, playground and kiosks (6 km). Overlooking the river 35 km south of Ilha Solteira is restored **Fort Itapura**, built during the War of the Triple Alliance, with beach and restaurants nearby. There are a few hotels in Três Lagoas town, including cheap and safe options like **Novo**, near the rodoviária. The bus to Campo Grande leaves at 0800, 1200, 2230, US$12.50.

Campo Grande to the Paraguayan border

Ponta Porã → *Phone code: 067. Colour map 3, C2. Population: 54,000.*

Ponta Porã is separated from Pedro Juan Caballero in Paraguay by only a broad avenue. With paved streets, good public transport and smart shops, Ponta Porã is

decidedly more prosperous than its neighbour, although Brazilian visitors flock across the border to play the casino and buy cheaper 'foreign' goods. At the **Parque das Exposições**, by the rodoviária, an animal show is held each October.

Border with Paraguay

There are no border posts between the two towns and people pass freely for local visits. For entry/exit visas, go to the **Brazilian Federal Police office** ⓘ *R Marechal Floriano 1483 (2nd floor of the white engineering supply company building), T4311428, Mon-Fri 0730-1130, 1400-1700.*

The two nations' consulates face each other on Rua Internacional (border street), a block west of Ponta Porã's local bus terminal; some nationalities require a visa from the **Paraguayan consul** ⓘ *R Internacional, next to Hotel Internacional, Mon-Fri 0800-1200*. Check requirements carefully, and ensure your documents are in order; without the proper stamps you will inevitably be sent back somewhere later on in your travels. Taking a taxi between offices can speed things up if pressed for time, drivers know border crossing requirements, US$4.25.

Into Paraguay There are frequent buses and flights from Pedro Juan Caballero to Asunción. A road also runs to Concepción on the Rio Paraguay, where boat connections can be made. For more details, see the *South American Handbook*.

Bonito and around → *Phone code: 067. Colour map 3, C2. Population: 17,000.*

A beautiful area of plunging waterfalls and deep caves makes up the municipality of Bonito, in the **Serra do Bodoquena**, which yields granite and marble and is clad in forest. Although there are walks through mountains and forest, rafting and snorkelling in clear rivers and wildlife such as birds, monkeys, caiman and anaconda, Bonito is a full-scale resort for Brazilian families and there are far fewer animals here than there were in the early years. This is no place to come and contemplate the beauties of nature. Brazilian nature-based tourism is all about fun in a natural environment – with lots of noise and accompanying music and beer. Attractions are nearly all on private land and require authorization. As there is no public transport, it is advisable to go on an organized tour. Owners also enforce limits on the number of daily visitors so, at busy times, pre-booking is essential. Bonito is very popular with Brazilian holidaymakers, especially during December to January, Carnival, Easter, and July (at these times advance booking is essential) and prices are high. The wet season is January to February; December to February is hottest, July to August coolest. There's a tourist office, **Setuma** ⓘ *R Col Pilad Rebuá 1780, T2551351 ext 215.*

Lagoa Azul ⓘ *US$5 municipal tax*, 26 km from Bonito, is a cave with a lake 50 m long and 110 m wide, 75 m below ground level. The water, 20°C, is a jewel-like blue as light from the opening is refracted through limestone and magnesium. Prehistoric animal bones have been found in the lake. The light is at its best January to February, 0700-0900, but is fine at other times. A 25-ha park surrounds the cave. **Nossa Senhora Aparecida cave** has superb stalactites and stalagmites and can be visited, although there is no tourism infrastructure.

The **Balneário Municipal** ⓘ *US$5*, on the Rio Formoso (7 km on road to Jardim), has changing rooms, toilets, camping, swimming in clear water and plenty of colourful fish to see. Strenuous efforts are made to keep the water and shore clean. **Horminio waterfalls** ⓘ *US$0.20*, 13 km, consist of eight falls on the Rio Formoso, suitable for swimming; bar and camping. You can go **rafting on the Rio Formoso** ⓘ *US$15 per person, minimum 4 people, arranged by Hapakany Tour and many other agencies, see Tour operators, page 660*. The 2½-hour trip is a mixture of floating peacefully downriver, swimming and shooting four waterfalls (lifejackets available).

The **Aquário Natural** ⓘ *US$25*, is one of the springs of the Rio Formoso; to visit you must have authorization from **Hapakany Tour** (see page 660). Here you can swim and snorkel with five types of fish (remove suntan oil before swimming). Birdwatching and swimming or snorkelling in crystal-clear water from the springs of the **Rio Sucuri** to its meeting with the Formoso makes for a peaceful tour (permission from Hapakany or **TapeTur**). Other tours include **Aquidaban**, a series of limestone/marble waterfalls in dense forest, and **Rio da Prata** ⓘ *US$24*, a beautiful spring with underground snorkelling for 2 km. Parrots and animals can be seen on the trip. There are also plenty of chances for walking along ecological trails, horse riding and fishing trips. The **fishing** season is from 1 March to 31 October. In late October and early November is the *piracema* (fish run). The fish return to the spawning grounds and hundreds can be seen jumping the falls.

Jardim

Jardim, reached by paved road, has a wide, tree-lined main street. A few blocks uphill is **Panificadora Massa Pura**, clean and bright, and other eating places. There is a rodoviária for Cruzeiro do Sul buses. From Bonito a road leads to **Porto Murtinho**, where a boat crosses to Isla Margarita in Paraguay (entry stamp available on the island).

Campo Grande to Corumbá

The BR-262 is paved most of the way from Campo Grande to Corumbá and the Bolivian border; rail service along this route has been suspended indefinitely. It is best to make this journey during the day to take advantage of the marvellous scenery.

Aquidauana → *Colour map 3, C2. Population: 41,000.*

Some 131 km west of Campo Grande, Aquidauana has several daily buses from Campo Grande. The BR-412 heads south from here to Jardim, with connections to Paraguay (see above). The Ibama-controlled *jacaré* farm, **Olhos d'Água**, is not open to visitors. Aquidauana is one of the smaller gateways to the Pantanal (see below), excursions in fishing boats negotiable (around US$50 per person a day), or via **Chalanatuor** ⓘ *T2413396*; six-day trips are recommended.

Miranda → *Colour map 3, B2. Population: 23,000.*

Some 77 km further west is Miranda, another entrance to the Pantanal (see below). Here too is a *jacaré* farm, **Granja Caimã** ⓘ *US$1*, which is open to visitors. A road heads south to Bodoquena and on to Bonito.

Corumbá → *Phone code: 067. Colour map 3, B1. Population: 95,000.*

Corumbá is the best starting point for the southern part of the Pantanal, with boat and jeep trips and access to the major hotel and farm accommodation. Situated on the south bank by a broad bend in the Rio Paraguai, just 15 minutes from the Bolivian border, the city offers beautiful views of the river, especially at sunset. Corumbá is hot (particularly between September and January), with 70% humidity; June and July are cooler. Mosquitoes can be a real problem from December to February.

Corumbá was one of South America's most important river ports in the 19th century and the **port area** is worth a visit. The compact streets include the spacious **Praça da Independência** and Avenida General Rondon, between Frei Mariano and 7 de Septembro, which has a palm-lined promenade that comes to life in the evenings. The **Forte Junqueira**, the city's most historic building which may be visited, was built in 1772. In the hills to the south is the world's greatest reserve of manganese, now being worked.

 The municipal tourist office, **Emcotur** ⓘ *R América 969, T2316996*, provides general information and city maps. The combination of economic hard times since 1994 and drug-running make the city unsafe late at night.

Border with Bolivia

Immigration Immigration formalities are constantly changing, so check procedures in advance. You need not have your passport stamped to visit Quijarro or Puerto Suárez only for the day. Otherwise, get your passport stamped by **Brazilian Polícia Federal** ⓘ *Praça da Republica 37*. The visa must be obtained on the day of departure. If exiting Brazil just to get a new visa, remember that exit and entry must not be on the same day.

Transport Leaving Brazil, take Canarinho city bus marked 'Fronteira' from the port end of Rua Antônio Maria Coelho to the Bolivian border (15 minutes, US$0.35), walk over the bridge to Bolivian immigration (blue building), then take a *colectivo* to Quijarro or Puerto Suárez.

When travelling from Quijarro, take a taxi or walk to the Bolivian border to go through formalities. Just past the bridge, on a small side street to the right, is the bus stop for Corumbá. Take bus marked Fronteira or Tamengo to Praça da República (US$0.80, every 45 minutes between 0630 and 1915); don't believe taxi drivers who say there is no bus. Taxi to centre US$6. Find a hotel then take care of Brazilian immigration formalities at Polícia Federal, address above.

Into Bolivia Over the border from Corumbá are Arroyo Concepción, Puerto Quijarro and Puerto Suárez. From Puerto Quijarro a 650-km railway runs to Santa Cruz de la Sierra. There is a road of sorts. A better road route is from Cáceres to San Matías, thence to San Ignacio (see page 667). There are internal flights from Puerto Suárez. For more details, see the *Bolivia Handbook* or the *South American Handbook*.

Money Money changers at the border and in Quijarro offer the same rates as in Corumbá.

Health If you arrive in Brazil without a yellow fever vaccination certificate, you may have to go to Rua 7 de Setembro, Corumbá, for an inoculation.

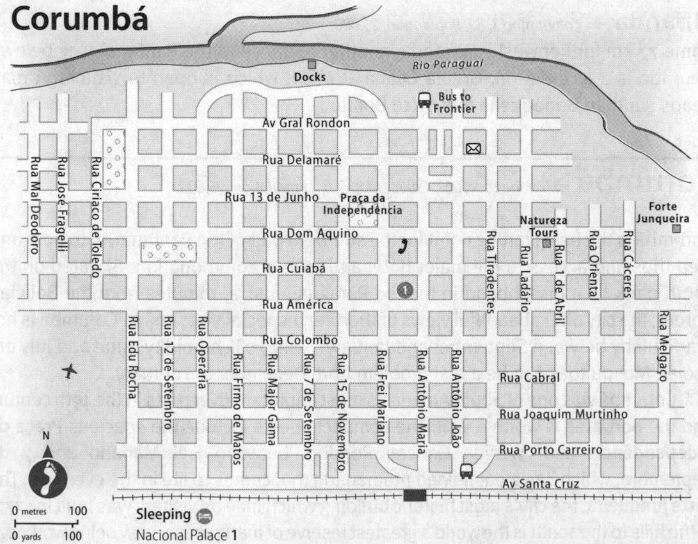

Pantanal

ⓘ *Ibama, R Rubens de Mendonça, Cuiabá, CEP 78008, T6441511/1581, will grant permission to visit the Pantanal. See also Ecology and conservation, page 652.*

Wildlife

The animals and birds found here are similar in many ways to those of the Amazon basin, but because of the more open land, they are easier to see than in the dense jungle growth. You are pretty much guaranteed to see lots of birds, many of them very large. The enormous jabiru stork (*tuiuíu*) is the height of a child at around 1.2 m, and the symbol of the Pantanal. The 300 or so species of bird include the hyacinth macaw, plumbeous ibis, both blue-throated and red-throated piping guans and roseate spoonbill.

Easy to see on the riverbanks are the ubiquitous and bizarre capybara, a kind of giant aquatic guinea pig, and the caiman (*jacaré*). You may also come across otters, anteaters, opossums, armadillos, bare-eared marmosets, black-and-gold howler monkeys and marsh deer. Harder to spot are the maned wolf, South American coati, ocelot, margay, jaguarundi and even the puma, jaguar and yellow anaconda. There are also around 230 varieties of fish, from the giant *pintado*, weighing up to 80 kg, to the tiny, voracious *piranha*. Fishing here is exceptionally good (best May-October). The extraordinary thing is that man and his domesticated cattle thrive, together with the wildlife, with seemingly little friction, and local farmers protect the area jealously.

Ins and outs

Getting there The edges of the Pantanal are relatively easy to visit. The heartland is mostly inaccessible to those without very deep pockets. The best starting points are Corumbá, Cuiabá and, to a lesser extent, Campo Grande, from where there is public transport all around the perimeter, but none at all within. Wild camping is possible if you have some experience and your own transport. Remember that the longer you stay and the further you go from the edges (where most of the hotels are located), the more likely you are to see rare wildlife.

From Corumbá there is access to the Pantanal by both road and river, offering a variety of day trips, luxury houseboat excursions, and connections to many surrounding *fazendas*. Along the road from Corumbá to Campo Grande (BR-262) are Miranda and Aquidauana, both gateways to various fishing and tourist lodges. The BR-163, which connects Campo Grande and Cuiabá, skirts the east edge of the Pantanal; Coxim, 242 km north of Campo Grande, offers access via the Rio Taquari but few facilities. From Cuiabá there is year-round road access to Barão de Melgaço and Poconé, both of which can be starting points for excursions. The **Transpantaneira Highway** runs south from Poconé to Porto Jofre, through the heart of the Pantanal, providing access to many different lodges, but does not have any bus service. During the rainy season, access is restricted between Pixiam and Porto Jofre. Finally, Cáceres, 215 km west of Cuiabá at the northwest corner of the Pantanal, offers access along the Rio Paraguai to one of the least developed parts of the region.

Another access to the Pantanal from the east is Coxim, see page 647.

Tourist facilities Tourist facilities in the Pantanal cater to four main categories of visitor. **Sports fishermen** usually stay at one of the numerous speciality lodges scattered throughout the region, which provide guides, boats, bait, ice and other related amenities. Bookings can be made locally or in any of Brazil's major cities. **All-inclusive tours**, combining air and ground transportation, accommodation at the most elaborate *fazendas*, meals, guided river and land tours, can be arranged from abroad or through travel agencies in Brazil's gateway cities. This is the most expensive

The plight of the Guaraní

"On my land, cattle is worth more than Indians. The cattle stomp on their gardens and tractors knock down their houses. The rivers are dirty with the waste from large farms in the region; pesticides, mercury. They finished with our forests, they are finishing with what is left of our savannahs. For this reason young Guarani are killing themselves, they are searching for the end, hanging themselves." (Marta Silva Vito Guarani, President of the Kaguateca Association for Diplaced Indians in an address to the US House of Representatives, 10 May 1994.)

The Guaraní in Brazil, one of the country's largest indigenous groups are suffering terribly from the theft of almost all their land. Nowhere is their plight more urgent than in the Pantanal, where thousands of Guaraní Kaiowa live crowded onto tiny plots hemmed in by ranches and plantations. The surrounding ranch land has long been hunted and farmed by the tribe but has been forcibly taken from them by gunmen hired by ranch owners. One community, which has a federal act recognizing its right to 1,240 ha of land, is crammed into an area of barely 60 ha, hemmed in by electric fences and patrolled by armed guards. They are forced by these men to work the land stolen from them as cheap labour. The situation has proved intolerable for many young Guaraní. More than 300 have committed suicide since 1986, drinking a mixture of rum and pesticide. The youngest was only nine years old.

In desperation the tribe began to campaign internationally in the 1990s and one group was granted land rights by the Brazilian government in 2002. But the law has not been upheld. Many Guaraní groups were forced from the little land they had, their homes were burnt and in early 2003, Marcos Veron, a 70-year-old shaman, leader of the Guarani-Kaiowá tribe and land rights campaigner, was beaten to death by thugs employed by the ranchers who had taken over his homeland, Takuára.

In January 2004 a group of several thousand Indians, enraged by lack of activity from the government, invaded several farms close to Brazil's border with Paraguay. The ranch owners fled in fear. The invasions were widely reported in the international press, forcing the Brazilian government to promise to review the tribe's land rights in Matto Grosso do Sul. What will happen remains to be seen.

option. **Moderately priced tours**, using private guides, camping or staying at more modest *fazendas*, can be arranged locally in Cuiabá (where guides await arrivals at the airport) or through the more reputable agencies in Corumbá. The **lowest priced tours** are offered by independent guides in Corumbá, some of whom are unreliable; some travellers have reported serious problems here (see Choosing a tour, below). For those with the barest minimum of funds, a glimpse of the Pantanal and its wildlife can be had on the bus ride from Campo Grande to Corumbá, by lodging or camping near the ferry crossing over the Rio Paraguai (Porto Esperança), and by staying in Poconé and day-walking or hitching south along the Transpantaneira.

When to go The Pantanal is good for seeing wildlife year-round. However, the dry season between July and October is the ideal time as animals and birds congregate at the few remaining areas of water. During these months you are very likely to see jaguars. This is the nesting and breeding season, when birds form vast nesting areas, with thousands crowding the trees, creating an almost unbearable cacophony of sounds. The white-sand river beaches are exposed, *jacarés* bask in the sun, and capybaras frolic in the grass. July sees lots of Brazilian visitors and the increased noise decreases the chances of sightings. From the end of November to the end of March (wettest in February), most of the area, which is crossed by many rivers, floods. At this time mosquitoes abound and cattle crowd onto the few islands remaining above water. In the southern part, many wild animals leave the area, but in the north, which is slightly higher, the animals do not leave.

What to take Most tours arrange for you to leave your baggage in town, so you need only bring what is necessary for the duration of the tour. In winter (June-August), temperatures fall to 10°C; warm clothing and covers or sleeping bag are needed at night. It's very hot and humid during summer and a hat and sun protection is vital. Wear long sleeves and long trousers and spray clothes as well as skin with insect repellent. Insects are less of a problem July-August. Take insect repellent from home as mosquitoes, especially in the North Pantanal, are becoming immune to local brands. Drinks are not included in the price of packages and tend to be overpriced, so if you are on a tight budget bring your own. Most importantly, make sure you take a pair of binoculars.

Choosing a tour

Most tours combine 'safari' jeep trips, river-boat trips, piranha fishing and horse riding with accommodation in lodges. Excursions often take place at sunset and sunrise as these are the best times for spotting birds and wildlife. A two-day trip, with a full day taken up with travel each way, allows you to experience most of what is on offer. Longer tours tend to have the same activities spread out over a longer period of time. The best way to enjoy a tour is not to have fixed expectations about what you will see, but to take in the whole experience that is the Pantanal.

Many budget travellers en route to or from Bolivia make Corumbá their base for visiting the Pantanal. They are often approached, in the streets and at the cheaper hotels, by salesmen who speak foreign languages and promise complete tours for low prices; they then hand their clients over to agencies and/or guides, who often speak only Portuguese, and may deliver something quite different. Similarly, guides at the airport may give the impression that they will lead the tour, but this may not be so. Always ask who will lead the party and how big it will be. Less than four is not economic and a guide will make cuts in boats or guides. Some travellers have reported very unpleasant experiences and it is important to select a guide with great care. By far the best way is to speak with other travellers who have just returned from a Pantanal tour. Most guides also have a book containing comments from their former clients. Do not rush to sign up when first approached, always compare several available alternatives. Discuss the planned itinerary carefully and try to get it in writing (although this is seldom possible – threaten to go to someone else if necessary). Do not pay everything in advance of departure, and try to deal directly with agencies or guides, not salesmen (it can be difficult to tell who is who). Always get an itemized receipt. Bear in mind that a well-organized three-day tour can be more rewarding than four days with an ill-prepared guide. There is fierce competition between guides who provide similar services, but with very different styles. Although we list a few of the most reputable guides, there are other good ones and most economy travellers enjoy a pleasant if spartan experience. (Once guides are recommended by a guidebook, they often cease to guide themselves and set up their own businesses using other guides to work under their names.) Travellers share part of the responsibility for the current chaotic guiding situation in Corumbá. Act responsibly and don't expect to get something for nothing.

▸▸ *See also Tour operators, page 659.*

Ecology and conservation

Only one area is officially a national park, the **Parque Nacional do Pantanal Matogrossense** in the municipality of Poconé, 135,000 ha of land and water, only accessible by air or river. You can obtain permission to visit at **Ibama** ⓘ *Rua Rubens de Mendonça, Cuiabá, CEP 78008, T6441511/1581*. Hunting in any form is strictly forbidden throughout the Pantanal and is punishable by four years' imprisonment. Fishing is allowed with a licence, currently US$25. Application forms from **Banco Brasil** or **Ibama Campo** ⓘ *T37822966, wwwsema.ms.gov.br*, or ask travel agents for latest details; see Fishing, page 64. It is not permitted in the spawning season or *piracema* (1 October to 1 February in Mato Grosso do Sul; 1 November to 1 March in Mato Grosso). There are also restrictions on sizes of fish species that can legally be caught. Catch and release is the only kind of fishing allowed on rivers Abobral, Negro, Perdido and Vermelho. Like other wilderness areas, the Pantanal faces important threats to its integrity. Agro-chemicals and *garimpo* mercury, washed down from the neighbouring *planalto*, are a hazard to wildlife.

Visitors can make an important contribution to protecting the Pantanal by acting responsibly and choosing guides accordingly. Take your rubbish away with you, don't fish out of season, don't let guides kill or disturb fauna, don't buy products made from endangered species, don't buy live birds or monkeys, and report any violation of these norms to the authorities. The practice of catching caymans, even though they are then released, is traumatizing for the animals and has potentially disruptive long-term effects.

The International Union for the Conservation of Nature is concerned at the amount of poaching, particularly of *jacaré* skins, birds and capybaras. The Forestry Police have built control points on all major access roads to the Pantanal. Biologists interested in research projects in the area should contact the **Coordenador de Estudos do Pantanal** ⓘ *Departamento de Biologia, Universidade Federal do Mato Grosso do Sul, Caixa Postal 649, Campo Grande, CEP 79070-900, T067-7873311 ext 2113, F067-7875317*.

Further reading *The Pantanal: Brazil's Forgotten Wilderness*, Vic Banks. Sierra Club Books, 1991, 730 Polk Street, San Francisco, CA 94100.

The Transpantaneira from Cuiabá

The Transpantaneira Highway, built in 1976, was originally projected to connect Cuiabá (see page 663) with Corumbá, but currently goes only as far as Porto Jofre on the Rio Cuiabá. Work has been suspended indefinitely because of difficulties, costs and ecological considerations. » *For Tour operators in Cuiabá, see page 673.*

Poconé → *Phone code: 065. Colour map 3, A2. Population: 31,500.*

A paved road turns south off the main Cuiabá to Cáceres road to Poconé, founded in 1781 and known as the Cidade Rosa (pink city). Until 1995 there was much *garimpo* activity north of town and many slag heaps can be seen from the road.

Pixaim → *Colour map 3, B2.*

Pixaim is 63 km south of Poconé, a journey of two hours in the dry season and up to five in the wet. It is the only easily accessible settlement in the Pantanal with any tourist infrastructure. It is located where a bridge crosses the Rio Pixaim and has two hotels, a fuel station (all types available, check that the pump is set to zero) and a tyre-repair shop (*borracheria*). Next to the Pousada Pantaneira (see Sleeping) is a private **Jaguar Ecological Reserve**, owned by *pantaneiros*, funded by donation. Further details, donations and reservations can be made through *Focus Tours* (see page 26), who helped to set up the reserve.

Porto Jofre → *Colour map 3, B2*

From Poconé, the Transpantaneira runs 146 km south to Porto Jofre, where there is just a gas station, gasoline and diesel, but no alcohol fuel is available. At the entrance to the Pantanal there is a gate across the road where drivers are given a list of rules of conduct. The road is of earth, in poor condition, with ruts, holes and many bridges that need care in crossing. The easiest access is in the dry season (July to September), which is also the best time for seeing birds and, in September, the trees are in bloom. In the wet, especially January to February, there is no guarantee that the Transpantaneira will be passable. The wet season, however, is a good time to see many of the more shy animals because more fruit, new growth and other high calorie foods are available, and there are fewer people.

Campos de Jofre

Campos de Jofre, about 20 km north of Porto Jofre, is magnificent between August and October, with very large concentrations of birds and animals. In Poconé you can hitch (not much traffic, bumpy, especially in a truck) to Porto Jofre, or hire a vehicle in Cuiabá. You will get more out of this part of the Pantanal by going with a guide; a lot can be seen from the Transpantaneira in a hired car, but guides can take you into *fazendas* and will point out wildlife. Recommended guides are listed on page 659 and, in Cuiabá, on page 670. Although there are gas stations in Pixaim and Porto Jofre, they are not always well stocked, so it is best to carry extra fuel.

Barão de Melgaço and around → *Colour map 3, A2.*

Situated on Rio Cuiabá, 130 km from Cuiabá (**TUT** bus leaves Cuiabá at 0730 and 1500, US$6.50), Barão de Melgaço is reached by two roads. The shorter, via Santo Antônio de Leverger, is unpaved from Santo Antônio to Barão (closed in the wet season); via São Vicente is longer, but has more pavement. The way to see the Pantanal from here is by boat down the Rio Cuiabá. Boat hire, for example from **Restaurant Peixe Vivo** on waterfront, costs up to US$85 for a full day; or enquire with travel agencies in Cuiabá. The best time of day is sunset, but it would need some organizing to be in the best part at the best time without too much boating in the dark. Remember to protect against the sun when on the water.

Initially farms and small habitations line the riverbanks, but they become more forested, with lovely combinations of flowering trees (best seen September to October). After a while, a small river to the left leads to the Baia and Lakes Chacororé and Sia Mariana, which join each other. Boats can continue beyond the lakes to the Rio Mutum, but a guide is essential because there are many dead ends. The area is rich in birdlife and the waterscapes are beautiful.

Sleeping

Campo Grande *p644, map p645, phone code 067*

Large, mid-market hotels, many with small pools and restaurants, and all very traditional, are found along Av Calógeras, away from the bus station and its budget options.

There is a wide variety of hotels in the streets around the rodoviária so it is easy to leave bags in the *guarda volumes* and shop around. This area is not safe at night.

A Buriti, Av A M Coelho 2301, T/F3212211. Large, and a little past its best but with a pool, sauna, parking, restaurant.

A Exceler Plaza, Av Afonso Pena 444, T3210102, F3215666. Very comfortable, traditional hotel that caters to tourists and businesss visitors. Small pool, tennis.

A Vale Verde, Av Afonso Pena 106, T3213355. Pleasant and well maintained with a small pool. Recommended.

A-B Internacional, Allan Kardec 223, near the rodoviária, T3844677, F3212729. Modern, comfortable and with a small pool. Cheaper with fan.

B Saigali, Barão do Rio Branco 356, near the rodoviária, T3845775. A/c, minibar, parking, cheaper with fan, comfortable. Recommended.

B-C Advanced, Av Calógeras 1909, T3215000, F3257744. A little dowdy and with a very small pool. A/c rooms, cheaper with fan.

B-C Palace, R Dom Aquino 1501, near the rodoviária, T3844741. A/c rooms with a fridge (cheaper with fan), some are very small.

B-C Paris, Av Costa e Silva 4175, T3871795, F3257744. A/c rooms, al with a minibar, cheaper with fan.

C Central, R 15 de Novembro 472, T3846442. Basic fan-cooled rooms cheaper with a shared bath.

C Concord, Av Calógeras 1624, T3843081, F3824987. Smart, standard town hotel with a pool. All rooms are a/c with a minibar.

D-E Iguaçu, R Dom Aquino 761, T3844621, F3213215. A/c, fridge, bar, cheaper with fan, modern, pleasant. Internet US$4 per hr. Recommended.

D-E Nacional, R Dom Aquino 610, near the rodoviária, T3832461. A/c, cheaper with fan, shared bath, or single. Busy, includes breakfast, real bargain.

E Americano, R 14 de Julho 2311 and Mcal Rondón, T3211454. Frayed hotel with a/c rooms all with a fridge and cheaper options with a fan. In the main shopping area.

E Youth hostel, large block opposite rodoviária. Laundry, kitchen, reception open 24 hrs. Recommended. Offers Pantanal trips from office next door.

E-F Pousada LM, R 15 de Novembro 201, By Praça Ari Coelho, T3215207, lmhotel@enersulnet.com.br. Nice motel-style rooms around a courtyard, all with a TV, fridge and terraces overlooking a busy road. Cheaper with fan (**G** for a single room), also rents by the month. Recommended.

F Cosmos, R Dom Aquino 771, near the rodoviária, T3844270. Quieter than others in area, good value. Recommended.

Ponta Porã *p645, phone code 067*

Brazilian hotels include breakfast in tariff; Paraguayan ones do not.

B Porta do Sol Palace, R Paraguai 2688, T4313341, F4311193. A/c rooms with a pool, very nice.

C Alvorada, Av Brasil 2977, T4315866. With a good café, close to post office, good value but often full.

C-D Internacional, R Internacional 1267, T4311243, cheaper without a/c. Hot water, good breakfast. Recommended.

E Dos Viajantes, across park opposite railway station. Very basic and only for those on the tightest budget.

Bonito *p646, phone code 067*

A Canaã, R Col Pilad Rebuá 1376, T2551255, F2551282. Smart, standard town hotel with a/c rooms, parking and a restaurant and *churrascaria*.

A-B Pousada Olho d'Água, Rod Três Morros, Km 1, T2551430, olhodagua@vip2000.net. Comfortable accommodation in fan-cooled cabins, set in a fruit tree garden next to a small lake. Horse riding, bike rental, solar-powered hot water and great food from the vegetable garden. Recommended.

A Tapera, Estrada Ilha do Padre, Km 10, on hill above Shell station on road to Jardim, T/F2551700. Peaceful location with fine views and cool breezes. Very comfortable, but own transport an advantage.

B Bonanza, R Col Pilad Rebuá (main street) 628, T2551315, F2551235. Suites and family rooms available, a/c. Recommended. Opposite is parking lot, with bar from 1800, darts and *churrascaria* on Fri.

C Pousadinha da Praça, R Col Pilad Rebuá 2097, T2551135. Rooms with 2-4 beds (the latter cramped), fan and hot water.

D Pousada Muito Bonito, R Col Pilad Rebuá 1448, T/F2551645. Price per person in en suites or dorm-style rooms with bunk beds all with a nice shared patio. Clean, excellent and with helpful owners. The price includes breakfast. Mario Doblack at the *pousada's* tour office speaks English, French and Spanish. Warmly recommended.

E Bonito, R Lúcio Borralho 716, Vila Donária, T/F2551462, www.ajbonito.com.br. IYHA youth hostel. Pool, kitchen and laundry facilities. English spoken, very friendly. Price per person. Recommended.

Camping

Ilha do Padre, 12 km north of Bonito, T/F2551430. On island with natural pools, very pleasant, no regular transport, although Hapakany's raft trip ends here. 4 rustic cabins with either 4 bunk beds, or 2 bunks and a double, US$10 per person. Youth hostel with dorms, US$6 per person, same price for camping. Toilets, showers, clothes washing,

meals available, bar, electricity, lots of trees. You can swim anywhere, to enter the island for a day US$3.
Poliana, on Rio Formosa, 100 m past Ilha do Padre, T2551267. Very nice camping.

Jardim *p647*
E **Eldorado**. Basic but friendly, clean and with good food.

Aquidauana *p647, phone code 067*
AL-A **Fazenda Toca da Onça**, see p656; take taxi, owner also has a campsite.
D **Fluminense**, in town near the railway station. Basic with fan-cooled rooms and breakfast, a/c is more expensive.
D **Lord**, R Manoel Paes de Barros 739, T2411857. Shared bathroom with single rooms, private bathrooms for the double rooms. Recommended.

Corumbá *p647, map p648, phone code 067*
Although there are hostels around the bus station, this is a 10-min walk from the centre of town, close to the river. The best of the accommodation as well as all the travel agents and restaurants are here.
B **Carandá**, R Dom Aquino 47, T2312023. Helpful and with a pool and restaurant.
B **Internacional Palace**, R Dom Aquino Corrêa 1457, T2316247, F2316852. With a pool, sauna, parking and a café.
B **Nacional Palace**, R América 936, T2316868, F2310202. Decent hotel with a good pool and parking.
B **Pousada do Cachimbo**, R Allan Kardec 4, outside town, on the way to the Bolivian border, T2313910. A range of rooms in a farm setting by the river. Peaceful and set in pretty gardens. With a pool.
C **Premier**, R Antônio Maria Coelho 389, T2314937. Basic *pousada* with small a/c rooms.
C-E **Salette**, R Delamaré 893, T2313768, F2314948. Cheap and cheerful with a range of rooms, the cheapest with fans and shared bathrooms. Recommended.
D **Beira Rio**, R Manoel Cavassa 109, by the port, T2312554. A/c and cheaper fan-cooled rooms. Popular with fishermen.
D **Nelly**, Delamaré 902, T2316001, F2317396. A/c rooms and cheaper fan-cooled options with a shared bath. Good breakfast.
D-E **Angola**, R Antônio Maria 124, T2317233. A/c rooms with very plain decoration, cheaper with a fan. Modest restaurant.
E **Campus**, R Antônio João 1333. Basic fan-cooled rooms, all very spartan. Cheaper with shared bath, good value.
E **Pantanal**, R Antônio Maria Coelho 677, T2312305, F2317740. IYHA youth hostel with dorms and doubles. The owner, Pontis, organizes jungle trips. Price per person. Cheaper for a group, negotiate price. Recommended.
E-F **City**, R Cabral 1031, between rodoviária and centre, T2314187. A/c or fan-cooled rooms with en suites or shared bath.

Pantanal *p649, phone code 067*
The inexperienced are cautioned not to strike out on their own. There are many lodges with fair to good accommodation, some only approachable by air or river; most are relatively expensive. One option is to hire a car and check accommodation for yourself: in Jun-Sep, especially Jul, it is necessary to book accommodation in advance. An ordinary vehicle should be able to manage the Transpantaneira out of Cuiabá throughout most of the year, but in the wet season you should be prepared to get stuck, and muddy, pushing your car from time to time. Camping away from areas of human activity can allow you to see more wildlife, but is potentially dangerous. Protection against mosquitoes is essential. Care should also be taken to avoid dangerous animals: snakes (especially in the rainy season), *piranhas* (especially in the dry season), killer bees and the larger *jacarés*.

From Campo Grande
LL **Pousada São Francisco**, 135 km from Aquidauana in the Rio Negro area of Nhecolândia, T2413494. Accessible only by air during the wet, with bath, fan, screening, horse riding, full board, price includes transport, meals, tours. Bookings through **Impacto Turismo**, Campo Grande, T/F7243167/7243616.
LL **Refúgio Ecológico Caiman**, 36 km from Miranda, 236 km from Campo Grande. Full board. First class, full board, excursions, T6872102, F6872103, or São Paulo T011-8836622, member of the **Roteiros de Charme** group (see p47).
L **Pousada Aguapé**, Fazenda São José, 59 km north of Aquidauana, 202 km from Campo

Grande, T6861036. Full board in a farmhouse hotel, screened rooms, some with a/c, pool, horse riding, boat trips, trekking, meals and tours included, bookings through **Impacto Turismo**, as above, or T2412889, F2413494.

L **Cabana do Pescador**, 65 km from Aquidauana on the Rio Miranda, T2413697, F2412406, access by Bonito bus from Campo Grande (see p661). Fishing lodge, includes breakfast.

AL **Fazenda Rio Negro**, 13,000-ha farm on the shores of the Rio Negro, farmhouse dating to 1920, tours, horses, fishing, T37257853, F37249345, or São Paulo T011-2142777.

AL **Fazenda Salobra**, T2421162, 6 km from Miranda, 209 km from Corumbá, 198 from Campo Grande. Recommended. With bath, including all meals; tours, boat rentals and horses are extra. By the Rio Salobra (clear water) and Rio Miranda, with birds and animals easily seen. Take bus from Campo Grande to Miranda, and alight 50 m from the bridge over Rio Miranda, turn left for 1,200 m to the *fazenda*.

AL **Pousada Mangabal**, in Nhecolândia, T2413494. A farm with horse and walking. tours. Book through **Panbratur**, Aquidauana, see p660.

A **Toca da Onça**, 10 km from Aquidauana on the shores of the Rio Aquidauana. A/c cabins, a restaurant and boat tours. Bookings through **Panbratur**, Aquidauana, see p660.

B **Pousada Águas do Pantanal**, Av Afonso Pena 367, Miranda, T/F2421242, contact Fátima or Luís Cordelli. Very good accommodation, tours and food.

Camping and self drive There is a good campsite 30 km past Miranda. Alternatively, hire a car in Corumbá and drive to Miranda, but note that the dirt road is bad after rain (consequently not much traffic and more wildlife can be seen). Car with driver can be hired at Salobra for US$25. There are several camping possibilities along the shores of the Rio Aquidauana, including **Camping Baía**, 50 km from Aquidauana, on a bay on the river, trees for shade, boats; **Pequi Camping**, 48 km from Aquidauana, with toilets, electricity; **Camping Itajú**, sandy beach, cabins, *lanchonete*, shower, electricity, boat rental.

From Corumbá

LL **Pousada do Pantanal**, T7255267, 125 km from Corumbá near the Campo Grande road at **Fazenda Santa Clara**. Working cattle ranch, very comfortable, easy access by bus. Reservations from all agencies in Corumbá; full board, US$190 per person for 3 days/2 nights, minimum 2 persons, good food, drinks not included. Excursions on horse (US$8), car (US$20) and boat (US$20), guides included, canoes, simple fishing gear, motor boats for rent. Try bargaining for reduced rates in the offseason.

LL **Hotel Fazenda Xaraes**, T2316777, T011-8704600, Rio Abobral, 130 km from Corumbá. Full board, luxurious with a pool, restaurant and horse and boat trips.

L **Pousada Do Castelo**, 3 hrs by boat from Corumbá, T2313736, F2315040. One of the least visited with plenty of birdlife. Comfortable accommodation.

AL-A **Fazenda Leque**, Roberto Kassan (contact through R América 262, Corumbá, T2311598). Take mosquito coils, unlimited use of horses and boats, on small lake behind the farm, good food, plenty of wildlife to be seen.

A **Fazenda Santa Blanca**, on the Rio Paraguai, 15 mins by boat south of Porto Esperança (where the BR-262 crosses the Rio Paraguai). Full board, good kayak excursions, horse riding, information from R 15 de Novembro 659, Corumbá, T2311460, or **Flins Travel** (Walter Zoss), R do Acre 92, 6th floor, 602, CEP 20081, Rio de Janeiro, T021-2538588/0195 or **Safari Fotográfico**, R Frei Mariano 502, Corumbá, T2315797.

Photo and fishing safaris

The going rate for a 3-day camping photo safari by jeep is US$100 per person for 4-6 people; US$110-120 per person for 4 days. Fishing trips in luxurious floating hotels for 8 (eg **Tuiuiú** T/F2312052 and **Cabexy II** T2314683, from **Pantanal Tours**, Corumbá – must be booked in advance), US$1,200-2,000 per day, minimum 5 days.

LL **Pesqueiro da Odila**, on the Rio Paraguai, reservations T2315623, from Belo Horizonte T031-2214003. Full board. Specializes in fishing, reached from Corumbá by road. Restaurant.

LL **Porto Morrinho**, on the Rio Paraguai, T2311360. Full board. Specializes in fishing, reached from Corumbá by road. Pool.

LL **Pesqueiro Paraiso dos Dourados**, 72 km from Corumbá, Rios Paraguai and Miranda, Corumbá office at R Antônio João, T/F2313021. Full board. Fishing and tours.
L **Pantanal Park**, 20 mins by boat from Porto Esperança (where the BR-262 crosses the Rio Paraguai), T0182-215332. Specializes in fishing. Restaurant.
L **Pesqueiro Cabana do Lontra**, including meals, T3834532, 180 km from Aquidauana on the Corumbá Rd. Specializes in fishing.
L **Pesqueiro Tarumã**, Rio Paraguai, 65 km from Corumbá, Corumbá office at RM Cavassa 109, T/F2314771. Full board. Specializes in fishing.

Poconé *p652, phone code 065*
E ***Hotel Joá***, just south of town. Basic with en suite baths.

Pixaim *p652, phone code 065*
L **Pantanal Mato Grosso**, T/F065- 3219445, Modern cabins, 35 rooms for 3-6 people, with full board, fan, clean, hot water (also family-size apartments with a/c), good home-grown food, in radio contact with office on R Barão de Melgaço in Cuiabá, camping possible, boat rental with driver US$30 per hr.
AL **Hotel-Fazenda Cabanas do Pantanal**, 142 km from Cuiabá, 50 km from Poconé by the Rio Pixaim, on the northern edge of the Pantanal. 10 chalet bedrooms with bath, restaurant, boat trips (few in dry season), horse riding, fishing, helpful proprietor and staff, everything except boat trips and bar drinks included in price. Book through **Confiança**, Cuiabá, T6234141, see p673.
A **Pousada Pixaim**, On the opposite bank of the Rio Pixaim from **Pantanal Mato Grosso**, T37211899. Full board (meals also available separately), built on stilts, rooms with a/c or fan, mosquito-netted windows, hot water, electricity 24 hrs, pleasant setting, boat trips – US$30 per hr with driver, camping possible, US$10 per tent or free if you eat in the restaurant. Recommended. Reservations through **Focus Tours**, see p).
A **Pousada Araras**, Km 32 on Transpantaneira, T6822800, F6821260. 14 rooms with bath, a pool, good food, homemade *cachaça* and a walkway over a private patch of swampland filled with capybara and cayman.
A **Pouso Alegre**, Km 40 on Transpantaneira, www.pousoalegre.com.br, alegre.p@terra.com.br. A working farm with simple accommodation but some of the best tours in the Pantanal. Overflowing with wildlife. Wonderful staff.
A **Pousada Pantaneira**, about 45 km from Pixaim. Reservations through **Focus Tours** see p26), full board, 7 rooms with 2-3 bunk beds each, bath, simple, owned and operated by *pantaneiros*.
L **Sapé Pantanal Lodge**, Caixa Postal 2241 – CEP 78020-970, Cuiabá, T3911442, www.sapehotel.com.br. Rustic wooden accommodation on stilts aimed at luxury market. A complete programme includes road transport from Cuiabá airport to Barão de Melgaço (wet season) or Porto Cercado (dry season), with onward river transportation (around 1½ hrs). Specializes in sport fishing. Outboard powered boats with experienced guides at guests' disposal; optional trekking and horse riding in dry season, paddling in wet. English, French, Spanish spoken. Closed 20 Dec-31 Jan.

Barão de Melgaço and around *p653, phone code 065*
L **Pousada Passárgada**, Sia Mariana. Programmes from 3 days up, full board, boat, car and trekking expeditions, transport from Barão de Melgaço, owner speaks English, French and German, food excellent. Highly recommended, closed Dec-Feb; reservations T37131128, in Barão de Melgaço on riverside, through **Nature Safaris**, Av Marechal Rondon, Barão de Melgaço, or São Paulo T011-2845434, or Rio de Janeiro T021-2873390. Much cheaper if booked direct with the owner, Maré Sigaud, Mato Grosso, CEP 786807, **Pousada Passárgada**, Barão de Melgaço.
B **Pousada do Barão**, Sia Mariana. 6 chalets with bath, swimming pool, first class, boat and trekking expeditions.
B **Restaurant Flamingo**, Sia Mariana. Simple food, rooms, camping with permission, popular with fishermen.
C **Barão Tour Hotel**, in the town. Apartments with a/c, restaurant, boat trips and excursions (Cuiabá T3221568). There are a handful of cheaper options near the waterfront.

Eating

Campo Grande *p644, map p645, phone code 067*
Local specialities include *caldo de piranha* (soup), *chipa* (Paraguayan cheese bread), sold on the streets, delicious when hot, and the local liqueur, *pequi com caju*, which contains *cachaça*.

Cantina Romana, R da Paz, 237. Established over 20 years, Italian and traditional cuisine, good atmosphere.

Casa Colonial, Av Afonso Pena, 3997, on corner with R Paraíba. Traditional, regional and Italian cuisine, with large dessert menu.

Dom Leon, Av Afonso Pena, 1907. Large *churrascaria*, pizzeria and restaurant, self-service lunch. Live music evenings.

Largo de Ouro, R 14 de Julho, 1345. No-frills, large pizzeria and restaurant that does a brisk trade.

Morada dos Bais, Av Noroeste, 5140, corner with Afonso Pena, behind tourist office. Pretty courtyard, Brazilian and Italian dishes.

Shopping Campo Grande has a wide selection of restaurants in this category, including **Pão de Queijo Express**. There are also lots of good, cheap options around the bus station and Praça Ari Coelho, and several self-service restaurants on R Candido Mariano, Nos 1660-2512.

Bonito *p646, phone code 067*

Comida Caseira, Luís da Costa Leite and Santana do Paraíso. Good local food, lunch and dinner, not open Sun afternoon.

Tapera, Pilad Rebuá 480, T2551110. Good, home-grown vegetables, breakfast, lunch, pizzas, meat and fish dishes, opens 1900 for evening meal.

Verdo-Frutos e Sucos Naturais, Pilad Rebuá 1853, next to **Bonanza** car park. Good juices and fruits. Cheap.

Corumbá *p647, map p648, phone code 067*
Local specialities include *peixadas corum-baenses*, a variety of fish dishes prepared with the catch of the day; as well as ice cream, liquor and sweets made of *bocaiúva*, a small yellow palm fruit, in season Sep-Feb.

There are a range of decent restaurants in R Frei Mariano including a number of *churrascarias* and pasta restaurants. You'll find plenty of simple but good fish restaurant bars on the waterfront.

Almanara, R America 964, next to **Hotel Nacional**. Reasonable Arabic food.

Peixaria do Lulú, R Antônio João 410. Good fish and local dishes.

Viva Bella, R Arthur Mangabeira 1, behind **Clube Corumbaense**, 1 block from Gen Rondon. Fish, meat, pizza, home- made pastas, drinks, magnificent views over the river especially at sunset, live music Wed-Sat, opens at 1700, good food and atmosphere. Recommended.

Barril de Ouro, 556 R Frei Mariano. One of the better per-kilo lunchtime restaurants.

Churrascaria Rodéio, 13 de Junho 760. Decent *churrascaria* and excellent lunchtime buffet. Recommended.

Portal do Pantanal. On the waterfront. Good fish.

Bars and clubs

Campo Grande *p644, map p645, phone code 067*

Morada dos Bais, see above. Restaurant and *choperia*, live music in courtyard nightly from 2030, free.

Opera Rock Café, R Candido Mariano, corner with Joao Crippa.

Stones Blues Bar, Av Ceara, 2124, T3264957. Large venue with Rock 'n' Roll, Fri is main night.

Tango, R Candido Mariano, 2181. Techno club, US$7.

Topogigio, Alfonso, corner with Julho. *Lanchonete*/bar, popular, basic, local hang-out, open 24 hrs.

Festivals

Corumbá *p647, map p648, phone code 067*

2 Feb Festa de Nossa Senhora da Candelária, Corumbá's patron saint, all offices and shops are closed.

24 Jun Festa do Arraial do Banho de São João, fireworks, parades, traditional food stands, processions and the main event, the bathing of the image of the saint in the Rio Paraguai.

21 Sep Corumbá's anniversary, includes a Pantanal **fishing festival** held on the eve.

Shopping

Campo Grande *p644, map p645, phone code 067*
Local native crafts, including ceramics, tapestry and jewellery, are of good quality. A local speciality is *Os Bugres da Conceição*, squat wooden statues covered in moulded wax. Very good selections are found at:
Casa do Artesão, Av Calógeras 2050, on corner with Av Afonso Pena, in a historic building. Mon-Fri 0800-2000, Sat 0800-1200.
Barroarte, Av Afonso Pena, 4329.
Arte do Pantanal, Av Afonso Pena 1743.

There is a market (*Feira Livre*) on Wed and Sat. **Shopping Campo Grande**, Av Afonso Pena, is the largest shopping mall in the city, on its eastern edge.

Corumbá *p647, map p648, phone code 067*
Shops tend to open early and close by 1700.
Casa do Artesão, R Dom Aquino 405, in a converted prison. Mon-Fri 0800-1200, 1400-1800, Sat 0800-1200, good selection of handicrafts and a small bookshop, friendly staff but high prices.
CorumbArte, Av Gen. Rondon 1011, for good silk-screen T-shirts with Pantanal motifs.
Livraria Corumbaense, R Delamaré 1080, for state maps.
Ohara, Dom Aquino 621, corner Antônio João. Supermarket.
Frutal, R 13 de Junho 538. Open 0800-2000. Supermarket.

Activities and tours

One-day river trips are available on boats with a capacity of 80 passengers, US$25 half-day; US$50 full day, including transfers and hot fish meal. Smaller boats US$15 per person for 3 hrs. Tickets at travel agents and by port. Boats may be hired, with fishing tackle and guide, at the port (US$100 per day, up to 3 people, in season only). Cattle boats will on occasion take passengers on their round trips to farms in the Pantanal, but take your own food – it is not always possible to disembark. Ask at Bacia da Prata, 10 mins out of Corumbá on the Ladário bus. Some of Corumbá's many agencies are listed below. Tours out of Corumbá are of 3-4 days, costing up to US$100 (includes all food, accommodation and transport). Travel is in the back of a pick-up (good for seeing animals), maximum 6 people. Accommodation is in a hammock under a palm thatch on a *fazenda*. Food can be good and guides provide bottled mineral water (make sure enough is carried). If you want flushing toilets, showers or luxury cabins, approach an agency. Some guides go to *fazendas* without permission, have unreliable vehicles, or are inadequately equipped, so try to check their credentials. Agencies sometimes subcontract to guides over whom they have no control. If you are asked to pay half the money directly to the guide, check him out as if he were independent and ask to see his equipment. Guides will generally not make the trip with fewer than 5 people, so if you have not already formed a group, stay in touch with several guides (most important during Mar-Oct, when fewer tourists are around). We list below those guides who have received positive reports from most travellers.

Campo Grande *p644, map p645, phone code 067*

Tour operators
Asteco Turismo, R 13 de Maio, 3192, T3210077, www.ecotur-ms.com.br/com/as. 2-day (1-night) trips from US$60-75, depending on activities and hotel.
Ecological Expeditions, R Joaquim Nabuco 185, T3210505, www.pantanaltrekking.com. Attached to youth hostel at bus station. Budget camping trips (sleeping bag needed) for 3, 4 or 5 days ending in Corumba. First day travel by public bus free. Recommended.
Impacto, R Padre João Crippa 496, sala 101, T3251333, www.impactotur.com.br. Helpful Pantanal and Bonito tour operators established over 10 years. Prices vary according to standard of accommodation; a wide range is offered. 2-day packages for 2 people from US$190-600. Transfers and insurance included.
Open Door, R Barão do Rio Branca 314, T3218303, www.opendoortur.com.br. Specialists for the Pantanal and Amazon.
Time Tour, R Joaquim Murtinho 386, T3122500, F37212879, American Express representative.
Vox Tour, R Cândido Mariano 1777, T3843335, F37258663, English and Spanish spoken, very helpful.

Bonito and around *p646, phone code 067*

Tour operators and guides

Hapakany Tour, Pilad Rebuá 628, T/F2551315. Jason and Murilo, for all local tours. Diving trips US$40 per day. Recommended.

Henrique Ruas, T/F2551430, see **Ilha do Padre**, p654, or **Pousada Olho d'Água**, p654. For information in English and French.

Sérgio Ferreira Gonzales, R Col Pilad Rebuá 628, T2551315 (opposite **Bonanza**), is an authority on the caves. Recommended.

TapeTur, next to *Tapera* restaurant. Guides, information, tours, clothes shop. Also recommended.

Aquidauana *p647, phone code 067*

Buriti Viagens e Turismo, R Manoel Paes de Barros 720, 79200, T2412718, F2412719.

Cordon Turismo, R Búzios, CEP 79003-101, T3841483. Organizes fishing trips into the Pantanal.

Lucarelli Turismo, R Manoel Paes de Barros 552, T2413410.

Panbratur, R Estevão Alves Correa 586, T/F2413494. Tour operator in southern Pantanal.

Corumbá *p647, map p648, phone code 067*

Corumbatur, Antônio M Coelho 852, T/F2311532. Combined Pantanal/Bonito tours.

JMS Turismo, RM Cavassa 215, T2315235. Small fishing boats for rent US$60 per day for 3 persons, minivans for trips to Bolivia US$10 per person.

Mutum Turismo, R Frei Mariano 17, T2311818, F2313027. For airline tickets, tours, helpful.

Pantanal Service, R Dom Aquino 700, T/F2315998. Fishing and photo trips by boat, agents for **Hotel Porto Vitória Régia**.

Pantanal Tours/Sairú Turismo, RM Cavassa 61A, T2315410, F2313130. Fishing trips, agents for *Cabexy I* and *II*, luxurious floating hotels, day trips on land, US$55 per person, river trips US$15 per person per 3 hrs. Recommended.

Pérola do Pantanal, RM Cavassa 255, T2311470, F2316585. River and land tours, good 1-day river tour with *Lancha Pérola*.

Taimã, R Antônio M Coelho 786, T/F2312179, river trips, flights over Pantanal, airline tickets.

Pantur, R América 969, T2312000, F2316006. Tours, agents for **Hotel Fazenda Xaraés** in Nhecolândia.

Receptivo Pantanal, R Frei Mariano 502, T2315795. Helpful, 1-day tour US$50, 3-day US$100, 4-day US$130.

Colibri Pantanal Safari, in **Hotel City**, R Cabral 1031, T2313934. Swiss owner Claudine.

Green Track, R Delamaré s/n, between Tiradentes e Antônio João, T2312258, greentk@brasinet.com.br. Recommended for those who like trips without game fishing.

Katu, R Dom Aquino 220, T2311987. Recommended.

Saldanha Tour, R Porto Carreiro 896B, T23116891, saldanha_v@hotmail.com. Owner Eliane is very helpful to travellers.

Tucan Tours, R Delamaré 576, T2313569. Guide William Chaparro speaks English, Hebrew and Spanish, contact him at w_chaparro@hotmail.com.

There are many other guides not listed here, some have similar names, lots have received criticisms (some repeatedly) from correspondents.

Transport

Campo Grande *p644, map p645, phone code 067*

Air

Airport, Av Duque de Caxias, 7 km, T37632444. Flights to Cuiabá, Londrina and São Paulo. City bus No 158, 'Popular' stops outside airport. Taxi to airport, US$6. It is safe to spend the night at the airport. Banco do Brasil at airport exchanges dollars. Post office, fax and phones in same office.

Airline offices TAM, airport, T3630000. **Varig**, R Barão do Rio Branco 1356, Centro, T3254070, at airport, T3634870. **Vasp**, R Cândido Mariano, 1837, T3218277.

Bus

The rodoviária is in the block bounded by R Barão do Rio Branco, R Vasconcelos Fernandes, R Dom Aquino and R Joaquim Nabuco, T3831678, all offices on 2nd floor. At the R Vasconcelos Fernandes end are town buses, at the R Joaquim Nabuco end state and interstate buses. 8 blocks' walk from Praça República. Taxi to rodoviária, US$3.60. There are shops, *lanchonetes* and a cinema, US$1.25.

Campo Grande has good connections throughout the country. To **São Paulo**, US$32, 14 hrs, 9 buses daily, first at 0800, last at 2400, 3 *leito* buses US$40. To **Cuiabá**, US$20, 10 hrs, 12 buses daily, *leito* at 2100 and 2200, US$50. To **Brasília**, US$32, 23 hrs at 1000 and 2000. To **Goiânia**, São Luís company 1100, 2000, 15 hrs on 1900 service, US$32, others 24 hrs, US$1 cheaper. **Rio de Janeiro**, US$54, 21 hrs, 4 buses daily, *leito* at 1540, US$64. To **Belo Horizonte**, 22 hrs, US$35. To **Corumbá**, with **Andorinha**, 8 daily from 0600, 6 hrs, US$12. Campo Grande-Corumbá buses connect with those from Rio and São Paulo, similarly those from Corumbá through to Rio and São Paulo. Good connections to all major cities. To **Ponta Porã**, 5 hrs, 9 buses daily, US$10. To **Dourados**, 4 hrs, 14 daily (Queiroz), US$7. Beyond Dourados is Mundo Novo, from where buses go to Ponta Porã (0530) and to Porto Frajelli (very frequent). From Mundo Novo, ferries for cars and passengers go to Guaíra for US$1. Twice daily direct service to **Foz do Iguaçu** (17 hrs) with **Integração**, 1600, US$27; same company goes to Cascavel, US$20. To **Pedro Juan Caballero** (Paraguay), **del Amambay** company, 0600, US$8.50. **Amambay** goes every Sun morning to **Asunción**.

Car

Car hire Localiza, Av Afonso Pena 318, T3828786, at airport, T0800- 992000. **Hertz**, Av Afonso Pena 2620, T3835331. **Locagrande**, Av Afonso Pena 466, T37213282, F37213282. **Unidas**, Av Afonso Pena 829, T3845626, F3846115, at airport, T3632145.

Ponta Porã *p645, phone code 067*

Air Services to São Paulo, Dourados, Marília and Presidente Prudente.

Bus To **Campo Grande**, 9 a day from 0100-2130, 4 hrs, US$5. The rodoviária is 3 km out on the Dourados road ('São Domingos' bus, taxi US$3).

Bonito *p646, phone code 067*

Bus Rodoviária is on the edge of town. From **Campo Grande**, US$11, 5½-6 hrs, 1500, returns at 0530. Bus uses MS-345, with a stop at Autoposto Santa Cruz, Km 60, all types of fuel, food and drinks available. For **Aquidauana**, take Campo Grande bus. Bus Corumbá-Miranda-Bonito-Jardim-Ponta Porã, Mon-Sat, leaves either end at 0600, arriving Bonito 1230 for Ponta Porã, 1300 for Miranda; can change in Jardim (1400 for 1700 bus) or Miranda (better connections) for Campo Grande; fare Corumbá-Bonito US$12.50. Also connections on 1230 route in Bela Vista at 2000 for **Asunción** and **Col Oviedo**. Ticket office opens at 1200.

Car hire Yes Rent a Car, R Senador Filinto Muller 656, T2551702. **Unidas**, R das Flores s/n, T2551066.

Jardim *p647*

Bus To **Campo Grande**, 0530, 1200, 1600 and 2 in middle of night, US$10, 5 hrs. To **Aquidauana**, 0730 and 1700. To **Bonito** (US$3.50), **Miranda** and **Corumbá** at 1130. To **Dourados**, 0600. To **Bela Vista** (Paraguayan border) 0200, 1030, 1500, 1930. To **Porto Murtinho**, 0010 and 1530 (bus from Bonito connects). To **Ponta Porã**, 0600, 1500; Sun only at 1400 to **São Paulo**.

Miranda *p647, phone code 067*
Bus **Campo Grande**-Miranda, 7 a day with Expresso Mato Grosso, US$8.50, and others.

Car The Campo Grande-Corumbá road crosses the Rio Miranda bridge (2 service stations before it), then carries on, mostly paved, to cross the Rio Paraguai.

Corumbá *p647, map p648, phone code 067*
Air
Airport, R Santos Dumont, 3 km, T2313322. Flights to Campo Grande, Cuiabá, Londrina and São Paulo (via Campo Grande). Check whether flights between Corumbá and Santa Cruz, Bolivia, are still operating. If in doubt, fly from Puerto Suárez in Bolivia. No public transport from airport to town, you have to take a taxi.

Airline offices TAM, T2317299. Visa, T2311745.

Boat
The *Acurí*, a luxury vessel, sails between **Cáceres** and Corumbá, once a week, US$600 including return by air. (See p675, under Cáceres.)

Bus
The rodoviária is on R Porto Carreiro at the south end of R Tiradentes, next to the railway station. City bus to rodoviária from Praça da República, US$0.80. Taxis are extortionate, but moto-taxis charge only US$0.65.

Andorinha services to all points east. To **Campo Grande**, 7 hrs, US$22, 13 buses daily, between 0630 and 2400, interesting journey ('an excursion in itself') – take an early bus to see plentiful wildlife, connections from Campo Grande to all parts of Brazil. To **São Paulo** direct, 22 hrs, US$50, 1100 and 1500, confirm bus times in advance as these change (T2312033). To **Rio de Janeiro** direct, 30 hrs, US$55, daily 1100. **Cruzeiro do Sul** operates the route south to the Paraguayan border. To **Ponta Porã**, 12 hrs, US$20, via Bonito (6 hrs, US$12.50) and Jardim (9 hrs, US$15), Mon-Sat at 0600; ticket office open 0500-0600 only, at other times call T2312383.

Car
Car hire Localiza, airport and R Cabral 2064, T2316000. **Unidas**, R Frei Mariano 633, T/F2313124.

Poconé *p652, phone code 065*
Bus From **Cuiabá** US$7.50 by TUT, T3224985, 6 a day between 0600 and 1900.

Car Poconé has a 24-hr gas station with all types of fuel, but closed on Sun.

Directory

Campo Grande *p644, map p645, phone code 067*
Banks ATMs at **Banco do Brasil**, 13 de Maio and Av Afonso Pena, open 1100-1600, commission US$10 for cash, US$20 for TCs, regardless of amount exchanged, and Bradesco, 13 de Maio and Av Afonso Pena. HSBC, R 13 de Maio, 2837, ATM. **Banco 24 horas**, R Maracaju, on corner with 13 de Junho. Also at R Dom Aquino and Joaquim Nabuco. **Overcash Câmbio**, R Rui Barbosa, 2750, Mon-Fri 1000-1600. **Embassies and consulates** Bolivia, R João Pedro de Souza 798, T3822190. **Paraguay**, R 26 Agosto 384, T3244934. **Internet** Cyber Café Iris, Av Alfonso Pena 1975. **Medical services** Yellow and dengue fevers are both present in Mato Grosso do Sul. There is a clinic at the railway station, but it's not very hygienic, best to get your immunizations at home. **Post office** On corner of R Dom Aquino and Av Calógeras 2309, and Barão do Rio Branco on corner of Ernesto Geisel, both locations offer fax service, US$2.10 per page within Brazil. **Telephone** Telems, R 13 de Maio e R 15 de Novembro, daily 0600-2200.

Ponta Porã *p645, phone code 067*
Banks Banco do Brasil changes TCs. Many in the centre of town (but on Sun change money in hotels).

Bonito *p646, phone code 067*
Banks Banco do Brasil, R Luís da Costa Leite 2279 for Visa. There are no **Banco 24 Horas**. Some hoteliers and taxi drivers may change money. **Post office** R Col Pilad Rebuá. **Telephone** Santana do Paraíso.

Jardim *p647, phone code 067*
Banks Elia, a taxi driver, will change money.

Corumbá *p647, map p648, phone code 067*
Banks Banco do Brasil, R 13 de Junho 914, ATM. HSBC, R Delamare 1068, ATM. HSBC, R

Delamare 1068, ATM. Câmbio Mattos, R 15 de Novembro 140, Mon-Fri 0800-1700, good rates for US$ cash, US$5 commission on TCs. Câmbio Rau, R 15 de Novembro 212, Mon-Fri 0800-1700, Sat 0900-1200, cash only, good rates. **Embassies and consulates** Bolivia, R Antônio Maria Coelho 881, T2315605, Mon-Fri 0700-1100, 1500-1730. A fee is charged to citizens of those countries which require a visa. A yellow fever vaccination certificate is also required. **Internet** Pantanalnet, R América 430, Centro, US$2.50 per hr. **Laundry** Apae, R 13 de Junho 1377, same day service. **Post office** Main office at R Delamaré 708, fax service. Branch at R 15 de Novembro 229. **Telephone** R Dom Aquino 951, near Praça da Independência, daily 0700-2200. To phone Quijarro/Puerto Suárez, Bolivia, it costs slightly more than a local call, dial 214 + the Bolivian number.

Mato Grosso and Tocantins

Mato Grosso, immediatley to the north of Matto Grosso do Sul, shares much of the Pantanal with that state and has equally well-developed tourism facilities. Although there are just as many opportunities for seeing wildlife, trips to the Pantanal near the state capital, Cuiabá, tend to be less backpackery than those leaving from Corumbá in Mato Grosso do Sul. Rather than camping, there is accommodation in rustic but comfortable ranch houses. The state also has abundant though rapidly depleting areas of Amazon forest and Alto Floresta, in the north, has an excellent birding and wildlife lodge. The much-vaunted Chapada dos Guimarães hills near Cuiabá have reasonable hill walking and birdwatching although the natural landscape has been greatly damaged by farming and development.

Although the area that is now Mato Grosso and Mato Grosso do Sul was demarcated as Spanish territory, it was the Portuguese Aleixo Garcia who was the first to explore it in 1525. Jesuits and then bandeirantes *entered the Mato Grosso for their different ends during the 17th and early 18th centuries, and when gold was discovered near Cuiabá a new influx of explorers began. Mato Grosso became a captaincy in 1748 and the borders between Portuguese and Spanish territories were resolved in the following years. Throughout the 19th century, after the decline in gold extraction, the province's economy stagnated and its population dwindled. This trend was reversed when the rubber boom brought immigrants in the early 20th century to the north of the region. Getúlio Vargas's 'March to the West' in the 1940s brought added development, accompanied first by the splitting off of Rondônia and, some 80 years later, by the formation of Mato Grosso do Sul in 1977.*

Tocantins is not yet on the tourist track, other than for its share in the fishing bonanza around the Ilha do Bananal, one of the largest river islands in the world. There are some opportunities for ecotourism in the Parque Nacional do Araguaia (park entrance is at Santa Terezinha in Mato Grosso, see page 669). However, most visitors to this state are likely to be only passing through on the long road journey between Brasília and Belém. ▸▸ *For Sleeping, Eating and other listings, see pages 670-676.*

Cuiabá

→ *Phone code: 065. Colour map 3, A2. Population: 470,000.*

An important starting point for trips into the Pantanal, Cuiabá is the state capital and a visibly wealthy city. It has a number of leafy *praças* and is known as the Cidade Verde (green city). Situated on the Rio Cuiabá, an upper tributary of the Rio Paraguai, it is in fact two cities: Cuiabá on the east bank of the river and Várzea Grande, where the airport is located, on the west. It is very hot; the coolest months for a visit are June, July and August in the dry season.

Ins and outs

Getting there Flights arrive at the airport in Várzea Grande. There are buses and taxis to the centre. Take any white **Tuiuiú** bus, name written on the side, in front of the airport to Avenida Tenente Coronel Duarte. Interstate buses arrive at the rodoviária north of the centre. Town buses (see below) stop at the entrance. ▸▸ *See also Transport, page 675.*

> *The port area is best avoided, even in daylight.*

Getting around Many bus routes have stops in the vicinity of Praça Ipiranga. Bus 501 or 505 (Universidade) to University museums and zoo (ask for 'Teatro') goes from Avenida Tenente Coronel Duarte by Praça Bispo Dom José, a triangular park just east of Praça Ipiranga. To rodoviária, no 202 from Rua Joaquim Murtinho behind the cathedral, about 20 minutes.

Tourist offices Secretaria de Desenvolvimento do Turismo, **Sedtur** ⓘ *Praça da República 131, next to the post office building, T/F6249060, Mon-Fri 0700-1800*. Good maps, friendly, helpful regarding general information, hotels and car hire, some English and Spanish spoken. Also very helpful in settling disputes with local tour companies. **Ramis Bucair** ⓘ *R Pedro Celestino 280*, is good for detailed maps of the region.

Sights

Cuiabá has an imposing government palace and other fine buildings around the green **Praça da República**. On the square is the **cathedral**, with a plain, imposing exterior, two clock towers and, inside, coloured glass mosaic windows and doors. Behind the altar is a huge mosaic of Christ in majesty, with smaller mosaics in side chapels. Beside the cathedral is another leafy square, **Praça Alencastro**.

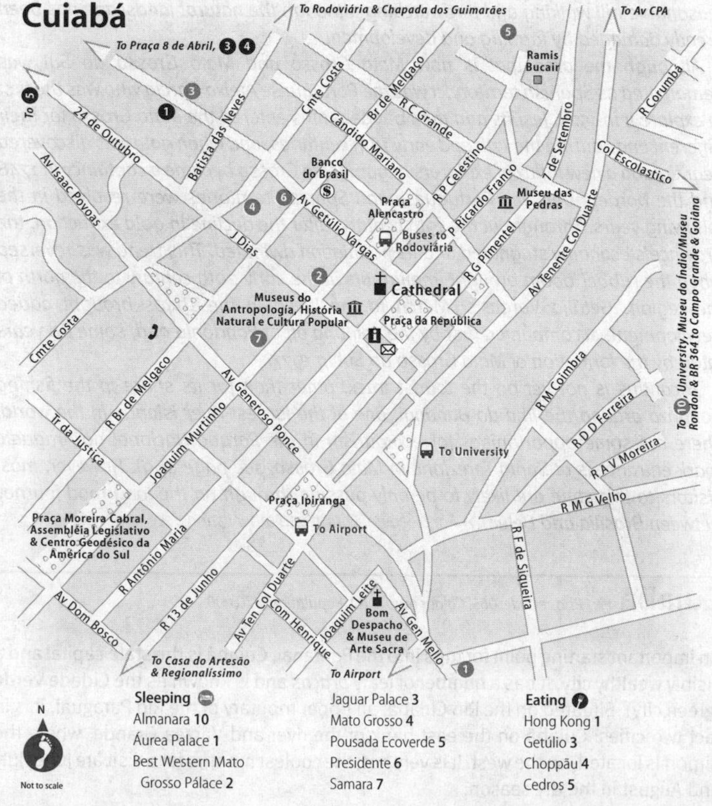

Guaraná

"In order to obtain *guaraná*, their favourite stimulant, the inhabitants of Cuiabá organized canoe expeditions lasting more than six months along the Tapajoz. The paste is compressed into a sausage shape and grated on the horny tongue of a *pirarucu* fish, which is kept in a deerskin pouch. These details are significant, because it is believed that the use of a metal grater or a different kind of leather pouch would cause the precious substance to lose its peculiar properties."

Thus Claude Levi-Strauss described the harvesting of *guaraná* in the 1930s. Today you can still buy the *pirarucu* tongues in markets in the Amazon region.

Guaraná is prepared into a paste from the fruit of the creeper *Paullinia sorbilis*. The Maué people of Cuiabá used to be the only ones to appreciate it as a stimulant but it is now world renowned. *Guaraná* is everywhere, consumed as a soft drink in such quantities that it rivals Coca-Cola in popularity, with massive advertising campaigns and sponsorship deals to boost sales. Taken in its powder form and made into an infusion, it is a natural pick-me-up with similar properties to coffee. It is even available now as a sports drink, consumed by fitness-crazy Brazilians after a long game of *futevolei* on the beach or a session in the gym. You can also buy it in chewing-gum form in Europe, where it is popular as an energizer after a hard night's clubbing.

Whether or not it really works is another matter; but it remains a popular drink today and some people combine it with alcohol to make cocktails with a distinctly Brazilian flavour. But to enjoy the real effects, perhaps you need to use the same method as the Cuiabans did in the 1930s.

On **Praça Ipiranga**, at the junction of Avenidas Isaac Póvoas and Tenente Coronel Duarte, a few blocks southwest of the central squares, there are market stalls and an iron bandstand from Huddersfield in the UK, or Hamburg in Germany, depending on which story you believe.

On a hill beyond the square is the extraordinary church of **Bom Despacho**, built in the style of Notre Dame. It is best viewed from afar as it is sadly run down and not open to visitors. In front of the Assembléia Legislativa, Praça Moreira Cabral, is a point marking the **Geogedesic Centre of South America** (see also under Chapada dos Guimarães, below).

The rather dusty **Museus de Antropologia, História Natural e Cultura Popular** ⓘ *Fundação Cultural de Mato Grosso, Praça da República 151, Mon-Fri 0800-1730, US$0.50*, are worth a look. There are interesting historical photos, a contemporary art gallery, indigenous weapons, archaeological finds and pottery. The section of stuffed wildlife from the Pantanal is disturbingly compelling.

At the entrance to Universidade de Mato Grosso by the swimming pool, 10 minutes by bus from the centre, is the small **Museu do Índio/Museu Rondon** with well-displayed exhibits. Carrying on along the road through the campus, signed on the left before a right turn in the road, is the **Zoológico** ⓘ *Tue-Sun 0800-1100, 1330-1700, free*. The *jacaré*, capybara, tortoise and tapir pen can be seen at any time, but are best in the early morning or late afternoon. It also has coatis, otters, emu, monkeys, peccaries, birds, etc. Opposite the zoo is the theatre.

The **Águas Quentes** hot springs, 86 km (9 km south of the BR-163, 77 km east of Cuiabá), can be visited.

Monsoons

Although the Brazilian Monsoons (*monções*) were given their name in association with the weather, they were not, in fact, rainy seasons. They were, like their predecessors, the *bandeirantes*, another breed of pioneer who expanded Brazil's frontiers. In Portuguese, the *monções* were winds that determined the seasons which were best for sailing. When the term reached Brazil it was applied to the rainy seasons, rather than the winds, because the rain determined whether journeys into the interior could be made. From about the second decade of the 18th century, the expeditions that penetrated into the far west of Brazil took to the rivers, rather than going on foot. The people who made these trips acquired the name Monsoons.

Taking the Rio Tietê out of São Paulo, the Monsoons sailed to the heart of the continent. Their main destination was the gold mines of Senhor Bom Jesus do Cuiabá and the alluvial deposits on the Rio Coxipó-Mirim. Various routes were tried until the best way was found of getting from the Tietê to Mato Grosso. When this route had been established convoys would set out once a year to trade with the miners and bring the gold back to São Paulo. It was not an easy journey. Everything, including animals, had to be taken to Cuiabá on boats that were modelled on the Indian *pirogue*, using navigation which was also borrowed from the indigenous people. The remoteness of Cuiabá was only matched by the legends of vast wealth which drew the Monsoons to the area. It took longer to get from São Paulo to Cuiabá than it did from Rio de Janeiro to Lisbon; the journey time was about five months, as long as it took to get from Lisbon to India. Many lives and a great deal of merchandise was lost on the rivers, but this remained the only form of communication between São Paulo and Mato Grosso until the third decade of the 19th century. In the same way that the *bandeirantes* extended Brazil's boundaries and established Portuguese rule over the south and southwest, so the Monsoons brought the far west into Portuguese possession.

Taken from Sérgio Buarque de Holanda, 'The Monsoons', chapter 10 of Richard M Morse (ed), *The Bandeirantes*.

Chapada dos Guimarães

→ *Phone code: 065. Colour map 3, A2. Population: 13,500.*

Although greatly damaged by agriculture and careless tourism development, the Chapada dos Guimarães is one of the oldest plateaus on earth and one of the most scenic areas of Brazil. It retains much of the mystery attributed to it for centuries, and is still often described as as a mystical, energizing place. In the 1920s, Colonel Fawcett was told of many strange things hidden in its depths, and an unusual local magnetic force that reduces the speed of cars has been documented. The whole area is studded with waterfalls and caves, the birdwatching is very good and mammals, such as puma, giant river otter and black-tailed marmoset, live here.

The pleasant town of Chapada dos Guimarães, 68 km northeast of Cuiabá, is a base for many beautiful excursions in this area. It has the oldest church in the Mato Grosso, **Nossa Senhora de Santana** (1779), a bizarre blending of Portuguese and French baroque styles, and a huge springwater public **swimming pool** ⓘ *R Dr Pem Gomes, behind the town.*

Formerly the centre of an important diamond-prospecting region, today Chapada is a popular place for Cuiabanos to escape the heat of the city on weekends and holidays. It is a full-day excursion from Cuiabá with many birds, butterflies and flora on the way. The **Festival de Inverno** is held in the last week of July, and **Carnival** is very busy. Accommodation is scarce and expensive at these times. The **tourist office** ⓘ *R Quinco Caldas 100, near the praça*, provides a useful map of the region and organizes tours.

The Chapada is an immense geological formation rising to 700 m, with rich forests, curiously eroded rocks and many lovely grottoes, peaks and waterfalls. A **national park** has been established in the area just west of the town, where the Salgadeira tourist centre offers bathing, camping and a restaurant close to the **Salgadeira waterfall**. The beautiful 85-m **Véu da Noiva** waterfall (Bridal Veil), 12 km before the town near Buriti (well signposted, ask bus from Cuiabá to let you off), is reached either by a short route, or a long route through forest. Other sights include the **Mutuca** beauty spot, **Rio Claro**, the viewpoint over the breathtaking 80-m-deep **Portão do Inferno** (Hell's Gate), and the falls of **Cachoeirinha** (small restaurant), and **Andorinhas**.

About 8 km east of town is the **Mirante do Ponto Geodésico**, a monument officially marking the Geodesic Centre of South America. It overlooks a great canyon with views of the surrounding plains, the Pantanal and Cuiabá's skyline on the horizon.

Some 45 km east of Chapada is the access for **Caverna do Francês** or Caverna Aroe Jari ('dwelling of the souls' in the Bororo language), a sandstone cave over 1 km long, the second largest in Brazil. It is a 2-km walk to the cave which contains **Lagoa Azul**, a lake with crystalline blue water. Latest reports say visitors are not allowed to go to the lake. Take your own torch/flashlight (guides' lamps are sometimes weak). A guide is only really necessary to get through *fazenda* property to the cave.

Other excursions are to the **Cidade de Pedra** rock formations, 25 km from town along the road to the diamond prospecting town of Água Fria. Nearby is a 300-m wall formed by the Rio Claro. About 60 km from town are the **Pingador** and **Bom Jardim** archaeological sites – caverns with petroglyphs dating back some 4,000 years.

Hiring a car in Cuiabá is the most convenient way to see many of the scattered attractions, although access to several of them is via rough dirt roads which may deteriorate in the rainy season; drive carefully as the area is prone to dense fog. Hitchhiking from Chapada town to the national park is feasible on weekends and holidays, but expect crowds at the swimming holes.

Cáceres → *Phone code: 065. Colour map 3, A1. Population: 86,000.*

Cáceres is a very hot but clean and hospitable town on the banks of the Rio Paraguai, 200 km west of Cuiabá. It has many well-maintained 19th-century buildings painted in pastel colours and is known for its many bicycles. Until 1960, Cáceres used to have regular boat traffic; today it is limited to a few tour boats and pleasure craft. River trips from Cuiabá to Corumbá are very difficult since boats on the Cuiabá river are few and irregular, but you can sometimes get to Corumbá by river from here.

The **Museu de Cáceres** ⓘ *R Antônio Maria by Praça Major João Carlos*, is a small local history museum. Exhibits include indigenous funerary urns. The main square, **Praça Barão de Rio Branco**, has one of the original border markers from the Treaty of Tordesillas, which divided South America between Spain and Portugal; it is pleasant and shady during the day. In the evenings between November and March the trees are packed with thousands of chirping swallows (*andorinhas*), beware of droppings. The square is full bars, restaurants and ice-cream parlours and comes to life at night.

The beautiful **Serra da Mangabeira** is about 15 km east crossed by the road from Cuiabá; the town is also at the edge of the Pantanal. Vitória Regia lilies can be seen north of town, just across the bridge over the Rio Paraguai along the BR-174. There are archaeological sites on the river's edge north of the city.

Border with Bolivia

An unpaved road runs from Cáceres to the Bolivian border at San Matías. **Brazilian immigration** ⓘ *R Col Farías, Cáceres*, for exit and entry formalities; when closed (for example Sunday), go to **Polícia Federal** ⓘ *Av Rubens de Medarca 909*.

Into Brazil Leaving Bolivia, get your passport stamped at Bolivian immigration (1000-1200, 1500-1700), then get your passport stamped at Cáceres; nowhere in between, but there are three luggage checks for drugs.

Into Bolivia San Matías is a busy little town with hotels, restaurants and a bank. The next major town in Bolivia is San Ignacio de Velasco, which is on the road route to Santa Cruz de la Sierra. There are buses from San Matías to San Ignacio and San Ignacio to Santa Cruz; also flights. For more details, see *Footprint Bolivia* or the *South American Handbook*.

North of Cuiabá

Alta Floresta → *Phone code: 065. Colour map 1, B4. Population: 71,500.*

The road due north from Cuiabá to Santarém (1,777 km) has been completed and is all-weather, through **Sinop**, with a branch west to Colíder and Alta Floresta (daily bus from Cuiabá with *São Luís* at 2000, 12 hours, US$45). Outside Alta Floresta, the **Cristalino Jungle Lodge** on the Cristalino river is a basic lodge, with shared baths, in a very rich and well-preserved section of southern Amazônia. Many rare mammals are found here (including the short-eared dog), as well as five species of macaw, harpy eagle and a few hundred other bird species. **Anaconda Operators** in Cuiabá run tours to **Cristalino Jungle Lodge**, US$100 per person per day plus airfare (US$200 return).

When travelling north of Cuiabá, yellow fever vaccination is obligatory; if you do not have a certificate, you will be (re)vaccinated.

East of Cuiabá

São Félix do Araguaia → *Colour map 1, C5, Population: 14,500.*

This is a large town with a high population of Carajás Indians; a depot of their handicrafts is between the pizzeria and **Mini Hotel** (good view but not recommended) on Avenida Araguaia. There is some infrastructure for fishing. Mosquito nets are highly recommended since there is a high incidence of malaria.

Many river trips are available for fishing or to see wildlife. Juracy Lopes, a very experienced guide, can be contacted through **Hotel Xavante**; he has many friends, including the chief and council, in Santa Isabela (see below). Morning or afternoon trips to the village or to see wildlife cost US$15 for two; longer trips can be made to the meeting of the waters with the Rio das Mortes, or spending a night in the jungle sleeping in hammocks. **Icuryala** is recommended (ToXX62-2239518, Goiâna), excellent food, drink, and service, US$100 per day, independent visitors also welcomed. *Fazenda* owners may invite you as their guest – do not abuse this, and remember to take a gift.

Tocantins

Palmas → *Phone code: 063. Colour map 1, B5. Population: 130,000.*

Brazil's newest city is an interesting detour on the highway between Belém (1,282 km away) and Brasília (973 km). There are waterfalls in the surrounding mountains and beaches on the River Tocantins, which make for a relaxing stop on an otherwise long drive. The BR-153 is close to the city and provides a good road connection, both north to Maranhão, Pará, and south to Goiás.

The new capital is a planned city, with wide, long avenues and modern public buildings. Construction began in 1989 and the state government was transferred a year later. The choice of name was partly influenced by the large numbers of palm trees in the area. The city is divided into four sectors: **Noroeste** (NO), **Nordeste** (NE), **Sudoeste** (SO) and **Sudeste** (SE). Like Brasília, the different blocks are named by use and location. Some address abbreviations are **Área Central** (AC), **Área de Comércio** and **Serviço Urbano** (ACSU) and **Área Administrativa** (AA).

The **Palácio Araguaia** ⓘ *Praça dos Girassóis*, is an impressive modern building. The **Catedral de Nossa Senhora das Mercês** was built by the Dominicans from rocks from the Rio Tocantins. The **Parque da Cidade** is south of the city centre. See also **Praça do Bosque** ⓘ *ARSE 51*. The **Cachoeira de Taquarussu**, located near the city in the Serra do Carmos, is worth visiting. **Tourist office** ⓘ *ACSE 1, Conj 4, Lt 10, Edif Jamir Resende, 2nd floor, CEP 77100-100, T2151481, F2151494*.

Excursions from Palmas

About 8 km away at Canelas is **Praia da Graciosa**, a river beach on the Rio Tocantins. Popular at weekends, there are floating bars, sports courts, shows, and camping is possible. Along the Estrada do Rio Negro at Km 18 is the **Reserva Ecológica do Lajeado**, 1,500 sq km of *caatinga*, *cerrado* and humid forest. The Morro do Governador, near the entrance, offers good views. Further along the road at Km 36 there are trails along the river **Brejo da Lagoa** until the 60 m-high **Cachoeira do Roncador** and other waterfalls are reached.

Ilha do Bananal

→ *Colour map 1, B5. Phone code 062.*

ⓘ *Permission to visit the park should be obtained in advance from Ibama, Rua 219, No 95, Setor Universitário, 74605-800 Goiânia.*

Bananal is the world's largest river island and is located on the northeastern border of Mato Grosso. The island is formed by a division in the south of the Rio Araguaia and is approximately 320 km long. The entire island was originally a national park (called **Parque Nacional Araguaia**), which was then cut in half and later further reduced to its current size of 562,312 ha. The island and park are subject to seasonal flooding and contain several permanent lakes. The island, and especially the park, form one of the more spectacular wildlife areas on the continent, in many ways similar to the Pantanal. The vegetation is a transition zone between the

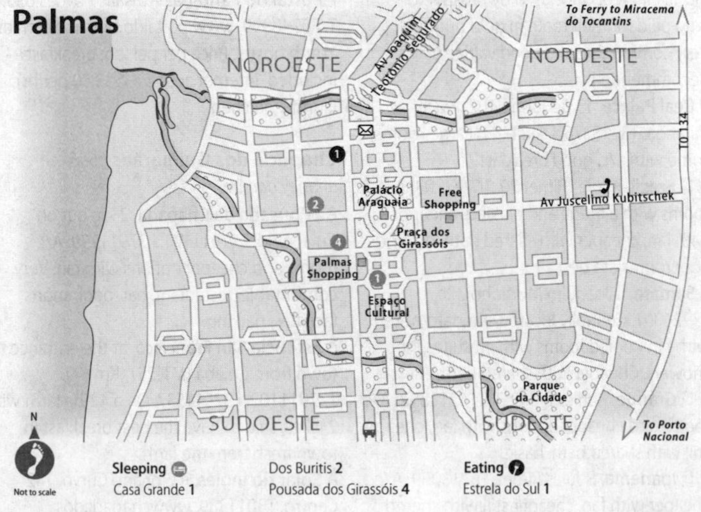

cerrado (woody savannah) and Amazon forests, with gallery forests along the many waterways. There are several marshlands throughout the island.

The fauna is also transitional. More than 300 bird species are found here, including the hoatzin, hyacinthine macaw, harpy eagle and black-fronted piping guan. The giant anteater, maned wolf, bush dog, giant otter, jaguar, puma, marsh deer, pampas deer, American tapir, yellow anaconda and South American river turtle also occur here. The island is flooded most of the year, with the prime visiting (dry) season being from June to early October, when the beaches are exposed. Unfortunately, the infrastructure for tourism aside from fishing expeditions (the island is a premier spot for big fish) is very limited.

Access to the park is through the small but pleasant town of **Santa Teresinha**, which is north of São Félix do Araguaia (see page 668) and is the gateway to the park.

Sleeping

Cuiabá *p663, map p664, phone code 065*

L **Áurea Palace**, Gen Mello 63, T/F3223377. Pleasant rooms, restaurant, pool, good.

L **Best Western Mato Grosso Palace**, Joaquim Murtinho 170, T6247747, F3212386. Central, sedate and very popular, restaurant but no pool.

L **Hotel Águas Quentes** at Águas Quentes spring, 86 km from Cuiabá, see p665. All meals included, reservations through **Hotel** Mato Grosso Palace, T6246637. The waters fill pools of 42°C and 36°C; no buses go there, arrange transport through hotel.

A **Skala Palace**, R Jules Rimet 26, T3224347. Restaurant, smart lobby, front rooms, noisy.

B **Jaguar Palace**, Av G Vargas 600, T6244404, jaguarph@zaz.com.br. New extension with rooms around large pool. Older rooms are large with sofas and wonderfully old-fashioned. Once used by prospectors who paid for their room in gold nuggets. Very comfortable and good value. Recommended.

B **Real Palace**, 13 de Junho 102, Praça Ipiranga, T3215375, F6111141. Large rooms, some with a/c, good breakfast.

B-D **Brazil**, R Jules Rimet 20, T6212703. A/c rooms with a fridge and parking, cheaper with fan, cheaper with shared bath, ground floor rooms are best.

C **Samara**, R Joaquim Murtinho 270, T3226001. Centrally located standard hotel with fan-cooled rooms with en suites, hot showers. Cheaper with shared bath.

C-D **Grande**, R Jules Rimet 30, T6213852. A/c rooms and cheaper options with fan, cheaper still with shared bath, basic.

C-D **Ipanema**, R Jules Rimet, T6213069. A/c, cheaper with fan, cheaper still with shared bath, good value, good breakfast. Recommended.

C-D **Mato Grosso**, R Comandante Costa 2522, T6147777, bwmt@zaz.com.br. Excellent value, friendly, central, with a/c rooms, cheaper with fan. Good restaurant. Recommended.

E **Pousada Ecoverde**, R Pedro Celestino 391, T6241386. 5 rooms with shared bath around a courtyard in colonial family house. **F** for singles. Kitchen, laundry facilities and lovely walled garden with hammocks. Highly recommended.

E-F **Presidente**, Barão de Melgaço and Av G Vargas 155A, T6241386. On a busy central corner with lots of traffic outside. A/c rooms. Popular and cheap but very badly run down. Cheaper with fan, fridge, cheaper still with shared bath.

F **Portal do Pantanal**, Av Isaac Póvoas 655, T/F6248999, www.portaldopantanal.com.br. Youth hostel. Price per person, breakfast included, internet access (US$2.50 per hr), laundry, kitchen.

Chapada dos Guimarães *p666, phone code 065*

AL **Pousada da Chapada**, 2 km out on Cuiabá Rd, T37911171, F37911299. A/c rooms and cheaper options with fan. Very comfortable, restaurant, bar, pool, sports facilities, parking.

A **Estância San Francisco**, at the entrance to town from Cuiabá (MT-251, Km 61), T37911102, F37911537. On a 42-ha farm with 2 lakes, said to have the best breakfast in town fresh from the farm.

A **Solar do Inglês**, R Cipriano Curvo, 142 Centro, T3011389, wwwchapadados guimaraes.com.br. In an old converted house near town centre with 6 rooms each with private bathroom, TV and frigobar. Garden, swimming pool and sauna. Breakfast and afternoon tea included.

B **Turismo**, R Fernando Corrêa 1065, a block from rodoviária, T37911176, F37911383. A/c rooms with a fridge, cheaper with fan, restaurant, breakfast and lunch excellent, very popular, German-run; Ralf Goebel, the owner, is very helpful in arranging excursions.

B-C **Rio's Hotel**, R Tiradentes 333, T37911126. A/c rooms with a fridge, cheaper with fan, cheaper with shared bath, good breakfast. Recommended.

C **Pousada Bom Jardim**, Praça Bispo Dom Wunibaldo, T37911244. Comfortable fan-cooled rooms with parking and good breakfast. Recommended.

D **São José**, R Vereador José de Souza 50, T37911152. Fan-cooled rooms. Cheaper with a shared bath and no fan, hot showers, basic, good, owner Mário sometimes runs excursions.

Camping

Aldeia Velha, in the Aldeia Velha neighbourhood at the entrance to town from Cuiabá, T3227178 (Cuiabá). Fenced area with bath, hot shower, some shade, guard.

Salgadeira, unorganized camping 16 km from town at the tourist centre, watch your belongings.

Cáceres *p667, phone code 065*

A **Caiçaras**, R dos Operários 745 corner R Gen Osório, T2233187, F2232692. Modern town hotel with a/c rooms and cheaper options without a fridge.

A **Ipanema**, R Gen Osório 540, T2231177, F2231743. Simple town hotel with a/c rooms, a garage and a good restaurant.

A **Turbo**, Av São Luiz 1399 by BR 070, T2231984. One of the town's most luxurious hotels with a restaurant and pool.

B **Fênix**, R dos Operários 600, T2231027, F2212243. Comfortable a/c rooms.

B-D **Rio**, Praça Major João Carlos 61, T2233387, F2233084. A range of rooms – the cheapest with no a/c and shared bathrooms.

C-D **Charm**, Col José Dulce 405, T/F2234949. A/c and fan-cooled rooms, with or without a shared bath.

D **Rio Doce**, R 7 de Setembro. A/c rooms and cheaper options with shared bath, good value.

D-E **União**, R 7 de Setembro 340. Fan-cooled rooms, cheaper with shared bath, basic but good value.

Alta Floresta *p668, phone code 065*

L **Cristalino Jungle Lodge**, (Administration), Av Perimetral Oeste 2001, T5127100, www.cristalinolodge.com.br. A beautifully situated and well-run lodge. Trips from the lodge include canoe and snorkel trips on clear water rivers and the usual gammut of caimun spotting and piranha fishing. Also more adventurous options such as rapelling and canyoning. Superb birdwatching, the lodge also has a lookout with a view over the canopy.

B **Floresta Amazônica**, Av Perimetral Oeste 2001, T5213601, F5213801. In the park with lovely views, pool, sports, all facilities.

C **Italian Palace**, Av das Figueras 493, Sinop, T5312109. With a restaurant, bar, sauna.

C **Pirâmide Palace**, Av do Aeroporto 445, T5212400. A/c rooms with fridges, restaurant.

D **Grande Hotel Coroados**, R F 1 118, T5213022. Not too well kept but has a/c, pool and bar.

São Félix do Araguaia *p668, phone code 062*

C **Xavante**, Av Severiano Neves 391, T5221305. A/c, frigobar, excellent breakfast, delicious *cajá* juice, Sr e Sra Carvalho are very hospitable. Recommended.

Palmas *p668, map p668, phone code 063*

A **Dos Buritis**, Av JK (ACNO 1), Conj 1, Lt 4/6, T/F2153666. Business hotel with a restaurant and pool.

A **Rio do Sono**, Av Teotônio Segurado (ACSUSO 10), Conj 1, Lt 10, T/F2151733. Business hotel with a restaurant and pool and convention centre.

B **Pousada dos Girassóis**, ACSO 1, Conj 3, Lt 43, T2151187, www.pousadadosgirassois.com.br. A/c rooms in a hotel with a restaurant, pool and sauna.

C **Casa Grande**, Av Joaquim Teotônio Segurado, 201-s (ACSUSO 20), Conj 1, Lt 1, T/F2151813. A/c rooms in a basic hotel with a restaurant and pool.

Ilha do Bananal *p669, phone code 062*
A **Bananal**, Praça Tarcila Braga 106, CEP 78395 (Mato Grosso), with full board. There is only room for 10; reserve well in advance, either by mail, allowing several months for the mail to get through, or by phoning the town's telephone operator, asking the hotel to call you back and hoping that you hear from them.

There is some simple accommodation for scientists at the park, which can sometimes be reserved at the address above or from the national parks department in Brasília. Bring your own food and bedding, and the severely underpaid but dedicated staff would appreciate any extra food or financial help, although it will not be solicited. A boat to the park can be lined up at the **Hotel** Bananal.

Eating

Cuiabá *p663, map p664, phone code 065*
Lots of restaurants in the very centre are only open for lunch. On Av CPA are many good restaurants and small snack bars. There are several cheap restaurants and *lanchonetes* on R Jules Rimet across from the rodoviária.

TTT **Getúlio**, Av Getúlio Vargas 1147. Somewhat pretentious a/c restaurant with pavement tables, dance floor and sushi bar. Excellent food, with meat specialities and pizza.

TT **Cedros**, Praça 8 de Abril 750, Goiabeiras. Fan-cooled, friendly and very popular place offering wide selection of Arabic food, including *tabule* salad and 'pizza' made with pitta bread. Delivery service, T6249134. Recommended.

TT **China in Box**, Av Lavapés 70, T6238400. Chinese food with a Brazilian twist, also fish dishes and desserts. Open daily for lunch and dinner; delivery service.

TT **Chopão**, Praça 8 de Abril. Established 30 years, this local institution and is buzzing at any time of the day or night. Go for huge portions of delicious food or just for *chopp* served by fatherly waiters. The house dish of chicken soup promises to give diners drinking strength in the early hours and is a meal in itself. Warmly recommended.

TT **Lig-China**, R Presidente Marques 960. Sophisticated, a/c restaurant with standard Chinese and Japanese menu. Open daily for lunch and dinner until 2400, also delivers.

T **Hong Kong**, Av G Vargas 647, opposite Jaguar Hotel. Self-service Chinese, good quality for price.

T **Lanchonete Presidente**, next to hotel of same name. Hamburgers and sandwiches. Open late for eating, drinking and TV watching.

Chapada dos Guimarães *p666, phone code 065*
Pequi is a regional palm fruit with a deadly spiky interior used to season many foods; *arroz com pequi* is a popular local rice and chicken dish.

TT **Nivios**, Praça Dom Wunibaldo 631. The best place for good regional food.

TT **O Mestrinho**, R Quinco Caldas 119. Meat, regional dishes, *rodízio* at weekends.

TT **Trapiche**, R Cipriano Curvo 580. Pizza, drinks, regional dishes.

T **Choppada** (**O Chopp da Chapada**), R Cipriano Curvo near *praça*. Drinks and meals, regional dishes, live music at weekends.

T **Fogão da Roça**, Praça Dom Wunibaldo 488. Good *comida mineira* in generous portions. Recommended.

Cáceres *p667, phone code 065*

TT **Corimbá**, R 15 de Novembro s/n, on riverfront. Fish dishes and general Brazilian food.

T **Gulla's**, R Cel José Dulce 250. Buffet by kg, good quality and variety. Recommended.

T **Panela de Barro**, R Frei Ambrósio 34, near rodoviária. Brazilian home cooking (*comida caseira*) with the usual gamut of meat dishes with squash, rice, black beans and salads.

São Félix do Araguaia *p668, phone code 062*

TT **Pizzeria Cantinho da Peixada** , Av Araguaia, next to the Texaco station, overlooking the river. The owner, Klaus, rents rooms, **E** , better than hotels, T5221320, he also arranges fishing trips. Recommended.

Palmas *p668, map p669, phone code 063*

T **Bela Palma**, ACSUSO 40, Conj 1, Lt 19. Bog-standard pizzas and Italian food.

T **Estrela do Sul**, ACNO II, Conj 4, Lt 38/42. *Churrasco* serving at lunchtime only.

Bars and clubs

Palmas p668, map p669, phone code 063

Boulevard, Av JK.
Carangueijos Bar, Av Joaquim Teotônio Segurado (ACSUSE 40).
Consulado, ACSO 1.
Phaeton Club, ACSE 1, Conj 3, Lt 19.

Entertainment

Cuiabá *p663, map p664, phone code 065*

Cuiabá is quite lively at night, bars with live music and dance on Av CPA. **Bierhaus**, Isaac Póvoas 1200. Large, sophisticated, semi open-air bar/restaurant with music.
Chopão, see Eating above.
Tucano Av CPA, bar/restaurant specializing in pizza with beautiful view, open daily 1800-2300. 4 cinemas in town.

Cáceres *p667, phone code 065, phone code 065*

Traditional folkloric dance groups: **Chalana**, T2233317, and **Tradição**, T2234505, perform shows at different locations.

Palmas *p668, map p669, phone code 063*

Cinema
Cine Blue, Palmas Shopping, ACSU 10.

Theatre
Espaço Cultural, Av Teotônio Segurado, also has a library.

Festivals

Cáceres *p667, phone code 065*

Mid-Mar Piranha Festival.
Mid-Sep International Fishing Festival. There's also an annual cattle fair.

Shopping

Cuiabá *p663, map p664, phone code 065*

Handicrafts in wood, straw, netting, leather, skins, Pequi liquor, crystallized *caju* fruit, compressed *guaraná* fruit, indigenous crafts on sale at the airport, rodoviária, craft shops in centre, and daily market, Praça da República, interesting. The **Casa de Artesão**, Praça do Expedicionário 315, T3210603, sells all types of local crafts in a restored building. Fish and vegetable market, picturesque, at the riverside.

Chapada dos Guimarães *p666, phone code 065*

Crafts, indigenous artefacts, sweets and locally made honey from **Casa de Artes e Artesanato Mato Grossense**, Praça Dom Wunibaldo. Regional sweets from **Doceria Olho de Sogra**, Praça Dom Wunibaldo 21. João Eloy de Souza Neves is a local artist, his paintings, music and history about Chapada (*Chapada dos Guimarães da descoberta aos dias atuais*) are on sale at **Pousada Bom Jardim**.

Cáceres *p667, phone code 065*

Náutica Turismo, R Bom Jardim 119A, by the waterfront, for fishing/camping supplies and boat repairs.

Palmas *p668, map p669, phone code 063*

Free Shopping, Av JK.
Palm Blue Shopping, ACSUSO 10, Conj 2.

Activities and tours

Cuiabá *p663, map p664, phone code 065*

Tour operators
You should expect to pay US$60-90 per person per day for tours in the Pantanal. All these agencies arrange trips to the Pantanal. For longer or special programmes, book in advance.
Ametur, R Joaquim Murtinho 242, T/F6241000. Very helpful, good for air tickets.
Anaconda, R Mal Deodoro 2142, T6244142, www.anacondapantanal.com.br. Upmarket agency providing airport transfers, all meals and high standard of accommodation both in Cuiabá before departure and on trips. Pantanal 1-, 2- and 3-day tours to Pantanal, day tour to Chapada dos Guimarães or Águas Quentes, Amazon trips to Alta Floresta/Rio Cristalino region (price does not include airfare). Recommended.
Ararauna Turismo Ecológica, Av Lavapes 500, loja 07, T/F6261067. Adriana Coningham is highly recommended.
Confiança, R Cândido Mariano 434, T6234141. Very helpful travel agency, tours to Pantanal US$75 per day.
Focus Tours (see p26) specializes in tours in this part of the Pantanal and, starting from Cuiabá, to the southern Amazon, with bases at Alta Floresta and on the Rio Cristalino (see page 668).

Pantanal Explorers, Av Gov Ponce de Arruda 670, T6822800, sightseeing, fishing trips for 4-5 days by boat.

Recommended guides

In alphabetical order: all guides work freelance for other companies as well as employing other guides for trips when busy. Most guides await incoming flights at the airport; compare prices and services in town if you don't wish to commit yourself at the airport. The tourist office recommends guides; this is not normal practice and their advice is not necessarily impartial.

Sérgio Alves, F6235258, speaks English, birdwatching and other tours.

Paulo Boute, R Getúlio Vargas 64, Várzea Grande, near airport, T6862231, speaks Portuguese, English, French, also sells Pantanal publications.

Marcus W Kramm, R Franklin Cassiano da Silva 63, Cuiabá, T/F3218982, speaks Portuguese, English, German.

Djalma dos Santos Moraes, R Arnaldo Addor 15, Coophamil, 78080 Cuiabá, T/F6251457, US$100 per person per day.

Laércio Sá, FaunaTour, T99837475 (mob; 24 hrs), faunatur@zaz.com.br. Very well informed, helpful and knowledgable about environmental issues. Speaks English, Spanish and Italian, 2 and 3-day Pantanal tours (including transport, accommodation in farmhouses rather than hotels, meals, trekking, horse riding, boat trips, fishing). Has own car, can arrange longer tours and camping (Aug-Oct) on request, also excursions to Chapada dos Guimarães. Warmly recommended.

Joel Souza, owner of Pousada Ecoverde, see p670. Can be contacted at Av Getúlio Vargas 155A, next to Hotel Presidente, T6461852, T99567229 (mob; 24 hrs). Speaks English, German and Italian, enthusiastic, very helpful, checklists for flora and fauna provided. Tends to employ other guides, rather than take trips himself.

Chapada dos Guimarães *p666, phone code 065*

Tour operators and guides

Travel agencies in Chapada and Cuiabá offer expensive tours to all the sights.

José Paulino dos Santos is a guide working with the tourist office (Mon-Fri 0800-1100, 1300-1800, T37911245).

Ecoturismo Cultural, Praça Dom Wunibaldo 464, T/F37911393. Recommended tours with Jorge Belfort Mattos who speaks English and knows the area well; several 4-to 6-hr itineraries from US$20-50 per person (minimum 4 people or prices increase).

AC Tour, R Tiradentes 28, T37911122. Cássio Martins often waits at the rodoviária. 4-hr tours are about US$20 per person, minimum 5 persons; 7-8-hr tours, US$25 per person, minimum 5; horse riding day tour, US$25 per person, minimum 2; an 8-to 10-km hike with a guide, US$20 per person, minimum 2; bicycle tour with guide, US$20 per person, minimum 2. Tours from Cuiabá cost US$35-40 per person.

Cáceres *p667, phone code 065*

Tour operators

Cáceres, Av Getúlio Vargas 408, T2231428, F2232440. Fishing and photo tours to Pantanal, boat rentals, Cláudio Duarte helpful guide.

Pantanal Tour, R Col Fária 180, T2231200. Boat rentals, fishing trips, tickets.

Vereda Turismo, R Padre Cassemiro 1121, T2234360. Tours, boat rentals, fishing.

Palmas *p668, map p669, phone code 063*

Gym

Academia Corpus, ACNO 1 Conj 2, Lt 11.

Tour operators

Batista Pereira Turismo, ACSO 1, Conj 1, Lt 41, T2151228, F2151414.

Ilha do Bananal *p669, phone code 062*

Focus Tours, see Specialist tour operators p23, will arrange tours.

Bananal can be visited from São Félix do Araguaia – see above (with permission from Funai in the town) by crossing the river to the Carajá village of **Santa Isabela de Morra** and asking to see the chief, who can tell you the history of the tribe. The island can be crossed from São Félix to **São Miguel de Araguaia** by taking an 8-hr trip (contact the Bar Beira). From São Miguel, a 5-hr bus trip brings you to **Porangatu** (D **Hotel Mauriti**, shower, restaurant) on the Belém-Brasília highway.

Transport

Cuiabá *p663, map p664, phone code 065*
See also Ins and outs, page 664.

Air
Airport in Várzea Grande, T6822213. Flights to Alta Floresta, Brasília, Campo Grande, Itaituba, Rio Branco, Santarém, São Paulo and Sinop. Taxi from centre US$15, 'Aeroporto' bus from Praça Ipiranga, US$0.50. ATMs outside include Banco do Brasil for Visa, MasterCard, Cirrus and Maestro. There is a post office and a **Sedtur** office (not always open). **Airline offices** Varig, R 15 de Novembro 230, Bairro Porto, T6246498, at airport T6821140.

Bus
Rodoviária, R Jules Rimet, Bairro Alvorada, north of the centre.

Comfortable buses (toilets) to **Campo Grande**, 10 hrs, US$20, 12 buses daily, *leito* at 2000 and 2100, US$50. To **Goiânia**, 14 hrs, US$25. Direct to **Brasília**, 24 hrs, US$30, *leito* US$60. To **Porto Velho**, 6 União Cascavel buses a day, US$45, 21 hrs. **Andorinha** 1700 bus São Paulo-Cuiabá connects with Porto Velho service. Several to **São Paulo**, eg Motta, US$42. To **Rio de Janeiro**, US$57. To **Barra do Garças**, **Xavante** 0800, 1300 and 2030, US$15, also **Barattur**. Connections to all major cities.

Car
Car hire Unidas, airport, T6824062. **Localiza**, Av Dom Bosco 965, T6247979, and at airport, T6827900. **Atlântida**, Av Isaac Póvoas, T6230700. Cheapest at **Vitória**, R Comandante Costa 1350, T3227122.

Chapada dos Guimarães *p666, phone code 065*
Bus 7 departures daily to and from **Cuiabá** (**Rubi**, 0700-1900, last back to Cuiabá 1800), 1½ hrs, US$.75.

Cáceres *p667, phone code 065*
Air
Aeroporto de Nível Internacional, Av Tancredo Neves, T2236474.

Bus
Colibrí/União Cascavel buses **Cuiabá**-Cáceres, US$9, many daily between 0630-2400 from rodoviária, Terminal da Japonesa, T2241261 (book in advance, very crowded), 3½ hrs. Cáceres-**Porto Velho**, US$32.

Boat
The **Acurí**, a luxury tourist vessel, sails to **Corumbá**, 1-week cruise including return by air from Corumbá to Cuiabá, US$600 per person. For information on other boat sailings, ask at the Capitânia dos Portos, on the corner of the main square at the waterfront. If possible phone in advance to Cáceres, Posto Arrunda, T2211707, to find out if any boats are going. Also Portobrás on the outskirts at the waterfront (T2211728). In the dry season there are practically no boats to Corumbá. At the waterfront you can hire a boat for a day trip, US$5 per person per hr, minimum 3 people; on holidays and some weekends there are organized day trips on the river.

Car
Car hire Localiza, R Padre Cassimiro 630, T2231330, and at airport. **Locavel**, Av São Luiz, 300, T2231212.

Border with Bolivia *p668*
Bus The bus fare from Cáceres to **San Matías** is US$9 with **Transical-Velásquez**, Mon-Sat at 0630 and 1500, Sun 1500 only (return at same times). **Trans Bolivia** to San Matías, Sun, Mon, Fri at 1500, Tue, Wed, Thu and Sat at 0700.

São Félix do Araguaia *p668, phone code 062*
Air Access to both São Félix and Santa Teresinha (see below) is by **Brasil Central/TAM** flights, unreliable and, as the planes hold just 15 passengers, it is common to get delayed up to several days. There is a daily **Votec** flight from São Felix to Belém, stopping at Redenção, Tucumã and many other places.

Bus Rodoviária is 3 km from the centre and waterfront, taxi US$5. To **Barra do Garças** at 0500, arrive 2300, or 1730, arrive 1100 next day. Also to **Tucumã**, 6-8 hrs, and to **São José do Xingu**, 10 hrs. No buses to Marabá.

Palmas *p668, map p669, phone code 063*
Air airport, Av NS 5, 2 km from centre, T2161237. Air taxi with **Nobre**, T2161500, and **Aeropalmas** T2161716. Flights to Belém

and Brasília, Goiânia, São Paulo.

Airline offices Passeredo, T2161515. TAM, T2193777.

Boat Port is 9 km from the city. Ferries to **Miracema do Tocantins** and **Paraíso do Tocantins**.

Bus City buses are plentiful and cheap. Bus station, ACSUSO 40, T2161603.

Car hire Hertz, Av Nossa Senhora, T9781900, F2151900, and **Localiza**, ACSO 11-CL02, lote 41, Setor comercial, T2161104, and airport. **Rentauto**, Av Joaquim Teotônio Segurado (ASUSE10), Conj 1, Lt 6, T/F2151900.

Taxi Rádio Táxi Palmas, T2132001.

Directory

Cuiabá *p663, map p664, phone code 065*

Banks Banco do Brasil, Av Getúlio Vargas and R Barão de Melgaço, commission US$10 for cash, US$20 per transaction for TCs, very slow for TCs, but best rates. **Incomep Câmbio**, R Gen Neves 155, good rates. The following travel agents or gold dealers change cash only at poor rates (generally open Mon-Fri): **Mattos-Tur**, R Cândido Mariano 465. **Goldmine**, R Cândido Mariano 400, 0800-1600. **Ourominas**, R Cândido Mariano 401, 0800-1700, may change on Sat 0800-1200 if cash is available, enquire first, T6249400. **Portobello**, R Comandante Costa 555, 0900-1600. It is difficult to get cash advances on credit cards especially MasterCard; for Visa try **Banco do Brasil** or **Bradesco**. **Embassies and consulates** Bolivia, Av Isaac Póvoas 117, T6235094, Mon-Fri. **Internet** Copy Grafic, Praça Alencastro 32, fax and email, English spoken, friendly. **Post office** Main branch at Praça da República, fax service. **Telephone** R Barão de Melgaço 3209, 0700-2200, also at rodoviária, 0600-2130, international service.

Chapada dos Guimarães *p666, phone code 065*

Post office R Fernando Corrêa 848.

Cáceres *p667, phone code 065*

Banks Banco do Brasil, R Cel Jose Dulcé, 234. HSBC, R Cel Jose Dulcé, 145. **Casa de Câmbio Mattos**, Comte Bauduino 180, next to main *praça*, changes cash and TCs at good rates. **Telephone** Praça Barão de Rio Branco.

Palmas *p668, map p669, phone code 065*

Medical services Dentist Dra Adriana Helena Toledo, ACNO 11, Conj 3, Lt 38, T2153201. **Hospitals** Hospital Regional, Praça ARSE, Quadra 51, Setor Serrano, T2141424. **Post office** Av Joaquim Teotônio Segurado. **Telephone** Av JK.

Background

Footprint features

History

Indigenous peoples

Origins

Some 50,000 years ago the very first peoples crossed the temporary land bridge spanning Asia and America at the Bering Straits, and began a long migration southwards. They were hunters and foragers, following in the path of huge herds of now extinct animals, such as mammoth, giant ground sloth and antecedents of the camel and horse. The first signs that these people had reached South America date from around 10,000 BC, if not earlier.

Archaeological evidence

The major handicap to archaeological study of tropical cultures is that most material remains deteriorate rapidly in the warm, humid climate. Since the majority of cultural output from Brazil was in perishable materials such as feathers, wood, baskets, and woven textiles, little has survived for modern analysis. Nevertheless various artefacts have been discovered from all around the country, showing considerable artistic and technical skill. The pottery produced by the early peoples was of a high standard, admired by the European newcomers. Early ceramics have been found on Marajó island at the mouth of the Amazon. The Annatuba culture lived here in small villages by the river. Most of their ceramics found are round bowls and jars, including huge funeral urns, which have been dated with increasing antiquity; the earliest to date from around 980 BC. Textile production was done mainly with hand-twisted fibres, using both cotton and bast. Objects found in Rio Grande do Sul, dating from 550 AD or earlier, included twined bags, nets and ropes. Most of the textiles found throughout Brazil were simple everyday items, such as hammocks and straps, with little decoration.

It was assumed that the first humans in Brazil came down to the lowlands from the Andean chain, following the east-facing river valleys. Some very early human remains have been found in central and northeastern Brazil. In Pedra Furada, in northeast Brazil, a rock-shelter named Toca do Boquirão has yielded evidence of human presence from as early as 47,000 years ago. The cave, in a region well-known for its prehistoric rock paintings, is known to have been occupied by hunters about 8,000 years ago. However, French archaeologist Niède Guidon made deeper probings into the ground and claims to have found evidence of much earlier human presence. Guidon's claims sparked hot debate among other experts, many of whom argued that what she described as ash from fireplaces was in fact the remains of naturally caused forest fires. In Monte Alegre, opposite Santarém on the Rio Solimões, recent studies have been made of human remains, dating from around 15,000 BC, also predating previous estimates. These, and other controversial claims from sites in the mid-Amazon region, have led some experts to raise the theory of original human migration from across the Pacific Ocean. However, In general, the most authoritative studies of the first humans in Brazil point to a much later date, between 10,000-5,000 BC.

Amazon lifestyles

The earliest people soon learnt to make the most of the rich food sources provided by the rivers of the Amazon basin. They lived on the flood plain and caught fish and manatee (large sea mammals, related to dugongs and sea cows) using spears thrown from the shore, or from dugout canoes. Besides fishing, these people also cultivated manioc and other plants found on the forest floor. They kept turtles in corrals at the river's edge, for eating and also for making tools and other artefacts from their shells.

Their nomadic lifestyle was carefully planned, and they followed planting and harvesting seasons in accordance with the periodic rising and falling river levels. Worship of multiple deities, of the weather and agriculture for instance, was very important. The gods had to be appeased to prevent excessive fluctuations in the level of the river. At first, as hunters and gatherers, they built simple, temporary houses out of tree trunks and palm leaves, and slept in hammocks made from plant fibres. Clothing was equally simple; a large, ankle-length tunic called a *kushma* was the main garment worn. Although this may sound impractical wear for people living in a warm, humid climate, the *kushma* provided much-needed protection against biting insects. Compensating for their plain clothing, the people painted their bodies and wore colourful jewellery, such as feather head-dresses. Little has remained of the perishable adornments, but cylindrical and flat ceramic stamps have been found throughout Amazônia, which may have been used to apply ink designs onto the face and other parts of the body, still common today among ethnic groups.

Migration to the coast

Around 7000-4000 BC a climatic change increased the temperature throughout the south of Brazil, drawing people down from the inland *planalto* region to the coasts, and leading to an upsurge in population here. These coastal inhabitants lived on shellfish collected from the water's edge, as evidenced by *sambaquis* (huge shell mounds), discovered on the coast. In rare cases they also fed on whales that had probably been beached, but they did not go far out to sea to fish. Some of the *sambaquis* found measure up to 25 m high; many of them also served as dwellings, with floors and fireplaces, and as burial sites, with graves often underneath the houses. The dead were buried with personal adornments and some domestic artefacts.

Settlement and political structure

By about 100-200 BC, people throughout Brazil were settled in structured, fixed communities by the coasts and rivers, living increasingly by farming instead of nomadic hunting and gathering. The subsequent population growth spread communities further along river courses and into seasonally flooded savannah lands.

Unlike the great empires of the Andes, the lowland peoples did not form political groupIngs much larger than a few villages. However, by the 16th century AD, there was a very large population of different peoples spread throughout Brazil, some of them settled in chiefdoms. These structured groups contained several hundred individuals. One chieftain led a province composed of several villages, each of which was led by a lower-ranking chieftain. The first European explorers reported that there was at least one case of the title or name of one chief being the same as the local word for god, and as such the chief was revered far from his people's territory. One such chiefdom was at the village of Teso dos Bichos on Marajó island at the mouth of the Amazon. The oval-shaped village was built on a mound some 7 m high and covering 2½ ha. It is thought that the site was inhabited continuously for about 900 years, by 500-1,000 people living in houses made of earth, wooden poles and thatch. The village appeared to have been kept very clean and tidy and communal life was well organized, with duties divided between men and women.

Linguistic groups

The most widespread linguistic grouping in Brazil at the time of the European conquest was the **Tupi-Guarani**. These people originated from the Atlantic coast and rivers around 500-700 AD. They lived off slash-and-burn farming, cultivating tropical plants, but when they began moving inland and south they took over from resident hunters and gatherers. By the 1500s the Tupi-Guarani, who often moved from place to place, following a prophet, could be found from north of the Amazon south to Rio de la Plata, and west into Paraguay and Bolivia.

Another large, organized group of people were the **Tupinambá**. They lived on the coast, from the mouth of the Amazon south to São Paulo state. The Tupinambá lived by cultivating crops, such as manioc, sweet potato, yams, as well as cotton, gourds and tobacco. They lived in villages of four to eight large, rectangular, thatched houses, each containing up to 30 families. They usually built their villages on an elevation to catch the breeze, and moved to new sites every five years or so. A chief, the patrilineal head, enforced various social customs, such as marriages and puberty rites. Burial ceremonies were elaborate, with the body wrapped in a hammock and squeezed into a huge ceramic urn. The head of a family was usually buried under his house, others elsewhere within the village. Sometimes a hut was built over the grave, and a fire lit nearby to ward off evil spirits.

Cannibalism was also an important custom for the Tupinambá, as it had been for many other peoples throughout South America for thousands of years. The practice was highly ritualized, using prisoners of war. The victims were kept as slaves, often for long periods, being well fed and looked after; in some cases even marrying the owner's daughter or sister, who had their children. But all such slaves were eventually eaten, after an elaborate ceremony with much singing and dancing. An appointed executioner would kill them with a club and they were then cooked and different parts of the body divided up among various participants in the ritual. There have been many theories as to why people practised cannibalism; since they tended to eat victims of war it was thought that it gave them power over the spirits of their dead enemies. It is most commonly argued that human flesh supplemented the diet for large populations who had scarce resources. But this was not the case for the Tupinambá, who had ample food supplies. When the Tupinambá themselves were asked why they ate human meat they simply said they liked the taste of it.

European colonization

Arrival of the Portuguese

Pedro Álvares Cabral is believed to be the first Portuguese explorer to land on the Brazilian coast, having been blown off his course to India and making landfall on 22 April 1500. He claimed the territory for Portugal as a result of agreements with Spain under the papal bull of 1493 and the Treaty of Tordesillas (1494), but it was some years before the Portuguese realized that this was not just another island as the Spanish had found in the Caribbean, and that in reality they had stumbled across a huge new continent. Further expeditions were sent out in 1501 and 1503-04 and a few trading stations were set up to export the only commodity they felt was of commercial interest: a species of dyewood known as 'pau do brasil'. Little attention was paid to the new colony, as the Portuguese concentrated on the more lucrative trade with Africa, India and the Far East. Some settlers, often banished criminals as well as merchants, gained acceptance with the local Indian tribes and intermarried, fathering the first hybrid cultural Brazilians.

Colonization

The coastal trading stations at Salvador da Bahia, Pernambuco, São Vicente and Cabo Frio soon attracted the attention of French and British traders, who seized Portuguese ships and started to trade directly with the Indians. The French even proclaimed the right to trade in any part of Brazil not occupied by the Portuguese. This forced the Portuguese Crown to set up a colony and in 1530, Martim Afonso de Sousa was sent out with about 400 men. Faced with the impossibly huge task of colonizing the Brazilian coastline, the Crown turned to private enterprise to stake its claim. In 1534 the coast was divided into 15 captaincies, each of which was donated to an individual captain and governor to develop on behalf of the Crown. Although successful settlements were established in Pernambuco in the north and São Vicente in the south, the problems faced in most captaincies, Indian resistance, lack of capital and the difficulty of attracting settlers, led to the reassertion of Crown control in 1549. The Indians had been happy to barter brazil wood with the Portuguese and had helped in the logging and transporting of timber, but the introduction of sugar plantations was a different matter and the hunter-gatherers had no experience of such exhausting work. When they refused to co-operate in this profitable enterprise, the Portuguese took Indians as slaves on a massive scale, which destroyed the good relations previously enjoyed and led to attacks on Portuguese settlements.

The Jesuits

Tomé de Sousa was sent out as Governor-General to the vacant captaincy of Bahia in 1549. He established his seat at Salvador, which became the first capital of Brazil. With him travelled six Jesuit priests, the first of what was to become a hugely powerful missionary and educational order in Brazil. Their role was to smooth the path between Indians and Europeans, convert and educate the Indians in Christian ways and organize them into special villages, or *aldeias*. This last move brought them into conflict with the settlers, however, for their control over the labour market, and with the clergy, who regarded the Indians as savages who could be enslaved. As a result of disagreements with the first Bishop of Brazil, Fernandes Sardanha, the Jesuits moved in 1554 from Bahia to the captaincy of São Vicente, where they set up an *aldeia* at Piratininga, which later became the city of São Paulo. In 1557 a new governor was appointed, Mem de Sá, who was more sympathetic to the Jesuits and their aims and the *aldeias* began to spread.

French and Dutch incursions

The Crown still had difficulties in consolidating its hold on Brazil and other European powers continued to encroach on its territory. A Protestant French expedition found an area which had not been settled by the Portuguese and stayed there from the mid-1550s until they were finally ousted in 1567. Their colony was replaced by a new royal captaincy and a town was founded: Rio de Janeiro. São Luís was also occupied by the French in 1612-15, but it was the Dutch who posed the greatest threat on both sides of the Atlantic (see The Dutch in Brazil, see page 444). They seized Pernambuco in 1630, Portuguese Angola in 1641 and dominated the Atlantic trading routes until the Portuguese managed to regain Angola in 1648-49 and Pernambuco in 1654.

Sugar and slaves

Throughout the colonial period Brazil produced raw materials for Portugal. The colonial economy experienced a succession of booms and recessions, the first of these based on sugar: during the 17th century the northeastern provinces of Pernambuco, Bahia and Paraíba were the world's main producers of sugar. As European settlement had led to the death of much of the native population (over a third of the Indians in coastal areas died in epidemics in 1562-63 alone) and Indian slavery was unsuccessful, the Portuguese imported African slaves to meet the demand for labour on the sugar plantations (*engenhos*). "The most solid properties in Brazil are slaves", wrote the Governor in 1729, "for there are lands enough, but only he who has slaves can be master of them." As many as 10 million African slaves may have survived the dreadful conditions of the Atlantic crossing before the trade was abolished in 1854.

The gold rush

As the sugar industry declined in the late 17th century in the face of competition from British, French and Dutch Caribbean colonies, gold was discovered inland in 1695 in Minas Gerais, Mato Grosso and other areas. Despite the lack of communications, prospectors rushed in from all over Europe. Shortly afterwards, diamonds were found in the Serra do Frio. The economy was largely driven by gold until the 1760s and a revival of world demand for sugar in the second half of the 18th century. Thereafter, there was diversification into other crops such as cacao, rice, cotton and coffee, all of which were produced for export by large numbers of slaves.

The gold rush shifted the power centre of Brazil from the Northeast to the centre, in recognition of which new captaincies were created in Minas Gerais in 1720, Goiás in 1744 and Mato Grosso in 1748, and the capital was moved from Salvador to Rio de Janeiro in 1763. Legacies of the period can be seen today in the colonial towns of Mariana, Congonhas, São João del Rei, Diamantina and, above all, in the exceptionally beautiful city of Ouro Preto, a national monument full of glorious buildings, paintings and sculpture.

Marquês de Pombal

The decline of gold in the mid-18th century made economic reform necessary and the Marquês de Pombal was the minister responsible for a new programme for Portugal and her empire. Imbalances had arisen particularly in trade with Britain. Portugal imported manufactured goods and wheat but her exports of oil and wine left her in deficit, which for a while was covered by Brazilian gold. Pombal was a despotic ruler from 1750 to 1777, modernizing and reforming society, education, politics and the economy. In order to revive Portugal he concentrated on expanding the economy of Brazil, increasing and diversifying exports to cover the deficit with Britain. Cacao, cotton and rice were introduced by the new monopoly company of Grão Pará e Maranhão in the North and a similar company for Paraíba and Pernambuco revitalized the sugar industry in the Northeast. The monopoly companies led to high prices and were not entirely successful so were closed in 1778-79, but the effects of Pombal's reforms were felt in the latter part of the 18th century and Portugal's trade with Britain turned into a surplus. From 1776 when the American colonies revolted, Britain was constantly at war and Portugal was able to supply rising British demand.

Rebellion

Pombal's influence on society enabled the Portuguese Empire to last much longer than the Spanish Empire. He deliberately offered posts in the militia and the bureaucracy to Brazilians and was careful not to alienate the Brazilian élites. White Brazilians were on the same standing as the Portuguese and identified strongly with the mother country. Rebellion was therefore rare but did occur, influenced partly by the turmoil that was going on in Europe with the French Revolution. In 1788-89 a famous plot was uncovered in Minas Gerais called the *inconfidência mineira* (see page 248), which aimed to establish an independent republic in protest at the decline of the gold industry and high taxes. The rebels, who included many of the local hierarchy, were punished and the most prominent leader, Tiradentes (the teeth-puller), was hanged. Other plots were discovered in Rio de Janeiro in 1794, Pernambuco in 1801 and Bahia in 1807, but they were all repressed.

The Brazilian empire

At the beginning of the 19th century, **Napoleon Bonaparte** caused a major upheaval in the monarchies of Europe. His expansion into the Iberian peninsula caused panic in both Spain and Portugal. In August 1807 he demanded that Portugal close its ports to British ships but the British sent a fleet to Lisbon and threatened to attack Brazil if that happened. In November of the same year the French invaded and occupied Portugal. The Prince Regent decided to evacuate the court to Brazil and under British escort sailed to Rio de Janeiro, which became the capital of the empire in 1808. The court stayed there even after 1814 when Napoleon was defeated and Portugal was ruled by a Regency Council, but King João VI was forced to return to Portugal in 1820 after a series of liberal revolts in the mother country, leaving his son Dom Pedro as Prince Regent in Brazil.

Independence from Portugal

Dom Pedro oversaw a growing rift between Portugal and Brazil as the liberals in Lisbon tried to return Brazil to its former colonial status, cancelling political equality and the freedom of trade granted when the King left Portugal in the hands of the French. In October 1821 the government in Lisbon recalled the Prince Regent but Brazilians urged him not to go. Encouraged by his chief minister, José Bonifácio de Andrada e Silva, a conservative monarchist, Dom Pedro announced on 9 January 1822 that he would stay in Brazil, thereby asserting his autonomy. After another attempt to recall the Prince Regent, Dom Pedro made the final break with Portugal, proclaiming Brazil's independence on 7 September 1822. He was crowned emperor and Brazil became a constitutional monarchy in its own right. There was resistance in the North and Northeast, particularly from the militia, but by 1824 violence had subsided. In 1825, under pressure from Britain, Portugal recognized the independent state of Brazil.

The first years of independence were unsettled, partly because of the Emperor's perceived favouritism for the Portuguese faction at court and lack of attendance to the needs of the local oligarchy. De Andrada e Silva resigned as opposition grew. In 1823 Dom Pedro dissolved the constituent assembly amidst fears that he had absolutist designs. However, he set up a royal commission to draft a new constitution which lasted from 1824 until the fall of the monarchy in 1889. This gave the emperor the right to appoint and dismiss cabinet ministers, veto legislation and dissolve parliament and call for elections. The parliamentary government consisted of two houses, a senate appointed by the monarch and a legislature indirectly elected by a limited male suffrage. A Council of State advised the monarch and ensured the separation of the executive, the legislature and the judiciary. Catholicism remained the official religion and the monarchy was supported by the Church.

Abdication

Dom Pedro still failed to gain the trust of all his people. A **republican rebellion** broke out in Pernambuco in 1824, where the élite were suffering from the declining sugar industry, and there was further resentment from all the planter oligarchy as a result of the Anglo-Brazllian Treaty of 1826. This treaty granted British recognition of the independent Brazil in return for certain trading privileges, but, almost more importantly, stipulated that the Atlantic slave trade should come to an end in three years. There was also a **territorial dispute** in 1825 with the Argentine provinces over the left bank of the Río de la Plata, called the Banda Oriental, which flared up into war and was only settled in 1828 with the creation of Uruguay as a buffer state. The mistrust between the Portuguese and the Brazilians became even more pronounced. Portuguese merchants were blamed for the rising cost of living and in 1831 rioting broke out in Rio de Janeiro. Dom Pedro shuffled and reshuffled his cabinet to appease different factions but nothing worked and on 7 April he abdicated in favour of his five-year-old son, **Dom Pedro II**, choosing to leave Brazil a week later on a British warship.

Regency and rebellion

During the 10 years of the young prince's boyhood, there were many separatist movements and uprisings by the oppressed lower classes. In 1832-35 there was the **War of the Cabanos**, in Pernambuco, a guerrilla war against the slave-owning plantocracy of the Northeast; in 1835 the **Cabanagem rebellion** of free Indians and mestizos took place in Pará after a white secessionist revolt and sporadic fighting continued until 1840 (see page 556); in 1837-38 in Bahia there was a federalist rebellion; in 1835 Rio Grande do Sul proclaimed itself a republic, remaining independent for nearly 10 years, with the movement spreading into Santa Catarina, which also declared itself a republic. By 1840 there was a general consensus that

Slavery

For over three centuries African slavery was a central feature of the economy and society of Brazil. Slave labour was a key part of the production of agricultural exports from the mid-16th century through to the abolition of slavery in 1888. slaves also provided much of the labour needed in the gold rush of the 18th century. In the 19th century, at a time when slavery was being abolished in the rest of South America, the demand for slaves increased in Brazil as they became the labour force on the new coffee *fazendas* of the South.

Although the first African slaves arrived in Brazil around 1550, it was only after 1580 with the expansion of sugar *engenhos* in the Northeast that slave labour became common. Faced with a shortage of labour and the resistance of the indigenous population who tended to die of diseases, as well as the attitude of the Church, which opposed indigenous slavery, *engenho* owners soon resorted to African slave labour. The Church had few moral qualms about African slavery. By the 18th century, when slavery was introduced on a large scale in the mining areas of Minas Gerais, Goiás and Mato Grosso, slave ownership was common in most strata of white society and had spread north to Amazônia and south to Río Grande do Sul. The importance of slaves in this society was noted by local people and visitors alike; in 1729 Governor Luís Vahia Monteiro commented "the most solid properties in Brazil are slaves and a man's wealth is measured by having more or fewer for there are lands enough, but only he who has slaves can be masters of them".

While no one knows how many Africans survived the terrible 'middle passage' between Africa and the Brazilian ports, let alone how many died, estimates of three to four million are common. Most came from two areas of West Africa, corresponding roughly to the modern states of Ghana and Angola. Slaves were employed in a surprising range of roles: they were often the cowboys who drove herds of cattle to the coastal towns for slaughter,

although he had not come of age, it was imperative that the 14-year old, Pedro, should ascend the throne. He was duly crowned. Administration of the country was centralized again, the powers of provincial assemblies were curtailed, a national police force set up and the Council of State restored.

The second empire

It took a couple of years for the balance of power to be worked out between the conservative élites of Rio de Janeiro and the liberal élites of São Paulo and Minas Gerais, but once the interests of different groups had been catered for, the constitutional monarchy worked smoothly for 20 years. *Coffee* was now the major crop in São Paulo and Minas Gerais and it was important that the wealthy oligarchy who produced it shared in the power structure of the nation in order to prevent secessionist movements.

Abolition of slavery

Despite the Anglo-Brazilian Treaty of 1826, the slave trade continued until the British Royal Navy put pressure on Brazilian ships carrying slaves in 1850 and the trade was halted soon afterwards. As slaves in Brazil did not reproduce at a natural rate because of the appalling conditions in which they lived and worked, it was clear that an alternative source of labour would eventually have to be found. Anti-slavery the sailors who navigated the rivers and coast, the stevedores who loaded ships bound for Europe and they were frequently domestic workers, midwives and retailers. Despite this, the vast majority were labourers who worked under such poor conditions that there was a continual demand for more imported slaves.

Regardless of the overwhelming odds, slave resistance was continual; whites constantly complained about the reluctance of slaves to work hard and slaves often escaped and formed *quilombos* or *mocambos*, communities of escaped slaves. Though these were usually in impenetrable parts of the interior, they were sometimes on the outskirts of town or near plantations, from where they could launch raids for supplies. Though many *quilombos* were small and short-lived, the most famous, known as Palmares, survived from around 1630 until its final defeat in 1694. Though slave rebellions took place throughout the period of slavery, they were more common in certain parts of the country and occurred with greater frequency in the 19th century. There were over 20 rebellions around Bahia between 1809 and 1835, some of them led by slaves who were Muslim preachers.

By the late 19th century the days of slavery were clearly numbered; the slave trade to Brazil was finally ended by British pressure in 1850. The defeat of the South in the Civil War put a finish to slavery in the USA, leaving Brazil as one of only two states in the Americas where slavery was legal (the other was Cuba). Though there had been an abolitionist movement since the 1830s, it made little headway until the 1860s. In 1871 the children of slaves were freed, a move which, when combined with the abolition of the slave trade, meant slavery would eventually end. Though plantation owners complained of labour shortages and bought slaves from the towns, they were forced to consider new sources of labour and from about 1880 they began to encourage European immigration, especially from Portugal and Italy. Thus, in 1888, when Congress finally debated the issue, there were only nine votes against abolition.

movements gathered strength and in 1871 the first steps towards abolition were taken. A new law gave freedom to all children born to slaves from that date and compensation was offered to masters who freed their slaves. During the 1870s large numbers of European immigrants, mostly from Italy and Portugal, came to work on the coffee plantations, and as technology and transport improved, so the benefits of slavery declined. During the 1880s the abolition movement became unstoppable and, after attempts to introduce compensation for slave owners failed, a law abolishing slavery immediately was passed on 13 May 1888. Some plantation owners went bankrupt, but the large majority survived by paying immigrant workers and newly freed slaves a pittance. Those freed slaves who left the plantations to find employment in the cities were equally exploited and lived in poverty.

Proclamation of the Republic

The first Republic: 1889-1930

The monarchy did not long survive the end of slavery. The São Paulo coffee producers resented abolition and resented their under-representation in the structures of power nationwide, while being called upon to provide the lion's share of the Treasury's revenues. The republican movement started in the early 1870s in cities all over Brazil, but grew strongest in São Paulo. It gradually attracted the support of the military, who also felt under-represented in government, and on 15 November 1889 a bloodless military coup d'état deposed the monarchy and instituted a federal system. The constitution of the new republic established 20 states with wide powers of self-government, a directly elected president of a national government with a senate and a chamber of deputies. Suffrage was introduced for literate adult males (about 3% of the population) and the Church and state were separated. Although the birth of the Republic was bloodless, there were pockets of resistance in rural areas such as the Northeast, where the sugar estates were in recession. In the 1890s O Conselheiro led tens of thousands of followers against the secular republic at Canudos, nearly all of whom were eventually killed by government troops. In 1911 there was another rebellion in the southern states of Paraná and Santa Catarina, led by a Catholic visionary in defence of the monarchy. The **Contestado movement** lasted until 1915, when it too was destroyed by the military.

Brazilian politics were now dominated by an alliance known as *café com leite* (coffee with milk), of the coffee growers of São Paulo and the cattle ranchers of Minas Gerais, occasionally challenged by Rio Grande do Sul, with periodic involvement of the military. The first two presidents of the republic were military: Marshal Deodoro da Fonseca (1889-91) and Marshal Floriano Peixoto (1891-94). In some ways the military took the place of the Crown in mediating between the states' oligarchies, but its interventions were always unconstitutional and therefore gave rise to political instability. By the 1920s tensions between São Paulo and Minas Gerais had come out into the open with the cattle ranchers resenting the way in which the coffee growers used their position to keep the price of coffee artificially high at a time when there was an oversupply. Other social groups also became restive and unsuccessful coup attempts were launched by junior army officers in 1922, 1924 and 1926.

The end of the First World War saw the **rise of the USA** as an industrial power and the decline of Britain's traditional supremacy in trade with Latin America. Although Brazil was still exporting its raw materials to Europe at ever lower prices, it now imported its manufactured goods from the USA, leading to difficulties with finance and fluctuating exchange rates. Brazil's terms of trade had therefore deteriorated and the profitability of its export-led economy was declining before the crash of Wall Street in 1929. The cost of stockpiling excess coffee had led to a rise in debt and by 1930 the government was spending a third of its budget on debt servicing. The growth of nationalism was a key feature of this period as well as the emergence of new political factions and parties such as fascists and communists.

Vargas and the Estado Nôvo: 1930-45

The **Wall Street crash** led to a sudden decline in demand for coffee and the São Paulo élite saw its hegemony wiped out. The elections of 1930 saw another win for the São Paulo candidate but the results were disputed by a coalition of opposition forces. After several months of tension and violence, the army intervened, deposed the outgoing president and installed the alternative candidate of Rio Grande do Sul, Getúlio Vargas, a wealthy rancher, as provisional president. Vargas in fact held office until 1954, with only one break in 1945-50. Vargas' main aim when he took office was to redress the balance of power away from São Paulo and in favour of his own state. However, the effects of his reforms were more far-reaching. He governed by decree, replacing all state governors with 'interventors' who reduced the state militias, and reorganized the system of patronage within the states in favour of Vargas. São Paulo naturally resisted and there was a rebellion in 1932, but it was soon put down by federal troops, effectively wiping out the threat to Vargas' authority. In 1934 a constituent assembly drew up a new constitution which reduced the power of the states and gave more power to the president. The assembly then elected Vargas as president for a four-year term.

With the decline of traditional oligarchic blocs came the rise of political parties. The first to fill the vacuum were the **fascists** and the **communists**, which frequently took to street violence against each other. The fascists, called Integralists, were founded by Plínio Salgado in 1932. The Aliança Libertadora Nacional (ALN), a popular front including socialists and radical liberals, was founded by the Brazilian Communist Party in 1935. The ALN attempted to gain power by infiltrating the junior ranks of the army and encouraging rebellions, but Vargas clamped down on the movement, imprisoning its leaders. The fascists aimed to take power in 1938, the year elections were due, at which Vargas was not eligible to stand. However, in October 1937, Vargas declared a state of siege against an alleged communist plot and suspended the constitution which had prevented him being re-elected. Instead, he proclaimed a new constitution and a new state, *Estado Nôvo*. The fascists tried to oust him but failed, leaving Vargas with no effective opposition whatsoever.

The *Estado Nôvo* was also a response to an **economic crisis**, brought on by a fall in coffee prices, rising imports, a resulting deficit in the balance of payments, a high level of debt and soaring inflation. Vargas assumed dictatorial powers to deal with the economic crisis, censoring the press, banning political parties, emasculating trade unions and allowing the police unfettered powers. There followed a transition from export-led growth to import substitution and industrialization with heavy state intervention. Agricultural resources were channelled into industry and the government became involved in mining, oil, steel, electricity, chemicals, motor vehicles and light aircraft. The military were allowed free rein to develop their own armaments industry. As **war** approached in Europe, Vargas hedged his bets with both Nazi Germany and the USA, to see who would provide the greatest assistance for Brazil's industrialization. It turned out to be the USA, and in return for allowing US military bases to be built in northern Brazil he secured loans, technical assistance and other investments for a massive steel mill at Volta Redonda and infrastructure projects. Brazil did not declare war on Germany until 1944, but it was the only Latin American country to send troops to join the allies, with a force of 25,000 men going to Italy.

The elections of 1943 had been postponed during the War, but Vargas scheduled a vote for December 1945 in an attempt to dispel his fascist image. He allowed the formation of political parties, which included two formed by himself: the Social Democratic Party (PSD), supported by industrialists and large farmers, and a Labour Party (PTB), supported by pro-Vargas trade unions. There was also the National Democratic Union (UDN), opposed to Vargas, and the newly legalized Communist Party. However, there were growing fears that Vargas would not relinquish power, and when he appointed his brother as chief of police in Rio de Janeiro, the military intervened. Faced with the prospect of being deposed, Vargas chose to resign in October 1945, allowing the elections to take place as planned in the December. They were won by the PSD, led by General Eurico Dutra, a former supporter of the *Estado Nôvo*, who had encouraged Vargas to resign.

The second Republic: 1946-64

Yet another constitution was drafted by a constituent assembly in 1946, this one based on the liberal principles of the 1891 constitution but including the labour code and the social legislation of the *Estado Nôvo*. Industrialization through state planning was retained, the foreign-owned railways were nationalized, hydroelectric power was developed, but deflation was necessary to bring down spiralling prices. The Communist Party was banned again in 1947. Meanwhile Vargas was elected Senator for Rio Grande do Sul, his home state, and kept active in politics, eventually being elected as candidate for the PSD and PTB alliance in the 1950 presidential elections. Although it was his third presidency, it was only his first by direct elections.

The third Vargas presidency was beset by the problems of fulfilling populist election promises while grappling with **debt** and **inflation**. Rapid industrialization required levels of investment which could only be raised abroad, but the nationalists were opposed to foreign investment. He failed to reconcile the demands of the USA and the nationalists, particularly with regards to oil and energy, and he failed to control inflation and stabilize the economy. There were rumours of corruption, and after the president's bodyguard was implicated in a plot to kill a journalist which went wrong and another man was shot, the army issued him with another ultimatum to resign or be ousted. Instead, on 24 August 1954, Vargas shot himself, leaving a suicide note denouncing traitors at home and capitalists abroad.

The next president was **Juscelino Kubitschek**, who took office in January 1956 with the aim of achieving economic growth at any cost, regardless of inflation and debt. He is best known for building the new capital of Brazil, Brasília, nearly 1,000 km northwest of Rio de Janeiro in the state of Goiás. This massive modernist project served in the short term to expand the debt and in 1961, the next president, Jânio Quadros, inherited huge economic problems which brought his government down after only seven months and Congress unexpectedly accepted his resignation. Power passed to his vice-president, João Goulart, a populist and former labour minister under Vargas, who was mistrusted by the armed forces and the right wing. His powers were curtailed with the appointment of a prime minister and cabinet who would be jointly answerable to Congress. The 1960s were a turbulent time in Brazil as elsewhere, with the universities a hotbed of revolutionary socialism after the Cuban Revolution, Trotskyist and Communist agitators encouraging land occupations, strikes in industry and a move to secure trade union rights for the armed forces. A nationalist Congress passed legislation cutting foreign companies' annual profit remittances to 10% of profits, which sparked a massive outflow in foreign capital and a halving of US aid. Goulart was forced to print money to keep the economy going, which naturally put further pressure on an already soaring inflation rate. When Goulart clashed with Congress over approval of an economic adjustment programme and tried to strengthen his position by appealing for popular support outside Congress, he alarmed the middle classes, who unexpectedly supported a military coup in March 1964. Goulart took refuge in Uruguay.

Military rule: 1964-85

The 1964 coup was a turning point in Brazilian political history. This time the armed forces did not return to barracks as they had before. Opposition leaders were arrested, the press censored, labour unions purged of anyone seen as left wing, and the secret police were given wide powers. The political parties were outlawed and replaced by two officially approved parties: the government Aliança Renovadora Nacional (ARENA) and the opposition Movimento Democrático Brasileiro (MDB). Congress, consisting only of members of these two parties, approved a succession of military presidents nominated by the armed forces. A new constitution, introduced in 1967, gave the president broad powers over the states and over Congress. The worst period of repression occurred between 1968 and 1973 with a wave of urban **guerrilla warfare**. Around this time, the military government's economic adjustment programme paid dividends and the economy began to grow, making life easier for the middle classes and reducing any potential support for guerrilla groups. In 1968-74 the economy grew at over 10% a year, which became known as the Brazilian **'economic miracle'**. This spectacular growth, achieved because of the authoritarian nature of the regime, masked a widening gulf between the rich and poor, with the blacks and mulattos, always at the bottom in Brazilian society, suffering the most. Edwin Williamson (*The Penguin History of Latin America*) quotes statistics showing that in 1960 the richest 10% of the population received 40% of the national income; by 1980 they received 51%, while the poorest 50% received only 13%. In the shanty towns, or *favelas*, which had mushroomed around all the large cities, but especially São Paulo, disease, malnutrition and high mortality rates were prevalent and their citizens battled constantly in appalling housing lacking sewerage, running water and electricity.

By 1973 some military officers and their civilian advisors had become alarmed at the rising level of opposition. Arguing that repression alone would merely lead to further opposition and even to attempted revolution, they pressed for 'decompression': policies to relax the repression while remaining in power. The attempt to carry out this policy by legalizing political parties, permitting freer trade unions and strikes and reducing censorship, gave greater space for the opposition to demand an end to military rule. Attempts to introduce elections to Congress which were less controlled faced the same obstacle: they tended to result in victories for candidates who favoured civilian rule.

One of the main reasons for the military deciding to return to their barracks was the dire state of the economy. The armed forces had taken over in 1964 when the economy had hit rock bottom, their authoritarian regime had allowed rapid expansion and change which brought about the 'economic miracle', yet by 1980 the economy had gone full circle. Inflation was running at 100% a year and was set to go through the roof, foreign debt was the highest in Latin America, estimated at over US$87 bn, and unemployment was soaring. When international interest rates rose sharply in 1982, Brazil was no longer able to service its debt and it suspended interest payments. Unwilling to go through another round of authoritarianism and repression, the military decided to let the civilians have a go. Elections in 1982 produced a majority for the pro-government Social Democratic Party (PDS) in the electoral college which was to elect the next president, but splits in the PDS led to the election in January 1985 of the opposition candidate, (see under São João del Rei, page 256).

The return to democracy

Corruption and impeachment

In 1985 Tancredo Neves was elected as the first civilian president for 21 years. Before he could take office he fell ill and died. His vice-president José Sarney became president at a time of economic crisis, with inflation at 300%. Sarney introduced the Cruzado Plan in 1986, freezing prices and wages, but inflation exploded when the freeze was lifted.

A new constitution brought direct presidential elections in November 1989. After two rounds of voting Fernando Collor de Melo, of the small Partido da Reconstrução Nacional, won 53% of the vote to narrowly defeat his left-wing rival, Luís Inácio da Silva (popularly known as Lula). Collor launched controversial economic reforms, including opening the economy to imports, privatisation and a freeze on savings and bank accounts. The policies failed; by 1991 inflation reached 1,500% and foreign debt payments were suspended.

Just over half way through his term, Collor was suspended from office after Congress voted overwhelmingly to impeach him for corruption. He avoided impeachment by resigning on 29 December 1992. Vice-president Itamar Franco took over, but had scant success in tackling poverty and inflation until the introduction of an anti-inflation package that introduced the *real* as the new currency.

The Plano Real

The architect of the *Real* plan was finance minister **Fernando Henrique Cardoso**. Three decades earlier he had been a high-profile leftist and opponent of military rule, forced into exile after the 1964 military coup. The success of the *Real* plan led to his election as president in October 1994. After trailing Lula (see above) of the Workers Party (PT), Cardoso gained such popularity that he won the election in the first round of voting. However, his alliance of the Brazilian Social Democrat Party (PSDB), the Liberal Front (PFL) and the Labour Party (PTB) failed to gain a majority in either house of Congress. This severely hampered plans to reform the tax and social security systems and the civil service. The government was also criticized for its slowness in addressing social problems. Such problems ranged from the need for land reform and violence associated with landlessness, to the slave-like working conditions in agricultural areas and the human rights of Indians and of street children in large cities.

Towards the end of 1997 the financial crisis in Asia sapped investor confidence throughout the world, and threatened Brazil's currency and economic stability. The failure to cut public spending had swollen the budget deficit and the *real* was exposed to speculation. Cardoso was obliged to take actions to prevent an upsurge in inflation and devaluation of the currency, but at the cost of slowing down economic growth. Crisis was avoided and inflation remained in single figures, in contrast to the hyperinflation of earlier periods.

The government still faced the serious social imbalances that it had failed to redress. However, Cardoso managed to beat Lula again in October 1998 without the need for a second poll. In doing so he became the first Brazilian president to be elected for a second term.

Cardoso's second term

Cardoso and his PSDB party emerged victorious from the 1998 elections with 99 Deputies, but they needed allies both in the 513 seat Chamber of Deputies and in the Senate. Political opponents had also won many powerful state governorships. The PSDB's relations with its major ally the PFL came under increasing strain. Unlike the PSDB, the PFL is a conservative group dominated by old-style politicians, typified by its leader Antônio Carlos Magalhães, who increasingly controlled Congress. There were rumours of corruption in Cardoso's government, with not even the president himself above implication. Another financial crisis threatened, which was averted by an IMF loan of US$18 bn at the end of 1998, but the delayed social security reforms had still not been passed. Finally when ex-president Itamar Franco, governor of Minas Gerais, refused to pay his state's debts to the Federal Government in January 1999, foreign investors lost confidence. The pressures on the *real* became too great and the central bank had to let it float freely against the dollar. It lost 50% of its value in the process. Two more stable years followed, but with its economic credibility eroded and shifting alliances in Congress the Cardoso government made little progress with its policies.

The 2002 elections

As in the USA, Brazilian presidents cannot run for a third term. Four front-runners emerged in the 2002 elections. Taking an early commanding lead in the opinion polls was Luiz Inácio Lula da Silva, best known as Lula, who was making his fourth bid for the presidency. With a refurbished image, a new suit, moderated policies and a millionaire running mate, the veteran firebrand, gained support from all classes.

Against a backdrop of global crises, the *real* again lost some 50% of its value in less than a year. Foreign investors were concerned about repeated budget deficits, and the prospect that a more left-wing government might default on debts. In August 2002 the IMF again came to the rescue, this time with a record US$30 bn loan, subject to tough conditions. On 27 October 2002 Lula won a convincing victory against government-backed José Serra. The new president – once shoe-shine boy, ex-leader of the Metal Workers' Union and head of the Workers' Party –set out to lead the first left-wing government in Brazil for 40 years. So far Lula has presided over no apparent change in Brazil – but only Brazilians would expect quick change to a country with so many entrenched difficulties. What is remarkable is perhaps what has not happened. Lula was bequeathed a legacy of rising debt, foreign exchange shortages, an unplanned 50% devaluation in the Real, and an upsurge in inflation. But his government have brought this under control. The country has not plummeted into economic crisis – its economy although growing very slowly, is growing and inflation is under control. Lula has also introduced reforms which run against the grain of Brazilian society and political practice – in other words they take money from the elite

The Landless

The acclaimed Brazilian photographer, Sebastião Salgado, published a book in 1997 entitled *Terra – Struggle for the Landless* (Phaidon Press) which documents the plight of a portion of Brazilian society which calls itself the Movimento Sem Terra, the Landless Movement. In one of the pictures, the horizon between half-tilled land and the sky is obliterated by an army of people raising flags, hoes and machetes to the clouds. It looks like an unstoppable force and yet conjures up images of the futile peasant revolts of bygone eras. In view of the many unkept promises by successive politicians to speed up the redistribution of unused land, 'unstoppable force' may be wishful thinking. Yet for the thousands who marched on Brasília in 1997, for the squatters who have reclaimed empty property, and for those who have been killed in disputes with landowners, the fight for somewhere to settle and grow crops is a reality. It is one of Brazil's biggest contradictions that so much potentially productive farmland is owned by a tiny proportion of the population and yet 42% of privately owned land is unused. For the millions of families who have little or no land to work, such inequality has been the spur for Sem Terra. The demand for land also encompasses the desire no longer to be at the outer margins of the economic and social progress that is taking place elsewhere in the country.

The trek of over 1,000 km that the Movement made from São Paulo to Brasília in 1997 took two months and, as a sign of the popular support for the marchers, they were greeted like heroes by 120,000 people. Top politicians attended, announcements were made of new credit lines for settlements and of land confiscations, even a US$400 mn World Bank loan for land reform. But would the landowners who have set up private armies to keep Sem Terra out be convinced? Would the political system be radically altered?

In late 1999 the government said that it had acquired unused farmland for 370,000 families since 1994. Critics claimed, though, that the number of landless was still growing. History has not been on their side and another part of their reality is not to believe in anything until the land rights are in their hands. Even when a landowner is found not to have valid title to a property, the legal process to reallocate the land is lengthy and slows the progress of land reform. Such delays have led to the radicalization of Sem Terra, with some loss of its romantic appeal in Brazil.

and public servants and their results will take a long time to manifest. Brazil's public services are among the most cumbersome, financially draining, bureaucratic and corrupt in the world. And none are more so than the pension system. Many public sector professionals collect several pensions and many retire on pensions higher than their final salary. Judges for example receive an average £1,700 per month. Army officers do even better and pass on their pensions to the second generation after their death. In contrast state pensions to the private sector average £80 per month. In 2002 the state pension ran a deficit worth 4.3% of GDP or £12bn.

One of Lula's greatest achievements was to get the Senate to pass a bill on pensions reform, capping public pensions at £500 per month (still two times higher than the average middle class salary), raising the retirement age and introducing new pension taxes. This resulted in strikes by half of the country's federal workers. Judges tried to block the bill through the courts.

In mid-2004 Lula published an impressive proposed bill on Agrarian Reform which promised far more than any Brazilian government ever has: 400,000 families are to be settled via expropriation, 200,000 to be settled on land purchased by a renamed Banco da Terra – now called Credito Fundiario, which will then sell to small farmers at subsidised interest rates and 400,000 families that have received land but nothing else will be given financial support.

His Fome Zero – or no hunger program, designed to give all poor Brazilians enough to eat has been encumbered by the incompetence of a number of his ministers whose intentions have proved better than their abilities. Other problems are intrinsically Brazilian. Municipal governments – principally individual mayors have been trying to control the disbursement of funds. Raking off public money has long been a way of life in Brazil; its most famous exponent, São Paulo politician Paulo Maluf, boasts about it openly on TV and yet stood in October 2004's municipal elections and received a respectable count of votes. However these same elections showed that the Brazilian people are still enamoured of Lula who nearly doubled the number of municipal councils under PT control and those involved with the Fome Zero campaign say these teething problems are being ironed out, and that 1.3 million families are now benefiting.

Culture

People

Indigenous peoples

There were probably between three and five million indigenous people in Brazil when the Portuguese arrived. Today there are between 200,000 and 300,000. The effects of European colonization were devastating; with whole tribes wiped out completely under the Portuguese Amazon slave trade and others set to fight against each other for Portuguese advantage. Present-day tribal groups number about 220; each has a unique dialect, but most languages belong to four main linguistic families, Tupi-Guarani, Gê, Carib and Arawak. A few tribes remain uncontacted, others are exclusively nomadic, others are semi-nomadic hunter-gatherers and farmers, while some are settled groups in close contact with non-Indian society. There is no agreement on precisely how many tribes are extant, but the Centro Ecumênico da Documentação e Informação (CEDI) of São Paulo said that of the 200 or so groups it documented, 40% have populations of less than 200 people and 77% have populations of less than 1,000. Hemming underlines this depressing statistic when he reports that tribes contacted in recent decades have, as have others in previous centuries, suffered catastrophic reductions in numbers as soon as they encounter diseases which are common to non-indigenous people, but to which their bodies have no immunity.

Most of Brazil's indigenous people live in the Amazon region; they are affected by deforestation, encroachment from colonizers, small- and large-scale mining, and the construction of hydroelectric dams. Besides the Yanomami, other groups include the Xavante, Ticuna, Tukano, Kreen-Akrore, Kaiapó, Bororo and Arara. The struggle of groups such as the Yanomami to have their land demarcated in order to secure title is well-documented. The goal of the Statute of the Indian (Law 6.001/73), for demarcation of all Indian land by 1978, is largely unmet. It was feared that a new law introduced in January 1996 would slow the process even more. However all is not bleak. The populations of many indigenous groups have grown over the last decade and a number have their land rights have been protected under Brazilian Law, by Fernando Henrique Cardoso and by Lula (although the latter is alleged to have reneged on a promise to enshrine an important area territory in Roraima into law at the 11th hour in exchange for support by powerful members of the state elite. On occasion indigenous land rights are even enforced. A Flight out over the Xingu in northern Mato Grosso shows this starkly, with the indigenous territory a huge green island in a sea of soya and cattle plantations. Funai, the National Foundation for the Support of the Indian, a part of the Interior Ministry, is charged with representing the Indians' interests, but lacks resources and support. There is no nationwide, representative body for indigenous people, although the Amazon indigenous lobbying group, COIAB is increasingly powerful and Manoel Moura's FIUPAM (seepage 548) is growing daily.

Mestiços

At first the Portuguese colony grew slowly. From 1580 to 1640 the population was only about 50,000 apart from the million or so indigenous Indians. In 1700 there were some 750,000 non-indigenous people in Brazil. Early in the 19th century Humboldt computed there were about 920,000 whites, 1.96 million Africans, and 1.12 million Indians and people of mixed Portuguese and Indian origin (*mestiços*): after three centuries of occupation a total of only four million, and over twice as many Africans as there were whites.

The arid wastes of the *sertão* remain largely uncultivated. Its inhabitants are *mestiço*; most live off a primitive but effective method of cultivation known as 'slash and burn', which involves cutting down and burning the brushwood for a small patch of ground which is cultivated for a few years and then allowed to grow back.

Afro-Brazilians

Racism is culturally rife in Brazil; an often openly expressed in all-white company. Though there is no legal discrimination against black people, the economic and educational disparity – by default rather than intent of the Government – is such that successful Afro-Brazilians are active almost exclusively in the worlds of sport, entertainment and the arts.

Brazilian culture, however would be nothing without its African influences. Those interested in the development of Afro-Brazilian music, dance, religion, arts and cuisine will find the cities of Rio de Janeiro, Bahia and São Luís which retain the greatest African influences particularly fascinating. Black Pride movements are particularly strong in Bahia.

After the rigours of transatlantic shipment in tiny rat-infested spaces, the Africans suffered further trauma on arrival at the Brazilian ports. They were often sold in groups which were segregated to avoid slaves from the same family or speaking the same language being together. By breaking all cultural and sentimental ties, the Portuguese hoped to eradicate ethnic pride and rebellions on the estates. As a result African spiritual cults became mixed and syncretistic even before they mixed with Portuguese Catholicism and Indian spirituality. In what is now modern day Nigeria, for instance, there were different groups of people, each with its own divinity or Orixá (pronounced 'Orisha'). These Orixás were normally the spirit of a distinguished ancestor or a legendary hero and were worshipped only in a particular region. As the slaves went to Brazilian estates in groups made up of people from different African regions, they soon started to worship all the Orixás, instead of just one. As a result uniquely Afro-Brazilian religions were born out of the template of African spirituality: notably Candomblé, Umbanda, and Macumba.

Europeans

Modern immigration did not begin effectively until after 1850. Of the 4.6 million immigrants from Europe between 1884 and 1954, 32% were Italians, 30% Portuguese, 14% Spanish, 4% German, and the rest of various nationalities. Since 1954 immigrants have averaged 50,000 a year.

The cult of the Orixás

In Candomblé, the figure of God, the Creator is called Olorum. But this figure is almost never mentioned. To some degree, this is because Olorum is too busy to care about mankind's small problems. These are taken care of by the Orixás, the spiritual guides responsible for all sorts of matters concerning our lives. According to Candomblé, from the moment of birth, every person has one or two Orixás to act as protector and tutor. The personality and the temperament of everyone is directly influenced by his or her Orixá. For example, a son or daughter of Ogun (the Orixá of war) is likely to be an impulsive and combative person, while the sons and daughters of Oxun (the Orixá of waterfalls and love) tend to be charming and coquettish.

To discover who your protector Orixá is, you must go to a *Pai de Santo* (male priest) or a *Mãe de Santo* (woman priest) and ask him or her to use the *Jogo de Buzios*. This is an oracle using 16 sea shells by which the priests can predict the future and answer questions related to material or spiritual matters. It is also very common to make offerings to the Orixás, consisting of special foods (every Orixá has his or her own preferences), alcoholic beverages, cigars, flowers, pop-corn, candles, toys and even ritually sacrificed animals such as cockerels, goats and pigeons. These offerings are delivered in different places, according to the Orixá. For example, offerings to Oxossi, the hunter, are delivered in a forest or a bush, and so on. The offerings are always associated with a wish being made, or by way of thanks to the Orixá for a favour received.

The religious ceremonies take place in *terreiros*, with much singing and drumming. The *Pais de Santo* and *Mães de Santo* enter into a trance and each is possessed by his or her protector Orixá, being able to communicate with humans, answer questions, give advice and predict the future.

It is very difficult to estimate the exact number of Brazilians who follow Candomblé, Macumba and Umbanda. One of the main reasons is that many of their followers also profess themselves to be Catholics and regard themselves as such. For many years the Afro-Brazilian religions were officially forbidden and only recently are people becoming more open in admitting their beliefs in public. The greatest concentration of these cults is in the cities of Salvador da Bahia and Rio de Janeiro. Many writers, academic and otherwise, have written on the subject, notably the novelist Jorge Amado, who was a member of the Candomblé cult until he died in 2001 (see his book, *The War of the Saints*, 1993).

Important Orixás

Exu (pronounced Eshoo) is considered the messenger between people and the Orixás. Sometimes associated with the Christian Devil, Exu is always represented with a trident and his colours are black and red. Offerings to this Orixá are always made at crossroads and normally consist of cigars, *cachaça* and red and black candles. His day is Monday.

Most of the German immigrants settled in Santa Catarina, Rio Grande do Sul, and Paraná. The Germans (and the Italians and Poles and other Slavs who followed them) did not in the main go as wage earners on the big estates, but as cultivators of their own small farms. Here there is a settled agricultural population cultivating the soil intensively.

Ogum the Orixá of war, thunder, lightning and iron. His colour is deep blue and he is always represented with an iron sword. The sons and daughters of Ogum are very combative and impulsive. His day is Tuesday.

Oxossi (pronounced Oshossee) is the hunter and protector of wild animals. This Orixá lives in the forest and is represented with a bow, arrows and a leather hat. His colour is green and sometimes blue. His day is Thursday and all his offerings, including raw tobacco and fruits, must be made in wooded places. People protected by this Orixá are normally very independent and solitary.

Xangô (pronounced Shango) is the Orixá of truth and justice. His colours are red and white and his day is Wednesday. He is represented with a double-headed axe, the African symbol of justice.

Oxum (pronounced Oshoon) is a feminine Orixá, associated with love and the family, found in waterfalls and whitewater. Pretty and extremely coquettish, she is sometimes represented as a siren with a golden mirror. Her colour is yellow and offerings to her should be delivered close to a waterfall. Her sons and daughters are very dedicated to the family. Her day is Saturday.

Yemanjá , the mother of the seas and saltwater. Her principal day is 31 December, New Year's Eve, and on this day people offer her white flowers, champagne and small boats full of candles and gifts placed in the sea. Her colour is light blue.

Iansã (pronounced Iansan) is a female Orixá related to tempests and storms. Very impulsive, Iansã is the only Orixá who can command the **Eguns**, the spirits of the dead. She wears red and her day is Wednesday.

Omolu a strange Orixá who never shows his face (severely disfigured by smallpox), is always invoked in cases of disease and illness as he has the power to cure. Often referred as the 'doctor of the poor', he is represented as a strong man covered by a straw coat and holding a straw box full of herbs and medicines.

Two other terms are sometimes used in relation to Afro-Brazilian religions: **Macumba** used to be employed, mainly in Rio de Janeiro, as a generic term to describe all Afro-Brazilian cults. It was a popular expression at the beginning of the 20th century, but has become a derogatory term, not very politically correct. To call someone a 'macumbeiro/a' is offensive. The other term is **Quimbanda**. This is the dark side of Afro-Brazilian religion. It is associated with black magic and sorcery. A 'trabalho de quimbanda' is a ritual designed to hurt someone through offerings or sacrifices. Perhaps performed in cemeteries or at crossroads, these 'trabalhos' may use wax models of the intended victim (like in voodoo), or may involve imaginative and weird practices such as writing the enemy's name on a piece of paper, putting it in a frog's mouth, then sewing up the mouth. The victim is supposed to die a death as slow and painful as the frog's. Quimbanda is a taboo subject and no one will profess to being involved with it.

Asians

There are some one million Japanese-descended Brazilians; they grow a fifth of the coffee, 30% of the cotton, all the tea, and are very active in market gardening. Today the whites and near-whites are about 53% of the population, people of mixed race about 34%, and Afro Brazilians 11%; the rest are either Indians or Asians. There are large regional variations in the distribution of the races: the whites predominate greatly in the South, which received the largest flood of European immigrants.

Arts and crafts

Woodcarving

Woodworking has two principal origins, the African and the Jesuit. In northeastern Brazil, many woodcarving and sculpting techniques are inherited from the African slaves who were brought across the Atlantic to work the sugar plantations. One of the most prominent examples is the *carranca*, the grotesque figurehead that was placed on a boat's prow to ward off evil spirits. *Carrancas* are an adaptation of the African mask-making tradition and other carved and sculpted masks can be found in the Northeast. The Jesuits passed on skills in the carving and painting of religious figures in wood. Originally they encouraged their Indian converts in the techniques, but today others practice the art. Woodcarving is widespread in Pernambuco and Bahia in the Northeast. In Rio de Janeiro many contemporary artists work in wood and Embu, near São Paulo (see page 190), is a centre for wooden sculptures and furniture making.

Ceramics

In northeastern Brazil, religious figures are also made in clay, for instance the unglazed, life-sized saints made from red clay in Tracunhaém, near Recife. Another centre for similar work is Goiana, also in Pernambuco. A third place from which the ceramics are even more famous is Alto da Moura, near Caruaru (Pernambuco – see page 452). Here Mestre Vitalino began modelling scraps of clay into little figures depicting everyday life (work, festivals, dancing, political events). He died in 1963, but the tradition that he started has continued and is known throughout Brazil.

The pots that are made in the Amazon region come in various styles, some of them quite strange. Bahian and other northeastern pottery shows African influence.

Textiles, clothing and leather

Ceará, in the North, is famous for its lace-making, and beautiful pieces are sold all over Brazil. In other parts of the North hammocks and other woven items are found. The hammock is, of course, an essential household item and you may well need to buy one if you are travelling up the Amazon on a boat. Other utilitarian articles which have become craft items are the rugs and capes made in the highlands further south, such as Minas Gerais, to keep out the night-time cold.

In the Northeast, traditional costumes have their roots in the rituals of the African religions that came to Brazil with the slave trade. In southern areas where European immigration was heaviest, many traditional costumes can be seen, usually at the festivals and dances that have survived. Another type of clothing from the South is that associated with the *gaúchos*, the Brazilian cowboys of Rio Grande do Sul. As well as the clothes, which normally use hide in their manufacture, you may also buy saddlery, stirrups, silverware and the gourds used for drinking *maté*.

Leatherwork is not confined to the South, but can be found in any region where cattle are raised.

Musical instruments

The most popular instruments that tourists like to buy are those connected with African music, especially the drums, shakers and the *berimbau*, the one-stringed bow that is twanged in accompaniment to Capoeira. Here again, the best places to look are in the Northeast where the African heritage is strongest. You can also purchase guitars and other stringed instruments.

Basketware

In Amazônia, a huge variety of raw materials are available for making baskets, nets, hammocks, slings for carrying babies, masks and body adornments. In the Northeast,

Brazilian cinema

My first encounter with Brazil came through the medium of its cinema when in the early 1980s I saw Hector Babenco's controversial drama Pixote, *a Lei do Mais Fraco*. This left a lasting impression and curiosity that I was never to satisfy until my first visit to São Paulo nearly 15 years later. Hopefully the current resurgence of Oscar-nominated films such as Walter Salles's *Central do Brasil* (Central Station) will inspire more people to explore the country where they were filmed rather sooner than I did!

No one knows for sure when the first film was made in Brazil but a travelling Italian showman, Vittorio di Maio, was to claim this when he exhibited four films in Petrópolis in 1897. The industry developed steadily at the beginning of the last century with often-repeated adaptations of literary texts such as *O Guaraní* before later specializing in light entertainment musicals known as *chanchadas* during the 1930s and 1940s. A national star, Carmen Miranda, grew out of these before moving to Hollywood where she quickly became America's stereotype of the exotic Latin woman.

During the 1950s more serious films such as Nelson Perreira dos Santos's *Rio 40 Graus* began to appear before Anselmo Duarte's *O Pagador de Promessas* won best film at Cannes. This golden age continued in the 1960s with the birth of *Cinema Novo*. Glauber Rocha's *Deus e o Diabo no Terra do Sol* reinterpreted the popular theme of Lampião and the bandits of the northeast previously used in Lima Barreto's 1953 epic *O Cangaçeiro*. Other films such as *O Barravento* also by Glauber Rocha challenged the previously passive role of the viewing public.

In the 1970s and 1980s under the military dictatorship the national film industry led by the state-run *Embrafilme* lost its way as *porno-chanchadas* and comedies like *Os Trapalhões* dominated the box office. There were however some films such as Bruno Barreto's *Dona Flor e Seus Dois Maridos* that combined both commercial and critical success and helped to push actress Sonia Braga to international fame.

The return came in the 1990s with Fabio Barreto's *O Quatrilho*, showing the life of Brazil's Italian immigrants, and Bruno Barreto's *O Que é Isso Companheiro,* based on the 1969 kidnap of the American ambassador. Other good films, including *Anahy de las Missiones* based on a Gaúcho legend, and *Terra Estrangeira* exploring the life of a Brazilian immigrant in Portugal, have displayed both excellent photography and innovative plots.

Brazilian cinema has come increasingly to the fore since *Central Station*. Walter Salles who made that film has received increasing critical success; first with his bleak, Hardy-esque tragedy *Behind the Sun*, and most recently with his Che Guevara biopic, *The Motorcycle Diaries*. Hot on his heels is Hector Babenco, an Argentinian naturalized as a Brazilian, who caused a big splash in 2004 with his rather sentimen-talized account of life in Sao Paulo's notorious gaol, *Carandiru*. But the greatest acclaim has gone to Fernando Meirelles who received an Oscar nomination for his stunningly shot, brutal portrayal of life in one of Rio's most violent *favelas*, the *Cidade de Deus* or *City of God*. This is a remarkable picture; perhaps the greatest ever to come out of Brazil. And Meirelles went from there to direct his first English-language feature, John Le Carre's *The Constant Gardener*.

 too, baskets come in all shapes and sizes, especially in Bahia, Pernambuco and Paraíba. Another northeastern craft, which does not fit into the above categories, is pictures made in bottles with coloured sands (Lençóis, Bahia, and Natal, Rio Grande do Norte, are good places to buy them). In Minas Gerais, two very common things to see and buy are soapstone carvings (for instance birds and animals) and the cooking pots used in *mineira* kitchens.

Gemstones

Legends of rich deposits, even mountains of precious stones preceded their discovery in the interior of the country. Prospectors looked for diamonds and emeralds as well as gold and silver to make them wealthy. The existence of gems was known about almost from the earliest days of the Portuguese colony, from the reports given to the new arrivals by the Indians and from scattered discoveries of different stones. But there was nothing to bring riches on the scale of the silver and gold found in the Spanish colonies. Gold was found in Minas Gerais in the 17th century and diamonds in 1725 at Diamantina (Minas Gerais) and thus Brazil's mineral wealth began to appreciate. The search for new deposits has never flagged.

Some of the commercially mined stones are: **diamonds**, found in Minas Gerais, Roraima, Bahia, Tocantins, Mato Grosso and Mato Grosso do Sul. Brazil was the world's largest producer of diamonds until South Africa entered the market in the 19th century. **Emeralds** were not discovered in Brazil until 1963 (many green beryls had been mined before then, but were known not to be true emeralds); they are now mined in Bahia, Minas Gerais and Goiás. **Aquamarine** is a clear blue beryl from Rio Grande do Norte, Paraíba, Bahia, Minas Gerais and Espírito Santo. **Ruby** and **sapphire** are two shades of the same mineral, corundum, the former rich red, the latter a deep blue. Rubies are found in Santa Catarina, sapphires in Minas Gerais. The two most valued forms of *topaz* found are the rare Imperial Topaz from Ouro Preto (Minas Gerais), which comes in a range of colours from honey-coloured through shades of red to pink, and Blue Topaz from Minas Gerais and Rondônia.

Tourmalines come from Minas Gerais, Ceará and Goiás; they have the widest range of colours of any gemstone, from colourless (white) to red, yellow, greens, blues, lilac and black. They even come in bi- and tricoloured varieties. **Opals**, unique for their rainbow flecks, are mined in Piauí and Rio Grande do Sul. **Amethyst**, a quartz which ranges in colour from pale lilac to deep purple, is mined in Tocantins, Pará, Bahia, Mato Grosso do Sul and Rio Grande do Sul. From the last three states, plus Minas Gerais, comes **citrine**, another quartz which is predominantly yellow. Less well-known, but equally beautiful are **kunzite**, a rare pinkish-violet stone, and **chrysoberyl**, both found in Minas Gerais. Chrysoberyl is found in a variety of forms, a golden-yellow-brown, 'cat's eye' chrysoberyl which has an luminous thread running through it, and the very rare **alexandrite**, which changes colour according to the light. Its most spectacular form changes from green in daylight to red in artificial light.

Music

Contemporary Brazilian music

Brazil has by far the most interesting and varied musical scene in Latin America, with a range of genres as rich as the USA's or the UK's, or perhaps even richer. As well as international standards like rock, rap and jazz, there are a panoply of uniquely Brazilian styles – samba, choro, frevo, forró, axé, bossa nova, guitarrada, mangue-beat... in fact there is so much choice it is hard to know where to begin.

The music scene in Brazil can perhaps be roughly divided into two categories: music to dance to and music for listening to, though there is a great deal of cross over.

Capoeira and berimbau

One of the most exciting sounds to be heard in the streets of Salvador, Bahia, is that of the *berimbau*, the instrument that accompanies the dance-cum-martial arts form called Capoeira. The *berimbau* is a vertical wooden bow with a resonator at the lower end and a single steel string played with a thin stick. The player also holds a *caxixi*, a small rattle, in the stick hand and coin held against the string to modulate the pitch in the other. The *berimbau* is accompanied by one of a number of '*toques*' or chants, such as the São Bento Grande, Angola, Benguela or Cavalaria. Although the objective of the Capoeirista is to knock his opponent off his hands or feet, what the bystander will most appreciate is the wonderful grace with which the two bodies of the opponents whirl and cartwheel around one another, as though participating in some physically powerful ballet, never actually touching until a 'fall' is engineered by one of them. Undeniably of African origin, the Capoeira was practised much more violently in the past and did not acquire respectability until the celebrated Mestre Bimba opened the first Academy in 1932.

Music to dance to

The most famous of the country's dance rhythms is **samba**; a complex and infectious 2/4 rhythm which came to Rio from Angola via the Brazilian state of Bahia and reached its full fruition in the Rio Carnival of the 1930s. Samba sounds wonderfully happy but is in reality invariably bittersweet, with rhythms filled with joy and optimism and lyrics as sad as a lament. Offshoots of samba include **samba canção** (see below) – which is more sedate and highbrow and **pagode** which is the opposite.

As popular as samba in Brazil is **axé**, which is twice as fast and twice as frenetic and played principally at Brazil's other great and even more hedonistic Carnival – in Salvador. Axé sounds like salsa sexed-up, fused with rock and roll and overdosing on speed. Less frantic is **forró**, another dance rhythm from the Northeast which was invented at 'For All' barn dances thrown for Brazilian railway workers by their English bosses. 'For all' was rendered 'For Haw' by the northeastern palate which in Brazil is spelt 'Forró'. It is a beach bar dance with yokely lyrics, powered by a pulsating drum and accordion and danced far closer than anything you will find in Hispanic America. Its offspring, **lambada**, which is danced even closer, has all but disappeared in Brazil nowadays. Other dance music styles include **frevo**, a fast 2/4 instrumental style which evolved from the polka, **guitarrada**, electric guitar driven, from the Amazon and sounding a little like Dick Dale on a cocktail of speed and acid and **samba rock** which sounds like neither rock nor samba, is very, very funky and is very in vogue in Rio nowadays.

Music to listen to

That the pedigree of Brazil's serious artists is second to none can be easily seen by a casual look at the guest musicians on their CDs. Names like Herbie Hancock, Joe Henderson, Stan Getz, Stevie Wonder, Wayne Shorter, Billy Cobham and Larry Coryell are commonplace. Serious contemporary music has a long and distinguished pedigree in Brazil. Whilst Scott Joplin was inventing early jazz, Rio musicians were inventing their own kind of ragtime, **choro** which like jazz was a fusion of Africa and Europe born out of the abolition of the slave trade. Choro never went away and can still be heard in Brazil; it bore children, notably a sit down, more harmonically sophisticated from of guitar samba called **samba canção**. And in the 1950s when this was slowed down and garnished with chord progressions inspired by US jazz, **bossa** nova was born. Bossa will forever be associated with one song in the minds of most non-Brazilians, *The Girl from Ipanema*, which is as integral to Brazilian music as *Norwegian Wood* is to English and played about as often.

Choro, Samba Canção and Bossa were all acoustically driven. When the Beatles and Hendrix rose to global stardom in the 1960s and even Dylan picked up an electric guitar, there was something of a revolution in Brazil. Conservatives wanted to keep the country's music 'authentic' and unpolluted by foreign influences. Liberals, spearheaded by pop crooner Roberto Carlos and a group of Bahian musicians led by Gilberto Gil and Caetano Veloso and known as the **tropicalistas** embraced electric instruments and fused Bossa and Jazz to produce a new set of Brazilian sounds collectively known as **música popular brasileira** or **MPB**. What followed was a golden age in Brazil with a fluorescence of talent that ran in parallel with the explosion of new music in the UK and US and encapsulated as wide a diversity of styles. MPB spread like a wave throughout Brazil and spawned all kinds of regional expressions. There were the melancholy, contemplative and richly complex songs of groups of musicians from the inland state of Minas called the **clube da esquina** and headed by Milton Nascimento, the numerous jazzy, poppy records of Gil, Caetano and the other Tropicalistas, the funky catchy Carioca anthems of Jorge Ben, the sophisticated Brazilian soul of Djavan and the pensive anthems of Almir Satir and Zé Ramalho, alongside many more...

Other genres

In recent years **rap**, particularly **hip hop**, which is known as funk or **rap Brasileiro** in Brazil has grown immensely in popularity. But despite all the MTV posturing on the videos it would be mistake to think that Brazilian hip hop is a pale imitation of the US. It is more melodic, funkier and more socially aware and is as strongly influenced by Brazilian musical genres and northeastern **repentista** spontaneous street poetry as it is by Grandmaster Flash and the Furious Five. But like US hip hop, Brazilian hip hop has long been seen as the voice of the voiceless; many of the stars are quite literally from the *favelas*. Many were or are gangsters. And like US hip hop, Brazilian hip hop represents a politically motivated alternative to crime and violence. But, unlike it, Brazilian stars actually put their rap into words. Bands like Grupo Afro-Reggae run active social programmes in the very worst Rio *favelas* and many of their ever-rotating teenaged band members have quite literally been weaned off guns and drugs. On the back of the hip hop scene and further north in Recife came **mangue-beat** – a fusion of electronic sounds, Brazilian rhythms rap and signing headed by the charismatic and short-lived Chico Science, whose legacy is continued today by the likes of Otto and DJ Dolores.

Concurrent with the rise in popularity of rap has been the rise of all manner of **club** music and **electronica**. The centre of the club scene in Brazil is São Paulo. But world famous name DJs like Marky and Patife who hail from there frequently play in Rio (see Bars and clubs page 118) as do São Paulo electronica stars like Fernanda Porto. The most famous international name in Brazilian electronica, Bebel Gilberto is still little known in Brazil. Her father may be the co-inventor of bossa nova, João Gilberto, but Bebel lives and was musically created in New York.

A brief guide to Brazilian genres

Most CD shops will allow you to listen to a CD before buying it.

Carnaval samba Buy a compilation of the best songs from this year's Rio Carnival

Pagode Look out for CDs by Beth Carvalho or Zeca Pagodinho

Axé Daniela Mercury is the most famous international name – and although she hasn't released a CD in years, *Feijão Com Arroz* is easy to find abroad. Chiclete com Banana are currently the biggest band of any genre in Brazil whilst Band Beijo's *Ao Vivo* captures the raw energy of live axé like no other.

Repentistas and cordel

A fascinating experience in the Nordeste is to come across a pair of '*Violeiros*' or '*Repentistas*', *troubadours* who accompany themselves on the melodious *Viola Nordestina*, developed from the Portuguese seven-string guitar, generally to be found in markets. They will sing, jokingly but flatterlngly, about individual members of the audience, expecting a tip in return. They also have a large repertoire of the ballads that deal with regional themes and personalities which are to be found in the '*Folhetos*', or pamphlets known under the generic title of '*Literatura de Cordel*' (String Literature), because they are traditionally displayed for sale hung from a string. Both the ballads and the pamphlets are of archaic Portuguese origin. The ballads are made up of innumerable verse forms, such as the Mourão, Galope, Martelo, Sextilha and Quadrão. The celebrated bandit, Lampião, is a favourite subject and the compiling of long lists of words or names is popular too.

Forró The most traditional names and inventors of modern forró are Luiz Gonzaga and Sivuca. For something that would be played in north eastern beach clubs look out for CDs by northeastern bands like Mastruz com Leite or Mel Com Terra.

Lambada Kaoma and Beto Barbosa are well-known names – though their CDs can be hard to find outside of Bahia.

Frevo Many Brazilian singers and bands from Alceu Valença to Zé ramalho have sung some frevo but Claudionor Germano e Expedito Baracho are two of the few who are specialists in the genre.

Guitarrada The most famous exponents are Aldo Sena and Mestre Vieira, both from the Amazon.

Samba rock This style is irresistibly danceable and very popular in Rio de Janeiro. Its godfather is Jorge Ben who wrote one of the country's most famous songs *Mas Que Nada*. He always plays free concerts over New Year on Copacabana. You can find many of his best songs on *Brazilian Hits* and *Funky Classics*. Other names to look out for are Seu Jorge, Ivo Mereilles and jazz-funksters Acid X– all Cariocas. *Favela* Chic is an excellent compilation.

Brazilian jazz fusion The most famous of all Brazilian Fusion tracks is Deodato's funked up 1970s *Also Spracht Zarathustra* (the 2001 theme) on his CD Prelude. Airto Moreira's Identity is a wonderful CD, as is Flora Purim's *Flight*. Other classics include Egberto Gismonti's Circense and Delia Fischer's Antônio. For something altogether more off the wall look out for CDs by multi-instrumentalist eccentric Hermeto Pascoal.

Choro Choro's most legendary figure is flautist Pixinguinha; his recordings although re-issued are as scratchy and ancient as Robert Johnson but nonetheless show a musician equally as great. For something less gramophone try the James Dean of the choro world Raphael Rabello; a brilliant violinist who died in the 1980s when still in his 30s. There is plenty of live choro throughout Brazil – see **Aprazível** page 115, **Clan Café,** page 119, and **Toca do Vinicus**, page 121.

Samba canção There are many great names in this genre and perhaps the greatest are João Bosco and Baden Powell; two of Brazil's very best guitarists, composers and singers. Bosco's classic albums are Galos De Briga and *Caça À Raposa* . *Nosso Baden* is a good Powell compilation. Other names to look out for are Nelson Gonçalves and Paulinho da Viola.

Bossa nova There are three great bossa nova names – João Gilberto, Tom Jobim and Vinícius de Moraes, all of whom have such a distinguished pedigree that selecting any one CD from any of them would be an impossible task. Go for a compilation.

Tropicalismo This group of Bahians includes some of Brazil's best known international names – Gilberto Gil, Caetano Veloso, Tom Zé, Maria Bethania and Gal Costa. All have been prolific in their output and continue to be but their best work comes from the 1970s; notably Caetano Velosos' *Bicho* and Gil's *Refazenda*. *Doces Bárbaros* with Caetano, Gil, Gal Costa and Maria Bethânia is an excellent compilation.

Música popular brasileira (MPB) There are a vast panoply of MPB musicians in Brazil. A roll call of the greatest names would have to include Milton Nascimento, the golden voice of Brazil and perhaps the country's greatest ever songwriter, Djavan, Brazil's Stevie Wonder and a master of harmonic complexity, Elis Regina the country's great, tragic diva and Chico Buraque, considered by some to be Brazil's greatest living poet and its foremost protest singer. More modern names include silky-voiced Marisa Monte and Bahian Timabalada percussionist and eccentric, Carlinhos Brown.

Hip hop Artists here include funky Rappin' Hood, Gabriel o Pensador, and Grupo Afro-Reggae and Planet Hemp from Rio. The *Rough Guide to Brazilian Hip-Hop* is an excellent introduction.

Mangue-beat The key names here are Chico Science and Nação Zumbi, whose best CD is *Afrociberdelia* and their one time band member, Otto, whose *Sem Gravidade* is a dreamy tour de force of percussion, lyrical singing and samples.

Club music Brazil's big name DJs are Patife and Marky. More interesting than either is DJ Dolores – who fuses traditional Brazilian and international sounds and who won the BBC World Music Awards in 2004.

Electronica Bebel Gilberto is undoubtedly the most famous name here. But she is atypical – more New York than Brazil. For something homegrown checkout Suba and Fernanda Porto.

Miscellaneous Marlui Miranda, a musicologist and jazz musician has more than any living person done more to show the world the complexity and beauty of Amazon Indian music. Her *Todos os Sons* is an absolute must. The music of master percussionist Naná Vasconcelos defies categorisation – orchestral, folkloric, technically awe-inspiring and completely original.

Brazilian classical composers

Ever since the Catholic church and its missionaries arrived in all parts of present-day Latin America, appropriate religious music was being composed locally, particularly by the Jesuits, and this led on to Baroque and other classical music. Brazil was no exception and Carlos Gomes' opera 'Il Guarany' achieved great popularity after its first performance in 1870. During the present century, Brazilian composers (together with those of Mexico and Argentina) are at the forefront of Latin American classical music and have produced many works based on folk and popular themes. The figure of Heitor Villa-Lobos (1857-1959) towers above all others and achieved world renown well within his lifetime. Largely self-taught, his prodigious output included the celebrated nine '*bachianas Brasileiras*' and six choros. Given to bold experimentation, he composed two pieces of which the melodic line was based on the skyline of New York and that of the Serra da Piedade mountains near Belo Horizonte, respectively. Other major names among the so-called 'nationalist' composers are Francisco Mignone, Camargo Guarnieri, Radames Gnatalli and Cesar Guerra Peixe (who found inspiration in the regional music of the Northeast).

Festivals

Brazilians love a party and the mixing of different ethnic groups has resulted in some particularly colourful and varied celebrations. The difficulties of daily life are often relieved by the fantasy and release of Carnival as well as the many other popular festivals held through the year. Wherever you go you will find street vendors selling ice cold beer and the smell of *churrasco* coming from improvised barbecues accompanied by loud vibrant music and dancing in the streets.

Carnival

Almost all Brazilian towns have some form of Carnival festivities. Although the most famous is Rio de Janeiro, there are equally spectacular and different traditions in Bahia and Pernambuco as well as a number of other good locations for those who wish only to party. The colonial mining towns of Diamantina and Ouro Preto in the interior of Minas Gerais are good locations to spend Carnival in atmospheric surroundings. Florianópolis and Laguna on the coast of Santa Catarina have less traditional but still very popular and lively carnivals.

Out of season carnivals

Street carnivals with *trios eléctricos* in the style of Bahia are held throughout Brazil at various times of the year. Some of the most popular are *Micareta* in Feira de Santana (April), *Fortal* in Fortaleza (July) and *Carnatal* in Natal (December). Although by no means traditional they are nonetheless exuberant and enjoyable.

Other popular festivities

There are several other festivals which are almost as important to Brazilians as Carnival. *Reveillon* (New Year's Eve) is a significant event and is generally celebrated on beaches. This can be either a hedonistic party as at Copacabana and Arraial D'Ajuda with the revellers dressed in white for luck, or as a respectful Candomblé ceremony in which flowers are launched into the sea at midnight as an offering to Yemanjá.

The *Fiestas Juninhas* (São João) are extremely popular especially in the Northeast and are held around 24 June (St John's day). Fires are built and forró is the music of choice with the festivities lasting for over a week at times. Fireworks and the co-ordinated dancing of groups called *quadrilhas* are also part of the celebrations.

In the North, the African and Indian cultures have mixed to form the *Boi-Bumba* tradition. In Amazonas, the Festa do Boi has become more commercialized but is still very impressive and popular. In Maranhão, where it is known as *Bumba-meu-boi*, the festivities are more traditional but equally as popular.

There are many Catholic saints' days that are sometimes celebrated in conjunction with African deities (especially in Bahia). Every town has a patron saint and his or her day will be an excuse for civic festivities, in addition to those of the foundation day of the town.

Immigrants from Europe to the south of Brazil and elsewhere have brought festivals from their own cultures such as the Oktoberfest held in Blumenau, believed to be second only to Munich.

Literature

The colonial period

Some of the major differences between Brazil and Spanish America spring from the history of colonization in the two areas. There were no great empires with large cities like those of the Incas or the Aztecs, and Portuguese exploitation concentrated first on extractive, then on cultivated export products (brazil-wood, then sugar). Although cities like Recife, Bahia and Rio de Janeiro did finally develop, there was, incredible as it may seem, no printing press in Brazil until the flight of the Regent, later King João VI to Rio in 1808. This is not to say that there was no colonial literature, though scholars can still quarrel about how 'Brazilian' it was. When the Portuguese set foot in Brazil in 1500, the letter sent back to King Manuel by Pero Vaz de Caminha, already wondering at the tropical magnificence of the country and the nakedness of the inhabitants, set themes which would recur in many later works. The first plays to be put on in Brazil were religious dramas, staged in three languages – Portuguese, Spanish, and Tupi – by the Jesuit José de Anchieta (1543-97). The most notable 17th-century poet is **Gregório de Matos** (1636-96), famous for his sharp satires on the corrupt life of the city of Salvador, and its tempting black and mulatta women. In the late 18th century, a group of poets from the gold-mining area of Minas, foremost among them **Tomás Antônio Gonzaga** (1744-1810), were at the centre of the early, abortive move for independence, the *Inconfidência* (1789 – see page 248). Although best known as a lyric poet, Gonzaga has been proved to be the author of the anonymous satirical poem *Cartas chilenas*, which gives a vivid portrait of colonial society.

The 19th century

It is helpful to understand Brazilian literature, even long after political independence, as a gradual and to some extent contradictory process of emancipation from foreign models. Every European literary movement – Romanticism, Realism, Symbolism, etc – had its Brazilian followers, but in each there was an attempt to adjust the model to local reality. A good example is the first of these, Indianism, which flourished in the mid-19th century, and produced two central figures: the poet **Antônio Gonçalves Dias** (1823-64), himself partly of Indian descent, and the novelist **José de Alencar** (1829-77). It is a form of Romanticism, idealizing the noble savage, and with plots adapted from Walter Scott, and it happily ignored what was happening to real Indians at the time. However, it does express national aspirations and feelings, if in nothing else, in the nostalgia for a kind of tropical Eden expressed in perhaps the most famous Brazilian poem, Gonçalves Dias *Canção do exílio*: "My land has palm-trees/ where the sabiá sings./ The birds that sing here/ don't sing like those back home." Alencar's novels, not all of them about Indians, are a systematic attempt to portray Brazil in its various settings, including the city. *O guarani* (1857), turned into a famous opera by Carlos Gomes, and *Iracema* (1865) are his most popular. The latter is perhaps the most complete mythical version of the Portuguese conquest, allegorized as a love affair between a native woman and an early colonist, Martim Soares. Iracema, "the virgin with the honeyed lips" dies in childbirth at the end, but the future lies with their mixed-blood son, Moacir.

After his death, Alencar was succeeded as the chief figure in Brazilian letters by **Joaquim Maria Machado de Assis** (1839-1908). Perhaps Brazil's best writer, and certainly the greatest to appear in Latin America until well into the 20th century, he had to fight against formidable obstacles: he was of relatively poor origins, was mulatto, stammered and in later life was subject to epileptic fits. He wrote nine novels and more than 200 short stories as well as poetry and journalism. He ended his life as an establishment figure, founder of the Brazilian Academy of Letters, but his novels, especially those written after 1880, when he published *Memórias póstumas de Brás Cubas*, and the best of his stories are surprisingly subversive, covert attacks on slavery and on male power, for instance. He avoided detection by not using his own voice, hiding behind quirky, digressive narrators who are not always trustworthy. All the novels and most of the stories are set in Rio, which he hardly left, and give a remarkably varied account of the city and its different social levels. His most famous novel, *Dom Casmurro* (1900) is one of the best-disguised cases of an unreliable narrator in the history of the novel, and still arouses critical polemics.

Machado's atmosphere is predominantly that of the empire, which fell in 1889, a year after the abolition of slavery. In the Republic, a younger generation, more overtly rebellious in their aims, and affected by new scientific ideas from Europe, came to the fore. If Machado is the most famous Brazilian author, perhaps *Os sertões*, by **Euclides da Cunha** (1866-1909) is the most famous book. It is an account of the Canudos campaign in the interior the state of Bahia in 1896-97. The campaign was a horrific failure, victory being won only at a huge cost in casualties, and Euclides, sent to cover it as a journalist, turned this failure into an indictment of a social system which excluded huge groups of people. Written in a dramatic, somewhat self-indulgent style, with extensive use of scientific words, it has been excellently translated as *Rebellion in the Backlands*.

The other important prose writer of this period, the novelist **Afonso Lima Barreto** (1881-1922), was mulatto like Machado, but there resemblances end. Much more openly rebellious and less of a conscious artist than Machado, his novels, the most notable of which is *Triste fim de Policarpo Quaresma*, are overt attacks on intellectual mediocrity, and the corruption and despotism into which the Republic soon fell. A passing mention ought to be made, too, of one of the 'unclassifiable' books in which Brazilian literature abounds: **Helena Morley**'s *Minha vida de menina* (translated by Elizabeth Bishop as *The Diary of Helena Morley*), and only published in 1942, it is the precocious, funny, and remarkably perceptive teenager's diary, written in Diamantina, Minas Gerais, at the end of the 19th century.

The 20th century

In general, the poetry of the turn of the century was imitative and stuffy: renewal did not come until the early 1920s, when a group of intellectuals from São Paulo, led by **Mário de Andrade** (1893-1945) and **Oswald de Andrade** (1890-1954) (unrelated) began the movement known as modernism. This is conveniently supposed to have begun in 1922, the centenary of political independence, with a Week of Modern Art in São Paulo; in fact it began earlier, and took until the mid-1920s to spread to the provinces. In great part, modernism's ideology was nationalist, and though the word spanned the political spectrum, at its best it simply meant the discovery of a real Brazil behind stereotypes: Mário travelled throughout the country, attempting to understand its variety, which he embodied in his major prose-work, the comic 'rhapsody' *Macunaíma* (1928), which in its plot and language attempts to construct a unity out of a complex racial and regional mix. Also in 1928, Oswald launched the 'anthropophagist', or cannibalist programme, which proclaimed that Brazilian writers should imitate their native predecessors, and fully digest European culture: a new kind of Indianism, perhaps ...

The most enduring artistic works to have emerged from modernism, however, are poetic: two of Brazil's major modern poets, **Manuel Bandeira** (1886-1968) and **Carlos Drummond de Andrade** (1902-87) were early enthusiasts of modernism, and corresponded at length with Mário. Bandeira, the older man, made a slow transition to the new, freer style; his poems, often short and based on everyday events or images, nevertheless have a power and rhythmic accuracy which are deceptively simple. Drummond's poetry is more self-conscious, and went through a complex intellectual development, including a period of political enthusiasm during the Second World War, followed by disillusionment with the beginning of the Cold War. His themes, including some remarkable love-poetry addressed by a 50-year old to a younger woman, and a lifelong attachment to Itabira, the small town in Minas Gerais where he was born, are very varied. Readers without Portuguese can best approach Drummond, widely regarded as Brazil's greatest poet, through an excellent anthology, *Traveling in the Family*.

The 1930s were a crucial decade. With increasing political mobilization, the growth of cities, and of an aspiring middle class, literature began to look to a wider audience; however, at first, it still reflected the dominance of rural life. The realism of this period, which often had a strong regionalist bias, had its raison d'être in a society still divided by huge social and/or geographical differences, and indeed played its part in diminishing those differences. Many of the first group came from the economically and socially backward Northeast. **José Lins do Rego** (1901-57) is perhaps the most characteristic figure. He was highly influenced by the ideas of **Gilberto Freyre** (1900-87), whose *Casa grande e sensually* (The Masters and the Slaves), published in 1933, one of the most important and readable of Brazilian books. It is a study of the slave-based, sugar-plantation society, and one of the first works to appreciate the contribution made by Blacks to Brazil's culture. It remains, however, very paternalist, and Lins do Rego's fiction, beginning with the semi-autobiographical *Menino de engenho*, reflects that, commenting on the poverty and filth of the (ex-)slave-quarters as if they were totally natural. His 'Sugar-cane cycle' sold in large editions, in part because of its unaffected, simple style.

A greater novelist belonging to the same group is **Graciliano Ramos** (1892-1953). His fiction is much more aggressive, and in later life he became a communist. His masterpiece, turned into an excellent film in the 1960s, is *Vedas secas*, which returns to the impoverished interior of *Os sertões*, but concentrates on an illiterate cowhand and his family, forced from place to place by drought and social injustice; it is a courageous attempt to enter the mental world of such people. *Memórias do cárcere*, published after Ramos's death, is his unflinching account of his imprisonment for a year during the Vargas regime.

The essential novelist to read for anyone visiting the south of Brazil is **Érico Veríssimo** (1905-75), especially his epic trilogy collectively entitled *O tempo e o vento* (O continente [1949], *O retrato* [1951], and *O arquipélago* [1961]) spread over two centuries of the turbulent history of Rio Grande do Sul.

Gradually, in the 1940s and 1950s, a subtler and more adventurous fiction began to be published alongside the regionalist realism that was the major heritage of the 1930s. Three writers stand out: João Guimarães Rosa, Clarice Lispector and João Cabral de Melo Neto. **João Guimarães Rosa** (1908-67) published his major novel, *Grande sertão: veredas* in 1956. Almost Joycean in its aspirations and linguistic innovations, it is a kind of mixture of a cowboy story and a modern version of Faustian pact with the devil. For those without stamina (and excellent Portuguese), the translation (*The Devil to Pay in the Backlands*) is unfortunately not an adequate alternative. Rosa is best approached through his stories, those of Sagarana (particularly "*A hora e vez de Augusto Matraga*") being perhaps the best.

The stories and novels of **Clarice Lispector** (1920-77) now have a considerable audience outside Brazil, as well as a huge one inside it. Her stories, especially those of *Laços de família* (1960), are in general set in middle-class Rio, and usually have women as their central characters: the turbulence, family hatreds, and near-madness hidden beneath routine lives are conveyed in unforgettable ways, with a language and symbolism that is poetic and adventurous without being exactly difficult (she said she fought with the Portuguese language daily). Some of her novels have over-ambitious metaphysical superstructures, and may not be to some readers' tastes – *A paixão segundo G H*, for instance, concerns a housewife's confrontation with a dead cockroach in her maid's room, and her final decision to eat it, seen as a kind of "communion". At her best, in some of her journalism, in her late, deliberately semi-pornographic stories, and above all in the posthumous novel, *A hora da estrela*, which approaches the poor in an utterly unsentimental way; Lispector can stimulate and move like no one else.

The greatest poet of this generation is **João Cabral de Melo Neto** (born 1920 in Pernambuco, died 1999), whose best poetry concerns his home state. The drought-ridden interior, the lush but oppressive landscape of the sugar-plantations, and the city slums are all present in the verse-play *Morte e vida severina* (1956), and his tight, spare poetry often returns to the same places, or analogous ones in the several countries (most importantly, in Spain) in which he has resided as a diplomat.

The 1964 military coup, and the increasing use of torture and censorship in the late 1960s and early 1970s, had profound effects on literature, especially as they were accompanied by vast economic changes (industrialization, a building boom, huge internal migration, the opening up of the Amazon). At first, censorship was haphazard, and the 1960s liberation movements had their – increasingly desperate – Brazilian equivalents. Protest theatre had a brief boom, with *Arena conta Zumbi*, about a 17th-century rebel slave leader, produced by **Augusto Boal** (born 1931), being one of the most important. The best fictional account of those years can be found in two novels by **Antônio Callado** (born 1917), *Quarup* (1967), set in the Northeast and centred on a left-wing priest, and *Bar Don Juan* (1971), whose focus is on the contradictions of a group of middle-class guerrillas; and in **Ivan Ângelo**'s *A festa* (1976), set in Belo Horizonte, a funny and hard-hitting account of a varied set of people, which chronicles the impact of the 'sex and drugs' revolution alongside its political concerns. A remarkable documentary account of the period is ex- guerrilla (subsequently leader of the Green Party) **Fernando Gabeira**'s *O que é isso companheiro?* (1982), which chronicles his involvement in the kidnapping of the American ambassador in 1969. Poetry at this time went through a crisis of self-confidence, and it was widely thought that it had emigrated into the (marvellous) lyrics of such popular composers as **Chico Buarque de Holanda** and **Caetano Veloso,** who were also the foremost standard-bearers of political protest in the 1970s.

It is impossible in the space available to give more than a few suggestions of some of the best work published in recent decades, concentrating on books which have been translated. A brilliant satirical novel by **Paulo Emílio Salles Gomes** (1916-77) about the São Paulo upper middle class is *Três mulheres e três pppês* (1977); **Darcy Ribeiro** (born 1922), an anthropologist and politician, took time off to write *Maíra* (1978), an updating of Indianism, but with real Indians and a threatened Amazon environment; **Rubem Fonseca** (born 1925), whose story *Feliz ano novo* (1973) created a scandal because of its brutal treatment of class differences, has dedicated himself to the writing of hardnosed thrillers like *A grande arte* (1983); **Caio Fernando Abreu** (1948-96) is a short-story writer of considerable talent, dealing with the alienated urban young in such books as *Morangos mofados* and *Os dragões não conhecem o paraíso*; finally, **Milton Hatoum**'s *Relato de um certo oriente* (1989) is a vivid novel set in Manaus, amongst the Lebanese immigrant community.

Recommended reading

Essays and books which can be wholeheartedly recommended for those who want more information are: Ray Keenoy, David Treece and Paul Hyland, *The Babel Guide to the Fiction of Portugal, Brazil and Africa in English Translation* (London: Boulevard Books, 1995). Irwin Stern (ed) *Dictionary of Brazilian Literature* (New York: Greenwood Press, 1988). Mike González and David Treece, *The Gathering of Voices* (Verso, 1992) (on 20th-century poetry). Elizabeth Bishop and Emanuel Brasil (eds) *An Anthology of Twentieth-Century Brazilian Poetry* (Wesleyan University Press, 1972). John Gledson, *Brazilian Fiction: Machado de Assis to the Present*, in John King (ed), *Modern Latin American Fiction: A Survey* (Faber, 1987). Many of the essays in Roberto Schwarz, *Misplaced Ideas: Essays on Brazilian Culture* (Verso, 1992), especially those on *Machado de Assis*, and *Culture and Politics in Brazil, 1964-69* are very stimulating.

» See also Books, page 722, for further recommended reading.

Fine art and sculpture

The colonial era: 16th and 17th centuries

No visitor to Brazil should miss visiting a colonial church. During the colonial period in Brazil the Church dominated artistic patronage, with the religious orders vying with each other to produce ever more lavish interiors. In the 17th century the Benedictines included several notable sculptors among their ranks. Much of the magnificent gilded interior of the monastery of São Bento in Rio de Janeiro is by **Frei Domingos da Conceição** (circa 1643-1718), who worked there during the 1660s. His *Crucifixion* of 1688 in the monastery of São Bento in Olinda sets up a deliberately shocking contrast between the sinuous elegance of Christ's body and the terrible lacerations of his flesh. **Frei Agostinho de Piedade** (died 1661) of the Benedictine community in

Salvador produced some old-fashioned terracotta reliquary busts during the 1630s and 1640s (Museu de Arte Sacra, Salvador) but the powerful *Penitent Peter* in Salvador's Nossa Senhora do Monte (circa 1636), also attributed to him, prefigures the emotional intensity of subsequent generations.

A distinctive feature of colonial interiors is the incorporation of decorative scenes in blue and white painted tiles, *azulejos*, around the walls. These were imported from Portugal from the earlier 17th century onwards, with subject matter as often secular as religious. Good examples include the Franciscan foundations in Olinda, Salvador and Recife, and the church of Nossa Senhora da Glória in Rio de Janeiro, which has hunting scenes in the sacristy, Old Testament figures in the choir, and in the nave, astonishingly, scenes of pastoral love loosely based on the *Song of Songs*.

The 18th century

Although 17th-century church decoration is often lavish there is little warning of the extraordinary theatricality which characterizes the work of the 18th century. Behind their sober façades churches open out like theatres, with the equivalent of balconies and boxes for the privileged, and a stage for the high altar with a proscenium arch and wings of carved and gilded wood. Cherubs whisper to each other or gesticulate from their perches amongst the architectural scrolls; angels, older and more decorous, recline along a cornice or flutter in two dimensions across an illusionistic ceiling. The object of devotion is usually placed high above the altar on a tiered dais, surrounded by a Bernini-esque sunburst of gilded rays. A skilled exponent of this type of design was the sculptor **Francisco Xavier de Brito** (died 1751), as in Nossa Senhora do Pilar, Ouro Preto and São Francisco de Penitência, Rio.

This theatricality reaches its climax in the work of **Aleijadinho**, the 'Little Cripple' (1738-1814) a mulatto artist who worked in the province of Minas Gerais. As by far the most famous artist in the colonial period in the whole of Latin America it is perhaps not surprising to find his name attached to an impossible number of projects, but a consideration even of the securely documented reveals a man of extraordinary passion and energy who worked as a painter, architect and above all sculptor. The church at Congonhas do Campo offers the most dramatic example of Aleijadinho's art. Pilgrims paying homage to the miracle-working Bom Jesus do Matozinhos approach the church along a penitential road winding up the hill between six small chapels, each housing scenes from Christ's Passion represented by lifesize expressive statues of polychrome wood. The final ascent is up an imposing double staircase under the stony gaze of 12 judgmental prophets who variously lament, threaten or cajole, addressing the heavens, the distant horizon, each other, or the faithful on the stone steps below them. In a building beside the church a fascinating display of drawings and photographs of the many accidents and emergencies from which the Good Jesus has saved people testifies to the continuing popularity of this shrine.

The painterly equivalent to Aleijadinho's sculptures can be found in the work of his contemporary, **Manuel da Costa Ataíde** (1762-1830) from Mariana, whose vividly colourful narrative scenes decorate numerous churches in Minas Gerais. Ataíde's rococo settings are populated with solidly-built saints and angels whose rolling eyes and exaggerated gestures give them an earthy vigour sometimes at odds with the spirituality of the subject matter, as in the illusionistic ceiling of São Francisco de Assis, Ouro Preto, a church whose design is traditionally attributed to Aleijadinho.

In Bahia, **José Joaquim da Rocha** (1737-1807) (see page 372) was one of the most successful artists of his day and his slightly Italianate ceiling paintings survive in many churches in Salvador. The best sculptor of the late colonial period in Bahia was **Manuel Inácio da Costa** (1763-1857) whose figures, often dramatically gaunt with protruding veins and large eyes, are reminiscent of Aleijadinho's work (see, for example, his *Christ at the Column* in the Museu de Arte Sacra in Salvador). It is in Rio that sculpture first begins to sober up again, as for example in the work of the sculptor Valentim de Fonseca e Silva, known as **Mestre Valentim** (circa 1750-1813) which can be seen in several churches including São Francisco de Paula and Nossa Senhora da Glória. Valentim also designed the first public gardens in Rio: the *Passeio Público* was inaugurated in 1783 and included walks, seats decorated with *azulejos* and pavilions. A unique series of six painted views of Rio and Guanabara Bay by **Leandro Joaquim** (1738-1798), originally made for one of the pavilions, are now in the Museu Histórico Nacional in Rio.

French influence in Imperial Brazil

After the transfer of the Imperial court to Rio in 1808 João VI made a determined effort to renovate Brazilian culture, and in 1816 the French Artistic Mission – a boatload of painters, sculptors, architects, musicians and craftsmen – arrived from France to found what was to become the Imperial Academy. Two artists were particularly influential: **Nicolas-Antoine Taunay** (1755-1830) and **Jean-Baptiste Debret** (1768-1848). Taunay's luminous landscapes of the area around Rio and Debret's lively street scenes helped to open up new areas of secular Brazilian subject matter, and inspired artists throughout the 19th century. The Academy provided scholarships to send promising young artists to Paris, so reinforcing the French influence, and there are echoes of Delacroix in the work of **Vítor Meireles** (1832-1903) as for example, in his *Battle of the Guararapes* of 1879 in the Museu Nacional de Belas Artes, Rio, and of Ingres in *La Carioca* (1882) of **Pedro Américo** (1843-1905) in the same museum. The influence of Courbet can be seen in the so-called belle époque of the first republican years (1889-1922), in particular in the work of Meireles' pupil, **José Ferraz de Almeida Júnior** (1850-1899).

The 20th century, towards a Brazilian vision

Brazil moved from this essentially academic tradition straight into the radicalism of the early 20th century, and movements such as Cubism, Futurism, Fauvism and Constructivism were quickly translated into distinctively Brazilian idioms. **Lasar Segall** (1891-1957), **Anita Malfatti** (1896-1964) and the sculptor **Vitor Brecheret** (1894-1955) were pioneers of modernism, working in relative isolation before the Semana da Arte Moderna (Modern Art Week) in São Paulo in 1922 drew together a group of artists and intellectuals whose influence on Brazilian culture can still be felt today. They sought to challenge established bourgeois attitudes, to shake off the traditional cultural subservience to Europe, and to draw attention to the cultural diversity and social inequality of contemporary Brazil. **Emilio di Cavalcanti** (1897-1976) mocked the artificiality of middle class socialites (examples in the Museu de Arte Contemporânea, São Paulo). **Tarsila do Amaral** (1886-1973) borrowed her loud colours from popular art while her imagery includes ironic reworkings of European myths about the savage cannibalistic Indians supposed to inhabit the Brazilian jungle. **Cândido Portinari** (1903-62) used murals to expose the exploitation and injustice suffered by workers and peasants while **Osvaldo Goeldi** (1895-1961) explored similar themes in his powerful wood engravings. Portinari, in an interesting revival of the colonial use of *azulejos*, created murals in blue and white painted tiles for modern building such as the MES building by Costa and Niemeyer of Rio, begun in 1937, and Niemeyer's church of São Francisco in Pampulha, Belo Horizonte (1943).

The economic strength of the middle years of the century encouraged state patronage of the arts. President Getúlio Vargas recognized that art and architecture could be used to present an image of Brazil as a modern industrialized nation, with Brasília being the culmination of this vision. Museums of Modern Art were founded in São Paulo and Rio, and in 1951 São Paulo hosted its first Bienal Internacional which attracted abstract artists from Europe and the US and confirmed Abstraction – symbol of progress and technological modernization – as the dominant mode in Brazil during the 1950s. Rivalry between the artistic communities of Rio and São Paulo helped to produce some outstanding avant-garde art. In the 1950s **Waldemar Cordeiro** (1925-73), leader of the São Paulo Grupo Ruptura, painted what at first sight appear to be rather simple geometric patterns in bright, contrasting colours, but on closer attention the flat surface seems to break up, suggesting recession, space and restless movement, in some ways prefiguring the British Op Art movement of the 1960s. The Neo-Concrete group of artists of Rio argued for the integration of art into daily life, and experimented with art which makes sensory and emotional demands on the 'spectator' whose participation leads in turn to creation. During the early 1960s **Lygia Clark** (1920-88) made *bichos* (*animals*) out of hinged pieces of metal which, as the name implies, are like creatures with a life of their own: they can be rearranged indefinitely but because of their complexity it is impossible to predetermine what shape will result from moving a particular section. Nowadays, unfortunately, they are displayed in museums where touching is not encouraged (as in the Pinacoteca do Estado, São Paulo). **Hélio Oiticica** (1937-80) took the idea further, working with people (poor and often black) from the samba schools in the Rio *favelas* to create artistic 'happenings' involving dance, music and flamboyant costumes called *parangolés* (capes). The notion that a key function of art should be to shock the bourgeoisie was first voiced by in the 1922 Week of Modern Art. Oiticica often succeeded, and he and other artists of the 1960s also realized another of the aims of the first modernists: to create a Brazilian modern art that was not the poor relation of developments in Europe or the US. A museum of his work has recently opened in Rio. Other important figures of this generation include the neo-concretist painter **Ivan Serpa** (1923-73), **Sérgio Camargo** (1930-90), who produced textured rhythmic constructions of white on white but because they are made with off-cuts of wood they suggest the tensions between form and material, geometry and nature; and **Amílcar de Castro** (born 1920) whose deceptively simple sculptures are often cut from one large panel of cast iron.

The military coup of 1964 marked the beginning of a period of political repression and of renewed artistic energy, with figurative tendencies re-emerging. In 1970 **Antônio Enrique Amaral** (born 1935) took as his theme the banana, so often used in dismissive references to Latin America, and in an extended series of paintings monumentalized it into an extraordinary symbol of power and fruitfulness. In an ironic neo-colonial altarpiece (circa 1966) installed in the Museu de Arte de São Paulo, **Nelson Leirner** (born 1932) makes the object of devotion the neon-lit head of pop star Robert Carlos. Conceptual art offers different ways of confronting the dominant ideology. Both **Cildo Meireles** (born 1948) and **Jac Lierner** (born 1961) have used, misused or forged banknotes, for example, and both they and **Waltercio Caldas** (born 1946) and **Tunga** (born 1952) have created installations which draw attention, directly and indirectly to environmental issues. The painter **Siron Franco** (born 1947) also often addresses the issue of the destruction of the Amazon rainforest, but his disturbing surreal images explore many other areas – industrial pollution, sexual fantasy, political corruption, national identity – making him one of the most exciting artists in Brazil today.

Architecture

Brazilian colonial style: houses and civic buildings

The earliest Portuguese colonizers to arrive in Brazil in the 16th century faced many problems in building their houses, forts, churches and other necessary structures. First of all there was a lack of building materials, such as bricks, roof tiles and mortar. Second, there were few trained craftsmen, such as carpenters and bricklayers, in the colony. They therefore had to improvise by developing unusual building techniques and trying different materials. In the hinterland, in places like São Paulo, Goiás and Minas Gerais the majority of the houses were built with *taipa de pilão*. This technique consisted in using a wooden form to build thick walls. These forms were filled with a mixture of clay, vegetable fibres, horsehair, ox blood and dung. This paste was then compacted with a pestle and allowed to dry for two to three days before the next layer was added. The roof tiles were often moulded on a female slave's thigh and dried in the sun.

It is quite easy to identify a house in Brazilian colonial style. Their shapes, colours and building techniques remained virtually unchanged for almost three centuries. Firstly, they always had large, visible roofs, made with red clay tiles, finishing in eaves extending beyond the walls. All the buildings were painted in a white wash, with bright colours used only on window and door frames. These were made of wood and had, mostly, elegant arches at the top. In the 19th century, sash windows with squared 10 cm by 10 cm pieces of glass were added in many houses, as can be seen in cities like Paraty, Ouro Preto and Salvador.

Urban colonial houses had doors and windows opening directly onto the street. Courtyards were never placed in front of the house, but internally, forming airy patios which protected the privacy of the family. The furniture was extremely simple and rough. Often, the only pieces of furniture in a bedroom would be the bed itself and a leather box to store clothes and personal belongings. In the colonial period, the highest status symbol was to live in a *sobrado* (a house with more than one floor, usually two). The ground floor was normally a commercial business and above it the residence of the owner's family.

Churches, convents and religious buildings: the Baroque in Brazil

Houses, public buildings and other colonial civic edifices were generally unelaborate. All the refinement, style and sophistication in art, architecture and decoration was lavished on churches, convents and monasteries. The great religious orders, such as the Jesuits, Franciscans, Carmelites and Benedictines brought to Brazil the latest artistic trends from Europe, mainly the Baroque and Rococo.

Two separate strands in Brazilian religious architecture evolved. In the most important cities, close to the seaboard and more influenced by European culture, the churches and convents were built according to designs brought from Portugal, Italy and Spain. Some were merely copies of Jesuit or Benedictine temples in Europe. Examples of this can be found in Salvador (the main cathedral, the São Francisco church), Rio de Janeiro (the Mosteiro de São Bento, the Convento de Santo Antônio) and Olinda (church and convent of Nossa Senhora das Neves).

Brazilian Baroque

At the end of the 17th century gold was found in the region of Minas Gerais. One of the first administrative acts of the Portuguese crown in response to this discovery was to banish the traditional European orders from the mining region. The royal administration wanted to control the mining itself, taxation and traffic in gold and, as the friars were regarded as among the most shameless of smugglers of the metal, the orders in this instance were denied the support they were given elsewhere in the Portuguese colonies. Therefore the majority of the churches in cities like Ouro Preto, Mariana, Congonhas and Sabará were built by local associations, the so-called 'third orders'. These lay orders had the gold and the will to build magnificent temples but, although they wanted their projects to be as European as possible, the original designs were hard to obtain in such out-of-the-way places. So the local artists had to find their own way. Inspired by descriptions and second-hand information, they created their own interpretation of the Baroque, thoroughly infused with regional influences and culture. This is the reason why the 'Barroco Mineiro' is so original.

Curved churches and the decline of the Gold Era

At the beginning of the 18th century, when gold was easily found in Minas Gerais, the main attraction was the inside of the church, richly and heavily decorated in carved wood and gold. Many of the churches built in this period will be a total surprise for the visitor. Their façades and exteriors are so simple and yet the naves and altars are so highly and artistically decorated. As the mines started to decline, the outside of the buildings became more sophisticated, with curves, round towers and sinuous walls, such as the churches of São Francisco de Assis and Rosário, in Ouro Preto. As the gold for covering walls ran out, it was replaced by paintings and murals.

The 19th century and the Neoclassic style

The beginning of 19th century brought a major change in the history of Brazilian architecture. When Napoleon invaded Portugal in 1808, the Portuguese royal family and some 15,000 nobles and wealthy families fled to Rio de Janeiro, bringing with them their own view of what was sophisticated in the arts. In 1816 the king, Dom João VI, invited a group of French artists (The French Artistic Mission) to Brazil to introduce the most recent European trends in painting, sculpture, decoration and architecture. This was the beginning of the Neoclassic style in Brazil. An Imperial Academy of Fine Arts was created and all the new government buildings were built in Neoclassic style. The great name of this period as the French architect Grandjean de Montigny , who planned and built many houses and public buildings throughout the city of Rio de Janeiro.

The rich and famous also wanted their houses in this newly fashionable style, which revolutionized the Brazilian way of building. The large roofs were now hidden by a small wall, the plat band. Windows and doors acquired round arches and walls were painted in ochres and light tones of pink. Public buildings and churches started to look like ancient Greek temples, with triangular pediments and columns. This new style was not best suited Brazil's climate. The earlier, large colonial roofs were much more efficient in dealing with heavy tropical rains and, in consequence, the Neoclassic style never became popular in the countryside.

Even when the coffee planters, in the second half of 19th century, started to become extremely rich and fond of imported fashions, they would build their urban mansions in the Neoclassic style, but still keep their farm houses with large roofs, sometimes adding small Neoclassic details in windows, doors and internal decoration. Good examples of this 19th-century rural architecture can be found very close to Rio de Janeiro, in cities like Vassouras, Valença, Barra do Piraí and Bananal, where some of the old farm houses are open to visitors.

There are many examples of urban Neoclassic building in Rio de Janeiro, such as the Museu Nacional, the Santa Casa da Misericórdia, the Casa de Rui Barbosa and the Instituto Benjamin Constant. Also very close to Rio, in Petrópolis, the Museu Imperial (formerly the Emperor's summer palace) is also a perfect example of the style. This Neoclassic remained popular in Brazil until the end of the 19th century, being also the 'official' style of the First and the Second Brazilian Empires.

The early 20th century and the eclectic style

After the Republic, in 1889, the Neoclassic style lost favour since it had been serving the king and the emperors for such a long time. A new style, or better, a new harmony of different styles started to gain popularity, also under the influence of Paris and the Belle Époque. There were elements of neoclassic architecture, but also an excess of decoration and adornment on the façades. A broad 'boulevard' was constructed in Rio de Janeiro in 1906, the Avenida Central (today Avenida Rio Branco), with the idea of creating 'a Paris in the Tropics'. There are many examples of buildings in the Eclectic style on this avenue: the Biblioteca Nacional, the Teatro Municipal (Opera House) and the Museu Nacional de Belas Artes, all of them built in the first decade of

20th century. Also in Manaus, during the rubber boom, many buildings adopted this style, such as the Teatro Amazonas (the Opera House). During the first two decades of this century, the Eclectic style remained very popular.

The 'Modern Art Week' of 1922 and national pride

In 1922 a group of artists, painters, poets and architects organized in São Paulo 'A Semana da Arte Moderna' or the Modern Art Week, during which they exhibited their distaste at the influence of foreign standards in Brazilian art. They considered their role to be a quest for a genuine Brazilian form of expression. This resulted in the rejection of all imported standards and, as far as architecture was concerned, two main currents emerged.

The Neocolonial

The first movement sought its true Brazilian style in the past, in the colonial period. Architects like Lúcio Costa, studied the techniques, materials and designs of the 16th, 17th and 18th centuries, soon producing houses with a colonial look, but also combining elements which were only previously found in Baroque churches. These included pediments and decorated door frames. The style was called Neocolonial and remained popular until the 1940s, especially in Rio de Janeiro and São Paulo.

In search of greater authenticity, many architects employed original materials brought from demolished old houses. A good example of thls can be found in Rio de Janeiro, in the Largo do Boticário (very close to the train station for Corcovado, in Cosme Velho), a small square surrounded by Neocolonial houses painted in fancy, bright colours.

Modernism

The other current generated by the Semana da Arte Moderna looked to the future for its inspiration for Brazilian-ness. Architects such as Oscar Niemeyer, Lúcio Costa, Affonso Eduardo Reidy, the landscape designer Roberto Burle Marx and many others started to design functional and spacious buildings, with large open areas and *pilotis* (pillars carrying a building, leaving the ground floor open). The use of concrete and glass was intense and the masterpiece of the Brazilian architectural Modernism is Brasília, the capital, planned from scratch in the 1950 by Lúcio Costa and Oscar Niemeyer.

Many examples of Modernist building can be found all over Brazil: in Brasília, the Cathedral, the National Congress, the Palácio do Planalto (the presidential palace), in fact the whole city, with its broad freeways and spacious urban blocks, called *quadras*; in Belo Horlzonte, the church of São Francisco de Assis, in Pampulha; in São Paulo, the MASP (Museum of Art of São Paulo), the Memorial da América Latina, and many commercial buildings along the Avenida Paulista; in Rio de Janeiro, the Ministério da Educação e Saúde, the Museu de Arte Moderna, the Catedral Metropolitana, the Petrobrás building (Brazilian State Petrol Company), the BNDES building (National Bank of Social and Economic Development), all in the central area of the city.

Brazilian contemporary architecture

The most recent trend is the post-modern. Many business centres, shopping malls and residential buildings are being designed in a style which uses coloured mirror glass, granite and stylized structures reminiscent of classical temples.

Brazilian architects are also famous worldwide for their techniques in designing houses for construction on steeply-inclined hills. In Rio de Janeiro, if you are driving along the coastal road in the neighbourhoods of Barra and São Conrado you can see many of these astonishing projects, homes of the very wealthy.

Land and environment

Geography

Brazil is the largest country in South America and the fifth largest in the world, almost as large as the USA. It is over 4,300 km from north to south and the same from east to west, with land borders of 15,700 km and an Atlantic coastline of 7,400 km. It has a common frontier with all the other South American countries except Chile and Ecuador and occupies almost half the total area of the continent. Its population of 162 million is now, after the recent break-up of the USSR, also the fifth largest in the world, and over half that of South America.

Geology

Although Brazil is dominated by the vast river basins of the Amazon and the Paraná which account for about three-fifths of the country, not much of it is 'lowlands'. Ancient rock structures, some of the oldest in the world, underlie much of the area creating resistant plateaux and a rounded hilly landscape. These ancient Pre-Cambrian rocks culminate in the Guiana highlands to the north and the crystalline ranges which run close to the coastline all the way from near the Amazon to the Uruguayan frontier.

It is believed that South America and Africa were joined in the geologic past, and there is a tolerable fit between the easterly bulge of Brazil and the Gulf of Guinea. Persuasive evidence has been found of identical ostracod fossils (freshwater fish) in corresponding Cretaceous rocks in both Brazil and Gabon, overlain by salt deposits that could have been the first appearance of the South Atlantic Ocean. This suggests that the split began some 125 million years ago. What is now accepted is that the South American Plate continues to move westwards with the consequent elevation of the Andes on the other side of the continent where it meets the Pacific Plates.

The Amazon Basin

The Amazon River is the greatest in the world in area of drainage, about 7,000,000 sq km, and in volume of discharge into the sea averaging 180,000 cu m per second (or 170 billion gallons per hour), 10 times that of the Mississippi, and more than all the rivers of Europe put together. Such is the flow that the salinity of the Atlantic Ocean is affected for 250 km out from the river delta. It is 6,400 km long (marginally shorter than the Nile) from its sources in the Andes of Peru, and still has over 3,000 km to go through Brazil when it leaves Leticia on the Colombia/Brazil border, yet with only a fall of 80 m to sea level. Unlike most major world rivers, the basin is reduced in width near its mouth, indeed hills come down to the river near Monte Alegre only 200 km from the delta. Some 200 km above this at Óbidos, the river is over 75 m deep, that is the bottom is well below sea level. This reflects the more recent geological history of the basin which until the latter part of the Tertiary Period (say 25 million years ago) was connected to the Pacific and drained through what is now Ecuador. With the uplift of the Andes, this route was closed off, and a huge inland sea was formed, helped by a downward folding of the older rocks (some geologists believe there was also significant rifting of the strata) to create a huge geosyncline. Eventually the water broke through the crystalline rocks to the east and made the new connection to the Atlantic. Deep layers of sediment were laid down and have been added to ever since, with today's heavy tropical rains continuing to erode the surrounding mountains. This gives the largest more or less level area in Brazil, but it is so heavily forested and the soils so continually leached by the climate, with vast expanses frequently under floodwaters, that the potential for agriculture is strictly limited.

A characteristic of virtually all the tributaries which join the Amazon from the south is that upstream navigation ends where the rivers tumble off the plateaux of central Brazil creating dramatic waterfalls and in many cases now providing hydroelectric power.

The Centre West

South of the Amazon basin is a large area of undulating highlands, a dissected plateau mostly between 200 m and 800 m. These are ancient rocks, back as far as Pre-Cambrian crystallines. They produce poor soils but sufficient to provide the grasslands or *cerrado* (see box) of the Mato Grosso, Goiás, western Paraná and adjacent areas, widely used for ranching, though now increasingly found suitable for soya bean production, one of Brazil's foremost exports.

From Minas Gerais southwards, the rivers drain into the second largest basin of Brazil, the Paraná, which eventually reaches the Atlantic by way of the River Plate of Argentina/Uruguay. This is another large river system, 4,000 km long, of which about half is in Brazil. A principal tributary of the Paraná is the Rio Paraguay which, in its early stages, flows into a wide depression now filled with many thousands of metres of sediments and known in Brazil as the Pantanal. Further south, the swamps continue into the Chaco of Paraguay and Argentina. To the east of this, again the rivers fall off the old highland strata to form rapids and waterfalls, the largest of which was the former Sete Quedas Falls (Salto de Guaíra) on the Paraná, sadly drowned by the Itaipu Dam lake in 1982. Nearby however are the Iguaçu Falls, the most impressive of South America, created by very resistant layers of basalt.

The coast and escarpment

Highlands follow the coastline, only a short distance inland, for 3,000 km. The ancient crystalline/granite ridges, known as *serras*, stretch from Porto Alegre in the South to near Belém in the North, just short of the Amazon estuary. Long stretches are in the form of a single or stepped escarpment, abrupt in the east and sloping more gently inland to the west. They are not high in South American terms – the highest point, Pico da Bandeira is only 2,890 m – but it is no more than 120 km from the ocean near Vitória. The narrowness of the coastal strip has had a profound effect on the history of settlement. Until comparatively recent times, the lack of natural access to the hinterland confined virtually all economic activity to this area, and today most of the major cities of Brazil and 80% of the population are on or near the coast.

Because of varying erosion over many millions of years, there are a number of interesting natural features in these highlands. The many granite 'peaks' in and around Rio de Janeiro are the resistant remnants of very hard rocks providing spectacular viewpoints, Pico da Tijuca (the highest, 1,012 m), Corcovado (710 m) and Pão de Açúcar (396 m) the best known. There are others in the neighbouring state of Espírito Santo. Near Curitiba are the eroded sandstones of Vila Velha and the wild scenery through the Serra do Mar towards the coast. In the state of Bahía, there are remarkable caves and waterfalls in the Chapada da Diamantina National Park. In many places, what rivers there are flowing eastwards necessarily have to lose height quickly so that gorges and waterfalls abound. There are also many kilometres of spectacular coastline and fine beaches. South of Porto Alegre, eroded material moved down the coast by the southerly ocean currents added to alluvials brought north from the River Plate by subsidiary currents, have created long sand bars to form several large freshwater lagoons. The longest, Lagoa dos Patos, is over 250 km long.

The Rio São Francisco

The escarpment forces most of the rain run-off to flow west into the interior to feed the Amazon and Paraná river systems. However, one major river breaks through the barrier to flow into the Atlantic. The São Francisco rises south of Belo Horizonte – one

The sertão

The *sertão* (plural *sertões*) covers almost three-quarters of northeastern Brazil, extending into the north of Minas Gerais. Of the states in the Northeast, only Maranhão lacks this geographic zone. It is hot, semi-arid and subject to frequent droughts. The soil is stony and the trees and bushes are twisted, covered in thorns. There is also a great variety of cacti. The vegetation is typical of the *caatinga*, adapted to land which can be parched, sometimes for years at a time. In the drought, the plants appear to die, the inhabitants and their animals face hunger and misery, and all life awaits the return of the rain.

The *caatinga* is "not an impenetrable barrier. Its unique vegetation makes it more like a labyrinth, with a multitude of paths and clearings, always alike, and transformed as if by magic, to revive for a day, only when a chance rain fills the merciless sky. If the peril of virgin forest is solitude without trails or egress, the terror of the *caatinga* is the bewilderment which their multiplicity never fails to cause. The beast, led by instinct, can range to the uttermost parts and reach his destination without straying; but once a man enters the *caatinga* and his memory falters in choosing a trail, he is a victim whom only a miracle will save." (Quoted from *The Bandeirantes*, edited by Richard M Morse, page 42.)

To the Portuguese colonists, the *sertão* was a region of legends. Unlike the routes along the Amazon in the North and the routes taken by the *bandeirantes* along the Tietê in the South, the trackless Northeast was full of mystery because settlers were not tempted into it. The source of the only major river to run through it, the São Francisco, was a cause for speculation; the indigenous people were described as giants, or dwarves, or deformed in a bewildering variety of ways and all were believed to be savage fighters. And, of course, in this dangerous interior there were said to be great riches awaiting the intrepid explorer: silver mines, gold and mountains of emeralds.

In the 20th century the *sertão* has inspired some of the greatest Brazilian literature, but the geographical and human landscape portrayed is not the mythical *sertão* of the 16th and 17th centuries. Graciliano Ramos in *Vidas secas* (Barren Lives, 1938), João Guimarães Rosa in *Grande sertão: veredas* (The Devil to Pay in the Backlands, 1956) and Antônio Torres in *Essa terra* (The Land, 1976), among others, have all presented the region in memorable ways (see Literature, page 703, for notes on Ramos and Guimarães Rosa). The direct realism of Ramos' *Vidas secas* emphasizes the harshness of the *sertão*, the family driven from their land by drought, by the "enemy vegetation". Yet there is an ambiguity to the flight. They head for the city, where the children will learn "difficult, necessary things", but that too is an alien world, unknown, civilized and it, like the climate they have left, will imprison them.

important tributary starts only 250 km from the sea – but flows, north then east, for 2,900 km before it gets there. Almost 500 km of rapids through the escarpment culminate in the 75 m Paulo Afonso falls, before completing the final 240 km to the sea. Where it turns east is one of the driest areas of the country, known as the *sertão*. The river is therefore of great significance particularly as the rains here are so unreliable. Together with the link it provides to so much of the interior and its course wholly within the country (unlike the Amazon and the Paraná), the São Francisco is revered by the Brazilians as the 'river of national unity'. Its value for irrigation, hydroelectric power, fish and navigation above the rapids is inestimable, but because of sand bars at its mouth and close proximity to the fall line, the river has not proved useful for shipping or access generally to the ocean in spite of being the third largest river system on the continent.

The Northern Highlands

After sinking below the Amazon estuary, the Brazilian Highlands reappear to the north and sweep round to the west to form the border with the Guianas and Venezuela. The highest tabular uplands are near where Guyana, Venezuela and Brazil meet at Monte Roraima (2,810 m) and further west along the border where a national park has been set up focussed on Pico de Neblina, 3,014 m, the highest point in Brazil.

Climate

The climate of Brazil is a function of latitude and altitude. The average annual temperature exceeds 26°C along the northeast coast and in the central Amazon with little variation throughout the year. The highlands are cooler and further south there are seasonal variations: Brazil extends to 34° south which is equivalent to the latitude of North Carolina. High summer temperatures can occur almost anywhere here, yet frosts are not uncommon in July and August as coffee producers know only too well. Rainfall is more complicated. The northeast Trades bring moist air to the coast north of the Amazon, where there is heavy precipitation all year round. The same winds push saturated air into the Amazon basin where rainfall is progressively greater from east to west throughout the year and virtually on a daily basis. The abrupt rise of the Andes beyond the borders of Brazil increases the precipitation and feeds the many tributaries.

During the period December-May, the northeast Trades move north and Brazil between Belém and Recife receives less rain-bearing winds. From Salvador, the southeast Trades bring moisture from the South Atlantic and it is the gap between these two systems, known as the 'doldrums', that explains the dry areas of northeast Brazil. On average there is significant rainfall here, but sometimes it fails to arrive causing prolonged periods of drought. Precipitation in the southern states of Brazil is concentrated in the escarpment thus feeding the Paraná system and is well distributed throughout the year.

Although there are occasional storms causing local damage, for example in the *favelas* (shanties) of Rio, Brazil is not subject to hurricanes or indeed to other natural disasters common elsewhere in Latin America such as earthquakes, volcanic eruptions or unexpected widespread and catastrophic floods.

Flora and fauna

The neotropical realm is a land of superlatives, it contains the most extensive tropical rainforest in the world; drained by the Amazon which has by far the largest volume of any river. The fauna and flora are to a large extent determined by the influence of the great rivers and mountains – the Andes, which are the longest uninterrupted mountain chain in the world. Although not part of Brazil they dramatically affect the climate and hence the animals and plants that can inhabit the country. There are also huge expanses of open terrain, the Pantanal – a huge wet wilderness, vast mountain grasslands and tree-covered savannahs. It is this wide range of habitats which makes Brazil one of the greatest regions of biological diversity.

This diversity arises not only from the wide range of habitats available, but also from the history of the continent. South America has essentially been an island for some 70 million years joined only by a narrow isthmus to Central and North America. Land passage played a significant role in the gradual colonization of South America by species from the north. When the land-link closed these colonists evolved to a wide variety of forms free from the competitive pressures that prevailed elsewhere. When the land-bridge was re-established some four million years ago a new invasion of species took place from North America, adding to the diversity but also leading to numerous extinctions. Comparative stability has ensued since then and has guaranteed the survival of many primitive groups including a group of pouched mammals, the opossums.

Brazil can be divided into biogeographical zones; two huge river basins comprising the River Amazon and the River Plate, mountains – the Guiana highlands to the north and the Brazilian highlands to the south, and a coastal strip of Atlantic rainforest.

Atlantic rain forest

The Atlantic rainforest used to cover 2,600,000 sq km in a coastal strip 160 km wide and 4,200 km long. The coastal rainforest is bounded inland by a series of mountain ranges which contribute to the varied landscape and hence species diversity. It is one of the Earth's biological hotspots. Now critically fragmented and reduced to less than 5% of its original extent, it remains home to a very high proportion of unique species. For example 17 of the 21 primate species found there are unique to that region, and of those, 13 species, including the golden lion tamarin (see box, page 141), are endangered. Populations of South America's largest primate, the woolly spider monkey, locally known as *muriqui*, were decimated by European colonists who first settled along this coastal zone.

Along the coast, mangroves provide a breeding ground for numerous species of fish including many that are commercially important. Further inland is the *restinga*, a zone of shrub forest, coastal sand dunes, ponds and wetlands. The lush coastal rainforest itself extends to 800 m in elevation and grades into cloud forest between 800 m and 1,700 m. Drenching by mist, fog and rain leads to a profusion of plant growth, trees and shrubs which are covered with a great variety of epiphytes – orchids, mosses lichens and bromeliads. At the highest elevations, the forest gives way to mountain grasslands or *campos de altitude*. In the southern zone of the Atlantic forest there are large stands of monkey puzzle tree, *araucária*, which is characterized by its own parrot community, many of which are also endemic.

The Amazon River and rainforest

The Amazon basin contains the largest area of tropical rainforest in the world, 6,000,000 sq km, 60% of which is located in Brazil. It is home to 20% of the world's plant and bird species; perhaps 10% of mammal species; an inestimable number of insects and perhaps some 2,000 species of fish inhabiting the 1,000 tributaries of the Amazon. When in flood the great river inundates the forest for a short period in its upper reaches to create a unique habitat called *várzea*; in the lower reaches this flooding may last for four to seven months forming *igapó* swamp forest.

The rivers of the Amazon are either classified as blackwater or whitewater rivers. The former are highly coloured due to the brown humic acids derived from the decomposing materials on the forest floor but contain little suspended material. The whitewaters owe their colour to the suspended soil particles which originate in the run-off from the Andes. Each has its characteristic fish. Within a 30 km radius of Manaus, there are estimated to be over 700 species of fish. The largest of these species is the *arapaima* reaching over 3 m and weighing in at over 150 kg. It gulps air at the surface and is harpooned by fishermen. The *pacu* or silver-dollar fish feeds on fruit falling from trees of the flooded forest. The voracious *piranha* normally feeds on other fishes although they are quite capable of removing the flesh from larger animals. They probably benefit the ecosystem by removing diseased and dying individuals as well as disposing of carrion. A greater risk is posed by the electric eels and sting rays found in turbid waters. An electrical shock of 650 volts has been recorded from a captive electric eel; these electric fields are used to locate and kill prey. The ray does not inject poison but its 10 cm long spine can puncture and lacerate flesh.

Várzea and Igapó

Várzea is a highly productive seasonally inundated forest found along the banks of the whitewater rivers; it is very rich as a consequence of the huge amount of silt and nutrients washed out of the mountains and trapped by the massive buttress-rooted trees. This lakeland swamp forest is flooded for relatively short periods of time. One of the commonest trees of the *várzea*, the Pará rubber tree, is the source of latex. The Brazilian rubber industry foundered in the 19th century when seeds of this tree were illegally taken to Asia to form the basis of huge rubber plantations and flourished in the absence of pest species.

In contrast the *igapó* forests are characteristic of the blackwater rivers with little silt deposition leading to sandy beaches fringing the forest. Despite being flooded for up to seven months of the year to a possible depth of 15 m, palms dominate this swampy habitat, although massive kapok trees are also typical. During the wet season, these flooded forests are inhabited by turtles and small fish, and the predators that feed upon them – otters and caiman.

Flooded meadows are frequently found in the still-flowing reaches of the *várzea*. These vast carpets of floating waterlilies, waterlettuce and waterhyacInth are home to the Amazonian manatee, a large herbivorous aquatic mammal which is the freshwater relative of the dugong of the Caribbean. Vast numbers of spectacled caiman populate the lakes feeding on the highly productive fish community.

The river corridors are often the best places to observe wildlife. Caiman and turtles are commonly seen basking on the riverbanks. Neotropical cormorants, roseate spoonbills and jabiru storks are commonly observed fishing in the shallow waters. The hoatzin is generally found along waterways where it feeds on leaves, and fruit. The newly hatched chicks of this primitive bird have claws at the tip of each wing which enable them to crawl around in the foliage.

In the relatively constant climatic conditions, animal and plant life has evolved to an amazing diversity over the millennia. It has been estimated that 4 sq km of forest can harbour some 1,200 vascular plants, 600 species of tree, and 120 woody plants. Here in these relatively flat lands a soaring canopy some 45 m overhead is the power-house of the forest. It is a habitat choked with strangling vines and philodendrons amongst which mixed troupes of squirrel monkeys and *capuchins* forage. In the high canopy small groups of spider monkeys perform their lazy aerial acrobatics, whilst lower down, clinging to epiphyte-clad trunks and branches, groups of tamarins and marmosets forage for gums, blossom, fruit and the occasional insect prey.

Caiman are South American alligators. They are relatively small, usually growing to no more than 2½ m in length. They are found in areas of relatively still water, ranging form marshland to lakes and slow-flowing rivers. Youngsters feed mainly on aquatic invertebrates while adults also take larger prey, including wild pigs and small travellers. During the dry season when pools dry up caimans can stop feeding altogether and burrow into the mud at the bottom of a pool waiting for the return of the rains.

The **giant otter** is found along the tributaries of the Amazon. It can measure up to 2 m in length. They are active by day when they hunt for food, often in small groups. They are not rare but are rarely seen as they are shy and submerge quickly at the slightest hint of danger. They feed on fish, molluscs and crustaceans, also small mammals and birds. They can be tamed easily and are often raised as pets by some tribes.

Pantanal

This ecologically diverse zone includes the largest area of wetlands in the world when flooded between December to March. In addition it includes dry savannahs or *cerrado*, chaco scrublands as well as gallery rainforest. The area is very flat and flooded by the rising rivers leaving isolated islands (*cordilheiras*) between vast lakes (*bahias*) which become saline as the waters evaporate. This mixed ecosystem supports a highly diverse fauna characteristic of the constituent habitat types which includes 200 species of mammal. Capybara (see below), tapir and peccaries are common along the waters edge as are marsh deer. Jaguar, more commonly associated with the forest, prey on these herbivores and the cattle and feral pigs which graze here. Spectacular assemblages of wading birds – egrets, jabiru storks, ibises, spoonbills and herons prey on the abundant invertebrate and fish fauna. Anacondas and caiman are still common, although the black caiman has been hunted out.

Jaguars are the largest of the New World cats. Jaguars are great wanderers, roaming even further than pumas. Usually they haunt forests where they hunt for deer, agoutis and especially peccaries. They follow the herds of these South American swine and pounce on the stragglers. They also attack capybara. Unlike most cats, jaguars are often found beside rivers and frequently enter the water. It attacks the tapir as it comes down to drink and will even scoop fish from the water with its paws.

The **tapir** is a shy, nocturnal animal which confines itself to an intricate network of trails in the forests of the marshy lowlands of Bolivia, Brazil, Colombia, Venezuela, Ecuador, Peru and the north of Argentina.

Water is essential for its survival; it drinks a great deal and is an excellent swimmer. It is herbivorous, eating waterplants and the leaves and twigs of trees. Its only enemies are jaguars and alligators against which its only defence is to use its teeth.

The **capybara** is a large aquatic rodent that looks like a cross between a guinea pig and a hippopotamus. It is the largest of all the rodents at over 1 m long and weighing over 50 kg. They live in large groups along the riverbanks, where they graze on the lush grasses. It comes out onto dry land to rest and bask in the sun, but at the first hint of danger the whole troop dashes into the water. Its greatest enemy is the jaguar. They are rather vocal for rodents often emitting a series of strange clicks, squeaks and grunts.

National parks

Ecotourism is the international passion of this decade, but it is also a question of survival. It is modern and urgent to be a conservationist, to respect flora and fauna, not to pollute the beaches or the forests, to respect local populations, to value our cultural heritage, customs and traditions. *Guia do Turismo*, 10, 1997, page 25.

Different countries have different approaches to the relationship between national parks and tourism. In Brazil, the system which protects areas of outstanding beauty and unique flora and fauna has the dual role of providing centres of scientific research and places which are open to the public as an alternative form of recreation and education. **Ibama** (Instituto Brasileiro do Meio Ambiente e dos Recursos Naturais Renováveis – the Brazilian Institute for the Environment and Renewable Natural Resources) has in its care 35 national parks (Parques Nacionais, or PARNA). They are by no means the whole picture, though. They form part of a system of protected areas which go under different titles and which have varying degrees of public access. The network comprises, in addition to the national parks: *estações ecológicas* (ecological stations), *reservas biológicas* (biological reserves), *reservas ecológicas* (ecological reserves), *áreas de relevante interesse ecológico* (areas of relevant ecological interest), *reservas particulares do patrimônio nacional* (private national heritage reserves) and *áreas sob proteção especial* (areas of special protection). In all these entities, the exploitation of natural resources is completely forbidden. They are for research, education and recreation only. Three other types of entity are designed to allow the sustainable use of natural resources, while still preserving their

Ecotourism

Ecoturismo is a very popular word in Brazil nowadays. But with a mere handful of notable exceptions, it never means the same as it does in English and is never up to the standard of the best of Brazil's Spanish-speaking neighbours. Brazilian ecotourism is adventure tourism in natural surroundings – abseiling, rafting, rock climbing or mountain biking; usually accompanied by lots of noise. Such trips are often great fun. But they are not ecotourism and they leave many foreign tourists angry and disappointed.

The problem is cultural and stems from Brazil's age old utilitarian attitude to its natural landscape. In the early 20th century a Brazilian statesman famously said: 'our greatest assets have been our greatest obstacles, namely our rivers and our hills'. Grand projects which have brought the country to the point of economic collapse and ruined much of the forest stem from a desire to remove these obstacles, coupled with a propensity for grandiosity which is a characteristic of the country's powerful elite. Most infamous of these projects are the opening up of the Amazon in the 1970s under the slogan – 'the land without people for the people without land' and the carving up of the forest into sections separated by roads which continues to this day at a time when Federal Highways throughout Brazil are crumbling into potholes.

Nor has Brazil begun to grasp that many tourists come to the country precisely because of its natural heritage. The head of the tourist office in Belém in the heart of the Brazilian Amazon once assured us that tourists were not interested in the city because of its proximity to the Amazon, which was just '*mata e bichos*', a pejorative way of saying trees and animals. They came, she said, to see the city's historic museums. We looked aghast, but came to learn that her attitude was typical. Very, very few educated Brazilians are aware of the animals that live in their national parks and forests and even fewer realize how rare they are. The Federal and state governments and the larger companies are unaware and uninterested in what their neighbours offer. Whilst Bolivia, Peru, Colombia, Ecuador and even tiny Guyana offer genuine and exciting ecotourism packages you will be hard pushed to find a company in Brazil whose guides can identify animals beyond knowing they are a 'parrot' or a 'monkey'. Where there is tourism in Nature it considers the wild a playground for raising adrenaline levels. Requests for contemplative or wildlife orientated tours from foreigners often meet with a perplexed response. But they go a long way towards helping Brazilians to realize how much of a demand there is for genuine ecotourism from foreign visitors.

biodiversity: *florestas nacionais* (national forests), *áreas de proteção ambiental* (areas of environmental protection) and *reservas extrativas* (extractive reserves – such as the rubber tapping zones in Acre state). A new initiative is the **Projeto Corredores Ecológicos** (Ecological Corridors Project), which aims to create avenues of forest between isolated protected areas so that fauna may move over a greater area to breed, thus strengthening the stock of endangered animals which might otherwise suffer the ills of inbreeding. An example of this is project to link the Mata Atlântica of Poço das Antas (see page 142) with other pockets of coastal forest to help the survival of the golden lion tamarin.

Ibama was created in 1989, under Law No 7.735 of the 5 October 1988 Constitution. The Institute was formed by uniting four separate bodies, the environmental secretariat (SEMA), the Brazilian Institute of Forest Development (IBDF), and the superintendencies for the development of fishing and rubber (SUDEPE and SUDHEVEA). Brazil has a long history of passing laws to protect natural resources, such as that of 1808 which excluded from international trade the export of pau-brasil and other woods. At the same time, though, enforcement of such laws has not been easy. Today, the achievement of Ibama's goals is determined by resources, but funds are insufficient to commit either enough money or staff to the job of protecting the areas that have been designated for preservation. Sad though this is, there are still a large number of parks open to the visitor which can give a good idea of the variety of Brazil's natural resources and the value that they hold for the country.

This Handbook does not describe all Brazil's national parks or other conservation entities, only those which have easy access. Nor does the book list all the offices of Ibama or its related departments throughout the country, but those nearest to the parks described are given and it is to these that readers should apply if a permit is needed to visit a specific park.

For more information, contact Ibama at its local addresses, its national headquarters, SAIN, Avenida L-4, bloco "B", Térreo, Edifiço Sede do Ibama, CEP 70.800-200, Brasília DF, T061-2268221/9014, F061-3221058, or at its website, www.ibama.gov.br.

Information can also be obtained from the Ministério do Meio Ambiente (MMA – the environment ministry), Esplanada dos Ministérios, bloco "B", 5-9 andar (5th to 9th floors), CEP 70068-900, Brasília DF, or at its website www.mma.gov.br. See also the book *Nacionais Brasil*, Guias Philips (1999), with a good map, beautiful photographs, sections on history, flora and fauna and tourist services, US$15.

Books

History and anthropology

Hemming, J, *Red Gold, Amazon Frontier* and *Die if You Must, Pan*. The little-known history of Brazil's indigenous people is alternatively shocking and inspiring. This wonderful, scholarly and beautifully written account is as readable and exciting as Prescott's Conquest of Peru and will in time rank alongside it. A must for anyone with an interest in Brazil.

Reichel-Dolmatoff, G, *Rainforest Shamans*, Themis books. The best introduction to the thought of an Amazon people available in English.

Literature

Ângelo, I, *The Celebration*, Avon Books. Much the best novel and about the political, social and economic crisis at the end of the 1960s, the worst period of the military regime.

Amado, J, et al, *Gabriela, Clove and Cinnamon, Dona Flor and her two Husbands*, Avon Books. Very poor translations of these captivating novels almost all of which are set in Bahia and which read like a cross between Poldark and Angelique. Romps through 19th and 20th Century Bahia. Ripping yarns though not literary masterpieces. Over a long career Amado published many best-sellers, many others of which are available in English. He is often criticized for producing an overly optimistic, sexily tropical view of the country, and of Bahia, his home state.

Buarque, C, *Turbulence*, and *Budapest*, Bloomsbury. The first is a short, pacey allegory of modern Brazil, the second which has only just been translated, is a labyrinthine Borgesian magic realist novel set in Budapest. It was top of the best sellers list in Brazil for many months – something unusual for literary fiction. Buarque is the son of a distinguished social historian and is most famous as a singer and composer.

da Cunha, E, *Rebellion in the Backlands*, University of Chicago Press. The book which inspired Mario Vargas Llosa and which is the country's most famous piece of sustained journalistic writing – Brazil's *Seven Pillars of Wisdom*.

Gilberto, F, *Macunaíma* (1988) Quartet. A central figure, still controversial: this account of racial mixture, and of sugar-plantation society in the northeast of Brazil in colonial times, is very readable.

Guimarães Rosa, J, *The Jaguar and Other Stories*, Boulevard Books. Decent translations of Brazil's greatest novelist are hard to come by. There are none at all of his masterpiece, *Grande sertão, veredas: As trilhas de amor e guerra de Riobaldo*. Guimarães Rosa is, in a sense, the first great magic realist author is by far the most respected author within Brazil and is credited with having invented a new kind of poetically colloquial literary Portuguese. This draws its inspiration from the mystical, lyrical language of the interior of Brazil, a region which evolved cut off from the rest of the country. The jaguar is little more than an introduction to his writing. As difficult to translate as Joyce.

Lins do Rego, J, *The Masters and the Slaves*, University of California Press. Highly influenced by Gilberto Freyre, this is an evocative account of childhood on a northeastern sugar plantation.

Llspector, C, *Family Ties, The Hour of the Star* and *Soulstorm*, University of Texas Press, Carcanet Press and New Directions. Brazil's other great modernist and the country's most highly revered woman's writer.

Llosa, M V, *The War of the End of the World*, Penguin. An enthralling dramatisation of the Canudos rebellion. Very hard to put down and beautifully structured.

Machado de Assis, J M, The Posthumous Memoirs of Bras Cubas, *Dom Casmurro*, Oxford University Press and *Philosopher or Dog*, Bloomsbury. At last some modern, decent translations of Brazil's most acerbic and witty literary social commentator. With a black mother and white Portuguese descended father, Machado de Assis was a bridge between the two Brazil's – the haves and the have nots.

Morley, H, *The Patriot*, London: Rex Collings. The diary of a girl's life in Diamantina, in Minas Gerais. Translated by the great American poet Elizabeth Bishop who lived in Brazil for many years. A delightfully intimate and frank portrait of small-town life.

Ramos, G, *São Bernardo* (Peter Owen) *Anguish* (Knopf, 1972) and *Barren Lives* (University of Texas Press, 1965). The greatest of the novelists of the 1930s and 1940s: a harsh realist. *Andrade, Mário de* (1893-1945) Written in the 1920s: a comic statement in picaresque form about Brazilian nationality, by the leader of Modernism.

Torres, A, *Blues for a Lost Childhood*, (1989) Readers International. An idealistic Brazilian journalist leaves his rural town for Rio only to be crushed by the realities of the city. Sobering and not very cheerful reading.

Ubaldo Ribeiro, J, *The Lost Manuscript*, Bloomsbury. A panoramic historical novel, entitled *Long Live the Brazilian People* in the original.

Poetry

Bandeira, M, *This Earth, that Sky: Poems by Manuel Bandeira*, University of California Press. The oldest member of the Modernist movement, and one of Brazil's greatest poets, master of the short, intense lyric.

Drummond de Andrade, C, *Plantation Boy*, New York: Knopf. Perhaps Brazil's greatest poet, with a varied, lyrical, somewhat downbeat style.

Photography

Salgado, S, *Migrations*, Aperture. The most recent volume from the world's most highly respected photojournalist renowned for transcendental images of the world's silent majority and their daily lives. Incredible.

Social comment

Bellos, A, *Futebol: The Brazilian Way of Life*, (2003) Bloomsbury. A loving look at the beautiful game, its history, its players, supporters and its legendary feats. Alex Bellos is one of the UK's leading Brazilian experts and was the Guardian correspondent based in Rio.

Castro, R, *Rio de Janeiro*, (2004) Bloomsbury. An anecdotal history and profile of Rio de Janeiro written by a Carioca.

Fausto, B, *A Concise History of Brazil*, Cambridge University Press. Dry as dust but

the only readily available, reliable history of the country available in English.
Harvey, **Constable** and **Robinson**, *Liberators*, (2002). A wonderful romp through the Liberation of South America from Europe with a colourful section on imperial Brazil. How all history should be written.
McGowan, C and **Pessanha, R**, *The Brazilian Sound: Samba, Bossa Nova and the Popular Music of Brazil*, (1998) Temple University Press. An encyclopaedic survey of Brazilian popular music with interviews from many of the key players.
Page, J, *The Brazilians*, (1995) Da Capo Press. One of the few popular books on Brazil which really gets under the country's skin. With excellent chapters on Carnival, football, Brazilian society and character and plenty of information on Rio.

Travel writing

Davis, W, *One River* is a remarkable travel book – Hunter S Thompson meets George Forrest and Levi Strauss in the heart of the Amazon.
Fawcett, P, *Exploration Fawcett*, (2001) Weidenfeld & Nicholson. The diaries of the intrepid explorer who disappeared in Matto Grosso in the 1920s and whose descriptions of the table-top mountains there inspired Conan Doyle to write *The Lost World*. Some beautiful writing on the Amazon, Rio de Janeiro and the Andes.
Fleming, P, *Brazilian Adventure*, (1998) Pimlico. The sparkling, delightfully humorous account of a 1930s expedition in search of Colonel Percy Fawcett.
Robb, P, *A Death in Brazil*, (2004) Bloomsbury. A poetic odyssey through Brazil's history, culture and landscape.

Wildlife field guides

General

Kricher, J, *A Neotropical Companion*, Princeton University Press. A very clear, intelligent introduction to the ecosystems, biology and botany of the neotropical region.
Pearson, D & **Beletsky, L** *Brazil - Amazon & Pantanal*, Academic Press. By far the best of the introductory wildlife and botanical guides.

Birds

de la Peña, M & **Rumboll, M**, *Birds of Southern South America and Antarctica*, Harper Collins & Princeton University Press. A slim volume, but with comprehensive information on almost all of Brazil's non-neotropical species.
Hilty, S and **Brown, W** *Birds of Colombia*. The best book for the northern Amazon region.
Ridgely, R & **Tudor, G**, *The Birds of South America, Volume 1 & II*, University of Texas Press & Oxford University Press (UK). One of the most important bird books of the century. Voted 'Best Bird Book of the 20th Century' and the only truly comprehensive guide.
Sick, H, *The Birds of Brazil*, Princeton University Press. Currently the only widely available book covering almost all Brazil's species (there are more species added almost monthly).
Wheatley, N, *Where to Watch Birds in South America*, Princeton University Press. A little out of date but with an interesting list of places and useful bird inventories.
Zimmer, K & **Whittaker, A**, *Birds of Brazil*, Princeton University Press. The first comprehensive, modern illustrated field guide to the birds of Brazil. Due out in 2005/6.

Mammals

Eisenberg, J F & **Redford, K**, *Mammals of the Neotropics Vol. 3: The Central Neotropics - Ecuador, Peru, Bolivia, Brazil*.
Emmons, L H, *Neotropical Rainforest Mammals: A Field Guide*, University of Chicago Press. Excellent illustrated field guides which between them cover pretty much everything in tropical Brazil.

Reptiles and Amphibians

Bartlett, R D & **Pope Bartlett, P**, *Reptiles and Amphibians of the Amazon: An Ecotourist's Guide*, University of Florida Press. With 250 common species.

Plants

Henderson, A, **Galeano, G** & **Bernal, R**, *A Field Guide to the Palms of the Americas*, Princeton University Press. A comprehensive illustrated guide. Well worth having.

Footnotes

Basic Portuguese for travellers

Learning Portuguese is a useful part of the preparation for a trip to Brazil and no volume of dictionaries, phrase books or word lists will provide the same enjoyment as being able to communicate directly with the people of the country you are visiting. It is a good idea to make an effort to grasp the basics before you go. As you travel you will pick up more of the language and the more you know, the more you will benefit from your stay. ▸▸ *See also Language in Essentials, page 28.*

General pronunciation

Within Brazil itself, there are variations in pronunciation, intonation, phraseology and slang. This makes for great richness and for the possibility of great enjoyment in the language. A couple of points which the newcomer to the language will spot immediately are the use of the tilde (~) over 'a' and 'o'. This makes the vowel nasal, as does a word ending in 'm' or 'ns', or a vowel followed by 'm' + consonant, or by 'n' + consonant. Another important point of spelling is that for words ending in 'i' and 'u' the emphasis is on the last syllable, though (unlike Spanish) no accent is used. This is especially relevant in place names like Buriti, Guarapari, Caxambu, Iguaçu. Note also the use of 'ç', which changes the pronunciation of c from hard [k] to soft [s].

Personal pronouns

In conversation, most people refer to 'you' as *você*, although in the south and in Pará *tu* is more common. To be more polite, use *O Senhor/A Senhora*. For 'us', *gente* (people, folks) is very common when it includes you too.

Portuguese words and phrases

Greetings and courtesies

hello	*oi*
good morning	*bom dia*
good afternoon	*boa tarde*
good evening/night	*boa noite*
goodbye	*adeus/tchau*
see you later	*até logo*
please	*por favor/faz favor*
thank you	*obrigado* (if a man is speakinng) /*obrigada* (if a woman is speaking)
thank you very much	*muito obrigado/muito obrigada*
How are you?	*Como vai você tudo bem?/tudo bom?*
I am fine	*vou bem/tudo bem*
pleased to meet you	*um prazer*
no	*não*
yes	*sim*
excuse me	*com licença*
I don't understand	*não entendo*
Please speak slowly	*fale devagar por favor*
What is your name?	*Qual é seu nome?*
my name is...	*O meu nome é...*
Go away!	*Vai embora!*

Basic questions

where is?	*onde está/onde fica?*
why?	*por que?*
how much does it cost?	*quanto custa?*
what for?	*para que?*
how much is it?	*quanto é?*
how do I get to...?	*para chegar a...?*
when?	*quando?*
I want to go to...	*quero ir para...*
when does the bus leave?/arrive?	*a que hor sai/chega o ônibus?*
is this the way to the church?	*aquí é o caminho para a igreja?*

Basics

bathroom/toilet	*banheiro*
police (policeman)	*a polícia (o polícia)*
hotel	*o (a pensão, a hospedaria)*
restaurant	*o restaurante (o lanchonete)*
post office	*o correio*
telephone office	*(central) telefônica*
supermarket	*o supermercado*
market	*o mercado*
bank	*o banco*
bureau de change	*a casa de câmbio*
exchange rate	*a taxa de câmbio*
notes/coins	*notas/moedas*
traveller's cheques	*os travelers/os cheques de viagem*
cash	*dinheiro*
breakfast	*o caféde manh*
lunch	*o almoço*
dinner/supper	*o jantar*
meal	*a refeição*
drink	*a bebida*
mineral water	*a água mineral*
soft fizzy drink	*o refrigerante*
beer	*a cerveja*
without sugar	*sem açúcar*
without meat	*sem carne*

Getting around

on the left/right	*à esquerda/à direita*
straight on	*direto*
to walk	*caminhar*
bus station	*a rodoviária*
bus	*o ônibus*
bus stop	*a parada*
train	*a trem*
airport	*o aeroport*
aeroplane/airplane	*o avião*
flight	*o vôa*
first/second class	*primeira/segunda clase*
train station	*a ferroviária*
combined bus and train station	*a rodoferroviária*
ticket	*o passagem/o bilhete*
ticket office	*a bilheteria*

Accommodation

room	*quarto*
noisy	*barulhento*
single/double room	*(quarto de) solteiro/(quarto para) casal*
room with two beds	*quarto com duas camas*
with private bathroom	*quarto com banheiro*
hot/cold water	*água quente/fria*
to make up/clean	*limpar*
sheet(s)	*o lençol (os lençóis)*
blankets	*as mantas*
pillow	*o travesseiro*
clean/dirty towels	*as toalhas limpas/sujas*
toilet paper	*o papel higiêico*

Health

chemist	*a farmacia*
doctor	*o coutor/a doutora*
(for) pain	*(para) dor*
stomach	*o esômago (a barriga)*
head	*a cabeça*
fever/sweat	*a febre/o suor higiênicas*
diarrhoea	*a diarréia*
blood	*o sangue*
condoms	*as camisinhas/os preservativos*
contraceptive (pill)	*anticonceptional (a pílula)*
period	*a menstruação/a regra*
sanitary towels/tampons	*toalhas absorventes/absorventes internos*
contact lenses	*lentes de contacto*
aspirin	*a aspirina*

Time

at one o'clock (am/pm)	*a uma hota (da manhã/da tarde)*
at half past two/two thirty	*as dois e meia*
at a quarter to three	*quinze para as três*
it's one o'clock	*é uma*
it's seven o'clock	*são sete horas*
it's twenty past six/six twenty	*são seis e vinte*
it's five to nine	*são cinco para as nove*
in ten minutes	*em dez minutos*
five hours	*cinco horas*
does it take long?	*sura muito?*

Days

Monday	*segunda feiro*
Tuesday	*terça feira*
Wednesday	*quarta feira*
Thursday	*quinta feira*
Friday	*sexta feira*
Saturday	*sábado*
Sunday	*domingo*

Months

January	*janeiro*
February	*fevereiro*

March	*março*
April	*abril*
May	*maio*
June	*junho*
July	*julho*
August	*agosto*
September	*setembro*
October	*outubro*
November	*Novembro*
December	*dezembro*

Numbers

one	*um/uma*
two	*dois/duas*
three	*três*
four	*quatro*
five	*cinco*
six	*seis* ('*meia*' half, is frequently used for number 6 ie half-dozen)
seven	*sete*
eight	*oito*
nine	nove
ten	*dez*
eleven	*onze*
twelve	*doze*
thirteen	*treze*
fourteen	*catorze*
flfteen	*quinze*
sixteen	*dezesseis*
seventeen	*dezessete*
eighteen	*dezoito*
nineteen	*dezenove*
twenty	*vinte*
twenty-one	*vente e um*
thirty	*trinta*
forty	*cuarenta*
fifty	*cinqüe*
sixty	*sessenta*
seventy	*setenta*
eighty	*oitenta*
ninety	*noventa*
hundred	*cem, cento*
thousand	*mil*

Useful slang

that's great/cool	*que legal*
bloke/guy/geezer	*cara* (literally 'face')
biker slang for bloke/guy	*mano*
cheesy/tacky	*brega*
posh, spoilt girl/boy with rich parents	*patricinha/mauricinho*
in fashion/cool	*descolado*

Index

Complete title listing

Footprint publishes travel guides to over 150 destinations worldwide. Each guide is packed with practical, concise and colourful information for everybody from first-time travellers to travel aficionados. The list is growing fast and current titles are noted below.
Available from all good bookshops and online at www.footprintbooks.com

(P) denotes pocket guide

Latin America and Caribbean
Antigua & Leeward Islands (P)
Argentina
Barbados (P)
Bolivia
Brazil
Caribbean Islands
Central America & Mexico
Chile
Colombia
Costa Rica
Cuba
Cusco & the Inca Trail
Dominican Republic
Dominican Republic (P)
Ecuador & Galápagos
Guatemala
Havana (P)
Jamaica (P)
Mexico
Nicaragua
Patagonia
Peru
Rio de Janeiro
Rio de Janeiro (P)
South American Handbook
St Lucia (P)
Venezuela

North America
Vancouver (P)
New York (P)
Western Canada

Africa
Cape Town (P)
East Africa
Egypt
Libya
Marrakech (P)
Morocco
Namibia
South Africa
Tunisia
Uganda

Middle East
Dubai (P)
Israel
Jordan
Syria & Lebanon

Australia
Australia
East Coast Australia
New Zealand
Sydney (P)
West Coast Australia

Asia
Bali
Bangkok & the Beaches
Bhutan
Cambodia
Goa
Hong Kong (P)
India
Indian Himalaya
Indonesia
Laos
Malaysia
Nepal
Northern Pakistan
Pakistan
Rajasthan & Gujarat
Singapore
South India
Sri Lanka
Sumatra
Thailand
Tibet
Vietnam

Europe
Andalucía
Barcelona (P)
Berlin (P)
Bilbao (P)
Bologna (P)
Britain
Copenhagen (P)
Cardiff (P)
Croatia
Dublin
Dublin (P)
Edinburgh
Edinburgh (P)
England
Glasgow (P)
Ireland
Lisbon (P)
London
London (P)
Madrid (P)
Naples (P)
Northern Spain
Paris (P)
Reykjavík (P)
Rajasthan
Scotland
Scotland Highlands & Islands
Seville (P)
South India
Spain
Tallinn (P)
Turin (P)
Turkey
Valencia (P)
Verona (P)

Lifestyle guides
Surfing Britain
Surfing Europe

Also available:
Traveller's Handbook (WEXAS)
Traveller's Healthbook (WEXAS)
Traveller's Internet Guide (WEXAS)

Map index

Advertisers' index

Credits

Footprint credits
Text editor: Felicity Laughton
Assistant editors: Angus Dawson, Nicola Jones
Map editor: Sarah Sorensen
Picture editor: Kevin Feeney
Proofreaders: Adrian Dixon, Tim Jollands

Publisher: Patrick Dawson
Editorial: Alan Murphy, Sophie Blacksell, Sarah Thorowgood, Claire Boobbyer, Laura Dixon
Cartography: Robert Lunn, Claire Benison, Kevin Feeney, Melissa Lin
Series development: Rachel Fielding
Design: Mytton Williams and Rosemary Dawson (brand)
Advertising: Debbie Wylde
Finance and administration: Sharon Hughes, Elizabeth Taylor, Lindsay Dytham

Photography credits
Front cover: Powerstock
Inside: Alamy, Powerstock, Alex Robinson
Back cover: Alamy

Print
Manufactured in Italy by LegoPrint
Pulp from sustainable forests

Footprint feedback
We try as hard as we can to make each Footprint guide as up to date as possible but, of course, things always change. If you want to let us know about your experiences – good, bad or ugly – then don't delay, go to **www.footprintbooks.com** and send in your comments.

Publishing information
Footprint Brazil
4th edition

November 2004
ISBN 1 904777 15 5

CIP DATA: A catalogue record for this book is available from the British Library

Published by Footprint
6 Riverside Court
Lower Bristol Road
Bath BA2 3DZ, UK
T +44 (0)1225 469141
F +44 (0)1225 469461
discover@footprintbooks.com
www.footprintbooks.com

Distributed in the USA by
Publishers Group West

Neither the black and white nor colour maps are intended to have any political significance.

Every effort has been made to ensure that the facts in this guidebook are accurate. However, travellers should still obtain advice from consulates, airlines etc about travel and visa requirements before travelling. The authors and publishers cannot accept responsibility for any loss, injury or inconvenience however caused.

Acknowledgements

Many thanks to: Gardênia for doing almost all the maps and the research in the Amazon Chapter. Ben Box, Alan Murphy and Felicity Laughton for patience with the steep learning curve and for encouragement. Sarah Sorensen for her diligence on the maps. Rachel Fielding and Alan Murphy for the commission. There are many people to thank within Brazil: Ben Box and Mick Day for the thorough research in the previous editions on which this book was built; Manoel Fernandes Moura (Axketo) in Tabatinga for his incredible work; Danielle Migueletto in Rio who put up with so much with so much patience; Elizabeth Robinson for help and company in Iguaçu, Tiradentes and São João del Rey; Mike and Christine for help company in Búzios and São Paulo; Aragão and Maria Eliza in Rio for the nightlife in Gávea and Lapa; Alessandra Santos in São Paulo – for her help and time with all things fashionable; Casas Brancas in Búzios who helped me find my feet there; Richard at Trivium for his wonderful work and wonderful conscience; all at Regua; Aidan at Body and Soul Adventures in Ilha Grande; Gisele and Marcelo in Goiás for showing me their beautiful state; Ion and Tattoo in the Chapada dos Veadeiros, Rodrigo in Pirenópolis, Moacyr the Ayrton Senna of Goiânia; Eduardo and Felipe at Manary in Natal for their support and professionalism; everyone at Areia Branca in Rio Grande do Norte; Toca da Coruja in Pipa – what a great restaurant; Conor in Salvador for being so helpful; Haroldo Aragão in Bahia for great company and assistance; William in Praia do Forte; Boqueirão in Salvador, for their good taste; Vila Sereiea and Santa Clara on Boipeba for great food and accommodation; Norma Mattos; Silvia Luz for her incredible treatments; Pousada Mata Nativa in Trancoso – what a beautiful place; Fazenda Vila Guaiamú for great fish and massage; The people of Campina Grande for showing me their festival; the very helpful staff in the Paranaguá tourist office; Stephen Thompson for Lençóis and for his company in Rio and Raphael Robinson for reviewing things for small children in Itaúnas.

For readers letters and info I must thank the following: Matthias Fehrenbach in Immenstaad; Ingve Taksdal in Oslo; Robert Manley of Manley Burke in Cincinnati; Daniel and Daniela in Trancoso and Richard Dye.

The health section was written by Dr Charlie Easmon, MBBS, MRCP, Msc Public Health, DTM&H, DoccMed, Director of Travel Screening Services.

Brazil

VENEZUELA
GUYANA
SURI-NAME
GUYANE
COLOMBIA
ECUADOR
PERU
BOLIVIA
PARAGUAY
CHILE
ARGENTINA
URUGUAY
Pacific Ocean
Atlantic Ocean
Lago Titicaca
Shown at smaller scale
Macapá
Belém
Manaus
São Luís
Fortaleza
Natal
João Pessoa
Recife
Maceió
Aracaju
Salvador
Porto Velho
Rio Branco
Cuiabá
BRASÍLIA
Goiânia
Campo Grande
Belo Horizonte
Vitória
Rio de Janeiro
São Paulo
Curitiba
Florianópolis
Porto Alegre
1
2
3
4
5
N
0 km 300
0 miles 300
Altitude in metres
1000
500
200
0
Neighbouring Country
Federal highway
Primary route
Main road
Minor road
Unpaved road
BR285
Route number
International border
State border

Map 1
VENEZUELA
COLOMBIA
PERU
PERU
BOLIVIA
RORAIMA
AMAZONAS
ACRE
RONDÔNIA
Santa Elena de Uairén
Pacaraima
Normandia
BR174
Bonfim
Lethem
Alto Alegre
Boa Vista
Serra Parima
Floresta Nacional de Roraima
Caracaraí
Novo Paraiso
São Luís
Rio Branco
Cucuí
Parque Nacional Pico da Neblima
São Gabriel da Cachoeira
Uaimiri Atroari Reserve
Represa de Balbina
Parque Nacional do Jaú
Figueiredo
Rio Preto da Eva
Negro
Novo Airão
Manaus
Manacapuru
Careiro da Várzea
Careiro
Codajás
Foz do Mamaria
Santo Antônio do Içá
Rio Içá
Tonantins
Fonte Boa
Mamirauá
Tefé
Rio Solimões
Coari
Monte Cristo
São Paulo de Olivença
Al Tikuna Evare
Leticia
Tabatinga
Benjamin Constant
Rio Javari
Borba
Rio Madeira
Reserva Biológica de Abufari
BR319
Manicoré
Rodovia Transamazônica
Lábrea
Humaitá
Maici
Calama
Japim
Cruzeiro do Sul
BR364
Feijó
Parque Nacional Serra do Divisor
Boco do Acre
Porto Velho
Represa de Samuel
Tabajara
Abunã
Rio Abunã
Rio Branco
Taquaras
Ariquemes
Aripuanã
Assis Brasil
Xapuri
Brasiléia
Parque Nacional dos Pacaás Novos
Jaru
Ouro Preto d'Oeste
Ji Paraná
Presidente Médici
Cacoal
Pimento Bueno
Rolim de Moura
Guajará Mirim
Costa Marques
Principe da Beira
Reserva Biológica do Guaporé
Vilhena
Colorado do Oeste
Comodoro
Vila Bela da Sma Trindade
Pontes e Lacerda
Bala Grande
San Ma
L Orión (Provident
Lake Titicaca
Pacific Ocean
N
0 km 100
0 miles 100
A
B
C
1
2
3

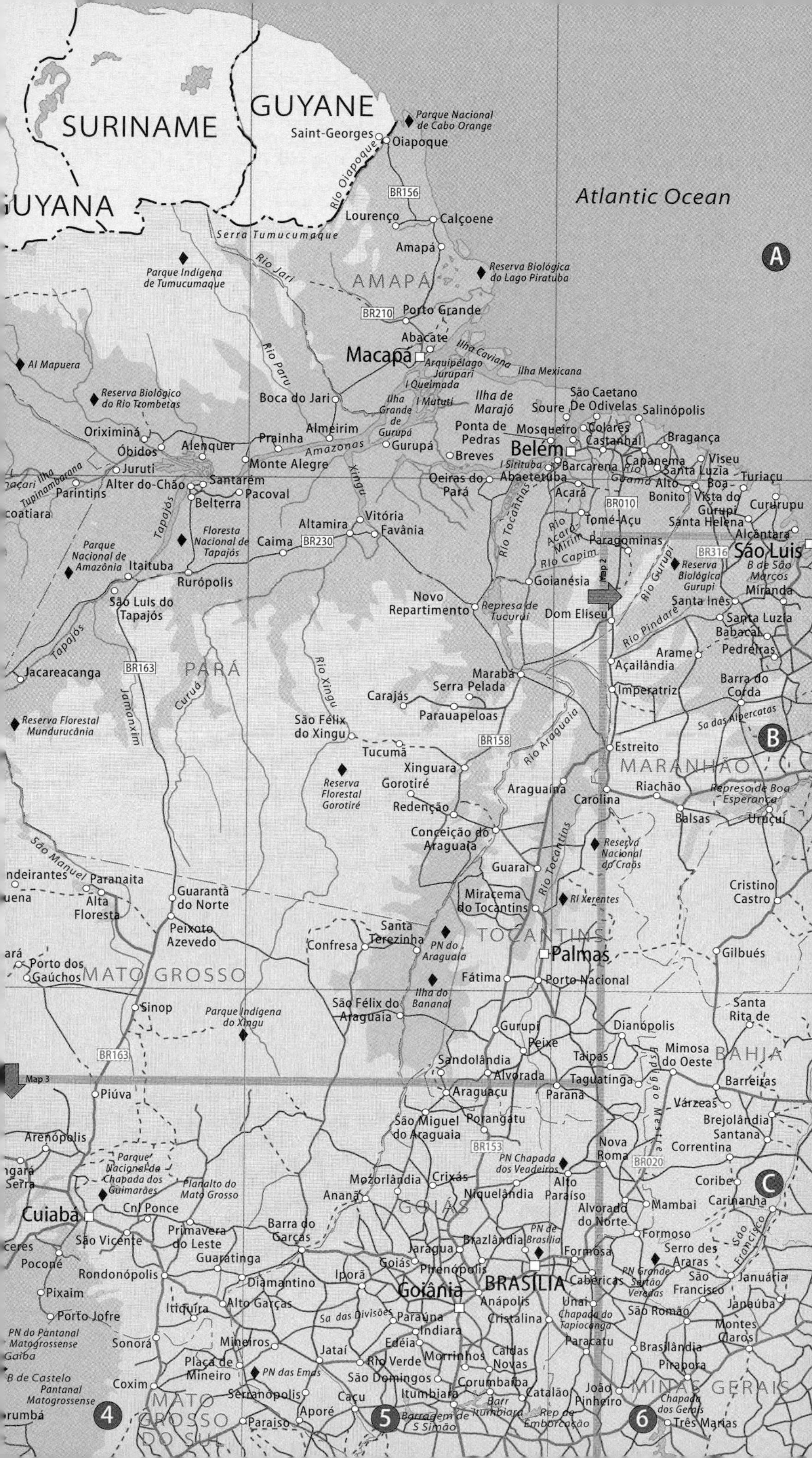
SURINAME
GUYANE
GUYANA
Atlantic Ocean
A
B
C
4
5
6
Parque Nacional de Cabo Orange
Saint-Georges
Oiapoque
Rio Oiapoque
BR156
Lourenço
Calçoene
Serra Tumucumaque
Amapá
Parque Indígena de Tumucumaque
Rio Jari
AMAPÁ
Reserva Biológica do Lago Piratuba
BR210
Porto Grande
Abacate
Macapá
Ilha Caviana
Arquipélago Jurupari
I Queimada
Ilha Mexicana
Al Mapuera
Rio Paru
Reserva Biológico do Rio Trombetas
Boca do Jari
Ilha Grande de Gurupá
I Mututi
Ilha de Marajó
São Caetano De Odivelas
Soure
Salinópolis
Ponta de Pedras
Mosqueiro
Colares
Castanhal
Bragança
Oriximiná
Almeirim
Prainha
Óbidos
Alenquer
Amazonas
Gurupá
Breves
Belém
Capanema
Viseu
Juruti
Monte Alegre
Xingu
I Sirituba
Barcarena
Rio Guamá
Santa Luzia
Alter do-Chão
Santarém
Oeiras do Pará
Abaetetuba
Alto Bonito
Boa Vista do Gurupi
Turiaçu
Ilha Tupinambarana
Parintins
Pacoval
Belterra
Acará
BR010
Cururupu
Tapajós
Altamira
Vitória
Favânia
Tomé-Açu
Santa Helena
Floresta Nacional de Tapajós
Rio Acará-Mirim
Paragominas
Alcântara
Parque Nacional de Amazônia
Caima
BR230
Rio Tocantins
Rio Capim
BR316
São Luís
Itaituba
Rurópolis
Goianésia
Reserva Biológica Gurupi
B de São Marcos
Map 2
Rio Gurupi
Miranda
São Luís do Tapajós
Novo Repartimento
Represa de Tucuruí
Dom Eliseu
Santa Inês
Santa Luzia
Rio Pindaré
Babacal
Pedreiras
Tapajós
Arame
Jacareacanga
BR163
PARÁ
Rio Xingu
Marabá
Açailândia
Curuá
Serra Pelada
Imperatriz
Barra do Corda
Jamanxim
Carajás
Parauapeloas
Sa das Alpercatas
Reserva Florestal Mundurucânia
São Félix do Xingu
BR158
Rio Araguaia
Estreito
Tucumã
Xinguara
MARANHÃO
Reserva Florestal Gorotiré
Gorotiré
Araguaína
Riachão
Represo de Boa Esperança
Carolina
Redenção
Balsas
Uruçuí
Conceição do Araguaia
Reserva Nacional do Craos
Rio Tocantins
São Manuel
Guaraí
Paranaita
Cristino Castro
Alta Floresta
Guarantã do Norte
Miracema do Tocantins
RI Xerentes
Peixoto Azevedo
Santa Terezinha
PN do Araguaia
TOCANTINS
Confresa
Palmas
Gilbués
Porto dos Gaúchos
MATO GROSSO
Ilha do Bananal
Fátima
Porto Nacional
Sinop
Parque Indígena do Xingu
São Félix do Araguaia
Santa Rita de
Gurupi
Dianópolis
Peixe
Mimosa do Oeste
BAHIA
BR163
Sandolândia
Taipas
Espigão Mestre
Map 3
Alvorada
Taguatinga
Barreiras
Piúva
Araguaçu
Paranã
Várzeas
São Miguel do Araguaia
Porangatu
Brejolândia
Arenópolis
Santana
Nova Roma
BR153
Correntina
Parque Nacional de Chapada dos Guimarães
PN Chapada dos Veadeiros
BR020
Planalto do Mato Grosso
Mozorlândia
Crixás
Alto Paraíso
Coribe
Cuiabá
Cnl Ponce
Anana
Niquelândia
Mambai
Carinhanha
GOIÁS
Alvorado do Norte
São Vicente
Primavera do Leste
Barra do Garças
Formoso
PN de Brasília
Brazlândia
São Francisco
Poconé
Jaraguá
Formosa
Serro des Araras
Guaratinga
Goiás
Pirenópolis
BRASÍLIA
Rondonópolis
Diamantino
Iporá
Cabeceiras
PN Grande Sertão Veredas
São Francisco
Januária
Pixaim
Goiânia
Anápolis
Unaí
Itiquira
Alto Garças
Sa das Divisões
Paraúna
Cristalina
Chapada do Tapiocanga
São Romão
Janaúba
Porto Jofre
Indiara
PN do Pantanal Matogrossense
Montes Claros
Sonorá
Mineiros
Edéia
Caldas Novas
Paracatu
Brasilândia
Jataí
Rio Verde
Morrinhos
Placa de Mineiro
Pirapora
PN das Emas
São Domingos
B de Castelo Pantanal Matogrossense
Coxim
Corumbaíba
Catalão
Serranópolis
Itumbiara
Barr Itumbiara
João Pinheiro
MINAS GERAIS
Caçu
Chapada dos Gerais
Aporé
Rep de Emborcação
Barragem de S Simão
MATO GROSSO DO SUL
Paraiso
Três Marias
Corumbá

Map 2
São Luís
Alcântara
Pinheiro
São Bento
B de São José
B de São Marcos
Primeira Cruz
Ribamar
Morros
Rosário
Parque Nacional Lençois Maranhenses
Barreirinhas
Paulino Neves
Ilha do Caju
Tutóia
Luís Correia
Parnaíba
Paragominas
Reserva Biológica Gurupi
Rio Gurupi
Rio Paraná
Rio Pindaré
Vargem Grande
Miranda do Norte
Santa Inês
Santa Luzía
Entroncamento
Brejo
Rio Paranaíba
Luzilândia
Cocal
Chapadinha
Porto
Viçosa do Ce
BR316
BR135
BR222
Babacal
Caxuxa
Coroatá
Timbiras
Miguel Alves
Batalha
Piracuruca
PN Sete Cidades
Peritoró
Pedreiras
Coelho Neto
Barras
Arame
Codó
União
Piripiri
Açailândia
MARANHÃO
Tocaia
Caxias
Campo Maior
Presidente Dutra
Imperatriz
BR010
BR226
Barra do Corda
Teresina
PIAUÍ
Alto Longa
Rio Itapecuru
Santana
Beneditinos
Sa das Alpercatas
Porto Franco
Colinas
Água Branca
Barro Duro
Estreito
São Gonçalo do Piauí
Chapada Grande
Amarante
Pastos Bons
Valença do Piauí
S Domingos
Pimenteira
Carolina
Riachão
Represo Boa Esperança
Floriano
Nazaré do Piaui
Goiatins
Balsas
Uruçuí
BR343
Oeiras
Picos
CE3
Bertolínia
Itaueira
Flores do Paul
Formosa
Itainópolis
Elisau Martins
Canto do Buriti
Simplício Mendes
Parque Nacional Serra da Capivara
São João do Piauí
Paulistana
Cristino Castro
Map 1
Alto Parnaíba
Bom Jesus
Afrânio
Redenção de Gurguéia
São Raimundo Nonato
Casa Nova
Gilbués
Remanso
TOCANTINS
Pilão Arcado
Sento Sé
Barragem de Sobradinho
Corrente
Amaniú
Sta Rita de Cássia
Ibiraba
Xique-Xique
Dianopolis
Barra
Boqueirão
Espigão Mestre
Juçara
Copixaba
Irecê
Rio Grande
Taipas
Mimosa do Oeste
Rio São Francisco
BR020
Taguatinga
Barreiras
Javi
Brotas
Ibotirama
Roda Velha
Várzeas
BAHIA
Brejolândia
Campos Belos
BR242
Map 4
Palmeiras
Lençóis
Parque Nacional da Chapada
A
B
C
1
2
3

Atlantic Ocean
A
B
C
4
5
6
N
0 km 50
0 miles 50
Nova Tatajuba
Jericoacoara
Barinha
Camocim
Jijoca
Cruz
Almofala
Granja
Marco
CE165
Senador Sá
Moraújo
Meruoca
Alcântara
Aprazival
Sobral
PN de Ubajara
Ubajara
Ibiapina
São Benedito
Carnaubal
Itapipoca
Mundaú
Fleixeiras
Paracuru
Taíba
Tururu
Trairi
Pecém
Cumbuco
Tabuba
BR222
Patos
Icaraí
Fortaleza
CEARÁ
Maranguape
Ponta do Mucuripe
Praia Futuro
Porto das Dunas
Barro Preto
Aquiraz
Iguape
Caponga
Cascavel
Varjota
Santa Quitéria
Açude Araras
Canindé
Pacoti
Morro Branco & Praia das Fontes
CE032
Ipueiras
Guaramiranga
CE021
Beberibe
Sucatinga
Poranga
Nova Russas
Baturité
BR116
Ararendá
Targinos
Boqueirão do Cesário
Canoa Quebrada
Aracati
BR304
Majorlândia
CE044
BR122
Itaiçaba
CE075
Icapuí
Crateús
Boa Viagem
Quixadá
Ibicutinga
Jaguaruana
Ibicuitaba
Russas
Tibau
CE021
Independencia
Limoeiro do Norte
Grossos
São Joaquim do Salgado
Quixeramobim
Morada Nova
Novo Oriente
Açude Bariabuiu
Areia Branca
Tabuleiro do Norte
Mossoró
Macau
Mineirolândia
CE02
Rio Jaguaribe
Guamaré
Jaguaretama
RN117
Rio Assu
Parazinho
Touros
Mombaça
Senador Pompeu
BR 405
Pendências
CE020
Piquet Carneiro
RG DO NORTE
BR406
Tauá
Apodi
João Câmara
Acopiara
Novo Floresta
BR116
Caraúbas
Assu
Angicos
Bento Fernandes
Muriú
Parambu
Ceará-Mirim
Catarina
Itaú
Paraú
São Rafael
Redinha
Açude Orós
Pereiro
Barragem Armando R Gonçalves
BR304
Riachuelo
Natal
Orós
Pau de Ferros
Patu
Rio Potengi
Bom Jesus
Jucás
Iguatu
Pirangi do Norte
Antonina do Norte
Brejo da Cruz
Rio Piranhas
Currais Novas
Santa Cruz
Icó
Alexandria
Florânia
Búzios
Cedro
Tangará
Tibau do Sul
Campos Sales
CE184
Assaré
Várzea Alegre
BR 230
Mangabeira
Uiraúna
Brejo dos Santos
Caicó
BR427
Acari
Goianinha
Praia da Barra de Cunhaú
Souza
Novo Olinda
Aratama
Farias Brito
Lavras da Mangabeira
Cajazeiras
Pombal
Serra Negra Do Norte
Canguaretama
Araripe
Picuí
Cuité
Baía Formosa
Juazeiro do Norte
Araruna
Tacima
Chapada do Araripe
Santana do Cariri
Crato
Missão Velha
São José das Piranhas
Santa Luzia
Barra de Camaratuba
BR104
Belém
BR101
Araripina
Barbalha
BR361
Patos
BR230
Arara
Guarabira
Rio Tinto
Mamanguape
Exu
Jardim
Itaporanga
Teixeira
PARAÍBA
Alagoa Grande
Campina
Planalto da Borborema
Campina Grande
Sapé
Cabedelo
João Pessoa
Bela Vista
Bodocó
Jati
Conceição
São João do Cariri
Ouricuri
Cabo Branco
Ingá
Itabaiana
Jacumá
BR316
BR412
BR122
Salgueir
Triunfo
Sumé
Boqueirão
Queimadas
Pitimbu
BR232
Timbaúba
Itambé
Tambaba
Santa Cruz
Flores
Jabitacá
BR104
Caraúbas
Goiana
Pontas de Pedra
Serra Talhada
PERNAMBUCO
Taquaritinga do Norte
Surubim
Carpina
Reserva Biológica de Serra Negra
Sítio dos Nunes
Sertânia
PE090
I de Itamaracá
BR110
Limoeira
Igarassu
Paulista
Fazenda Nova
Olinda
Cruzeiro de Nordeste
Lagao Grande
Ibo
Floresta
Rio São Francisco
Belo Jardim
Gravatá
Jaboatão
Caruaru
Recife
PE360
Arcoverde
Pesqueira
Bezerros
Vitória de Sto Antão
Gaibu
RB da Pedra Talhada
Barragem de Itaparica
Pau Ferro
Tupanatinga
PE180
Cabo
Petrolândia
Venturosa
Lajedo
RB de Saltinho
Porto de Galinhas
Petrolina
Catende
BR424
Barra de Sirinhaém
Itaiba
Palmares
Juazeiro
Garanhuns
PE177
Tamandaré
Águas Belas
Bom Conselho
Quipapá
Barreiros
São José da Coroa Grande
BR423
Paulo Afonso
Delmiro Gouveia
S José de Laje
União de Palmares
Maragogi
Santana do Ipanema
Palmeira dos Índios
To Fernando de Noronha
BR407
Uauá
S Luís do Qitunde
AL110
Taquarana
BR101
Pão de Açúcar
Barra de Santo Antônio
ALAGOAS
Canudos
Campo Alegre
Feira Nova
Arapiraca
Maceió
Jeremoaba
NS da Glória
Marechal Deodoro
Traipu
Junqueiro
São Miguel dos Campos
Praia do Francês
Senhor do Bonfim
Porto Real do Colégio
Euclides da Cunha
BR110
Monte Santo
Carira
SERGIPE
Propriá
Coruripe
Cansanção
Penedo
Rebeirópolis
NS das Dores
Neópolis
EE Foz de São Francisco
Heliópolis
Simão Dias
Itabaiana
Japaratuba
Pacatuba
Piaçabuçu
Poço Verde
Tucano
Laranjeiras
RB de Santa Isabel
Lagarto
Pirambu
324
Capim Grosso
Cipó
NS do Socorro
Aracaju
BR116
Riachão do Dantas
Salgado
São Cristóvão
Vázea de Poco
Tobias Barreto
Mosqueiro
Itapicuru
Itabaianinha
Estância
Serrinha
Cristinápolis
Barra de Estância
Inhambupe
Indiaroba
Mangue Seco
Esplanada
Feira de Santana
BR101
Sítio de Conde
Alagoinhas
BR099
Cachoeira
Conceiçao

Map 3
MATO GROSSO
Piúva
Nova Mutum
Arenápolis
Tangará da Serra
A
Pontas e Lacerda
Parque Nacional da Chapada dos Guimarães
Jangada
Chapada dos Guimarães
Planalto do Mato Grosso
Rio Mortes
Rio Paraguí
Várzea Grande
Cuiabá
BR070
Primavera do este
Cnl Ponce
São Vicente
Alto Coité
Sto Antônio do Leverger
Rio Chacororé
Jaciara
Cáceres
Poconé
Rio Cuiabá
Barão de Melgaço
San Matías
Guaratinga
Rio Claro
Rondonópolis
Diamantino
Pixaim
Rio São Lourenço
BR163
Alto Garças
Porto Jofre
Itiquira
Alto Araguaia
L Uberaba
Parque Nacional do Pantanal Matogrossense
Pantanal do São Lourenço
Sonora
L Gaiba
BOLIVIA
B
Rio Negro
Pantanal do Taquari
Placa de Mineiros
B de Castelo
Coxim
Silvolândia
Costa Rica
Rio Paraguay
Pantanal do Rio Negro
Rio Verde de Mato Grosso
Puerto Suárez
Corumbá
Paraíso
Map 1
MATO GROSSO DO SUL
Morrinho
Camapuã
Porto Esperança
Guaicurus
Capim Verde
Rochedo
Miranda
Bonfim
Bodoquena
Aquidauana
Campo Grande
N
Sidrolândia
Bonito
Nioaque
Serra de Bodoquena
Serra de Maracajú
PN Serra da Bodoquena
Porto Murtinho
Guia Lopes da Laguna
Sta Rita do Pardo
Novo Alvorada
0 km 50
0 miles 50
Jardim
Maracaju
C
Boqueirão
Rio Apá
Bela Vista
Cabeceira do Apá
Itaum
Itaporã
Antônio João
Dourados
BR376
Pedro Juan Caballero
Ponta Porã
Ivinhema
Caarapó
PARAGUAY
Rio Paraná
Amambaí
Map 5
1
2
3
Eldorado
Umuarama

Sandolândia
Alvorada
Paranã
São Salvador do Tocantins
Araguaçu
Palmeirópolis
Arraias
Luis Alves
Bandeirantes
RI Pimental Barbosa
São Miguel do Araguaia
Novo Planalto
Porangatu
Rio Paranã
Serra Dourada
Rio Mortes
Rio Cristalinho
Mundo Novo
Xixá
Mutunópolis
Água Boa
Novo Crixás
Estrela do Norte
Parque Nacional de Chapada dos Veadeiros
Teresina de Goiás
Nova Roma
Mara Rosa
Barragem da Serra da Mesa
Colinas
Cocalinho
Peixe
Campinorte
A
Areões
Alto Paraíso
Nova Xavantina
Crixás
Map 4
Niquelândia
Mozarlândia
Uruaçu
Pindaíba
Aruanã
Rio Tocantins
Britânia
Araguapaz
Rio Araguaia
Dois Irmãos
Ceres
Goianésia
Serra Bonita
Jacilândia
Parque Nacional de Brasília
Santa Fe
Barro do Garças
Juçara
Jaraguá
Brazlândia
Cidade de Goiás
Aragarças
Sobradinho
Formosa
Aparecida do Rio Claro
BRASÍLIA
Planaltina
Buritis
Bom Jardim de Goiás
Pirenópolis
Taguatinga
Cabeceiras
Gama
Iporã
Abadiânia
Luziânia
Amorinópolis
Anápolis
Garapuava
Doverlândia
Trindade
Unaí
Leopoldo de Bulhões
Palestina
Goiânia
Chapada do Tapiocanga
Caiapônia
Sa das Divisões
Paraúna
Aparecida de Goiânia
Bela Vista
Cristalina
Portelândia
Indiara
Edéia
Mineiros
GOIÁS
Piracanjuba
Pires do Rio
Paracatu
Pontalina
Jataí
Rio Verde
BR040
Caldas Novas
Morrinhos
Rio Quente
B
Parque Nacional das Emas
S Domingos
Aparecida do Rio Doce
Corumbaíba
João Pinheiro
Serranópolis
Catalão
Quirinópolis
Caçu
Barragem de S Simão
Itumbiara
Barr Itumbiara
Barragem de Embarcação
Aporé
Coromandel
Araguari
Patos de Minas
BR365
Uberlândia
Patrocínio
Raimundo
Prata
BR452
Paranaíba
Rio Grande
Barragem Agua Vermelha
Iblá
Aparecida do Taboado
Uberaba
Araxá
Santa Fe do Sul
Jales
Igarapava
Fernandópolis
Colombia
BR050
Parque Nacional da Serra da Canastra
Votuporanga
Ituverava
Icém
Rio Grande
Três Lagoas
Castilho
Nhandeara
Barretos
Franca
Represa Peixoto
São Roque de Minas
Andradina
Rio Tietê
José do Río Preto
Cassia
Mirandópolis
Bebedouro
Batatais
Passos
Panorama
Aracatuba
Represa do Furnas
Guararapes
Birigui
Cantanduva
São Sebastião do Paraíso
Penápolis
Sertãozinho
Ribeirão Preto
Bataguassu
Adamantina
Promissão
Represa Promissão
Cajuru
Guaxupé
C
Osvaldo Cruz
Lins
Matão
Mococa
Tupã
Icanga
Ibitinga
São José do Rio Pardo
Alfenas
Planalto do Sul
Rancheria
Pirajui
Araraquara
Poços de Caldas
Presidente Prudente
Marília
Garça
Bariri
São Carlos
Pirassununga
Rio Paranapanema
Paraguaçu Paulista
Gália
Bauru
Leme
São João da Boa Vista
Santo Inácio
Assis
Jaú
Ubirajara
Araras
Rep Capivari
Río Claro
Moji-Guaçu
Barra Bonita
Pouso Alegre
Lençóis Paulista
Moji-Mirim
Bela Vista do Paraíso
Limeira
Ourinhos
Piracicaba
Americana
Cornélio Procópio
Londrina
Botucatu
Sumaré
Jacarezinho
Sta Bárbara d'Oeste
4
5
6
Avaré
SÃO PAULO
Maringá
Arapongas
Bandeirantes
Piraju
Campinas
Sto Antonio de Platina
Jundiai
Atibaia
Tatuí
São Jos

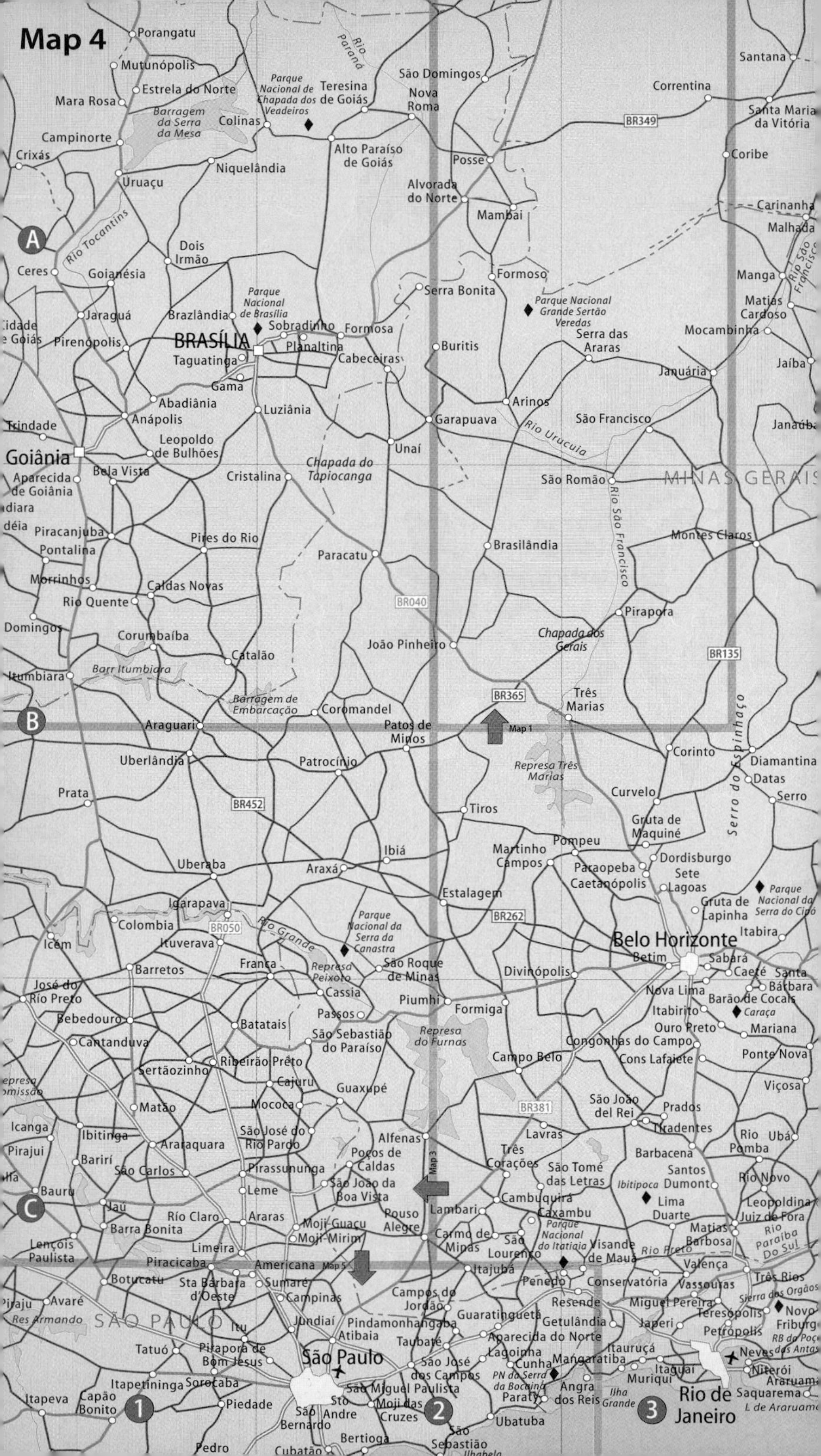
Map 4
Porangatu
Mutunópolis
Estrela do Norte
Mara Rosa
Barragem da Serra da Mesa
Campinorte
Crixás
Uruaçu
Niquelândia
Colinas
Parque Nacional de Chapada dos Veadeiros
Rio Paraná
Teresina de Goiás
Alto Paraíso de Goiás
São Domingos
Nova Roma
Posse
Alvorada do Norte
Mambaí
Formoso
Serra Bonita
Correntina
BR349
Santana
Santa Maria da Vitória
Coribe
Carinanha
Malhada
Rio São Francisco
Manga
Matias Cardoso
Mocambinha
Jaíba
Januária
Janaúba
A
Rio Tocantins
Dois Irmão
Ceres
Goianésia
Jaraguá
Cidade de Goiás
Pirenópolis
Brazlândia
Parque Nacional de Brasília
BRASÍLIA
Sobradinho
Planaltina
Formosa
Cabeceiras
Taguatinga
Gama
Abadiânia
Anápolis
Luziânia
Trindade
Goiânia
Leopoldo de Bulhões
Aparecida de Goiânia
Bela Vista
Cristalina
Chapada do Tapiocanga
Unaí
Garapuava
Buritis
Arinos
Parque Nacional Grande Sertão Veredas
Serra das Araras
São Francisco
Rio Urucuia
São Romão
MINAS GERAIS
Rio São Francisco
Piracanjuba
Pontalina
Morrinhos
Pires do Rio
Caldas Novas
Rio Quente
Domingos
Corumbaíba
Catalão
Paracatu
Brasilândia
Montes Claros
BR040
Pirapora
João Pinheiro
Chapada dos Gerais
BR135
Itumbiara
Barr Itumbiara
Barragem de Embarcação
Coromandel
BR365
Três Marias
B
Araguari
Patos de Minas
Map 1
Serro do Espinhaço
Uberlândia
Patrocínio
Represa Três Marias
Corinto
Diamantina
Datas
Prata
BR452
Tiros
Curvelo
Serro
Gruta de Maquiné
Ibiá
Martinho Campos
Pompeu
Uberaba
Araxá
Paraopeba
Caetanópolis
Dordisburgo
Sete Lagoas
Parque Nacional da Serra do Cipó
Estalagem
Igarapava
Gruta de Lapinha
BR050
Colombia
Parque Nacional da Serra da Canastra
BR262
Itabira
Rio Grande
Icém
Ituverava
Belo Horizonte
Betim
Barretos
Franca
Represa Peixoto
São Roque de Minas
Divinópolis
Sabará
Caeté
Santa Bárbara
José do Rio Preto
Cassia
Piumhi
Nova Lima
Barão de Cocais
Passos
Formiga
Itabirito
Caraça
Bebedouro
Batatais
Represa do Furnas
Ouro Preto
Mariana
Cantanduva
São Sebastião do Paraíso
Congonhas do Campo
Ribeirão Preto
Campo Belo
Cons Lafaiete
Ponte Nova
Sertãozinho
Represa Promissão
Cajuru
Guaxupé
Viçosa
Matão
Mococa
BR381
São João del Rei
Prados
Icanga
Ibitinga
São José do Rio Pardo
Tiradentes
Lavras
Pirajui
Araraquara
Alfenas
Rio Pomba
Ubá
Barirí
Poços de Caldas
Três Corações
Barbacena
São Carlos
Pirassununga
Map 3
São Tomé das Letras
Santos Dumont
Bauru
Leme
São João da Boa Vista
Cambuquirá
Ibitipoca
Lima Duarte
Rio Novo
C
Jaú
Caxambu
Leopoldina
Rio Claro
Araras
Moji-Guaçu
Pouso Alegre
Lambari
Juiz de Fora
Barra Bonita
Moji-Mirim
Carmo de Minas
São Lourenço
Parque Nacional do Itatiaia
Matias Barbosa
Lençóis Paulista
Limeira
Visande de Mauá
Rio Preto
Rio Paraíba Do Sul
Piracicaba
Americana
Map 5
Itajubá
Valença
Botucatu
Sta Bárbara d'Oeste
Sumaré
Penedo
Conservatória
Vassouras
Três Rios
Campinas
Campos do Jordão
Resende
Miguel Pereira
Serra dos Orgãos
Piraju
Avaré
Guaratinguetá
Getulândia
Teresópolis
Nova Friburgo
Res Armando
SÃO PAULO
Itu
Jundiaí
Pindamonhangaba
Japeri
Petrópolis
RB do Poço das Antas
Atibaia
Aparecida do Norte
Tatuí
Pirapora de Bom Jesus
Taubaté
Lagoinha
Itauruçá
Cunha
Mangaratiba
São Paulo
São José dos Campos
Muriqui
Itaguaí
Neves
Niterói
Itapetininga
Sorocaba
PN da Serra da Bocaina
Araruama
Angra dos Reis
Ilha Grande
Itapeva
Capão Bonito
São Miguel Paulista
Paraty
Saquarema
1
Piedade
Sto Andre
Moji das Cruzes
2
3
Rio de Janeiro
L de Araruama
São Bernardo
Ubatuba
São Sebastião
Pedro
Cubatão
Bertioga
Ilhabela

Map 2
Palmeiras
Lençóis
BR242
Parque Nacional da Chapada Diamantina
Feira de Santana
Esplanada
BR101
Sítio de Conde
Conceiçao do Jacuipe
Alagoinhas
BR099
Itaberaba
Cachoeira
Catu
Imbassaí
Praia do Forte
Bom Jesus da Lapa
São Félix
Santo Amaro
BAHIA
Castro Alves
Santo Candeias
Camaçari
Baía De Todos Os Santos
Arembepe
Simões Filha
Rio de Contas
Iramaia
Santo Antônio de Jesus
Itaparica
Salvador
Maracás
Nazaré das Farinhas
Jaguaripe
Guanambi
Caetité
BR116
Valença
Morro de São Paulo
Rio das Contas
Jequié
BR101
Ilha de Tinharé
Brumado
Ituberá
Boipeba
Camamu
A
Ubaitaba
Maraú
Itacaré
Espinosa
Condeúba
Vitória do Conquista
Itabuna
Ilhéus
BR415
Olivença
Itapetinga
Macarani
Porteirinha
Camacã
Una
Rio Pardo
Caveira
Salinas
Pedra Azul
Canavieiras
Salto da Divisa
Belmonte
Rio Jequitinhonha
Almenara
Santa Cruz Cabrália
Itaobim
Eunápolis
Porto Seguro
Araçuaí
Arraial da Ajuda
Itabela
Trancoso
Caraíva
Sierra do Chifre
PN Monte Pascoal
Catuji
Itamaraj
Capelinha
Cumuruxatiba
BR101
Prado
Teixeira de Freitas
B
Teófilo Otoni
Alcobaça
Nanuque
BR116
Caravelas
Parque Nacional Marinho dos Abrolhos
Nova Viçosa
Reserva Biológica do Córrego Grande
Mucuri
Reserva Biológica do Córrego do Veado
Itaúnas
Governador Valadares
Conceição da Barra
São Mateus
Reserva Biológica de Sooretama
Rio Doce
ESPIRITO SANTO
Reserva Biológica Linhares
Linhares
Colatina
Caratinga
Reserva Biológica Dr Augusto Ruschi
Reserva Biológica Comboios
Ibiraçu
Aracruz
Manhuaçu
Sta Teresa
Santa Cruz
BR262
Manhumirim
Fundão
Parque Nacional Caparaó
Sta Leopoldina
Serra
N
Vitória
Pedra Azul
Domingos Martins
Vila Velha
Guarapari
Cachoeiro do Itapemirim
0 km 50
0 miles 50
Bom Jesus do Itabapoana
Itaperuna
Marataízes
Atlantic Ocean
C
Santo Antônio de Pádua
São Fidelis
Itaocara
S João da Barra
Campos
Lagoa Feia
Macaé
Rio das Ostras
Barra de São João
Búzios
Cabo Frio
Arraial do Cabo
4
5
6

Map 5
Map 3
Inácio
PARAGUAY
ARGENTINA
URUGUAY
A
B
C
1
2
3
Rio Paraná
Maringá
Umuarama
Cianorte
Eldorado
Parque Nacional da Ilha Grande
Mundo Novo
Guaíra
Palotina
Campo Mourão
Termas de Jurema
Campina
Iretama
Toledo
PARANÁ
Represa de Itaipu
Cascavel
Pitanga
Medeaneira
Catanduvas
Ciudade del Este
Foz do Iguaçu
Parque Nacional Foz do Iguaçu
Laranjeiras do Sul
Guarapuava
Iguaçu Falls
Rio Iguaçu
Represa de Salto Santiago
Represa de Foz Areia
Campo Erê
Pato Branco
São Lourenço d'Oeste
São Miguel d'Oeste
Horizonte
Bom Jesus
Xanxerê
SANTA
Itapiranga
Chapecó
Treze Tílias
Salto do Yucumã
Iraí
Concórdia
Joaçaba
Federico Westphalen
Campos Novo
Erexim
Tupitanga
Barragem Passo Fundo
Santa Rosa
Porto Xavier
RIO GRANDE DO SUL
São Luís Gonzaga
Santo Ângelo
Carazinho
Passo Fundo
Santo Tomé
Ijuí
BR285
Lagoa Vermelha
São Borja
São Miguel das Missões
Cruz Alta
Encruzilhada
Soledade
Itaqui
Santiago
Caxia do Su
Bento Gonçalves
Farroupilha
Paso de las Letras
Manuel Viana
Garibaldi
Novo Petrópoli
Lajeado
Uruguaiana
Alegrete
Santa María
Novo Hamburgo
Candelária
Santa Cruz do Sul
Sapucaia do Sul
São Leopoldo
Barra do Quaraí
Rio Jacuí
Esteio
Canoas
Guaíba
Bella Unión
Rosário do Sul
São Gabriel
Porto Alegre
BR290
Caçapava do Sul
Barra do Ribeiro
Santana do Livramento
Encruzilhada do Sul
Aguas Brancas
Tapes
Rivera
Camaquã
Lagoa dos Patos
Arambaré
Santa Rita
Bagé
Mostarda
São Lourenço do Sul
Tavares
Parque Nacional Lagoa do Peixe
Canguçu
BR293
Pelotas
Dunas
Bojuru
Aceguá
Estreito
São José do Norte
Rio Grande
Cassino
Jaguarão
Rio Branco
Estação Ecológica do Taim
Lagoa Mirim
Curral Alto
Laguna Mangabeira
Santa Vitória do Palmar
Chuí